The United States Government Manual 2016

Office of the Federal Register
National Archives and Records Administration

ISBN 1-59804-828-7

Published and for sale by:
CLAITOR'S PUBLISHING DIVISION
P.O. Box 261333, Baton Rouge, LA 70826-1333
800-274-1403 (In LA 225-344-0476)
Fax: 225-344-0480
Internet address:
e mail: claitors@claitors.com
World Wide Web: http://www.claitors.com

*We acknowledge the input and assistance of the National Archives and Records Administration since the following is extracted from their web site at http://www.usgovernmentmanual.gov

Preface

As the official handbook of the Federal Government, *The United States Government Manual* provides comprehensive information on the agencies of the legislative, judicial, and executive branches. The *Manual* also includes information on quasi-official agencies; international organizations in which the United States participates; and boards, commissions, and committees.

A typical agency description includes a list of principal officials, a summary statement of the agency's purpose and role in the Federal Government, a brief history of the agency, including its legislative or executive authority, a description of its programs and activities, and a "Sources of Information" section. This last section provides information on consumer activities, contracts and grants, employment, publications, and many other areas of public interest.

The *Manual* is also available and periodically updated on its own website. The U.S. Government Manual website (usgovernmentmanual.gov) is jointly administered by the Office of the Federal Register (OFR)/Government Printing Office (GPO) partnership. The website offers three ways to and information about Government agencies and organizations by entering a term in the keyword search box, browsing categories, or using "The Government of the United States" site map for an overview of the Government. For more information and to view The *Manual* online, go to *www.usgovernmentmanual.gov*.

The 2016 *Manual* was prepared by the Presidential and Legislative Publications Unit, Office of the Federal Register. Alfred W. Jones was Team Leader; Joseph Frankovic was Managing Editor; assisted by Lois Davis, Joshua Liberatore, Joseph Vetter, Edgar G. Gibbs, Ryan R. Nolan, and Todd Goodman.

The Federal Register and Its Special Editions

The *Manual* is published as a special edition of the *Federal Register* (see 1 CFR 9.1). Its focus is on programs and activities. Persons interested in detailed organizational structure, the regulatory documents of an agency, or Presidential documents should refer to the Federal Register or one of its other special editions, described below. Issued each Federal working day, the *Federal Register* provides a uniform system for publishing Presidential documents, regulatory documents with general applicability and legal effect, proposed rules, notices, and documents required to be published by statute. For more information and to look at the Federal Register online, go to *www.federalregister.gov*.

The Code of Federal Regulations is an annual codification of the general and permanent rules published in the Federal Register. The Code is divided into 50 titles that represent broad areas subject to Federal regulation. The Code is kept up to date by the individual issues of the Federal Register. For more information and to look at the Code of Federal Regulations online, go to *www.gpo.gov/fdsys/browse/collectionCfr.action?collectionCode=CFR*.

The *Compilation of Presidential Documents* serves as a timely, up-to-date reference source for the public policies and activities of the President. It contains remarks, news conferences, messages, statements, and other Presidential material of a public nature issued by the White House. The *Compilation of Presidential Documents* collection is composed of the *Daily Compilation of Presidential Documents* and its predecessor, the *Weekly Compilation of Presidential Documents.* For more information and to look at the Presidential documents online, go to *www.gpo.gov/fdsys/browse/collection.action?collectionCode=CPD.* The Compilation of Presidential Documents now has a free mobile application at *www.gpo.gov/mobile.*

A companion publication to the Compilation of Presidential Documents is the Public Papers of the Presidents, which contains public Presidential documents and speeches in convenient book form. Volumes of the Public Papers have been published for every President since Herbert Hoover, with the exception of Franklin D. Roosevelt, whose papers were published privately. For more information and to view the Public Papers online, go to *www.gpo.gov/fdsys/browse/collection.action?collectionCode=PPP.*

Other Office of the Federal Register Publications

The Office of the Federal Register publishes slip laws, which are pamphlet prints of each public and private law enacted by Congress. Slip laws are compiled annually as the *United States Statutes at Large.* For more information and to look at the slip laws online, go to *www.gpo.gov/fdsys/browse/collection.action?collectionCode=PLAW.* The *Statutes* at Large volumes contain all public and private laws and concurrent resolutions enacted during a session of Congress; recommendations for executive, legislative, and judicial salaries; reorganization plans; proposed and ratified amendments to the Constitution; and Presidential proclamations. Included with many of these documents are sidenotes, *U.S. Code* and statutes citations, and a summary of their legislative histories. For more information and to look at the Statutes at Large online, go to *www.gpo.gov/fdsys/browse/collection.action?collectionCode=STATUTE.*

Electronic Services

The Office of the Federal Register maintains an Internet site for the Federal Register's public inspection list, and information on the Office and its activities at *www.ofr.gov.* This site also contains links to the texts of *The United States Government Manual,* public laws, the *Compilation of Presidential Documents,* the *Federal Register,* and the *Code of Federal Regulations* (both as officially published on a quarterly basis and an unofficial, daily updated version, the e-CFR) in electronic format through the GPO's Federal Digital System (FDsys) at *www.fdsys.gov.* For more information, contact the GPO Customer Contact Center, U.S. Government Printing Office. Phone, 202–512–1800, or 866–512–1800 (toll-free). Email, gpo@custhelp.com, Online, *www.gpo.gov/askgpo.*

Inquiries

For inquiries concerning *The United States Government Manual* and other publications of the Office of the Federal Register, call 202–741–6000, write to the Director, Office of the Federal Register, National Archives and Records Administration, Washington, DC 20408, or email fedreg.info@nara.gov.

Sales

The publications of the Office of the Federal Register are available for sale by writing to the Superintendent of Documents, P.O. Box 371954, Pittsburgh, PA 15250–7954. Publications are also available for sale through the GPO's online bookstore at *http://bookstore.gpo.gov,* the GPO bookstore located in Washington, DC, and the retail sales outlet in Laurel, MD. Telephone inquiries should be directed to 202–512–1800, 866–512–1800 (toll-free), or 202–512–2104 (fax).

Contents

Declaration of Independence

Action of Second Continental Congress, July 4, 1776

IN CONGRESS, JULY 4, 1776.

THE UNANIMOUS DECLARATION of the thirteen united STATES OF AMERICA,

WHEN in the Course of human events, it becomes necessary for one people to dissolve the political bands which have connected them with another, and to assume among the powers of the earth, the separate and equal station to which the Laws of Nature and of Nature's God entitle them, a decent respect to the opinions of mankind requires that they should declare the causes which impel them to the separation.

We hold these truths to be self-evident, that all men are created equal, that they are endowed by their Creator with certain unalienable Rights, that among these are Life, Liberty and the pursuit of Happiness.—That to secure these rights, Governments are instituted among Men, deriving their just powers from the consent of the governed,—That whenever any Form of Government becomes destructive of these ends, it is the Right of the People to alter or to abolish it, and to institute new Government, laying its foundation on such principles and organizing its powers in such form, as to them shall seem most likely to effect their Safety and Happiness. Prudence, indeed, will dictate that Governments long established should not be changed for light and transient causes; and accordingly all experience hath shewn, that mankind are more disposed to suffer, while evils are sufferable, than to right themselves by abolishing the forms to which they are accustomed. But when a long train of abuses and usurpations, pursuing invariably the same Object evinces a design to reduce them under absolute Despotism, it is their right, it is their duty, to throw off such Government, and to provide new Guards for their future security.—Such has been the patient sufferance of these Colonies; and such is now the necessity which constrains them to alter their former Systems of Government. The history of the present King of Great Britain is a history of repeated injuries and usurpations, all having in direct object the establishment of an absolute Tyranny over these States. To prove this, let Facts be submitted to a candid world.—He has refused his Assent to Laws, the most wholesome and necessary for the public good.—He has forbidden his Governors to pass Laws of immediate and pressing importance, unless suspended in their operation till his Assent should be obtained; and when so suspended, he has utterly neglected to attend to them.—He has refused to pass other Laws for the accommodation of large districts of people, unless those people would relinquish the right of Representation in the Legislature, a right inestimable to them and formidable to tyrants only.—He has called together legislative bodies at places unusual, uncomfortable, and distant from the depository of their public Records, for the sole purpose of fatiguing them into compliance with his measures.—He has dissolved Representative Houses repeatedly, for opposing with manly firmness his invasions on the rights of the people.—He has refused for a long time, after such dissolutions, to cause others to be elected; whereby the Legislative powers, incapable of Annihilation, have returned to the People at large for their exercise; the State remaining in the mean time exposed to all the dangers of invasion from without, and convulsions within.—He has endeavoured to prevent the population of these States; for that purpose obstructing the Laws for Naturalization of Foreigners; refusing to pass others to encourage their migrations hither, and raising the conditions of new Appropriations of Lands.—He has obstructed the Administration of Justice, by refusing his Assent to Laws for establishing Judiciary powers.—He has made Judges dependent on his Will alone, for the tenure of their offices, and the amount and payment of their salaries.—He has erected a multitude of New Offices, and sent hither swarms of Officers to harrass our people, and eat out their substance.—He has kept among us, in times of peace, Standing Armies without the Consent of our legislatures.—He has affected to render the Military independent of and superior to the Civil power.—He has combined with others to subject us to a jurisdiction foreign to our constitution, and unacknowledged by our laws; giving his Assent to their Acts of pretended Legislation:—For Quartering large bodies of armed troops among us:—For protecting them, by a mock Trial, from punishment for any Murders which they should commit on the Inhabitants of these States:—For cutting off our Trade with all parts of the world:—For imposing Taxes on us without our Consent:—For depriving us in many cases, of the benefits of Trial by Jury:—For transporting us beyond Seas to be tried for pretended offences—For abolishing the free System of English Laws in a neighbouring Province, establishing therein an Arbitrary government, and enlarging its Boundaries so as to render it at once an example and fit instrument for introducing the same absolute rule into these Colonies:—For taking away our Charters, abolishing our most valuable Laws, and altering fundamentally the Forms of our Governments:—For suspending our own Legislatures, and declaring themselves invested with power to legislate for us in all cases whatsoever.—He has abdicated Government here, by declaring us out of his Protection and waging War against us.—He has plundered our seas, ravaged our Coasts, burnt our towns, and destroyed the lives of our people.—He is at this time transporting large Armies of foreign Mercenaries to compleat the works of death, desolation and tyranny, already begun with circumstances of Cruelty & perfidy scarcely paralleled in the most barbarous ages, and totally unworthy the Head of a civilized nation.—He has constrained our fellow Citizens taken Captive on the high Seas to bear Arms against their Country, to become the executioners of their friends and Brethren, or to fall themselves by their Hands.—He has excited domestic insurrections amongst us, and has endeavoured to bring on the inhabitants of our frontiers, the merciless Indian Savages, whose known rule of warfare, is an undistinguished destruction of all ages, sexes and conditions.—In every stage of these Oppressions We have Petitioned for Redress in the most humble terms: Our repeated Petitions have been answered only by repeated injury. A Prince whose character is thus marked by every act which may define a Tyrant, is unfit to be the ruler of a free people.—Nor have We been wanting in attentions to our Brittish brethren. We have warned them from time to time of attempts by their legislature to extend an unwarrantable jurisdiction over us. We have reminded them of the circumstances of our emigration and settlement here. We have appealed to their native justice and magnanimity, and we have conjured them by the ties of our common kindred to disavow these usurpations, which, would inevitably interrupt our connections and correspondence. They too have been deaf to the voice of justice and of consanguinity. We must, therefore, acquiesce in the necessity, which denounces our Separation, and hold them, as we hold the rest of mankind, Enemies in War, in Peace Friends.

WE, THEREFORE, the Representatives of the UNITED STATES OF AMERICA, in General Congress, Assembled, appealing to the Supreme Judge of the world for the rectitude of our intentions, do, in the Name, and by Authority of the good People of these Colonies, solemnly publish and declare, That these United Colonies are, and of Right ought to be **FREE AND INDEPENDENT STATES;** that they are Absolved from all Allegiance to the British Crown, and that all political connection between them and the State of Great Britain, is and ought to be totally dissolved; and that as Free and Independent

States, they have full Power to levy War, conclude Peace, contract Alliances, establish Commerce, and to do all other Acts and Things which Independent States may of right do. And for the support of this Declaration, with a firm reliance on the protection of divine Providence, we mutually pledge to each other our Lives, our Fortunes and our sacred Honor.

The 56 signatures on the Declaration appear in the positions indicated:

Column 1

Georgia:
Button Gwinnett
Lyman Hall
George Walton

Column 2

North Carolina:
William Hooper
Joseph Hewes
John Penn

South Carolina:
Edward Rutledge
Thomas Heyward, Jr.
Thomas Lynch, Jr.
Arthur Middleton

Column 3

Massachusetts:
John Hancock

Maryland:
Samuel Chase
William Paca
Thomas Stone
Charles Carroll of Carrollton

Virginia:
George Wythe
Richard Henry Lee
Thomas Jefferson
Benjamin Harrison
Thomas Nelson, Jr.
Francis Lightfoot Lee
Carter Braxton

Column 4

Pennsylvania:
Robert Morris
Benjamin Rush
Benjamin Franklin
John Morton
George Clymer
James Smith
George Taylor
James Wilson
George Ross

Delaware:
Caesar Rodney
George Read
Thomas McKean

Column 5

New York:
William Floyd
Philip Livingston
Francis Lewis
Lewis Morris

New Jersey:
Richard Stockton
John Witherspoon
Francis Hopkinson
John Hart
Abraham Clark

Column 6

New Hampshire:
Josiah Bartlett
William Whipple

Massachusetts:
Samuel Adams
John Adams
Robert Treat Paine
Elbridge Gerry

Rhode Island:
Stephen Hopkins
William Ellery

Connecticut:
Roger Sherman
Samuel Huntington
William Williams
Oliver Wolcott

New Hampshire:
Matthew Thornton

For more information on the Declaration of Independence and the Charters of Freedom, see http://archives.gov/exhibits/charters/declaration.html

Constitution of the United States

Note: The following text is a transcription of the Constitution in its original form. Items that are underlined have since been amended or superseded.

Preamble

WE THE PEOPLE of the United States, in order to form a more perfect union, establish justice, insure domestic tranquility, provide for the common defense, promote the general welfare, and secure the blessings of liberty to ourselves and our posterity, do ordain and establish this Constitution for the United States of America.

Article I

Section 1. All legislative powers herein granted shall be vested in a Congress of the United States, which shall consist of a Senate and House of Representatives.

Section 2. The House of Representatives shall be composed of members chosen every second year by the people of the several states, and the electors in each state shall have the qualifications requisite for electors of the most numerous branch of the state legislature.

No person shall be a Representative who shall not have attained to the age of twenty five years, and been seven years a citizen of the United States, and who shall not, when elected, be an inhabitant of that state in which he shall be chosen.

Representatives and direct taxes shall be apportioned among the several states which may be included within this union, according to their respective numbers, which shall be determined by adding to the whole number of free persons, including those bound to service for a term of years, and excluding Indians not taxed, three fifths of all other Persons. The actual Enumeration shall be made within three years after the first meeting of the Congress of the United States, and within every subsequent term of ten years, in such manner as they shall by law direct. The number of Representatives shall not exceed one for every thirty thousand, but each state shall have at least one Representative; and until such enumeration shall be made, the state of New Hampshire shall be entitled to chuse three, Massachusetts eight, Rhode Island and Providence Plantations one, Connecticut five, New York six, New Jersey four, Pennsylvania eight, Delaware one, Maryland six, Virginia ten, North Carolina five, South Carolina five, and Georgia three.

When vacancies happen in the Representation from any state, the executive authority thereof shall issue writs of election to fill such vacancies.

The House of Representatives shall choose their speaker and other officers; and shall have the sole power of impeachment.

Section 3. The Senate of the United States shall be composed of two Senators from each state, chosen by the legislature thereof, for six years; and each Senator shall have one vote.

Immediately after they shall be assembled in consequence of the first election, they shall be divided as equally as may be into three classes. The seats of the Senators of the first class shall be vacated at the expiration of the second year, of the second class at the expiration of the fourth year, and the third class at the expiration of the sixth year, so that one third may be chosen every second year; and if vacancies happen by resignation, or otherwise, during the recess of the legislature of any state, the executive thereof may make temporary appointments until the next meeting of the legislature, which shall then fill such vacancies.

No person shall be a Senator who shall not have attained to the age of thirty years, and been nine years a citizen of the United States and who shall not, when elected, be an inhabitant of that state for which he shall be chosen.

The Vice President of the United States shall be President of the Senate, but shall have no vote, unless they be equally divided.

The Senate shall choose their other officers, and also a President pro tempore, in the absence of the Vice President, or when he shall exercise the office of President of the United States.

The Senate shall have the sole power to try all impeachments. When sitting for that purpose, they shall be on oath or affirmation. When the President of the United States is tried, the Chief Justice shall preside: And no person shall be convicted without the concurrence of two thirds of the members present.

Judgment in cases of impeachment shall not extend further than to removal from office, and disqualification to hold and enjoy any office of honor, trust or profit under the United States: but the party convicted shall nevertheless be liable and subject to indictment, trial, judgment and punishment, according to law.

Section 4. The times, places and manner of holding elections for Senators and Representatives, shall be prescribed in each state by the legislature thereof; but the Congress may at any time by law make or alter such regulations, except as to the places of choosing Senators.

The Congress shall assemble at least once in every year, and such meeting shall be on the first Monday in December, unless they shall by law appoint a different day.

Section 5. Each House shall be the judge of the elections, returns and qualifications of its own members, and a majority of each shall constitute a quorum to do business; but a smaller number may adjourn from day to day, and may be authorized to compel the attendance of absent members, in such manner, and under such penalties as each House may provide.

Each House may determine the rules of its proceedings, punish its members for disorderly behavior, and, with the concurrence of two thirds, expel a member.

Each House shall keep a journal of its proceedings, and from time to time publish the same, excepting such parts as may in their judgment require secrecy; and the yeas and nays of the members of either House on any question shall, at the desire of one fifth of those present, be entered on the journal.

Neither House, during the session of Congress, shall, without the consent of the other, adjourn for more than three days, nor to any other place than that in which the two Houses shall be sitting.

Section 6. The Senators and Representatives shall receive a compensation for their services, to be ascertained by law, and paid out of the treasury of the United States. They shall in all cases, except treason, felony and breach of the peace, be privileged from arrest during their attendance at the session of their respective Houses, and in going to and returning from the same; and for any speech or debate in either House, they shall not be questioned in any other place.

No Senator or Representative shall, during the time for which he was elected, be appointed to any civil office under the authority of the United States, which shall have been created, or the emoluments whereof shall have been increased during such time: and no person holding any office under the United States, shall be a member of either House during his continuance in office.

Section 7. All bills for raising revenue shall originate in the House of Representatives; but the Senate may propose or concur with amendments as on other Bills.

Every bill which shall have passed the House of Representatives and the Senate, shall, before it become a law, be presented to the President of the United States; if he approve he shall sign it, but if not he shall return it, with his objections to that House in which it shall have originated, who shall enter the objections at large on their journal, and proceed to reconsider it. If after such reconsideration two thirds of that House shall agree to pass the bill, it shall be sent, together with the objections, to the other House, by which it shall likewise be reconsidered, and if approved by two thirds of that House, it shall become a law. But in all such cases the votes of both Houses shall be determined by yeas and nays, and the names of the persons voting for and against the bill shall be entered on the journal of each House respectively. If any bill shall not be returned by the President within ten days (Sundays excepted) after it shall have been presented to him, the same shall be a law, in like manner as if he had signed it, unless the Congress by their adjournment prevent its return, in which case it shall not be a law.

Every order, resolution, or vote to which the concurrence of the Senate and House of Representatives may be necessary (except on a question of adjournment) shall be presented to the President of the United States; and before the same shall take effect, shall be approved by him, or being disapproved by him, shall be repassed by two thirds of the Senate and House of Representatives, according to the rules and limitations prescribed in the case of a bill.

Section 8. The Congress shall have power to lay and collect taxes, duties, imposts and excises, to pay the debts and provide for the common defense and general welfare of the United States; but all duties, imposts and excises shall be uniform throughout the United States;

To borrow money on the credit of the United States;

To regulate commerce with foreign nations, and among the several states, and with the Indian tribes;

To establish a uniform rule of naturalization, and uniform laws on the subject of bankruptcies throughout the United States;

To coin money, regulate the value thereof, and of foreign coin, and fix the standard of weights and measures;

To provide for the punishment of counterfeiting the securities and current coin of the United States;

To establish post offices and post roads;

To promote the progress of science and useful arts, by securing for limited times to authors and inventors the exclusive right to their respective writings and discoveries;

To constitute tribunals inferior to the Supreme Court;

To define and punish piracies and felonies committed on the high seas, and offenses against the law of nations;

To declare war, grant letters of marque and reprisal, and make rules concerning captures on land and water;

To raise and support armies, but no appropriation of money to that use shall be for a longer term than two years;

To provide and maintain a navy;

To make rules for the government and regulation of the land and naval forces;

To provide for calling forth the militia to execute the laws of the union, suppress insurrections and repel invasions;

To provide for organizing, arming, and disciplining, the militia, and for governing such part of them as may be employed in the service of the United States, reserving to the states respectively, the appointment of the officers, and the authority of training the militia according to the discipline prescribed by Congress;

To exercise exclusive legislation in all cases whatsoever, over such District (not exceeding ten miles square) as may, by cession of particular states, and the acceptance of Congress, become the seat of the government of the United States, and to exercise like authority over all places purchased by the consent of the legislature of the state in which the same shall be, for the erection of forts, magazines, arsenals, dockyards, and other needful buildings;—And

To make all laws which shall be necessary and proper for carrying into execution the foregoing powers, and all other powers vested by this Constitution in the government of the United States, or in any department or officer thereof.

Section 9. The migration or importation of such persons as any of the states now existing shall think proper to admit, shall not be prohibited by the Congress prior to the year one thousand eight hundred and eight, but a tax or duty may be imposed on such importation, not exceeding ten dollars for each person.

The privilege of the writ of habeas corpus shall not be suspended, unless when in cases of rebellion or invasion the public safety may require it.

No bill of attainder or ex post facto Law shall be passed.

No capitation, or other direct, tax shall be laid, unless in proportion to the census or enumeration herein before directed to be taken.

No tax or duty shall be laid on articles exported from any state.

No preference shall be given by any regulation of commerce or revenue to the ports of one state over those of another: nor shall vessels bound to, or from, one state, be obliged to enter, clear or pay duties in another.

No money shall be drawn from the treasury, but in consequence of appropriations made by law; and a regular statement and account of receipts and expenditures of all public money shall be published from time to time.

No title of nobility shall be granted by the United States: and no person holding any office of profit or trust under them, shall, without the consent of the Congress, accept of any present, emolument, office, or title, of any kind whatever, from any king, prince, or foreign state.

Section 10. No state shall enter into any treaty, alliance, or confederation; grant letters of marque and reprisal; coin money; emit bills of credit; make anything but gold and silver coin a tender in payment of debts; pass any bill of attainder, ex post facto law, or law impairing the obligation of contracts, or grant any title of nobility.

No state shall, without the consent of the Congress, lay any imposts or duties on imports or exports, except what may be absolutely necessary for executing it's inspection laws: and the net produce of all duties and imposts, laid by any state on imports or exports, shall be for the use of the treasury of the United States; and all such laws shall be subject to the revision and control of the Congress.

No state shall, without the consent of Congress, lay any duty of tonnage, keep troops, or ships of war in time of peace, enter into any agreement or compact with another state, or with a foreign power, or engage in war, unless actually invaded, or in such imminent danger as will not admit of delay.

Article II

Section 1. The executive power shall be vested in a President of the United States of America. He shall hold his office during the term of four years, and, together with the Vice President, chosen for the same term, be elected, as follows:

Each state shall appoint, in such manner as the Legislature thereof may direct, a number of electors, equal to the whole number of Senators and Representatives to which the State may be entitled in the Congress: but no Senator or Representative, or person holding an office of trust or profit under the United States, shall be appointed an elector.

The electors shall meet in their respective states, and vote by ballot for two persons, of whom one at least shall not be an inhabitant of the same state with themselves. And they shall make a list of all the persons voted for, and of the number of votes for each; which list they shall sign and certify, and transmit sealed to the seat of the government of the United States, directed to the President of the Senate. The President of the Senate shall, in the presence of the Senate and House of Representatives, open all the certificates, and the votes shall then be counted. The person having the greatest number of votes shall be the President, if such number be a majority of the whole number of electors appointed; and if there be more than one who have such majority, and have an equal number of votes, then the House of Representatives shall immediately choose by ballot one of them for President; and if no person have a majority, then from the five highest on the list the said House shall in like manner choose the President. But in choosing the President, the votes shall be taken by States, the representation from each state having one vote; A quorum for this purpose shall consist of a member or members from two thirds of the states, and a majority of all the states shall be necessary to a choice. In every case, after the choice of the President, the person having the greatest number of votes of the electors shall be the Vice President. But if there should remain two or more who have equal votes, the Senate shall choose from them by ballot the Vice President.

The Congress may determine the time of choosing the electors, and the day on which they shall give their votes; which day shall be the same throughout the United States.

No person except a natural born citizen, or a citizen of the United States, at the time of the adoption of this Constitution, shall be eligible to the office of President; neither shall any person be eligible to that office who shall not have attained to the age of thirty five years, and been fourteen Years a resident within the United States.

In case of the removal of the President from office, or of his death, resignation, or inability to discharge the powers and duties of the said office, the same shall devolve on the Vice President, and the Congress may by law provide for the case of removal, death, resignation or inability, both of the President and Vice President, declaring what officer shall then act as President, and such officer shall act accordingly, until the disability be removed, or a President shall be elected.

The President shall, at stated times, receive for his services, a compensation, which shall neither be increased nor diminished during the period for which he shall have been elected, and he shall not receive within that period any other emolument from the United States, or any of them.

Before he enter on the execution of his office, he shall take the following oath or affirmation:—"I do solemnly swear (or affirm) that I will faithfully execute the office of President of the United States, and will to the best of my ability, preserve, protect and defend the Constitution of the United States."

Section 2. The President shall be commander in chief of the Army and Navy of the United States, and of the militia of the several states, when called into the actual service of the United States; he may require the opinion, in writing, of the principal officer in each of the executive departments, upon any subject relating to the duties of their respective offices, and he shall have power to grant reprieves and pardons for offenses against the United States, except in cases of impeachment.

He shall have power, by and with the advice and consent of the Senate, to make treaties, provided two thirds of the Senators present concur; and he shall nominate, and by and with the advice and consent of the Senate, shall appoint ambassadors, other public ministers and consuls, judges of the Supreme Court, and all other officers of the United States, whose appointments are not herein otherwise provided for, and which shall be established by law: but the Congress may by law vest the appointment of such inferior officers, as they think proper, in the President alone, in the courts of law, or in the heads of departments.

The President shall have power to fill up all vacancies that may happen during the recess of the Senate, by granting commissions which shall expire at the end of their next session.

Section 3. He shall from time to time give to the Congress information of the state of the union, and recommend to their consideration such measures as he shall judge necessary and expedient; he may, on extraordinary occasions, convene both Houses, or either of them, and in case of disagreement between them, with respect to the time of adjournment, he may adjourn them to such time as he shall think proper; he shall receive ambassadors and other public ministers; he shall take care that the laws be faithfully executed, and shall commission all the officers of the United States.

Section 4. The President, Vice President and all civil officers of the United States, shall be removed from office on impeachment for, and conviction of, treason, bribery, or other high crimes and misdemeanors.

Article III

Section 1. The judicial power of the United States, shall be vested in one Supreme Court, and in such inferior courts as the Congress may from time to time ordain and establish. The judges, both of the supreme and inferior courts, shall hold their offices during good behaviour, and shall, at stated times, receive for their services, a compensation, which shall not be diminished during their continuance in office.

Section 2. The judicial power shall extend to all cases, in law and equity, arising under this Constitution, the laws of the United States, and treaties made, or which shall be made, under their authority;—to all cases affecting ambassadors, other public ministers and consuls;—to all cases of admiralty and maritime jurisdiction;—to controversies to which the United States shall be a party;—to controversies between two or more states;—between a state and citizens of another state;—between citizens of different states;—between citizens of the same state claiming lands under grants of different states, and between a state, or the citizens thereof, and foreign states, citizens or subjects.

In all cases affecting ambassadors, other public ministers and consuls, and those in which a state shall be party, the Supreme Court shall have original jurisdiction. In all the other cases before mentioned, the Supreme Court shall have appellate jurisdiction, both as to law and fact, with such exceptions, and under such regulations as the Congress shall make.

The trial of all crimes, except in cases of impeachment, shall be by jury; and such trial shall be held in the state where the said crimes shall have been committed; but when not committed within any state, the trial shall be at such place or places as the Congress may by law have directed.

Section 3. Treason against the United States, shall consist only in levying war against them, or in adhering to their enemies, giving them aid and comfort. No person shall be convicted of treason unless on the testimony of two witnesses to the same overt act, or on confession in open court.

The Congress shall have power to declare the punishment of treason, but no attainder of treason shall work corruption of blood, or forfeiture except during the life of the person attainted.

Article IV

Section 1. Full faith and credit shall be given in each state to the public acts, records, and judicial proceedings of every other state. And the Congress may by general laws prescribe the manner in which such acts, records, and proceedings shall be proved, and the effect thereof.

Section 2. The citizens of each state shall be entitled to all privileges and immunities of citizens in the several states.

A person charged in any state with treason, felony, or other crime, who shall flee from justice, and be found in another state, shall on demand of the executive authority of the state from which he fled, be delivered up, to be removed to the state having jurisdiction of the crime.

No person held to service or labor in one state, under the laws thereof, escaping into another, shall, in consequence of any law or regulation therein, be discharged from such service or labor, but shall be delivered up on claim of the party to whom such service or labor may be due.

Section 3. New states may be admitted by the Congress into this union; but no new states shall be formed or erected within the jurisdiction of any other state; nor any state be formed by the junction of two or more states, or parts of states, without the consent of the legislatures of the states concerned as well as of the Congress.

The Congress shall have power to dispose of and make all needful rules and regulations respecting the territory or other property belonging to the United States; and nothing in this Constitution shall be so construed as to prejudice any claims of the United States, or of any particular state.

Section 4. The United States shall guarantee to every state in this union a republican form of government, and shall protect each of them against invasion; and on application of the legislature, or of the executive (when the legislature cannot be convened) against domestic violence.

Article V

The Congress, whenever two thirds of both houses shall deem it necessary, shall propose amendments to this Constitution, or, on the application of the legislatures of two thirds of the several states, shall call a convention for proposing amendments, which, in either case, shall be valid to all intents and purposes, as part of this Constitution, when ratified by the legislatures of three fourths of the several states, or by conventions in three fourths thereof, as the one or the other mode of ratification may be proposed by the Congress; provided that no amendment which may be made prior to the year one thousand eight hundred and eight shall in any manner affect the first and fourth clauses in the ninth section of the first article; and that no state, without its consent, shall be deprived of its equal suffrage in the Senate.

Article VI

All debts contracted and engagements entered into, before the adoption of this Constitution, shall be as valid against the United States under this Constitution, as under the Confederation.

This Constitution, and the laws of the United States which shall be made in pursuance thereof; and all treaties made, or which shall be made, under the authority of the United States, shall be the supreme law of the land; and the judges in every state shall be bound thereby, anything in the Constitution or laws of any State to the contrary notwithstanding.

The Senators and Representatives before mentioned, and the members of the several state legislatures, and all executive and judicial officers, both of the United States and of the several states, shall be bound by oath or affirmation, to support this Constitution; but no religious test shall ever be required as a qualification to any office or public trust under the United States.

Article VII

The ratification of the conventions of nine states, shall be sufficient for the establishment of this Constitution between the states so ratifying the same.

Signers

Done in convention by the unanimous consent of the states present the seventeenth day of September in the year of our Lord one thousand seven hundred and eighty seven and of the independence of the United States of America the twelfth. *In witness whereof We have hereunto subscribed our Names,*

G^{o} Washington—Presid^{t}
and deputy from Virginia

New Hampshire	John Langdon Nicholas Gilman
Massachusetts	Nathaniel Gorham Rufus King
Connecticut	W^{m}: Saml Johnson Roger Sherman
New York	Alexander Hamilton
New Jersey	Wil: Livingston David Brearly Wm Paterson Jona: Dayton
Pennsylvania	B. Franklin Thomas Mifflin Robt Morris Geo. Clymer

	Thos FitzSimons Jared Ingersoll James Wilson Gouv Morris
Delaware	Geo: Read Gunning Bedford jun John Dickinson Richard Bassett Jaco: Broom
Maryland	James McHenry Dan of St Thos Jenifer Danl Carroll
Virginia	John Blair— James Madison Jr.
North Carolina	Wm Blount Richd Dobbs Spaight Hu Williamson
South Carolina	J. Rutledge Charles Cotesworth Pinckney Charles Pinckney Pierce Butler
Georgia	William Few Abr Baldwin

Amendments

Note: The first ten Amendments were ratified December 15, 1791, and form what is known as the Bill of Rights.

Amendment 1

Congress shall make no law respecting an establishment of religion, or prohibiting the free exercise thereof; or abridging the freedom of speech, or of the press; or the right of the people peaceably to assemble, and to petition the government for a redress of grievances.

Amendment 2

A well regulated militia, being necessary to the security of a free state, the right of the people to keep and bear arms, shall not be infringed.

Amendment 3

No soldier shall, in time of peace be quartered in any house, without the consent of the owner, nor in time of war, but in a manner to be prescribed by law.

Amendment 4

The right of the people to be secure in their persons, houses, papers, and effects, against unreasonable searches and seizures, shall not be violated, and no warrants shall issue, but upon probable cause, supported by oath or affirmation, and particularly describing the place to be searched, and the persons or things to be seized.

Amendment 5

No person shall be held to answer for a capital, or otherwise infamous crime, unless on a presentment or indictment of a grand jury, except in cases arising in the land or naval forces, or in the militia, when in actual service in time of war or public danger; nor shall any person be subject for the same offense to be twice put in jeopardy of life or limb; nor shall be compelled in any criminal case to be a witness against himself, nor be deprived of life, liberty, or property, without due process of law; nor shall private property be taken for public use, without just compensation.

Amendment 6

In all criminal prosecutions, the accused shall enjoy the right to a speedy and public trial, by an impartial jury of the state and district wherein the crime shall have been committed, which district shall have been previously ascertained by law, and to be informed of the nature and cause of the accusation; to be confronted with the witnesses against him; to have compulsory process for obtaining witnesses in his favor, and to have the assistance of counsel for his defense.

Amendment 7

In suits at common law, where the value in controversy shall exceed twenty dollars, the right of trial by jury shall be preserved, and no fact tried by a jury, shall be otherwise reexamined in any court of the United States, than according to the rules of the common law.

Amendment 8

Excessive bail shall not be required, nor excessive fines imposed, nor cruel and unusual punishments inflicted.

Amendment 9

The enumeration in the Constitution, of certain rights, shall not be construed to deny or disparage others retained by the people.

Amendment 10

The powers not delegated to the United States by the Constitution, nor prohibited by it to the states, are reserved to the states respectively, or to the people.

Amendment 11

(Ratified February 7, 1795)

The judicial power of the United States shall not be construed to extend to any suit in law or equity, commenced or prosecuted against one of the United States by citizens of another state, or by citizens or subjects of any foreign state.

Amendment 12

(Ratified July 27, 1804)

The electors shall meet in their respective states and vote by ballot for President and Vice-President, one of whom, at least, shall not be an inhabitant of the same state with themselves; they shall name in their ballots the person voted for as President, and in distinct ballots the person voted for as Vice-President, and they shall make distinct lists of all persons voted for as President, and of all persons voted for as Vice-President, and of the number of votes for each, which lists they shall sign and certify, and transmit sealed to the seat of the government of the United States, directed to the President of the Senate;—The President of the Senate shall, in the presence of the Senate and House of Representatives, open all the certificates and the votes shall then be counted;—the person having the greatest number of votes for President, shall be the President, if such number be a majority of the whole number of electors appointed; and if no person have such majority, then from the persons having the highest numbers not exceeding three on the list of those voted for as President, the House of Representatives shall choose immediately, by ballot, the President. But in choosing the President, the votes shall be taken by states, the representation from each state having one vote; a quorum for this purpose shall consist of a member or members from two-thirds of the states, and a majority of all the states shall be necessary to a choice. And if the House of Representatives shall not choose a President whenever the right of choice shall devolve upon them, before the fourth day of March next following, then the Vice-President shall act as President, as in the case of the death or other constitutional disability of the President. The person having the greatest number of votes as Vice-President, shall be the Vice-President, if such number be a majority of the whole number of electors appointed, and if no person have a majority, then from the two highest numbers on the list, the Senate shall choose the Vice-President; a quorum for the purpose shall consist of two-thirds of the whole number of Senators, and a majority of the whole number shall be necessary to a choice. But no person constitutionally ineligible to the office of President shall be eligible to that of Vice-President of the United States.

Amendment 13

(Ratified December 6, 1865)

Section 1. Neither slavery nor involuntary servitude, except as a punishment for crime whereof the party shall have been duly convicted, shall exist within the United States, or any place subject to their jurisdiction.

Section 2. Congress shall have power to enforce this article by appropriate legislation.

Amendment 14

(Ratified July 9, 1868)

Section 1. All persons born or naturalized in the United States, and subject to the jurisdiction thereof, are citizens of the United States and of the state wherein they reside. No state shall make or enforce any law which shall abridge the privileges or immunities of citizens of the United States; nor shall any state deprive any person of life, liberty, or property, without due process of law; nor deny to any person within its jurisdiction the equal protection of the laws.

Section 2. Representatives shall be apportioned among the several states according to their respective numbers, counting the whole number of persons in each state, excluding Indians not taxed. But when the right to vote at any election for the choice of electors for President and Vice President of the United States, Representatives in Congress, the executive and judicial officers of a state, or the members of the legislature thereof, is denied to any of the male inhabitants of such state, being twenty-one years of age, and citizens of the United States, or in any way abridged, except for participation in rebellion, or other crime, the basis of representation therein shall be reduced in the proportion which the number of such male citizens shall bear to the whole number of male citizens twenty-one years of age in such state.

Section 3. No person shall be a Senator or Representative in Congress, or elector of President and Vice President, or hold any office, civil or military, under the United States, or under any state, who, having previously taken an oath, as a member of Congress, or as an officer of the United States, or as a member of any state legislature, or as an executive or judicial officer of any state, to support the Constitution of the United States, shall have engaged in insurrection or rebellion against the same, or given aid or comfort to the enemies thereof. But Congress may by a vote of two-thirds of each House, remove such disability.

Section 4. The validity of the public debt of the United States, authorized by law, including debts incurred for payment of pensions and bounties for services in suppressing insurrection or rebellion, shall not be questioned. But neither the United States nor any state shall assume or pay any debt or obligation incurred in aid of insurrection or rebellion against the United States, or any claim for the loss or emancipation of any slave; but all such debts, obligations and claims shall be held illegal and void.

Section 5. The Congress shall have power to enforce, by appropriate legislation, the provisions of this article.

Amendment 15

(Ratified February 3, 1870)

Section 1. The right of citizens of the United States to vote shall not be denied or abridged by the United States or by any state on account of race, color, or previous condition of servitude.

Section 2. The Congress shall have power to enforce this article by appropriate legislation.

Amendment 16

(Ratified February 3, 1913)

The Congress shall have power to lay and collect taxes on incomes, from whatever source derived, without apportionment among the several states, and without regard to any census or enumeration.

Amendment 17

(Ratified April 8, 1913)

The Senate of the United States shall be composed of two Senators from each state, elected by the people thereof, for six years; and each Senator shall have one vote. The electors in each state shall have the qualifications requisite for electors of the most numerous branch of the state legislatures.

When vacancies happen in the representation of any state in the Senate, the executive authority of such state shall issue writs of election to fill such vacancies: Provided, that the legislature of any state may empower the executive thereof to make temporary appointments until the people fill the vacancies by election as the legislature may direct.

This amendment shall not be so construed as to affect the election or term of any Senator chosen before it becomes valid as part of the Constitution.

Amendment 18

(Ratified January 16, 1919. Repealed December 5, 1933 by Amendment 21)

Section 1. After one year from the ratification of this article the manufacture, sale, or transportation of intoxicating liquors within, the importation thereof into, or the exportation thereof from the United States and all territory subject to the jurisdiction thereof for beverage purposes is hereby prohibited.

Section 2. The Congress and the several states shall have concurrent power to enforce this article by appropriate legislation.

Section 3. This article shall be inoperative unless it shall have been ratified as an amendment to the Constitution by the legislatures of the several states, as provided in the Constitution, within seven years from the date of the submission hereof to the states by the Congress.

Amendment 19

(Ratified August 18, 1920)

The right of citizens of the United States to vote shall not be denied or abridged by the United States or by any state on account of sex.

Congress shall have power to enforce this article by appropriate legislation.

Amendment 20

(Ratified January 23, 1933)

Section 1. The terms of the President and Vice President shall end at noon on the 20th day of January, and the terms of Senators and Representatives at noon on the 3d day of January, of the years in which such terms would have ended if this article had not been ratified; and the terms of their successors shall then begin.

Section 2. The Congress shall assemble at least once in every year, and such meeting shall begin at noon on the 3d day of January, unless they shall by law appoint a different day.

Section 3. If, at the time fixed for the beginning of the term of the President, the President elect shall have died, the Vice President elect shall become President. If a President shall not have been chosen before the time fixed for the beginning of his term, or if the President elect shall have failed to qualify, then the Vice President elect shall act as President until a President shall have qualified; and the Congress may by law provide for the case wherein neither a President elect nor a Vice President elect shall have qualified, declaring who shall then act as President, or the manner in which one who is to act shall be selected, and such person shall act accordingly until a President or Vice President shall have qualified.

Section 4. The Congress may by law provide for the case of the death of any of the persons from whom the House of Representatives may choose a President whenever the right of choice shall have devolved upon them, and for the case of the death of any of the persons from whom the Senate may choose a Vice President whenever the right of choice shall have devolved upon them.

Section 5. Sections 1 and 2 shall take effect on the 15th day of October following the ratification of this article.

Section 6. This article shall be inoperative unless it shall have been ratified as an amendment to the Constitution by the legislatures of three-fourths of the several states within seven years from the date of its submission.

Amendment 21

(Ratified December 5, 1933)

Section 1. The eighteenth article of amendment to the Constitution of the United States is hereby repealed.

Section 2. The transportation or importation into any state, territory, or possession of the United States for delivery or use therein of intoxicating liquors, in violation of the laws thereof, is hereby prohibited.

Section 3. This article shall be inoperative unless it shall have been ratified as an amendment to the Constitution by conventions in the several states, as provided in the Constitution, within seven years from the date of the submission hereof to the states by the Congress.

Amendment 22

(Ratified February 27, 1951)

Section 1. No person shall be elected to the office of the President more than twice, and no person who has held the office of President, or acted as President, for more than two years of a term to which some other person was elected President shall be elected to the office of the President more than once. But this article shall not apply to any person holding the office of President when this article was proposed by the Congress, and shall not prevent any person who may be holding the office of President, or acting as President, during the term within which this article becomes operative from holding the office of President or acting as President during the remainder of such term.

Section 2. This article shall be inoperative unless it shall have been ratified as an amendment to the Constitution by the legislatures of three-fourths of the several states within seven years from the date of its submission to the states by the Congress.

Amendment 23

(Ratified March 29, 1961)

Section 1. The District constituting the seat of government of the United States shall appoint in such manner as the Congress may direct:

A number of electors of President and Vice President equal to the whole number of Senators and Representatives in Congress to which the District would be entitled if it were a state, but in no event more than the least populous state; they shall be in addition to those appointed by the states, but they shall be considered, for the purposes of the election of President and Vice President, to be electors appointed by a state; and they shall meet in the District and perform such duties as provided by the twelfth article of amendment.

Section 2. The Congress shall have power to enforce this article by appropriate legislation.

Amendment 24

(Ratified January 23, 1964)

Section 1. The right of citizens of the United States to vote in any primary or other election for President or Vice President, for electors for President or Vice President, or for Senator or Representative in Congress, shall not be denied or abridged by the United States or any state by reason of failure to pay any poll tax or other tax.

Section 2. The Congress shall have power to enforce this article by appropriate legislation.

Amendment 25

(Ratified February 10, 1967)

Section 1. In case of the removal of the President from office or of his death or resignation, the Vice President shall become President.

Section 2. Whenever there is a vacancy in the office of the Vice President, the President shall nominate a Vice President who shall take office upon confirmation by a majority vote of both Houses of Congress.

Section 3. Whenever the President transmits to the President pro tempore of the Senate and the Speaker of the House of Representatives his written declaration that he is unable to discharge the powers and duties of his office, and until he transmits to them a written declaration to the contrary, such powers and duties shall be discharged by the Vice President as Acting President.

Section 4. Whenever the Vice President and a majority of either the principal officers of the executive departments or of such other body as Congress may by law provide, transmit to the President pro tempore of the Senate and the Speaker of the House of Representatives their written declaration that the President is unable to discharge the powers and duties of his office, the Vice President shall immediately assume the powers and duties of the office as Acting President.

Thereafter, when the President transmits to the President pro tempore of the Senate and the Speaker of the House of Representatives his written declaration that no inability exists, he shall resume the powers and duties of his office unless the Vice President and a majority of either the principal officers of the executive department or of such other body as Congress may by law provide, transmit within four days to the President pro tempore of the Senate and the Speaker of the House of Representatives their written declaration that the President is unable to discharge the powers and duties of his office. Thereupon Congress shall decide the issue, assembling within forty-eight hours for that purpose if not in session. If the Congress, within twenty-one days after receipt of the latter written declaration, or, if Congress is not in session, within twenty-one days after Congress is required to assemble, determines by two-thirds vote of both Houses that the President is unable to discharge the powers and duties of his office, the Vice President shall continue to discharge the same as Acting President; otherwise, the President shall resume the powers and duties of his office.

Amendment 26

(Ratified July 1, 1971)

Section 1. The right of citizens of the United States, who are 18 years of age or older, to vote, shall not be denied or abridged by the United States or any state on account of age.

Section 2. The Congress shall have the power to enforce this article by appropriate legislation.

Amendment 27

(Ratified May 7, 1992)

No law, varying the compensation for the services of the Senators and Representatives, shall take effect, until an election of Representatives shall have intervened.

For more information on the Constitution of the United States and the Charters of Freedom, see http://archives.gov/exhibits/charters/constitution.html

THE GOVERNMENT OF THE UNITED STATES

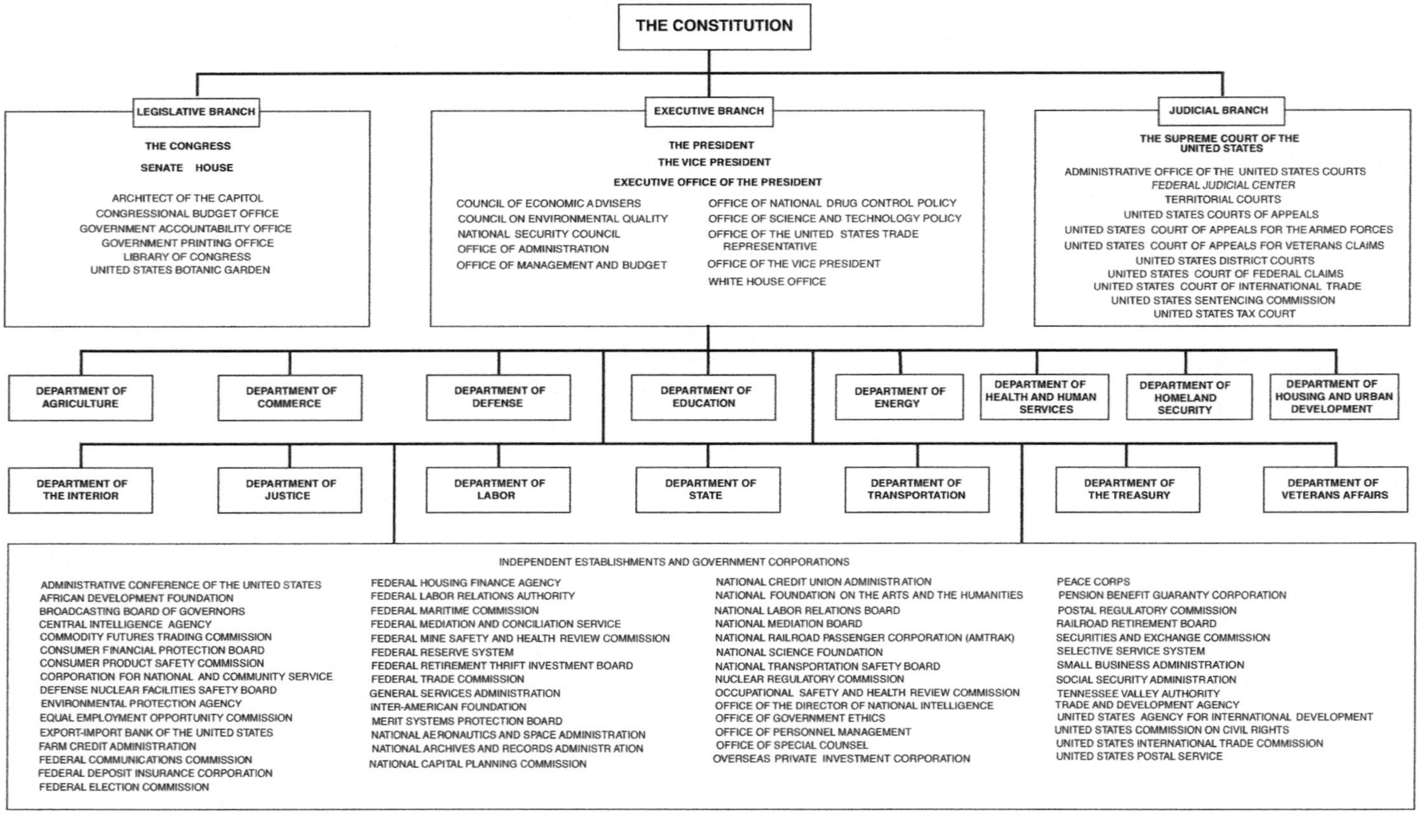

Legislative Branch

Congress

One Hundred and Thirteenth Congress, Second Session

The Congress of the United States was created by Article I, section 1, of the Constitution, adopted by the Constitutional Convention on September 17, 1787, providing that "All legislative Powers herein granted shall be vested in a Congress of the United States, which shall consist of a Senate and House of Representatives."

The first Congress under the Constitution met on March 4, 1789, in the Federal Hall in New York City. The membership then consisted of 20 Senators and 59 Representatives. [1]

Congressional Record

Proceedings of Congress are published in the Congressional Record, which is issued each day when Congress is in session. Publication of the Record began March 4, 1873. It was the first record of debate officially reported, printed, and published directly by the Federal Government. The Daily Digest of the Congressional Record, printed in the back of each issue of the Record, summarizes the proceedings of that day in each House and each of their committees and subcommittees, respectively. The Digest also presents the legislative program for each day and, at the end of the week, gives the program for the following week. Its publication was begun March 17, 1947.

Sessions

Section 4 of Article I of the Constitution makes it mandatory that "The Congress shall assemble at least once in every Year. . . ." Under this provision, also, the date for convening Congress was designated originally as the first Monday in December, "unless they shall by Law appoint a different Day." Eighteen acts were passed, up to 1820, providing for the meeting of Congress on other days of the year. From 1820 to 1934, however, Congress met regularly on the first Monday in December. In 1934 the 20th amendment changed the convening of Congress to January 3, unless Congress "shall by law appoint a different day." In addition, the President, according to Article II, section 3, of the Constitution "may, on extraordinary Occasions, convene both Houses, or either of them, and in Case of Disagreement between them, with Respect to the Time of Adjournment, he may adjourn them to such Time as he shall think proper. . . ."

Powers of Congress

Article I, section 8, of the Constitution defines the powers of Congress. Included are the powers to assess and collect taxes—called the chief power; to regulate commerce, both interstate and foreign; to coin money; to establish post offices and post roads; to establish courts inferior to the Supreme Court; to declare war; and to raise and maintain an army and navy. Congress is further empowered "To provide for calling forth the Militia to execute the Laws of the Union, suppress Insurrections and repel Invasions;" and "To make all Laws which shall be necessary and proper for carrying into Execution the foregoing Powers, and all other Powers vested by this Constitution in the Government of the United States, or in any Department or Officer thereof."

Amendments to the Constitution

Another power vested in the Congress is the right to propose amendments to the Constitution, whenever two-thirds of both Houses shall deem it necessary. Should two-thirds of the State legislatures demand changes in the Constitution, it is the duty of Congress to call a constitutional convention. Proposed amendments shall be valid as part of the Constitution when ratified by the legislatures or by conventions of three-fourths of the States, as one or the other mode of ratification may be proposed by Congress.

1. New York ratified the Constitution on July 26, 1788, but did not elect its Senators until July 15 and 16, 1789. North Carolina did not ratify the Constitution until November 21, 1789; Rhode Island ratified it on May 29, 1790.

Prohibitions Upon Congress

Section 9 of Article I of the Constitution also imposes prohibitions upon Congress. "The Privilege of the Writ of Habeas Corpus shall not be suspended, unless when in Cases of Rebellion or Invasion the public Safety may require it." A bill of attainder or an ex post facto law cannot be passed. No export duty can be imposed. Ports of one State cannot be given preference over those of another State. "No money shall be drawn from the Treasury, but in Consequence of Appropriations made by Law. . . ." No title of nobility may be granted.

Rights of Members

According to section 6 of Article I, Members of Congress are granted certain privileges. In no case, except in treason, felony, and breach of the peace, can Members be arrested while attending sessions of Congress "and in going to and returning from the same. . . ." Furthermore, the Members cannot be questioned in any other place for remarks made in Congress. Each House may expel a Member of its body by a two-thirds vote.

Enactment of Laws

In order to become law, all bills and joint resolutions, except those proposing a constitutional amendment, must pass both the House of Representatives and the Senate and either be signed by the President or be passed over the President's veto by a two-thirds vote of both Houses of Congress. Section 7 of Article I states: "If any Bill shall not be returned by the President within ten Days (Sundays excepted) after it shall have been presented to him, the Same shall be a Law, in like Manner as if he had signed it, unless the Congress by their Adjournment prevent its Return, in which Case it shall not be a Law." When a bill or joint resolution is introduced in the House, the usual procedure for its enactment into law is as follows: assignment to House committee having jurisdiction; if favorably considered, it is reported to the House either in its original form or with recommended amendments; if the bill or resolution is passed by the House, it is messaged to the Senate and referred to the committee having jurisdiction; in the Senate committee the bill, if favorably considered, may be reported in the form as received from the House, or with recommended amendments; the approved bill or resolution is reported to the Senate, and if passed by that body, is returned to the House; if one body does not accept the amendments to a bill by the other body, a conference committee comprised of Members of both bodies is usually appointed to effect a compromise; when the bill or joint resolution is finally approved by both Houses, it is signed by the Speaker (or Speaker pro tempore) and the Vice President (or President pro tempore or acting President pro tempore) and is presented to the President; and once the President's signature is affixed, the measure becomes a law. If the President vetoes the bill, it cannot become a law unless it is re-passed by a two-thirds vote of both Houses.

The Senate

The Capitol, Washington, DC 20510

202-224-3121, *http://www.senate.gov*

PRESIDENT OF THE SENATE / VICE PRESIDENT OF THE UNITED STATES	Michael R. Pence
President pro tempore	Orrin G. Hatch
Majority Leader	Mitch McConnell
Assistant Majority Leader	John Cornyn
Minority Leader	Charles E. Schumer
Assistant Minority Leader	Patty Murray
Secretary of the Senate	Julie E. Adams
Sergeant at Arms	Frank J. Larkin
Secretary for the Majority	Laura C. Dove
Secretary for the Minority	Gary B. Myrick
Chaplain	Barry C. Black

Overview

The Senate comprises 100 Members, 2 from each State. Senators are elected to serve for a term of 6 years. There are three classes of Senators, and a new class is elected every 2 years. Senators were originally chosen by the State legislatures. The 17th amendment, which became part of the Constitution in 1913, made their election a function of the people.

A Senator must be a resident of the State that he or she represents. A Senator also must be at least 30 years of age and have been a U.S. citizen for at least 9 years.

Officers

The Vice President of the United States is the Presiding Officer of the Senate. In the Vice President's absence, the duties are taken over by a President pro tempore, elected by that body, or someone designated by the President pro tempore.

The positions of Senate Majority and Minority Leader have been in existence only since the early years of the 20th century. Leaders are elected at the beginning of each new Congress by a majority vote of the Senators in their political party. In cooperation with their party organizations, Leaders are responsible for the design and achievement of a legislative program. This involves managing the flow of legislation, expediting noncontroversial measures, and keeping Members informed regarding proposed action on pending business. Each Leader serves as an ex officio member of his party's policymaking and organizational bodies and is aided by an assistant floor leader (whip) and a party secretary.

The Secretary of the Senate, elected by vote of the Senate, performs the duties of the Presiding Officer of the Senate in the absence of the Vice President and pending the election of a President pro tempore. The Secretary is the custodian of the seal of the Senate, draws requisitions on the Secretary of the Treasury for moneys appropriated for the compensation of Senators, officers, and employees, and for the contingent expenses of the Senate, and is empowered to administer oaths to any officer of the Senate and to any witness produced before it. The Secretary's executive duties include certification of extracts from the Journal of the Senate; the attestation of bills and joint, concurrent, and Senate resolutions; in impeachment trials, issuance, under the authority of the Presiding Officer, of all orders, mandates, writs, and precepts authorized by the Senate; and certification to the President of the United States of the advice and consent of the Senate to ratification of treaties and the names of persons confirmed or rejected upon the nomination of the President.

The Sergeant at Arms, elected by vote of the Senate, serves as the executive, chief law enforcement, and protocol officer and is the principal administrative manager for most support services in the Senate. As executive officer, the Sergeant at Arms has custody of the Senate gavel; enforces Senate rules and regulations as they pertain to the Senate Chamber, the Senate wing of the Capitol, and the Senate office buildings; and subject to the Presiding Officer, maintains order on the Senate floor, Chamber, and galleries. As chief law enforcement officer of the Senate, the Sergeant at Arms is authorized to maintain security in the Capitol and all Senate buildings, as well as to protect Senators; to arrest and detain any person violating Senate rules; and to locate absentee Senators for a quorum. The Sergeant at Arms serves as a member of the Capitol Police Board and as its chairman each odd year. As protocol officer, the Sergeant at Arms escorts the President and other heads of state or official guests of the Senate who are attending official functions in the Capitol; makes arrangements for funerals of Senators who die in office; and assists in planning the inauguration of the President and organizing the swearing-in and orientation programs for newly elected Senators.

Committees

The work of preparing and considering legislation is done largely by committees of both Houses of Congress. There are 16 standing committees in the Senate. The standing committees of the Senate are shown in the list below. In addition, there are two select committees in each House and various congressional commissions and joint committees composed of Members of both Houses. Each House may also appoint special investigating committees. The membership of the standing committees of each House is chosen by a vote of the entire body; members of other committees are appointed under the provisions of the measure establishing them.

Each bill and resolution is usually referred to the appropriate committee, which may report a bill out in its original form, favorably or unfavorably, recommend amendments, report original measures, or allow the proposed legislation to die in committee without action.

Standing Committees of the Senate

Senate Committee	**Room**
Agriculture, Nutrition, and Forestry	SR328A
Appropriations	S128
Armed Services	SR228
Banking, Housing, and Urban Affairs	SD534
Budget	SD624
Commerce, Science, and Transportation	SD512
Energy and Natural Resources	SD304
Environment and Public Works	SD410
Finance	SD219
Foreign Relations	SD423
Health, Education, Labor, and Pensions	SD428
Homeland Security and Governmental Affairs	SD340
Judiciary	SD224
Rules and Administration	SR305
Small Business and Entrepreneurship	SR428A
Veterans' Affairs	SR412

Rooms are in the Senate wing of the Capitol Building if preceded by S, in the Dirksen Office Building if preceded by SD, and in the Russell Office Building if preceded by SR.

Special Powers

Under the Constitution, the Senate is granted certain powers not accorded to the House of Representatives. The Senate approves or disapproves certain Presidential appointments by majority vote, and treaties must be concurred in by a two-thirds vote.

Senators

Name	State	Room
Alexander, Lamar (R)	Tennessee	SD455
Ayotte, Kelly A. (R)	New Hampshire	SR144
Baldwin, Tammy (D)	Wisconsin	SH717
Barrasso, John A. (R)	Wyoming	SD307
Bennet, Michael F. (D)	Colorado	SR261
Blumenthal, Richard (D)	Connecticut	SH706
Blunt, Roy (R)	Missouri	SR260
Booker, Cory A. (D)	New Jersey	SD359
Boozman, John (R)	Arkansas	SH141
Boxer, Barbara (D)	California	SH112
Brown, Sherrod (D)	Ohio	SH713
Burr, Richard (R)	North Carolina	SR217
Cantwell, Maria (D)	Washington	SH511
Capito, Shelley Moore (R)	West Virginia	SR172
Cardin, Benjamin L. (D)	Maryland	SH509
Carper, Thomas R. (D)	Delaware	SH513
Casey, Robert P., Jr. (D)	Pennsylvania	SR393
Cassidy, Bill (R)	Louisiana	SH703
Coats, Daniel (R)	Indiana	SR493
Cochran, Thad (R)	Mississippi	SD113
Collins, Susan M. (R)	Maine	SD413
Coons, Christopher A. (D)	Delaware	SR127A
Corker, Bob (R)	Tennessee	SD425
Cornyn, John (R)	Texas	SH517
Cotton, Tom (R)	Arkansas	SR124
Crapo, Mike (R)	Idaho	SD239
Cruz, Ted (R)	Texas	SR404
Daines, Steve (R)	Montana	SH320
Donnelly, Joe (D)	Indiana	SH720
Durbin, Richard J. (D)	Illinois	SH711
Enzi, Michael B. (R)	Wyoming	SR379A
Ernst, Joni (R)	Iowa	SR111
Feinstein, Dianne (D)	California	SH331
Fischer, Deb (R)	Nebraska	SR454
Flake, Jeff (R)	Arizona	SR413
Franken, Al (D)	Minnesota	SH309
Gardner, Cory (R)	Colorado	SR354
Gillibrand, Kirsten E. (D)	New York	SR478
Graham, Lindsey (R)	South Carolina	SR290
Grassley, Chuck (R)	Iowa	SH135

Name	State	Room
Hatch, Orrin G. (R)	Utah	SH104
Heinrich, Martin (D)	New Mexico	SH303
Heitkamp, Heidi (D)	North Dakota	SH110
Heller, Dean (R)	Nevada	SH324
Hirono, Mazie K. (D)	Hawaii	SH330
Hoeven, John (R)	North Dakota	SR338
Inhofe, James M. (R)	Oklahoma	SR205
Isakson, Johnny (R)	Georgia	SR131
Johnson, Ron (R)	Wisconsin	SH328
Kaine, Tim (D)	Virginia	SR231
King, Angus S., Jr. (I)	Maine	SH133
Kirk, Mark S. (R)	Illinois	SH524
Klobuchar, Amy (D)	Minnesota	SH302
Lankford, James (R)	Oklahoma	SH316
Leahy, Patrick J. (D)	Vermont	SR437
Lee, Michael S. (R)	Utah	SR361A
Manchin, Joe, III (D)	West Virginia	SH306
Markey, Edward J. (D)	Massachusetts	SD255
McCain, John (R)	Arizona	SR218
McCaskill, Claire (D)	Missouri	SH730
McConnell, A. Mitch (R)	Kentucky	SR317
Menendez, Robert (D)	New Jersey	SH528
Merkley, Jeff (D)	Oregon	SH313
Mikulski, Barbara A. (D)	Maryland	SH503
Moran, Jerry (R)	Kansas	SD521
Murkowski, Lisa (R)	Alaska	SH709
Murphy, Christopher (D)	Connecticut	SH136
Murray, Patty (D)	Washington	SR154
Nelson, Bill (D)	Florida	SH716
Paul, Rand (R)	Kentucky	SR167
Perdue, David (R)	Georgia	SR383
Peters, Gary C. (D)	Michigan	SH724
Portman, Rob (R)	Ohio	SR448
Reed, Jack (D)	Rhode Island	SH728
Reid, Harry M. (D)	Nevada	SH522
Risch, James E. (R)	Idaho	SR483
Roberts, Pat (R)	Kansas	SH109
Rounds, Mike (R)	South Dakota	SH502
Rubio, Marco (R)	Florida	SR284
Sanders, Bernard (I)	Vermont	SD332
Sasse, Ben (R)	Nebraska	SR386A
Schatz, Brian (D)	Hawaii	SH722
Schumer, Charles E. (D)	New York	SH322
Scott, Tim (R)	South Carolina	SH520
Sessions, Jeff (R)	Alabama	SR326
Shaheen, Jeanne (D)	New Hampshire	SH506
Shelby, Richard C. (R)	Alabama	SR304
Stabenow, Debbie (D)	Michigan	SH731

Name	State	Room
Sullivan, Dan (R)	Arkansas	SH702
Tester, Jon (D)	Montana	SH311
Thune, John (R)	South Dakota	SD511
Tillis, Thom (R)	North Carolina	SD185
Toomey, Patrick J. (R)	Pennsylvania	SR248
Udall, Tom (D)	New Mexico	SH531
Vitter, David (R)	Louisiana	SH516
Warner, Mark R. (D)	Virginia	SR475
Warren, Elizabeth (D)	Masschusetts	SH317
Whitehouse, Sheldon (D)	Rhode Island	SH530
Wicker, Roger F. (R)	Mississippi	SD555
Wyden, Ron (D)	Oregon	SD221

Republicans are 54; Democrats are 44; and Independents are 2. The total number of Senators is 100. Please note: Senate.gov is a more up-to-date electronic source of information.

Rooms are in the Dirksen Office Building if their numbers are preceded by SD, in the Hart Office Building if their numbers are preceded by SH, and in the Russell Office Building if their numbers are preceded by SR.

Sources of Information

Art

The Senate's collections of ephemera, decorative art, graphic art, paintings, and sculpture can be viewed online.

Career Opportunities

Information on fellowships, internships, and job openings is available online.

Committees

Information on Senate committees is available online.

Contact a Senator

Phone numbers, postal addresses, and online forms are available for contacting a Senator.

An online list of States also provides web forms for contacting a Senator via email.

Glossary

A Senate glossary is available online.

History

The Senate Historical Office has told the history of the Senate, from the First Federal Congress of 1789 through the early 21st century; explained its traditions; described the individuals who served in its Chamber, and examined the major issues that confronted these national leaders.

Legislation and Records

Research guides and resources are available online.

Publications

The Congressional Directory, the Senate Manual, and telephone directory for the U.S. Senate are available from the Government Publishing Office's bookstore. Phone, 202-512-0132.

Web Sites

More information on legislation and the Senate is available on Congress.gov and on the Government Publishing Office's Federal Digital System (FDsys) Web site.

For further information, contact the Secretary of the Senate, The Capitol, Washington, DC 20510. Phone, 202-224-2115.

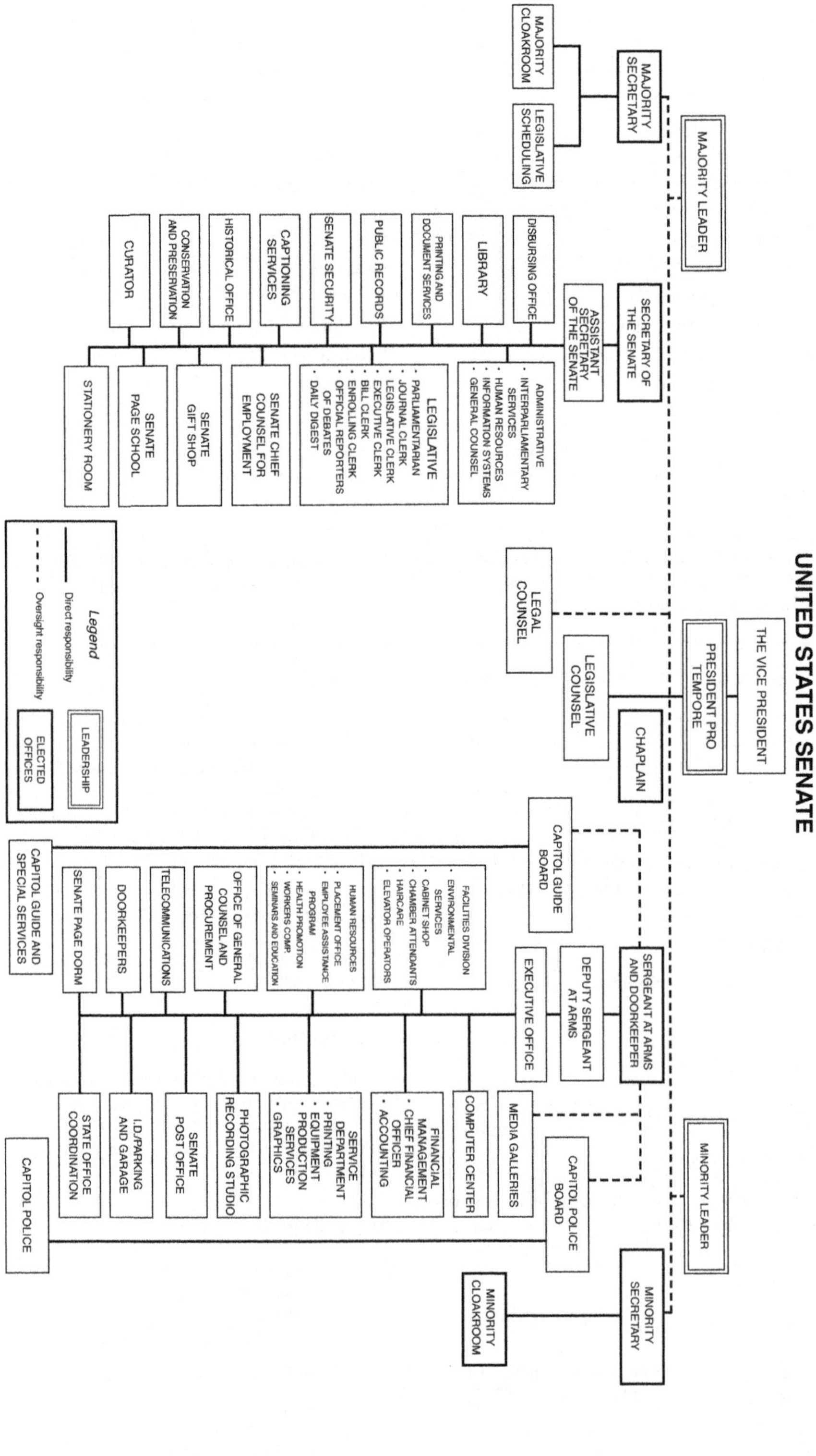
UNITED STATES SENATE
THE VICE PRESIDENT
PRESIDENT PRO TEMPORE
CHAPLAIN
LEGISLATIVE COUNSEL
LEGAL COUNSEL
MAJORITY LEADER
MAJORITY SECRETARY
MAJORITY CLOAKROOM
LEGISLATIVE SCHEDULING
SECRETARY OF THE SENATE
ASSISTANT SECRETARY OF THE SENATE
DISBURSING OFFICE
LIBRARY
PRINTING AND DOCUMENT SERVICES
PUBLIC RECORDS
SENATE SECURITY
CAPTIONING SERVICES
HISTORICAL OFFICE
CONSERVATION AND PRESERVATION
CURATOR
ADMINISTRATIVE
· INTERPARLIAMENTARY SERVICES
· HUMAN RESOURCES
· INFORMATION SYSTEMS
· GENERAL COUNSEL
LEGISLATIVE
· PARLIAMENTARIAN
· JOURNAL CLERK
· LEGISLATIVE CLERK
· EXECUTIVE CLERK
· BILL CLERK
· ENROLLING CLERK
· OFFICIAL REPORTERS OF DEBATES
· DAILY DIGEST
SENATE CHIEF COUNSEL FOR EMPLOYMENT
SENATE GIFT SHOP
SENATE PAGE SCHOOL
STATIONERY ROOM
Legend
Direct responsibility
Oversight responsibility
LEADERSHIP
ELECTED OFFICES
CAPITOL GUIDE BOARD
CAPITOL GUIDE AND SPECIAL SERVICES
SERGEANT AT ARMS AND DOORKEEPER
DEPUTY SERGEANT AT ARMS
EXECUTIVE OFFICE
FACILITIES DIVISION
· ENVIRONMENTAL SERVICES
· CABINET SHOP
· CHAMBER ATTENDANTS
· HAIRCARE
· ELEVATOR OPERATORS
HUMAN RESOURCES
· PLACEMENT OFFICE
· EMPLOYEE ASSISTANCE PROGRAM
· HEALTH PROMOTION
· WORKERS COMP
· SEMINARS AND EDUCATION
OFFICE OF GENERAL COUNSEL AND PROCUREMENT
TELECOMMUNICATIONS
DOORKEEPERS
SENATE PAGE DORM
MEDIA GALLERIES
COMPUTER CENTER
FINANCIAL MANAGEMENT
· CHIEF FINANCIAL OFFICER
· ACCOUNTING
SERVICE DEPARTMENT
· PRINTING
· EQUIPMENT
· PRODUCTION SERVICES
· GRAPHICS
PHOTOGRAPHIC RECORDING STUDIO
SENATE POST OFFICE
I.D./PARKING AND GARAGE
STATE OFFICE COORDINATION
CAPITOL POLICE BOARD
CAPITOL POLICE
MINORITY LEADER
MINORITY SECRETARY
MINORITY CLOAKROOM

The House of Representatives

The Capitol, Washington, DC 20515

202-225-3121, *http://www.house.gov*

THE SPEAKER	Paul D. Ryan
Majority Leader	Kevin McCarthy
Minority Leader	Nancy Pelosi
Clerk	Karen L. Haas
Sergeant at Arms	Paul D. Irving
Chief Administrative Officer	Will Plaster
Chaplain	Patrick J. Conroy

Overview

The House of Representatives comprises 435 Representatives. The number representing each State is determined by population, but every State is entitled to at least one Representative. Members are elected by the people for 2-year terms, all terms running for the same period. Representatives must be residents of the State from which they are chosen. In addition, a Representative must be at least 25 years of age and must have been a citizen for at least 7 years.

A Resident Commissioner from Puerto Rico (elected for a 4-year term) and Delegates from American Samoa, the District of Columbia, Guam, the Northern Mariana Islands, and the Virgin Islands complete the composition of the Congress of the United States. Delegates are elected for a term of 2 years. The Resident Commissioner and Delegates may take part in the floor discussions, but have no vote in the full House. They do, however, vote in the committees to which they are assigned.

Officers

The Presiding Officer of the House of Representatives, the Speaker, is elected by the House. The Speaker may designate any Member of the House to act in the Speaker's absence.

The House leadership is structured essentially the same as the Senate, with the Members in the political parties responsible for the election of their respective leader and whips.

The elected officers of the House of Representatives include the Clerk, the Sergeant at Arms, the Chief Administrative Officer, and the Chaplain.

The Clerk is custodian of the seal of the House and administers the primary legislative activities of the House. These duties include accepting the credentials of the Members-elect and calling the Members to order at the commencement of the first session of each Congress; keeping the Journal; taking all votes and certifying the passage of bills; and processing all legislation. Through various departments, the Clerk is also responsible for floor and committee reporting services; legislative information and reference services; the administration of House reports pursuant to House rules and certain legislation including the Ethics in Government Act and the Lobbying Disclosure Act of 1995; and the distribution of House documents. The Clerk is also charged with supervision of the offices vacated by Members due to death, resignation, or expulsion.

The Sergeant at Arms maintains the order of the House under the direction of the Speaker and is the keeper of the Mace. As a member of the U.S. Capitol Police Board, the Sergeant at Arms is the chief law enforcement officer for the House and serves as Board Chairman each even year. The ceremonial and protocol duties parallel those of the Senate Sergeant at Arms and include arranging the inauguration of the President of the United States, Joint

Sessions of Congress, visits to the House of heads of state, and funerals of Members of Congress. The Sergeant at Arms enforces the rules relating to the privileges of the Hall of the House, including admission to the galleries, oversees garage and parking security of the House, and distributes all House staff identification cards.

Committees

The work of preparing and considering legislation is done largely by committees of both Houses of Congress. There are 19 standing committees in the House of Representatives. The standing committees of the House of Representatives are shown in the list below. In addition, there are two select committees in the House and various congressional commissions and joint committees composed of Members of both Houses. Each House may also appoint special investigating committees. The membership of the standing committees of each House is chosen by a vote of the entire body; members of other committees are appointed under the provisions of the measure establishing them.

Each bill and resolution is usually referred to the appropriate committee, which may report a bill out in its original form, favorably or unfavorably, recommend amendments, report original measures, or allow the proposed legislation to die in committee without action.

Standing Committees of the House of Representatives

House Committee	Room
Agriculture	1301
Appropriations	H305
Armed Services	2216
Budget	207
Education and the Workforce	2176
Energy and Commerce	2125
Ethics	1015
Financial Services	2129
Foreign Affairs	2170
Homeland Security	H2-176
House Administration	1309
House Administration (Franking Office)	1216
Judiciary	2138
Natural Resources	1324
Oversight and Government Reform	2157
Rules	H312
Rules (Minority)	1627
Science, Space, and Technology	2321
Small Business	2361
Transportation and Infrastructure	2165
Veterans' Affairs	335
Ways and Means	1102

Rooms with three-digit numbers are in the Cannon House Office Building, with four-digit numbers beginning with 1 are in the Longworth House Office Building, and with four-digit numbers beginning with 2 are in the Rayburn House Office Building. Rooms with numbers preceded by H or HT are in the House wing of the Capitol Building, and those with numbers preceded by H2 are in the Ford House Office Building.

Special Powers

The House of Representatives is granted the power of originating all bills for the raising of revenue. Both Houses of Congress act in impeachment proceedings, which, according to the Constitution, may be instituted against the President, Vice President, and all civil officers of the United States. The House of Representatives has the sole power of impeachment, and the Senate has the sole power to try impeachments.

Representatives, Delegates, and Resident Commissioners

Name	State (District) / Territory	Room
Abraham, Ralph Lee (R)	Louisiana (5)	417
Adams, Alma S. (D)	North Carolina (12)	222
Aderholt, Robert B. (R)	Alabama (4)	235
Aguilar, Pete (D)	California (31)	1223
Allen, Rick W. (R)	Georgia (12)	513
Amash, Justin (R)	Michigan (3)	114
Amodei, Mark E. (R)	Nevada (2)	332
Ashford, Brad (D)	Nebraska (2)	107
Babin, Brian (R)	Texas (36)	316
Barletta, Lou (R)	Pennsylvania (11)	115
Barr, Andy (R)	Kentucky (6)	1432
Barton, Joe (R)	Texas (6)	2107
Bass, Karen (D)	California (37)	408
Beatty, Joyce (D)	Ohio (3)	133
Becerra, Xavier (D)	California (34)	1226
Benishek, Dan (R)	Michigan (1)	514
Bera, Ami (D)	California (7)	1535
Beyer, Donald S., Jr. (D)	Virginia (8)	431
Bilirakis, Gus M. (R)	Florida (12)	2112
Bishop, Mike (R)	Michigan (8)	428
Bishop, Rob (R)	Utah (1)	123
Bishop, Sanford D., Jr. (D)	Georgia (2)	2407
Black, Diane (R)	Tennessee (6)	1131
Blackburn, Marsha (R)	Tennessee (7)	2266
Blum, Rod (R)	Iowa (1)	213
Blumenauer, Earl (D)	Oregon (3)	1111
Bonamici, Suzanne (D)	Oregon (1)	439
Bordallo, Madeleine Z. (D)	Guam (Delegate)	2441
Bost, Mike (R)	Illinois (12)	1440
Boustany, Charles W., Jr. (R)	Louisiana (3)	1431
Boyle, Brendan F. (D)	Pennsylvania (13)	118
Brady, Kevin (R)	Texas (8)	301
Brady, Robert A. (D)	Pennsylvania (1)	102
Brat, Dave (R)	Virginia (7)	330
Bridenstine, Jim (R)	Oklahoma (1)	216
Brooks, Mo (R)	Alabama (5)	1230
Brooks, Susan W. (R)	Indiana (5)	1505
Brown, Corrine (D)	Florida (5)	2111
Brownley, Julia (D)	California (26)	1019
Buchanan, Vern (R)	Florida (16)	2104
Buck, Ken (R)	Colorado (4)	416
Bucshon, Larry (R)	Indiana (8)	1005
Burgess, Michael C. (R)	Texas (26)	2336

Name	State (District) / Territory	Room
Bustos, Cheri (D)	Illinois (17)	1009
Butterfield, G.K. (D)	North Carolina (1)	2305
Byrne, Bradley (R)	Alabama (1)	119
Calvert, Ken (R)	California (42)	2205
Capps, Lois (D)	California (24)	2231
Capuano, Michael E. (D)	Massachusetts (7)	1414
Cárdenas, Tony (D)	California (29)	1510
Carney, John C., Jr. (D)	Delaware (At Large)	1406
Carson, André (D)	Indiana (7)	2453
Carter, Earl L. "Buddy" (R)	Georgia (1)	432
Carter, John R. (R)	Texas (31)	2110
Cartwright, Matt (D)	Pennsylvania (17)	1419
Castor, Kathy (D)	Florida (14)	205
Castro, Joaquin (D)	Texas (20)	212
Chabot, Steve (R)	Ohio (1)	2371
Chaffetz, Jason (R)	Utah (3)	2236
Chu, Judy (D)	California (27)	2423
Cicilline, David N. (D)	Rhode Island (1)	2244
Clark, Katherine M. (D)	Massachusetts (5)	1721
Clarke, Yvette D. (D)	New York (9)	2351
Clawson, Curt (R)	Florida (19)	228
Clay, W. Lacy (D)	Missouri (1)	2428
Cleaver, Emanuel (D)	Missouri (5)	2335
Clyburn, James E. (D)	South Carolina (6)	242
Coffman, Mike (R)	Colorado (6)	2443
Cohen, Steve (D)	Tennessee (9)	2404
Cole, Tom (R)	Oklahoma (4)	2467
Collins, Chris (R)	New York (27)	1117
Collins, Doug (R)	Georgia (9)	1504
Comstock, Barbara (R)	Virginia (10)	226
Conaway, K. Michael (R)	Texas (11)	2430
Connolly, Gerald E. (D)	Virginia (11)	2238
Conyers, John, Jr. (D)	Michigan (13)	2426
Cook, Paul (R)	California (8)	1222
Cooper, Jim (D)	Tennessee (5)	1536
Costa, Jim (D)	California (16)	1314
Costello, Ryan A. (R)	Pennsylvania (6)	427
Courtney, Joe (D)	Connecticut (2)	2348
Cramer, Kevin (R)	North Dakota (At Large)	1032
Crawford, Eric A. (R)	Arkansas (1)	1711
Crenshaw, Ander (R)	Florida (4)	2161
Crowley, Joseph (D)	New York (14)	1436
Cuellar, Henry (D)	Texas (28)	2209
Culberson, John Abney (R)	Texas (7)	2372
Cummings, Elijah E. (D)	Maryland (7)	2230
Curbelo, Carlos (R)	Florida (26)	1429
Davis, Danny K. (D)	Illinois (7)	2159
Davis, Rodney (R)	Illinois (13)	1740

Name	State (District) / Territory	Room
Davis, Susan A. (D)	California (53)	1214
DeFazio, Peter A. (D)	Oregon (4)	2134
DeGette, Diana (D)	Colorado (1)	2368
Delaney, John K. (D)	Maryland (6)	1632
DeLauro, Rosa L. (D)	Connecticut (3)	2413
DelBene, Suzan K. (D)	Washington (1)	318
Denham, Jeff (R)	California (10)	1730
Dent, Charles W. (R)	Pennsylvania (15)	2211
DeSantis, Ron (R)	Florida (6)	308
DeSaulnier, Mark (D)	California (11)	327
DesJarlais, Scott (R)	Tennessee (4)	413
Deutch, Theodore E. (D)	Florida (21)	2447
Diaz-Balart, Mario (R)	Florida (25)	440
Dingell, Debbie (D)	Michigan (12)	116
Doggett, Lloyd (D)	Texas (35)	2307
Dold, Robert J. (R)	Illinois (10)	221
Donovan, Daniel M., Jr. (R)	New York (11)	1725
Doyle, Michael F. (D)	Pennsylvania (14)	239
Duckworth, Tammy (D)	Illinois (8)	104
Duffy, Sean P. (R)	Wisconsin (7)	1208
Duncan, Jeff (R)	South Carolina (3)	106
Duncan, John J., Jr. (R)	Tennessee (2)	2207
Edwards, Donna F. (D)	Maryland (4)	2445
Ellison, Keith (D)	Minnesota (5)	2263
Ellmers, Renee L. (R)	North Carolina (2)	1210
Emmer, Tom (R)	Minnesota (6)	503
Engel, Eliot L. (D)	New York (16)	2462
Eshoo, Anna G. (D)	California (18)	241
Esty, Elizabeth H. (D)	Connecticut (5)	405
Farenthold, Blake (R)	Texas (27)	1027
Farr, Sam (D)	California (20)	1126
[Fattah, Chaka] (D)	Pennsylvania (2)	2301
Fincher, Stephen Lee (R)	Tennessee (8)	2452
Fitzpatrick, Michael G. (R)	Pennsylvania (8)	2400
Fleischmann, Charles J. (R)	Tennessee (3)	230
Fleming, John (R)	Louisiana (4)	2182
Flores, Bill (R)	Texas (17)	1030
Forbes, J. Randy (R)	Virginia (4)	2135
Fortenberry, Jeff (R)	Nebraska (1)	1514
Foster, Bill (D)	Illinois (11)	1224
Foxx, Virginia (R)	North Carolina (5)	2350
Frankel, Lois (D)	Florida (22)	1037
Franks, Trent (R)	Arizona (8)	2435
Frelinghuysen, Rodney P. (R)	New Jersey (11)	2306
Fudge, Marcia L. (D)	Ohio (11)	2344
Gabbard, Tulsi (D)	Hawaii (2)	1609
Gallego, Ruben (D)	Arizona (7)	1218
Garamendi, John (D)	California (3)	2438

Name	State (District) / Territory	Room
Garrett, Scott (R)	New Jersey (5)	2232
Gibbs, Bob (R)	Ohio (7)	329
Gibson, Christopher P. (R)	New York (19)	1708
Gohmert, Louie (R)	Texas (1)	2243
Goodlatte, Bob (R)	Virginia (6)	2309
Gosar, Paul A. (R)	Arizona (4)	504
Gowdy, Trey (R)	South Carolina (4)	1404
Graham, Gwen (D)	Florida (2)	1213
Granger, Kay (R)	Texas (12)	1026
Graves, Garret (R)	Louisiana (6)	204
Graves, Sam (R)	Missouri (6)	1415
Graves, Tom (R)	Georgia (14)	2442
Grayson, Alan (D)	Florida (9)	303
Green, Al (D)	Texas (9)	2347
Green, Gene (D)	Texas (29)	2470
Griffith, H. Morgan (R)	Virginia (9)	1108
Grijalva, Raúl M. (D)	Arizona (3)	1511
Grothman, Glenn (R)	Wisconsin (6)	501
Guinta, Frank C. (R)	New Hampshire (1)	326
Guthrie, Brett (R)	Kentucky (2)	2434
Gutiérrez, Luis V. (D)	Illinois (4)	2408
Hahn, Janice (D)	California (44)	404
Hanna, Richard L. (R)	New York (22)	319
Hardy, Cresent (R)	Nevada (4)	430
Harper, Gregg (R)	Mississippi (3)	307
Harris, Andy (R)	Maryland (1)	1533
Hartzler, Vicky (R)	Missouri (4)	2235
Hastings, Alcee L. (D)	Florida (20)	2353
Heck, Denny (D)	Washington (10)	425
Heck, Joseph J. (R)	Nevada (3)	132
Hensarling, Jeb (R)	Texas (5)	2228
Herrera Beutler, Jaime (R)	Washington (3)	1130
Hice, Jody B. (R)	Georgia (10)	1516
Higgins, Brian (D)	New York (26)	2459
Hill, J. French (R)	Arkansas (2)	1229
Himes, James A. (D)	Connecticut (4)	1227
Hinojosa, Rubén (D)	Texas (15)	2262
Holding, George (R)	North Carolina (13)	507
Honda, Michael M. (D)	California (17)	1713
Hoyer, Steny H. (D)	Maryland (5)	1705
Hudson, Richard (R)	North Carolina (8)	429
Huelskamp, Tim (R)	Kansas (1)	1110
Huffman, Jared (D)	California (2)	1630
Huizenga, Bill (R)	Michigan (2)	1217
Hultgren, Randy (R)	Illinois (14)	2455
Hunter, Duncan (R)	California (50)	2429
Hurd, Will (R)	Texas (23)	317
Hurt, Robert (R)	Virginia (5)	125

Name	State (District) / Territory	Room
Israel, Steve (D)	New York (3)	2457
Issa, Darrell E. (R)	California (49)	2269
Jackson Lee, Sheila (D)	Texas (18)	2252
Jeffries, Hakeem S. (D)	New York (8)	1607
Jenkins, Evan H. (R)	West Virginia (3)	502
Jenkins, Lynn (R)	Kansas (2)	1526
Johnson, Bill (R)	Ohio (6)	1710
Johnson, Eddie Bernice (D)	Texas (30)	2468
Johnson, Henry C., Jr. (D)	Georgia (4)	2240
Johnson, Sam (R)	Texas (3)	2304
Jolly, David W. (R)	Florida (13)	1728
Jones, Walter B. (R)	North Carolina (3)	2333
Jordan, Jim (R)	Ohio (4)	1524
Joyce, David P. (R)	Ohio (14)	1124
Kaptur, Marcy (D)	Ohio (9)	2186
Katko, John (R)	New York (24)	1123
Keating, William R. (D)	Massachusetts (9)	315
Kelly, Mike (R)	Pennsylvania (3)	1519
Kelly, Robin L. (D)	Illinois (2)	1239
Kelly, Trent (R)	Mississippi (1)	1427
Kennedy, Joseph P., III (D)	Massachusetts (4)	306
Kildee, Daniel T. (D)	Michigan (5)	227
Kilmer, Derek (D)	Washington (6)	1520
Kind, Ron (D)	Wisconsin (3)	1502
King, Peter T. (R)	New York (2)	339
King, Steve (R)	Iowa (4)	2210
Kinzinger, Adam (R)	Illinois (16)	1221
Kirkpatrick, Ann (D)	Arizona (1)	201
Kline, John (R)	Minnesota (2)	2439
Knight, Stephen (R)	California (25)	1023
Kuster, Ann M. (D)	New Hampshire (2)	137
Labrador, Raúl R. (R)	Idaho (1)	1523
LaHood, Darin (R)	Illinois (18)	2464
LaMalfa, Doug (R)	California (1)	322
Lamborn, Doug (R)	Colorado (5)	2402
Lance, Leonard (R)	New Jersey (7)	2352
Langevin, James R. (D)	Rhode Island (2)	109
Larsen, Rick (D)	Washington (2)	2113
Larson, John B. (D)	Connecticut (1)	1501
Latta, Robert E. (R)	Ohio (5)	2448
Lawrence, Brenda L. (D)	Michigan (14)	1237
Lee, Barbara (D)	California (13)	2267
Levin, Sander M. (D)	Michigan (9)	1236
Lewis, John (D)	Georgia (5)	343
Lieu, Ted (D)	California (33)	415
Lipinski, Daniel (D)	Illinois (3)	2346
LoBiondo, Frank A. (R)	New Jersey (2)	2427
Loebsack, David (D)	Iowa (2)	1527

Name	State (District) / Territory	Room
Lofgren, Zoe (D)	California (19)	1401
Long, Billy (R)	Missouri (7)	1541
Loudermilk, Barry (R)	Georgia (11)	238
Love, Mia B. (R)	Utah (4)	217
Lowenthal, Alan S. (D)	California (47)	108
Lowey, Nita M. (D)	New York (17)	2365
Lucas, Frank D. (R)	Oklahoma (3)	2405
Luetkemeyer, Blaine (R)	Missouri (3)	2440
Luján, Ben Ray (D)	New Mexico (3)	2446
Lujan Grisham, Michelle (D)	New Mexico (1)	214
Lummis, Cynthia M. (R)	Wyoming (At Large)	2433
Lynch, Stephen F. (D)	Massachusetts (8)	2369
MacArthur, Thomas (R)	New Jersey (3)	506
Maloney, Carolyn B. (D)	New York (12)	2308
Maloney, Sean Patrick (D)	New York (18)	1529
Marchant, Kenny (R)	Texas (24)	2313
Marino, Tom (R)	Pennsylvania (10)	410
Massie, Thomas (R)	Kentucky (4)	314
Matsui, Doris O. (D)	California (6)	2311
McCarthy, Kevin (R)	California (23)	2421
McCaul, Michael T. (R)	Texas (10)	131
McClintock, Tom (R)	California (4)	2331
McCollum, Betty (D)	Minnesota (4)	2256
McDermott, Jim (D)	Washington (7)	1035
McGovern, James P. (D)	Massachusetts (2)	438
McHenry, Patrick T. (R)	North Carolina (10)	2334
McKinley, David B. (R)	West Virginia (1)	412
McMorris Rodgers, Cathy (R)	Washington (5)	203
McNerney, Jerry (D)	California (9)	2265
McSally, Martha (R)	Arizona (2)	1029
Meadows, Mark (R)	North Carolina (11)	1024
Meehan, Patrick (R)	Pennsylvania (7)	434
Meeks, Gregory W. (D)	New York (5)	2234
Meng, Grace (D)	New York (6)	1317
Messer, Luke (R)	Indiana (6)	508
Mica, John L. (R)	Florida (7)	2187
Miller, Candice S. (R)	Michigan (10)	320
Miller, Jeff (R)	Florida (1)	336
Moolenaar, John R. (R)	Michigan (4)	117
Mooney, Alexander X. (R)	West Virginia (2)	1232
Moore, Gwen (D)	Wisconsin (4)	2245
Moulton, Seth (D)	Massachusetts (6)	1408
Mullin, Markwayne (R)	Oklahoma (2)	1113
Mulvaney, Mick (R)	South Carolina (5)	2419
Murphy, Patrick (D)	Florida (18)	211
Murphy, Tim (R)	Pennsylvania (18)	2332
Nadler, Jerrold (D)	New York (10)	2109
Napolitano, Grace F. (D)	California (32)	1610

Name	State (District) / Territory	Room
Neal, Richard E. (D)	Massachusetts (1)	341
Neugebauer, Randy (R)	Texas (19)	1424
Newhouse, Dan (R)	Washington (4)	1641
Noem, Kristi L. (R)	South Dakota (At Large)	2422
Nolan, Richard M. (D)	Minnesota (8)	2366
Norcross, Donald (D)	New Jersey (1)	1531
Norton, Eleanor Holmes (D)	District of Columbia (Delegate)	2136
Nugent, Richard B. (R)	Florida (11)	1727
Nunes, Devin (R)	California (22)	1013
Olson, Pete (R)	Texas (22)	2133
O'Rourke, Beto (D)	Texas (16)	1330
Palazzo, Steven M. (R)	Mississippi (4)	331
Pallone, Frank, Jr. (D)	New Jersey (6)	237
Palmer, Gary J. (R)	Alabama (6)	206
Pascrell, Bill, Jr. (D.)	New Jersey (9)	2370
Paulsen, Erik (R)	Minnesota (3)	127
Payne, Donald M., Jr. (D)	New Jersey (10)	103
Pearce, Stevan (R)	New Mexico (2)	2432
Pelosi, Nancy (D)	California (12)	233
Perlmutter, Ed (D)	Colorado (7)	1410
Perry, Scott (R)	Pennsylvania (4)	1207
Peters, Scott H. (D)	California (52)	1122
Peterson, Collin C. (D)	Minnesota (7)	2204
Pierluisi, Pedro R. (D)	Puerto Rico (Resident Commissioner)	2410
Pingree, Chellie (D)	Maine (1)	2162
Pittenger, Robert (R)	North Carolina (9)	224
Pitts, Joseph R. (R)	Pennsylvania (16)	420
Plaskett, Stacey E. (D)	Virgin Islands (Delegate)	509
Pocan, Mark (D)	Wisconsin (2)	313
Poe, Ted (R)	Texas (2)	2412
Poliquin, Bruce (R)	Maine (2)	426
Polis, Jared (D)	Colorado (2)	1433
Pompeo, Mike (R)	Kansas (4)	436
Posey, Bill (R)	Florida (8)	120
Price, David E. (D)	North Carolina (4)	2108
Price, Tom (R)	Georgia (6)	100
Quigley, Mike (D)	Illinois (5)	2458
Radewagen, Aumua Amata Coleman (R)	American Samoa (Delegate)	1339
Rangel, Charles B. (D)	New York (13)	2354
Ratcliffe, John (R)	Texas (4)	325
Reed, Tom (R)	New York (23)	2437
Reichert, David G. (R)	Washington (8)	1127
Renacci, James B. (R)	Ohio (16)	328
Ribble, Reid J. (R)	Wisconsin (8)	1513
Rice, Kathleen M. (D)	New York (4)	1508
Rice, Tom (R)	South Carolina (7)	223
Richmond, Cedric L. (D)	Louisiana (2)	240
Rigell, E. Scott (R)	Virginia (2)	418

Name	State (District) / Territory	Room
Roby, Martha (R)	Alabama (2)	442
Roe, David P. (R)	Tennessee (1)	407
Rogers, Harold (R)	Kentucky (5)	2406
Rogers, Mike (R)	Alabama (3)	324
Rohrabacher, Dana (R)	California (48)	2300
Rokita, Todd (R)	Indiana (4)	1717
Rooney, Thomas J. (R)	Florida (17)	2160
Roskam, Peter J. (R)	Illinois (6)	2246
Ros-Lehtinen, Ileana (R)	Florida (27)	2206
Ross, Dennis A. (R)	Florida (15)	229
Rothfus, Keith J. (R)	Pennsylvania (12)	1205
Rouzer, David (R)	North Carolina (7)	424
Roybal-Allard, Lucille (D)	California (40)	2330
Royce, Edward R. (R)	California (39)	2310
Ruiz, Raul (D)	California (36)	1319
Ruppersberger, C.A. Dutch (D)	Maryland (2)	2416
Rush, Bobby L. (D)	Illinois (1)	2188
Russell, Steve (R)	Oklahoma (5)	128
Ryan, Paul D. (R)	Wisconsin (1)	1233
Ryan, Tim (D)	Ohio (13)	1421
Sablan, Gregorio Kilili Camacho (D)	Northern Mariana Islands (Delegate)	423
Salmon, Matt (R)	Arizona (5)	2349
Sánchez, Linda T. (D)	California (38)	2329
Sanchez, Loretta (D)	California (46)	1211
Sanford, Mark (R)	South Carolina (1)	2201
Sarbanes, John P. (D)	Maryland (3)	2444
Scalise, Steve (R)	Louisiana (1)	2338
Schakowsky, Janice D. (D)	Illinois (9)	2367
Schiff, Adam B. (D)	California (28)	2411
Schrader, Kurt (D)	Oregon (5)	2431
Schweikert, David (R)	Arizona (6)	409
Scott, Austin (R)	Georgia (8)	2417
Scott, David (D)	Georgia (13)	225
Scott, Robert C. (D)	Virginia (3)	1201
Sensenbrenner, F. James, Jr. (R)	Wisconsin (5)	2449
Serrano, José E. (D)	New York (15)	2227
Sessions, Pete (R)	Texas (32)	2233
Sewell, Terri A. (D)	Alabama (7)	1133
Sherman, Brad (D)	California (30)	2242
Shimkus, John (R)	Illinois (15)	2217
Shuster, Bill (R)	Pennsylvania (9)	2268
Simpson, Michael K. (R)	Idaho (2)	2312
Sinema, Kyrsten (D)	Arizona (9)	1530
Sires, Albio (D)	New Jersey (8)	2342
Slaughter, Louise McIntosh (D)	New York (25)	2469
Smith, Adam (D)	Washington (9)	2264
Smith, Adrian (R)	Nebraska (3)	2241
Smith, Christopher H. (R)	New Jersey (4)	2373

Name	State (District) / Territory	Room
Smith, Jason (R)	Missouri (8)	1118
Smith, Lamar (R)	Texas (21)	2409
Speier, Jackie (D)	California (14)	2465
Stefanik, Elise M. (R)	New York (21)	512
Stewart, Chris (R)	Utah (2)	323
Stivers, Steve (R)	Ohio (15)	1022
Stutzman, Marlin A. (R)	Indiana (3)	2418
Swalwell, Eric (D)	California (15)	129
[Takai, Mark] (D)	Hawaii (1)	422
Takano, Mark (D)	California (41)	1507
Thompson, Bennie G. (D)	Mississippi (2)	2466
Thompson, Glenn (R)	Pennsylvania (5)	124
Thompson, Mike (D)	California (5)	231
Thornberry, Mac (R)	Texas (13)	2208
Tiberi, Patrick J. (R)	Ohio (12)	1203
Tipton, Scott R. (R)	Colorado (3)	218
Titus, Dina (D)	Nevada (1)	401
Tonko, Paul (D)	New York (20)	2463
Torres, Norma J. (D)	California (35)	516
Trott, David A. (R)	Michigan (11)	1722
Tsongas, Niki (D)	Massachusetts (3)	1714
Turner, Michael R. (R)	Ohio (10)	2239
Upton, Fred (R)	Michigan (6)	2183
Valadao, David G. (R)	California (21)	1004
Van Hollen, Chris (D)	Maryland (8)	1707
Vargas, Juan (D)	California (51)	1605
Veasey, Marc A. (D)	Texas (33)	414
Vela, Filemon (D)	Texas (34)	437
Velázquez, Nydia M. (D)	New York (7)	2302
Visclosky, Peter J. (D)	Indiana (1)	2328
Wagner, Ann (R)	Missouri (2)	435
Walberg, Tim (R)	Michigan (7)	2436
Walden, Greg (R)	Oregon (2)	2185
Walker, Mark (R)	North Carolina (6)	312
Walorski, Jackie (R)	Indiana (2)	419
Walters, Mimi (R)	California (45)	236
Walz, Timothy J. (D)	Minnesota (1)	1034
Wasserman Schultz, Debbie (D)	Florida (23)	1114
Waters, Maxine (D)	California (43)	2221
Watson Coleman, Bonnie (D)	New Jersey (12)	126
Weber, Randy K., Sr. (R)	Texas (14)	510
Webster, Daniel (R)	Florida (10)	1039
Welch, Peter (D)	Vermont (At Large)	2303
Wenstrup, Brad R. (R)	Ohio (2)	1318
Westerman, Bruce (R)	Arkansas (4)	130
Westmoreland, Lynn A. (R)	Georgia (3)	2202
Whitfield, Ed (R)	Kentucky (1)	2184
Williams, Roger (R)	Texas (25)	1323

Name	State (District) / Territory	Room
Wilson, Frederica S. (D)	Florida (24)	208
Wilson, Joe (R)	South Carolina (2)	2229
Wittman, Robert J. (R)	Virginia (1)	2454
Womack, Steve (R)	Arkansas (3)	1119
Woodall, Rob (R)	Georgia (7)	1724
Yarmuth, John A. (D)	Kentucky (3)	403
Yoder, Kevin (R)	Kansas (3)	215
Yoho, Ted S. (R)	Florida (3)	511
Young, David (R)	Iowa (3)	515
Young, Don (R)	Alaska (At Large)	2314
Young, Todd C. (R)	Indiana (9)	1007
Zeldin, Lee M. (R)	New York (1)	1517
Zinke, Ryan K. (R)	Montana (At Large)	113
Davidson, Warren (R)	Ohio (8)	1011

Republicans are 247; Democrats are 188. The total number of Members is 435. (The Resident Commissioner and five Delegates are not counted as Members.) Please note: House.gov is a more up-to-date electronic source of information.

Rooms with three-digit numbers are in the Cannon House Office Building (New Jersey and Independence Avenues), with four-digit numbers beginning with 1 are in the Longworth House Office Building (between South Capitol Street and New Jersey Avenue on Independence Avenue), and with four-digit numbers beginning with 2 are in the Rayburn House Office Building (between First and South Capitol Streets on Independence Avenue). Square brackets enclosing a Member's name indicate that he or she resigned from or died in office.

Sources of Information

Career Opportunities

The House Vacancy Announcement and Placement Service assists House Members, committees, and leadership by posting job vacancies and maintaining a resume bank. The Service provides confidential referral of resumes when House offices request them. Information on submitting a resume is available online.

To apply for positions with House organizations, read the individual vacancy announcements and follow the instructions.

Committees

Information on House committees is available on House.gov.

Additional information is available on the Office of the Clerk's Web site.

Congressional Art Competition

Each spring, the Congressional Institute sponsors a nationwide high school visual art competition to recognize and encourage artistic talent. Students submit their entries to their Representative's office, and panels of district artists select the winning artwork, which is displayed at the U.S. Capitol for 1 year.

Contact a Representative

Phone numbers are available on House.gov for contacting Representatives, as well as links leading to their House.gov Web pages.

A Zip code-based search tool is available on House.gov for finding a representative.

Educational Resources

The Office of the Clerk's Web site features educational and entertaining information on the legislative branch of the Government for students of all ages. Its Kids in the House Web site explains the role of the House of Representatives, describes the legislative process, and covers House history.

Adults seeking to learn about commissions, committees, House history, House leadership, Representatives, rules, or a Representative's schedule may benefit from "The House Explained" section on House.gov.

Glossary

The Office of the Clerk's Web site features a short glossary for children.

House.gov features a glossary of terms related to congressional records.

House.gov features a glossary of records management terms.

The "Statement of Disbursements" is a quarterly public report of all receipts and expenditures for U.S. House of Representatives committees, leadership, Members, and officers and offices. House.gov features a glossary to help readers of this public report.

Publications

The Congressional Directory, Rules and Manual of the House of Representatives, and telephone directory for the House of Representatives are available from the Government Publishing Office's bookstore. Phone, 202-512-0132.

Schedule

The House's schedule and related resources are available in the "Legislative Activity" section on House.gov.

Site Map

House.gov features a site map that allows visitors to look for a specific topic or to browse for content that aligns with their interests.

Web Sites

More information on legislation and the House of Representatives is available on Congress.gov and House.gov, and on the Government Publishing Office's Federal Digital System (FDsys) Web site and on the Office of the Clerk's Web site.

http://clerk.house.gov

For further information, contact the Clerk, The Capitol, Washington, DC 20515. Phone, 202-225-7000.

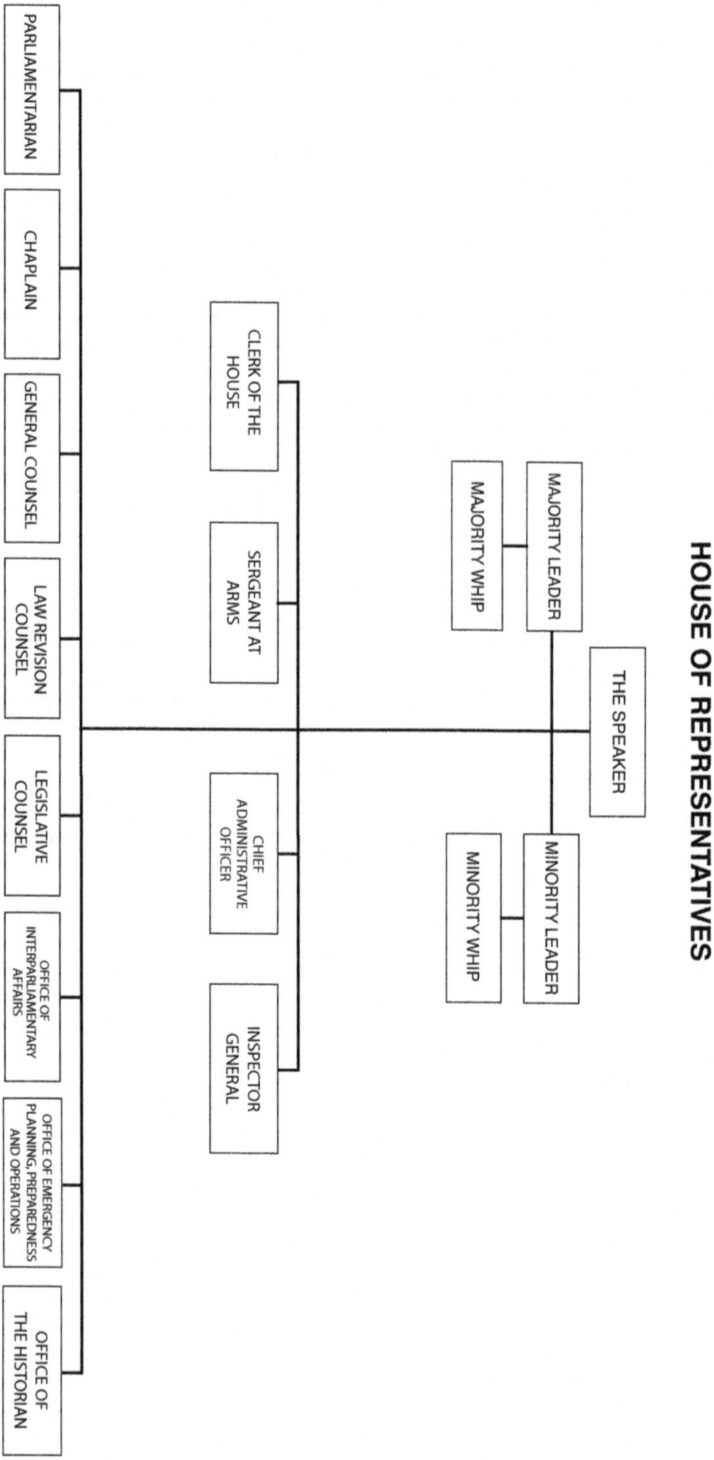
HOUSE OF REPRESENTATIVES
THE SPEAKER
MAJORITY LEADER
MAJORITY WHIP
MINORITY LEADER
MINORITY WHIP
CLERK OF THE HOUSE
SERGEANT AT ARMS
CHIEF ADMINISTRATIVE OFFICER
INSPECTOR GENERAL
PARLIAMENTARIAN
CHAPLAIN
GENERAL COUNSEL
LAW REVISION COUNSEL
LEGISLATIVE COUNSEL
OFFICE OF INTERPARLIAMENTARY AFFAIRS
OFFICE OF EMERGENCY PLANNING, PREPAREDNESS AND OPERATIONS
OFFICE OF THE HISTORIAN

Architect of the Capitol

U.S. Capitol Building, Washington, DC 20515, 202-228-1793, *http://www.aoc.gov*

ARCHITECT OF THE CAPITOL	Stephen T. Ayers
Chief Operating Officer	Christine A. Merdon
Assistant Architect of the Capitol	Michael G. Turnbull
General Counsel	Jason Baltimore
Inspector General	Kevin Mulshine
Chief Administrative Officer	Dan Cassil, Acting
Chief Executive Officer, Visitor Services	Beth Plemmons
Chief Financial Officer	Thomas Carroll
Director, Communications and Congressional Relations	Mary Anne Bittner
Director, Planning and Project Management	Peter W. Mueller
Director, Safety, Fire and Environmental Programs	Susan Adams
Director, Security Programs	Kenneth A. Eads
Director, Utilities and Power Plant Operations	Christopher Potter
Executive Director, U.S. Botanic Garden	Ari Novy
Facility Manager, Supreme Court Buildings and Grounds	Trent Wolfersberger
Superintendent, Capitol Building	Mark Reed
Superintendent, Capitol Grounds	Theodore R. Bechtol, Jr.
Superintendent, House Office Buildings	William M. Weidemeyer
Superintendent, Library Buildings and Grounds	Larry D. Brown
Superintendent, Senate Office Buildings	Takis Tzamaras

The Architect of the Capitol maintains the U.S. Capitol and the buildings and grounds of the Capitol campus.

Permanent authority for the care and maintenance of the U.S. Capitol was established by the act of August 15, 1876 (40 U.S.C. 162, 163). The title Architect of the Capitol (AOC) is the official title of both the agency and the person.

Historically, the President appointed the Architect of the Capitol for an indefinite term. Legislation enacted in 1989, however, provides that the President, with the advice and consent of the Senate, appoints the Architect for a 10-year term from a list of three candidates whom a congressional commission recommends. Upon confirmation by the Senate, the Architect becomes an official of the legislative branch as an officer of Congress. The Architect is eligible for reappointment at the end of his or her 10-year term. While overseeing the agency, the Architect also serves as the Acting Director of the U.S. Botanic Garden.

The Architect of the Capitol serves the Congress and Supreme Court in its capacity as the builder and steward of the landmark buildings and grounds of Capitol Hill. AOC staff preserves and maintains the art, historic buildings, monuments, and inspirational gardens on the Capitol campus. The AOC team, which comprises more than 2,000 employees who provide around the clock service, creates a safe environment and inspiring experiences for all who visit and work on Capitol Hill.

The AOC traces its beginnings to the laying of the Capitol cornerstone in 1793. The agency oversees the operations and care of more than 17.4 million square feet of facilities, 580 acres of grounds, and thousands of works of art. The Capitol campus accommodates 30,000 daily occupants and hosts more than 3 million visitors annually.

Sources of Information

Blog

AOC experts write on the architecture, art, and work on the Capitol Hill.

Business Opportunities

Information for contractors and small businesses—delivery instructions, procedures, procurement opportunities, and programs—is accessible online.

Employment

Information on working with the AOC, open positions, and the application process is available on the "Careers" Web page.

Gallery

A multimedia gallery is available online.

History

President George Washington appointed commissioners to provide buildings and accommodations for Congress. The commissioners hired the French artist and engineer Major Pierre Charles L'Enfant, a Revolutionary War veteran, to lay out the new city. They also staged a competition for the design of the Capitol. Dr. William Thornton's entry won the competition. To learn more about the first "architect of the capitol" and the Architects that followed, visit the AOC's history Web pages.

Planning a Visit

Information on accessibility services, activities, tours, visiting hours, and where to shop and eat is available online.

Publications

The AOC publishes a variety of publications that are accessible online.

Site Map

The Web site map allows visitors to look for specific topics or to browse content that aligns with their interests.

For further information, contact the Office of the Architect of the Capitol, U.S. Capitol Building, Washington, DC 20515. Phone, 202-228-1793.

Congressional Budget Office

Second and D Streets SW., Washington, DC 20515, 202-226-2600, *http://www.cbo.gov*

DIRECTOR	Keith Hall
Deputy Director	Mark P. Hadley
OFFICE OF THE DIRECTOR	
Associate Director, Communications	Deborah Kilroe
Associate Director, Economic Analysis	Wendy Edelberg
Associate Director, Economic Analysis	Jeffrey Kling
Associate Director, Legislative Affairs	Leigh Angres
General Counsel	(vacancy)
Senior Advisor	Robert A. Sunshine
OTHER DIVISIONS	
Assistant Director, Budget Analysis	Theresa A. Gullo
Assistant Director, Financial Analysis	Damien Moore
Assistant Director, Health, Retirement, and Long-Term Analysis	Linda Bilheimer
Assistant Director, Macroeconomic Analysis	Jeffrey F. Werling
Assistant Director, Microeconomic Studies	Joseph Kile
Assistant Director, National Security	David E. Mosher
Assistant Director, Tax Analysis	(vacancy)

Chief Administrative Officer, Management, Business, and Information Services	Joseph E. Evans, Jr.

The Congressional Budget Office produces independent analyses of budgetary and economic issues to support the congressional budget process.

The Congressional Budget Office (CBO) was established by the Congressional Budget Act of 1974 (2 U.S.C. 601), which also created a procedure by which the Congress considers and acts on the annual Federal budget. This process enables the Congress to have an overview of the Federal budget and to make overall decisions on spending and taxation levels and on the deficit or surplus these levels generate.

Activities

The CBO assists the congressional budget committees with drafting and enforcing the annual budget resolution, which serves as a blueprint for total levels of Government spending and revenues in a fiscal year. Once completed, the budget resolution guides the action of other congressional committees in drafting subsequent spending and revenue legislation within their jurisdiction.

To support this process, the CBO makes budgetary and economic projections, analyzes the proposals set forth in the President's budget request, and details alternative spending and revenue options for lawmakers to consider. The CBO also provides cost estimates of bills approved by congressional committees and tracks the progress of spending and revenue legislation in a scorekeeping system. CBO cost estimates and scorekeeping help the budget committees determine whether the budgetary effects of individual proposals are consistent with the most recent spending and revenue targets.

Upon congressional request, the CBO also produces reports analyzing specific policy and program issues that are significant for the budget. In keeping with the Office's nonpartisan role, its analyses do not include policy recommendations, and they routinely disclose their underlying assumptions and methods. This open and nonpartisan stance has been instrumental in preserving the credibility of the Office's analyses.

Analysis of the President's Budget

The CBO estimates the budgetary impact of the proposals in the President's budget using its own economic forecast and assumptions. The CBO's independent reestimate allows Congress to compare the administration's spending and revenue proposals with the CBO's baseline projections and other proposals using a consistent set of economic and technical assumptions.

Baseline Budget Projections and Economic Forecasts

Each year, the CBO issues reports on the budget and economic outlook that cover the 10-year period used in the congressional budget process. Those reports present and explain the CBO's baseline budget projections and economic forecast, which are generally based on current law regarding Federal spending and revenues. The reports also describe the differences between the current projections and previous ones, compare the CBO's economic forecast with those of other forecasters, and show the budgetary impact of some alternative policy assumptions.

Budgetary and Economic Policy Issues

The CBO also analyzes specific program and policy issues that affect the Federal budget and the economy. Generally, requests for these analyses come from the chair or ranking minority member of a committee or subcommittee or from the leadership of either party in the House or Senate.

Cost Estimates for Bills

The CBO provides cost estimates of every bill to show how it would affect spending or revenues over the next 5 or 10 years, depending on the type of spending involved. The CBO also provides informal estimates at the committee level and other stages in the legislative process.

Federal Mandates

As required by the Unfunded Mandates Reform Act of 1995, the CBO analyzes the costs that proposed legislation would impose on State, local, and tribal governments and on the private sector. The CBO produces mandate statements with its cost estimates for each committee-approved bill.

Scorekeeping

The CBO provides the budget and appropriations committees with frequent tabulations of congressional action affecting spending and revenues. Those scorekeeping reports provide information on whether legislative actions are consistent with the spending and revenue levels set by the budget resolution.

Sources of Information

Blog

The CBO Web site features a blog.

Business Opportunities

Information to help vendors is available online.

Cost Estimates

The CBO Web site features an online tool for searching cost estimates.

Employment

A career at the CBO offers opportunities to analyze public policies and their budgetary and economic effects, to work with policy analysis experts, to support the Congress, and to provide nonpartisan and objective analysis.

Frequently Asked Questions (FAQs)

The CBO posts answers to the most common questions that people ask.

Glossary

The glossary is available online in Portable Document Format (PDF). It defines terms that are commonly used in CBO reports. Many of the entries conform to those published in "A Glossary of Terms Used in the Federal Budget Process" (Government Accountability Office, 2005).

Information Products

CBO informational, nonpartisan products include baseline projections for selected programs, budget and economic data, and major recurring reports.

Internships

Interns attend seminars, participate in an educational program, and contribute to the agency's output of analysis.

Press Center

The CBO posts news and upcoming events online, as well as SlideShare presentations and YouTube videos. It also disseminates information via an RSS feed and by tweeting on Twitter.

Site Map

The CBO site map allows Internet visitors to look for keywords or to browse for content that aligns with their interests.

Topics

The CBO Web sites allows visitors to browse topics of analysis or to search for them with an online search tool. Topic categories include agriculture, budget, climate and environment, economy, education, energy and natural resources, health care, housing, immigration, income distribution, poverty and income security, social security, taxes, and more.

Visiting Scholars

The CBO welcomes applications from analysts and scholars in all fields; however, it has a special interest in collaborating with experts in macroeconomics and financial, health, and public economics.

For further information, contact the Management, Business, and Information Services Division, Congressional Budget Office, Second and D Streets SW., Washington, DC 20515. Phone, 202-226-2600. Fax, 202-226-2714.

CONGRESSIONAL BUDGET OFFICE

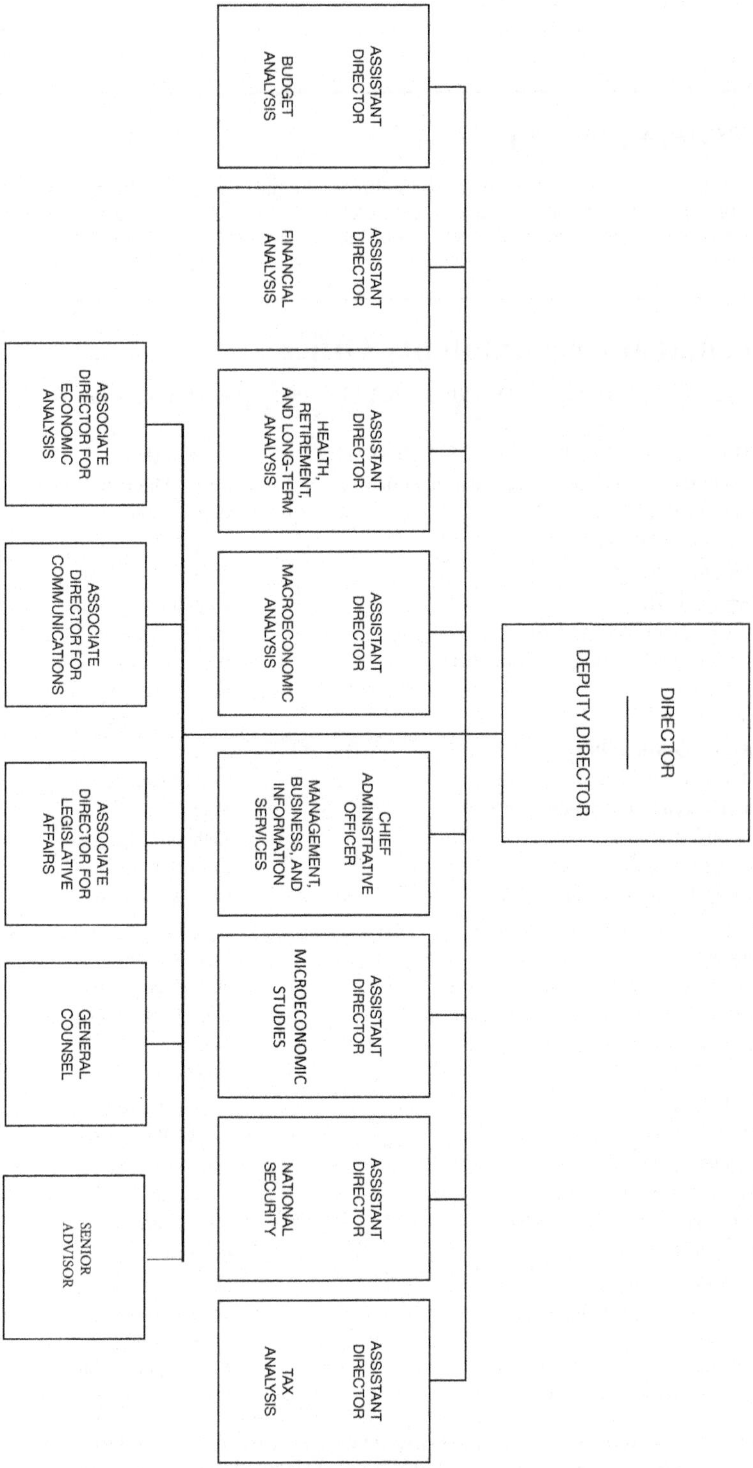

EDITORIAL NOTE

The Government Accountability Office did not meet the publication deadline for submitting updated information of its activities, functions, and sources of information as required by the automatic disclosure provisions of the Freedom of Information Act (5 U.S.C. 552(a)(1)(A)).

Government Accountability Office

441 G Street NW., Washington, DC 20548, 202-512-3000, *http://www.gao.gov*

COMPTROLLER GENERAL OF THE UNITED STATES	Gene L. Dodaro
Chief Administrative Officer / Chief Financial Officer	Karl J. Maschino
Chief Human Capital Officer	William White
Chief Information Officer	Howard Williams, Jr.
Chief Operating Officer	Patricia A. Dalton
Chief Quality Officer	Timothy P. Bowling
Deputy Chief Administrative Officer	Paul R. Johnson
Deputy Chief Financial Officer / Controller	William L. Anderson
General Counsel	Susan A. Poling
Inspector General	Adam Trzeciak
MANAGING DIRECTORS	
Acquisition and Sourcing Management	Paul L. Francis
Applied Research and Methods	Nancy Kingsbury
Congressional Relations	Katherine Siggerud
Continuous Process Improvement	Thomas Williams
Defense Capabilities and Management	Cathleen A. Berrick
Education, Workforce, and Income Security	Barbara D. Bovbjerg
Field Operations	Linda Calbom
Financial Management and Assurance	Gary Engel
Financial Markets and Community Investment	Orice Williams Brown
Forensic Audits and Investigative Service	Johana R. Ayers
Health Care	Nikki Clowers
Homeland Security and Justice	George A. Scott
Information Technology	Joel C. Willemssen
Infrastructure Operations	Terrell Dorn
International Affairs and Trade	Loren Yager
Natural Resources and Environment	Mark Gaffigan
Opportunity and Inclusiveness	Reginald E. Jones
Physical Infrastructure	Phillip Herr
Professional Development Program	Teresa Rivera Russell
Public Affairs	Charles Young
Strategic Issues	J. Christopher Mihm
Strategic Planning and External Liaison	James-Christian Blockwood

The Government Accountability Office helps the Congress fulfill its constitutional responsibilities and heightens the Federal Government's accountability and performance.

The Government Accountability Office (GAO) is an independent, nonpartisan agency that works for the Congress. The GAO is often called the "congressional watchdog" because it investigates how the Federal Government spends taxpayer dollars. The GAO was established as the General Accounting Office by the Budget Accounting Act of 1921 (31 U.S.C. 702). It was renamed the Government Accountability Office pursuant to the GAO Capital Reform Act of 2004 (31 U.S.C. 702 note).

Activities

The GAO gathers information that the Congress uses to determine how effective executive branch agencies are at carrying out their missions. Its efforts routinely center on answering basic questions: Are Government programs meeting their objectives? Are they providing services of value to the public? Ultimately, the GAO ensures that the Government is accountable to the American people.

To help Senators and Representatives make informed policy decisions, the GAO provides them with accurate, balanced, and timely information. The Office supports congressional oversight by evaluating Government policies and programs; auditing agency operations to ensure effective, efficient, and appropriate spending of Federal funds; investigating allegations of illegal and improper activities; and issuing legal decisions and opinions.

With virtually the entire Federal Government subject to its review, the GAO issues a steady stream of products, including hundreds of reports and testimonies by GAO officials each year. Its reports or "blue books" meet short-term, immediate needs for information on a wide range of Government operations. These reports help Members of Congress understand emerging, long-term issues with far-reaching effects. The GAO's work supports a wide variety of improvements in Government operations and legislative actions that save the American people billions of dollars.

Sources of Information

At a Glance

The "GAO at a Glance" Web page offers a profile of the agency, including information on the scope and nature of its activities.

Blog

The GAO's Web site features "WatchBlog: Following the Federal Dollar." To receive electronic notifications of new posts, sign up by entering an email address in the appropriate text box on the "WatchBlog" Web page.

Career Opportunities

The GAO relies on attorneys, communications analysts, criminal investigators, economists, financial auditors, information technology analysts, and other professionals to carry out its mission.

The GAO offers an intern program for students. Appointments for intern positions are 10–16 weeks in length and normally held during summer months. A student must be enrolled on at least a half-time basis, as determined by his or her college or university. A GAO student intern receives an appointment on a nonpermanent basis; however, after completing 400 hours of service and meeting degree requirements, he or she may be eligible for a permanent position. Internships are open to undergraduate and graduate students.

The GAO was named again as one of the top places to work in the Federal Government. It ranked third in the Partnership for Public Service's 2015 list of the Best Places To Work among midsize agencies.

Freedom of Information Act (FOIA)

The GAO is not subject to the FOIA; however, its disclosure policy adheres to the spirit of the act while remaining consistent with its duties and functions as an agency whose primary responsibility is to the Congress. Fax, 202-512-5806.

Good Governance

The Center for Audit Excellence promotes good governance and builds the capacity of domestic and international accountability organizations. It provides high-quality training, technical assistance, and related products and services.

Key Issues

The "Key Issues" Web pages contain information on GAO's work on a range of national issues, and they highlight the agency's most relevant reports.

Podcast Gallery

Recorded, hosted, and produced by GAO staff, the "Watchdog Report" features interviews with agency officials on significant issues and new reports.

Products

The best known GAO products—correspondence, legal decisions and opinions, reports, and testimonies—are available to the press and the public.

Publications

Most GAO products and publications are available online, free of charge. Charges for printed copies cover the printing, shipping, and handling costs. Phone, 202-512-6000 or 866-801-7077. TDD, 202-512-2537.

The GAO's Web site allows visitors to browse reports and testimonies by date and topic and by agency alphabetically or hierarchically.

The "Principles of Federal Appropriations Law," also known as the "Red Book," is a multivolume treatise on Federal fiscal law. It provides text discussions with references to specific legal authorities to illustrate legal principles, their applications, and exceptions. These references include GAO decisions and judicial decisions, opinions, statutory provisions, and other relevant sources.

Recommendations Database

The recommendations database contains report recommendations that still need to be addressed. GAO's recommendations help congressional and agency leaders prepare for appropriations and oversight activities, as well as improve Government operations. Recommendations remain open until designated as "closed-implemented" or "closed-not implemented." The public can explore open recommendations online by browsing or searching.

Resources

The GAO Web site features resources that auditors and others promoting accountability may find useful.

The GAO Web site features resources that Members of Congress and and their staff may find useful.

The GAO Web site features resources that Federal agency managers may find useful.

The GAO Web site features resources that journalists may find useful.

The GAO Web site features resources—search tips for locating GAO products on its website, information on using the data and images contained in them, suggestions for additional informational sources—that researchers may find useful.

Social Media

The GAO has a Facebook account.

The GAO tweets announcements, news, and other noteworthy items on Twitter.

The GAO posts videos on its YouTube channel.

The GAO posts informational graphics and photographs on Flickr.

Site Map

The Web site map allows visitors to look for specific topics or to browse content that aligns with their interests.

Telephone Directory

The "Organizational Telephone Directory" (June 2016), a document that is updated often, contains contact information for agency personnel and is available online in Portable Document Format (PDF).

Updates

A subscription form is available on the GAO's Web site to sign up for email updates on the latest reports. Daily or monthly electronic updates are options, too, as well as notifications about correspondence, reports, and testimony that fall within a specific topic area.

Video Gallery

The GAO Web site features a video collection that is diverse and extensive, educational and informative.

Widgets

Snippets of HTML code for embedding small news widgets that refresh automatically are available on the GAO Web site. Pasting the code into the desired location on a Web site makes the most recent reports and testimonies and legal decisions from GAO locally accessible.

For further information, contact the Office of Public Affairs, Government Accountability Office, 441 G Street NW., Washington, DC 20548. Phone, 202-512-4800.

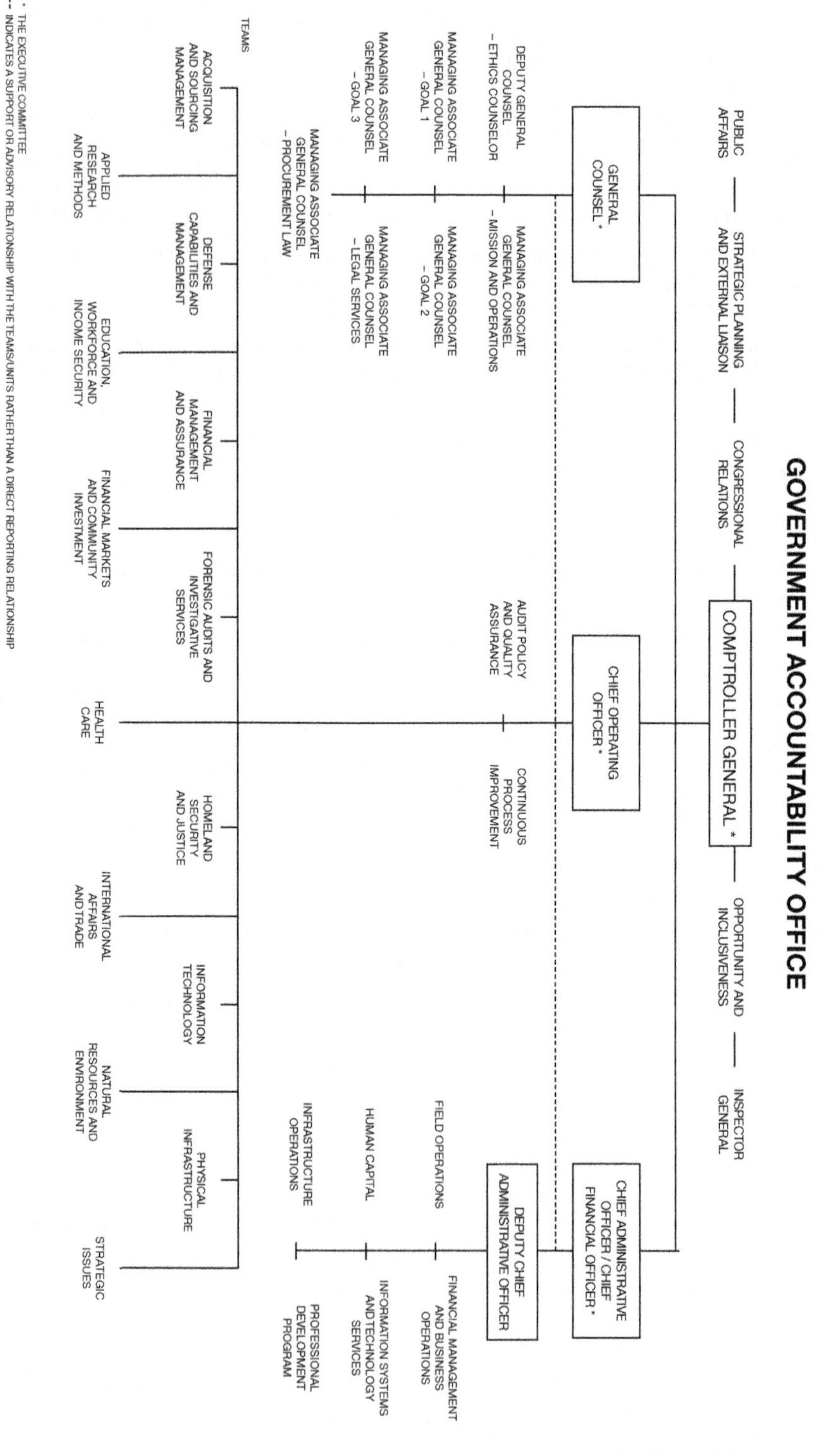
GOVERNMENT ACCOUNTABILITY OFFICE
COMPTROLLER GENERAL *
PUBLIC AFFAIRS
STRATEGIC PLANNING AND EXTERNAL LIAISON
CONGRESSIONAL RELATIONS
OPPORTUNITY AND INCLUSIVENESS
INSPECTOR GENERAL
GENERAL COUNSEL *
CHIEF OPERATING OFFICER *
CHIEF ADMINISTRATIVE OFFICER / CHIEF FINANCIAL OFFICER *
DEPUTY CHIEF ADMINISTRATIVE OFFICER
DEPUTY GENERAL COUNSEL – ETHICS COUNSELOR
MANAGING ASSOCIATE GENERAL COUNSEL – MISSION AND OPERATIONS
MANAGING ASSOCIATE GENERAL COUNSEL – GOAL 1
MANAGING ASSOCIATE GENERAL COUNSEL – GOAL 2
MANAGING ASSOCIATE GENERAL COUNSEL – GOAL 3
MANAGING ASSOCIATE GENERAL COUNSEL – LEGAL SERVICES
MANAGING ASSOCIATE GENERAL COUNSEL – PROCUREMENT LAW
AUDIT POLICY AND QUALITY ASSURANCE
CONTINUOUS PROCESS IMPROVEMENT
FIELD OPERATIONS
FINANCIAL MANAGEMENT AND BUSINESS OPERATIONS
HUMAN CAPITAL
INFORMATION SYSTEMS AND TECHNOLOGY SERVICES
INFRASTRUCTURE OPERATIONS
PROFESSIONAL DEVELOPMENT PROGRAM
TEAMS
ACQUISITION AND SOURCING MANAGEMENT
APPLIED RESEARCH AND METHODS
DEFENSE CAPABILITIES AND MANAGEMENT
EDUCATION, WORKFORCE AND INCOME SECURITY
FINANCIAL MANAGEMENT AND ASSURANCE
FINANCIAL MARKETS AND COMMUNITY INVESTMENT
FORENSIC AUDITS AND INVESTIGATIVE SERVICES
HEALTH CARE
HOMELAND SECURITY AND JUSTICE
INTERNATIONAL AFFAIRS AND TRADE
INFORMATION TECHNOLOGY
NATURAL RESOURCES AND ENVIRONMENT
PHYSICAL INFRASTRUCTURE
STRATEGIC ISSUES
* THE EXECUTIVE COMMITTEE
--- INDICATES A SUPPORT OR ADVISORY RELATIONSHIP WITH THE TEAMS/UNITS RATHER THAN A DIRECT REPORTING RELATIONSHIP

Government Publishing Office

732 North Capitol Street NW., Washington, DC 20401, 202-512-1800, *http://www.gpo.gov*

DIRECTOR	Davita Vance-Cooks
Deputy Director	Jim C. Bradley
Chief Administrative Officer	Herbert H. Jackson, Jr.
Chief of Staff	Andrew M. Sherman
General Counsel	Drew Spalding
Inspector General	Michael A. Raponi
Superintendent of Documents	Laurie Hall, Acting
Chief Financial Officer	Steven T. Shedd
Chief Human Capital Officer	Ginger T. Thomas
Chief Information Officer	Charles Riddle
Chief Public Relations Officer	Gary Somerset
Chief Technology Officer	Richard G. Davis
Chief of Acquisition Services	Lorna Baptiste-Jones
MANAGING DIRECTORS	
Customer Services	Bruce Seger
Equal Employment Opportunity	Juanita M. Flores
Labor Relations	Melissa Hatfield
Library Services and Content Management	Laurie Hall
Official Journals of Government	Lyle Green
Plant Operations	John Crawford
Security and Intelligent Documents	Stephen G. LeBlanc
Security Services	Lamont Vernon

The Government Publishing Office produces, procures, and disseminates printed and electronic publications of the Congress, executive departments, and Federal agencies and establishments.

The Government Publishing Office (GPO) was created on June 23, 1860, by Congressional Joint Resolution 25. The Office opened for business on March 4, 1861. Its duties are defined in title 44 of the U.S. Code. The President appoints the Director, who is then confirmed by the Senate.

Activities

Headquartered in Washington, DC, with a total employment of approximately 1,700, the Office is responsible for the production and distribution of information products and services for the three branches of the Federal Government. It is the Federal Government's primary centralized resource for producing, procuring, cataloging, indexing, authenticating, disseminating, and preserving the official information products of the U.S. Government in digital and tangible forms.

While many of the informational products, such as the "Congressional Record" and "Federal Register," are produced at the main GPO plant, most of the Government's printing is done in partnership with America's printing industry. The Office procures 75 percent of all printing orders through private sector vendors across the country, competitively buying products and services from thousands of businesses in all 50 States. The contracts cover the entire spectrum of printing and publishing services and are suitable for companies of all sizes.

The Office disseminates Federal information products through a sales program, distribution network of more than 1,200 Federal libraries nationwide, and the

Federal Digital System (FDsys). The public can access more than 800,000 Federal Government document titles online by using the FDsys Web site.

Sources of Information

Bookstore

Printed copies of many documents, ranging from Supreme Court opinions to reports from the Bureau of Labor Statistics, may be purchased. To order in person, visit the GPO Main Bookstore at 710 North Capitol Street NW., Washington, DC (corner of North Capitol Street NW. and G Street), 8 a.m.–4 p.m. To order online, use the link below. To order by phone or inquire about an order, call 866-512-1800 or 202-512-1800 (Washington, DC–metropolitan area), 8 a.m.–5:30 p.m., eastern standard time. All orders require prepayment by an American Express, Discover/NOVUS, MasterCard, or VISA credit card; check or money order; or Superintendent of Documents (SOD) deposit account, which customers who purchase Government products on a recurring basis can open with the GPO. Fax, 202-512-2104.

Business Opportunities

Acquisition Services obtains the equipment, services, and supplies that GPO needs from external sources to accomplish its mission. Phone, 202-512-0937.

Commercial printers seeking contract opportunities should contact Customer Services, Government Publishing Office, Washington, DC 20401. Phone, 202-512-0526.

Congressional Relations

The Office of Congressional Relations responds to congressional inquiries and requests. Phone, 202-512-1991. Fax, 202-512-1293.

Employment

GPO vacancy announcements and information on benefits, career paths, and the application process are accessible online.

Federal Digital System (FDsys)

The FDsys makes official publications from the executive, judicial, and legislative branches of Government accessible. The GPO provides user support for the System. Phone, 866-512-1800 or 202-512-1800 (Washington, DC–metropolitan area).

Frequently Asked Questions (FAQs)

Answers to FAQs are available on the GPO Web site.

Learning Resources

Ben's Guide is an educational Web site for children and young adults. It features learning adventures for the apprentice level (ages 4–8), journeyperson level (ages 9–13), and master level (ages 14 and older).

Newsroom

The newsroom features high resolution images for downloading, news reports, press releases, and a video chronicling GPO from its beginnings to the digital future. Phone, 202-512-1957. Fax, 202-512-1998.

Regional Offices

A list of regional offices, with contact information, is available on the GPO Web site.

Site Map

The Web site map allows visitors to look for specific topics or to browse content that aligns with their interests.

For further information, contact Public Relations, Government Publishing Office, 732 North Capitol Street NW., Washington, DC 20401. Phone, 202-512-1957. Fax, 202-512-1998.

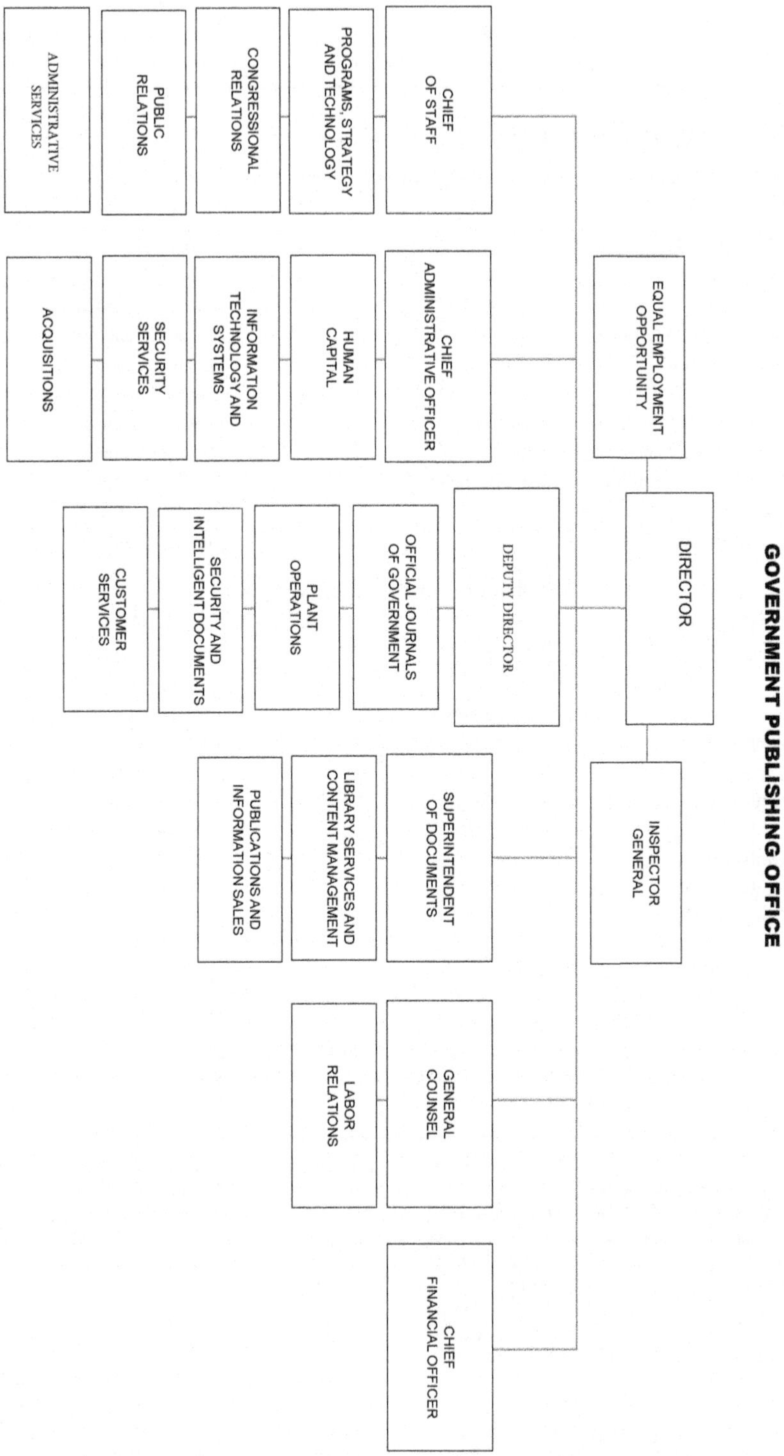
GOVERNMENT PUBLISHING OFFICE
DIRECTOR
EQUAL EMPLOYMENT OPPORTUNITY
INSPECTOR GENERAL
CHIEF OF STAFF
PROGRAMS, STRATEGY AND TECHNOLOGY
CONGRESSIONAL RELATIONS
PUBLIC RELATIONS
ADMINISTRATIVE SERVICES
CHIEF ADMINISTRATIVE OFFICER
HUMAN CAPITAL
INFORMATION TECHNOLOGY AND SYSTEMS
SECURITY SERVICES
ACQUISITIONS
DEPUTY DIRECTOR
OFFICIAL JOURNALS OF GOVERNMENT
PLANT OPERATIONS
SECURITY AND INTELLIGENT DOCUMENTS
CUSTOMER SERVICES
SUPERINTENDENT OF DOCUMENTS
LIBRARY SERVICES AND CONTENT MANAGEMENT
PUBLICATIONS AND INFORMATION SALES
GENERAL COUNSEL
LABOR RELATIONS
CHIEF FINANCIAL OFFICER

Library of Congress

101 Independence Avenue SE., Washington, DC 20540, 202-707-5000, *http://www.loc.gov*

LIBRARIAN OF CONGRESS	Carla D. Hayden
Deputy Librarian	David S. Mao
Chief of Staff	Robert R. Newlen
Chief Operating Officer	Edward R. Jablonski
General Counsel	Elizabeth Pugh
Inspector General	Kurt W. Hyde
Associate Librarian for Library Services	J. Mark Sweeney
Director of Human Resources Services	Rachel Bouman
Director of National International Outreach	Jane McAuliffe
Law Librarian	Roberta I. Shaffer
Register of Copyrights	Maria A. Pallante

Library of Congress Trust Fund Board

CHAIR (Librarian of Congress)	Carla D. Hayden
(Fiscal Assistant Secretary of the Treasury)	David A. Lebryk
(Chair, Joint Committee on the Library)	Charles E. Schumer
(Vice Chair, Joint Committee on the Library)	Gregg Harper
Member	Kathleen L. Casey
Member	J. Richard Fredericks
Member	Thomas Girardi
Member	Barbara Guggenheim
Member	Joan W. Harris
Member	James V. Kimsey
Member	Christopher G. Long
Member	George Marcus
Member	Sally Susman
Member	(vacancy)

The Library of Congress is the national library of the United States, offering diverse materials for research, including the world's most extensive collections in areas such as American history, music, and law.

The Library of Congress was established by Act of April 24, 1800 (2 Stat. 56), appropriating $5,000 "for the purchase of such books as may be necessary for the use of Congress . . . ." The Library's scope of responsibility has been widened by subsequent legislation (2 U.S.C. 131-168d). The Librarian, appointed by the President with the advice and consent of the Senate, directs the Library.

The Library's first responsibility is service to Congress. Its Congressional Research Service provides Congress with legislative research and analysis that is authoritative, confidential, objective, and timely during all stages of the legislative process. The Library's Congress.gov Web site serves as a source of legislative information for both Congress and the general public.

As the Library has developed, its range of service has expanded to include the entire governmental establishment and the public at large. The Library serves as a national library for the United States, and its online presence makes it a global resource.

Activities

Collections

The Library's extensive collections are universal in scope. They include books, serials, and pamphlets on every subject and in more than 470 languages, and research materials in many formats, including maps, photographs, manuscripts, motion pictures, and sound recordings. Among them are the most comprehensive collections of books outside Asia and the former Soviet Union; the largest collection of published aeronautical literature; and the most extensive collection of books in the Western Hemisphere.

The manuscript collections relate to various aspects of American history and civilization and include the personal papers of most of the Presidents from George Washington to Calvin Coolidge. The music collections contain volumes and pieces—manuscript and published—from classic works to the newest popular compositions. Other materials available for research include maps and views; photographic records; recordings, prints, drawings, and posters; government documents, newspapers, and periodicals; and motion pictures, microforms, audio and video tapes, and digital and online materials.

Reference Resources

Admission to the various research facilities of the Library is free. The Library's reading rooms are open to persons age 16 and older. Readers must register by presenting valid photo identification with a current address. For some collections, there are additional requirements. While priority is given to inquiries about special materials or to unique resources, the Library provides helpful responses to all inquirers. Online reference service is also available through the "Ask a Librarian" Web page.

Copyrights

With the enactment of the second general revision of the U.S. copyright law by Act of July 8, 1870 (16 Stat. 212–217), all activities relating to copyright, including deposit and registration, were centralized in the Library of Congress. The Copyright Act of 1976 (90 Stat. 2541) brought all forms of copyrightable authorship, both published and unpublished, under a single statutory system which gives authors protection upon creation of their works. Exclusive rights granted to authors under the statute include the right to reproduce and prepare derivative works, distribute copies or phonorecords, perform and display the work publicly, and in the case of sound recordings, to perform the work publicly by means of a digital audio transmission. Works eligible for copyright include literary works (books and periodicals), musical works, dramatic works, pantomimes and choreographic works, pictorial, graphic, and sculptural works, motion pictures, sound recordings, vessel hull designs, mask works, and architectural works.

The Copyright Office serves as a National registry for creative works, registering more than 500,000 claims annually. It is also a major source of acquisitions for the Library's collections. Most paper information is also accessible on its Web site.

Extension of Service

The Library offers duplication services; the sale of sound recordings, cataloging data and tools; the exchange of duplicates with other institutions; development of classification schemes; preparation of bibliographic lists for Government and research; maintenance and publication of cooperative publications; and publication of catalogs, bibliographic guides, and lists, and texts of original manuscripts and rare books. It has items for circulation in traveling exhibitions; books in Braille, as well as "talking books on the Internet, and books on tape. The Library distributes electronic materials and provides research and analytical services for a fee. The Library also manages the following programs: centralized and cooperative cataloging; cataloging-in-publication for unpublished books; interlibrary loan system; and the U.S. International Standard Serial Number (ISSN) Center.

Furthermore, the Library provides for the following: the preparation of bibliographical lists responsive to the needs of Government and research; the maintenance and the publication of cooperative publications; the publication of catalogs, bibliographical guides, and lists, and of texts of original manuscripts and rare books in the Library of Congress; the circulation in traveling exhibitions of items from the Library's collections; the provision of books in Braille, electronic access to Braille books on the Internet, "talking books," and books on tape for the blind and the physically handicapped through more than 100 cooperating libraries throughout the Nation; the distribution of its electronic materials via the Internet; and the provision of research and analytical services on a fee-for-service basis to agencies in the executive and judicial branches.

American Folklife Center

The American Folklife Center was established in the Library of Congress by Act of January 2, 1976 (20 U.S.C. 2102 et seq.). It supports, preserves, and presents American folklife by receiving and maintaining folklife collections, scholarly research, field projects, performances, exhibitions, festivals, workshops, publications, and audiovisual presentations. The Center administers the Veterans History Project, which records and preserves the first-person accounts of war veterans. It collaborates with the Smithsonian Institution's National Museum of African American History and Culture to maintain the Civil Rights History Project and its resulting collection of interviews with leaders and participants in the Civil Rights movement. The Center also maintains and administers the American Folklife Center Archive, which is an extensive multi-format collection of ethnographic materials from this country and around the world, and serves as the national repository for folk-related field recordings, manuscripts, and other unpublished materials. The Archive also contains the collections of StoryCorps, a program to record and collect oral histories from people from all walks of life.

The Center's reading room contains over 4,000 books and periodicals; a sizable collection of magazines, newsletters, unpublished theses, and dissertations; field notes; and many textual and some musical transcriptions and recordings. Information on the Center's blog, social media, publications, and collections is available online.

For further information, call 202-707-5510.

Center for the Book

The Center was established in the Library of Congress by an Act of October 13, 1977 (2 U.S.C. 171 et seq.), to stimulate public interest in books, reading, and libraries, and to encourage the study of books and print culture. The Center promotes and explores the vital role of books, reading, and libraries, nationally and internationally. As a partnership between the Government and the private sector, the Center for the Book depends on tax-deductible contributions from individuals and corporations to support its programs.

The Center's activities are directed toward the general public and scholars. The overall program includes reading promotion projects with television and radio networks, symposia, lectures, exhibitions, special events, and publications. More than 80 national education and civic organizations participate in the Center's annual reading promotion campaign.

The Center provides leadership for 52 affiliated State—including the District of Columbia and the Virgin Islands—centers for the book and nonprofit reading-promotion partners. It oversees the Library's read.gov Web site, administers the Library's Young Readers Center and its Poetry and Literature Center, and plays a key role in the Library's annual National Book Festival. The Center also administers the position of Poet Laureate Consultant in Poetry, as well as, in collaboration with the Children's Book Council, the position of the National Ambassador for Young People's Literature.

For further information, contact the Center for the Book. Phone, 202-707-5221. Fax, 202-707-0269.

National Film Preservation Board

The National Film Preservation Board, established by the National Film Preservation Act of 1988 (102 Stat. 1785) and reauthorized by the National Film Preservation Act of 2005 (2 U.S.C. 1791 note), serves as a public advisory group to the Librarian of Congress. The Board works to ensure the survival, conservation, and increased public availability of America's film heritage, including advising the Librarian on the annual selection of films to the National Film Registry and counseling the Librarian on development and implementation of the national film preservation plan.

For further information, call 202-707-5912.

National Sound Recording Preservation Board

The National Recording Preservation Board, established by the National Recording Preservation Act of 2000 (2 U.S.C. 1701 note) reviews nominated sound recordings for inclusion in the National Recording Registry and advises the Librarian on the inclusion of such recordings in the Registry to preserve sound recordings that are culturally, historically, or aesthetically significant. The Board comprises three major components: a National Recording Preservation Advisory Board, which brings together experts in the field; a National Recording Registry; and a fundraising foundation, all of which are conducted under the auspices of the Library of Congress. The Board implements a national plan for the long-term preservation and accessibility of the Nation's audio heritage. The national recording preservation program sets standards for future private and public preservation efforts in conjunction with the Library's National Audio-Visual Conservation Center in Culpeper, VA.

For further information, call 202-707-5856.

Preservation

The Library provides technical information related to the preservation of library and archival material. The Library's Preservation Directorate includes three preservation science laboratories, a Center for the Library's Analytical Science Samples, and a Collections Recovery Room. Information on publications and various preservation and conservation topics is available online.

For further information, call 202-707-1840.

Sources of Information

Books for the Blind and Physically Handicapped

Braille and talking books and magazines, including music materials, are distributed through more than 100 regional and subregional libraries to residents of the United States and its territories who are blind or have a physical disability. Eligible Americans living abroad are also able to participate. Users may also register for the Braille and Audio Reading Download (BARD) online service, enabling them to use the BARD mobile app to read on smart devices. Information is available from the National Library Service for the Blind and Physically Handicapped, Library of Congress, 1291 Taylor Street NW., Washington, DC 20542-4960. Phone, 202-707-5100 or 1-888-NLS-READ (1-888-657-7323).

Business Opportunities

To learn about business opportunities, visit the "Doing Business With the Library" Web page.

Cataloging Distribution Services

Cataloging and bibliographic information in the form of microfiche catalogs, book catalogs, magnetic tapes, CD-ROM cataloging tools, bibliographies, and other technical publications is distributed to libraries and other institutions. Information about ordering materials is available from the Cataloging Distribution Service, Library of Congress, Washington, DC 20541-4910. Phone, 202-707-6100. TDD, 202-707-0012. Fax, 202-707-1334. Email, cdsinfo@mail.loc.gov. Card numbers for new publications and Electronic Preassigned Control Numbers for publishers are available from the Cataloging in Publication Division, Library of Congress, Washington, DC 20541-4910. Phone, 202-707-6345.

Copyright Services

Information about the copyright law (title 17 of the U.S. Code), the method of securing copyright, and copyright registration procedures may be obtained by writing to the Copyright Office, Library of Congress, 101 Independence Avenue SE., Washington, DC 20559-6000. Phone, 202-707-3000. Registration application forms may be ordered by calling the forms hotline at 202-707-9100. Copyright records may be researched and reported by the Copyright Office for a fee; for an estimate, call 202-707-6850. Members of the public may use the copyright card catalog in the Copyright Office without charge. The database of Copyright Office records cataloged from January 1, 1978, to the present is available online at http://cocatalog.loc.gov/. The Copyright Information Office is located in Room LM-401, James Madison Memorial Building, 101 Independence Avenue SE., Washington, DC 20559-6000. It is open to the public Monday through Friday, 8:30 a.m. to 5 p.m., except for Federal holidays.

Employment

The Library offers many opportunities for those seeking employment, fellowships or internships, or volunteer positions. Job vacancy announcements and application information are posted online and also available from the Employment Office, Room LM-107, 101 Independence Avenue SE., Washington, DC 20540. Phone, 202-707-4315.

Duplication Services

Copies of manuscripts, prints, photographs, maps, and book material not subject to copyright and other restrictions are available for a fee. Order forms for photo reproduction and price schedules are available from Duplication Services, Library of Congress, 101 Independence Avenue SE., Washington, DC 20540-4570. Phone, 202-707-5640.

Exhibitions

Throughout the year, the Library offers free exhibitions featuring items from its collections. Library exhibitions may be viewed Monday through Saturday, 8:30 a.m. to 4:30 p.m., in the Thomas Jefferson Building. For more information, call 202-707-4604. To view current and past exhibitions online, use the link below.

Federal Agency Research Services

Federal agencies can procure research and analytical products on foreign and domestic topics using the collections of the Library of Congress through the Federal Research Division. Science, technology, humanities, and social science research are conducted by staff specialists exclusively on behalf of Federal agencies on a fee-for-service basis. Research requests should be directed to the Federal Research Division, Marketing Office, Library of Congress, Washington, DC 20540-4840. Phone, 202-707-9133. Fax, 202-707-3920.

Publications

Library of Congress publications are available online. The Library of Congress Magazine (LCM) is published 6 times a year and may be viewed online at http://www.loc.gov/lcm/. The calendar of public events is also available online at www.loc.gov/loc/events and is available by mail to persons within 100 miles of Washington, DC. To be added to the calendar mailing list, send a request to Office Systems Services, Mail and Distribution Management Section, Library of Congress, 101 Independence Avenue SE., Washington, DC 20540-9441 or send an email to pao@loc.gov.

Reference and Bibliographic Services

Guidance is offered to readers in identifying and using the material in the Library's collections, and reference service is provided to those with inquiries who have exhausted local, State, and regional resources. Persons requiring services that cannot be performed by the Library staff can be supplied with names of private researchers who work on a fee-for-service basis. Requests for information should be directed to the Reference Referral Service, Library of Congress, 101 Independence Avenue SE., Washington, DC 20540-4720. Phone, 202-707-5522. Fax, 202-707-1389. Questions may also be submitted online at the "Ask a Librarian" Web site.

Research and Reference Services in Science and Technology

Requests for reference services should be directed to the Science, Technology, and Business Division, Library of Congress,

Science Reference Section, 101 Independence Avenue SE., Washington, DC 20540-4750. Phone, 202-707-5639.

Tours

Guided tours of the Library are available on weekdays, 10:30 a.m.–3:30 p.m., and on Saturdays at 10:30 and 11:30 a.m. and at 1:30 and 2:30 p.m. For more information on scheduling a tour for a group of 10 or more, contact the Visitor Services Office. Phone, 202-707-0919.

For further information, contact the Public Affairs Office, Library of Congress, 101 Independence Avenue SE., Washington, DC 20540-8610. Phone, 202-707-2905. Fax, 202-707-2905. Fax, 202-707-9199.

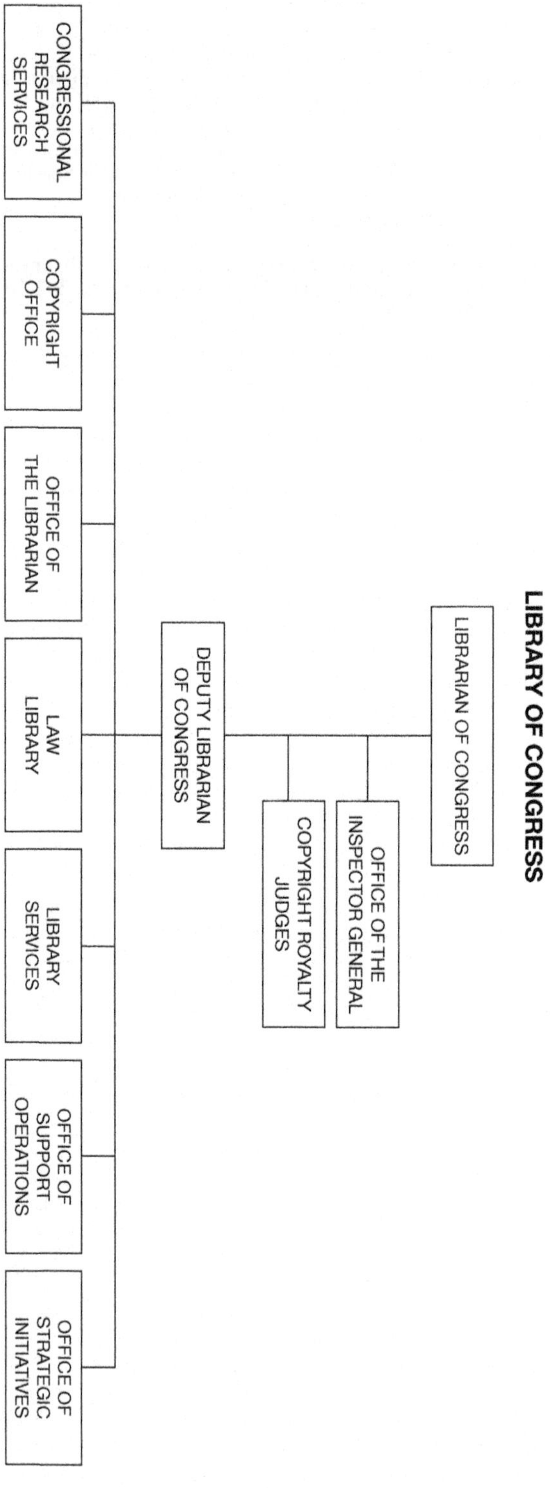
LIBRARY OF CONGRESS
LIBRARIAN OF CONGRESS
OFFICE OF THE INSPECTOR GENERAL
COPYRIGHT ROYALTY JUDGES
DEPUTY LIBRARIAN OF CONGRESS
CONGRESSIONAL RESEARCH SERVICES
COPYRIGHT OFFICE
OFFICE OF THE LIBRARIAN
LAW LIBRARY
LIBRARY SERVICES
OFFICE OF SUPPORT OPERATIONS
OFFICE OF STRATEGIC INITIATIVES

Congressional Research Service

101 Independence Avenue SE., Washington, DC 20540, 202-707-5000

Director, Congressional Research Service	Mary B. Mazanec

The Congressional Research Service (CRS) provides comprehensive research and analysis on all legislative and oversight issues of interest to Congress. The CRS assists Congress by responding to specific questions and by preparing reports on legislative topics in anticipation of questions and emerging issues. The CRS works with Members, committees, and congressional staff to identify and clarify policy problems and assess the implications of proposed policy alternatives. CRS experts play a role in every stage of the legislative process.

Sources of Information

Employment

Current vacancies and entry-level opportunities are posted online, as well as information on internship programs.

For further information, call 202-707-5700.

United States Botanic Garden

Office of Executive Director, 245 First Street SW., Washington, DC 20024, 202-226-8333, *http://www.usbg.gov*

Conservatory, 100 Maryland Avenue SW., Washington, DC 20001

Production Facility, 4700 Shepherd Parkway SW., Washington, DC 20032, 202-226-4780

ACTING DIRECTOR	Stephen T. Ayers
Executive Director	Ari Novy

The United States Botanic Garden informs visitors of the importance and value of plants to humankind and to Earth's ecosystems.

The U.S. Botanic Garden (USBG) has a long history that reaches back to the Founding Fathers. In October of 1796, President George Washington suggested that "a Botanic Garden would be a good appendage" to a Federal university. Twenty-four years later, President James Madison helped establish a botanic garden in the U.S. Capital under the auspices of the Columbian Institute, a society dedicated to promoting the arts and sciences. This early botanic collection served as the cornerstone of what would become the Nation's future botanic garden.

Congress also supported establishing a national botanic garden. By an act of August 26, 1842, it made provision for the safekeeping and arrangement of dried and living specimens that Lieutenant Charles Wilkes's expedition had collected while exploring the Pacific Rim. Congress placed the enlarged collection under the stewardship of its Joint Committee on the Library.

When the old Patent Office was expanded in 1849, a new location for the plants and greenhouse had to be found. Congress again intervened and, by an act of May 15, 1850, funded the construction of a new greenhouse and the collection's relocation. The Joint Committee on the Library, with assistance from the

Commissioner of Public Buildings, managed the project. A new national botanic garden opened on the National Mall, at the west end of the Capitol Grounds, later that year.

By 1856, the collection officially had been named the United States Botanic Garden, Congress was providing an annual appropriation for its upkeep, and the Joint Committee on the Library had assumed responsibility for both its direction and maintenance. To satisfy the McMillan Commission's plan for a large, open mall, the USBG was moved in 1933, one block south, to its present site. The Joint Committee on the Library maintains oversight of the USBG through the Architect of the Capitol, who holds the title of Acting Director.

Activities

The USBG highlights botanical diversity worldwide, as well as the aesthetic, cultural, ecological, economic, and therapeutic significance of plants. The agency promotes appreciation of plants and stimulates interest in botany through artistic plant displays, education programs, exhibits, and curation of a large plant collection. It supports conservation by serving as a repository for endangered plant species. It also encourages the exchange of ideas and disseminates mission-relevant information to national and international visitors and policymakers.

Three USBG sites are open year-round to the public: the Conservatory, the National Garden, and Bartholdi Park. The production facility is periodically open for public programs and tours.

Sources of Information

America's Agricultural Experience

Based on a meeting that the the U.S. Botanic Garden helped to organize of the Nation's leading agricultural and botanical educators, "Agriculture and the Future of Food: The Role of Botanic Gardens" presents a series of educational narratives that promote the reconnection of people and plants through the American agricultural experience. The document is available on the USBG Web site in Portable Document Format (PDF).

Employment

Information on career and volunteer opportunities is available online.

Exhibits

Information on current and upcoming exhibits is available online.

Factsheets

Gardening factsheets are available on the USBG's Web site.

Kids

The USBG is a child-friendly living plant museum.

Living Collections Database

An online tool is available to search the USBG's living collections database.

Plant Hotline

Questions about a garden plant? Call the Plant Hotline. Phone, 202-226-4785.

Pollinators

Learn about the role birds and bees, as well as other creatures like bats, beetles, butterflies, flies, moths, and even wasps, play in the life cycle of plants.

Production Facility

The production facility opens periodically for public programs and tours. An annual open house allows visitors to meet the gardeners, ask questions, and explore the facility.

For further information concerning the United States Botanic Garden, contact the Public Program Division, 245 First Street SW., Washington, DC 20515. Phone, 202-225-8333.

Judicial Branch

The Supreme Court of the United States

United States Supreme Court Building, One First Street NE., Washington, DC 20543, 202-479-3000, *http://www.supremecourt.gov*

MEMBERS

CHIEF JUSTICE OF THE UNITED STATES	John G. Roberts, Jr.
Associate Justice	Anthony M. Kennedy
Associate Justice	Clarence Thomas
Associate Justice	Ruth Bader Ginsburg
Associate Justice	Stephen G. Breyer
Associate Justice	Samuel A. Alito, Jr.
Associate Justice	Sonia Sotomayor
Associate Justice	Elena Kagan
Associate Justice	(vacancy)

OFFICERS

COUNSELOR TO THE CHIEF JUSTICE	Jeffrey P. Minear
Clerk	Scott S. Harris
Court Counsel	Ethan V. Torrey
Curator	Catherine E. Fitts
Director of Information Technology	Robert J. Hawkins
Librarian	Linda Maslow
Marshal	Pamela Talkin
Public Information Officer	Kathleen L. Arberg
Reporter of Decisions	Christine L. Fallon

Article III, section 1, of the Constitution of the United States provides that "[t]he judicial Power of the United States, shall be vested in one supreme Court, and in such inferior Courts as the Congress may from time to time ordain and establish."

The Supreme Court of the United States was created in accordance with this provision and by authority of the Judiciary Act of September 24, 1789 (1 Stat. 73). It was organized on February 2, 1790. Article III, section 2, of the Constitution defines the jurisdiction of the Supreme Court.

The Supreme Court comprises the Chief Justice of the United States and such number of Associate Justices as may be fixed by Congress, which is currently fixed at eight (28 U.S.C. 1). The President nominates the Justices with the advice and consent of the Senate. Article III, section 1, of the Constitution further provides that "[t]he Judges, both of the supreme and inferior Courts, shall hold their Offices during good Behaviour, and shall, at stated Times, receive for their Services, a Compensation, which shall not be diminished during their Continuance in Office."

Court officers assist the Court in the performance of its functions. They include: the Counselor to the Chief Justice, the Clerk, the Court Counsel, the Curator, the Director of Information Technology, the Librarian, the Marshal, the Public Information Officer, and the Reporter of Decisions.

Appellate Jurisdiction

Various statutes, derived from the authority that the Constitution has given to Congress, confer appellate jurisdiction upon the Supreme Court. The basic statute effective at this time in conferring and controlling jurisdiction of the Supreme Court may be found in 28 U.S.C. 1251,

1253, 1254, 1257-1259, and various special statutes. Congress has no authority to change the original jurisdiction of this Court.

Court Term

The term of the Court begins on the first Monday in October and lasts until the first Monday in October of the next year. Over the course of a term, approximately 10,000 petitions are filed for cases to be briefed before the Court. Moreover, each year, about 1,200 applications that can be acted upon by a single Justice while serving in the capacity of a Circuit Justice are filed.

Rulemaking

From time to time, Congress has conferred upon the Supreme Court power to prescribe rules of procedure to be followed by the lower courts of the United States.

Sources of Information

Exhibitions

The Office of the Curator develops exhibitions to highlight the work of the Nation's highest Court, the lives of individual Justices, and the architecture of the Supreme Court building.

News Media

Media advisories, press releases, speeches, and Year-End Reports on the Federal judiciary are accessible online. Information on the requirements and procedures for issuing Supreme Court press credentials is also available.

Public Access

The Supreme Court is open to the public from 9 a.m. to 4:30 p.m., weekdays, except on Federal holidays. Unless the Court or Chief Justice orders otherwise, the Clerk's office is open from 9 a.m. to 5 p.m., weekdays, except on Federal holidays. The library is open to members of the bar of the Court, attorneys for the various Federal departments and agencies, and Members of Congress.

For further information concerning the Supreme Court, contact the Public Information Office, United States Supreme Court Building, One First Street NE., Washington, DC 20543. Phone, 202-479-3211.

Lower Courts

Article III of the Constitution declares, in section 1, that the judicial power of the United States shall be invested in one Supreme Court and in "such inferior Courts as the Congress may from time to time ordain and establish." The Supreme Court has held that these constitutional courts ". . . share in the exercise of the judicial power defined in that section, can be invested with no other jurisdiction, and have judges who hold office during good behavior, with no power in Congress to provide otherwise."

United States Courts of Appeals

The courts of appeals are intermediate appellate courts created by act of March 3, 1891 (28 U.S.C. ch. 3), to relieve the Supreme Court of considering all appeals in cases originally decided by the Federal trial courts. They are empowered to review all final decisions and certain interlocutory decisions (18 U.S.C. 3731; 28 U.S.C. 1291, 1292) of district courts. They also are empowered to review and enforce orders of many Federal administrative bodies. The decisions of the courts of appeals are final except as they are subject to review on writ of certiorari by the Supreme Court.

The United States is divided geographically into 12 judicial circuits, including the District of Columbia. Each circuit has a court of appeals (28 U.S.C. 41, 1294). Each of the 50 States is assigned to one of the circuits. The territories and the Commonwealth of Puerto Rico are assigned variously to the first, third, and ninth circuits. There is also a Court of Appeals for the Federal Circuit, which has nationwide jurisdiction defined by subject matter. At present each court of appeals has from 6 to

28 permanent circuit judgeships (179 in all), depending upon the amount of judicial work in the circuit. Circuit judges hold their offices during good behavior as provided by Article III, section 1, of the Constitution. The judge senior in commission who is under 70 years of age (65 at inception of term), has been in office at least 1 year, and has not previously been chief judge, serves as the chief judge of the circuit for a 7-year term. One of the Justices of the Supreme Court is assigned as circuit justice for each of the 13 judicial circuits. Each court of appeals normally hears cases in panels consisting of three judges but may sit en banc with all judges present.

The judges of each circuit (except the Federal Circuit) by vote determine the size of the judicial council for the circuit, which consists of the chief judge and an equal number of circuit and district judges. The council considers the state of Federal judicial business in the circuit and may "make all necessary and appropriate orders for [its] effective and expeditious administration . . ." (28 U.S.C. 332).

The chief judge of each circuit may summon periodically a judicial conference of all judges of the circuit, including members of the bar, to discuss the business of the Federal courts of the circuit (28 U.S.C. 333). The chief judge of each circuit and a district judge elected from each of the 12 geographical circuits, together with the chief judge of the Court of International Trade, serve as members of the Judicial Conference of the United States, over which the Chief Justice of the United States presides. This is the governing body for the administration of the Federal judicial system as a whole (28 U.S.C. 331).

To obtain a complete list of judges, court officials, and official stations of the United States Courts of Appeals for the Federal Circuit, as well as information on opinions and cases before the court, consult the Judicial Circuit Web sites listed below.

List of Judicial Circuit Web Sites—United States Courts of Appeals

Circuit	URL
District of Columbia Circuit	http://www.cadc.uscourts.gov
First Circuit	http://www.ca1.uscourts.gov
Second Circuit	http://www.ca2.uscourts.gov
Third Circuit	http://www.ca3.uscourts.gov
Fourth Circuit	http://www.ca4.uscourts.gov
Fifth Circuit	http://www.ca5.uscourts.gov
Sixth Circuit	http://www.ca6.uscourts.gov
Seventh Circuit	http://www.ca7.uscourts.gov
Eighth Circuit	http://www.ca8.uscourts.gov
Ninth Circuit	http://www.ca9.uscourts.gov
Tenth Circuit	http://www.ca10.uscourts.gov
Eleventh Circuit	http://www.ca11.uscourts.gov

United States Court of Appeals for the Federal Circuit

This court was established under Article III of the Constitution pursuant to the Federal Courts Improvement Act of 1982 (28 U.S.C. 41, 44, 48), as successor to the former United States Court of Customs and Patent Appeals and the United States Court of Claims. The jurisdiction of the court is nationwide (as provided by 28 U.S.C. 1295) and includes appeals from the district courts in patent cases; appeals from the district courts in contract, and certain other civil actions in which the United States is a defendant; and appeals from final decisions of the U.S. Court of International Trade, the U.S. Court of Federal Claims, and the U.S. Court of Appeals for Veterans Claims. The jurisdiction of the court also includes the review of administrative rulings by the Patent and Trademark Office, U.S. International Trade Commission, Secretary of Commerce, agency boards of contract appeals, and the Merit Systems Protection Board, as well as rulemaking of the Department of Veterans Affairs; review of decisions of the U.S. Senate Committee on Ethics concerning discrimination claims of

Senate employees; and review of a final order of an entity to be designated by the President concerning discrimination claims of Presidential appointees.

The court consists of 12 circuit judges. It sits in panels of three or more on each case and may also hear or rehear a case en banc. The court sits principally in Washington, DC, and may hold court wherever any court of appeals sits (28 U.S.C. 48).

United States District Courts

The Nation's district courts are the trial courts of general Federal jurisdiction. These courts resolve disputes by determining the facts and applying legal principles to decide which party is right. Each State has at least one district court, and large States have as many as four. There are 89 district courts in the 50 States, plus one in the District of Columbia and another in the Commonwealth of Puerto Rico. Three other U.S. Territories also have courts that hear Federal cases: Guam and the Northern Mariana and Virgin Islands.

At present, each district court has from 2 to 28 Federal district judgeships, depending upon the amount of judicial work within its territory. Only one judge is usually required to hear and decide a case in a district court, but in some limited cases it is required that three judges be called together to comprise the court (28 U.S.C. 2284). The judge senior in commission who is under 70 years of age (65 at inception of term), has been in office for at least 1 year, and has not previously been chief judge, serves as chief judge for a 7-year term. There are 645 permanent district judgeships in the 50 States and 15 in the District of Columbia. There are seven district judgeships in Puerto Rico. District judges hold their offices during good behavior as provided by Article III, section 1, of the Constitution. However, Congress may temporary judgeships for a court with the provision that when a future vacancy occurs in that district, such vacancy shall not be filled. Each district court has one or more United States magistrate judges and bankruptcy judges, a clerk, a United States attorney, a United States marshal, probation officers, court reporters, and their staffs. The jurisdiction of the district courts is set forth in title 28, chapter 85, of the United States Code and at 18 U.S.C. 3231.

Cases from the district courts are reviewable on appeal by the applicable court of appeals.

Territorial Courts

Pursuant to its authority to govern the Territories (Art. IV, sec. 3, clause 2, of the Constitution), Congress has established district courts in the territories of Guam and the Virgin Islands. The District Court of the Canal Zone was abolished on April 1, 1982, pursuant to the Panama Canal Act of 1979 (22 U.S.C. 3601 note). Congress has also established a district court in the Northern Mariana Islands, which is administered by the United States under a trusteeship agreement with the United Nations. These Territorial courts have jurisdiction not only over the subjects described in the judicial article of the Constitution, but also over many local matters that, within the States, are decided in State courts. The District Court of Puerto Rico, by contrast, is established under Article III, is classified like other "district courts," and is called a "court of the United States" (28 U.S.C. 451). There is one judge each in Guam and the Northern Mariana Islands, and two in the Virgin Islands. The judges in these courts are appointed for terms of 10 years.

For further information concerning the lower courts, contact the Administrative Office of the United States Courts, Thurgood Marshall Federal Judiciary Building, One Columbus Circle NE., Washington, DC 20544. Phone, 202-502-2600.

United States Court of International Trade

This court was originally established as the Board of United States General Appraisers by act of June 10, 1890, which conferred upon it jurisdiction theretofore held by the district and circuit courts in actions arising under the tariff acts (19 U.S.C. ch. 4). The act of May 28, 1926 (19 U.S.C. 405a), created the United States Customs Court to supersede the Board; by acts of August 7, 1939, and June 25, 1948 (28 U.S.C. 1582, 1583), the court was integrated into the United States court structure, organization, and procedure. The act of July 14, 1956 (28 U.S.C. 251), established the court as a court of record of the United States under Article III of the Constitution. The Customs Court Act of 1980 (28 U.S.C. 251) constituted the court as the United States Court of International Trade.

The Court of International Trade has jurisdiction over any civil action against the United States arising from Federal laws governing import transactions. This includes classification and valuation cases, as well as authority to review certain agency determinations under the Trade Agreements Act of 1979 (19 U.S.C. 2501) involving antidumping and countervailing duty matters. In addition, it has exclusive jurisdiction of civil actions to review determinations as to the eligibility of workers, firms, and communities for adjustment assistance under the Trade Act of 1974 (19 U.S.C. 2101). Civil actions commenced by the United States to recover customs duties, to recover on a customs bond, or for certain civil penalties alleging fraud or negligence are also within the exclusive jurisdiction of the court.

The court is composed of a chief judge and eight judges, not more than five of whom may belong to any one political party. Any of its judges may be temporarily designated and assigned by the Chief Justice of the United States to sit as a court of appeals or district court judge in any circuit or district. The court has a clerk and deputy clerks, a librarian, court reporters, and other supporting personnel. Cases before the court may be tried before a jury. Under the Federal Courts Improvement Act of 1982 (28 U.S.C. 1295), appeals are taken to the U.S. Court of Appeals for the Federal Circuit, and ultimately review may be sought in appropriate cases in the Supreme Court of the United States.

The principal offices are located in New York, NY, but the court is empowered to hear and determine cases arising at any port or place within the jurisdiction of the United States.

For further information, contact the Clerk, United States Court of International Trade, One Federal Plaza, New York, NY 10278-0001. Phone, 212-264-2814.

Judicial Panel on Multidistrict Litigation

The Panel, created by act of April 29, 1968 (28 U.S.C. 1407), and consisting of seven Federal judges designated by the Chief Justice from the courts of appeals and district courts, is authorized to temporarily transfer to a single district, for coordinated or consolidated pretrial proceedings, civil actions pending in different districts that involve one or more common questions of fact.

For further information, contact the Clerk, Judicial Panel on Multidistrict Litigation, Room G–255, Thurgood Marshall Federal Judiciary Building, One Columbus Circle NE., Washington, DC 20002-8041. Phone, 202-502-2800.

Special Courts

United States Court of Appeals for the Armed Forces

450 E Street NW., Washington, DC 20442-0001, 202-761-1448, 202-761-4672, http://www.armfor.uscourts.gov

This court was established under Article I of the Constitution of the United States pursuant to act of May 5, 1950, as amended (10 U.S.C. 867). Subject only to certiorari review by the Supreme Court of the United States in a limited number of cases, the court serves as the final appellate tribunal to review court-martial convictions of all the Armed Forces. It is exclusively an appellate criminal court, consisting of five civilian judges who are appointed for 15-year terms by the President with the advice and consent of the Senate.

The court is called upon to exercise jurisdiction to review the record in all cases extending to death; certified to the court by a Judge Advocate General of one of the Armed Forces; or petitioned by accused who have received a sentence of confinement for 1 year or more and/or a punitive discharge.

The court also exercises authority under the All Writs Act (28 U.S.C. 1651(a)).

In addition, the judges of the court are required by law to work jointly with the senior uniformed lawyer from each of the Armed Forces and two members of the public appointed by the Secretary of Defense to make an annual comprehensive survey, to report annually to the Congress on the operation and progress of the military justice system under the Uniform Code of Military Justice, and to recommend improvements wherever necessary.

Sources of Information

Employment

Job openings and available clerkships are posted online.

For further information, contact the Clerk, United States Court of Appeals for the Armed Forces, 450 E Street NW., Washington, DC 20442-0001. Phone, 202-761-1448. Fax, 202-761-4672.

United States Court of Appeals for Veterans Claims

Suite 900, 625 Indiana Avenue NW., Washington, DC 20004-2950, 202-501-5970, 202-501-5848, http://www.uscourts.cavc.gov

The United States Court of Appeals for Veterans Claims, a court of record under Article I of the Constitution, was established on November 18, 1988 (38 U.S.C. 7251) and given exclusive jurisdiction to review decisions of the Board of Veterans' Appeals. Appeals concern veteran disability benefits, dependent educational assistance, survivor benefits, and pension benefits claims. In addition to its review authority, the Court has contempt authority, as well as the authority to compel action by the Secretary of Veterans Affairs, the authority to grant a petition for extraordinary relief under the All Writs Act (28 U.S.C. 1651), and the authority to make attorney fee determinations under the Equal Access to Justice Act (28 U.S.C. 2412). Decisions of the Court of Appeals for Veterans Claims are subject to review by the United States Court of Appeals for the Federal Circuit on questions of law and on writ of certiorari by the United States Supreme Court.

The Court consists of nine judges whom the President appoints with the advice and consent of the Senate for 15-year terms. One of the judges serves as chief judge.

The Chief Judge generally conducts a judicial conference every 2 years. The primary purpose of the conference, which involves the active participation of members of the legal community, attorneys, and practitioners admitted to practice before the Court, is to consider the business of the Court and to recommend means of improving the administration of justice within the Court's jurisdiction.

The Court is located in Washington, DC, but it is a court of national jurisdiction and may sit at any location within the United States.

Opinions issued by the Court, case information, and a current list of judges and officials of the United States Court of Appeals for Veterans Claims are available online.

Sources of Information

Employment

Job opportunities are posted online.

For further information, contact the Clerk, United States Court of Appeals for Veterans Claims, Suite 900, 625 Indiana Avenue NW., Washington, DC 20004-2950. Phone, 202-501-5970. Fax, 202-501-5848

United States Court of Federal Claims

717 Madison Place NW., Washington, DC 20439, 202-357-6400, http://www.uscfc.uscourts.gov

The United States Court of Federal Claims has jurisdiction over claims seeking money judgments against the United States. A claim must be founded upon the Constitution, an act of Congress, an Executive order, a contract with the United States, or Federal regulations. Judges are appointed by the President for 15-year terms, subject to Senate confirmation. Appeals are to the U.S. Court of Appeals for the Federal Circuit.

Sources of Information

Employment

Information on job opportunities and internships is available online.

For further information, contact the Clerk's Office, United States Court of Federal Claims, 717 Madison Place NW., Washington, DC 20439. Phone, 202-357-6400.

United States Tax Court

400 Second Street NW., Washington, DC 20217-0002, 202-521-0700, http://www.ustaxcourt.gov

The United States Tax Court is a court of record under Article I of the Constitution of the United States (26 U.S.C. 7441). The court was created as the United States Board of Tax Appeals by the Revenue Act of 1924 (43 Stat. 336). The name was changed to the Tax Court of the United States by the Revenue Act of 1942 (56 Stat. 957). The Tax Reform Act of 1969 (83 Stat. 730) established the court under Article I and then changed its name to the United States Tax Court.

The court comprises 19 judges who are appointed by the President to 15-year terms and subject to Senate confirmation. The court also has varying numbers of both senior judges (who may be recalled by the chief judge to perform further judicial duties) and special trial judges (who are appointed by the chief judge and may hear and decide a variety of cases). The court's jurisdiction is set forth in various sections of title 26 of the U.S. Code.

The offices of the court and its judges are in Washington, DC. However, the court has national jurisdiction and schedules trial sessions in more than 70 cities in the United States. Each trial session is conducted by one judge, senior judge, or special trial judge. Court proceedings are open to the public and are conducted in accordance with the court's rules of practice and procedure and the rules of evidence applicable in trials without a jury in the U.S. District Court for the District of Columbia. A fee of $60 is charged for the filing of a petition. Practice before the court is limited to practitioners admitted under the court's rules of practice and procedure.

Decisions entered by the court, other than decisions in small tax cases, may be appealed to the regional courts of appeals and, thereafter, upon the granting of a writ of certiorari, to the Supreme Court of the United States. At the option of petitioners, simplified procedures may be used in small tax cases. Small tax cases are final and not subject to review by any court.

Sources of Information

Employment

Vacancy announcements and information on the court's law clerk program are available online.

Forms

Applications, certificates, notices, and other forms can be completed online and then printed.

Taxpayer Information

An online guide provides information—not legal advice—that may be helpful for those representing themselves before the Tax Court. It answers frequent questions that taxpayers ask and explains the process of filing a petition to begin a Tax Court case and things that occur before, during, and after trial. It also features a glossary.

For further information, contact the Office of the Clerk of the Court, United States Tax Court, 400 Second Street NW., Washington, DC 20217-0002. Phone, 202-521-0700.

Administrative Office of the United States Courts

One Columbus Circle NE., Washington, DC 20544, 202-502-2600, http://www.uscourts.gov

DIRECTOR	James C. Duff
Deputy Director	Jill C. Sayenga
ASSOCIATE DIRECTORS	
Department of Administrative Services	James R. Baugher
Department of Program Services	Laura C. Minor
Department of Technology Services	Joseph R. Peters, Jr.
General Counsel	Sheryl L. Walter
Judicial Conference Secretariat Officer	Katherine H. Simon
Legislative Affairs Officer	Cordia A. Strom
Public Affairs Officer	David A. Sellers

The Administrative Office of the United States Courts supports and serves the nonjudicial, administrative business of the United States Courts.

The Administrative Office of the United States Courts was created by act of August 7, 1939 (28 U.S.C. 601). It was established on November 6, 1939. The Chief Justice of the United States, after consultation with the Judicial Conference, appoints the Director and Deputy Director of the Administrative Office.

Administering the Courts

The Director is the administrative officer of the courts of the United States—except of the Supreme Court. Under the guidance of the Judicial Conference of the United States, the Director supervises all administrative matters relating to the offices of clerks and other clerical and administrative personnel of the courts; examines the state of the dockets of the courts, secures information as to the courts' need of assistance, and prepares statistical data and reports each quarter and transmits them to the chief judges of the circuits; submits an activities report of the Administrative Office and the courts' state of business to the annual meeting of the Judicial Conference of the United States; fixes the compensation of court employees whose compensation is not otherwise fixed by law; regulates and pays annuities to widows and surviving dependent children of judges; disburses moneys appropriated for the maintenance and operation of the courts; examines accounts of court officers; regulates travel of judicial personnel; provides accommodations and supplies for the courts and their clerical and administrative personnel; establishes and maintains programs for the certification and utilization of court interpreters and the provision of special interpretation services in the courts; and performs such other duties as may be assigned by the Supreme Court or the Judicial Conference of the United States.

The Director also prepares and submits the budget of the courts, which the Office of Management and Budget transmits to Congress without change.

Probation Officers

The Administrative Office exercises general supervision of the accounts and practices of the Federal probation offices, which are subject to primary control by the respective district courts that they serve. The Administrative Office publishes, in cooperation with the Department of Justice's Bureau of Prisons, the "Federal Probation Journal." This online, quarterly publication presents current thought, research, and practice in corrections, community supervision, and criminal justice.

In accordance with the Pretrial Services Act of 1982 (18 U.S.C. 3152), the Director establishes pretrial services in the district courts. The offices of these district courts report information on pretrial release of persons charged with Federal offenses and supervise such persons who are released to their custody.

Bankruptcy

According to the Bankruptcy Amendments and Federal Judgeship Act of 1984 (28 U.S.C. 151), the bankruptcy judges for each judicial district constitute a unit of the district court known as the bankruptcy court. The courts of appeals appoint bankruptcy judges in such numbers as authorized by Congress. These judges serve for a term of 14 years as judicial officers of the district courts.

This act placed jurisdiction in the district courts over all cases under title 11, United States Code, and all proceedings arising in or related to cases under that title (28 U.S.C. 1334). The district court may refer such cases and proceedings to its bankruptcy judges (as authorized by 28 U.S.C. 157).

The Director of the Administrative Office recommends to the Judicial Conference the duty stations of bankruptcy judges and the places they hold court, surveys the need for additional bankruptcy judgeships to be recommended to Congress, and determines the staff needs of bankruptcy judges and the clerks of the bankruptcy courts.

Federal Magistrate Judges

The Director of the Administrative Office exercises general supervision over administrative matters in offices of U.S. magistrate judges, compiles and evaluates statistical data relating to such offices, and submits reports thereon to the Judicial Conference. The Director reports annually to Congress on the business that has come before U.S. magistrate judges and also prepares legal and administrative manuals for the magistrate judges. In compliance with the act, the Administrative Office conducts surveys of the conditions in the judicial districts to make recommendations as to the number, location, and salaries of magistrate judges. The Judicial Conference then determines their number, location, and salaries, subject to the availability of appropriated funds.

Federal Defenders

The Criminal Justice Act (18 U.S.C. 3006A) establishes the procedure for the appointment of private panel attorneys in Federal criminal cases for individuals who are unable to afford adequate representation, under plans adopted by each district court. The act also permits the establishment of Federal public defender or Federal community defender organizations by the district courts in districts where at least 200 persons annually require the appointment of counsel. Two adjacent districts may be combined to reach this total.

Each defender organization submits to the Director of the Administrative Office an annual report of its activities along with a proposed budget or, in the case of community defender organizations, a proposed grant for the coming year. The Director is responsible for the submission of the proposed budgets and grants to the Judicial Conference for approval. The Director also makes payments to the defender organizations out of appropriations in accordance with the approved budgets and grants, as well as compensating private counsel appointed to defend criminal cases in the United States courts.

Sources of Information

Budget, Accounting, and Procurement

Phone, 202-502-2000.

Court Services

Phone, 202-502-1500.

Defender Services

Phone, 202-502-3030.

Educational Resources

Learning resources for students are available online.

Electronic Filing

Attorneys and others may submit files online using the Federal courts' Case Management and Electronic Case Files system.

Frequently Asked Questions (FAQs)

Answers to FAQs on the Federal Judiciary are available online.

General Counsel

Phone, 202-502-1100.

Glossary

A glossary of legal terms is available online.

Human Resources

Phone, 202-502-3100.

Judicial Conference Executive Secretariat

Phone, 202-502-2400.

Judicial Services

Phone, 202-502-1800.

Judiciary Reporting and Analysis

Phone, 202-502-1440.

Legislative Affairs

Phone, 202-502-1700.

Probation and Pretrial Services

Phone, 202-502-1600.

Public Affairs

Phone, 202-502-2600.

Publications

The Federal judiciary and Administrative Office produce publications for the Congress, the public, and others to educate and inform about the work of the courts.

Statistical Data

Statistical data on the business of the Federal Judiciary are available online.

For further information, contact the Administrative Office of the United States Courts, Thurgood Marshall Federal Judiciary Building, One Columbus Circle NE., Washington, DC 20544. Phone, 202-502-2600.

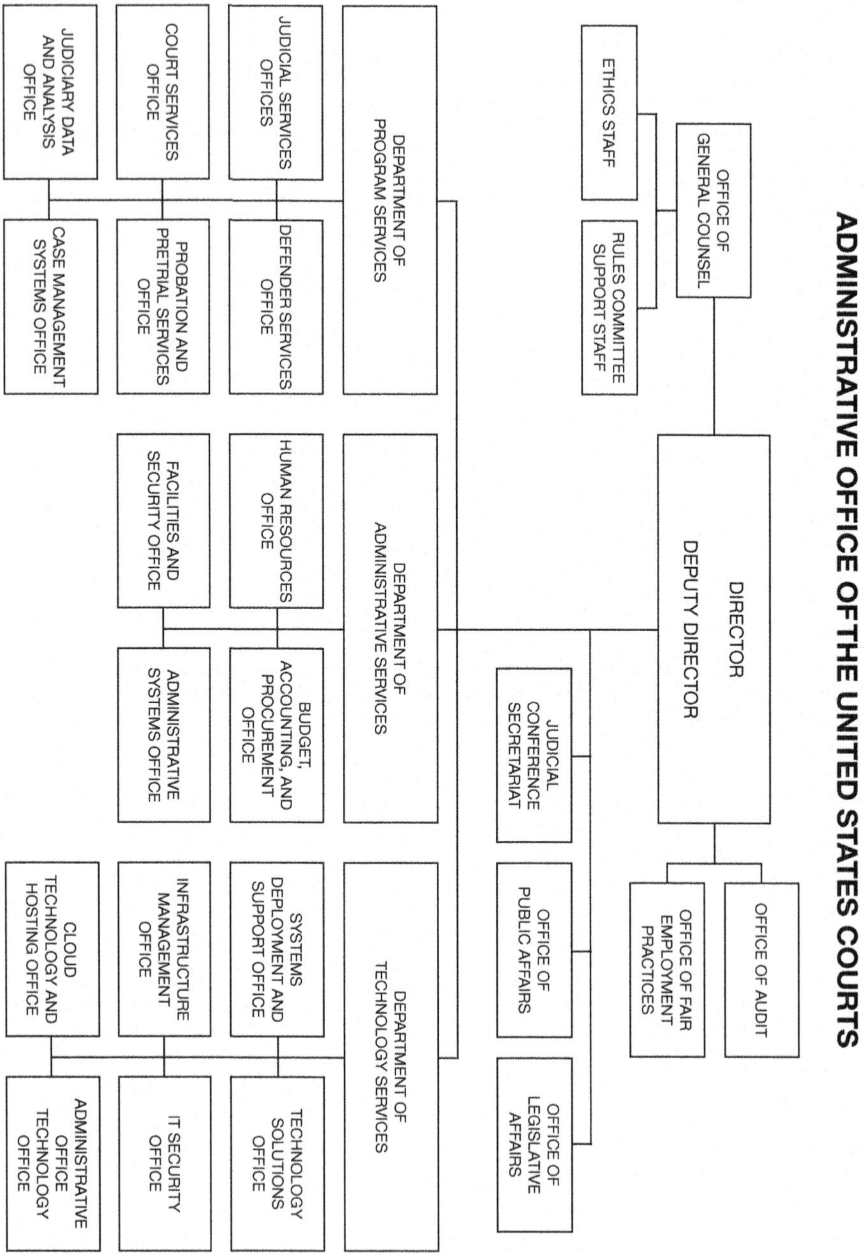
ADMINISTRATIVE OFFICE OF THE UNITED STATES COURTS
DIRECTOR
DEPUTY DIRECTOR
OFFICE OF GENERAL COUNSEL
ETHICS STAFF
RULES COMMITTEE SUPPORT STAFF
OFFICE OF AUDIT
OFFICE OF FAIR EMPLOYMENT PRACTICES
JUDICIAL CONFERENCE SECRETARIAT
OFFICE OF PUBLIC AFFAIRS
OFFICE OF LEGISLATIVE AFFAIRS
DEPARTMENT OF PROGRAM SERVICES
JUDICIAL SERVICES OFFICES
DEFENDER SERVICES OFFICE
COURT SERVICES OFFICE
PROBATION AND PRETRIAL SERVICES OFFICE
JUDICIARY DATA AND ANALYSIS OFFICE
CASE MANAGEMENT SYSTEMS OFFICE
DEPARTMENT OF ADMINISTRATIVE SERVICES
HUMAN RESOURCES OFFICE
BUDGET, ACCOUNTING, AND PROCUREMENT OFFICE
FACILITIES AND SECURITY OFFICE
ADMINISTRATIVE SYSTEMS OFFICE
DEPARTMENT OF TECHNOLOGY SERVICES
SYSTEMS DEPLOYMENT AND SUPPORT OFFICE
TECHNOLOGY SOLUTIONS OFFICE
INFRASTRUCTURE MANAGEMENT OFFICE
IT SECURITY OFFICE
CLOUD TECHNOLOGY AND HOSTING OFFICE
ADMINISTRATIVE OFFICE TECHNOLOGY OFFICE

Federal Judicial Center

Thurgood Marshall Federal Judiciary Building, One Columbus Circle NE., Washington, DC 20002-8003, 202-502-4000, *http://www.fjc.gov*

DIRECTOR	Jeremy D. Fogel
Deputy Director	John S. Cooke
Director, Editorial and Information Services Office	John S. Cooke, Acting
Director, Education Division	Dana K. Chipman
Director, Federal Judicial History Office	Clara Altman
Director, Information Technology Office	Esther DeVries
Director, International Judicial Relations Office	Mira Gur-Arie
Director, Research Division	James B. Eaglin

The Federal Judicial Center is the judicial branch's agency for policy research and continuing education.

The Federal Judicial Center was created by act of December 20, 1967 (28 U.S.C. 620), to further the development and adoption of improved judicial administration in the courts of the United States.

The Center's basic policies and activities are determined by its Board, which is composed of the Chief Justice of the United States, who is permanent Chair of the Board by statute, and two judges of the U.S. courts of appeals, three judges of the U.S. district courts, one bankruptcy judge, and one magistrate judge, all of whom are elected for 4-year terms by the Judicial Conference of the United States. The Director of the Administrative Office of the United States Courts is also a permanent member of the Board.

The organization of the Center reflects its primary statutory mandates. The Education Division plans education and produces training—including curriculum packages for in-district training, in-person programs, publications, video programs, and web-based programs and resources—for judges and court staff. The Research Division examines and evaluates current and alternative Federal court practices and policies. Its research assists Judicial Conference committees in developing policy recommendations. The research also contributes substantially to the Center's educational programs. The Federal Judicial History Office helps courts and others study and preserve Federal judicial history. The International Judicial Relations Office provides information to judicial and legal officials from foreign countries and informs Federal judicial personnel of developments in international law and other court systems that may affect their work. Two units of the Director's Office—the Information Technology Office and the Editorial and Information Services Office—support the agency's mission through editorial and design assistance, organization and dissemination of Center resources, and technology.

Sources of Information

Annual Reports

Annual Reports, from 1969 to the present, are available to download as Portable Document Format (PDF) files.

Educational Materials

Materials that the Center produces as part of its educational programs for judges and court employees are accessible online.

Employment

The Center posts job openings online. Contact the Human Resources Office for more information. Phone, 202-502-4165.

Federal Judicial History

Questions about the history of the Federal

judiciary? Submit them to the experts at the Federal Judicial History Office. Phone, 202-502-4180. Fax, 202-502-4077.

Publications

Single copies of most Federal Judicial Center publications are available free of charge. Phone, 202-502-4153. Fax, 202-502-4077.

Teaching Resources

Teaching and civic outreach resources are available online.

Visiting Foreign Judicial Fellows

Foreign judges, court officials, and scholars may apply for the opportunity to conduct research at the Center on topics concerning the administration of justice in the United States.

For further information, contact the Federal Judicial Center, Thurgood Marshall Federal Judiciary Building, One Columbus Circle NE., Washington, DC 20002-8003. Phone, 202-502-4000.

United States Sentencing Commission

Suite 2-500, One Columbus Circle NE., Washington, DC 20002-8002, 202-502-4500, *http://www.ussc.gov*

CHAIR	Patti B. Saris
Vice Chair	Charles R. Breyer
Vice Chair	(vacancy)
Vice Chair	(vacancy)
Commissioner	Rachel E. Barkow
Commissioner	Dabney L. Friedrich
Commissioner	Wiiliam H. Pryor, Jr.
Commissioner (ex officio)	Michelle Morales
Commissioner (ex officio)	J. Patricia Wilson Smoot
Staff Director	Kenneth P. Cohen
Director, Office of Administration and Planning	Susan M. Brazel
Director, Office of Education and Sentencing Practice	Raquel Wilson
Director, Office of Legislative and Public Affairs	Christine M. Leonard
Director, Office of Research and Data	Glenn R. Schmitt
General Counsel	Kathleen C. Grilli

The United States Sentencing Commission develops sentencing guidelines and policies for the Federal court system.

The United States Sentencing Commission was established as an independent agency in the judicial branch of the Federal Government by the Sentencing Reform Act of 1984 (28 U.S.C. 991 et seq. and 18 U.S.C. 3551 et seq.). The Commission establishes sentencing guidelines and policies for the Federal courts, advising them of the appropriate form and severity of punishment for offenders convicted of Federal crimes.

The Commission comprises seven voting members and two nonvoting members. The President appoints the voting members with the advice and consent of the Senate for 6-year terms. The President also appoints one of the voting members as the Chair and designates three others as Vice Chairs.

The Commission evaluates the effects of the sentencing guidelines on the criminal justice system, advises Congress on the modification or enactment of statutes pertaining to criminal law and sentencing matters, establishes a research and development program on sentencing issues, and performs other related duties.

In executing its duties, the Commission promulgates and distributes to Federal courts and to the U.S. probation system guidelines for determining sentences to be imposed in criminal cases, general policy statements regarding the application of guidelines, and policy statements on the appropriate use of probation and supervised release revocation provisions. These sentencing guidelines and policy statements are intended to support the principles of just punishment, deterrence, incapacitation, and rehabilitation; provide fairness in meeting the purposes of sentencing; avoid unwarranted disparity; and reflect advancement in the knowledge of human behavior as it relates to the criminal justice process.

The Commission also provides training, conducts research on sentencing-related issues, and serves as an information resource for Congress, criminal justice practitioners, and the public.

Sources of Information

Education

The Commission offers courses that fulfill continuing legal education requirements in several jurisdictions.

Employment

The Commission posts job announcements on its Web site.

Guidelines Manual

The current "USSC Guidelines Manual" is available in Portable Document Format on the Commission's Web site. An electronic archive of the yearly manual starts with the year 1987.

Helpline

Attorneys, judges, and probation officers who have questions may call the Commission's helpline for assistance. The helpline also handles data requests. Its hours of operations are 8:30 a.m.–5 p.m., eastern standard time, Monday–Friday, excluding Federal holidays. Phone, 202-502-4545.

News

Press releases are available on the Commission's Web site.

The Commission also posts amicus curiae briefs, reports, speeches, statements, and testimonies online.

Publications

A topical index of publications is available online.

Reports

The Commission posts reports to the Congress on its Web site.

Annual overviews of Federal criminal cases are available online.

The Office of Research and Data publishes periodic reports on Federal sentencing practices. The reports include information on the types of crimes committed, offenders who commit those crimes, the punishments imposed, and the manner in which the sentencing guidelines were applied.

Site Map

The Web site map allows visitors to look for specific topics or to browse for content that aligns with their interests.

Updates

An online subscription form is available to sign up for regular email updates from the USSC.

For further information, contact the Office of Legislative and Public Affairs, U.S. Sentencing Commission, Suite 2–500, One Columbus Circle NE., Washington, DC 20002-8002. Phone, 202-502-4500.

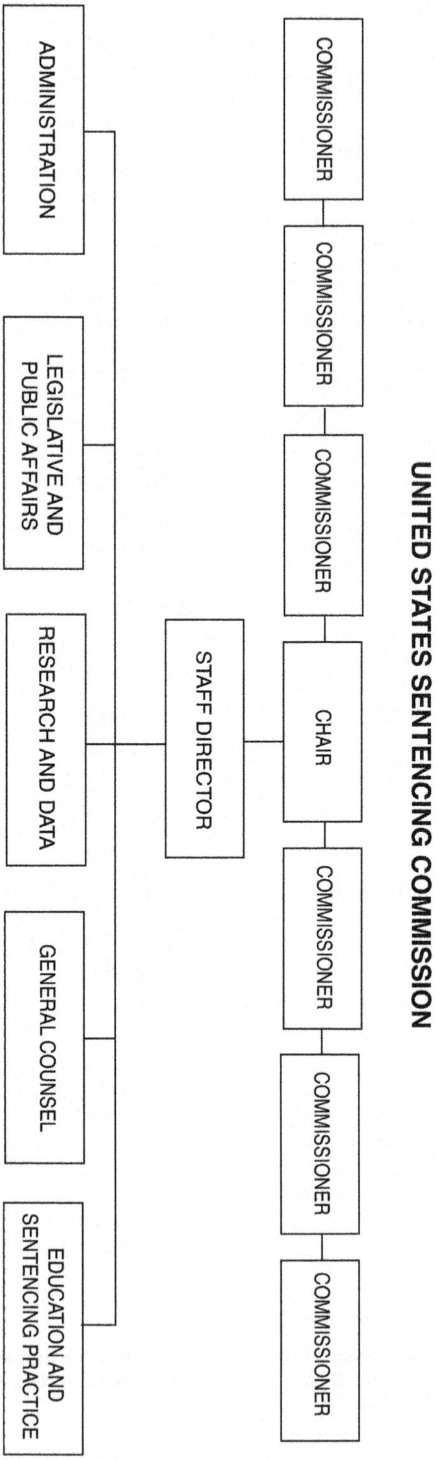
UNITED STATES SENTENCING COMMISSION
COMMISSIONER
COMMISSIONER
COMMISSIONER
CHAIR
COMMISSIONER
COMMISSIONER
COMMISSIONER
STAFF DIRECTOR
ADMINISTRATION
LEGISLATIVE AND PUBLIC AFFAIRS
RESEARCH AND DATA
GENERAL COUNSEL
EDUCATION AND SENTENCING PRACTICE

Executive Branch: The President

The President

THE PRESIDENT OF THE UNITED STATES — Barack Obama

Article II, section 1, of the Constitution provides that "[t]he executive Power shall be vested in a President of the United States of America. He shall hold his Office during the Term of four Years, . . . together with the Vice President, chosen for the same Term . . . ." In addition to the powers set forth in the Constitution, the statutes have conferred upon the President specific authority and responsibility covering a wide range of matters (United States Code Index).

The President is the administrative head of the executive branch of the Government, which includes numerous agencies, both temporary and permanent, as well as the 15 executive departments.

The Cabinet

The Cabinet, a creation of custom and tradition dating back to George Washington's administration, functions at the pleasure of the President. Its purpose is to advise the President upon any subject, relating to the duties of the respective offices, on which he requests information (pursuant to Article II, section 2, of the Constitution).

The Cabinet is composed of the Vice President and the heads of the 15 executive departments--the Secretaries of Agriculture, Commerce, Defense, Education, Energy, Health and Human Services, Homeland Security, Housing and Urban Development, Interior, Labor, State, Transportation, Treasury, and Veterans Affairs, and the Attorney General. Additionally, in the Obama administration, Cabinet-level rank has been accorded to the Chief of Staff to the President; the Administrator, Environmental Protection Agency; the Chair, Council of Economic Advisers; the Director, Office of Management and Budget; the U.S. Permanent Representative to the United Nations; and the U.S. Trade Representative.

The Vice President

THE VICE PRESIDENT — Joseph R. Biden, Jr.

Article II, section 1, of the Constitution provides that the President "shall hold his Office during the Term of four Years, . . . together with the Vice President . . . ." In addition to his role as President of the Senate, the Vice President is empowered to succeed to the Presidency, pursuant to Article II and the 20th and 25th amendments to the Constitution.

The executive functions of the Vice President include participation in Cabinet meetings and, by statute, membership on the National Security Council and the Board of Regents of the Smithsonian Institution.

The Executive Office of the President

Under authority of the Reorganization Act of 1939 (5 U.S.C. 133-133r, 133t note), various agencies were transferred to the Executive Office of the President by the President's Reorganization Plans I and II of 1939 (5 U.S.C. app.), effective July 1, 1939. Executive Order 8248 of September 8, 1939, established the divisions of the Executive Office and defined their functions. Subsequently, Presidents have used Executive orders, reorganization plans, and legislative initiatives to reorganize the Executive Office to make its composition compatible with the goals of their administrations.

White House Office

1600 Pennsylvania Avenue NW., Washington, DC 20500, 202-456-1414, *http://www.whitehouse.gov*

ASSISTANTS TO THE PRESIDENT

CHIEF OF STAFF	Denis R. McDonough
Cabinet Secretary	Broderick D. Johnson
Chief of Staff to the First Lady	Christina M. Tchen
Counsel to the President	W. Neil Eggleston
Deputy Chief of Staff for Implementation	Kristie A. Canegallo
Deputy Chief of Staff for Operations	Anita Decker Breckenridge
Deputy National Security Adviser	Avril D. Haines
Deputy National Security Adviser for Strategic Communications and Speechwriting	Benjamin J. Rhodes
Director of the White House Military Office	Emmett S. Beliveau
Director of Communications	Jennifer R. Psaki
Director of Presidential Personnel	Valerie E. Green
Director of Scheduling and Advance	Chase M. Cushman
Director of Speechwriting	Cody S. Keenan
Director of the Office of Legislative Affairs	Amy Rosenbaum
Director of the Office of Political Strategy and Outreach	David M. Simas
National Security Adviser	Susan E. Rice
Press Secretary	Joshua R. Earnest
Assistant to the President for Homeland Security and Counterterrorism	Lisa O. Monaco
Assistant to the President for Management and Administration	Katy A. Kale
Counselor to the President	(vacancy)

SENIOR ADVISORS

Assistant to the President for Climate, Conservation and Energy Policy	Brian C. Deese
Assistant to the President for Intergovernmental Affairs and Public Engagement	Valerie B. Jarrett
Assistant to the President for Strategy and Communications	Shailagh Murray

The White House Office serves the President in the performance of the many detailed activities incident to his immediate office.

The President's staff facilitates and maintains communication with the Congress, the heads of executive agencies, the press and other information media, and the general public. The various Assistants to the President aid the President in such matters as he may direct.

Office of the Vice President

Eisenhower Executive Office Building, Washington, DC 20501, 202-456-7549, https://www.whitehouse.gov/administration/vice-president-biden

CHIEF OF STAFF / ASSISTANT TO THE PRESIDENT	Steve Ricchetti
Chief of Staff to Dr. Jill Biden / Deputy Assistant to the President	Sheila Nix

Assistant	Kathy Chung
Counsel	John McGrail
Counselor / Deputy Assistant to the President	Donet Graves
Deputy Chief of Staff to Dr. Jill Biden / Special Assistant to the President	Anthony Bernal
DIRECTORS	
Administration	Cynthia Bernstein
Advance	Sam Salk
Communications	Kate Bedingfield
Intergovernmental Affairs / Special Assistant to the President	Michael Schrum
Legislative Affairs	Tonya Williams
Scheduling	Virginia Lance
Speechwriting / Special Assistant to the President	Vinay Reddy
National Security Advisor / Deputy Assistant to the President	Colin Kahl
Senior Advisor / Special Assistant to the President	Gregory Schultz
Senior Advisor for Operations and Implementation / Special Assistant to the President	John Flynn

The Office of the Vice President serves the Vice President in the performance of the many activities incident to his immediate office.

Council of Economic Advisers

Seventeenth and Pennsylvania Avenue NW., Washington, DC 20502, 202-456-4779, http://www.whitehouse.gov/cea

CHAIR	Jason L. Furman
Member	Sandra Black
Member	Jay Shambaugh

The Council of Economic Advisers analyzes and appraises the national economy to make policy recommendations to the President.

The Council of Economic Advisers (CEA) was established in the Executive Office of the President by the Employment Act of 1946 (15 U.S.C. 1023). It now functions under that statute and Reorganization Plan No. 9 of 1953 (5 U.S.C. app.), effective August 1, 1953.

The Chair and the two members govern the Council. The President appoints the Chair, whom the Senate must confirm, and the two members.

The Council analyzes the national economy and its various segments; advises the President on economic developments; appraises the economic programs and policies of the Federal Government; recommends policies for economic growth and stability to the President; assists in the preparation of the President's economic reports to the Congress; and prepares the Annual Report of the Council of Economic Advisers.

Sources of Information

Blog

The Council's Web site features a blog.

Career Opportunities

To learn about career opportunities, visit the "Jobs and Internships" Web page.

History

Photographs and brief professional bios of former Council Chairs, beginning with Edwin G. Nourse, who served as the Chair from 1946 to 1949, are available online.

Brief professional bios of former Council members, beginning with John D. Clark, who served as a member from 1946 to 1950 and then as the Vice Chair, are available online.

Publications

Reports and briefs are available in Portable Document Format (PDF) on the Council's Web site.

A monthly publication prepared by the Council for the Joint Economic Committee, "Economic Indicators" provides Congress and the public with information on business activity; credit, money, and prices; Federal finance; gross domestic product; employment, income, and production; international statistics; and security markets.

A yearly report written by the Council's Chair, the "Economic Report of the President" presents the administration's domestic and international economic policies. The report surveys the Nation's economic progress with text and data appendices. The full report and individual chapters are accessible in Portable Document Format (PDF) for download on the Council's Web site. Statistical tables are also available for download in Portable Document and Excel formats.

Speeches / Testimony

The Council posts Op-Ed pieces, prepared testimonies for congressional hearings, and speeches on its Web site.

For further information, contact the Council of Economic Advisers, Seventeenth and Pennsylvania Avenue NW., Washington, DC 20502. Phone, 202-456-4779.

Council on Environmental Quality

722 Jackson Place NW., Washington, DC 20503, 202-395-5750, 202-456-6224, 202-456-2710, http://www.whitehouse.gov/administration/eop/ceq

CHAIR	(vacancy)
Chief of Staff	Christopher Adamo
ASSOCIATE DIRECTORS	
Climate Preparedness	Jainey Bavishi
Communications	Noreen Nielson
Conservation and Wildlife	Timothy Male
Energy and Climate Change	Richard Duke
Lands and Water Ecosystems	Michael Degnan
Legislative Affairs	Stephenne Harding
NEPA Oversight	Edward Boling
Ocean and Coastal Policy	Whitley Saumweber
Deputy Associate Director, Public Engagement and Communications	Mark Antoniewicz
General Counsel	Brenda Mallory
Managing Director	Christina Goldfuss

The Council on Environmental Quality formulates and recommends national policies and initiatives for improving the environment.

The Council on Environmental Quality (CEQ) was established within the Executive Office of the President by the National Environmental Policy Act of 1969 (NEPA) (42 U.S.C. 4321 et seq.). The Environmental Quality Improvement Act of 1970 (42 U.S.C. 4371 et seq.) established the Office of Environmental Quality (OEQ) to provide professional and administrative support for the Council. The CEQ and OEQ are referred to, collectively, as the Council on Environmental Quality. The CEQ Chair, whom the President appoints and the Senate confirms, serves as Director of the OEQ.

The Council develops policies that bring

together the Nation's economic, social, and environmental priorities to improve Federal decisionmaking. As required by NEPA, the CEQ also evaluates, coordinates, and mediates Federal activities. It advises and assists the President on both national and international environmental policy matters. It oversees Federal agency and departmental implementation of NEPA.

Sources of Information

Blog

The CEQ Web site features a blog.

Freedom of Information Act (FOIA)

Requests may be submitted by email (without an attachment) or fax or sent by postal mail to the Freedom of Information Officer, Council on Environmental Quality, 722 Jackson Place NW., Washington, DC 20503. Fax, 202-456-0753.

Internships

Most interns work a semester-based schedule (May–August, September–December, or January–April). A position may be customized, however, to accommodate applicant availability and project needs. Application deadlines are February 1 for the summer, June 13 for the fall, and October 1 for the spring.

Open Government

The CEQ supports the Open Government initiative by promoting the principles of collaboration, participation, and transparency.

Participation

The CEQ maintains a social media presence on Twitter and Facebook. An online subscription form is available to sign up for email updates from the CEQ and opportunities to get involved.

Press Releases

The CEQ posts announcements, factsheets, memoranda, statements, and other newsworthy items on its Web site.

For further information, contact the Information Office, Council on Environmental Quality, 722 Jackson Place NW., Washington, DC 20503. Phone, 202-395-5750. Fax, 202-456-2710.

National Security Council

Eisenhower Executive Office Building, Washington, DC 20504, 202-456-1414, http://www.whitehouse.gov/nsc

MEMBERS

THE PRESIDENT	Barack Obama
The Vice President	Joseph R. Biden, Jr.
Secretary of State	John F. Kerry
Secretary of Defense	Ashton B. Carter

STATUTORY ADVISERS

Director of National Intelligence	James R. Clapper Jr.
Chairman, Joint Chiefs of Staff	Gen. Joseph F. Dunford, Jr., USMC

STANDING PARTICIPANTS

Secretary of the Treasury	Jacob J. Lew
Chief of Staff to the President	Denis R. McDonough
Counsel to the President	W. Neil Eggleston
National Security Adviser	Susan E. Rice
Director of the National Economic Council	Jeffrey D. Zients

OFFICIALS

National Security Adviser	Susan E. Rice
Deputy National Security Adviser	Avril D. Haines

The National Security Council was established by the National Security Act of 1947, as amended (50 U.S.C. 402). The Council was placed in the Executive Office of the President by Reorganization Plan No. 4 of 1949 (5 U.S.C. app.).

The President chairs the National Security Council. Its statutory members, in addition to the President, are the Vice President and the Secretaries of State and Defense. The Chairman of the Joint Chiefs of Staff is the statutory military adviser to the Council, and the Director of National Intelligence serves as its intelligence adviser. The Secretary of the Treasury, the U.S. Representative to the United Nations, the Assistant to the President for National Security Affairs, the Assistant to the President for Economic Policy, and the Chief of Staff to the President are invited to all meetings of the Council. The Attorney General and the Director of National Drug Control Policy are invited to attend meetings pertaining to their jurisdictions, and other officials are invited, as appropriate.

The Council advises and assists the President in integrating all aspects of national security policy as it affects the United States—domestic, foreign, military, intelligence, and economic—in conjunction with the National Economic Council.

For further information, contact the National Security Council, Eisenhower Executive Office Building, Washington, DC 20504. Phone, 202-456-1414.

Office of Administration

Eisenhower Executive Office Building, 1650 Pennsylvania Avenue, NW., Washington, DC 20503, 202-456-2861, http://www.whitehouse.gov/oa

DIRECTOR / DEPUTY ASSISTANT TO THE PRESIDENT	Catherine G. Solomon
Chief Administrative Officer	Kristie L. Mark
Chief Financial Officer	Faisal Amin
Chief Logistics Officer	Stephen E. Pearson, Acting
General Counsel	Hugh L. Brady

The Office of Administration was formally established within the Executive Office of the President by Executive Order 12028 of December 12, 1977.

The Office is exclusively dedicated to assisting the President in providing uniform administrative support services to all units within the Executive Office of the President. The services provided include facilities, information, personnel, technology, and financial management; digital solutions, library, and research services; security; legislative liaisons; and general office operations such as mail, messenger, printing, procurement, and supply services.

Sources of Information

Employment

The Office of Administration relies on professionals who come from diverse backgrounds and posses a rare blend of education, experience, and skill. The Office announces job vacancies on USAJobs.gov.

Photo Gallery

The Office of Administration contributes to the architectural and historic preservation of the properties associated with the Executive Office of the President. Images of current and past preservation projects are available online.

For further information, contact the Office of the Director, Office of Administration, Washington, DC 20503. Phone, 202-456-2861.

Office of Management and Budget

New Executive Office Building, Washington, DC 20503, 202-395-3080, http://www.whitehouse.gov/omb

DIRECTOR	Shaun L.S. Donovan
Deputy Director	(vacancy)
Controller, Office of Federal Financial Management	David A. Mader
Deputy Director, Management	(vacancy)
Executive Associate Director	Sara Aviel
General Counsel	Ilona Cohen
Intellectual Property Enforcement Coordinator	Daniel H. Marti
ADMINISTRATORS	
Office of Federal Procurement Policy	Anne E. Rung
Office of Information and Regulatory Affairs	Howard A. Shelanski

DIRECTORS

ASSISTANT DIRECTORS	
Budget	Courtney B. Timberlake
Legislative Reference	Matthew J. Vaeth
Management and Operations	Lauren E. Wright
ASSOCIATE DIRECTORS	
Communications	Shannon Buckingham
Economic Policy	Devin O'Connor
Education, Income Maintenance and Labor	Sharon Parrott
General Government Programs	Scott Nathan
Health	Adaeze Enekwechi
Information Technology and E–Government	Tony Scott
Legislative Affairs	Tamara L. Fucile
Management and Operations	Julie L. Miller
National Security Programs	Jonathan S. Lachman
Natural Resource Programs	Ali A. Zaidi
Performance Management	Lisa E. Danzig

The Office of Management and Budget evaluates, formulates, and coordinates management procedures and program objectives within and among Federal departments and agencies. It also controls the administration of the Federal budget, while routinely providing the President with recommendations regarding budget proposals and relevant legislative enactments.

The Office of Management and Budget (OMB), formerly the Bureau of the Budget, was established in the Executive Office of the President pursuant to Reorganization Plan No. 1 of 1939 (5 U.S.C. app.).

The Office's primary functions are diverse and many: to assist the President in developing and maintaining effective government by reviewing the organizational structure and management procedures of the executive branch to ensure that the intended results are achieved; to assist in developing efficient coordinating mechanisms to implement Government activities and to expand interagency cooperation; to assist the President in preparing the budget and in formulating the Government's fiscal program; to supervise and control the administration of the budget; to assist the President by clearing and coordinating departmental advice on proposed legislation and by making recommendations effecting Presidential action on legislative enactments, in accordance with past practice; to assist in developing regulatory reform proposals and programs for paperwork reduction, especially reporting burdens of the public; to assist in considering, clearing, and, where necessary, preparing proposed Executive orders and proclamations; to plan and develop information systems that provide the President with program performance data; to plan, conduct, and promote evaluation efforts that assist the President in assessing program objectives, performance, and efficiency; to keep the President informed of the progress of activities by Government agencies with respect to work proposed, initiated, and completed, together with the relative timing of work between the several agencies of the Government, all to the end that the work programs of the several agencies of the executive branch of the Government may be coordinated and that the moneys appropriated by the Congress may be expended in the most economical manner, barring overlapping and duplication of effort; and to improve the efficiency and effectiveness of the procurement processes by providing overall direction of procurement policies, regulations, procedures, and forms.

Sources of Information

Employment

The "Join OMB" Web page has links to learn more about career and detail opportunities, student internships, and applying for OMB positions. Questions may be addressed to the Human Resources Division, Office of Administration, Washington, DC 20500. Phone, 202-395-1088.

Freedom of Information Act (FOIA)

Information on how to submit a FOIA request is available online. The OMB's FOIA Request Service Center also provides assistance. Phone, 202-395-3642.

Publications

A copy of the "Budget of the United States Government" may be downloaded from the OMB Web site or purchased from the Government Publishing Office bookstore. Phone, 202-512-0132.

For further information, contact the Office of Management and Budget, New Executive Office Building, Washington, DC 20503. Phone, 202-395-3080.

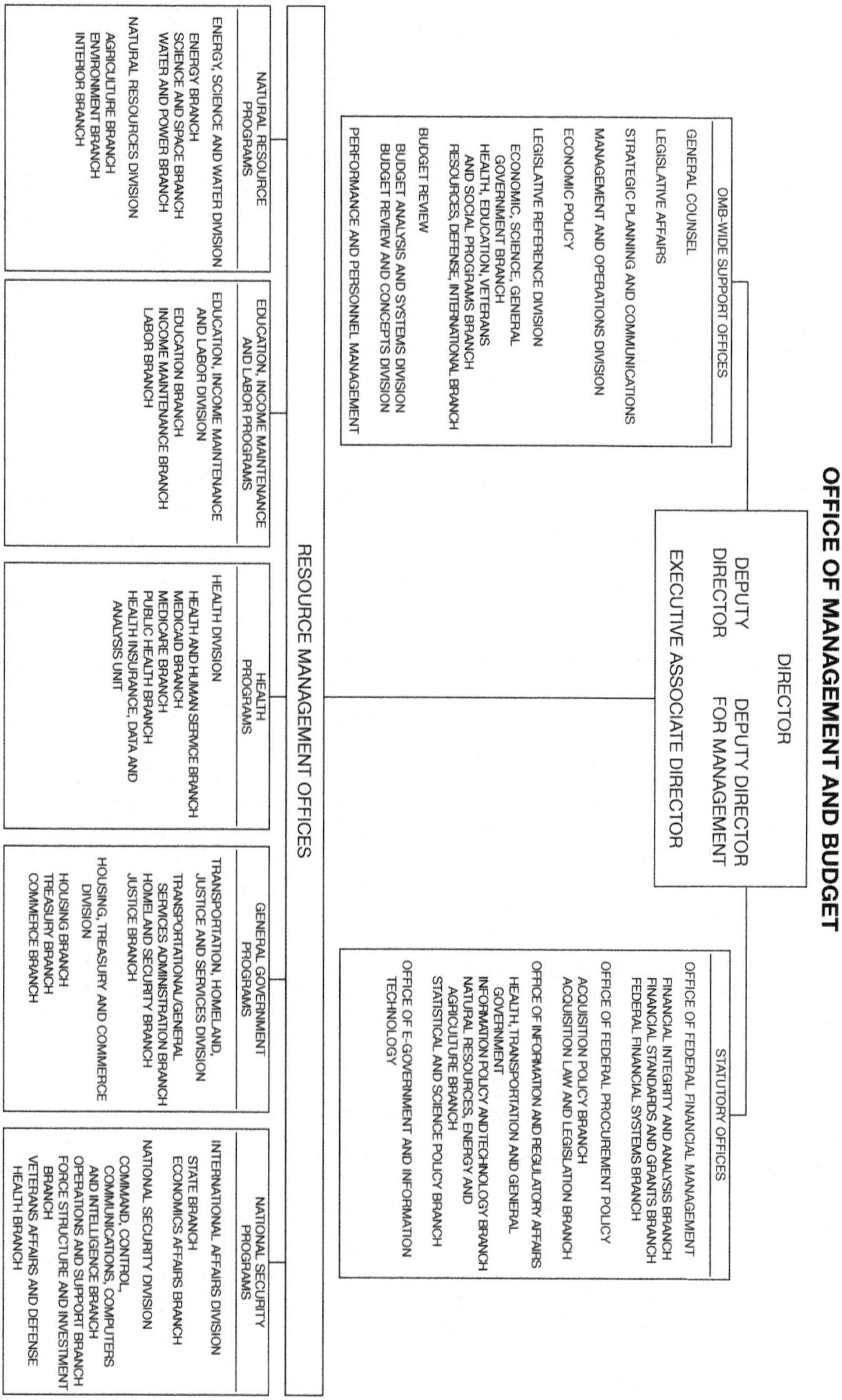
OFFICE OF MANAGEMENT AND BUDGET
DIRECTOR
DEPUTY DIRECTOR
DEPUTY DIRECTOR FOR MANAGEMENT
EXECUTIVE ASSOCIATE DIRECTOR
OMB-WIDE SUPPORT OFFICES
GENERAL COUNSEL
LEGISLATIVE AFFAIRS
STRATEGIC PLANNING AND COMMUNICATIONS
MANAGEMENT AND OPERATIONS DIVISION
ECONOMIC POLICY
LEGISLATIVE REFERENCE DIVISION
ECONOMIC, SCIENCE, GENERAL GOVERNMENT BRANCH
HEALTH, EDUCATION, VETERANS AND SOCIAL PROGRAMS BRANCH
RESOURCES, DEFENSE, INTERNATIONAL BRANCH
BUDGET REVIEW
BUDGET ANALYSIS AND SYSTEMS DIVISION
BUDGET REVIEW AND CONCEPTS DIVISION
PERFORMANCE AND PERSONNEL MANAGEMENT
STATUTORY OFFICES
OFFICE OF FEDERAL FINANCIAL MANAGEMENT
FINANCIAL INTEGRITY AND ANALYSIS BRANCH
FINANCIAL STANDARDS AND GRANTS BRANCH
FEDERAL FINANCIAL SYSTEMS BRANCH
OFFICE OF FEDERAL PROCUREMENT POLICY
ACQUISITION POLICY BRANCH
ACQUISITION LAW AND LEGISLATION BRANCH
OFFICE OF INFORMATION AND REGULATORY AFFAIRS
HEALTH, TRANSPORTATION AND GENERAL GOVERNMENT
INFORMATION POLICY AND TECHNOLOGY BRANCH
NATURAL RESOURCES, ENERGY AND AGRICULTURE BRANCH
STATISTICAL AND SCIENCE POLICY BRANCH
OFFICE OF E-GOVERNMENT AND INFORMATION TECHNOLOGY
RESOURCE MANAGEMENT OFFICES
NATURAL RESOURCE PROGRAMS
ENERGY, SCIENCE AND WATER DIVISION
ENERGY BRANCH
SCIENCE AND SPACE BRANCH
WATER AND POWER BRANCH
NATURAL RESOURCES DIVISION
AGRICULTURE BRANCH
ENVIRONMENT BRANCH
INTERIOR BRANCH
EDUCATION, INCOME MAINTENANCE AND LABOR PROGRAMS
EDUCATION, INCOME MAINTENANCE AND LABOR DIVISION
EDUCATION BRANCH
INCOME MAINTENANCE BRANCH
LABOR BRANCH
HEALTH PROGRAMS
HEALTH DIVISION
HEALTH AND HUMAN SERVICE BRANCH
MEDICAID BRANCH
MEDICARE BRANCH
PUBLIC HEALTH BRANCH
HEALTH INSURANCE, DATA AND ANALYSIS UNIT
GENERAL GOVERNMENT PROGRAMS
TRANSPORTATION, HOMELAND, JUSTICE AND SERVICES DIVISION
TRANSPORTATIONAL/GENERAL SERVICES ADMINISTRATION BRANCH
HOMELAND SECURITY BRANCH
JUSTICE BRANCH
HOUSING, TREASURY AND COMMERCE DIVISION
HOUSING BRANCH
TREASURY BRANCH
COMMERCE BRANCH
NATIONAL SECURITY PROGRAMS
INTERNATIONAL AFFAIRS DIVISION
STATE BRANCH
ECONOMICS AFFAIRS BRANCH
NATIONAL SECURITY DIVISION
COMMAND, CONTROL, COMMUNICATIONS, COMPUTERS AND INTELLIGENCE BRANCH
OPERATIONS AND SUPPORT BRANCH
FORCE STRUCTURE AND INVESTMENT BRANCH
VETERANS AFFAIRS AND DEFENSE HEALTH BRANCH

Office of National Drug Control Policy

Executive Office of the President, Washington, DC 20503, 202-395-6700, 202-395-6708, http://www.ondcp.gov

DIRECTOR	Michael P. Botticelli
Chief of Staff	Regina M. LaBelle
Deputy Director, Office of Policy, Research and Budget	Mary Lou Leary
General Counsel	Jeffrey J. Teitz
ASSOCIATE DIRECTORS	
Office of Intelligence	Gerard K. Burns
Office of Intergovernmental Public Liaison	Dalen A. Harris
Office of Legislative Affairs	Leopold Luberecki
Office of Management and Administration	Michele C. Marx
Office of Public Affairs	William D. Jenkins
Office of Research / Data Analysis	Terry S. Zobeck

The Office of National Drug Control Policy helps the President establish his National Drug Control Strategy objectives, priorities, and policies and makes budget, program, and policy recommendations affecting National Drug Control Program agencies.

The Office of National Drug Control Policy (ONDCP) was established by the National Narcotics Leadership Act of 1988 (21 U.S.C. 1501 et seq.), effective January 29, 1989, reauthorized through the Office of National Drug Control Policy Reauthorization Act of 1988 (21 U.S.C. 1701 et seq.), and again reauthorized through the Office of National Drug Control Policy Reauthorization Act of 2006 (21 U.S.C. 1701 et seq.).

The President appoints the Director of National Drug Control Policy with the advice and consent of the Senate.

The Director establishes policies, objectives, priorities, and performance measurements for the National Drug Control Program. Each year, the Director promulgates the President's National Drug Control Strategy, other related drug control strategies, supporting reports, and a program budget that the President submits to Congress. The Director advises the President on necessary changes in the organization, management, budgeting, and personnel allocation of Federal agencies that monitor drug activities. The Director also notifies Federal agencies if their policies do not comply with their responsibilities under the National Drug Control Strategy. The ONDCP also has direct programmatic responsibility for the Drug-Free Communities Support and the High Intensity Drug Trafficking Areas programs.

Sources of Information

Employment

Contact the Personnel Section, Office of National Drug Control Policy. Phone, 202-395-6695. Information on student opportunities is available on the "Working at ONDCP" Web page.

Publications

To receive publications on drugs and crime control policies, to access specific drug-related data, to access customized bibliographic searches, and to learn more about data availability and other resources, visit the ONDCP Web site.

For further information, contact the Office of National Drug Control Policy, Executive Office of the President, Washington, DC 20503. Phone, 202-395-6700. Fax, 202-395-6708.

Office of Policy Development

The Office of Policy Development comprises the Domestic Policy and the National Economic Councils, which advise and assist the President in the formulation, coordination, and implementation of domestic and economic policy. The Office of Policy Development also supports other policy development and implementation activities as directed by the President.

Domestic Policy Council

Room 469, Eisenhower Executive Office Building, Washington, DC 20502, 202-456-5594, https://www.whitehouse.gov/administration/eop/dpc

DOMESTIC POLICY COUNCIL

DIRECTOR / DOMESTIC POLICY ADVISOR TO THE PRESIDENT	Cecilia Muñoz

The Domestic Policy Council was established August 16, 1993, by Executive Order 12859. The Council oversees development and implementation of the President's domestic policy agenda and ensures coordination and communication among the heads of relevant Federal offices and agencies.

National Economic Council

Room 235, Eisenhower Executive Office Building, Washington, DC 20502, 202-456-2800, https://www.whitehouse.gov/administration/eop/nec

NATIONAL ECONOMIC COUNCIL

DIRECTOR / ASSISTANT TO THE PRESIDENT FOR ECONOMIC POLICY	Jeffrey D. Zients

The National Economic Council was created January 25, 1993, by Executive Order 12835, to coordinate the economic policymaking process and advise the President on economic policy. The Council also ensures that economic policy decisions and programs remain consistent with the President's stated goals and monitors the implementation of the President's economic goals.

Office of Science and Technology Policy

Eisenhower Executive Office Building, 1650 Pennsylvania Avenue NW., Washington, DC 20502, 202-456-4444, 202-456-6021, http://www.ostp.gov/

DIRECTOR	John P. Holdren
Chief of Staff	Cristin Dorgelo
Assistant Director, Federal Research and Development	Kei Koizumi
Assistant Director, Legislative Affairs	Donna Pignatelli
Communications Director / Senior Policy Analyst	Kristin Lee
Deputy Chief of Staff / Assistant Director	Ted M. Wackler
General Counsel	Rachael Leonard
OFFICE OF THE CHIEF TECHNOLOGY OFFICER	
Chief Technology Officer	Megan Smith
Deputy Chief Technology Officer	Alexander Macgillivray

Deputy Chief Technology Officer	Corinna Zarek
Deputy Chief Technology Officer	Edward W. Felten
Deputy Chief Technology Officer, Data Policy / Chief Data Scientist	Dhanuray Patil
ENVIRONMENT AND ENERGY DIVISION	
Associate Director	(vacancy)
Assistant Director, Clean Energy and Transportation	Austin Brown
Assistant Director, Climate Adaptation and Ecosystems	Laura Petes
Assistant Director, Climate Resilience and Information	Amy Luers
Assistant Director, Climate Resilience and Land Use	Rich Pouyat
Assistant Director, Climate Science	Donald Wuebbles
Assistant Director, Earth Observations	David Hermreck
Assistant Director, Environmental Health	Bruce Rodan
Assistant Director, Natural Disaster Resilience	Jacqueline Meszaros
Assistant Director, Polar Sciences	Martin Jeffries
Assistant Director, Space Weather	William Murtagh
Principal Assistant Director, Environment and Energy	Tamara Dickinson
NATIONAL SECURITY AND INTERNATIONAL AFFAIRS DIVISION	
Associate Director	(vacancy)
Assistant Director, Biosecurity and Emerging Technologies	Gerald Epstein
Assistant Director, Cybersecurity	Timothy Polk
Assistant Director, Cybersecurity Strategy	Gregory Shannon
Assistant Director, Defense Programs	Chris Fall
Assistant Director, Global Security	Matthew J. Heavner
Assistant Director, Special Programs	Mark LeBlanc
Principal Assistant Director, National Security and International Affairs	Steve Fetter
SCIENCE DIVISION	
Associate Director	Jo Emily Handelsman
Assistant Director, Bioethics and Privacy	Melissa Goldstein
Assistant Director, Broadening Participation	Wanda Ward
Assistant Director, Education and Learning Science	Danielle Carnival
Assistant Director, Education and Physical Sciences	Meredith Drosback
Assistant Director, Research Infrastructure	Altaf Carim
Assistant Director, Scientific Data and Information	Jerry Sheehan
TECHNOLOGY AND INNOVATION DIVISION	
Associate Director	(vacancy)
Assistant Director, Behavioral Science	Maya Shankar
Assistant Director, Biological Innovation	Robbie Barbero
Assistant Director, Civil and Commercial Space	Benjamin Roberts
Assistant Director, Education and Telecommunications Innovation	Aadil Ginwala
Assistant Director, Entrepreneurship	Douglas Rand
Assistant Director, Innovation for Growth	Jennifer Erickson
Assistant Director, Learning and Innovation	Kumar Garg
Assistant Director, Nanotechnology and Advanced Materials	Lloyd Whitman
Assistant Director, Open Innovation	Christofer Nelson
Deputy Director for Technology and Innovation	Thomas Kalil
BUDGET AND ADMINISTRATION	
Operations Manager and Security Officer	Stacy Murphy

COUNCILS

PRESIDENT'S COUNCIL OF ADVISORS ON SCIENCE AND TECHNOLOGY	
Executive Director	Ashley Predith
NATIONAL SCIENCE AND TECHNOLOGY COUNCIL	
Executive Director	Afua Bruce
Director, National Nanotechnology Coordination Office	Michael Meador
Director, Networking and Information Technology Research and Development National Coordination Office	Bryan Biegel
Director, U.S. Global Change Research Program National Coordination Office	Michael Kuperberg
Director, U.S. Group on Earth Observation Program	Timothy Stryker

The Office of Science and Technology Policy (OSTP) was established within the Executive Office of the President by the National Science and Technology Policy, Organization, and Priorities Act of 1976 (42 U.S.C. 6611).

The Office supports the President by serving as a source of engineering, scientific, and technological analysis and judgment on plans, policies, and programs of the Federal Government. OSTP experts advise the President on scientific and technological matters that affect areas of national concern like the economy, environment, foreign relations, health, and national security; evaluate the effectiveness, quality, and scale of the Federal effort in science and technology; advise and assist the President, the Office of Management and Budget, and Federal agencies throughout the Federal budget development process; and help the President with leading and coordinating the Federal Government's research and development programs.

Sources of Information

Blog

The OSTP's Web site features a blog.

Freedom of Information Act (FOIA)

Instructions for submitting a FOIA request are available online.

Internships

Internships offer a unique opportunity to work with senior White House officials and science and technology policy analysts in the OSTP's topic-based divisions or on the OSTP legal team. Applicants may apply for one of three terms: Fall, Spring, or Summer. Each term lasts no more than 90 days; interns receive no remuneration; and students may be eligible to receive academic credit.

Library

The OSTP's resource library is an expanding collection of agency materials that includes compliance guidelines, documents, presentations, reports, speeches, and testimonies. An archival section contains materials from past administrations.

Press Room

White House factsheets and science and technology-related remarks, statements, weekly addresses, and other Presidential items are available on the OSTP's Web site.

For further information, contact the Office of Science and Technology Policy, Eisenhower Executive Office Building, 1650 Pennsylvania Avenue NW., Washington, DC 20502. Phone, 202-456-4444. Fax, 202-456-6021.

Office of the United States Trade Representative

600 Seventeenth Street NW., Washington, DC 20508, 202-395-3230, http://www.ustr.gov

UNITED STATES TRADE REPRESENTATIVE	Michael Froman

Deputy U.S. Trade Representative–Geneva	Michael Punke
Deputy U.S. Trade Representative–Washington	Robert Holleyman
Deputy U.S. Trade Representative–Washington	(vacancy)
Chief Agricultural Negotiator	Darci Vetter
Chief of Staff	Matthew Vogel
Director, Interagency Center on Trade Implementation, Monitoring and Enforcement	Bradford Ward
General Counsel	Timothy Reif

ASSISTANT U.S. TRADE REPRESENTATIVES

Administration	Fed Ames
African Affairs	Florizelle Liser
Agricultural Affairs	Sharon Bomer Lauritsen
Central and South Asian Affairs	Michael Delaney
China Affairs	Jeffrey Moon
Congressional Affairs	J. Mike Harney
Environment and Natural Resources	Jennifer Prescott
Europe and Middle East Affairs	Daniel Mullaney
Innovation and Intellectual Property	Probir Mehta
Intergovernmental Affairs and Public Engagement	Omar Khan
Japan, Korea, and Asia Pacific Economic Cooperation (APEC) Affairs	Bruce Hirsh
Labor	Lewis Karesh
Monitoring and Enforcement	Juan Millan, Acting
Private Sector Engagement	M. Ashley Jones
Public and Media Affairs	Matthew McAlvanah
Services and Investment	(vacancy)
Small Business, Market Access and Industrial Competitiveness	James Sanford
Southeast Asia and Pacific Affairs	Barbara Weisel
Textiles	William Jackson
Trade Policy and Economic Affairs	Edward Gresser
Western Hemisphere	John Melle
World Trade Organization (WTO) and Multilateral Affairs	Mark Linscott

The United States Trade Representative formulates trade policy for and directs all trade negotiations of the United States.

The Office of the U.S. Trade Representative was created as the Office of the Special Representative for Trade Negotiations by Executive Order 11075 of January 15, 1963. The Trade Act of 1974 (19 U.S.C. 2171) established the Office as an agency of the Executive Office of the President charged with administering the trade agreements program.

The Office sets and administers overall trade policy. The U.S. Trade Representative heads the Office and serves as the President's principal adviser, negotiator, and spokesperson on international trade and investment issues. The Representative acts as the chief representative of the United States in all General Agreement on Tariffs and Trade activities; in Organization for Economic Cooperation and Development discussions, meetings, and negotiations that deal primarily with commodity issues and trade; in U.N. Conference on Trade and Development negotiations and other multilateral institution negotiations that deal primarily with commodity issues and trade; in other bilateral and multilateral negotiations that deal primarily with commodities or trade, including East-West trade; in negotiations under sections 704 and 734 of the Tariff Act of 1930 (19 U.S.C. 1671c and 1673c); and in negotiations on direct investment incentives and disincentives and on bilateral investment issues concerning barriers to investment.

The Omnibus Trade and Competitiveness Act of 1988 codified these authorities and added additional authority, including the implementation of section 301 actions that enforce U.S. rights under international trade agreements.

The U.S. Trade Representative serves as a Cabinet-level official with the rank of Ambassador and reports directly to the President. The Chief Agricultural Negotiator and three Deputy U.S. Trade Representatives also hold the rank of Ambassador—two of the deputies are located in Washington, DC, and the other serves in Geneva, Switzerland.

The U.S. Trade Representative is also an ex officio member on the boards of directors of the Export-Import Bank and the Overseas Private Investment Corporation. The Representative also serves on the National Advisory Council on International Monetary and Financial Policy.

Sources of Information

Blog

"Tradewinds" is the official blog of the U.S. Trade Representative.

Factsheets

The U.S. Trade Representative releases factsheets on trade issues.

Freedom of Information Act (FOIA)

Requests must be made in writing: Freedom of Information Officer, Office of the U.S. Trade Representative, 1724 F Street NW., Washington, DC 20508. Security procedures can slow down mail receipt and processing. Sending a request by email or fax avoids security-related delays. To facilitate finding the desired information, a record description must contain key details—author, date, recipient, subject matter, title or name. The Office of the U.S. Trade Representative operates a FOIA requestor service center. Phone, 202-395-3419. Fax, 202-395-9458.

The electronic reading room contains information that is made available on a routine basis to the public. It also features documents that are frequently requested under the FOIA. This collection of online documents continues to grow as records in which the public expresses an interest are added.

History

In 1963, President John F. Kennedy created a new Office of the Special Trade Representative in the Executive Office of the President and designated two new Deputies, one in the Nation's capital and the other in Geneva, Switzerland. The rest of the story is available on the Web site of the Office of the U.S. Trade Representative.

The Office of the U.S. Trade Representative posted "Facts About Trade" to commemorate its 50th anniversary.

Key Issues

The Office of the U.S. Trade Representative focuses it's trade policy on 14 issue areas: agriculture, economy and trade, enforcement, environment, government procurement, industry and manufacturing, intellectual property, labor, preference programs, services and investment, small business, textiles and apparel, trade and development, and trade organizations.

Map

The United States has trade relations with more than 75 countries worldwide.

North American Free Trade Agreement (NAFTA)

The Web site of the Office of the U.S. Trade Representative features facts on the NAFTA.

Open Government

The Office of the U.S. Trade Representative supports the Open Government initiative by promoting the principles of collaboration, participation, and transparency.

Press Releases

The Office of the U.S. Trade Representative posts press releases on its Web site.

Reports / Publications

The Office of the U.S. Trade Representative posts reports and publications on its Web site.

Social Media

The U.S. Trade Representative tweets announcements and other newsworthy items on Twitter.

The Office of the U.S. Trade Representative has a Facebook account.

Speeches / Transcripts

The Office of the U.S. Trade Representative posts transcriptions of public remarks made by its senior staff.

Transatlantic Trade and Investment Partnership (T–TIP)

The Web site of the Office of the U.S. Trade Representative features a T–TIP issue-by-issue information center.

Trans-Pacific Partnership (TPP)

The Office of the U.S Trade Representative has answered frequently asked questions regarding the TPP on its Web site.

For further information, contact the Office of Public and Media Affairs, Office of the U.S. Trade Representative, 600 Seventeenth Street NW., Washington, DC 20508. Phone, 202-395-3230.

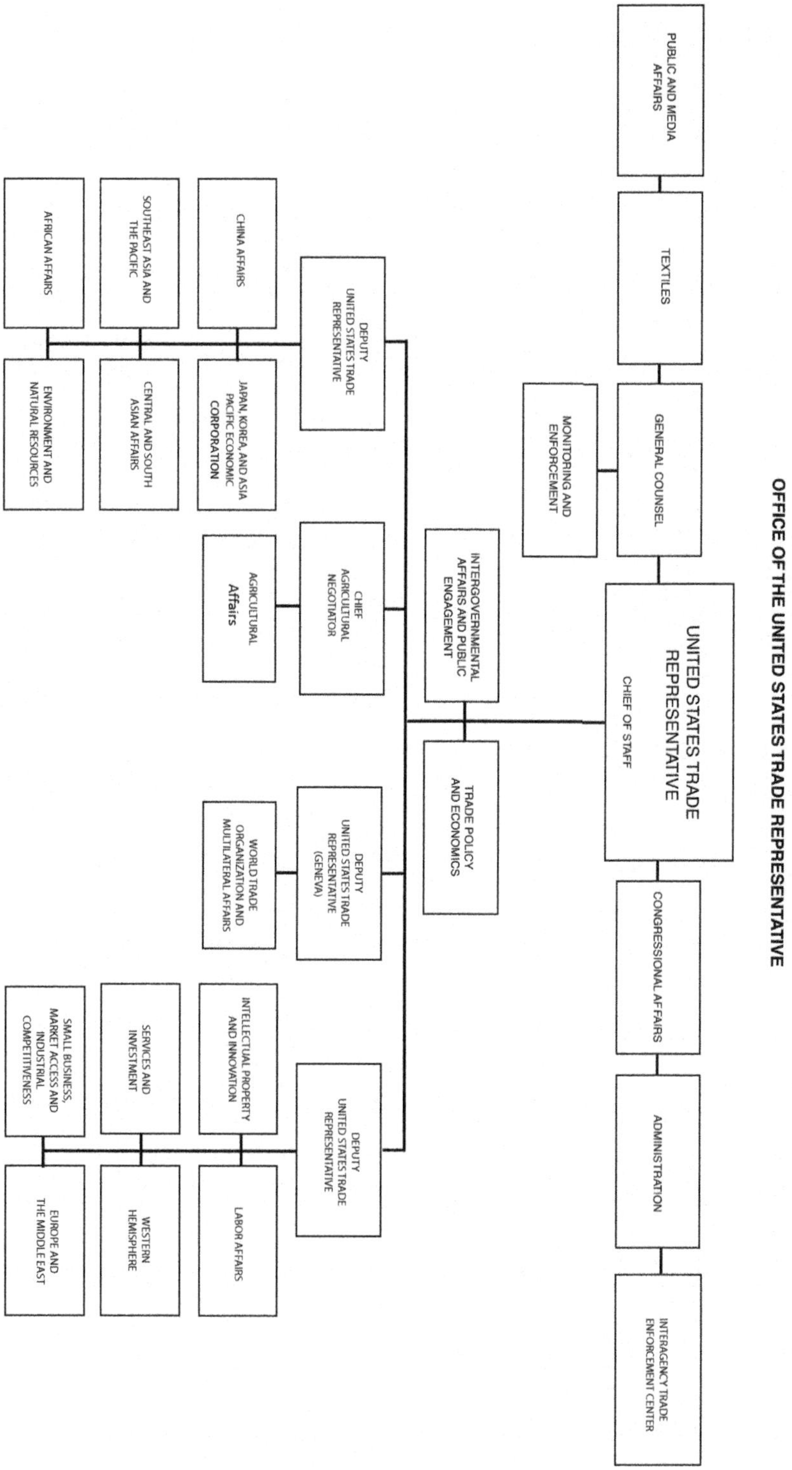
OFFICE OF THE UNITED STATES TRADE REPRESENTATIVE
UNITED STATES TRADE REPRESENTATIVE
CHIEF OF STAFF
PUBLIC AND MEDIA AFFAIRS
TEXTILES
GENERAL COUNSEL
MONITORING AND ENFORCEMENT
CONGRESSIONAL AFFAIRS
ADMINISTRATION
INTERAGENCY TRADE ENFORCEMENT CENTER
INTERGOVERNMENTAL AFFAIRS AND PUBLIC ENGAGEMENT
TRADE POLICY AND ECONOMICS
DEPUTY UNITED STATES TRADE REPRESENTATIVE
CHINA AFFAIRS
SOUTHEAST ASIA AND THE PACIFIC
AFRICAN AFFAIRS
JAPAN, KOREA, AND ASIA PACIFIC ECONOMIC CORPORATION
CENTRAL AND SOUTH ASIAN AFFAIRS
ENVIRONMENT AND NATURAL RESOURCES
CHIEF AGRICULTURAL NEGOTIATOR
AGRICULTURAL Affairs
DEPUTY UNITED STATES TRADE REPRESENTATIVE (GENEVA)
WORLD TRADE ORGANIZATION AND MULTILATERAL AFFAIRS
DEPUTY UNITED STATES TRADE REPRESENTATIVE
INTELLECTUAL PROPERTY AND INNOVATION
SERVICES AND INVESTMENT
SMALL BUSINESS, MARKET ACCESS AND INDUSTRIAL COMPETITIVENESS
LABOR AFFAIRS
WESTERN HEMISPHERE
EUROPE AND THE MIDDLE EAST

Executive Branch: Departments

Department of Agriculture

1400 Independence Avenue SW., Washington, DC 20250, 202-720-2791, http://www.usda.gov

SECRETARY OF AGRICULTURE	Thomas J. Vilsack
Deputy Secretary	Michael Scuse, Acting
AGENCY HEADS	
FARM AND FOREIGN AGRICULTURAL SERVICES	
Under Secretary	Michael Scuse
Administrator, Foreign Agricultural Service	Phil Karsting
Administrator, Farm Service Agency	Val Dolcini
Administrator, Risk Management Agency	Brandon Willis
FOOD, NUTRITION AND CONSUMER SERVICES	
Under Secretary	Kevin Concannon
Administrator, Food and Nutrition Service	Audrey Rowe
Executive Director, Center for Nutrition Policy and Promotion	Angela Tagtow
FOOD SAFETY	
Under Secretary for Food Safety	(vacancy)
Administrator, Food Safety and Inspection Service	Alfred V. Almanza, Acting
MARKETING AND REGULATORY PROGRAMS	
Under Secretary	Edward M. Avalos
Administrator, Agricultural Marketing Service	Elanor Starmer
Administrator, Animal and Plant Health Inspection Service	Kevin Shea
Administrator, Grain Inspection, Packers and Stockyards Administration	Larry Mitchell
NATURAL RESOURCES AND ENVIRONMENT	
Under Secretary	Robert Bonnie
Chief, Forest Service	Thomas Tidwell
Chief, Natural Resources Conservation Service	Jason Weller
RESEARCH, EDUCATION AND ECONOMICS	
Under Secretary	Catherine Woteki
Administrator, Agricultural Research Service	Chavonda Jacobs-Young
Administrator, Economic Research Service	Mary Bohman
Administrator, National Agricultural Statistics Service	Joseph T. Reilly
Director, National Institute of Food and Agriculture	Sonny Ramaswamy
RURAL DEVELOPMENT	
Under Secretary	Lisa Mensah
Administrator, Rural Business-Cooperative Service	Samuel H. Rikkers
Administrator, Rural Housing Service	Tony Hernandez
Administrator, Rural Utilities Service	Brandon McBride
OFFICE HEADS	
Assistant Secretary for Administration	Gregory Parham
Assistant Secretary for Civil Rights	Joseph Leonard, Jr.
Assistant Secretary for Congressional Relations	Todd A. Batta
Chief Economist	Robert Johansson
Chief Financial Officer	Jon M. Holladay

Chief Information Officer	Jonathan Alboum
Director, Advocacy and Outreach	Carolyn Parker
Director, Budget and Program Analysis	Michael Young
Director, Communications	Matthew Herrick
Director, National Appeals Division	Steven C. Silverman
General Counsel	Jeff Prieto
Inspector General	Phyllis K. Fong

[For the Department of Agriculture statement of organization, see the Code of Federal Regulations, Title 7, Part 2]

The Department of Agriculture develops agricultural markets, fights hunger and malnutrition, conserves natural resources, and ensures food quality standards.

The Department of Agriculture (USDA) was created by an act of Congress on May 15, 1862 (7 U.S.C. 2201). In carrying out its work in the program mission areas, the USDA relies on the support of departmental administration staff, as well as on the Offices of Communications, Congressional Relations, the Chief Economist, the Chief Financial Officer, the Chief Information Officer, the General Counsel, and the Inspector General.

FARM AND FOREIGN AGRICULTURAL SERVICES

This mission area centers on helping America's farmers and ranchers deal with the unpredictable nature of weather and markets. These services deliver commodity, conservation, credit, disaster, and emergency assistance programs to strengthen and stabilize the agricultural economy.

Farm Service Agency (FSA)

The Farm Service Agency administers farm commodity, disaster, and conservation programs for farmers and ranchers. It also makes and guarantees farm emergency, ownership, and operating loans through a network of State and county offices.

Commodity Credit Corporation

The Commodity Credit Corporation, an agency and instrumentality of the United States within the USDA, is under the supervision of the Secretary of Agriculture. The Corporation does not have any employees, but relies on various Federal agencies, principally those in the USDA, to conduct its operations. It carries out a wide array of functions as authorized by the Commodity Credit Corporation Charter Act and as specifically authorized by the Congress in numerous statutes. Corporation funds are used to offer marketing assistance loans to producers of certain commodities, fund conservation programs to protect or enhance natural resources, support the export of agricultural commodities, provide humanitarian assistance abroad, and further economic progress in developing countries.

Commodity Operations

FSA facilitates the purchase, storage, transportation, and disposition of U.S.-origin commodities acquired as a result of commodity loan forfeiture or through procurement for humanitarian food aid programs. FSA administers the United States Warehouse Act, which authorizes the Secretary of Agriculture to license warehouse operators who store agricultural products. The FSA also enters into agreements with warehouse operators to store commodities owned by the Commodity Credit Corporation or pledged by farmers as security for Commodity Credit Corporation marketing assistance loans.

Conservation Programs

FSA's conservation programs include the Conservation Reserve Program, which is the Federal Government's largest environmental improvement program on private lands. It safeguards millions of acres of topsoil from erosion, improves air quality, increases wildlife habitat, and reduces water runoff and sedimentation. In return for planting a protective cover of grass or trees on environmentally sensitive land, participants receive an annual rental payment. Cost-share payments are available to help establish conservation practices such as the planting of native grass, trees, windbreaks, or plants that improve water quality and give shelter and food to wildlife.

Farm Commodity Programs

FSA manages farm safety net programs for America's farmers and ranchers. Its Commodity Credit Corporation stabilizes, supports, and protects farm income and prices; helps maintain balanced and adequate supplies of agricultural commodities; and aids in their orderly distribution.

Farm Loan Programs

FSA makes and guarantees loans to family farmers and ranchers to purchase farmland and finance agricultural production. These programs offer credit on reasonable rates and terms to farmers—those who have suffered financial setbacks from natural disasters, those with limited resources for establishing and maintaining profitable farming operations, and beginners.

Noninsured Crop Disaster Assistance Program

The Noninsured Crop Disaster Assistance Program gives financial assistance to producers of noninsurable crops when yields are low, inventory is lost, or natural disasters prevent planting.

Other Emergency Assistance

In counties that are declared disaster areas, low-interest loans for eligible farmers help cover physical and production losses. Eligible producers can be compensated for crop losses, livestock feed losses, tree damage, and for the cost of rehabilitating certain farmlands damaged by natural disaster.

For further information, contact the Office of External Affairs, Farm Service Agency, Department of Agriculture, Stop 0506, 1400 Independence Avenue SW., Washington, DC 20250. Phone, 202-720-7807. Or, contact the Information Division, Foreign Agricultural Service, Department of Agriculture, Stop 1004, 1400 Independence Avenue SW., Washington, DC 20250. Phone, 202-720-7115. Fax, 202-720-1727.

Foreign Agricultural Service (FAS)

The Foreign Agricultural Service improves foreign market access for U.S. products, builds new markets, improves the competitive position of U.S. agriculture in the global marketplace, and provides food aid and technical assistance to foreign countries.

FAS has the primary responsibility for USDA's activities in the areas of international marketing, trade agreements and negotiations, and the collection and analysis of international statistics and market information. It also administers the USDA's export credit guarantee and food aid programs. FAS helps increase income and food availability in developing nations by mobilizing expertise for agriculturally led economic growth.

FAS also enhances U.S. agricultural competitiveness through a global network of agricultural economists, marketing experts, negotiators, and other specialists. FAS agricultural counselors, attaches, trade officers, and locally employed staff are stationed in over 93 countries to support U.S. agricultural interests and cover 171 countries.

In addition to agricultural affairs offices in U.S. embassies, trade offices operate in a number of key foreign markets. They function as service centers for U.S. exporters and foreign buyers seeking market information.

Reports prepared by FAS overseas offices cover changes in policies and other developments that could affect U.S. agricultural exports. FAS staff in U.S. embassies worldwide assess U.S. export marketing opportunities and respond to the daily informational needs of those who develop, initiate, monitor, and evaluate U.S. food and agricultural policies and programs.

The Service also maintains a worldwide

agricultural reporting system based on information from U.S. agricultural traders, remote sensing systems, and other sources. Analysts in Washington, DC, prepare production forecasts, assess export marketing opportunities, and track changes in policies affecting U.S. agricultural exports and imports.

FAS programs help U.S. exporters develop and maintain markets for hundreds of food and agricultural products, from bulk commodities to brand-name items. Formal market promotion activities are carried out chiefly in cooperation with agricultural trade associations, State-regional trade groups, small businesses, and cooperatives that plan, manage, and contribute human and financial resources to these efforts. The Service also advises exporters on locating buyers and provides assistance through a variety of other methods, including supporting U.S. participation in trade shows and single-industry exhibitions each year.

For further information, contact the Public Affairs Division, Foreign Agricultural Service, Stop 1004, 1400 Independence Avenue SW., Department of Agriculture, Washington, DC 20250-1004. Phone, 202-720-7115. Fax, 202-720-1727.

Risk Management Agency (RMA)

The Risk Management Agency, on behalf of the Federal Crop Insurance Corporation (FCIC), oversees and administers the Federal crop insurance program under the Federal Crop Insurance Act.

Federal crop insurance is offered to qualifying producers through 17 private sector crop insurance companies. Under the Standard Reinsurance Agreement (SRA), RMA provides reinsurance, pays premium subsidies, reimburses insurers for administrative and operating expenses, and oversees the financial integrity and operational performance of the delivery system. RMA bears much of the noncommercial insurance risk under the SRA, allowing insurers to retain commercial insurance risks or reinsure those risks in the private market.

In 2016, the Federal crop insurance program provided producers with more than $100 billion in protection. Twenty-four insurance plans are available, covering 547 commodities and types, 37 reinsured privately developed products, and 18 RMA-developed pilot programs in various stages of operation.

RMA also works closely with the private sector to find innovative ways to expand coverage. The expansion affects risk protection for specialty crops, livestock and forage, and rangeland and pasture. Thus, RMA is able to reduce the need for ad hoc disaster assistance, while providing coverage for production declines that result from adverse weather in many areas.

Additional information is available on the RMA Web site, which features agency news, State profiles, publications, and announcements on current issues. It also has summaries of insurance sales, pilot programs, downloadable crop policies, and agency-sponsored events. Online tools, calculators, and applications are also part of the Web site.

For further information, contact the Office of the Administrator, Risk Management Agency, Department of Agriculture, Stop 0801, 1400 Independence Avenue SW., Washington, DC 20250. Phone, 202-690-2803.

FOOD, NUTRITION AND CONSUMER SERVICES

The mission area of the food, nutrition, and consumer services centers on harnessing the Nation's agricultural abundance to reduce hunger and improve health in the United States. Its agencies administer Federal domestic nutrition assistance programs and the Center for Nutrition Policy and Promotion, which links scientific research to the nutrition needs of consumers through science-based dietary guidance, nutrition policy coordination, and nutrition education.

Center for Nutrition Policy and Promotion (CNPP)

The Center for Nutrition Policy and Promotion improves the health and well-being of Americans by developing and promoting dietary guidance that links the latest evidence-based scientific research to consumers' nutrition needs. Initiatives range from setting Federal dietary guidance to consumer-based nutrition education (MyPlate), to cutting-edge personalized electronic tools (SuperTracker), to "report cards" on the status of the American diet.

For further information, contact the Office of Public Information, Center for Nutrition Policy and Promotion, Suite 200, 1120 20th Street NW., Washington, DC 20036-3406. Phone, 202-418-2312.

Food and Nutrition Service (FNS)

The Food and Nutrition Service administers the USDA domestic nutrition assistance programs, serving one in four Americans in the course of a year. The FNS works in partnership with States and local agencies to increase food security and reduce hunger by providing children and low-income people with access to food, a healthy diet, and nutrition education.

FNS administers the following nutrition assistance programs:

The Supplemental Nutrition Assistance Program (SNAP) gives nutrition assistance to millions of eligible low-income individuals and families, and it provides economic benefits to communities. SNAP is the largest program in the domestic hunger safety net. FNS also works with State partners and the retail community to improve program administration and ensure program integrity.

The Special Supplemental Nutrition Program for Women, Infants, and Children (WIC) provides Federal grants to States for supplemental foods, health care referrals, and nutrition education for low-income pregnant, breastfeeding, and nonbreastfeeding postpartum women, and to infants and children up to age 5 who are found to be at nutritional risk. WIC and the Seniors' Farmers' Market Nutrition Programs provide WIC participants and senior citizens with increased access to fresh produce through coupons to purchase fresh fruits and vegetables from authorized farmers.

The Farmers' Market Nutrition Program is linked to WIC, which provides supplemental foods, health care referrals, and nutrition education at no cost to low-income pregnant, breastfeeding, and nonbreastfeeding post partum women, and to infants and children who are up to 5 years of age and found to be at nutritional risk.

The Senior Farmers' Market Nutrition Program awards grants to States, U.S. Territories, and federally recognized Indian tribal governments for coupons that low-income seniors can use to purchase eligible foods at farmers' markets, roadside stands, and community-supported agriculture programs.

The Commodity Supplemental Food Program improves the health of low-income pregnant and breastfeeding women, nonbreastfeeding mothers up to 1 year postpartum, infants, and children up to age 6. The program supplements their diets with nutritious USDA commodity foods. It also provides food and administrative funds to States to supplement the diets of these groups.

School districts and independent schools that choose to take part in the National School Lunch Program receive cash subsidies and donated commodities from the USDA. In return, they must serve lunches that meet Federal requirements and must offer free or reduced-price lunches to eligible children. School food authorities can also be reimbursed for snacks served to children through age 18 in afterschool educational or enrichment programs.

The School Breakfast Program operates like the National School Lunch Program. School districts and independent schools that choose to take part in the breakfast program receive cash subsidies from the USDA for each meal they serve. In return, they must serve breakfasts that meet Federal requirements and must offer free or reduced-price breakfasts to eligible children.

The Special Milk Program provides milk to schoolchildren and children in childcare institutions who do not participate in other Federal meal service programs. The program reimburses schools for the milk that they serve. Schools in the National School Lunch or School Breakfast Programs may participate so that milk is available to prekindergarten and kindergarten children who may not have access to school meal programs.

The Child and Adult Care Food Program helps child and adult care institutions and family or group day care homes provide nutritious foods to promote the health and wellness of young children, older adults, and chronically impaired disabled persons.

The Summer Food Service Program ensures that low-income children receive nutritious meals when they are not attending school.

The Emergency Food Assistance Program helps low-income and elderly Americans access free emergency food and nutrition assistance. The program provides food and administrative funds to States to supplement the diets of these groups.

The Food Distribution Program on Indian Reservations helps low-income households—including the elderly living on Indian reservations—and Native American families residing in designated areas in Oklahoma and near reservations elsewhere to access USDA foods.

The Fresh Fruit and Vegetable Program helps make fruits and vegetables available to students free of charge, during the schoolday, in participating elementary schools. The program is a tool for reducing childhood obesity: It exposes schoolchildren to fresh produce that they otherwise might not have the opportunity to sample.

For further information, contact the Public Information Officer, Food and Nutrition Service, Department of Agriculture, 3101 Park Center Drive, Alexandria, VA 22302. Phone, 703-305-2286.

FOOD SAFETY

This mission area centers on the labeling and packaging, safety, and wholesomeness of the Nation's commercial supply of egg, poultry, and meat. It also contributes significantly to the President's Council on Food Safety and has helped coordinate a nationwide food safety strategic plan.

Food Safety and Inspection Service (FSIS)

The Food Safety and Inspection Service was established by the Secretary of Agriculture on June 17, 1981, pursuant to authority contained in 5 U.S.C. 301 and Reorganization Plan No. 2 of 1953 (5 U.S.C. app.). FSIS monitors the Nation's commercial supply of meat, poultry, and processed egg products.

Meat, Poultry, and Processed Egg Products Inspection

FSIS is the public health regulatory agency in the U.S. Department of Agriculture that ensures meat, poultry, and processed egg products are safe, wholesome, accurately labeled, and properly packaged. FSIS enforces the Federal Meat Inspection Act (FMIA), the Poultry Products Inspection Act (PPIA), and the Egg Products Inspection Act (EPIA), which require Federal inspection and regulation of meat, poultry, and processed egg products prepared for distribution in commerce for use as human food. FSIS is also responsible for administering the Humane Methods of Slaughter Act, which requires that livestock are handled and slaughtered humanely at the FSIS-inspected establishment.

FSIS administers FMIA, PPIA, and EPIA by developing and implementing data-driven regulations, including inspection, testing, and enforcement activities for the products under FSIS's jurisdiction. In addition to mandatory inspection of meat, poultry, and processed egg products, FSIS tests samples of these products for microbial and chemical residues to monitor trends for enforcement purposes and to understand, predict, and prevent contamination. FSIS also ensures that only meat, poultry, and processed egg products that meet U.S. requirements are imported into the United States, and it certifies meat, poultry, and processed egg products for export.

FSIS also monitors meat, poultry, and processed egg products throughout storage, distribution, and retail channels, and it ensures regulatory compliance to protect the public, including detention of products, voluntary product recalls, court-ordered seizures of products, administrative suspension and withdrawal of inspection, and referral of violations for criminal and civil prosecution. To protect against intentional contamination, the Agency conducts food defense activities, as well.

FSIS maintains a toll-free Meat and Poultry Hotline (phone, 888-674-6854; TTY, 800-256-7072) and chat feature to answer questions in English and Spanish about the safe handling of meat, poultry, and egg products. The Hotline's hours are weekdays, from 10 a.m. to 4 p.m., EST, year round. An extensive selection of food safety messages in English and Spanish is available at the same number at all hours of the day. Questions can also be submitted anytime to MPHotline.fsis@usda.gov.

"Ask Karen," an online virtual representative, provides answers to consumer questions on preventing foodborne illness, safe food handling and storage, and safe preparation of meat, poultry, and egg products (http://www.fsis.usda.gov/wps/portal/informational/askkaren).

For further information, contact the Assistant Administrator, Office of Public Affairs and Consumer Education, Department of Agriculture, 1400 Independence Avenue SW., Washington, DC 20250. Phone, 202-720-3884.

MARKETING AND REGULATORY PROGRAMS

The scope of the marketing and regulatory mission area includes marketing and regulatory programs other than those concerned with food safety.

Agricultural Marketing Service (AMS)

The Agricultural Marketing Service was established by the Secretary of Agriculture on April 2, 1972, under the authority of Reorganization Plan No. 2 of 1953 (5 U.S.C. app.) and other authorities. The Service facilitates the fair and efficient marketing of U.S. agricultural products. It supports agriculture through a variety of programs: cotton and tobacco; dairy; fruit and vegetable; livestock, poultry, and seed; organic products; transportation and marketing, and science and technology. The Service's activities support American agriculture in the global marketplace and help ensure the availability of wholesome food.

Audit and Accreditation Services

AMS audit and accreditation programs give producers and suppliers of agricultural products the opportunity to assure customers of their ability to provide consistent quality products and services. The AMS verifies their documented programs through independent, third-party audits. AMS audit and accreditation programs are voluntary and paid through hourly user-fees.

Commodity Purchasing

The AMS purchases a variety of domestically produced and processed commodity food products through a competitive process involving approved vendors. The purchasing supports American agriculture by providing an outlet for surplus products and encouraging domestic consumption of domestic foods. The wholesome, high quality products, collectively called USDA Foods, are delivered to schools, food banks, and households across the country and constitute a vital component of the Nation's food safety net.

Farmers Markets and Direct-to-Consumer Marketing

The AMS regularly collects data and analyzes farmers market operations and other direct-to-consumer marketing outlets—Community Supported Agriculture, food hubs, on-farm markets—to help market managers, planners, and researchers better understand the effect of these outlets on food access and local economic development, and to help the public find sources of fresh, local food.

Food Quality Assurance

Under a Governmentwide quality assurance program, the Service is responsible for the development and revision of specifications used by Federal agencies in procuring food for military and civilian uses. The Service coordinates and approves certification programs designed to ensure that purchased products conform to the specification requirements.

Grant Programs

The AMS administers a series of grant programs that make over $100 million available to support local food, organic operations, ranchers, and specialty crop growers. These grant programs improve domestic and international opportunities for growers and producers and help support rural America.

Laboratory Testing and Approval Services

The AMS oversees the National Science Laboratories (NSL), a fee-for-service lab network. NSL scientists and technicians conduct chemical, microbiological, and biomolecular analyses on food and agricultural commodities. The network provides testing services for AMS commodity programs, other USDA agencies, Federal and State agencies, research institutions, private sector food and agricultural industries, and the U.S. military. The AMS also approves or accredits labs to perform testing services in support of domestic and international trade. At the request of industry, other Federal agencies, or foreign governments, it develops and administers laboratory approval programs to verify that the analysis of food and agricultural products meet country or customer-specified requirements.

Marketing Agreements and Orders

Marketing agreements and orders are initiated by industry to stabilize markets for dairy products, fruits, vegetables, and specialty crops. An agreement is binding only for handlers who sign the agreement. Marketing orders are a binding regulation for the entire industry in the specified geographical area, once the producers and the Secretary of Agriculture have approved it.

Market News

Market News issues thousands of reports each year, providing the agricultural industry with important wholesale, retail, and shipping data. The reports give farmers, producers, and other agricultural businesses the information they need to evaluate market conditions, identify trends, make purchasing decisions, monitor price patterns, evaluate transportation equipment needs, and accurately assess movement.

National Organic Program

The National Organic Program is a regulatory program housed within the AMS. It develops national standards for organically-produced agricultural products. The "USDA ORGANIC" seal means that a product met consistent and uniform standards. USDA organic regulations do not address food safety or nutrition. Organic production integrates cultural, biological, and mechanical practices to increase cycling of resources, biodiversity, and ecological balance.

Pesticide Data Program

The Pesticide Data Program (PDP) monitors pesticide residue nationwide. It produces the most comprehensive pesticide residue database in the Nation. The PDP administers the sampling, testing, and reporting of pesticide residues on agricultural commodities in the U.S. food supply—with an emphasis on those commodities regularly consumed by infants and children. The AMS implements the program in cooperation with State agriculture departments and other Federal agencies. The Environmental Protection Agency relies on PDP data to assess dietary exposure, and Food and Drug Administration and other government experts use them for making informed decisions.

Plant Variety Protection Program

The Plant Variety Protection Office protects the intellectual property of breeders of new seed and tuber varieties. Implementing the Plant Variety Protection Act, the Office examines new applications and grants certificates that protect varieties for 20 or 25 years. Certificate owners have exclusive rights to market and sell their varieties, manage the use of their varieties by other breeders, and benefit from legal protection of their work.

Regulatory Programs

The AMS administers several regulatory programs designed to protect producers, handlers, and consumers of agricultural commodities from financial loss or personal injury resulting from careless, deceptive, or fraudulent marketing practices. These regulatory programs encourage fair trading practices in the marketing of fruits and vegetables, and they require accuracy in seed labeling and in advertising. The AMS also enforces the Country of Origin Labeling law, which requires retailers—full-line grocery stores, supermarkets, club warehouse stores—to notify their customers with information regarding the source of certain foods. The law covers food products such as muscle cut and ground meats.

Research and Promotion Programs

The AMS monitors certain industry-sponsored research, promotion, and information programs authorized by Federal laws. These programs give farmers and processors a means to finance and operate various research, promotion, and information activities for agricultural products.

Standardization, Grading, and Classing

Nearly 600 grade standards have been established for some 230 agricultural commodities to help buyers and sellers trade on agreed-upon quality levels. Standards are developed with assistance from individuals outside the Department, particularly from those involved with the industries directly affected. The AMS also participates in developing international commodity standards to facilitate trade. Grading and classing services are provided to certify the grade and quality of products. These grading services are provided to buyers and sellers of live cattle, swine, sheep, meat, poultry, eggs, rabbits, fruits, vegetables, tree nuts, peanuts, dairy products, tobacco, and other miscellaneous food products. Classing services are provided to buyers and sellers of cotton and cotton products. These services are mainly voluntary and are provided upon request and for a fee. The AMS is also responsible for testing seed.

Transportation Research and Analysis

The Transportation Services Division (TSD) of the AMS serves as the definitive source for economic analysis of agricultural transportation. TSD experts support domestic and international agribusinesses by giving technical assistance and releasing reports and offering analysis. They track developments in truck, rail, barge, and ocean transportation and provide information on and analysis of these modes of moving food from farm to table, from port to market.

For further information, contact the Public Affairs Staff, Agricultural Marketing Service, Department of Agriculture, Room 2532, South Agriculture Building, Stop 0273, 1400 Independence Ave, SW., Washington, DC 20250. Phone, 202-720-8998.

Animal and Plant Health Inspection Service (APHIS)

[For the Animal and Plant Health Inspection Service statement of organization, see the Code of Federal Regulations, Title 7, Part 371]

The Animal and Plant Health Inspection Service was originally established in 1972 and reestablished by the Secretary of Agriculture on March 14, 1977, pursuant to authority contained in 5 U.S.C. 301 and Reorganization Plan No. 2 of 1953 (5 U.S.C. app.). The APHIS was established to conduct regulatory and control programs to protect and improve animal and plant health for the benefit of agriculture and the environment. In cooperation with State governments, industry stakeholders, and other Federal agencies, the APHIS works to prevent the entry and establishment of foreign animal and plant pests and diseases. It also regulates certain genetically engineered organisms and supports healthy international agricultural trade and exports of U.S. agricultural products. The agency also works to ensure the humane treatment of certain animals and carries out research and operational activities to mitigate damage caused by birds, rodents, and other wildlife.

Animal Care

Animal Care upholds and enforces the Animal Welfare Act and the Horse Protection Act. The Animal Welfare Act requires that federally established standards of care and treatment be provided for certain warmblooded animals bred for commercial sale, used in research, transported commercially, or publicly exhibited. The Horse Protection Act seeks to end soring by preventing sored horses from participating in auctions, exhibitions, sales, and shows. The Center for Animal Welfare collaborates with other animal welfare entities to help the USDA build partnerships domestically and internationally, improve regulatory practices, and develop outreach, training, and educational resources. Animal Care's emergency response component provides national leadership on the safety and well-being of pets during disasters—supporting animal safety during emergencies is a significant factor in ensuring the well-being of pet owners.

Biotechnology Regulatory Services

To protect plant health, Biotechnology Regulatory Services implements APHIS regulations affecting the importation, movement, and field release of genetically engineered plants and certain other genetically engineered organisms that may pose a risk to plant health. The APHIS coordinates these responsibilities along with the other designated Federal agencies as part of the Federal coordinated framework for the regulation of biotechnology.

International Services

APHIS protects the health and value of American agriculture and natural resources. Its International Services supports this mission in an international environment. The Services collaborate with foreign partners to control pests and diseases, facilitate safe agricultural trade, ensure effective and efficient management of internationally-based programs, and invest in international capacity-building with foreign counterparts to build technical and regulatory skills that prevent diseases and pests from spreading.

Plant Protection and Quarantine

APHIS oversees Plant Protection and Quarantine. The program protects U.S. agriculture and natural resources against the entry, establishment, and spread of economically and environmentally significant pests. It also facilitates the safe trade of agricultural products.

Veterinary Services

Veterinary Services supports APHIS' efforts to protect and improve the health, quality, and marketability of the Nation's animals, animal products, and veterinary biologics. The Service is organized strategically into four sections: surveillance, preparedness, and response; national import export services; science, technology, and analysis; and program support services.

Wildlife Services

Wildlife Services provides Federal leadership and expertise for resolving conflicts between wildlife and people to allow coexistence. It conducts program delivery, research, and other activities through regional and State offices, the National Wildlife Research Center and field stations, as well as through national programs. Contact the APHIS customer service call center for more information. Phone, 844-820-2234.

For further information, contact Legislative and Public Affairs, Animal and Plant Health Inspection Service, Department of Agriculture, 1400 Independence Avenue SW., Washington, DC 20250. Phone, 202-799-7030.

Grain Inspection, Packers and Stockyards Administration (GIPSA)

The Grain Inspection, Packers and Stockyards Administration was established in 1994 to facilitate the marketing of livestock, poultry, meat, cereals, oilseeds, and related agricultural products, and to promote fair and competitive trading practices for the overall benefit of consumers and American agriculture. The Packers and Stockyards Program protects fair trade practices, financial integrity, and competitive markets for livestock, meat, and poultry. The Federal Grain Inspection Service facilitates the marketing of U.S. grains, oilseeds, and related agricultural products through its grain inspection and weighing system. The Service also maintains the integrity of the grain marketing system by developing unbiased grading standards and methods for assessing grain quality.

Inspection

The United States Grain Standards Act requires most U.S. export grain to be inspected. At export port locations, GIPSA or State agencies that have been delegated authority by the Administrator carry out inspections. For domestic grain marketed at inland locations, the Administrator designates private and State agencies to provide official inspection services upon request. Both export and domestic services are provided on a fee-for-service basis.

Methods Development

GIPSA's methods development activities include applied research or tests to produce new or improved techniques for measuring grain quality. Examples include knowledge gained through the study of how to establish real-time grain inspection, develop reference methods in order to maintain consistency and standardization in the grain inspection system, as well as the comparison of different techniques for evaluation of end-use quality in wheat.

Packers and Stockyards Activities

GIPSA prohibits deceptive, discriminatory, and unfair practices by market agencies, dealers, stockyards, packers, swine contractors, and live poultry dealers in the livestock, meat packing, and poultry industries. According to the provisions of the Packers and Stockyards Act, it fosters fair competition and ensures payment protection for growers and farmers through regulatory activities: investigating alleged violations of the act, auditing regulated entities, verifying the accuracy of scales, and monitoring industry trends to protect consumers and members of the livestock, meat, and poultry industries. The Administration also has certain responsibilities derived from the Truth-in-Lending and the Fair Credit Reporting Acts. GIPSA carries out the Secretary's responsibilities under section 1324 of the Food Security Act of 1985 pertaining to State-established central filing systems to prenotify buyers, commission merchants, and selling agents of security interests against farm products. GIPSA administers the section of the act commonly referred to as the "Clear Title" provision and certifies qualifying State systems.

Standardization

Official inspections of grains, oilseeds, and other agricultural and processed commodities are based on established official U.S. standards. The inspections also rely on sound, proven, and standardized procedures, techniques, and equipment. The official standards and accompanying procedures, techniques, and equipment produce consistent test results and services, from elevator to elevator and State to State.

Weighing

GIPSA or State agencies that have been delegated authority the Administrator officially weigh U.S. export grain at port locations. For domestic grain marketed at inland locations, GIPSA or designated private or State agencies provide the weighing services. Weighing services are provided on a fee-for-service basis.

For further information, contact the Grain Inspection, Packers, and Stockyards Administration, Department of Agriculture, 1400 Independence Avenue SW., Washington, DC 20250. Phone, 202-720-0219.

NATURAL RESOURCES AND ENVIRONMENT

This mission area centers on stewardship of 75 percent of the Nation's total land area. The USDA's operating philosophy in this mission area places a premium on collaboration with diverse partners and on the health and sustainability of ecosystems to maximize stewardship of the Nation's natural resources. This approach ensures that the necessary requirements for maintaining healthy and sustainable systems are in balance with people's priorities and the products and services that they desire.

Forest Service (FS)

[For the Forest Service statement of organization, see the Code of Federal Regulations, Title 36, Part 200.1]

In 1876, Congress created the Office of Special Agent in the Department of

Agriculture to assess the condition of the forests in the United States. The Forest Service was created decades later by the Transfer Act of February 1, 1905 (16 U.S.C. 472), which transferred the Federal forest reserves and the responsibility for their management to the USDA from the Department of the Interior. The mission of the Forest Service is to achieve quality land management under the sustainable, multiple-use management concept to meet the diverse needs of people. The Service advocates a conservation ethic in promoting the health, productivity, diversity, and beauty of forests and associated lands; listens to people and responds to their diverse needs in making decisions; protects and manages the National Forests and Grasslands to best demonstrate the sustainable, multiple-use management concept; provides technical and financial assistance to State, tribal, and private forest landowners, encouraging them to become better stewards and quality land managers; helps cities and communities improve their natural environment by planting trees and caring for their forests; provides international technical assistance and scientific exchanges to sustain and enhance global resources and to encourage quality land management; assists States and communities in using the forests wisely to promote rural economic development and a quality rural environment; develops and disseminates scientific and technical knowledge that helps protect, manage, and improve use of forests and rangelands; and offers employment, training, and educational opportunities to the unemployed, underemployed, disadvantaged, elderly, and youth.

Forest Research

The Service performs basic and applied research to develop the scientific information and technology needed to protect, manage, use, and sustain the natural resources of the Nation's forests and rangelands, including those on private and tribal lands. Its forest research strategy focuses on three major program components: understanding the structure and functions of forest and range ecosystems; understanding how people perceive and value the protection, management, and use of natural resources; and determining which protection, management, and utilization practices are most suitable for sustainable production and use of natural resources worldwide.

National Forest System

Using the principles of multiple-use and sustained yield, the Service manages 154 National Forests, 20 National Grasslands, 1 tall grass prairie, and 8 national monuments on approximately 193 million acres of land in 44 States, the U.S. Virgin Islands, and Puerto Rico. The Nation's need for wood and paper products must be balanced against the other vital, renewable resources or benefits that the National Forests and Grasslands provide: recreation and natural beauty, wildlife habitat, livestock forage, and water supplies. As a guiding principle, the Service tries to achieve greatest good for the greatest number in the long run.

These lands are managed to promote resiliency against catastrophic wildfire, epidemics of disease and insect pests, erosion, and other threats. Burned areas receive emergency seeding treatment to prevent massive erosion and stream siltation. Roads and trails are built where needed to give the public access to outdoor recreation areas and provide scenic drives and hikes. Picnic, camping, skiing, water sport and other recreational areas feature facilities for public convenience and enjoyment. Vegetative management methods protect the land and streams, ensure rapid renewal of the forest, provide food and cover for wildlife and fish, and mitigate human impact on scenic and recreation assets. Local communities benefit from activities on National Forest lands. These lands also provide needed oil, gas, and minerals. Millions of livestock and game animals benefit from improved rangelands. The National Forests serve as a refuge for many species of endangered birds, animals, and fish. Some 34.6 million acres are set aside as wilderness and 175,000 acres as primitive areas where timber will not be harvested.

State and Private Forestry

The State and Private Forestry organization of the Forest Service reaches across the boundaries of National Forests to States, tribes, communities, and nonindustrial private landowners. The organization is the Federal leader in giving technical and financial assistance to landowners and resource managers to help sustain the Nation's forests and protect communities and the environment from wildland fires. National priorities for State and private forestry promote four core actions: conserving and managing working forest landscapes for multiple values and uses, protecting forests from threats, enhancing public benefits from trees and forests, and increasing organizational effectiveness. The State and Private Forestry organization supports sustainable stewardship of non-Federal forest land nationwide, including 423 million acres of private forest land, 69 million acres of State forest land, 18 million acres of tribal forests, and over 130 million acres of urban and community forests. The organization offers leadership in wildland fire management, operations, methods development, risk mapping, forest products utilization, and advanced survey and monitoring, as well as geospatial technologies.

Natural Resources Conservation Service (NRCS)

[For the Natural Resources Conservation Service statement of organization, see the Code of Federal Regulations, Title 7, Parts 600 and 601]

The Natural Resources Conservation Service, formerly known as the Soil Conservation Service, helps America's farmers, ranchers, and other private landowners develop and implement voluntary efforts to conserve and protect the Nation's natural resources.

Agricultural Conservation Easement Program

The Agricultural Conservation Easement Program helps conserve agricultural lands and wetlands by offering financial and technical assistance. Under the program's Agricultural Land Easements component, NRCS supports Indian tribes, State and local governments, and nongovernmental organizations in their efforts to protect working agricultural lands and to limit agricultural land use for nonagricultural purposes. Under the program's Wetlands Reserve Easements component, NRCS supports efforts to restore, protect, and enhance enrolled wetlands.

Agricultural Management Assistance

Agricultural Management Assistance, by giving financial and technical assistance to agricultural producers, encourages them to incorporate conversation practices into their farming operations to improve water management and quality, to reduce erosion, and to mitigate risk through production diversification. The assistance supports producers' in their efforts to plant trees for windbreaks, construct irrigation structures, use integrated pest management, and transition to organic farming. NRCS administers the program's conservation components, while AMS and RMA handle the others.

Conservation Stewardship Program

The Conservation Stewardship Program helps agricultural producers maintain and improve their existing conservation systems and adopt additional conservation practices that address resource concerns of high priority. Participants earn program payments for conservation performance: Payments are directly proportional to performance. The program offers two types of payments through 5-year contracts: annual payments for adopting new conservation practices and maintaining current ones, and supplemental payments for initiating a resource-conserving crop rotation. Producers may be able to renew a contract if they met the obligations of the initial contract and agree to achieve additional conservation goals.

Conservation Technical Assistance

Conservation Technical Assistance makes conservation technology and the delivery system needed to achieve the benefits of a healthy and productive landscape available to land users. The program reduces the loss of soil from erosion; offers solutions for agricultural waste management, air quality, soil, and water conservation and quality problems; mitigates potential water, sedimentation, or drought damage; improves fish and wildlife habitat; assists others in facilitating changes in land use for natural resource protection and sustainability; and increases the long term sustainability of all lands—cropland, forestland, grazing lands, coastal lands, and developing or developed lands. Technical Assistance supports clients in their efforts to address concerns and problems and explore opportunities related to the use of natural resources. NRCS staff and the employees of other agencies or entities under the technical supervision of

NRCS provide the assistance.

Emergency Watershed Protection Program

The Emergency Watershed Protection Program safeguards lives and property in jeopardy due to sudden watershed impairment caused by natural disasters. Emergency assistance includes quickly establishing a protective plant cover on denuded land and stream banks, opening dangerously restricted channels, and repairing diversions and levees. To be eligible for assistance under this program, an emergency area does not need to be declared a national disaster area. NRCS may bear up to 75 percent of the construction cost of emergency measures. The remaining cost must come from local sources. Funding is subject to Congressional approval.

Environmental Quality Incentives Program

The Environmental Quality Incentives Program assists agricultural producers by offering contracts up to a maximum term of 10 years in length. These contracts provide financial assistance for planning and implementing conservation practices that address natural resource concerns and for improving air, animal, plant, soil, water, and related resources on agricultural land and nonindustrial private forestland. Sixty percent of the available funds are for conservation activities related to livestock production. The program also helps producers meet Federal, State, tribal and local environmental regulations.

Healthy Forests Reserve Program

The Healthy Forests Reserve Program helps landowners restore, enhance, and protect forestland resources on private lands through easements, 30-year contracts, and 10-year cost-share agreements. The program supports the efforts of landowners to promote the recovery of endangered or threatened species, increase plant and animal biodiversity, and improve carbon sequestration.

National Cooperative Soil Survey

The National Cooperative Soil Survey, a nationwide partnership of Federal, State, regional, and local agencies and private entities and institutions, works cooperatively to investigate, inventory, document, classify, interpret, disseminate, and publish soil information. It informs the public about the uses and capabilities of local soils. The published survey for a county or other designated area includes maps and interpretations that are essential for farm planning, other private land use decisions, and governmental policy development and resource planning.

Plant Materials Program

The Plant Materials Program selects conservation plants and develops innovative planting technology for addressing natural resource challenges and maintaining healthy and productive farms and ranches. It focuses on using plants as a natural solution for conservation issues and reestablishing ecosystem function; collects, selects, and releases grasses, legumes, wildflowers, trees and shrubs, working with commercial, private, public, and tribal partners and land managers to apply new plant-based conservation methods; provides plant materials and new applied technologies for national initiatives; offers plant solutions to fight invasive species, heal lands damaged by natural disasters, reduce drought effects, promote air and water quality, and produce alternative energy; and assists Native American tribes with producing and protecting culturally significant plants.

Regional Conservation Partnership Program

The Regional Conservation Partnership Program promotes coordination between NRCS and its partners for the delivery of conservation assistance to producers and landowners. NRCS assists producers through partnership agreements and program contracts or easement agreements. The program combines the authorities of four previous programs: the Cooperative Conservation Partnership Initiative, the Agricultural Water Enhancement, the Chesapeake Bay Watershed, and the Great Lakes Basin Programs.

Small Watershed Program

The Small Watershed Program relies on local government sponsors to help participants solve natural resource and related economic problems on a watershed basis. Projects include efforts to protect watersheds, prevent floods, control erosion and sedimentation, improve water supply and quality, enhance fish and wildlife habitat, create and restore wetlands, and support public recreation in watersheds of 250,000 or fewer acres. The program offers both financial and technical assistance. Through the Small Watershed Program, NRCS maps flood hazard areas, solves local flooding problems, evaluates potential greenbelts along streams, develops guidelines for erosion control and runoff management, helps farmers control erosion in high priority watersheds, and improves the water quality of ground water and water bodies.

Snow Survey and Water Supply Forecasts

The Snow Survey is conducted by NRCS to make information on future water supplies available to residents of Alaska and Western States. At more than 1,800 mountain sites, NRCS personnel collect and analyze data on snowpack depth and its water equivalent to estimate annual water availability, spring runoff, and summer streamflows. Federal and State agencies, organizations, and individuals rely on these forecasts for agricultural production, fish and wildlife management, municipal and industrial water supply, urban development, flood control, recreation power generation, and water quality management. The National Weather Service includes the forecasts in their river forecasting function.

Watershed Surveys and Planning

The Watershed Surveys and Planning program supports Federal, State, and local agencies and tribal governments in their efforts to protect watersheds from damage caused by erosion, floodwater, and sediment and to conserve and develop water and land resources. The program addresses a number of resource concerns: agricultural drought problems, municipal and industrial water needs, rural development, upstream flood damages, water quality and conservation, wetland and water storage capacity, and water needs for fish, wildlife, and forest-based industries.

RESEARCH, EDUCATION AND ECONOMICS

This mission area centers on creating, applying, and transferring knowledge and technology to make available affordable food and fiber, ensure food safety and nutrition, and support rural development and people's natural resource needs. The creation, application, and transfer of this knowledge and technology are achieved by conducting integrated national and international research and by providing information, education, and statistical programs and services.

Agricultural Research Service (ARS)

The Agricultural Research Service conducts research on agricultural problems of high national priority. It provides information access and dissemination to ensure high-quality, safe food and other agricultural products; to assess the nutritional needs of Americans; to sustain a competitive agricultural economy; to enhance the natural resource base and the environment; and to promote economic opportunities for rural citizens, communities, and society as a whole.

Research activities are carried out at 96 domestic locations, including Puerto Rico and the U.S. Virgin Islands, and five overseas locations. ARS conducts much of this research in cooperation with partners in State universities and experiment stations, other Federal agencies, and private organizations. National Programs, headquartered in Beltsville, MD, plans and coordinates the research programs, and five area offices carry out the day-to-day management of the respective programs for specific field locations.

The National Agricultural Library, the primary resource in the United States for information on food, agriculture, and natural resources, serves as an electronic gateway to a widening array of scientific literature, printed text, and agricultural images. The library supports the USDA and a broad customer base of policymakers, agricultural specialists, research scientists, and the general public. It works with other agricultural libraries and institutions to advance open and democratic access specifically to the Nation's agricultural knowledge and to agricultural information in general.

For further information, contact the Agricultural Research Service, Department of Agriculture, 1400 Independence Avenue SW., Washington, DC 20250. Phone, 202-720-3656. Fax, 202-720-5427.

The National Institute of Food and Agriculture (NIFA)

The National Institute of Food and Agriculture invests in and advances agricultural education, extension, and research to address societal challenges. The Institute works with academic institutions, land-grant universities, and other science organizations nationwide. With its partners and customers, NIFA promotes a global system of research, extension, and higher education in the food and agricultural sciences and related environmental and human sciences for the good of people, communities, and the Nation.

The Institute collaborates with scientists, policymakers, experts, and educators in organizations worldwide to find innovative solutions to pressing local and global problems. Scientific discovery and application advance the competitiveness of American agriculture, strengthen the U.S. economy, make the Nation's food supply safer, improve the nutrition and well-being of American citizens, sustain natural resources and the environment, and build energy independence. Partnering with other Federal science agencies, NIFA also makes important contributions to science policy decisionmaking.

For further information, contact the Communications Staff, The National Institute of Food and Agriculture, Department of Agriculture, 1400 Independence Avenue SW., Washington, DC 20250-2207. Phone, 202-720-4651. Fax, 202-690-0289.

Economic Research Service (ERS)

The Service informs and strengthens public and private decisionmaking on economic and policy issues affecting agriculture, food, rural development, and the environment. ERS also serves as a primary source of economic information and research in the USDA.

Using a variety of means, ERS disseminates economic information and research results. It produces agency-published research reports, economic briefs, data products, and market analysis and outlook reports. "Amber Waves," its award-winning online magazine features articles on the economics of food, farming, natural resources, and rural America (www.ers.usda.gov/amber-waves). The ERS Web site allows access to all agency products, and it connects users directly with ERS analysts. The agency delivers oral briefings, written staff analyses, and congressionally mandated studies to executive and legislative branch policymakers and program administrators. Its experts also write articles for professional journals and present papers at academic conferences and meetings.

For further information, contact the Information Services Division, Economic Research Service, Department of Agriculture, 1400 Independence Avenue SW., Washington, DC 20250. Phone, 202-694-5100. Fax, 202-245-4781.

National Agricultural Statistics Service (NASS)

The National Agricultural Statistics Service prepares estimates and reports on production, supply, price, chemical use, and other items necessary for the orderly operation of the U.S. agricultural economy.

NAAS reports include statistics on field crops, fruits and vegetables, dairy, cattle, hogs, sheep, poultry, aquaculture, and related commodities or processed products. Estimates concern farm numbers, farm production expenditures, agricultural chemical use, prices received by farmers for products sold, prices paid for commodities and services, indexes of prices received and paid, parity prices, farm employment, and farm wage rates.

NASS prepares these estimates through a complex system of sample surveys of producers, processors, buyers, and others associated with agriculture. Information is gathered by mail, electronic data reporting, telephone, and personal interviews.

The Service conducts the Census of Agriculture, which is taken every 5 years and provides comprehensive data on the agricultural economy down to the county level. It also conducts follow-on studies on aquaculture, irrigation, horticultural energy, and organic agriculture.

NASS performs reimbursable survey work and statistical consulting services for other Federal and State agencies. It also helps other countries develop agricultural data systems by offering technical assistance.

For further information, contact the Customer Service Center, National Agricultural Statistics Service, Department of Agriculture, 1400 Independence Avenue SW., Washington, DC 20250-2000. Phone, 202-720-3878.

RURAL DEVELOPMENT

The rural development mission area centers on increasing the economic opportunities of rural Americans and improving their quality of life. To achieve these goals, the USDA creates and fosters cooperative relationships among Government, industry, and communities. As a capital investment bank, the USDA provides financing for rural housing and community facilities, business and cooperative development, telephone and high-speed Internet access, and electric, water, and sewer infrastructure. Approximately 400 rural development field offices, staffed by 3,500 employees, deliver rural development loan and grant programs at the local level.

Advanced Biofuel Repayment Program

The program provides payments to producers to support and expand production of advanced biofuels refined from sources other than corn kernel starch.

Biorefinery, Renewable Chemical, and Biobased Product Manufacturing Assistance Program

This program assists in the development, construction, and retrofitting of new and emerging technologies for developing advanced biofuels, renewable chemicals, and biobased product manufacturing by giving loan guarantees.

Business and Industry Guaranteed Loan Program

This program creates jobs and stimulates the rural economy by financially backing rural businesses. It bolsters the existing private credit structure through the guaranteeing of loans for rural businesses, allowing private lenders to increase the credit that they extend. Borrowers use loan proceeds for working capital, machinery and equipment, buildings, real estate, and certain types of debt refinancing. A borrower may be a cooperative organization, corporation, partnership, nonprofit corporation, Native American tribe, federally recognized tribal group, public body, or individual.

Cooperative Programs

USDA Cooperative Programs is the Nation's major source for information on cooperatives. Its library of more than 150 co-op publications—many of which are available in hardcopy, as well as online—range from co-op primers, such as "Co-ops 101," to reports on technical topics, such as "Tax Law for Cooperatives," to reports focusing on co-op economic theory, such as "The Nature of the Cooperative." These publications may be accessed on the "Publications for Cooperatives" Web page.

Delta Health Care Services Grant Program

This program provides financial assistance to meet ongoing health needs in the Delta Region through cooperation among health care professionals, institutions of higher education, research institutions, and others in the Delta Region.

Intermediary Relending Program

This program provides capital to rural areas through low-interest and direct loans made to nonprofit corporations, public agencies, Native American groups, and certain corporations (intermediaries). These intermediaries establish revolving loan funds so they can relend the money to businesses in economically and socially disadvantaged rural communities. The process creates a source of capital that promotes job growth and economic development.

Repowering Assistance Program

This program funds up to 50 percent of the total eligible costs for biorefineries to install renewable biomass systems for heating and power or to produce new energy from renewable biomass.

Rural Business Development Grant Program

This program provides grants for rural projects that promote small and emerging business development, business incubators, employment, and related adult education programs. It also provides grants for sustainable economic development in rural communities with exceptional needs. Recipients use the grants to fund community- and technology-based economic development projects, feasibility studies, leadership and entrepreneur training, rural business incubators, and long-term business strategic planning. Eligible organizations include Native American tribes, nonprofit corporations, and rural public entities.

Rural Business-Cooperative Service

To meet business credit needs in underserved rural areas, USDA's Rural Business-Cooperative Service provides loan guarantees, direct loans, and grants to rural businesses, cooperatives, farmers, and ranchers, often in partnership with private sector lenders. The following is a list and description of USDA's Rural Development business and cooperative programs.

Rural Cooperative Development Grant Program

This program improves rural economic conditions by assisting individuals and businesses in the startup, expansion or operational improvement of rural cooperatives and other mutually-owned businesses through Cooperative Development Centers.

Rural Economic Development (RED) Loan and Grant Program

The RED Loan and Grant programs provide funding to rural projects through local utility organizations. Under the loan program, USDA gives zero-interest loans that local utilities pass through to local businesses for projects that create and retain employment in rural areas. Under the grant program, USDA gives grant funds to local utility organizations that use them to establish revolving loan funds.

Rural Energy for America Program

Grant recipients assist rural small businesses and agricultural producers by conducting and promoting energy audits and assisting in the development of renewable energy.

Rural Housing Programs

USDA Rural Development improves the quality of life in rural America. Its Rural Housing Service offers loans, grants, and loan guarantees to support essential services such as housing, economic development, health care, first-responder equipment and personnel, and water, electric and communications infrastructure. It also helps rural residents buy or rent safe and affordable housing, and make home repairs to improve safety and to create healthier living environments.

Rural Microentrepreneur Assistance Program

This program makes loans and gives grants to Microenterprise Development Organizations. These organizations then provide microloans for microenterprise startups and growth through a rural microloan revolving fund. They also offer training and technical assistance to microloan borrowers and microentrepreneurs.

Rural Utilities Programs

USDA Rural Development strengthens rural economies and makes life better for Americans living in rural areas. Its Rural Utilities Service administers programs that provide infrastructure or infrastructure improvements to nonurban communities. These programs include water and waste treatment and electric power and telecommunications services. Utilities programs connect residents to the global community and its economy by increasing access to broadband and 21st-century telecommunications services, funding sustainable renewable energy development and conservation, financing reliable and affordable electric systems, working to integrate electric smart grid technologies, and developing reliable and affordable rural water and wastewater systems.

Socially-Disadvantaged Groups Grant Program

This program gives technical assistance to small socially-disadvantaged agricultural producers in rural areas.

Value-Added Producer Grant Program

This program helps agricultural producers engage in value-added activities related to the processing and marketing of bio-based, value-added products. The program is designed to generate new products, create and expand marketing opportunities, and increase producer income.

For further information, contact the Rural Development Legislative and Public Affairs Staff, Department of Agriculture, Stop 0705, 1400 Independence Avenue SW., Washington, DC 20250-0320. Phone, 800-670-6553.

Sources of Information

Ask the Expert

This tool helps Web site visitors locate the answers to their USDA-related questions.

Blog

The USDA Web site features a blog that includes contributions on conservation, energy, food and nutrition, forestry, knowing your farmer and your food, rural development, and other topics.

Business Opportunities

Marketing to the USDA can be a daunting task. To assist businessmen and women who seek to sell their products and services to the agency, the USDA has collected all of the necessary information and packaged it in one place—in the "Doing Business with USDA Kit" (2005 edition).

The USDA awards over 50 percent of eligible contracting dollars to small businesses nationwide. Information on contracting or subcontracting opportunities, attending small business outreach events, or how to do business with the USDA is available on the "Office of Small and Disadvantaged Business Utilization" Web site. Phone, 202-720-7117.

Employment

For information on vacant positions within the USDA and opportunities for students, recent graduates, and veterans, visit the "Careers and Jobs" Web page.

Freedom of Information Act (FOIA)

Departmental Management oversees the USDA's FOIA program. Twenty-one USDA FOIA officers at the mission area and agency levels work to increase Government transparency through proactive disclosures and the use of technology.

Agency reading rooms are updated frequently and contain commonly requested records. Information seekers should visit the relevant reading rooms before submitting a FOIA request.

The FOIA public access link (PAL) is a web portal that allows information seekers to create and submit a FOIA request and to check its status. Registration, which requires creating a user name and password, is the first step for using PAL.

Glossary

The USDA maintains a glossary of agency acronyms.

Newsroom

Announcements, factsheets, reports, and statements are accessible online.

The USDA tweets events, news items,

and other information on Twitter.

Open Government

The USDA supports the Open Government initiative by promoting the principles of collaboration, participation, and transparency.

Organic Agriculture

The USDA is committed to increasing organic agriculture. It operates many programs that serve the growing organic sector. The USDA Organic Seal, which has been in use nearly 15 years, is a leading global standard. Visit the "Organic Agriculture" Web pages to learn more.

Instructions for becoming a certified organic operation are available online.

To receive "USDA Organic Insider" updates via email, use the online subscription form.

Plain Language

In support of the Plain Writing Act of 2010, USDA editors and writers strive to provide the public with information that is clear, understandable, and useful in forms, instructions, letters, notices, and publications. If a USDA document or content on the Department's Web site is unclear or difficult to understand, contact the USDA via email.

Program Discrimination

The Office of the Assistant Secretary for Civil Rights investigates and resolves complaints of discrimination in programs operated or assisted by the USDA. Information on what to include in a letter of complaint is available online. For information on the discrimination complaint process, contact the information research service in the Office of the Assistant Secretary. Phone, 202-260-1026 or 866-632-9992. Federal Relay Service, 800-877-8339 (English) or 800-845-6136 (Spanish).

Reports

Agency reports, data, and forecasts and outlooks are accessible online.

Site Map

The Web site map allows visitors to look for specific topics or to browse for topics that align with their interests.

The USDA Web site also features an A–Z index of topics.

Speakers

Contact the nearest USDA office or county extension agent. In the District of Columbia, contact the Office of the Chief Economist, U.S. Department of Agriculture, 1400 Independence Avenue SW., Washington, DC 20250. Phone, 202-720-4623.

Whistleblower Hotline

To file a complaint of alleged improprieties—employee misconduct, conflicts of interest, criminal activity, mismanagement or wasteful use of funds, workplace violence—visit the "OIG Hotline" Web page and use the "Submit a Complaint" feature. Or, contact a regional office or the Office of the Inspector General, U.S. Department of Agriculture, P.O. Box 23399, Washington, DC 20026. Phone, 800-424-9121 or 202-690-1622. TDD, 202-690-1202. Fax, 202-690-2474.

For further information concerning the Department of Agriculture, contact the Office of Communications, Department of Agriculture, 1400 Independence Avenue SW., Washington, DC 20250. Phone, 202-720-4623.

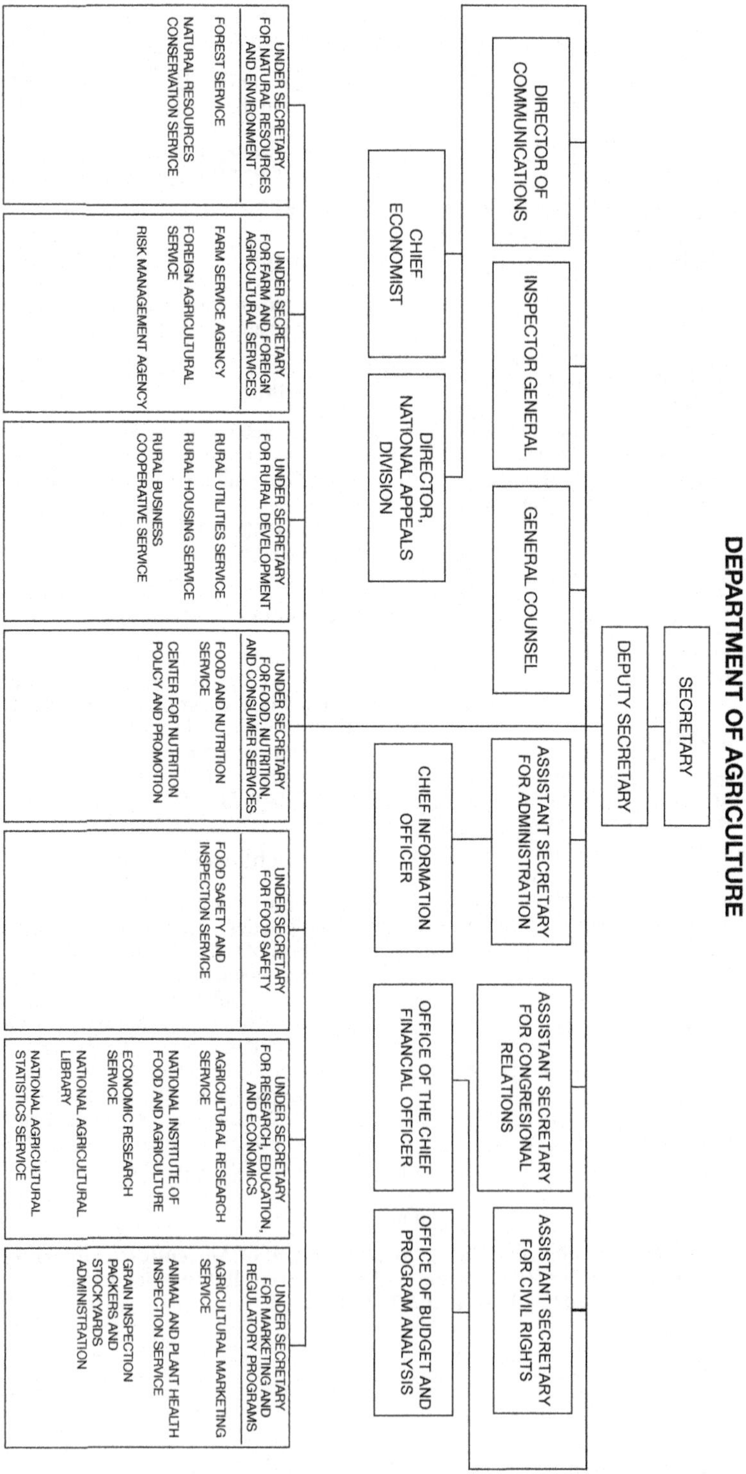
DEPARTMENT OF AGRICULTURE
SECRETARY
DEPUTY SECRETARY
DIRECTOR OF COMMUNICATIONS
INSPECTOR GENERAL
GENERAL COUNSEL
CHIEF ECONOMIST
DIRECTOR, NATIONAL APPEALS DIVISION
ASSISTANT SECRETARY FOR ADMINISTRATION
CHIEF INFORMATION OFFICER
ASSISTANT SECRETARY FOR CONGRESIONAL RELATIONS
OFFICE OF THE CHIEF FINANCIAL OFFICER
ASSISTANT SECRETARY FOR CIVIL RIGHTS
OFFICE OF BUDGET AND PROGRAM ANALYSIS
UNDER SECRETARY FOR NATURAL RESOURCES AND ENVIRONMENT
FOREST SERVICE
NATURAL RESOURCES CONSERVATION SERVICE
UNDER SECRETARY FOR FARM AND FOREIGN AGRICULTURAL SERVICES
FARM SERVICE AGENCY
FOREIGN AGRICULTURAL SERVICE
RISK MANAGEMENT AGENCY
UNDER SECRETARY FOR RURAL DEVELOPMENT
RURAL UTILITIES SERVICE
RURAL HOUSING SERVICE
RURAL BUSINESS COOPERATIVE SERVICE
UNDER SECRETARY FOR FOOD, NUTRITION, AND CONSUMER SERVICES
FOOD AND NUTRITION SERVICE
CENTER FOR NUTRITION POLICY AND PROMOTION
UNDER SECRETARY FOR FOOD SAFETY
FOOD SAFETY AND INSPECTION SERVICE
UNDER SECRETARY FOR RESEARCH, EDUCATION, AND ECONOMICS
AGRICULTURAL RESEARCH SERVICE
NATIONAL INSTITUTE OF FOOD AND AGRICULTURE
ECONOMIC RESEARCH SERVICE
NATIONAL AGRICULTURAL LIBRARY
NATIONAL AGRICULTURAL STATISTICS SERVICE
UNDER SECRETARY FOR MARKETING AND REGULATORY PROGRAMS
AGRICULTURAL MARKETING SERVICE
ANIMAL AND PLANT HEALTH INSPECTION SERVICE
GRAIN INSPECTION PACKERS AND STOCKYARDS ADMINISTRATION

Department of Commerce

Fourteenth Street and Constitution Avenue NW., Washington, DC 20230, 202-482-2000, http://www.doc.gov

SECRETARY OF COMMERCE	Penny S. Pritzker
Deputy Secretary	Bruce H. Andrews
Assistant Secretary, Administration / Chief Financial Officer	Ellen Herbst
Assistant Secretary, Legislative and Intergovernmental Affairs	Steven M. Haro
Chief Information Officer	Steve Cooper
Director, Office of Business Liaison	Theodore Johnston
Director, Office of Policy and Strategic Planning	John Ratliff
Director, Office of Public Affairs	Marni Goldberg
Director, Office of the Executive Secretariat	James Slattery
Director, Office of White House Liaison	Lauren Leonard
General Counsel	Kelly R. Welsh
Inspector General	Todd J. Zinser

The Department of Commerce promotes the Nation's domestic and international trade, economic growth, and technological advancement by fostering free enterprise worldwide, supporting fair trade, compiling social and economic statistics, protecting Earth's physical resources, granting patents and registering trademarks, and assisting small and minority-owned businesses.

The Department of Commerce was designated as such by act of March 4, 1913 (15 U.S.C. 1501). The act reorganized the Department of Commerce and Labor, created by act of February 14, 1903 (15 U.S.C. 1501), by transferring labor activities into a new, separate Department of Labor.

Office of the Secretary

Secretary

The Secretary is responsible for the administration of all functions and authorities assigned to the Department of Commerce and for advising the President on Federal policy and programs affecting the industrial and commercial segments of the national economy. The Secretary is served by the offices of Deputy Secretary, Inspector General, General Counsel, and the Assistant Secretaries of Administration, Legislative and Intergovernmental Affairs, and Public Affairs. Other offices whose public purposes are widely administered are detailed below.

Business Liaison

The Office of Business Liaison directs the business community to the offices and policy experts who can best respond to their needs by promoting proactive, responsive, and effective outreach programs and relationships with the business community. It also informs the Secretary and Department officials of the critical issues facing the business community, informs the business community of Department and administration initiatives and priorities, as well as information regarding Department resources, policies, and programs, and provides general assistance to the business community.

For further information, call 202-482-1360.

Sources of Information

Business Opportunities

Contact the Office of Small and Disadvantaged Business Utilization. Phone, 202-482-1472.

Data

Age and sex and citizenship data are available online and from the Personal Census Search Unit, Bureau of the Census, National Processing Center, P.O. Box 1545, Jeffersonville, IN 47131. Phone, 812-218-3046.

Economic Development Information

The Economic Development Administration maintains a clearinghouse for economic development information on its Web site.

Employment

For information on internships and career opportunities throughout the Department, visit the "Career Opportunities and Internships" Web page.

Environment

The National Oceanic and Atmospheric Administration conducts research and gathers data on the atmosphere, oceans, space, and Sun, and it applies this knowledge to science and public service: warning of dangerous weather, charting seas and skies, guiding the use and protection of ocean and coastal resources, and improving stewardship of the environment. For more information, contact the Office of Communications, National Oceanic and Atmospheric Administration, Room 6013, Fourteenth Street and Constitution Avenue NW., Washington, DC 20230. Phone, 202-482-6090. Fax, 202-482-3154.

Inspector General Hotline

The Office of Inspector General promotes economy, efficiency, and effectiveness and prevents and detects fraud, waste, abuse, and mismanagement in departmental programs and operations. To file a complaint, contact the Hotline, Inspector General, Complaint Intake Unit, Mail Stop 7886, 1401 Constitution Avenue, NW., Washington, DC 20230. Phone, 202-482-2495 or 800-424-5197. TTD, 202-482-5923 or 856-860-6950. Fax, 855-569-9235.

Publications

The Department's "Find Data" Web page features recent releases of key economic indicators and the "Commerce Data Hub," which allows the general public to access an abundance of data. The titles of selected publications are noted in the appropriate sections below dealing with the operating units responsible for their issuance. These publications and others are announced in the weekly "Business Service Checklist": Contact the Government Publishing Office's Superintendent of Documents. Phone, 202-512-1800.

For further information concerning the Department of Commerce, contact the Office of Public Affairs, Department of Commerce, Fourteenth Street and Constitution Avenue NW., Room 5040, Washington, DC 20230. Phone, 202-482-3263.

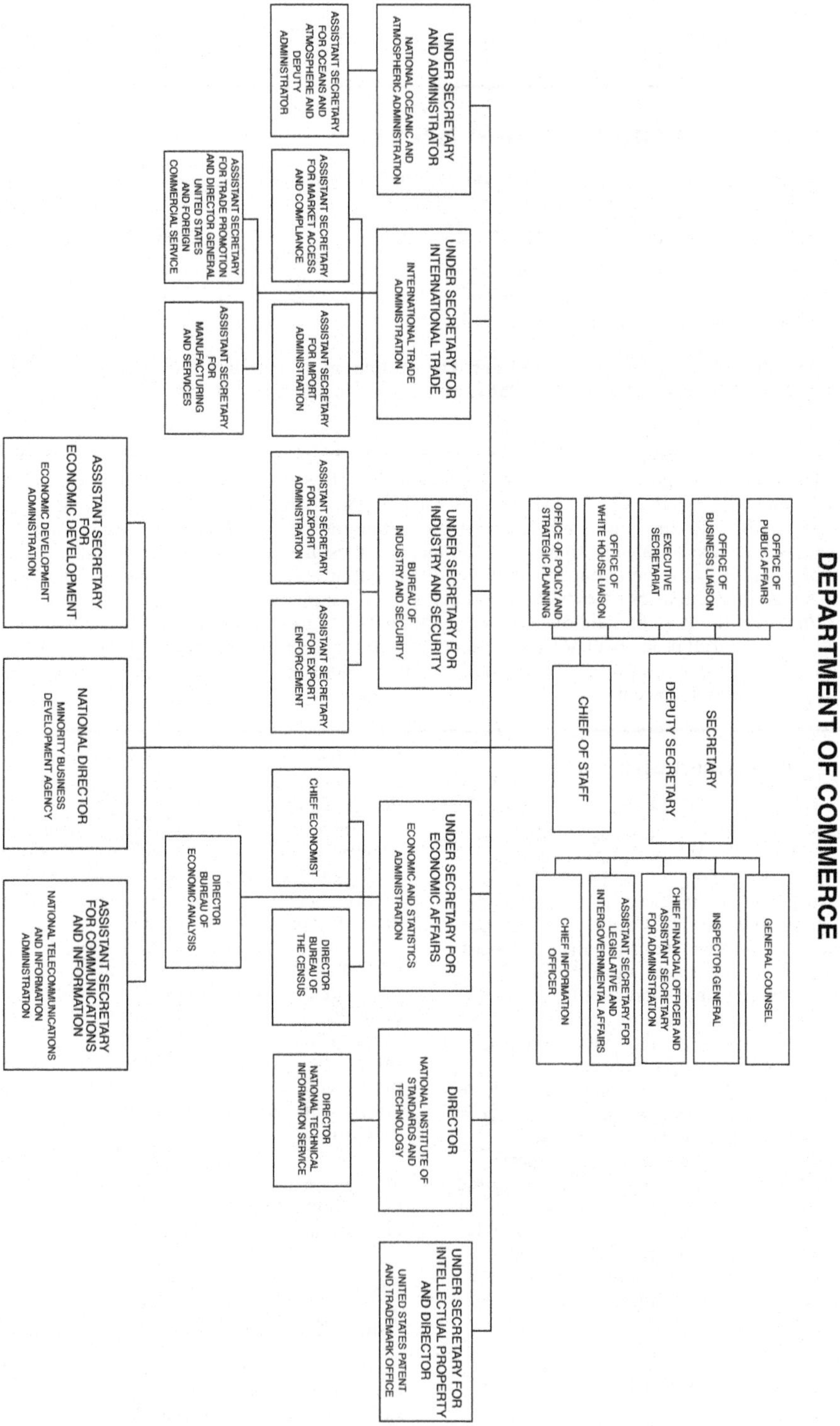
DEPARTMENT OF COMMERCE
SECRETARY DEPUTY SECRETARY
CHIEF OF STAFF
OFFICE OF PUBLIC AFFAIRS
OFFICE OF BUSINESS LIAISON
EXECUTIVE SECRETARIAT
OFFICE OF WHITE HOUSE LIAISON
OFFICE OF POLICY AND STRATEGIC PLANNING
GENERAL COUNSEL
INSPECTOR GENERAL
CHIEF FINANCIAL OFFICER AND ASSISTANT SECRETARY FOR ADMINISTRATION
ASSISTANT SECRETARY FOR LEGISLATIVE AND INTERGOVERNMENTAL AFFAIRS
CHIEF INFORMATION OFFICER
UNDER SECRETARY AND ADMINISTRATOR NATIONAL OCEANIC AND ATMOSPHERIC ADMINISTRATION
ASSISTANT SECRETARY FOR OCEANS AND ATMOSPHERE AND DEPUTY ADMINISTRATOR
UNDER SECRETARY FOR INTERNATIONAL TRADE INTERNATIONAL TRADE ADMINISTRATION
ASSISTANT SECRETARY FOR MARKET ACCESS AND COMPLIANCE
ASSISTANT SECRETARY FOR IMPORT ADMINISTRATION
ASSISTANT SECRETARY FOR TRADE PROMOTION AND DIRECTOR GENERAL UNITED STATES AND FOREIGN COMMERCIAL SERVICE
ASSISTANT SECRETARY FOR MANUFACTURING AND SERVICES
UNDER SECRETARY FOR INDUSTRY AND SECURITY BUREAU OF INDUSTRY AND SECURITY
ASSISTANT SECRETARY FOR EXPORT ADMINISTRATION
ASSISTANT SECRETARY FOR EXPORT ENFORCEMENT
UNDER SECRETARY FOR ECONOMIC AFFAIRS ECONOMIC AND STATISTICS ADMINISTRATION
CHIEF ECONOMIST
DIRECTOR BUREAU OF THE CENSUS
DIRECTOR BUREAU OF ECONOMIC ANALYSIS
DIRECTOR NATIONAL INSTITUTE OF STANDARDS AND TECHNOLOGY
DIRECTOR NATIONAL TECHNICAL INFORMATION SERVICE
UNDER SECRETARY FOR INTELLECTUAL PROPERTY AND DIRECTOR UNITED STATES PATENT AND TRADEMARK OFFICE
ASSISTANT SECRETARY FOR ECONOMIC DEVELOPMENT ECONOMIC DEVELOPMENT ADMINISTRATION
NATIONAL DIRECTOR MINORITY BUSINESS DEVELOPMENT AGENCY
ASSISTANT SECRETARY FOR COMMUNICATIONS AND INFORMATION NATIONAL TELECOMMUNICATIONS AND INFORMATION ADMINISTRATION

Bureau of Industry and Security

Department of Commerce, Washington, DC 20230, 202-482-2721, *http://www.bis.doc.gov*

UNDER SECRETARY, INDUSTRY AND SECURITY	Eric L. Hirschhorn
Deputy Under Secretary, Industry and Security	Daniel O. Hill
Assistant Secretary, Export Administration	Kevin J. Wolf
Assistant Secretary, Export Enforcement	David W. Mills

[For the Bureau of Industry and Security statement of organization, see the Federal Registers of June 7, 1988, 53 FR 20881, and April 26, 2002, 67 FR 20630]

The Bureau of Industry and Security (BIS) advances U.S. national security, foreign policy, and economic objectives by ensuring an effective export control and treaty compliance system and promoting continued U.S. strategic technology leadership. BIS activities include regulating the export of sensitive goods and technologies in an effective and efficient manner; enforcing export control, antiboycott, and public safety laws; cooperating with and assisting other countries on export control and strategic trade issues; assisting U.S. industry to comply with international arms control agreements; monitoring the viability of the U.S. defense industrial base; evaluating the effects on national security of foreign investments in U.S. companies; and supporting continued U.S. technology leadership in industries that are essential to national security.

Export Administration

The Office of the Assistant Secretary for Export Administration is responsible for export licenses, treaty compliance, treaty obligations relating to weapons of mass destruction, and the defense industrial and technology base. The Office regulates the export of dual-use items requiring licenses for national security, nonproliferation, foreign policy, and short supply; ensures that approval or denial of license applications is consistent with economic and security concerns; promotes an understanding of export control regulations within the business community; represents the Department in interagency and international forums relating to export controls, particularly in multilateral regimes; monitors the availability of industrial resources of national defense; analyzes the impact of export controls on strategic industries; and assesses the security consequences of certain foreign investments.

Export Enforcement

The Office of the Assistant Secretary for Export Enforcement enforces dual-use export controls. This enables exporters to take advantage of legal export opportunities while ensuring that illegal exports will be detected and either prevented or investigated and sanctioned. The Office also ensures prompt, aggressive action against restrictive trade practices; and conducts cooperative enforcement activities on an international basis. Export Enforcement also enforces U.S. antiboycott laws and regulations by advising U.S. exporters on potential prohibited requests contained in foreign contracts; investigating violations such as the furnishing of boycott-related information, refusing to deal with blacklisted businesses; and pursuing criminal and administrative sanctions for violations.

Contact information for the nine export enforcement field offices is available on the "Investigations" Web page.

Management and Policy Coordination

The Management and Policy Coordination (MPC) unit establishes and evaluates the Bureau's overall policy agenda, priorities, goals, unit objectives, and key metrics. MPC performs oversight of program operations and expenditures; executes or supervises the President's Management Agenda; and adjudicates appeals of licensing and enforcement decisions as part of an extended legal process involving administrative law judges and the Office of General Counsel. MPC provides guidance and coordination for the Bureau's participation in the Export Control and Related Border Security Assistance Program, which provides technical assistance to strengthen the export and transit control systems of nations that are identified as potential locations for the exporting of weapons of mass destruction, missile delivery systems, or the commodities, technologies, and equipment that can be used to design and build them.

Sources of Information

Business Information

U.S. business information—export news, updates to Export Administration Regulations, export license and enforcement information, compliance and training information, Bureau program information, e-FOIA information, export seminar event schedules, and Denied Persons List information—is available on the Bureau's Web site.

Employment

BIS career opportunities are posted on USAJobs, a free web-based job board that serves as the Federal Government's official source of Federal job listings and employment opportunity information.

Enforcement

For enforcement-related questions, contact the partnership-in-security hotline. Phone, 800-424-2980.

Outreach / Education

The Outreach and Educational Services Division has offices in Washington, DC (phone, 202-482-4811); Irvine, CA (phone, 949-660-0144); and San Jose, CA (phone, 408-998-8806).

Publications

Publications available on the Bureau's Web site include the BIS's Annual Report to Congress, the guidance on the Commerce Department's Reexport Controls, and the Exporter User Manual and Licensing FAQ.

Rules

Subscribers to the Export Administration Regulations can stay informed of the latest rules. Subscriptions typically cost $199 per year. Phone, 301-208-0700 (ext. 112).

For further information, contact the Bureau of Industry and Security, Office of Public Affairs, Room 3895, Fourteenth Street and Constitution Avenue NW., Washington, DC 20230. Phone, 202-482-2721.

Economic Development Administration

Department of Commerce, Washington, DC 20230, 202-482-5081, *http://www.eda.gov*

ASSISTANT SECRETARY, ECONOMIC DEVELOPMENT	Jay Williams
Deputy Assistant Secretary, Economic Development	Matthew Erskine

The Economic Development Administration (EDA) was created in 1965 under the Public Works and Economic Development Act (42 U.S.C. 3121) as part of an effort to target Federal resources to economically distressed areas and to help develop local economies in the United States. It was mandated to assist rural and urban communities that were outside the mainstream economy and that lagged in economic development, industrial growth, and personal income.

EDA provides grants to States, regions, and communities nationwide to generate wealth and minimize poverty by promoting an attractive business environment for private capital investment and higher skill, higher wage jobs through capacity building, planning, infrastructure, research grants, and strategic initiatives. Through its grant program, EDA uses public sector resources to cultivate an environment where the private sector risks capital and job opportunities are created.

Contact information for the Administration's six regional offices—Atlanta, Austin, Chicago, Denver, Philadelphia, Seattle—is available on the "Contact" Web page.

Sources of Information

Employment

For information on career opportunities, visit the "EDA Job Opportunities" Web page.

Newsroom

The online newsroom features blog posts, press releases, an archive of newsletters, and the latest media.

For further information, contact the Economic Development Administration, Department of Commerce, Washington, DC 20230. Phone, 202-482-5081. Fax, 202-273-4781.

Economics and Statistics Administration

Department of Commerce, Washington, DC 20230, 202-482-3727, *http://www.esa.doc.gov*

UNDER SECRETARY, ECONOMIC AFFAIRS	Justin Antonipillai
Deputy Under Secretary, Economic Affairs	Kenneth A. Arnold
Chief Economist	Ellen Hughes-Cromwick
Director, Bureau of Economic Analysis	Brian C. Moyer
Director, Bureau of the Census	John H. Thompson

The Economics and Statistics Administration (ESA), headed by the Under Secretary for Economic Affairs, has three principal components: the Office of the Chief Economist, the Bureau of the Census, and the Bureau of Economic Analysis. ESA develops policy options, analyzes economic developments, manages economic data systems, and produces a major share of U.S. economic and demographic statistics, including the national economic indicators. The Under Secretary is the chief economic adviser to the Secretary and provides leadership and executive management for the Office of the Chief Economist and the Bureaus of Economic Analysis and of the Census.

Bureau of Economic Analysis

[For the Bureau of Economic Analysis statement of organization, see the Federal Register of Dec. 29, 1980, 45 FR 85496]

The Bureau of Economic Analysis (BEA) provides the most accurate, relevant, and timely economic accounts data in an objective and cost-effective manner. BEA's economic statistics offer a comprehensive picture of the U.S. economy. BEA prepares national, regional, industry, and international accounts that present essential information on such issues in the world economy.

BEA's national economic statistics provide a comprehensive look at U.S. production, consumption, investment, exports and imports, and income and saving. The international transactions accounts provide information on trade in goods and services (including the balance of payments and trade), investment income, and government and private finances. In addition, the accounts measure the value of U.S. international assets and liabilities and direct investment by multinational companies.

The regional accounts provide data on total and per capita personal income by region, State, metropolitan area, and county, and on gross State product. The industry economic account provides a detailed view of the interrelationships between U.S. producers and users and the contribution to production across industries.

For further information, contact the Public Information Office, Bureau of Economic Analysis, Department of Commerce, Washington, DC 20230. Phone, 202-606-9900. Fax, 202-606-5310.

Bureau of the Census

[For the Bureau of the Census statement of organization, see the Federal Register of Sept. 16, 1975, 40 FR 42765]

The Bureau of the Census was established as a permanent office by act of March 6, 1902 (32 Stat. 51). The major functions of the Census Bureau are authorized by the Constitution, which provides that a census of population shall be taken every 10 years, and by laws codified as title 13 of the United States Code. The law also provides that the information collected by the Census Bureau from individual persons, households, or establishments be kept strictly confidential and be used only for statistical purposes.

The Census Bureau is responsible for the decennial censuses of population and housing; the quinquennial censuses of State and local governments, manufacturers, mineral industries, distributive trades, construction industries, and transportation; current surveys that provide information on many of the subjects covered in the censuses at monthly, quarterly, annual, or other intervals; compilation of current statistics on U.S. foreign trade, including data on imports, exports, and shipping; special censuses at the request and expense of State and local government units; publication of estimates and projections of the population; publication of current data on population and housing characteristics; and current reports on manufacturing, retail and wholesale trade, services, construction, imports and exports, State and local government finances and employment, and other subjects.

The Census Bureau makes available statistical results of its censuses, surveys, and other programs to the public through the Internet, mobile applications, and other media. The Bureau also prepares special tabulations sponsored and paid for by data users. It also produces statistical compendia, catalogs, guides, and directories that are useful in locating information on specific subjects. Upon request, the Bureau makes searches of decennial census records and furnishes certificates to individuals for use as evidence of age, relationship, or place of birth. A fee is charged for searches.

Contact information for the Census Bureau's six regional offices—Atlanta, Chicago, Denver, Los Angeles, New York, Philadelphia—is available on the "Regional Offices" Web page.

For further information, contact the Public Information Office, Bureau of the Census, Department of Commerce, Washington, DC 20233. Phone, 301-763-3030. Fax, 301-763-3762.

Office of the Chief Economist

The economists and analysts of the Office of the Chief Economist analyze domestic and international economic developments and produce in-depth reports, factsheets, briefings, and social media postings. These tools cover policy issues and current economic events, as well as economic and demographic trends. Department of Commerce and White House policymakers, American businessmen, State and local governments, and news organizations worldwide rely on these tools.

Sources of Information

Data

Monthly and quarterly economic indicators are posted online. To receive the most current economic indicators by email, subscribe using the online form.

Employment

For information on employment opportunities at the Bureaus of Economic Analysis or the Census, visit the "Working at BEA" or "Census Careers" Web page.

Publications

The BEA posts research papers, its

customer guide, and the monthly journal "Survey of Current Business" under the "Publications" section on its Web site. The Census Bureau's most recently released publications are part of its online library.

For further information, contact the Economics and Statistics Administration, Department of Commerce, Washington, DC 20230. Phone, 202-482-6607.

International Trade Administration

Department of Commerce, Washington, DC 20230, 202-482-3917, *http://www.trade.gov*

UNDER SECRETARY, INTERNATIONAL TRADE	Kenneth E. Hyatt, Acting
Deputy Under Secretary, International Trade	Thomas McGinty, Acting
Assistant Secretary, Enforcement and Compliance	Paul Piquado
Assistant Secretary, Global Markets / Director General of the U.S. and Foreign Commercial Service	Arun M. Kumar
Assistant Secretary, Industry and Analysis	Marcus D. Jadotte

[For the International Trade Administration statement of organization, see the Federal Register of Jan. 25, 1980, 45 FR 6148]

The International Trade Administration (ITA) was established on January 2, 1980, by the Secretary of Commerce to promote world trade and to strengthen the international trade and investment position of the United States.

The International Trade Administration (ITA) was established on January 2, 1980, by the Secretary of Commerce to promote world trade and to strengthen the international trade and investment position of the United States. The Under Secretary for International Trade heads the ITA, coordinating all issues concerning trade promotion, international commercial policy, market access, and trade law enforcement. The Administration is responsible for U.S. Government nonagricultural trade operations, and it supports the U.S. Trade Representative's efforts to negotiate trade policy.

Enforcement / Compliance

The Office of Enforcement and Compliance defends American industry against injurious and unfair trade practices by administering U.S. antidumping and countervailing duty trade laws. The Office also ensures the proper administration of foreign trade zones and advises the Secretary on establishment of new ones; oversees the administration of the Department's textiles program; and administers programs governing watch assemblies and other statutory import programs.

Global Markets

The Global Markets unit assists and advocates for U.S. businesses in international markets. Relying on a network of trade promotion and policy professionals located in over 70 countries and 100 U.S. locations, the unit promotes U.S. exports, especially those of small and medium-sized enterprises; advances and protects U.S. commercial interests overseas; and attracts investment from abroad into the United States.

Industry / Analysis

The Manufacturing and Services unit advises on domestic and international trade and investment policies affecting the competitiveness of U.S. industry. It also researches and analyzes manufacturing and services. Based on this analysis and interaction with U.S. industry, the unit Secretary develops strategies, policies, and programs to strengthen U.S. industry competitiveness domestically and globally.

The unit manages an integrated program that includes industry and economic analysis, trade policy development and multilateral, regional, and bilateral trade agreements for manufactured goods and services; administers trade arrangements with foreign governments in product and service areas; and develops and provides business information and assistance to the United States on its rights and opportunities under multilateral and other agreements.

Sources of Information

Data

Trade data and export and import statistics are available online.

Employment

For information on career opportunities, visit the "Jobs" Web page.

Publications

The ITA has an online bookstore.

For further information, contact the International Trade Administration, Department of Commerce, Washington, DC 20230. Phone, 202-482-3917.

Minority Business Development Agency

Department of Commerce, Washington, DC 20230, 202-482-2332, *http://www.mbda.gov*

NATIONAL DIRECTOR	Alejandra Y. Castillo
National Deputy Director	Albert K. Shen

[For the Minority Business Development Agency statement of organization, see the Federal Register of Mar. 17, 1972, 37 FR 5650, as amended]

The Minority Business Development Agency was established by Executive order in 1969. The Agency develops and coordinates a national program for minority business enterprise.

The Agency was created to help minority businesses achieve effective and equitable participation in the American free enterprise system and overcome social and economic disadvantages that limited past participation. The Agency provides policies and leadership supporting a partnership of business, industry, and government with the Nation's minority businesses.

Business development services are provided to the minority business community through three vehicles: the minority business opportunity committees, which disseminate information on business opportunities; the minority business development centers, which provide management and technical assistance and other business development services; and electronic commerce, which includes a Web site that shows how to start a business and use the service to find contract opportunities.

The Agency promotes and coordinates the efforts of other Federal agencies in assisting or providing market opportunities for minority business. It coordinates opportunities for minority firms in the private sector. Through such public and private cooperative activities, the Agency promotes the participation of Federal, State, and local governments, and business and industry in directing resources for the development of strong minority businesses.

Sources of Information

Internships

Information on student eligibility and how to apply is available online.

Library

An online research library serves as a repository for factsheets, reports, statistical data, and other publications.

Newsletter

A free, monthly newsletter is accessible online.

For information on scheduling a speaker for an organized event, visit the "Speaker Request Form" Web page.

Speakers

For further information, contact the Office of the National Director, Minority Business Development Agency, Department of Commerce, Washington, DC 20230. Phone, 202-482-2332.

National Oceanic and Atmospheric Administration

Department of Commerce, Washington, DC 20230, 202-482-2985, *http://www.noaa.gov*

UNDER SECRETARY, OCEANS AND ATMOSPHERE / ADMINISTRATOR	Kathryn D. Sullivan
Assistant Secretary, Conservation and Management / Deputy Administrator	Christine Blackburn, Acting
Assistant Secretary, Environmental Observation and Prediction / Deputy Administrator	Manson K. Brown
Chief Scientist	Richard W. Spinrad

[For the National Oceanic and Atmospheric Administration statement of organization, see the Federal Register of Feb. 13, 1978, 43 FR 6128]

The National Oceanic and Atmospheric Administration (NOAA) was formed on October 3, 1970, by Reorganization Plan No. 4 of 1970 (5 U.S.C. app.).

NOAA's mission centers on environmental assessment, prediction, and stewardship. It monitors and assesses the state of the environment to make accurate and timely forecasts to protect life, property, and natural resources; to promote the Nation's economic health; and to enhance its environmental security. The agency protects America's ocean, coastal, and living marine resources while promoting sustainable economic development.

National Environmental Satellite, Data, and Information Service

The National Environmental Satellite, Data, and Information Service operates the Nation's civilian geostationary and polar-orbiting environmental satellites. It also manages the largest collection of atmospheric, climatic, geophysical, and oceanographic data in the world. The Service develops and provides, through various media, environmental data for forecasts, national security, and weather warnings to protect life and property. These data are also used for energy distribution, global food supplies development, natural resources management, and rescuing downed pilots and mariners in distress.

For further information, contact the National Environmental Satellite, Data, and Information Service, 1335 East-West Highway, Silver Spring, MD 20910-3283. Phone, 301-713-3578. Fax, 301-713-1249.

National Marine Fisheries Service

The National Marine Fisheries Service supports the management, conservation, and sustainable development of domestic and international living marine resources and the protection and restoration of ecosystems. The Service helps assess the stock of the Nation's multi-billion-dollar marine fisheries, protect marine mammals and threatened species, conserve habitats, assist trade and industry, and conduct fishery enforcement activities.

For further information, contact the National Marine Fisheries Service, 1315 East-

West Highway, Silver Spring, MD 20910. Phone, 301-713-2239. Fax, 301-713-1940.

National Ocean Service

The National Ocean Service helps balance the Nation's use of coastal resources through research, management, and policy. The Service monitors the health of U.S. coasts by examining how human use and natural events affect coastal ecosystems. Coastal communities rely on the Service for information on natural hazards so they can reduce or eliminate destructive effects of coastal hazards. The Service assesses the damage caused by hazardous material spills and tries to restore or replace the affected coastal resources. The Service also protects beaches, water quality, wetlands, and wildlife. It provides a wide range of navigational products and data that help vessels move safely through U.S. waters, and it supplies the basic information for establishing the latitude, longitude, and elevation framework necessary for the Nation's mapping, navigation, positioning, and surveying activities.

For further information, contact the National Ocean Service, Room 13231, SSMC 4, 1305 East-West Highway, Silver Spring, MD 20910. Phone, 301-713-3074. Fax, 301-713-4307.

National Weather Service

The National Weather Service (NWS) provides weather, water, and climate warnings and forecasts and data for the United States, its territories, and adjacent waters and ocean areas. Government agencies, the private sector, the general public, and the global community rely on NWS data and products to protect life and property. Working with partners in Government, academic and research institutions, and private industry, the Service responds to the needs of the American public through its products and services. NWS data and information support aviation, maritime activities, and other sectors of the economy, as well as wildfire suppression. The Service also helps national security efforts with long- and short-range forecasts, air quality and cloud dispersion forecasts, and broadcasts of warnings and critical information over the 800-station NOAA Weather Radio network.

For further information, contact the National Weather Service–Executive Affairs, 1325 East-West Highway, Silver Spring, MD 20910-3283. Phone, 301-713-0675. Fax, 301-713-0049.

Office of Marine and Aviation Operations

The Office of Marine and Aviation Operations manages the aviation safety, the small boat, and the NOAA diving programs. It also operates a fleet of specialized ships and aircraft that collect data and carry out research to support NOAA's mission, the Global Earth Observation System, and the Integrated Ocean Observing System—including flying "hurricane hunter" aircraft into the most turbulent storms to collect data critical for research.

For further information, contact Office of Marine and Aviation Operations, Suite 500, 8403 Colesville Rd., Silver Spring, MD 20910. Phone, 301-713-7600. Fax, 301-713-1541.

Office of Oceanic and Atmospheric Research

The Office of Oceanic and Atmospheric Research conducts research on air quality and composition, climate variability and change, weather, and coastal, marine, and Great Lakes ecosystems. The Office uses its own laboratories and offices to run research programs in atmospheric, coastal, marine, and space sciences, as well as relying on networks of university-based programs across the country.

For further information, contact the Office of Oceanic and Atmospheric Research, Room 11458, 1315 East-West Highway, Silver Spring, MD 20910. Phone, 301-713-2458. Fax, 301-713-0163.

Sources of Information

Employment

For information on career and volunteer opportunities, contracting and partnering, and grants, visit the "Working with NOAA" Web page.

Facilities

Information on NOAA facilities, programs, and activities nationwide is available on the "NOAA in Your State and Territory" Web page.

News

News and features—explainers, stories, and videos—are available online.

Weather

The NOAA Weather Radio All Hazards network broadcasts continuous weather information nationwide from the nearest National Weather Service office. The network broadcasts official Weather Service forecasts, warnings, watches, and other hazard information around the clock every day.

For further information, contact the Office of Communications and External Affairs, National Oceanic and Atmospheric Administration, Department of Commerce, Washington, DC 20230. Phone, 202-482-6090. Fax, 202-482-3154.

National Telecommunications and Information Administration

Department of Commerce, Washington, DC 20230, 202-428-1840, *http://www.ntia.doc.gov*

ASSISTANT SECRETARY, COMMUNICATIONS AND INFORMATION / ADMINISTRATOR	Lawrence E. Strickling
Deputy Assistant Secretary, Communications and Information	Angela Simpson

[For the National Telecommunications and Information Administration statement of organization, see the Federal Register of June 5, 1978, 43 FR 24348]

The National Telecommunications and Information Administration (NTIA) was established in 1978 by Reorganization Plan No. 1 of 1977 (5 U.S.C. app.) and Executive Order 12046 of March 27, 1978 (3 CFR, 1978 Comp., p. 158), by combining the Office of Telecommunications Policy of the Executive Office of the President and the Office of Telecommunications of the Department of Commerce to form a new agency reporting to the Secretary of Commerce. NTIA operates under the authority of the National Telecommunications and Information Administration Organization Act (47 U.S.C. 901).

NTIA serves as the principal executive branch adviser to the President on telecommunications and information policy; develops and presents U.S. plans and policies at international communications conferences and related meetings; prescribes policies for and manages Federal use of the radio frequency spectrum; serves as the principal Federal telecommunications research and engineering laboratory—NTIA's Institute for Telecommunication Sciences; promotes broadband deployment and adoption through BroadbandUSA (www2.ntia.doc.gov); and assists the First Responder Network Authority (www.firstnet.gov) develop and operate a nationwide broadband network dedicated to public safety.

Sources of Information

Employment

To see current NTIA career opportunities on USAJobs, click on the link below, scroll down, and select "NTIA Jobs."

Publications

Since 1954, NTIA and its predecessors

have published several hundred technical reports and memoranda, special publications, contractor reports, and other information products. For more information, call the Office of Spectrum Management in Washington, DC, at 202-482-1850. Or, contact the publications officer at the Institute for Telecommunication Sciences–Department of Commerce, 325 Broadway, MC ITS.D, Boulder, CO 80305. Phone, 303-497-3572.

Speakers

A speaker request form is available online.

Telecommunications Research

For information on telecommunications research and engineering services, visit the "Institute for Telecommunication Sciences" Web page. Phone, 303-497-3571.

For further information, contact the National Telecommunications and Information Administration, Department of Commerce, Washington, DC 20230. Phone, 202-482-1551.

National Institute of Standards and Technology

100 Bureau Drive, Gaithersburg, MD 20899, 301-975-2000, *http://www.nist.gov*

UNDER SECRETARY, STANDARDS AND TECHNOLOGY / DIRECTOR — Willie E. May

The National Institute of Standards and Technology (NIST) operates under the authority of the National Institute of Standards and Technology Act (15 U.S.C. 271), which amends the Organic Act of March 3, 1901 (ch. 872), which created the National Bureau of Standards (NBS) in 1901. In 1988, the Congress renamed NBS as NIST and expanded its activities and responsibilities.

NIST is a nonregulatory Federal agency within the Department of Commerce. To carry out its mission, NIST relies on research laboratories, user facilities, innovative manufacturing programs, and its participation in collaborative institutes and centers. NIST research laboratories conduct world-class research to advance the Nation's technological infrastructure and help U.S. companies improve products and services. The Baldrige Performance Excellence Program (www.nist.gov/baldrige) also helps them and other organizations increase operational performance and quality. NIST user facilities include the Center for Nanoscale Science and Technology (www.nist.gov/cnst) and NIST Center for Neutron Research (www.ncnr.nist.gov).

Sources of Information

Employment

For information on career opportunities, visit the "Careers at NIST" Web page.

Publications

The "Journal of Research of the National Institute of Standards and Technology" and other publications are available online.

For further information, contact the National Institute of Standards and Technology, 100 Bureau Drive, Mail Stop 1070, Gaithersburg, MD 20899-1070. Phone, 301-975-6478. Fax, 301-926-1630.

National Technical Information Service

5301 Shawnee Road, Alexandria, VA 22312, 703-605-6050, 888-584-8332, *http://www.ntis.gov*

DIRECTOR — Avi Bender

The National Technical Information Service (NTIS) is the largest central resource for business-related, engineering, Government-funded, scientific, and technical information available. For more than 60 years, the Service has assured businesses, Government, universities, and the public timely access to approximately 3 million publications covering over 350 subject areas. The Service supports the Department of Commerce's mission by providing access to information that stimulates innovation and discovery. The Service receives no appropriations and recovers its costs through fees charged for products and services.

The NTIS promotes economic growth, progress, and science and information. On behalf of the Secretary of Commerce, the Service operates a permanent clearinghouse of scientific and technical information and makes it readily available to industry, business, and the general public—codified as chapter 23 of Title 15 of the United States Code (15 U.S.C. 1151-1157). The Service collects scientific and technical information; catalogs, abstracts, indexes, and permanently archives the information; disseminates information through electronic and other media; and provides information processing services to other Federal agencies.

NTIS also provides information management services to other Federal agencies to help them interact with and better serve the information needs of their own constituents. It develops, plans, evaluates, and implements business strategies for information management and dissemination services and Internet-based service business opportunities for Federal agencies; uses new and existing technologies to ensure optimal access to Government online information services; and manages service projects using in-house capabilities and through joint public-private partnerships. NTIS provides eTraining and Knowledge Management, Web services and cloud computing, distribution and fulfillment, digitization and scanning services for Federal Government agencies.

Sources of Information

Employment

Approximately 150 NTIS employees work in Northern Virginia. The Service hires professionals with skills in administration, information technology, and program management.

Freedom of Information Act (FOIA)

The Office of Director handles Freedom of Information Act (FOIA) requests. The FOIA contact reviews, coordinates, and responds to requests within 20 days under the requirements of the Freedom of Information Act.

Products

For general information or to place a telephone order, call the Customer Contact Center, 8 a.m.–6 p.m., eastern standard time. Phone, 800-553-6847. TDD, 703-487-4639. Fax, 703-605-6900.

Services

To learn more about NTIS information services for Federal agencies, call the Office of Federal Services at 703-605-6800.

For further information, contact the National Technical Information Service, 5301 Shawnee Road, Alexandria, VA 22312. Phone, 703-605-6000 or 800-553-6847.

United States Patent and Trademark Office

600 Dulany Street, Alexandria, VA 22314, 571-272-8700, *http://www.uspto.gov*

UNDER SECRETARY, INTELLECTUAL PROPERTY / DIRECTOR	Michelle K. Lee
Deputy Under Secretary, Intellectual Property / Deputy Director	Russell D. Slifer

[For the Patent and Trademark Office statement of organization, see the Federal Register of Apr. 14, 1975, 40 FR 16707]

The United States Patent and Trademark Office (USPTO) was established by the act of July 19, 1952 (35 U.S.C. 1) "to promote the progress of science and useful arts, by securing for limited times to authors and inventors the exclusive right to their respective writings and discoveries" (U.S. Constitution Art. I, sec. 8). The commerce clause provides the constitutional basis for the registration of trademarks.

USPTO examines and issues patents. There are three major patent categories: utility patents, design patents, and plant patents. USPTO also issues statutory invention registrations and processes international patent applications.

Through the registration of trademarks, USPTO assists businessmen and women in protecting their investments, promoting goods and services, and safeguarding consumers against confusion and deception in the marketplace. A trademark includes any distinctive word, name, symbol, device, or any combination thereof adopted and used or intended to be used by a manufacturer or merchant to identify his or her goods or services and distinguish them from those manufactured or sold by others. Trademarks are examined by the Office for compliance with various statutory requirements to prevent unfair competition and consumer deception.

In addition to the examination of patent and trademark applications, issuance of patents, and registration of trademarks, USPTO advises and assists government agencies and officials in matters involving all domestic and global aspects of intellectual property. USPTO also promotes an understanding of intellectual property protection.

USPTO provides public access to patent, trademark, and related scientific and technical information. Patents and trademarks may be reviewed and searched online or at designated Patent and Trademark Depository Libraries. There are 80 Patent and Trademark Depository Libraries located within the United States and Puerto Rico. Additionally, USPTO's Scientific and Technical Information Center in Alexandria, VA, houses over 120,000 volumes of scientific and technical books in various languages; 90,000 bound volumes of periodicals devoted to science and technology; the official journals of 77 foreign patent organizations; and over 40 million foreign patents on paper, microfilm, microfiche, and CD–ROM.

Sources of Information

Data

Monthly summaries for patents data and quarterly summaries for trademark data are available online.

Employment

Information on employment opportunities is available on the "Careers" Web page.

Patents

Information on getting started and applying for and maintaining a patent is available online.

Publications

The "Official Gazette" journal, "Inventors Eye" newsletter, and other publications are accessible online.

Speakers

A speaker request form is available online.

Trademarks

Information on getting started and applying for and maintaining a trademark is available online.

For further information, contact the Office of the Chief Communications Officer, United States Patent and Trademark Office, 600 Dulany Street, Alexandria, VA 22314. Phone, 571-272-8400.

Department of Defense

Office of the Secretary, The Pentagon, Washington, DC 20301-1155, 703-545-6700, http://www.defense.gov

SECRETARY OF DEFENSE	Ashton B. Carter
Deputy Secretary of Defense	Robert O. Work
Under Secretary of Defense for Acquisition, Technology and Logistics	Frank Kendall III
Under Secretary of Defense Comptroller / Chief Financial Officer	Michael J. McCord
Under Secretary of Defense for Intelligence	Marcel J. Lattre II
Under Secretary of Defense for Personnel and Readiness	Peter K. Levine, Acting
Under Secretary of Defense for Policy	Christine E. Wormuth
Principal Deputy Under Secretary of Defense Comptroller / DOD Chief Financial Officer	John Conger
Principal Deputy Under Secretary of Defense for Acquisition, Technology and Logistics	Alan F. Estevez
Principal Under Secretary of Defense for Intelligence	(vacancy)
Principal Under Secretary of Defense for Personnel and Readiness	(vacancy)
Principal Under Secretary of Defense for Policy	Brian P. McKeon
Assistant Secretary of Defense for Acquisition	Darlene Costello, Acting
Assistant Secretary of Defense for Asian and Pacific Security Affairs	David B. Shear
Assistant Secretary of Defense for Health Affairs	Jonathan Woodson
Assistant Secretary of Defense for Homeland Defense and Global Security	Thomas Atkin, Acting
Assistant Secretary of Defense for International Security Affairs	Elissa Slotkin, Acting
Assistant Secretary of Defense for Legislative Affairs	Stephen C. Hedger
Assistant Secretary of Defense for Logistics and Materiel Readiness	David Berteau
Assistant Secretary of Defense for Manpower and Reserve Affairs	(vacancy)
Assistant Secretary of Defense for Nuclear, Chemical, and Biological Defense Programs	(vacancy)
Assistant Secretary of Defense for Operational Energy Plans and Programs	Thomas E. Morehouse, Acting
Assistant Secretary of Defense for Personnel and Readiness	(vacancy)
Assistant Secretary of Defense for Research and Engineering	Stephen Welby
Assistant Secretary of Defense for Special Operations/Low-Intensity Conflict	(vacancy)
Chief Information Officer	Terry Halvorsen
Chief Operating Officer	Anthony A. Aldwell
Director, Administration and Management	Michael L. Rhodes
Director, Cost Assessment and Program Evaluation	Jamie M. Morin
Director, Operational Test and Evaluation	J. Michael Gilmore
General Counsel	Jennifer M. O'Connor
Inspector General	Glenn A. Fine, Acting
Assistant to the Secretary of Defense for Public Affairs	Peter Cook, Acting
Deputy Chief Management Officer	David Tillotson

JOINT CHIEFS OF STAFF

CHAIR	Gen. Joseph F. Dunford, Jr., USMC

Vice Chair	Gen. Paul J. Selva, USAF
Senior Enlisted Advisor to the Chair	CSM John W. Troxwell, USMC
Chief of Naval Operations	Adm. John Richardson, USN
Chief of Staff, Air Force	Gen. David L. Goldfein, USAF
Chief of Staff, Army	Gen. Mark A. Milley, USA
Chief of the National Guard Bureau	Gen. Joseph L. Lengyel, USAF
Commandant of the Marine Corps	Gen. Robert B. Neller, USMC

[For the Department of Defense statement of organization, see the Code of Federal Regulations, Title 32, Chapter I, Subchapter R]

The Department of Defense provides the military forces needed to deter war and protect the security of our country. The major elements of these forces are the Army, Navy, Marine Corps, and Air Force, consisting of approximately 1.3 million men and women on active duty. Under the President, who also serves as Commander in Chief, the Secretary of Defense directs and exercises authority and control over the Department, which comprises the separately organized departments of Army, Navy, and Air Force; the Joint Chiefs of Staff, who serve as advisers; the combatant commands; and defense agencies and field activities established for specific purposes.

The National Security Act Amendments of 1949 redesignated the National Military Establishment as the Department of Defense (DOD) and established it as an executive department (10 U.S.C. 111) headed by the Secretary of Defense.

Structure

The Department of Defense is composed of the Office of the Secretary of Defense; the military departments and the military services within those departments; the Chairman of the Joint Chiefs of Staff and the Joint Staff; the combatant commands; the defense agencies; DOD field activities; and such other offices, agencies, activities, and commands as may be established or designated by law or by the President or the Secretary of Defense.

Each military department is separately organized under its own Secretary and functions under the authority, direction, and control of the Secretary of Defense. The Secretary of each military department is responsible to the Secretary of Defense for the operation and efficiency of his department. Orders to the military departments are issued through the Secretaries of these departments or their designees, by the Secretary of Defense, or under authority specifically delegated in writing by the Secretary of Defense or provided by law.

The commanders of the combatant commands are responsible to the President and the Secretary of Defense for accomplishing the military missions assigned to them and exercising command authority over forces assigned to them. The operational chain of command runs from the President to the Secretary of Defense, to the commanders of the combatant commands. The Chairman of the Joint Chiefs of Staff functions within the chain of command by transmitting the orders of the President or the Secretary of Defense to the commanders of the combatant commands.

Office of the Secretary of Defense

Secretary of Defense

The Secretary of Defense is the principal defense policy adviser to the President and is responsible for the formulation of general defense policy and policy related to DOD and for the execution of approved policy. Under the direction of the President, the Secretary exercises authority, direction, and control over the Department of Defense.

Acquisition, Technology and Logistics

The Under Secretary of Defense for Acquisition, Technology and Logistics is the principal staff assistant and adviser to the Secretary of Defense for all matters relating to the DOD Acquisition System; research and development; modeling and simulation; systems engineering; advanced technology;

developmental test and evaluation; production; systems integration; logistics; installation management; military construction; procurement; environment, safety, and occupational health management; utilities and energy management; business management modernization; document services; and nuclear, chemical, and biological defense programs.

Intelligence

The Under Secretary of Defense for Intelligence is the principal staff assistant and adviser to the Secretary and Deputy Secretary of Defense for intelligence, intelligence-related matters, counterintelligence, and security. The Under Secretary of Defense for Intelligence supervises all intelligence and intelligence-related affairs of DOD.

Networks and Information Integration

The Assistant Secretary of Defense for Networks and Information Integration is the principal staff assistant and adviser to the Secretary and Deputy Secretary of Defense for achieving and maintaining information superiority in support of DOD missions, while exploiting or denying an adversary's ability to do the same. The Assistant Secretary of Defense for Networks and Information Integration also serves as the Chief Information Officer.

Personnel and Readiness

The Under Secretary of Defense for Personnel and Readiness is the principal staff assistant and adviser to the Secretary of Defense for policy matters relating to the structure and readiness of the total force. Functional areas include readiness; civilian and military personnel policies, programs, and systems; civilian and military equal opportunity programs; health policies, programs, and activities; Reserve component programs, policies, and activities; family policy, dependents' education, and personnel support programs; mobilization planning and requirements; language capabilities and programs; and the Federal Voting Assistance Program. The Under Secretary of Defense for Personnel and Readiness also serves as the Chief Human Capital Officer.

Policy

The Under Secretary of Defense for Policy is the principal staff assistant and adviser to the Secretary of Defense for policy matters relating to overall international security policy and political-military affairs and represents the Department at the National Security Council and other external agencies involved with national security policy. The Under Secretary's areas of activity include homeland defense; NATO affairs; foreign military sales; arms limitation agreements; international trade and technology security; regional security affairs; special operations and low-intensity conflict; stability operations; integration of departmental plans and policies with overall national security objectives; drug control policy, requirements, priorities, systems, resources, and programs; and issuance of policy guidance affecting departmental programs.

Special Staff

A special staff assists the Secretary and Deputy Secretary of Defense. This special staff of assistants includes the Assistant Secretaries of Defense for Legislative Affairs and for Public Affairs; the Under Secretary of Defense (Comptroller), who also functions as the Chief Financial Officer; the General Counsel; the Inspector General; the Assistant to the Secretary of Defense for Intelligence Oversight; the Directors of Administration and Management, of Operational Test and Evaluation, of Business Transformation, of Net Assessment, of Program Analysis and Evaluation; and other officers whom the Secretary of Defense determines are necessary to help carry out his or her duties and responsibilities.

Joint Chiefs of Staff

The Joint Chiefs of Staff consist of the Chairman, the Vice Chairman, the Chief of Staff of the Army, the Chief of Naval Operations, the Chief of Staff of the Air Force, and the Commandant of the Marine Corps. The Chairman of the Joint Chiefs of Staff is the principal military adviser to the President, the National Security Council, and the Secretary of Defense. The other members of the Joint Chiefs of Staff are military advisers who may provide additional information upon request from the President, the National Security Council, or the Secretary of Defense. They may also submit their advice when it does not agree with that of the Chairman. Subject to the authority of the President and the Secretary of Defense, the Chairman of the Joint Chiefs of Staff is responsible for assisting the President and the Secretary of Defense in providing strategic direction and planning for the Armed Forces; making recommendations for the assignment of responsibilities within the Armed Forces; comparing the capabilities of American and allied Armed Forces with those of potential adversaries; preparing and reviewing contingency plans that conform to policy guidance; preparing joint logistic and mobility plans; and recommending assignment of logistic and mobility responsibilities.

The Chairman, while so serving, holds the grade of general or admiral and outranks all other officers of the Armed Forces.

The Vice Chairman of the Joint Chiefs performs duties assigned by the Chairman, with the approval of the Secretary of Defense. The Vice Chairman acts as Chairman when there is a vacancy in the office of the Chairman or in the absence or disability of the Chairman. The Vice Chairman, while so serving, holds the grade of general or admiral and outranks all other officers of the Armed Forces except the Chairman of the Joint Chiefs of Staff.

Joint Staff

The Joint Staff, under the Chairman of the Joint Chiefs of Staff, assists the Chairman and the other members of the Joint Chiefs of Staff in carrying out their responsibilities.

The Joint Staff is headed by a Director who is selected by the Chairman in consultation with the other members of the Joint Chiefs of Staff and with the approval of the Secretary of Defense. Officers assigned to serve on the Joint Staff are selected by the Chairman in approximately equal numbers from the Army, Navy, Marine Corps, and Air Force.

Combatant Commands

The combatant commands are military commands with broad continuing missions maintaining the security and defense of the United States against attack; supporting and advancing the national policies and interests of the United States and discharging U.S. military responsibilities in their assigned areas; and preparing plans, conducting operations, and coordinating activities of the forces assigned to them in accordance with the directives of higher authority. The operational chain of command runs from the President to the Secretary of Defense, to the commanders of the combatant commands. The Chairman of the Joint Chiefs of Staff serves as the spokesman for the commanders of the combatant commands, especially on the administrative requirements of their commands.

Field Activities

Counterintelligence Field Activity

The DOD Counterintelligence Field Activity was established in 2002 to build a Defense counterintelligence (CI) system that is informed by national goals and objectives and supports the protection of DOD personnel and critical assets from foreign intelligence services, foreign terrorists, and other clandestine or covert threats. The desired end is a transformed Defense CI system that integrates and synchronizes the counterintelligence activities of the military departments, defense agencies, Joint Staff, and combatant commands.

Defense Health Agency

The Defense Health Agency (DHA) manages the activities of the Military Health System. It is also the market manager for the National Capital Region enhanced Multi-Service Market, which includes Walter Reed National Military Medical Center and Fort Belvoir Community Hospital.

Defense Media Activity

Defense Media Activity (DMA) gathers Defense news and information from all departmental levels and reports that news and information to DOD audiences worldwide through American Forces Network online, radio, television, and through publications. DMA reports news on individual airmen, marines, sailors, soldiers, and DOD civilian employees to the American public through the Hometown News Service. DMA provides World Wide Web infrastructure and services for DOD organizations. It collects, processes, and stores DOD imagery products created by the

Department and makes them available to the American public. It trains the Department's public affairs and visual information military and civilian professionals. DMA also operates Stars and Stripes, a news and information organization, free of Government editorial control and censorship, for military audiences overseas.

Defense Prisoner of War / Missing in Action Accounting Agency

The Defense POW / MIA Accounting Agency (DPAA) provides centralized management of prisoner of war and missing personnel affairs within the DOD. DPAA's primary responsibilities include leadership for and policy oversight over all efforts to account for Americans still missing from past conflicts and the recovery of and accounting for those who may become isolated in hostile territory in future conflicts. DPAA also provides administrative and logistical support to the U.S.-Russia Joint Commission on POW / MIAs, conducts research and analysis to help resolve cases of those unaccounted for, examines DOD documents for possible public disclosure, and maintains viable channels of communications on POW / MIA matters between the DOD and Congress, the families of the missing, and the American public.

Defense Technical Information Center

The Defense Technical Information Center (DTIC) is a field activity in the Office of the Under Secretary of Defense for Acquisition, Technology and Logistics. It operates under the authority, direction, and control of the Director of Defense Research and Engineering. DTIC provides defense scientific and technical information, offers controlled access to defense information, and designs and hosts more than 100 DOD Web sites. DTIC's collections include technical reports, summaries of research in progress, independent research and development material, defense technology transfer agreements, and DOD planning documents.

Defense Technology Security Administration

The Defense Technology Security Administration (DTSA) is the central DOD point of contact for development and implementation of technology security policies governing defense articles and services and dual-use commodities. DTSA administers the development and implementation of DOD technology security policies on international transfers of defense-related goods, services, and technologies. It does so to ensure that critical U.S. military technological advantages are preserved, transfers that could prove detrimental to U.S. security interests are controlled and limited, weapons of mass destruction and their means of delivery do not proliferate, diversion of defense-related goods to terrorists is prevented, legitimate defense cooperation with foreign friends and allies is supported, and the health of the defense industrial base is assured.

Education Activity

The Department of Defense Education Activity (DODEA) was established in 1992. It consists of two subordinate organizational entities: the Department of Defense Dependents Schools (DODDS) and the Department of Defense Domestic Dependent Elementary and Secondary Schools (DDESS). DODEA formulates, develops, and implements policies, technical guidance, and standards for the effective management of Defense dependents education activities and programs. It also plans, directs, coordinates, and manages the education programs for eligible dependents of U.S. military and civilian personnel stationed overseas and stateside; evaluates the programmatic and operational policies and procedures for DODDS and DDESS; and provides education activity representation at meetings and deliberations of educational panels and advisory groups.

Human Resources Field Activity

The Department of Defense Human Resources Activity (DODHRA) enhances the operational effectiveness and efficiency of a host of dynamic and diverse programs supporting the Office of the Under Secretary of Defense for Personnel and Readiness. The Field Activity supports policy development, performs cutting-edge research and expert analysis, supports readiness and reengineering efforts, manages the largest automated personnel data repositories in the world, prepares tomorrow's leaders through robust developmental programs, supports recruiting and retaining the best and brightest, and delivers both benefits and critical services to warfighters and their families.

Office of Economic Adjustment

The Office of Economic Adjustment (OEA) assists communities that are adversely affected by base closures, expansions, or realignments and Defense contract or program cancellations. OEA provides technical and financial assistance to those communities and coordinates other Federal agencies' involvement through the Defense Economic Adjustment Program.

Test Resource Management

The Test Resource Management Center (TRMC) is a DOD Field Activity under the authority, direction, and control of the Under Secretary of Defense for Acquisition, Technology and Logistics. The Center develops policy, plans for, and assesses the adequacy of the major range and test facility base to provide adequate testing in support of development, acquisition, fielding, and sustainment of defense systems. TRMC develops and maintains the test and evaluation resources strategic plan, reviews the proposed DOD test and evaluation budgets, and certifies the adequacy of the proposed budgets and whether they provide balanced support of the strategic plan. TRMC manages the Central Test and Evaluation Investment Program, the Test and Evaluation Science and Technology Program, and the Joint Mission Environment Test Capability Program.

Washington Headquarters Services

Washington Headquarters Services (WHS), established as a DOD Field Activity on October 1, 1977, is under the authority and control of the Deputy Chief Management Officer. WHS provides a range of administrative and operational services to the Office of the Secretary of Defense, specified DOD components, the general public, and for Federal Government activities. WHS services include contracting and procurement; data systems and information technology support; Defense facilities, directives and records, and financial management; enterprise information technology infrastructure, human resource, legal, library, and personnel security services; evaluation and planning functions; Pentagon renovation and construction; and support for advisory boards and commissions.

Sources of Information

Budget Data

The Defense Technical Information Center (DTIC) sponsors a Web site that features congressional budget data pertaining to the DOD. The DTIC posts data from each budget report once it is filed and made available on the Library of Congress' Web site. The data are accessible in Portable Document Format (PDF) and Excel spreadsheet format.

Business Opportunities

Information on and resources for acquisition, business, contracting, and subcontracting opportunities are available on the DOD's Web site.

The Office of Small Business Programs supports the participation of small businesses in the acquisition of goods and services for the DOD.

Dictionary

The Defense Technical Information Center's Web site features the "DOD Dictionary of Military and Associated Terms," which is commonly called the "DOD Dictionary." The dictionary facilitates communication and mutual understanding within the DOD, with external Federal agencies, and between the United States and its international partners by standardizing military and associated terminology.

Employment

The DOD employs over 718,000 civilian personnel. For additional information on applying for DOD job opportunities, contact Washington Headquarters Services–Human Resources Servicing Team. Phone, 614-692-0252.

Freedom of Information Act (FOIA)

Approved by President Lyndon B. Johnson in 1966, the statute generally provides that any person has the right to request access to Federal agency information or records. Upon receiving a written request, the Federal agency holding the desired document or record must disclose it. Some records, however, are shielded from disclosure by one of the FOIA's nine exemptions or three exclusions.

History

A short history of the Pentagon, from construction to completion, is available on the Pentagon Tours Office's Web site.

Joint Chiefs of Staff

The Joint Chiefs of Staff maintain a Web site.

News

The DOD posts news releases on its Web site.

Plain Language

The DOD aims to write documents in readable English by adhering to Federal plain language guidelines.

Popular Resources

A page of popular DOD resources is available on the DOD Web site.

Social Media

The DOD tweets announcements and other newsworthy items on Twitter.

The DOD has a Facebook account.

The DOD posts videos on its YouTube channel.

Site Index

The Web site index allows visitors to look for specific topics or to browse content that aligns with their interests.

Speakers

Civilian and military officials from the DOD are available to speak to public and private sector groups interested in defense-related topics, including the global war on terrorism. Requests for speakers should be addressed to the Director for Community Relations and Public Liaison, 1400 Defense Pentagon, Room 2C546, Washington, DC 20310-1400.

Today in the DOD

The "Today in the Department of Defense" Web page features contracts, news and casualty releases, photos, press advisories, speeches, and transcripts on a daily basis.

Tours

For information on guided tours of the Pentagon, contact the Pentagon Tours Office. Phone, 703-697-1776.

Web Sites

A list of DOD Web site links is available online.

An A–Z list of DOD Web site links is available online.

For further information concerning the Department of Defense, contact the Director, Directorate for Public Inquiry and Analysis, Office of the Assistant Secretary of Defense for Public Affairs, 1400 Defense Pentagon, Washington, DC 20301-1400. Phone, 703- 697-9312.

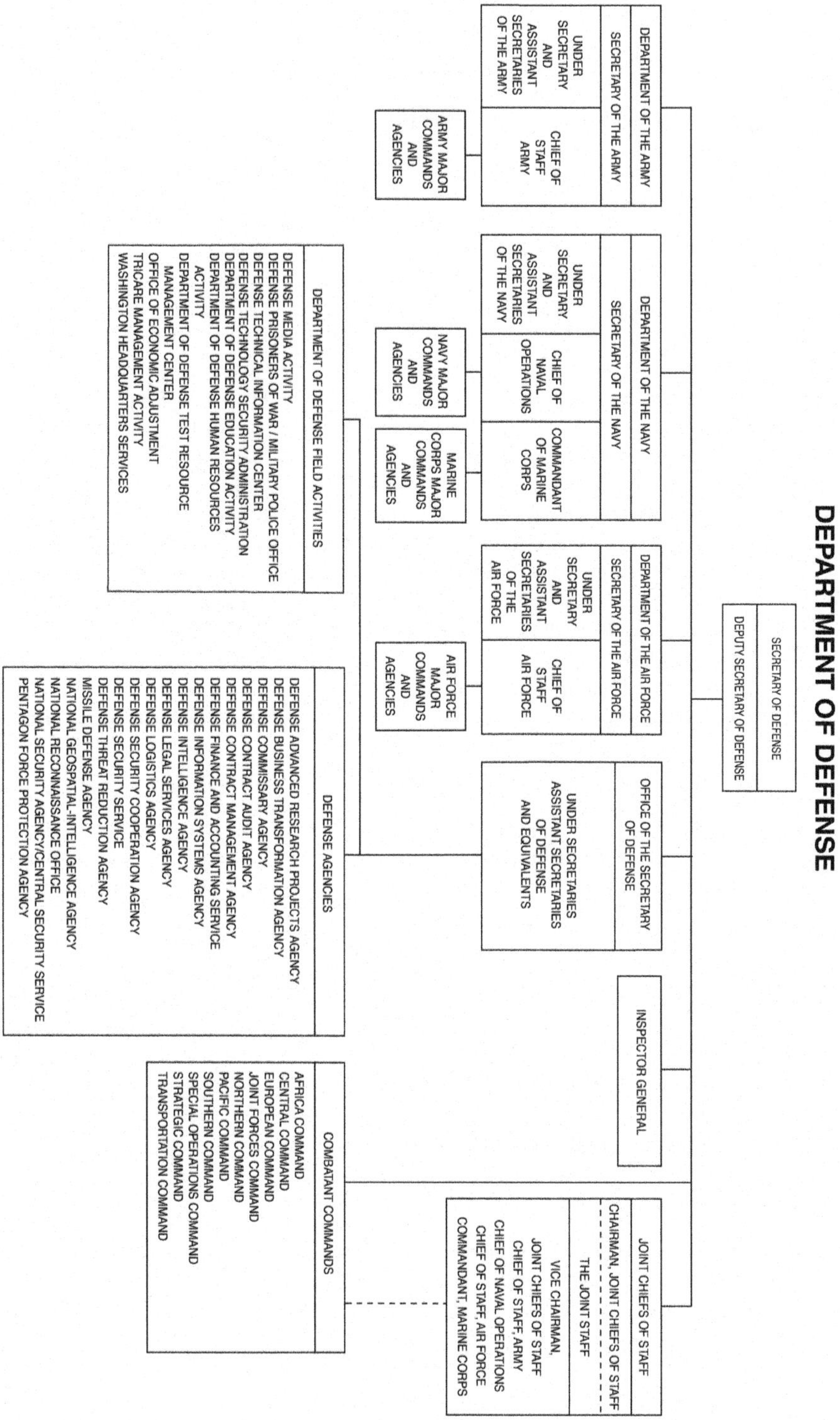
DEPARTMENT OF DEFENSE
SECRETARY OF DEFENSE
DEPUTY SECRETARY OF DEFENSE
DEPARTMENT OF THE ARMY
SECRETARY OF THE ARMY
UNDER SECRETARY AND ASSISTANT SECRETARIES OF THE ARMY
CHIEF OF STAFF ARMY
ARMY MAJOR COMMANDS AND AGENCIES
DEPARTMENT OF THE NAVY
SECRETARY OF THE NAVY
UNDER SECRETARY AND ASSISTANT SECRETARIES OF THE NAVY
CHIEF OF NAVAL OPERATIONS
COMMANDANT OF MARINE CORPS
NAVY MAJOR COMMANDS AND AGENCIES
MARINE CORPS MAJOR COMMANDS AND AGENCIES
DEPARTMENT OF THE AIR FORCE
SECRETARY OF THE AIR FORCE
UNDER SECRETARY AND ASSISTANT SECRETARIES OF THE AIR FORCE
CHIEF OF STAFF AIR FORCE
AIR FORCE MAJOR COMMANDS AND AGENCIES
OFFICE OF THE SECRETARY OF DEFENSE
UNDER SECRETARIES ASSISTANT SECRETARIES OF DEFENSE AND EQUIVALENTS
INSPECTOR GENERAL
JOINT CHIEFS OF STAFF
CHAIRMAN, JOINT CHIEFS OF STAFF
THE JOINT STAFF
VICE CHAIRMAN, JOINT CHIEFS OF STAFF
CHIEF OF STAFF, ARMY
CHIEF OF NAVAL OPERATIONS
CHIEF OF STAFF, AIR FORCE
COMMANDANT, MARINE CORPS
DEPARTMENT OF DEFENSE FIELD ACTIVITIES
DEFENSE MEDIA ACTIVITY
DEFENSE PRISONERS OF WAR / MILITARY POLICE OFFICE
DEFENSE TECHNICAL INFORMATION CENTER
DEFENSE TECHNOLOGY SECURITY ADMINISTRATION
DEPARTMENT OF DEFENSE EDUCATION ACTIVITY
DEPARTMENT OF DEFENSE HUMAN RESOURCES ACTIVITY
DEPARTMENT OF DEFENSE TEST RESOURCE MANAGEMENT CENTER
OFFICE OF ECONOMIC ADJUSTMENT
TRICARE MANAGEMENT ACTIVITY
WASHINGTON HEADQUARTERS SERVICES
DEFENSE AGENCIES
DEFENSE ADVANCED RESEARCH PROJECTS AGENCY
DEFENSE BUSINESS TRANSFORMATION AGENCY
DEFENSE COMMISSARY AGENCY
DEFENSE CONTRACT AUDIT AGENCY
DEFENSE CONTRACT MANAGEMENT AGENCY
DEFENSE FINANCE AND ACCOUNTING SERVICE
DEFENSE INFORMATION SYSTEMS AGENCY
DEFENSE INTELLIGENCE AGENCY
DEFENSE LEGAL SERVICES AGENCY
DEFENSE LOGISTICS AGENCY
DEFENSE SECURITY COOPERATION AGENCY
DEFENSE SECURITY SERVICE
DEFENSE THREAT REDUCTION AGENCY
MISSILE DEFENSE AGENCY
NATIONAL GEOSPATIAL-INTELLIGENCE AGENCY
NATIONAL RECONNAISSANCE OFFICE
NATIONAL SECURITY AGENCY/CENTRAL SECURITY SERVICE
PENTAGON FORCE PROTECTION AGENCY
COMBATANT COMMANDS
AFRICA COMMAND
CENTRAL COMMAND
EUROPEAN COMMAND
JOINT FORCES COMMAND
NORTHERN COMMAND
PACIFIC COMMAND
SOUTHERN COMMAND
SPECIAL OPERATIONS COMMAND
STRATEGIC COMMAND
TRANSPORTATION COMMAND

Department of the Air Force

1690 Air Force Pentagon, Washington, DC 20330-1670, 703-697-6061, *http://www.af.mil*

AIR FORCE SECRETARIAT

SECRETARY OF THE AIR FORCE	Deborah Lee James
Under Secretary of the Air Force	Lisa S. Disbrow
Administrative Assistant	Patricia J. Zarodkiewicz
Auditor General	Daniel F. McMillin
General Counsel	Gordon O. Tanner
Information Dominance and Chief Information Officer (A6)	Lt. Gen. William J. Bender
Inspector General	Lt. Gen. Gregory Biscone
Legislative Liaison	Maj. Gen. Thomas W. Bergeson
Assistant Secretary, Acquisition	William A. LaPlante, Jr.
Assistant Secretary, Financial Management and Comptroller	Ricardo Aguilera
Assistant Secretary, Installations, Environment, and Energy	Miranda Ballentine
Assistant Secretary, Manpower and Reserve Affairs	Daniel R. Sitterly
Deputy Chief Management Officer	Marilynn M. Thomas
Deputy Under Secretary, International Affairs	Heidi H. Grant
Deputy Under Secretary, Space	Winston Beauchamp
Director, Air Force Small Business Programs	Mark S. Teskey
Director, Public Affairs	Brig. Gen. Kathleen A. Cook

AIR STAFF

Chief of Staff	Gen. David L. Goldfein
Vice Chief of Staff	Gen. Stephen W. Wilson
Chief Master Sergeant of the Air Force	CMSAF James A. Cody
Assistant Vice Chief of Staff	Lt. Gen. Stayce D. Harris
Judge Advocate General	Lt. Gen. Christopher F. Burne
Surgeon General	Lt. Gen. Mark A. Ediger
Chief of Air Force Reserve	Lt. Gen. Maryanne Miller
Chief of Chaplains	Maj. Gen. Dondi Constin
Chief of Safety	Maj. Gen. Andrew Mueller
Chief of Staff, Strategic Deterrence and Nuclear Integration (A10)	Lt. Gen. Jack Weinstein
Chief Scientist	Greg L. Zacharias
Deputy Chief of Staff, Intelligence, Surveillance and Reconnaissance (A2)	Lt. Gen. Robert P. Otto
Deputy Chief of Staff, Logistics, Engineering and Force Protection (A4)	Lt. Gen. John B. Cooper
Deputy Chief of Staff, Manpower, Personnel and Services (A1)	Lt. Gen. Gina Grosso
Deputy Chief of Staff, Operations, Plans and Requirements (A3)	Lt. Gen. John W. Raymond
Deputy Chief of Staff, Strategic Plans and Requirements (A5/8)	Lt. Gen. James M. Holmes
Director, Air Force Sexual Assault Prevention and Response	Maj. Gen. James C. Johnson
Director, Air National Guard	Lt. Gen. L. Scott Rice
Director, History and Museums Policies and Programs	Walter A. Grudzinskas
Director, Studies and Analyses, Assessments and Lessons Learned	Kevin E. Williams

(A9)	
Director, Test and Evaluation	Devin Cate
MAJOR COMMANDS	
Air Combat Command	Gen. Herbert J. Carlisle
Air Education and Training Command	Lt. Gen. Darryl L. Roberson
Air Force Global Strike Command	Gen. Robin Rand
Air Force Materiel Command	Gen. Ellen M. Pawlikowski
Air Force Reserve Command	Lt. Gen. James F. Jackson
Air Force Space Command	Gen. John H. Hyten
Air Force Special Operations Command	Lt. Gen. Bradley A. Heithold
Air Mobility Command	Gen. Carlton D. Everhart
Pacific Air Forces	Gen. Lori J. Robinson
U.S. Air Forces in Europe	Gen. Frank Gorenc

The Department of the Air Force defends the United States by providing air, space, and cyberspace capabilities.

The Department of the Air Force (USAF) was established as part of the National Military Establishment by the National Security Act of 1947 (61 Stat. 502) and came into being on September 18, 1947. The National Security Act Amendments of 1949 redesignated the National Military Establishment as the Department of Defense, established it as an executive department, and made the Department of the Air Force a military department within the Department of Defense (63 Stat. 578). The Department of the Air Force is separately organized under the Secretary of the Air Force. It operates under the authority, direction, and control of the Secretary of Defense (10 U.S.C. 8010). The Department comprises the Office of the Secretary of the Air Force, the Air Staff, and field organizations.

Secretary

The Secretary and Secretariat Staff oversee matters of organization, training, logistical support, maintenance, welfare of personnel, administrative, recruiting, research and development, and other activities that the President or Secretary of Defense prescribes.

Air Staff

The Air Staff assists the Secretary, the Under Secretary, the Assistant Secretaries, and the Chief of Staff in carrying out their responsibilities.

Field Organizations

The major commands, field operating agencies, and direct reporting units constitute the field organizations of the Air Force. They are organized primarily on a functional basis in the United States and on a geographic basis overseas. These commands are responsible for accomplishing certain phases of the Air Force's worldwide activities. They also organize, administer, equip, and train subordinate elements to accomplish assigned missions.

MAJOR COMMANDS: CONTINENTAL U.S. COMMANDS

Air Combat Command

The Air Combat Command operates CONUS-based, combat-coded fighter and attack aircraft. It organizes, trains, equips, and maintains combat-ready forces for rapid deployment and employment while ensuring strategic air defense forces are ready to meet the challenges of peacetime air sovereignty and wartime air defense.

Air Education and Training Command

The Air Education and Training Command recruits, assesses, commissions, educates, and trains Air Force enlisted and officer personnel. It provides basic military training, initial and advanced technical training, flying training, and professional military and post-secondary education. The Command also conducts Air Force security assistance, joint, medical service, and readiness training.

Air Force Global Strike Command

The Air Force Global Strike Command is responsible for the Nation's three intercontinental ballistic missile wings; the Air Force's bomber force, including the B–1, B–2, and B–52 wings; the Long Range Strike Bomber program; and operational and maintenance support to organizations within the nuclear enterprise.

Air Force Materiel Command

The Air Force Materiel Command delivers expeditionary capabilities through research, development, test, evaluation, acquisition, modernization, and sustainment of aerospace weapon systems throughout their life cycles. Those weapon systems include Air Force fighter, bomber, cargo, and attack fleets and armament. They also include net-centric command and control assets; intelligence, surveillance, and reconnaissance assets; and combat support information systems. The command oversees basic research and development that support air, space, and cyberspace capabilities. The command relies on an integrated, efficient life cycle management approach to ensure the best possible support to warfighters.

Air Force Reserve Command

The Air Force Reserve Command provides the Air Force with approximately 14 percent of the total force and approximately 4 percent of the manpower budget. Reservists support air, space, and cyberspace superiority; command and control; global integrated intelligence surveillance reconnaissance; global precision attack; nuclear deterrence operations; special operations; rapid global mobility; and personnel recovery. They also perform aircraft flight testing, space operations, and aerial port operations, as well as communications, civil engineer, military training, mobility support, security forces, services, and transportation missions.

Air Force Space Command

The Air Force Space Command provides space and cyberspace capabilities such as missile warning, space control, spacelift, satellite operations, and designated cyberspace activities.

Air Force Special Operations Command

The Air Force Special Operations Command provides the air component of U.S. Special Operations Command. The command deploys specialized air power and delivers special operations combat power wherever and whenever needed. It provides agile combat support, combat search and rescue, information warfare, precision aerospace fires, psychological operations, and specialized aerospace mobility and refueling to unified commands.

Air Mobility Command

The Air Mobility Command provides airlift, air refueling, special air missions, and aeromedical evacuation for U.S. forces. It also airlifts forces to theater commands to support wartime tasking.

MAJOR COMMANDS: OVERSEAS COMMANDS

Pacific Air Forces

The Pacific Air Forces deliver rapid and precise air, space, and cyberspace capabilities to protect the United States, its territories, and its allies and partners; provide integrated air and missile warning and defense; promote interoperability throughout the Pacific area of responsibility; maintain strategic access and freedom of movement across all domains; and posture to respond across the full spectrum of military contingencies to restore regional security.

U.S. Air Forces in Europe

The U.S. Air Forces in Europe (USAFE) execute the Air Force, European Command, and Africa Command missions with forward-based air power and infrastructure to conduct and enable theater and global operations. The USAFE direct air operations in a theater that spans three continents, covers more than 19 million square miles, contains 104 independent states, produces more than a quarter of the world's gross domestic product, and comprises more than a quarter of Earth's population.

FIELD OPERATING AGENCIES

Air Force Agency for Modeling and Simulation

The Air Force Agency for Modeling and Simulation provides seamless integration of cross-functional live, virtual, and constructive operational training environments that allow war fighters to maximize performance and optimize decisionmaking. The agency works with combatant commands, major commands, the Air Force Reserve Command, the Air National Guard, the Air Force headquarters, direct reporting units, and field operating agencies to provide the necessary development and implementation standards for common access and interoperability within the live, virtual, and constructive domains for efficient and secure global operations.

Air Force Audit Agency

The Air Force Audit Agency provides all levels of Air Force management with independent, objective, and quality audit services by reviewing and promoting operational economy, effectiveness, and efficiency; evaluating programs and activities to achieve intended results; and assessing and improving financial reporting.

Air Force Cost Analysis Agency

The Air Force Cost Analysis Agency performs nonadvocate cost analyses for major space, aircraft, and information system programs. The agency supports the departmentwide cost analysis program by developing and maintaining cost-estimating tools, techniques, and infrastructure. It provides guidance, analytical support, quantitative risk analyses, and special studies to improve long-range planning, force structure, analysis of alternatives, and lifecycle cost analyses.

Air Force Flight Standards Agency

The Air Force Flight Standards Agency performs worldwide inspection of airfields, navigation systems, and instrument approaches. It provides flight standards to develop Air Force instrument requirements and certifies procedures and directives for cockpit display and navigation systems. It also provides air traffic control and airlift procedures and evaluates air traffic control systems and airspace management procedures.

Air Force Historical Research Agency

The Air Force Historical Research Agency serves as a repository for Air Force historical records and maintains research facilities for scholars and the general public.

Air Force Inspection Agency

The Air Force Inspection Agency provides independent inspection, evaluation, oversight, training and analysis to improve the effectiveness and efficiency of the Air Force.

Air Force Legal Operations Agency

The Air Force Legal Operations Agency includes all senior defense, senior trial, appellate defense, and Government counsel in the Air Force, as well as all Air Force civil litigators who defend the Air Force against civil lawsuits that claim damages and seek other remedies in contracts, environmental, labor, and tort litigation.

Air Force Manpower Analysis Agency

The Air Force Manpower Analysis Agency provides analysis and develops tools for helping Air Force and Department of Defense senior leaders make decisions affecting total force manpower requirements. The agency supports the Under Secretary of the Air Force for Management's efforts to improve processes and carries out departmentwide transformation initiatives. It also oversees human capital planning and training to develop and sustain manpower-specific capabilities at adequate levels.

Air Force Medical Operations Agency

The Air Force Medical Operations Agency assists the Air Force Surgeon

General in developing plans, programs, and policies for aerospace medicine, bioenvironmental engineering, clinical investigations, family advocacy, health promotion, military public health, quality assurance, radioactive material management, and the medical service.

Air Force Medical Support Agency

The Air Force Medical Support Agency provides consultative support and policy development for the Air Force Surgeon General in medical force management. It also supports ground and air expeditionary medical capabilities used in global, homeland security, and force health protection, as well as all aspects of medical and dental services, aerospace medicine operations, and medical support functions.

Air Force Mortuary Affairs Operations

The Air Force Mortuary Affairs Operations, a field operating agency of the Deputy Chief of Staff for Manpower, Personnel and Services, works to support the entire Department of Defense and other Federal entities ensuring dignity, honor and respect to the fallen, and care, service, and support to their families.

Air Force Office of Special Investigations

The Air Force Office of Special Investigations identifies, exploits, and neutralizes criminal, terrorist, and intelligence threats to the U.S. Air Force, Department of Defense, and U.S. Government. Its primary responsibilities are criminal investigations and counterintelligence services. It also protects critical technologies and information, detects and mitigates threats, provides global specialized services, conducts major criminal investigations, and offensively engages foreign adversaries and threats.

Air Force Operations Group

The Air Force Operations Group collects, processes, analyzes, and communicates information, enabling situational awareness of USAF operations worldwide. This awareness facilitates timely, responsive, and effective decisionmaking by senior USAF leaders and combatant commanders.

Air Force Personnel Center

The Air Force Personnel Center ensures that commanders around the world have enough skilled Air Force personnel to carry out the mission. The center also runs programs affecting the entire life cycle of military and civilian Air Force personnel from accession through retirement.

Air Force Program Executive Offices

The Air Force Program Executive Offices (PEOs) oversee the execution of a program throughout its entire lifecycle. While the PEOs are not part of USAF headquarters, they report on acquisition and program-specific issues directly to the Air Force Service Acquisition Executive and the Assistant Secretary of the Air Force for Acquisition. Air Force PEOs are currently responsible for diverse programs in a range of areas: aircraft, command and control and combat support systems, Joint Strike Fighter, and weapons.

Air Force Public Affairs Agency

The Air Force Public Affairs Agency manages the Air Force media center. The center collects, archives, and distributes Air Force imagery; manages licensing and branding of Air Force trademarks; provides policy guidance and oversight for the Air Force's Web site and social media programs; operates the Air Force's official social media program; composes original musical arrangements for Air Force regional bands; and develops training curricula and requirements for the Air Force's nearly 6,000 public affairs practitioners.

Air Force Review Boards Agency

The Air Force Review Boards Agency manages various military and civilian appellate processes for the Secretary of the Air Force.

Air Force Safety Center

The Air Force Safety Center promotes safety to reduce the number and severity of mishaps. It also supports combat readiness by developing, implementing, executing, and evaluating Air Force aviation, ground, weapons, nuclear surety, space, and system programs.

Air National Guard Readiness Center

The Air National Guard Readiness Center performs the operational and technical tasks associated with manning, equipping, and training Air National Guard units to meet required readiness levels.

National Air and Space Intelligence Center

The National Air and Space Intelligence Center (NASIC) assesses foreign air and space threats. It creates integrated, predictive intelligence in the domains of air, space, and cyberspace to support military operations, force modernization, and policymaking. NASIC analyzes data on foreign aerospace forces and weapons systems to determine performance characteristics, capabilities, vulnerabilities, and intentions. These assessments are used to shape national security and defense policies. NASIC personnel also play a role in weapons treaty negotiations and verification.

DIRECT REPORTING UNITS

Air Force District of Washington

The Air Force District of Washington supports Headquarters Air Force and other Air Force units in the National Capital Region.

Air Force Operational Test and Evaluation Center

The Air Force Operational Test and Evaluation Center plans and conducts test and evaluation procedures to determine operational effectiveness and suitability of new or modified USAF systems and their capacity to meet mission needs.

U.S. Air Force Academy

The U.S. Air Force Academy provides academic and military instruction and experience to prepare future USAF career officers. The Academy offers Bachelor of Science degrees in 31 academic majors, and upon completion, graduates receive commissions as second lieutenants.

Sources of Information

Employment

Members of the Air Force civilian service work side by side with active duty airmen. They are a diverse group of professionals: contract specialists, engineers, human resources specialists, intelligence experts, mechanics, scientists, teachers, and more.

Factsheets

Factsheets contain current information and statistics on Air Force careers, organizations, inventory, and equipment—including aircraft and weapons.

Freedom of Information Act (FOIA)

The Freedom of Information and Privacy Act Office manages the policy and procedural guidance for the Freedom of Information and Privacy Acts.

Links to FOIA requester service centers are available online. The service centers are grouped, by base and by command, in two lists.

Frequently Asked Questions (FAQs)

The Air Force provides answers to FAQs on its Web site.

History

For over a century, the Air Force has relied on the bravery and skill of American airmen to protect the United States in the air, space, and cyberspace. An overview of that history is available online.

Inspector General (IG)

The IG receives and investigates complaints of abuse, fraud, and waste involving Air Force personnel or programs. Phone, 800-538-8429.

Intelligence, Surveillance, and Reconnaissance (ISR)

The Air Force's Web site features a section dedicated to ISR activities and news.

Joining the Air Force

To learn about its mission, how to join, and about educational, training, and career opportunities that enlistment offers, visit the Air Force's recruitment Web site.

Medal of Honor

Members of the Air Force and its predecessor organizations have earned Medals of Honor. The medal is awarded for conspicuous gallantry and intrepidity at the risk of life above and beyond the call of duty.

News

The Air Force posts announcements, art, commentaries, news items, and photos on its Web site. Air Force TV and radio news are also accessible online.

"Air Force Magazine" is posted online. Beginning in January 2013, full issues are available. Beginning in November 2015, HTML5 versions are available .

Reading List

The Air Force Chief of Staff's annual reading list (2016) is available on the Department's Web site. An archives of the reading list, starting with the year 2007, is also available online.

Sexual Assault

The "Sexual Assault Prevention and Response" (SAPR) Web page has information, policies, and reports on sexual assault, as well as links leading to additional resources within the Department of Defense (DOD) community and to external resources.

The "SAPR" Web page also provides access to the Safe Helpline—an anonymous, confidential, and free crisis support service for DOD community members who have been affected by sexual assault. Phone, 877-995-5247.

Site Map

The Web site map allows visitors to look for specific topics or to browse content that aligns with their interests.

Social Media

The Air Force has a blog and maintains a social media presence on Facebook, Flickr, Instagram, Twitter, and YouTube.

Strategic Documents

The "USAF Posture Statement 2016" (FEB 2016), "Air Force Future Operating Concept: A View of the Air Force in 2035" (SEP 2015), "USAF Strategic Master Plan" (MAY 2015), and other strategic documents are posted on the Air Force's Web site in Portable Document Format (PDF).

Suicide Prevention

The "Suicide Prevention" Web page promotes resources like the ACE (Ask, Care, and Escort) Card and provides access, by phone or confidential online chat, to the Military Crisis Line. Phone, 800-273-8255.

Web sites

A directory of all registered Air Force Web sites is available online.

For further information concerning the Department of the Air Force, contact the Office of the Director of Public Affairs, Department of the Air Force, 1690 Air Force Pentagon, Washington, DC 20330-1670. Phone, 703-697-6061.

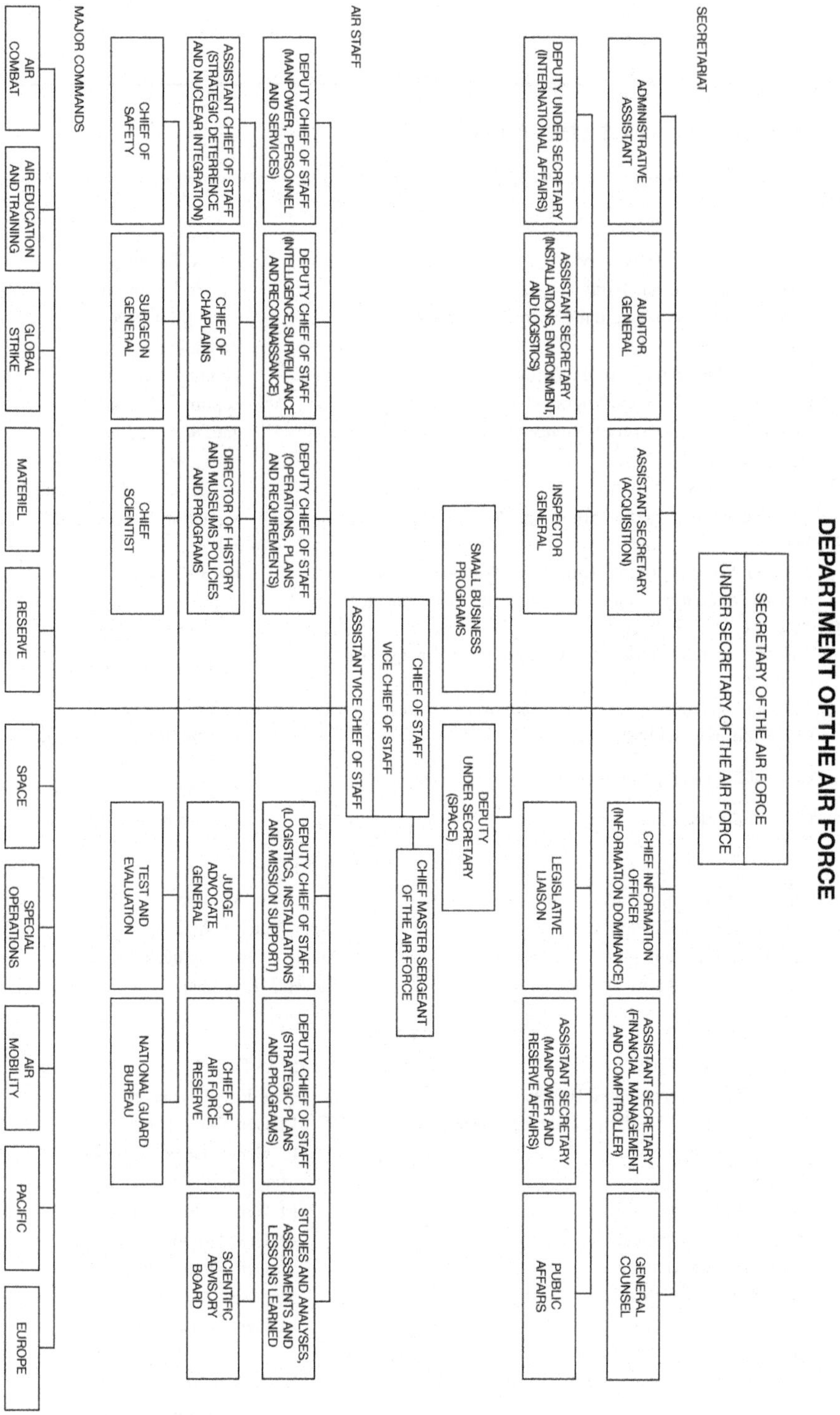
DEPARTMENT OF THE AIR FORCE
SECRETARY OF THE AIR FORCE
UNDER SECRETARY OF THE AIR FORCE
SECRETARIAT
ADMINISTRATIVE ASSISTANT
AUDITOR GENERAL
ASSISTANT SECRETARY (ACQUISITION)
CHIEF INFORMATION OFFICER (INFORMATION DOMINANCE)
ASSISTANT SECRETARY (FINANCIAL MANAGEMENT AND COMPTROLLER)
GENERAL COUNSEL
DEPUTY UNDER SECRETARY (INTERNATIONAL AFFAIRS)
ASSISTANT SECRETARY (INSTALLATIONS, ENVIRONMENT, AND LOGISTICS)
INSPECTOR GENERAL
LEGISLATIVE LIAISON
ASSISTANT SECRETARY (MANPOWER AND RESERVE AFFAIRS)
PUBLIC AFFAIRS
SMALL BUSINESS PROGRAMS
DEPUTY UNDER SECRETARY (SPACE)
CHIEF OF STAFF
VICE CHIEF OF STAFF
ASSISTANT VICE CHIEF OF STAFF
CHIEF MASTER SERGEANT OF THE AIR FORCE
AIR STAFF
DEPUTY CHIEF OF STAFF (MANPOWER, PERSONNEL AND SERVICES)
DEPUTY CHIEF OF STAFF (INTELLIGENCE, SURVEILLANCE AND RECONNAISSANCE)
DEPUTY CHIEF OF STAFF (OPERATIONS, PLANS AND REQUIREMENTS)
DEPUTY CHIEF OF STAFF (LOGISTICS, INSTALLATIONS AND MISSION SUPPORT)
DEPUTY CHIEF OF STAFF (STRATEGIC PLANS AND PROGRAMS)
STUDIES AND ANALYSES, ASSESSMENTS AND LESSONS LEARNED
ASSISTANT CHIEF OF STAFF (STRATEGIC DETERRENCE AND NUCLEAR INTEGRATION)
CHIEF OF CHAPLAINS
DIRECTOR OF HISTORY AND MUSEUMS POLICIES AND PROGRAMS
JUDGE ADVOCATE GENERAL
CHIEF OF AIR FORCE RESERVE
SCIENTIFIC ADVISORY BOARD
CHIEF OF SAFETY
SURGEON GENERAL
CHIEF SCIENTIST
TEST AND EVALUATION
NATIONAL GUARD BUREAU
MAJOR COMMANDS
AIR COMBAT
AIR EDUCATION AND TRAINING
GLOBAL STRIKE
MATERIEL
RESERVE
SPACE
SPECIAL OPERATIONS
AIR MOBILITY
PACIFIC
EUROPE

Department of the Army

The Pentagon, Washington, DC 20310, 703-695-6518, *http://www.army.mil*

EXECUTIVE OFFICE

SECRETARY OF THE ARMY	Eric K. Fanning
Under Secretary of the Army	Patrick J. Murphy
Administrative Assistant to the Secretary of the Army	Gerald B. O'Keefe
Auditor General	Randall L. Exley
Deputy Under Secretary of the Army	Thomas E. Hawley
Director, Small Business Programs	Tommy L. Marks
Executive Director, Army National Military Cemeteries	Patrick K. Hallinan
General Counsel	Alissa M. Starzak
Inspector General	Lt. Gen. David E. Quantock
Assistant Secretary of the Army, Acquisition, Logistics and Technology	Katharina G. McFarland, Acting
Assistant Secretary of the Army, Civil Works	Jo-Ellen Darcy
Assistant Secretary of the Army, Financial Management / Comptroller	Robert M. Speer
Assistant Secretary of the Army, Installations, Energy and Environment	Katherine G. Hammack
Assistant Secretary of the Army, Manpower and Reserve Affairs	Debra S. Wada
Chief Information Officer (G–6)	Lt. Gen. Robert S. Ferrell
Chief of Legislative Liaison	Maj. Gen. Laura E. Richardson
Chief of Public Affairs	Brig. Gen. Malcolm B. Frost

OFFICE OF THE CHIEF OF STAFF

Chief of Staff of the Army	Gen. Mark A. Milley
Vice Chief of Staff of the Army	Gen. Daniel B. Allyn
Director of the Army Staff	Lt. Gen. Gary H. Cheek
Vice Director of the Army Staff	Steven J. Redmann

ARMY STAFF

Sergeant Major of the Army	SMA Daniel A. Dailey
Chief of the National Guard Bureau	Gen. Joseph Lengyel
Assistant Chief of Staff, Installation Management	Lt. Gen. Gwen Bingham
Chief of Army Reserve	Lt. Gen. Charles D. Luckey
Chief of Chaplains	Maj. Gen. Paul K. Hurley
Chief of Engineers	Lt. Gen. Todd T. Semonite
Director, Army National Guard	Lt. Gen. Timothy J. Kadavy
Judge Advocate General	Lt. Gen. Flora D. Darpino
Provost Marshal General	Maj. Gen. Mark S. Inch
Surgeon General	Lt. Gen. Nadja Y. West
DEPUTY CHIEFS OF STAFF	
Financial Management (G–8)	Lt. Gen. John M. Murray
Intelligence (G–2)	Lt. Gen. Robert P. Ashley, Jr.
Logistics (G–4)	Lt. Gen. Gustave F. Perna

Operations (G–3/5/7)	Lt. Gen. Joseph Anderson
Personnel (G–1)	Lt. Gen. James C. McConville

COMMANDS

COMMANDING GENERALS	
U.S. Army Forces Command	Gen. Robert B. Abrams
U.S. Army Materiel Command	Gen. Gustave F. Perna
U.S. Army Training and Doctrine Command	Gen. David G. Perkins

ARMY SERVICE COMPONENT COMMANDS

COMMANDING GENERALS	
U.S. Army Africa / Southern European Task Force	Maj. Gen. Joseph P. Harrington
U.S. Army Central	Lt. Gen. Michael X. Garrett
U.S. Army Europe	Lt. Gen. Ben Hodges
U.S. Army North	Lt. Gen. Jeffrey S. Buchanan
U.S. Army Pacific	Gen. Robert B. Brown
U.S. Army South	Maj. Gen. Clarence K.K. Chinn
U.S. Army Military Surface Deployment and Distribution Command	Maj. Gen. Susan A. Davidson
U.S. Army Space and Missile Defense Command/Army Strategic Command	Lt. Gen. David L. Mann
U.S. Army Special Operations Command	Lt. Gen. Kenneth E. Tovo

DIRECT REPORTING UNITS

Commandant, U.S. Army War College	Maj. Gen. William E. Rapp
Commander, Second Army	Lt. Gen. Edward C. Cardon
Commander, U.S. Army Accessions Support Brigade	Col. Janet R. Holliday
Director, U.S. Army Acquisition Support Center	Craig A. Spisak
Executive Director, Arlington National Cemetery	Patrick K. Hallinan
Superintendent, U.S. Military Academy	Lt. Gen. Robert L. Caslen, Jr.
COMMANDING GENERALS	
U.S. Army Corps of Engineers	Lt. Gen. Todd T. Semonite
U.S. Army Criminal Investigation Command	Maj. Gen. Mark S. Inch
U.S. Army Installation Management Command	Lt. Gen. Kenneth R. Dahl
U.S. Army Intelligence and Security Command	Maj. Gen. Christopher S. Ballard
U.S. Army Medical Command	Lt. Gen. Nadja Y. West
U.S. Army Military District of Washington	Maj. Gen. Bradley A. Becker
U.S. Army Reserve Command	Lt. Gen. Charles D. Luckey
U.S. Army Test and Evaluation Command	Maj. Gen. Daniel L. Karbler

The Department of the Army equips, organizes, and trains active duty and reserve forces to maintain peace and security and to defend the Nation; administers programs to mitigate erosion and flooding, to develop water resources, to improve waterway navigation, and to protect the environment; and provides military and natural disaster relief assistance to Federal, State, and local government agencies.

The Continental Congress established the American Continental Army, now called the United States Army, on June 14, 1775, more than a year before the Declaration of Independence. The Department of War was established as an executive department at the seat of Government by act approved August 7, 1789 (1 Stat. 49). The Secretary of War was established as its head. The National Security Act of 1947 (50 U.S.C. 401) created the National Military Establishment, and the Department of War was designated the Department of the Army. The title of its Secretary became Secretary of the Army (5 U.S.C. 171). The National Security Act Amendments of 1949 (63 Stat. 578) provided that the Department of the Army be a military department within the Department of Defense.

Secretary

The Secretary of the Army is the senior official of the Department of the Army. Subject to the direction, authority, and control of the President as Commander in Chief and of the Secretary of Defense, the Secretary of the Army is responsible for and has the authority to conduct all affairs of the Department of the Army, including its organization, administration, operation, efficiency, and such other activities as may be prescribed by the President or the Secretary of Defense as authorized by law.

For further information, call 703-695-2422.

Army Staff

The Army Staff is the Secretary of the Army's military staff. It makes preparations for deploying the Army, including recruiting, organizing, supplying, equipping, training, mobilizing, and demobilizing it, to support the Secretary or the Chief of Staff in his or her executive capacity; investigates and reports on the efficiency of the Army and its preparation for military operations; acts as the agent of the Secretary of the Army and the Chief of Staff in coordinating the action of all organizations of the Department of the Army; and performs other nonstatutory duties that the Secretary of the Army may prescribe.

PROGRAM AREAS

Civil Functions

Civil functions of the Department of the Army include the administration of Arlington and the U.S. Soldiers' and Airmen's Home National Cemeteries and the Civil Works Program—the Nation's principal Federal water resources development activity involving dams, reservoirs, levees, harbors, waterways, locks, and other engineering structures.

History

This area includes advisory and coordination service provided to the Army Secretariat and staff on all historical matters: the formulation and execution of the Army historical program, the maintenance of the organizational history of Army units, the preparation and publication of histories that the Army requires, and historical properties.

Installations

This area consists of policies, procedures, and resources for the management of installations to ensure the availability of efficient and affordable base services and infrastructure in support of military missions. It includes the identification and validation of resource requirements, the review of facilities requirements and stationing, and program and budget development and justification. Other activities include support for base operations; base realignment and closure; competitive sourcing; energy security and sustainability; environmental programs; housing; military construction; morale, recreation, and welfare; and real property maintenance and repair.

Intelligence

This area includes management of Army intelligence with responsibility for policy formulation, planning, programming, budgeting, evaluation, and oversight of intelligence activities. The Army Staff is responsible for monitoring relevant foreign intelligence developments and foreign disclosure; imagery, signals, human, open-source, measurement, and signatures intelligence; counterintelligence; threat models and simulations; and security countermeasures.

Medical

This area includes management of health services for the Army and as directed for other services, agencies, and organizations;

health standards for Army personnel; health professional education and training; career management authority over commissioned and warrant officer personnel of the Army Medical Department; medical research, materiel development, testing, and evaluation; policies concerning health aspects of Army environmental programs and prevention of disease; and planning, programming, and budgeting for Armywide health services.

Military Operations and Plans

This includes Army forces strategy formation; mid-range, long-range, and regional strategy application; arms control, negotiation, and disarmament; national security affairs; joint service matters; net assessment; politico-military affairs; force mobilization, demobilization, and planning; programming structuring, development, analysis, requirements, and management; operational readiness; overall roles and missions; collective security; individual and unit training; psychological operations; information operations; unconventional warfare; counterterrorism; operations security; signal security; special plans; equipment development and approval; nuclear and chemical matters; civil affairs; military support of civil defense; civil disturbance; domestic actions; command and control; automation and communications programs and activities; management of the program for law enforcement, correction, and crime prevention for military members of the Army; special operations forces; foreign language and distance learning; and physical security.

Reserve Components

This area includes management of individual and unit readiness and mobilization for Reserve Components, which consist of the Army National Guard and U.S. Army Reserve.

Religious

This area includes departmentwide management of religious and moral leadership and chaplain support activities; religious ministrations, religious education, pastoral care, and counseling for Army military personnel; liaison with ecclesiastical agencies; chapel construction requirements and design approval; and career management of clergymen serving in the Chaplains Corps.

ARMY COMMANDS

U.S. Army Forces Command

Headquartered at Fort Bragg, NC, U.S. Army Forces Command (FORSCOM) prepares conventional forces to provide a sustained flow of trained and ready land power to combatant commanders in defense of the Nation at home and abroad.

For further information, contact the FORSCOM Public Affairs Office. Phone, 910-570-7200.

U.S. Army Materiel Command

U.S. Army Materiel Command (AMC) is the Army's premier provider of materiel readiness—technology, acquisition support, materiel development, logistics power projection, and sustainment—to the total force across the spectrum of joint military operations. Headquartered at Redstone Arsenal, Alabama, AMC's missions include the development of weapon systems, advanced research on future technologies, and maintenance and distribution of spare parts and equipment. AMC works closely with program executive offices, industry, academia, and other Military Services and Government agencies to develop, test, and acquire equipment that soldiers and units need to accomplish their missions.

For further information, contact the AMC Public Affairs Office. Phone, 256-450-7978.

U.S. Army Training and Doctrine Command

Headquartered in Fort Eustis, VA, U.S. Army Training and Doctrine Command (TRADOC) develops, educates, and trains soldiers, civilians, and leaders; supports unit training; and designs, builds, and integrates a versatile mix of capabilities, formations, and equipment to strengthen the U.S. Army as a force of decisive action.

For further information, contact the TRADOC Public Affairs Office. Phone, 757-501-5876.

ARMY SERVICE COMPONENT COMMANDS

U.S. Army Africa / Southern European Task Force

U.S. Army Africa (USARAF) / Southern European Task Force (SETAF) is the Army service component command for U.S. Africa Command. It supports U.S. Africa Command operations, employs Army forces as partners, builds sustainable capacity, and supports the joint force to disrupt transnational threats and promote regional security in Africa.

For further information, contact the USARAF / SETAF Public Affairs Office. Phone, 011-39-0444-71-8341 or 8342.

U.S. Army Central

U.S. Army Central (ARCENT) shapes the U.S. Central Command area of responsibility in 20 countries through forward land power presence and security cooperation engagements that ensure access, build partner capacity, and develop relationships. ARCENT also provides flexible options and strategic depth to the U.S. combatant commander and sets the conditions for improved regional security and stability.

For further information, contact the USARCENT Public Affairs Office. Phone, 803-885-8266.

U.S. Army Europe

U.S. Army Europe (USAREUR) provides the principal land component for U.S. European Command throughout a 51-country area. As the U.S. Army's largest forward-deployed expeditionary force, USAREUR supports NATO and U.S. bilateral, multinational, and unilateral objectives. It supports U.S. Army forces in the European Command area; receives and assists in the reception, staging, and onward movement and integration of U.S. forces; establishes, operates, and expands operational lines of communication; ensures regional security, access, and stability through presence and security cooperation; and supports U.S. combatant commanders and joint and combined commanders.

For further information, contact the USAREUR Public Affairs Office. Phone, 011-49-611-143-537-0005 or 0006.

U.S. Army North

U.S. Army North (USARNORTH) supports U.S. Northern Command, the unified command responsible for defending the U.S. homeland and coordinating defense support of civil authorities. USARNORTH helps maintain readiness to support homeland defense, civil support operations, and theater security cooperation activities.

For further information, contact the USARNORTH Public Affairs Office. Phone, 210-221-0015.

U.S. Army South

U.S. Army South (ARSOUTH) is the Army service component command of U.S. Southern Command. ARSOUTH conducts security cooperation and responds to contingencies as part of a whole-of-government approach in conjunction with partner national armies in the U.S. Southern Command area of responsibility, which encompasses 31 countries and 15 areas of special sovereignty in Central and South

America and the Caribbean. These activities counter transnational threats and strengthen regional security in defense of the homeland. ARSOUTH maintains a deployable headquarters at Fort Sam Houston, Texas, where it conducts strategic and operational planning.

For further information, contact the ARSOUTH Public Affairs Office. Phone, 210-295-6739.

U.S. Army Pacific

U.S. Army Pacific (USARPAC) prepares the force for unified land operations, responds to threats, sustains and protects the force, and builds military relationships that develop partner defense capacity to contribute to the stability and security of the U.S. Pacific Command area of responsibility. USARPAC commands soldiers in an area spanning from the Northwest Coast and Alaska to the Asia-Pacific region, including Japan. Since September 11, 2001, USARPAC soldiers have played a vital role in homeland defense for Alaska and Hawaii, Guam, and Japan, as well as in supporting operations with our allies elsewhere in the region.

For further information, contact USARPAC Public Affairs. Phone, 808-438-9761.

U.S. Army Military Surface Deployment and Distribution Command

U.S. Army Military Surface Deployment and Distribution Command (SDDC) delivers world-class, origin-to-destination distribution. It is the Army service component command of the U.S. Transportation Command and a subordinate command to the Army Materiel Command. This relationship links the Transportation Command's joint deployment and distribution enterprise with the Army Materiel Command's materiel enterprise. The SDDC also partners with the commercial transportation industry as the coordinating link between Department of Defense surface transportation requirements and the capability industry provides.

For further information, contact the SDDC Public Affairs Office. Phone, 618-220-6284.

U.S. Army Space and Missile Defense Command / Army Strategic Command

U.S. Army Space and Missile Defense Command (SMDC / ARSTRAT) conducts space and missile defense operations and provides planning, integration, control, and coordination of Army forces and capabilities in support of U.S. Strategic Command missions. SMDC / ARSTRAT also supports space, high-altitude, and global missile defense modernization efforts; serves as the Army operational integrator for global missile defense; and conducts mission-related research and development to support the Army's statutory responsibilities.

For further information, contact the SMDC Public Affairs Office. Phone, 256-955-3887.

U.S. Army Special Operations Command

U.S. Army Special Operations Command (USASOC) administers, deploys, educates, equips, funds, mans, mobilizes, organizes, sustains, and trains Army special operations forces to carry out missions worldwide, as directed. These special and diverse military operations support regional combatant commanders, American ambassadors, and other agencies.

For further information, contact the USASOC Public Affairs Office. Phone, 910-432-6005.

Sources of Information

Business Opportunities

For information on contract procurement policies and procedures, contact the Deputy Assistant Secretary of the Army, Procurement. Phone, 703-695-2488.

Assistance for small businesses and minority educational institutions to increase participation in the Army contracting program is available through the Office of Small Business Programs. Phone, 703-697-2868. Fax, 703-693-3898.

Cemeteries

Arlington National Cemetery is one of the two national military cemeteries that the Army maintains. This cemetery is the final resting place for more than 400,000 active duty servicemembers, veterans, and their families. For more information, visit its Web site or contact the cemetery. Phone, 877-907-8585.

The U.S. Soldiers' and Airmen's Home National Cemetery is one of the two national military cemeteries that the Army maintains. This cemetery is the final resting place for more than 14,000 veterans, including those that fought in the Civil War. For more information, visit its Web site or contact the Superintendent. Phone, 877-907-8585.

Environment

Information is available from the U.S. Army Environmental Command.

Information is also available from the Office of the Deputy Assistant Secretary of the Army for Environment, Safety and Occupational Health.

The Army Environmental Policy Institute posts publications on its Web site. "Army Water Security Strategy" (DEC 2011), the results of the first comprehensive study of Army water security management, is available in Portable Document Format (PDF). "Quantifying the Army Supply Chain Water Bootprint" (DEC 2011), an initial step to quantify the amount of water used by suppliers to produce the goods and services that the Army procures through the supply chain, is also available in PDF.

Employment

More than 330,000 Army civilians work in a wide range of diverse professions. These professionals are not active duty military, but serve as an integral part of the Army team to support the defense of the Nation.

Films

Address loan requests for Army-produced films to the Visual Information Support Centers of Army installations. Unclassified Army productions are available for sale from the National Audiovisual Center, National Technical Information Service, 5301 Shawnee Road, Alexandria, VA 22312. Phone, 800-553-6847.

Freedom of Information Act (FOIA)

Contact the appropriate information management officer associated with the Army installation or activity managing the desired information. Information is also available on the Records Management and Declassification Agency's Web site.

Frequently Asked Questions (FAQs)

The Army posts answers to FAQs on its Web site.

Gold Star Survivors

All Gold Star family members have made a sacrifice to the Nation. The Army recognizes that no one gives more for the Nation than a family member of the fallen. Gold Star Mother's and Family's Day is the last Sunday of September, and Gold Star Spouses Day is April 5.

Historical Resources

"Army History" magazine, the professional bulletin of Army history, is available online in Portable Document Format (PDF).

A directory of Army museums is available on the Center of Military History's Web site.

The Office of Historic Properties and Partnerships raises awareness of and explores and tests creative uses for the Army's historic buildings. Its staff also promotes partnerships between the Army and nonprofit organizations, public or private, to preserve, renovate, and restore.

Joining the Army

Information on Army life, assignments, benefits, pay, and enlisting or joining in other capacities is available online. Phone, 888-550-2769.

National Guard

The National Guard responds to domestic emergencies, counterdrug efforts, overseas combat missions, reconstruction missions, and more. The President or a State governor can call on the Guard in a moment's notice. Guard soldiers hold civilian jobs or attend college while maintaining their military training on a part-time basis, and their primary area of operation is their home state.

Public Affairs / Community Relations

For official Army and community relations information, contact the Office of the Chief of Public Affairs. Phone, 703-695-0616. Automated assistance is available after normal work hours. Phone, 201-590-6575.

Publications

To request a publication, contact either the proponent listed on the title page of the document or the information management officer of the Army activity that publishes the desired publication. If the requester does not know which Army activity published the document, contact the Publishing Division, Army Publishing Directorate. Phone, 703-693-1557.

Official texts published by Headquarters, Department of the Army, are available from the National Technical Information Service. Phone, 888-584-8332.

Ranks

Descriptions of officer, warrant officer, and enlisted ranks are available on the Army Web site.

Reading List

The U.S. Army Chief of Staff's professional reading list comprises three categories—Armies at war: battles and campaigns; the Army profession; and strategy and the strategic environment—and is accessible online.

Research

The Research, Development and Engineering Command is the Army's technology leader and largest technology developer. Its Web site features news on and resources related to long-range research and development plans for materiel requirements and objectives. Phone, 443-395-4006 (Public Affairs) or 3922 (Media Relations).

Reserve Officers' Training Corps (ROTC)

Available at over 1,100 colleges and universities nationwide, the ROTC offers merit-based scholarships that can cover the full cost of tuition and open educational opportunities.

Site Index

The Army's Web site features an A–Z index.

Specialized Careers

Information on how to become an Army chaplain, the chaplain candidate program, and chaplain corps careers and jobs is available online and from the U.S. Army Recruiting Command. Phone, 877-437-6572.

Health care professionals serving as officers in the Army's medical department benefit from a wide range of opportunities and financial incentives.

Members of the Army Judge Advocate General's corps often represent soldiers during courts-martial; however, they also engage in a wider range of legal activities that include civil litigation, international law, labor law, and tort claims. For more information, contact the Army Judge Advocate Recruiting Office. Phone, 866-276-9524.

The Army relies on talented musicians to assist with military ceremonies, boost morale, and provide entertainment.

Speakers

The Public Affairs Office nearest the event can help provide local Army speakers. The Office of the Chief of Public Affairs can assist with scheduling a general officer to address Army matters at public forums. To request a general officer speaker, writer to the Office of the Chief of Public Affairs, ATTN: Community Relations, Division (Speaker Request), 1500 Army Pentagon, Washington, DC 20310-1500. A lead time of at least 60–90 days is required. Phone, 703-614-1107.

U. S. Military Academy

West Point has been educating, training, and inspiring U.S. Army leaders for more than 200 years. The academy offers a 47-month leader-development program of academic rigor, military discipline, and physical challenges with adherence to a code of honor.

For further information concerning the Department of the Army, contact U.S. Army Public Affairs, Community Relations Division, Office of the Chief of Public Affairs, 1500 Army Pentagon, Washington, DC 20310-1500.

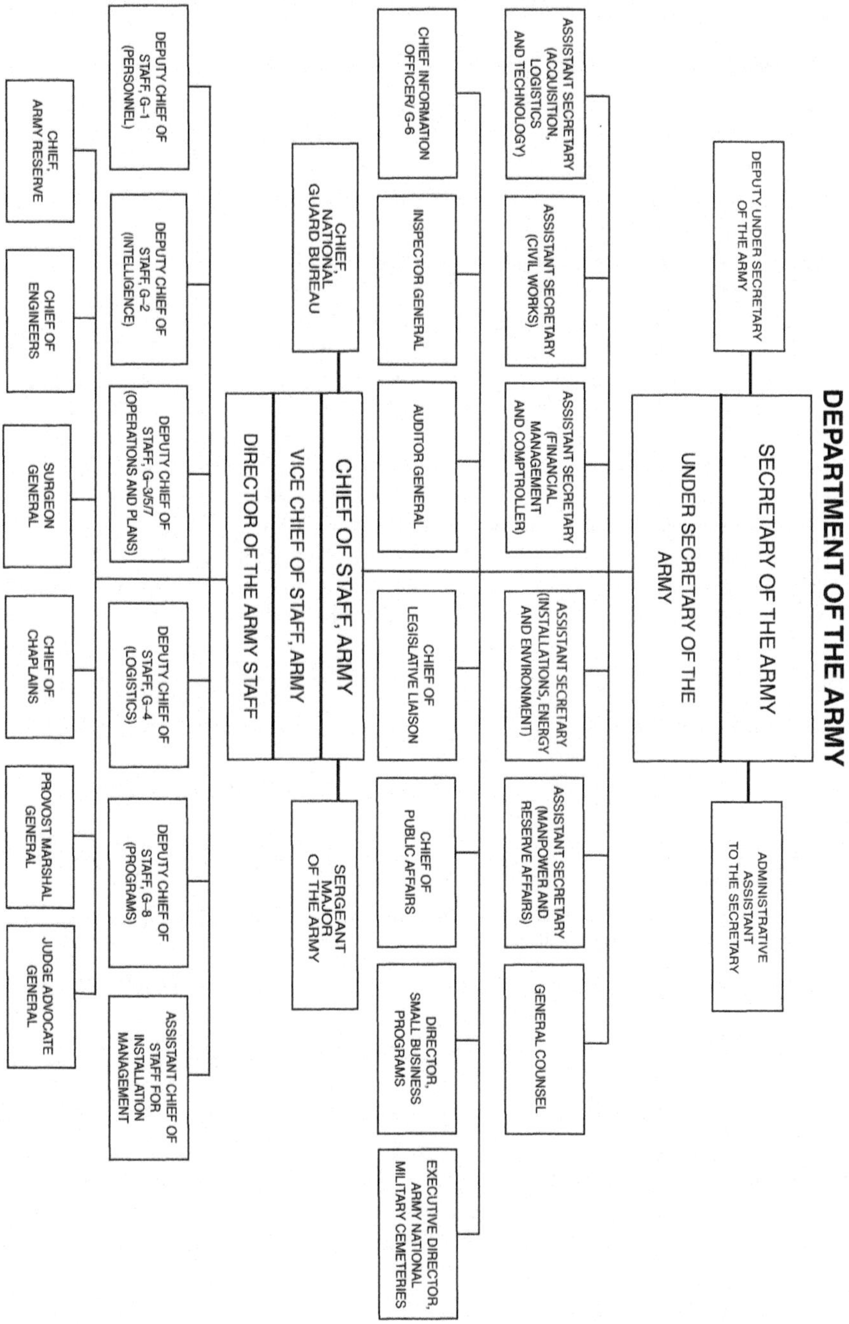
DEPARTMENT OF THE ARMY
SECRETARY OF THE ARMY
UNDER SECRETARY OF THE ARMY
DEPUTY UNDER SECRETARY OF THE ARMY
ADMINISTRATIVE ASSISTANT TO THE SECRETARY
ASSISTANT SECRETARY (ACQUISITION, LOGISTICS AND TECHNOLOGY)
ASSISTANT SECRETARY (CIVIL WORKS)
ASSISTANT SECRETARY (FINANCIAL MANAGEMENT AND COMPTROLLER)
ASSISTANT SECRETARY (INSTALLATIONS, ENERGY AND ENVIRONMENT)
ASSISTANT SECRETARY (MANPOWER AND RESERVE AFFAIRS)
GENERAL COUNSEL
CHIEF INFORMATION OFFICER/ G-6
INSPECTOR GENERAL
AUDITOR GENERAL
CHIEF OF LEGISLATIVE LIAISON
CHIEF OF PUBLIC AFFAIRS
DIRECTOR, SMALL BUSINESS PROGRAMS
EXECUTIVE DIRECTOR, ARMY NATIONAL MILITARY CEMETERIES
CHIEF, NATIONAL GUARD BUREAU
CHIEF OF STAFF, ARMY
VICE CHIEF OF STAFF, ARMY
DIRECTOR OF THE ARMY STAFF
SERGEANT MAJOR OF THE ARMY
DEPUTY CHIEF OF STAFF, G–1 (PERSONNEL)
DEPUTY CHIEF OF STAFF, G–2 (INTELLIGENCE)
DEPUTY CHIEF OF STAFF, G–3/5/7 (OPERATIONS AND PLANS)
DEPUTY CHIEF OF STAFF, G–4 (LOGISTICS)
DEPUTY CHIEF OF STAFF, G–8 (PROGRAMS)
ASSISTANT CHIEF OF STAFF FOR INSTALLATION MANAGEMENT
CHIEF, ARMY RESERVE
CHIEF OF ENGINEERS
SURGEON GENERAL
CHIEF OF CHAPLAINS
PROVOST MARSHAL GENERAL
JUDGE ADVOCATE GENERAL

Department of the Navy

The Pentagon, Washington, DC 20350, 703-697-7391, *http://www.navy.mil*

SECRETARY OF THE NAVY	Raymond E. Mabus
Under Secretary of the Navy	Janine Davidson
ASSISTANT SECRETARIES	
Energy, Installations and Environment	Dennis V. McGinn
Financial Management / Comptroller	Susan J. Rabern
Manpower and Reserve Affairs	Franklin Parker
Research, Development and Acquisition	Sean J. Stackley
Auditor General	Luther Bragg
Chief Information Officer	Robert Frost
Chief of Information	Rear Adm. Dawn Cutler, USN, Acting
Chief of Legislative Affairs	Rear Adm. Craig S. Faller, USN
Chief of Naval Research	Rear Adm. Mathias W. Winter, USN
Director, Naval Criminal Investigative Service	Andrew L. Traver
General Counsel	Paul L. Oostburg Sanz
Judge Advocate General	Vice Adm. James W. Crawford III, JAGC, USN
Naval Inspector General	Vice Adm. Herman Shelanski, USN

NAVAL OPERATIONS

Chief of Naval Operations	Adm. John M. Richardson, USN
Vice Chief of Naval Operations	Adm. William F. Moran, USN
DEPUTY CHIEFS OF NAVAL OPERATIONS	
Fleet Readiness and Logistics	Vice Adm. Philip H. Cullom, USN
Information Dominance	Vice Adm. Ted N. Branch, USN
Integration of Capabilities and Resources	Vice Adm. Joseph P. Mulloy, USN
Manpower, Personnel, Training Education	Vice Adm. Robert P. Burke, USN
Operations, Plans and Strategy	Vice Adm. John C. Aquilino, USN
DIRECTORS	
Naval Intelligence	Vice Adm. Ted N. Branch, USN
Naval Nuclear Propulsion Program	Adm. James F. Caldwell, USN
Navy Staff	(vacancy)
Test and Evaluation and Technology Requirements / Chief of Naval Research	Rear Adm. Mathias W. Winter, USN
Chief of Chaplains of the Navy	Rear Adm. Margaret G. Kibben, USN
Chief of Naval Reserve	Vice Adm. Robin R. Braun, USN
Master Chief Petty Officer of the Navy	Michael D. Stevens, USN
Oceanographer of the Navy / Navigator of the Navy	Rear Adm. Timothy C. Gallaudet, USN
Surgeon General of the Navy	Vice Adm. C. Forrest Faison III, USN

SHORE ESTABLISHMENT

Chief of Naval Operations	Adm. John M. Richardson, USN
COMMANDERS	
Naval Air Systems Command	Vice Adm. David Dunaway, USN
Naval Education and Training Command	Rear Adm. Michael S. White, USN
Naval Facilities Engineering Command	Rear Adm. Kate L. Gregory, USN
Naval Legal Service Command	Rear Adm. John G. Hannink, JAGC, USN
Naval Meteorology and Oceanography	Rear Adm. Brian Brown, USN
Naval Network Warfare Command	Capt. John W. Chandler, USN
Naval Sea Systems Command	Vice Adm. William H. Hilarides, USN
Naval Supply Systems Command	Rear Adm. Jonathan A. Yuen, SC, USN
Naval Warfare Development Command	Rear Adm. Scott B.J. Jerabek, USNR
Navy Installations Command	Vice Adm. Dixon Smith, USN
Space and Naval Warfare Systems Command	Rear Adm. David H. Lewis, USN
Chief, Bureau of Medicine and Surgery	Vice Adm. C. Forrest Faison III
Chief, Naval Personnel	Vice Adm. Robert P. Burke, USN
Director, National Maritime Intelligence-Integration Office / Commander, Office of Naval Intelligence	Rear Adm. Elizabeth L. Train, USN
Director, Strategic Systems Program	Rear Adm. Terry J. Benedict, USN
Superintendent, U.S. Naval Academy	Vice Adm. Michael H. Miller, USN

OPERATING FORCES

COMMANDERS	
U.S. Fleet Forces Command	Adm. Philip S. Davidson, USN
Pacific Fleet	Adm. Scott H. Swift, USN
Military Sealift Command	Rear Adm. Thomas K. Shannon, USN
Naval Forces Central Command	Vice Adm. John W. Miller, USN
Naval Forces Europe	Adm. Bruce W. Clingan, USN
Naval Reserve Forces Command	Rear Adm. Bryan Cutchen, USN
Naval Special Warfare Command	Rear Adm. Brian L. Losey, USN
Operational Test and Evaluation Force	Rear Adm. Jeffrey R. Penfield, USN

[For the Department of the Navy statement of organization, see the Code of Federal Regulations, Title 32, Part 700]

The Department of the Navy protects the United States and its interests by the prosecution of war at sea, including the seizure or defense of advanced naval bases with the assistance of its Marine Corps component; supports the forces of all military departments of the United States; and safeguards freedom of the seas.

The United States Navy was founded on October 13, 1775, when Congress enacted the first legislation creating the Continental Navy of the American Revolution. The Department of the Navy and the Office of Secretary of the Navy were established by act of April 30, 1798 (10 U.S.C. 5011, 5031). For 9 years prior to that date, by act of August 7, 1789 (1 Stat. 49), the Secretary of War oversaw the conduct of naval affairs.

The National Security Act Amendments of 1949 provided that the Department of the Navy be a military department within the Department of Defense (63 Stat. 578).

The President appoints the Secretary of the Navy as the head of the Department of the Navy. The Secretary is responsible to the Secretary of Defense for the operation and efficiency of the Navy (10 U.S.C. 5031). The Department of the Navy includes the U.S. Coast Guard when it is operating as a Service in the Navy.

Secretary

The Secretary of the Navy is the head of the Department of the Navy, responsible for the policies and control of the Department of the Navy, including its organization, administration, functioning, and efficiency. The members of the Secretary's executive administration assist in the discharge of the responsibilities of the Secretary of the Navy.

Legal

The Office of the Judge Advocate General provides all legal advice and related services throughout the Department of the Navy, except for the advice and services provided by the General Counsel. It also provides legal and policy advice to the Secretary of the Navy on military justice, ethics, administrative law, claims, environmental law, operational and international law and treaty interpretation, and litigation involving these issues. The Judge Advocate General provides technical supervision for the Naval Justice School at Newport, RI.

For further information, contact the Office of the Judge Advocate General, Department of the Navy, Washington Navy Yard, Suite 3000, 1322 Patterson Avenue SE., Washington Navy Yard, DC 20374-5066. Phone, 202-685-5190.

Criminal Investigations

The Naval Criminal Investigative Service investigates and neutralizes criminal, terrorist, and foreign intelligence threats to the United States Navy and Marine Corps. To carry out its mission, the Service relies on the professionalism and law enforcement expertise of administrative support personnel, forensic specialists, intelligence analysts, investigators, military personnel, security specialists, special agents, and technical investigative specialists.

For further information, contact the Naval Criminal Investigative Service, 27130 Telegraph Road, Quantico, VA 22134. Phone, 877-579-3648.

Research

The Office of Naval Research initiates, coordinates, plans, and promotes naval research, including the coordination of research and development conducted by other agencies and offices in the Department of the Navy. The Office researches, develops, and delivers decisive naval capabilities by investing in a balanced portfolio of promising scientific research, innovative technology, and talent. It also manages and controls activities within the Department concerning copyrights, inventions, manufacturing technology, patents, royalty payments, small businesses, and trademarks.

For further information, contact the Public Affairs Office, Office of Naval Research, One Liberty Center, 875 North Randolph Street, Arlington, VA 22203-1995. Phone, 703-696-5031.

Operating Forces

Operating forces carry out operations that enable the Navy to meet its responsibility to uphold and advance the national policies and interests of the United States. These forces include the several fleets; seagoing, fleet marine, and other assigned Marine Corps forces; the Military Sealift Command; Naval Reserve forces; and other forces and activities that the President or the Secretary of the Navy may assign. The Chief of Naval Operations administers and commands the operating forces of the Navy.

The Atlantic Fleet is composed of ships, submarines, and aircraft that operate throughout the Atlantic Ocean and Mediterranean Sea.

The Naval Forces Europe includes forces assigned by the Chief of Naval Operations or made available from either the Pacific or Atlantic Fleet to operate in the European theater.

The Pacific Fleet is composed of ships, submarines, and aircraft operating throughout the Pacific and Indian Oceans.

The Military Sealift Command provides ocean transportation for personnel and cargo of all components of the Department of Defense and, as authorized, for other Federal agencies; operates and maintains underway replenishment ships and other vessels providing mobile logistic support to elements of the combatant fleets; and operates ships in support of scientific projects and other programs for Federal agencies.

Other major commands of the operating forces of the Navy are the Naval Forces Central Command, Operational Test and Evaluation Force, Naval Special Warfare Command, and Naval Reserve Force.

Activities

Air Systems

The Naval Air Systems Command provides full life-cycle support of naval aviation aircraft, weapons, and systems operated by Sailors and Marines. This support includes research, design, development, and systems engineering; acquisition; test and evaluation; training facilities and equipment; repair and modification; and in-service engineering and logistics support. The Command comprises eight "competencies" or communities of practice: program management, contracts, research and engineering, test and evaluation, logistics and industrial operations, corporate operations, comptroller, and counsel. The Command also supports the affiliated naval aviation program executive officer and the assigned program managers, who are responsible for meeting the cost, schedule, and performance requirements of their assigned programs. It is the principal provider for the Naval Aviation Enterprise, while contributing to every warfare enterprise in the interest of national security.

For further information, contact the Commander, Naval Air Systems Command, 47123 Buse Road, Building 2272, Suite 540, Patuxent River, MD 20670-1547. Phone, 301-757-7825.

Coast Guard

The Commandant of the Coast Guard reports to the Secretary of the Navy and the Chief of Naval Operations when the Coast Guard is operating as a service in the Navy and represents the Coast Guard before the Joint Chiefs of Staff. During such service, Coast Guard operations are integrated and uniform with Department of the Navy operations to the maximum extent possible. The Commandant of the Coast Guard organizes, trains, prepares, and maintains the readiness of the Coast Guard for the performance of national defense missions as directed. The Commandant also maintains a security capability; enforces Federal laws and regulations on and under the high seas and waters subject to the jurisdiction of the United States; and develops, establishes, maintains, and operates aids to maritime navigation, as well as ice-breaking and rescue facilities, with due regard to the requirements of national defense.

Computers and Telecommunications

Naval Network Warfare Command operates the Navy's networks to achieve effective command and control through optimal alignment, common architecture, mature processes, and functions and standard terminology. The command enhances the Navy's network security posture and improves IT services through standardized enterprise-level management, network information assurance compliance, enterprise management, and root cause and trend analysis. Naval Network Warfare Command also delivers enhanced space products to operating forces by leveraging Department of Defense, national, commercial, and international space capabilities. The command serves as the Navy's commercial satellite operations manager; it executes tactical-level command and control of Navy networks and leverages Joint Space capabilities for Navy and Joint Operations.

For further information, contact Public Affairs, Naval Network Warfare Command, 112 Lake View Parkway, Suffolk, VA 23435. Phone, 757-203-0205.

Education and Training

The Naval Education and Training Command provides shore-based education and training for Navy, certain Marine Corps, and other personnel; develops specifically designated education and training afloat programs for the fleet; provides voluntary and dependents education; and participates with research and development activities in the development and implementation of the most effective teaching and training systems and devices for optimal education and training.

For further information, contact the NETC Office of Public Affairs, 250 Dallas Street, Pensacola, FL 32508-5220. Phone, 850-452-4858.

Facilities

The Naval Facilities Engineering Command provides material and technical support to the Navy and Marine Corps for shore facilities, real property and utilities, fixed ocean systems and structures, transportation and construction equipment, energy, environmental and natural resources management, and support of the naval construction forces.

For further information, contact the Commander, Naval Facilities Engineering Command and Chief of Civil Engineers, Washington Navy Yard, 1322 Patterson Avenue SE., Suite 1000, Washington, DC 20374-5065. Phone, 202-685-1423.

Intelligence

The Office of Naval Intelligence ensures the fulfillment of the intelligence requirements and responsibilities of the Department of the Navy.

For further information, contact the Office of Public Affairs, Office of Naval Intelligence, Department of the Navy, 4251 Suitland Road, Washington, DC 20395-5720. Phone, 301-669-5670.

Manpower

The Bureau of Naval Personnel directs the procurement, distribution, administration, and career motivation of the military personnel of the regular and reserve components of the U.S. Navy to meet the quantitative and qualitative manpower requirements determined by the Chief of Naval Operations.

For further information, contact the Bureau of Naval Personnel, Department of the Navy, Federal Office Building 2, Washington, DC 20370-5000. Phone, 703-614-2000.

Medicine

The Bureau of Medicine and Surgery directs the medical and dental services for Navy and Marine Corps personnel and their dependents; administers the implementation of contingency support plans and programs to effect medical and dental readiness capability; provides medical and dental services to the fleet, fleet marine force, and shore activities of the Navy; and ensures cooperation with civil authorities in matters of public health disasters and other emergencies.

For further information, contact the Bureau of Medicine and Surgery, Department of the Navy, 2300 E Street NW., Washington, DC 20373-5300. Phone, 202-762-3211.

Oceanography

The Naval Meteorology and Oceanography Command and the Naval Observatory are responsible for the science, technology, and engineering operations that are essential to explore the ocean and the atmosphere and to provide astronomical data and time for naval and related national objectives. To that end, the naval oceanographic program studies astrometry, hydrography, meteorology, oceanography, and precise time.

For further information, contact the Commander, Naval Meteorology and Oceanography Command, 1100 Balch Boulevard, Stennis Space Center, MS 39529-5005. Phone, 228-688-4384. Internet, http://www.navmetoccom.navy.mil. Or, contact the Oceanographer of the Navy, U.S. Naval Observatory, 3450 Massachusetts Avenue NW., Washington, DC 20392-1800. Phone, 202-762-1026.

Sea Systems

The Naval Sea Systems Command provides material support to the Navy and Marine Corps and to the Departments of Defense and Transportation for ships, submarines, and other sea platforms, shipboard combat systems and components, other surface and undersea warfare and weapons systems, and ordnance expendables not specifically assigned to other system commands.

For further information, contact the Office of Public Affairs, Naval Sea Systems Command, 1333 Isaac Hull Avenue SE., Washington Navy Yard, DC 20376-1010. Phone, 202-781-4123.

Space and Naval Warfare

The Space and Naval Warfare Systems Command develops, delivers, and sustains advanced cyber capabilities for naval warfighters. It helps provide the hardware and software needed to executive Navy missions. With nearly 10,000 active military and civilian professionals worldwide, the Command is at the forefront of research, engineering, and acquisition relevant for keeping U.S. military forces connected around the globe.

For further information, contact the Commander, Space and Naval Warfare Systems Command, 4301 Pacific Highway, San Diego, CA 92110-3127. Phone, 619-524-3428.

Strategic Systems

The Office of Strategic Systems Programs provides development, production, and material support to the Navy for fleet ballistic missile and strategic weapons systems, security, training of personnel, and the installation and direction of necessary supporting facilities.

For further information, contact the Director, Strategic Systems Programs, Department of the Navy, Nebraska Avenue Complex, 287 Somers Court NW., Suite 10041, Washington, DC 20393-5446. Phone, 202-764-1608.

Supply Systems

The Naval Supply Systems Command provides supply management policies and methods and administers related support service systems for the Navy and Marine Corps.

For further information, contact the Commander, Naval Supply Systems Command, 5450 Carlisle Pike, P.O. Box 2050, Mechanicsburg, PA 17055-0791. Phone, 717-605-3565.

Warfare Development

The Navy Warfare Development Command plans and coordinates experiments employing emerging operational concepts; represents the Department of the Navy in joint and other service laboratories and facilities and tactical development commands; and publishes and disseminates naval doctrine.

For further information, contact the Commander, Navy Warfare Development Command, 686 Cushing Road, Sims Hall, Newport, RI 02841. Phone, 401-841-2833.

Sources of Information

Business Opportunities

"Open for Business," a short video that gives an overview of the Navy's buying activities and small business programs, is available online. For more information, contact the Office of Small Business Programs. Phone, 202-685-6485.

Civilian Employment

The possibilities of a civilian career at the Department of the Navy are many and diverse. They include a full range of occupations: from aircraft mechanic to pipefitter, from electrician to engineer, from zoologist to physician, and more. The Navy offers hundreds of different occupations nationwide and around the world.

Environment

For information on Navy and Marine Corps environmental protection and natural resources management programs, contact the Deputy Assistant Secretary–Environment, 1000 Navy Pentagon, Room 4A674, Washington, DC 20350-1000. Phone, 703-614-5493.

The "U.S. Navy Climate Change Roadmap" (April 2010) is available in Portable Document Format (PDF) online.

The Navy has posted its environmental goals and descriptions of its strategies to achieve them.

Glossary

The origins of Navy terminology section explains nautical terminology that has become a part of everyday English.

Joining the Navy

Unparalleled opportunities, challenges, and experiences motivate bright and skilled people to join. America's Navy offers careers and jobs that match many backgrounds and interests. Hundreds of distinct roles in dozens of professional fields are part of what the Navy has to offer.

Naval Oceanography Portal

The U.S. Naval Meteorology and Oceanography Command provides information from the ocean depths to the distant reaches of space to meet the needs of civilian and the military and scientific communities.

The U.S. Naval Observatory offers a wide range of astronomical data and products, and it serves as the official source of time for the Department of Defense and as the official source of a standard of time for the entire United States.

"The Sky This Week" is a weekly set of pictures and descriptions of the planets, sky, and stars.

News

The Navy posts recent headline news stories on its Web site.

An online subscription form is available to sign up for updates from the Navy news service.

"All Hands" magazine is an electronic publication for sailors by sailors. It features articles, imagery, information, and videos that are relevant to sailors and their families.

Research Programs

Research programs of the Office of Naval Research cover a broad spectrum of scientific fields. The research is primarily for the needs of the Navy and Marine Corps, but some of these programs conduct research that has relevance for the general public. For information on specific research programs, contact the Office of Naval Research–Public Affairs, One Liberty Center 875 N. Randolph Street, Arlington, VA 22203-1995. Phone, 703-696-5031.

Ships

The Navy operates and relies on many types of ships to carry out its mission. Descriptions of these different ships—aircraft carriers, amphibious assault ships, cruisers, destroyers, littoral combat ships, and submarines—are available online.

Site Index

An A–Z information index is available on the Navy's Web site.

For further information concerning the Navy, contact the Office of Information, Department of the Navy, 1200 Navy Pentagon, Washington, DC 20350-1200. For press inquiries, phone 703-697-7391 or 703-697-5342.

United States Marine Corps

Commandant of the Marine Corps, Headquarters, U.S. Marine Corps, 3000 Pentagon, Washington, DC 20380-1775, 703-614-2500, *http://www.marines.mil*

COMMANDANT OF THE MARINE CORPS	Gen. Robert B. Neller, USMC
Assistant Commandant of the Marine Corps	Gen. Glenn M. Walters, USMC
Sergeant Major of the Marine Corps	Sgt. Maj. Ronald L. Green, USMC

The Continental Congress established the United States Marine Corps by resolution on November 10, 1775. Marine Corps composition and functions are detailed in 10 U.S.C. 5063.

The Marine Corps, which is part of the Department of the Navy, is the smallest of the Nation's combat forces. It also is the only service that the Congress has tasked specifically to be able to fight in the air, on land, and at sea. Although Marines fight in each of these dimensions, they are primarily a maritime force linked with the Navy, moving from the sea to fight on land.

The Marine Corps conducts entry-level training for its enlisted marines at two bases: Marine Corps Recruit Depot, Parris Island, SC; and Marine Corps Recruit Depot, San Diego, CA. Officer candidates are evaluated at Officer Candidate School, Marine Corps Combat Development Command, Quantico, VA. Marines train to be first on the scene to respond to attacks on the United States or its interests and to acts of political violence against Americans abroad, to provide disaster relief and humanitarian assistance, and to evacuate Americans from foreign countries.

Sources of Information

DSTRESS Line

The DSTRESS Line offers an around-the-clock anonymous phone, live chat, and referral service. The call center is staffed with veteran Marines, Fleet Marine Force Navy Corpsmen who were previously attached to the Marine Corps, Marine spouses and other family members, and licensed behavioral health counselors trained in Marine Corps culture. DSTRESS Line is designed to help callers improve overall fitness and to develop the necessary skills for coping with the challenges of life in the Marine Corps. Phone, 877-476-7734.

Electronic Publications

Authentic and current digital versions of publications issued by Headquarters Marine Corps staff agencies, major commands, and other Department of Defense and Federal agencies are available online.

Freedom of Information Act (FOIA)

Procedures for requesting records that the U.S. Marine Corps controls are available online. Phone, 703-614-4008.

Marine Corps Bands

Marine Corps bands perform at ceremonies, concerts, festivals, parades, professional sporting events, and other public events. Marine Corps bands perform six types of ensembles: brass/woodwind quintet, bugler, ceremonial band, concert band, jazz combo, and jazz/show band. Phone, 504-697-8184.

News

The Marine Corps posts press releases on its Web site.

Marines TV is accessible via the Marine Corps Web site.

Reading List

The Commandant's professional reading list is available online.

Sexual Assault

The Marine Corps' Sexual Assault Prevention and Response program lowers the incidence of sexual assault through preventative strategies and provides care to victims of the crime.

The Safe Helpline provides anonymous and confidential support for sexual assault survivors in the military. Phone, 877-995-5247.

Silent Drill Platoon

The Marine Corps Silent Drill Platoon is a 24-Marine rifle platoon that performs a precision drill exhibition. This disciplined platoon exemplifies the professionalism associated with the U.S. Marine Corps. It first performed in the Sunset Parades of 1948 and received such a favorable response that it became a regular part of the parades at Marine Barracks, Washington, DC. Performance requests for the Silent Drill Platoon should be made 30–90 days prior to the event. Phone, 504-697-8184.

Site Map

The Web site map allows visitors to look for specific topics or to browse for content that aligns with their interests.

Social Media

The Marine Corps maintains a social media presence and supports online communities where people can go to share and collect information and stories.

Speakers

The Marine Corps supports speaking engagements for community events nationwide, ranging from small-town civic organizations to big-city national conventions. The Marine Corps In the Community program helps business executives, educators, members of civic organizations, conference organizers, and others make contact with a Marine Corps public speaker. Phone, 504-697-8184.

Tattoo Regulations

The Marine Corps tattoo policy seeks to balance personal taste with the high standards of professional military appearance and heritage. The Marine Corps Bulletin 1020 (June 2016) explains the current tattoo policy, which replaces previous guidance on the subject.

Unit Directory

A complete list of Marine Corps units with links to their respective web pages is available online.

For further information regarding the Marine Corps, contact the Director of Public Affairs, Headquarters, U.S. Marine Corps, 2 Navy Annex–Pentagon 5D773, Washington, DC 20380-1775. Phone, 703-614-1492.

United States Naval Academy

Annapolis, MD 21402-5018, 410-293-1500, *http://www.usna.edu*

SUPERINTENDENT	Vice Adm. Michael H. Miller, USN
Commandant of Midshipmen	Capt. Robert E. Clark II, USN

The U.S. Naval Academy is the undergraduate college of the Naval Service. Through its comprehensive 4-year program, which stresses excellence in academics, physical education, professional training, conduct, and honor, the Academy prepares young men and women morally, mentally, and physically to be professional officers in the Navy and Marine Corps. All graduates receive a Bachelor of Science degree in 1 of 19 majors.

Sources of Information

Armel-Leftwich Visitor Center

From March to December, the visitor center is open daily, 9 a.m.–5 p.m. During January and February, the visitor center is open on weekdays, 9 a.m.–4 p.m. The gift shop, however, is open on the weekends, 9 a.m.–5 p.m.

Employment

Six sources of employment are associated with the Naval Academy and its supporting organizations.

Naval Academy Preparatory School

The Naval Academy Preparatory School prepares midshipman candidates for success at the U.S. Naval Academy. The 10-month course of instruction, August–May, centers on preparation in Chemistry, English Composition, Information Technology, Mathematics, and Physics. Phone, 401-841-6966 (administration). Phone, 401-841-2947 (academics).

Naval Academy Store

All Profits support the brigade of midshipmen.

Nimitz Library

An online tool is available to search the library's collection of articles, books, ebooks, and journals. Phone, 410-293-6945.

Site Index

An A–Z site index is available on the Naval Academy's Web site.

For further information concerning the U.S. Naval Academy, contact the Superintendent, U.S. Naval Academy, 121 Blake Road, Annapolis, MD 21402-5018.

DEPARTMENT OF THE NAVY

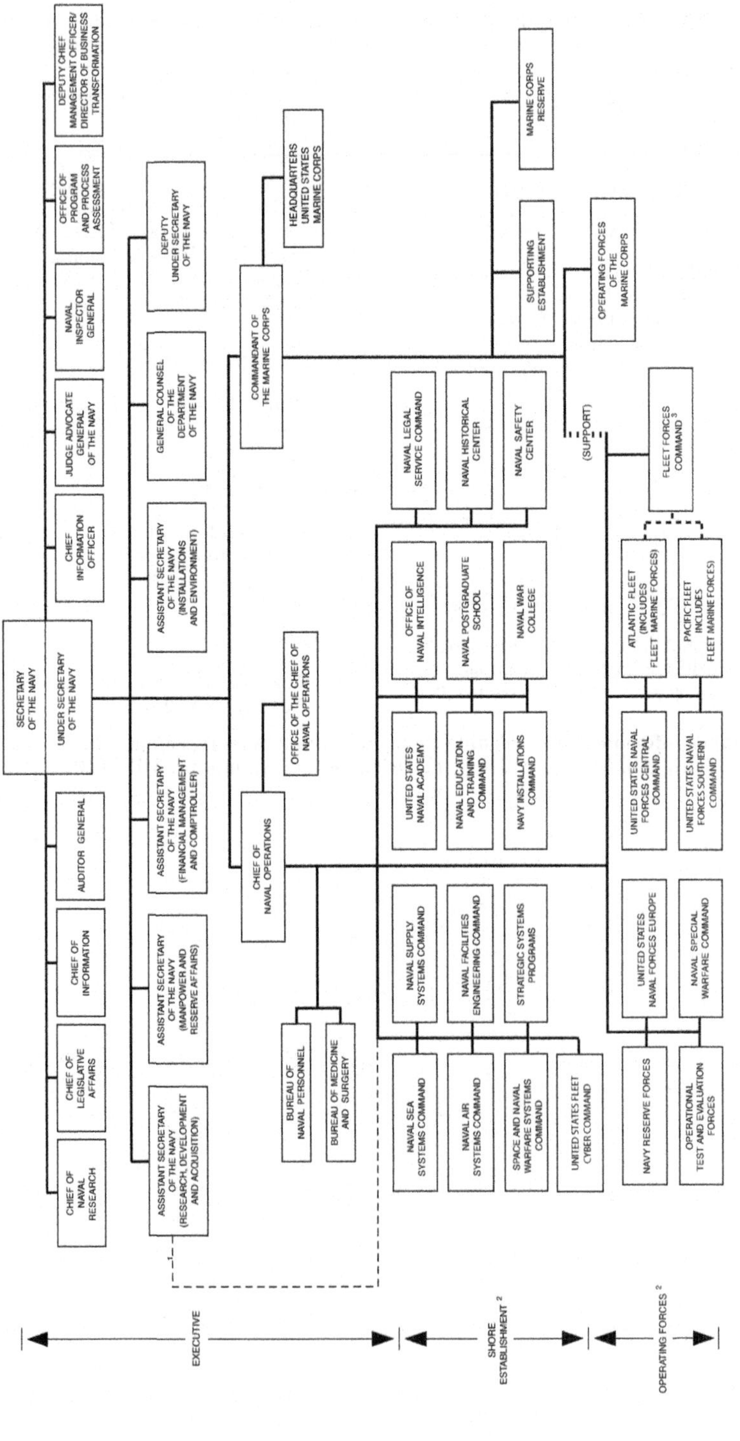

1 Systems commands and SSP report to ASN (RDA) for acquisition matters only.
2 Also includes other Echelon 2 commands and subordinate activities under the command or supervision of the designated organizations.
3 For Interdeployment Training Cycle purposes. Commander, Fleet Forces Command Controls LANFLT and PACFLT assets.

Defense Agencies

Defense Advanced Research Projects Agency

675 North Randolph Street, Arlington, VA 22203-2114, 703-526-6630, *http://www.darpa.mil*

DIRECTOR	Arati Prabhakar
Deputy Director	Steven H. Walker

The Defense Advanced Research Projects Agency is a separately organized agency within the Department of Defense and is under the authority, direction, and control of the Under Secretary of Defense (Acquisition, Technology and Logistics). The Agency serves as the central research and development organization of the Department of Defense with a primary responsibility to maintain U.S. technological superiority over potential adversaries. It pursues imaginative and innovative research and development projects, and conducts demonstration projects that represent technology appropriate for joint programs, programs in support of deployed forces, or selected programs of the military departments. To this end, the Agency arranges, manages, and directs the performance of work connected with assigned advanced projects by the military departments, other Government agencies, individuals, private business entities, and educational or research institutions, as appropriate.

For further information, contact the Defense Advanced Research Projects Agency, 675 North Randolph Street, Arlington, VA 22203-2114. Phone, 703-526-6630.

Defense Commissary Agency

1300 E Avenue, Fort Lee, VA 23801-1800, 804-734-8720, *http://www.commissaries.com*

DIRECTOR / CHIEF EXECUTIVE OFFICER	Joseph H. Jeu
Deputy Director / Chief Operating Officer	Michael J. Dowling

The Defense Commissary Agency (DeCA) was established in 1990 and is under the authority, direction, and control of the Under Secretary of Defense for Personnel and Readiness and the operational supervision of the Defense Commissary Agency Board of Directors.

DeCA provides an efficient and effective worldwide system of commissaries that sell quality groceries and household supplies at low prices to members of the Armed Services community. This benefit satisfies customer demand for quality products and delivers exceptional savings while enhancing the military community's quality of life. DeCA works closely with its employees, customers, and civilian business partners to satisfy its customers and to promote the commissary benefit. The benefit fosters recruitment, retention, and readiness of skilled and trained personnel.

Sources of Information

Employment information is available at www.commissaries.com or by calling the following telephone numbers: employment (703-603-1600); small business activities (804-734-8000, extension 4-8015/4-8529); contracting for resale items (804-734-8000, extension 4-8884/4-8885); and contracting for operations support and equipment (804-734-8000, extension 4-8391/4-8830).

For further information, contact the Defense Commissary Agency, 1300 E Avenue,

Fort Lee, VA 23801-1800. Phone, 804-734-8720

Defense Contract Audit Agency

8725 John J. Kingman Road, Suite 2135, Fort Belvoir, VA 22060-6219, 703-767-3265, http://www.dcaa.mil| Email: dcaaweb@dcaa.mil

DIRECTOR	Anita F. Bales
Deputy Director	Kenneth J. Saccoccia

The Defense Contract Audit Agency (DCAA) was established in 1965 and is under the authority, direction, and control of the Under Secretary of Defense (Comptroller)/Chief Financial Officer. DCAA performs all necessary contract audit functions for DOD and provides accounting and financial advisory services to all Defense components responsible for procurement and contract administration. These services are provided in connection with the negotiation, administration, and settlement of contracts and subcontracts to ensure taxpayer dollars are spent on fair and reasonable contract prices. They include evaluating the acceptability of costs claimed or proposed by contractors and reviewing the efficiency and economy of contractor operations. Other Government agencies may request the DCAA's services under appropriate arrangements.

DCAA manages its operations through five regional offices responsible for approximately 104 field audit offices throughout the United States and overseas. Each region is responsible for the contract auditing function in its assigned area. Point of contact information for DCAA regional offices is available at www.dcaa.mil.

For further information, contact the Executive Officer, Defense Contract Audit Agency, 8725 John J. Kingman Road, Suite 2135, Fort Belvoir, VA 22060-6219. Phone, 703-767-3265.

Defense Contract Management Agency

3901 A Avenue, Fort Lee, VA 23801, 703-428-1700, http://www.dcma.mil

DIRECTOR	Lt. Gen. Wendy M. Masiello, USAF
Deputy Director	James M. Russell

The Defense Contract Management Agency (DCMA) was established by the Deputy Secretary of Defense in 2000 and is under the authority, direction, and control of the Under Secretary of Defense (Acquisition, Technology, and Logistics). DCMA is responsible for DOD contract management in support of the military departments, other DOD components, the National Aeronautics and Space Administration, other designated Federal and State agencies, foreign governments, and international organizations, as appropriate.

For further information, contact the Public Affairs Office, Defense Contract Management Agency, 3901 A Avenue, Fort Lee, VA 23801. Phone, 703-428-1700.

Defense Finance and Accounting Service

4800 Mark Center Drive, Suite 08J25-01, Alexandria, VA 22350-3000, 571-372-7883, http://www.dfas.mil

DIRECTOR	Teresa A. McKay

Principal Deputy Director	Audrey Y. Davis

The Defense Finance and Accounting Service (DFAS) was established in 1991 under the authority, direction, and control of the Under Secretary of Defense (Comptroller)/Chief Financial Officer to strengthen and reduce costs of financial management and operations within DOD. DFAS is responsible for all payments to servicemembers, employees, vendors, and contractors. It provides business intelligence and finance and accounting information to DOD decisionmakers. DFAS is also responsible for preparing annual financial statements and the consolidation, standardization, and modernization of finance and accounting requirements, functions, processes, operations, and systems for DOD.

For further information, contact Defense Finance and Accounting Service Corporate Communications, 4800 Mark Center Drive, Suite 08J25-01, Alexandria, VA 22350-3000. Phone, 571-372-7883.

Defense Information Systems Agency

P.O. Box 549, Command Building, Fort Meade, MD 20755, 301-225-6000, http://www.disa.mil | Email: dia-pao@dia.mil

DIRECTOR	Lt. Gen. Alan R. Lynn, USAF
Vice Director	Maj. Gen. Sarah E. Zabel, USAF

The Defense Information Systems Agency (DISA), established originally as the Defense Communications Agency in 1960, is under the authority, direction, and control of the Assistant Secretary of Defense (Networks and Information Integration). DISA is a combat support agency responsible for planning, engineering, acquiring, fielding, operating, and supporting global net-centric solutions to serve the needs of the President, Vice President, Secretary of Defense, and other DOD components.

For further information, contact the Public Affairs Office, Defense Information Systems Agency, P.O. Box 549, Command Building, Fort Meade, MD 20755. Phone, 301-225-6000.

Defense Intelligence Agency

200 MacDill Boulevard, Washington DC 20340-5100, 202-231-0800, http://www.dia.mil | Email: dia-pao@dia.mil

DIRECTOR	Lt. Gen. Vincent R. Stewart, USMC
Deputy Director	Melissa A. Drisko

The Defense Intelligence Agency (DIA) was established in 1961 and is under the authority, direction, and control of the Under Secretary of Defense for Intelligence. DIA provides timely, objective, and cogent military intelligence to warfighters, force planners, as well as defense and national security policymakers. DIA obtains and reports information through its field sites worldwide and the Defense Attache System; provides timely intelligence analysis; directs Defense Human Intelligence programs; operates the Joint Intelligence Task Force for Combating Terrorism and the Joint Military Intelligence College; coordinates and facilitates Measurement and Signature Intelligence activities; manages and plans collections from specialized technical sources; manages secure DOD intelligence networks; and coordinates required intelligence support for the Secretary of Defense, Joint Chiefs of Staff, Combatant Commanders, and Joint Task Forces.

For further information, contact the Public Affairs Office, Defense Intelligence Agency, 200 MacDill Boulevard, Washington DC 20340-5100. Phone, 202-231-0800.

Defense Legal Services Agency

The Pentagon, Washington, DC 20301-1600, 703-695-3341, http://www.dod.mil/dodgc

DIRECTOR / GENERAL COUNSEL OF THE DEPARTMENT OF DEFENSE	Jennifer M. O'Connor
Principal Deputy General Counsel of the Department of Defense	Robert S. Taylor

The Defense Legal Services Agency (DLSA) was established in 1981 and is under the authority, direction, and control of the General Counsel of the Department of Defense, who also serves as its Director. DLSA provides legal advice and services for specified DOD components and adjudication of personnel security cases for DOD and other assigned Federal agencies and departments. It also provides technical support and assistance for development of the Department's legislative program; coordinates positions on legislation and Presidential Executive orders; provides a centralized legislative and congressional document reference and distribution point for the Department; maintains the Department's historical legislative files; and administers programs governing standards of conduct and alternative dispute resolution.

For further information, contact the Administrative Office, Defense Legal Services Agency, Room 3A734, Washington, DC 20301-1600. Phone, 703-697-8343.

Defense Logistics Agency

8725 John J. Kingman Road, Suite 2533, Fort Belvoir, VA 22060-6221, 703-767-5264, http://www.dla.mil

DIRECTOR	Lt. Gen. Andrew E. Busch, USAF
Vice Director	Edward J. Case

The Defense Logistics Agency (DLA) is under the authority, direction, and control of the Under Secretary of Defense for Acquisition, Technology, and Logistics. DLA supports both the logistics requirements of the military services and their acquisition of weapons and other materiel. It provides logistics support and technical services to all branches of the military and to a number of Federal agencies. DLA supply centers consolidate the requirements of the military services and procure the supplies in sufficient quantities to meet their projected needs. DLA manages supplies in eight commodity areas: fuel, food, clothing, construction material, electronic supplies, general supplies, industrial supplies, and medical supplies. Information on DLA's field activities and regional commands is available at www.dla.mil/ataglance.aspx.

Sources of Information

Employment

For the Washington, DC, metropolitan area, all inquiries and applications concerning job recruitment programs should be addressed to Human Resources, Customer Support Office, 3990 East Broad Street, Building 11, Section 3, Columbus, OH, 43213-0919. Phone, 877-352-4762.

Environmental Program

For information on the environmental program, contact the Staff Director, Environmental and Safety, Defense Logistics Agency, Attn: DSS-E, 8725 John J. Kingman Road, Fort Belvoir, VA 22060-6221. Phone, 703-767-6278.

Procurement / Small Business Activities

For information on procurement and small business activities, contact the Director, Small and Disadvantaged Business Utilization, Defense Logistics Agency, Attn:

DB, 8725 John J. Kingman Road, Fort Belvoir, VA 22060-6221. Phone, 703-767-0192.

Surplus Sales Program

Questions concerning this program should be addressed to DOD Surplus Sales, International Sales Office, 74 Washington Avenue North, Battle Creek, MI 49017-3092. Phone, 877-352-2255.

For further information, contact the Defense Logistics Agency, 8725 John J. Kingman Road, Fort Belvoir, VA 22060-6221. Phone, 703-767-5264.

Defense Security Cooperation Agency

201 Twelfth Street South, Suite 203, Arlington, VA 22202-5408, 703-604-6605, http://www.dsca.mil | Email: info@dsca.mil

DIRECTOR	Vice Adm. Joseph W. Rixey, USN
Deputy Director	James Worm, Acting

The Defense Security Cooperation Agency (DSCA) was established in 1971 and is under the authority, direction, and control of the Under Secretary of Defense (Policy). DSCA provides traditional security assistance functions such as military assistance, international military education and training, and foreign military sales. DSCA also has program management responsibilities for humanitarian assistance, demining, and other DOD programs.

For further information, contact the Defense Security Cooperation Agency, 201 Twelfth Street South, Suite 203, Arlington, VA 22202-5408. Phone, 703-604-6605.

Defense Security Service

27130 Telegraph Road, Quantico, VA 22134, 703-617-2352, http://www.dss.mil

DIRECTOR	Daniel E. Payne
Deputy Director	James J. Kren

The Defense Security Service (DSS) is under the authority, direction, and control of the Under Secretary of Defense for Intelligence. DSS ensures the safeguarding of classified information used by contractors on behalf of the DOD and 22 other executive branch agencies under the National Industrial Security Program. It oversees the protection of conventional arms, munitions, and explosives in the custody of DOD contractors; evaluates the protection of selected private sector critical assets and infrastructures (physical and cyber-based systems) and recommends measures needed to maintain operations identified as vital to DOD. DSS makes clearance determinations for industry and provides support services for DOD Central Adjudicative Facilities. It provides security education, training, and proactive awareness programs for military, civilian, and cleared industry to enhance their proficiency and awareness of DOD security policies and procedures. DSS also has a counterintelligence office to integrate counterintelligence principles into security countermeasures missions and to support the national counterintelligence strategy. Information on DSS operating locations and centers is available at www.dss.mil/isp/dss_oper_loc.html.

For further information, contact the Defense Security Service, Office of Public Affairs, 27130 Telegraph Road, Quantico, VA 22134. Phone, 703-617-2352.

Defense Threat Reduction Agency

8725 John J. Kingman Road, MS 6201, Fort Belvoir, VA 22060-6201, 703-767-7594, http://www.dtra.mil

DIRECTOR	Shari Durand, Acting
Deputy Director	Rear Adm. Scott Jerabek, USN

The Defense Threat Reduction Agency (DTRA) was established in 1998 and is under the authority, direction, and control of the Under Secretary of Defense for Acquisition, Technology, and Logistics. DTRA's mission is to reduce the threat posed by weapons of mass destruction (WMD). DTRA covers the full range of WMD threats (chemical, biological, nuclear, radiological, and high explosive), bridges the gap between the warfighters and the technical community, sustains the nuclear deterrent, and provides both offensive and defensive technology and operational concepts to warfighters. DTRA reduces the threat of WMD by implementing arms control treaties and executing the Cooperative Threat Reduction Program. It uses combat support, technology development, and chemical-biological defense to deter the use and reduce the impact of such weapons. DTRA also prepares for future threats by developing the technology and concepts needed to counter new WMD threats and adversaries.

For further information, contact the Public Affairs Office, Defense Threat Reduction Agency, 8725 John J. Kingman Road, MS 6201, Fort Belvoir, VA 22060-5916. Phone, 703-767-7594. Email, dtra.publicaffairs@dtra.mil.

Missile Defense Agency

5700 Eighteenth Street, Bldg 245, Fort Belvoir, VA 22060-5573, 703-695-6420, http://www.mda.mil | Email: mda.info@mda.mil

DIRECTOR	Vice Adm. James D. Syring, USN
Deputy Director	Maj. Gen. Ole A. Knudson, USA
Executive Director	John H. James, Jr.

[For the Missile Defense Agency statement of organization, see the Code of Federal Regulations, Title 32, Part 388]

The Missile Defense Agency's (MDA) mission is to establish and deploy a layered ballistic missile defense system to intercept missiles in all phases of their flight and against all ranges of threats. This capability will provide a defense of the United States, deployed forces, and allies. MDA is under the authority, direction, and control of the Under Secretary of Defense for Acquisition, Technology, and Logistics. MDA manages and directs DOD's ballistic missile defense acquisition programs and enables the Services to field elements of the overall system as soon as practicable. MDA develops and tests technologies and, if necessary, uses prototype and test assets to provide early capability. Additionally, MDA improves the effectiveness of deployed capabilities by implementing new technologies as they become available or when the threat warrants an accelerated capability.

For further information, contact the Human Resources Directorate, Missile Defense Agency, 5700 Eighteenth Street, Bldg 245, Fort Belvoir, VA 22060-5573. Phone, 703-695-6420. Email, mda.info@mda.mil.

National Geospatial-Intelligence Agency

7500 Geoint Drive, MS N73-OCCAE, Springfield, Virginia 22150, 571-557-7300, http://www.nga.mil

DIRECTOR	Robert Cardillo
Deputy Director	Susan Gordon

The National Geospatial-Intelligence Agency (NGA), formerly the National Imagery and Mapping Agency, was established in 1996 and is under the authority, direction, and control of the Under Secretary of Defense for Intelligence. NGA is a DOD combat support agency and a member of the national intelligence community. NGA's mission is to provide timely, relevant, and accurate geospatial intelligence in support of our national security. Geospatial intelligence means the use and analysis of imagery to describe, assess, and visually depict physical features and geographically referenced activities on the Earth. Headquartered in Bethesda, MD, NGA has major facilities in the Washington, DC, Northern Virginia, and St. Louis, MO, areas with NGA support teams worldwide.

For further information, contact the Public Affairs Office, National Geospatial-Intelligence Agency,. 7500 Geoint Drive, MS N73-OCCAE, Springfield, Virginia 22150. Phone, 571-557-7300.

National Security Agency / Central Security Service

Fort Meade, MD 20755-6248, 301-688-6524, 301-688-6198, http://www.nsa.gov

DIRECTOR	Adm. Michael S. Rogers, USN
Deputy Director	Richard H. Ledgett, Jr.

The National Security Agency (NSA) was established in 1952 and the Central Security Service (CSS) was established in 1972. NSA/CSS is under the authority, direction, and control of the Under Secretary of Defense for Intelligence. As the Nation's cryptologic organization, NSA/CSS employs the Nation's premier codemakers and codebreakers. It ensures an informed, alert, and secure environment for U.S. warfighters and policymakers. The cryptologic resources of NSA/CSS unite to provide U.S. policymakers with intelligence information derived from America's adversaries while protecting U.S. Government signals and information systems from exploitation by those same adversaries.

For further information, contact the Public Affairs Office, National Security Agency/ Central Security Service, Fort Meade, MD 20755-6248. Phone, 301-688-6524. Fax, 301-688-6198.

Pentagon Force Protection Agency

9000 Defense Pentagon, Washington, DC 20301, 703-697-1001, http://www.pfpa.mil

DIRECTOR	Jonathan H. Cofer
Deputy Director	Daniel P. Walsh, Acting

The Pentagon Force Protection Agency (PFPA) was established in May 2002 in response to the events of September 11, 2001, and subsequent terrorist threats facing the DOD workforce and facilities in the National Capital Region (NCR). PFPA is under the authority, direction, and control of the Director, Administration and Management, in the Office of the Secretary of Defense. PFPA provides force protection, security, and law enforcement for the people, facilities, infrastructure, and other resources at the Pentagon and for DOD activities and facilities within the NCR that are not under the jurisdiction of a military department. Consistent with the national strategy on combating terrorism, PFPA addresses threats, including chemical, biological, and radiological agents, through a strategy of prevention, preparedness, detection, and response to ensure that the DOD workforce and facilities in the NCR are secure and protected.

For further information, contact the Pentagon Force Protection Agency, 9000 Defense Pentagon, Washington, DC 20301. Phone, 703-697-1001.

Joint Service Schools

Defense Acquisition University

9820 Belvoir Road, Fort Belvoir, VA 22060-5565, 703-805-2764, http://www.dau.mil

PRESIDENT James P. Woosley

The Defense Acquisition University (DAU), established pursuant to the Defense Acquisition Workforce Improvement Act of 1990 (10 U.S.C. 1701 note), serves as the DOD center for acquisition, technology, and logistics training; performance support; continuous learning; and knowledge sharing. DAU is a unified structure with five regional campuses and the Defense Systems Management College-School of Program Managers, which provides executive and international acquisition training. DAU's mission is to provide the training, career management, and services that enable the acquisition, technology, and logistics community to make smart business decisions and deliver timely and affordable capabilities to warfighters.

For further information, contact the Director, Operations Support Group, Defense Acquisition University, 9820 Belvoir Road, Fort Belvoir, VA 22060-5565. Phone, 800-845-7606.

National Intelligence University

Defense Intelligence Analysis Center, Washington, DC 20340-5100, 202-231-5466, http://www.ni-u.edu

PRESIDENT Rear Adm. David R. Ellison, USN (retired)

The National Intelligence University, formerly the Joint Military Intelligence College, was established in 1962. The College is a joint service interagency educational institution serving the intelligence community and operates under the authority of the Director, Defense Intelligence Agency. Its mission is to educate military and civilian intelligence professionals, conduct and disseminate relevant intelligence research, and perform academic outreach regarding intelligence matters. The College is authorized by Congress to award the bachelor of science in intelligence, master of science and technology intelligence, and master of science of strategic intelligence. Courses are offered to full-time students in a traditional daytime format and for part-time students in the evening, on Saturday, and in an executive format (one weekend per month and a 2-week intensive summer period).

For further information, contact the Admissions Office, National Intelligence University, 200 MacDill Blvd (MCA-2), Washington, DC 20340-5100. Phone, 202-231-5466 or 202-231-3319.

National Defense University

300 Fifth Avenue, Building 62, Fort McNair, DC 20319-5066, 202-685-2649, *http://www.ndu.edu*

College of International Security Affairs: 260 Fifth Avenue, Building 64, Fort McNair, DC 20319-5066, 202-685-3870, *http://cisa.ndu.edu*

Dwight D. Eisenhower School for National Security and Resource Strategy: 408 Fourth Avenue, Building 59, Fort McNair, DC 20319-5062, 202-685-4333, *http://es.ndu.edu/Home.aspx*

Information Resources Management College: 300 Fifth Avenue, Building 62, Fort McNair, DC 20319-5066, 202-685-6300, *http://icollege.ndu.edu*

Joint Forces Staff College: 7800 Hampton Boulevard, Norfolk, VA 23511-1702, 757-443-6124, *http://jfsc.ndu.edu*

National War College: 300 D Street SW., Building 61, Fort McNair, DC 20319-5078, 202-685-3674, 202-685-6461, *http://nwc.ndu.edu*

PRESIDENT	Maj. Gen. Frederick M. Padilla, USMC
Commandant, Dwight D. Eisenhower School for National Security and Resource Strategy	Col. Paul H. Fredenburgh III, USA
Commandant, Joint Forces Staff College	Rear Adm. Jeffrey Ruth, USN
Commandant, National War College	Brig. Gen. Darren E. Hartford, USAF
Chancellor, College of International Security Affairs	Col. Michael S. Bell, USA (retired)
Chancellor, Information Resources Management College	Rear Adm. Janice Hamby, USN (retired)

National Defense University

The mission of the National Defense University is to prepare military and civilian leaders from the United States and other countries to evaluate national and international security challenges through multidisciplinary educational and research programs, professional exchanges, and outreach.

The National Defense University was established in 1976 and comprises the following colleges and programs: the Dwight D. Eisenhower School for National Security and Resource Strategy, National War College, Joint Forces Staff College, Information Resources Management College, College of International Security Affairs, Institute for National Strategic Studies, Center for the Study of Weapons of Mass Destruction, Center for Technology and National Security Policy, International Student Management Office, Joint Reserve Affairs Center, CAPSTONE, Security of Defense Corporate Fellows Program, NATO Education Center, Institute for National Security Ethics and Leadership, Center for Joint Strategic Logistics Excellence, Center for Applied Strategic Leaders, and Center for Complex Operations.

For further information, contact the Human Resources Directorate, National Defense University, 300 Fifth Avenue, Building 62, Fort McNair, DC 20319-5066. Phone, 202-685-2169.

College of International Security Affairs

The College of International Security Affairs (CISA) is one of NDU's five colleges. CISA educates students from across the international, interagency, and interservice communities. CISA's primary areas of concentration include counterterrorism, conflict management of stability of operations, homeland security, and defense and international security studies. CISA is also home to NDU's International Counterterrorism Fellowship Program.

For further information, contact the Office of Academic Affairs, College of International Security Affairs, 260 Fifth Avenue, Building 64, Fort McNair, DC 20319-5066. Phone, 202-685-7774.

Dwight D. Eisenhower School for National Security and Resource Strategy

The Dwight D. Eisenhower School for National Security and Resource Strategy provides graduate level education to senior members of the U.S. Armed Forces, Government civilians, foreign nationals, and professionals from the private industrial sector. The School prepares students to contribute to national security strategy and policy, emphasizing the evaluation, marshaling, and managing of national resources. Students who fulfill the degree requirements receive a Master of Science degree in national resource strategy.

For further information, contact the Director of Operations, Dwight D. Eisenhower School for National Security and Resource Strategy, 408 Fourth Avenue, Building 59, Fort McNair, DC 20319-5062. Phone, 202-685-4333.

Information Resources Management College

The Information Resources Management College provides graduate-level courses in information resources management. The College prepares leaders to direct the information component of national power by leveraging information and information technology for strategic advantage. The College's primary areas of concentration include policy, strategic planning, leadership/management, process improvement, capital planning and investment, performance- and results-based management, technology assessment, architecture, information assurance and security, acquisition, domestic preparedness, transformation, e-Government, and information operations.

For further information, contact the Office of Student Services, Information Resources Management College, 300 Fifth Avenue, Building 62, Fort McNair, DC 20319-5066. Phone, 202-685-6300.

Joint Forces Staff College

The Joint Forces Staff College (JFSC) is an intermediate- and senior-level joint college in the professional military education system dedicated to the study of the principles, perspectives, and techniques of joint operational-level planning and warfare. The mission of JFSC is to educate national security professionals in the planning and execution of joint, multinational, and interagency operations in order to instill a primary commitment to joint, multinational, and interagency teamwork, attitudes, and perspectives. The College accomplishes this mission through four schools: the Joint Advanced Warfighters School, the Joint and Combined Warfighting School, the Joint Continuing and Distance Education School, and the Joint Command, Control, and Information Operations School.

For further information, contact the Public Affairs Officer, Joint Forces Staff College, 7800 Hampton Boulevard, Norfolk, VA 23511-1702. Phone, 757-443-6212. Fax, 757-443-6210.

National War College

The National War College provides education in national security policy to selected military officers and career civil service employees of Federal departments and agencies concerned with national security. It is the only senior service college with the primary mission of offering a course of study that emphasizes national security policy formulation and the planning and implementation of national strategy. Its 10-month academic program is an issue-centered study in U.S. national security. The elective program is designed to permit each student to tailor his or her academic experience to meet individual professional development needs.

For further information, contact the Office of Administration, National War College, 300 D Street SW., Building 61, Fort McNair, DC 20319-5078. Phone, 202-685-3674.

Uniformed Services University of the Health Sciences

4301 Jones Bridge Road, Bethesda, MD 20814-4799, 301-295-3190, *http://www.usuhs.mil*

PRESIDENT — Maj. Gen. Richard W. Thomas, USA (retired)

Authorized by act of September 21, 1972 (10 U.S.C. 2112), the Uniformed Services University of the Health Sciences was established to educate career-oriented medical officers for the Military Departments and the Public Health Service. The University currently incorporates the F. Edward Hebert School of Medicine (including graduate and continuing education programs) and the Graduate School of Nursing.

Students are selected by procedures recommended by the Board of Regents and prescribed by the Secretary of Defense. The actual selection is carried out by a faculty committee on admissions and is based upon motivation and dedication to a career in the uniformed services and an overall appraisal of the personal and intellectual characteristics of the candidates without regard to sex, race, religion, or national origin. Applicants must be U.S. citizens.

Medical school matriculants will be commissioned officers in one of the uniformed services. They must meet the physical and personal qualifications for such a commission and must give evidence of a strong commitment to serving as a uniformed medical officer. The graduating medical student is required to serve a period of obligation of not less than 7 years, excluding graduate medical education.

Students of the Graduate School of Nursing must be commissioned officers of the Army, Navy, Air Force, or Public Health Service prior to application. Graduate nursing students must serve a commitment determined by their respective service.

For further information, contact the President, Uniformed Services University of the Health Sciences, 4301 Jones Bridge Road, Bethesda, MD 20814-4799. Phone, 301-295-3013.

Department of Education

400 Maryland Avenue SW., Washington, DC 20202, 202-401-2000, TTY, 800-437-0833, *http://www.ed.gov*

SECRETARY OF EDUCATION	John B. King, Jr.
Deputy Secretary	James Cole, Jr.
Under Secretary	Theodore R. Mitchell
OFFICE OF THE SECRETARY	
Assistant Deputy Secretary and Director, Office of English Language	Libia Gil

Acquisition	
Assistant Deputy Secretary, Office of Innovation and Improvement	Nadya Chinoy Dabby, Acting
Assistant Secretary, Office for Civil Rights	Catherine E. Lhamon
Assistant Secretary, Office of Communication and Outreach	Jonathan Schorr, Acting
Assistant Secretary, Office of Elementary and Secondary Education	Ann Whalen, Acting
Assistant Secretary, Office of Legislation and Congressional Affairs	Lloyd Horwich, Acting
Assistant Secretary, Office of Planning, Evaluation and Policy Development	Amy McIntosh, Acting
Assistant Secretary, Office of Special Education and Rehabilitative Services	(vacancy)
Chief of Staff	Emma Vadehra
Director, International Affairs Office	Maureen A. McLaughlin
Director, Institute of Education Sciences	Ruth Neild, Acting
Inspector General	Kathleen S. Tighe
OFFICE OF THE DEPUTY SECRETARY	
Assistant Secretary, Office of Management	Andrew Jackson
Chief Financial Officer	(vacancy)
Chief Information Officer	Jason K. Gray
Director, Office of Educational Technology	Joseph Smith
General Counsel	James Cole, Jr.
OFFICE OF THE UNDER SECRETARY	
Assistant Secretary, Office of Career, Technical, and Adult Education	Johan Uvin, Acting
Assistant Secretary, Office of Postsecondary Education	Jamienne Studley, Acting
Chief Operating Officer for Federal Student Aid	James W. Runcie
Director, Center for Faith-Based and Neighborhood Partnerships	Brenda Girton-Mitchell
Executive Director, White House Initiative on American Indian and Alaska Native Education	William Mendoza
Executive Director, White House Initiative on Asian Americans and Pacific Islanders	Kiran Ahuja
Executive Director, White House Initiative on Educational Excellence for African Americans	David J. Johns
Executive Director, White House Initiative on Educational Excellence for Hispanic Americans	Alejandra Ceja
Executive Director, White House Initiative on Historically Black Colleges and Universities	Kim Hunter Reed, Acting

The Department of Education ensures equal access to education; promotes educational excellence; and administers, coordinates, and makes policy for most Federal assistance to education with the aim of raising levels of student achievement and readiness for the global future.

The Department of Education was created by the Department of Education Organization Act (20 U.S.C. 3411) and is administered under the supervision and direction of the Secretary of Education.

Secretary

The Secretary of Education advises the President on education plans, policies, and programs of the Federal Government and serves as the chief executive officer of the Department, supervising all Department activities, providing support to States and localities, and focusing resources to ensure equal access to educational excellence throughout the Nation.

Activities

Career, Technical, and Adult Education

The Office of Career, Technical, and Adult Education (OCTAE) administers grant, contract, and technical assistance programs for vocational-technical education and for adult education and literacy. It promotes programs that enable adults to acquire the basic literacy skills necessary to function in today's society. The Office also helps students acquire challenging academic and technical skills and prepare for high-skill, high-wage, and high-demand occupations in the 21st-century global economy. OCTAE provides national leadership and works to strengthen the role of community colleges in expanding access to postsecondary education for youth and adults in advancing workforce development.

Education Sciences

The Institute of Education Sciences was formally established by the Education Sciences Reform Act of 2002 (20 U.S.C. 9501 note). The Institute includes national education centers focused on research, special education, statistics, and evaluation and is the mechanism through which the Department supports the research activities needed to improve education policy and practice.

Elementary and Secondary Education

The Office of Elementary and Secondary Education directs, coordinates, and formulates policy relating to early childhood, elementary, and secondary education. Included are grants and contracts to State educational agencies and local school districts, postsecondary schools, and nonprofit organizations for disadvantaged, migrant, and Indian children; enhancement of State student achievement assessment systems; improvement of reading instruction; economic impact aid; technology; safe and healthy schools; and after-school learning programs. The Office also focuses on improving K–12 education, providing children with language and cognitive development, early reading, and other readiness skills, and improving the quality of teachers and other instructional staff.

English Language Acquisition

The Office of English Language Acquisition helps children who are limited in their English, including immigrant children and youth, attain English proficiency, develop high levels of academic attainment in English, and meet the same challenging State academic content and student academic achievement standards that all children are expected to meet.

Federal Student Aid

Federal Student Aid partners with postsecondary schools and financial institutions to deliver programs and services that help students finance their education beyond high school. This includes administering postsecondary student financial assistance programs authorized under Title IV of the Higher Education Act of 1965, as amended.

Innovation and Improvement

The Office of Innovation and Improvement (OII) oversees competitive grant programs that support innovations in the educational system and disseminates the lessons learned from these innovative practices. OII administers, coordinates, and recommends programs and policy for improving the quality of activities designed to support and test innovations throughout the K–12 system in areas such as parental choice, teacher quality, use of technology in education, and arts in education. OII encourages the establishment of charter schools through planning, start-up funding, and approaches to credit enhancement for charter school facilities. OII also serves as the Department's liaison and resource to the nonpublic education community.

Postsecondary Education

The Office of Postsecondary Education (OPE) formulates Federal postsecondary education policy and administers programs that address critical national needs in support of the mission to increase access to quality postsecondary education. OPE develops policy for Federal student financial programs and support programs that reach out to low-income, first-generation college students and communities. OPE also supports programs that strengthen the capacity of colleges and universities serving a high percentage of disadvantaged students and improve teacher quality. OPE recognizes accrediting agencies that monitor academic quality, promote innovation in higher education, and expand American educational resources for international studies and services.

Special Education and Rehabilitative Services

The Office of Special Education and Rehabilitative Services (OSERS) provides leadership and resources to help ensure that people with disabilities have equal opportunities to learn, work, and live as fully integrated and contributing members of society. OSERS has three components: The Office of Special Education Programs administers the Individuals with Disabilities Education Act legislation, which helps States meet the early intervention and educational needs of infants, toddlers, children, and youth with disabilities. The Rehabilitation Services Administration supports State vocational rehabilitation, independent living, and assistive technology programs that provide people with disabilities the services, technology, and job training and placement assistance they need to gain meaningful employment and lead independent lives. The National Institute on Disability and Rehabilitation Research supports research and development programs that improve the ability of individuals with disabilities to work and live in a barrier-free, inclusive society. OSERS also supports Gallaudet University, the National Technical Institute for the Deaf, the American Printing House for the Blind, and the Helen Keller National Center.

Sources of Information

Blog

"Homeroom" is the official blog of the Department of Education.

Business Opportunities

Contact the Office of Small and Disadvantaged Business Utilization. Phone, 202-245-6301.

College Scorecard

The Department of Education's Web site features a tool to help college bound students find colleges and universities based upon their location, size, and the programs and degrees that they offer.

Data / Statistics

Information on school accreditation and data on the academic achievement of U.S. students are available on the "Data and Research" Web page. The National Center for Education Statistics collects and analyzes data related to education. Phone, 202-403-5551.

Employment

For information on employment and the college recruitment program, contact Human Capital and Client Services. Phone, 202-401-0553.

Freedom of Information Act (FOIA)

The FOIA generally provides that any person has the right to request access to Federal agency records or information; all agencies of the Government are required to disclose records upon receiving a written request for them; nine exemptions to the FOIA protect certain records from disclosure; and three special protection provisions or record exclusions authorize Federal law enforcement agencies, under exceptional circumstances, to exclude records from FIOA requirements. The Federal FOIA does not provide access to records held by State or local government agencies, or by private businesses or individuals.

Before submitting a request, browse the electronic FOIA Library and search the Department of Education's Web site. The desired records and information may be immediately available online and not require a FOIA request to access them.

Frequently Asked Questions (FAQs)

The Department of Education provides answers to FAQs on its Web site.

Glossaries

The Department of Education's Web site features a glossary of reading terms.

The Department of Education's Web site features a glossary of terms related to Federal student aid.

The Department of Education's Web site features a glossary of terms related to education research.

The Department of Education's Web site features a glossary of terms related to education statistical standards.

Language Assistance

Education resources for Spanish speakers are available on the Department's Web site.

Free language assistance services—Chinese, Korean, Spanish, Vietnamese, Tagalog—are available to the public. Phone, 800-872-5327.

News

The Department of Education posts media advisories, press releases, and speeches on its Web site.

Press releases in Spanish are also available on the Department's Web site.

Open Government

The Department of Education supports the Open Government initiative by promoting the principles of collaboration, participation, and transparency.

Plain Language

Department of Education writers and editors are committed to using Federal plain language guidelines. Publishing clear, useful information on programs and services is a priority and an ongoing effort. To comment on the clarity of a written product or to offer a suggestion for improvement, please communicate via email.

Regional Offices

Each regional office serves as a center for the dissemination of information and provides technical assistance to State and local educational agencies and other institutions and individuals interested in Federal educational activities. Offices are located in Boston, MA; New York, NY; Philadelphia, PA; Atlanta, GA; Chicago, IL; Cleveland, OH; Dallas, TX; Kansas City, MO; Denver, CO; San Francisco, CA; and Seattle, WA.

Site Map

The Web site map allows visitors to look for specific topics or to browse content that aligns with their interests.

Student Loans

Information on student loans is available online.

For further information, contact the Information Resources Center, Department of Education, Room 5E248 (FB–6), 400 Maryland Avenue SW., Washington, DC 20202. Phone, 800-872-5327.

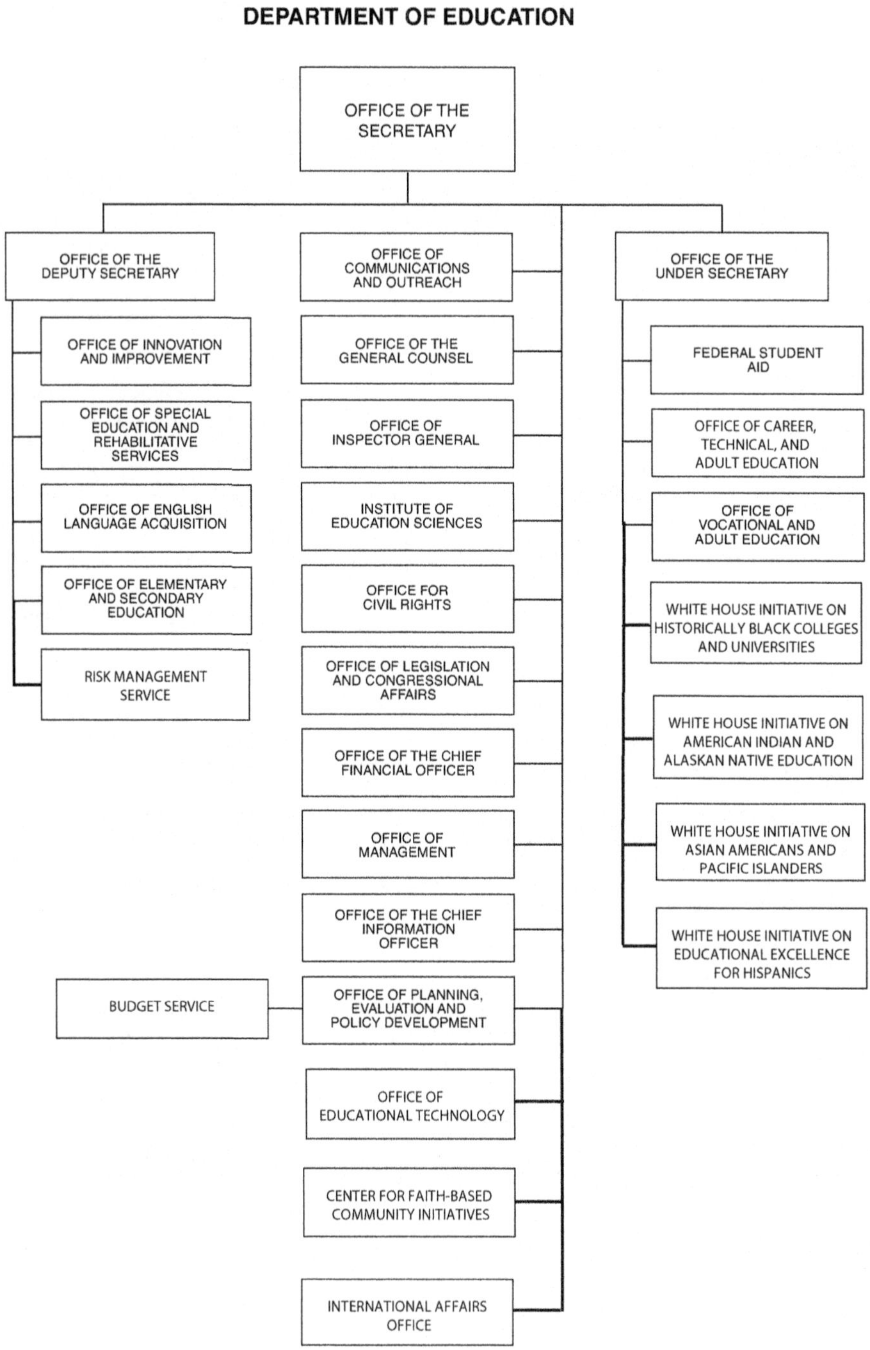
DEPARTMENT OF EDUCATION
OFFICE OF THE SECRETARY
OFFICE OF THE DEPUTY SECRETARY
OFFICE OF INNOVATION AND IMPROVEMENT
OFFICE OF SPECIAL EDUCATION AND REHABILITATIVE SERVICES
OFFICE OF ENGLISH LANGUAGE ACQUISITION
OFFICE OF ELEMENTARY AND SECONDARY EDUCATION
RISK MANAGEMENT SERVICE
OFFICE OF COMMUNICATIONS AND OUTREACH
OFFICE OF THE GENERAL COUNSEL
OFFICE OF INSPECTOR GENERAL
INSTITUTE OF EDUCATION SCIENCES
OFFICE FOR CIVIL RIGHTS
OFFICE OF LEGISLATION AND CONGRESSIONAL AFFAIRS
OFFICE OF THE CHIEF FINANCIAL OFFICER
OFFICE OF MANAGEMENT
OFFICE OF THE CHIEF INFORMATION OFFICER
BUDGET SERVICE
OFFICE OF PLANNING, EVALUATION AND POLICY DEVELOPMENT
OFFICE OF EDUCATIONAL TECHNOLOGY
CENTER FOR FAITH-BASED COMMUNITY INITIATIVES
INTERNATIONAL AFFAIRS OFFICE
OFFICE OF THE UNDER SECRETARY
FEDERAL STUDENT AID
OFFICE OF CAREER, TECHNICAL, AND ADULT EDUCATION
OFFICE OF VOCATIONAL AND ADULT EDUCATION
WHITE HOUSE INITIATIVE ON HISTORICALLY BLACK COLLEGES AND UNIVERSITIES
WHITE HOUSE INITIATIVE ON AMERICAN INDIAN AND ALASKAN NATIVE EDUCATION
WHITE HOUSE INITIATIVE ON ASIAN AMERICANS AND PACIFIC ISLANDERS
WHITE HOUSE INITIATIVE ON EDUCATIONAL EXCELLENCE FOR HISPANICS

Federally Aided Corporations

American Printing House for the Blind

P.O. Box 6085, Louisville, KY 40206, 502-895-2405, *http://www.aph.org*

PRESIDENT	Tuck Tinsley III
Chair of the Board	W. Barrett Nichols

Founded in 1858 as a nonprofit organization, the American Printing House for the Blind (APH) received its Federal charter in 1879 when Congress passed the Act to Promote Education of the Blind. This Act designates APH as the official supplier of educational materials adapted for students who are legally blind and who are enrolled in formal educational programs below the college level. Materials produced and distributed by APH include textbooks in Braille and large type, educational tools such as Braille typewriters and computer software and hardware, teaching aides such as tests and performance measures, and other special supplies. The materials are distributed through allotments to the States to programs serving individuals who are blind.

Sources of Information

Business Opportunities

Requests for proposals are posted online.

Employment

The APH is the world's largest manufacturer of products for people who are blind and visually impaired. It is a drug-free workplace: New hires must pass a drug screening test and background check.

For further information, contact the American Printing House for the Blind, P.O. Box 6085, Louisville, KY 40206. Phone, 502-895-2405.

Gallaudet University

800 Florida Avenue NE., Washington, DC 20002, 202-651-5000, *http://www.gallaudet.edu*

PRESIDENT	T. Alan Hurwitz
Chair, Board of Trustees	Heather Harker

Gallaudet University received its Federal charter in 1864 and is currently authorized by the Education of the Deaf Act of 1986, as amended. Gallaudet is a private, nonprofit educational institution providing elementary, secondary, undergraduate, and continuing education programs for persons who are deaf. The University offers a traditional liberal arts curriculum for students who are deaf and graduate programs in fields related to deafness for students who are deaf and students who are hearing. Gallaudet also conducts a wide variety of basic and applied deafness research and provides public service programs for persons who are deaf and for professionals who work with persons who are deaf.

Gallaudet University is accredited by a number of organizations, among which are the Middle States Association of Colleges and Secondary Schools, the National Council for Accreditation of Teacher Education, and the Conference of Educational Administrators of Schools and Programs for the Deaf.

Laurent Clerc National Deaf Education Center

Gallaudet's Laurent Clerc National Deaf Education Center operates elementary and secondary education programs on the main campus of the University. These programs are authorized by the Education of the Deaf Act of 1986 (20 U.S.C. 4304, as amended) for the primary purpose of developing, evaluating, and disseminating model curricula, instructional strategies, and materials in order to serve individuals who are deaf or hard of hearing. The Education of the Deaf Act requires the programs to include students preparing for postsecondary opportunities other than college and students with a broad spectrum of needs, such as students who are academically challenged, come from non-English-speaking homes, have secondary disabilities, are members of minority groups, or are from rural areas.

Model Secondary School for the Deaf

The school was established by act of October 15, 1966, which was superseded by the Education of the Deaf Act of 1986. The school provides day and residential facilities for secondary-age students from across the United States from grades 9 to 12, inclusively.

Kendall Demonstration Elementary School

The school became the Nation's first demonstration elementary school for the deaf by the act of December 24, 1970 (20 U.S.C. 695), which was also later superseded by the Education of the Deaf Act of 1986. The school is a day program for students from the Washington, DC, metropolitan area from the age of onset of deafness to age 15, inclusively, but not beyond the eighth grade or its equivalent.

Sources of Information

Campus Tour

A virtual tour of the University's campus is available online.

Employment

Serving deaf and hard of hearing students from many different backgrounds, Gallaudet University seeks to develop a workforce that reflects its diversity. The University is an equal employment opportunity and affirmative action employer, and it encourages members of traditionally underrepresented groups, persons with disabilities, veterans, and women to apply for vacancies.

For further information, contact the Public Relations Office, Gallaudet University, 800 Florida Avenue NE., Washington, DC 20002. Phone, 202-651-5505.

Howard University

2400 Sixth Street NW., Washington, DC 20059, 202-806-6100, *http://www.howard.edu*

PRESIDENT	Wayne A.I. Frederick

Howard University was established by Congress by the act of March 2, 1867 (14 Stat. 438). It offers instruction in 12 schools and colleges, as follows: the colleges of arts and sciences; dentistry; engineering, architecture, and computer sciences; medicine; pharmacy, nursing, and allied health sciences; the graduate school; the schools of business; communications; divinity; education; law; and social work. In addition, Howard University has research institutes, centers, and special programs in the following areas: cancer, child development, computational science and engineering, international affairs, sickle cell disease, and the national human genome project.

Sources of Information

Employment

Information is available on the "Career Opportunities" Web page.

Libraries

The Howard University Libraries are

accessible online.

For further information, contact the Office of University Communications, Howard University, 2400 Sixth Street NW., Washington, DC 20059. Phone, 202-806-0970.

National Technical Institute for the Deaf / Rochester Institute of Technology

52 Lomb Memorial Drive, Rochester, NY 14623, 585-475-6317, *http://www.ntid.rit.edu*

PRESIDENT, ROCHESTER INSTITUTE OF TECHNOLOGY	William W. Destler
President, National Technical Institute for the Deaf / Vice President, Rochester Institute of Technology	Gerard J. Buckley

The National Technical Institute for the Deaf (NTID) was established by act of June 8, 1965 (20 U.S.C. 681) to promote the employment of persons who are deaf by providing technical and professional education. The National Technical Institute for the Deaf Act was superseded by the Education of the Deaf Act of 1986 (20 U.S.C. 4431, as amended). The U.S. Department of Education contracts with the Rochester Institute of Technology (RIT) for the operation of a residential facility for postsecondary technical training and education for individuals who are deaf. The purpose of the special relationship with the host institution is to give NTID's faculty and students access to more facilities, institutional services, and career preparation options than could be provided otherwise by a national technical institute for the deaf operating independently.

NTID offers a variety of technical programs at the certificate, diploma, and associate degree levels. Degree programs include majors in business, engineering, science, and visual communications. In addition, NTID students may participate in approximately 200 educational programs available through RIT.

NTID also conducts applied research in occupational- and employment-related aspects of deafness, communication assessment, demographics of NTID's target population, and learning processes in postsecondary education. In addition, NTID conducts training workshops and seminars related to deafness. These workshops and seminars are offered nationwide to professionals who employ, work with, teach, or serve persons who are deaf.

Sources of Information

Campus Tour

A virtual tour of the college's campus is available online.

For further information, contact the Rochester Institute of Technology, National Technical Institute for the Deaf, Department of Recruitment and Admissions, Lyndon Baines Johnson Building, 52 Lomb Memorial Drive, Rochester, NY 14623-5604. Phone, 716-475-6700.

Department of Energy

1000 Independence Avenue SW., Washington, DC 20585, 202-586-5000, *http://www.energy.gov*

OFFICE OF THE SECRETARY	
SECRETARY OF ENERGY	Ernest J. Moniz
Deputy Secretary / Chief Operating Officer	Elizabeth Sherwood-

	Randall
Associate Deputy Secretary	John MacWilliams
Chief of Staff	Kevin Knobloch
Inspector General	Rickey R. Hass, Acting
Administrator, U.S. Energy Information Administration	Adam Sieminski
Assistant Secretary, Congressional and Intergovernmental Affairs	Bradley R. Crowell
Assistant Secretary, International Affairs	Jonathan H. Elkind
Chief Financial Officer	Joseph S. Hezir
Director, Advanced Research Projects Agency–Energy	Ellen Dudley Williams
Director, Energy Policy and System Analysis	Melanie Kenderdine
Director, Enterprise Assessment	Glenn S. Podonsky
Director, Intelligence and Counterintelligence	Steven Black
Executive Director, Loan Programs Office	Mark A. McCall
General Counsel	Steven P. Croley
OFFICE OF THE UNDER SECRETARY FOR MANAGEMENT AND PERFORMANCE	
Under Secretary	(vacancy)
Deputy Under Secretary	David M. Klaus
Assistant Secretary, Environmental Management	Monica C. Regalbuto
Associate Under Secretary, Environment, Health, Safety and Security	Matthew Moury
Chief Human Capital Officer	Robert Gibbs
Chief Information Officer	Michael Johnson
Director, Economic Impact and Diversity	Ladoris G. Harris
Director, Legacy Management	(vacancy)
Director, Management	Ingrid Kolb
Director, Project Management Oversight and Assessment	Paul Bosco
OFFICE OF THE UNDER SECRETARY FOR SCIENCE AND ENERGY	
Under Secretary	Franklin M. Orr
Deputy Under Secretary	Adam Cohen
Assistant Secretary, Electricity Delivery and Energy Reliability	Patricia A. Hoffman
Assistant Secretary, Energy Efficiency and Renewable Energy	David Friedman, Acting
Assistant Secretary, Fossil Energy	Christopher Smith
Assistant Secretary, Nuclear Energy	John Kotek, Acting
Director, Indian Energy Policy and Programs	Christopher C. Deschene
Director, Science	Cherry Murray
Director, Technology Transitions	Jetta Wong
OFFICE OF THE UNDER SECRETARY FOR NUCLEAR SECURITY / NATIONAL NUCLEAR SECURITY ADMINISTRATION	
Under Secretary, Nuclear Security / Administrator, National Nuclear Security	Frank G. Klotz
Principal Deputy Administrator, National Nuclear Security	Madelyn Creedon
Deputy Under Secretary, Counterterrorism and Counterproliferation	Jay Tilden
Deputy Administrator, Defense Nuclear Nonproliferation	Anne Harrington
Deputy Administrator, Defense Programs	Brig. Gen. Stephen L. Davis, USAF

Deputy Administrator, Naval Reactors	Adm. James F. Caldwell, Jr., USN
Associate Administrator, Counterterrorism and Counterproliferation	Jay Tilden
Associate Administrator, Defense Nuclear Security	Jeffrey Johnson
Associate Administrator, Emergency Operations	Debra A. Wilber
Associate Administrator Safety, Infrastructure and Operations	James McConnell

The Department of Energy addresses the Nation's energy, environmental, and nuclear challenges, using transformative science and technology to ensure national security and prosperity.

The Department of Energy (DOE) was established by the Department of Energy Organization Act (42 U.S.C. 7131), effective October 1, 1977, pursuant to Executive Order 12009 of September 13, 1977. The act consolidated the major Federal energy functions into one Cabinet-level department.

Secretary

The Secretary decides major energy policy and planning issues; acts as the principal spokesperson for the Department; and ensures effective communication and working relationships with the public and with Federal, State, local, and tribal governments. The Secretary also serves as the President's principal adviser on energy policies, plans, and programs.

Enterprise Assessments

The Office of Enterprise Assessments functions as an autonomous organization that assesses nuclear and industrial safety performance, cyber and physical security performance, and other critical functions as directed by the Secretary and his or her leadership team. The Office implements congressionally-mandated enforcement functions, manages the National Training Center, serves as an important check-and-balance that meets the DOE's self-regulating responsibilities.

For further information, contact the Office of Resources, Communications and Congressional Affairs. Phone, 301-903-3272.

Environment, Health, Safety, and Security

The Office of the Associate Under Secretary for Environment, Health, Safety and Security increases the effectiveness and efficiency of DOE primary mission-support organizations and initiates enterprisewide responses to common, widespread challenges. The Office serves as the central organization responsible for health, safety, environment, and security and for coordinating and integrating these vital programs. It develops policy and assists with technical matters, provides safety analysis, and oversees corporate safety and security programs.

For further information, contact the Office of Resources Management. Phone, 301-903-5139.

Intelligence and Counterintelligence

The Office of Intelligence and Counterintelligence safeguards national security information and technologies that comprise intellectual property of incalculable value. The Office has the ability to leverage the Department's scientific and technological expertise to assist policymakers, as well as national security missions in cyber, energy, and homeland security, and in defense and intelligence.

For further information, contact the Office of Intelligence and Counterintelligence. Phone, 202-586-2610.

Operations, Field, and Site Offices

The Administration of Government-owned, contractor-operated facility contracts is the principal responsibility of the operations, field, and site offices. Contractors who operate Government-owned facilities do most of the DOE's energy and physical research and development, environmental restoration, and waste management.

Department operations offices act as a formal link between Department headquarters and the field laboratories and other operating facilities. They manage programs and projects that the lead headquarters program offices assign. The appropriate assistant secretary, office director, or program officer provides daily, specific program direction for the operations offices. He or she also provides management guidance and coordination for and oversight of them and the field and site offices.

Project Management Oversight and Assessments

The Office of Project Management Oversight and Assessments is the Department of Energy's central management organization providing leadership and assistance in developing and implementing departmentwide policies, procedures, programs, and management systems pertaining to project management, and independently monitors, assesses, and reports on project execution performance.

ENERGY PROGRAMS

Advanced Research Projects Agency–Energy

The Advanced Research Projects Agency–Energy (ARPA–E) advances high-potential, high-impact energy technologies before they attract private-sector investment. ARPA-E awardees pursue new ways of generating, storing, and using energy. The Agency focuses on transformational energy projects that can be advanced with a small investment over a defined period of time. A streamlined awards process allows quick action to stimulate cutting-edge energy research.

For further information, contact the Office of the Director. Phone, 202-287-1004.

Efficiency and Renewable Energy

The Office of Energy Efficiency and Renewable Energy leads the Department's efforts to develop and deliver market-driven solutions for sustainable transportation, renewable electricity generation, and energy-saving homes, buildings, and manufacturing. It supports research and development and technology transfer activities to improve energy efficiency in the transportation, building, industrial, and utility sectors. The Office also administers programs providing financial assistance for State energy planning, weatherizing homes owned by the poor and disadvantaged, implementing State and local energy conservation initiatives, and promoting energy efficient construction and renovation of Federal facilities.

For further information, contact the Director of Information and Business Management Systems. Phone, 202-586-7241.

Electricity Delivery and Energy Reliability

The Office of Electricity Delivery and Energy Reliability comprises five divisions: Advanced Grid Integration, Energy Infrastructure Modeling and Analysis, Infrastructure Security and Energy Restoration, National Electricity Delivery, and Power Systems Engineering Research and Development. It promotes electric grid modernization and energy infrastructure resiliency and leads the Department's efforts to ensure a resilient, reliable, and flexible electricity system.

For further information, contact the Office of the Director. Phone, 202-586-1411.

Energy Information

The Energy Information Administration collects, processes, and disseminates data on energy consumption, demand, distribution, production, resource reserves, and technology. It also helps government and nongovernment energy users understand trends by offering analyses of the data.

For further information, contact the Director, National Energy Information Center. Phone, 202-586-6537.

Fossil Energy

The Office of Fossil Energy helps the Nation meet its need for secure, reasonably priced, and environmentally sound fossil energy supplies. It ensures that the Nation can rely on traditional resources for clean, secure and affordable energy while enhancing environmental protection. The office supports clean coal research, maintains the Strategic Petroleum and the Northeast Home Heating Oil Reserves, promotes responsible development of the Nation's oil and gas reserves, and regulates imports and exports of natural gas and liquefied natural gas.

For further information, contact the Office of Communications. Phone, 202-586-6803.

Indian Energy Policy and Programs

The Office of Indian Energy Policy and Programs coordinates, directs, fosters, and implements energy planning, education, management, and programs to assist Tribes with energy development, capacity building, energy infrastructure, energy costs, and electrification of Indian lands and homes. The Office works within the Department, across Government agencies, and with tribes and organizations to promote Indian energy policies and initiatives.

For further information, contact the Director. Phone, 202-586-1272.

Loan Programs Office

The Loan Programs Office accelerates the domestic commercial deployment of innovative and advanced clean energy technologies at a scale that contributes significantly to achieving national clean energy objectives: enhanced American global economic competitiveness, job creation, reduced dependency on foreign oil, and an improved environmental legacy. It fulfills this mission by guaranteeing loans to eligible clean energy projects and by providing direct loans to eligible manufacturers of advanced technology vehicles and components.

For further information, contact Loan Programs Office. Phone, 202-586-8335.

Nuclear Energy

The Office of Nuclear Energy advances nuclear power as a resource capable of meeting the Nation's energy, environmental, and national security needs. It relies on research, development, and demonstration to resolve barriers of cost, proliferation resistance, safety, security, and technology. Four research objectives guide the Office's efforts: developing technologies and other solutions to improve the reliability, maintain the safety, and extend the life of current reactors; making new reactors more affordable so that nuclear energy can play a bigger role in meeting energy security and climate change goals; developing sustainable fuel cycles; and understanding and minimizing the risks of nuclear proliferation and terrorism.

For further information, contact the Director, Corporate Communications and External Affairs. Phone, 301-903-1636.

Science

The Office of Science delivers scientific discoveries and tools to transform our understanding of nature and to advance national security, including the Nation's economic and energy security. The Office is the lead Federal agency supporting fundamental scientific research for energy and the Nation's largest supporter of basic research in the physical sciences. It supports scientific research and the development, construction, and operation of open-access, state-of-the-art facilities for researchers. For example, it supports research in all 50 States and the District of Columbia—at DOE laboratories and more than 300 universities and institutions of higher learning nationwide.

For further information, contact the Director of Human Resources. Phone, 301-903-5705.

Technology Transitions

The Office of Technology Transitions oversees and advances the DOE's mission by expanding the commercial impact of its portfolio of research, development, demonstration, and deployment activities in the short, medium, and long term. The Office develops the Department's policy and vision for expanding the commercial results of its research investments, and it streamlines information and access to DOE's national labs and sites to foster partnerships that will move innovations from the labs into the marketplace.

ENVIRONMENTAL QUALITY PROGRAMS

Environmental Management

The Office of Environmental Management completes the safe cleanup of the environmental legacy after decades of nuclear weapons development and Government-sponsored nuclear energy research. The Office adheres to a mission philosophy based on reducing risk and harm to the environment. Current activities include fulfilling commitments to lower risk and complete cleanup across all sites; constructing and operating facilities treating radioactive liquid tank waste in a safe, stable form; securing and storing nuclear material in a safe, stable manner in secure locations; transporting and disposing transuranic and low-level wastes in a safe, cost-effective way; decontaminating and decommissioning facilities without further value; remediating soil and ground water containing radioactive and hazardous contaminants; and planning a facility to manage and store mercury.

For further information, contact the Director of Communication/External Affairs. Phone, 202-287-5591.

Legacy Management

The Office of Legacy Management manages DOE post-closure responsibilities and ensures the future protection of human health and the environment. The Office has control and custody for legacy land, structures, and facilities that it maintains at levels consistent with DOE long-term plans. Its activities include protecting human health and the environment through long-term surveillance and maintenance; preserving, protecting, and making accessible legacy records and information; supporting a workforce structured to accomplish DOE missions; implementing departmental policy affecting continuity of worker pension and medical benefits; managing legacy land and assets with an emphasis on safety, reuse, and disposition; mitigating community impacts from the cleanup of legacy waste and changing departmental missions; and coordinating policy issues with appropriate departmental organizations.

For further information, contact the Director of Business Operations. Phone, 202-586-7388.

NUCLEAR SECURITY PROGRAMS

Defense Programs

The Office of Defense Programs ensures that the U.S. nuclear arsenal meets national security requirements and continues to serve as a deterrent. In partnership with the Department of Defense, the Office provides the research, development, secure transportation, and production activities necessary to support the U.S. nuclear weapons stockpile.

For further information, contact the Associate Administrator for Management and Budget. Phone, 202-586-5753.

Naval Nuclear Propulsion

The Naval Reactors Office administers the Naval Nuclear Propulsion Program, which provides militarily effective nuclear propulsion plants and maintains their operational safety, reliability, and longevity. This program relies on trained U.S. Navy personnel, fast and stealthy ships, and supply-chain independence to carry out its mission.

For further information, contact the Deputy Administrator for Naval Reactors. Phone, 202-781-6174.

Nuclear Nonproliferation

The Office of Defense Nuclear Nonproliferation works closely with a range of international partners, U.S. Federal agencies, the U.S. national laboratories, and the private sector. It secures and safeguards or disposes of dangerous nuclear and radiological material and monitors and controls the proliferation of weapons-of-mass-destruction technology and expertise.

For further information, contact the Associate Administrator for Management and Budget. Phone, 202-586-5753.

Nuclear Security Administration

The National Nuclear Security Administration (NNSA) was created by Congress through the National Defense Authorization Act for Fiscal Year 2000 (113 Stat. 512) to bring focus to the management of the Nation's defense nuclear security programs. Three existing organizations within the Department of Energy—Defense Programs, Defense Nuclear Nonproliferation, and Naval Reactors—were combined into a new, separately managed agency, headed by an Administrator who reports to the Secretary of Energy. The NNSA seeks to strengthen national security through military application of nuclear energy and by reducing the global threat from terrorism and weapons of mass destruction.

The Administration's service center and eight site offices provide operations oversight and contract administration for NNSA site activities. Federally-run site offices oversee the management and operating contractors for each of NNSA's eight sites. These offices provide the necessary communication between Federal and contractor employees as well as oversight to improve management procedures.

For further information, contact the Associate Administrator for Management and Budget. Phone, 202-586-5753.

POWER ADMINISTRATIONS

The Department's four Power Administrations market and transmit electric power produced at Federal hydroelectric projects and reservoirs. The Deputy Secretary provides management oversight of the Power Administrations.

Bonneville Power Administration

This Administration markets power produced by the Federal Columbia River Power System at the lowest rates consistent with sound business practices and gives preference to public entities.

It also is responsible for energy conservation, renewable resource development, and fish and wildlife enhancement under the provisions of the Pacific Northwest Electric Power Planning and Conservation Act of 1980 (16 U.S.C. 839 note).

For further information, contact the Bonneville Power Administration, 905 Eleventh Avenue NE., Portland, OR 97232-4169. Phone, 503-230-3000 or 800-282-3713.

Southeastern Power Administration

This Administration transmits and disposes of surplus electric power and energy generated at reservoir projects in Alabama, Florida, Georgia, Kentucky, Mississippi, North and South Carolina, Tennessee, Virginia, and West Virginia.

It sets the lowest possible rates for consumers consistent with sound business practices and gives preference to public entities.

For further information, contact the Southeastern Power Administration, 1166 Athens Tech Road, Elberton, GA 30635-4578. Phone, 706-213-3800.

Southwestern Power Administration

This Administration sells and disposes of electric power and energy in Arkansas, Kansas, Louisiana, Missouri, Oklahoma, and Texas.

It transmits and disposes of the electric power and energy generated at Federal reservoir projects, supplemented by power purchased from public and private utilities, in such a manner as to encourage the most widespread and economical use. It sets the lowest possible rates for consumers consistent with sound business practices and gives preference to public entities. It also conducts and participates in the comprehensive planning of water resource development in the Southwest.

For further information, contact the Southwestern Power Administration, Suite 1600, Williams Center Tower One, One West Third Street, Tulsa, OK 74103-3532. Phone, 918-595-6600.

Western Area Power Administration

This Administration markets and transmits wholesale electricity in 15 Central and Western States, encompassing a geographic area of 1.3 million square miles. It sells power to cooperatives, municipalities, public utility districts, private utilities, Federal and State agencies, and irrigation districts. The wholesale power customers, in turn, provide service to millions of retail consumers in Arizona, California, Colorado, Iowa, Kansas, Minnesota, Montana, Nebraska, Nevada, New Mexico, North Dakota, South Dakota, Texas, Utah, and Wyoming.

It operates and maintains transmission lines, substations, and various auxiliary power facilities in the 15-State region. It also plans, constructs, operates, and maintains additional Federal transmission facilities that may be authorized in the future.

For further information, contact the Western Area Power Administration, 12155 West Alameda Parkway, Lakewood, CO 80228-1213. Phone, 720-962-7000.

Sources of Information

Business Opportunities

To learn about the Office of Small and Disadvantaged Business Utilization and its mission or to find information on the services that it offers and its programs, visit the Office's Web site. Phone, 202-586-7377.

Useful external links for small businesses are available on the Office of Small and Disadvantaged Business Utilization's Web site.

Employment

The DOE offers career opportunities that span a broad, diverse range of professions: accounting and contracting, administration, business, communications and information technology, computer science, engineering, mathematics, national security and international affairs, public affairs, science and technology, and more. Most Federal jobs require U.S. citizenship; however, noncitizens may apply for some opportunities at the National Laboratories.

Information on opportunities for students and recent graduates, veterans, and those with disabilities is available on the DOE Web site. For more information, contact the Chief Human Capital Officer. Phone, 202-586-1234.

Energy Saver

Energy Saver is the DOE's consumer resource on saving energy and using renewable energy technologies at home.

When deciding whether or not to invest in more energy efficiency, consumers can benefit from knowing electricity usages and the associated costs. The online energy use calculator estimates annual energy use and costs associated with operating appliances and home electronics.

Energy Simulation Software

EnergyPlus is cross-platform, free, and open-source software that runs on the Windows, Mac OS X, and Linux operating systems. It is a whole building energy simulation program that architects, engineers, and researchers use to model energy consumption and water use in buildings. The DOE's Building Technologies Office funded the development of EnergyPlus, and the National Renewable Energy Laboratory manages it.

Freedom of Information Act (FOIA)

The Office of Information Resources administers policies, procedures, and programs to ensure DOE compliance with the FOIA. The DOE provides resources on its Web site to assist information seekers with finding answers to questions about DOE programs and with locating information that is already publicly available and does not require a FOIA request to access. Information seekers should use these resources before submitting a FOIA request for DOE records.

Contact information for FOIA requester service centers and FOIA public liaisons and officers is available online.

The DOE Web site features an electronic FOIA request form.

Glossaries

The Bioenergy Technologies Office maintains an online biomass glossary. Its short descriptions are intended to help students and researchers understand biomass terminology.

The waterpower program maintains an online hydropower glossary. It is intended to help readers understand terminology associated with hydroturbine and hydropower plant components.

History

The DOE history timeline provides the public with easy access to information on the Department's history and its predecessor agencies. The timeline includes links to press releases, reports, speeches, and other documentation.

Maps

The DOE Web site features maps depicting a variety of energy-related topics and trends: alternative fueling stations, carbon capture, climate vulnerabilities, per capita energy expenditure, renewable energy production, solar energy potential, and more.

National Laboratories

For more than 60 years, these Laboratories have been leading institutions for scientific innovation in the United States. To learn more about the Ames Laboratory, Princeton Plasma Physics Laboratory, Thomas Jefferson National Accelerator Facility, and the other 14 National Laboratories, visit the DOE's "About the National Labs" Web page.

News

The DOE posts news stories, photos, speeches, and videos on its Web site, which also features a blog.

The DOE's online photo galleries are diverse and extensive, as well as captivating for browsers who have an interest in America's energy future.

An online subscription form is available to sign up for DOE advisories and press releases.

Office of Inspector General (OIG)

The OIG maintains electronic and telephone hotlines to facilitate the reporting of allegations of abuse, fraud, mismanagement, or waste in DOE programs or operations. Phone, 202-586-4073 or 800-541-1625.

An online complaint form for reporting allegations is also available on the OIG Web site.

The early alert system is a distribution list used to inform subscribers of significant press releases, publications, and reports the moment that the OIG posts them online. Subscription is free and available to anyone who has an email address and an interest in the OIG's work.

Open Government

The DOE supports the Open Government initiative to create a more open and transparent Government by promoting the principles of collaboration, participation, and transparency.

Phonebook

A departmentwide phonebook with a text box for entering search requests is available on the DOE Web site.

Program and Staff Offices

The "Offices" Web page features links to the program and staff offices' Web sites. It also includes links to the Web sites of the laboratories and technology centers, power marketing administrations, field sites, and Energy Information and National Nuclear Security Administrations.

Renewable Energy

The steady expansion of the U.S. renewable energy sector indicates that a clean energy revolution is underway nationwide. The DOE Web site features charts that graphically illustrates trends that will shape America's energy future.

Scientific and Technical Information

The Office of Scientific and Technical Information (OSTI) advances science and sustains technological creativity by making research and development findings available to and useful for DOE researchers and the public. The OSTI Web site provides access to DOE science resources and to U.S. Federal science (Science.gov) and global science (WorldWideScience.org) information.

Social Media

The DOE tweets announcements and other newsworthy items on Twitter.

The DOE has a Facebook page.

For further information, contact the Office of Public Affairs, Department of Energy, 1000 Independence Avenue SW., Washington, DC 20585. Phone, 202-586-4940.

DEPARTMENT OF ENERGY

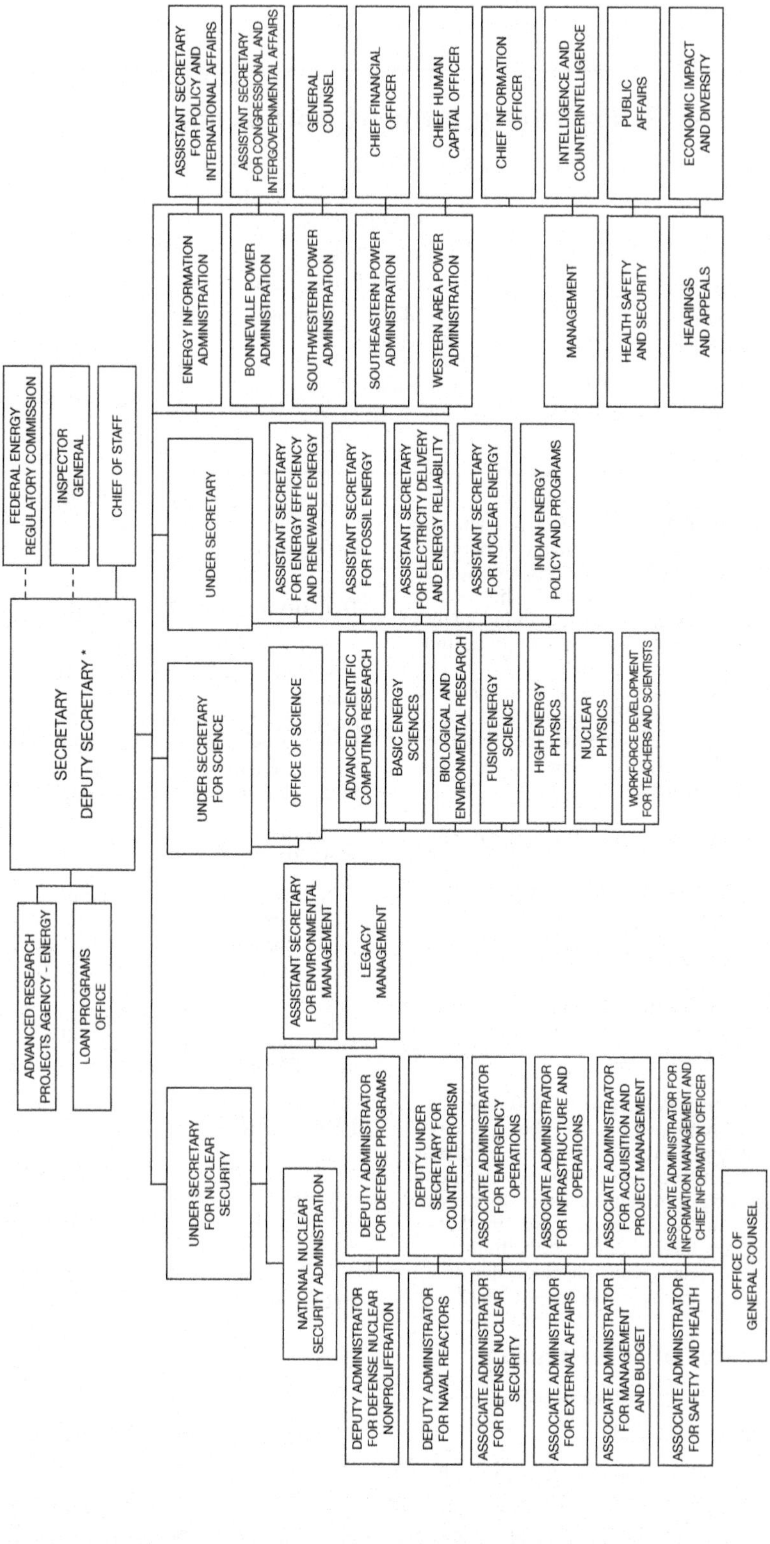

* The Deputy Secretary also serves as the Chief Operating Officer.

Federal Energy Regulatory Commission

888 First Street NE., Washington, DC 20426, 202-502-8055, *http://www.ferc.gov*

CHAIR	Norman C. Bay
Commissioner	Tony Clark
Commissioner	Colette D. Honorable
Commissioner	Cheryl A. LaFleur
Commissioner	(vacancy)

The Federal Energy Regulatory Commission helps consumers obtain efficient, reliable, and sustainable energy services at fair and reasonable rates through regulatory and market means.

The Federal Energy Regulatory Commission (FERC) is an independent agency within the Department of Energy that regulates the interstate transmission of electricity, natural gas, and oil. The Commission comprises five members whom the President appoints with the advice and consent of the Senate. FERC Commissioners serve 5-year terms and have an equal vote on regulatory matters. The President designates one member to serve as both the Commission's Chair and its administrative head.

Under the authority of the Federal Power, the Natural Gas, and the Interstate Commerce Acts, the FERC regulates the interstate transmission of electricity, natural gas, and oil. That authority also includes review of proposals to build interstate natural gas pipelines, natural gas storage facilities, and liquefied natural gas terminals, and licensing of nonfederal hydropower dams.

The Energy Policy Act of 2005 gave additional responsibilities to the Commission. Under the authority of that act, the FERC enforces regulatory requirements by imposing civil penalties and other means, monitors and investigates energy markets, and protects the reliability of the high voltage interstate transmission system through mandatory reliability standards.

Sources of Information

Critical Energy Infrastructure Information (CEII)

The FERC protects energy facilities by restricting public access to CEII. An electronic CEII request form is available on the Commission's Web site.

Decisionmaking Participation

Citizens who may be affected by a proposed natural gas or hydroelectric project that the Commission regulates have certain rights. These rights range from being able to look at project correspondence to becoming an intervener and being able to appeal FERC decisions in Federal court.

Employment

Information on college recruitment and internship programs, reasons for pursuing career opportunities at the FERC, and a list of job vacancies are available online.

In 2015, the FERC was ranked as one of the best midsize agencies at which to work in the Federal Government.

FERC Online

FERC Online serves as a portal to documents and dockets and provides an easy and efficient way to communicate and do business with the Commission.

Freedom of Information Act (FOIA)

An electronic FOIA request form is available on the Commission's Web site.

Frequently Asked Questions (FAQs)

A topical list of FAQ's is available on the

Commission's Web site.

Glossary

The FERC maintains a glossary and list of acronyms on its Web site.

Media

The Commission posts headlines, news releases, photographs, and statements, as well as videos of testimonies before congressional committees, speeches, and interviews.

Open Government

The FERC supports the principles of collaboration, participation, and transparency to expand the openness of the Federal Government.

Phone Book

The 2016 employee phone directory is available online in Portable Document Form (PDF).

Plain Language

The Commission is committed to the Plain Writing Act of 2010 and adheres to Federal plain language guidelines. The Commission, however, needs assistance from the public to comply with this Act. FERC editors and writers want to know if a document or section of the Web site is difficult to understand.

Speakers

An online form is available to initiate a request for a FERC representative to serve as a speaker at an organized event.

For further information, contact the Office of External Affairs. Phone, 202-502-8004 or 866-208-3372. Fax, 202-208-2106.

Department of Health and Human Services

200 Independence Avenue SW., Washington, DC 20201, 202-690-6343, *http://www.hhs.gov*

SECRETARY OF HEALTH AND HUMAN SERVICES	Sylvia Mathews Burwell
Deputy Secretary	Mary K. Wakefield, Acting
Chief of Staff	Alastair M. Fitzpayne
Chair, Departmental Appeals Board	Constance B. Tobias
Chief Administrative Law Judge, Office of Medicare Hearings and Appeals	Nancy J. Griswold
Executive Secretary	Madhura Valverde
General Counsel	Peggy Dotzel, Acting
Inspector General	Daniel R. Levinson
National Coordinator for Health Information Technology	Karen B. DeSalvo
Surgeon General	Vivek H. Murthy
ASSISTANT SECRETARIES	
Administration	Colleen Barros, Acting
Financial Resources	Ellen G. Murray
Global Affairs	Jimmy Kolker
Health	Karen B. DeSalvo, Acting
Legislation	Jim R. Esquea
Planning and Evaluation	Kathryn Martin, Acting
Preparedness and Response	Nicole Lurie
Public Affairs	Kevin Griffis

DIRECTORS	
Center for Faith-Based and Neighborhood Partnerships	Acacia Bamberg Salatti
Office for Civil Rights	Jocelyn Samuels
Office of Health Reform	Meena Seshamani
Office of Intergovernmental and External Affairs	Emily Barson

The Department of Health and Human Services strengthens the public health and welfare of the American people by making affordable and quality health care and childcare accessible, ensuring the safety of food products, preparing for public health emergencies, and advancing the diagnosis, treatment, and curing of life-threatening illnesses.

The Department of Health and Human Services (HHS) was created as the Department of Health, Education, and Welfare on April 11, 1953 (5 U.S.C. app.).

Secretary

The Secretary of Health and Human Services advises the President on health, welfare, and income security plans, policies, and programs of the Federal Government and directs Department staff in carrying out the programs and activities of the Department and promotes general public understanding of the Department's goals, programs, and objectives.

Office of Intergovernmental and External Affairs

The Office of Intergovernmental and External Affairs (IEA) supports the Secretary by serving as the primary liaison between the Department and external stakeholders and governments at the State, local, territorial, and tribal levels. The Office facilitates communication regarding HHS initiatives as they relate to external stakeholders and governments at the State, local, territorial, and tribal levels. The IEA both represents the State, territorial, and tribal perspective in the process of Federal policymaking and clarifies the Federal perspective to State, territorial and tribal representatives.

For further information, contact the Office of Intergovernmental and External Affairs. Phone, 202-690-6060.

Office of the Assistant Secretary for Preparedness and Response

The Office of the Assistant Secretary for Preparedness and Response (ASPR) provides national leadership in the prevention of, preparation for, and response to the adverse health effects of public health emergencies and disasters. It acts as the primary advisor to the HHS Secretary on bioterrorism and other public health emergency matters, strengthens the Nation's health and response systems, and enhances national health security. The ASPR leads a collaborative policy approach to the Department's preparedness, response, and recovery portfolio. It works with partners across Federal, State, local, tribal, and international bodies, in communities, and in the private sector to promote a unified and strategic approach to the challenges of public health and medical preparedness, response, and recovery through programs like the Hospital Preparedness Program. The ASPR coordinates public health and medical support available from across the Federal Government to help prepare communities and to augment local capabilities of overwhelmed communities during and after disasters, which includes providing medical professionals through the ASPR's National Disaster Medical System and the Medical Reserve Corps. The ASPR provides an integrated, systematic approach to the advanced development and acquisition of the necessary vaccines, drugs, therapies, and diagnostic tools for public health medical emergencies. It also coordinates within the Department and among Federal partners on the policy, prioritization, funding, acquisition, and distribution of these medical countermeasures. In addition, offices within the ASPR coordinate within the division, within the Department and with Federal, State, local, territorial, tribal and international bodies on emergency communications, science preparedness, and administrative management to support decisionmakers in emergencies.

For further information, contact the Office of the Assistant Secretary for Preparedness and Response. Phone, 202-205-2882.

Office of the Assistant Secretary for Health

The Office of the Assistant Secretary for Health (ASH) comprises 12 offices and 10 Presidential and secretarial advisory committees. The Assistant Secretary for Health heads the Office and serves as the Secretary's senior public health advisor. ASH provides assistance in implementing and coordinating secretarial decisions for the Public Health Service and coordination of population-based health clinical divisions; provides oversight of research conducted or supported by the Department; implements programs that provide population-based public health services; and provides direction and policy oversight, through the Office of the Surgeon General, for the Public Health Service Commissioned Corps. ASH administers a wide array of interdisciplinary programs related to disease prevention, health promotion, the reduction of health disparities, women's health, HIV/ AIDS, vaccine programs, physical fitness and sports, bioethics, population affairs, blood supply, research integrity, and human research protections.

For further information, contact the Office of the Assistant Secretary for Health. Phone, 202-690-7694.

Sources of Information

A–Z Index

The HHS Web site features an alphabetical index to help visitors search for specific topics or browse content that aligns with their interests.

Bullying

The HHS manages StopBullying.gov, a Web site that provides resources for defining, preventing, and responding to bullying, and for identifying who may be at risk. The Web site also features sections for children and teens, educators, parents, and communities.

Information on identifying, preventing, and reporting cyberbullying is also available on the Web site.

Business Opportunities

The HHS relies on its contractors and grantees to help protect the health of Americans and provide essential human services.

The Office of Small and Disadvantaged Business Utilization helps develop and implement outreach programs to raise awareness of HHS contracting opportunities within the small business community. For information on programs, contact the Office of Small and Disadvantaged Business Utilization. Phone, 202-690-7300.

Civil Rights

The Office for Civil Rights improves people's health and well-being, ensures equal access to health care and services without discrimination, and protects the privacy and security of people's health information. For information on enforcement of civil rights laws, contact the Director, Office for Civil Rights, 200 Independence Avenue SW.,Room 515–F Washington, DC 20201. Phone, 800-368-1019. TDD, 800-537-7697.

Departmental Appeals Board

For information, contact the Departmental Appeals Board Immediate Office, MS 6127, Wilbur J. Cohen Building, 330 Independence Avenue SW., Room G–644, Washington, DC 20201. Phone, 202-565-0200.

Employment

For information on training opportunities and opportunities for recent graduates and students or to view current job openings, visit the "Why a Career at HHS?" Web page.

Freedom of Information Act (FOIA)

The FOIA allows individuals to request access to Federal agency records. The statute contains, however, nine exemptions that exempt some records or portions of them from disclosure. The Assistant Secretary for Public Affairs also serves as the Agency Chief FOIA Officer.

Frequently Asked Questions (FAQs)

The HHS posts answers to FAQs on its Web site.

Glossary

In the world of organ donation and transplantation, terms are used and topics discussed that many may not recognize. The OrganDonor.gov Web site features a glossary of organ donation terms.

Inspector General

Contact the Office of Inspector General, Wilbur J. Cohen Building, 330 Independence Avenue SW., Washington, DC 20201.

To report fraud, waste, or abuse in Department programs, contact the Office of Inspector General, OIG Hotline Operations, P.O. Box 23489, L'Enfant Plaza Station, Washington, DC 20026-3489. TIPS Line, 800-447-8477. OIG Fugitive Line, 888-476-4453. TTY, 800-377-4950. Fax, 800-223-8164.

Medicare Hearings / Appeals

For information on Medicare hearings before administrative law judges, regarding Medicare coverage and payment determinations that Medicare contractors, Medicare Advantage Organizations, or Part D plan sponsors have made, as well as information on determinations related to Medicare beneficiary eligibility and entitlement, Part B late enrollment penalties, and income-related monthly adjustment amounts that the Social Security Administration has made, contact the Office of Medicare Hearings and Appeals. Phone, 703-235-0635 or 855-556-8475.

Open Government

The HHS supports the Open Government initiative by promoting the principles of collaboration, participation, and transparency.

Privacy Rights

For information on the HIPAA privacy, security, and breach notification rules or the Patient Safety Act, contact the Office for Civil Rights. Phone, 800-368-1019. TDD, 800-537-7697.

Public Health Service Commissioned Corps Officer Program

Information on the Commissioned Corps Officer programs is available at the Public Health Service Commissioned Corps Officer Web site.

Regional Offices

Visit the "Regional Offices" Web page for contact information.

Support Services (Fee-for-Service Activities)

The Program Support Center provides support services to all components of the Department and Federal agencies worldwide. For information concerning fee-for-service activities in the areas of acquisitions, occupational health, information technology support and security, human resource systems, financial management, and administrative operations, contact the Program Support Center, 5600 Fishers Lane, Rockville, MD 20857. Phone, 301-443-0034.

Surgeon General

For information on the benefits of active living, healthy eating, mental and emotional well-being, and tobacco-free living, visit the "Surgeon General" Web site. Phone, 240-276-8853.

For further information, contact the U.S. Department of Health and Human Services, 200 Independence Avenue SW., Washington, DC 20201. Phone, 877-696-6775.

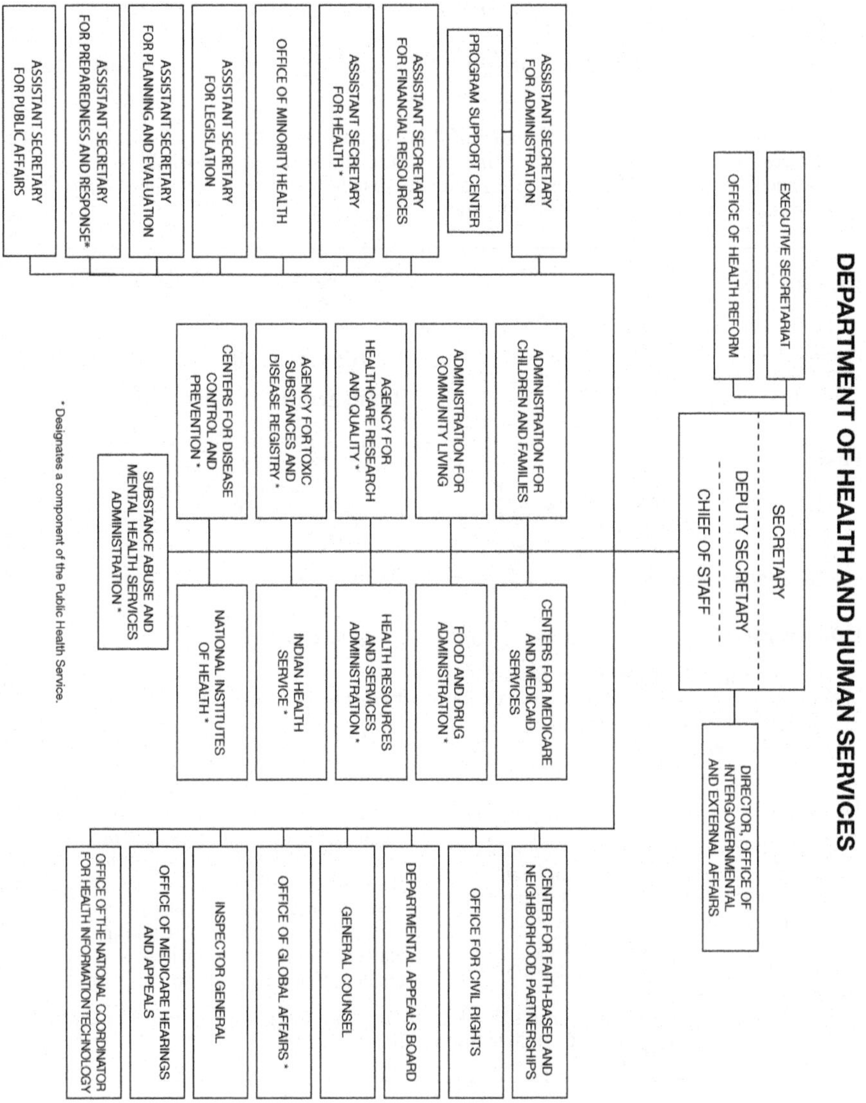
DEPARTMENT OF HEALTH AND HUMAN SERVICES
EXECUTIVE SECRETARIAT
OFFICE OF HEALTH REFORM
SECRETARY
DEPUTY SECRETARY
CHIEF OF STAFF
DIRECTOR, OFFICE OF INTERGOVERNMENTAL AND EXTERNAL AFFAIRS
ASSISTANT SECRETARY FOR ADMINISTRATION
PROGRAM SUPPORT CENTER
ASSISTANT SECRETARY FOR FINANCIAL RESOURCES
ASSISTANT SECRETARY FOR HEALTH*
OFFICE OF MINORITY HEALTH
ASSISTANT SECRETARY FOR LEGISLATION
ASSISTANT SECRETARY FOR PLANNING AND EVALUATION
ASSISTANT SECRETARY FOR PREPAREDNESS AND RESPONSE*
ASSISTANT SECRETARY FOR PUBLIC AFFAIRS
ADMINISTRATION FOR CHILDREN AND FAMILIES
ADMINISTRATION FOR COMMUNITY LIVING
AGENCY FOR HEALTHCARE RESEARCH AND QUALITY *
AGENCY FOR TOXIC SUBSTANCES AND DISEASE REGISTRY *
CENTERS FOR DISEASE CONTROL AND PREVENTION *
SUBSTANCE ABUSE AND MENTAL HEALTH SERVICES ADMINISTRATION *
CENTERS FOR MEDICARE AND MEDICAID SERVICES
FOOD AND DRUG ADMINISTRATION *
HEALTH RESOURCES AND SERVICES ADMINISTRATION *
INDIAN HEALTH SERVICE *
NATIONAL INSTITUTES OF HEALTH *
CENTER FOR FAITH-BASED AND NEIGHBORHOOD PARTNERSHIPS
OFFICE FOR CIVIL RIGHTS
DEPARTMENTAL APPEALS BOARD
GENERAL COUNSEL
OFFICE OF GLOBAL AFFAIRS *
INSPECTOR GENERAL
OFFICE OF MEDICARE HEARINGS AND APPEALS
OFFICE OF THE NATIONAL COORDINATOR FOR HEALTH INFORMATION TECHOLOGY
* Designates a component of the Public Health Service.

Administration for Children and Families

330 C Street SW., Washington, DC 20201, 202-401-9200, *http://www.acf.hhs.gov*

ASSISTANT SECRETARY FOR CHILDREN AND FAMILIES	Mark Greenberg, Acting
Chief of Staff	S. Jeffrey Hild

The Administration for Children and Families administers programs and provides advice to the Secretary on issues relevant to children, youth, and families; child support enforcement; community services; developmental disabilities; family assistance; Native American assistance; and refugee resettlement.

Employment

The Administration employs professionals with diverse academic and social backgrounds in a broad range of career fields and positions.

History

The Administration for Children and Families was created on April 15, 1991. A short history of the Administration is available on its Web site.

Homelessness

The Administration's Web site features information on its programs and services for the homeless and for those at risk of becoming homeless.

Hotlines

The Administration supports nationwide crisis hotlines for child abuse, domestic violence, human trafficking, and runaways. The Health Insurance Marketplace Call Center assists callers with choosing coverage that provides the best protection and benefits for them and family members, as well as for their businesses.

Lesbian, Gay, Bisexual, and Transgender (LGBT) Assistance

The Administration's Web site features information on its programs and services for the LGBT community, especially for LGBT families and youth.

News

The Administration posts press releases on its Web site.

Programs / Services

The Administration's Web site features a page showcasing by topic the programs and services that it provides to support families, children, individuals, and communities. Topics include children and youth, communities, emergency response and recovery, families, financial security, global populations, Hispanic outreach, homelessness, human trafficking, LGBT, Native Americans and tribes, and unaccompanied children.

For further information, contact the Administration for Children and Families, 330 C Street SW., Washington, DC 20201. Phone, 202-401-9200.

Administration for Community Living

330 C Street SW., Washington, DC 20201, 202-401-4634, TTY, 800-877-8339, *http://www.acl.gov*

ADMINISTRATOR	Edwin Walker, Acting
Principal Deputy Administrator	James D. Toews, Acting

The Administration for Community Living administers programs and advises the Secretary on issues relevant to people with disabilities, their families and caregivers, and the independence, well-being, and health of older adults.

Blog

The Administration's Blog presents diverse perspectives on trends and issues related to older adults and people with disabilities.

Data / Statistics

Data and statistics on older adults, as well as on persons with intellectual, physical, and developmental disabilities, are available on the Administration's Web site.

Elder Care Services

The elder care locator is a public service that provides information on services for older adults and their families. Online chat with an information specialist is also available Monday–Friday, 9 a.m.–8 p.m., eastern time. Phone, 800-677-1116.

Employment

For information on employment opportunities, visit the "Career Opportunities" Web page.

Help / Resources

The Administration's Web site features resources for connecting caregivers, families, older adults, people with disabilities, and professionals to Federal, national, and local programs and information.

For further information, contact the Administration for Community Living, 330 C Street SW., Washington, DC 20201. Phone, 202-401-4634. TTY, 800-877-8339.

Agency for Healthcare Research and Quality

5600 Fishers Lane, Rockville, MD 20857, 301-427-1364, *http://www.ahrq.gov*

DIRECTOR	Andrew Bindman
Deputy Director	Sharon B. Arnold

The Agency for Healthcare Research and Quality produces evidence to make health care affordable, equitable, more accessible, of a higher quality, and safer. It also works within the Department of Health and Human Services and with other partners to ensure that the evidence is understood and used.

Data

Statistical portraits of health care delivery in the United States are available on the Agency's Web site.

Employment

For information on employment opportunities, visit the "Job Opportunities" Web page.

Frequently Asked Questions (FAQs)

The Agency posts answers to FAQs on is Web site.

Site Map

The Web site map allows visitors to look for specific topics or to browse content that aligns with their interests.

For further information, contact the Agency for Healthcare Research and Quality, 5600 Fishers Lane, Rockville, MD 20857. Phone, 301-427-1364.

Agency for Toxic Substances and Disease Registry

MS E–61, 4770 Buford Highway NE., Atlanta, GA 30341, 770-488-0604, *http://www.atsdr.cdc.gov*

ADMINISTRATOR	Thomas R. Frieden

The Agency for Toxic Substances and Disease Registry (ATSDR), as part of the Public Health Service, tries to prevent exposure to toxic substances—exposure to substances from wastesites, unplanned releases, and other pollution sources present in the environment—which produces adverse health effects and diminishes the quality of life.

A–Z Index

The Agency's Web site features an alphabetical index to help visitors search for specific topics or browse content that aligns with their interests.

ATSDR in 60 Seconds

The ATSDR protects people from the health effects of chemical exposures. The Agency's Web site features the 60-second video "Dangerous Discovery" that communicates the importance of its mission.

Internships / Training

Information on internships and educational and training opportunities is available on the ATSDR Web site.

Toxic Frequently Asked Questions (ToxFAQs)

ToxFAQs features a series of summaries on hazardous substances that the Agency's Division of Toxicology developed. ATSDR toxicological profiles and public health statements are the on which the series relies. Each factsheet serves as a guide that is quick to read and easy to understand. ToxFAQs also answers FAQs on exposure to hazardous substances that are encountered near wastesites and their effects on human health.

Toxic Substances Portal

The portal offers convenient access to the most relevant information on toxic substances and their effects on human health. The portal's Web pages feature an alphabetical ordering of documents on specific substances, toxicological information by health effect or chemical class, and toxicological information for specific audiences (community members, emergency responders, toxicological and health professionals, and health care providers).

For further information, contact the Agency for Toxic Substances and Disease Registry, 4770 Buford Highway NE., Atlanta, GA 30341. Phone, 770-488-0604.

Centers for Disease Control and Prevention

1600 Clifton Road, Atlanta, GA 30333, 800-232-4636, *http://www.cdc.gov*

DIRECTOR	Thomas R. Frieden
Principal Deputy Director	Anne Schuchat

The Centers for Disease Control and Prevention (CDC), as part of the Public Health Service, protect the public health of the Nation by providing leadership and direction in the prevention and control of diseases and other preventable conditions and by responding to public health emergencies. Within the CDC, the following seven centers, institutes, and offices lead prevention, diagnosis, and treatment efforts for public health concerns.

Center for Global Health

The Center leads the CDC global health strategy, working in partnership with foreign governments and international organizations to help countries worldwide evaluate, manage, and plan global health care programs. The Center works to eradicate chronic diseases and life-threatening injuries, expanding global health care programs to address the leading causes of disability, morbidity, and mortality.

National Institute for Occupational Safety and Health

The Institute coordinates, directs, and plans a national program to develop and establish recommended occupational safety and health standards and to conduct research and training, offer technical assistance, and engage in related activities to assure safe and healthy work conditions for every working person.

Office of Infectious Diseases

The Office facilitates research, programs, and policies to reduce the national and international burden of infectious diseases. The Office includes the following organizational components: the National Center for HIV/AIDS, Viral Hepatitis, STD and TB Prevention; the National Center for Immunization and Respiratory Diseases; and the National Center for Emerging and Zoonotic Infectious Diseases.

Office of Noncommunicable Diseases, Injury, and Environmental Health

The Office provides strategic direction and leadership for the prevention of noncommunicable diseases, injuries, disabilities, and environmental health hazards. The Office includes the following organizational components: the National Center on Birth Defects and Developmental Disabilities; the National Center for Chronic Disease Prevention and Health Promotion; the National Center for Environmental Health; and the National Center for Injury Prevention and Control.

Office of Public Health Preparedness and Response

The Office helps the Nation prepare for and respond to urgent public health threats by providing strategic direction, coordination, and support for CDC's terrorism preparedness and emergency response activities.

Office of Public Health Scientific Services

The Office provides scientific services, knowledge, and resources to promote public health, prepare for potential health threats, and prevent disease, disability, and injury. It includes the following organizational components: the National Center for Health Statistics; the Laboratory Science, Policy and Practice Program Office; the Public Health Informatics and Technology Program Office; the Public Health Surveillance Program Office; the Epidemiology and Analysis Program Office; and the Scientific Education and Professional Development Program Office.

Office of State, Tribal, Local, and Territorial Support

The Office provides guidance, strategic direction, oversight, and leadership in support of State, local, territorial, and tribal public health agencies, initiatives, and priorities to improve the capacity and performance of a comprehensive public health system.

Sources of Information

Climate Change

Climate change threatens human health and well-being in many ways. Information on the steps that the CDC is taking to mitigate and adapt to the health effects of climate change is available online.

Disease of the Week

The "Disease of the Week" Web page features key facts on, prevention tips for, and a quiz to test one's knowledge of common, serious diseases.

Employment

The CDC is the leading national public

health protection agency in the United States. It relies on professionals with scientific and nonscientific expertise to protect Earth's human population from the threat of deadly diseases like Ebola, HIV/AIDS, influenza, malaria, and tuberculosis. Most scientific and technical positions at the CDC are filled through the Commissioned Corps of the Public Health Service, a uniformed service of the U.S. Government.

Freedom of Information Act (FOIA)

The CDC posts answers to frequently asked FOIA questions on its Web site.

The CDC posts frequently requested agency records in its electronic reading room.

Influenza (Flu)

The CDC Web site features of trove of influenza information and resources.

Library

The Stephen B. Thacker CDC Library helps the advancement of science and public health and safety through information. It provides a full range of information services and products to support public health research, policy, and action. The Library, which comprises the headquarters library in Atlanta and six branches, serves CDC employees nationwide, as well as employees working in international locations.

Museum

The David J. Sencer CDC Museum features award-winning permanent and changing exhibitions that focus on public health topics, as well as on the history of the CDC. The museum is located in Atlanta, GA, and admission is free. It is open to the public on weekdays, excluding Federal holidays. Phone, 404-639-0830.

Podcasts

CDC podcasts provide reliable health and safety information.

Publications

Many publications are accessible on the CDC's Web site.

The monthly report "CDC Vital Signs" is released on the first Tuesday of every month. Past editions have addressed topics like colorectal and breast cancer screening, obesity, alcohol and tobacco use, HIV testing, motor vehicle safety, cardiovascular disease, teen pregnancy and infections associated with health care, foodborne disease, and more.

Social Media

The CDC tweets announcements and other newsworthy items on Twitter.

The CDC has a Facebook account.

The CDC posts videos on its YouTube channel.

Stress

The CDC's Web site provides information on managing stress after a traumatic event.

Travel Health Notices

The CDC posts travel health notices on its Web site.

For further information, contact the Centers for Disease Control and Prevention, 1600 Clifton Road, Atlanta, GA 30333. Phone, 800-232-4636. TTY, 888-232-6348.

Centers for Medicare and Medicaid Services

7500 Security Boulevard, Baltimore, MD 21244, 410-786-3000, *http://www.cms.gov*

ADMINISTRATOR	Andrew Slavitt, Acting
Principal Deputy Administrator	Patrick H. Conway, Acting
Chief Operating Officer / Chief of Staff	Mandy Cohen

The Centers for Medicare and Medicaid Services (CMS) provides health coverage to more than 100 million people through Medicare, Medicaid, the Children's Health Insurance Program, and the Health Insurance Marketplace. The CMS seeks to strengthen and modernize the Nation's health care system, to provide access to high quality care and improved health at lower costs.

Sources of Information

Blog

The CMS maintains an official blog on its Web site.

Employment

For information on career opportunities, visit the "Careers at CMS" Web page.

Forms

Many CMS forms are accessible on the agency's Web site.

Frequently Asked Questions (FAQs)

The CMS posts answers to FAQs on its Web site.

Glossary

The CMS maintains a glossary that explains terms found on its Web site.

History

The CMS Web site features the agency's program history.

Medicaid

The CMS manages the Medicaid.gov Web site.

Medicare

The CMS manages the Medicare.gov Web site.

The Medicare Coverage Database contains all national coverage determinations and local coverage determinations, local articles, and proposed national coverage determination decisions. The database also includes several other types of national coverage policy-related documents, including national coverage analyses, coding analyses for labs, Medicare Evidence Development and Coverage Advisory Committee proceedings, and Medicare coverage guidance documents.

The CMS manages the "STOP Medicare Fraud" Web site. To report Medicare fraud, call 800-447-8477. TTY, 800-377-4950.

Newsroom

The CMS posts news items on its Web site.

Social Media

The CMS tweets announcements and other newsworthy items on Twitter.

The CMS posts videos on its YouTube channel.

For further information, contact the Centers for Medicare and Medicaid Services, Department of Health and Human Services, 7500 Security Boulevard, Baltimore, MD 21244. Phone, 410-786-3000.

Food and Drug Administration

10903 New Hampshire Avenue, Silver Spring, MD 20993, 888-463-6332, *http://www.fda.gov*

COMMISSIONER	Robert M. Califf
Chief of Staff	Thomas Kraus

The Food and Drug Administration (FDA) protects the public health by ensuring the safety, security, and efficacy of human and veterinary drugs, biological products, medical devices, the Nation's food supply, cosmetics, and products that emit radiation. The FDA also advances the public health by accelerating innovations to make medicines more effective and by providing the public with accurate, science-based information on medicines and food to improve health. The agency plays a significant role in the Nation's counterterrorism capability by ensuring the security of the food supply.

Sources of Information

Animal and Veterinary Recalls

The FDA posts animal and veterinary recall information—brand name, date of recall, company name, product description, and the reason or problem—on its Web site.

A–Z Index

The FDA's Web site features an alphabetical index to help visitors search for specific topics or browse content that aligns with their interests.

Cigarettes

The FDA describes cigarettes with three words: attractive, addictive, and deadly. Cigarettes are designed to be attractive and addictive. The FDA's infographic "How a Cigarette is Engineered" explains the role design plays in attraction and addiction.

Cosmetics

The FDA posts answers to the questions that consumers frequently ask about cosmetic safety and regulation.

Employment

The FDA relies on attorneys, biologists, chemists, consumer safety officers, engineers, information technology specialists, medical officers, microbiologists, pharmacists, pharmacologists, statisticians, and other professionals to carry out its mission.

Foodborne Illnesses

The FDA regulates human and animal food. It posts information on recent foodborne illness outbreaks on its Web site.

Recalls / Safety Alerts

Information gathered from press releases and other public notices on certain recalls of FDA-regulated products is available online.

For further information contact the Food and Drug Administration, 10903 New Hampshire Avenue, Silver Spring, MD 20993. Phone, 888-463-6332.

Health Resources and Services Administration

5600 Fishers Lane, Rockville, MD 20857, 301-443-3376, *http://www.hrsa.gov*

ADMINISTRATOR	James Macrae, Acting
Deputy Administrator	Diana Espinosa

The Health Resources and Services Administration (HRSA) improves access to health care by strengthening the health care workforce, building healthy communities, and achieving health equity. HRSA programs make health care accessible to people who are geographically isolated or economically or medically vulnerable. It supports the training of health professionals, the distribution of providers to areas where they are needed most, and improvements in health care delivery. The agency also oversees organ, bone marrow, and cord blood donations; compensates individuals harmed by vaccination; and maintains databases that protect against health care abuse, fraud, malpractice, and waste.

Sources of Information

Data

The HRSA maintains an online data warehouse.

Employment

The HRSA posts career opportunities on

its Web site.

Freedom of Information Act (FOIA)

The FOIA requires the HRSA to disclose documents or records that any person properly requests in writing. Certain documents or records, or parts of them, may be protected, however, from disclosure by one of the nine exemptions contained in the statute.

Organ Donation and Transplantation

The HRSA manages the OrganDonor.gov Web site, which provides the public with U.S. Government information on organ donation and transplantation.

Social Media

The HRSA tweets announcements and other newsworthy items on Twitter.

The HRSA has a Facebook account.

The HRSA posts videos on its YouTube channel.

For further information, contact the Office of Communications, Health Resources and Services Administration, 5600 Fishers Lane, Rockville, MD 20857. Phone, 301-443-3376.

Indian Health Service

5600 Fishers Lane Rockville, MD 20857, 301-443-3593, *http://www.ihs.gov*

DIRECTOR	(vacancy)
Principal Deputy Director	Mary L. Smith
Deputy Director	Christopher Buchanan

The Indian Health Service, as part of the Public Health Service, provides a comprehensive health services delivery system for American Indians and Alaska Natives. It helps Native American tribes develop their health programs; facilitates and assists tribes in coordinating health planning and obtaining and utilizing health resources available through Federal, State, and local programs, in operating comprehensive health programs and evaluating them; and provides comprehensive health care services, including hospital and ambulatory medical care, preventive and rehabilitative services, and development of community sanitation facilities.

Sources of Information

A–Z Index

The Indian Health Service's Web site features an alphabetical index to help visitors search for specific topics or browse content that aligns with their interests.

Employment

For information on employment, visit the "Career Opportunities" Web page.

Freedom of Information Act (FOIA)

The Indian Health Service's Web site features an electronic FOIA requester center.

Newsroom

The Newsroom features announcements, congressional testimony, factsheets, press releases, and speeches.

Social Media

The Indian Health Service has a Facebook account.

The Indian Health Service posts videos on its YouTube channel.

For further information, contact the Management Policy and Internal Control Staff, Indian Health Service, 5600 Fishers Lane Rockville, MD 20857. Phone, 301-443-3593.

National Institutes of Health

1 Center Drive, Bethesda, MD 20892, 301-496-4000, *http://www.nih.gov*

DIRECTOR	Francis S. Collins
Principal Deputy Director	Lawrence A. Tabak

The National Institutes of Health (NIH) support biomedical and behavioral research domestically and abroad, conduct research in NIH laboratories and clinics, train research scientists, and develop and disseminate credible, science-based health information to the public.

Aging

The National Institute on Aging (NIA) conducts and supports research on the aging process, age-related diseases, and other special problems and needs of older people. It is also the lead NIH Institute for research on age-related cognitive change and Alzheimer's disease. The NIA provides information on aging to the scientific community, health care providers, and the public.

For further information, contact the National Institute on Aging. Phone, 301-496-1752.

Alcohol Abuse and Alcoholism

The National Institute on Alcohol Abuse and Alcoholism leads the national effort to reduce alcohol-related problems by conducting and supporting biomedical and behavioral research into the causes, consequences, prevention, and treatment of alcohol-use disorders.

For further information, contact the National Institute on Alcohol Abuse and Alcoholism. Phone, 301-443-3885.

Allergy and Infectious Diseases

The National Institute of Allergy and Infectious Diseases conducts and supports research to study the causes of infectious diseases and immune-mediated diseases and to develop better means of preventing, diagnosing, and treating these diseases.

For further information, contact the National Institute of Allergy and Infectious Diseases. Phone, 866-284-4107 or 301-496-5717.

Arthritis and Musculoskeletal and Skin Diseases

The National Institute of Arthritis and Musculoskeletal and Skin Diseases supports research on the causes, treatment, and prevention of arthritis and musculoskeletal and skin diseases; the basic and clinical training of scientists to carry out this research; and the dissemination of information on research progress.

For further information, contact the National Institute of Arthritis and Musculoskeletal and Skin Diseases. Phone, 877-226-4267 or 301-496-8190.

Behavioral and Social Sciences Research

The Office of Behavioral and Social Sciences Research supports and coordinates health-related behavioral and social sciences research that the NIH conducts or supports, and it integrates these sciences within the larger NIH research enterprise. It also communicates and disseminates research findings to stakeholders within and outside the Federal Government, thereby increasing understanding and improving treatment and prevention of disease.

For further information, contact the Office of Behavioral and Social Sciences Research. Phone, 301-402-1146.

Biomedical Imaging and Bioengineering

The National Institute of Biomedical Imaging and Bioengineering supports research, training, and the dissemination of research advances for accelerating the development and application of biomedical technologies to improve the detection, treatment, and prevention of disease. It integrates the physical and engineering sciences with the life sciences to advance basic research and medical care.

For further information, contact the National Institute of Biomedical Imaging and Bioengineering. Phone, 301-496-3500.

Cancer

The National Cancer Institute (NCI) is the Federal Government's principal agency for cancer research and training. It coordinates the National Cancer Program, which conducts and supports research, training, health information dissemination, and other activities associated with diagnosing, preventing, treating, and finding the cause of cancer and with the continuing care of cancer patients and their families.

For further information, contact the Cancer Information Service. Phone, 800-422-6237.

Center for Information Technology

The Center for Information Technology provides, coordinates, and manages information technology to advance computational science.

For further information, contact the Center for Information Technology. Phone, 301-496-5703.

Child Health and Human Development

The Eunice Kennedy Shriver National Institute of Child Health and Human Development conducts and supports basic, clinical, and epidemiological research on the reproductive, rehabilitative, neurobiological, developmental, and behavioral processes that determine the health of children, adults, families, and communities.

For further information, contact the Eunice Kennedy Shriver National Institute of Child Health and Human Development. Phone, 800-370-2943.

Clinical Center

The Clinical Center is the clinical research hospital for the NIH. By doing clinical research, investigators translate laboratory discoveries into better treatments, therapies, and interventions to improve the Nation's health. The Center conducts clinical and laboratory research and trains future clinical investigators. Nearly 500,000 volunteers from across the Nation have participated in clinical research studies since the Center opened in 1953. About 1,500 clinical research studies are currently in progress.

For further information, contact the Clinical Center. Phone, 301-496-4000.

Communications

The Office of Communications and Public Liaison communicates information on consumer health, scientific results, and NIH accomplishments, issues, and research and training programs to the public, media, scientific and medical communities, and other interested groups.

For further information, contact the Office of Communications and Public Liaison. Phone, 301-496-5787

Complementary and Integrative Health

The National Center for Complementary and Integrative Health defines the utility and safety of complementary and integrative health interventions and their roles in improving health and health care. This science-based information helps the public, health care professionals, and health policymakers make decisions on the use and integration of complementary and integrative health approaches.

For further information, contact the National Center for Complementary and Integrative Health. Phone, 888-644-6226.

Deafness and Other Communication Disorders

The National Institute on Deafness and Other Communication Disorders conducts and supports biomedical and behavioral research and training on normal and disordered processes of hearing, balance, taste, smell, voice, speech, and language. The Institute also makes science-based health information publicly available, and it supports efforts to create devices that substitute for lost or impaired sensory and communication function.

For further information, contact the National Institute on Deafness and Other Communication Disorders. Phone, 800-241-1044. TTY, 800-241-1055.

Dental and Craniofacial Research

The National Institute of Dental and Craniofacial Research funds research on dental, oral, and craniofacial health and disorders. It also conducts research in its own laboratories and clinic, supports research training, and promotes the timely transfer of research-based knowledge and its implications for health to researchers, to health professionals, to patients, and to the general public.

For further information, contact the National Institute of Dental and Craniofacial Research. Phone, 301-496-4261.

Diabetes and Digestive and Kidney Diseases

The National Institute of Diabetes and Digestive and Kidney Diseases conducts, supports, and coordinates research and research training. It also offers science-based information on diabetes and other endocrine and metabolic diseases; on digestive diseases, nutritional disorders, weight control, and obesity; and on kidney, urologic and blood diseases.

For further information, contact the National Institute of Diabetes and Digestive and Kidney Diseases. Phone, 301-496-3583.

Drug Abuse

The National Institute on Drug Abuse supports and conducts basic and clinical research on drug use, its consequences, and the underlying neurobiological, behavioral, and social mechanisms. The Institute also ensures effective translation and dissemination of scientific findings to improve the prevention and treatment of substance-use disorders, and it works at raising the public's awareness that addiction is a type of brain disorder.

For further information, contact the National Institute on Drug Abuse. Phone, 877-643-2644.

Environmental Health Sciences

The National Institute of Environmental Health Sciences supports research that explores how the environment affects people's health. Its research centers on environmental exposures and understanding their effects on human biology and health with an emphasis on disease and disability prevention. The Institute also houses the national toxicology program, a cross-agency organization that coordinates toxicity testing across the Federal Government.

For further information, contact the National Institute of Environmental Health Sciences. Phone, 919-541-3345.

Eye and Vision Diseases

The National Eye Institute conducts, fosters, and supports research on the causes, natural history, prevention, diagnosis, and treatment of disorders of the eye and visual system. It also directs the National Eye Health Education Program.

For further information, contact the National Eye Institute. Phone, 301-496-5248.

Fogarty International Center

The Fogarty International Center addresses global health challenges through innovative and collaborative research and training programs. It also supports and advances the NIH mission through international partnerships.

For further information, contact the Fogarty International Center. Phone, 301-496-2075.

General Medical Sciences

The National Institute of General Medical Sciences (NIGMS) supports basic research that increases understanding of biological processes and lays the foundation for advances in disease diagnosis, treatment, and prevention. NIGMS-funded scientists investigate how living systems work at a range of levels, from molecules and cells to tissues, to whole organisms and populations. The Institute also supports research in clinical areas, primarily those that affect multiple organ systems. To assure the vitality and productivity of the research enterprise, the NIGMS provides leadership in training the next generation of scientists, in diversifying the scientific workforce, and in developing research capacities throughout the country.

For further information, contact the National Institute of General Medical Sciences. Phone, 301-496-7301.

Heart, Lung, and Blood Diseases

The National Heart, Lung, and Blood Institute provides leadership for a global program in sleep disorders, blood resources, and diseases of the heart, blood vessels, blood, and lungs. It conducts, fosters, and supports a comprehensive program of basic research, clinical investigations and trials, observational and implementation science studies, as well as demonstration and education projects.

For further information, contact the National Heart, Lung, and Blood Institute. Phone, 301-592-8573.

Human Genome Research

The National Human Genome Research Institute supports research to uncover the role that the genome plays in human health and disease; studies on the ethical, legal, and social implications of genomics research for individuals, families, and communities; and the application of genomics research to medical care.

For further information, contact the National Human Genome Research Institute. Phone, 301-402-0911.

Library of Medicine

The National Library of Medicine, the world's largest biomedical library, serves as the Nation's principal medical information source, providing medical library services and extensive online information resources to scientists, practitioners, and the general public. It conducts, fosters, and supports research and training in biomedical informatics and supports development and dissemination of clinical terminology standards.

For further information, contact the National Library of Medicine. Phone, 301-496-6308.

Mental Health

The National Institute of Mental Health works to transform the understanding and treatment of mental illnesses. Through basic and clinical research, it advances the prevention, recovery, and cure of mental conditions that disable many Americans.

For further information, contact the National Institute of Mental Health. Phone, 866-615-6464.

Minority Health and Health Disparities

The National Institute on Minority Health and Health Disparities leads scientific research to improve minority health and eliminate health disparities. The Institute plans, reviews, coordinates, and evaluates all minority health and health disparities research and activities of the NIH; conducts and supports research on minority health and health disparities; promotes and supports the training of a diverse research workforce; translates and disseminates research information; and fosters innovative collaborations and partnerships.

For further information, contact the National Institute on Minority Health and Health Disparities. Phone, 301-402-1366.

Neurological Disorders and Stroke

The National Institute of Neurological Disorders and Stroke works to better understand the brain and spinal cord and to use that knowledge to mitigate the effects of neurological disease. It conducts, promotes, coordinates, and guides research and training on the causes, prevention, diagnosis, and treatment of neurological disorders and stroke. It also supports basic, translational, and clinical research in related scientific areas.

For further information, contact the National Institute of Neurological Disorders and Stroke. Phone, 301-496-5751.

Nursing Research

The National Institute of Nursing Research supports clinical and basic research and research training to build the scientific foundation for clinical practice, to prevent disease and disability, to manage and eliminate symptoms caused by illness, to enhance end-of-life and palliative care, and to train the next generation of nurse scientists.

For further information, contact the National Institute of Nursing Research. Phone, 301-496-0207.

Program Coordination, Planning, and Strategic Initiatives

The Division of Program Coordination, Planning, and Strategic Initiatives coordinates trans-NIH programs, planning, and strategic scientific initiatives in the Office of the NIH Director. The Division includes major programmatic offices that coordinate and support research and research infrastructure. The Division also serves as a portfolio analysis resource, coordinates evaluation reporting and agency activities under the Government Performance and Results Act, and supports science education partnership awards.

For further information, contact the Division of Program Coordination, Planning, and Strategic Initiatives. Phone, 301-402-9852.

Scientific Review

The Center for Scientific Review (CSR) organizes the peer review groups that evaluate the majority of grant applications submitted to the NIH. These groups include experienced and respected researchers from across the country and abroad. Since 1946, CSR has ensured that NIH grant applications receive fair, independent, expert, and timely reviews—free from inappropriate influences—so the NIH can fund the most promising research. CSR also receives all incoming applications and assigns them to the appropriate Centers and Institutes that fund grants.

For further information, contact the Center for Scientific Review. Phone, 301-435-1111.

Translational Sciences

The National Center for Advancing Translational Sciences focuses on what is common across diseases and the translational process. The Center emphasizes innovation and deliverables, relying on data and new technologies to develop, demonstrate, and disseminate advances in translational science that tangibly improve human health.

For further information, contact the National Center for Advancing Translational Sciences. Phone, 301-435-0888.

Sources of Information

Employment

For information on employment opportunities, visit the "Jobs at NIH" Web page.

Events

The NIH posts upcoming events on its Web site.

Freedom of Information Act (FOIA)

The FOIA gives a right to access documents or records in the possession of the Federal Government to any person. The Government may withhold, however, information pursuant to the statute's nine exemptions and three exclusions. For more information, contact the NIH FOIA Office. Phone, 301-496-5633. Fax, 301-402-4541.

Frequently Asked Questions (FAQs)

The NIH posts answers to FAQs on its Web site.

History

The story of the agency begins in 1887, and a brief retelling of it is available online.

The DeWitt Stetten, Jr., Museum of Medical Research, also known as the NIH Stetten Museum, preserves and interprets the material culture of the NIH's scientific work through physical and virtual exhibits.

News

The NIH posts news releases on its Web site.

The monthly newsletter "NIH News In Health" features practical consumer health news and information that is based on NIH research.

Social Media

The NIH tweets announcements and other newsworthy items on Twitter.

The NIH has a Facebook account.

The NIH posts videos on its YouTube channel.

Spanish

Important health information is available in Spanish.

Staff Directory

The NIH enterprise directory allows users to search for staff members by email address, name, or phone number.

Visitor Information

Maps and information on access and security, parking, tours, the campus shuttle, and more are available on the NIH Web site.

Weight Management

The National Institute of Diabetes and Digestive and Kidney Diseases' Web site has a trove of weight management information and resources.

The online body weight planner allows users to make personalized calorie and physical activity plans for reaching a target weight within a specific time period—and for maintaining it afterwards.

For further information, contact the National Institutes of Health, 1 Center Drive, Bethesda, MD 20892. Phone, 301-496-4000.

Substance Abuse and Mental Health Services Administration

5600 Fishers Lane Rockville, MD 20857, 240-276-2130, *http://www.samhsa.gov*

ADMINISTRATOR	Kana Enomoto, Acting
Chief of Staff	Tom Coderre

The Substance Abuse and Mental Health Services Administration mitigates the effects of substance abuse and mental illness on communities nationwide. It provides national leadership, serving as a voice for behavioral health; funds State and local service agencies through grants and formulas; collects data and makes available surveillance reports on the effect of behavioral health on Americans; leads efforts to offer public education on mental illness and substance abuse prevention, treatment, and recovery; regulates and oversees national behavioral health programs; and promotes practice improvement in community-based, primary, and specialty care settings.

Sources of Information

Blog

The Administration's Web site features a blog.

Data

The Administration maintains five collections of data: Center for Behavioral Health Statistics and Quality reports, client level data, mental health facilities data, population data, and substance abuse facilities data.

Employment

For information on career opportunities, visit the "Jobs and Internships" Web page.

Help / Treatment

Resources for help and treatment are available on the Administration's Web site.

KSOC–TV

KSOC–TV is a web-based technical assistance program featuring behavioral health experts discussing leading issues in children's mental health.

Newsroom

Press announcements, quarterly newsletters, and media highlights of initiatives and other activities are available in the newsroom.

Offices / Centers

The agency's offices and centers provide leadership and assistance for quality behavioral health services, as well as support States, territories, tribes, communities, and local organizations through grants and contract awards. Contact information for these offices and centers is available online.

Publications

Hundreds of publications are available on the Administration's Web site.

Site Map

The Web site map allows visitors to look for specific topics or to browse content that aligns with their interests.

Social Media

The Administration uses various forms of social media to connect with the Internet community and engage people.

Suicide Prevention

The Administration funds the National Suicide Prevention Lifeline. Phone, 800-273-8255.

Treatment Services Locator

The behavioral health treatment services locator is a confidential and anonymous source of information for persons seeking treatment facilities in the United States or U.S. Territories for substance abuse, addiction, mental health problems, or a combination of the three. Phone, 800-662-4357. TDD, 800-487-4889.

Underage Drinking

Underage drinking accounts for 11 percent of all the alcohol consumed in the United States. Alcohol is the most widely misused substance among America's youth. The Administration disseminates information on the dangers of underage drinking and offers prevention tips.

For further information, contact the Substance Abuse and Mental Health Services Administration, 5600 Fishers Lane Rockville, MD 20857, Rockville, MD 20857. Phone, 240-276-2130.

Department of Homeland Security

Washington, DC 20528, 202-282-8000, *http://www.dhs.gov*

Secretary of Homeland Security	Jeh Charles Johnson
Deputy Secretary	Alejandro N. Mayorkas
Chief of Staff	Paul M. Rosen
Executive Secretary	Kimberly O'Connor
General Counsel	Stevan E. Bunnell
Under Secretary, Management	Russell C. Deyo
Under Secretary, National Protection and Programs Directorate	Suzanne E. Spaulding
Assistant Secretary, Cybersecurity and Communications	Andy Ozment
Assistant Secretary, Infrastructure Protection	Caitlin Durkovich
Director, Federal Protective Service	L. Eric Patterson
Under Secretary, Science and Technology	Reginald Brothers
Under Secretary, Intelligence and Analysis	Francis X. Taylor
Assistant Secretary, Policy	(vacancy)
Assistant Secretary, International Affairs / Chief Diplomatic Officer	Alan D. Bersin
Director, Office for Community Partnerships	George Selim
Assistant Secretary, Partnership and Engagement	Philip A. McNamara
Director, U.S. Citizenship and Immigration Services	León Rodríguez
Commandant, U.S. Coast Guard	Adm. Paul F. Zukunft
Commissioner, U.S. Customs and Border Protection	R. Gil Kerlikowske
Director, U.S. Immigration and Customs Enforcement	Sarah Saldaña
Administrator, Federal Emergency Management Agency	W. Craig Fugate
Director, U.S. Secret Service	Joseph P. Clancy
Administrator, Transportation Security Administration	Peter V. Neffenger
Ombudsman, Citizenship and Immigration Services	Maria M. Odom
Officer, Civil Rights and Civil Liberties	Megan H. Mack

Director, Domestic Nuclear Detection Office	L. Wayne Brasure, Acting
Director, Federal Law Enforcement Training Center	Connie L. Patrick
Assistant Secretary, Health Affairs / Chief Medical Officer	Kathryn Brinsfield
Inspector General	John Roth
Assistant Secretary, Legislative Affairs	M. Tia Johnson
Director, Operations Coordination	Richard Chávez
Chief Privacy Officer	(vacancy)
Assistant Secretary, Public Affairs	J. Todd Breasseale
Deputy Under Secretary, Management / Chief Financial Officer	Chip H. Fulghum

The Department of Homeland Security prevents terrorism and enhances security, secures and manages the Nation's borders, enforces and administers its immigration laws, safeguards and secures cyberspace, and ensures resilience to disasters.

The Department of Homeland Security (DHS) was established by the Homeland Security Act of 2002 (6 U.S.C. 101 note). The Department came into existence on January 24, 2003, and is administered under the supervision and direction of the Secretary of Homeland Security.

OFFICE OF THE SECRETARY

The Office of the Secretary oversees activities in collaboration with other Federal, State, local, and private entities to carry out the Department's overall mission. The Office of the Secretary comprises 10 smaller offices that support the Secretary in fulfilling his or her responsibilities.

Secretary

The Secretary is responsible for developing and coordinating a comprehensive national strategy to protect the United States against terrorist attacks. The Secretary advises the President on how to strengthen U.S. borders, to provide for intelligence analysis and infrastructure protection, to improve the use of science and technology to counter weapons of mass destruction, and to create a comprehensive response and recovery division.

Office for Civil Rights and Civil Liberties

The Office provides legal and policy advice to Department leadership on civil rights and civil liberties issues, investigates and resolves complaints, and provides leadership to DHS Equal Employment Opportunity Programs.

Office for Community Partnerships

The Office for Community Partnerships serves as the Department's lead in the countering violent extremism (CVE) mission space. It coordinates, expands, improves, and supports the Department's existing community-based CVE efforts by working with key stakeholders at Federal, State, local, tribal, and territorial levels. The Office's major objectives are to increase access to grants for CVE initiatives, engage DHS leadership with communities, engage the tech sector to empower credible voices in communities, train DHS field staff to better support local communities and law enforcement involved in CVE efforts, and engage the philanthropic community to facilitate long-term partnerships with communities.

Office of General Counsel

The Office of General Counsel (OGC) is responsible for ensuring that departmental activities comply with applicable legal requirements. OGC provides legal advice on areas such as national security, immigration, litigation, international law, maritime safety and security, transportation security, border security law, cybersecurity, fiscal and appropriations law, environmental law, and many others. It also ensures that the Department's efforts to secure the Nation are consistent with the civil rights and civil liberties of its citizens and follow the rule of law. OGC also provides legal services in several areas where the law intersects with the achievement of mission goals, such as the coordination of the Department's rulemaking activities, managing interdepartmental clearance of proposed legislation, and providing legal training for law enforcement officers.

Office of Inspector General

The Office of Inspector General (OIG) conducts and supervises audits, investigations, and inspections relating to the Department's programs and operations. The OIG examines, evaluates, and where necessary, critiques these operations and activities, recommending ways for DHS to carry out its responsibilities in the most economical, efficient, and effective manner possible. The OIG also reviews recommendations regarding existing and proposed legislation and regulations relating to the Department's programs and operations.

Office of Legislative Affairs

The Office of Legislative Affairs (OLA) serves as the Department's primary liaison to Congress. It advocates for the policy interests of the administration and the Secretary. OLA also ensures that all DHS components are actively engaged with Congress in their specific areas of responsibility. The Office articulates views on behalf of DHS components and their legislative initiatives. It responds to requests and inquiries from congressional committees, individual Members of Congress, and their staffs. OLA also participates in the Senate confirmation process for each DHS Presidential nominee.

Office of Partnership and Engagement

The Office of Partnership and Engagement includes the following offices and programs: the Office for State and Local Law Enforcement, Private Sector Office, Office of Academic Engagement, Committee Management Office, Homeland Security Advisory Council, and the "If You See Something, Say Something" public awareness campaign. The Office comprises stakeholder engagement offices that communicate with State, local, tribal, and territorial governments, and with law enforcement, the private sector, academia and Federal advisory committees. These offices also coordinate DHS programs and policies with these same stakeholders. The Office also serves as the liaison between these stakeholders and the Office of the Secretary. It promotes an integrated national approach to homeland security by coordinating and advancing Federal interaction with external stakeholders, and it is responsible for continuing the homeland security dialogue with those partners and with the national associations that represent them.

Office of Public Affairs

The Office of Public Affairs manages external and internal communications. The Office responds to national media inquiries, maintains the Department's Web site, and writes speeches for senior Department officials. The Office manages DHS's organizational identity program, which includes usage of the DHS seal and related guidelines. Also, the Office oversees the Department's employee communication activities, which include coordinating communications for departmentwide initiatives, townhall meetings between management and employees, and the operation and management of an intranet site. Per Presidential directive, the Office's incident communications program guides overall Federal incident communication activity and coordinates with State, local, and international partners to ensure accurate and timely information is provided to the public during a crisis.

Office of the Chief Financial Officer

The Chief Financial Officer oversees all financial management activities relating to the programs and operations of DHS, develops and maintains an integrated accounting and financial management system, and is responsible for financial reporting and internal controls.

Office of the Citizenship and Immigration Services Ombudsman

The Office of the Citizenship and Immigration Services Ombudsman (CISOMB) helps individuals and employers resolve problems with the delivery of immigration services and benefits issued by U.S. Citizenship and Immigration Services. The CISOMB identifies trends and proposes changes to mitigate problems and improve the delivery of immigration services. It is a confidential, independent, and neutral office where stakeholders can submit requests for assistance and provide feedback. The CISOMB delivers an annual report directly to Congress each year.

Office of the Executive Secretary

The Office of the Executive Secretary (ESEC) provides analytical and administrative support to the Office of the Secretary and the Office of the Deputy Secretary. ESEC manages the Secretary's internal and external correspondence, prepares classified and unclassified briefing materials, and oversees development of departmental testimony, questions for the record, and congressional reports. ESEC also facilitates departmental communications with Federal departments and agencies, the National Security Council, and other White House executive offices.

Office of the Military Advisor

The Senior Military Advisor provides counsel to the Secretary and DHS Components relating to the facilitation, coordination, and execution of policy, procedures, and preparedness activities and operations between DHS and the Department of Defense.

Privacy Office

The Privacy Office protects the collection, use, and disclosure of personally identifiable information and departmental information. It ensures that appropriate access to information is consistent with the vision, strategic mission, and core values of DHS. The Office also implements the policies of the Department to defend and protect the individual rights, liberties, and information interests of our citizens. The Office has oversight of all privacy and disclosure policy matters, including compliance with the Privacy Act of 1974, the Freedom of Information Act, and the completion of privacy impact statements on all new programs and systems, as required by the E-Government Act of 2002 and Section 222 of the Homeland Security Act.

OPERATIONAL AND SUPPORT COMPONENTS

Directorate for Management

The Directorate for Management is responsible for accounting and finance, appropriations, budget, expenditure of funds, and procurement; equipment, facilities, property, and other material resources; human resources, personnel, and their security; identification and tracking of performance measurements relating to the responsibilities of the Department, and information technology and communication systems.

The Directorate for Management ensures that the Department's employees have well-defined responsibilities and that managers and their employees have effective means of communicating with one another, with other governmental and nongovernmental bodies, and with the public they serve.

Directorate for Science and Technology

The Science and Technology Directorate is the primary research and development arm of the Department. The Directorate provides Federal, State, and local officials with the technology and capabilities to protect the homeland. Its strategic objectives are to develop and deploy systems to prevent, detect, and mitigate the consequences of chemical, biological, radiological, nuclear, and explosive attacks; develop equipment, protocols, and training procedures for response to and recovery from those attacks; enhance the Department's and other Federal, State, local, and tribal agencies' technical capabilities to fulfill their homeland security-related functions; and develop technical standards and establish certified laboratories to evaluate homeland security and emergency responder technologies for SAFETY Act certification.

Domestic Nuclear Detection Office

The Domestic Nuclear Detection Office is the primary entity in the U.S. Government for developing the global nuclear detection architecture, implementing its domestic portion, and integrating nuclear forensics programs. In coordination with Federal, State, local, tribal, and territorial governments, as well as with the private sector, the Office is responsible for developing, acquiring, and supporting the deployment of an enhanced domestic system to detect and report attempts to import, possess, store, transport, develop, or use an unauthorized nuclear explosive device, fissile material, or other radioactive material in the United States. It also improves that domestic system over time.

The Office further serves as steward of an enduring national technical nuclear forensics capability and leads efforts to improve national nuclear forensics expertise. Working with the international community, the Office promotes the development of nuclear detection architectures and nuclear forensics guidance.

Federal Emergency Management Agency

Federal Emergency Management Agency (FEMA) manages and coordinates the Federal response to and recovery from major domestic disasters and emergencies of all types. FEMA coordinates programs to improve the effectiveness of emergency response providers at all levels of the government to respond to terrorist attacks, major disasters, and other emergencies. FEMA also initiates proactive mitigation activities, trains first responders, and manages the National Flood Insurance Program and U.S. Fire Administration.

Federal Law Enforcement Training Centers

The Federal Law Enforcement Training Centers serves as an interagency law enforcement training organization for more than 90 Federal agencies and provides strategically designed training to State, local, tribal, and international law enforcement agencies.

National Protection and Programs Directorate

The National Protection and Programs Directorate executes the DHS operational mission of securing the Nation's infrastructure and enhancing its resilience against cyber and physical threats. Secure and resilient infrastructure advances public health and safety, promotes economic vitality, and safeguards national security. The National Protection and Programs Directorate collaborates with Federal, State, local, tribal, and territorial, as well as international and private-sector entities, to maintain situational awareness of both physical and cyber events, to share information about risks that may disrupt critical infrastructure, and to build capabilities to reduce those risks.

Office of Health Affairs

The Office of Health Affairs (OHA) serves as the principal adviser to the Secretary on medical and public health issues. OHA leads the Department's workforce health protection and medical support activities. The Office also manages and coordinates the Department's biological and chemical defense programs and provides medical and scientific expertise to support DHS preparedness and response efforts.

Office of Intelligence and Analysis

The Office of Intelligence and Analysis, as a member of the U.S. Intelligence Community, is the nexus between the Nation's intelligence apparatus and DHS components and other State, local, and private sector partners. The Office ensures that information is gathered from all relevant DHS field operations and other State, local, and private sector partners and that this information is shared with appropriate stakeholders to produce accurate, timely, and actionable analytical intelligence products and services.

Office of Operations Coordination

The Office of Operations Coordination provides decision support and enables the Secretary's execution of responsibilities across the homeland security enterprise by promoting situational awareness and information sharing, integrating and synchronizing strategic operations, and administering the DHS continuity program. At the strategic level, the Office provides a joint operations coordination capability to support DHS operational decisionmaking, departmental leadership, and participation in interagency operations throughout the homeland security enterprise and across all mission areas.

Office of Policy

The Office of Policy coordinates departmentwide policies, programs, and planning to ensure consistency. The Office provides a centralized coordination point for developing and communicating policies across the multiple internal and external components of the Homeland Security network. The Office also interacts with other government entities, academia, and includes risk management functions for DHS.

Transportation Security Administration

The Transportation Security Administration protects the Nation's transportation systems to ensure freedom of movement for people and commerce.

United States Citizenship and Immigration Services

U.S. Citizenship and Immigration Services (USCIS) ensures that information and decisions on citizenship and immigration benefits are provided to customers in a timely, accurate, consistent, courteous, and professional manner, while also helping to safeguard our national security. USCIS is also responsible for enhancing the integrity of our country's legal immigration system by deterring, detecting, and pursuing immigration-related fraud, combating the unauthorized practice of immigration law, and helping to combat unauthorized employment in the workplace.

United States Coast Guard

The U.S. Coast Guard protects those on the sea, protects the Nation from seaborne threats, and ensures the safety, security, and stewardship of the Nation's ports, waterways, coasts, and far-reaching maritime regions of economic and national security interest. Coast Guard missions include search and rescue; maritime safety; ports, waterways, and coastal security; drug interdiction; defense readiness; ice operations; aids to navigation; marine environmental protection; living marine resources; and other law enforcement activities.

United States Customs and Border Protection

The U.S. Customs and Border Protection secures America's borders to protect the public from terrorists and terrorist weapons, while enabling legitimate trade and travel to enhance the Nation's global economic competitiveness.

United States Immigration and Customs Enforcement

U.S. Immigration and Customs Enforcement (ICE) is the principal investigative arm of DHS. ICE's primary mission is to promote homeland security and public safety through the criminal and civil enforcement of Federal laws governing border control, customs, trade, and immigration.

United States Secret Service

The U.S. Secret Service carries out a dual mission of protection and investigation. It protects the President, Vice President, and their families; major Presidential and Vice Presidential candidates; visiting heads of state and government; and National Special Security Events, as well as the White House and other designated buildings within the Washington, DC, area. The Secret Service also safeguards the Nation's financial infrastructure and payments systems to preserve the integrity of the economy.

Sources of Information

Blog

The DHS maintains a blog on its Web site.

Data

The DHS and its components provide Internet access to statistical reports and datasets: Coast Guard maritime information, Customs and Border Protection intellectual property rights recordations, Federal Emergency Management Agency disaster declarations, immigration data, and more.

Employment

To search DHS job postings and to learn how to apply, visit the "Careers" Web page.

Flood Insurance Rate Maps (FIRMs)

Flooding can occur anywhere in the United States; however, certain areas are prone to serious flooding. To help communities understand their risk, flood maps or FIRMs have been created to show the locations of high-risk, moderate-to-low risk, and undetermined-risk areas. Banks, citizens, insurance agents, and all levels of government rely on FIRMs to determine whether flood insurance is required.

Freedom of Information Act (FOIA)

The FOIA provides for the full disclosure of agency records and information to the public as long as those records and information are not exempted under clearly delineated statutory language. Instructions for submitting a FOIA request, filing a Privacy Act request, and information on other FOIA-related matters are available on the DHS Web site.

The DHS maintains a FOIA library on its Web site. Information seekers should use the library's online resources to determine if the desired document or record is immediately available and, therefore, does not require a FOIA request to access it.

Green Card

A person may obtain authorization to live and work in the United States on a permanent basis in several ways: A family member or employer in the United States may sponsor the Green Card applicant; refugee or asylee status and other humanitarian programs offer additional pathways; and, in some cases, a person may be eligible to file on his or her own initiative for permanent residency.

How Do I?

The DHS Web site features a comprehensive section that organizes answers to "how do I" questions according to audience: DHS employees, businessmen and women, travelers, and the general public. Entrepreneurs can learn how to apply for grants, find forms for exporting and importing, and verify employment eligibility; travelers can learn how to check wait times at airports and border crossings; and members of the public can learn how to adopt a child internationally, become a citizen, check the status of an immigration case, prepare for a disaster, and report cyber incidents and suspicious activity.

Keywords

The DHS Web site features a long list of keywords that are linked to pages containing information on the DHS, its components, and its mission.

Multilingual Resources

The Office of Civil Rights and Civil Liberties identifies documents containing information that is particularly important to diverse communities of limited English proficiency. These documents are often translated into Arabic, Chinese, French, Haitian-Creole, Portuguese, Russian, Somali, Spanish, and Vietnamese.

News

The DHS posts audio items, congressional testimony, factsheets, photos and videos, press releases, and speeches on its Web site. It also posts news items on national security in Spanish.

Open Government

The DHS supports the Open Government initiative by promoting the principles of collaboration, participation, and transparency.

Operational Components

The DHS comprises nine operational components: the U.S. Department of Homeland Security, U.S. Customs and Border Protection, Federal Emergency Management Agency, Federal Law Enforcement Training Center, U.S. Immigration and Customs Enforcement, U.S. Secret Service, Transportation Security Administration, U.S. Coast Guard, and U.S. Citizenship and Immigration Services. The DHS Web site offers easy access to all of their home pages.

Publications

The DHS publications library contains brochures, guidance and policy papers, guidelines, program regulations, reports, strategies, and more.

Report Cyber Incidents

To protect the Nation's cybersecurity, the DHS has organizations dedicated to collecting information and reporting on cyber incidents, phishing, malware, and other vulnerabilities.

Site Map

The Web site map allows visitors to look for specific topics or to browse content that aligns with their interests.

The DHS Web site features an A–Z index to help visitors navigate its content.

Social Media

The DHS maintains accounts on Facebook, Flickr, Instagram, and Twitter. An online subscription form also is available to sign up for email updates.

Terrorist Threats

The National Terrorism Advisory System provides detailed, timely information on terrorist threats to the American public.

Transportation Security

The "Transportation Security" Web page provides information on transportation and travel: aviation security, cargo screening, domestic travel, electronic passports, visas, and more.

Travel Alerts

The DHS Web site offers convenient access to alerts and wait times: airport security checkpoint wait times from the Transportation Security Administration, airport wait times from the U.S. Customs and Border Protection, international travel warnings from the Department of State, and health alerts from the Centers for Disease Control and Prevention.

For further information, contact the Office of Public Affairs, Department of Homeland Security, Washington, DC 20528. Phone, 202-282-8010.

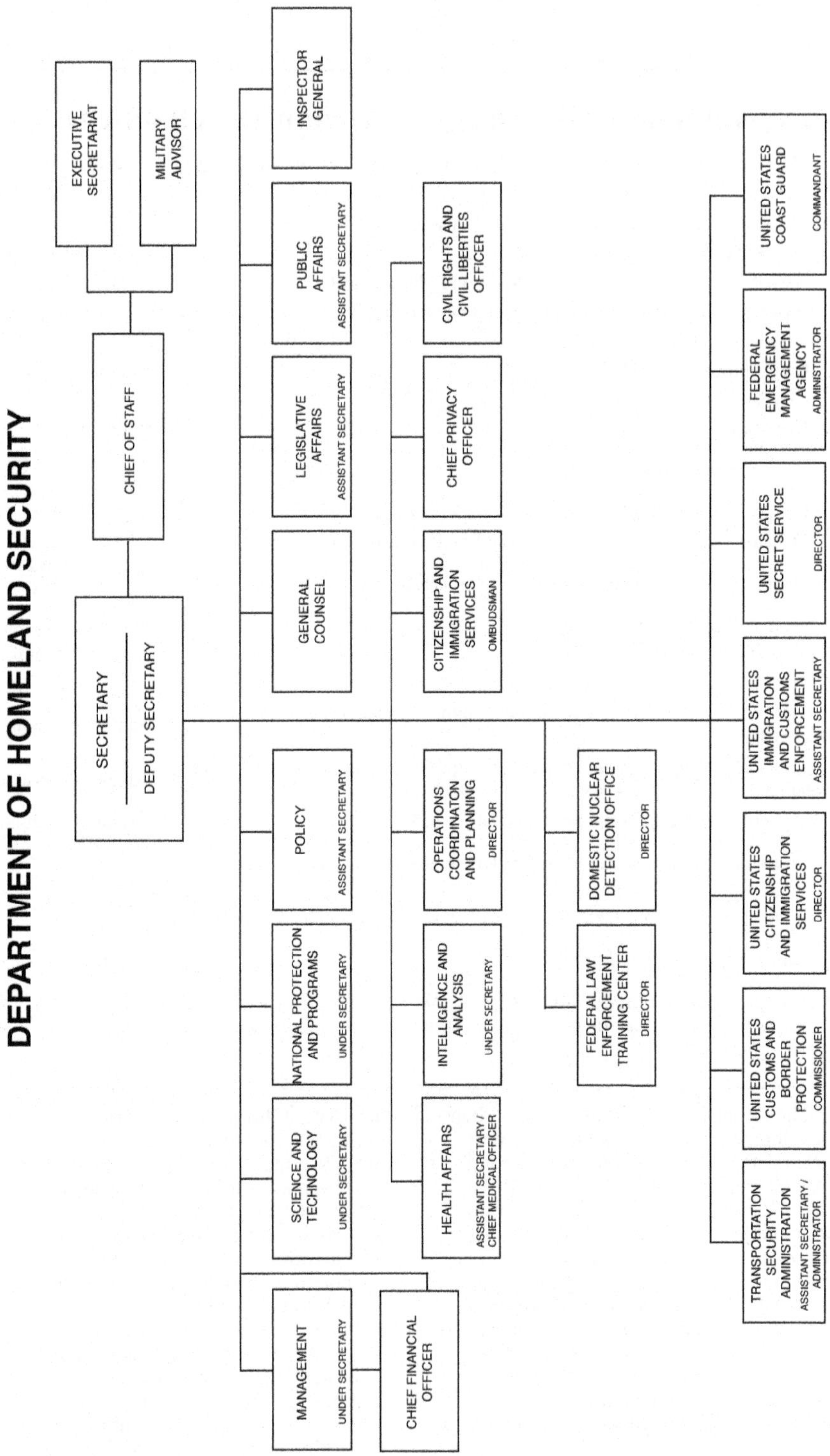
DEPARTMENT OF HOMELAND SECURITY
EXECUTIVE SECRETARIAT
MILITARY ADVISOR
CHIEF OF STAFF
SECRETARY
DEPUTY SECRETARY
INSPECTOR GENERAL
PUBLIC AFFAIRS ASSISTANT SECRETARY
LEGISLATIVE AFFAIRS ASSISTANT SECRETARY
GENERAL COUNSEL
POLICY ASSISTANT SECRETARY
NATIONAL PROTECTION AND PROGRAMS UNDER SECRETARY
SCIENCE AND TECHNOLOGY UNDER SECRETARY
MANAGEMENT UNDER SECRETARY
CHIEF FINANCIAL OFFICER
CIVIL RIGHTS AND CIVIL LIBERTIES OFFICER
CHIEF PRIVACY OFFICER
CITIZENSHIP AND IMMIGRATION SERVICES OMBUDSMAN
OPERATIONS COORDINATON AND PLANNING DIRECTOR
INTELLIGENCE AND ANALYSIS UNDER SECRETARY
HEALTH AFFAIRS ASSISTANT SECRETARY / CHIEF MEDICAL OFFICER
DOMESTIC NUCLEAR DETECTION OFFICE DIRECTOR
FEDERAL LAW ENFORCEMENT TRAINING CENTER DIRECTOR
UNITED STATES COAST GUARD COMMANDANT
FEDERAL EMERGENCY MANAGEMENT AGENCY ADMINISTRATOR
UNITED STATES SECRET SERVICE DIRECTOR
UNITED STATES IMMIGRATION AND CUSTOMS ENFORCEMENT ASSISTANT SECRETARY
UNITED STATES CITIZENSHIP AND IMMIGRATION SERVICES DIRECTOR
UNITED STATES CUSTOMS AND BORDER PROTECTION COMMISSIONER
TRANSPORTATION SECURITY ADMINISTRATION ASSISTANT SECRETARY / ADMINISTRATOR

Department of Housing and Urban Development

451 Seventh Street SW., Washington, DC 20410, 202-708-1422, *http://www.hud.gov*

SECRETARY OF HOUSING AND URBAN DEVELOPMENT	Julián Castro
Deputy Secretary	Nani A. Coloretti
Assistant Deputy Secretary, Field Policy and Management	Mary McBride
Assistant Secretary, Fair Housing and Equal Opportunity	Gustavo F. Velasquez
Assistant Secretary, Public Affairs	Jamie Castillo
Chief Human Capital Officer	Towanda Brooks
Chief Information Officer	Rafael Diaz
Chief of Staff	Neilin Parker
Chief Procurement Officer	Keith W. Surber, Acting
Deputy Chief Financial Officer	Joseph Hungate
Director, Office of Departmental Equal Employment Opportunity	John P. Benison
Director, Office of Lead Hazard Control and Healthy Homes	Michelle Miller, Acting
General Counsel	Helen R. Kanovsky
Inspector General	David A. Montoya
President, Government National Mortgage Association–Ginnie Mae	Theodore W. Tozer
Principal Deputy Assistant Secretary, Community Planning and Development	Harriet Tregoning
Principal Deputy Assistant Secretary, Congressional and Intergovernmental Relations	Erika L. Moritsugu
Principal Deputy Assistant Secretary, Office of Housing	Edward L. Golding
Principal Deputy Assistant Secretary, Office of Public and Indian Housing	Lourdes Castro Ramirez
Principal Deputy Assistant Secretary, Policy Development and Research	Katherine M. O'Regan
Senior Advisor to the Secretary	Jennifer Ho

The Department of Housing and Urban Development oversees housing needs nationwide, ensures fair housing opportunities, and creates strong, sustainable, and inclusive communities.

The Department of Housing and Urban Development (HUD) was established in 1965 by the Department of Housing and Urban Development Act (42 U.S.C. 3532–3537). It was created to administer the principal programs that provide assistance for housing and the development of communities; to promote finding solutions to housing and community development problems through States and localities; and to maximize contributions of the homebuilding and mortgage lending industries to housing, community development, and the national economy.

HUD administers many programs; however, it has six core functions: insuring mortgages for single-family and multifamily dwellings and extending loans for home improvement and for the purchasing of mobile homes; channeling funds from investors to the mortgage industry through the Government National Mortgage Association–Ginnie Mae; making direct loans for construction or rehabilitation of housing projects that benefit the elderly and handicapped; providing Federal housing subsidies for low- and moderate-income families; giving community development grants to States and communities; and promoting and enforcing fair housing and equal housing opportunity.

Secretary

The Secretary formulates policy recommendations affecting housing and community development; encourages the participation of private enterprise in housing and community development; promotes the growth of cities and States and the efficient and effective use of housing and community and economic development resources by stimulating private sector initiatives, public-private sector partnerships, and public entrepreneurship; ensures equal access to housing and affirmatively prevents housing discrimination; and oversees the Federal National Mortgage Association–Fannie Mae.

To learn more about the powers of the Secretary, visit HUD's Web site:

Program Areas

Community Planning and Development

The Office of Community and Planning Development administers grant programs to help communities plan and finance growth and development, to increase their governing capacity, and to shelter and provide services for the homeless. The Office is responsible for implementing Community Development Block Grant (CDBG) programs for entitlement communities; the State- and HUD-administered Small Cities Program; community development loan guarantees; special purpose grants for insular areas and historically black colleges and universities; Appalachian Regional Commission grants; the Home Investment in Affordable Housing Program, which provides Federal assistance for housing rehabilitation, tenant-based assistance, first-time homebuyers, and new construction when a jurisdiction is determined to need new rental housing; the Department's programs to address homelessness; the John Heinz Neighborhood Development Program; community outreach partnerships; the joint community development plan that assists institutions of higher education working in concert with State and local governments to undertake activities under the CDBG program; community adjustment and economic diversification planning grants; empowerment zones and enterprise communities; efforts to improve the environment; and community planning and development efforts of other departments and agencies, public and private organizations, private industry, financial markets, and international organizations.

For further information, contact the Office of Community Planning and Development. Phone, 202-708-2690.

Fair Housing and Equal Opportunity

The Office of Fair Housing and Equal Opportunity administers fair housing laws and regulations prohibiting discrimination in public and private housing; equal opportunity laws and regulations prohibiting discrimination in HUD-assisted housing and community development programs; the fair housing assistance grants program to provide financial and technical assistance to State and local government agencies to implement local fair housing laws and ordinances; and the Community Housing Resources Boards program to provide grants for fair housing activities, including outreach and education, identification of institutional barriers to fair housing, and telephone hotlines for complaints.

For further information, contact the Office of Fair Housing and Equal Opportunity. Phone, 202-708-4252.

Government National Mortgage Association–Ginnie Mae

This Government corporation supports expanded affordable housing by providing an efficient, Government-guaranteed secondary market vehicle to link the capital markets with Federal housing markets. Ginnie Mae guarantees mortgage-backed securities composed of FHA-insured or VA-guaranteed mortgage loans that private lenders issued and Ginnie Mae guaranteed with the full faith and credit of the United States. These programs allow Ginnie Mae to increase the overall supply of credit available for housing by providing a vehicle for channeling funds from the securities market into the mortgage market.

For further information, contact the Government National Mortgage Association. Phone, 202-708-0926.

Housing

The Office of Housing oversees aid for construction and financing of new and rehabilitated housing and for preservation of existing housing. The Office underwrites single-family, multifamily, property improvement, and manufactured home loans; administers special purpose programs designed for the elderly, handicapped, and chronically mentally ill; administers housing assistance programs for low-income families having difficulties affording standard housing; administers grants to fund resident ownership of multifamily house properties; and protects consumers against fraudulent land development and promotional practices.

For further information, contact the Office of Housing. Phone, 202-708-3600.

Lead Hazard Control and Healthy Homes

The Office of Lead Hazard Control and Healthy Homes is responsible for lead hazard control policy development, abatement, training, regulations, and research. Activities of the Office include increasing public and building-industry awareness of the dangers of lead-based paint poisoning and the options for detection, risk reduction, and abatement; encouraging the development of safer, more effective, and less costly methods for detection, risk reduction, and abatement; and encouraging State and local governments to develop lead-based paint programs covering contractor certification, hazard reduction, financing, enforcement, and primary prevention, including public education.

For further information, contact the Office of Lead Hazard Control and Healthy Homes. Phone, 202-755-1785.

Public and Indian Housing

The Office of Public and Indian Housing administers public and Indian housing programs; assists technically and financially with planning, developing, and managing low-income projects; subsidizes the operations of public housing agencies (PHAs) and Indian housing authorities (IHAs) and provides procedures for reviewing the management of public housing agencies; administers the comprehensive improvement assistance and comprehensive grant programs for modernizing low-income housing projects; administers programs for resident participation, resident management, home ownership, economic development and supportive services, and drug-free neighborhood programs; protects low-income tenants from lead-based paint poisoning by requiring PHAs and IHAs to comply with HUD regulations for the testing and removal of lead-based paint; implements and monitors program requirements related to program eligibility and admission of families to public and assisted housing, as well as tenant income and rent requirements for continued occupancy; administers the HOPE VI and vacancy reduction programs; administers voucher and certificate programs and the Moderate Rehabilitation Program; coordinates all departmental housing and community development programs for Indian and Alaskan Natives; and awards grants to PHAs and IHAs for the construction, acquisition, and operation of public and Indian housing projects.

For further information, contact the Office of Public and Indian Housing. Phone, 202-708-0950.

Sources of Information

Business Opportunities

To learn about contracting opportunities, programs, and resources, use the link below. The Office of the Chief Procurement Officer can provide additional information. Phone, 202-708-1290. TDD, 202-708-1455.

Data / Research

The Office of Policy Development and

Research posts datasets, publications, research, and information on initiatives on its "HUD User" Web site.

Directory Locator

To locate a HUD employee or to send a HUD employee an email, visit the "Search for HUD Employees" Web page. An automated phone locator service is also available. Phone, 202-708-1112. TDD, 202-708-1455.

Employment

Information on career opportunities—including opportunities for veterans, students, and people with disabilities—is available online. Information is also available from the Personnel Division at the nearest regional office and from the Office of Human Resources in Washington, DC. Phone, 202-708-0408.

Field Offices

Visit HUD's online local office directory to find contact information for its field offices.

Freedom of Information Act (FOIA)

Many HUD documents are available online. Before submitting a written request, see the "Frequently Requested Materials" and "E-FOIA Reading Room" links on HUD's FOIA Web page. Send written requests to the Director, Executive Secretariat, Department of Housing and Urban Development, Room 10139, 451 Seventh Street SW., Washington, DC 20410. For information on inspecting documents or records, contact the Freedom of Information Officer. Phone, 202-708-3054.

Hotline

The Office of the Inspector General maintains the Hotline to report fraud, mismanagement, and waste. Phone, 202-708-4200 or 800-347-3735. TDD, 202-708-2451.

Library

The library is located at HUD headquarters in Washington, DC. Visitors must schedule an appointment to use the library. It is open weekdays, except Federal holidays, from 9:30 a.m. to 5 p.m. Phone, 202-402-2680.

Property Disposition

For single-family properties, contact the Chief Property Officer at the nearest HUD regional office or the Property Disposition Division. Phone, 202-708-0614. For multifamily properties, contact the Regional Housing Director at the nearest HUD regional office or the Property Disposition Division. Phone, 202-708-0614.

Site Map

The Web site map allows visitors to look for specific topics or to browse content that aligns with their interests.

An index of topics in alphabetical order is also available on the HUD Web site.

Social Media

HUD's social media directory provides links to all of its official blogs and social media platforms on Facebook, Flickr, Instagram, Twitter, and YouTube.

For further information, contact the Office of Public Affairs, Department of Housing and Urban Development, 451 Seventh Street SW., Washington, DC 20410. Phone, 202-708-0980.

DEPARTMENT OF HOUSING AND URBAN DEVELOPMENT

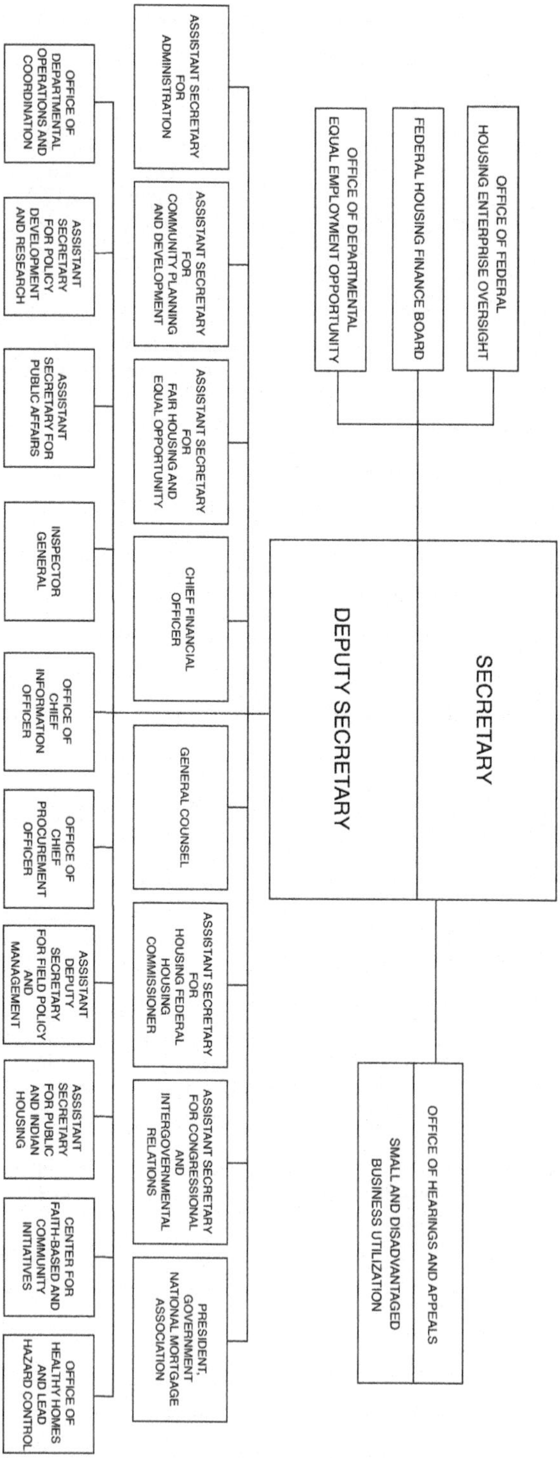

Department of the Interior

1849 C Street NW., Washington, DC 20240, 202-208-3100, *http://www.doi.gov*

SECRETARY OF THE INTERIOR	Sally Jewell
Deputy Secretary	Michael L. Connor
ASSISTANT SECRETARIES	
Indian Affairs	Lawrence S. Roberts, Acting
Insular Areas	Esther Kia'aina
Land and Minerals Management	Janice M. Schneider
PRINCIPAL DEPUTY ASSISTANT SECRETARIES	
Fish and Wildlife and Parks	Michael J. Bean
Policy, Management and Budget	Kristen Sarri
Water and Science	Jennifer Gimbel
Chief Information Officer	Sylvia Burns
Deputy Inspector General	Mary L. Kendall
Solicitor	Hilary C. Tompkins
Special Trustee for American Indians	Vincent G. Logan

The Department of the Interior protects America's heritage and natural resources, honors its cultures and tribal communities, and supplies energy for powering its future.

The Department of the Interior was created by act of March 3, 1849 (43 U.S.C. 1451), which transferred the Office of Indian Affairs and the General Land, the Patent, and the Pension Offices to the new Department. It was reorganized by Reorganization Plan No. 3 of 1950, as amended (5 U.S.C. app.).

The Department manages the Nation's public lands and minerals, national parks, national wildlife refuges, and western water resources and upholds Federal trust responsibilities to Indian tribes and Alaska Natives. It is also responsible for endangered species and migratory wildlife conservation; historic preservation; surface-mined lands protection and restoration; mapping geological, hydrological, and biological science; and giving financial and technical assistance to the insular areas.

Secretary

The Secretary of the Interior reports directly to the President. She directs and supervises all operations and activities of the Department, which has over 70,000 employees and serves as steward of approximately one-fifth of the Nation's lands.

Fish and Wildlife and Parks

The Office of the Assistant Secretary for Fish and Wildlife and Parks oversees natural resources use, management, and conservation programs; National Park and National Refuge Systems lands and cultural facilities; and fish, wildlife, and habitat conservation and enhancement. The Office represents the Department in the coordination and oversight of ecosystems restoration and biological resources programs with States and tribes and other Federal agencies. It also exercises secretarial direction and supervision over the U.S. Fish and Wildlife and the National Park Services.

Indian Affairs

The Office of the Assistant Secretary for Indian Affairs establishes and implements Indian policy and programs; maintains the Federal-tribal Government-to-government relationship; assists the Secretary of the Interior with carrying out the Department's Federal trust and treaty responsibilities; directs and supervises the Bureau of Indian Affairs and the Bureau of Indian Education; supervises the Offices of Federal Acknowledgement, of Self-Governance, of

Indian Gaming, of Indian Economic Development, and all administrative and financial resource management activities; and maintains liaison coordination between the Department and other Federal agencies that provide services or funding to the federally recognized tribes and to the eligible American Indians and Alaska Natives.

The Office of the Special Trustee for American Indians oversees departmentwide Indian trust reform efforts to increase the Secretary of the Interior's effectiveness at carrying out trust responsibilities to American Indian Tribes, individual American Indians, and Alaska Natives. The Office also has programmatic responsibility for the management of financial trust assets, appraisals, and fiduciary trust beneficiary services.

Insular Areas

The Office of the Assistant Secretary for Insular Areas gives financial and technical assistance to the territories of American Samoa, Guam, the U.S. Virgin Islands, and the Commonwealth of the Northern Mariana Islands to promote better governance. It plays a role in the management of relations between the United States and the insular areas by developing and promoting appropriate Federal policies. The Office also carries out the Secretary's responsibilities that are related to the three freely associated states (the Federated States of Micronesia, the Republic of the Marshall Islands, and the Republic of Palau), the Palmyra Atoll excluded areas, and Wake Atoll's residual administration.

Land and Minerals Management

The Office of the Assistant Secretary for Land and Minerals Management oversees the Bureaus of Land Management, of Ocean Energy Management, of Safety and Environmental Enforcement, and the Office of Surface Mining Reclamation and Enforcement. These bureaus run programs associated with public land management; operations management and leasing of public lands for energy resources and mineral extraction, including the Outer Continental Shelf to the outer limits of U.S. economic jurisdiction; mineral operations management on Indian lands; and surface mining reclamation and enforcement functions.

Water and Science

The Office of the Assistant Secretary for Water and Science oversees the U.S. Geological Survey, the Bureau of Reclamation, and the Central Utah Project Completion Act Office. It guides policy and oversees program areas dealing with water project operations, facility security, natural resource management, and research involving geology, hydrology, cartography, biology, and technology. It also guides the development of national water and science policies and supports environmental improvement.

For further information, contact the Department of the Interior, 1849 C Street NW., Washington, DC 20240. Phone, 202-208-3186.

Sources of Information

Blog

The Department of the Interior has a blog.

Bureaus and Offices

The Department's Web site features a web page that provides easy access to the numerous bureau and office web sites.

Business Opportunities

The Department of the Interior is helping America establish a new foundation for economic prosperity by supporting the transition to a clean energy economy, stimulating local economic growth through stewardship, and procuring goods and services from American businesses. The Department relies on American businesses for bridge, irrigation system, office building, reservoir, road, school, and other types of maintenance.

Additional information is available from the Office of Acquisition and Property Management, 1849 C Street NW., Rm. 4262, Washington, DC 20240. Phone, 202-513-7554.

Climate Science

The Department of the Interior posts news items from its Climate Science Centers on its Web site.

Diversity Inclusion

A list of resources is available on the Department's Web site.

Employment

Information to assist persons with disabilities, students and recent graduates, veterans, and others interested in career opportunities is available on the Department's Web site.

Information on voluntarism and service is available on the Department's Web site.

Freedom of Information Act (FOIA)

Thirteen bureaus and offices support the Department's FOIA operations. The Department's Web site features a single web page that allows convenient access to those bureaus and offices and to their electronic FOIA libraries. From the same web page, an information seeker may file a request, track the status of a request, learn about the FOIA program's structure, and review FOIA-related guidance and resources. Please note: the Department and its bureaus and offices post a great deal of information online; therefore, an information seeker should visit the appropriate electronic libraries and search for the desired information before submitting a FOIA request. That information already may be accessible, immediately and without charge.

Library

The Interior Library's holdings and its reference and research services support the mission of the Department and its agencies and bureaus. Its holdings cover American history, geology, law, national parks, Native American culture and history, nature, and public lands and wildlife management. The library offers subscription databases and other online data sources that give Interior employees and external researchers nationwide access. A holdings catalog and descriptions of educational programs and training opportunities are available on the library's Web site. Please note: A temporary library is now open in Room 2262 of the Stewart Lee Udall Department of Interior Building. Phone, 202-208-5815.

Wing 1 of the Stewart Lee Udall Department of the Interior Building is undergoing a 2-year modernization project. On May 30, 2014, the Interior Library closed its historic reading room and stack areas. More information is available online to help patrons understand how the modernization project will affect their access to library resources.

Museum

The Interior Museum offers exhibits on the history and mission of the Department. Programs highlight bureau management of cultural and natural resources. Museum guides conduct tours of the Interior Building's New Deal era art and architecture. Phone, 202-208-4743.

News

The Department posts press releases online.

Open Government

The Department of the Interior supports the Open Government initiative by promoting the principles of collaboration, participation, and transparency. Beyond meeting Open Government requirements, the agency intends to create better relationships between citizens and their Government; to become better at understanding citizens' demands for services and more responsive to their needs; to accelerate the rate of innovation by leveraging public knowledge; to increase the Department's ability to carry out its mission more effectively and efficiently by transparently engaging the public in decisionmaking; and to encourage the development of Open Government programs.

Site Map

The Web site map allows visitors to look for specific topics or to browse content that aligns with their interests.

Sustainability Programs

The Department of the Interior is dedicated to conserving and protecting the Nation's natural and cultural resources now and for future generations. Its employees are passionate about their stewardship responsibility for the resources and properties that they manage for the American People.

Water Conservation

The WaterSMART program improves water conservation and helps water-resource managers make sound decisions about water use. It identifies strategies to ensure that this and future generations will have sufficient supplies of clean water for drinking, economic activities, ecosystem health, and recreation. The program also identifies adaptive measures to address climate change and its effect on future water demands.

For further information, contact the Department of the Interior, 1849 C Street NW., Washington, DC 20240. Phone, 202-208-3100.

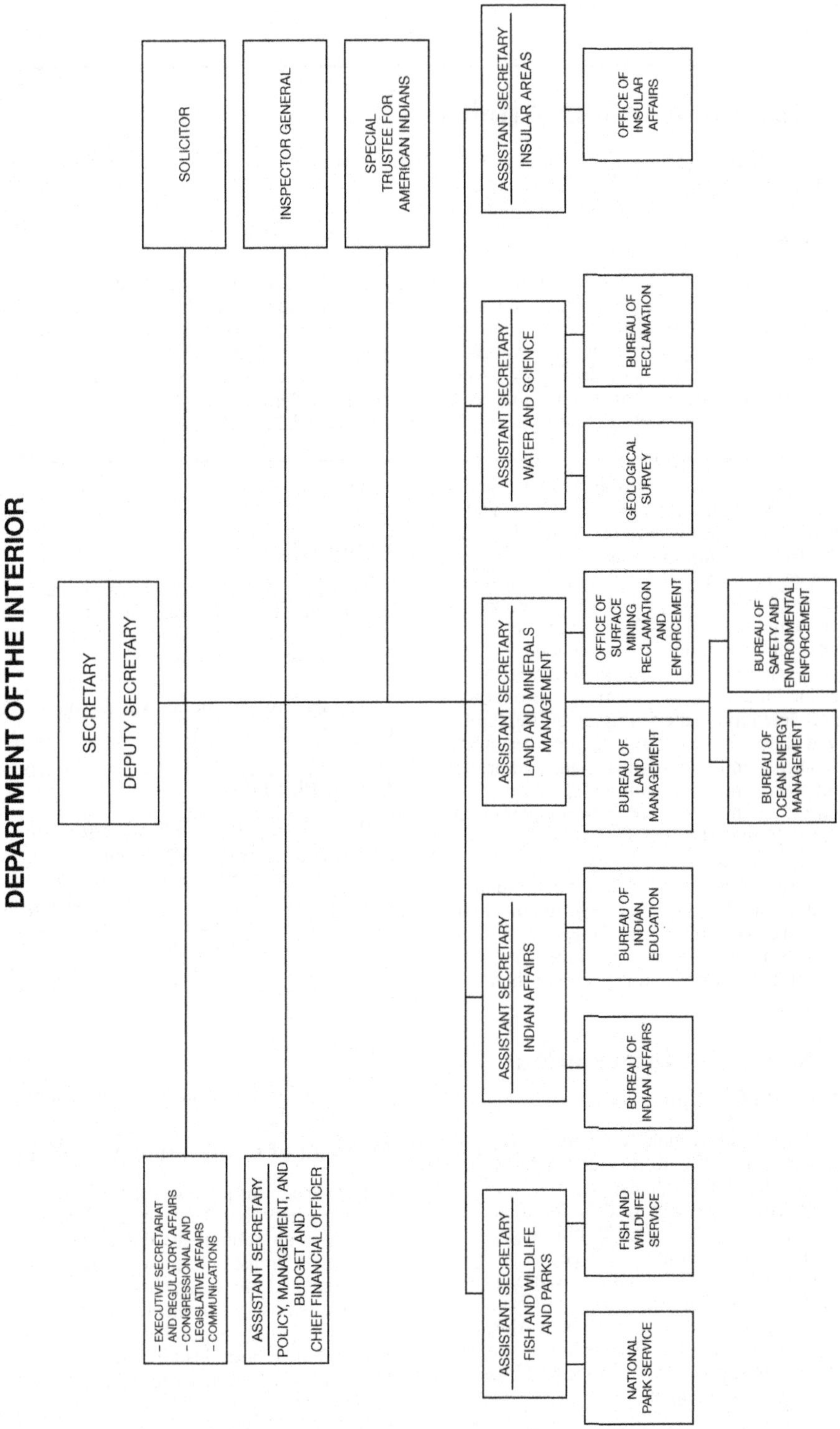
DEPARTMENT OF THE INTERIOR
SECRETARY
DEPUTY SECRETARY
- EXECUTIVE SECRETARIAT AND REGULATORY AFFAIRS
- CONGRESSIONAL AND LEGISLATIVE AFFAIRS
- COMMUNICATIONS
SOLICITOR
ASSISTANT SECRETARY
POLICY, MANAGEMENT, AND BUDGET AND CHIEF FINANCIAL OFFICER
INSPECTOR GENERAL
SPECIAL TRUSTEE FOR AMERICAN INDIANS
ASSISTANT SECRETARY
FISH AND WILDLIFE AND PARKS
NATIONAL PARK SERVICE
FISH AND WILDLIFE SERVICE
ASSISTANT SECRETARY
INDIAN AFFAIRS
BUREAU OF INDIAN AFFAIRS
BUREAU OF INDIAN EDUCATION
ASSISTANT SECRETARY
LAND AND MINERALS MANAGEMENT
BUREAU OF LAND MANAGEMENT
OFFICE OF SURFACE MINING RECLAMATION AND ENFORCEMENT
BUREAU OF OCEAN ENERGY MANAGEMENT
BUREAU OF SAFETY AND ENVIRONMENTAL ENFORCEMENT
ASSISTANT SECRETARY
WATER AND SCIENCE
GEOLOGICAL SURVEY
BUREAU OF RECLAMATION
ASSISTANT SECRETARY
INSULAR AREAS
OFFICE OF INSULAR AFFAIRS

Bureau of Indian Affairs

Department of the Interior, 1849 C Street NW., Washington, DC 20240, 202-208-3710, *http://www.bia.gov*

DIRECTOR Michael S. Black

The Bureau of Indian Affairs (BIA) was created as part of the War Department in 1824 and transferred to the Department of the Interior when the latter was established in 1849. The BIA's mission is to fulfill its trust responsibilities and promote self-determination on behalf of federally recognized tribal governments, American Indians, and Alaska Natives. The Bureau provides services directly or through contracts, grants, and compacts to members of 566 federally recognized Indian tribes in the 48 contiguous United States and Alaska—approximately 1.9 million American Indians and Alaska Natives.

BIA programs cover the entire range of State and local government services. These programs, administered by either tribes or the Bureau, support the following activities: managing natural resources on 55 million acres of trust land, providing fire protection and emergency natural disaster relief, developing economically isolated and depressed areas of the United States, law enforcement and administrating tribal courts and detention centers, implementing land and water claim settlements, building and repairing and maintaining roads and bridges, repairing and maintaining high-hazard dams, and managing irrigation systems and agriculture on Federal Indian lands.

The BIA works with American Indian and Alaska Native tribal governments and organizations, other Federal agencies, State and local governments, and other groups to develop programs and implement them effectively.

Sources of Information

Climate Change

The Tribal Climate Resilience program mainstreams climate considerations at the project level through leadership engagement, delivery of data and tools, training, and tribal capacity building. Mainstreaming climate change considerations into all BIA activities is a high priority. Climate change will bring new challenges to Indian Country and Alaska Native Villages. The BIA serves as the lead agency to support tribes as they address changes in the climate.

Tribal Climate Resilience Resources are available online.

Employment

BIA job opportunities, common job documents, and hiring information for American Indian and Alaska Native veterans are available online.

The BIA tweets Indian Affairs job opportunities on Twitter.

Estate Planning

The American Indian Probate Reform Act of 2004 (AIPRA) made many changes to the way trust or restricted land and property is inherited. It also made changes that affected land management and purchases. The BIA Web site provides information describing how AIPRA affects wills and inheritance.

Events

A calendar of events is available online.

Freedom of Information Act (FOIA)

Before submitting a written FOIA request, verify that the desired information is not already publicly available. "FOIA REQUEST" must be clearly written on the envelope, and the requester should be as specific as possible in identifying the record or records being sought. He or she should also include a brief description of the reason for the request because the Department of the Interior may use it as a basis for fee reduction or discretionary release of otherwise exempt materials. Requests made under the FOIA become part of the public record and may be placed in BIA public files. A FOIA request should be addressed to the Indian Affairs FOIA Officer, Assistant Secretary–Indian Affairs, 1849 C Street NW., MS 3070–MIB, Washington, DC 20240. Phone, 202-208-3135 or 202-208-5097. Fax, 202-208-6597.

Frequently Asked Questions (FAQs)

The BIA posts answers to FAQs on its Web site.

The BIA Web site also features a "How Do I" informational Web page.

Library

An online document library features frequently requested documents and links.

News

The BIA posts joint statements, statements, and other news items on its Web site.

The BIA maintains a social media presence on Facebook.

Regional Offices

Contact information for the 12 BIA regional offices is available online.

Site Map

The Web site map allows visitors to look for specific topics or to browse content that aligns with their interests.

For further information, contact the Office of the Assistant Secretary for Indian Affairs, Office of Public Affairs, Department of the Interior, MS–3658–MIB, 1849 C Street NW., Washington, DC 20240. Phone, 202-208-3710.

Bureau of Indian Education

Department of the Interior, 1849 C Street NW., Washington, DC 20240, 202-208-3710, *http://www.bie.edu*

DIRECTOR Ann Marie Bledsoe Downes, Acting

The Bureau of Indian Education (BIE) provides quality educational opportunities for eligible American Indian and Alaska Native elementary, secondary, and postsecondary students from federally recognized tribes. The Bureau directs and manages education functions, including forming policies and procedures, supervises program activities, and approves the expenditure of funds appropriated for education functions.

The BIE educates approximately 48,000 American Indian and Alaska Native children at 183 elementary and secondary schools on 64 reservations in 23 States. The Bureau operates 57 of these schools. The other 126 schools are tribally operated under the Indian Self-Determination and Education Assistance Act of 1975 (25 U.S.C. 450 et seq.) or the Tribally Controlled Schools Act of 1988 (25 U.S.C. 2501 et seq.). The BIE oversees two postsecondary schools—Haskell Indian Nations University in Lawrence, KS, and Southwestern Indian Polytechnic Institute in Albuquerque, NM—and it funds the Navajo and United Tribes Technical Colleges.

Sources of Information

Directory

The BIE "National Directory" (SEP 2016) is available in Portable Document Format (PDF) online.

Divisions and Programs

The BIE Web site features a web page with a list of the agency's divisions and programs and links to their web sites.

Employment

American Indian children deserve a quality education—and that starts with highly qualified, dedicated staff and educators. The BIE employees nearly 4,500 professionals in careers that offer unique and diverse cultural and lifestyle experiences. Phone, 505-563-5304.

Freedom of Information Act (FOIA)

FOIA requests for BIE records should be sent to the Indian Affairs FOIA Officer. Phone, 202-208-3135 or 202-208-5097.

News

The BIE posts news items on its Web site.

The BIE has a Facebook page.

The BIE tweets on Twitter.

Reports

Performance and special education reports and school report cards are accessible online.

Resources

BIE education line officers, school superintendents, principals, teachers, and staff can access program guidance, handbooks, templates, and training provided in various formats—WebEx or PowerPoint—to refresh professional skills. These online documents and presentations are provided to supplement staff training throughout the school year.

Scholarships

The BIE Web site provides information on scholarship opportunities for American Indian students.

Site Map

The Web site map allows visitors to look for specific topics or to browse content that aligns with their interests.

For further information, contact the Office of the Assistant Secretary for Indian Affairs, Office of Public Affairs, Department of the Interior, 1849 C Street NW., MS–3658–MIB, Washington, DC 20240. Phone, 202-208-3710.

Bureau of Land Management

Department of the Interior, 1849 C Street NW., Washington, DC 20240, 202-208-3801, *http://www.blm.gov*

DIRECTOR	Neil G. Kornze

The Bureau of Land Management (BLM) was established July 16, 1946, by the consolidation of the General Land Office (created, 1812) and the Grazing Service (formed, 1934).

The Bureau sustains the diversity, health, and productivity of America's public lands for the benefit of present and future generations through a mandate of multiple-use and sustained-yield. It manages 1 of every 10 acres of land across the United States, about 245 million acres of land, most of which is located in Alaska and 11 other Western States. The Bureau also manages about 30 percent or 700 million acres of the Nation's subsurface mineral estate. The Bureau oversees conventional and renewable energy development, livestock grazing, recreation, and timber harvesting, and it protects cultural, historical, and natural resources. Many of these resources are found on National Conservation Lands, a subset of BLM lands that are federally designated, that cover 32 million acres, and that include 223 wilderness areas and 25 national monuments.

BLM management responsibilities and activities are broad in scope and diverse. It manages Federal onshore coal, gas, and oil operations—and also vast stretches of public lands that will play a significant role in the Nation's emerging renewable energy portfolio. The BLM is already 75 percent of the way to reaching President Obama's

Climate Action Plan goal of approving projects that will generate 20,000 megawatts of renewable energy by 2020. The Bureau also contributes to wildland fire management to protect the public and the Nation's natural resource landscape, recreational areas, and wildlife habitat.

The Bureau manages livestock on 155 million acres of land, administering nearly 18,000 permits and leases held by ranchers who graze mostly cattle and sheep. Under the Wild Free-Roaming Horses and Burros Act of 1971, it also manages herds of wild horses and burros on public rangelands.

Recreation is also part of the BLM's portfolio. Birdwatchers, campers, hang gliders, horseback riders, hunters, mountain bikers, photographers, whitewater rafters, and visitors to cultural and natural heritage sites recreate on hundreds of millions of acres of public lands. The Bureau estimates that it receives approximately 62 million recreational visits per year.

The Bureau's broad management responsibilities require balancing public land uses and protection of public land resources. Working with State and local and tribal governments, stakeholder groups, and the public, the BLM creates land use plans, referred to as Resource Management Plans, to guide decisions for approved uses of and actions affecting public lands.

Sources of Information

Adoption Schedule

The BLM offers wild horses and burros for adoption or purchase at events nationwide throughout the year. The most current adoption event schedule is accessible online.

Business Opportunities

The National Operations Center in Denver, Colorado, and the Oregon/ Washington State Office handle most procurements over $150,000 and also award and administer all Indefinite Delivery / Indefinite Quantity (IDIQ) contracts that are national in scope.

Government contracting and financial assistance information and resources for small businesses are available online.

Employment

The BLM relies on people with diverse skills and professional backgrounds—administration and management, biological sciences, business services, cadastral survey and geological sciences, fire and aviation, law and realty, petroleum engineering, and more—to carry out its mission.

Information on BLM Pathways programs for students and recent graduates is available online.

Freedom of Information Act (FOIA)

Instructions to submit a FOIA request for agency records are available on the BLM Web site.

General Land Office Records

The General Land Office Records Automation Web site provides access to Federal land conveyance records for the Public Land States, including image access to more than five million Federal land title records issued between 1820 and the present. The Web site also has survey plat- and field note-related images that date back to 1810. Please note: The Web site does not currently contain every Federal title record issued for the Public Land States.

Reading Rooms

State offices provide facilities where visitors may examine status records, tract books, and other records of public lands and their resources.

Recreation

The National Conservation Lands program offers online recreational guides for a convenient connection to public lands.

The BLM Web site provides resources for mountain bikers. These resources include the BLM Top 20 Mountain Biking Opportunities list and interactive mountain biking maps for trails on BLM lands.

Renewable Energy

The BLM Web site features a table that

contains the locations and other details of the renewable energy projects approved since 2009 on public lands.

Site Maps

An index of BLM site maps is available online. A site map allows Internet visitors to look for specific topics or to browse content that aligns with their interests.

Speakers

Upon request from organizations within their areas of jurisdiction, local offices will arrange for speakers to explain BLM programs.

Statistics

Public Land Statistics documents according to year and starting with 1996 are accessible online.

Tables and spreadsheets with data that include the numbers of BLM-administered oil and gas leases, of applications for permit to drill, and of oil and gas wells are accessible on the BLM Web site. Most of the statistics presented cover Fiscal Years 1988–2015.

For further information, contact the Office of Public Affairs, Bureau of Land Management, Department of the Interior, 1849 C Street NW., Washington, DC 20240. Phone, 202-208-3801.

Bureau of Ocean Energy Management

Department of the Interior, 1849 C Street NW., Washington, DC 20240-0001, 202-208-6474, *http://www.boem.gov*

DIRECTOR Abigail Ross Hopper

The Bureau of Ocean Energy Management (BOEM) was created on October 1, 2011, as directed by Secretarial Order No. 3299, as amended.

The Bureau assesses marine-related activities on the Outer Continental Shelf (OCS) and the nature, extent, recoverability, and value of energy resources and minerals located there. It promotes responsible marine-related activities, including exploring, inventorying, and developing energy and mineral resources; analyzes the potential environmental effects of proposed resource management operations; conducts and oversees environmental studies to inform policy decisions on OCS energy and marine mineral resources management; develops and implements leasing and resource evaluation and management regulations; and oversees the financial accountability of lessees, operators, and operating-rights holders to ensure that they meet financial and contractual commitments.

The Bureau promotes cooperation among the Federal Government, State and tribal governments, and native communities on national, regional, and local issues relevant to the scope of its responsibilities. BOEM activities also support national policy priorities: energy security, environmental protection, and social and economic development.

Sources of Information

Business Opportunities

Information on doing business with the Bureau is available online.

Calendar

The BOEM Web site features a calendar of upcoming events.

Educational Resources

BOEM teacher resources are available online.

Employment

The BOEM relies on professionals with

engineering and science backgrounds for ensuring the safe and environmentally responsible development of the Nation's offshore energy and marine mineral resources.

The BOEM posts vacancy announcements on its Web site.

Freedom of Information Act (FOIA)

Instructions for submitting a request for BOEM records under the FOIA are available online. The BOEM operates a FOIA requester service center. Phone, 703-787-1818.

Glossary

The BOEM maintains an online resource evaluation glossary.

Library

The BOEM Web site has an electronic library.

Marine Minerals

Mineral resources from the OCS are used in coastal restoration projects to address erosion. The BOEM has conveyed rights to millions of cubic yards of OCS sand for coastal restoration projects in multiple States. These projects have restored hundreds of miles of the Nation's coastline, protecting both infrastructure and ecological habitat. The BOEM posts key marine mineral statistics on its Web site.

Newsroom

The BOEM newsroom features congressional testimony, factsheets, Frequently Asked Questions (FAQs), leadership presentations, media advisories, notes to stakeholders, science notes, statistics and facts, technical announcements, and videos.

Oil and Gas Energy

The BOEM has posted the 2012–2017 lease sale schedule and information on specific lease sales on its Web site.

Posters

Colorful BOEM posters that promote maritime history, ocean science and stewardship, and awareness of marine animals and their habitats are available from the Gulf of Mexico Public Information Office. Phone, 800-200-4853.

Renewable Energy

The offshore renewable energy guide provides background information on ocean renewable energy resources, the Outer Continental Shelf, and alternate uses for oil and gas platforms.

A list of leases that the BOEM has executed since the inception of its renewable energy program is available online.

The BOEM collaborates with States on offshore energy development and is in the process of coordinating Federal-State task forces in certain coastal States. A summary of the status of activity in the various States is available online.

Regional Offices

The BOEM operates three regional offices, one for the Alaska Outer Continental Shelf (OCS) region, one for the Pacific OCS region, and one for the Gulf of Mexico and Atlantic OCS regions. Phone, 907-334-5200 (Alaska). Phone, 805-384-6305 (Pacific). Phone, 800-200-4853 (Gulf of Mexico and Atlantic).

Shipwrecks

The BOEM Alaskan shipwreck table is the most comprehensive compilation of Alaskan shipwrecks to date. The table offers a list of wrecks that occurred in Alaskan waters from 1741 to 2011. The "Shipwrecks Off Alaska's Coast" Web page also features maritime history, ship, and shipwreck links to external Web sites.

Site Map

The Web site map allows visitors to look for specific topics or to browse content that aligns with their interests.

For further information, contact the Office of Public Affairs, Bureau of Ocean Energy Management, Department of the Interior, 1849 C Street NW., Washington, DC 20240-0001. Phone, 202-208-6474.

Bureau of Reclamation

Department of the Interior, 1849 C Street NW., Washington, DC 20240, 202-513-0575, *http://www.usbr.gov*

COMMISSIONER — Estevan López

The Bureau of Reclamation was established pursuant to the Reclamation Act of 1902 (43 U.S.C. 371 et seq.). The Bureau is the largest wholesale water supplier and the second largest producer of hydroelectric power in the United States, with operations and facilities in the 17 Western States. Its operations and facilities also support recreation and flood control and benefit fish and wildlife.

Sources of Information

Business Opportunities

The Bureau of Reclamation purchases a wide range of products and services and supports various Federal socioeconomic development programs by reaching out to and assisting businesses. The Bureau also provides financial assistance for programs related to conservation, Endangered Species Act mitigation, rural water, and water management and reclamation and reuse.

The Acquisition and Assistance Management Division is responsible for the Bureau's acquisition and financial assistance policy, acquisition and financial assistance operations, and property programs. Phone, 303-445-2431.

Employment

The Bureau relies on professionals with expertise in administration, engineering and design, environmental protection, research, wildlife management, and other disciplines to carry out its mission. Career-related information is available from the nearest regional office or the Diversity and Human Resources Office, Denver, CO. Phone, 303-445-2684.

Environment

The Bureau maintains a list of links to online resources that provide environmental information.

Freedom of Information Act (FOIA)

Contact information for the Bureau's regional FOIA coordinators is available online.

The Bureau maintains an electronic reading room that contains frequently requested records and documents that are currently of special interest.

Glossary

Definitions for terms commonly used by the Bureau are accessible in its online glossary.

The Bureau maintains a separate online glossary of recreation-related terms.

News

The Bureau posts news releases and stories on its Web site, which also features congressional testimony, factsheets, photos, and speeches.

Publications

Publications for sale are available through the National Technical Information Service. Phone, 800-553-6847.

Reclamation Manual

The Bureau's Web site has an online tool that allows users to search for keywords and terms in the "Reclamation Manual." The manual comprises a series of policy and directives and standards, which collectively assign program responsibility and establish and document agencywide methods of doing business.

Recreation

Recreation.gov provides information on all recreation facilities on Federal lands, including those owned and managed by the Bureau of Reclamation or one of its partners. Internet visitors can use Recreation.gov to make reservations at facilities that require them.

The Bureau's Web site features a list of publications on recreation-related topics.

Regional Offices

Contact information for the Washington, DC, and Denver, CO, based offices and Upper Colorado, Great Plains, Lower Colorado, Mid-Pacific, and Pacific Northwest regional offices is available on the "Addresses and Contacts" Web page.

Water Conservation

The WaterSMART program allows all Department of the Interior bureaus to work with States, tribes, local governments, and nongovernmental organizations to pursue a sustainable water supply for the Nation by establishing a framework that provides Federal leadership and assistance on the efficient use of water, that integrates water and energy policies to support the sustainable use of all natural resources, and that coordinates the water conservation activities of the various Department offices.

For further information, contact the Office of Public Affairs, Bureau of Reclamation, Department of the Interior, 1849 C Street NW., Washington, DC 20240-0001. Phone, 202-513-0575.

Bureau of Safety and Environmental Enforcement

Department of the Interior, 1849 C Street NW., Washington, DC 20240, 202-208-3985, *http://www.bsee.gov*

DIRECTOR	Brian M. Salerno

The Bureau of Safety and Environmental Enforcement (BSEE) was created on May 19, 2010, by Secretarial Order No. 3299, as amended.

The BSEE promotes safety, protects the environment, and conserves resources on the Outer Continental Shelf (OCS) through regulatory oversight and enforcement. The Offshore Regulatory Program develops standards and regulations to improve operational safety and to strengthen environmental protection. The Oil Spill Preparedness Division develops standards and guidelines for offshore operators. It also collaborates with sister agencies on spill response technologies and capabilities.

Three regional offices support the Bureau. Their personnel inspect gas and oil drilling rigs and production platforms to ensure compliance with safety requirements. Inspection teams are multiperson, and the expertise of their members spans a range of disciplines.

Sources of Information

Business Opportunities

Information on doing business with the BSEE is available online.

Employment

The BSEE relies on professionals with backgrounds in biology, geology, geophysics, engineering, and other fields to carry out its mission.

Freedom of Information Act (FOIA)

The FOIA gives the public the right to request Federal agency records and requires Federal agencies to make certain records available. The BSEE Web site serves as the portal to the agency's FOIA program. The FOIA is based on the principle of openness in Government: Any person has a right of access to Federal agency records, except to the extent that such records or portions of them are protected from disclosure by exemption or by special law-enforcement record exclusion.

The BSEE maintains an electronic FOIA reading room.

Frequently Asked Questions (FAQs)

The BSEE promotes safety, protects the environment, and conserves resources offshore through regulatory oversight and enforcement. To accomplish this mission, the Bureau relies on a wide range of world-class professionals. The Frequently Asked Questions (FAQs) Web page offers a sample of the questions that BSEE experts address and answers that they have provided.

Glossary

This glossary contains common oil and gas exploration and leasing terms, many of which are unique to the drilling industry.

News

The BSEE newsroom contains feature stories, media advisories, news briefs, photos and videos, press releases, and posts from the Director. The briefing room contains annual reports, congressional testimony, factsheets, speeches, statements, and technical presentations.

The BSEE tweets announcements and other newsworthy items on Twitter.

Offshore Statistics

The BSEE Web sites features a section dedicated to offshore statistics and facts.

Reading Room

The Bureau's Deepwater Horizon electronic reading room contains documents that deal with the BP/Deepwater Horizon explosion and ensuing oil spill and that have been cleared for public release.

Regional Offices

Information on the BSEE's three geographic regions—Alaska OCS, Gulf of Mexico OCS, and Pacific OCS—and their respective regional offices is available on the "BSEE Regions" Web page.

Site Map

The Web site map allows visitors to look for specific topics or to browse content that aligns with their interests.

For further information, contact the Office of Public Affairs, Bureau of Safety and Environmental Enforcement, Department of the Interior, 1849 C Street NW., Washington, DC 20240-7000. Phone, 202-208-3985.

National Park Service

Department of the Interior, 1849 C Street NW., Washington, DC 20240, 202-208-6843, *http://www.nps.gov*

DIRECTOR — Jonathan B. Jarvis

The National Park Service (NPS) was established in the Department of the Interior on August 25, 1916 (16 U.S.C. 1).

The National Park Service protects the natural and cultural resources and values of the National Park System for the benefit of present and future generations. The National Park System comprises 401 units. These units include national parks, monuments and memorials, battlefield sites and national military parks, scenic parkways, preserves and reserves, trails and riverways, rivers and lakeshores and seashores, recreation areas, and historic sites of American or international importance. The Service also manages a variety of national and international programs to promote natural and cultural resource conservation and to expand the benefits of outdoor recreation.

The NPS develops and implements park management plans and staffs the areas under its administration. Through exhibits, films, publications talks, tours, and other interpretive media, it promotes the natural values of these areas and communicates their historical significance to the public. The NPS operates a range of visitor facilities, including campgrounds, and provides a variety of food, lodging, and transportation services.

The National Park Service also administers the State portion of the Land and Water Conservation Fund, State comprehensive outdoor recreation planning, nationwide outdoor recreation coordination and information, the National Register of Historic Places and the National Trails System, natural area programs, national historic landmarks and historic preservation, technical preservation services, the historic American engineering record and buildings survey, interagency archeological services, and planning and technical assistance for the national wild and scenic rivers system.

Sources of Information

America the Beautiful Passes

A pass may be used at more than 2,000 federal recreation sites. A pass covers entrance fees at national parks and national wildlife refuges, as well as standard amenity fees and day use fees at national forests and grasslands and at lands managed by the Bureaus of Land Management and Reclamation and the U.S. Army Corps of Engineers. Five types of passes are available: access, annual, annual fourth grade, senior, and volunteer.

Business Opportunities

Visit the "Doing Business With Us" Web page to find information on commercial tours, contracts and procurement, National Park concessions, and special park uses, including commercial filming.

Directories

An online text box allows Internet visitors to search for NPS employees by last name.

A park directory (SEP 2016) that includes park addresses, codes, phone numbers, and superintendents is available online in Portable Document Format (PDF).

Employment

To find permanent and seasonal NPS career opportunities online, visit USAJobs, the Federal Government's official source for Federal job listings.

Additional information on internships, permanent careers, seasonal opportunities, and volunteering is available on the "Work With Us" Web page.

Find a Park

Visitors to the NPS Web site may search for a park by name or by State.

Freedom of Information Act (FOIA)

Instructions for submitting a FOIA request to obtain NPS records are available online.

The NPS Web site features an electronic FOIA library.

Frequently Asked Questions (FAQs)

The NPS Web site has answers to these questions.

Glossaries

The NPS's National Center for Preservation Technology and Training maintains an extensive glossary of building stone terms.

The online series "Defining the Southwest" includes a glossary of terms that are often encountered in discussions of the cultures and environments of the American Southwest.

A glossary of geologic terms that the NPS and U.S. Geological Survey western Earth surface processes team compiled is available on the NPS Web site.

Grants

Information is available online for grants authorized under the Land and Water

Conservation Fund. Phone, 202-354-6900.

Information is also available online for grants authorized under the Historic Preservation Fund. Phone, 202-354-2067.

News

The NPS posts new releases online.

The NPS Web site features a multimedia section that includes audio, photographs, videos, and webcam.

The NPS tweets announcements and other newsworthy items on Twitter.

The NPS maintains a Facebook page.

Publications

To explain decisions, document information, and disseminate knowledge, the NPS uses a variety of publications, many of which are accessible online. For example, "The National Parks: Index 2012–2016" can be downloaded as a PDF. The "Publications" Web page offers online access to contemporary and historic reports, periodicals, virtual stacks, and public databases.

Some publications are available for purchase in hardcopy from the U.S. Government Bookstore. Phone, 202-512-1800. Phone, 866-512-1800.

Regional Offices

Contact information is available online for NPS regional offices and parks and the Washington office.

For further information, contact the Office of Communications, National Park Service, Department of the Interior, 1849 C Street NW., Washington, DC 20240. Phone, 202-208-6843.

Office of Surface Mining Reclamation and Enforcement

Department of the Interior, 1951 Constitution Avenue NW., Washington, DC 20240, 202-208-2565, TDD, 202-208-2694, *http://www.osmre.gov*

DIRECTOR Joseph Pizarchik

The Office of Surface Mining Reclamation and Enforcement (OSMRE) was established in the Department of the Interior by the Surface Mining Control and Reclamation Act of 1977 (30 U.S.C. 1211).

The OSMRE carries out the requirements of the Surface Mining Control and Reclamation Act in cooperation with States and tribes. The Office protects people and the environment from the adverse effects of coal mining. The OSMRE assures that land is restored to beneficial use after mining operations cease, and it mitigates the effects of past operations by reclamation of abandoned coal mines. The Office mainly oversees State mining regulatory and abandoned-mine reclamation programs, assists States in meeting the objectives of surface mining law, and regulates mining and reclamation activities on Federal and Indian lands and in those States opting not to assume primary responsibility for regulating coal mining and reclamation activities within their borders.

The Office establishes national policy for the surface mining control and reclamation program, reviews and approves amendments to previously approved State programs, and reviews and recommends approval of new State program submissions. It also manages the collection, disbursement, and accounting of abandoned-mine land reclamation fees; administers civil penalties programs; establishes technical standards and regulatory policy for reclamation and enforcement; offers guidance for environmental considerations, research, training, and technology transfers; and monitors and evaluates State and tribal regulatory programs, cooperative agreements, and abandoned-mine land reclamation programs.

Sources of Information

Abandoned Mine Land Inventory System

To provide information for implementing the Surface Mining Control and Reclamation Act of 1977, the OSMRE maintains an inventory of land and water affected by past mining. The inventory contains information on the location, type, and extent of abandoned mine land impacts, as well as information on the reclamation costs. The inventory is based on field surveys by State, tribal, and OSMRE program officials.

Business Opportunities

Information to assist small business operators and owners is available online. For additional information, contact the Acquisition Management Branch. Phone, 202-208-2902.

Employment

To find employment opportunities at the OSMRE, visit the "Jobs at OSMRE" Web page and click on the USAJobs quick link.

Freedom of Information Act (FOIA)

A FOIA request for OSMRE records may be submitted via electronic or postal mail or by using the Department of the Interior's electronic request form and selecting "Office of Surface Mining" in the drop-down menu.

Frequently Asked Questions (FAQs)

The OSMRE posts answers to FAQs on its Web site.

The OSMRE Web site also features a "How Do I?" section.

Grants

Information on regulatory program grants and abandoned mine land grants is available on the OSMRE Web site.

Library

The general public may use the OSMRE online library catalog to locate legal and technical information.

Mine Maps

The National Mine Map Repository collects and maintains mine map information and images for the entire country.

An index that includes over 180,000 maps of closed and abandoned mines is available online. The index serves as an inventory for determining which maps are available. To obtain actual copies of maps, contact the National Mine Map Repository. Fax, 412-937-2888.

Most Requested Content

The OSMRE Web site features a collection of links to its most frequently requested Web pages.

Newsroom

The newsroom features OSMRE stories and news releases.

The OSMRE tweets announcements and other newsworthy items on Twitter.

The OSMRE has a Facebook page.

Regional Offices

Appalachian Region Office

Mid-Continent Region Office

Western Region Office

Resources

The OSMRE Web site features a section dedicated to electronic, informational resources.

Site Map

The Web site map allows visitors to look for specific topics or to browse content that aligns with their interests.

An A–Z Index is also available to help visitors find the information that they seek on the OSMRE Web site.

Top Priorities

The OSMRE Web site features a section on the agency's top priorities.

For further information, contact the Office of Communications, Office of Surface Mining Reclamation and Enforcement, Department of the Interior, 1951 Constitution Avenue NW., Washington, DC 20240. Phone, 202-208-2565. TDD, 202-208-2694.

United States Fish and Wildlife Service

Department of the Interior, 1849 C Street NW., Washington, DC 20240, 703-358-4545, *http://www.fws.gov*

DIRECTOR	Daniel M. Ashe

[For the United States Fish and Wildlife Service statement of organization, see the Code of Federal Regulations, Title 50, Subchapter A, Part 2]

The U.S. Fish and Wildlife Service (USFWS) is the principal Federal agency dedicated to fish and wildlife conservation. The Service's history spans 145 years, dating from the establishment of its predecessor agency, the Bureau of Fisheries, in 1871. First created as an independent agency, the Bureau of Fisheries was later placed in the Department of Commerce. A second predecessor agency, the Bureau of Biological Survey, was established in 1885 in the Department of Agriculture. In 1939, the two Bureaus and their functions were transferred to the Department of the Interior. In 1940, they were consolidated into one agency and redesignated the Fish and Wildlife Service by Reorganization Plan No. 3 (5 U.S.C. app.).

The USFWS works with others to conserve, protect, and enhance fish, wildlife and plants and their habitats for the continuing benefit of the American people. The Service manages the 150-million-acre National Wildlife Refuge System, which comprises 563 refuges and 38 wetland management districts. It operates 72 national fish hatcheries, a historic national fish hatchery, 65 fishery resource offices, and 81 ecological service field stations. The USFWS enforces Federal wildlife laws, administers the Endangered Species Act, manages migratory bird populations, restores nationally significant fisheries, conserves and restores wildlife habitats, and assists foreign governments with conservation. It also collects excise taxes on fishing and hunting equipment and distributes the revenues to State fish and wildlife agencies.

The Service improves and maintains fish and wildlife resources by proper management of wildlife and habitat. It also helps meet public demand for wildlife dependent recreational activities by maintaining public lands and restoring native fish and wildlife populations.

Wildlife and fishery resource programs support the management of wildlife refuges on public lands. Wildlife-related activities include population control, migration and harvest surveys, and law and gaming enforcement for migratory and nonmigratory birds and mammals. Fishery-related activities include hatchery production monitoring, stocking, and fishery management. Fishery resource programs also provide technical assistance for coastal anadromous, Great Lakes, and other inland fisheries.

The USFWS identifies, protects, and restores endangered fish, wildlife, and plant species. It maintains Federal lists of endangered and threatened wildlife and plants that are published in the Code of Federal Regulations (50 CFR 17.11 et seq.), conducts status surveys, prepares recovery plans, and coordinates national and international wildlife refuge operations.

The Service protects and improves land and water environments to benefit living natural resources and to enhance the quality of human life. It administers grant programs that help imperiled species, assists private landowners restore habitat, asses environmental impact and reviews potential environmental threats, manages Coastal Barrier Resource System mapping, monitors potential wildlife contaminants, and studies fish and wildlife population trends.

Public use and information activities include preparing informational brochures and maintaining public Web sites; coordinating environmental studies on USFWS lands; operating visitor centers, self-guided nature trails, observation towers, and display ponds; and promoting birdwatching, fishing, hunting, wildlife photography, and other forms of wildlife-dependent outdoor recreation.

The Wildlife and Sport Fish Restoration Program supports the conservation and enhancement of the Nation's fish and wildlife resources. Excise taxes on sporting arms and fishing equipment fund these efforts.

Sources of Information

Blog

The USFWS Web site features "Open Spaces—A Talk on the Wild Side."

Business Opportunities

An online guide explains how to find business opportunities and to compete for them. Information is also available from regional offices and from the Division of Contracting and General Services in Falls Church, VA. Phone, 703-358-2500.

Climate Change

The USFWS Web site provides a collection of links and informational sources for learning about climate science and conservation in a changing climate.

Contaminants

The USFWS Web site features a section dedicated to contaminants—for example, metals and pesticides—and their effects on wildlife.

Employment

Information on careers in conservation is available on the USFWS Web site. Additional information is available from USFWS regional offices and the Human Capital Office in Falls Church, VA. Phone, 703-358-1743.

Endangered Species

The USFWS Web site features a search tool for learning about and identifying endangered species. The text boxes can search for an endangered species based on the State, U.S. Territory, or county where it lives, or according to its common or scientific name.

An online subscription form is available to receive breaking news affecting endangered species, endangered species news stories, and the "Endangered Species Bulletin" via email.

Energy Development

The USFWS Web site features a section dedicated to the development of domestic energy sources and its effect on wildlife.

Freedom of Information Act (FOIA)

The USFWS makes records available to the public to the greatest extent possible. The records that are being sought already may be posted online. If the information cannot be found online or if the location of the desired records is uncertain, consider contacting the USFWS FOIA public liaison before submitting a FOIA request.

The USFWS does not have a centralized records system. Most data and records are kept in field offices. Instructions on where to send a FOIA request for USFWS records are available online.

Glossaries

Ecological Services maintains an online glossary of terms found in environmental legislation.

The Midwest Region maintains an online glossary of terms associated with endangered species.

The Midwest Region also maintains a glossary of terms associated with freshwater mussels of the Upper Mississippi River System.

The USFWS Web site features a short glossary of National Environmental Policy Act (NEPA) terms in Portable Document Format (PDF).

National Wildlife Refuges

For information on the National Wildlife Refuge System, including information on specific wildlife refuges and wetland management districts, visit the "National Wildlife Refuge System" Web site. Phone, 800-344-9453.

News Media Inquiries

Journalists, reporters, and other media professionals seeking information or to arrange an interview should contact a regional public affairs officer or the Division of Public Affairs in Falls Church, VA. Phone, 703-358-2220.

Newsroom

The USFWS posts news releases online.

Permits

Visit the "Do I Need a Permit" Web page to learn the rules for importing, exporting, and reexporting protected species. Information on Convention on International Trade in Endangered Species of Wild Fauna and Flora (CITES) permits and certificates is also available from the Division of Management Authority. Phone, 800-358-2104 or 703-358-2093.

Publications

The USFWS national publications unit is headquartered at the National Conservation Training Center in Shepherdstown, WV. It is the primary distribution center for printed material published by the USFWS. The publications unit handles requests from Federal and State agencies, businesses, educators, and the general public. USFWS publications include booklets, brochures, posters, and reports. Phone, 800-344-9543.

Some publications may need to be ordered from the U.S. Government

Bookstore, which the Government Publishing Office operates. Phone, 866-512-1800 (customer contact center). Phone, 202-512-0132 (store phone).

Regional Offices

USFWS has regional offices that represent each of its eight geographic regions: Pacific, Southwest, Midwest, Southeast, Northeast, Mountain-Prairie, Alaska, and Pacific Southwest. Contact information for each of these regional offices is available on the USFWS Web site.

The Office of Law Enforcement, in addition to its national office in Falls Church, VA, maintains a regional office in each of the eight regions. Contact information for these offices is available on the USFWS Web site.

A State list of other USFWS offices and their contact information is also available online.

Report a Violation

To report a violation of wildlife laws or to learn about enforcement of them, visit the "Office of Law Enforcement" Web site, contact the nearest regional law enforcement office, or call the Office of Law Enforcement in Falls Church, VA. Phone, 703-358-1949.

Social Media

The USFWS uses social media to communicate and connect with Internet users worldwide. The agency tweets from its Twitter accounts; maintains an Instagram feed and Pinterest board; posts videos on its YouTube channel and photographs on Flickr; and has Facebook, LinkedIn, and Google+ pages.

Water Resource Development

The USFWS Web site features a section dedicated to the development of water resources and its effect on wildlife.

For further information, contact the Division of Marketing Communications–External Affairs, U.S. Fish and Wildlife Service, Department of the Interior, 1849 C Street NW., Washington, DC 20240. Phone, 703-358-2613.

United States Geological Survey

12201 Sunrise Valley Drive, Reston, VA 20192, 703-648-4000, *http://www.usgs.gov* | Email: *ASK@usgs.gov*

DIRECTOR	Suzette Kimball

The United States Geological Survey (USGS) was established by the Organic Act of March 3, 1879 (43 U.S.C. 31). Since March 3, 1879, the Survey has provided the United States with science information needed to make important land use and resource management policy decisions.

The USGS serves as the Earth and natural science research bureau for the Department of the Interior. It is the only integrated natural resources research agency in the Federal Government. USGS research and data support the Department's resource and land management information needs. Other Federal, State, tribal, and local government agencies rely on USGS research and data for their biological, climate, energy, mineral resources, natural hazards, and water information needs. Emergency response organizations, natural resource managers, land use planners, and other customers use USGS research and data to protect lives and property, to address environmental health issues, and to promote the public weal.

The USGS conducts research, monitoring, and assessments to increase understanding of America's biological, land, and water resources. The Service informs American citizens and members of the global community by producing data, maps, and reports containing analyses and interpretations. These analyses and interpretations cover a range of topics: biological, energy, mineral, and water resources; land surfaces; marine environments; geologic structures; natural hazards; and dynamic processes of the Earth. Citizens, managers, and planners regularly use USGS data, analytical, and interpretive products to respond to and plan for changes in ecosystems and the environment.

The USGS has 135 years of experience generating science-based data. In more than 400 science centers across the United States, the Service employs 8,000 science and science-support staff, who work on locally, regionally, and nationally scaled studies, on research projects, and at sampling and monitoring sites.

Sources of Information

Business Opportunities

Contact information for USGS small business specialists and information on contracting with the USGS are available on the agency Web site. Information is also available from the Office of Acquisition and Grants. Phone, 703-648-7376.

Earthquakes for Kids

Earthquakes for kids provides online resources to help children and adults learn about earthquakes and earthquake science.

Employment

The USGS relies on professionals with a range of expertise and diverse skills to carry out its mission. Many of these professionals were educated and trained in the sciences: biology, chemistry, cartography, ecology, geology, geography, hydrology, and physics.

Information on opportunities for students and recent graduates is available on the USGS Web site.

Freedom of Information Act (FOIA)

The FOIA electronic reading room contains documents related to the Flow Rate Technical Group in response to the Deepwater Horizon oil spill. These documents have been cleared for public release, and the USGS expects to publish additional documents to this collection. Before submitting a FOIA request for agency records, an information seeker should search this reading room and other Federal Government Deepwater Horizon electronic reading rooms for documents and information.

Frequently Asked Questions (FAQs)

The USGS posts answers to FAQs on its Web site.

Glossaries

The volcano hazards program includes an online glossary.

The earthquake hazards program includes an online glossary.

Grants

Information on financial assistance programs is available on the USGS Web site.

Landsat

The Landsat Web site features colorful images spanning the globe.

Libraries

Maps, publications, reports, and a variety of biological and Earth information resources and historical documents are available through the USGS library system. The USGS Web site features a tool for searching the library's catalog.

National Map

The National Map Web site offers Internet users a trove of topographical information.

Natural Hazards

Information on the programs and activities of the natural hazards mission—including information on earthquakes, volcanoes, and landslides—is available online.

News

USGS national and State news items are posted online.

The USGS tweets on Twitter and has a Facebook page.

Publications

The USGS publications warehouse provides access to over 130,000 publications written by USGS scientists throughout the agency's history.

Report a Landslide

An online form is available on the USGS Web site to report a landslide.

Science Snippets

The USGS posts fun facts and interesting snippets of science on its Web site.

Site Map

The Web site map allows visitors to look for specific topics or to browse content that aligns with their interests.

USGS Store

Educational materials, Federal recreation passes, maps, scientific reports, and more are available from the online USGS Store.

Volcano Notification Service

This electronic notification service keeps subscribers abreast of volcanic activity at U.S. monitored volcanoes.

Water Data

Reliable, impartial, and timely information on the Nation's water resources is available on the USGS Web site. Phone, 888-275-8747.

The USGS manages water information at local water resources offices located nationwide. The offices are linked through a computer network; however, each office collects data and conducts studies in a particular area. Local information is best found at a local site or at neighboring sites.

For additional information, contact the U.S. Geological Survey, Department of the Interior, 12201 Sunrise Valley Drive, Reston, VA 20192. Phone, 703-648-4000.

Department of Justice

950 Pennsylvania Avenue NW., Washington, DC 20530, 202-514-2000, *http://www.justice.gov*

ATTORNEY GENERAL	Loretta E. Lynch
Deputy Attorney General	Sally Quillian Yates
Associate Attorney General	William J. Baer, Acting
Counsel, Office of Professional Responsibility	Robin C. Ashton
Inspector General	Michael E. Horowitz
Pardon Attorney	Robert A. Zauzmer, Acting
Solicitor General	Donald B. Verrilli, Jr.
ASSISTANT ATTORNEYS GENERAL	
Criminal Division	Leslie Ragon Caldwell
Environment and Natural Resources Division	John C. Cruden
Justice Management Division / Chief Financial Officer	Lee J. Lofthus
National Security Division	John P. Carlin
Office of Legislative Affairs	Peter J. Kadzik
Tax Division	Caroline D. Ciraolo, Acting
DIRECTORS	
Community Relations Service	Paul Monteiro, Acting
Executive Office for Organized Crime and Drug Enforcement Task Force	Bruce G. Ohr

Executive Office for U.S. Attorneys	Monty Wilkinson
Executive Office for U.S. Trustees	Clifford J. White III
Office for Access to Justice	Lisa Foster
Office of Information Policy	Melanie Ann Pustay
Office of Public Affairs	Melanie Newman
Office of Tribal Justice	Tracy Toulou
Professional Responsibility Advisory Office	Stacy Ludwig
PRINCIPAL DEPUTY ASSISTANT ATTORNEYS GENERAL	
Antitrust Division	Renata B. Hesse
Civil Division	Benjamin C. Mizer
Civil Rights Division	Vanita Gupta
Office of Legal Counsel	Karl Remón Thompson
Office of Legal Policy	Jonathan Wroblewski

[For the Department of Justice statement of organization, see the Code of Federal Regulations, Title 28, Chapter I, Part 0]

The Department of Justice serves as counsel for U.S citizens and represents them by enforcing the law in the public interest. It deters criminality and subversion, ensures healthy business competition, safeguards consumers, and enforces drug, immigration, and naturalization laws.

The Department of Justice was established by act of June 22, 1870 (28 U.S.C. 501, 503, 509 note), with the Attorney General as its head. The affairs and activities of the Department of Justice are generally directed by the Attorney General.

Attorney General

The Attorney General represents the United States in legal matters generally and gives advice and opinions to the President and to the heads of the executive departments of the Government when so requested. The Attorney General appears in person to represent the Government before the U.S. Supreme Court in cases of exceptional gravity or importance.

Community Relations Service

The Service offers assistance to communities in resolving disputes relating to race, color, or national origin and facilitates the development of viable agreements as alternatives to coercion, violence, or litigation. It also assists and supports communities in developing local mechanisms as proactive measures to prevent or reduce ethnic and racial tensions.

A list of Community Relations Service regional offices—including contact information—is available online.

For further information, contact any regional office or the Director, Community Relations Service, Department of Justice, Suite 2000, 600 E Street NW., Washington, DC 20530. Phone, 202-305-2935.

Pardon Attorney

The Office of the Pardon Attorney assists the President in the exercise of his pardon power under the Constitution. Generally, all requests for pardon or other forms of executive clemency, including commutation of sentences, are directed to the Pardon Attorney for investigation and review. The Pardon Attorney prepares the Department's recommendation to the President for final disposition of each application.

For further information, contact the Office of the Pardon Attorney, Department of Justice, Suite 5E–508, 145 N Street NE., Washington, DC 20530. Phone, 202-616-6070.

Solicitor General

The Office of the Solicitor General represents the U.S. Government in cases before the Supreme Court. It decides what cases the Government should ask the Supreme Court to review and what position the Government should take in cases before the Court. It also supervises the preparation of the Government's Supreme Court briefs and other legal documents and the conduct of the oral arguments in the Court. The Solicitor General also decides whether the United States should appeal in cases that it loses before the lower courts.

For further information, contact the Executive Officer, Office of the Solicitor General, Room 5142, 950 Pennsylvania Avenue NW., RFK Justice Building (Main), Washington, DC 20530-0001.

U.S. Attorneys

The Executive Office for U.S. Attorneys was created on April 6, 1953, to provide liaison between the Department of Justice in Washington, DC, and the U.S. attorneys. It gives general executive assistance to the 94 offices of the U.S. attorneys and coordinates the relationship between the U.S. attorneys and the organization components of the Department of Justice and other Federal agencies.

For further information, contact the Executive Office for U.S. Attorneys, Department of Justice, Room 2261, 950 Pennsylvania Avenue NW., Washington, DC 20530. Phone, 202-514-1020.

U.S. Trustee Program

The Program was established by the Bankruptcy Reform Act of 1978 (11 U.S.C. 101 et seq.) as a pilot effort in 10 regions comprising 18 Federal judicial districts to promote the efficiency and protect the integrity of the bankruptcy system by identifying and helping to investigate bankruptcy fraud and abuse. It now operates nationwide except in Alabama and North Carolina. The Bankruptcy Abuse Prevention and Consumer Protection Act of 2005 (11 U.S.C. 101 note) significantly expanded the Program's responsibilities and provided additional tools to fight bankruptcy fraud and abuse. The Executive Office for U.S. Trustees provides day-to-day policy and legal direction, coordination, and control.

For further information, contact the Executive Office for U.S. Trustees, Department of Justice, Suite 6150, 441 G Street NW., Washington, DC 20530. Phone, 202-307-1391.

Divisions

Antitrust Division

The Assistant Attorney General in charge of the Antitrust Division is responsible for promoting and maintaining competitive markets by enforcing the Federal antitrust laws. This involves investigating possible antitrust violations, conducting grand jury proceedings, reviewing proposed mergers and acquisitions, preparing and trying antitrust cases, prosecuting appeals, and negotiating and enforcing final judgments. The Division prosecutes serious and willful violations of antitrust laws by filing criminal suits that can lead to large fines and jail sentences. Where criminal prosecution is not appropriate, the Division seeks a court order forbidding future violations of the law and requiring steps by the defendant to remedy the anticompetitive effects of past violations.

The Division also is responsible for acting as an advocate of competition within the Federal Government as well as internationally. This involves formal appearances in Federal administrative agency proceedings, development of legislative initiatives to promote deregulation and eliminate unjustifiable exemptions from the antitrust laws, and participation on executive branch policy task forces and in multilateral international organizations. The Division provides formal advice to other agencies on the competitive implications of proposed transactions requiring Federal approval, such as mergers of financial institutions.

For further information, contact the Office of the Assistant Attorney General, Antitrust Division, Department of Justice, 950 Pennsylvania Avenue NW., Washington, DC 20530. Phone, 202-514-2401.

Civil Division

The Civil Division represents the United States, its departments and agencies, Members of Congress, Cabinet officers, and other Federal employees. Its litigation reflects the diversity of Government activities involving, for example, the defense of challenges to Presidential actions; national security issues; benefit programs; energy policies; commercial issues such as contract disputes, banking, insurance, fraud, and debt collection; all manner of accident and liability claims; and violations of the immigration and consumer protection laws. The Division confronts significant policy issues, which often rise to constitutional dimensions, in defending and enforcing various Federal programs and actions. Each year, Division attorneys handle thousands of cases that collectively involve billions of dollars in claims and recoveries.

The Division litigates cases in the following areas:

Commercial litigation, litigation associated with the Government's diverse financial involvements including all monetary suits involving contracts, express or implied; actions to foreclose on Government mortgages and liens; bankruptcy and insolvency proceedings; suits against guarantors and sureties; actions involving fraud against the Government, including false or fraudulent claims for Federal insurance, loans, subsidies, and other benefits such as Medicare, false or fraudulent claims for payment under Federal contracts, whistleblower suits, and Government corruption; patent, copyright, and trademark cases and suits arising out of construction, procurement, service contracts, and claims associated with contract terminations; claims for just compensation under the Fifth Amendment; claims for salary or retirement by civilian and military personnel; cases assigned by congressional reference or special legislation; and litigation involving interests of the United States in any foreign court, whether civil or criminal in nature.

Consumer litigation, including civil and criminal litigation and related matters arising under various consumer protection and public health statutes.

Federal programs, including constitutional challenges to statutes, suits to overturn Government policies and programs, challenges to the legality of Government decisions, allegations that the President has violated the Constitution or Federal law, suits to enforce regulatory statutes and to remedy or prevent statutory or regulatory violations.

The areas of litigation include:

Suits against the heads of Federal departments and agencies and other Government officials to enjoin official actions, as well as suits for judicial review of administrative decisions, orders, and regulations; suits involving national security, including suits to protect sensitive intelligence sources and materials; suits to prevent interference with Government operations; litigation concerning the constitutionality of Federal laws; and suits raising employment discrimination claims and Government personnel issues.

Immigration litigation, involving civil litigation under the Immigration and Nationality Act and related laws; district court litigation, habeas corpus review and general advice; petitions for removal order review and immigration-related appellate matters; cases pertaining to the issuance of visas and passports; and litigation arising under the legalization and employer sanction provisions of the immigration laws.

Torts, including the broad range of tort litigation arising from the operation of the Federal Government, constitutional tort claims against Federal Government officials throughout the Government, aviation disasters, environmental and occupational disease, and radiation and toxic substance exposure. It defends petitions filed pursuant to the Vaccine Injury Compensation Program and is responsible for administering the Radiation Exposure Compensation Program. It also handles maritime litigation and suits that seek personal monetary judgments against individual officers or employees.

Appellate, having primary responsibility for the litigation of Civil Division cases in the courts of appeal, and on occasion, State appeal courts. The Appellate Staff prepares Government briefs and presents oral arguments for these cases. Additionally, the Appellate Staff works with the Solicitor General's office to prepare documents filed for these cases in the Supreme Court, including briefs on the merits, petitions for certiorari, and jurisdictional statements. The Appellate Staff also works with the Solicitor General's office to obtain authorization for appellate review.

For further information, contact the Office of the Assistant Attorney General, Civil Division, Department of Justice, Tenth Street and Pennsylvania Avenue NW., Washington, DC 20530. Phone, 202-514-3301.

Civil Rights Division

The Civil Rights Division, headed by an Assistant Attorney General, was established in 1957 to secure effective Federal enforcement of civil rights. The Division is the primary institution within the Federal Government responsible for enforcing Federal statutes prohibiting discrimination on the basis of race, sex, disability, religion, citizenship, and national origin. The Division has responsibilities in the following areas:

Coordination and review of various civil rights statutes that prohibit discrimination on the basis of race, color, national origin, sex, and religion in programs and activities that receive Federal financial assistance by Federal agencies.

Criminal cases involving conspiracies to interfere with federally protected rights; deprivation of rights under color of law; the use of force or threat of force to injure or intimidate someone in their enjoyment of specific rights (such as voting, housing, employment, education, public facilities, and accommodations); interference with the free exercise of religious beliefs or damage to religious property; the holding of a worker in a condition of slavery or involuntary servitude; and interference with persons seeking to obtain or provide reproductive services.

Disability rights cases, achieving equal opportunity for people with disabilities in the United States by implementing the Americans with Disabilities Act (ADA). ADA mandates are carried out through enforcement, certification, regulatory, coordination, and technical assistance activities, combined with an innovative mediation program and a technical assistance grant program. The Division also carries out responsibilities under sections 504 and 508 of the Rehabilitation Act, the Help America Vote Act of 2002, the Small Business Regulatory Enforcement Fairness Act, and Executive Order 12250.

Educational opportunities litigation, involving title IV of the Civil Rights Act of 1964, the Equal Educational Opportunities Act of 1974, and title III of the Americans with Disabilities Act. In addition, the Division is responsible for enforcing other statutes such as title VI of the Civil Rights Act of 1964, title IX of the Education Amendments of 1972, section 504 of the Rehabilitation Act of 1973, title II of the Americans with Disabilities Act, and the Individuals with Disabilities Education Act upon referral from other governmental agencies.

Employment litigation enforcing against State and local government employers the provisions of title VII of the Civil Rights Act of 1964, as amended, and other Federal laws prohibiting employment practices that discriminate on grounds of race, sex, religion, and national origin. The Division also enforces against State and local government and private employers the provisions of the Uniformed Services Employment and Reemployment Rights Act of 1994, which prohibits employers from discriminating or retaliating against an employee or applicant for employment because of such person's past, current, or future military obligation.

Housing and Civil Enforcement statutes enforcing the Fair Housing Act, which prohibits discrimination in housing; the Equal Credit Opportunity Act, which prohibits discrimination in credit; title II of the Civil Rights Act of 1964, which prohibits discrimination in certain places of public accommodation, such as hotels, restaurants, nightclubs and theaters; title III of the Civil Rights Act of 1964, which prohibits discrimination in public facilities; and the Religious Land Use and Institutionalized Persons Act, which prohibits local governments from adopting or enforcing land use regulations that discriminate against religious assemblies and institutions or which unjustifiably burden religious exercise.

Immigration-related unfair employment practices enforcing the antidiscrimination provisions of the Immigration and Nationality Act, which protect U.S. citizens and legal immigrants from employment discrimination based upon citizenship or immigration status and national origin, unfair documentary practices relating to the employment eligibility verification process, and retaliation.

Special litigation protecting the constitutional and statutory rights of persons confined in certain institutions owned or operated by State or local governments, including facilities for individuals with mental and developmental disabilities, nursing homes, prisons, jails, and juvenile detention facilities where a pattern or practice of violations exist; civil enforcement of statutes prohibiting a pattern or practice of conduct by law enforcement agencies that violates Federal law; and protection against a threat of force and physical obstruction that injures, intimidates, or interferes with a person seeking to obtain or provide reproductive health services, or to exercise the first amendment right of religious freedom at a place of worship.

Voting cases enforcing the Voting Rights Act, the Help America Vote Act of 2002, the National Voter Registration Act, the Voting Accessibility for the Elderly and Handicapped Act, the Uniformed and Overseas Citizens Absentee Voting Act, and other Federal statutes designed to safeguard citizens' rights to vote. This includes racial and language minorities, illiterate persons, individuals with disabilities, overseas citizens, persons who change their residence shortly before a Presidential election, and persons 18 to 20 years of age.

For further information, contact the Executive Officer, Civil Rights Division, Department of Justice, 950 Pennsylvania Avenue NW., Washington, DC 20035. Phone, 202-514-4224.

Criminal Division

The Criminal Division develops, enforces, and supervises the application of all Federal criminal laws, except those specifically assigned to other divisions. In addition to its direct litigation responsibilities, the Division formulates and implements criminal enforcement policy and provides advice and assistance, including representing the United States before the United States Courts of Appeal. The Division engages in and coordinates a wide range of criminal investigations and prosecutions, such as those targeting individuals and organizations that engage in international and national drug trafficking and money laundering systems or organizations and organized crime groups. The Division also approves or monitors sensitive areas of law enforcement such as participation in the Witness Security Program and the use of electronic surveillance; advises the Attorney General, Congress, the Office of Management and Budget, and the White House on matters of criminal law; provides legal advice, assistance, and training to Federal, State, and local prosecutors and investigative agencies; provides leadership for coordinating international and national law enforcement matters; and provides training and development assistance to foreign criminal justice systems. Areas of responsibility include the following:

Asset forfeiture and money laundering, including the prosecution of complex, sensitive, multidistrict, and international cases; formulating policy and conducting training in the money laundering and forfeiture areas; developing legislation and regulations; ensuring the uniform application of forfeiture and money laundering statutes; participating in bilateral and multilateral initiatives to develop international forfeiture and money laundering policy and promote international cooperation; adjudicating petitions for remission or mitigation of forfeited assets; distributing forfeited funds and properties to appropriate domestic and foreign law enforcement agencies and community groups within the United States; and ensuring that such agencies comply with proper usage of received funds.

Child exploitation and obscenity, including the prosecution of sexual predators, sex trafficking of children, U.S. citizens and resident aliens who travel abroad to sexually abuse foreign children (sex tourism), and the enforcement of sex offender registration laws; providing forensic assistance to Federal prosecutors and law enforcement agents in investigating and prosecuting child exploitation: coordinating nationwide operations targeting child predators; and developing policy and legislative proposals related to these issues.

Computer and intellectual property crimes, including cyberattacks on critical information systems (cyberterrorism); strengthening, domestic and international laws prosecute computer crimes; and directing multidistrict and transnational cyberinvestigations and prosecutions.

Enforcement, including the review of all Federal electronic surveillance requests and requests to apply for court orders permitting the use video surveillance; authorizing or denying the entry of applicants into the Federal Witness Security Program (WSP) and coordinating and administering its program components; reviewing requests for witness immunity ; transfer of prisoners to and from foreign countries to serve the remainder of their prison sentences; attorney and press subpoenas; applications for S-visa status; and disclosure of grand jury information.

Fraud, including the investigation and prosecution of white-collar crimes (corporate, securities, and investment fraud), government program and procurement fraud, and international criminal violations including the bribery of foreign government officials in violation of the Foreign Corrupt Practices Act.

International affairs, including making requests for international extradition and foreign evidence on behalf of Federal, State, and local prosecutors and investigators, fulfilling foreign requests for fugitives and evidence, and negotiating and implementing law enforcement treaties.

Narcotics and dangerous drugs, including domestic and international drug trafficking and narco-terrorism; enforcing laws that criminalize the extraterritorial manufacture or distribution of certain controlled substances; prosecuting drug traffickers who support a person or organization that engages in terrorist activity; and providing targeted intelligence support to the DEA and other law enforcement agencies worldwide.

Organized crime, including combining the resources and expertise of several Federal agencies in cooperation with the Tax Division, U.S. attorneys offices, and State and local law enforcement to identify, disrupt, and dismantle major drug supply and money laundering organizations through coordinated, nationwide investigations targeting the entire infrastructure of these enterprises.

Assistance to foreign law enforcement institutions, including the creation of new and reforming existing police forces in other countries and international peacekeeping operations; enhancing the capabilities of existing police forces in emerging democracies; and assisting nations that are combating terrorism.

Overseas prosecutorial development, assistance, and training for prosecutors and judicial personnel in other countries to develop and sustain democratic criminal justice institutions.

Policy and legislation, developing legislative proposals and reviewing pending legislation affecting the Federal criminal justice system; reviewing and developing proposed changes to the Federal sentencing guidelines and rules; and analyzing crime policy and program issues.

Public integrity efforts to combat corruption of elected and appointed public officials at all levels of government.

Human rights and special prosecutions, investigating and prosecuting human rights violations, international violent crime, immigration violations, and war crimes.

Appellate work, including drafting briefs and certiorari petitions for the Solicitor General for filing in the U.S. Supreme Court; making recommendations to the Solicitor General as to whether further review is warranted on adverse decisions in the district courts and courts of appeals; and preparing briefs and arguing cases in the courts of appeals.

Counterterrorism, including in

conjunction with the National Security Division, investigating and prosecuting terrorist financing and material support cases; establishing and maintaining an essential communication network between the Department of Justice and United States Attorneys' Offices for the rapid transmission of information on terrorism threats and investigative activity; providing and serving as trusted liaisons to the intelligence, defense, and immigration communities as well as to foreign government partners on counterterrorism issues and cases.

For further information, contact the Office of the Assistant Attorney General, Criminal Division, Department of Justice, Tenth Street and Pennsylvania Avenue NW., Washington, DC 20530. Phone, 202-514-2601.

Environment and Natural Resources Division

The Environment and Natural Resources Division is the Nation's environmental lawyer. The Division's responsibilities include enforcing civil and criminal environmental laws that protect America's health and environment. It also defends environmental challenges to Government activities and programs and ensures that environmental laws are implemented in a fair and consistent manner nationwide. It also represents the United States in all matters concerning the protection, use, and development of the Nation's natural resources and public lands, wildlife protection, Indian rights and claims, and the acquisition of Federal property. To carry out this broad mission, the Division litigates in the following areas:

Environmental crimes, prosecuting individuals and corporate entities violating laws designed to protect the environment.

Civil environmental enforcement, on behalf of EPA; claims for damages to natural resources filed on behalf of the Departments of the Interior, Commerce, and Agriculture; claims for contribution against private parties for contamination of public land; and recoupment of money spent to clean up certain oil spills on behalf of the U.S. Coast Guard.

Environmental defense, representing the United States in suits challenging the Government's administration of Federal environmental laws including claims that regulations are too strict or lenient and claims alleging that Federal agencies are not complying with environmental standards.

Wildlife and marine resources protection, including prosecution of smugglers and black-market dealers in protected wildlife.

Use and protection of federally owned public lands and natural resources across a broad spectrum of laws.

Indian resources protection, including establishing water rights, establishing and protecting hunting and fishing rights, collecting damages for trespass on Indian lands, and establishing reservation boundaries and rights to land.

Land acquisition for use by the Federal Government for purposes ranging from establishing public parks to building Federal courthouses.

For further information, contact the Office of the Assistant Attorney General, Environment and Natural Resources Division, Department of Justice, Tenth Street and Pennsylvania Avenue NW., Washington, DC 20530. Phone, 202-514-2701.

National Security Division

The National Security Division (NSD) develops, enforces, and supervises the application of all Federal criminal laws related to the national counterterrorism and counterespionage enforcement programs, except those specifically assigned to other divisions. NSD litigates and coordinates a wide range of prosecutions and criminal investigations involving terrorism and violations of the espionage, export control, and foreign agents registration laws. It administers the Foreign Intelligence Surveillance Act and other legal authorities for national security activities; approves and monitors the use of electronic surveillance; provides legal and policy advice regarding the classification of and access to national security information; performs prepublication review of materials written by present and former DOJ employees; trains the law enforcement and intelligence communities; and advises the Department and legislative and executive branches on all areas of national security law. NSD also serves as the Department's representative on interdepartmental boards, committees, and entities dealing with issues related to national security.

NSD also has some additional counterterrorism, counterespionage, and intelligence oversight responsibilities as follows: to promote and oversee national counterterrorism enforcement programs; develop and implement counterterrorism strategies, legislation, and initiatives; facilitate information sharing between and among the Department and other Federal agencies on terrorism threats; share information with international law enforcement officials to assist with international threat information and litigation initiatives; liaison with the intelligence, defense, and immigration communities and foreign governments on counterterrorism issues and cases; supervise the investigation and prosecution of cases involving national security, foreign relations, the export of military and strategic commodities and technology, espionage, sabotage, neutrality, and atomic energy; coordinate cases involving the application for the Classified Information Procedures Act; enforce the Foreign Agents Registration Act of 1938 and related disclosure laws; supervise the preparation of certifications and applications for orders under the Foreign Intelligence Surveillance Act (FISA); represent the United States before the Foreign Intelligence Surveillance Court; participate in the development, implementation, and review of United States intelligence policies; evaluate existing and proposed national security-related activities to determine their consistency with relevant policies and law; monitor intelligence and counterintelligence activities of other agencies to ensure conformity with Department objectives; prepare reports evaluating domestic and foreign intelligence and counterintelligence activities; and process requests to use FISA-derived information in criminal, civil, and immigration proceedings and to disseminate that information to foreign governments.

For further information, contact the Office of the Assistant Attorney General, National Security Division, Department of Justice, Tenth Street and Pennsylvania Avenue NW., Washington, DC 20530. Phone, 202-514-5600.

Tax Division

Tax Division ensures the uniform and fair enforcement of Federal tax laws in Federal and State courts. The Division conducts enforcement activities to deter specific taxpayers, as well as the taxpaying public at large, from conduct that deprives the Federal Government of its tax-related revenue. It represents the United States and its officers in all civil and criminal litigation arising under the internal revenue laws, other than proceedings in the U.S. Tax Court. Tax Division attorneys frequently join with assistant U.S. attorneys in prosecuting tax cases. Some criminal tax grand jury investigations and prosecutions are handled solely by Tax Division prosecutors, while others are delegated to assistant U.S. attorneys. Division attorneys evaluate requests by the Internal Revenue Service or U.S. attorneys to initiate grand jury investigations or prosecutions of tax crimes.

The Division handles a wide array of civil tax litigation, including the following: suits to enjoin the promotion of abusive tax shelters and to enjoin activities relating to aiding and abetting the understatement of tax liabilities of others; suits to enforce Internal Revenue Service administrative summonses that seek information essential to determine and collect taxpayers' liabilities, including summonses for records of corporate tax shelters and offshore transactions; suits brought by the United States to set aside fraudulent conveyances and to collect assets held by nominees and egos; tax refund suits challenging the Internal Revenue Service's determination of taxpayers' Federal income, employment, excise, and estate liabilities; bankruptcy litigation raising issues of the validity, dischargeability, and priority of Federal tax claims, and the feasibility of reorganization plans; suits brought by taxpayers challenging determinations made in the collection due process proceedings before the Internal Revenue Service's Office of Appeals; and suits against the United States for damages for the unauthorized disclosure of tax return information or for damages claimed because of alleged injuries caused by Internal Revenue Service employees in the performance of their official duties.

The Division also collects judgments in tax cases. To this end, the Division directs collection efforts and coordinates with, monitors the efforts of, and provides assistance to the various U.S. attorneys' offices in collecting outstanding judgments in tax cases.The Division also works with the Internal Revenue Service, U.S. attorneys, and other Government agencies on policy and legislative proposals to enhance tax administration and handling tax cases assigned to those offices.

For further information, contact the Office of the Assistant Attorney General, Tax Division, Department of Justice, Tenth Street and Pennsylvania Avenue NW., Washington, DC 20530. Phone, 202-514-2901.

Sources of Information

Americans With Disabilities Act

The Civil Rights Division maintains an Americans with disabilities hotline. Phone, 800-514-0301. TDD, 800-514-0383.

Business Opportunities / Grants

For information on business opportunities, grants, and small and disadvantaged business utilization, visit the "Business and Grants" Web page.

Drugs / Crime

The Bureau of Justice Statistics' Web page includes criminal justice statistics on drugs and crime.

Employment

For general information on career opportunities, visit the "Careers" Web page.

The "Legal Careers" Web page provides information that is of interest to experienced and entry-level attorneys and law students.

Freedom of Information Act (FOIA)

The Department manages the Web site FOIA.gov to make information on the FOIA accessible, interactive, and understandable.

Instructions for properly submitting a FOIA request to the Department are available online.

History

Historical information on the Attorneys General of the United States, the Department's motto and seal, and the art and architecture of the Robert F. Kennedy Department of Justice Building is available online.

Housing Discrimination

Contact the Civil Rights Division's Housing and Civil Enforcement Section. Phone, 800-896-7743.

Immigration-Related Employment Matters

The Civil Rights Division maintains a worker hotline. Phone, 800-255-7688. TDD, 800-237-2515. It also offers information for employers. Phone, 800-255-8155. TDD, 800-362-2735.

Publications

Each year, the Department publishes the U.S. Attorney General's annual report and posts it online.

Textbooks on citizenship—teacher manuals and student textbooks at various reading levels—are distributed free to public schools for citizenship applicants. Others may purchase them from the Superintendent of Documents, Government Publishing Office, Washington, DC 20402. Public schools or organizations under the supervision of public schools that are entitled to free textbooks should make their requests to the appropriate Immigration and Naturalization Service regional office. Phone, 202-514-3946.

The "Freedom of Information Act (FOIA) Guide" is updated on a rolling basis; the "DOJ FOIA Litigation and Compliance Report" is prepared annually; and both are available on the Department's Web site. The "Privacy Act Overview" is prepared biannually and may be accessed on the Department's Web site or acquired from the

Superintendent of Documents, Government Publishing Office, Washington, DC 20530.

"Guidelines for Effective Human Relations Commissions," "Annual Report of the Community Relations Service," "Community Relations Service Brochure," "CRS Hotline Brochure," "Police Use of Deadly Force: A Conciliation Handbook for Citizens and Police," "Principles of Good Policing: Avoiding Violence Between Police and Citizens," "Resolving Racial Conflict: A Guide for Municipalities," and "Viewpoints and Guidelines on Court-Appointed Citizens Monitoring Commissions in School Desegregation" are available from the Public Information Office, Community Relations Service, Department of Justice, Washington, DC 20530.

Reading Rooms

Reading rooms are located in Washington, DC, at the following locations:

Department of Justice, Room 5400, Tenth Street and Constitution Avenue NW., Washington, DC 20530. Phone, 202-514-3775.

Board of Immigration Appeals, Suite 2400, 5107 Leesburg Pike, Falls Church, VA 22041. Phone, 703-305-0168.

National Institute of Justice, 9th Floor, 633 Indiana Avenue NW., Washington, DC 20531. Phone, 202-307-5883.

http://www.justice.gov/contact-us

For further information, contact the Office of Public Affairs, Department of Justice, Tenth Street and Constitution Avenue NW., Washington, DC 20530. Phone, 202-514-2007. TDD, 202-786-5731.

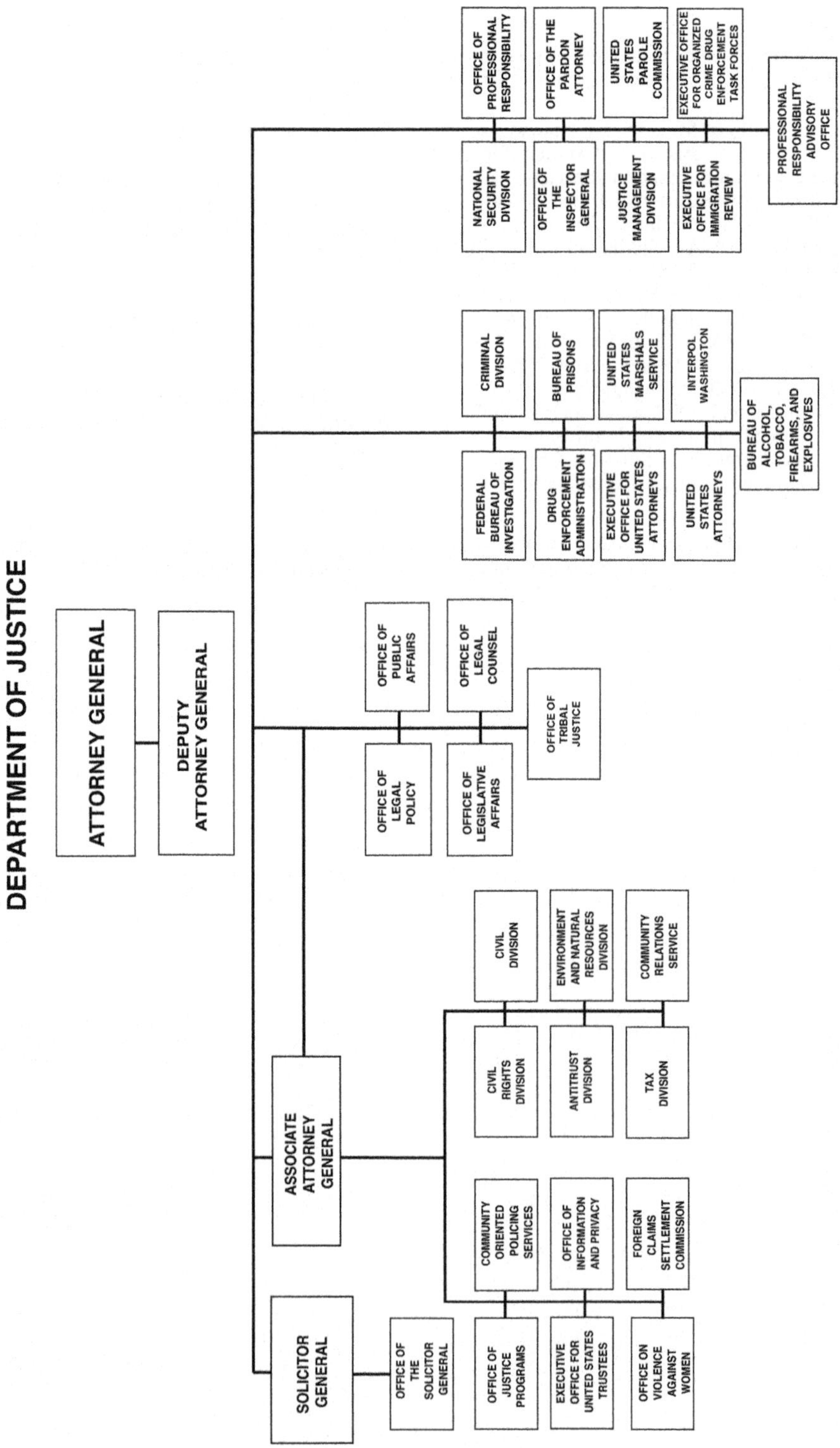
DEPARTMENT OF JUSTICE
ATTORNEY GENERAL
DEPUTY ATTORNEY GENERAL
ASSOCIATE ATTORNEY GENERAL
SOLICITOR GENERAL
OFFICE OF THE SOLICITOR GENERAL
OFFICE OF LEGAL POLICY
OFFICE OF PUBLIC AFFAIRS
OFFICE OF LEGISLATIVE AFFAIRS
OFFICE OF LEGAL COUNSEL
OFFICE OF TRIBAL JUSTICE
OFFICE OF JUSTICE PROGRAMS
EXECUTIVE OFFICE FOR UNITED STATES TRUSTEES
OFFICE ON VIOLENCE AGAINST WOMEN
COMMUNITY ORIENTED POLICING SERVICES
OFFICE OF INFORMATION AND PRIVACY
FOREIGN CLAIMS SETTLEMENT COMMISSION
CIVIL RIGHTS DIVISION
ANTITRUST DIVISION
TAX DIVISION
CIVIL DIVISION
ENVIRONMENT AND NATURAL RESOURCES DIVISION
COMMUNITY RELATIONS SERVICE
FEDERAL BUREAU OF INVESTIGATION
CRIMINAL DIVISION
DRUG ENFORCEMENT ADMINISTRATION
BUREAU OF PRISONS
EXECUTIVE OFFICE FOR UNITED STATES ATTORNEYS
UNITED STATES MARSHALS SERVICE
UNITED STATES ATTORNEYS
INTERPOL WASHINGTON
BUREAU OF ALCOHOL, TOBACCO, FIREARMS, AND EXPLOSIVES
NATIONAL SECURITY DIVISION
OFFICE OF PROFESSIONAL RESPONSIBILITY
OFFICE OF THE INSPECTOR GENERAL
OFFICE OF THE PARDON ATTORNEY
JUSTICE MANAGEMENT DIVISION
UNITED STATES PAROLE COMMISSION
EXECUTIVE OFFICE FOR IMMIGRATION REVIEW
EXECUTIVE OFFICE FOR ORGANIZED CRIME DRUG ENFORCEMENT TASK FORCES
PROFESSIONAL RESPONSIBILITY ADVISORY OFFICE

Bureaus

Bureau of Alcohol, Tobacco, Firearms and Explosives

99 New York Avenue NE., Washington, DC 20226, 202-648-8500, *http://www.atf.gov*

DIRECTOR	Thomas E. Brandon, Acting

The Bureau of Alcohol, Tobacco, Firearms and Explosives (ATF) is responsible for enforcing Federal criminal laws and regulating the firearms and explosives industries. ATF, formerly known as the Bureau of Alcohol, Tobacco, and Firearms, was initially established by Department of Treasury Order No. 221, effective July 1, 1972, which transferred the functions, powers, and duties arising under laws relating to alcohol, tobacco, firearms, and explosives from the Internal Revenue Service to ATF. The Homeland Security Act of 2002 (6 U.S.C. 531) transferred certain functions and authorities of ATF to the Department of Justice and established it under its current name. Directly and through partnerships, ATF investigates and deters violent crime involving arson, firearms and explosives, and trafficking of alcohol and tobacco products. The Bureau provides training and support to its Federal, State, local, and international law enforcement partners and works primarily in 25 field divisions across the 50 States, Puerto Rico, the U.S. Virgin Islands, and Guam. It also has foreign offices in Canada, Colombia, France, and Mexico.

Sources of Information

Employment

Information on career opportunities is available online.

Publications

FOIA and regulations libraries and factsheets are accessible online.

For further information, contact the Office of Public Affairs, Bureau of Alcohol, Tobacco, Firearms and Explosives, Department of Justice, 99 New York Avenue NE., Suite 10W.121, Washington, DC 20530. Phone, 202-648-8500.

Bureau of Prisons

320 First Street NW., Washington, DC 20534, 202-307-3198, *http://www.bop.gov*

DIRECTOR	Thomas R. Kane, Acting

The BOP was established in 1930 to provide more progressive and humane care for Federal inmates, to professionalize the prison service, and to ensure consistent and centralized administration of the 11 Federal prisons in operation at that time. Today, the Bureau comprises more than 100 institutions and 6 regional offices. The Bureau has its headquarters, also known as Central Office, in Washington, DC. The Central Office is divided into 10 divisions, including the National Institute of Corrections.

The Correctional Programs Division (CPD) is responsible for inmate classification and programming, including psychology and religious services, substance abuse treatment, case management, and programs for special needs offenders. CPD provides policy direction and daily operational oversight of institution security, emergency preparedness, intelligence gathering, inmate discipline, inmate sentence computations, receiving and discharge, and inmate transportation, as well as coordinating international treaty transfers and overseeing the special security needs of inmates placed in the Federal Witness Protection Program. CPD administers contracts and intergovernmental agreements for the confinement of offenders in community-based programs, community corrections centers, and other facilities, including privately managed facilities. CPD staff is also involved in the Bureau's privatization efforts.

The Industries, Education, and Vocational Training Division oversees Federal Prison Industries, or UNICOR, which is a wholly owned Government corporation that provides employment and training opportunities for inmates confined in Federal correctional facilities. Additionally, it is responsible for oversight of educational, occupational, and vocational training and leisure-time programs, as well as those related to inmate release preparation.

The National Institute of Corrections (NIC) provides technical assistance, training, and information to State and local corrections agencies throughout the country, as well as the Bureau. It also provides research assistance and documents through the NIC Information Center.

Sources of Information

Business Opportunities

Information is available on the "Let's Do Business" Web page.

Employment

Job openings are posted online. For additional career-related information, contact any regional or field office or the Central Office, 320 First Street NW., Washington, DC 20534. Phone, 202-307-3082.

Reading Room

The reading room is located at the Bureau of Prisons, 320 First Street NW., Washington, DC 20534. Phone, 202-307-3029.

For further information, contact the Public Information Office, Bureau of Prisons, 320 First Street NW., Washington, DC 20534. Phone, 202-514-6551.

Drug Enforcement Administration

8701 Morrissette Drive, Springfield, VA 22152, 202-307-1000, *http://www.dea.gov/index.shtml*

ADMINISTRATOR — Charles Rosenberg, Acting

The Drug Enforcement Administration (DEA) is the lead Federal agency in enforcing narcotics and controlled substances laws and regulations. The DEA also enforces the Federal money laundering and bulk currency smuggling statutes when the funds involved in the transactions or smuggling are derived from the sale of narcotics. It was created in July 1973 by Reorganization Plan No. 2 of 1973 (5 U.S.C. app.).

The DEA enforces the provisions of the controlled substances and chemical diversion and trafficking laws and regulations of the United States, operating on a worldwide basis. It presents cases to the criminal and civil justice systems of the United States—or any other competent jurisdiction—on those significant organizations and their members involved in cultivation, production, smuggling, distribution, laundering of proceeds, or diversion of controlled substances appearing in or destined for illegal traffic in the United States. The DEA disrupts and dismantles these organizations by arresting their members, confiscating their drugs, and seizing their assets; and it creates, manages, and supports enforcement-related programs—domestically and internationally—to reduce the availability of and demand for illicit controlled substances.

The DEA's responsibilities include: investigation of major narcotic, chemical, drug-money laundering, and bulk currency smuggling violators who operate at interstate and international levels; seizure and forfeiture of assets derived from, traceable to, or intended to be used for illicit drug trafficking; seizure and forfeiture of assets derived from or traceable to drug-money laundering or the smuggling of bulk currency derived from illegal drugs; enforcement of regulations governing the legal manufacture, distribution, and dispensing of controlled substances; management of an intelligence program that supports drug investigations, initiatives, and operations worldwide; coordination with Federal, State, and local law enforcement authorities and cooperation with counterpart agencies abroad; assistance to State and local law enforcement agencies in addressing their most significant drug and drug-related violence problems; leadership and influence over international counterdrug and chemical policy and support for institution building in host nations; training, scientific research, and information exchange in support of drug traffic prevention and control; and education and assistance to the public community on the prevention, treatment, and dangers of drugs.

The DEA maintains liaison with the United Nations, INTERPOL, and other organizations on matters relating to international narcotics control programs. It has 222 offices in 21 divisions throughout the United States and 86 foreign offices located in 67 countries.

Sources of Information

Controlled Substances Act Registration

For information on registration under the Controlled Substances Act, contact the Office of Diversion Control, 8701 Morrissette Drive, Springfield, VA 22152. Phone: 800-882-9539.

Employment

For career information, contact the nearest DEA field division recruitment office. To learn about searching for job vacancies online and applying, visit the "How To Apply" Web page.

Publications

A limited selection of pamphlets and brochures is available. The most frequently requested publication is "Drugs of Abuse," an identification manual intended for professional use. Single copies are free.

For further information, contact the Public Affairs Section, Drug Enforcement Administration, 8701 Morrissette Drive Springfield, VA 22152. Phone, 202-307-7977.

Federal Bureau of Investigation

935 Pennsylvania Avenue NW., Washington, DC 20535, 202-324-3000, *http://www.fbi.gov*

DIRECTOR	James B. Comey

The Federal Bureau of Investigation (FBI) is the Department of Justice's principal investigative arm. It is primarily charged with gathering and reporting facts, locating witnesses, and compiling evidence in cases involving Federal jurisdiction. It also provides law enforcement leadership and assistance to State and international law enforcement agencies.

The FBI was established in 1908 by the Attorney General, who directed that Department of Justice investigations be handled by its own staff. The Bureau is charged with investigating all violations of Federal law except those that have been assigned by legislative enactment or otherwise to another Federal agency. Its jurisdiction includes a wide range of responsibilities in the national security, criminal, and civil fields. Priority has been assigned to areas such as counterterrorism, counterintelligence, cybercrimes, internationally and nationally organized crime and drug-related activities, and financial crimes.

The FBI also offers cooperative services to local, State, and international law enforcement agencies. These services include fingerprint identification, laboratory examination, police training, the Law

Enforcement Online communication and information service for use by the law enforcement community, the National Crime Information Center, and the National Center for the Analysis of Violent Crime.

Sources of Information

Employment

The FBI relies on professionals with diverse expertise and skills to analyze data for the intelligence community, safeguard national security, and support the structure of the Bureau. Information on career opportunities, including student internships, is available online.

Publications

The "FBI Law Enforcement Bulletin," reports, and other publications are available online.

For further information, contact the Office of Public Affairs, Federal Bureau of Investigation, J. Edgar Hoover FBI Building, 935 Pennsylvania Avenue NW., Washington, DC 20535. Phone, 202-317-2727.

International Criminal Police Organization (INTERPOL)–Washington

Department of Justice, Washington, DC 20530, 202-616-9000, 202-616-8400, *http://www.justice.gov/interpol-washington*

DIRECTOR	Geoffrey S. Shank

INTERPOL–Washington is a separate component under the supervision of the Deputy Attorney General and comanaged with the Department of Homeland Security. It provides an essential communications link between the U.S. police community and their counterparts in the foreign member countries.

INTERPOL is an association of 190 countries that promotes mutual assistance among law enforcement authorities to prevent and suppress international crime. With no police force of its own, INTERPOL has no powers of arrest or search and seizure and, therefore, relies on the law enforcement authorities of its member countries. Each member country is required to have a national central bureau, such as INTERPOL–Washington, to act as the primary point of contact for police affairs. INTERPOL serves as a channel of communication for its member countries to cooperate in the investigation and prosecution of crime; provides a forum for discussions, working group meetings, and symposia to help police focus on specific areas of criminal activity affecting their countries; and issues information and maintains databases—supplied and used by member countries—on crime, fugitives, humanitarian concerns, missing persons, and stolen passports and vehicles.

INTERPOL–Washington has permanent staff and detailed special agents from numerous Federal law enforcement agencies. It is organized into seven divisions: the Alien and Fugitive, Counterterrorism, Drug, Economic Crimes, Human Trafficking and Child Protection, State and Local Police Liaison, and Violent Crimes Divisions.

Sources of Information

Employment

Information on career opportunities is available online.

For further information, contact the INTERPOL–Washington, Department of Justice, Washington, DC 20530. Phone, 202-616-9000.

Office of Justice Programs

810 Seventh Street NW., Washington, DC 20531, 202-307-0703, *http://www.ojp.gov* | Email: *askojp@ojp.usdoj.gov*

ASSISTANT ATTORNEY GENERAL	Karol V. Mason

The Office of Justice Programs (OJP) was established by the Justice Assistance Act of 1984 (42 U.S.C. 3711) and reauthorized in 1994 and 2005 to provide Federal leadership, coordination, and assistance needed to make the Nation's justice system more efficient and effective in preventing and controlling crime. OJP is responsible for collecting statistical data and conducting analyses; identifying emerging criminal justice issues; developing and testing promising approaches to address these issues; evaluating program results; and disseminating these findings and other information to State and local governments.

The OJP is comprised of the following bureaus and offices: the Bureau of Justice Assistance provides funding, training, and technical assistance to State and local governments to combat violent and drug-related crime and help improve the criminal justice system; the Bureau of Justice Statistics is responsible for collecting and analyzing data on crime, criminal offenders, crime victims, and the operations of justice systems at all levels of government; the National Institute of Justice sponsors research and development programs, conducts demonstrations of innovative approaches to improve criminal justice, and develops new criminal justice technologies; the Office of Juvenile Justice and Delinquency Prevention provides grants and contracts to States to help them improve their juvenile justice systems and sponsors innovative research, demonstration, evaluation, statistics, replication, technical assistance, and training programs to increase the Nation's understanding of and improve its response to juvenile violence and delinquency; the Office for Victims of Crime administers victim compensation and assistance grant programs and provides funding, training, and technical assistance to victim service organizations, criminal justice agencies, and other professionals to improve the Nation's response to crime victims; and the Office of Sex Offender Sentencing, Monitoring, Apprehending, Registering, and Tracking (SMART) maintains the standards of the Sex Offender Registration and Notification Act as defined by the Adam Walsh Act. The SMART Office also provides technical assistance and supports innovative and best practices in the field of sex offender management.

Sources of Information

Employment

For employment information, contact the Human Resources Division, 810 Seventh Street NW., Washington, DC 20531. Phone, 202-307-0730.

For further information, contact the Department of Justice Response Center. Phone, 800-421-6770.

United States Marshals Service

Department of Justice, Washington, DC 20530, 202-307-9000, *http://www.usmarshals.gov*

DIRECTOR	(vacancy)
Deputy Director	David Harlow

The United States Marshals Service is the Nation's oldest Federal law enforcement agency, having served as a vital link between the executive and judicial branches of the Government since 1789. The Marshals Service performs tasks that are essential to the operation of virtually every aspect of the Federal justice system.

The Marshals Service has these responsibilities: providing support and protection for the Federal courts, including security for 800 judicial facilities and nearly 2,000 judges and magistrates, as well as countless other trial participants such as jurors and attorneys; apprehending the majority of Federal fugitives; operating the Federal Witness Security Program and ensuring the safety of endangered Government witnesses; maintaining custody of and transporting thousands of Federal prisoners annually; executing court orders and arrest warrants; managing and selling seized property forfeited to the Government by drug traffickers and other criminals and assisting the Justice Department's asset forfeiture program; responding to emergency circumstances, including civil disturbances, terrorist incidents, and other crisis situations through its Special Operations Group; restoring order in riot and mob-violence situations; providing housing, transportation, and medical care of federal detainees; and operating the U.S. Marshals Service Training Academy.

Sources of Information

Business Opportunities

The Marshals Service posts online products and services that it purchases.

Employment

The Marshals Service hires administrative staff, aviation and detention enforcement officers, Deputy U.S. Marshals, and other types of professionals. Information on Deputy U.S. Marshal hiring programs is available online.

For further information, contact the Office of Public Affairs, U.S. Marshals Service, Department of Justice, Washington, DC 20530. Phone, 202-307-9065.

Offices / Boards

Executive Office for Immigration Review

Falls Church, VA 22041, 703-305-0289, *http://www.usdoj.gov/eoir*

DIRECTOR	Juan P. Osuna

The Executive Office for Immigration Review, under a delegation of authority from the Attorney General, is charged with adjudicating matters brought under various immigration statutes to its three administrative tribunals: the Board of Immigration Appeals, the Office of the Chief Immigration Judge, and the Office of the Chief Administrative Hearing Officer.

The Board of Immigration Appeals has nationwide jurisdiction to hear appeals from certain decisions made by immigration judges and by district directors of the Department of Homeland Security (DHS). In addition, the Board is responsible for hearing appeals involving disciplinary actions against attorneys and representatives before DHS and the Board.

Decisions of the Board are binding on all DHS officers and immigration judges unless modified or overruled by the Attorney General or a Federal court. All Board decisions are subject to judicial review in Federal court. The majority of appeals reaching the Board involve orders of removal and applications for relief from removal. Other cases before the Board include the removal of aliens applying for admission to the United States, petitions to classify the status of alien relatives for the issuance of preference immigrant visas, fines imposed upon carriers for the violation of the immigration laws, and motions for reopening and reconsideration of decisions previously rendered.

The Office of the Chief Immigration Judge provides overall direction for more than 200 immigration judges located in 53 immigration courts throughout the Nation.

Immigration judges are responsible for conducting formal administrative proceedings and act independently in their decisionmaking capacity. Their decisions are administratively final, unless appealed or certified to the Board.

In removal proceedings, an immigration judge determines whether an individual from a foreign country should be admitted or allowed to stay in the United States or be removed. Judges are located throughout the United States, and each judge has jurisdiction to consider various forms of relief available under the law, including applications for asylum.

The Office of the Chief Administrative Hearing Officer is responsible for the general supervision and management of administrative law judges who preside at hearings that are mandated by provisions of immigration law concerning allegations of unlawful employment of aliens, unfair immigration-related employment practices, and immigration document fraud.

Sources of Information

Library

A virtual law library that serves as a complement to the Law Library and Immigration Research Center is available online.

Statistics and Publications

Agency decisions and plans, instructions and manuals, meeting notes, and reports and updates are available on the "Statistics and Publications" Web page.

For further information, contact the Office of Legislative and Public Affairs, Executive Office for Immigration Review, Department of Justice, 5107 Leesburg Pike, Suite 1902, Falls Church, VA 22041. Phone, 703-305-0289. Fax, 703-605-0365.

Foreign Claims Settlement Commission of the United States

Suite 6002, 600 E Street NW., Washington, DC 20579, 202-616-6975, 202-616-6993, *http://www.justice.gov/fcsc*

COMMISSIONER	Anuj C. Desai
COMMISSIONER	Sylvia M. Becker

The Foreign Claims Settlement Commission of the United States is a quasi-judicial, independent agency within the Department of Justice, which adjudicates claims of U.S. nationals against foreign governments, either under specific jurisdiction conferred by Congress or the Department of State or pursuant to international claims settlement agreements. The decisions of the Commission are final and are not reviewable under any standard by any court or other authority. Funds for payment of the Commission's awards are derived from congressional appropriations, international claims settlements, or the liquidation of foreign assets in the United States by the Departments of Justice and the Treasury.

The Commission also has authority to receive, determine the validity and amount, and provide for the payment of claims by members of the U.S. Armed Services and civilians held as prisoners of war or interned by a hostile force in Southeast Asia during the Vietnam conflict or by the survivors of such servicemembers and civilians.

The Commission is also responsible for maintaining records and responding to inquiries related to the various claims programs it has conducted against the Governments of Albania, Bulgaria, China, Cuba, Czechoslovakia, Egypt, Ethiopia, the Federal Republic of Germany, the German Democratic Republic, Hungary, Iran, Italy, Panama, Poland, Romania, the Soviet Union, Vietnam, and Yugoslavia, as well as those authorized under the War Claims Act of 1948 and other statutes.

Sources of Information

Employment

General information on career opportunities is available on the Department of Justice's "Careers" Web page. For additional information on attorney positions, contact the Office of the Chief Counsel, 600 E Street NW., Suite 6002, Washington, DC 20579. Phone, 202-616-6975.

Publications

Annual reports, starting with the year 2008, are available on the "Publications" Web page.

Reading Room

The reading room is located at 600 E Street NW., Washington, DC 20579. Phone, 202-616-6975.

For further information, contact the Office of the Chairman, Foreign Claims Settlement Commission of the United States, Department of Justice, Suite 6002, 600 E Street NW., Washington, DC 20579. Phone, 202-616-6975. Fax, 202-616-6993.

Office of Community Oriented Policing Services

935 N. Street NE., Washington, DC 20530, 202-514-2058, *http://www.cops.usdoj.gov*

DIRECTOR	Ronald L. Davis

The Office of Community Oriented Policing Services (COPS) was established to assist law enforcement agencies in enhancing public safety through the implementation of community policing strategies. The Office gives assistance by providing training to enhance law enforcement officers' problem-solving and community interaction skills and helping law enforcement and community members develop initiatives to prevent crime; increasing the number of law enforcement officers directly interacting with communities; and supporting the development of new technologies to shift law enforcement's focus to preventing crime and disorder within communities.

Sources of Information

Employment

To sign up to receive email updates on COPS employment opportunities, visit the "Careers" Web page.

Grants and Funding

COPS grants and funding opportunities support State, local, and tribal law enforcement efforts to advance community policing. Current applicant and grantee information—announcements, fiscal year grant programs, current funding opportunities, and resources for grantees—is available online.

For further information, contact the Office of Community Oriented Policing Services (COPS), Department of Justice, 935 N Street NE., Washington, DC 20530. Phone, 202-514-2058.

Office on Violence Against Women

145 N Street NE., Suite 10W–121, Washington, DC 20530, Phone: 202-307-6026, *http://www.justice.gov/ovw*

PRINCIPAL DEPUTY DIRECTOR	Beatrice Hanson

The Office on Violence Against Women (OVW) was established in 2005 to reduce violence against women through the implementation of the Violence Against Women Act. The Office administers financial and technical assistance to communities that are developing programs, policies, and practices to end domestic and dating violence, sexual assault, and stalking.

Sources of Information

Employment

Information on employment and internship opportunities is available online.

Publications

Portable Document Format (PDF) files of selected publications are available online.

For further information, contact the Office on Violence Against Women, 145 N Street NE., Suite 10W–121, Washington, DC, 20530. Phone, 202-307-6026.

United States Parole Commission

90 K Street NE., Washington, DC 20530. Phone, 202-346-7000., *http://www.usdoj.gov/uspc*

CHAIR	J. Patricia Wilson Smoot, Acting

The U.S. Parole Commission (USPC) makes parole release decisions for eligible Federal and District of Columbia prisoners; authorizes methods of release and conditions under which release occurs; prescribes, modifies, and monitors compliance with the terms and conditions governing offenders' behavior while on parole or mandatory or supervised release; issues warrants for violation of supervision; determines probable cause for the revocation process; revokes parole, mandatory, or supervised release; releases from supervision those offenders who are no longer a risk to public safety; and promulgates the rules, regulations, and guidelines for the exercise of USPC's authority and the implementation of a national parole policy.

USPC has sole jurisdiction over the following: Federal offenders who committed offenses before November 1, 1987; DC Code offenders who committed offenses before August 5, 2000; DC Code offenders sentenced to a term of supervised release; Uniform Code of Military Justice offenders who are in Bureau of Prison's custody; transfer treaty cases; and State probationers and parolees in the Federal Witness Protection Program.

Sources of Information

Freedom of Information Act (FOIA)

The Commission maintains an online FOIA library. Information on Freedom of Information Act requests is available online.

Reading Room

The reading room is located at 90 K Street NE., Washington, DC 20530. Phone, 202-346-7000.

For further information, contact the U.S. Parole Commission, Department of Justice, 90 K Street NE., Washington, DC 20530. Phone, 202-346-7000.

Department of Labor

200 Constitution Avenue NW., Washington, DC 20210, 202-693-6000, *http://www.dol.gov*

SECRETARY OF LABOR	Thomas E. Perez
Deputy Secretary	Christopher P. Lu
Chief Economist	Heidi Shierholz
Chief of Staff	Seema Nanda
Executive Secretariat Director	Elizabeth Way, Acting

AGENCIES	
Administrator, Wage and Hour Division	David Weil
Chief Administrative Law Judge	Stephen R. Henley
Chief Financial Officer	Geoffrey Kenyon, Acting
Commissioner, Bureau of Labor Statistics	Erica L. Groshen
Deputy Undersecretary, Bureau of International Labor Affairs	Carol Pier
Inspector General	Scott S. Dahl
Ombudsman, Energy Employee Occupational Illness Compensation Program	Malcolm Nelson
Solicitor of Labor	M. Patricia Smith
ASSISTANT SECRETARIES	
Employee Benefits Security Administration	Phyllis Borzi
Employment and Training Administration	Portia Y. Wu
Mine Safety and Health Administration	Joseph A. Main
Occupational Safety and Health Administration	David Michaels
Office of Congressional and Intergovernmental Affairs	Adri Jayaratne, Acting
Office of Disability Employment Policy	Jennifer Sheehy, Acting
Office of Public Affairs	Dori Henry
Office of the Assistant Secretary, Administration and Management	T. Michael Kerr
Office of the Assistant Secretary, Policy	(vacancy)
Veterans' Employment and Training Services	Mike Michaud
CHIEF JUDGES / CHAIRS	
Administrative Review Board	Paul M. Igasaki
Benefits Review Board	Betty Jean Hall
Employees' Compensation Appeals Board	Christopher Godfrey
DIRECTORS	
Center for Faith-Based and Neighborhood Partnerships	Teresa W. Gerton
Office of Workers' Compensation Programs	Leonard Howie III
Office of Federal Contract Compliance Programs	Patricia A. Shiu
Office of Labor-Management Standards	Michael Hayes
Office of Public Engagement	(vacancy)
Women's Bureau	Latifa Lyles

The Department of Labor promotes the welfare of job seekers, wage earners, and retirees by improving working conditions, advancing opportunities for profitable employment, protecting retirement and health care benefits, matching workers to employers, strengthening free collective bargaining, and tracking changes in economic indicators on a national scale.

The Department of Labor (DOL) was created by act of March 4, 1913 (29 U.S.C. 551). Congress first created a Bureau of Labor in the Interior Department by act of June 24, 1884. The Bureau of Labor later became independent as a Department of Labor without executive rank by act of June 13, 1888. It returned to bureau status in the Department of Commerce and Labor, which was created by act of February 14, 1903 (15 U.S.C. 1501; 29 U.S.C. 1 note).

The Department administers a variety of Federal labor laws to guarantee workers' rights to fair, safe, and healthy working conditions, including minimum hourly wage and overtime pay, protection against employment discrimination, and unemployment insurance.

Secretary

The Secretary is the principal adviser to the President on the development and execution of policies and the administration and enforcement of laws relating to wage earners, their working conditions, and their employment opportunities.

Administrative Law

Administrative law judges from the Office of Administrative Law Judges preside over formal adversarial hearings involving labor-related matters: the Longshore and Harbor Workers' Compensation, the Defense Base, the Black Lung Benefits, the McNamara O'Hara Service Contract, and the Davis Bacon Acts; environmental, transportation, and securities whistleblower protection laws; permanent and temporary immigration; child labor law violations; employment discrimination; job training; seasonal and migrant workers; and Federal construction and service contracts. Headquartered in Washington, DC, the Office comprises seven district offices. Its judges are nonpolitical appointees: They are appointed under and guaranteed decisional independence by the Administrative Procedure Act. The Administrative Review Board or Benefits Review Board typically reviews appeals of the decisions made by the Office's judges. Depending upon the statute at issue, appeals then go to Federal district or appellate courts and, ultimately, may go to the U.S. Supreme Court.

For further information, call 202-693-7300.

Administration and Management

The Office of the Assistant Secretary for Administration and Management is responsible for the development and promulgation of policies, standards, procedures, systems, and materials related to the resource and administrative management of the Department and for the execution of such policies and directives at Headquarters and in the field.

For more information, call 202-693-4040.

Audits / Investigations

The Office of Inspector General conducts audits to review the economy, effectiveness, efficiency, and integrity of all DOL programs and operations, including those performed by its contractors and grantees. The Inspector General works to answer the following types of questions: Do Department programs and operations comply with the applicable laws and regulations; are departmental resources being utilized efficiently and economically; and are DOL programs achieving their intended results?

The Office also conducts administrative, civil, and criminal investigations relating to violations of Federal laws, regulations, or rules—including violations committed by DOL contractors and grantees—as well as investigations of allegations of misconduct on the part of DOL employees. In addition, by conducting criminal investigations, the Office weakens the influence of labor racketeering and organized crime in the Nation's labor unions. Labor racketeering investigations are conducted in three areas: employee benefit plans, internal union affairs, and labor-management relations.

For further information, call 202-693-5100.

Communications / Public Affairs

The Office of Public Affairs (OPA) directs and coordinates all public and employee communications activities. The Assistant Secretary of the Office acts as the chief adviser to the Secretary of Labor and his or her Deputy Secretary and to the agency heads and departmental staff for developing and implementing strategies that engage and connect with the public and educate it about the work and mission of the Department.

The Assistant Secretary also acts as the Secretary's chief adviser on crisis communications. The OPA serves as the first point of contact for news media inquiries, as the clearance and dissemination point for DOL public-facing materials, and it develops and maintains the Department's Web-based, audiovisual, and contact center communications. The OPA also administers "lock ups" when sensitive economic data are released to the press under an embargo.

For further information, call 202-693-4676.

Disability Employment Policy

The Office of Disability Employment Policy (ODEP) develops and seeks to influence policies and practices to increase employment opportunities for people with disabilities. ODEP promotes collaboration, policy and resource alignment, and the adoption and implementation of effective practices by Federal agencies, States, local, and nongovernmental entities, including businesses, to improve employment opportunities for the disabled.

For further information, call 202-693-7880. TTY, 202-693-7881.

Energy Employees Occupational Illness Compensation

The Office of the Ombudsman for the Energy Employees Occupational Illness Compensation Program was established in 2004 under Part E of the Energy Employees Occupational Illness Compensation Program Act (EEOICPA), as amended (42 U.S.C. 7385s-15). The EEOICPA is a system of Federal payments to compensate certain nuclear workers for occupational illnesses caused by exposure to toxic substances. This small and independent Office is headed by the Ombudsman, whom the Secretary of Labor appoints. It provides information to claimants on the benefits available under Parts B and E of the EEOICPA and issues annual reports to Congress detailing the complaints, grievances, and requests for assistance that the Office receives.

For further information, call 202-693-5890.

Federal Contract Compliance

The Office of Federal Contract Compliance Programs administers and enforces three equal employment opportunity laws: Executive Order 11246, Section 503 of the Rehabilitation Act of 1973, and the Vietnam Era Veterans' Readjustment Assistance Act of 1974. As amended, these laws prohibit Federal contractors and subcontractors from discriminating based on race, color, religion, sex, sexual orientation, gender identity, national origin, disability, or status as a protected veteran. Executive Order 11246 prohibits Federal contractors and subcontractors, with limited exceptions, from taking adverse employment actions against applicants and employees for asking about, discussing, or sharing information on their pay or the pay of their coworkers. These laws also require Federal contractors and subcontractors to take affirmative action to ensure equal employment opportunity.

For further information, call 800-397-6251.

Labor-Management Standards

The Office of Labor-Management Standards (OLMS) conducts criminal and civil investigations to safeguard the financial integrity of unions and to ensure union democracy. The Office conducts investigative audits of labor unions to uncover and remedy criminal and civil violations of the Labor-Management Reporting and Disclosure Act and related statutes. The Office also publishes the text of the Labor-Management Reporting and Disclosure Act and pamphlets that explain the reporting, election, bonding, and trusteeship provisions of the act. The pamphlets and reporting forms used by persons covered by the act are free and available, in limited quantities, online and from OLMS field offices and its national office in Washington, DC.

For further information, call 202-693-0123.

Legal Services

The Office of the Solicitor of Labor (SOL) provides comprehensive legal services to help the Department achieve its mission. More specifically, the Solicitor serves dual roles in the Department. The Solicitor is the Department's chief enforcement officer, pursuing affirmative litigation on behalf of the Secretary before administrative law judges, review boards and commissions, and in the Federal district courts and courts of appeals. The Solicitor is also the Department's general counsel, assisting in the development of regulations, standards, and legislative proposals; providing legal opinions and advice on all of the Department's activities; advising the Solicitor General on Supreme Court litigation; and coordinating with the Department of Justice, as appropriate, to defend the Department in litigation.

For further information, call 202-693-5260.

Policy and Rulemaking

The Office of the Assistant Secretary for Policy advises and assists the Secretary, Deputy Secretary, and Department on policy development, policy evaluation, regulation, and legislation that improves the lives of workers, retirees, and their families. The Office also serves as the DOL's regulatory policy officer to ensure that the Department complies with the regulatory and guidance development requirements of Executive Order 12866, as amended, and any other related Office of Management and Budget circular or bulletin. The Office leads special initiatives and manages departmentwide and interdepartmental activities. In its capacity as the DOL's policy innovation arm, it invests in research and analysis of current and emerging labor issues. At the moment, those issues include the growing wage gap for working families, ensuring protections and opportunity for all workers, promoting work and family balance, and labor standards for the rapidly changing 21st-century economy.

For further information, call 202-693-5959.

Workers' Compensation

The Office of Workers' Compensation Programs (OWCP) protects workers who are injured or become ill on the job by making decisions on claims, paying benefits, and helping workers return to their jobs. OWCP administers eight major disability compensation statutes: the Federal Employees' Compensation Act; the Longshore and Harbor Workers' Compensation Act; the Defense Base Act (DBA); the Nonappropriated Fund Instrumentalities Act; the Outer Continental Shelf Lands Act; the War Hazards Compensation Act; the Black Lung Benefits Act; and the Energy Employees Occupational Illness Compensation Act. OWCP serves specific employee groups that are covered under the relevant statutes and regulations by mitigating the financial burden resulting from workplace injury or illness and promoting return to work when appropriate. Dependents or survivors may also be eligible for benefits.

For further information, call 202-343-5580.

Boards

Administrative Review

The Administrative Review Board (ARB) consists of five members appointed by the Secretary. It issues final agency decisions for appeals cases under a wide range of worker protection laws, including the McNamara O'Hara Service Contract Act and the Davis Bacon Act. The appeals cases primarily address environmental, transportation, and securities whistleblower protection; H-1B immigration provisions; child labor law violations; employment discrimination; job training; seasonal and migrant workers; and Federal construction and service contracts. The Board's cases generally arise upon appeal from decisions of Department of Labor Administrative Law Judges or the Administrator of the Department's Wage and Hour Division. Depending upon the statute at issue, the parties may appeal the Board's decisions to Federal district or appellate courts and, ultimately, to the U.S. Supreme Court.

For further information, call 202-693-6234.

Benefits Review

The Benefits Review Board (BRB) consists of five members appointed by the

Secretary. In 1972, Congress created the Board to review and issue decisions on appeals of workers' compensation cases arising under the Longshore and Harbor Workers' Compensation Act, and its extensions, and the Black Lung Benefits amendments to the Federal Coal Mine Safety Act of 1969. Board decisions may be appealed to the U.S. Courts of Appeals and to the U.S. Supreme Court.

For further information, call 202-693-6234.

Employees' Compensation Appeals

The Employees' Compensation Appeals Board (ECAB) is a three-member quasi-judicial body appointed by the Secretary and delegated exclusive jurisdiction by Congress to hear and make final decisions on appeals filed by Federal workers arising under the Federal Employees' Compensation Act. The Board was created by Reorganization Plan No. 2 of 1946 (60 Stat. 1095). The Board's decisions are not reviewable and are binding upon the Office of Workers' Compensation Programs (OWCP).

For further information, call 202-693-6234.

Sources of Information

Agencies / Programs

The DOL carries out its mission through a number of offices and agencies, which are organized into major program areas. An Assistant Secretary, Director, or other official oversees each of these offices and agencies.

A–Z Index

The DOL Web sites features an alphabetical index to help visitors search for information or browse topics of interest.

Business Opportunities

The Office of Procurement Services is the primary procurement office for the DOL national office. It carries out most contracting, grants, and related activities. The Office procures a variety of goods and services on a recurring basis: auditors, expert witnesses, moving services, printing and graphics, support services, technical studies, and video productions. It also acts as the central procurement center for the Department's information technology needs. Phone, 202-693-4570.

The Office of Small and Disadvantaged Business Utilization administers the DOL's small business program in accordance with the Small Business Act. It seeks to ensure a fair share of procurement opportunities for small businesses, as well as for Historically Underutilized Business Zone (HUBZone) certified, service-disabled veteran-owned, small disadvantaged, and woman-owned small businesses. Phone, 202-603-7299.

Employment

Detailed information on job opportunities with the DOL—including the addresses and telephone numbers of personnel offices in the regions and in Washington, DC—is available online.

Find It!

The "Find It" Web page allows Internet visitors to look for information by audience or by topic. It also contains the following internal links: A–Z Index, DOL agencies, DOL forms, DOL services by location, and top 20 requested items.

Freedom of Information Act (FOIA)

The FOIA provides that anyone can request access to Federal agency records or information. The DOL must disclose records that are properly requested in writing by any person. Pursuant, however, to one or more of nine exemptions and three exclusions contained in the law, a Federal agency may withhold information. The FOIA applies only to Federal agencies and does not create a right of access to records held by Congress, the courts, State or local government agencies, and private entities.

Frequently Asked Questions (FAQs)

Answers to many FAQs are posted on the DOL's Web site.

History

A historical timeline is available on the DOL's Web site.

The history of the DOL in narrative form is available on its Web site.

Library

The Wirtz Labor Library maintains an online card catalog of holdings added to the library after January of 1975. The online catalog also includes collections of historical significance: for example, the Folio and James Taylor Collections. The library is open to the public from 8:15 a.m. to 4:45 p.m. on weekdays, excluding Federal holidays. If the purpose of a visit is to access research material, contact the library in advance: Wirtz Labor Library, 200 Constitution Avenue NW., Frances Perkins Building, Room N–2445, Washington, DC 20210. Phone, 202-693-6600.

Minimum Wage

The DOL Web site features a list of DOL Web pages that deal with the topic of minimum wage. The Wage and Hour Division administers and enforces the federal minimum wage law.

Newsroom

The newsroom features the DOL newsletter, news releases, and press resources, including national media contact information. Phone, 202-693-4676.

Office of Inspector General (OIG)

To file a complaint of abuse, fraud, or waste, use the online complaint form, call the OIG Hotline, or write to the Office of Inspector General, Department of Labor, 200 Constitution Avenue NW., Room S–5506, Washington, DC 20210. Phone, 202-693-6999 or 800-347-3756. Fax, 202-693-7020.

The OIG maintains a glossary of terms related to its activities and mission.

Open Government

The DOL has a comprehensive Open Government plan to support the making of a more accountable, responsive, and transparent Government.

Plain Language

The DOL is committed to producing documents whose content complies with Federal plain language guidelines. It trains its employees and has adopted an oversight process to ensure the use of plain language in any document that is necessary for obtaining Federal Government benefits or services or filing taxes, provides information on Federal Government benefits or services, or explains to the public how to comply with a requirement that the Federal Government administers or enforces.

Popular Topics

The DOL Web site features a topics page with links for convenient access to popular material.

Publications

The Office of Public Affairs distributes fact sheets that describe the activities of the major agencies within the Department.

Public Disclosure

The Office of Labor-Management Standards maintains a public disclosure room: 200 Constitution Avenue NW., Room N–5609, Washington, DC 20210. It also has an online disclosure room where collective bargaining agreements; union bylaws, constitutions, and reports; and other types of reports are accessible. Online visitors can search union annual financial reports starting with the year 2000; view and print reports filed by unions, union officers and employees, employers, and labor relations consultants starting with the year 2000; and order copies of reports for the years prior to 2000.

Spanish

The DOL supports the Hispanic workforce. An online list highlights some of the Department's Spanish resources. This list is intended for English-speakers who are looking for information in Spanish to share with the Hispanic community.

For further information concerning the Department of Labor, contact the Office of

Public Affairs, Department of Labor, Room S–1032, 200 Constitution Avenue NW., Washington, DC 20210. Phone, 202-693-4650.

Bureau of International Labor Affairs

200 Constitution Avenue NW., Washington, DC 20210, 202-693-4770, *http://www.dol.gov/ilab*

DEPUTY UNDER SECRETARY	Carol Pier
Associate Deputy Undersecretary	Eric Biel
Associate Deputy Undersecretary	Mark Mittelhauser

The Bureau of International Labor Affairs ensures that workers around the world are treated fairly and able to share in the benefits of the global economy. The Bureau uses all available international channels to improve working conditions, raise living standards, protect workers' rights, and address exploitation of children and other vulnerable populations in the workplace.

Sources of Information

Contracts / Grants

The Bureau collaborates with international organizations, nongovernmental organizations, research institutions, universities, and others to advance workers' rights and livelihoods. Project evaluations, research, and technical assistance projects are funded through grants, contracts, and cooperative agreements.

Laws / Regulations

The Bureau's Web site features a page of laws and regulations that are relevant to its work.

Newsroom

The Bureau posts news releases on its Web site.

Reports

The Bureau publishes three reports on international child labor and forced labor: The Department of Labor's "Findings on the Worst Forms of Child Labor"; the "List of Goods Produced by Child Labor or Forced Labor"; and the "List of Products Produced by Forced or Indentured Child Labor." Each report has a distinct mandate, focus, and set of implications—but taken collectively—they document the current situation of forced labor and child labor worldwide.

Research

The Bureau sponsors qualitative studies, quantitative surveys, impact evaluations, and other research products to study worker livelihoods, the incidences and root causes of child labor and worker rights violations, and the effectiveness of particular policies and projects.

Toolkit

The Bureau's Web sites features a toolkit to help responsible entrepreneurs reduce the chance that their products—and the raw materials from which they are made—are harvested, manufactured, or mined by children who should be in school or by workers who are locked in sweatshops or forced to work through threats or false promises.

For further information, contact the Bureau of International Affairs, Department of Labor, Room C–2235, Washington, DC 20201. Phone, 202-693-4770.

Bureau of Labor Statistics

2 Massachusetts Avenue NE., Washington, DC 20212, 202-691-7800, 800-877-8339

(TDD), *http://www.bls.gov*

COMMISSIONER	Erica L. Groshen
Deputy Commissioner	William Wiatrowski

The Bureau of Labor Statistics (BLS) was established, in the Department of the Interior, as the Bureau of Labor by the act of June 27, 1884 (23 Stat. 60). It was renamed the Bureau of Labor Statistics by the act of March 4, 1913 (37 Stat. 737). The BLS measures labor market activity, working conditions, and price changes in the economy. It also collects, analyzes, and disseminates essential economic information to support public and private decisionmaking.

The Bureau strives to have its data satisfy a number of criteria, including: relevance to current social and economic issues, timeliness in reflecting today's rapidly changing economic conditions, accuracy and consistently high statistical quality, and impartiality in both subject matter and presentation.

Basic data are issued in monthly, quarterly, and annual news releases; bulletins, reports, and special publications; and periodicals. Regional offices issue additional reports and releases, usually presenting locality or regional detail.

Sources of Information

Data Tools

Calculators, databases, and tables are available online.

Employment

Information on career opportunities is available online.

Frequently Asked Questions (FAQs)

The BLS posts answers to FAQs on its Web site.

Glossary

The BLS maintains a glossary on its Web site.

Publications

The BLS publishes bulletins and reports and economic news releases. Its major publications include "Beyond the Numbers," "Career Outlook," "Monthly Labor Review," "Occupational Outlook Handbook," "The Economics Daily", and "Spotlight on Statistics." These publications are available online. For more information, contact the Washington Information Office or one of the Bureau's regional offices.

Regional Information

Economic statistics and data according to geographic areas are available on the "Regional Information Offices" Web page.

Site Index

The BLS Web site features an A–Z index.

Unemployment / Employment

A local area unemployment statistics map is available on the BLS Web site.

An overview of statistics on unemployment is available on the BLS Web site.

An overview of statistics on employment is available on the BLS Web site.

Updates

The BLS Web site features an online subscription form to sign up for electronic updates.

For further information, contact the Bureau of Labor Statistics, Department of Labor, Room 4040, 2 Massachusetts Avenue NE., Washington, DC 20212. Phone, 202-691-7800.

Employee Benefits Security Administration

Department of Labor, Washington, DC 20210, 866-444-3272, *http://www.dol.gov/ebsa*

ASSISTANT SECRETARY	Phyllis C. Borzi
Deputy Assistant Secretary for Policy	Judith Mares
Deputy Assistant Secretary for Program Operations	Timothy Hauser

The Employee Benefits Security Administration (EBSA) promotes and protects the retirement, health, and other benefits of the over 141 million participants and beneficiaries in over 5 million private sector employee benefit plans. EBSA develops regulations; assists and educates workers, plan sponsors, fiduciaries, and service providers; and enforces the law. The Employee Retirement Income Security Act is enforced through 13 field offices nationwide and a national office in Washington, DC.

Sources of Information

Ask EBSA

EBSA's workers and families assistance Web page provides accessible information on programs and services, answers to questions, and assistance in cases where a health or retirement benefit has been denied inappropriately.

Key Topics

The EBSA Web site features a page with links to key topics: health and other employee benefits, reporting and filing, and retirement.

Offices

A list of EBSA regional and district offices is available online.

Publications

The EBSA distributes booklets, factsheets, and pamphlets on employer obligations and employee rights under the Employee Retirement Income Security Act. A list of publications is available online or from the Office of Outreach, Education, and Assistance. Phone, 866-444-3272.

Reading Room

The EBSA maintains a disclosure room at Room N–1513, 200 Constitution Avenue NW., Washington, DC 20210. Reports filed under the Employee Retirement Income Security Act may be examined in the public disclosure room and purchased for 15 cents per page. Phone, 202-693-8673.

Spanish

Information is available in Spanish.

For further information, contact the Employee Benefits Security Administration, Department of Labor, Room S-2524, Washington, DC 20210. Phone, 866-444-3272.

Employment and Training Administration

Department of Labor, Washington, DC 20520, 877-872-5627, *http://www.doleta.gov*

ASSISTANT SECRETARY	Portia Y. Wu
Deputy Assistant Secretary	Gerri Fiala
Deputy Assistant Secretary	Eric Seleznow
Deputy Assistant Secretary	Byron Zuidema

The Employment and Training Administration (ETA) provides quality job training, employment, labor market information, and income maintenance services, primarily through

State and local workforce development systems. ETA also administers programs to enhance employment opportunities and business prosperity.

Apprenticeship Programs

The Office of Apprenticeship oversees the National Apprenticeship System, sets standards for apprenticeship, and assists States, industry, and labor in developing apprenticeship programs that meet required standards while promoting equal opportunity and safeguarding the welfare of apprentices.

For more information, call 202-693-2796.

Contracts Management

The Office of Contracts Management (OCM) provides leadership and direction to ensure acquisition excellence, integrity, accountability, and sound management of procurement resources to support Employment and Training Administration (ETA) and Job Corps goals and guiding principles for the acquisition of goods and services. Job Corps contracts account for 75 percent of the Department's contracting activity. Non-Job Corps contract activity supports ETA grant programs through technical assistance and long-term studies and evaluations.

For further information, contact the Office of Contracts Management, Department of Labor, Suite N-4643, Washington, DC 20210. Phone, 202-693-3701.

Financial Administration

The Office of Financial Administration (OFA) is responsible for managing all ETA fiscal resources for programs and activities for which funds are appropriated through its functions of accounting, budget, and financial system oversight. OFA provides critical budgetary, accounting, audit, and internal control management. It coordinates with the Departmental Budget Center and the Office of the Chief Financial Officer to provide financial management supporting the accomplishment of all aspects of ETA's mission.

For further information, call 202-693-3162.

Foreign Labor Certification

The Office of Foreign Labor Certification (OFLC) carries out the delegated responsibility of the Secretary of Labor under the Immigration and Nationality Act, as amended, concerning the admission of foreign workers into the United States for employment.

In carrying out this responsibility, OFLC administers temporary nonimmigrant and permanent labor certification programs through ETA's National Processing Centers located, respectively, in Chicago and Atlanta.

OFLC also administers nationally the issuance of employer-requested prevailing wage determinations through ETA's National Prevailing Wage and Helpdesk Center located in Washington, DC. Prevailing wage determinations are issued for use in all nonagricultural temporary labor certification programs and the permanent labor certification program.

For more information, call 202-693-3010.

Job Training

The Office of Job Corps (OJC) teaches young adults relevant skills they need to become employable and independent and helps them secure meaningful jobs or opportunities for further education. OJC has six regional offices responsible for monitoring and oversight of Job Corps centers, outreach and admissions, and career transition services.

For further information, call 202-693-3000.

Management and Administrative Services

The Office of Management and Administrative Services (OMAS) is responsible for managing administrative and grant management programs for ETA. OMAS provides critical grant-making and human resources management, information technology services, controlled correspondence, emergency preparedness, Freedom of Information Act coordination, facilities management, and facilitates communication and coordination of activities providing strategic advice, counsel, and customer service to ETA's six regions. OMAS provides technological infrastructure and administrative support for critical ETA functions.

For further information, call 202-693-2800.

Policy Development and Research

The Office of Policy Development and Research (OPDR) supports ETA policies and investments to improve the public workforce system by analyzing, formulating, and recommending legislative changes and options for policy initiatives, including budget justifications. OPDR coordinates ETA's legislative and regulatory activities and their interactions with international organizations and foreign countries. OPDR maintains ETA's portion of the Department's regulatory agenda and disseminates advisories and publications to the public workforce system. OPDR provides ETA with strategic approaches to improve performance and outcomes through research, demonstrations, and evaluation of its major programs. OPDR manages the Workforce Investment Act performance accountability reporting system; oversees the maintenance of wage record exchange systems for State and other grantees; coordinates the development of ETA's Operating Plan; and disseminates workforce program performance results. OPDR also provides policy guidance and technical assistance on the Worker Adjustment and Retraining Notification Act.

For further information, call 202-693-3700.

Trade Adjustment Assistance

The Office of Trade Adjustment Assistance (TAA) is responsible for administering a workers assistance program for those who have lost or may lose their jobs because of foreign trade. The TAA program provides reemployment services and allowances for eligible individuals.

For further information, call 202-693-3560.

Unemployment Compensation

The Office of Unemployment Insurance (OUI) provides national leadership, oversight, policy guidance, and technical assistance to the Federal-State unemployment compensation system. OUI also interprets Federal legislative requirements.

For more information, call 202-693-3029.

Workforce Investment

The Office of Workforce Investment (OWI) is responsible for implementing an integrated national workforce investment system that supports economic growth and provides workers with the information, advice, job search assistance, supportive services, and training needed for employment. OWI also helps employers acquire skilled workers.

For further information, call 202-693-3980.

Sources of Information

Advisories

The ETA uses its advisory system to disseminate its interpretations of Federal laws; procedural, administrative, management, and program direction; and other information to the States, direct grant recipients, and other interested parties.

Data

Unemployment insurance data are available on the ETA Web site.

Program data from the Office of Foreign Labor Certification are available on the ETA Web site.

Statistics, charts, and other information used to analyze the Trade Adjustment Assistance for Workers program are available on the ETA Web site.

Job Corps

Answers to frequently asked questions are posted on the Job Corps Web site.

The six Job Corps regional offices oversee Job Corps centers nationwide. Contact information for these regional offices is available on the Job Corps Web site.

Job Corps trains more than 60,000 students at 125 centers nationwide. Contact information for these training centers is available on the Job Corps Web site. Phone, 800-733-5627.

Library

A large repository of information is available online at the ETA Library.

News

The ETA posts news releases on its Web site.

Regional Offices

Contact information for the ETA's six regional offices is available on its Web site.

Research

The research publication database provides access to a collection of research and evaluation reports. The ETA commissioned the research and evaluation reports to help guide the workforce investment system in administering effective programs that enhance employment opportunity and business.

Youth Services

The Division of Youth Services has a "Resources" Web page.

For further information, contact the Employment and Training Administration, Department of Labor, Washington, DC 20210. Phone, 877-872-5627.

Mine Safety and Health Administration

201 12th Street South, Suite 400, Arlington, Virginia 22202, 202-693-9400, *http://www.msha.gov*

ASSISTANT SECRETARY	Joseph A. Main
Deputy Assistant Secretary for Operations	Patricia W. Silvey
Deputy Assistant Secretary for Policy	Laura McClintock

The Mine Safety and Health Administration (MSHA) was created in 1978, when the Federal Mine Safety and Health Act of 1977 transferred the Federal mine safety program from the Department of the Interior to the Department of Labor.

The MSHA promotes safe and healthful workplaces for the Nation's miners. The MSHA develops and enforces safety and health rules for all U.S. mines. The MSHA also provides technical, educational, and other assistance to mine operators.

Sources of Information

Data

Mine safety and health data—information on accidents, air sampling, employment, injuries, illnesses, inspections, production totals, violations, and more—are available on the MSHA Web site. Compliance calculator tools that allow users to find a mine's history of key health and safety violations are also available the Web site.

Summaries of MSHA data on annual fatality and injury statistics, most frequently cited standards, number of citations and orders issued, total dollar amount of penalties assessed, and more are available on the MSHA Web site.

Employment

Information on employment opportunities is available online.

The MSHA seeks motivated professionals committed to ensuring the health and safety of the Nation's miners.

Frequently Asked Questions (FAQs)

The MSHA posts answers to FAQs on its Web site.

News / Media

The MSHA posts alerts and hazards, announcements, congressional testimonies, events, news releases, photographs and videos, and speeches on its Web site.

Offices

A complete listing of MSHA district and field offices is available online.

Reports

Current and historical preliminary accident reports, fatalgrams, and fatal investigation reports for metal, nonmetal, and coal mines are accessible on the MSHA Web site. Quarterly and annual summaries of mining fatalities along with associated best practices and preventative recommendations are also accessible.

Part 50 of Title 30 of the "Code of Federal Regulation" (30 CFR Part 50) requires mine operators to notify the MSHA of accidents, requires operators to investigate accidents, and restricts disturbance of accident related areas. This part also requires them to file reports with the MSHA pertaining to accidents, occupational injuries, and occupational illnesses, as well as employment and coal production data. These Data are summarized in quarterly and annual reports.

Resources / Tools

Mine emergency operations information, miners' resources, and technical resources and reports are available on the MSHA Web site.

Spanish

In the top right corner of the MSHA's home page are an Español option and an Inglés option. Using these options, visitors to the Web site can toggle between content in Spanish or English.

For further information, contact the Office of Program Education and Outreach Services, Mine Safety and Health Administration, Department of Labor, 201 12th Street South, Suite 400, Arlington, Virginia 22202. Phone, 202-693-9400.

Occupational Safety and Health Administration

Department of Labor, Washington, DC 20210, 800-321-6742, *http://www.osha.gov*

ASSISTANT SECRETARY	David Michaels
Deputy Assistant Secretary	Jordan Barab
Deputy Assistant Secretary	Dorothy Dougherty

The Occupational Safety and Health Administration (OSHA), created pursuant to the Occupational Safety and Health Act of 1970 (29 U.S.C. 651 et seq.), assures safe and healthful working conditions for men and women by promulgating common sense, protective health, and safety standards; enforcing workplace safety and health rules; providing training, outreach, education, and assistance to workers and employers in their efforts to control workplace hazards; prevent work-related injuries, illnesses, and fatalities; and partnering with States that run their own OSHA-approved programs.

Sources of Information

Enforcement Cases

The OSHA Web site features a nationwide map of enforcement cases with initial penalties above $40,000.

File a Complaint

Information on how to file a safety and health complaint and an electronic complaint form are available on the OSHA Web site. Phone, 800-321-6742.

Freedom of Information Act (FOIA)

The OSHA is required to disclose records that are properly requested in writing by any person. An agency may withhold information pursuant to one or more of nine exemptions and three exclusions contained in the FOIA. The act applies only to Federal agencies and does not create a right of access to records held by Congress, the courts, State or local government agencies, and private entities.

Frequently Asked Questions (FAQs)

The OSHA posts answers to FAQs on its Web site.

Injury and Illness Data

The OSHA Web site features a searchable, establishment-specific database for establishments that provided OSHA with valid data from 1996 through 2011.

Workplace injury, illness, and fatality statistics are available on the OSHA Web site.

Make a Report

Employers must notify OSHA when an employee is killed on the job or suffers a work-related amputation, hospitalization, or loss of an eye. A fatality must be reported within 8 hours; an amputation, in-patient hospitalization, or eye loss must be reported within 24 hours. An employer should be prepared to supply the name of the business, the names of employees who were affected, the location and time of the incident, a brief description of the incident, and a contact person and phone number.

News

The OSHA posts news releases, which can be sorted by subject, date, or region, on its Web site.

The "What's New" Web page features news items that are organized chronologically.

Offices

A complete listing of OSHA regional and area offices is available online.

Publications

OSHA publications are accessible online.

Site Index

An A–Z index is available on the OSHA Web site.

Spanish

In the top right corner of the OSHA's home page are an Español option and an Inglés option. Using these options, visitors to the Web site can toggle between content in Spanish or English.

Training / Education

Stand-alone, interactive, Web-based training tools—eTools and the eMatrix—are available on the OSHA Web site. These tools are highly illustrated and utilize graphical menus.

Prevention video training tools (v-tools) on construction hazards are available on the OSHA Web site. These videos show how workers can be injured suddenly or even killed on the job. The videos assist those who are in the construction industry with identifying, reducing, and eliminating hazards. The videos are presented in clear, accessible vocabulary; show common construction worksite activities; and most are 2–4 minutes long.

For further information, contact the Occupational Safety and Health Administration, Department of Labor, Washington, DC 20210. Phone, 202-693-2000 or 800-321-6742.

Veterans' Employment and Training Service

Department of Labor, Washington, DC 20210, 866-487-2365, *http://www.dol.gov/vets*

ASSISTANT SECRETARY	Mike Michaud
Deputy Assistant Secretary for Policy	Teresa W. Gerton
Deputy Assistant Secretary for Operations and Management	Sam Shellenberger

The Veterans' Employment and Training Service (VETS) is responsible for administering veterans' employment and training programs and compliance activities that help them and servicemembers succeed in their civilian careers. VETS also administers the Jobs for Veterans State Grant program, which provides grants to States to fund personnel dedicated to serving the employment needs of veterans. VETS field staff works closely with and provides technical assistance to State employment workforce agencies to ensure that veterans receive priority of service and gain meaningful employment. VETS has two competitive grants programs: the Homeless Veterans Reintegration Program, and the Incarcerated Veterans Transition Program. VETS also prepares separating servicemembers for the civilian labor market with its Transition Assistance Program Employment Workshop.

VETS has three distinct compliance programs: the Federal Contractor Program, Veterans' Preference in Federal hiring and the Uniformed Services Employment and Reemployment Rights Act of 1994 (USERRA). With respect to Federal contractors, VETS promulgates regulations and maintains oversight of the program by assisting contractors to comply with their affirmative action and reporting obligations. Although the Office of Personnel Management is responsible for administering and interpreting statutes and regulations governing veterans' preference in Federal hiring, VETS investigates allegations that veterans' preference rights have been violated. In addition, VETS preserves servicemembers' employment and reemployment rights through its administration and enforcement of the USERRA statute. VETS conducts thorough investigations of alleged violations and conducts an extensive USERRA outreach program.

Sources of Information

Directories

A national office directory is available online.

A regional and State directory is available online.

Freedom of Information Act (FOIA)

Any person has the right to request access to Federal agency records or information. VETS is required to disclose records that are properly requested in writing by any person. An agency may withhold information pursuant to nine exemptions and three exclusions contained in the FOIA. The act applies only to Federal agencies and does not create a right of access to records held by Congress, the courts, or by State or local government agencies. A FOIA request should be submitted to the appropriate national or regional VETS office by email, fax, or mail. The subject line, cover page, or envelope should be clearly labeled "Freedom of Information Act Request." The content of the request should indicate that it is a FOIA request, and it should contain as much information as possible describing the record or records being sought.

Frequently Asked Questions (FAQs)

VETS posts answers to FAQs on its Web site.

Grants

Information on grants and other opportunities is available online.

Hire a Veteran

Resources to help employers hire veterans are available online.

News / Media

VETS posts news releases and public service announcements on its Web site.

Updates / Reports

The VETS Web site features updates and reports, as well as congressional testimonies, factsheets, and infographics.

For further information, contact the Assistant Secretary for Veterans' Employment and Training, Department of Labor, Washington, DC 20210. Phone, 202-693-4700.

Wage and Hour Division

Department of Labor, Washington, DC 20210, 866-487-9243, *http://www.dol.gov/whd*

ADMINISTRATOR	David Weil
Deputy Administrator	Laura A. Fortman
Deputy Administrator for Program Operations	Patricia Davidson

The Wage and Hour Division (WHD) enforces Federal minimum wage, overtime pay, recordkeeping, and child labor law requirements of the Fair Labor Standards Act. WHD also enforces the Migrant and Seasonal Agricultural Worker Protection Act, the Employee Polygraph Protection Act, the Family and Medical Leave Act, wage garnishment provisions of the Consumer Credit Protection Act, and a number of employment standards and worker protections as provided in several immigration-related statutes. Additionally, WHD administers and enforces the prevailing wage requirements of the Davis Bacon Act and the Service Contract Act and other statutes applicable to Federal contracts for construction and for the provision of goods and services.

Sources of Information

Evaluations / Studies

The WHD posts evaluations and studies on its Web site in Portable Document Format (PDF).

File a Complaint

Instructions for filing a complaint are available online. Phone, 866-487-9243.

Freedom of Information Act (FOIA)

The WHD is required to disclose records that are properly requested in writing by any person. The WHD may withhold information pursuant to nine exemptions and three exclusions contained in the FOIA. The WHD does not require a special FOIA request form. A request must reasonably describe the desired record. Providing its name or title is not mandatory, but the more specific the record description, the more likely that WHD staff can locate it. A FOIA request must be made in writing and may be submitted by courier service, email, fax, or postal mail.

Frequently Asked Questions (FAQs)

The WHD provides answers to FAQs on its Web site.

News

The WHD posts national and State news releases on its Web site.

Offices

Contact information for WHD area, district, and regional offices is available on the "WHD Local Offices" Web page.

Resources

Resources for workers are available on the WHD Web site.

Resources for employers are available on the WHD Web site.

Resources for State and local governments are available on the WHD Web site.

For further information, contact the Office of the Administrator, Wage and Hour Division, Department of Labor, Room S-3502, Washington, DC 20210. Phone, 202-693-0051.

Women's Bureau

Department of Labor, Washington, DC 20210, 202-693-6710, *http://www.dol.gov/wb*

DIRECTOR	Latifa Lyles
Deputy Director	Joan Harrigan-Farrelly

The Women's Bureau develops policies and standards and conducts inquiries to safeguard the interests of working women, to advocate for their equality and the economic security of their families, and to promote quality work environments.

The Bureau identifies, researches, and analyzes topics that are relevant for working women; pioneers policies and programs to address those topics; and enhances public education and outreach efforts to raise awareness on key issues and developments affecting women in the workforce.

Sources of Information

Blog

The Bureau's Web site features a blog.

Data / Statistics

Current and historical statistics on a broad range of topics and subpopulations of women in the labor force are available online.

Regional Offices

A complete listing of Women's Bureau regional offices is available online.

Resources

Resources for women in the labor force produced by or in collaboration with the Bureau are available on its Web site.

For further information, contact the Women's Bureau, Department of Labor, Room S-3002, NW., Washington, DC 20210. Phone, 202-693-6710.

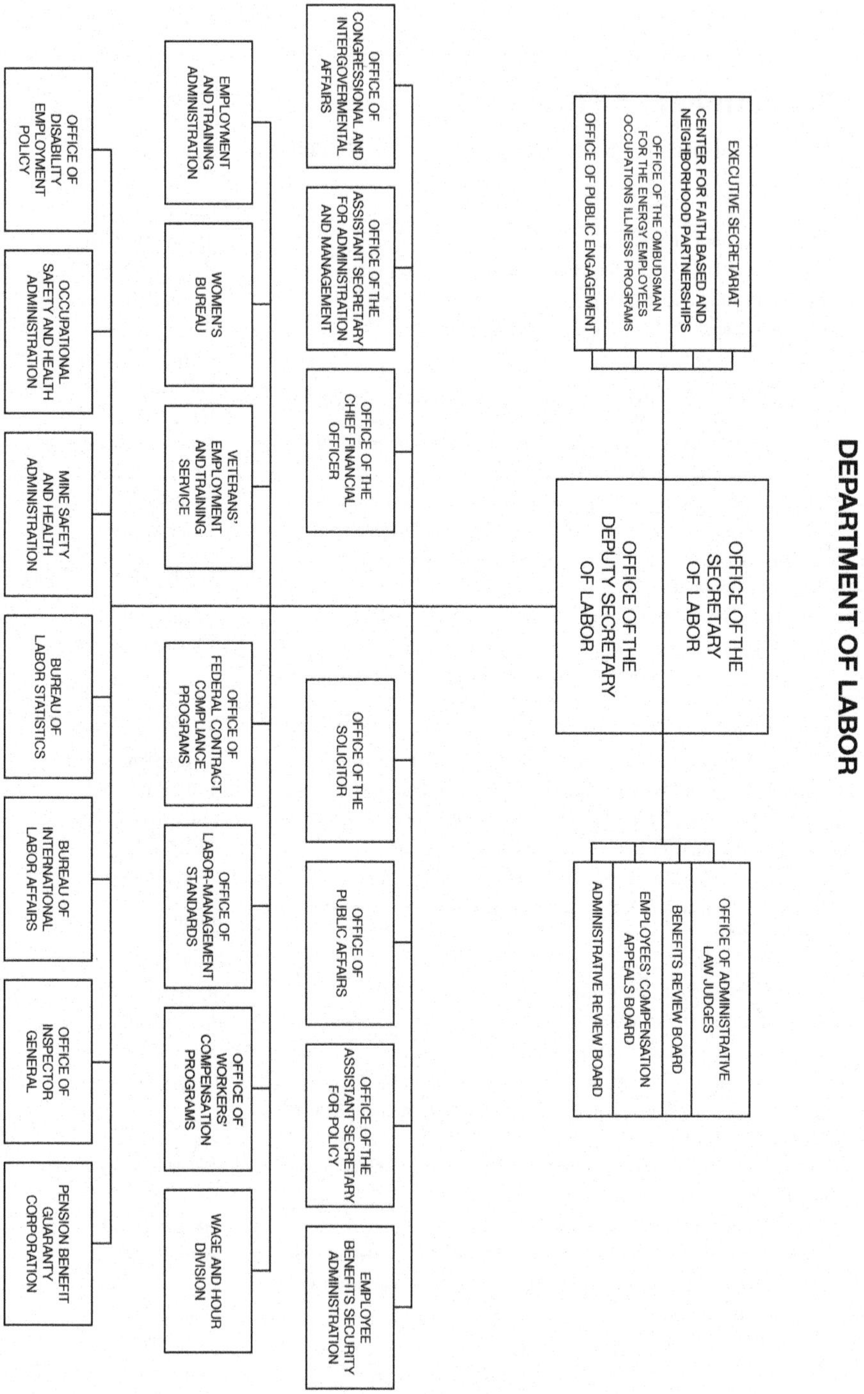
DEPARTMENT OF LABOR
OFFICE OF THE SECRETARY OF LABOR
OFFICE OF THE DEPUTY SECRETARY OF LABOR
EXECUTIVE SECRETARIAT
CENTER FOR FAITH BASED AND NEIGHBORHOOD PARTNERSHIPS
OFFICE OF THE OMBUDSMAN FOR THE ENERGY EMPLOYEES OCCUPATIONS ILLNESS PROGRAMS
OFFICE OF PUBLIC ENGAGEMENT
OFFICE OF ADMINISTRATIVE LAW JUDGES
BENEFITS REVIEW BOARD
EMPLOYEES' COMPENSATION APPEALS BOARD
ADMINISTRATIVE REVIEW BOARD
OFFICE OF CONGRESSIONAL AND INTERGOVERMENTAL AFFAIRS
OFFICE OF THE ASSISTANT SECRETARY FOR ADMINISTRATION AND MANAGEMENT
OFFICE OF THE CHIEF FINANCIAL OFFICER
OFFICE OF THE SOLICITOR
OFFICE OF PUBLIC AFFAIRS
OFFICE OF THE ASSISTANT SECRETARY FOR POLICY
EMPLOYEE BENEFITS SECURITY ADMINISTRATION
EMPLOYMENT AND TRAINING ADMINISTRATION
WOMEN'S BUREAU
VETERANS' EMPLOYMENT AND TRAINING SERVICE
OFFICE OF FEDERAL CONTRACT COMPLIANCE PROGRAMS
OFFICE OF LABOR-MANAGEMENT STANDARDS
OFFICE OF WORKERS' COMPENSATION PROGRAMS
WAGE AND HOUR DIVISION
OFFICE OF DISABILITY EMPLOYMENT POLICY
OCCUPATIONAL SAFETY AND HEALTH ADMINISTRATION
MINE SAFETY AND HEALTH ADMINISTRATION
BUREAU OF LABOR STATISTICS
BUREAU OF INTERNATIONAL LABOR AFFAIRS
OFFICE OF INSPECTOR GENERAL
PENSION BENEFIT GUARANTY CORPORATION

Department of State

2201 C Street NW., Washington, DC 20520, 202-647-4000, *http://www.state.gov*

SECRETARY OF STATE	John F. Kerry
Deputy Secretary of State	Antony Blinken
Deputy Secretary of State for Management and Resources	Heather Higginbottom
Counselor of the Department	Kristie A. Kenney
Director, Office of U.S. Foreign Assistance	Hari Sastry
Executive Secretary	Joseph E. Macmanus
Under Secretary for Arms Control and International Security Affairs	Thomas M. Countryman, Acting
Assistant Secretary for International Security and Nonproliferation	Thomas M. Countryman
Assistant Secretary for Political-Military Affairs	Tina Kaidanow, Acting
Assistant Secretary for Arms Control, Verification and Compliance	Frank Rose
Under Secretary for Civilian Security, Democracy, and Human Rights	Sarah B. Sewall
Ambassador-at-Large for the Office to Monitor and Combat Trafficking in Persons	Susan Coppedge Amato
Assistant Secretary for Conflict and Stabilization Operations	David Robinson
Assistant Secretary for Democracy, Human Rights, and Labor	Tomasz P. Malinowksi
Assistant Secretary for International Narcotics and Law Enforcement Affairs	William R. Brownfield
Assistant Secretary for Population, Refugees, and Migration	Anne C. Richard
Coordinator and Ambassador-at-Large for Counterterrorism	Justin Siberell, Acting
Special Coordinator for the Office of Global Criminal Justice	Todd Buchwald
Under Secretary for Economic Growth, Energy, and the Environment	Catherine A. Novelli
Assistant Secretary for Economic and Business Affairs	Charles H. Rivkin
Assistant Secretary for Energy Resources	Amos Hochstein
Assistant Secretary for Oceans and International Environmental and Scientific Affairs	Judith Garber, Acting
Office of the Chief Economist	Rodney Ludema
Under Secretary for Management	Patrick F. Kennedy
Assistant Secretary for Administration	Joyce A. Barr
Assistant Secretary for Consular Affairs	Michele Bond
Assistant Secretary for Diplomatic Security and Foreign Missions	Gregory B. Starr
Assistant Secretary for Information Resource Management / Chief Information Officer	Steven C. Taylor
Comptroller, Bureau of the Comptroller and Global Financial Services	Christopher H. Flaggs
Director, Budget and Planning	Douglas Pitkin
Director, Foreign Service Institute	Nancy McEldowney
Director, Human Resources / Director General of the Foreign Service	Arnold Chacon
Director, Office of Management Policy, Rightsizing and Innovation	Adam Namm
Director, Office of Medical Services	Gary D. Penner
Director, Overseas Buildings Operations	Lydia Muniz
Under Secretary for Political Affairs	Thomas A. Shannon, Jr.
Assistant Secretary for African Affairs	Linda Thomas-Greenfield
Assistant Secretary for East Asian and Pacific Affairs	Daniel R. Russel
Assistant Secretary for European and Eurasian Affairs	Victoria Nuland

Assistant Secretary for International Organization Affairs	Bathsheba Crocker
Assistant Secretary for Near Eastern Affairs	Anne Patterson
Assistant Secretary for South and Central Asian Affairs	Nisha Desai Biswal
Assistant Secretary for Western Hemisphere Affairs	Mari Aponte
Under Secretary for Public Diplomacy and Public Affairs	D. Bruce Wharton, Acting
Assistant Secretary for Educational and Cultural Affairs	Evan Ryan
Assistant Secretary for Public Affairs	John Kirby
Coordinator of International Information Programs	Macon Phillips
Assistant Secretary for Intelligence and Research	Daniel Smith
Assistant Secretary for Legislative Affairs	Julie Frifield
Ambassador-at-Large of the Office of Global Women's Issues	Catherine M. Russell
Chief of Protocol	Peter Selfridge
Coordinator, Office of U.S. Global AIDS	Deborah L. Birx
Director, Office of Civil Rights	John M. Robinson
Director, Office of Policy Planning	Jonathan Finer
Inspector General	Steve A. Linick
Legal Adviser	Brian Egan

UNITED STATES MISSION TO THE UNITED NATIONS
799 United Nations Plaza, New York, NY 10017

United States Permanent Representative to the United Nations and Representative in the Security Council	Samantha Power
Deputy United States Representative to the United Nations	Michele Sisson
United States Alternate Representative for Special Political Affairs in the United Nations	David Pressman
United States Representative to the Economic and Social Council	Richard W. Erdman, Acting
United States Representative for United Nations Management and Reform	Isobel Coleman

[For the Department of State statement of organization, see the U.S. Code of Federal Regulations, Title 22, Part 5.]

The Department of State advises the President on issues of foreign policy; supports democracy, freedom, and prosperity for all people; and fosters conditions that favor stability and progress worldwide.

The Department of State was established by act of July 27, 1789, as the Department of Foreign Affairs and was renamed Department of State by act of September 15, 1789 (22 U.S.C. 2651 note).

Secretary of State

The Secretary of State is responsible for the overall direction, coordination, and supervision of U.S. foreign relations and for the interdepartmental activities of the U.S. Government abroad. The Secretary is the first-ranking member of the Cabinet, is a member of the National Security Council, and is in charge of the operations of the Department, including the Foreign Service.

Regional Bureaus

Foreign affairs activities worldwide are handled by the geographic bureaus, which include the Bureaus of African Affairs, European and Eurasian Affairs, East Asian and Pacific Affairs, Near Eastern Affairs, South and Central Asian Affairs, and Western Hemisphere Affairs.

Administration

The Bureau of Administration provides support programs and services to

Department of State operations worldwide, as well as programs and services to other U.S. Government agencies represented at U.S. Embassies and consulates. These functions include administrative policy; domestic emergency management; management of owned or leased facilities in the United States; procurement, supply, travel, and transportation support; classified pouch, unclassified pouch, and domestic mail distribution; official records, publishing, library, and foreign language interpreting and translating services; and support to the schools abroad that educate dependents of U.S. Government employees assigned to diplomatic and consular missions. Direct services to the public include authenticating documents used abroad for legal and business purposes; responding to requests under the Freedom of Information and Privacy Acts; providing the electronic reading room for public reference to State Department records; and determining use of the diplomatic reception rooms of the Harry S. Truman headquarters building in Washington, DC.

For further information, contact the Bureau of Administration. Phone, 202-485-7000.

Arms Control, Verification and Compliance

The Bureau of Arms Control, Verification and Compliance is responsible for ensuring and verifying compliance with international arms control, nonproliferation, and disarmament agreements and commitments. The Bureau also leads negotiation and implementation efforts with respect to strategic arms control, most recently the new START Treaty and conventional forces in Europe. The Bureau is the principal policy representative to the intelligence community with regard to verification and compliance matters and uses this role to promote, preserve, and enhance key collection and analytic capabilities and to ensure that intelligence verification, compliance, and implementation requirements are met. The Bureau staffs and manages treaty implementation commissions, creates negotiation and implementation policy for agreements and commitments, and develops policy for future arms control, nonproliferation, and disarmament arrangements. It also provides secure government-to-government communication linkages with foreign treaty partners. The Bureau is also responsible for preparing verifiability assessments on proposals and agreements, and reporting these to Congress as required. The Bureau also prepares the "President's Annual Report to Congress on Adherence to and Compliance With Arms Control, Nonproliferation, and Disarmament Agreements and Commitments," as well as the reports required by the Iran, North Korea, and Syria Nonproliferation Act.

For further information, contact the Bureau of Arms Control, Verification and Compliance. Phone, 202-647-6830. Fax, 202-647-1321.

Budget and Planning

The Bureau of Budget and Planning manages budgeting and resource management for operation accounts.

For further information, contact the Bureau of Budget and Planning. Phone, 202-647-8517.

Comptroller and Global Financial Services

The Bureau of the Comptroller and Global Financial Services, led by the Chief Financial Officer, integrates strategic planning, budgeting, and performance to secure departmental resources. The Bureau manages all departmental strategic and performance planning; global financial services, including accounting, disbursing, and payroll; issuance of financial statements and oversight of the Department's management control program; coordination of national security resources and remediation of vulnerabilities within the Department's global critical infrastructure; and management of the International Cooperative Administrative Support Services Program.

For further information, contact the Bureau of the Comptroller and Global Financial

Services. Phone, 703-875-4364.

Conflict and Stabilization Operations

The Bureau of Conflict and Stabilization Operations advances U.S. national security by driving integrated, civilian-led efforts to prevent, respond to, and stabilize crises in priority states, setting conditions for long-term peace. The Bureau emphasizes sustainable solutions guided by local dynamics and actors and promotes unity of effort, strategic use of scarce resources, and burden sharing with international partners.

For further information, contact the Bureau of Conflict Stabilization Operations. Phone, 202-663-0299.

Consular Affairs

The Bureau of Consular Affairs is responsible for the protection and welfare of American citizens and interests abroad; the administration and enforcement of the provisions of the immigration and nationality laws insofar as they concern the Department of State and Foreign Service; the issuance of passports and visas; and related services. Approximately 18 million passports a year are issued by the Bureau's Office of Passport Services at the processing centers in Portsmouth, NH, and Charleston, SC, and the regional agencies in Boston, MA; Chicago, IL; Aurora, CO; Honolulu, HI; Houston, TX; Los Angeles, CA; Miami, FL; New Orleans, LA; New York, NY; Philadelphia, PA; San Francisco, CA; Seattle, WA; Norwalk, CT; Detroit, MI; Minneapolis, MN; and Washington, DC. In addition, the Bureau helps secure America's borders against entry by terrorists or narcotraffickers, facilitates international adoptions, and supports parents whose children have been abducted abroad.

More information is available online at the Bureau of Consular Affairs.

Counterterrorism

The Bureau of Counterterrorism leads the Department in the U.S. Government's effort to counter terrorism abroad and secure the United States against foreign terrorist threats. To carry out its mission, the Bureau develops and implements counterterrorism strategies, promotes international cooperation on counterterrorism issues, serves as the Department's key link on counterterrorism to the Department of Homeland Security, focuses efforts to counter violent extremism, and develops international partner counterterrorism capacity.

For further information, contact CT's Office of Public Affairs. Phone, 202-647-1845.

Democracy, Human Rights, and Labor

The Bureau of Democracy, Human Rights, and Labor (DRL) is responsible for developing and implementing U.S. policy on democracy, human rights, labor, religious freedom, monitoring and combating anti-Semitism, and advocating for inclusion of people with disabilities. DRL practices diplomatic engagement and advocacy to protect human rights and strengthen democratic institutions. Working with governments, civil society, and multilateral organizations to support democratic governance and human rights, the Bureau also participates in multi-stakeholder initiatives to encourage multinational corporations to adhere to human rights standards of conduct, including the elimination of child labor. DRL fulfills the USG reporting responsibilities on human rights and democracy, producing the annual "Country Reports on Human Rights Practices," the annual "International Religious Freedom" report, and the "Advancing Freedom and Democracy" report. Providing targeted program assistance through the Human Rights and Democracy Fund and other funding streams, the Bureau works to protect human rights and strengthen democratic institutions around the world. DRL programs help prosecute war criminals, promote religious freedom, support workers' rights, encourage accountability in governance, as well as facilitate freedom of expression and freedom to access information on the

Internet. The Bureau also has a Congressionally mandated responsibility to ensure that foreign military assistance and training is not provided to gross violators of human rights. DRL leads the Secretary of State's Task Force on Global Internet Freedom.

For further information, contact the Bureau of Democracy, Human Rights, and Labor. Phone, 202-647-2126.

Diplomatic Security

The Bureau of Diplomatic Security provides a secure environment to promote U.S. interests at home and abroad. The Bureau's mission includes protecting the Secretary of State and other senior Government officials, resident and visiting foreign dignitaries, and foreign missions in the United States; conducting criminal, counterintelligence, and personnel security investigations; ensuring the integrity of international travel documents, sensitive information, classified processing equipment, and management information systems; the physical and technical protection of domestic and overseas facilities of the Department of State; providing professional law enforcement and security training to U.S. and foreign personnel; and a comprehensive, multifaceted overseas security program serving the needs of U.S. missions and resident U.S. citizens and business communities. Through the Office of Foreign Missions, the Bureau regulates the domestic activities of the foreign diplomatic community in the areas of taxation, real property acquisitions, motor vehicle operation, domestic travel, and customs processing.

For further information, contact the Bureau of Diplomatic Security Office of Public Affairs. Phone, 571-345-2502.

Economic and Business Affairs

The Bureau of Economic and Business Affairs (EB) promotes international trade, investment, economic development, and financial stability on behalf of the American people. EB works to build prosperity and economic security at home and abroad by implementing policy related to the promotion of U.S. trade, investment and exports, international development and reconstruction, intellectual property enforcement, terrorism financing and economic sanctions, international communications and information policy, and aviation and maritime affairs. EB formulates and carries out U.S. foreign economic policy and works to sustain a more democratic, secure, and prosperous world.

For further information, contact the Bureau of Economic and Business Affairs. Phone, 202-647-9204.

Educational and Cultural Affairs

The Bureau of Educational and Cultural Affairs administers the principal provisions of the Mutual Educational and Cultural Exchange Act (the Fulbright-Hays Act), including U.S. international educational and cultural exchange programs. These programs include the prestigious Fulbright Program for students, scholars, and teachers; the International Visitor Leadership Program, which brings leaders and future leaders from other countries to the United States for consultation with their professional colleagues; and professional, youth, sports, and cultural exchanges. Programs are implemented through cooperative relationships with U.S. nongovernmental organizations that support the Bureau's mission.

For further information, contact the Bureau of Educational and Cultural Affairs. Phone, 202-632-6445. Fax, 202-632-2701.

Energy Resources

The Bureau of Energy Resources (ENR) leads the State Department in the U.S.

Government's promotion of U.S. and international energy policy. ENR works to ensure that international energy markets are secure and predictable in order to mitigate potential disruptions, while also working with international partners to diversify U.S. energy supplies. The Bureau also seeks to encourage the transformation of United States and world production and consumption of energy to confront the limits of a hydrocarbon-based society and rapid increases in energy demand. ENR works to promote good governance, transparency, and reform of energy sectors globally, which will help broaden energy access, further ensure stable energy supplies, and reduce political instability.

For further information, contact the Bureau of Energy Resources. Phone, 202-647-3423.

Foreign Service

To a great extent, the future of our country depends on the relations we have with other countries, and those relations are conducted principally by the U.S. Foreign Service. Trained representatives stationed worldwide provide the President and the Secretary of State with much of the raw material from which foreign policy is made and with the recommendations that help shape it.

Ambassadors are the personal representatives of the President and report to the President through the Secretary of State. Ambassadors have full responsibility for implementation of U.S. foreign policy by any and all U.S. Government personnel within their country of assignment, except those under military commands. Their responsibilities include negotiating agreements between the United States and the host country, explaining and disseminating official U.S. policy, and maintaining cordial relations with that country's government and people.

For a complete listing of Foreign Service posts, including addresses, telephone numbers, and key officials, use the link below.

Foreign Service Institute

The Foreign Service Institute of the Department of State is the Federal Government's primary foreign affairs-related training institution. In addition to the Department of State, the Institute provides training for more than 47 other Government agencies. The Institute has more than 700 courses, including some 70 foreign language courses, ranging in length from 1 day to 2 years. The courses are designed to promote successful performance in each professional assignment, to ease the adjustment to other countries and cultures, and to enhance the leadership and management capabilities of the foreign affairs community.

For further information, contact the Foreign Service Institute. Phone, 703-302-7144. Fax, 703-302-7152.

Information Resource Management

The Bureau of Information Resource Management (IRM) provides the Department with the information technology it needs to carry out U.S. diplomacy in the information age. The IRM Bureau is led by the Department's Chief Information Officer. IRM establishes effective information resource management planning and policies; ensures availability of information technology systems and operations, including information technology contingency planning, to support the Department's diplomatic, consular, and management operations; exercises management responsibility to ensure the Department's information resources meet the business requirements of the Department and provide an effective basis for knowledge sharing and collaboration within the Department and with other foreign affairs agencies and partners; exercises delegated approving authority for the Secretary of State for the development and administration of the Department's computer and information security programs and policies.

For further information, contact the Bureau of Information Resource Management. Phone, 202-647-2977.

Inspector General

The Office of Inspector General (OIG) conducts independent audits, inspections, and investigations to promote effective management, accountability, and positive change in the Department of State, the Broadcasting Board of Governors (BBG), and the foreign affairs community. OIG provides leadership to promote integrity, efficiency, effectiveness, and economy; prevents and detects waste, fraud, abuse, and mismanagement; identifies vulnerabilities and recommends constructive solutions; offers expert assistance to improve Department and BBG operations; communicates timely, useful information that facilitates decision-making and achieves measurable gains; and keeps the Department, BBG, and Congress informed.

For further information, contact the Office of Inspector General. Phone, 202-663-0340.

Intelligence and Research

The primary mission of the Bureau of Intelligence and Research (INR) is to harness intelligence to serve U.S. diplomacy. Drawing on all-source intelligence, INR provides value-added independent analysis of events to Department policymakers, ensures that intelligence activities support foreign policy and national security purposes, and serves as the focal point in the Department for ensuring policy review of sensitive counterintelligence and law enforcement activities. The Bureau also analyzes geographical and international boundary issues. INR is a member of the U.S. Intelligence Community and serves as the Community's Executive Agent for Analytical Outreach.

For further information, contact the Bureau of Intelligence and Research. Phone, 202-647-1080.

International Information Programs

The Bureau of International Information Programs (IIP) informs, engages, and influences international audiences about U.S. policy and society to advance America's interests. IIP is a leader in developing and implementing public diplomacy strategies that measurably influence international audiences through quality programs and cutting-edge technologies. IIP provides localized contact for U.S. policies and messages, reaching millions worldwide in English, Arabic, Chinese, French, Persian, Russian, and Spanish. IIP delivers America's message to the world through a number of key products and services. These programs reach, and are created strictly for, key international audiences, such as U.S. diplomatic missions abroad, the media, government officials, opinion leaders, and the general public in more than 140 countries around the world. They include Web and print publications, in-person and telecommunications-based speaker programs, and information resource services. IIP orchestrates the State Department's efforts to counter anti-American disinformation/propaganda and serves as the Department's chief link with other agencies in coordinating international public diplomacy programs.

For further information, contact the Bureau of International Information Programs. Phone, 202-632-9942.

International Narcotics and Law Enforcement

The Bureau of International Narcotics and Law Enforcement Affairs (INL) is responsible for developing policies and managing programs to combat and counter international narcotics production and trafficking, and for strengthening law enforcement and other rule of law institutional capabilities outside the United States. The Bureau also directs narcotics control coordinators at posts abroad and provides guidance on narcotics control, justice sector reform, and anticrime matters to the chiefs of missions. It supports the development of strong, sustainable criminal justice systems as well as training for police force and judicial officials. INL works closely with a broad range of other U.S. Government agencies.

For further information, contact the Bureau of International Narcotics and Law Enforcement Affairs. Phone, 202-647-2545. Fax, 202-736-4045.

International Organizations

The Bureau of International Organization Affairs provides guidance and support for U.S. participation in international organizations and conferences and formulates and implements U.S. policy toward international organizations, with particular emphasis on those organizations which make up the United Nations system. It provides direction in the development, coordination, and implementation of U.S. multilateral policy.

For further information, contact the Bureau of International Organization Affairs. Phone, 202-647-9600. Fax, 202-736-4116.

International Security and Nonproliferation

The Bureau of International Security and Nonproliferation (ISN), is responsible for managing a broad range of nonproliferation, counterproliferation, and arms control functions. ISN leads U.S. efforts to prevent the spread of weapons of mass destruction (nuclear, radiological, chemical, and biological weapons) related materials, and their delivery systems. It is responsible for spearheading efforts to promote international consensus on weapons of mass destruction proliferation through bilateral and multilateral diplomacy; addressing weapons of mass destruction proliferation threats posed by nonstate actors and terrorist groups by improving physical security, using interdiction and sanctions, and actively participating in the Proliferation Security Initiative; coordinating the implementation of key international treaties and arrangements, working to make them relevant to today's security challenges; working closely with the U.N., the G–8, NATO, the Organization for the Prohibition of Chemical Weapons, the International Atomic Energy Agency, and other international institutions and organizations to reduce and eliminate the threat posed by weapons of mass destruction; and supporting efforts of foreign partners to prevent, protect against, and respond to the threat or use of weapons of mass destruction by terrorists.

For further information, contact the Bureau of International Security and Nonproliferation. Phone, 202-647-9868. Fax, 202-736-4863.

Legal Adviser

The Office of the Legal Adviser advises the Secretary of State and other Department officials on all domestic and international legal matters relating to the Department of State, Foreign Service, and diplomatic and consular posts abroad. The Office's lawyers draft, negotiate, and interpret treaties, international agreements, domestic statutes, departmental regulations, Executive orders, and other legal documents; provide guidance on international and domestic law; represent the United States in international organization, negotiation, and treaty commission meetings; work on domestic and foreign litigation affecting the Department's interests; and represent the United States before international tribunals, including the International Court of Justice.

For further information, contact the Office of the Legal Adviser. Phone, 202-647-9598.

Legislative Affairs

The Bureau of Legislative Affairs coordinates legislative activity for the Department of State and advises the Secretary, the Deputy, as well as the Under Secretaries and Assistant Secretaries on legislative strategy. The Bureau facilitates effective communication between State Department officials and the Members of Congress and their staffs. Legislative Affairs works closely with the authorizing, appropriations, and oversight committees of the House and Senate, as well as with individual Members that have an interest in State Department or foreign policy issues. The Bureau also manages Department testimony before House and Senate hearings, organizes Member and staff briefings, facilitates congressional travel to overseas posts for Members and staff throughout the year, reviews proposed legislation, and coordinates Statements of Administration Policy on legislation affecting the conduct of U.S. foreign policy. The Legislative Affairs staff advises individual Bureaus of the Department on legislative and outreach strategies and coordinates those strategies with the Secretary's priorities.

For further information, contact the Bureau of Legislative Affairs. Phone, 202-647-1714.

Medical Services

The Office of Medical Services (MED) develops, manages, and staffs a worldwide primary health care system for U.S. Government employees and their eligible dependents residing overseas. In support of its overseas operations, MED approves and monitors the medical evacuation of patients, conducts pre-employment and in-service physical clearance examinations, and provides clinical referral and advisory services. MED also provides for emergency medical response in the event of a crisis at an overseas post.

For further information, contact the Office of Medical Services. Phone, 202-663-1649. Fax, 202-663-1613.

Oceans and International Environmental and Scientific Affairs

The Bureau of Oceans and International Environmental and Scientific Affairs (OES) serves as the foreign policy focal point for international oceans, as well as environmental and scientific efforts. OES projects, protects, and promotes U.S. global interests in these areas by articulating U.S. foreign policy, encouraging international cooperation, and negotiating treaties and other instruments of international law. The Bureau serves as the principal adviser to the Secretary of State on international environment, science, and technology matters and takes the lead in coordinating and brokering diverse interests in the interagency process, where the development of international policies or the negotiation and implementation of relevant international agreements are concerned. The Bureau seeks to promote the peaceful exploitation of outer space, develop and coordinate policy on international health issues, encourage government-to-government scientific cooperation, and prevent the destruction and degradation of the planet's natural resources and the global environment.

For further information, contact the Bureau of Oceans and International Environmental and Scientific Affairs. Phone, 202-647-3004.

Overseas Buildings Operations

The Bureau of Overseas Buildings Operations (OBO) directs the worldwide overseas buildings program for the Department of State and the U.S. Government community serving abroad under the authority of the chiefs of mission. Along with the input and support of other State Department bureaus, foreign affairs agencies, and Congress, OBO sets worldwide priorities for the design, construction, acquisition, maintenance, use, and sale of real properties and the use of sales proceeds. OBO also serves as the Single Real Property Manager of all overseas facilities under the authority of the chiefs of mission.

For further information, contact the Bureau of Overseas Buildings Operations. Phone, 703-875-4131. Fax, 703-875-5043.

Political-Military Affairs

The Bureau of Political-Military Affairs is the principal link between the Departments of State and Defense and is the Department of State's lead on operational military matters. The Bureau provides policy direction in the areas of international security, security assistance, military operations, defense strategy and policy, counterpiracy measures, and defense trade. Its responsibilities include coordinating the U.S. Government's response to piracy in the waters off the Horn of Africa, securing base access to support the deployment of U.S. military forces overseas, negotiating status of forces agreements, coordinating participation in coalition combat and stabilization forces, regulating arms transfers, directing military assistance to U.S. allies, combating illegal trafficking in small arms and light weapons, facilitating the education and training of international peacekeepers and foreign military personnel, managing humanitarian mine action programs, and assisting other countries in reducing the availability of man-portable air defense systems.

For further information, contact the Bureau of Political-Military Affairs. Phone, 202-647-9022. Fax, 202-736-4413.

Population, Refugees, and Migration

The Bureau of Population, Refugees, and Migration directs the Department's population, refugee, and migration policy development. It administers U.S. contributions to international organizations and nongovernmental organizations for humanitarian assistance- and protection-related programs on behalf of refugees, conflict victims, and internally displaced persons. The Bureau oversees the annual admissions of refugees to the United States for permanent resettlement, working closely with the Department of Homeland Security, the Department of Health and Human Services, and various State and private voluntary agencies. It coordinates U.S. international population policy and promotes its goals through bilateral and multilateral cooperation. It works closely with the U.S. Agency for International Development, which administers U.S. international population programs. The Bureau also coordinates the Department's international migration policy through bilateral and multilateral diplomacy. The Bureau oversees efforts to encourage greater participation in humanitarian assistance and refugee resettlement on the part of foreign governments and uses humanitarian diplomacy to increase access and assistance to those in need in the absence of political solutions.

For further information, contact the Bureau of Population, Refugees, and Migration. Phone, 202-453-9339. Fax, 202-453-9394.

Protocol

The Chief of Protocol is the principal adviser to the U.S. Government, the President, the Vice President, and the Secretary of State on matters of diplomatic procedure governed by law or international custom and practice. The Office is responsible for arranging visits of foreign chiefs of state, heads of government, and other high officials to the United States; organizing credential presentations of newly arrived Ambassadors, as presented to the President and to the Secretary of State; operating the President's guest house, Blair House; organizing delegations representing the President at official ceremonies abroad; conducting official ceremonial functions and public events; interpreting the official order of precedence; conducting outreach programs of cultural enrichment and substantive briefings of the Diplomatic Corps; accrediting of over 118,000 embassy, consular, international organization, and other foreign government personnel, members of their families, and domestics throughout the United States; determining entitlement to diplomatic or consular immunity; publishing of diplomatic and consular lists; resolving problems arising out of diplomatic or consular immunity, such as legal and police matters; and approving the opening of embassy and consular offices in conjunction with the Office of Foreign Missions.

For further information, contact the Office of the Chief of Protocol. Phone, 202-647-1735. Fax, 202-647-1560.

Public Affairs

The Bureau of Public Affairs (PA) supports U.S. foreign policy goals and objectives, advances national interests, and enhances National security by informing and influencing domestic and global public opinion about American interaction with the rest of the world. In addition, PA works to help Americans understand the importance of foreign affairs by conducting press briefings for the domestic and foreign press, pursuing media outreach by other means, arranging townhall meetings and community speakers, and preparing historical studies on U.S. diplomacy and foreign affairs matters.

For further information, contact the Bureau of Public Affairs. Phone, 202-647-6575.

Sources of Information

A–Z Index

The Department of State's Web site features an alphabetical subject index that allows visitors to look for specific topics or to browse content that aligns with their interests.

Business Opportunities

The Department of State and U.S. Embassies overseas post contract opportunities on the Federal Government business opportunities (FedBizOpps.gov) and the commodities marketplace service (FedBid.com) Web sites. The Office of Acquisitions Management offers professional procurement and grant services—acquisition planning, contract negotiations and administration, and cost and price analysis—to customers worldwide. Phone, 703-516-1706. Fax, 703-875-6085.

The Office of Small and Disadvantaged Business Utilization's Web site features information and resources that support businesses falling into one or more of the legislatively specified small business categories in their efforts to secure prime contracts and subcontracts. Phone, 703-875-6822.

Data

To support the Open Government Initiative, the Department of State publishes datasets online.

Diplomatic and Official Passports

Those inquiring about these types of passports should contact their respective travel offices. The U.S. Government only issues these types of passports to individuals traveling abroad in connection with official employment. Additional information is available online at Consular Affairs.

Emergencies Abroad

For information on missing persons, emergencies, travel warnings, overseas voting, judicial assistance, and arrests or deaths of Americans abroad, contact the Office of American Citizens Services and Crisis Management, Department of State. Phone, 888-407-4747 or 202-501-4444 (international). Address correspondence to Overseas Citizens Services, Bureau of Consular Affairs, Department of State, SA–29, 2201 C Street NW., Washington, DC 20520. Inquiries regarding international parental child abduction should be directed to the Office of Children's Issues, Bureau of Consular Affairs, Department of State, SA–29, 2201 C Street NW., Washington, DC 20520-4818. Phone, 888-407-4747 or 202-501-4444 (international).

Employment

To learn about joining the Civil Service, becoming a Foreign Service Specialist, or the Consular Fellows Program, visit the "Careers" Web page. Information of interest to students, recent graduates, veterans, and persons with disabilities is also accessible online. State Department personnel are available to answer questions on Federal workdays, 8:30 a.m.–4:30 p.m., eastern standard time. Phone, 202-663-2176.

The Department of State consistently ranks high among large agencies in the Partnership for Public Service's "Best Places To Work Agency Rankings."

Freedom of Information Act (FOIA)

To request records, write to the Director, Office of Information Programs and Services, A/GIS/IPS/RL, Department of State, SA–2, Washington, DC 20522-8100. Many documents are accessible online in the virtual reading room. For more information, contact the FOIA Requester Service Center. Phone, 202-261-8484.

Frequently Asked Questions (FAQs)

The Department of State posts answers to FAQs on its Web site.

International Adoptions

For information on adoption of foreign children by private U.S. citizens, contact the Office of Children's Issues, Bureau of Consular Affairs, Department of State, SA–29, 2201 C Street NW., Washington, DC 20520-4818. Phone, 888-407-4747 or 202-501-4444 (international).

News

The Department of State maintains an online media center.

Passports

Passport information, including where to apply, is available online at the Bureau of Consular Affairs. For passport questions, travel emergencies, or to make an appointment at any regional passport agency, call the National Passport Information Center. Phone, 877-487-2778. TDD/TTY, 888-874-7793. Passport information is available around the clock, 7 days a week; customer service representatives are available on weekdays, 8 a.m.–10 p.m., eastern standard time, excluding Federal holidays. Correspondence may be submitted online, or direct it to the appropriate regional agency (http://travel.state.gov/passport) or to the Correspondence Branch, Passport Services, Room 510, 1111 Nineteenth Street NW., Washington, DC 20524.

Publications

Publications that are produced on a regular basis include "Background Notes" and the "Foreign Relations" series. The Bureau of Public Affairs also occasionally publishes brochures and other publications to inform the public of U.S. diplomatic efforts.

Social Media

The Department of State tweets announcements and other newsworthy items on Twitter.

The Department of State has a Facebook account.

The Department of State posts videos on its YouTube channel.

Telephone Directory

The Department's telephone directory can be accessed online.

Tips for U.S. Travelers

Information for Americans traveling abroad—including a traveler's checklist and tips on destinations, personal safety, health, and other topics—is available online from the Bureau of Consular Affairs.

Travel Alerts / Warnings

The Bureau of Consular Affairs Web site provides travel warnings and other information designed to help Americans travel safely abroad, as well as information on U.S. passports, visas, and downloadable applications.

Visas

For information on visas for foreigners wishing to enter the United States, visit the Bureau of Consular Affairs online or call 603-334-0700.

For further information, contact the Office of Public Communication, Public Information Service, Bureau of Public Affairs, Department of State, Washington, DC 20520. Phone, 202-647-6575.

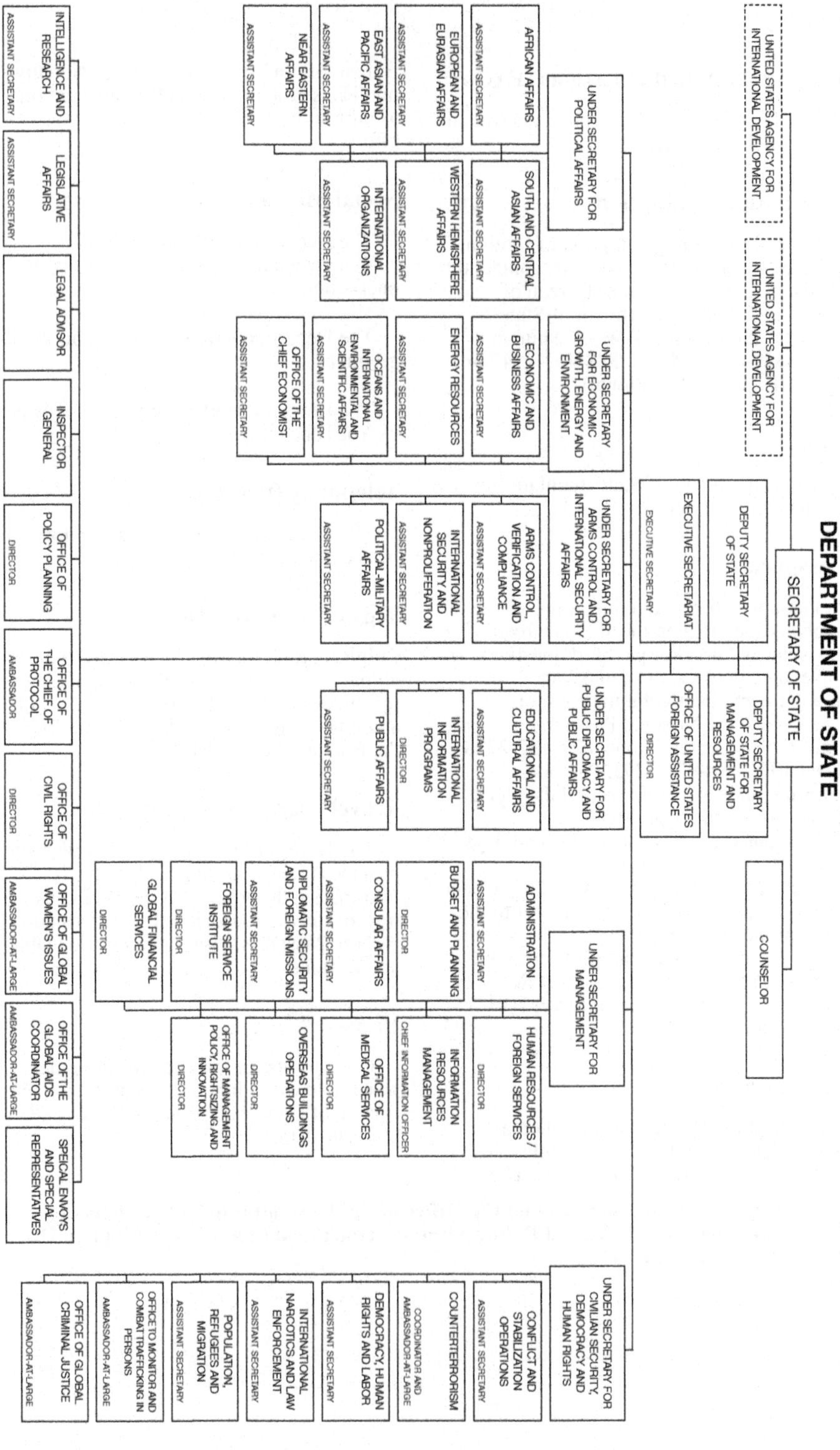
DEPARTMENT OF STATE
SECRETARY OF STATE
UNITED STATES AGENCY FOR INTERNATIONAL DEVELOPMENT
UNITED STATES AGENCY FOR INTERNATIONAL DEVELOPMENT
DEPUTY SECRETARY OF STATE
DEPUTY SECRETARY OF STATE FOR MANAGEMENT AND RESOURCES
COUNSELOR
EXECUTIVE SECRETARIAT EXECUTIVE SECRETARY
OFFICE OF UNITED STATES FOREIGN ASSISTANCE DIRECTOR
UNDER SECRETARY FOR POLITICAL AFFAIRS
AFRICAN AFFAIRS ASSISTANT SECRETARY
EUROPEAN AND EURASIAN AFFAIRS ASSISTANT SECRETARY
EAST ASIAN AND PACIFIC AFFAIRS ASSISTANT SECRETARY
NEAR EASTERN AFFAIRS ASSISTANT SECRETARY
SOUTH AND CENTRAL ASIAN AFFAIRS ASSISTANT SECRETARY
WESTERN HEMISPHERE AFFAIRS ASSISTANT SECRETARY
INTERNATIONAL ORGANIZATIONS ASSISTANT SECRETARY
UNDER SECRETARY FOR ECONOMIC GROWTH, ENERGY AND ENVIRONMENT
ECONOMIC AND BUSINESS AFFAIRS ASSISTANT SECRETARY
ENERGY RESOURCES ASSISTANT SECRETARY
OCEANS AND INTERNATIONAL ENVIRONMENTAL AND SCIENTIFIC AFFAIRS ASSISTANT SECRETARY
OFFICE OF THE CHIEF ECONOMIST ASSISTANT SECRETARY
UNDER SECRETARY FOR ARMS CONTROL AND INTERNATIONAL SECURITY AFFAIRS
ARMS CONTROL, VERIFICATION AND COMPLIANCE ASSISTANT SECRETARY
INTERNATIONAL SECURITY AND NONPROLIFERATION ASSISTANT SECRETARY
POLITICAL-MILITARY AFFAIRS ASSISTANT SECRETARY
UNDER SECRETARY FOR PUBLIC DIPLOMACY AND PUBLIC AFFAIRS
EDUCATIONAL AND CULTURAL AFFAIRS ASSISTANT SECRETARY
INTERNATIONAL INFORMATION PROGRAMS DIRECTOR
PUBLIC AFFAIRS ASSISTANT SECRETARY
UNDER SECRETARY FOR MANAGEMENT
ADMINISTRATION ASSISTANT SECRETARY
BUDGET AND PLANNING DIRECTOR
CONSULAR AFFAIRS ASSISTANT SECRETARY
DIPLOMATIC SECURITY AND FOREIGN MISSIONS ASSISTANT SECRETARY
FOREIGN SERVICE INSTITUTE DIRECTOR
GLOBAL FINANCIAL SERVICES DIRECTOR
HUMAN RESOURCES / FOREIGN SERVICES DIRECTOR
INFORMATION RESOURCES MANAGEMENT CHIEF INFORMATION OFFICER
OFFICE OF MEDICAL SERVICES DIRECTOR
OVERSEAS BUILDINGS OPERATIONS DIRECTOR
OFFICE OF MANAGEMENT POLICY, RIGHTSIZING AND INNOVATION DIRECTOR
UNDER SECRETARY FOR CIVILIAN SECURITY, DEMOCRACY AND HUMAN RIGHTS
CONFLICT AND STABILIZATION OPERATIONS ASSISTANT SECRETARY
COUNTERTERRORISM COORDINATOR AND AMBASSADOR-AT-LARGE
DEMOCRACY, HUMAN RIGHTS AND LABOR ASSISTANT SECRETARY
INTERNATIONAL NARCOTICS AND LAW ENFORCEMENT ASSISTANT SECRETARY
POPULATION, REFUGEES AND MIGRATION ASSISTANT SECRETARY
OFFICE TO MONITOR AND COMBAT TRAFFICKING IN PERSONS AMBASSADOR-AT-LARGE
OFFICE OF GLOBAL CRIMINAL JUSTICE AMBASSADOR-AT-LARGE
INTELLIGENCE AND RESEARCH ASSISTANT SECRETARY
LEGISLATIVE AFFAIRS ASSISTANT SECRETARY
LEGAL ADVISOR
INSPECTOR GENERAL
OFFICE OF POLICY PLANNING DIRECTOR
OFFICE OF THE CHIEF OF PROTOCOL AMBASSADOR
OFFICE OF CIVIL RIGHTS DIRECTOR
OFFICE OF GLOBAL WOMEN'S ISSUES AMBASSADOR-AT-LARGE
OFFICE OF THE GLOBAL AIDS COORDINATOR AMBASSADOR-AT-LARGE
SPEICAL ENVOYS AND SPECIAL REPRESENTATIVES

Department of Transportation

1200 New Jersey Avenue SE., Washington, DC 20590, 202-366-4000, *http://www.dot.gov*

SECRETARY OF TRANSPORTATION	Anthony R. Foxx
Deputy Secretary	Victor M. Mendez
Under Secretary of Transportation, Policy	Blair C. Anderson
Chief of Staff	Daniel E. Katz
General Counsel	Molly J. Moran, Acting
Inspector General	Calvin L. Scovel III
ASSISTANT SECRETARIES	
Administration	Jeff M. Marootian
Aviation and International Affairs	Jenny T. Rosenberg, Acting
Budget and Programs / Chief Financial Officer	Shoshana M. Lew
Governmental Affairs	Dana G. Gresham
Transportation Policy	Vincent G. White, Acting
Research and Technology	Gregory D. Winfree
DIRECTORS	
Departmental Office of Civil Rights	Leslie M. Proll, Acting
Executive Secretariat	Shawn G. Skelly
Office of Intelligence, Security and Emergency Response	Michael W. Lowder
Office of Small and Disadvantaged Business Utilization	Torre J. Jessup
Office of the Chief Information Officer	Richard L. McKinney
Public Affairs	Susan P. Lagana

[For the Department of Transportation statement of organization, see the Code of Federal Regulations, Title 49, Part 1, Subpart A]

The Department of Transportation establishes national transportation policy for highway planning and construction, motor carrier safety, urban mass transit, railroads, aviation, and the safety of waterways, ports, highways, and pipelines.

The Department of Transportation (DOT) was established by act of October 15, 1966, as amended (49 U.S.C. 102 and 102 note), "to assure the coordinated, effective administration of the transportation programs of the Federal Government" and to develop "national transportation policies and programs conducive to the provision of fast, safe, efficient, and convenient transportation at the lowest cost consistent therewith." It became operational in April 1967 and comprised elements transferred from eight other major departments and agencies.

Secretary

The Secretary of Transportation, who serves as the principal adviser to the President in all Federal transportation program matters, administers the DOT.

Under Secretary

The Under Secretary for Policy serves as a principal policy adviser to the Secretary and provides leadership in policy development for the DOT.

Aviation and International Affairs

The Office of the Assistant Secretary for Aviation and International Affairs develops, reviews, and coordinates policy for international transportation and develops, coordinates, and implements policy on economic regulation of the airline industry. The Office licenses U.S. and foreign carriers to serve in international air transportation and conducts carrier fitness determinations for carriers serving the United States. The Office participates in negotiations with foreign governments to develop multilateral and bilateral aviation and maritime policies on international transportation and trade and to coordinate cooperative agreements for the exchange of scientific and technical information. The Office also resolves complaints of unfair competitive practices in domestic and international air transportation, establishes international and intra-Alaska mail rates, determines the disposition of requests for approval and immunization from the antitrust laws of international aviation agreements, and administers the essential air service program.

For further information, contact the Office of the Assistant Secretary for Aviation and International Affairs. Phone, 202-366-8822.

Drug and Alcohol Policy and Compliance

The Office of Drug and Alcohol Policy and Compliance ensures that the Secretary's national and international drug and alcohol policies and goals are developed and implemented in a consistent, efficient, and effective manner within the transportation industry. Experts from the Office advise, counsel, and give recommendations on drugs and alcohol, as they pertain to the DOT and testing within the industry, to the Secretary.

For further information, contact the Office of Drug and Alcohol Policy and Compliance. Phone, 202-366-3784.

Intelligence, Security and Emergency Response

The Office of Intelligence, Security and Emergency Response ensures development, coordination, and execution of plans and procedures for the DOT to balance transportation security requirements with safety, mobility, and the Nation's economic needs. The Office monitors the Nation's transportation network on a continuous basis; advises the Secretary on incidents affecting transportation systems; leads on issues of national preparedness, response, and transportation security; briefs the Secretary on transportation-related intelligence; performs the DOT's National Response Framework Emergency Support Function responsibilities; coordinates departmental participation in emergency preparedness and response exercises under the National Training and Exercise Program; administers the DOT's Continuity of Government and Continuity of Operations programs; and serves as the DOT representative for emergency planning for civil aviation support to NATO and other allies.

For further information, contact the Office of Intelligence, Security and Emergency Response. Phone, 202-366-6525.

Transportation Policy

The Office of the Assistant Secretary for Transportation Policy analyzes, develops, articulates, and reviews policies and plans for all transportation modes. It also develops, coordinates, and evaluates public policy on safety, energy, and environmental initiatives that affect air, surface, marine, and pipeline transportation. It maintains policy and economic oversight of DOT regulatory programs and legislative initiatives. The Office also analyzes the economic and institutional implications of current and emerging transportation policy issues, transportation infrastructure finances, and new transportation technologies.

For further information, contact the Office of Transportation Policy. Phone, 202-366-8979.

Research and Technology

The Office of the Assistant Secretary for Research and Technology (OST–R) was created by title I, division L, of the Department of Transportation Appropriations Act, 2014 (49 USC 112 note), which transferred the authorities, functions, personnel, and powers and duties of the former Research and Innovative Technology Administration to the OST–R. The Office coordinates, facilitates, and reviews DOT research and development programs and activities; performs transportation statistics research, analysis, and reporting; and promotes innovative technologies for improving transportation systems. The OST–R is composed of the staff from the Bureau of Transportation Statistics, the Volpe National Transportation Systems Center, the Transportation Safety Institute, and the Office of Research, Development, and Technology.

Sources of Information

Administrations

The "Our Administrations" Web page provides convenient Internet access to the home pages of the DOT's administrations.

Aviation Consumer Protection

For information on air travelers' rights or for assistance in resolving consumer problems with providers of commercial air transportation services, contact the Consumer Affairs Division. Phone, 202-366-2220.

The Office of Aviation Enforcement and Proceedings produces the "Air Travel Consumer Report" each month. The report makes information on the quality of airline services accessible to consumers. Issues of the consumer report are posted on the DOT's Web site in Portable Document Format (PDF). Phone, 202-366-2220. TTY, 202-366-0511.

Blog

"Fast Lane" is the DOT's official blog.

Business Opportunities

Contact the Office of the Senior Procurement Executive. Phone, 202-366-4263. Information is also available on the "Small Business" Web page.

Civil Rights

For information on equal employment opportunity, nondiscrimination in DOT employment and transportation services, or the Department's disadvantaged business enterprise certification appeals program, contact the Director, Departmental Office of Civil Rights. Phone, 202-366-4648.

Employment

The DOT employs administrators and managers, air traffic controllers, aviation safety specialists, clerical staff, electronics maintenance technicians, and engineers—aeronautical, automotive, civil, electrical, highway, and general. For further information, contact the Office of the Secretary–Human Resource Operations, 1200 New Jersey Avenue SE., Room W75–340, Washington, DC 20590. Phone, 202-366-9391 or 800-525-2878.

Freedom of Information Act (FOIA)

The FOIA gives information seekers the right to access DOT records, unless the Departement reasonably foresees that the release of the information would harm an interest protected by one or more of the nine FOIA exemptions or the release is prohibited by law. The DOT's responsibility is to provide an information seeker with copies of the documents or records or the portions of them that he or she is entitled to receive under the law.

Motor Vehicle Safety

To report vehicle safety problems, get motor vehicle and highway safety information, or request consumer information publications, visit the National Highway Traffic Safety Administration's SafeCar.gov Web site or call its vehicle safety hotline. Phone, 888-327-4236. TTY, 800-424-9153. Complaints also can be filed online.

News

The DOT posts press releases on its Web site.

Office of Inspector General (OIG)

To report abuse, fraud, or waste, contact the DOT Inspector General, 1200 New Jersey Avenue SE., West Building–7th floor, Washington, DC 20590. Phone, 202-366-1461 or 800-424-9071.

Open Government

The DOT supports the Open Government initiative by promoting the principles of collaboration, participation, and transparency.

Plain Language

The DOT seeks to comply with the Plain Writing Act of 2010. If a DOT document or Web page is difficult to understand, please contact the Department via email and point out the lack of clarity.

Policy Initiatives

The DOT posts current policy initiatives on its Web site.

Publications

The DOT and its operating agencies issue publications on a variety of subjects. Some of these publications are available from the issuing administration or from the Government Publishing Office.

Other publications are available from the National Technical Information Service, 5285 Port Royal Road, Springfield, VA 22151.

Reading Rooms

Contact the Public Docket, Room W12–140, 1200 New Jersey Avenue SE., Washington, DC 20590. Phone, 800-647-5527. DOT administrations and their regional offices maintain reading rooms for public use. Contact the appropriate administration at the address or phone number indicated in the relevant section above or below. Other reading rooms are located at the Technical and Law Libraries: Technical Library, Room 2200, 1200 New Jersey Avenue SE., Washington, DC 20590. Phone, 202-366-0745. Law Library, Room W12–300, 1200 New Jersey Avenue SE., Washington, DC 20590. Phone, 202-366-0746.

Social Media

The DOT has a YouTube channel and maintains Facebook, Flickr, Instagram, LinkedIn, and Twitter accounts.

For further information, contact the Department of Transportation, Office of Public Affairs, 1200 New Jersey Avenue SE., Washington, DC 20590. Phone, 202-366-5580.

Federal Aviation Administration

800 Independence Avenue SW., Washington, DC 20591, 202-366-4000, 866-835-5322, *http://www.faa.gov*

ADMINISTRATOR	Michael P. Huerta
Deputy Administrator	Victoria B. Wassmer, Acting
Chief of Staff	Michelle D. Schwartz

The Federal Aviation Administration (FAA), formerly the Federal Aviation Agency, was established by the Federal Aviation Act of 1958 (72 Stat. 731). The Administration became a component of the Department of Transportation in 1967, pursuant to the Department of Transportation Act (49 U.S.C. 106). The FAA regulates civil aviation and U.S. commercial space transportation, maintains and operates air traffic control and navigation systems for civil and military aircraft, and develops and administers programs involving aviation safety and the National Airspace System.

Activities

Air Navigation Facilities

The FAA locates and positions, constructs or installs, maintains, operates, and assures the quality of Federal air navigation electronic and visual aids. At flight service stations, airport traffic control towers, and air route traffic control centers, the Administration operates and maintains computer systems, radar facilities, and voice-data communications and visual display equipment.

Airport Programs

The Administration maintains a national plan of airport requirements, administers a grant program for development of public-use airports to assure and improve safety and to meet current and future airport capacity needs, evaluates the environmental effects of airport development, and administers an airport noise compatibility program. It also develops standards for and technical guidance on airport planning, design, operations, and safety and provides grants to assist public agencies in airport system and master planning and airport development and improvement.

Airspace and Air Traffic Management

FAA activities center on the safe and efficient utilization of the navigable airspace. To achieve this goal, the Administration operates a network of airport traffic control towers, air route traffic control centers, and flight service stations. It develops air traffic rules and regulations and allocates airspace use. It also provides air traffic security control that meets national defense requirements.

Civil Aviation Abroad

Under the Federal Aviation Act of 1958 and the International Aviation Facilities Act (49 U.S.C. app. 1151), the FAA promotes aviation safety and supports civil aviation abroad. FAA experts exchange aeronautical information with foreign counterparts; certify foreign airmen, mechanics, and repair shops; provide technical aid and training; negotiate bilateral airworthiness agreements with other countries; and participate in international conferences.

Commercial Space Transportation

The Administration regulates and supports the U.S. commercial space transportation industry. It licenses commercial space launch facilities and private sector launches of space payloads on expendable vehicles. It also sets insurance requirements for the protection of persons and property and ensures that space transportation activities comply with U.S. domestic and foreign policy.

Registration

The Aircraft Registry establishes and maintains the record of every U.S. civil aircraft. Buyers seeking information on aircraft they want to acquire, banks that finance aircraft purchases, aviation historians, and law enforcement and security agencies rely on the registry. An aircraft record contains information on the aircraft's registered owner, its airworthiness, and on recorded aircraft security interests.

Research, Engineering, and Development

The research, engineering, and development activities of the FAA provide the systems, procedures, facilities, and devices needed for a safe and efficient air navigation and air traffic control system for civil aviation and air defense. The Administration also performs an aeromedical research function: It applies knowledge gained from its research program and the work of others to improve civil aviation safety and the safety, health, and efficiency of FAA employees. The Administration also supports the development and testing of aircraft and their parts.

Safety Regulation

The FAA issues and enforces regulations and minimum standards affecting the manufacture, operation, and maintenance of aircraft. It also certifies airmen and airports that serve air carriers.

Test and Evaluation

The FAA tests and evaluates specified items such as aviation systems, subsystems, equipment, devices, materials, concepts, or procedures at any phase in the cycle of their development from conception to acceptance, to implementation. At key decision points, it also carries out assigned independent testing.

Other Programs

The FAA administers the Aviation Insurance Program, which provides insurance products to cover U.S. domestic air transportation industry needs that are not adequately met by the commercial insurance market. The Administration develops specifications for the preparation of aeronautical charts. It also publishes current information on airways and airport service; issues technical publications for the improvement of in-flight safety, airport planning and design, and other aeronautical activities; and serves as the executive administration for the operation and maintenance of the DOT automated payroll and personnel systems.

Contact information for field and regional offices is available on the "Offices" Web page.

Sources of Information

A–Z Index

The FAA Web site features an alphabetical index to help visitors browse its content or search for information.

Aircraft Registry

The FAA maintains a registry that allows users to search aircraft registration information online.

Airlines

The Air Traffic Control System Command Center Web site features a list of links for the Web sites of airlines.

Airmen Certification

The FAA posts answers to frequently asked questions dealing with airmen certification on its Web site.

Business Opportunities

Registration with the System for Award Management is required for doing business with the FAA.

The FAA's small business development program supports the procurement of goods and services from qualified small businesses.

Contact the FAA

Information for finding the appropriate point of contact or reporting an issue to the FAA is available online.

Data / Research

The FAA conducts research on commercial and general aviation. It posts information on how the research is carried out, the resulting data and statistics, and grant data and funding information.

Employment

The FAA offers civil aviation career opportunities in air traffic control, acquisition, contracts, engineering, information technology, safety and security, and other fields.

Field and Regional Offices

Contact information for field and regional offices is available on the FAA Web site.

Flight Delays

The FAA's Air Traffic Control System Command Center provides status information, which is not flight specific, for general airport conditions nationwide.

Email, personal digital assistants (PDAs), pagers, phones, and wireless devices can be used to monitor the real-time operating status of the Nation's largest airports and receive delay information from the FAA.

Freedom of Information Act (FOIA)

The FOIA gives anybody the right to access information from the Federal Government. The law requires agencies to disclose information that is requested, unless that information is protected from public disclosure.

FAA posts a lot of information on its Web site. Before making a formal FOIA request, first look through what is immediately available, particularly through the contents of the FAA's electronic FOIA library. The desired information already may be accessible.

Frequently Asked Questions (FAQs)

The FAA posts answers to FAQs on its Web site.

Glossary

The Air Traffic Control System Command Center maintains a glossary of air traffic control management acronyms and terms.

History

The FAA's Web site features a timeline of aerospace history that starts on December 17, 1903, with Orville and Wilbur Wright's first self-propelled airplane flight.

News

The FAA posts factsheets, news items and updates, press releases, speeches, and testimony on its Web site.

NextGen

NextGen is a comprehensive suite of state-of-the-art technologies and procedures that enable aircraft to move more directly between two distant points. These technologies will help passengers reach their destinations on schedule and mitigate environmental damage by reducing fuel consumption. To learn more about NextGen and the improvements that it will bring to air travel in the United States, visit its Web site.

Social Media

The FAA has accounts on Facebook, Flickr, Instagram, LinkedIn, and Twitter, as well as a channel on YouTube.

Wildlife Strikes

Aircraft and wildlife in the United States collide on occasion. Wildlife strikes almost always involve birds; however, the FAA also has received reports of alligator, bat, coyote, deer, skunk, and turtle strikes. The most frequently struck birds are gulls, but ducks and geese cause more damage per strike. The FAA's National Wildlife Strike Database contains the information needed for telling the full story of collisions involving aircraft and animals.

The wildlife strike reporting system helps the FAA collect the information used to build the National Wildlife Strike Database. An online form is available for submitting a strike report.

For further information, contact the Federal Aviation Administration, Office of Communications, 800 Independence Avenue SW., Washington, DC 20591. Phone, 202-267-3883. Fax, 202-267-5039.

Federal Highway Administration

1200 New Jersey Avenue SE., Washington, DC 20590, 202-366-0650, *http://www.fhwa.dot.gov*

ADMINISTRATOR	Gregory G. Nadeau
Deputy Administrator	David S. Kim
Executive Director	Walter C. Waidelich, Jr.

The Federal Highway Administration (FHWA) was established as an agency of the Department of Transportation by the Department of Transportation Act (49 U.S.C. 104). Title 23 of the United States Code and other supporting legislation authorize the Administration's various activities.

The FHWA improves mobility on our Nation's highways through national leadership, innovation, and program delivery. The Administration works with Federal, State, and local agencies as well as with other stakeholders and partners to maintain and improve the National Highway System, which includes the Interstate System and other roads of importance for national defense and mobility. The FHWA works to increase the National Highway System's safety and to minimize its traffic congestion. The FHWA ensures that America's roads and highways remain safe, technologically up-to-date, and environmentally friendly.

Through surface transportation programs, innovative and traditional financing mechanisms, and new types of pavement and operational technology, the FHWA helps people and goods move more efficiently throughout the Nation. The Administration also improves the efficiency of highway and road connections to other modes of transportation. The Federal-aid Highway Program's budget is primarily divided between Federal-aid funding and the Federal Lands Highway Program.

Activities

Federal-aid Highway Program

The Federal-Aid Highway Program supports State highway systems, providing financial assistance for the construction, maintenance and operations of the Nation's 3.9 million-mile highway network, which includes the Interstate Highway System, primary highways, and secondary local roads. The FHWA implements the Federal-aid Highway Program in cooperation with State and local governments.

Federal Lands Highway Program

The Office of Federal Lands Highway promotes effective, efficient, and reliable administration for a coordinated program of Federal public roads and bridges; protects and enhances the Nation's natural resources; and gives transportation access to Native Americans. The Office provides financial resources and engineering assistance for public roads that meet the transportation needs of Federal and Indian lands. These services are provided in all 50 States, Puerto Rico, U.S. Territories, and the District of Columbia through the Office's Headquarters and its eastern, central, and western Federal Lands Highway division offices.

Sources of Information

All-American Roads / National Scenic Byways

America's Byways—which include the National Scenic Byways and All-American Roads—is an umbrella term referring to the collection of 150 roads that the Secretary of Transportation selects for inclusion based on distinctiveness and diverseness.

Business Opportunities

FHWA programs generate a large number of contracting and procurement opportunities.

The Office of Acquisition and Grants Management manages most FHWA contracting opportunities. Phone, 202-366-4232.

Core Topics

The "Core Highway Topics" Web page features a topical, alphabetical list. The topics are categorized according to nine headings: environment, Federal and Indian lands, highway funding, international, research and technologies, road operations and congestion, roads and bridges, road users, and safety.

Employment

The FHWA operates offices throughout the country and hires professionals with expertise in a variety of fields to carry out its mission.

The FHWA consistently ranks high among agency subcomponents in the Partnership for Public Service's "Best Places To Work in the Federal Government" list.

Environment

The "Air Quality and Climate Change Highlights" newsletter is available on the FHWA Web site.

Federal-Aid Essentials

Federal-aid Essentials offers an online library of informational videos and resources for local public agencies. Each video addresses a single topic and condenses the complex regulations and requirements of the Federal-aid Highway Program into basic concepts and illustrated examples.

Field and Division Offices

The FHWA comprises a headquarters office in Washington, DC; a Federal-aid division office in each State, Puerto Rico, and the District of Columbia; four metropolitan offices—Chicago, Los Angeles, New York City, Philadelphia—that serve as extensions of the corresponding Federal-aid division offices; and three Federal Lands Highway division offices.

Freedom of Information Act (FOIA)

The FOIA establishes a presumption that records in the possession of agencies and departments of the Federal Government's executive branch are available to the public. The statute sets standards for determining when Government records must be made available and which records may be withheld. It also gives information seekers specific legal rights and provides administrative and judicial remedies when access is denied. Most importantly, the FOIA requires that Federal agencies provide, to the fullest extent possible, access to and disclosure of information pertaining to the Government's business.

The FHWA maintains an electronic FOIA reading room. It contains records that are often requested under the statute.

Glossary

The FHWA Web site features a glossary of transportation planning terms and acronyms.

History

The FHWA Web site features a general highway history.

Infrastructure

The FHWA's Web site offers a trove of information on the following infrastructure topics: asset management, bridges and structures, construction, design, Federal-aid Program administration, Federal-aid programs and special funding, geotechnical, hydraulics, pavement, preservation, and transportation performance management.

Libraries

The FHWA research library is located in the Turner-Fairbank Highway Research Center in McLean, VA. It is open on weekdays, excluding Federal holidays, 7:30–4 p.m. Phone, 202-493-3172. Fax, 202-493-3495.

Each FHWA office maintains accessibility information that relates to its own program. The accessibility resource library supports the effort to organize information relating to the Americans with Disabilities Act and other accessibility resources that may affect FHWA projects.

Newsroom

The FHWA posts press releases, as well as photos and videos, speeches and testimony, on its Web site and YouTube channel.

Resource Center / Technical Service Teams

The FHWA's technical service teams are organized into 12 activity areas: air quality, civil rights, construction and program management, environment and realty, finance services, geotechnical, hydraulics, operations, pavement and materials, planning, safety and design, and structures. Contact information for these teams and information on their activities, products, and services are available online in the Resource Center.

Social Media

The FHWA tweets announcements and other newsworthy items on Twitter.

The FHWA maintains a page on Facebook.

The FHWA posts videos on its YouTube channel.

Staff Directories

The headquarters organizational directory, key field personnel directory, and Washington headquarters fax numbers are available on the FHWA's Web site.

For further information, contact the Federal Highway Administration, Office of Public Affairs, 1200 New Jersey Avenue, SE., Washington, DC 20590. Phone, 202-366-0660.

Federal Motor Carrier Safety Administration

1200 New Jersey Avenue SE., Washington, DC 20590, 202-366-2519, *http://www.fmcsa.dot.gov*

ADMINISTRATOR	T.F. Scott Darling III
Deputy Administrator	Daphne Y. Jefferson
Chief Safety Officer / Assistant Administrator	John Van Steenburg

The Federal Motor Carrier Safety Administration (FMCSA) was established within the Department of Transportation on January 1, 2000, pursuant to the Motor Carrier Safety Improvement Act of 1999 (49 U.S.C. 113).

Formerly a part of the Federal Highway Administration, the FMCSA reduces commercial motor vehicle-related fatalities and injuries. Administration activities increase the safety of motor carrier operations by enforcing safety regulations—targeting high-risk commercial drivers and carriers; improving safety information systems and commercial motor vehicle technologies; strengthening equipment and operating standards; and increasing safety awareness. When carrying out these activities, the Administration works with representatives of the motor carrier industry, labor safety interest groups, and Federal, State, and local enforcement agencies.

Activities

Commercial Licensing

The FMCSA develops standards to test and license commercial motor vehicle drivers.

Data / Analysis

The FMCSA collects and disseminates data on motor carrier safety and directs resources to improve motor carrier safety.

Regulatory Compliance / Enforcement

The FMCSA operates a program to improve safety performance and remove high-risk carriers from the Nation's highways.

Research / Technology

The FMCSA coordinates research and development to improve the safety of motor carrier operations and commercial motor vehicles and drivers.

Safety Assistance

The FMCSA provides States with financial assistance for roadside inspections and other commercial motor vehicle safety programs.

Other Activities

The FMCSA supports the development of unified motor carrier safety requirements and procedures throughout North America. It participates in international technical organizations and committees to help share best-practices in motor carrier safety worldwide. It enforces regulations ensuring safe highway transportation of hazardous materials and maintains a task force to identify and investigate carriers of household goods that exhibit an unmistakable pattern of consumer abuse.

Sources of Information

Bicyclists / Pedestrians

Bicyclists and pedestrians share roads with large trucks and buses. The FMCSA Web site features resources promoting safety issues affecting riders, walkers, and drivers.

Certified Medical Examiners

Inclusion in the National Registry of Certified Medical Examiners is limited to medical professionals who complete training and pass an exam on the FMCSA's physical qualification standards.

Commercial Carriers

The FMCSA Web site features resources to help carrier companies with registration and safety and regulatory matters.

The FMCSA Web site features resources—regulatory information and safety publications—to help passenger carriers comply with regulations and operate safely.

Commercial Drivers

The FMCSA Web site features driver resources to promote safety and for registration and licensing.

Company Safety Records

The FMCSA maintains Web sites that provide convenient access to safety-related information. To perform a search, a user must know a company's name, USDOT number, or motor carrier number.

Data / Statistics

The annual "Pocket Guide to Large Truck and Bus Statistics" highlights the FMCSA's role in collecting and analyzing data on large trucks and buses. The pocket guide is a compilation of statistics from the overall state of the industry to enforcement activity, details on traffic violations and other incidents, the costs of crashes, and more.

The Analysis Division compiles the information used for "Large Truck and Bus Crash Facts," an annual report containing descriptive statistics on fatal, injurious, and property-damage-only crashes involving large trucks and buses.

Employment

The FMCSA posts job announcements on the USAJobs Web site. Application tips, information for students and recent graduates, and reasons for pursuing a career at the FMCSA are available on its Web site. Phone, 800-832-5660.

Freedom of Information Act (FOIA)

The FMCSA supports efforts to create a more open and transparent Federal Government, and it conscientiously carries out its FOIA responsibilities. The FMCSA ensures that nonexempt documents or records are accessible to anyone who properly files a FOIA request. Phone, 202-366-2960. Fax, 202-385-2335.

The FMCSA's electronic reading room contains frequently requested records, as well as final opinions and orders, policy statements, and staff manuals.

Frequently Asked Questions (FAQs)

The FMCSA provides answers to FAQs on its Web site.

Grants

State and local government agencies in the 50 States and the District of Columbia, as well as in American Samoa, Guam, Puerto Rico, and the Northern Mariana and the U.S. Virgin Islands may apply for safety grant funding.

Look Before You Book

The FMCSA Web site features resources to assist travel planners or those chartering buses for sport events, field trips, or other group activities. Safety tips and information, software applications (apps) to research bus operators, and information on reporting safety violations are available on the "Look Before You Book" Web pages.

Bus travel safety kits for seniors, students, and those traveling to faith-based events are available on "Look Before You Book."

Newsroom

The FMCSA posts events, news releases, speeches, and testimony on its Web site.

Protect Your Move

The "Protect Your Move" Web pages feature a trove of information on and resources for planning a move, selecting a mover, and filing a moving fraud complaint.

Safety Violations

Safety, service, or discrimination issues involving a bus or truck or moving company or a cargo tank facility? If so, file a complaint on the National Consumer Complaint Database Web site or by phone on weekdays, 8 a.m.–8 p.m., eastern time. Phone, 888-368-7238.

Service Centers / Field Offices

Contact information for service centers and field offices is available on the FMCSA Web site. Phone, 800-832-5660.

Social Media

The FMCSA tweets announcements and other newsworthy items on Twitter.

The FMCSA has a Facebook account.

USDOT Numbers

The FMCSA Web site features an interactive tool that can determine whether or not a commercial vehicle requires a USDOT number.

Veterans

The FMCSA helps veterans find employment in the motor carrier industry. Several provisions in the Fixing America's Surface Transportation (FAST) Act support this effort.

For further information, contact the Federal Motor Carrier Safety Administration, 1200 New Jersey Avenue SE., Washington, DC 20590. Phone, 202-366-2519.

Federal Railroad Administration

1200 New Jersey Avenue, SE., West Building, Washington, DC 20590, 202-493-6014, *http://www.fra.dot.gov*

ADMINISTRATOR	Sarah E. Feinberg
Deputy Administrator	Amitabha Bose
Executive Director	Patrick T. Warren, Acting

The Federal Railroad Administration (FRA) was created pursuant to section 3(e)(1) of the Department of Transportation Act of 1966 (49 U.S.C. 103). The Administration promulgates and enforces rail safety regulations, administers railroad financial assistance programs, conducts research and development to improve railroad safety and national rail transportation policy, provides for the rehabilitation of Northeast Corridor rail passenger service, and consolidates Government support of rail transportation activities.

Activities

Passenger and Freight Services

The FRA's passenger rail activities include administering Federal grants and loans to Amtrak, Alaska Railroad, and high-speed rail; supporting the Secretary of Transportation in his or her role as a member of Amtrak's board of directors; providing guidance and analysis of intercity passenger rail services and high-speed rail. Its freight rail activities include supporting current freight rail market share and growth and developing strategies to attract 50 percent of all shipments 500 miles or more to intermodal rail. The Administration's Office of Railroad Policy and Development implements programs that provide financial support, research and development, and analysis and guidance for the freight rail industry and its stakeholders.

Railroad Safety

The Administration administers and enforces the Federal laws and regulations that promote railroad safety, and it exercises jurisdiction over all areas of rail safety under the Rail Safety Act of 1970—track maintenance, inspection standards, equipment standards, operating practices.

Railroad and related industry equipment, facilities, and records are inspected and required reports are reviewed. The Administration also educates the public about safety at highway rail grade crossings and the danger of trespassing on rail property.

Research and Development

The FRA's research and development program relies on basic and applied research and on the development of innovations and solutions to ensure the efficient, reliable, and safe movement of people and goods. Safety is the principal driver of the research and development program.

Transportation Test Center

The Administration tests and evaluates conventional and advanced railroad systems and components at the Transportation Test Center, Inc. Private sector companies and the Governments of Canada, Japan, and the United States use the facility to study the operation of conventional and advanced systems under controlled conditions. Amtrak tests new high-speed locomotives and trains at the Center, and the Federal Transit Administration uses it for testing urban rapid transit vehicles.

A list of the Federal Railroad Administration's eight regional offices—California, Georgia, Illinois, Massachusetts, Missouri, Pennsylvania, Texas, and the District of Columbia —is available on the "Regional Offices" Web page.

Sources of Information

Business Opportunities

The FRA's Web site explains how to become eligible for doing business and how to identify business opportunities with the FRA. The Web site also features a database of small business vendors.

Electronic Library (E-library)

An e-library offers convenient access to all the documents that are found on the FRA's public Web site.

Employment

The FRA relies heavily on railroad safety inspectors—hazardous materials, motive power and equipment, operating practices, signals and train control, and track inspectors—to carry out its mission. Safety inspectors inspect for compliance with Federal laws, regulations, rules, and standards; conduct accident investigations and report on their findings; and seek correction of unsafe conditions. They also testify as expert witnesses in civil suits. These jobs require skill in evaluation, factfinding, and report writing; comprehension and application of technical and regulatory standards; an ability to build rapport with individuals and organizations; and knowledge of methods used in installation, operation, and maintenance or manufacturing of railroad equipment and systems.

Freedom of Information Act (FOIA)

Any person—U.S. citizens, foreign nationals, as well as those representing organizations, associations, and universities—can file a FOIA request. All FOIA requests must be submitted in writing and are processed in the Office of Chief Counsel at FRA headquarters in Washington, DC.

To comply with the Electronic Freedom of Information Act (E–FOIA) Amendments of 1996, agencies must make some categories of records available to the public on an ongoing basis.

Horn Noise

Noise from transportation systems, including rail operations, often produces adverse environmental effects. The FRA posts answers to frequently asked questions on horn noise.

Maps

The FRA Web site features a Geographic Information System safety map.

News

The FRA posts news items on its Web site.

Railroad Crossings / Trespassing

FRA programs have helped to reduce the number of railroad crossing and trespassing fatalities by 54% over the last two decades. The Railroad Crossing Safety and Trespasser Prevention Division seeks to continue this trend. Information on and resources for railroad crossing safety and preventing trespassing along railroad rights-of-way are available online.

Railroad Safety

The Office of Safety Analysis posts railroad safety information—data related to railroad accidents and incidents, including highway-rail grade crossing accidents, rail equipment accidents, and employee injuries and illnesses—on its Web site.

The FRA monitors the occurrence of train accidents and incidents and investigates serious events to determine their cause and to assess compliance with safety laws and regulations. Detailed information on these investigations is available on the FRA's Web site.

Regional Offices

Contact information for the FRA's eight regional offices is available on its Web site.

Research / Development

The Office of Research and Development is organized into four divisions and works in 10 program areas. An online table shows where the four divisions and 10 program areas intersect with the most frequent causes of railroad accidents and incidents.

Social Media

The FRA posts photographs and tweets announcements and other newsworthy items on Twitter.

The FRA has a Facebook page.

The FRA posts videos on its YouTube channel.

For further information, contact the Federal Railroad Administration, Office of Public Affairs, 1200 New Jersey Avenue SE., Washington, DC 20590. Phone, 202-493-6024. Fax, 202-493-6481.

Federal Transit Administration

1200 New Jersey Avenue SE., Washington, DC 20590, 202-366-4043, *http://www.fta.dot.gov*

ADMINISTRATOR	Carolyn Flowers, Acting
Deputy Administrator	Carolyn Flowers
Executive Director	Matthew J. Welbes

[For the Federal Transit Administration statement of organization, see the Code of Federal Regulations, Title 49, Part 601]

The Federal Transit Administration (FTA), formerly the Urban Mass Transportation Administration, was established as an operating administration of the U.S. Department of Transportation by section 1 of Reorganization Plan No. 2 of 1968 (5 U.S.C. app. 1), effective July 1, 1968. The FTA helps America's communities by developing improved public transportation and providing financial assistance to State and local governments to finance public transportation systems and carry out national transit goals and policy.

Programs

Alternatives Analysis

The Alternatives Analysis program provides grants to help identify public transportation needs and the costs and benefits of various transportation strategies for a defined travel corridor. The results of these studies may be the selection of a locally preferred transportation alternative, which is the first step for developing viable projects for possible future funding under the New Starts and Small Starts program.

For further information, call the Office of Program Management. Phone, 202-366-2053.

Capital Investment

The Capital Investment program helps finance the acquisition, construction, reconstruction, and improvement of facilities and equipment for public transportation service in urban areas. The Capital Investment program makes available three types of funds: fixed guideway modernization funds for rolling stock renewal, safety-related improvements, and signal and power modernization; new and small starts funds for construction of new fixed guideway systems or extensions to existing fixed guideway systems or corridor based rapid bus systems; and bus and bus facilities funds for the acquisition of buses and rolling stock, ancillary equipment, and the construction of bus facilities.

For further information, call the Office of Program Management. Phone, 202-366-2053.

Clean Fuels Grants

The Clean Fuels Grants program helps nonattainment and maintenance areas achieve or maintain the National Ambient Air Quality Standards for ozone and carbon monoxide, and it supports emerging clean fuel and advanced propulsion technologies for transit buses and markets for those technologies. The program funds purchasing or leasing clean fuel buses, including buses that employ a lightweight composite primary structure and vans for use in revenue service; constructing or leasing clean fuel bus facilities, including electrical recharging facilities and related equipment; and projects involving clean fuel, biodiesel, hybrid electric, or zero emissions technology buses.

For further information, call the Office of Program Management. Phone, 202-366-2053.

Elderly Persons and Persons With Disabilities

The Transportation for Elderly Persons and Persons With Disabilities program provides financial assistance to private nonprofit agencies for the transportation needs of elderly persons and persons with disabilities in places where public services are unavailable, insufficient, or inappropriate; to public bodies approved by the State to coordinate services for elderly persons or persons with disabilities; and to public bodies that certify to the Governor that no nonprofit corporation or association is readily available in an area to provide the service. Funds are allocated by formula to the States. Local organizations apply for funding through a designated State agency.

For further information, call the Office of Program Management. Phone, 202-366-2053.

Job Access and Reverse Commuting

The Job Access and Reverse Commute program addresses the transportation challenges faced by welfare recipients and low-income persons seeking or maintaining employment. The program provides capital and planning and operating expenses for projects that transport low income individuals to and from jobs and employment-related activities and for projects that support reverse commuting. Many new entry level jobs are located in suburban areas: Low-income individuals have difficulty accessing these jobs from their inner city, urban, or rural neighborhoods. Many entry level-jobs also require working late or on weekends when conventional transit services are either reduced or nonexistent. Many employment related-trips also are complex, involving multiple destinations.

For further information, call the Office of Program Management. Phone, 202-366-2053.

New Freedom

The New Freedom formula grants program supports new public transportation services that surpass the requirements of the Americans with Disabilities Act (ADA) of 1990. The program makes capital and operating funding available to private nonprofit organizations, State and local governmental authorities, and operators of public transportation services, including private operators of public transportation services. Eligible projects must benefit individuals with disabilities: Projects must assist them with transportation—including transportation to and from jobs and employment services—and remove barriers to transportation.

For further information, call the Office of Program Management. Phone, 202-366-2053.

Nonurban Area Assistance

The Other Than Urbanized Areas formula grants program provides funding to States to support public transportation in rural areas—with populations under 50,000. The program enhances people's access in nonurbanized areas to health care, shopping, education, employment, public services, and recreation; assists in the maintenance, development, improvement, and use of public transportation systems in nonurbanized areas; encourages and facilitates the most efficient use of all transportation funds used to provide passenger transportation in nonurbanized areas through the coordination of programs and services; helps develop and support intercity bus transportation; and promotes the participation of private transportation providers in nonurbanized transportation.

For further information, call the Office of Program Management. Phone, 202-366-2053.

Planning

The Office of Planning and Environment supports the development of information that Federal, State, and local officials use to make transportation investment decisions. With FHWA partners, the Office co-administers a national planning program that provides funding, guidance, oversight, and technical support to State and local transportation agencies. The FTA's 10 region offices and FHWA's 52 division offices work to convey the program to State and local governments and other transportation agencies.

For further information, call the Office of Planning and Environment. Phone, 202-366-4033.

Research and Technology

The FTA conducts research, development, demonstration, deployment, and evaluation projects to improve public transportation services. The FTA administers the Bus Testing, International Public Transportation, National Research and Technology, and Transit Cooperative Research Programs. Through the Transit Investments for Greenhouse Gas and Energy Reduction (TIGGER) program, the Administration works with public transportation agencies to implement new strategies for lowering greenhouse gas emissions and to reduce energy use within transit operations. The FTA has five priority research areas: bicycles and transit, bus rapid transit, environmental sustainability, livable and sustainable communities, and state of good repair.

For further information, call the Office of Research, Demonstration and Innovation. Phone, 202-366-4052.

Rural Transit Assistance

The Rural Transit Assistance Program provides a funding source to help design and implement training and technical assistance projects and other support services tailored to meet the needs of transit operators in nonurbanized areas. States, local governments, and providers of rural transit services can receive program funds. States may use the funds to support nonurbanized transit activities in four areas: training, technical assistance, research, and related support services.

For further information, call the Office of Program Management. Phone, 202-366-2053.

Safety

The Office of Transit Safety and Oversight administers a national safety program and oversees compliance with it. Based on FTA legislative, policy, and regulatory requirements, the program helps further the nationwide provision of transit service that is equitable, reliable, and safe.

For further information, call the Office of Transit Safety and Oversight. Phone, 202-366-1783.

Training and Technical Assistance

The Administration funds the National Transit Institute at Rutgers, The State University of New Jersey. Working with the Institute, the FTA develops and offers training courses on transit operations, planning, workforce performance, and productivity. Institute courses are offered at locations nationwide on a variety of subjects. Current course offerings are posted online.

For further information, call the Office of Research, Demonstration and Innovation. Phone, 202-366-4052.

Transit in Parks

The Paul S. Sarbanes Transit in Parks Program provides funding for alternative transportation projects in and around National Parks and other Federal recreation areas. Alternative transportation includes bicycle, ferry, pedestrian trail, shuttle bus, and other forms of public or nonmotorized transportation. These projects reduce congestion, protect sensitive natural and cultural treasures, and enhance visitor experience. Funding is awarded through a competitive process to units of Federal land management agencies and to State, local and tribal government agencies.

For further information, call the Office of Program Management. Phone, 202-366-2053.

Sources of Information

Business Opportunities

Procurement-related information and resources are available on the FTA Web site.

Employment

FTA fills vacancies in its Washington, DC, headquarters and regional offices. The FTA relies on attorneys, congressional relations specialists, engineers, environmental specialists, planners, program management specialists, research program specialists, and other professionals to carry out its mission.

Environmental Justice

The FTA posts answers to questions related to environmental justice on its Web site.

Events

The FTA has a calendar of events on its Web site.

Freedom of Information Act (FOIA)

The FOIA grants public access to the content of certain records that are held by the offices, agencies, corporations, administrations, commissions, boards, and services of the Federal Government's executive branch. Some records that contain sensitive commercial, governmental, and personal information are protected from disclosure.

The FTA maintains an electronic reading room. Before submitting a FOIA request, information seekers should search for the desired document or record in the reading room to determine whether it is accessible immediately, without charge.

Glossary

The FTA maintains a National Transit Database glossary on its Web site.

Grants

The FTA provides grants to local public transit systems. It invests billions of dollars each year to support and to expand public transit services. It provides annual formula grants to transit agencies nationwide, as well as discretionary funding in competitive processes.

History

A brief history of mass transit is available on the FTA Web site.

National Transit Database

U.S. transit ridership has grown by more than 20 percent in the last decade. To keep track of the industry and provide public information and statistics as growth continues, the National Transit Database records the asset, financial, and operating conditions of transit systems. Phone, 888-252-0936.

News

The FTA posts news releases on its Web site.

Regional Offices

Contact information for the 10 regional offices is available on the FTA's Web site.

Research / Innovation

Research projects assess new operational processes, expand public-private partnerships, fund demonstration grants for low or no emissions buses, improve traveler experiences, and test systems that monitor safety. Research and innovation reports and publications are available on the FTA Web site.

Social Media

The FTA maintains a channel on YouTube, as well as accounts on Facebook, LinkedIn, and Twitter.

Updates

A subscription form is available on the FTA Web site to sign up for email updates.

For further information, contact the Federal Transit Administration, Office of Communications and Congressional Affairs, 1200 New Jersey Avenue SE., Washington, DC 20590. Phone, 202-366-4043.

Maritime Administration

1200 New Jersey Avenue SE., Washington, DC 20590, 202-366-5807, 800-996-2723, *http://www.marad.dot.gov*

ADMINISTRATOR	Paul N. Jaenichen, Sr.
Deputy Administrator	Michael J. Rodriquez
Executive Director	Joel Szabat

The Maritime Administration was established by Reorganization Plan No. 21 of 1950 (5 U.S.C. app.). The Maritime Act of 1981 (46 U.S.C. 1601) transferred the Maritime Administration to the DOT. The Administration manages programs that help develop and promote the U.S. merchant marine and its operations. It also organizes and directs emergency merchant ship operations.

The Administration serves as the DOT's waterborne transportation agency. Its programs promote waterborne transportation use, the seamless integration of waterborne transportation with other parts of the transportation system, and U.S. merchant marine viability. The Administration's activities involve ships and shipping, shipbuilding, port operations, vessel operations, national security, safety, and the environment. It also maintains the health of the merchant marine—commercial mariners, vessels, and intermodal facilities contribute significantly to national security. The Administration, therefore, supports current mariners, helps educate future mariners, and informs Americans about the maritime industry and how it benefits them. Recently, the Administration realigned its functions to be more effective as an industry promoter and to focus more attention on the environment and safety.

The Administration administers the Maritime Security Program, which maintains a core fleet of U.S.-flag, privately-owned ships that operate in international commerce. Under agreement, these ships are available to provide needed capacity, during war and national emergencies, to meet Department of Defense requirements.

It also administers the Ready Reserve Force program to facilitate deployment of U.S. military forces—rapidly and worldwide. The Force primarily supports transport of Army and Marine Corps unit equipment and combat support equipment. The Force also supports initial resupply during the critical surge period before commercial ships become available. The program provides nearly one-half of the Government-owned surge sealift capability.

For information on the Administration's 10 Gateway Offices, visit the "Gateway Presence" Web page.

Sources of Information

Business Opportunities

Links to business services are available on the Administration's Web site.

The Administration uses FedBizOpps.Gov for announcing solicitations and requests for comments.

Data / Statistics

The Administration's Web site features an open data portal that provides access to maritime data and statistics.

Educational Resources

The Adopt a Ship program allows a class of students to partner with a ship's crew. During the school year, the class and crew correspond and share experiences. The correspondence stimulates interest in English, geography, history, math, science, trade, and transportation. It gives children a unique opportunity for responding to their natural curiosity of the sea and introduces them to the men and women of the American Merchant Marine.

A video archives is available on the Administration's Web site.

Employment

For information on career opportunities, visit the "Careers" Web page.

Exhibits / Virtual Tours

A shipbuilding exhibit and virtual tours inside cargo and crew spaces and engine rooms are part of the Administration's Web site.

Freedom of Information Act (FOIA)

Instructions for submitting a FOIA request are available on the Administration's Web site. Fax, 202-366-7485.

The Administration maintains an electronic reading room. Before submitting a FOIA request, an information seeker should search for the desired document or record in the reading room to determine whether it may be available immediately, without charge.

Frequently Asked Questions (FAQs)

The Administration posts answers to FAQs on its Web site.

History

Historical documents and resources are available on the Administration's Web site.

National Maritime Resource and Education Center

The Center serves as a major information source and facilitator within the Government for the maritime industry by providing expertise, information, and reference material on commercial shipbuilding.

Newsroom

News items and releases, as well as advisories, events, photographs, and speeches, are accessible in the newsroom.

Ports

Information on the importance of ports to the Nation's economy and the Strong Ports program is available on the Administration's Web site.

Publications

Factsheets, policy papers, and reports are available on the Administration's Web site.

Ship Disposal

The Administration's Web site provides information on four methods of ship disposal: artificial reefing, domestic recycling, ship donations, and naval sink at sea live-fire training exercises (SINKEX).

For further information, contact the Maritime Administration, Office of Congressional and Public Affairs, 1200 New Jersey Avenue SE., Washington, DC 20590. Phone, 202-366-5807 or 800-996-2723.

National Highway Traffic Safety Administration

1200 New Jersey Avenue SE., Washington, DC 20590, 202-366-9550, 888-327-4236, *http://www.nhtsa.gov*

ADMINISTRATOR	Mark R. Rosekind
Deputy Administrator	Terry Shelton, Acting
Executive Director	Jack Danielson

[For the National Highway Traffic Safety Administration statement of organization, see the Code of Federal Regulations, Title 49, Part 501]

The National Highway Traffic Safety Administration (NHTSA) was established by the Highway Safety Act of 1970 (23 U.S.C. 401 note) to reduce the number of deaths, injuries, and economic losses resulting from motor vehicle crashes on the Nation's highways.

The Administration administers motor vehicle and related equipment safety performance programs; co-administers the State and community highway safety program; regulates the Corporate Average Fuel Economy program; issues Federal Motor Vehicle Safety Standards (FMVSS) that prescribe safety features and levels of safety-related performance for vehicles and vehicular equipment; rates the safety of passenger vehicles in the New Car Assessment Program; monitors and participates in international vehicle safety forums to harmonize the FMVSS where appropriate; investigates and prosecutes odometer fraud; administers the National Driver Register Program; conducts studies and operates programs to reduce economic losses in motor vehicle crashes and repairs; performs studies, conducts demonstration projects, and issues regulations requiring manufacturers to provide motor vehicle consumer information; promotes programs to reduce impaired driving, to reduce risky driver behaviors, and to increase seat belt use; and issues theft prevention standards for passenger motor vehicles.

Activities

Research and Program Development

The Administration helps develop motor vehicle and highway safety program standards. It analyzes data and researches, develops, tests, and evaluates motor vehicles, motor vehicle equipment, and advanced technologies, and it collects and analyzes crash data. NHTSA activities are broad in scope with respect to safety: The Administration encourages industry to adopt advanced motor vehicle safety designs, increases public awareness of safety issues, and provides a base for vehicle safety information.

Regional Operations and Program Delivery

The NHTSA administers State highway safety grant programs that the Safe, Accountable, Flexible, Efficient Transportation Equity Act: A Legacy for Users authorized. The Highway Safety formula grant program provides funds to States, Indian nations, and the territories each year to support safety programs, particularly in the following priority areas: data and traffic records, emergency medical services, impaired driving, motorcycle safety, occupant protection, pedestrian and bicycle safety, police traffic services, roadway safety, and speed control. Incentive grants are also used to encourage States to implement effective data improvement, impaired driving, motorcycle safety, and occupant protection programs.

Rulemaking

The Administration issues FMVSS that prescribe safety features and levels of safety-related performance for vehicles and vehicular equipment. The Administration participates in the United Nations World Forum for the Harmonization of Vehicle Regulations (WP.29). It also oversees the New Car Assessment Program and the Government's Five Star Safety Rating Program, which evaluates the safety performance of light trucks, passenger cars, vans, and child seats (www.safercar.gov/Safety+Ratings). These evaluations are highly publicized—star ratings must be visible on the price labels of new vehicles. The Administration also educates consumers on topics such as driving while distracted, as well as the proper use of vehicle safety features and child restraint seats. To promote fuel economy, it manages a program establishing and revising fleet average fuel economy standards for passenger car and light truck manufacturers (www.nhtsa.gov/fuel-economy). The Administration also runs an antitheft program. Under this program the NHTSA issues rules requiring that certain passenger motor vehicles meet parts-marking requirements, and it calculates and publishes annual motor vehicle theft rates.

Enforcement

The Administration's Office of Enforcement assures that all new vehicles sold in the U.S. meet applicable FMVSS. Under its compliance program, the Office conducts random tests and collects consumer complaints to identify and investigate problems with motor vehicles and vehicular equipment. If a vehicle or equipment suffers from a safety-related defect or does not meet all applicable FMVSS, the Office seeks a recall, which requires manufacturers to notify owners and to remedy the defect free of charge. The Office monitors recalls to ensure that owners are notified in a timely manner and that the scope of the recall and the remedy are adequate. The Office also assures that all motor vehicles subject to the Corporate Average Fuel Economy (CAFE) regulations meet their respective targets, and it enforces violations of Federal odometer fraud regulations by criminally prosecuting offenders.

National Center for Statistics and Analysis

The NHTSA maintains a collection of scientific and technical information on motor vehicle safety. It also operates the National Center for Statistics and Analysis, whose activities include the development and maintenance of national highway-crash data collection systems and related statistical and economic analyses. The public and the private sector and universities and Federal, State, and local agencies rely on these motor vehicle safety information resources for documentation.

Communications and Consumer Information

The Office of Communications and Consumer Information develops, directs, and implements communication strategies based on NHTSA policy and programs, including campaigns to support high visibility enforcement efforts. It promotes safety messages for NHTSA vehicle-related issues. The Office also manages NHTSA Web sites and the toll-free Vehicle Safety Hotline. Information received from calls to the hotline forms the basis of investigations, which can lead to recalls if safety-related defects are identified.

Contact information for the NHTSA's 10 regional offices is available on the "Regional Offices" Web page.

Sources of Information

Car Seats

A car seat glossary is available on the Parents Central Web site.

The car seat finder is an online tool that uses date of birth, height, and weight to find a car seat type that properly fits a child.

Data

The NHTSA posts factsheets, reports, research notes, statistics, and studies on its Web site.

Driving Safety

The NHTSA Web site features a trove of safety information and resources. Disabled, older, and teen drivers, as well as motorcyclists and others can find Web pages dedicated to improving their driving habits and addressing their safety needs.

Employment

Information on job openings is available on the "Jobs at NHTSA" Web page.

Events

The NHTSA hosts meetings and forums to explore new approaches to highway safety. Information and materials from these event are available online.

Freedom of Information Act (FOIA)

The NHTSA is required to disclose records that are properly requested in writing by any person. A Government agency may withhold information pursuant to one or more of nine exemptions and three exclusions contained in the FOIA. The act applies only to Federal agencies and does not give a right of access to records held by Congress, the courts, State or local government agencies, and private entities.

The NHTSA maintains an electronic reading room. Before submitting a FOIA request, an information seeker should search for the desired document or record in the reading room to determine whether it may be available immediately, without charge. The NHTSA also operates a service center for answering FOIA-related questions. Phone, 202-366-2870.

News

The NHTSA posts press releases on its Web site.

The NHTSA posts speeches, press events, and testimonies on its Web site.

Publications

The NHTSA disseminates information on traffic safety programs in "Traffic Techs." The publication, starting with the year 1995, is available online. Staring with the years 2005 and 2006, "Traffic Techs" becomes available in Portable Document Format (PDF).

Recalls

The Recalls Spotlight monitors high-profile recalls and provides resources finding and addressing vehicle recalls.

The NHTSA's Web site features a search tool that allows the user to enter a vehicle's identification number (VIN) to learn whether it has been repaired as part of a safety recall in the last 15 years.

Research

The Office of Vehicle Safety Research strategizes, plans, and implements research programs to reduce crashes, fatalities, and injuries. The NHTSA's Web site contains a trove of information related to these programs.

Resources for Parents

The Parents Central Web site features resources to help parents protect their children and educate them on car and road safety and becoming responsible drivers.

Vehicle Safety

The NHTSA Web site features a trove of information on and resources for vehicle safety. Topics include defects and recalls, odometer fraud, theft protection, and tires.

To report suspected safety defects in vehicles, vehicle equipment, and child restraint seats, call the Vehicle Safety Hotline. English- and Spanish-speaking representatives are available on weekdays, excluding Federal holidays. Phone, 888-327-4236. TTY, 800-424-9153.

For further information, contact the National Highway Traffic Safety Administration, Office of Communications and Consumer Information, 1200 New Jersey Avenue SE., Washington, DC 20590. Phone, 202-366-9550.

Pipeline and Hazardous Materials Safety Administration

1200 New Jersey Avenue SE., Washington, DC 20590, 202-366-4433, *http://www.phmsa.dot.gov*

ADMINISTRATOR	Marie Therese Dominguez
Deputy Administrator	John W. Drake
Executive Director	(vacancy)

The Pipeline and Hazardous Materials Safety Administration (PHMSA) was established on February 20, 2005. It is responsible for hazardous materials transportation and pipeline safety.

Hazardous Materials

The Office of Hazardous Materials Safety develops and issues regulations for the safe and secure transportation of hazardous materials by all modes, except bulk transportation by water. The regulations cover shipper and carrier operations, packaging and container specifications, and hazardous materials definitions. The Office provides training and outreach to help shippers and carriers meet hazardous material regulatory requirements. The Office enforces regulations other than those applicable to a single mode of transportation. It manages a fee-funded grant program to help States plan for hazardous materials emergencies and to assist them and Indian tribes with training for hazardous materials emergencies. The Office also maintains a national safety program to safeguard food and other products from contamination during motor or rail transportation.

For further information, call the Hazardous Materials Information Center. Phone, 800-467-4922.

Pipelines

The Office of Pipeline Safety (OPS) ensures the safety, security, and environmental protection of the Nation's pipeline transportation system. The Office establishes and enforces safety and environmental standards for pipeline transportation of gas and hazardous liquids. The Office analyzes data, educates and trains, promotes damage prevention, and conducts research and development for pipeline safety. Through OPS administered grants, States that voluntarily assume regulatory jurisdiction of pipelines can receive funding for up to 50 percent of the costs for their intrastate pipeline safety programs. OPS engineers inspect most interstate pipelines and other facilities not covered by State programs. In accordance with the Oil Pollution Act of 1990, the Office also approves and tests oil pipeline spill response plans.

For further information, call the Pipeline Safety Information Center. Phone, 202-366-4595. Fax, 202-493-2311.

Sources of Information

Business Opportunities

Information on the acquisition vehicles that the PHMSA uses to fulfill the requirements for goods and services of its program offices is available online.

Data / Statistics

The Office of Pipeline Safety makes available data on federally regulated and State regulated natural gas pipelines, hazardous liquid pipelines, and liquefied natural gas plants. The operators of these pipeline facilities report this data in accordance with PHMSA pipeline safety regulations. The PHMSA provides downloads of the raw data, yearly summaries, multiyear trends of safety performance metrics, and inventories tracking the removal of aging and other higher-risk infrastructure.

Employment

The PHMSA relies on accident investigators, accountants, attorneys, auditors, budget analysts, economists, engineers, finance analysts, geographic information systems specialists, grant specialists, human resource specialists, information technology specialists, and other professionals to carry out its mission.

Environmental Justice

The PHMSA Web site provides information for promoting environmental justice and ensuring nondiscrimination in communities.

Events

A calendar of PHMSA events is available online.

Freedom of Information Act (FOIA)

The FOIA establishes the public's right to obtain information from Federal Government agencies. Any person may file a FOIA request, including citizens and foreign nationals, as well as associations, organizations, and universities.

Frequently Asked Questions (FAQs)

The PHMSA posts answers to FAQs on its Web site.

Glossary

The PHMSA's Web site features an online glossary.

History

Millions of miles of transportation pipelines deliver the energy products that the American public uses to keep homes and businesses running. While rare, pipeline incidents can be fatal and cost millions of dollars in property damage. The Office of Pipeline Safety participated in the investigations of major pipeline incidents in San Bruno, CA; Allentown, PA; and Marshall, MI. In its commitment to safety awareness and outreach, the Office offers a historical look at high-profile pipeline incidents.

Library

The electronic library contains an accessible collection of public documents related to the safe transport of hazardous materials.

The Pipeline Library is an online resource containing electronic files that stakeholders and pipeline safety industry professionals regularly use. These files include archives, forms, frequently asked questions, glossaries, and Freedom of Information Act information.

Mapping System

The National Pipeline Mapping System public map viewer is a Web-based application designed to assist the general public with displaying and querying data related to gas transmission and hazardous liquid pipelines, liquefied natural gas plants, and breakout tanks under the jurisdiction of the PHMSA.

News

The PHMSA posts announcements, congressional testimony, events, press releases, speeches, videos, and more in its electronic briefing room.

Site Map

The Web site map allows visitors to look for specific topics or to browse content that aligns with their interests.

For further information, contact the Pipeline and Hazardous Materials Safety Administration, Office of Governmental, International and Public Affairs, Suite 84061200 New Jersey Avenue SE., Washington, DC 20590. Phone: 202-366-4831.

Saint Lawrence Seaway Development Corporation

55 M Street SE., Suite 930, Washington, DC 20003., 202-366-0091, 202-366-7147, *http://www.seaway.dot.gov*

Departmental Postal Address: Saint Lawrence Seaway Development Corporation, 1200 New Jersey Avenue SE., Washington, DC 20590. Email: *slsdc@dot.gov*

Postal and Physical Address: Saint Lawrence Seaway Development Corporation–Operations, 180 Andrews Street, Massena, NY 13662, 315-764-3200, 315-764-3235

POLICY HEADQUARTERS—WASHINGTON, DC

ADMINISTRATOR	Betty Sutton
Deputy Administrator	Craig H. Middlebrook

OPERATIONAL HEADQUARTERS—MASSENA, NY

Associate Administrator, Seaway Operations	Thomas A. Lavigne

The Saint Lawrence Seaway Development Corporation (SLSDC) was established by the Saint Lawrence Seaway Act of May 13, 1954 (33 U.S.C. 981-990) and became an operating administration of the DOT in 1966.

The SLSDC, working jointly with the Saint Lawrence Seaway Management Corporation (SLSMC) of Canada, operates and maintains a safe, reliable, and efficient deep draft waterway between the Great Lakes and the Atlantic Ocean. It ensures the safe transit of commercial and noncommercial vessels through the two U.S. locks and the navigation channels of the Saint Lawrence Seaway System and engages in economic and trade development activities to stimulate trade and employment in the eight States of the Great Lakes region. The SLSDC and SLSMC work together on all matters related to rules and regulations, overall operations, vessel inspections, traffic control, navigation aids, safety, operating dates, and trade development programs.

The Great Lakes-Saint Lawrence Seaway System extends from the Atlantic Ocean to the Lake Superior ports of Duluth and Superior, a distance of 2,342 miles. The Corporation's main customers are vessel owners and operators, Midwest States and Canadian Provinces, Great Lakes port communities, shippers and receivers of domestic and international cargo, and the maritime and related service industries of the Great Lakes and Saint Lawrence Seaway systems.

Sources of Information

Employment

The SLSDC relies on professionals with expertise in administration, engineering, information technology, management, marine operations, public policy, and other fields.

Events

Upcoming events are posted on the SLSDC's Web site.

Freedom of Information Act (FOIA)

Any person has the right to a copy of certain records possessed by the Government's executive administrations, agencies, boards, commissions, corporations, offices, and services. Some records, however, are protected from disclosure.

Grants

The SLSDC has an easy-to-use Federal grants toolkit that offers a snapshot of the essential information, resources, and tools needed to identify Federal agencies and processes offering financial assistance to maritime stakeholders seeking to carry out environmental, infrastructural, intermodal, and other development projects.

Map

An interactive map of vessels transiting the Great Lakes-St. Lawrence Seaway System is available online.

News

The SLSDC's quarterly newsletter "Seaway Compass" is available online. It features current information and recent news on the Great Lakes-St. Lawrence Seaway System.

Publications

The "Great Lakes-St. Lawrence Seaway System Directory" is a comprehensive publication on the ports and shipping-related businesses that are critical throughout the region and beyond. It features extensive photography and serves as an excellent resource for readers who are interested in the Great Lakes Seaway maritime industry.

The SLSDC's marketing brochure offers comprehensive information on the waterway and its significance to the Great Lakes region. It is available online in Portable Document Format (PDF).

Reports

The SLSDC posts annual reports on its Web site.

The SLSDC posts Asset Renewal Program reports on its Web site.

Social Media

The SLSDC maintains a Facebook account.

Studies

The "Environmental and Social Impacts of Marine Transport in the Great Lakes-St. Lawrence Seaway Region" study provides marine stakeholders, transportation planners, and government policymakers with an assessment of the potential environmental and social consequences that could occur if cargo carried by marine vessels on the Seaway navigation system shifted to rail and road modes of transport.

Videos

The SLSDC's Web site features a video gallery.

Visitors' Center

The Seaway Visitors' Center at the Eisenhower Lock provides tourists and ship watchers with an observation deck where they can view commercial vessels and cruise ships transiting the lock. Each year, hundreds of ships from all over the globe make thousands of transits through the St. Lawrence Seaway. They carry a wide variety of cargoes: coal, grains, iron ore, steel, steel slabs, stone, and more.

For further information, contact the Saint Lawrence Seaway Development Corporation, Director of Congressional and Public Relations, 1200 New Jersey Avenue SE., Washington, DC 20590. Phone, 202-366-0091. Fax, 202-366-7147.

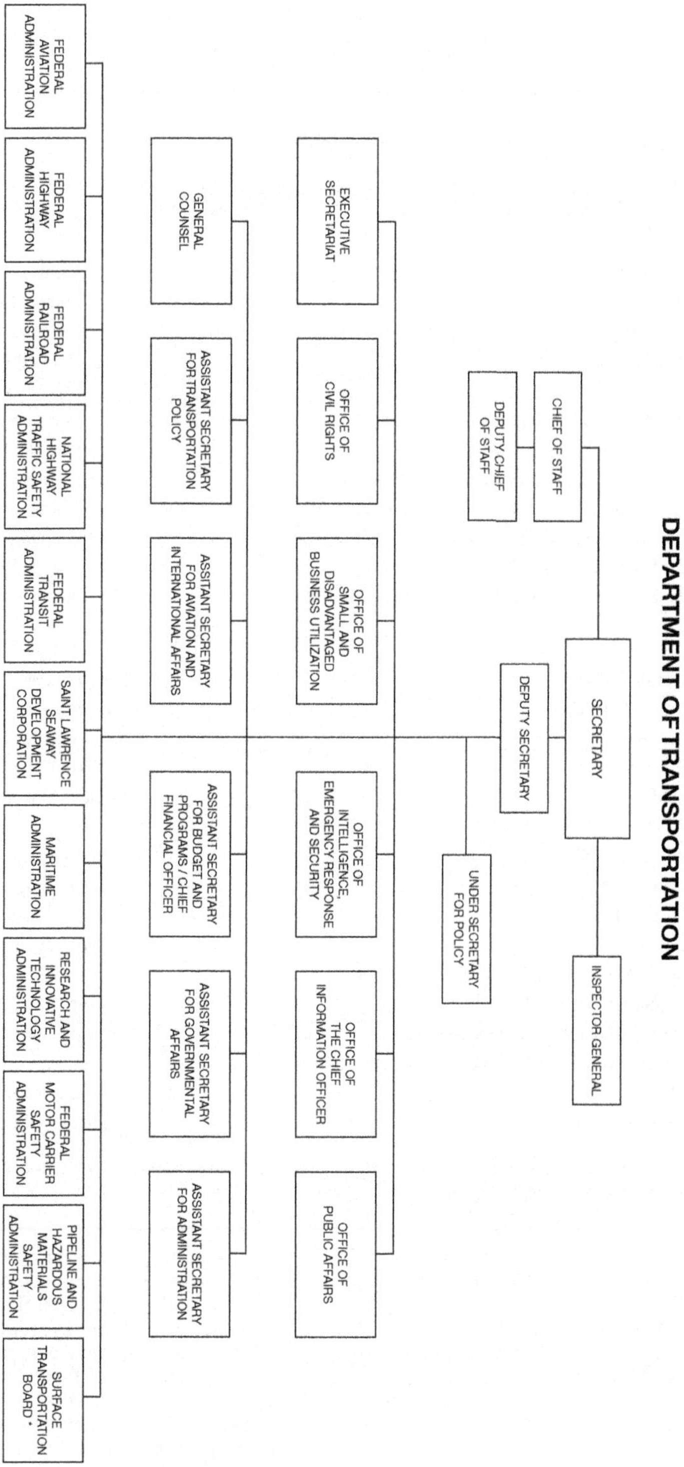

* The Surface Transportation Board is administratively affiliated with the Department of Transportation.

Department of the Treasury

1500 Pennsylvania Avenue NW., Washington, DC 20220, 202-622-2000, *http://www.treasury.gov*

SECRETARY OF THE TREASURY	Jacob J. Lew
Deputy Secretary of the Treasury	Sarah Bloom Raskin
Chief of Staff	Christian A. Weideman
Chief Risk Officer	Kenneth Phelan
General Counsel	Priya Aiyar, Acting
Treasurer of the United States	(vacancy)
Inspector General	Eric M. Thorson
Treasury Inspector General, Tax Administration	J. Russell George
Treasury Special Inspector General, Troubled Asset Relief Program	Christy Romero
Under Secretary, Domestic Finance	(vacancy)
Under Secretary, International Affairs	Nathan Sheets
Under Secretary, Terrorism and Financial Intelligence	Adam Szubin, Acting

ASSISTANT SECRETARIES

Economic Policy	Karen Dynan
Legislative Affairs	(vacancy)
Management	Kody Kinsley
Public Affairs	Victoria Esser
Tax Policy	Mark J. Mazur
DOMESTIC FINANCE	
Financial Institutions	Amias Gerety, Acting
Financial Markets	Daleep Singh, Acting
Financial Stability	(vacancy)
Fiscal Assistant Secretary	David A. Lebryk
INTERNATIONAL AFFAIRS	
International Finance	Ramin Toloui
International Markets and Development	Marisa Lago
TERRORISM / FINANCIAL INTELLIGENCE	
Intelligence / Analysis	S. Leslie Ireland
Terrorist Financing	Daniel L. Glaser

The Department of the Treasury enforces financial laws, manufactures coins and currency, and recommends economic, fiscal, and tax policies.

The Treasury Department was created by act of September 2, 1789 (31 U.S.C. 301 and 301 note). Many subsequent acts have figured in the development of the Department, delegating new duties to its charge and establishing the numerous bureaus and divisions that now constitute the Treasury.

Secretary

As a major policy adviser to the President, the Secretary recommends domestic and international financial, economic, and tax policy; formulates broad fiscal policies that have general significance for the economy; and manages the public debt. The Secretary oversees the activities of the Department in carrying out its major law enforcement responsibility; in serving as the financial agent for the U.S. Government; and in manufacturing coins, currency, and other products for customer agencies. The Secretary also acts as the Government's chief financial officer.

Activities

Domestic Finance

The Office of Domestic Finance maintains confidence in the U.S. Treasury market, manages Federal fiscal operations, and strengthens financial institutions and markets; promotes access to credit; and improves financial access and education in service of America's long-term economic strength and stability.

Economic Policy

The Office of the Assistant Secretary for Economic Policy helps policymakers determine economic policies. The Office analyzes domestic and international economic issues and developments in the financial markets, assists in forming official economic projections, and works closely with Federal Government agencies to make economic forecasts supporting the yearly budget process.

Enforcement

The Department's law enforcement activities are carried out by its offices and bureaus, including the Alcohol and Tobacco Tax and Trade Bureau, the Internal Revenue Service, and the Office of Terrorism and Financial Intelligence (TFI). The Office of Foreign Assets Control, which is part of the TFI, plays an important role in controlling the assets of "blocked" countries in the United States and restricting the flow of funds and trade with these countries.

Financial Institutions

The Office of Financial Institutions coordinates the Department's efforts regarding financial institutions legislation and regulation, legislation affecting Federal agencies that regulate or insure financial institutions, and securities markets legislation and regulation. The Office also coordinates the Department's financial education policy efforts and ensures the resiliency of the financial services sector.

Financial Markets

The Office of Financial Markets serves to formulate policy on Federal debt management, State and local finance (including the Federal debt), Federal Government credit policies, and lending and privatization. This Office also oversees the Federal Financing Bank, and the Assistant Secretary serves as the senior member of the Treasury Financing Group and coordinates the President's Working Group on Financial Markets.

Financial Stability

The Office of Financial Stability within the U.S. Treasury was created by the Emergency Economic Stabilization Act of 2008 (12 U.S.C. 5201 et seq.) to administer the Troubled Asset Relief Program (TARP). The purpose of the TARP was to help restore liquidity and stability to the U.S. financial system following the 2008 financial crisis. The Treasury's authority to make financial commitments under TARP ended on October 3, 2010. The Office continues to wind down the TARP investments in a manner that balances exit speed with maximizing taxpayer returns. It also helps homeowners prevent avoidable foreclosures.

Fiscal Affairs

The Office of the Fiscal Assistant Secretary provides policy oversight of the Fiscal Service bureaus and develops policy on payments, collections, debt financing operations, electronic commerce, Governmentwide accounting, Government investment fund management, and other related issues. The Office also performs two critical functions for the Department: It manages the daily cash position of the Government, and it produces the cash and debt forecasts used to determine the size and timing of the Government's financing operations.

International Finance

The Office of the Assistant Secretary for International Finance conducts macroeconomic analyses to advise the Under Secretary for International Affairs and other policymakers. The Office also helps them formulate and execute financial and economic policy affecting or involving the International Monetary Fund, the U.S.-

China Strategic and Economic Dialogue, the G–20, and other major multilateral and bilateral engagements.

International Markets and Development

The Office of the Assistant Secretary of International Markets and Development manages the work of the Committee on Foreign Investment in the United States and the Treasury's Office of Technical Assistance. The Office also advises the Under Secretary for International Affairs and other policymakers on financial and economic policies relevant to major bilateral and multilateral engagements, and it assists them with these engagements. The Office plays a similar role in the formulation and execution of policies affecting export finance, financial services, trade, and multilateral development, including the World Bank, the regional development banks, and emerging global issues like food security and climate finance.

Tax Policy

The Office of the Assistant Secretary for Tax Policy advises and assists the Secretary and the Deputy Secretary in the formulation and execution of domestic and international tax policies and programs. These functions include analysis of proposed tax legislation and tax programs; projections of economic trends affecting tax bases; studies of effects of alternative tax measures; preparation of official estimates of Government receipts for the President's annual budget messages; legal advice and analysis on domestic and international tax matters; assistance in the development and review of tax legislation and domestic and international tax regulations and rulings; and participation in international tax treaty negotiations and in maintenance of relations with international organizations on tax matters.

Treasurer of the United States

The Office of the Treasurer of the United States was established on September 6, 1777. The Treasurer was originally charged with the receipt and custody of Government funds, but many of these functions have been assumed by different bureaus of the Department. In 1981, the Treasurer was assigned responsibility for oversight of the Bureau of Engraving and Printing and the United States Mint. The Treasurer reports to the Secretary through the Assistant Secretary for Management.

Treasury Inspector General for Tax Administration

The Treasury Inspector General for Tax Administration (TIGTA), in accordance with the Internal Revenue Service Restructuring and Reform Act of 1998 (26 U.S.C. 1 note), independently oversees Internal Revenue Service programs and activities. TIGTA monitors the Nation's tax laws to ensure that the Internal Revenue Service (IRS) acts with efficiency, economy, and effectiveness; ensures compliance with applicable laws and regulations; prevents, detects, and deters fraud, waste, and abuse; investigates activities or allegations related to fraud, waste, and abuse by IRS personnel; and protects the IRS against attempts to corrupt or threaten its employees.

Sources of Information

Blog

Senior officials and staff post announcements, information, and news items on the Department's official blog "Treasury Notes."

Bureaus

The Bureaus carry out specific operations assigned to the Department of the Treasury. Bureau employees constitute 98% of the Treasury workforce. The Department's Web site features a "Bureaus" Web page that provides easy access to the Web sites of each of the Bureaus.

Business Opportunities

The Office of the Procurement Executive oversees the Department's acquisition system. It supports the use of best value, cost effective, streamlined procurement strategies and encourages achievement of socioeconomic participation goals in the Nation's business activities. For more information, contact the Senior Procurement Executive, 1500 Pennsylvania Avenue NW., Suite 400–W, Washington, DC 20220. Phone, 202-622-1039.

For information on small and disadvantaged business activities, contact the Director, Office of Small and Disadvantaged Business Utilization,1500 Pennsylvania Avenue NW., Mail Code 655, 15th Street, 6th Floor, Washington, DC 20220. Phone, 202-622-0530.

Careers

The Department of the Treasury employs over 100,000 professionals nationwide and around the world.

Data / Charts

A trove of economic information—charts, data, and tables—is available on the Department of the Treasury's Web site.

Educational Resources

The Department of the Treasury's Web site features learning resources that are suitable for children and parents, for students and teachers, as well as college students and other curious adults.

Environment

The most recent "Office of Management and Budget Scorecard on Sustainability/ Energy" (JAN 2016) is accessible online in Portable Document Format (PDF).

The most recent "Strategic Sustainability Performance Plan" (JUN 2016) was released by the Office of Real Estate and Facilities Management in Portable Document Format (PDF).

To learn about the Department's role in supporting U.S. efforts to improve the environment and to facilitate a transition to a national and global economy powered by clean energy, see the Office of Environment and Energy's Web page.

Freedom of Information Act (FOIA)

The FOIA gives the right to request access to records of the U.S. Government's executive branch to any person. The records must be disclosed unless they are shielded from request by one or more of the exempt categories of information found in the statute.

The Department of the Treasury's Web site features an electronic reading room whose holdings are governed by the FOIA.

An electronic FOIA request form is available on the Department of the Treasury's Web site.

Frequently Asked Questions (FAQs)

The Department of the Treasury posts answers to FAQs on its Web site.

Glossary

The Department of the Treasury maintains a list of acronyms and terms that recur on its Web site.

History

A trove of historical information on the Department of the Treasury and its building is available online.

Inspector General

For general information, contact the Assistant Inspector General for Management at 202-927-5200 or visit the Office of Inspector General (OIG) Web site. To report the possible existence of a Treasury activity constituting mismanagement, gross waste of funds, abuse of authority, a substantial and specific danger to the public health and safety, or a violation of law, rules, or regulations—not including the Internal Revenue Service, which reports to the Treasury Inspector General for Tax Administration—contact the Treasury OIG Hotline, Office of Inspector General, 1500 Pennsylvania Avenue NW., Washington, DC 20220. Phone, 800-359-3898.

Library / Reading Room

The reading room is located in the Treasury Library, Room 1428, Main Treasury Building, 1500 Pennsylvania Avenue NW., Washington, DC 20220. Phone, 202-622-0990.

Tax Legislation

For information on tax legislation, contact the Assistant Secretary for Tax Policy, Departmental Offices, Treasury Department, Washington, DC 20220. Phone,

202-622-0050.

Treasury Inspector General for Tax Administration

To report abuse or fraud against or by Internal Revenue Service employees, or waste, contact the Treasury Inspector General for Tax Administration, P.O. Box 589, Ben Franklin Station, Washington, DC 20044-0589. Phone, 800-366-4484.

For further information, contact the Public Affairs Office, Department of the Treasury, 1500 Pennsylvania Avenue NW., Washington, DC 20220. Phone, 202-622-2960.

Alcohol and Tobacco Tax and Trade Bureau

1310 G Street NW., Box 12, Washington, DC 20005, 202-453-2000, *http://www.ttb.gov*

ADMINISTRATOR	John J. Manfreda
Deputy Administrator	Mary G. Ryan

The Alcohol and Tobacco Tax and Trade Bureau (TTB) was established on January 24, 2003, by the Homeland Security Act of 2002 (6 U.S.C. 531). TTB collects Federal alcohol, tobacco, firearms, and ammunition excise taxes; regulates the production, labeling, and advertising of alcohol beverages; and investigates unfair or unlawful trade in alcohol and tobacco products. TTB regulates alcohol and tobacco producers, importers, and wholesalers. Regulation of retailers takes place on State and local levels.

Sources of Information

Advertising, Labeling, and Formulation

For information on the advertising, labeling, and formulation of alcohol beverages, contact the Advertising, Labeling and Formulation Division. Phone, 202-453-2250 or 866-927-2533.

Consumer Complaints

Contact the Market Compliance Office. Phone, 866-927-2533 or 202-453-2250. Fax, 202-453-2984.

Fraud Tipline

To report fraud, diversion, and illegal activity by producers, importers, or wholesalers of alcohol and tobacco, contact the Bureau's tipline. Phone, 855-882-8477. TTD, 202-882-9914.

Freedom of Information Act (FOIA)

The TTB adheres to the policy and disclosure regulations of the Department of the Treasury for implementing the Freedom of Information Act (FOIA) consistently and uniformly and for providing maximum allowable disclosure of agency records upon request. Requests are processed within the time limits defined by the FOIA.

The TTB's Web site features an electronic reading room containing materials that the FOIA requires the Bureau to maintain. Some records are available in the public reading room located at 1310 G Street NW., Washington, DC 20005. Phone, 202-882-9904.

Frequently Asked Questions (FAQs)

The TTB posts answers to FAQs on its Web site.

Glossary

The TTB maintains a glossary on its Web site.

National Revenue Center

The National Revenue Center operates a call center that is open on weekdays, 8 a.m.–11:30 a.m. and 12:30 p.m.–5 p.m., eastern standard time. It can provide information on applications, claims, filing excise tax returns, permits, and other tax collection topics. Phone, 877-882-3277.

Site Map

The Web site map allows visitors to look for specific topics or to browse content that aligns with their interests.

The Web site also features an A–Z Index to help visitors navigate its content.

For further information, contact the Administrator's Office, Alcohol and Tobacco Tax and Trade Bureau. Phone, 202-453-2000.

Bureau of Engraving and Printing

Fourteenth and C Streets SW., Washington, DC 20228, 202-874-4000, *http://www.moneyfactory.com*

DIRECTOR	Leonard R. Olijar
Deputy Director	(vacancy)

The Bureau of Engraving and Printing operates on basic authorities conferred by act of July 11, 1862 (31 U.S.C. 303), and on additional authorities contained in past appropriations made to the Bureau that are still in force. A revolving fund established in 1950, in accordance with Public Law 81–656, finances the Bureau's operations. The Secretary of the Treasury selects the Director who heads the Bureau.

The Bureau designs, prints, and finishes all of the Nation's paper currency and many other security documents, including White House invitations and military identification cards. It also is responsible for advising and assisting Federal agencies in the design and production of other Government documents that, because of their innate value or for other reasons, require security or counterfeit-deterrence characteristics.

The Bureau also operates a second currency manufacturing plant at 9000 Blue Mound Road, Fort Worth, TX. Phone, 817-231-4000.

Sources of Information

Business Opportunities

For information on contracts and small business activities, visit the "Doing Business with the BEP" Web page or contact the Office of Acquisition. Phone, 202-874-2065.

Career Opportunities

The BEP relies on acquisition specialists, administrative staff, attorneys, chemists, engineers, police officers, security specialists, and other professionals to carry out its mission.

Currency Production

The production of U.S. currency involves highly trained and skilled craftspeople, specialized equipment, and a combination of traditional old world printing techniques merged with sophisticated, cutting edge technology. To learn more about the process, visit the "How Money is Made" Web page.

Educational Resources

The U.S. currency education program offers free educational and training resources online.

Freedom of Information Act (FOIA)

All Federal agencies, including the BEP, create and receive records when carrying out their missions. The FOIA gives the right to access executive branch agency records to the public. The BEP makes available, upon written request, records or extracts of records in accordance with the FOIA, the Privacy Act, and certain regulations of the Department of the Treasury. The FOIA contains, however, exemptions that shield some records from request and disclosure. Phone, 202-874-2500. Fax, 202-874-2951.

The BEP maintains an electronic FOIA library on its Web site.

History

A history of the BEP and U.S. Currency is available online.

Mail Order Sales

Uncut sheets of currency, engraved Presidential portraits, historical engravings of national landmarks, and other souvenirs and mementos are available for purchase by phone and online. Phone, 800-456-3408.

News

The BEP posts press releases on its Web site.

Tours

Tours of the Bureau's facilities are provided year-round according to the schedules listed below. Up-to-the-minute tour information is available online.

WASHINGTON, DC—During peak season, from March through August, 9 a.m.–10:45 a.m. and 12:30 p.m.–2 p.m., tickets are required for all tours. Tours begin every 15 minutes, with the last tour beginning at 2 p.m. The times between 11 a.m. and 12:15 p.m. are reserved for school and other groups. The ticket booth is located on Raoul Wallenberg Place (formerly Fifteenth Street) and opens at 8 a.m. Tour tickets are free. The ticket booth remains open for the morning and evening tours until all tickets have been distributed. Lines form early, and tickets go quickly, typically by 9 a.m. during peak season. Tickets are distributed on a first-come, first-served basis. Lines form on Raoul Wallenberg Place. Evening tours, running from April through August, 5 p.m.–7 p.m., are offered every 15 minutes. During nonpeak season, from September through February, 9 a.m.–2 p.m., tickets are not necessary for tours. Lines form on Fourteenth Street. No tours are given on weekends, Federal holidays, or between Christmas and New Year's Day. Phone, 202-874-2330 or 866-874-2330.

FORT WORTH, TX—During peak season, June and July, 11 a.m.–5 p.m., a new tour starts every 30 minutes. The Tour and Visitor Center opens at 10:30 a.m. and closes at 6:30 p.m. During nonpeak season, from August through May, 9 a.m.–2 p.m., the Visitor Center opens at 8:30 a.m. and closes at 3:30 p.m. No tours are given on weekends, Federal holidays, or between Christmas and New Year's Day. Phone, 817-231-4000 or 866-865-1194.

For further information, contact the Office of External Relations, Bureau of Engraving and Printing, Department of the Treasury, Room 533–M, Fourteenth and C Streets SW., Washington, DC 20228. Phone, 202-874-3019. Fax, 202-874-3177.

Bureau of the Fiscal Service

401 Fourteenth Street SW., Washington, DC 20227, 202-874-6950, *http://www.fiscal.treasury.gov*

COMMISSIONER	Sheryl R. Morrow
Deputy Commissioner	Wanda J. Rogers
Deputy Commissioner	Kimberly McCoy

The Bureau of the Fiscal Service provides central payment services to Federal program agencies, operates the Federal Government's collections and deposit systems, provides Governmentwide accounting and reporting services, manages the collection of delinquent debt owed to the Federal Government, borrows the money needed to operate the Federal Government, accounts for the resulting public debt, and gives reimbursable support to Federal agencies.

Accounting

The Fiscal Service gathers and publishes Governmentwide financial information that is used by the public and private sectors to monitor the Government's financial status and establish fiscal and monetary policies. These publications include the "Daily Treasury Statement," "Monthly Treasury Statement," "Treasury Bulletin," "U.S.

Government Annual Report," and "Financial Report of the U.S. Government."

Collections

The Fiscal Service administers the world's largest collection system, processing more than 400 million transactions through the support of six Federal Reserve Banks and a network of over 100 financial institutions. In Fiscal Year 2012, the Fiscal Service collected over $3.16 trillion in Federal revenues from individual and corporate income tax deposits, customs duties, loan repayments, fines, proceeds from leases, as well as from other revenue sources.

The Fiscal Service and Internal Revenue Service manage the Electronic Federal Tax Payment System (EFTPS), which allows individuals and businesses to pay Federal taxes online. The EFTPS Web site features printable acknowledgments for documenting transactions, advance payment scheduling, and payment history access.

The Treasury Offset Program is one of the methods used to collect delinquent debt. The Fiscal Service uses the program to withhold Federal payments, such as Federal income tax refunds, Federal salary payments, and Social Security benefits, to recipients with delinquent debts, including past-due child support obligations and State and Federal income tax debt.

Debt Financing

The Bureau auctions and issues Treasury bills, notes, and bonds and manages the sales and redemption of savings bonds. It provides daily and other periodic reports to account for the composition and size of the debt. In addition, the Bureau implements the regulations for the Government securities market. These regulations provide for investor protection while maintaining a fair and liquid market for Government securities.

Do Not Pay

The Do Not Pay Business Center has a two-part vision for programs administered or funded by the Federal Government: to help prevent and stop improper payments from being made and to identify and mitigate fraud, waste, and abuse. The goal of the program is to integrate Do Not Pay into existing business processes by providing agencies with access to current data that are relevant for making an award or payment decision.

Electronic Commerce

Through its electronic money programs, the Fiscal Service offers new payment and collection technologies to help Federal agencies modernize their cash management activities. Examples include stored-value cards used on military bases, point-of-sale check conversion, and online credit card collection programs.

Payments

Each year, the Fiscal Service disburses more than one billion non-Defense payments to a wide variety of recipients, such as those individuals who receive Social Security, IRS tax refunds, and veterans' benefits. In Fiscal Year 2012, the Fiscal Service issued more than $2.4 trillion in payments, 88 percent of which were issued electronically.

Shared Services

The Administrative Resource Center delivers franchise services on a reimbursable basis to more than 85 Treasury and Federal Government agencies. The Center provides services in six areas: financial management, investment accounting, human resources, information technology, procurement, and travel.

Sources of Information

A–Z Index

The Fiscal Service's Web site features an alphabetical and comprehensive list of links to the Bureau's major programs and services.

Do Not Pay

The Do Not Pay Business Center supports Federal agencies in their efforts to reduce the number of improper payments. Data, information, and resources are available on its Web site.

Electronic Federal Tax Payment

System (EFTPS)

The EFTPS provides answers to frequently asked questions (FAQs) on its Web site.

The EFTPS Web site features a glossary of terms and common acronyms.

Employment

The Fiscal Service relies on accountants, administrators, business and finance experts, information technology specialists, and others to carry out mission.

Freedom of Information Act (FOIA)

The FOIA gives the right to request information from the Federal Government's executive branch agencies to any person. It is sometimes referred to as the law that keeps citizens in the know about their Government. The Fiscal Service posts a lot of information on its Web site for the public's benefit and convenience. Before submitting a FOIA request in writing, information seekers should search the Web site for the desired information. It may be accessible immediately and free of charge.

The Fiscal Service maintains an electronic reading room to support the FOIA.

Glossary

The Fiscal Service's Web site contains acronyms and abbreviations, which are unpacked in the glossary and defined along with other technical terms.

The TreasuryDirect Web site features a glossary of terms.

Government-to-Government Shared Services

The Administrative Resource Center provides Federal agencies with cost-effective, customer-focused, responsive administrative support.

History

A short history of the Fiscal Service is available on its Web site.

The TreasuryDirect Web site features a history that relies on historical images to tell the story of U.S. Savings Bonds from their introduction in 1935 to the second decade of the 21st century.

News

The Fiscal Service posts news items and press releases on its Web site.

Public Debt Outstanding

The TreasuryDirect Web site features an online tool that allows users to access the data on total public debt outstanding on a daily basis from January 4, 1993, onward. For example, on November 8, 2016, the total public debt outstanding was $19,806,239,858,606.

Reports / Publications

The monthly "Statement of the Public Debt of the United States" and "Treasury Statement of Receipts and Outlays of the U.S. Government," as well as the annual "Financial Report of the U.S. Government" and other publications are available on the Fiscal Service's Web site.

Savings Bonds

Savings bonds may be purchased and held in an online account. Current rate information is available online or by calling 800-487-2663. Requests for information on all series of savings bonds, savings notes, and retirement plans or individual retirement bonds should be addressed to the Bureau of the Fiscal Service, Division of Customer Assistance, PO Box 7012, Parkersburg, WV 26106-7012. Phone, 304-480-7711.

Treasury Securities

For information on the purchase of Treasury bills, bonds, and notes, contact the Bureau of the Fiscal Service, Division of Customer Assistance, PO Box 7015, Parkersburg, WV 26106-7015. Phone, 800-722-2678.

For further information, contact the Office of Legislative and Public Affairs, Bureau of the Fiscal Service, Department of the Treasury, 401 Fourteenth Street SW., Washington, DC 20227. Phone, 202-874-6750.

Internal Revenue Service

1111 Constitution Avenue NW., Washington, DC 20224, 202-622-5000, *http://www.irs.gov*

COMMISSIONER OF INTERNAL REVENUE	John A. Koskinen
Chief of Staff	Crystal Philcox
DEPUTY COMMISSIONERS	
Operations Support	Jeffrey Tribiano
Services and Enforcement	John M. Dalrymple
Chief, Appeals	Kirsten Wielobob
Chief, Communications and Liaison	Terry L. Lemons
Chief Counsel	William J. Wilkins
Director, Research, Applied Analytics and Statistics	Benjamin Herndon
Executive Director, Office of Equity, Diversity and Inclusion	Elita Christiansen
National Taxpayer Advocate	Nina E. Olson

The Office of the Commissioner of Internal Revenue was established by act of July 1, 1862 (26 U.S.C. 7802). The Internal Revenue Service (IRS) administers and enforces the internal revenue laws and related statutes, except those relating to alcohol, tobacco, firearms, and explosives. It collects the proper amount of tax revenue, at the least cost to the public, by efficiently applying the tax law with integrity and fairness. The IRS aims for the highest possible degree of voluntary compliance in accordance with the tax laws and regulations; advises the public of their rights and responsibilities; determines the extent of compliance and the causes of noncompliance; properly administers and enforces the tax laws; and continually searches for and implements new, more efficient ways of accomplishing its mission. The IRS ensures satisfactory resolution of taxpayer complaints; provides taxpayer service and education; determines, assesses, and collects internal revenue taxes; determines pension plan qualifications and exempt organization status; and prepares and issues rulings and regulations to supplement the provisions of the Internal Revenue Code.

Most of the collected revenues depend on the individual income tax and the social insurance and retirement taxes. Other major revenue sources are corporate income, excise, estate, and gift taxes. The 16th Amendment of the Constitution, ratified on February 3, 1913, gave Congress the authority to levy taxes on the income of individuals and corporations.

Sources of Information

Business Opportunities

Information on and resources for doing business with the IRS are available on its "Procurement" Web page.

Charities / Nonprofits

Tax information for charities and nonprofit organizations is available on the IRS Website.

Employment

The IRS relies on accountants, appeals officers, artificial intelligence analysts, attorneys, budget analysts, computer research analysts, contact representatives, data transcribers, engineers, human resources specialists, information technology specialists, internal revenue agents and officers, mathematical statisticians, operations research analysts, policy analysts, program analysts, risk analysts, special agents, tax compliance officers, tax examiners, tax law specialists, and other professionals to carry out its mission.

Forms / Publications

Current forms, instructions, and publications may be downloaded from the IRS's Web site.

Freedom of Information Act (FOIA)

In 1966, President Lyndon B. Johnson's approval of the FOIA gave the right to access documents or records belonging to the executive branch of the Federal Government to any person. The statute is based on the presumption that the Government and its information belong to the public. The IRS may withhold, however, documents or records shielded from disclosure by one of the statute's nine exemptions, and it must withhold them when disclosure is prohibited by law.

The IRS Web site features an electronic reading room whose contents are arranged by subject category.

Frequently Asked Questions (FAQs)

The IRS posts answers to FAQs on its Web site.

Identity Theft

The IRS responds to tax-related identity theft with an aggressive strategy of prevention, detection, and victim assistance. The IRS continues to make progress against this crime, and it remains one of the agency's highest priorities. The IRS is committed to helping victims of identity theft resolve their cases as quickly as possible.

Language Resources

The home page of the IRS's Web site features a drop-down menu that allows visitors to access information in Chinese, Korean, Russian, Spanish, and Vietnamese.

News

The IRS posts news items on its Web site.

Reading Rooms

Public reading rooms are located in the national office and in each territory office.

Retirement Plans

The IRS Web site features resources for and a trove of information on retirement plans.

Tax Assistance

The Internal Revenue Service provides taxpayers with year-round tax information and assistance, primarily through its Web site and toll-free telephone system. Answers to many tax-related questions can be found on the IRS's Web site. The toll-free telephone numbers are listed in local telephone directories and in the annual tax form packages. The telephone system can accommodate the needs of taxpayers who are deaf or hearing-impaired. Taxpayers may also visit IRS offices to find answers to their tax questions. Individual preparation is available for handicapped or other individuals unable to use the group preparation method. Tax assistance in a foreign language is also available at many locations.

To find the nearest taxpayer assistance center, type a ZIP Code in the text box of the online locator tool. Before going to a taxpayer assistance center for help, call and schedule an appointment.

Tax Statistics

The IRS posts articles, data, and tables that describe and measure elements of the U.S. tax system.

Taxpayer Advocate Service

Each district has problem resolution personnel to address taxpayer complaints that cannot be resolved through regular channels.

Taxpayer Rights

The taxpayer bill of rights is available on the IRS's Web site.

Topics Asked About Most

Information on the asked-about-most topics is available on the IRS's Web site.

Where's My Refund?

Once the IRS processes a tax filer's return and approves a refund, he or she can check the refund date online. The IRS usually issues a refund in fewer than 21 days after receiving a tax filer's return. Some returns, however, require additional review and, therefore, additional time to process.

For further information, contact the Internal Revenue Service, Department of the

Treasury, 1111 Constitution Avenue NW., Washington, DC 20224. Phone, 202-622-5000.

Office of the Comptroller of the Currency

400 7th Street SW., Washington, DC 20219, 202-649-6800, *http://www.occ.gov*

COMPTROLLER	Thomas J. Curry
Senior Deputy Comptroller / Chief of Staff	Paul M. Nash
Senior Deputy Comptroller / Chief Counsel	Amy S. Friend

[For the Office of the Comptroller of the Currency statement of organization, see the Code of Federal Regulations, Title 12, Part 4]

The Office of the Comptroller of the Currency (OCC) was created February 25, 1863 (12 Stat. 665), as a bureau of the Department of the Treasury. Its primary mission is to regulate national banks. The Office is headed by the Comptroller, whom the President appoints for a 5-year term with the Senate's advice and consent. In July 2011, the Office of Thrift Supervision was integrated into the OCC, along with the responsibility for the supervision of Federal savings associations.

The OCC regulates national banks and Federal savings associations through its power to examine banks; to approve or deny applications for new bank charters, branches, or mergers; to take enforcement actions such as bank closures against banks that are not in compliance with laws and regulations; and to issue rules, regulations, and interpretations on banking practices.

The OCC supervises approximately 1,900 national banks, Federal savings associations, and Federal branches, including their trust activities and overseas operations. Each bank is examined by a nationwide staff of approximately 2,500 bank examiners who are supervised by four district offices. The OCC is independently funded through assessments of bank assets.

Sources of Information

Alerts

The OCC posts alerts—counterfeiting, fictitious correspondence, fraudulent issuances, misrepresentation, unauthorized banking activity—on its Web site.

Answers / Solutions

The "HelpWithMyBank" Web site features information and resources to help customers of national banks and Federal savings associations find answers to their questions and solutions for their problems.

The "HelpWithMyBank" Web site answers frequently asked questions on checking accounts, credit cards, credit reports, mortgages, overdraft fees, and more.

Bulletins

The OCC posts bulletins on its Web site.

Business Opportunities

The OCC's annual procurement awards comprise about 1,500 contracts and total approximately $150 million. Awards typically fall within the following categories of services: computer-related services; computer facilities management services; computer systems design services; data processing, hosting, and related services; real estate agent and broker services; insurance agency and brokerage services; and administrative management and general management consulting services.

Consumer Protection

The OCC's Web site features information and resources to protect consumers.

Customer Complaints

An electronic customer complaint form is available on the OCC's Web site.

District and Field Offices

Contact information for district and field offices is available on the OCC's Web site.

Employment

The OCC relies on accountants, attorneys, economists, financial analysts, human resources specialists, information technology specialists, project management analysts, and other professionals, particularly bank examiners, to carry out its mission. Examiners help ensure the safety and soundness of America's national banking system; they help provide fair access to financial services and equal treatment; and they help establish and maintain a flexible regulatory framework that allows the Nation's banks to be competitive. National bank examiners are generally hired at the entry level through college recruitment. For more information, contact the Director for Human Resources Operations. Phone, 202-649-6590. Fax, 202-649-5998.

The OCC ranks consistently high among agency subcomponents in the Partnership for Public Service's "Best Places To Work in the Federal Government."

Forms / Software / Tools

For bankers, the OCC offers forms, search tools, and software. For consumers and job seekers, it offers forms and job search tools. It also provides links to external Web sites that offer banking-related software and other tools.

Freedom of Information Act (FOIA)

The FOIA is the vehicle for obtaining Federal agency documents or records. The statute does contain, however, nine exemptions and three special law enforcement exclusions that shield some documents or records or parts of them from disclosure.

History

The OCC celebrated its 153d anniversary in 2016. A trove of historical information is available on the OCC's Web site.

News

The OCC posts news releases on its Web site.

Publications

OCC publications are available online. Copies of certain publications are available in print from the Communications Division. Phone, 202-649-6759. Fax, 202-649-6168.

An alphabetical list of OCC publications is available online.

Public Information on Banks

The Federal bank regulators post public information on individual banks online. The OCC's Web site provides convenient access to the Web sites of these regulators.

Site Map

The Web site map allows visitors to look for specific topics or to browse content that aligns with their interests.

Social Media

The OCC tweets announcements and other newsworthy items on Twitter.

The OCC has a Facebook account.

For further information, contact the Communications Division, Office of the Comptroller of the Currency, 400 7th Street SW., Washington, DC 20219. Phone, 202-649-6700.

United States Mint

801 Ninth Street NW., Washington, DC 20220, 202-354-7200, *http://www.usmint.gov*

DIRECTOR	(vacancy)
Principal Deputy Director	M. Rhett Jeppson

Chief Counsel	Jean Gentry
Chief of Staff	Elisa Basnight
Deputy Director, Management	David A. Motl, Acting
Deputy Director, Manufacturing and Quality / Chief Operating Officer	Richard A. Peterson

The establishment of a mint was authorized by act of April 2, 1792 (1 Stat. 246). The Bureau of the Mint was established by act of February 12, 1873 (17 Stat. 424), and recodified on September 13, 1982 (31 U.S.C. 304, 5131). The name was changed to United States Mint by Secretarial order on January 9, 1984.

The primary mission of the Mint is to produce an adequate volume of circulating coinage for the Nation to conduct its trade and commerce. The Mint also produces and sells numismatic coins, American Eagle gold and silver bullion coins, and national medals. The Fort Knox Bullion Depository is the primary storage facility for the Nation's gold bullion.

The U.S. Mint maintains sales centers at the Philadelphia and Denver Mints and at its headquarters on 9th Street in Washington, DC. Public tours are conducted, with free admission, at the Philadelphia and Denver Mints.

Sources of Information

Artists

The artistic infusion program enriches and invigorates coin and medal designs by contracting with a pool of American artists from diverse backgrounds and having a variety of interests. These artists collaborate with the Mint's sculptor-engravers to create and submit new designs for U.S. coins and medals.

Bullion Dealers

The Mint's Web site features a locator tool for finding U.S. Mint bullion sellers by city and State or by ZIP Code.

Business Opportunities

Contact the facility head of the appropriate field office or call the contracting and vendor department. Phone, 202-354-7820.

Educational Resources

The Mint's Web site offers learning resources for children, educators, and parents.

Employment

The Mint offers a wide range of career opportunities. An innovative, progressive bureau in the Department of the Treasury, it operates six facilities nationwide and employees professionals with backgrounds in financial management, information technology, manufacturing, protection, sales and marketing, workforce solutions, and other fields.

Facilities

The U.S. Mint operates four mints (CA, CO, NY, PA), one depository (KY), and maintains its headquarters in Washington, DC.

Freedom of Information Act (FOIA)

The FOIA gives the right of requesting access to documents or records maintained by the Mint to any person. Some information, however, is shielded from request and disclosure by the statute.

The Mint's electronic reading room contains records that are commonly requested under the FOIA.

Glossary

The H.I.P. Pocket Change Web site features a glossary.

History

The Mint's Web site features a section on the Mint's history and work.

The bureau's Web site features a timeline of the Mint that stretches from the 18th to 21st century.

How Are Coins Made?

The Mint's Web site features an animated overview of the six-step coin manufacturing process: blanking, annealing, upsetting, striking, inspecting, and counting and bagging.

Image Libraries

High-resolution images of coins and medals are available on the Mint's Web site. For information on the use of these images, contact the Office of Licensing. Phone, 202-354-7350. Fax, 202-756-6585.

The high-resolution images in the historical image library represent commemorative, circulating, and bullion coins from current and previous programs. For information on the use of these images, contact the Office of Licensing. Phone, 202-354-7350. Fax, 202-756-6585.

Medals

National medals commemorate significant historical events or sites and honor individuals whose superior deeds and achievements have enriched American history or the world. Some national medals are bronze duplicates of Congressional Gold Medals that Congress authorizes under separate Public Laws, and others are produced under the Secretary of the Treasury's authority to strike them.

News

The Mint posts news releases on its Web site.

Numismatic Services

The United States Mint maintains public exhibit and sales areas at the Philadelphia and Denver Mints and at its headquarters in Washington, DC. Brochures and order forms for official coins, medals, and other numismatic items are available online.

Production / Sales

The Mint produces circulating coins for commerce, numismatic coins for collectors, and bullion coins for investors. Quantities are measured in terms of production figures when referring to circulating coins, sales figures when referring to numismatic products, and sales and mintage figures when referring to bullion.

Reports

Annual reports are available online in Portable Document Format (PDF).

Special reports are available online in Portable Document Format (PDF).

Seigniorage

The Mint returned $550 million in seigniorage—the difference between the face value and the manufacturing cost of circulating coins—to the Department of the Treasury's general fund in 2015, which was more than double the amount that it returned to the fund in 2014. The Mint publishes the amount that it returns in seigniorage each year in its annual report.

Site Map

The Web site map allows visitors to look for specific topics or to browse content that aligns with their interests.

Sustainability

The Mint has made significant progress toward achieving sustainability goals. Achievements include reducing its direct greenhouse gas emissions and water consumption and increasing its solid waste diversion rate.

For further information, contact the United States Mint, Department of the Treasury, 801 Ninth Street NW., Washington, DC 20220. Phone, 202-354-7200.

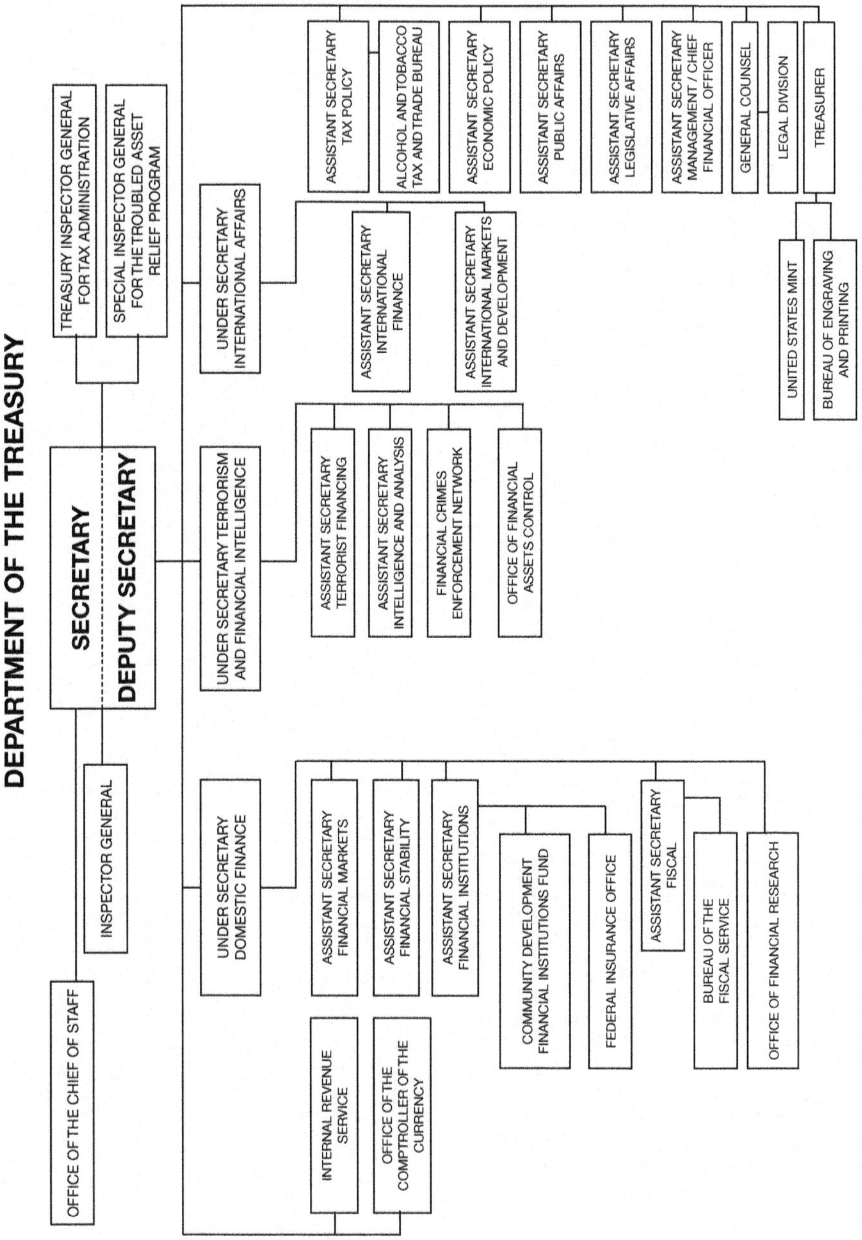
DEPARTMENT OF THE TREASURY
SECRETARY
DEPUTY SECRETARY
TREASURY INSPECTOR GENERAL FOR TAX ADMINISTRATION
SPECIAL INSPECTOR GENERAL FOR THE TROUBLED ASSET RELIEF PROGRAM
INSPECTOR GENERAL
OFFICE OF THE CHIEF OF STAFF
UNDER SECRETARY INTERNATIONAL AFFAIRS
ASSISTANT SECRETARY INTERNATIONAL FINANCE
ASSISTANT SECRETARY INTERNATIONAL MARKETS AND DEVELOPMENT
UNDER SECRETARY TERRORISM AND FINANCIAL INTELLIGENCE
ASSISTANT SECRETARY TERRORIST FINANCING
ASSISTANT SECRETARY INTELLIGENCE AND ANALYSIS
FINANCIAL CRIMES ENFORCEMENT NETWORK
OFFICE OF FINANCIAL ASSETS CONTROL
UNDER SECRETARY DOMESTIC FINANCE
ASSISTANT SECRETARY FINANCIAL MARKETS
ASSISTANT SECRETARY FINANCIAL STABILITY
ASSISTANT SECRETARY FINANCIAL INSTITUTIONS
COMMUNITY DEVELOPMENT FINANCIAL INSTITUTIONS FUND
FEDERAL INSURANCE OFFICE
ASSISTANT SECRETARY FISCAL
BUREAU OF THE FISCAL SERVICE
OFFICE OF FINANCIAL RESEARCH
INTERNAL REVENUE SERVICE
OFFICE OF THE COMPTROLLER OF THE CURRENCY
ASSISTANT SECRETARY TAX POLICY
ALCOHOL AND TOBACCO TAX AND TRADE BUREAU
ASSISTANT SECRETARY ECONOMIC POLICY
ASSISTANT SECRETARY PUBLIC AFFAIRS
ASSISTANT SECRETARY LEGISLATIVE AFFAIRS
ASSISTANT SECRETARY MANAGEMENT / CHIEF FINANCIAL OFFICER
GENERAL COUNSEL
LEGAL DIVISION
TREASURER
UNITED STATES MINT
BUREAU OF ENGRAVING AND PRINTING

Department of Veterans Affairs

810 Vermont Avenue NW., Washington, DC 20420, 202-461-4800, *http://www.va.gov*

SECRETARY OF VETERANS AFFAIRS	Robert A. McDonald
Deputy Secretary	Sloan D. Gibson
Chair, Board of Veterans' Appeals	Laura Eskenazi
Chief of Staff	Robert D. Snyder
Executive Director, Office of Acquisition, Logistics, and Construction	Gregory L. Giddens
General Counsel	Leigh A. Bradley
Inspector General	Michael J. Missal
UNDER SECRETARIES	
Benefits	Thomas J. Murphy, Acting
Health	David J. Shulkin
Memorial Affairs	Ronald E. Walters
ASSISTANT SECRETARIES	
Congressional and Legislative Affairs	Christopher E. O'Connor, Acting
Human Resources and Administration	Meghan Flanz, Acting
Information and Technology / Chief Information Officer	LaVerne H. Council
Management / Chief Financial Officer	Edward Murray, Acting
Operations, Security and Preparedness	Kevin T. Hanretta
Policy and Planning	Linda Spoonster Schwartz
Public Affairs	Rosemary Freitas Williams
Chief Veterans Experience Officer	Thomas Allin

The Department of Veterans Affairs operates programs benefiting veterans and members of their families: It offers education opportunities and rehabilitation services and provides compensation payments for disabilities or death related to military service, home loan guaranties, pensions, burials, and health care that includes the services of nursing homes, clinics, and medical centers.

The Department of Veterans Affairs (VA) was established as an executive department by the Department of Veterans Affairs Act (38 U.S.C. 201 note). It is comprised of three organizations that administer veterans programs: the Veterans Health Administration, the Veterans Benefits Administration, and the National Cemetery Administration. Each organization has field facilities and a central office component. Staff offices support the overall function of the Department and its Administrations.

Activities

Advisory Committee Management Office

The Advisory Committee Management Office serves as the coordinating office for the Department's 25 Federal advisory committees. It is responsible for establishing clear and uniform goals, standards, and procedures for advisory committee activities. It is also responsible for ensuring that VA advisory committee operations are in compliance with the provisions of the Federal Advisory Committee Act.

Office of Acquisition, Logistics, and Construction

The Office of Acquisition, Logistics, and Construction (OALC) is a multifunctional organization responsible for directing the acquisition, logistics, construction, and leasing functions within the VA. The

Executive Director, OALC, is also the Chief Acquisition Officer for the VA.

Cemeteries

The National Cemetery Administration (NCA) is responsible for the management and oversight of 131 national cemeteries in the United States and Puerto Rico, as well as 33 soldiers' lots, Confederate cemeteries, and monument sites. Burial in a national cemetery is available to eligible veterans and their spouses and dependent children. At no cost to the family, a national cemetery burial includes the gravesite, graveliner, opening and closing of the grave, headstone or marker, and perpetual care as part of a national shrine. If a veteran is buried in an unmarked grave in a private cemetery anywhere in the world, NCA will provide a headstone or marker. If a veteran died on or after November 1, 1990, and is buried in a grave marked with a privately purchased headstone, NCA will provide a headstone or marker to supplement the grave or a medallion to be affixed to the permanent headstone. NCA's State Cemetery Grants Program provides funds to State and tribal governments to establish, expand, or improve veterans' cemeteries. NCA issues Presidential Memorial Certificates to recognize the service of honorably discharged servicemembers or veterans.

Center for Minority Veterans

The Center for Minority Veterans (CMV), established by the Veterans' Benefits Improvement Act of 1994, promotes the use of VA benefits, programs, and services by minority veterans. The CMV focuses on the unique and special needs of African Americans, Hispanics, Asian Americans, Pacific Islanders, and Native Americans, which include American Indians, Native Hawaiians, and Alaska Natives.

Center for Women Veterans

The Center for Women Veterans (CWV), established by the Veterans' Benefits Improvement Act of 1994, reports to the Secretary's Office and oversees the Department's programs for women veterans. The CWV Director serves as the primary advisor to the Secretary on all matters related to policies, legislation, programs, issues, and initiatives affecting women veterans. The CWV ensures that women veterans receive benefits and services on par with male veterans; VA programs are responsive to gender-specific needs of women veterans; outreach is performed to improve women veterans' awareness of services, benefits, and eligibility criteria; and women veterans are treated with dignity and respect.

Health Services

The Veterans Health Administration (VHA) is home to the largest integrated health care system in the United States. It provides hospital, nursing home, domiciliary, and outpatient medical and dental care to eligible veterans of military service in the Armed Forces. VHA conducts both individual medical and health care delivery research projects and multihospital research programs, to include assisting in the education of physicians, dentists, and the training of many other health care professionals through affiliations with educational institutions and organizations. VHA treated over 6 million patients in 2010, and has over 1,600 sites of care which include: 152 hospitals, 965 outpatient clinics, 133 community living centers, and 293 Vet Centers. In 2010, VA hospitals also had approximately 680,000 inpatient admissions and more than 75 million outpatient visits. The number of women veterans using VA health care doubled from 160,000 in 2000 to 315, 000 in 2010. VA hospitals provide more public data about quality and safety than any health care system in the world and held academic affiliations with more than 1,200 educational institutions. More than 100,000 health care students receive clinical training from VA each year.

Historically, VHA has been at the forefront in developing new devices, treatments, and tools for various conditions and diseases, including the first electronic health record, cardiac pacemaker, bionic ankle, and successful liver transplant. It has also developed new drugs and treatments for acquired immune deficiency syndrome/ human immunodeficiency virus, diabetes, Alzheimer's disease, and osteoporosis. Currently, VHA medical centers provide a wide range of services including traditional hospital-based services such as critical care, mental health, orthopedics, pharmacy, radiology, and physical therapy. Furthermore, most VA medical centers offer additional medical and surgical specialties services including pathology, dermatology, dental, geriatrics, neurology, oncology, prosthetics, urology, and vision care. Some medical centers also offer advanced services such as organ transplants and plastic surgery. VHA also distinguishes itself as the Nation's largest provider of graduate medical education and a major contributor to medical research.

Operations, Security, and Preparedness

The Assistant Secretary for Operations, Security, and Preparedness (OSP) coordinates the Department's emergency management, preparedness, personal identity verification, physical security, personnel security and suitability, police services, law enforcement activities, and ensures compliance and resource management in the OSP, so the Department can continue to perform the mission-essential functions under all circumstances across the spectrum of threats. OSP directs and provides oversight for the VA's overall operations for planning, response, and security and law enforcement programs in support of the National Response Framework, Homeland Security Presidential Directive 12, and other related Executive orders and Federal regulations.

Veterans Benefits

The Veterans Benefits Administration provides information, advice, and assistance to veterans, their dependents, beneficiaries, representatives, and others applying for VA benefits. It also cooperates with the Department of Labor and other Federal, State, and local agencies in developing employment opportunities for veterans and referral for assistance in resolving socioeconomic, housing, and other related problems.

The Compensation and Pension Service is responsible for claims for disability compensation and pension, specially adapted housing, accrued benefits, adjusted compensation in death cases, and reimbursement for headstone or marker; allowances for automobiles and special adaptive equipment; special clothing allowances; emergency officers' retirement pay; survivors' claims for death compensation, dependency and indemnity compensation, death pension, and burial and plot allowance claims; forfeiture determinations; and a benefits protection program for minors and incompetent adult beneficiaries.

The Education Service administers the Montgomery GI Bill program and other programs which provide education benefits to qualified active-duty members, veterans, certain dependents of veterans, and members of the Selected and Ready Reserve. The Service also checks school records to ensure that they comply with the pertinent law, approves courses for the payment of educational benefits, and administers a work-study program. Additional details are available at www.gibill.va.gov.

The Insurance Service's operations for the benefit of servicemembers, veterans, and their beneficiaries are available through the regional office and insurance center (phone, 800-669-8477) in Philadelphia, PA, which provides the full range of activities necessary for a national life insurance program. Activities include the complete maintenance of individual accounts, underwriting functions, life and death insurance claims awards, and any other insurance-related transactions. The Service also administers the Veterans Mortgage Life Insurance Program for those disabled veterans who receive a VA grant for specially adapted housing and supervises the Servicemembers' Group Life Insurance Program and the Veterans' Group Life Insurance Program.

The Loan Guaranty Service is responsible for operations that include appraising properties to establish their values; approving grants for specially adapted housing; supervising the construction of new residential properties; establishing the eligibility of veterans for the program; evaluating the ability of a veteran to repay a loan and the credit risk; making direct loans to Native American veterans to acquire a home on trust land; servicing and liquidating defaulted loans; and disposing of real estate acquired as the consequence of defaulted loans.

The Vocational Rehabilitation and Employment Service provides outreach, motivation, evaluation, counseling, training, employment, and other rehabilitation services to service-connected disabled veterans. Vocational and educational counseling, as well as the evaluation of abilities, aptitudes, and interests are provided to veterans and servicepersons. Counseling, assessment, education programs, and in some cases, rehabilitation services are available to spouses and children of totally and permanently disabled veterans as well as surviving orphans, widows, and widowers of certain deceased veterans.

Vocational training and rehabilitation services are available to children with spina bifida having a parent who served in the Republic of Vietnam during the Vietnam era or who served in certain military units in or near the demilitarized zone in Korea between September 1, 1967 and August 31, 1971.

Veterans' Appeals

The Board of Veterans' Appeals (BVA) renders final decisions on behalf of the Secretary on appeals from decisions of local VA offices. The Board reviews all appeals for entitlement to veterans' benefits, including claims for service connection, increased disability ratings, total disability ratings, pension, insurance benefits, educational benefits, home loan guaranties, vocational rehabilitation, dependency and indemnity compensation, health care delivery, and fiduciary matters. The Board has jurisdiction over appeals arising from the VA regional offices, VA medical centers, the National Cemetery Administration, and the Office of General Counsel. The Board's mission is to conduct hearings and issue timely, understandable, and quality decisions for veterans and other appellants in compliance with the requirements of law. Final BVA decisions are appealable to the U.S. Court of Appeals for Veterans Claims.

Field Facilities

The Department's operations are handled through the following field facilities: cemeteries, domiciliaries, medical centers, outpatient clinics, and regional offices. Cemeteries provide burial services to veterans, their spouses, and dependent children. Domiciliaries provide the least intensive level of inpatient medical care, including necessary ambulatory medical treatment, rehabilitation, and support services, in a structured environment to veterans who are unable because of their disabilities to provide adequately for themselves in the community. Medical centers provide eligible beneficiaries with medical and other health care services equivalent to those provided by private sector institutions, augmented in many instances by services to meet the special requirements of veterans. Outpatient clinics provide eligible beneficiaries with ambulatory care. Regional offices grant benefits and services provided by law for veterans, their dependents, and beneficiaries within an assigned territory; furnish information regarding VA benefits and services; adjudicate claims and make awards for disability compensation and pension; conduct outreach and information dissemination; provide support and assistance to various segments of the veteran population to include former prisoners of war, minority, homeless, women, and elderly veterans; supervise payment of VA benefits to incompetent beneficiaries; provide vocational rehabilitation and employment training; administer educational benefits; guarantee loans for purchase, construction, or alteration of homes; process grants for specially adapted housing; process death claims; and assist veterans in exercising rights to benefits and services.

For information on key staff and VA facilities nationwide or to locate facilities in a particular State, visit the "Find Locations" Web page.

Sources of Information

Blog

"VAntage Point" is the VA's official blog.

Business Opportunities

Information for doing business with the VA is available on the Office of Acquisition and Logistics' Web pages.

For information on small and veteran-owned business programs, call 800-949-8387 or 202-461-4300. More information is available from the Office of Small and Disadvantaged Business Utilization's Web pages.

Business Ownership Services

The Center for Verification and Evaluation is a program office in the Office of Small and Disadvantaged Business

Utilization. The center provides verification to veteran-owned and service-disabled veteran-owned small businesses. Phone, 866-584-2344.

Construction / Design Projects

Construction projects for VA medical centers and other facilities in excess of $4 million are managed and controlled at the VA central office, located in Washington, DC. Projects requiring design, construction, and other related services are advertised on the Web site USA.Gov. Submit project-specific qualifications (SF 254/SF 255) to the Director, A/E Evaluation and Program Support Team (181A), 810 Vermont Avenue NW., Washington, DC 20420. Additional information on the selection process can be found on the Office of Construction and Facilities Management Web page. Construction projects for VA medical centers and other facilities that cost less than $4 million are managed and controlled locally at the medical centers. For information on specific projects, contact the appropriate local Acquisition and Materiel Management office.

Data / Statistics

The Web site of the National Center for Veterans Analysis and Statistics features reports, statistics, surveys, and other information.

Employment

Under its excepted merit system, the VA employs certified respiratory technicians, dentists, expanded-function dental auxiliaries, licensed nurses, licensed physical therapists, optometrists, nurse anesthetists, occupational therapists, pharmacists, physician assistants, physicians, podiatrists, and registered respiratory therapists. This system does not require civil service eligibility. Other administrative, clerical, and technical occupations that require civil service eligibility—such as management analyst, secretary, and veterans claims examiner—do exist in the VA. For information on employment, contact the human resources services office at the nearest VA facility. Or, use the VA's online, career-building resources.

Freedom of Information Act (FOIA)

A FOIA request should be addressed to one of the approximately 400 geographically dispersed components where the desired document or record is kept. A request may be sent by email, fax, or postal mail. If the information seeker does not know which office or component maintains the desired document or record, he or she should contact the Director, FOIA Service, (005R1C), 810 Vermont Avenue NW., Washington, DC 20420. Phone, 877-750-3642. Fax 202-273-0487.

Glossaries

The VA Web site features a glossary of HIV and AIDS terms.

The VA National Center for Patient Safety maintains an online glossary of patient safety terms.

The VA Web site features a health benefits glossary.

Health Topics

The veterans health A–Z index is an informational and navigational tool that helps users find and retrieve veterans health information. Popular topics, frequent inquiries, and items of critical importance to veterans and their caregivers are included in it.

History

The Department's Web site features a history of the VA.

Homeless Veterans

Information and resources to help a homeless veteran find a home are available on the VA Web site.

Media Room

The VA posts news releases on its Web site.

The VA posts speeches on its Web site.

National Gravesite Locator

The National Cemetery Administration's Web site features a database of burial information that is updated each day. The online locator allows users to search for the burial locations of veterans and their family members in VA National Cemeteries, State veterans cemeteries, and various other military and Department of Interior cemeteries, as well as for the interment sites of veterans who were buried in private cemeteries and whose graves are marked with Government grave markers.

Our Doctors

The VA Web site features an online directory that lists dentists, nurse practitioners, physicians, and other licensed independent practitioners.

Public Affairs / News Media

Contact the the nearest regional Office of Public Affairs: Atlanta (404-929-5880); Chicago (312-980-4235); Dallas (817-385-3720); Denver (303-914-5855); Los Angeles (310-268-4207); New York (212-807-3429); or Washington, DC (202-530-9360). Representatives of the national media may prefer contacting the Office of Public Affairs in the VA Central Office, 810 Vermont Avenue NW., Washington, DC 20420. Phone, 202-461-7400.

Publications

Information on books, factsheets, and other publications is available on the Office of Public and Intergovernmental Affairs Web page.

Office of Inspector General (OIG)

Public documents and information are available on the OIG's Web site. Complaints may be sent to the VA Inspector General (53E), P.O. Box 50410, Washington, DC 20091-0410. Hotline phone, 800-488-8244.

Site Map

The Web site map allows visitors to look for specific topics or to browse content that aligns with their interests.

Social Media

The VA tweets announcements and other newsworthy items on Twitter.

The VA has a Facebook account.

The VA posts photos on Flickr.

The VA posts videos on its YouTube channel.

Veterans Service Organizations

The VA's Web site features a directory of veterans services organizations.

For further information, contact the Office of Public and Intergovernmental Affairs, Department of Veterans Affairs, 810 Vermont Avenue NW., Washington, DC 20420. Phone, 202-273-6000.

Executive Branch: Independent Agencies and Government Corporations

Administrative Conference of the United States

1120 Twentieth Street NW., Suite 706 South, Washington, DC 20036, 202-480-2080, 202-386-7190, *http://www.acus.gov*

CHAIR	(vacancy)
Executive Director	Matthew L. Wiener
Chief Financial and Operations Officer	Harry M. Seidman
Deputy General Counsel	David M. Pritzker
General Counsel	Shawne C. McGibbon
Public Affairs Coordinator	Abigail Price
Research Chief	Reeve T. Bull

COUNCIL

VICE CHAIR	Steven P. Croley
Member	Ronald A. Cass
Member	Danielle C. Gray
Member	Ilona R. Cohen
Member	Ronald A. Klain
Member	Theodore B. Olson
Member	Edith Ramirez
Member	Geovette E. Washington
Member	Jonathan Sallet
Member	Jane C. Sherburne

The Administrative Conference of the United States develops recommendations for improving the fairness and effectiveness of procedures by which Federal agencies administer regulatory, benefit, and other Government programs.

The Administrative Conference of the United States was established as a permanent independent agency by the Administrative Conference Act (5 U.S.C. 591-596) enacted in 1964. The Conference is the successor to two temporary Administrative Conferences during the Eisenhower and Kennedy administrations.

The Conference ceased operations on October 31, 1995, due to termination of funding by Congress. Congress reauthorized the Conference in 2004 and again in 2008. The 2004 legislation expanded its responsibilities to include specific attention to achieving more effective public participation and efficiency, reducing unnecessary litigation, and improving the use of science in the rulemaking process. Funding was approved in 2009, and the Conference was officially reestablished in March 2010.

By statute, the Administrative Conference has no fewer than 75 and no more than 101 members, a majority of whom are Government officials. The President appoints the Chair of the Conference with the advice and consent of the Senate for a 5-year term. The Council, which acts as an executive board, comprises the Chair and 10 other members whom the President appoints for 3-year terms. Federal officials named to the Council may not constitute more than half of the total Council membership. The Chair, the only full-time, compensated member of the Conference, appoints members representing the private sector with the approval of the Council for 2-year terms.

The entire membership is divided into committees. Each committee is assigned a broad area of interest such as adjudication, administration and management, judicial review, regulation, or rulemaking. The membership meeting in plenary session constitutes the Assembly of the Conference, which by statute must meet at least once, and customarily meets twice, each year.

Activities

Subjects for inquiry are developed by the Chair and approved by the Council, often based on input from government and nongovernment experts in administrative procedure. The committees conduct thorough studies of these subjects and propose recommendations, based on supporting reports, ordinarily prepared for the Conference by expert consultants. Recommendations are evaluated by the Council and, if ready for Assembly consideration, are distributed to the membership with the supporting reports and placed on the agenda of the next plenary session for discussion and a final vote. The general public may attend committee and Assembly deliberations.

Recommendations adopted by the Conference may be addressed to administrative agencies, Congress, the President, or the Judicial Conference. Most recommendations call for action on the part of affected agencies or for new legislation. While a substantial number of recommendations have been implemented, implementation activities are continually ongoing.

The Chair may make independent inquiries into procedural matters, including matters proposed by individuals inside or outside the Government. These inquiries help determine whether the problems should be made the subject of Conference study in the interest of developing fairer or more effective or efficient procedures.

Upon the request of a department or agency head, the Chair is authorized to advise and assist on matters of administrative procedure. The Conference may collect information and statistics from departments and agencies and publish reports that it considers useful for evaluating and improving administrative processes. The Conference also serves as a forum for the interchange among departments and agencies of information that may be useful for improving administrative practices and procedures.

Sources of Information

Blog

The blog "Administrative Fix" is available on the Conference's Web site.

Calendar

A calendar of meetings and events is available online.

Employment

Current job openings and information on internships and the research fellow program are accessible online.

Freedom of Information Act (FOIA)

FOIA requests may be submitted using the online request form. Phone, 202-480-2080.

Newsroom

An online newsroom features blog articles and news releases.

Publications

Articles, books, papers, reports, and bibliographies are accessible online.

Resources

The "Resources For" Web pages provide convenient access to the electronic resources that are available on the Conference's Web site.

Site Map

The Web site map allows visitors to look for specific topics or to browse content that aligns with their interests.

For further information, contact the Office of the Chairman, Administrative Conference of the United States, 1120 Twentieth Street NW., Suite 706 South, Washington, DC 20036. Phone, 202-480-2080. Fax, 202-386-7190.

African Development Bank

Avenue Jean-Paul II, 01 BP 1387, Abidjan 01, Côte d'Ivoire, +225 20 26 10 20, *http://www.afdb.org* | Email: *afdb@afdb.org*

PRESIDENT Akinwumi Adesina

The African Development Bank stimulates sustainable economic development and social progress in regional member countries to mitigate poverty and its effects.

The African Development Bank (AFDB) was established in 1964. By charter amendment, the AFDB expanded its membership to include nonregional countries in 1982. The admission of nonregional countries boosted AFDB capital resources by more than twofold.

The Bank's mandate centers on the economic development and social progress of its regional members. On May 31, 2015, AFDB membership totaled 80 countries: 54 African and 26 nonregional countries. In 1998, at the time of the fifth general capital increase, African countries controlled 60 percent and nonregional countries controlled 40 percent of AFDB shares.

The African Development Fund, established in 1972 and operational in 1974, complements AFDB operations by providing concessional financing for high-priority development projects. Comprising 27 contributing countries, the Fund improves economic and social conditions in 40 beneficiary countries. These beneficiaries include countries that are increasing in economic capacity and en route to becoming the new emerging markets or that are regarded as fragile states and require special assistance for basics levels of service delivery.

Sources of Information

Employment

Grade and salary data and information on current job vacancies are available online.

Documents

The AFDB posts documents on its Web site.

Field Offices

Contact information for AFDB field offices is available online.

Frequently Asked Questions (FAQs)

The AFDB posts answers to FAQs on its Web site.

Glossary

The AFDB Web site features a glossary of acronyms.

News / Events

The AFDB Web site features events, interviews, loan and grant announcements, multimedia, news, press releases, project stories, and speeches.

Site Map

The Web site map allows visitors to look for specific topics or to browse content that aligns with their interests.

Web TV

The AFDB's Web TV features programs in English and French.

Where the AFDB Works

The AFDB's Web site features a list of African countries where the Bank is active.

Social Media

The AFDB tweets announcements and newsworthy items in English and French on Twitter.

The AFDB has a Facebook account.

Broadcasting Board of Governors

330 Independence Avenue SW., Washington, DC 20237, 202-203-4545, *http://www.bbg.gov*

BOARD	
Chair	Jeffrey Shell
Member	Matthew C. Armstrong
Member	Leon Aron
Member	Ryan C. Crocker
Member	Michael Kempner
Member	Karen Kornbluh
Member	Kenneth Weinstein
Member	(vacancy)
Ex Officio Member	Secretary of State John F. Kerry
MANAGEMENT	
Chief Executive Officer and Director	John F. Lansing
Chief of Staff	Robert Fallon
Director, International Broadcasting Bureau	(vacancy)
Deputy Director, International Broadcasting Bureau	Jeffrey N. Trimble
Chief Financial Officer	Grant Turner
Chief Information Officer / Chief Technology Officer	André Mendez
Director, Congressional Affairs	Ellona Fritschie
Director, Internet Freedom Program Office	Nnake Nweke
Director, Management Services	Marie Lennon
General Counsel	Elizabeth Parish, Acting
NETWORKS	
Director, Office of Cuba Broadcasting	Maria González
Director, Voice of America	Amanda Bennett
President, Middle East Broadcasting Networks	Brian T. Conniff
President, Radio Free Asia	Libby Liu
President, Radio Free Europe / Radio Liberty	Thomas Kent

The Broadcasting Board of Governors informs, engages, and connects people around the world in support of freedom and democracy.

The Broadcasting Board of Governors (BBG) became an independent agency on October 1, 1999, by authority of the Foreign Affairs Reform and Restructuring Act of 1998 (22 U.S.C. 6501 note). It is composed of nine members. The President appoints eight of the members, and the Senate confirms them. The ninth member, an ex officio member, is the Secretary of State.

The BBG serves as the governing body for all civilian U.S. international media and provides programming in 61 languages via radio, television, and the Internet. The BBG broadcast services comprise Voice of America, Radio Free Europe/Radio Liberty, Radio Free Asia, the Office of Cuba Broadcasting, and the Middle East Broadcasting Networks. The BBG relies on the International Broadcasting Bureau for transmission and technical support of its broadcast services.

All BBG broadcast services adhere to the broadcasting standards and principles of the International Broadcasting Act of 1994. These principles and standards support reliable, accurate, and comprehensive news; balanced and comprehensive presentations of U.S. thought, institutions, and policies, as well as discussions on those policies; information on developments throughout the world; and a variety of opinions from nations around the world.

Activities

International Broadcasting Bureau

The International Broadcasting Bureau (IBB) provides program delivery and essential support services for U.S. international media. The IBB is responsible for the Agency's strategic planning and for integrating activities across the Federal and grantee broadcasters for greater organizational efficiency. The IBB manages a global network of transmitting sites, an extensive system of leased satellite and fiber optic circuits, and an increasing variety of rapidly growing Internet and mobile audience platforms and services. It is responsible for program placement services and marketing for all BBG broadcast organizations. It provides research and evaluations of broadcasts. The IBB manages the Agency's financial operations, legal support, and communications, and also provides information technology, human resources, equal employment opportunity, procurement, security, and other administrative support.

Voice of America

The Voice of America (VOA) is a multimedia international broadcasting service funded by the U.S. Government through the Broadcasting Board of Governors. It began broadcasting in 1942 and now reaches more than 172 million people worldwide. The VOA provides accurate, comprehensive, and trustworthy news and information, as well as informed discussion on the United States and the world. It engages audiences in regions deemed critical to the United States through whatever medium—radio, television, Internet, or digital media—the people of those regions prefer. It broadcasts approximately 1,800 hours of news, information, educational, and cultural programming every week to a global audience. Programs are produced in nearly 50 languages.

Radio Free Europe/Radio Liberty

Radio Free Europe/Radio Liberty (RFE/RL) is a private nonprofit multimedia broadcasting corporation whose funding comes from a BBG grant. It reaches more than 23 million people in 24 countries and 29 languages, including Afghanistan, Iran, Iraq, Pakistan, and Russia. Its journalists provide what many people cannot get locally: uncensored news, responsible discussion, and open debate. RFE/RL uses the latest digital technologies—the Internet, SMS text messaging, online video, satellite radio, and popular social media networks—and trusted broadcast radio to reach people in some of the most closed societies on Earth. With 65 years of surrogate broadcasting experience, it continues to bring diverse, immediate, and interactive content to audiences.

Radio Free Asia

Radio Free Asia (RFA) is a private nonprofit news organization that operates under a grant from the BBG. Broadcasting daily in nine languages to Asian audiences whose governments restrict media, RFA delivers award-winning, reliable news and information. It also allows a range of voices and opinions from within Asia to be heard as a demonstration of freedom of expression over the airwaves, on television, and online. Through shortwave, medium wave, satellite and transmission television, social media, and the Internet, RFA broadcasts in Mandarin, Cantonese, Uyghur, three Tibetan dialects, Burmese, Vietnamese, Korean, Lao, and Khmer. Headquartered in Washington, DC, it has seven overseas bureaus and a network of correspondents around the world.

Middle East Broadcasting Networks

The Middle East Broadcasting Networks, Inc. (MBN) is a nonprofit news organization that operates Alhurra Television, Radio Sawa, and MBN Digital under a grant from the BBG. Alhurra Television, Radio Sawa, and MBN Digital offer an open line of communication between the people of the Middle East and the United States. These networks deliver accurate information on the United States, its policies, and its people from a range of perspectives and with an exchange of ideas on relevant issues. They reach an audience of more than 30 million people in 22 countries in the Middle East and North Africa.

Office of Cuba Broadcasting

The Office of Cuba Broadcasting operates the Martís from its headquarters in

Miami, FL. The Martís are a multimedia hub of news, information, and analysis that provides the people of Cuba with interactive programs each day of the week. To broadcast their message, the Martís rely on a combination of high- and low-tech approaches: DVDs, emails, flash drives, Internet, satellite television, shortwave and AM radio, and SMS text. Combined with martinoticias.com, they constitute a unique service that brings objective information to the Cuban people.

Sources of Information

Awards

The BBG has won awards for its productions in a variety of categories: documentary, education, investigative journalism, promotional programming, special reporting, video, and more.

Business Opportunities

Information on contract opportunities and instructions on how to do business with the BBG are available online.

Employment

The BBG work environment is diverse, multicultural, and professional. In addition to American citizens, the agency also hires non-U.S. citizens for positions that require foreign language skills.

Freedom of Information Act (FOIA)

The FOIA provides a statutory basis for public access to official agency information previously restricted from public view. Through the FOIA, Congress affirmed that citizens have the right to know what their Government does. Under the act, official information is available to "any person" without regard to need for or interest in the material. The BBG and its FOIA staff are committed to ensuring the fullest possible disclosure that is consistent with the letter and spirit of the law. The Office of the General Counsel manages FOIA and Privacy Act requests. Typical requests are for audience survey reports, Board of Governors records, lists of credit card purchase holders, personnel and security files, and procurement records.

The FOIA requires agencies to disclose, proactively and electronically, certain categories of records to the public. Records that the BBG has previously released to the public under the FOIA and that are the subject of subsequent requests or likely to be the subject of subsequent requests are proactively disclosed in the BBG's electronic reading room for public access. Records that the BBG determines are of sufficient public interest to warrant automatic disclosure are also proactively disclosed in the electronic reading room.

Frequently Asked Questions (FAQs)

The BBG posts answers to FAQs on its Web site.

History

The BBG's Web site features a timeline of important events in the agency's history.

Learn English

The Voice of America's Web site features resources for learning American English.

Networks

The BBG's Web site provides convenient access to the home pages of all of its networks.

News

News and information are available on the BBG's Web site.

An online subscription form is available for the BBG newsletter, events, media highlights, press releases, and the VOA Buzz.

Office of Inspector General (OIG)

Report allegations of abuse, fraud, mismanagement, or waste involving employees and programs of the BBG or Department of State to the OIG hotline. Phone, 800-409-9926.

Open Government

The BBG supports the Open Government initiative by promoting collaboration, participation, and transparency.

Site Map

The Web site map allows visitors to look for specific topics or to browse content that aligns with their interests.

The BBG provides training opportunities for reporters and students of media on five continents.

Training Opportunities

For further information, contact the Office of Communications and External Affairs, Broadcasting Board of Governors, 330 Independence Avenue SW., Washington, DC 20237. Phone, 202-203-4400. Fax, 202-203-4961.

BROADCASTING BOARD OF GOVERNORS

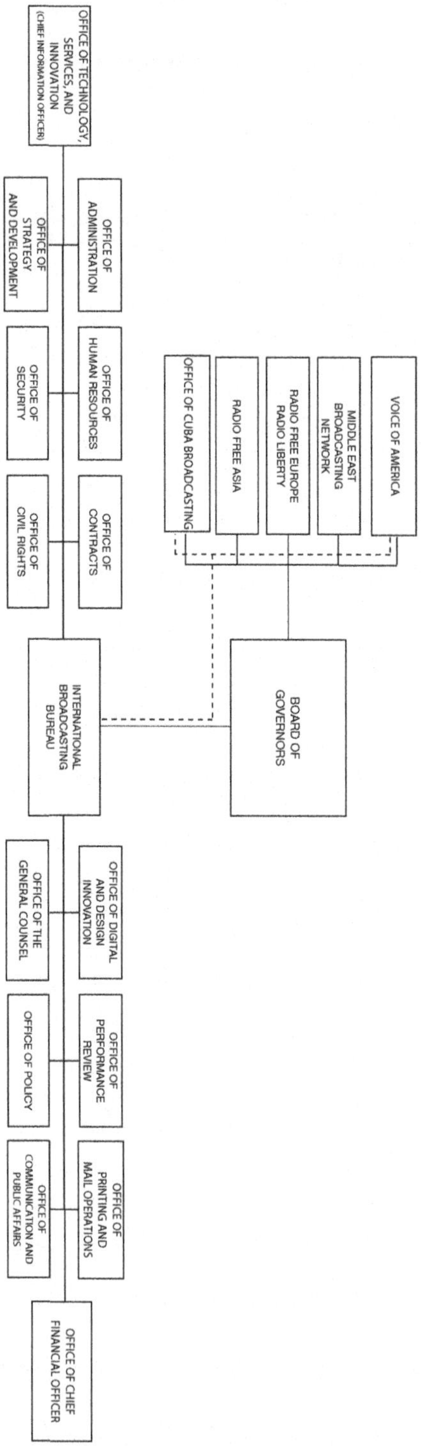

Central Intelligence Agency

Washington, DC 20505, 703-482-0623, *http://www.cia.gov*

DIRECTOR	John O. Brennan
Deputy Director	David S. Cohen

[For the Central Intelligence Agency statement of organization, see the Code of Federal Regulations, Title 32, Part 1900]

The Central Intelligence Agency collects, evaluates, and disseminates vital information on economic, military, political, scientific, and other developments abroad to safeguard national security.

The Central Intelligence Agency was established by the National Security Act of 1947, as amended (50 U.S.C. 401 et seq.). It now functions under that statute, Executive Order 12333 of December 4, 1981, the Intelligence Reform and Terrorism Prevention Act of 2004 (50 U.S.C. 401 note), and other laws, Executive orders, regulations, and directives.

The Director, whom the President appoints with the advice and consent of the Senate, serves as the head of the Central Intelligence Agency. The Director reports to the Director of National Intelligence (DNI) regarding the activities of the Agency.

The Central Intelligence Agency uses human source collection and other means to gather intelligence; however, it neither carries out internal security functions nor exercises police, subpoena, or other law enforcement powers. The Agency correlates, evaluates, and disseminates national security intelligence. It also directs and coordinates intelligence collecting outside the United States by U.S. intelligence community elements authorized to engage in human source collection.

In coordination with other departments, agencies, and authorized elements of the U.S. Government, the Agency ensures that resources are used effectively and that adequate consideration is given to the risks, both to the United States and to those involved in collecting intelligence abroad. The Agency carries out other intelligence-related tasks that are necessary for safeguarding national security, as the President or the DNI may indicate. Under the direction of the DNI and consistent with section 207 of the Foreign Service Act of 1980, the Agency coordinates relationships between elements of the U.S. intelligence community and the security or intelligence services of foreign governments or international organizations in matters of national security and clandestine intelligence.

Sources of Information

Employment

Career and student opportunities, as well as information on benefits, diversity, military transitioning, and the application process, are posted on the "Careers and Internships" Web page.

Library

The Agency posts millions of pages of documents, including many items of public interest, on its Web site each year. Its online library contains a wealth of information that ranges from unclassified publications to basic references, reports, and maps.

For further information, contact the Central Intelligence Agency, Office of Public Affairs, Washington, DC 20505. Phone, 703-482-0623.

Commodity Futures Trading Commission

1155 Twenty-first Street NW, Washington, DC 20581, 202-418-5000, 202-418-5514 (TTY), 202-418-5521, *http://www.cftc.gov/index.htm*

CHAIR	Timothy G. Massad
Commissioner	Sharon Y. Bowen
Commissioner	J. Christopher Giancarlo
Commissioner	(vacancy)
Commissioner	(vacancy)
EXECUTIVE DIRECTOR	Anthony C. Thompson
Chief Economist	Sayee Srinivasan
Chief Information Officer	John L. Rogers
Director, Division of Clearing and Risk	Jeffrey M. Bandman, Acting
Director, Division of Enforcement	Aitan Goelman
Director, Division of Market Oversight	Vincent A. McGonagle
Director, Division of Swap Dealer and Intermediary Oversight	Eileen T. Flaherty
Director, Office of International Affairs	Eric J. Pan
General Counsel	Jonathan L. Marcus
Inspector General	A. Roy Lavik

[For the Commodity Futures Trading Commission statement of organization, see the Code of Federal Regulations, Title 17, Part 140]

The Commodity Futures Trading Commission avoids systemic risk; fosters open, transparent, competitive, and financially sound markets; and protects the market users and their funds, consumers, and the public from fraud, manipulation, and abusive practices related to derivatives and other products that are subject to the Commodity Exchange Act.

The Commodity Futures Trading Commission was established by the Commodity Futures Trading Commission Act of 1974 (7 U.S.C. 2). The Commission began operation in April 1975, and its authority to regulate futures trading was renewed by Congress in 1978, 1982, 1986, 1992, 1995, 2000, and 2008. In 2010, the Dodd-Frank Wall Street Reform and Consumer Protection Act (Public Law 111–203, Title VII) gave the Commission new and expanded responsibilities and authorities for regulation of the swaps marketplace.

The Commission comprises five Commissioners whom the President appoints with the advice and consent of the Senate. One Commissioner is designated by the President to serve as the Chair. The Commissioners serve staggered 5-year terms, and no more than three of them may belong to the same political party.

The Commission has nine major operating components: the Divisions of Market Oversight, Clearing and Risk, Swap Dealer and Intermediary Oversight, Enforcement, and the Offices of the Executive Director, the General Counsel, the Chief Economist, International Affairs, and Data and Technology. The Office of Inspector General is an independent organizational unit at the Commission.

Activities

The Commission regulates trading on the U.S. futures and options markets that offer commodity futures and options contracts, as well as the swaps marketplace in the United States. This oversight of the derivatives marketplace is carried out through the various activities of the Commission.

The Commission oversees derivatives clearing organizations and other market participants in the clearing process, including futures commission merchants, swap dealers, major swap participants, and large traders. The Commission oversees the registration and compliance of intermediaries and futures industry self-regulatory organizations, including U.S. derivatives exchanges and the National Futures Association. It also oversees trade execution facilities and data repositories, conducts surveillance, reviews new exchange applications, and examines existing exchanges to ensure compliance with applicable core principles. Under the Dodd-Frank Act, the Commission is responsible for developing and monitoring compliance with regulations addressing registration, business conduct standards, capital adequacy, and margin requirements for swap dealers and major swap participants.

Exercising the Commission's authority, its staff also investigates and prosecutes alleged violations of the Commodity Exchange Act and Commission regulations. Potential violations include fraud, manipulation, and other abuses concerning commodity derivatives and swaps that threaten market integrity, market participants, and the general public.

Sources of Information

Business Opportunities

The Commission has recurring requirements for the following goods: furniture, office equipment and supplies, and telecommunications equipment and supplies. It also has recurring requirements for copying and printing services and minor construction.

Electronic Updates

An online subscription form is available to receive email updates.

Employment

The Commission hires professionals with strong academic records and superior analytical and problem solving skills.

Freedom of Information Act (FOIA)

Information on how to submit a FOIA request is available online.

Glossary

The online glossary defines some of the specialized words and phrases heard in the futures industry. Standard reference works do not include many of them.

Press Room

The press room features events, press releases, remarks, statements, and testimonies.

Regional Offices

The Commission maintains regional offices in Chicago, IL, and New York, NY, where many of the Nation's designated contract markets are located. Phone, 312-596-0700 (IL); Phone, 646-746-9700 (NY). A third regional office is located in Kansas City, MO. Phone, 816-960-7700.

Transparency

The Commission demonstrates its commitment to transparency by posting data, information on activities and rulemaking matters, and records and reports online.

Whistleblower Program

The Commission gives monetary incentives to whistleblowers who report possible Commodity Exchange Act violations that lead to a successful enforcement action. The Commission also provides antiretaliation protections, confidentiality, and privacy.

For further information, contact the Office of Public Affairs, Commodity Futures Trading Commission, 1155 Twenty-first Street NW., Washington, DC 20581. Phone, 202-418-5080. TTY, 202-418-5514. Fax, 202-418-5521.

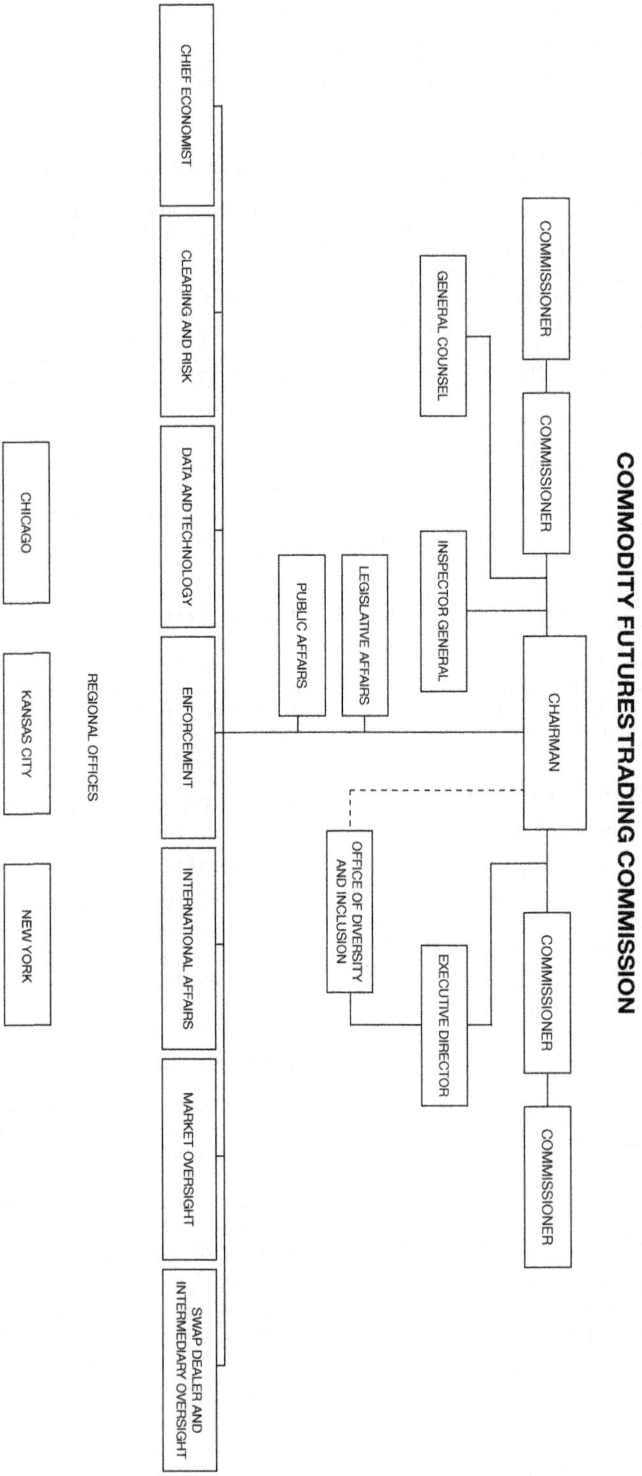
COMMODITY FUTURES TRADING COMMISSION
COMMISSIONER
COMMISSIONER
CHAIRMAN
COMMISSIONER
COMMISSIONER
GENERAL COUNSEL
INSPECTOR GENERAL
EXECUTIVE DIRECTOR
LEGISLATIVE AFFAIRS
PUBLIC AFFAIRS
OFFICE OF DIVERSITY AND INCLUSION
CHIEF ECONOMIST
CLEARING AND RISK
DATA AND TECHNOLOGY
ENFORCEMENT
INTERNATIONAL AFFAIRS
MARKET OVERSIGHT
SWAP DEALER AND INTERMEDIARY OVERSIGHT
REGIONAL OFFICES
CHICAGO
KANSAS CITY
NEW YORK

Consumer Financial Protection Bureau

1700 G Street NW., Washington, DC 20552, 202-435-7000, *http://www.consumerfinance.gov*

DIRECTOR	Richard Cordray
Deputy Director	David Silberman, Acting
Administrative Law Judge	Christine Kirby
Assistant Director, Card Markets	William Wade-Gery
Assistant Director, Communications	Jennifer Howard
Assistant Director, Community Affairs	Chris Vaeth
Assistant Director, Consumer Engagement	Gene Koo
Assistant Director, Deposits, Liquidity Lending, and Reporting Markets	Gary Stein, Acting
Assistant Director, Enforcement	Anthony Alexis
Assistant Director, Fair Lending and Equal Opportunity	Patrice Ficklin
Assistant Director, Financial Education	Janneke Ratcliffe
Assistant Director, Financial Empowerment	Daniel Dodd-Ramirez
Assistant Director, Installment Lending and Collections Markets	Jeffrey Langer
Assistant Director, Intergovernmental Affairs	Cheryl Parker Rose
Assistant Director, Legislative Affairs	Catherine Galicia
Assistant Director, Mortgage Markets	Patricia McClung
Assistant Director, Office of Civil Rights	M. Stacey Bach
Assistant Director, Office of Consumer Response	Christopher Johnson
Assistant Director, Office of Equal Opportunity and Fairness	Stuart Ishimaru
Assistant Director, Office of Financial Institutions and Business Liaison	Daniel Smith
Assistant Director, Office of Minority and Women Inclusion	Stuart Ishimaru
Assistant Director, Office of Supervision Examinations	Paul Sanford
Assistant Director, Office of Supervision Policy	Peggy Twohig
Assistant Director, Older Americans	Nora Dowd Eisenhower
Assistant Director, Regulations	Kelly Cochran
Assistant Director, Research	Ron Borzekowski
Assistant Director, Servicemember Affairs	Hollister Petraeus
Assistant Director, Students	Seth Frotman
Associate Director, Consumer Education and Engagement	Gail Hillebrand
Associate Director, External Affairs	Zixta Martinez
Associate Director, Research, Markets and Regulations	David Silberman
Associate Director, Supervision, Enforcement, and Fair Lending	David Bleicken, Acting
Chief Administrative Officer	Suzanne Tosini
Chief Financial Officer	Stephen Agostini
Chief Human Capital Officer	Jeffrey Sumberg
Chief Information Officer	Ashwin Vasan
Chief of Staff	Christopher D'Angelo
Chief Operating Officer	Sartaj Alag
Chief Procurement Officer	David Gragan
Deputy General Counsel, General Law and Ethics	Richard Lepley
Deputy General Counsel, Law and Policy	Stephen Van Meter
Deputy General Counsel, Litigation and Oversight	To-Quyen Truong

General Counsel	Mary McLeod
Ombudsman	Wendy Kamenshine
Principal Deputy General Counsel	(vacancy)
Staff Director, Consumer Advisory Board and Councils	Delicia Hand

The Consumer Financial Protection Bureau (CFPB) helps consumer finance markets work by making rules more effective, by consistently and fairly enforcing those rules, and by empowering consumers to take more control over their economic lives.

The Consumer Financial Protection Bureau (CFPB) is an independent Federal agency established by title X of the Dodd-Frank Wall Street Reform and Consumer Protection Act of 2012 (12 U.S.C. 5491). The CFPB is headed by a Director whom the President appoints and the Senate confirms.

Activities

The Bureau regulates the offering and provision of consumer financial products and services under Federal consumer financial laws. It gives consumers the information they need to understand the terms of their agreements with financial companies. It also makes regulations and guidance as clear and streamlined as possible so providers of consumer financial products and services can understand and follow the rules without assistance.

The CFPB's principal activities center on writing rules, supervising companies, and enforcing Federal consumer financial protection laws; restricting unfair, deceptive, or abusive acts or practices; taking consumer complaints; promoting financial education; researching consumer behavior; monitoring financial markets for new risks to consumers; and enforcing laws that prohibit discrimination and other unfair treatment in consumer finance.

Sources of Information

Business Opportunities

Information on doing business with the CFPB is available online.

Consumer Help

The CFPB forwards financial product or service complaints to the company offering the product or service and then works to get an appropriate response. A form for filing a complaint and a searchable complaint database are accessible online. Assistance by phone is available on weekdays, excluding Federal holidays, 8 a.m.–8 p.m., eastern standard time. Phone, 855-411-2372. TTY/TDD, 855-729-2372.

The CFPB posts clear, impartial answers to financial questions on its Web site.

Data

The CFPB publishes research and posts consumer financial marketplace information online.

Educational Resources

Resources for educators, librarians, parents, and those who manage someone else's money are available online.

Employment

The CFPB posts new job openings online, as well as information on the application process and opportunities for students and recent graduates.

Freedom of Information Act (FOIA)

A FOIA request may be submitted by email, fax, or letter. The CFPB recommends using email for making a submission.

Newsroom

Blog posts, press releases, and speeches are accessible online. An online subscription form is available to receive press releases via email.

Open Government

The CFPB adheres to Open Government policies.

Plain Writing

CFPB editors and writers apply plain

language principles in all of their consumer-oriented materials. They want to know if something on the CFPB Web site or in its printed materials is unclear.

Publications

CFPB publications, in English and Spanish, may be ordered in bulk online.

Whistleblowers

The CFPB wants to know about companies that may be breaking Federal consumer financial laws. A current or former employee of such a company, an industry insider who knows of such a company, or a competitor being unfairly undercut by such a company—people like these should report alleged violations to the CFPB. Phone, 855-695-7974.

For further information, contact the Consumer Financial Protection Bureau, 1700 G Street NW., Washington, DC 20552. Phone, 202-435-7000.

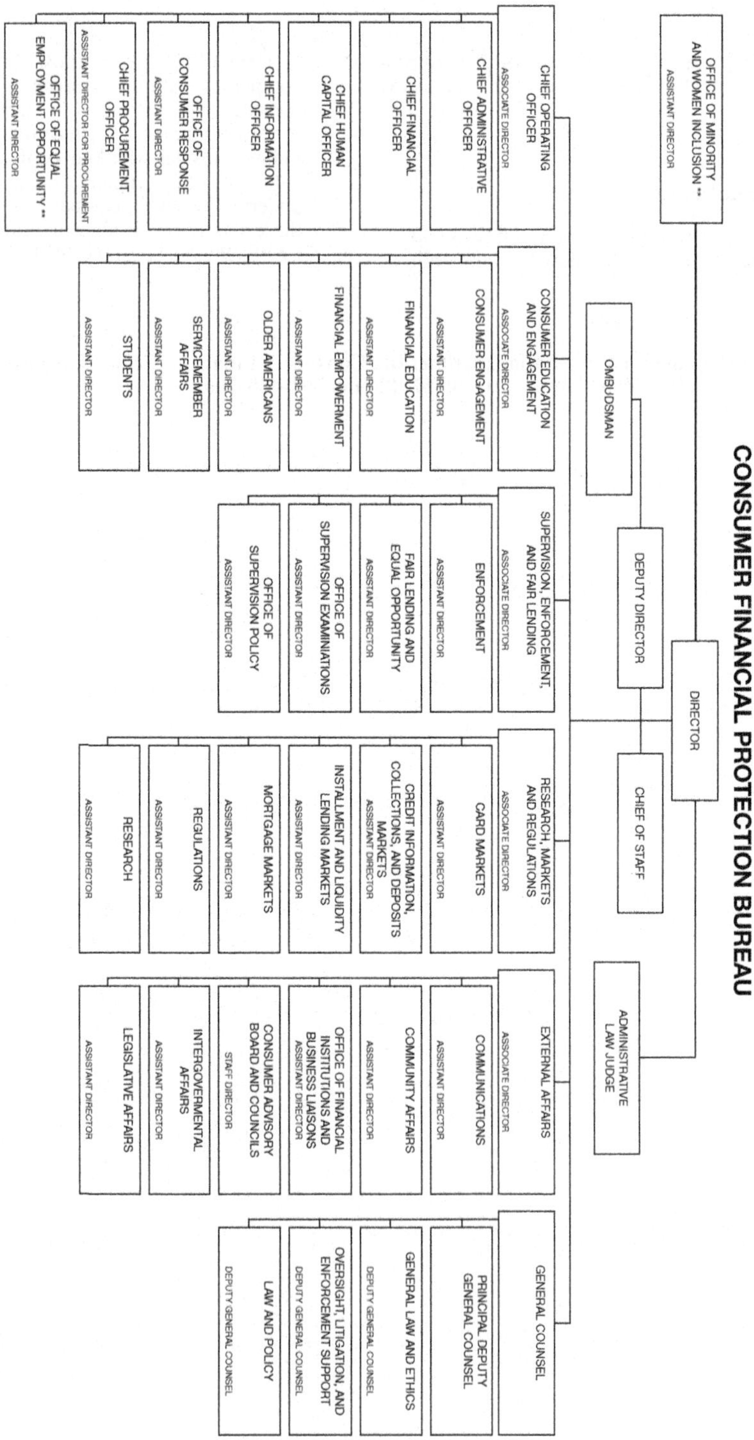

** Position has direct reporting responsibilities to the Director.

Consumer Product Safety Commission

4330 East-West Highway, Bethesda, MD 20814, 301-504-7923, *http://www.cpsc.gov*

CHAIR	Elliot F. Kaye
Commissioner	Robert S. Adler
Commissioner	Ann Marie Buerkle
Commissioner	Joseph P. Mohorovic
Commissioner	Marietta Robinson
EXECUTIVE DIRECTOR	Patricia Adkins
Assistant Executive Director, Office of Hazard Identification and Reduction	George Borlase
Chief Financial Officer	Jay Hoffman
Chief Information Officer	James C. Rolfes
Deputy Executive Director, Operations Support	DeWane Ray
Deputy Executive Director, Safety Operations	Jay Howell
Director, Office of Communications	Scott J. Wolfson
Director, Office of Compliance and Field Operations	Carol Cave
Director, Office of Equal Employment Opportunity and Minority Enterprise	Kathleen V. Buttrey
Director, Office of Facilities Services	Douglas Brown
Director, Office of Human Resources Management	Donna M. Simpson
Director, Office of Import Surveillance	James Joholske
Director, Office of International Programs	Richard O'Brien
Director, Office of Legislative Affairs	Julia E. Richardson
Director, Office of the Secretary	Todd A. Stevenson
General Counsel	Mary Boyle, Acting
Inspector General	Christopher W. Dentel
Small Business Ombudsman	William Cusey, Acting

[For the Consumer Product Safety Commission statement of organization, see the Code of Federal Regulations, Title 16, Part 1000]

The Consumer Product Safety Commission protects the public by reducing the risk of injury and death from consumer products.

The Consumer Product Safety Commission (CPSC) was established as an independent regulatory agency by the Consumer Product Safety Act (15 U.S.C. 2051 et seq.) in 1973 and reauthorized by the Consumer Product Safety Improvement Act of 2008. The Commission comprises a maximum of five members whom the President appoints with the advice and consent of the Senate for 7-year terms.

The CPSC implements provisions of the Flammable Fabrics Act (15 U.S.C. 1191), Poison Prevention Packaging Act of 1970 (15 U.S.C. 1471), Federal Hazardous Substances Act (15 U.S.C. 1261), Children's Gasoline Burn Prevention Act (15 U.S.C. 2056 note), Virginia Graeme Baker Pool and Spa Safety Act (15 U.S.C. 8001 et seq.), and an act of 2 August 1956 (15 U.S.C. 1211) that prohibits the transportation of refrigerators without door safety devices.

Activities

To protect the public from risk of injury, the CPSC requires manufacturers to report defects in products presenting substantial hazards; conducts outreach programs for consumers, industry, and local governments; collects information on consumer product-related injuries and maintains the National Injury Information Clearinghouse; conducts research on consumer product hazards; and encourages and assists in the development of voluntary standards affecting the safety of consumer products. When appropriate, the CPSC requires manufacturers to correct hazards associated with specific consumer products already in circulation, establishes mandatory consumer product standards, and bans hazardous products.

The Commission also has a special project to reach as many Americans as possible with lifesaving safety information. The Neighborhood Safety Network disseminates safety information to hard-to-reach populations by partnering with other organizations already active within their communities.

Sources of Information

Employment

To carry out its mission, the CPSC relies on attorneys and paralegal specialists, compliance officers, economists, engineers, IT specialists, product safety investigators, program analysts, statisticians, toxicologists and pharmacologists and chemists, and other skilled professionals.

Hotline

The Commission operates a toll-free consumer product safety hotline in English and Spanish, on weekdays from 8 a.m. to 5:30 p.m. Phone, 800-638-2772. TTY, 301-595-7054.

Newsroom

The online newsroom features CPSC data, Freedom of Information Act documents, press statements, recent news releases, videos, and a public calendar.

Product Safety

Resources for U.S. Government recalls and information on ATV and pool safety are available online.

Reading Room

The CPSC maintains a public reference reading room in the public information center of its headquarters in Bethesda, MD.

For further information, contact the Office of Information and Public Affairs, Consumer Product Safety Commission, 4330 East-West Highway, Bethesda, MD 20814. Phone, 301-504-7908.

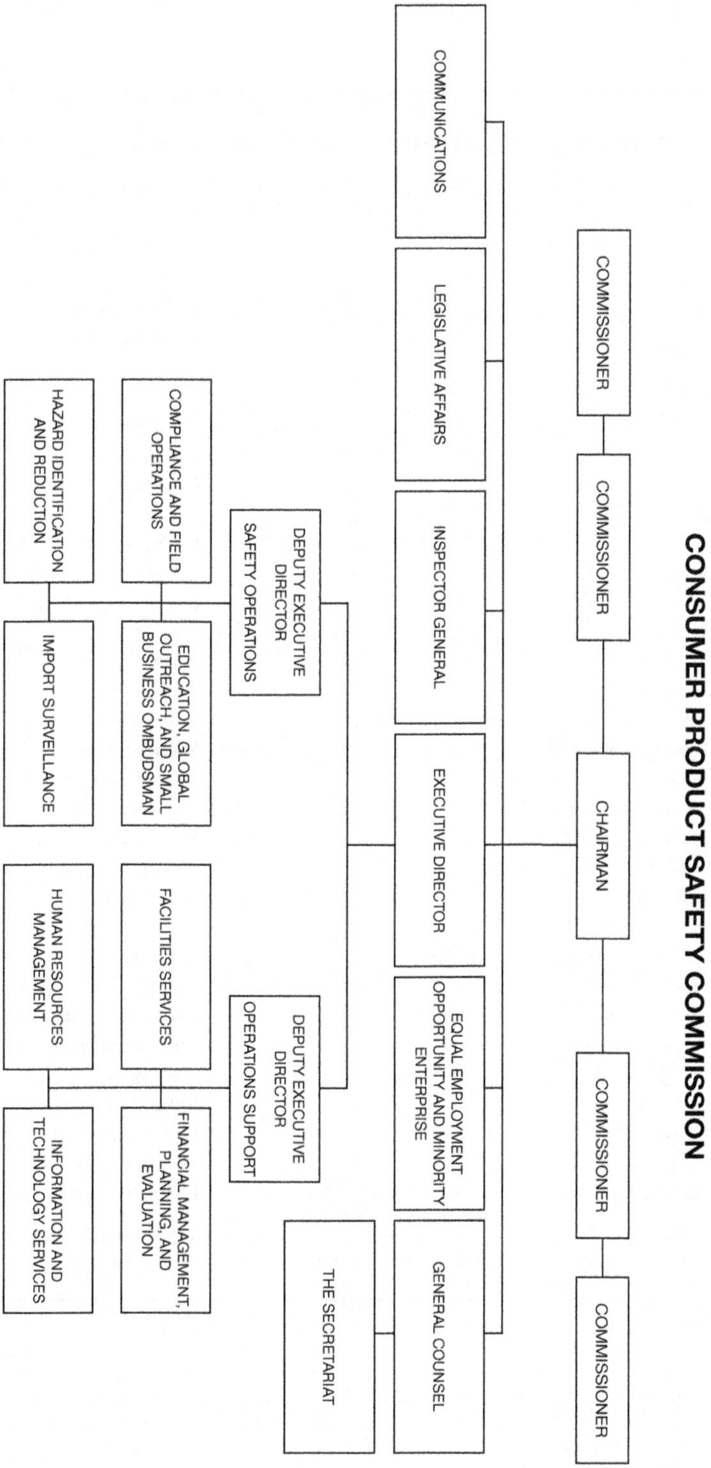
CONSUMER PRODUCT SAFETY COMMISSION
COMMISSIONER
COMMISSIONER
CHAIRMAN
COMMISSIONER
COMMISSIONER
COMMUNICATIONS
LEGISLATIVE AFFAIRS
INSPECTOR GENERAL
EXECUTIVE DIRECTOR
EQUAL EMPLOYMENT OPPORTUNITY AND MINORITY ENTERPRISE
GENERAL COUNSEL
THE SECRETARIAT
DEPUTY EXECUTIVE DIRECTOR SAFETY OPERATIONS
DEPUTY EXECUTIVE DIRECTOR OPERATIONS SUPPORT
COMPLIANCE AND FIELD OPERATIONS
HAZARD IDENTIFICATION AND REDUCTION
EDUCATION, GLOBAL OUTREACH, AND SMALL BUSINESS OMBUDSMAN
IMPORT SURVEILLANCE
FACILITIES SERVICES
HUMAN RESOURCES MANAGEMENT
FINANCIAL MANAGEMENT, PLANNING, AND EVALUATION
INFORMATION AND TECHNOLOGY SERVICES

Corporation for National and Community Service

250 E Street NW., Washington, DC 20525, 202-606-5000, *http://www.nationalservice.gov*

CHAIR	Shamina Singh
Vice Chair	Dean A. Reuter
Member	Richard Christman
Member	Romonia S. Dixon
Member	Victoria A. Hughes
Member	Eric P. Liu
Member	(vacancy)
Member	(vacancy)
Member	(vacancy)
Member	(vacancy)
Member	(vacancy)
Member	(vacancy)
Member	(vacancy)
Member	(vacancy)
Member	(vacancy)
Chief Executive Officer	Wendy Spencer
Chief Operating Officer / Chief Financial Officer	Jeffrey Page
Chief Human Capital Officer	Susan Bradberry
Chief Information Officer	Thomas Hanley
Chief of External Affairs	Theodore S. Miller
Chief of Program Operations	Kimberly Mansaray
Chief of Staff	Asim Mishra
Chief Risk Officer	Lori Giblin
Director, AmeriCorps NCCC	Gina Cross, Acting
Director, AmeriCorps State and National	William C. Basl
Director, AmeriCorps VISTA	Max Finberg
Director, Government Relations	Kimberly L. Allman
Director, Office of Field Liaison	Mikel Herrington
Director, Office of Research and Evaluation	Mary Hyde
Director, Senior Corps	Mikel Herrington, Acting
Director, Social Innovation Fund	Damian Thorman
General Counsel	Jeremy Joseph
Inspector General	Deborah J. Jeffrey

The Corporation for National and Community Service improves lives, strengthens communities, and fosters civic engagement through service and volunteering.

The Corporation for National and Community Service (CNCS) was established on October 1, 1993, by the National and Community Service Trust Act of 1993 (42 U.S.C. 12651 et seq.). The CNCS is a Federal corporation governed by a bipartisan board of directors whom the President appoints with the advice and consent of the Senate. The Board sets policies and direction for the Corporation and is responsible for all actions taken by the Chief Executive Officer with respect to standards, policies, procedures, programs, and initiatives as necessary to carry out the CNCS's mission.

As the Nation's largest grantmaker for service and volunteering, the CNCS engages millions of Americans in service through its core programs—AmeriCorps, Senior Corps, the Social Innovation Fund, and the Volunteer Generation Fund—and leads President Obama's nationwide service initiative, United We Serve. The CNCS harnesses America's most powerful resource: the energy and talents of its citizens. From grade school through retirement, the CNCS empowers Americans and fosters a lifetime of service to improve lives, strengthen communities, and foster civic engagement.

AmeriCorps

AmeriCorps provides opportunities for more than 75,000 Americans each year to serve their communities. AmeriCorps members recruit, train, and supervise community volunteers; tutor and mentor youth; build affordable housing; teach computer skills; clean parks and streams; run afterschool programs; help nonprofit groups become self-sustaining; and assist communities responding to disasters. In exchange for a year of full-time service, AmeriCorps members earn an education award that can be used for college or graduate school tuition or for repaying qualified student loans. Since 1994 nearly 1 million Americans have served in AmeriCorps, which includes AmeriCorps State and National, AmeriCorps NCCC, and AmeriCorps VISTA.

AmeriCorps State and National supports a wide range of local service programs that engage thousands of Americans in community service each year, providing grants to a network of local and national organizations and agencies committed to using national service to address critical community needs in education, public safety, health, and the environment. Each of these organizations and agencies, in turn, uses its AmeriCorps funding to recruit, place, and supervise AmeriCorps members nationwide.

AmeriCorps State and National operates through national and local nonprofit organizations, public agencies, and faith-based and community groups. More than three-quarters of AmeriCorps grant funding goes to Governor-appointed State service commissions, which in turn award grants to nonprofit groups to respond to local needs.

AmeriCorps NCCC (National Civilian Community Corps) is a team-based, residential program for men and women from age 18 to 24 that combines the best practices of civilian service, including leadership and team building. AmeriCorps VISTA (Volunteers in Service to America) members serve full-time for 1 year in nonprofit and faith-based organizations and public agencies to fight poverty, improve health services, increase housing opportunities, and bridge the digital divide.

Senior Corps

Senior Corps taps the skills, talents, and experience of more than 270,000 Americans age 55 and older to meet a wide range of community challenges through three programs: Retired and Senior Volunteers Program (RSVP), Foster Grandparents, and Senior Companions. RSVP volunteers help local police departments conduct safety patrols, participate in environmental projects, provide educational services to children and adults, respond to natural disasters, and recruit other volunteers. Foster Grandparents serve as tutors and mentors to young people with special needs. Senior Companions help homebound seniors and other adults maintain independence in their own homes. Senior Corps volunteers have served 1.5 million Americans, including 560,000 veterans and 300,000 children.

Social Innovation Fund

The Social Innovation Fund is an approach to transforming lives and communities that allows the Federal Government to serve as a catalyst for promoting community solutions with evidence of strong results. A key White House initiative and CNCS program, the Fund identifies solutions that work and makes them work for more people. It combines public and private resources to foster innovative community-based solutions that have produced results in low-income communities in three priority areas: economic opportunity, health, and youth development.

Other Initiatives

As the Federal agency for service and volunteerism, the CNCS carries out the Call to Service authority in multiple ways. CNCS initiatives include the Martin Luther King,

Jr., National Day of Service; September 11th National Day of Service and Remembrance; President's Higher Education Community Service Honor Roll; National Mentoring Month; and United We Serve, a nationwide effort launched with the White House in 2009 to engage Americans in service to meet community needs. As a result of United We Serve, hundreds of thousands of Americans have joined with friends and neighbors to replenish food banks, provide health services, support veterans and military families, restore public lands, and more. The CNCS has also partnered with other agencies and nonprofit organizations on Let's Read! to reduce summer reading loss and Let's Move! to combat childhood obesity. Other initiatives include the Task Force on Expanding National Service, Mayors Day of Recognition, County Day of Recognition, and Joining Forces, an effort led by First Lady Michelle Obama and Dr. Jill Biden to engage Americans in supporting veterans and military families.

Sources of Information

Blog

The National Service blog features posts of interest to students, recent graduates, retirees, senior citizens, veterans, and others. The range of discussion is expansive—conservation, disaster recovery, nonprofit sector career pathways, voluntarism, and more.

Data

The CNCS posts datasets and other information online to support the principles of open government.

Its Open Government Gallery is a demonstration of the CNCS's commitment to collaboration, participation, and transparency.

Employment

Most CNCS career opportunities are volunteer AmeriCorps and Senior Corps positions. The agency hires full-time employees at its Washington, DC, headquarters and at CNCS offices located across the country.

Grants

To find discretionary funding opportunities that Federal agencies have posted, visit the "Funding Opportunities" Web page.

Newsroom

The newsroom features media advisories, official statements, press releases, and proclamations.

Online Courses

Self-paced instructional courses that subject matter experts created on topics aligning with CNCS strategic initiatives are available online.

Site Map

The Web site map allows visitors to look for specific topics or to browse content that aligns with their interests.

For further information, contact the Corporation for National and Community Service, 250 E Street NW., Washington, DC 20525. Phone, 202-606-5000.

CORPORATION FOR NATIONAL AND COMMUNITY SERVICE

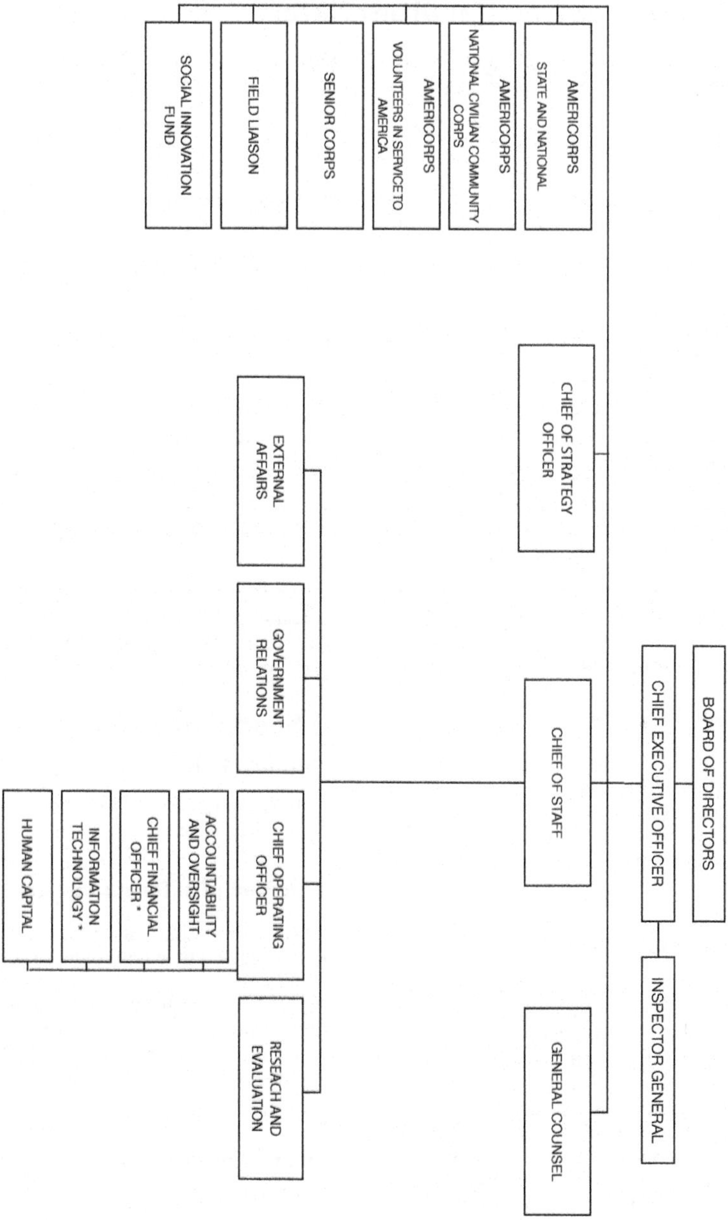

* Denotes staff that also have reporting line to the Chief Executive Officer.

Defense Nuclear Facilities Safety Board

625 Indiana Avenue NW., Suite 700, Washington, DC 20004, 202-694-7000, 202-208-6518, *http://www.dnfsb.gov*

CHAIR	Joyce L. Connery
Vice Chair	Jessie H. Roberson
Member	Bruce Hamilton
Member	Daniel J. Santos
Member	Sean P. Sullivan
General Counsel	James P. Biggins
General Manager	Mark T. Welch
Technical Director	Timothy Dwyer
Deputy General Counsel	Richard N. Reback
Deputy General Manager	Katherine Herrera
Deputy Technical Director	Richard E. Tontodonato

The Defense Nuclear Facilities Safety Board identifies the nature and consequences of public health and safety threats at the Department of Energy's defense nuclear facilities, elevates awareness of and information on such threats to the highest levels of governmental authority, and keeps the public informed.

The Defense Nuclear Facilities Safety Board was established as an independent agency on September 29, 1988, by the Atomic Energy Act of 1954, as amended (42 U.S.C. 2286 et seq.).

The Board comprises five members whom the President appoints with the advice and consent of the Senate. Appointees to the Board must be U.S. citizens and experts in the field of nuclear safety.

Activities

The Defense Nuclear Facilities Safety Board reviews and evaluates the content and implementation of standards for the design, construction, operation, and decommissioning of the Department of Energy's defense nuclear facilities; investigates any incident or practice at these facilities that may adversely affect public health and safety; and reviews and monitors their design, construction, and operation. The Board makes recommendations to the Secretary of Energy to ensure adequate protection of public health and safety. When the Board determines that any aspect of operations, practices, or occurrences at these Department of Energy defense nuclear facilities presents an imminent or severe threat to public health and safety, the Board transmits its recommendations directly to the President.

Sources of Information

Employment

Information on career opportunities is available online.

Freedom of Information Act (FOIA)

An information seeker may submit a FOIA request by email, mail, or telephone for records held or believed to be held by the Board. To make a request by mail, write to the Information / FOIA Officer, Defense Nuclear Facilities Safety Board, 625 Indiana Avenue NW., Suite 700, Washington, DC 20004. Phone, 202-694-7000.

Open Government

The Defense Nuclear Facilities Safety Board supports the Open Government initiative to strengthen the principles of collaboration, participation, and transparency.

Safety Management

The Victor Stello, Jr., Award was established by the Board to recognize Department of Energy employees for exemplary leadership in promoting safety management in the Department's defense nuclear complex.

Site Representative Offices

Site representatives produce a weekly report summarizing the pertinent activities and events that occurred during that week at their site. Five Defense Nuclear Facilities locations—Hanford, Los Alamos National Laboratory, Pantex, Savannah River Site, and Y–12 National Security Complex / Oak Ridge National Laboratory—have at least one site representative currently assigned to them.

For further information, contact the Defense Nuclear Facilities Safety Board, 625 Indiana Avenue NW., Suite 700, Washington, DC 20004. Phone, 202-694-7000.

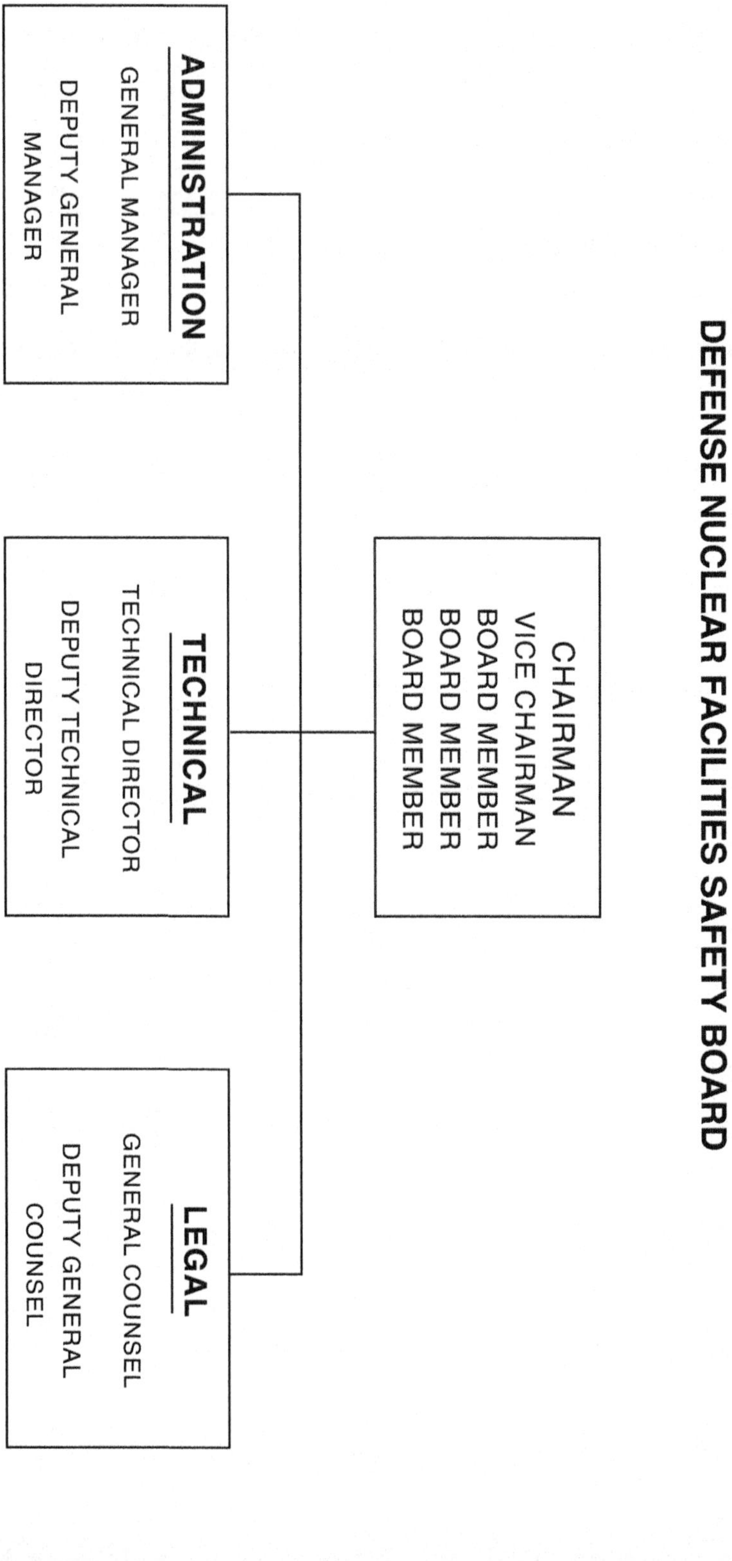
DEFENSE NUCLEAR FACILITIES SAFETY BOARD
CHAIRMAN
VICE CHAIRMAN
BOARD MEMBER
BOARD MEMBER
BOARD MEMBER
ADMINISTRATION
GENERAL MANAGER
DEPUTY GENERAL MANAGER
TECHNICAL
TECHNICAL DIRECTOR
DEPUTY TECHNICAL DIRECTOR
LEGAL
GENERAL COUNSEL
DEPUTY GENERAL COUNSEL

Environmental Protection Agency

1200 Pennsylvania Avenue NW., Washington, DC 20460, 202-272-0167, *http://www.epa.gov*

ADMINISTRATOR	Regina McCarthy
Deputy Administrator	Stan Meiburg, Acting
ASSISTANT ADMINISTRATORS	
Assistant Administrator, Office of Administration and Resources Management	Donna Vizian, Acting
Assistant Administrator, Office of Air and Radiation	Janet McCabe, Acting
Assistant Administrator, Office of Chemical Safety and Pollution Prevention	James J. Jones
Assistant Administrator, Office of Enforcement and Compliance Assurance	Cynthia Giles
Assistant Administrator, Office of International and Tribal Affairs	(vacancy)
Assistant Administrator, Office of Land and Emergency Management	Mathy V. Stanislaus
Chief Information Officer, Office of Environmental Information	Ann Dunkin
Chief Financial Officer, Office of the Chief Financial Officer	(vacancy)
Deputy Assistant Administrator, Office of Research and Development / Agency Science Advisor, Office of the Science Advisor	Thomas Burke
Deputy Assistant Administrator, Office of Water	Joel Beauvais
General Counsel, Office of General Counsel	Avi S. Garbow
Inspector General, Office of the Inspector General	Arthur A. Elkins, Jr.
REGIONAL ADMINISTRATORS	
Region 1	H. Curtis Spalding
Region 2	Judith A. Enck
Region 3	Shawn M. Garvin
Region 4	Heather McTeer Toney
Region 5	Robert A. Kaplan, Acting
Region 6	Ronald Curry
Region 7	Mark J. Hague
Region 8	Shaun McGrath
Region 9	Alexis Strauss, Acting
Region 10	Dennis McLerran

The Environmental Protection Agency protects human health and safeguards the environment.

The Environmental Protection Agency (EPA) was established in the executive branch as an independent agency pursuant to Reorganization Plan No. 3 of 1970 (5 U.S.C. app.), effective December 2, 1970.

The Agency facilitates coordinated and effective governmental action to protect the environment. It also serves as the public's advocate for a livable environment.

Core Functions

Air and Radiation

The Office of Air and Radiation develops air quality policies, programs, regulations, and standards, including emission standards for stationary sources, for mobile sources, and for hazardous air pollutants. It also conducts research and disseminates information on indoor air pollutants. This Office provides technical direction, support, and evaluation of regional air activities; offers training in the field of air pollution control; gives technical assistance to States and agencies operating radiation protection programs; and provides technical support and policy direction to international efforts to reduce global and transboundary air pollution and its effects.

For further information, call 202-564-7400.

Chemical Safety and Pollution Prevention

The Office of Chemical Safety and Pollution Prevention is responsible for EPA's strategies for implementation and integration of the pollution prevention, pesticides, and toxic substances programs and developing and operating Agency programs and policies for assessment and control of pesticides and toxic substances as well as recommending policies and developing operating programs for implementing the Pollution Prevention Act. The Office develops recommendations for EPA's priorities for research, monitoring regulatory and information gathering activities relating to implementation of the Pollution Prevention Act, to pesticides, and to toxic substances; and monitoring and assessing pollution prevention, pesticides and toxic substances program operations in EPA headquarters and regional offices.

For further information, call 202-564-2902.

Enforcement and Compliance Assurance

The Office of Enforcement and Compliance Assurance serves as the primary adviser to the Administrator in matters concerning enforcement, compliance assurance, and environmental-equity efforts. It also provides the direction and review of all administrative, civil and criminal enforcement, and compliance monitoring and assurance activities. The Office manages the national criminal enforcement program as well as regulatory, site remediation, and Federal facilities enforcement and compliance assurance programs. The Office manages both administrative and judicial activities in the enforcement and compliance programs and provides case preparation and investigative expertise for enforcement activities through the National Enforcement Investigations Center.

For further information, call 202-564-2440.

Land and Emergency Management

The Office of Solid Waste and Emergency Response provides agencywide policy, guidance, and direction for EPA's solid waste and emergency response programs. The Office's responsibilities include: development of guidelines and standards for the land disposal of hazardous wastes and for underground storage tanks; technical assistance in the development, management, and operation of solid waste management activities; analyses on the recovery of useful energy from solid waste; and development and implementation of a program to respond to hazardous waste sites and spills.

For further information, call 202-566-0200.

Research and Development

The Office of Research and Development conducts leading-edge research and fosters the sound use of science and technology to fulfill EPA's mission to protect human health and safeguard the natural environment. The Office of Research and Development is responsible for the research and development needs of EPA's operating programs and the conduct of an integrated research and development program for the Agency. The Assistant Administrator serves as the Agency's principal science adviser and is responsible for the development, direction, and conduct of a national environmental research, development, and demonstration program in health risk assessment, health effects, engineering and technology, processes and effects, acid rain deposition, monitoring systems, and quality assurance. The Office participates in the development of EPA's policy, standards, and regulations; provides for dissemination of scientific and technical knowledge, including analytical methods, monitoring techniques, and modeling methodologies; and provides technical and scientific advice on agencywide technical program issues.

For further information, call 202-564-6620.

Water

The Office of Water provides agencywide policy, guidance, and direction for EPA's water quality, drinking water, groundwater, wetlands protection, marine and estuarine protection, and other related programs. The Office's responsibilities include: program policy development and evaluation; environmental and pollution source standards development; program policy guidance and overview, technical support, and evaluation of regional activities as they relate to drinking water and water programs; development and implementation of programs for education, technical assistance and technology transfer; development of selected demonstration programs; long-term strategic planning and special studies; economic and long-term environmental analysis; and development and implementation of pollution prevention strategies.

For further information, call 202-564-5700.

Sources of Information

Blog

The EPA Web site features a blog.

Business Opportunities

Acquisition management information, the procurement status of projects across the Agency's procurement divisions, and an acquisition forecast database of future EPA procurement opportunities are available on the EPA Web site. Contact the Office of Acquisition Management for more information. Phone, 202-564-4310.

Education

Educators and students can access homework resources, lesson plans, and project ideas on the EPA's Web site. Environmental education incorporates a multidisciplinary approach to learning, builds critical thinking skills, and helps students make informed and responsible decisions that sustain Earth's ecosystems.

EJSCREEN

The EPA Web site features an environmental justice mapping and screening tool that is based on nationally consistent data and an approach that combines environmental and demographic indicators in maps and reports. The EPA developed the tool to make the Agency a more effective protector of public health and the environment.

Employment

The EPA relies on professionals from diverse backgrounds and with a wide range of skill sets to carry out its mission. The Agency posts current job openings on its Web site. For more information, contact the Office of Human Resources. Phone, 202-564-4606.

Freedom of Information Act (FOIA)

The EPA is required to disclose records that the public requests, unless they are protected from disclosure by certain FOIA exemptions.

The EPA participates in FOIAonline, an electronic search, submission, processing, and tracking tool.

The FOIA libraries contain frequently requested information. Before making a FOIA request, search the online FOIA libraries to see if the desired information is immediately available at no cost.

Frequently Asked Questions (FAQs)

Some EPA offices and programs have their own FAQs Web pages. The EPA maintains a list of FAQs pages that Internet users visit most often.

Glossary

A climate change glossary and links to other glossaries are accessible online.

Grants

Information to apply for, manage, and understand EPA grants is available online. Contact the Office of Grants and Debarment for more information. Phone, 202-564-5315.

Hotlines and Service Lines

Hotline and service line information for specific topics is available on the EPA Web site.

Region-specific, customer service line information is also available.

Newsroom

The EPA posts news stories on its Web site. It maintains a social media presence on Facebook and Twitter and uses RSS feeds to disseminate information.

The EPA produces public service announcements and materials.

Non-English Readers

The EPA provides information on its Web site in Chinese, Korean, Spanish, and Vietnamese. Language tags are visible in the top right corner of the EPA's home page.

Office of the Inspector General (OIG)

The OIG receives complaints of abuse, fraud, and waste in EPA programs. A complaint may be filed by email, fax, or phone. A person can expect confidentiality when filing his or her complaint by fax or phone—not by email. If the hotline is busy, leave a message and a Federal special agent will return the call. Phone, 888-546-8740. Fax, 202-566-2599.

Open Government

The EPA supports the Open Government initiative by promoting the principles of collaboration, participation, and transparency.

Plain Language

The EPA upholds the Plain Writing Act of 2010 by adhering to Federal plain language guidelines. EPA writers and editors want to know if a document or Web page contains content that was not written in plain language.

Regional Offices

Ten regional offices help develop local programs for pollution abatement.

Staff Directory

The EPA maintains an online staff directory.

Sustainability

The EPA posts information on the Agency's sustainable practices and offers suggestions for adopting habits that are environmentally friendly.

Sustainable practices science investigates the balance between the economy, the environment, and society.

For further information, contact the Office of External Affairs and Environmental Education, Environmental Protection Agency, 1200 Pennsylvania Avenue NW., Washington, DC 20460-0001. Phone, 202-272-0167.

ENVIRONMENTAL PROTECTION AGENCY

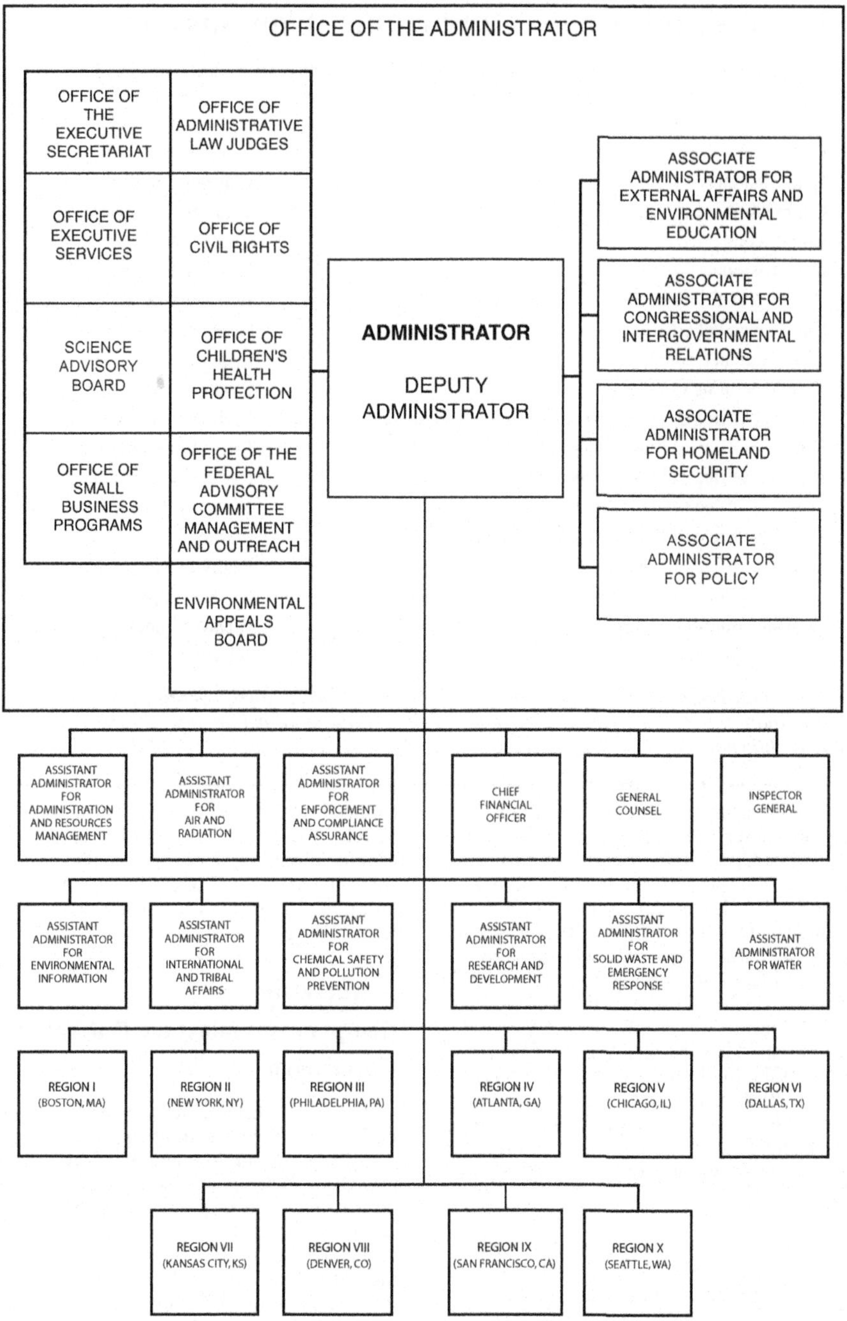

Equal Employment Opportunity Commission

131 M Street NE., Washington, DC 20507, 202-663-4900, TTY, 202-663-4444, *http://www.eeoc.gov*

CHAIR	Jenny R. Yang
Commissioner	Constance S. Barker
Commissioner	Charlotte A. Burrows
Commissioner	Chai R. Feldblum
Commissioner	Victoria A. Lipnic
EXECUTIVE OFFICER	Bernadette B. Wilson, Acting
Chief Financial Officer	Germaine P. Roseboro
Chief Human Capital Officer	Lisa Williams
Chief Operating Officer	Cynthia G. Pierre
Director, Office of Communications and Legislative Affairs	Brett Brenner, Acting
Director, Office of Equal Opportunity	Erica White-Dunston
Director, Office of Federal Operations	Carlton M. Hadden
Director, Office of Field Programs	Nicholas Inzeo
Director, Office of Information Technology	(vacancy)
Director, Office of Legal Counsel	Peggy R. Mastroianni
Director, Office of Research, Information and Planning	Deidre Flippen
General Counsel	P. David Lopez
Inspector General	Milton A. Mayo, Jr.

The Equal Employment Opportunity Commission enforces laws prohibiting employment discrimination based on race, color, gender, religion, national origin, age, disability, or genetic information.

The Equal Employment Opportunity Commission (EEOC) was created by Title VII of the Civil Rights Act of 1964 (42 U.S.C. 2000e-4) and became operational July 2, 1965. Laws enforced by EEOC include Title VII of the Civil Rights Act of 1964 (42 U.S.C. 2000e et seq.), the Age Discrimination in Employment Act of 1967 (29 U.S.C. 621 et seq.), sections of the Rehabilitation Act of 1973 (29 U.S.C. 791 et seq.) and Civil Rights Act of 1991 (105 Stat. 1071), the Equal Pay Act of 1963 (29 U.S.C. 206), Title I of the Americans with Disabilities Act of 1990 (42 U.S.C. 12101 et seq.), and Title II of the Genetic Information Non-Discrimination Act of 2008 (42 U.S.C. 2000ff et seq.).

The EEOC is a bipartisan commission comprising five members whom the President appoints with the advice and consent of the Senate to staggered 5-year terms. The President designates a Chair and Vice Chair. In addition to the Commission members, the President appoints a General Counsel, with the advice and consent of the Senate, to support the Commission and provide direction, coordination, and supervision of the EEOC's litigation program. The General Counsel serves for a term of 4 years.

Activities

Complaints Against the Federal Government

The EEOC establishes the procedures for Federal employees and job applicants to file complaints of employment discrimination or retaliation. The agency charged with discrimination is responsible for informal counseling and, if a complaint is filed and accepted, for investigating the claims raised therein. At the conclusion of the investigation, complainants may request a hearing before an EEOC administrative judge or that the agency issue a final decision on the matter. The agency's final decision or final action after a hearing may be appealed to the Commission.

In addition, the Office of Federal Operations provides oversight of and technical assistance for equal employment opportunity (EEO) complaint adjudication and Governmentwide maintenance of affirmative employment programs. Using the guidance and principles contained in the EEOC's EEO Management Directive 715, the Commission monitors and evaluates Federal agencies' affirmative employment programs under Title VII and section 501 of the Rehabilitation Act and ensures that all Federal employees compete on a fair and level playing field.

Enforcement

The EEOC enforces its statutory, regulatory, policy, and program responsibilities through its headquarters-based Office of General Counsel, Office of Field Programs, and its 53 field offices. The field offices receive charges of discrimination from the public and use a variety of resolution methods, including voluntary mediation and full-scale investigation and conciliation. The field staff is responsible for achieving a wide range of objectives that focus on the quality, timeliness, and appropriateness of individual, class, and systemic charges; for securing relief for victims of discrimination in accordance with Commission policies; for counseling individuals about their rights under the laws enforced by the EEOC; and for conducting outreach and technical assistance programs. The EEOC's Office of General Counsel litigates in U.S. District Courts and Courts of Appeal.

Other Activities

The Commission promotes voluntary compliance with EEO statutes through a variety of educational and technical assistance activities. Its outreach and education programs provide general information on the EEOC, its mission, rights and responsibilities under the statutes enforced by the Commission, and the charge/complaint process. EEOC representatives are available, on a limited basis and at no cost, to make presentations and participate in meetings, conferences, and seminars with employee and employer groups, professional associations, students, nonprofit entities, community organizations, and other members of the general public.

The Commission offers additional training tailored to employers for a fee. The EEOC Training Institute makes this more in-depth training available to private employers and State, local, and Federal government personnel. The EEOC Training Institute helps educate managers and employees on the laws enforced by the EEOC and how to prevent and eliminate discrimination in the workplace.

The Commission publishes data on the employment status of minorities and women through six employment surveys covering private employers, apprenticeship programs, labor unions, State and local governments, elementary and secondary schools, and colleges and universities. This collection of data is shared with selected Federal agencies and is made available, in appropriate form, for public use.

Sources of Information

District Offices

The EEOC operates 15 district offices. An office list and jurisdictional map are available online. A search tool allows EEOC Web site visitors to locate field offices by using Zip Codes.

Employment

The Commission hires in various job categories: attorneys, information intake representatives, investigators, mediators, office automation assistants, paralegals, program analysts, and social scientists. EEOC employment opportunities are posted on USAJobs—the Federal Government's official source for job listings and employment opportunity information. For more information, contact the Office of Human Resources. Phone, 202-663-4306.

Freedom of Information Act (FOIA)

Contact the requester service center for FOIA-related questions. Phone, 877-869-1802.

Internships

EEOC Internships offer high school, college, and graduate and law students the opportunity to gain experience working on projects or cases involving issues of Federal antidiscrimination law. Interns work closely with experienced attorneys and specialists on assignments. Work assignments include legal research and writing, research and analysis of public policy developments, correspondence with Commission stakeholders, and assistance with charge intake and investigations.

Media Inquiries

Representatives of the media should contact the Office of Communications and Legislative Affairs, 131 M Street NE., Washington, DC 20507. Phone, 202-663-4191. TTY, 202-663-4494.

Open Government

The EEOC supports the Open Government initiative by implementing principles of collaboration, participation, and transparency.

Publications

The EEOC's most popular publications may be downloaded in Portable Document Format (PDF) for easy reproduction. Publications that are unavailable online may be obtained by phone or fax. Phone, 800-669-3362. TTY, 800-800-3302. Fax, 513-489-8692.

Reading Room

Contact the EEOC Library, 131 M Street NE., Washington, DC 20507. Phone, 202-663-4630.

Reports and Surveys

The EEOC collects workforce data from employers with more than 100 employees. Employers who meet the reporting thresholds are required to provide the information. The data are used for enforcement, research, and self-assessment by employers. Data remain confidential; however, the public can access them in aggregate form.

Training Institute

For information on training programs and registration, contact the EEOC Training Institute. Phone, (703) 291-0880 or (866) 446-0940.

Speakers

An agency representative may be available to present an overview of the laws that the EEOC enforces and EEOC charge processing procedures—including mediation—at a conference or seminar. Contact an outreach program coordinator for more information. Phone, 800-669-4000.

Statistics

The EEOC posts data, reports, and statistics online.

For further information, contact the Office of Communications and Legislative Affairs, Equal Employment Opportunity Commission, 131 M Street NE., Washington, DC 20507. Phone, 202-663-4191.

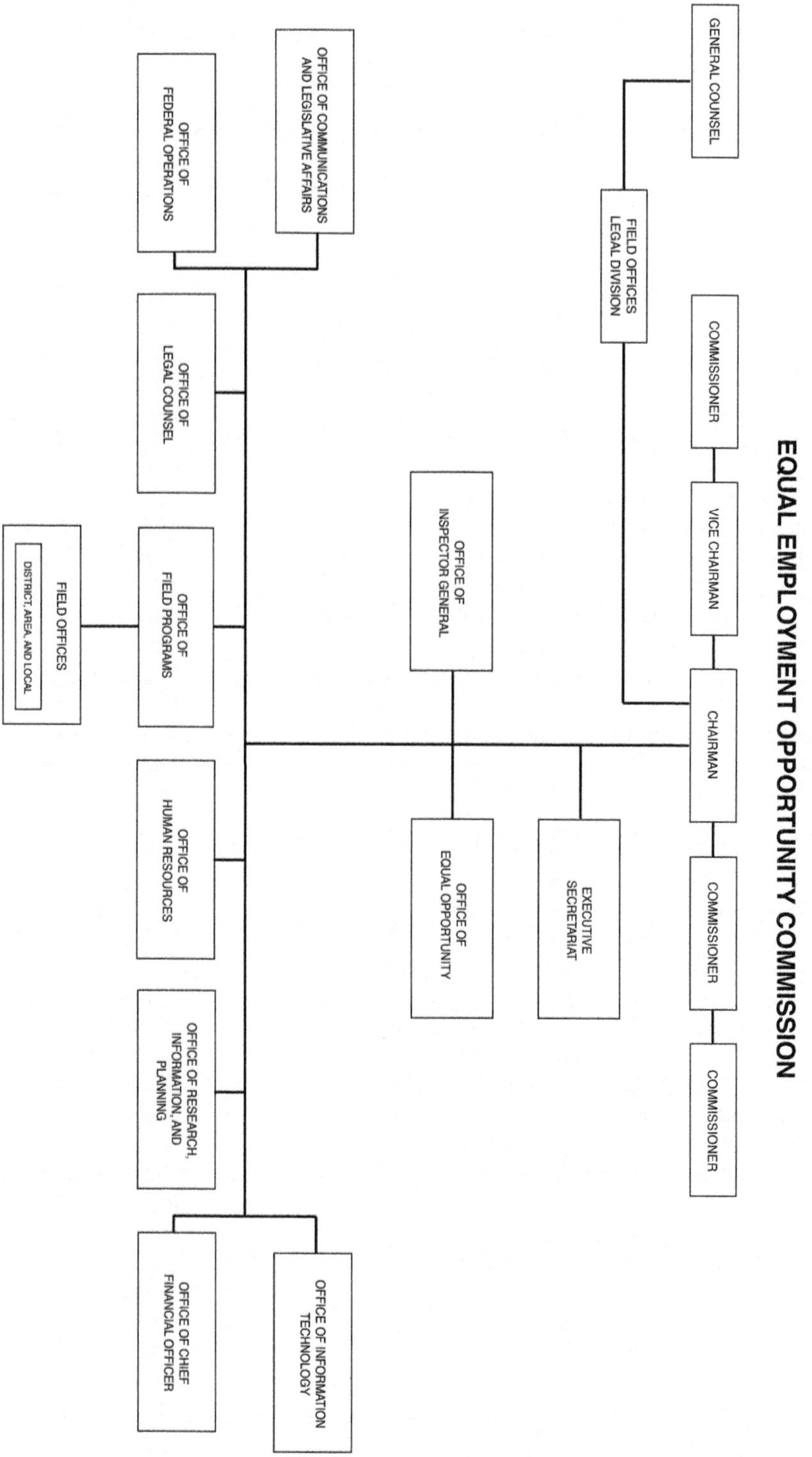
EQUAL EMPLOYMENT OPPORTUNITY COMMISSION
GENERAL COUNSEL
FIELD OFFICES LEGAL DIVISION
COMMISSIONER
VICE CHAIRMAN
CHAIRMAN
COMMISSIONER
COMMISSIONER
OFFICE OF INSPECTOR GENERAL
EXECUTIVE SECRETARIAT
OFFICE OF EQUAL OPPORTUNITY
OFFICE OF COMMUNICATIONS AND LEGISLATIVE AFFAIRS
OFFICE OF FEDERAL OPERATIONS
OFFICE OF LEGAL COUNSEL
OFFICE OF FIELD PROGRAMS
FIELD OFFICES
DISTRICT, AREA, AND LOCAL
OFFICE OF HUMAN RESOURCES
OFFICE OF RESEARCH, INFORMATION, AND PLANNING
OFFICE OF INFORMATION TECHNOLOGY
OFFICE OF CHIEF FINANCIAL OFFICER

Export-Import Bank of the United States

811 Vermont Avenue NW., Washington, DC 20571, 202-565-3946, 800-565-3946, *http://www.exim.gov*

PRESIDENT / CHAIR	Fred P. Hochberg
First Vice President / Vice Chair	Wanda Felton
Director	(vacancy)
Director	(vacancy)
Director	(vacancy)
Chief Financial Officer	David M. Sena
Chief Information Officer	Howard Spira
Chief Risk Officer / Executive Vice President	Charles J. Hall
Chief of Staff / Senior Vice President	Scott P. Schloegel
Deputy Chief of Staff	Matthew Bevens
General Counsel / Senior Vice President	Angela Mariana Freyre
Senior Vice President, Export Finance / Chief Banking Officer	Madolyn Phillips, Acting
Senior Vice President, Business and Product Development	Robert A. Morin
Senior Vice President, Communications	(vacancy)
Senior Vice President, Congressional and Intergovernmental Affairs	Erin Gulick
Senior Vice President, Credit and Risk Management	Kenneth M. Tinsley
Senior Vice President, Policy and Planning	James C. Cruse
Senior Vice President, Resource Management	Michael Cushing
Senior Vice President, Small Business	James Burrows
Senior Vice President, Strategy	(vacancy)
Vice President, Asset Management	Walter F. Keating
Vice President, Business Credit	Pamela S. Bowers
Vice President, Business Processes, Total Enterprise Modernization	Michele A. Kuester
Vice President, Communications	(vacancy)
Vice President, Congressional and Intergovernmental Affairs	Kevin Warnke
Vice President, Controller	Patricia Wolf
Vice President, Country Risk and Economic Analysis / Chief Economist	William A. Marsteller
Vice President, Credit Review and Compliance	Walter Hill, Jr.
Vice President, Credit Underwriting	David W. Carter
Vice President, Customer Experience	Stephanie Thum
Vice President, Engineering and Environment	James A. Mahoney, Jr.
Vice President, Finance / Treasurer	Nathalie Herman
Vice President, Global Business Development	Raymond J. Ellis
Vice President, International Relations	Isabel Galdiz
Vice President, Operations and Data Quality	Nicole M.B. Valtos
Vice President, Policy Analysis	Helene Walsh
Vice President, Public Affairs	Catrell Brown
Vice President, Small Business Operation	James Burrows
Vice President, Structured Finance	Michael S. Whalen
Vice President, Transportation	Robert F.X. Roy

The Export-Import Bank helps finance the export of U.S. goods and services to international markets.

The Export-Import Bank of the United States (Ex-Im Bank), established in 1934, operates as an independent agency of the U.S. Government under the authority of the Export-Import Bank Act of 1945, as amended (12 U.S.C. 635 et seq.). Its Board of Directors comprises the President and Chair, the First Vice President and Vice Chair, and three directors—a total of five members. With the advice and consent of the Senate, the President appoints all of them.

The Ex-Im Bank helps American exporters adjust to government-supported financing competition from other countries. The assistance allows U.S. exports to compete for overseas business on the basis of price, performance, and service, which protects U.S. jobs. The Bank also fills gaps in the availability of commercial financing for creditworthy export transactions by providing a variety of financing mechanisms, including working capital guarantees, export-credit insurance, and financing for the purchase of U.S. goods and services.

The Bank is required to find a reasonable assurance of repayment for each transaction it supports. Its legislation requires it to meet the financing terms of competitor export credit agencies, but not to compete with commercial lenders. Restrictions also apply to the Bank's support for military goods and services and to its operation in some countries.

The Ex-Im Bank operates at no cost to U.S. taxpayers and has earned nearly $7 billion above its operating costs over the past two decades. Its total authorizations support an estimated $50 billion in U.S. export sales and approximately 255,000 American jobs in communities across the country.

Activities

The Ex-Im Bank is authorized to have loans, guarantees, and insurance outstanding at any one time in aggregate amount not exceeding $120 billion. A variety of Ex-Im Bank programs offered under broad export financing categories—working capital guarantees, export credit insurance, loan guarantees, and direct loans—support U.S. exporters.

The Bank's regional offices focus on small business outreach and support. Its Small Business Committee makes recommendations on and coordinates and evaluates Bank functions necessary for an effective small-business strategy.

Sources of Information

Electronic Updates

An online subscription form is available to sign up for email updates from the Ex-Im Bank.

Employment

To carry out its mission, the Bank relies on professionals with a range of skills and expertise: attorney-advisors, business development and loan specialists, economists, engineers, and resource managers in accounting, finance, human resources, and information technology.

Freedom of Information Act (FOIA)

A FOIA request must be made in writing. It may be submitted using the online request form or by email, fax, or postal mail.

News

Ex-Im Bank posts board agendas and meeting minutes, reports, and speeches online.

The Chair writes a quarterly newsletter that includes information on the Bank's performance over the previous 3 months. The newsletter also includes analysis of global economic trends, customer stories, practical export tips, upcoming Bank events, and other resources.

Office of the Inspector General (OIG)

The OIG investigates complaints of abuse, fraud, and waste. Phone, 888-644-3946.

Open Government

The Ex-Im Bank is becoming more collaborative, participatory, and transparent by making data available in an open format and by providing a mechanism for the public to submit feedback.

Project Information and Concerns

The "Environmental and Social Project Information and Concerns" Web page provides an online form for expressing project-specific concerns, requesting project-specific information, or submitting information on a particular project.

Regional Offices

The Ex-Im Bank operates regional export finance centers and field offices nationwide. A List of these centers, with their contact information, is available online.

For further information, contact the Business Development Office, Export-Import Bank, 811 Vermont Avenue NW., Washington, DC 20571. Phone, 202-565-3946 or 800-565-3946.

Farm Credit Administration

1501 Farm Credit Drive, McLean, VA 22102-5090, 703-883-4000, 703-790-3260, *http://www.fca.gov*

CHAIR / CHIEF EXECUTIVE OFFICER	Kenneth A. Spearman
Member of the Board	Jeffery S. Hall
Member of the Board	Dallas P. Tonsager
Secretary to the Board	Dale L. Aultman
Chief Operating Officer	William J. Hoffman
Designated Agency Ethics Official	Philip J. Shebest
Director, Equal Employment and Inclusion	Thais Burlew
Director, Office of Agency Services	A. Jerome Fowlkes, Acting
Director, Office of Congressional and Public Affairs	Michael A. Stokke
Director, Office of Examination and Chief Examiner	S. Robert Coleman
Director, Office of Information Technology	Jerold Golley
Director, Office of Regulatory Policy	Gary K. Van Meter
Director, Office of Secondary Market Oversight	Laurie A. Rea
Director, Office of the Chief Financial Officer	Stephen G. Smith
General Counsel	Charles R. Rawls
Inspector General	Elizabeth Dean

[For the Farm Credit Administration statement of organization, see the Code of Federal Regulations, Title 12, Parts 600 and 611]

The Farm Credit Administration ensures the safe and sound operation of the banks, associations, affiliated service organizations, and other entities of the Farm Credit System, and protects the interests of the public and those who borrow from Farm Credit institutions or invest in Farm Credit securities.

The Farm Credit Administration (FCA) was established as an independent financial regulatory agency in the executive branch of the Federal Government by Executive Order 6084 on March 27, 1933. The FCA carries out its responsibilities by conducting examinations of the various Farm Credit lending institutions: Agricultural Credit Associations, Farm Credit Banks, Federal Land Credit Associations, and the Agricultural Credit Bank.

The FCA also examines the service organizations owned by the Farm Credit lending institutions, as well as the National Consumer Cooperative Bank.

FCA policymaking is vested in the Farm Credit Administration Board, whose three full-time members the President appoints to 6-year terms with the advice and consent of the Senate. One member of the Board is designated by the President as Chair and serves as the FCA's chief executive officer. The Board approves rules and regulations, provides for the examination and regulation of and reporting by Farm Credit institutions, and establishes the policies under which the Administration operates. Board meetings are regularly held on the second Thursday of the month and are subject to the Government in the Sunshine Act. Public announcements of these meetings are published in the "Federal Register."

Authority for the organization and activities of the Farm Credit System may be found in the Farm Credit Act of 1971, as amended.

The lending institutions of the Farm Credit System were established to provide adequate and dependable credit and closely related services to farmers, ranchers, and producers or harvesters of aquatic products; persons engaged in providing on-the-farm services; rural homeowners; and associations of farmers, ranchers, and producers or harvesters of aquatic products, or federations of such associations that operate on a cooperative basis and are engaged in marketing, processing, supply, or business service functions for the benefit of their members. Initially capitalized by the U.S. Government, the Farm Credit lending institutions are organized as cooperatives—their borrowers completely own them. The loan funds provided to borrowers by these institutions are obtained primarily through the sale of securities to investors in the Nation's capital markets.

The Agricultural Credit Act of 1987, as amended (12 U.S.C. 2279aa-1), established the Federal Agricultural Mortgage Corporation, commonly known as Farmer Mac. The Corporation, designated as part of the Farm Credit System, is a federally chartered instrumentality of the United States and promotes the development of a secondary market for agricultural real estate and rural housing loans. Farmer Mac also provides guarantees for the timely payment of principal and interest on securities representing interests in or obligations backed by pools of agricultural real estate loans. The Administration examines and regulates Farmer Mac to ensure the safety and soundness of its operations.

The FCA manages regulations under which Farm Credit institutions operate. These regulations implement the Farm Credit Act of 1971, as amended (12 U.S.C. 2001), and have the force and effect of law. Similar to the authorities of other Federal regulators of financial institutions, the Administration's authorities include the power to issue cease-and-desist orders, to levy civil monetary penalties, to remove officers and directors of Farm Credit institutions, and to establish financial and operating reporting requirements. Although it is prohibited from participation in routine management or operations of Farm Credit institutions, the Administration is authorized to become involved in these institutions' management and operations when the Farm Credit Act or its regulations have been violated, when taking an action to correct an unsafe or unsound practice, or when assuming a formal conservatorship over an institution.

The Administration does not operate on funds appropriated by Congress: It derives income from assessments collected from the institutions that it regulates and examines. In addition to its headquarters in McLean, VA, the Administration maintains four field offices located in Bloomington, MN; Greenwood Village, CO; Irving, TX; and Sacramento, CA.

Sources of Information

Business Opportunities

The Office of Agency Services manages the FCA's procurement opportunities. Phone, 703-883-4378. TTY, 703-883-4056.

Employment

To carry out its mission, the FCA relies on attorneys, examiners, information technology specialists, and other professionals. Examiners play a prominent role at the FCA: They plan, organize, and conduct examinations of Farm Credit System institutions. The FCA hires examiners with diverse college degrees. The ideal candidate understands agriculture, business, finance, or information technology. Adaptability, teamwork, and communication skills are essential. Contact the Office of Agency Services for more information. Phone, 703-883-4135. TTY, 703-883-4056.

Freedom of Information Act (FOIA)

A written submission must clearly indicate that it is a "FOIA Request." The FCA may require payment for searching for, reviewing, and reproducing a document. A submitter must provide a detailed description—date, subject matter, title—of the record sought and indicate the maximum amount he or she is willing to pay in fees. A request may be submitted by email or fax, or by mail and addressed to the Freedom of Information Act Officer, Farm Credit Administration, 1501 Farm Credit Drive, McLean, VA 22102-5090. Phone, 703-883-4020. TTY, 703-883-4056. Fax, 703-790-0052.

Glossary

The FCA maintains an online glossary.

News and Events

The FCA announces events and posts news releases, rulemaking factsheets, speeches and statements, and testimonies online.

Publications

FCA documents are posted online, including publications about the Farm Credit Administration and information on the Farm Credit System. To find an older document, one that is over 5 years old, search in the archives. More information is available from the Office of Congressional and Public Affairs. Phone, 703-883-4056 (voice and TTY). Fax, 703-790-3260.

Plain Writing

Providing feedback on the clarity of documents and other material on the FCA Web site helps improve the guidance that the FCA gives to institutions and the services that it offers to Americans. Contact the Office of Congressional and Public Affairs. Phone, 703-883-4056.

For further information, contact the Office of Congressional and Public Affairs, Farm Credit Administration, 1501 Farm Credit Drive, McLean, VA 22102-5090. Phone, 703-883-4056.

FARM CREDIT ADMINISTRATION

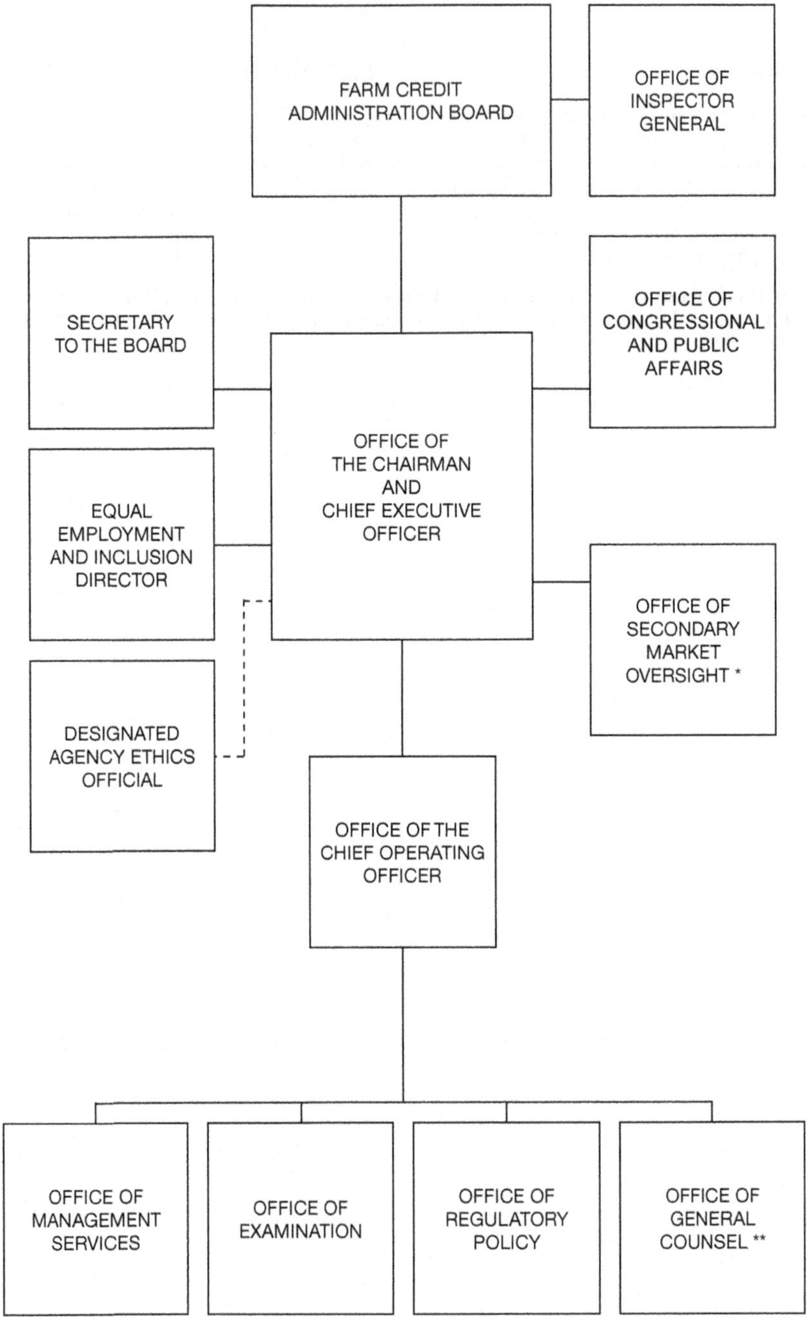

* Reports to the Board for policy and to the Chief Executive Officer for administration.
** Maintains a confidential advisory relationship with each of the Board members.

Federal Communications Commission

445 Twelfth Street SW., Washington, DC 20554, 888-225-5322, TTY, 888-835-5322, *http://www.fcc.gov*

CHAIR	Tom Wheeler
Commissioner	Mignon Clyburn
Commissioner	Michael O'Reilly
Commissioner	Ajit Pai
Commissioner	Jessica Rosenworcel
Managing Director	Mark Stephens, Acting
General Counsel	Jonathan Sallet
Inspector General	David L. Hunt
Chief, Consumer and Governmental Affairs Bureau	Alison Kutler
Chief, Enforcement Bureau	Travis LeBlanc
Chief, International Bureau	Mindel De La Torre
Chief, Media Bureau	William T. Lake
Chief, Office of Administrative Law Judges	Richard L. Sippel
Chief, Office of Engineering and Technology	Julius Knapp
Chief, Office of Strategic Planning and Policy Analysis	Elizabeth Biley Andrion, Acting
Chief, Public Safety and Homeland Security Bureau	David G. Simpson
Chief, Wireless Telecommunications Bureau	Jon Wilkins
Chief, Wireline Competition Bureau	Matthew DelNero
Director, Office of Communications Business Opportunities	Thomas Reed
Director, Office of Legislative Affairs	Mike Dabbs
Director, Office of Media Relations	Shannon Gilson
Director, Office of Workplace Diversity	Thomas Wyatt

[For the Federal Communications Commission statement of organization, see the Code of Federal Regulations, Title 47, Part 0]

The Federal Communications Commission regulates interstate and foreign communications by radio, television, wire, satellite, and cable.

The Federal Communications Commission (FCC) was established by the Communications Act of 1934 (47 U.S.C. 151 et seq.) and is charged with regulating interstate and foreign communications by wire and radio in the public interest. The scope of FCC regulation includes radio and television broadcasting; telephone and cable television operation; two-way radio and radio operators; and satellite communication.

The Commission comprises five members whom the President appoints with the advice and consent of the Senate. One of the members is designated by the President as the Chair.

Activities

Consumer and Governmental Affairs Bureau

The Consumer and Governmental Affairs Bureau develops and administers the FCC's consumer and governmental affairs policies and initiatives. The Bureau facilitates public participation in the Commission's decisionmaking process; represents the Commission on consumer and Government committees, working groups, task forces, and conferences; works with public, Federal, State, local, and tribal agencies to develop and coordinate policies; oversees the Consumer Advisory Committee, the

Disability Advisory Committee, and the Intergovernmental Advisory Committee; offers expert advice on applicable disability and accessibility requirements, rules, and regulations, and assists with compliance; resolves informal complaints; and conducts consumer outreach and education programs.

For further information, contact the Consumer and Governmental Affairs Bureau. Phone, 202-418-1400 or 888-225-5322.

Enforcement Bureau

The Enforcement Bureau serves as the FCC's primary agency for enforcing the Communications Act, other communications statutes, and the FCC's rules. The Bureau investigates and resolves complaints regarding common carriers (wireline, wireless, and international) and noncommon carriers subject to the Commission's jurisdiction under Title II of the Communications Act; radio frequency interference, equipment, and devices; accessibility to communications services and equipment for persons with disabilities; noncompliance with the lighting and marking of radio transmitting towers and pole attachment regulations; and unauthorized construction and operation of communication facilities and false distress signals.

For further information, contact the Enforcement Bureau. Phone, 202-418-7450 or 888-225-5322.

International Bureau

The International Bureau serves as the FCC's principal representative at international conferences and in international negotiations. The Bureau promotes procompetitive policies abroad, coordinating the FCC's global spectrum activities and advocating U.S. interests in international communications and competition. It provides advice and technical assistance to U.S. trade officials in the negotiation and implementation of telecommunications trade agreements. It also encourages the international coordination of spectrum allocation and of frequency and orbital assignments to minimize cases of international radio interference involving U.S. licenses.

For further information, contact the International Bureau. Phone, 202-418-0437 or 888-225-5322.

Media Bureau

The Media Bureau oversees broadcast radio, television, and cable policy and licensing, as well as post-licensing matters for satellite services. The Bureau also conducts rulemaking proceedings and studies, resolves waiver petitions, and processes applications for authorization, assignment, transfer, and renewal of radio, television, and cable television relay services.

For further information, contact the Media Bureau. Phone, 202-418-7200 or 888-225-5322.

Public Safety and Homeland Security Bureau

The Public Safety and Homeland Security Bureau develops, recommends, and administers the FCC's policies on public safety communication. This includes 911 and E911, operability and interoperability of public safety communications, communications infrastructure protection and disaster response, and network security and reliability. The Bureau also disseminates public safety communication information for emergency communication programs; alerting and warning U.S. citizens; continuity of government operations and operational planning; public safety outreach (e.g., first-responder organizations and hospitals); disaster management coordination and outreach; and studies and reports of public safety, homeland security, and disaster management issues.

For further information, contact the Public Safety and Homeland Security Bureau. Phone, 202-418-1300 or 888-225-5322.

Wireless Telecommunications Bureau

The Wireless Telecommunications Bureau administers all domestic commercial and private wireless communication programs and rules. It addresses present and future wireless communication and spectrum needs; promotes access, efficiency, and innovation in the allocation, licensing, and use of electromagnetic spectrum; ensures choice, opportunity, and fairness in the development of wireless communication services and markets; and encourages the development and widespread availability of wireless communication devices, facilities, and services. The Bureau also develops, recommends, administers, and coordinates policy for wireless communication services, including rulemaking, interpretations, and equipment standards; advises the public on FCC rules; serves as the FCC's principal policy and administrative resource for all spectrum auctions; and processes wireless service and facility authorization applications.

For further information, contact the Wireless Telecommunications Bureau. Phone, 202-418-0600 or 888-225-5322.

Wireline Competition Bureau

The Wireline Competition Bureau advises and makes recommendations to the FCC on policies affecting telephone landlines and fixed broadband. Its programs protect affordable communications access for health care providers, libraries, schools, and lifeline and rural consumers. The Bureau also ensures choice, opportunity, and fairness in the development of wireline communications; assesses the present and future wireline communication needs of the Nation; encourages the development and widespread availability of wireline communication services; and promotes investment in wireline communication infrastructure.

For further information, contact the Wireline Competition Bureau. Phone, 202-418-1500 or 888-225-5322.

Sources of Information

Business Opportunities

The FCC relies on contractors for goods and services to carry out its mission. Many of these procurements are suitable for small businesses, and some offer opportunities for subcontracting.

Consumer Assistance

For general information on FCC operations, contact the FCC Consumer Center, 445 Twelfth Street SW., Washington, DC 20554. Phone, 888-225-5322. TTY, 888-835-5322.

Employment

The FCC maintains a web-based recruitment system that allows employees and outside job seekers to apply for job opportunities online.

Equal Employment Practices by the Communications Industry

For more information, contact the FCC Consumer Center. Phone, 888-225-5322.

Ex-Parte Presentations

For more information, contact the Commission's Office of General Counsel. Phone, 202-418-1720.

Federal Advisory Committee Management

For more information, contact the Office of Managing Director. Phone, 202-418-2178.

Fees

Information on the FCC's fee programs is available online or from the Registration

System / Fee Filer Help Desk. Phone, 877-480-3201 (option 4).

Freedom of Information Act

For more information, contact the FOIA Requester Service Center. Phone, 202-418-1379.

Internal Equal Employment Practices

For more information, contact the Office of Workplace Diversity. Phone, 202-418-1799.

Internships

Information on FCC internships is available online.

Licensing

Information on the FCC's licensing systems is available online.

Public Inspection

Records that are deemed nonconfidential by law can be viewed on the FCC's Web site. Each broadcasting station maintains a current copy of its application for license, operational information, and nonconfidential FCC reports for public inspection.

Publications

The Office of Media Relations distributes public notices and press releases and makes them available online. The Consumer and Governmental Affairs Bureau maintains an online consumer publications library.

For further information, contact the Consumer Center, Federal Communications Commission, 445 Twelfth Street SW., Washington, DC 20554. Phone, 888-225-5322. TTY, 888-835-5322.

FEDERAL COMMUNICATIONS COMMISSION

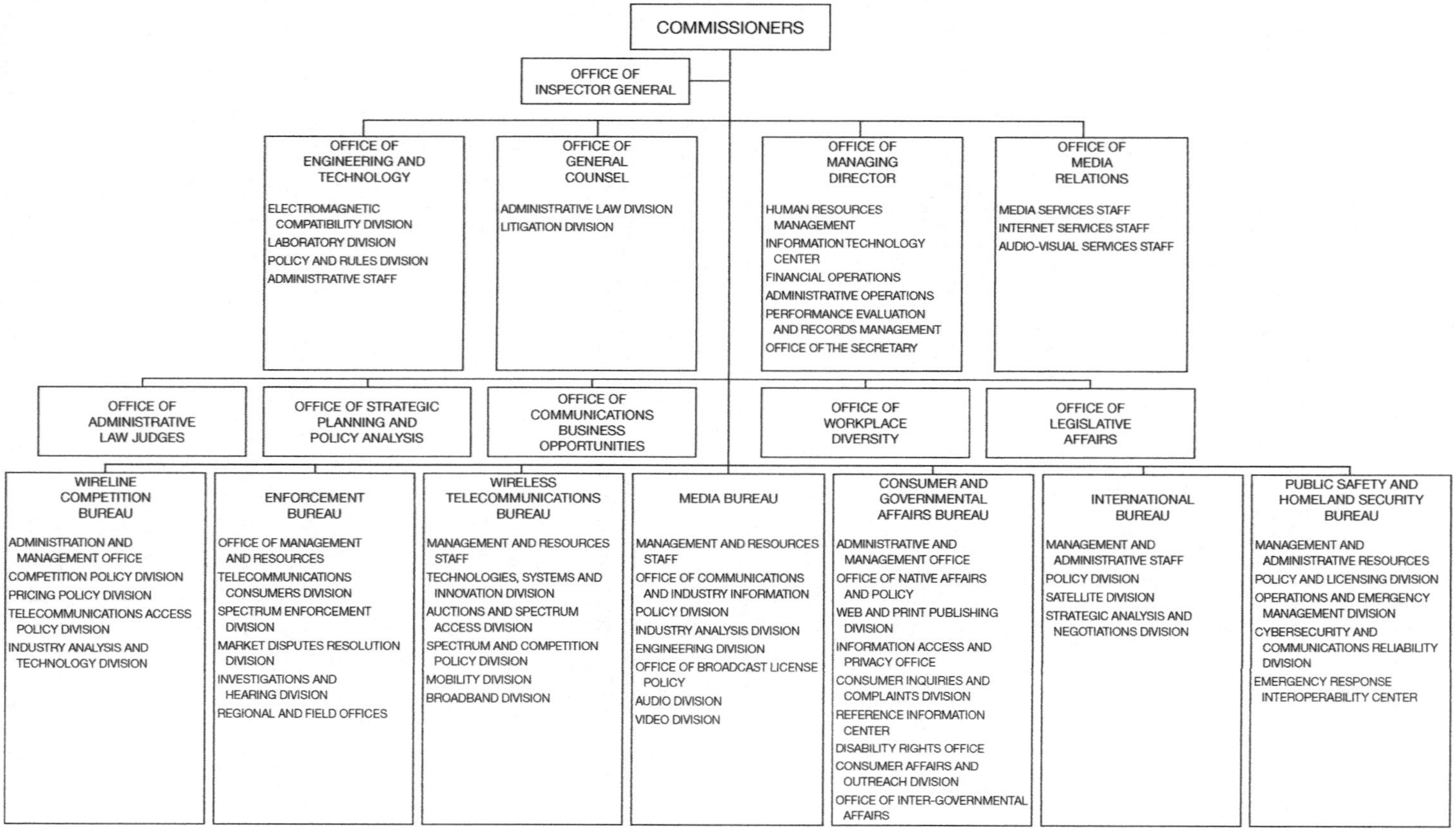

Federal Deposit Insurance Corporation

550 Seventeenth Street NW., Washington, DC 20429, 703-562-2222, *http://www.fdic.gov*

Board of Directors

CHAIR	Martin J. Gruenberg
Vice Chair	Thomas M. Hoenig
Director (Director, Consumer Financial Protection Bureau)	Richard A. Cordray
Director (Comptroller of the Currency)	Thomas J. Curry
Director	(vacancy)

Headquarters–Washington, DC

CHAIR	Martin J. Gruenberg
Vice Chair	Thomas M. Hoenig
Chief of Staff	Barbara A. Ryan
Senior Advisor to the Chair	David S. Hoelscher
Senior Advisor to the Chair	(vacancy)
DEPUTIES	
Deputy to the Chair	Kymberly K. Copa
Deputy to the Chair / Chief Financial Officer	Steven O. App
Deputy to the Chair / Chief Operating Officer	Barbara A. Ryan
Deputy to the Vice Chair	Karl Reitz
DIVISION HEADS	
Chief Information Officer / Chief Privacy Officer	Lawrence Gross, Jr.
Director, Administration	Arleas Upton Kea
Director, Corporate University / Chief Learning Officer	Suzannah L. Susser
Director, Depositor and Consumer Protection	Mark E. Pearce
Director, Finance	Craig R. Jarvill
Director, Information Technology	Russell G. Pittman
Director, Insurance and Research	Diane Ellis
Director, Resolution and Receiverships	Bret D. Edwards
Director, Risk Management Supervision	Doreen R. Eberley
General Counsel	Charles Yi
OFFICE HEADS	
Chief Risk Officer	Lee Price, Acting
Deputy to the Chair for Communications	Barbara Hagenbaugh
Director, Complex Financial Institutions	Arthur J. Murton
Director, Legislative Affairs	Andy Jiminez
Director, Minority and Women Inclusion	Avelino Rodriguez, Acting
Inspector General	Fred W. Gibson, Acting
Ombudsman	Gordon Talbot, Acting

The Federal Deposit Insurance Corporation preserves and promotes public confidence in U.S. financial institutions by insuring bank and thrift deposits, examining State-chartered banks, and liquidating assets of failed institutions.

The Federal Deposit Insurance Corporation (FDIC) was established under the Banking Act of 1933 after numerous banks failed during the Great Depression. FDIC began insuring banks on January 1, 1934. The basic insurance coverage per depositor at each insured bank and savings association is $250,000.

The FDIC is managed by a five-member Board of Directors, all of whom the President appoints and the Senate confirms. No more than three of the Directors can be affiliated with the same political party.

The FDIC insures approximately 6,100 institutions. It receives no congressional appropriations. FDIC funding comes from insurance premiums on deposits held by insured banks and savings associations and from interest on the investment of those premiums in U.S. Government securities. FDIC has authority to borrow up to $100 billion from the Treasury for insurance purposes.

Activities

The FDIC insures about $11 trillion of U.S. bank and thrift deposits. As required by law, the fund relies on two sources of income: premiums paid by banks and savings associations, and the interest on the investment of those premiums in U.S. Government securities. An institution's level of capitalization and potential risk to the insurance fund determines its premiums.

The FDIC examines about 3,600 State-chartered commercial and savings banks that are not members of the Federal Reserve System, called State nonmember banks. The FDIC also has authority to examine other types of FDIC-insured institutions for deposit insurance purposes. The two types of examinations conducted are for safety and soundness and for compliance with applicable consumer laws such as the Truth in Lending Act, the Home Mortgage Disclosure Act, the Equal Credit Opportunity Act, the Fair Housing Act, and the Community Reinvestment Act. FDIC examiners work onsite at the institution as well analyze bank data offsite.

A failed bank or savings association is generally closed by its chartering authority, and the FDIC is named receiver. The FDIC is required to resolve the closure in a manner that is least costly to its Deposit Insurance Fund. Ordinarily, the FDIC attempts to locate a healthy institution to acquire the failed entity. If such an entity cannot be found, the FDIC pays depositors the amount of their insured funds, usually by the next business day following the closure. Depositors with funds that exceed the insurance limit often receive an advance dividend, which is a portion of their uninsured funds that is determined by an estimate of the future proceeds from liquidating the failed institution's remaining assets. Depositors with funds in a failed institution that exceed the insurance limit receive a receivership certificate for those funds and partial payments of their uninsured funds as asset disposition permits.

As part of its insurance, supervisory, and receivership responsibilities, the FDIC approves or disapproves mergers, consolidations, and acquisitions where the resulting bank is an insured State nonmember; approves or disapproves proposals by banks to establish and operate a new branch, close an existing branch, or move its main office from one location to another; and approves or disapproves requests to engage as principal in activities and investments that are not permissible for a national bank. It also issues enforcement actions, including cease-and-desist orders, for specific violations or practices requiring corrective action and reviews changes in ownership or control of a bank.

Sources of Information

Assistance for Bank Customers

An electronic form is available for filing a complaint against a particular financial institution. The form also may be used to inquire about FDIC deposit insurance coverage or to ask a question about a particular financial institution.

Bank Failures

The FDIC maintains a failed bank list that contains information on how accounts and loans are affected, how vendors can file claims against the receivership, and the acquiring bank—if applicable. The list covers from October 1, 2000, to the present.

Starting with the year 2001, the FDIC maintains a brief summary of each bank failure. For additional information on recent failures, call the customer service hotline. Phone, 888-206-4662.

A search tool is available online to help the public find the point of contact information of failed institutions.

Detailed information on bank and thrift failures since 1934 is available on the FDIC Web site.

BankFind

The FDIC Web site features an online tool for locating insured banking institutions.

Call Center

The call center is open every day of the week: Monday–Friday, 8 a.m.–8 p.m., eastern standard time; Saturday and Sunday, 9 a.m.–5 p.m., eastern standard time. Phone, 877-275-3342. Phone, 800-925-4618 (hearing impaired).

Electronic Deposit Insurance Estimator (EDIE)

Consumers and bankers can use EDIE to determine, on a per-bank basis, how the insurance rules and limits apply to a depositor's specific group of deposit accounts—what is insured and what portion, if any, exceeds coverage limits.

Employment

FDIC job openings and information on career transition assistance, student employment opportunities, and submitting an application are available online.

In 2015, the FDIC was ranked number one among midsize Government agencies in the Best Places To Work Agency Rankings.

Freedom of Information Act (FOIA)

The FDIC operates a FOIA service center that is open on weekdays, 8:30 a.m.–5:00 p.m., excluding Federal holidays. Phone, 202-898-7021.

The FDIC's FOIA guide offers a concise explanation of the FOIA and how it can be used to access Government records. It also explains the process for submitting a request to the FDIC. The guide also provides links to helpful reference guides and describes how additional information may be obtained from the FDIC.

The FDIC accepts electronic FOIA requests.

News and Events

The FDIC posts conferences and events, financial institution letters, opinion editorials, press releases, speeches, and testimonies on its Web site.

The FDIC offers an online subscription service for email alerts. A subscriber may opt to receive various types of alerts: financial institution letters, news releases, statistical publications, and other types.

The FDIC disseminates information and news using RSS feeds.

The FCC tweets news items and other information on Twitter.

Office of Inspector General (OIG)

The OIG operates a toll-free, nationwide hotline to provide a way for FDIC employees, its contractors, financial institution staff, and other members of the public to report incidents of abuse, fraud, mismanagement, and waste within FDIC programs and activities or its contractor operations. A person can file a report anonymously, confidentially, or openly by using the hotline; however, filing a report by email guarantees neither anonymity nor confidentiality. Phone, 800-964-3342. Fax, 703-562-6444.

Open Government

The FDIC supports the Open Government initiative by promoting the principles of collaboration, participation, and transparency.

Plain Language

The FDIC welcomes comment on it's compliance with the Plain Writing Act of 2010 and suggestions for improving communication between the agency and the public.

Publications

The FDIC Web site features an online product catalog and ordering system.

Publications, press releases, congressional testimony, directives to financial institutions, and other documents are available through the Public Information

Center. Phone, 877-275-3342 (press 1, then press 5).

Site Map

The Web site map allows visitors to look for specific topics or to browse for content that aligns with their interests.

For further information and media inquiries, contact the Office of Communications, Federal Deposit Insurance Corporation, 550 Seventeenth Street NW., Washington, DC 20429. Phone, 202-898-6993.

FEDERAL DEPOSIT INSURANCE CORPORATION

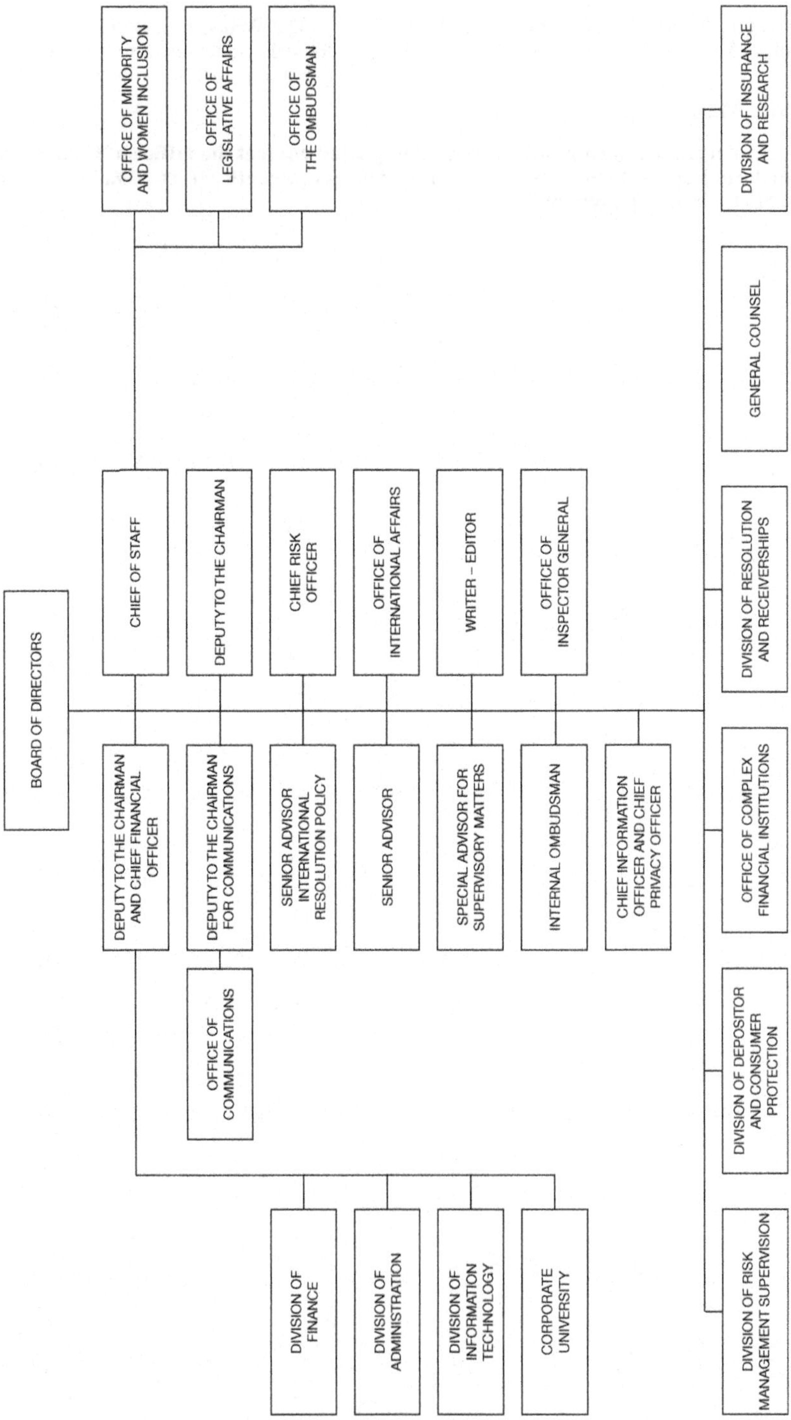

Federal Election Commission

999 E Street NW., Washington, DC 20463, 202-694-1100, 800-424-9530, *http://www.fec.gov*

CHAIR	Matthew S. Petersen
Vice Chair	Steven T. Walther
Commissioner	Lee E. Goodman
Commissioner	Caroline C. Hunter
Commissioner	Ann M. Ravel
Commissioner	Ellen L. Weintraub
Staff Director	Alec Palmer
Chief Financial Officer	Judy Berning, Acting
General Counsel	Daniel Petalas, Acting
Inspector General	Lynne A. McFarland

The Federal Election Commission provides public disclosure of campaign finance activities and ensures compliance with campaign finance laws and regulations.

The Federal Election Commission is an independent agency established by section 309 of the Federal Election Campaign Act of 1971, as amended (52 U.S.C. 30106). It comprises six Commissioners whom the President appoints with the advice and consent of the Senate. The Act also provides for three statutory officers—the staff director, the general counsel, and the inspector general—whom the Commissioners appoint.

Activities

The Commission administers and enforces the Federal Election Campaign Act of 1971, as amended (52 U.S.C. 30101 et seq.), and the Revenue Act, as amended (26 U.S.C. 1 et seq.). These laws provide for the public funding of Presidential elections, public disclosure of the financial activities of political committees involved in Federal elections, and limitations and prohibitions on contributions and expenditures made to influence Federal elections.

Public Funding of Presidential Elections

The Commission oversees the public financing of Presidential elections by certifying Federal payments to primary candidates and general election nominees. It also audits recipients of Federal funds and may require repayment to the U.S. Treasury if a committee has made nonqualified campaign expenditures.

Disclosure

The Commission ensures public disclosure of the campaign finance activities reported by political committees supporting Federal candidates. These committees regularly file reports disclosing the sources of campaign money and how that money is spent. The Commission places these reports on the public record within 48 hours after they are received and digitizes the data contained in them.

Sources of Information

Congressional Affairs

This Office of Congressional, Legislative, and Intergovernmental Affairs serves as the Commission's primary congressional and executive branch liaison. Phone, 202-694-1006.

Data

Data tables summarizing campaign financial activity by filer type, election cycle, and reporting period are available online.

Employment

The Commission posts available positions on its Web site. Sign up online to receive email updates regarding employment opportunities. Information is also available from the Office of Human Resources. Phone, 202-694-1080.

Filing

Information is available online to help filers comply with the disclosure requirements of the Federal campaign finance law.

Freedom of Information Act (FOIA)

FOIA requests may be submitted by email or fax or sent by mail to the Federal Election Commission, Attn: FOIA Requester Service Center, Room 408, 999 E Street NW., Washington, DC 20463. Fax, 202-219-1043.

General Inquiries

The Information Division informs and assists Federal candidates, political committees, and the public. It answers questions on campaign finance laws, conducts workshops and seminars on these laws, and distributes publications and forms. Phone, 202-694-1100 or 800-424-9530. TDD, 202-219-3336.

Law Library

The library contains a collection of basic legal research resources on political campaign financing, corporate and labor political activity, and campaign finance reform. It is open to the public on weekdays, 9 a.m.–5 p.m., except on Federal holidays. Phone, 202-694-1516 or 800-424-9530.

Media Inquiries

The Press Office answers questions from media sources, issues press releases on Commission actions and statistical data, responds to requests for information, and distributes other materials. Phone, 202-694-1220.

Public Records

The Public Records Branch, located at 999 E Street NW., Washington, DC, provides space for public inspection of campaign finance reports and statements after 1971. It is open to the public on weekdays, 9 a.m.–5 p.m., except on Federal holidays. Phone, 202-694-1120 or 800-424-9530.

For further information, contact the Information Division, Federal Election Commission, 999 E Street NW., Washington, DC 20463. Phone, 202-694-1100 or 800-424-9530 (option 6).

FEDERAL ELECTION COMMISSION

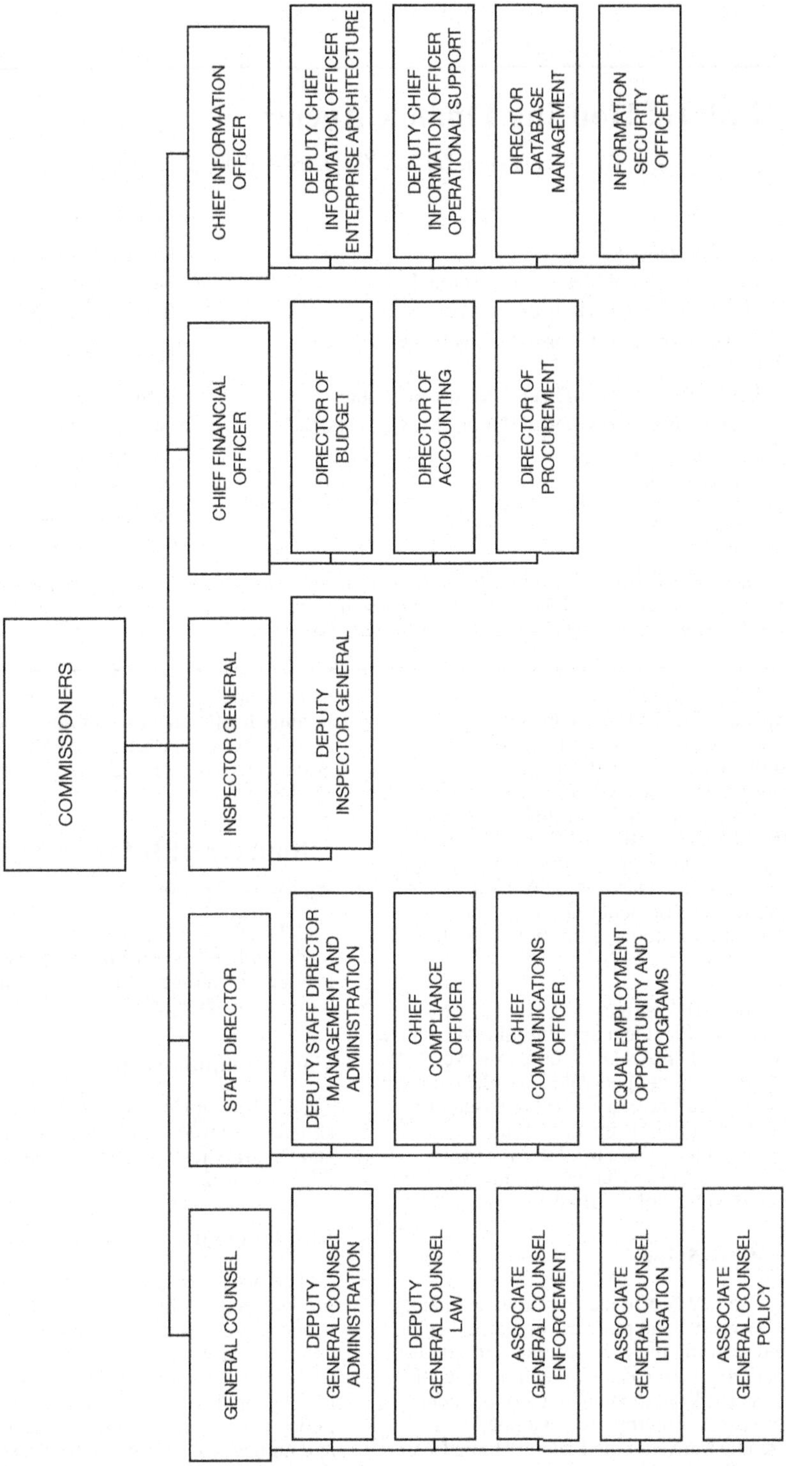

Federal Housing Finance Agency

400 7th Street SW., Washington, DC 20219, 202-649-3800, *http://www.fhfa.gov*

DIRECTOR	Melvin L. Watt
Chief Operating Officer	Lawrence Stauffer, Acting
Director, Office of Minority and Women Inclusion	Sharron P. A. Levine
Deputy Director, Division of Conservatorship	Bob Ryan, Acting
Deputy Director, Division of Federal Home Loan Bank Regulation	Fred C. Graham
Deputy Director, Division of Enterprise Regulation	Nina Nichols
Deputy Director, Division of Housing Mission and Goals	Sandra Thompson
General Counsel	Alfred M. Pollard
Inspector General	Laura S. Wertheimer
Obmbudsman	Janell Byrd-Chichester, Acting

The Federal Housing and Finance Agency ensures that the housing Government-Sponsored Enterprises operate safely and soundly and serve as a reliable source of liquidity and funding for housing finance and community investment.

The Federal Housing and Finance Agency (FHFA) was established by the Housing and Economic Recovery Act of 2008 (42 U.S.C. 4501 note) as an independent agency in the executive branch. The merger of the Federal Housing Finance Board and the Office of Federal Housing Enterprise Oversight, combined with the transfer of the Department of Housing and Urban Development's Government-Sponsored Enterprise mission team, formed the FHFA.

The FHFA is managed by a Director whom the President appoints and the Senate confirms. FHFA's Director also serves as the Chairman of the Federal Housing Oversight Board. The Secretary of the Treasury, the Secretary of Housing and Urban Development, and the Chairman of the Securities and Exchange Commission are also members of the Board.

Activities

The FHFA provides research and data, supervision, and policies for strengthening and securing the U.S. secondary mortgage markets. It oversees vital components of those markets: the housing Government-Sponsored Enterprises of Fannie Mae, Freddie Mac, and the Federal Home Loan Bank System. Combined, these entities make available more than $5.6 trillion in funding for financial institutions and the U.S. mortgage markets. The FHFA also acts as the conservator of Fannie Mae and Freddie Mac.

Sources of Information

Business Opportunities

FHFA Contracting Operations is responsible for procuring all goods and services, including information technology, required by the agency.

Congressional Affairs

Members of Congress or their staff may contact the Office of Congressional Affairs and Communications for assistance. Phone, 202-649-3802.

Employment

The Agency's mission-critical professionals include accountants, attorneys, economists, examiners, financial analysts, and information technology specialists. The FHFA regularly recruits other professionals to fill support positions: facilities managers, policy experts, and budget and procurement and human resource specialists, as well as student interns. The Agency advertises opportunities for employment on its "Careers" Web page and on USAJOBS, the Federal Government's free web-based job board. Questions and applications may be sent to the Office of Human Resources Management, FHFA, 400 7th Street SW., Washington, DC 20219. Phone, 202-649-3807.

Homeowner Assistance

The FHFA assists homeowners and home buyers. Information is available online. Phone, 202-649-3811. Fax, 202-649-1072.

Media Inquiries

The Office of Congressional Affairs and Communications maintains the Agency's Web site, answers questions from representatives of the media, issues press releases, and responds to requests for information. Phone, 202-649-3700.

Publications

The FHFA posts its publications online for download. The Agency generally does not mail hardcopies, but all requests are considered. Written requests for copies of publications may be addressed to the Office of Congressional Affairs and Communications, FHFA, 400 7th Street SW., Washington, DC 20219.

Public Records

FHFA public records are published online. Questions about other publicly accessible records, including those covered under the Freedom of Information Act, should be addressed to the Chief FOIA Officer.

For further information, contact the Office of Congressional Affairs and Communications, Federal Housing Finance Agency, 400 7th Street SW., Washington, DC 20219. Phone, 202-649-3802.

FEDERAL HOUSING FINANCE AGENCY

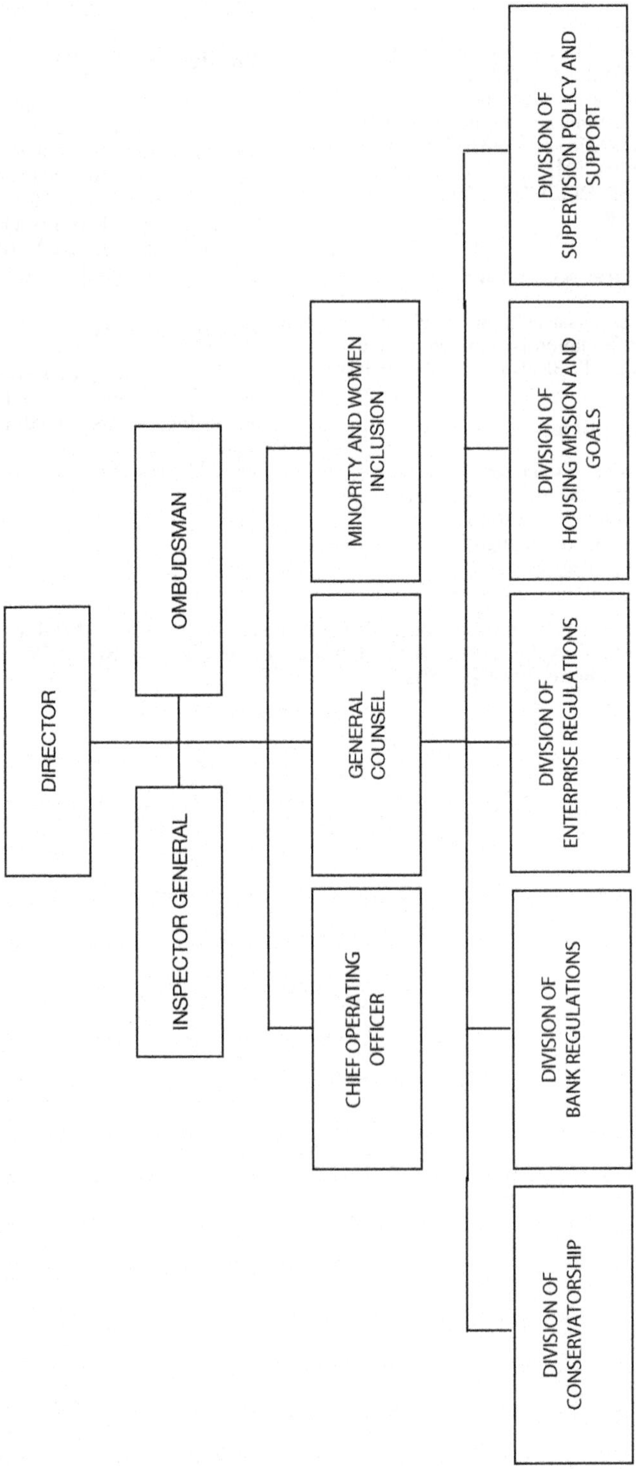

Federal Labor Relations Authority

1400 K Street NW., Washington, DC 20005, 202-218-7770, *http://www.flra.gov*

CHAIR	Carol Waller Pope
Member	Ernest DuBester
Member	Patrick Pizzella
Executive Director	Sarah Whittle Spooner
Chief Administrative Law Judge	Charles R. Center
Chief Counsel	David S. Eddy III
Chief, Case Intake and Publication	Cabrina S. Smith
General Counsel	Julia Akins Clark
Inspector General	Dana Rooney
Solicitor	Fred B. Jacob

FEDERAL SERVICE IMPASSES PANEL

CHAIR	Mary E. Jacksteit
Member	Barbara B. Franklin
Member	Marvin E. Johnson
Member	Edward F. Hartfield
Member	Martin H. Malin
Member	Donald S. Wasserman
Member	David E. Walker
Executive Director	Kimberly D. Moseley

FOREIGN SERVICE LABOR RELATIONS BOARD

CHAIR	Carol Waller Pope
Member	Herman J. Cohen
Member	Stephen R. Ledford

FOREIGN SERVICE IMPASSE DISPUTES PANEL

CHAIR	Mary E. Jacksteit
Member	Betty Bolden
Member	Shawn Hooper
Member	John C. Sullivan
Member	(vacancy)

The Federal Labor Relations Authority oversees labor-management relations between the Federal Government and its employees.

The Federal Labor Relations Authority (FLRA) was created as an independent establishment by Reorganization Plan No. 2 of 1978 (5 U.S.C. app.), effective January 1, 1979, pursuant to Executive Order 12107 of December 28, 1978, to consolidate the central policymaking functions in Federal labor-management relations. Its duties and authority are specified in Title VII (Federal Service Labor-Management Relations) of the Civil Service Reform Act of 1978 (5 U.S.C. 7101-7135).

The FLRA comprises three members whom the President nominates and Senate confirms to 5-year terms. The Chair of the Authority serves as the chief executive and administrative officer. The Chair also presides over the Foreign Service Labor Relations Board. The General Counsel investigates alleged unfair labor practices, files and prosecutes unfair labor practice complaints before the Authority, and exercises other powers that the Authority may prescribe.

Activities

The Authority adjudicates disputes arising under the Federal Labor-Management Relations Program, deciding cases concerning the negotiability of collective bargaining agreement proposals, appeals concerning unfair labor practices and representation petitions, and exceptions to grievance arbitration awards. It also assists Federal agencies and unions in understanding their rights and responsibilities under the program.

The Federal Service Impasses Panel, an entity within the FLRA, assists in resolving negotiation impasses between agencies and unions. The Panel can either recommend procedures to the parties for the resolution of the impasse or assist the parties in resolving the impasse through whatever methods and procedures it considers appropriate, including fact-finding and mediation-arbitration. If the parties do not arrive at a voluntary settlement after receiving Panel assistance, the Panel may take whatever action is necessary to resolve the impasse, including the imposition of contract terms.

The Foreign Service Labor Relations Board and the Foreign Service Impasse Disputes Panel administer provisions of chapter 2 of the Foreign Service Act of 1980 (22 U.S.C. 3921) concerning labor-management relations. This chapter establishes a statutory labor-management relations program for Foreign Service employees of the U.S. Government. Administrative and staff support is provided by the Federal Labor Relations Authority and the Federal Service Impasses Panel.

Sources of Information

Electronic Filing

To use the FLRA's electronic case filing system, register online and create a user profile. Email addresses are the case filing system's primary means of identifying electronic filers.

Employment

The FLRA posts announcements for job openings on USAJobs. For more information, contact the Human Resources Division. Phone, 202-218-7979.

The FLRA ranks among the best places to work in the Federal Government.

Freedom of Information Act (FOIA)

The FLRA maintains an electronic FOIA reading room.

If the desired information is unavailable in the reading room or elsewhere on the FLRA's Web site, then a written FOIA request may be necessary to access the information. To learn how to submit a FOIA request, consult the "Frequently Asked Questions" section.

Media

Members of the media should contact the Counsel for Regulatory and Public Affairs if they have questions or seek information. Phone, 202-218-7776.

News

The FLRA posts press releases on its Web site. The online archives contain press releases from 2009 through 2014.

Open Government

The FLRA supports the Federal Government's efforts to increase collaboration, participation, and transparency.

Plain Language

The FLRA adheres to Federal plain language guidelines. To comply with the Plain Writing Act of 2010, the agency relies on the general public. If a document or Web page is difficult to understand, alert the FLRA's writers and editors via email to the lack of clarity.

For further information, contact the Office of the Executive Director, Federal Labor Relations Authority, 1400 K Street NW., Washington, DC 20005. Phone, 202-218-7791.

FEDERAL LABOR RELATIONS AUTHORITY

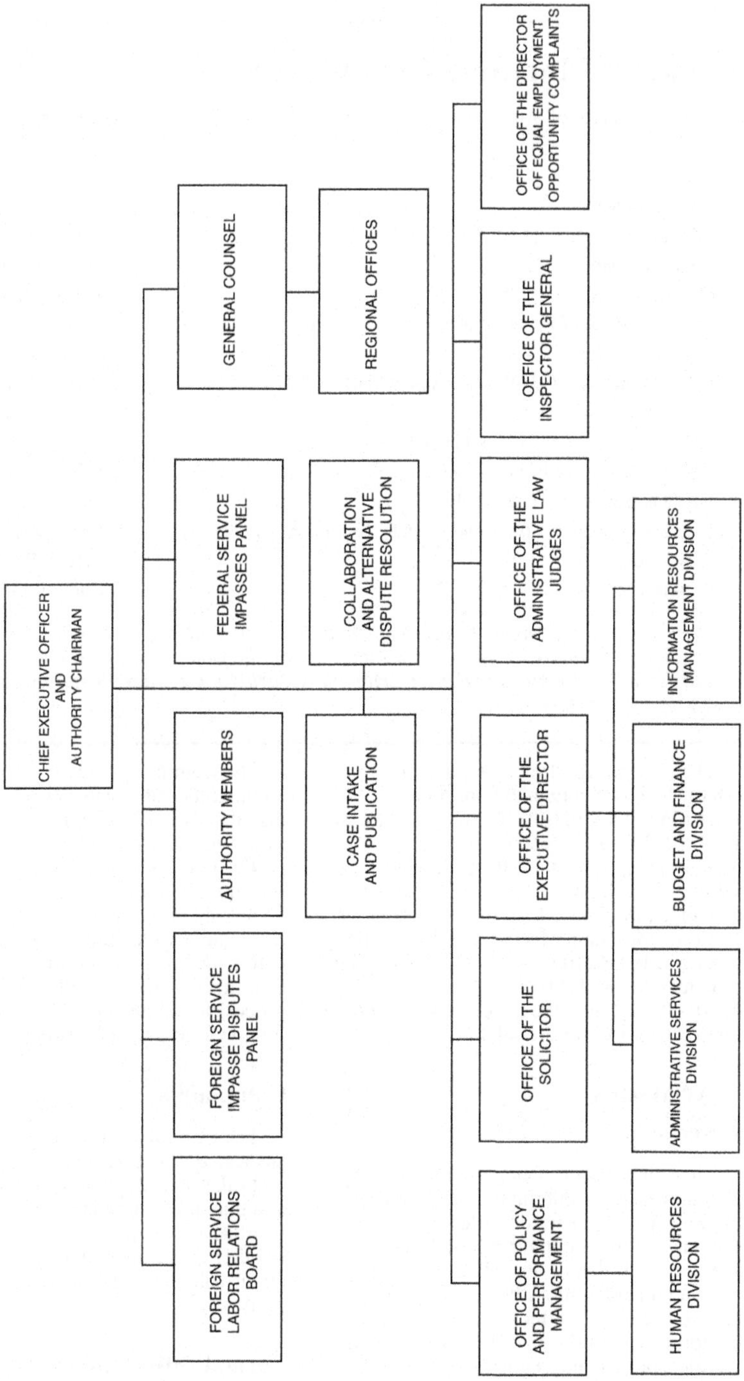

Federal Maritime Commission

800 North Capitol Street NW., Washington, DC 20573, 202-523-5707, *http://www.fmc.gov*

CHAIR	Mario Cordero
Commissioner	William P. Doyle
Commissioner	Rebecca F. Dye
Commissioner	Michael A. Khouri
Commissioner	Richard A. Lidinsky, Jr.
Director, Office of Equal Employment Opportunity	Howard F. Jimenez
Inspector General	Jonathan Hatfield
DIRECTOR, OFFICE OF MANAGING DIRECTOR	Vern W. Hill
Chief, Administrative Law Judge	Clay G. Guthridge
Director, Bureau of Certification and Licensing	Sandra L. Kusumoto
Director, Bureau of Enforcement	Peter J. King
Director, Bureau of Trade Analysis	Florence A. Carr
Director, Consumer Affairs and Dispute Resolution Services	Rebecca A. Fenneman
General Counsel	Tyler J. Wood
Secretary	Karen V. Gregory

The Federal Maritime Commission promotes an efficient, fair, and reliable system of international ocean transportation; protects the public from unfair, unlawful, and deceptive practices; and contributes to the integrity and security of the Nation's supply chain and transportation system.

The Federal Maritime Commission was established by Reorganization Plan No. 7 of 1961 (46 U.S.C. 301-307), effective August 12, 1961. It is an independent agency that regulates shipping under the following statutes: the Shipping Act of 1984, as amended (46 U.S.C. 40101-41309); Section 19 of the Merchant Marine Act, 1920 (46 U.S.C. 42101-42109); the Foreign Shipping Practices Act of 1988 (46 U.S.C. 42301-42307); and the act of November 6, 1966 (46 U.S.C. 44101-44106).

Activities

Agreements

The Commission reviews agreements by and among ocean common carriers and/or marine terminal operators, filed under section 5 of the Shipping Act of 1984, for statutory compliance as well as for likely impact on competition. It also monitors activities under all effective agreements for compliance with the provisions of law and its rules, orders, and regulations.

Alternative Dispute Resolution

The Commission reviews informal complaints and assists parties in resolving disputes. Mediation and other dispute resolution services are available to assist parties in achieving a more acceptable resolution to a dispute at less cost than may be possible in litigation. These services are available before and after the commencement of litigation. The Commission also provides an informal process to adjudicate certain complaints involving less than $50,000 in damages.

Complaints

The Commission reviews alleged or suspected violations of the shipping statutes and rules and regulations of the Commission and may take administrative action to institute formal proceedings, to refer matters to other governmental agencies, or to bring about voluntary agreement between the parties.

Formal Adjudicatory Procedures

The Commission conducts formal investigations and hearings on its own motion and adjudicates formal complaints in accordance with the Administrative Procedure Act (5 U.S.C. note prec. 551).

International Affairs

The Commission conducts investigations of foreign governmental and carrier practices that adversely affect the U.S. shipping trade. In consultation with other executive agencies, the Commission takes action to effect the elimination of discriminatory practices on the part of foreign governments against shipping in the United States foreign trade and to achieve comity between the United States and its trading partners.

Investigation and Economic Analyses

The Commission prescribes and administers programs to ensure compliance with the provisions of the shipping statutes. These programs include: education and outreach activities; the collection of information relating to field investigation of activities and practices of ocean common carriers, terminal operators, agreements among ocean common carriers and/or marine terminal operators, ocean transportation intermediaries, passenger vessel operators, and other persons subject to the shipping statutes; and rate analyses, studies, and economic reviews of current and prospective trade conditions, including the extent and nature of competition in various trade areas.

Licenses

The Commission issues licenses to those persons and entities in the United States who wish to carry out the business of providing freight forwarding services and non-vessel-operating common carrier services.

Non-Vessel-Operating Common Carrier Service Arrangements

The Commission receives and reviews service arrangements entered into by non-vessel-operating common carriers and their customers. Cargo moving under these service arrangements is exempt from the tariff publication and adherence requirements of the Shipping Act, on the condition that the service arrangements must be filed with the Commission.

Passenger Indemnity

The Commission administers the passenger indemnity provisions of the act of November 6, 1966, which require shipowners and operators to obtain certificates of financial responsibility to pay judgments for personal injury or death or to refund fares in the event of nonperformance of voyages.

Rulemaking

The Commission promulgates rules and regulations to interpret, enforce, and ensure compliance with shipping and related statutes by common carriers and other persons subject to the Commission's jurisdiction.

Service Contracts

The Commission receives and reviews filings of confidential service contracts between shippers and ocean common carriers. The Commission also monitors publication of certain essential terms of those service contracts.

Tariffs

The Commission monitors and prescribes requirements to ensure accessibility and accuracy of electronic tariff publications of common carriers engaged in the foreign commerce of the United States. Special permission applications may be submitted for relief from statutory and/or Commission tariff requirements.

Sources of Information

Consumer Affairs and Dispute Resolution

Contact the Office of Consumer Affairs and Dispute Resolution Services. Phone, 202-523-5807.

Electronic Reading Room

Decisions issued from July 1987 to the present and logs of all documents filed or issued in formal proceedings are accessible online.

Employment

Contact the Office of Human Resources, Federal Maritime Commission, 800 North Capitol Street NW., Washington, DC 20573-0001. Phone, 202-523-5773.

Freedom of Information Act (FOIA)

The Commission releases a lot of information into the public domain to reduce the number of official FOIA requests. When submitting a FOIA request by email, type the words "FOIA Request" in the subject line. Mailed requests must be addressed to the Secretary of the Commission–FOIA Request, Federal Maritime Commission, 800 North Capitol Street NW., Washington, DC 20573. Fax: 202-523-0014.

For further information, contact the Office of the Secretary, Federal Maritime Commission, 800 North Capitol Street NW., Washington, DC 20573-0001. Phone, 202-523-5725. Fax, 202-523-0014.

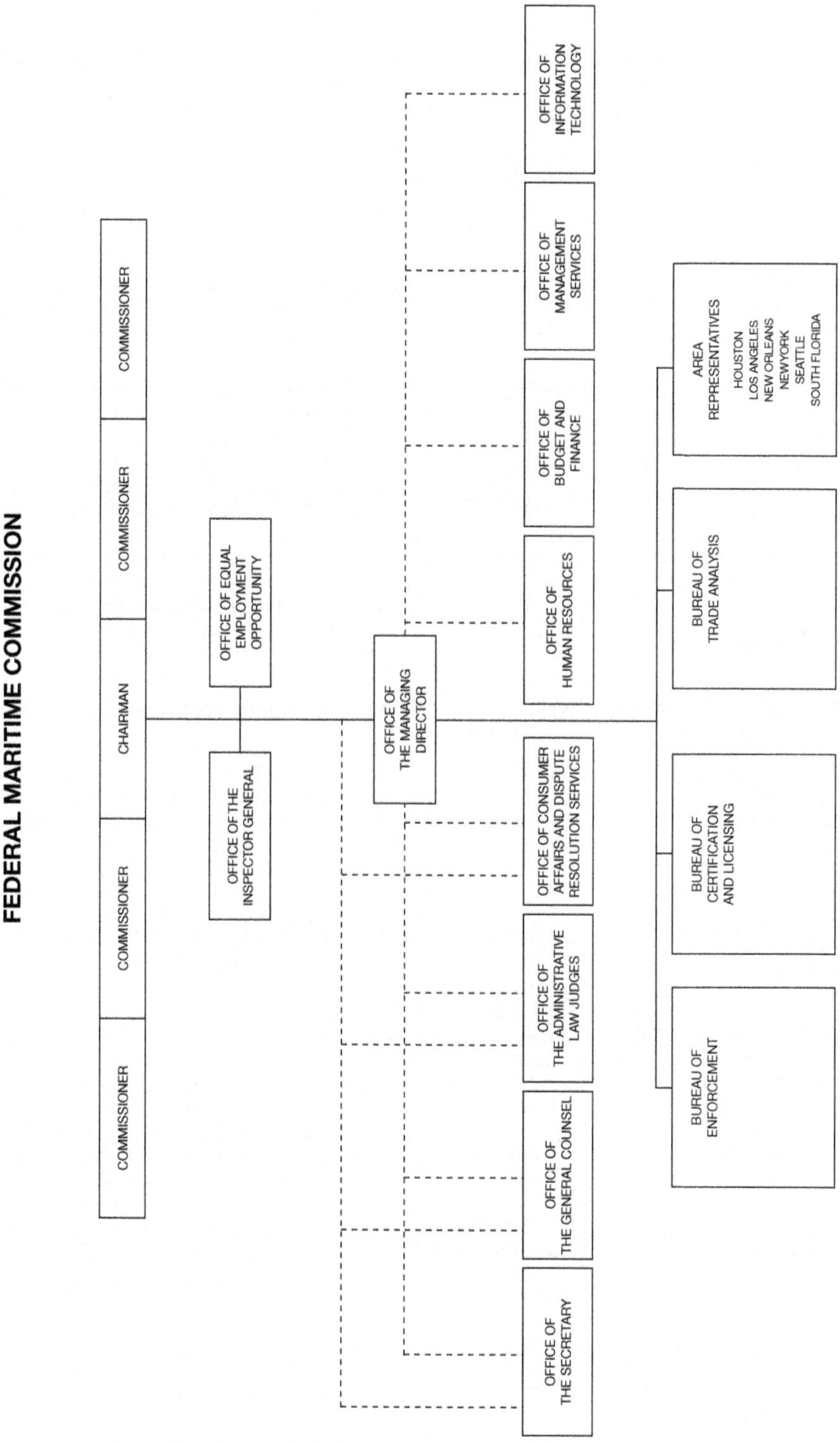
FEDERAL MARITIME COMMISSION
COMMISSIONER
COMMISSIONER
CHAIRMAN
COMMISSIONER
COMMISSIONER
OFFICE OF EQUAL EMPLOYMENT OPPORTUNITY
OFFICE OF THE INSPECTOR GENERAL
OFFICE OF THE MANAGING DIRECTOR
OFFICE OF INFORMATION TECHNOLOGY
OFFICE OF MANAGEMENT SERVICES
OFFICE OF BUDGET AND FINANCE
OFFICE OF HUMAN RESOURCES
OFFICE OF CONSUMER AFFAIRS AND DISPUTE RESOLUTION SERVICES
OFFICE OF THE ADMINISTRATIVE LAW JUDGES
OFFICE OF THE GENERAL COUNSEL
OFFICE OF THE SECRETARY
AREA REPRESENTATIVES
HOUSTON
LOS ANGELES
NEW ORLEANS
NEWYORK
SEATTLE
SOUTH FLORIDA
BUREAU OF TRADE ANALYSIS
BUREAU OF CERTIFICATION AND LICENSING
BUREAU OF ENFORCEMENT

Federal Mediation and Conciliation Service

2100 K Street NW., Washington, DC 20427, 202-606-8100, *http://www.fmcs.gov*

DIRECTOR	Allison Beck

The Federal Mediation and Conciliation Service helps labor and management resolve disputes in industries affecting commerce, offers training in cooperative processes to promote workplace stability and economic growth, and provides alternative dispute resolution services, training, negotiated rulemaking, and public policy facilitation to government entities.

The Federal Mediation and Conciliation Service (FMCS) was created by the Labor Management Relations Act, 1947 (29 U.S.C. 172). Subsequent laws amended the statute and expanded the scope of the agency's dispute resolution services. The President appoints the Director with the advice and consent of the Senate.

Activities

The FMCS reduces disruptions to interstate commerce and improves government efficiency by providing skilled mediators to resolve workplace disputes and conflicts arising under the statutory jurisdiction of government entities. FMCS mediators do not enforce laws: They rely on innovative mediation, communication, and relationship building techniques to help disputants achieve consensus.

The FMCS offers its labor mediation and training services in a variety of industries and sectors of the economy, including the private sector (except airlines and railroads), the Federal sector, and the public sector (in States without labor mediation agencies). The Labor-Management Cooperation Act of 1978 recognized the economic benefits of a more proactive approach to workplace stability. The FMCS awards grants to encourage the establishment of local, regional, and industrywide labor management committees to improve labor management relationships, organizational effectiveness, and economic development. The FMCS also promotes workplace innovation, productivity, and competitiveness through collaboration, good labor-management relationships, and problem solving between companies and their workers.

The Administrative Dispute Resolution and Negotiated Rulemaking Acts of 1996 recognized the broader value of FMCS conflict resolution services for government efficiency. The agency was designated as a key resource to help government entities resolve individual employment disputes, design conflict management systems, achieve stakeholder consensus on new regulations, and conduct more effective multi-stakeholder public policy dialogues.

Mediation and Training

FMCS mediators help parties resolve workplace disputes and establish sound, stable, and enduring labor-management relations. In addition to mediating collective bargaining disputes, mediators facilitate better day-to-day workplace relations through a variety of joint training programs. FMCS mediators also assist other government entities with resolving disputes arising under their jurisdictions.

Arbitration

Voluntary arbitration and factfinding are widely used in labor-management relations. Upon request, the FMCS can provide panels of arbitrators who are experienced in labor relations issues. Requests can be tailored, in terms of expertise, fees, geography, and other considerations, to accommodate a variety of requirements.

Sources of Information

Calendar

A day-by-day listing of important FMCS events is available on online.

Conflict Management

The FMCS Institute for Conflict Management offers practical and experience-based conflict resolution training for individuals and groups. Course descriptions and enrollment information are available online.

Documents and Data

Budgets and performance information, regulations and policies, speeches and presentations, publications (some in Spanish), and reports are available online. Collective bargaining notice data and work stoppage data are also posted online.

Electronic Updates

The FMCS uses email updates to disseminate information on its dispute resolution services and to announce training opportunities. A sign-up form is available online.

Employment

Stationed in offices nationwide, FMCS mediators are full-time excepted service employees of the Federal Government. They perform duties in five major areas: advocacy, education, and outreach; alternative dispute resolution services to government entities; collective bargaining mediation; grievance mediation; and relationship development training. The ideal applicant seeking to become an FMCS mediator has full-time experience in the collective bargaining process. U.S. citizenship is required.

Forms and Applications

Forms and applications needed to obtain FMCS services and funding—arbitration, Freedom of Information Act (FOIA) requests, labor-management cooperation grants, and notice of bargaining (F–7)—are available online.

Find a Mediator

An online search tool is available to find a mediator by city, State, or Zip Code, as well as by name, email, or phone number.

Regional Offices

Headquartered in Washington, DC, the FMCS delivers services nationwide through its 10 regional and numerous field offices. Contact information for the FMCS national office and its regional and field offices is available online.

For further information, contact the Public Affairs Office, Federal Mediation and Conciliation Service, 2100 K Street NW., Washington, DC 20427. Phone, 202-606-8100.

Federal Mine Safety and Health Review Commission

1331 Pennsylvania Avenue NW., Suite 520N, Washington, DC 20004-1710, 202-434-9900, *http://www.fmshrc.gov* | Email: *fmshrc@fmshrc.gov*

CHAIR	Mary Lucille Jordan
Commissioner	William I. Althen
Commissioner	Robert F. Cohen, Jr.
Commissioner	Patrick K. Nakamura
Commissioner	Michael G. Young
EXECUTIVE DIRECTOR	Lisa M. Boyd
Chief Administrative Law Judge	Robert J. Lesnick
General Counsel	Michael A. McCord
Senior Policy Advisor	John M. McWilliam

The Federal Mine Safety and Health Review Commission ensures compliance with occupational safety and health standards in the Nation's surface and underground coal, metal, and nonmetal mines.

The Federal Mine Safety and Health Review Commission is an independent, adjudicative agency established by the Federal Mine Safety and Health Act of 1977 (30 U.S.C. 801 et seq.), as amended. It provides administrative trial and appellate review of legal disputes arising from enforcement actions taken by the Department of Labor.

The Commission comprises five members whom the President appoints with the advice and consent of the Senate. Each Commissioner serves a 6-year term, and all the terms are staggered. The President appoints one of the Commissioners to serve as the Chair.

The Commission and its administrative law judges decide cases brought before it by the Department of Labor's Mine Safety and Health Administration, mine operators, and miners or their representatives. These cases generally involve review of the Administration's enforcement actions, including citations, mine-closure orders, and proposals for civil penalties issued for violations of the act or the mandatory safety and health standards promulgated by the Secretary of Labor. The Commission also has jurisdiction over discrimination complaints filed by miners or their representatives regarding their safety and health, complaints for compensation filed on behalf of miners idled as a result of mine closure orders issued by the Administration, and disputes involving mine emergency response plans.

Cases brought before the Commission are assigned to the Office of Administrative Law Judges, and hearings are conducted pursuant to the requirements of the Administrative Procedure Act (5 U.S.C. 554, 556) and the Commission's procedural rules (29 CFR 2700).

A judge's decision becomes a final, nonprecedential order of the Commission 40 days after issuance unless the Commission has directed the case for review in response to a petition or on its own motion. If a review is conducted, a decision of the Commission becomes final 30 days after issuance unless a party adversely affected seeks review in the U.S. Circuit Court of Appeals for the District of Columbia or the Circuit within which the mine subject to the litigation is located.

As far as practicable, hearings are held at locations convenient to the affected mines. In addition to its Washington, DC, offices, the Office of Administrative Law Judges maintains an office in the Colonnade Center, Room 280, 1244 Speer Boulevard, Denver, CO 80204.

Sources of Information

Decisions

Commission decisions are published bimonthly and are available through the Superintendent of Documents, U.S. Government Publishing Office, Washington, DC 20402. The Commission's Web site features audio recordings of recent public meetings, a searchable database of previous decisions, procedural rules, recent decisions, and other information.

Filing

For information on filing requirements, the status of cases before the Commission, or docket information, contact the Office of General Counsel or the Docket Office, Federal Mine Safety and Health Review Commission, 1331 Pennsylvania Avenue NW., Suite 520N, Washington, DC 20004-1710.

Freedom of Information Act (FOIA)

The FOIA Service Center assists those seeking information through the FOIA. For more information, write to the Federal Mine Safety and Health Review Commission, FOIA Service Center, 1331 Pennsylvania Avenue NW., Suite 520N, Washington, DC 20004-1710. Phone, 202-434-9935. Fax, 202-434-9944.

News

Recent Commission-related news is available online.

Reports

The Commission posts its reports to Congress—as well as budget and annual performance reports and performance accountability reports—online.

For further information, contact the Executive Director, Federal Mine Safety and Health Review Commission, 1331 Pennsylvania Avenue NW., Suite 520N, Washington DC 20004-1710. Phone, 202-434-9905. Fax, 202-434-9906.

FEDERAL MINE SAFETY AND HEALTH REVIEW COMMISSION

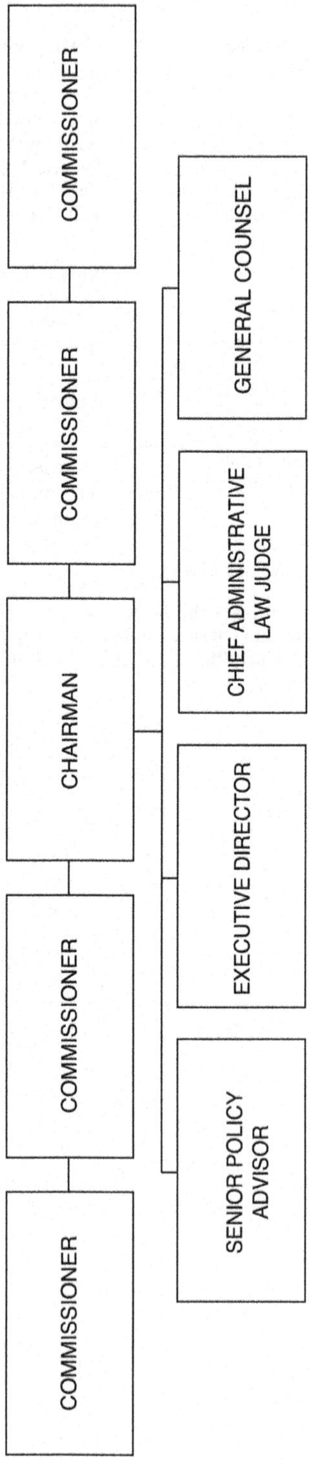

Federal Reserve System

Twentieth Street and Constitution Avenue NW., Washington, DC 20551, 202-452-3000, *http://www.federalreserve.gov*

CHAIR	Janet L. Yellen
Vice Chair	Stanley Fischer
Member	Lael Brainard
Member	Jerome H. Powell
Member	Daniel K. Tarullo
Member	(vacancy)
Member	(vacancy)
Director, Division of Banking Supervision and Regulation	Michael S. Gibson
Director, Division of Board Members	Michelle A. Smith
Director, Division of Consumer and Community Affairs	Eric Belsky
Director, Division of Federal Reserve Bank Operations and Payment Systems	Louise L. Roseman
Director, Division of Information Technology	Sharon L. Mowry
Director, Division of International Finance	Steven B. Kamin
Director, Division of Management	Michell C. Clark
Director, Division of Monetary Affairs	Thomas Laubach
Director, Division of Research and Statistics	David W. Wilcox
General Counsel	Scott G. Alvarez
Inspector General	Mark Bialek
Secretary	Robert deV. Frierson

The Federal Reserve System, the central bank of the United States, administers and formulates the Nation's credit and monetary policy.

The Federal Reserve System (FRS) was established by the Federal Reserve Act (12 U.S.C. 221), approved December 23, 1913. Its major responsibility is to implement monetary policy. It also performs other functions: transferring funds, handling Government deposits and debt issues, supervising and regulating banks, and acting as lender of last resort.

The FRS contributes to the strength and vitality of the U.S. economy. By influencing the lending and investing activities of depository institutions and the cost and availability of money and credit, the FRS promotes the full use of human and capital resources, the growth of productivity, relatively stable prices, and equilibrium in the Nation's international balance of payments. Through its supervisory and regulatory banking functions, the FRS helps maintain a commercial banking system that is responsive to the Nation's financial needs and objectives.

The FRS comprises the Board of Governors; the 12 Federal Reserve Banks and their 25 branches and other facilities; the Federal Open Market Committee; the Federal Advisory Council; the Consumer Advisory Council; the Thrift Institutions Advisory Council; and the Nation's financial institutions, including commercial banks, savings and loan associations, mutual savings banks, and credit unions.

Board of Governors

The Board comprises seven members whom the President appoints with the advice and consent of the Senate. The Chair of the Board of Governors is a member of the National Advisory Council on International Monetary and Financial

Policies. The Board determines general monetary, credit, and operating policies for the System as a whole and formulates the rules and regulations necessary to carry out the purposes of the Federal Reserve Act. The Board's principal duties consist of monitoring credit conditions; supervising the Federal Reserve Banks, member banks, and bank holding companies; and regulating the implementation of certain consumer credit protection laws.

The Board has the power, within statutory limitations, to fix the requirements for reserves to be maintained by depository institutions on transaction accounts or nonpersonal time deposits. The Board reviews and determines the discount rate charged by the Federal Reserve Banks. For the purpose of preventing excessive use of credit for the purchase or carrying of securities, the Board is authorized to regulate the amount of credit that may be initially extended and subsequently maintained on securities (with certain exceptions).

Supervision of Federal Reserve Banks

The Board is authorized to make examinations of the Federal Reserve Banks, require statements and reports from such Banks, supervise the issue and retirement of Federal Reserve notes, require the establishment or discontinuance of branches of Reserve Banks, and exercise supervision over all relationships and transactions of those Banks with foreign branches.

Supervision of Bank Holding Companies

The FRS supervises and regulates bank holding companies. It tries to maintain the separation between banking and commerce by controlling the expansion of bank holding companies, preventing the formation of banking monopolies, restraining certain trade practices in banking, and limiting the nonbanking activities of bank holding companies. A company that seeks to become a bank holding company must obtain prior approval from the FRS and, upon becoming a bank holding company, must register and file reports with it.

Supervision of Banking Organizations

The FRS supervises and regulates domestic and international activities of U.S. banking organizations. It supervises State-chartered banks that are members of the System, all bank holding companies, and Edge Act and agreement corporations (corporations chartered to engage in international banking).

The Board has jurisdiction over the admission of State banks and trust companies to membership in the FRS, membership termination for these banks, the establishment of branches by these banks, and the approval of bank mergers and consolidations where the resulting institution will be a State member bank. It receives copies of condition reports submitted to the Federal Reserve Banks. It has the power to examine all member banks and the affiliates of member banks and to require condition reports from them. It has the authority to require periodic and other public disclosure of information with respect to an equity security of a State member bank that is held by 500 or more persons. It establishes minimum standards with respect to installation, maintenance, and operation of security devices and procedures by State member banks. It can issue cease-and-desist orders in connection with violations of law or unsafe or unsound banking practices by State member banks and to remove directors or officers of such banks in certain circumstances. It also can suspend member banks from use of the Federal Reserve System's credit facilities for using bank credit for speculation or other purposes inconsistent with the maintenance of sound credit conditions.

The Board may grant authority to member banks to establish branches in foreign countries or dependencies or insular possessions of the United States, to invest in the stocks of banks or corporations engaged in international or foreign banking, or to invest in foreign banks. It also charters, regulates, and supervises certain corporations that engage in foreign or international banking and financial activities.

The Board is authorized to issue general regulations permitting interlocking relationships in certain circumstances between member banks and organizations dealing in securities or between member banks and other banks.

The Board prescribes regulations to ensure a meaningful disclosure of credit terms by lenders so that consumers can compare more readily the various credit terms available and be informed about rules governing credit cards, including their potential liability for unauthorized use.

The Board has authority to impose reserve requirements and interest rate ceilings on branches and agencies of foreign banks in the United States, grant loans to them, provide them access to Federal Reserve services, and limit their interstate banking activities.

Federal Open Market Committee

The Federal Open Market Committee comprises the Board of Governors and five of the presidents of the Reserve Banks. The Chair of the Board of Governors is traditionally the Chair of the Committee. The president of the Federal Reserve Bank of New York serves as a permanent member of the Committee. Four of the 12 Reserve Bank presidents rotate annually as members of the Committee.

Open market operations of the Reserve Banks are conducted under regulations adopted by the Committee and pursuant to specific policy directives issued by the Committee, which meets in Washington, DC, at frequent intervals. Purchases and sales of securities in the open market are undertaken to supply bank reserves to support the credit and money needed for long-term economic growth, to offset cyclical economic swings, and to accommodate seasonal demands of businesses and consumers for money and credit. These operations are carried out principally in U.S. Government obligations, but they also include purchases and sales of Federal agency obligations. All operations are conducted in New York, where the primary markets for these securities are located. The Federal Reserve Bank of New York executes transactions for the Federal Reserve System Open Market Account in carrying out these operations.

Under the Committee's direction, the Federal Reserve Bank of New York also undertakes transactions in foreign currencies for the Federal Reserve System Open Market Account. These operations are meant to safeguard the value of the dollar in international exchange markets and facilitate growth in international liquidity in accordance with the needs of an expanding world economy.

Federal Reserve Banks

The 12 Federal Reserve Banks are located in Atlanta, GA; Boston, MA; Chicago, IL; Cleveland, OH; Dallas, TX; Kansas City, MO; Minneapolis, MN; New York, NY; Philadelphia, PA; Richmond, VA; San Francisco, CA; and St. Louis, MO. Branch banks are located in Baltimore, MD; Birmingham, AL; Buffalo, NY; Charlotte, NC; Cincinnati, OH; Denver, CO; Detroit, MI; El Paso, TX; Helena, MT; Houston, TX; Jacksonville, FL; Little Rock, AR; Los Angeles, CA; Louisville, KY; Memphis, TN; Miami, FL; Nashville, TN; New Orleans, LA; Oklahoma City, OK; Omaha, NE; Pittsburgh, PA; Portland, OR; Salt Lake City, UT; San Antonio, TX; and Seattle, WA.

Reserves on Deposit

The Reserve Banks receive and hold on deposit the reserve or clearing account deposits of depository institutions. These banks are permitted to count their vault cash as part of their required reserve.

Extensions of Credit

The FRS is required to open its discount window to any depository institution that is subject to its reserve requirements on transaction accounts or nonpersonal time deposits. Discount window credit provides for Federal Reserve lending to eligible depository institutions under two basic programs: the adjustment credit program and another that supplies more extended credit for certain limited purposes.

Short-term adjustment credit is the primary type of Federal Reserve credit. It is available to help borrowers meet temporary requirements for funds. Borrowers are not permitted to use adjustment credit to take advantage of any spread between the discount rate and market rates.

Extended credit is provided through three programs designed to assist depository institutions in meeting longer term needs for funds. One provides seasonal credit, for periods running up to 9 months, to smaller depository institutions that lack access to market funds. A second program assists institutions that experience special difficulties arising from exceptional circumstances or practices involving only that institution. Lastly, in cases where more general liquidity strains are affecting a broad range of depository institutions, cases where institutional portfolios consist primarily of longer term assets, credit may be provided to address the problems of particular institutions being affected by the general situation.

Currency Issue

The Reserve Banks issue Federal Reserve notes, which constitute the bulk of money in circulation. These notes are obligations of the United States and are a prior lien upon the assets of the issuing Federal Reserve Bank. They are issued against a pledge by the Reserve Bank with the Federal Reserve agent of collateral security, including gold certificates, paper discounted or purchased by the Bank, and direct obligations of the United States.

Other Powers

The Reserve Banks are empowered to act as clearinghouses and as collecting agents for depository institutions in the collection of checks and other instruments. They are also authorized to act as depositories and fiscal agents of the United States and to exercise other banking functions specified in the Federal Reserve Act. They perform a number of important functions in connection with the issue and redemption of U.S. Government securities.

Sources of Information

Business Opportunities

Contact the Director, Division of Support Services, Board of Governors of the Federal Reserve System, Washington, DC 20551.

Employment

Written inquiries should be addressed to the Director, Division of Personnel, Board of Governors of the Federal Reserve System, Washington, DC 20551. A complete listing of job opportunities is available online.

Publications

An alphabetical list of publications is available online. For more information, contact Publications Fulfillment, 1709 New York Avenue NW., Washington, DC 20005. Phone, 202-452-3244.

Reading Room

A reading room for inspection of public records is open on weekdays from 9 a.m. to 5 p.m. It is located in room 3515 at 1801 K Street NW., Washington, DC 20551. Phone, 202-452-3684.

For further information, contact the Office of Public Affairs, Board of Governors, Federal Reserve System, Washington, DC 20551. Phone, 202-452-3204 or 202-452-3215.

Federal Retirement Thrift Investment Board

77 K Street NE., Washington, DC 20002, 202-942-1600, 202-942-1676, *http://www.frtib.gov*

CHAIR	Michael D. Kennedy
Member	Dana K. Bilyeu
Member	William S. Jasien
Member	David A. Jones
Member	Ronald D. McCray
EXECUTIVE DIRECTOR	Gregory T. Long
Chief Financial Officer	Susan C. Crowder

Chief Investment Officer	Ravindra Deo
Chief Operating Officer	Mark E. Walther
Chief Technology Officer	Scott Cragg
Director, Office of Communications and Education	James Courtney
Director, Office of Enterprise Planning	Renée Wilder Guerin
Director, Office of Enterprise Risk Management / Chief Risk Officer	Jay Ahuja
Director, Office of External Affairs	Kimberly A. Weaver
Director, Office of Participant Operations and Policy	Guadalupe Ramos
Director, Office of Resource Management	Gisile Goethe
General Counsel	Megan Grumbine

The Federal Retirement Thrift Investment Board administers the Thrift Savings Plan in the interest of its participants and beneficiaries.

The Federal Retirement Thrift Investment Board was established as an independent agency by the Federal Employees' Retirement System Act of 1986 (5 U.S.C. 8351 and 8401-79). The act vests responsibility for the Agency in six named fiduciaries: the five Board members and the Executive Director. The President, with the advice and consent of the Senate, appoints the five members of the Board, one of whom is designated as Chair. The members serve on a part-time basis, and they appoint the Executive Director, who is responsible for the management of the Agency and the Plan.

Activities

The Thrift Savings Plan is a tax-deferred, defined contribution plan that was established as one of the three parts of the Federal Employees' Retirement System. For employees covered under the System, savings accumulated through the Plan make an important addition to Social Security retirement benefits and the System's Basic Annuity. Civil Service Retirement System employees and members of the Uniformed Services may also take advantage of the Plan to supplement their annuities.

The Board operates the Thrift Savings Plan and manages the investments of the Thrift Savings Fund for the benefit of participants and their beneficiaries. As part of these responsibilities, the Board maintains an account for each Plan participant, makes loans, purchases annuity contracts, and provides for the payment of benefits.

Sources of Information

Employment

The Board relies on a wide range of professionals, including financial experts and attorneys, to carry out its mission.

Reading Room

Freedom of Information Act (FOIA) reports, regulations, reports to Congress, statements, and surveys are accessible online in the reading room.

For further information, contact the Office of External Affairs, Federal Retirement Thrift Investment Board, 77 K Street NE., Washington, DC 20002. Phone, 202-942-1640.

Federal Trade Commission

600 Pennsylvania Avenue NW., Washington, DC 20580, 202-326-2222, *http://www.ftc.gov*

CHAIR	Edith Ramirez
Commissioner	Terrell McSweeny
Commissioner	Maureen K. Ohlhausen
Commissioner	(vacancy)

Commissioner	(vacancy)
Chief of Staff	Heather Hippsley
Executive Director	David B Robbins
Chief Administrative Law Judge	D. Michael Chappell
Director, Bureau of Competition	Deborah L. Feinstein
Director, Bureau of Consumer Protection	Jessica L. Rich
Director, Bureau of Economics	Ginger Zhe Jin
Director, Office of Congressional Relations	Jeanne Bumpus
Director, Office of Equal Employment Opportunity	Kevin D. Williams
Director, Office of International Affairs	Randolph W. Tritell
Director, Office of Policy Planning	Marina Lao
Director, Office of Public Affairs	Justin Cole
General Counsel	David C. Shonka, Acting
Inspector General	Roslyn Mazer
Secretary of the Commission	Donald S. Clark

[For the Federal Trade Commission statement of organization, see the Code of Federal Regulations, Title 16, Part 0]

The Federal Trade Commission protects America's consumers and enforces laws prohibiting anticompetitive, deceptive, or unfair business practices.

The Federal Trade Commission (FTC) was established in 1914 by the Federal Trade Commission Act (15 U.S.C. 41-58). The Commission comprises five members whom the President appoints with the advice and consent of the Senate for 7-year terms. No more than three of the Commissioners may be members of the same political party. The President designates one of them as Chair of the Commission to oversee its administrative management.

Activities

The FTC protects consumers and promotes competition in broad sectors of the economy. It safeguards and strengthens free and open markets and helps consumers make informed choices. The FTC carries out its mission by using a variety of tools: consumer and business education, law enforcement, research, rulemaking, and studies of marketplace trends and legal developments. The FTC envisions a vigorously competitive U.S. economy offering accessible and accurate information to consumers, an economy yielding high-quality products at competitive prices and fostering efficiency, innovation, and consumer choice.

Competition

The FTC prevents anticompetitive mergers and works to keep the marketplace free from anticompetitive business practices. To promote competition, the FTC engages in six law enforcement-related activities: premerger notification, merger and joint venture enforcement, merger and joint venture compliance, nonmerger enforcement, nonmerger compliance, and antitrust policy. Policy initiatives, research, and business guidance and education also play a role in promoting competition.

Consumer Protection

The FTC brings a variety of consumer protection cases and works with State attorneys general and other State and local consumer protection officials. To protect consumers, it relies on five law enforcement functions: privacy and identity protection, financial practices, marketing practices, advertising practices, and enforcement. Policy initiatives, research, and business and consumer education also enhance protection.

Enforcement

The FTC's law enforcement activities foster voluntary compliance with the law, but also include formal administrative or Federal court litigation leading to mandatory orders against offenders.

The FTC can issue an administrative complaint or authorize the filing of a Federal district court complaint charging a person, partnership, or corporation with violating one or more of the statutes that the FTC enforces. If the charges are not contested, settled by consent of the parties, or found to be true after an administrative hearing or a Federal court trial, an administrative law judge or Federal court judge will issue an order requiring discontinuance of the unlawful practices. The FTC also may request that a U.S. district court issue preliminary relief to halt allegedly unfair or deceptive practices, to prevent an anticompetitive merger or unfair methods of competition from taking place, or to prevent violations of any statute that the FTC enforces, pending the full adjudication of the matter. In Federal court, the FTC may obtain other relief, including monetary redress. An order issued after an administrative or Federal court proceeding that requires the respondent to cease and desist or take other corrective action may be appealed.

International Affairs

With other nations and international organizations, the FTC promotes sound competition and consumer protection policies and provides technical assistance to nurture competition and enable consumer protection agencies to perform their missions.

Sources of Information

Antitrust Violations

To report an antitrust violation, contact the Bureau of Competition's Office of Policy and Coordination. Phone, 202-326-3300.

Business Opportunities

For information on contracts and procurement, contact the Assistant Chief Financial Officer for Acquisitions. Phone, 202-326-2339. Fax, 202-326-3529.

Consumer Complaints

The FTC relies on complaints from consumers to detect patterns of abuse and fraud. A complaint may be filed in English or Spanish and online or by phone. The FTC enters complaints into Consumer Sentinel, a secure online database that civil and criminal law enforcement agencies in the U.S. and abroad can access. Phone, 877-382-4357.

Credit Reports

The Fair Credit Reporting Act requires each of the nationwide credit reporting companies to provide a free credit report, upon request, once every 12 months.

Do Not Call Registry

Register a home or mobile phone for free on the National Do Not Call Registry to eliminate most telemarketing calls.

Employment

To carry out its mission, the FTC relies on attorneys, investigators, and specialists in financial management, information technology, public affairs, public policy, and in other fields. The agency posts current job vacancies on its Web site. Information on benefits, diversity, working at the FTC, and the application process is also accessible online. For additional information, contact the Human Capital Management Office. Phone, 202-326-2021. TTY, 202-326-3422.

Identity Theft

Use IdentiftyTheft.gov to report identity theft and formulate a personal recovery plan.

Publications

Blog updates, newsletters, and press releases are posted online. Free consumer and business education publications are available from the Consumer Response Center, Federal Trade Commission, Washington, DC 20580. Phone, 877-382-4357. TTY, 866-653-4261.

Regional Offices

A map of the seven FTC regions—East Central, Midwest, Northeast, Northwest, Southeast, Southwest, and Western—and contact information for the regional offices representing them are available online.

Scam Alerts

Stay abreast of new scams with the latest

information and practical tips. An online subscription form is available to receive scam alerts by email.

Workshops

Information on conferences and workshops is available online.

For further information, contact the Office of Public Affairs, Federal Trade Commission, 600 Pennsylvania Avenue NW., Washington, DC 20580. Phone, 202-326-2180. Fax, 202-326-3366.

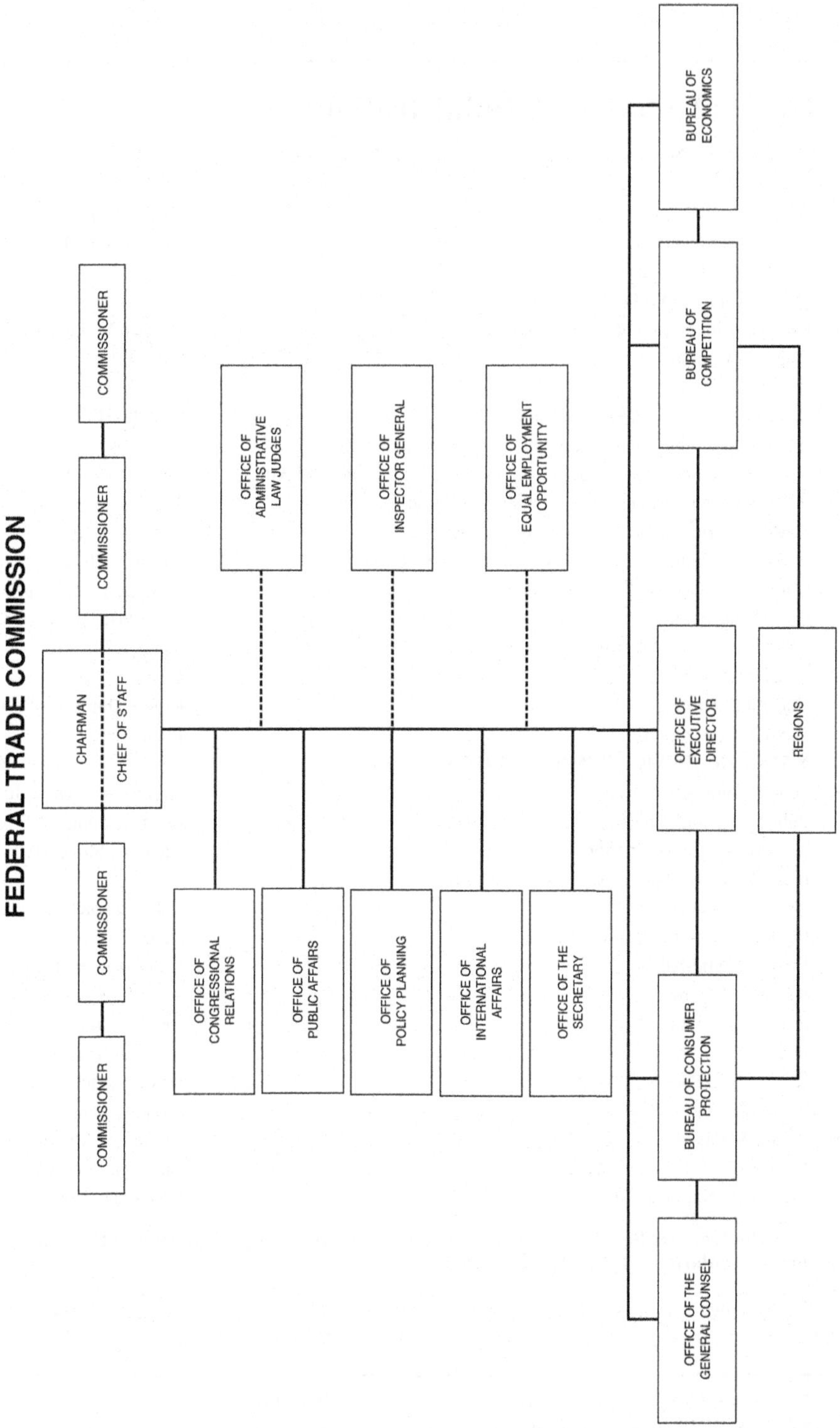
FEDERAL TRADE COMMISSION
COMMISSIONER
COMMISSIONER
CHAIRMAN
CHIEF OF STAFF
COMMISSIONER
COMMISSIONER
OFFICE OF ADMINISTRATIVE LAW JUDGES
OFFICE OF INSPECTOR GENERAL
OFFICE OF EQUAL EMPLOYMENT OPPORTUNITY
OFFICE OF CONGRESSIONAL RELATIONS
OFFICE OF PUBLIC AFFAIRS
OFFICE OF POLICY PLANNING
OFFICE OF INTERNATIONAL AFFAIRS
OFFICE OF THE SECRETARY
BUREAU OF ECONOMICS
BUREAU OF COMPETITION
OFFICE OF EXECUTIVE DIRECTOR
REGIONS
BUREAU OF CONSUMER PROTECTION
OFFICE OF THE GENERAL COUNSEL

General Services Administration

1800 F Street NW., Washington, DC 20405, *http://www.gsa.gov*

ADMINISTRATOR	Denise Turner Roth
Deputy Administrator	Adam Neufeld
Chief of Staff	Katy Kale
INDEPENDENT OFFICE HEADS	
Chair, Civilian Board of Contract Appeals	Stephen M. Daniels
Inspector General	Carol F. Ochoa
OFFICE HEADS	
Associate Administrator, Civil Rights	Madeline C. Caliendo
Associate Administrator, Communications and Marketing	Brett Prather
Associate Administrator, Congressional and Intergovernmental Affairs	Lisa A. Austin
Associate Administrator, Government-wide Policy	Troy Cribb
Associate Administrator, Mission Assurance	Robert J. Carter
Associate Administrator, Small Business Utilization	Jerome Fletcher
Chief Administrative Services Officer	Cynthia A. Metzler
Chief Financial Officer	Gerard Badorrek
Chief Human Capital Officer	Antonia T. Harris
Chief Information Officer	David A. Shive
General Counsel	Kris E. Durmer
White House Liaison	Jolene Lester
NATIONAL SERVICE COMMISSIONERS	
Federal Acquisition Service	Thomas A. Sharpe, Jr.
Public Buildings Service	Norman Dong
Technology Transformation Service	David A. Shive, Acting
REGIONAL SERVICE ADMINISTRATORS	
Region 1–New England	Robert Zarnetske
Region 2–Northeast and Caribbean	Denise L. Pease
Region 3–Mid-Atlantic	Sara Manzano-Diaz
Region 4–Southeast Sunbelt	Torre J. Jessup
Region 5–Great Lakes	Ann P. Kalayil
Region 6–Heartland	Jason O. Klumb
Region 7–Greater Southwest	Sylvia L. Hernandez
Region 8–Rocky Mountain	Susan B. Damour
Region 9–Pacific Rim	Andrew S. McMahon
Region 10–Northwest / Arctic	George E. Northcroft
Region 11–National Capital	Julia E. Hudson

[For the General Services Administration statement of organization, see the Code of Federal Regulations, Title 41, Part 105-53]

The General Services Administration strives to obtain the highest value in acquisition, real estate, and technology services for the Federal Government and the American people.

The General Services Administration (GSA) was established by section 101 of the Federal Property and Administrative Services Act of 1949 (40 U.S.C. 751).

Technology Transformation Service

The Technology Transformation Service (TTS) improves the public's experience with the Government by the application of modern methodologies and technologies. It offers services that exemplify accessibility, effectiveness, and efficiency, and it assists other Federal agencies with making their services more accessible, effective, and efficient. The TTS also builds technology applications, platforms, processes, and software solutions; it makes these products available to other agencies; and it shares technology personnel with them. The TTS comprises the Offices of Acquisitions and of Investment, the Presidential Innovation Fellowship, product and services teams, a product incubator, and the technology advisory-advocacy team.

USAGov helps Federal agencies develop consumer information, promote it, and disseminate it. The USAGov platform gives Americans greater ability to connect—via email, publications, social media, web sites and web chat, and phone calls to the contact center—with their Government and to access the services that it offers. USAGov makes Government information easily accessible to U.S. citizens and the public at large through a variety of resources. (See the Sources of Information below for additional USA.gov links.)

USA.GOV WEB SITES	DESCRIPTION OF CONTENT
https://www.usa.gov	General Government information
https://kids.usa.gov	Government information for kids
http://www.publications.usa.gov	Government informational publications
http://www.digitalgov.gov	Information to help Government agencies enhance customer experience
https://www.challenge.gov/list	Government challenges that are posted for the public to help solve and win prizes
http://www.data.gov	Accessible and readable Government datasets
https://gobierno.usa.gov	General Government information in Spanish

Contract Appeals

The Civilian Board of Contract Appeals hears and decides contract disputes between Government contractors and civilian executive agencies under the provisions of the Contract Disputes Act. The Board's authority extends to all agencies of the Federal Government except the Department of Defense and its constituent agencies, National Aeronautics and Space Administration, U.S. Postal Service, Postal Regulatory Commission, and Tennessee Valley Authority. The Board promotes alternative dispute resolution as a way of resolving contract disputes efficiently, inexpensively, and promptly. When jointly requested by an agency and its contractor, the Board also provides alternative dispute resolution services on contract-related matters not covered by the Contract Disputes Act to executive agencies.

The Board also hears and decides other classes of cases. These other classes include cases arising under the Indian Self-Determination Act, disputes between insurance companies and the Department of Agriculture's Risk Management Agency involving actions of the Federal Crop Insurance Corporation, claims by Federal employees for reimbursement of expenses incurred while on official temporary duty travel or in connection with relocation to a new duty station, claims by carriers or freight forwarders involving actions of the GSA regarding payment for transportation services, applications by prevailing private parties for recovery of litigation and other costs under the Equal Access to Justice Act, and requests for arbitration to resolve disputes between applicants and the Federal Emergency Management Agency as to funding for public assistance applications arising from damage caused by Hurricanes Katrina and Rita.

For further information, contact the Civilian Board of Contract Appeals, General Services Administration, Washington, DC 20405. Phone, 202-606-8800.

Governmentwide Policy

The Office of Government-wide Policy (OGP) collaborates with the Federal community to develop policies and guidelines for the management and efficient use of Government property, technology, and administrative services. OGP policymaking authority and policy support activities cover the following areas: electronic government and information technology, acquisition, real property and the workplace, travel, transportation, personal property, aircraft, the Federal motor vehicle fleet, mail, regulatory information, energy efficiency, and the use of Federal Advisory Committees. The OGP also provides leadership to interagency groups and promotes Governmentwide management reform. Its business lines include acquisition policy; asset and transportation policy; committee and regulatory management; information, integrity, and access; and Federal high-performance green buildings.

The Office of Acquisition Policy (OAP) leads positive change in acquisition policy through its role on the Federal Acquisition Regulation (FAR) Council as well as through GSA acquisition policy, guidance, and reporting to stakeholders. The OAP, in conjunction with the Department of Defense and NASA, writes the FAR, which serves as the rule book for all Federal agency procurements and governs the billions of dollars spent by the Federal Government every year. The OAP also hosts the Federal Acquisition Institute (FAI), which is charged with fostering and promoting the development of the Federal acquisition workforce, along with its training, certification, and warrant needs. The OAP also oversees acquisition integrity functions for the GSA. The Regulatory Secretariat Division staff prepares, compiles, and processes regulatory and general notices for publication in the "Federal Register." The OAP is headed by the Deputy Chief Acquisition Officer / Senior Procurement Executive and includes the Office of Government-wide Acquisition Policy; the Office of General Services Acquisition Policy, Integrity and Workforce; and the Federal Acquisition Institute.

The Office of Asset and Transportation Policy supports Federal agencies in the economic and efficient management of assets and specific services. It develops effective policies and guidance for travel, employee relocation allowances and entitlements, personal and real property, motor vehicles, aircraft, transportation, and mail. The Office maintains liaisons with State and local governments, industry, and professional organizations, and it participates in the work of boards, committees, and groups related to asset and transportation management. The Office also provides advice, guidance, and formal classroom training and consultation to agencies regarding establishing and managing Federal advisory committees, as mandated by the Federal Advisory Committee Act. The Office of Asset and Transportation Policy's divisions include: policy performance, aviation, transportation and mail, personal property, real property, travel and relocation, motor vehicle, and the Committee Management Secretariat.

The Office of Committee and Regulatory Management develops Governmentwide policies, guidance, performance measures, regulations, and training on the management and operation of the Federal advisory committees. It also gathers and publishes information about Federal regulations and their effect on society.

The Office of Information, Integrity, and Access develops, coordinates, and defines information technology business strategies that allow Federal agencies to improve services to American citizens. The Office also provides assistance for and develops policy in the following areas: data and acquisition management, identity credentialing and access management, information management and improvements of analysis capability and architecture development efforts on cross-agency priorities and enterprise data management strategies, Dot Gov domain registration and management, and Section 508 accessibility management.

The Office of Federal High-Performance Green Buildings helps the Federal Government operate more efficiently and effectively by minimizing the Federal footprint through efficient use of energy, water, and resources. It also helps create healthy and productive workspaces for Federal employees. Congress authorized this Office to increase Federal leadership in sustainable real property portfolio management and operations. The Office works to promote, coordinate, and stimulate environmentally friendly construction and building management practices across the entire Federal Government, which has over 400,000 owned or leased buildings containing over 3 billion square feet of space. The Office has three principal categories of activity: leading and coordinating the greening of the Federal real estate portfolio, supporting innovation and collaboration on the development of new technologies, and supplying the market with information and best practices. To accomplish its goals, the Office relies on an interdisciplinary team of energy, water, air quality, sustainable design, facilities management, budgeting, human behavior, organizational effectiveness, and communications experts.

The Office of Executive Councils coordinates with the Office of Management and Budget and Federal management councils to identify performance improvement initiatives to pursue Governmentwide, to lead working groups to drive these initiatives, to establish performance goals, and to facilitate the adoption of new processes by Federal agencies. The Office analyzes data, diagnoses challenges, identifies best practices, and documents the benefits delivered by the initiatives. This Office also provides technical and management services to the following Federal management councils: the Chief Acquisition Officers Council, the Chief Financial Officers Council, the Chief Information Officers Council, the Performance Improvement Council, and the President's Management Council.

For further information, contact the Office of Government-wide Policy. Phone, 202-501-8880.

Small Business Utilization

The Office of Small Business Utilization (OSBU) promotes increased access to the GSA's nationwide procurement opportunities for small, HUBZone, and minority-, veteran-, and women-owned businesses. the OSBU engages in activities that make it possible for the small business community to meet key contracting experts and be counseled on the procurement process. The OSBU monitors and implements small business policies and manages a range of programs mandated by law.

For further information, contact the Office of Small Business Utilization. Phone, 202-501-1021.

Federal Acquisition

The Federal Acquisition Service (FAS) provides acquisition and procurement support services for Federal agencies to increase overall Government efficiency. FAS programs include tools and resources that aid in the acquisition of products, services, and full-service programs in information technology, telecommunications, professional services, supplies, motor vehicles, travel and transportation, charge cards, and personal property utilization and disposal.

The FAS offers customers a variety of ways to acquire the products, services, and solutions they seek. Key acquisition programs include multiple awards schedules and Governmentwide acquisition contracts that provide customers easy access to information technology, telecommunications, and professional products and services. These products, services, and tools are accessible on the GSA's Web site: GSA Advantage!; eBuy and eOffer/eMod; Schedule Sales Query; GSA eLibrary; GSA Xcess, Transportation Management Services Solutions, and other electronic tools.

For further information, contact the Office of the Commissioner, Federal Acquisition Service. Phone, 703-605-5400.

Public Buildings

The Public Buildings Service (PBS) is the landlord for the civilian Federal Government, providing workspace solutions to more than one million Federal employees in 2,100 communities across the Nation, stimulating local economies by designing, building, managing, and maintaining public buildings, as well as leasing from the private sector. The PBS is a leader in sustainable design, energy conservation, and green building technologies. Its portfolio consists of 378 million square feet in over 9,000 assets across all 50 States, 6 U.S. Territories, and the District of Columbia. The Service preserves and maintains 471 historic properties and commissions the country's most talented artists to produce works of art for Federal buildings, as well as preserves artwork commissioned under the Works Progress Administration. PBS collects rent from Federal tenants, which is deposited into the Federal Buildings Fund, the principal funding mechanism for the PBS.

For further information, contact the Office of the Commissioner, Public Buildings Service. Phone, 202-501-1100.

Sources of Information

Auctions

GSA Auctions sells off Federal personal property assets—airplanes, furniture, heavy machinery, office equipment, vehicles, vessels, and other items—located nationwide to interested buyers irrespective of their location.

GSA Auctions is accessible on Facebook.

Business Opportunities

The GSA serves as the Federal Government's procurement arm. It offers facilities, products, and services that Federal agencies use to benefit the public. The GSA also gives businesses the opportunity to sell billions of dollars worth of products and services to those agencies.

The Office of Small Business Utilization Web pages feature information, opportunities, resources, and training for small business owners. Phone, 855-672-8472.

Employment

The GSA relies on professionals with diverse academic backgrounds, life experiences, and skills to carry out its mission. It encourages Federal and private sector employees, Peace Corps volunteers and staff, persons with disabilities, recent retirees, students and recent graduates, and others to apply for job openings. For more information, contact the national recruitment center. Phone, 816-823-2006.

Federal Relay (FedRelay)

FedRelay provides telecommunications services to Federal agencies and tribal governments for conducting official business with people who struggle with deafness, hearing impairments, or speech disabilities. The general public—those struggling with deafness, hearing impairments, or speech disabilities—also may use FedRelay for conducting business with Federal agencies.

For a free copy of the Federal Government TTY Directory, write to USAGov–TTY Directory, Pueblo, CO 81009. Phone, 844-872-4681. The directory is also available online.

Freedom of Information Act (FOIA)

The FOIA gives the public the right to request information from Federal agencies. The GSA participates in FOIAonline, which enables users to submit a FOIA request to all participating agencies, track the status of a request, search for requests submitted by others, access previously released records, and generate agency-specific FOIA processing reports.

A FOIA request also may be submitted to the GSA by fax or by sending it to the U.S. General Services Administration, FOIA Requester Service Center (H1F), 1800 F Street NW., Room 7308, Washington, DC 20405-0001. Phone, 855-675-3642. Fax, 202-501-2727.

Newsroom

The GSA Web site features an agency blog, congressional testimonies, news releases, and photo galleries.

RSS Feeds are available on the GSA Web site.

The GSA tweets announcements, news items, and other information on Twitter.

Office of the Inspector General (OIG)

The OIG operates a fraud hotline for reporting abuse, fraud, or waste in GSA programs and mismanagement or violations of law, regulations, or rules by GSA employees and contractors. Phone, 202-501-1780 or 800-424-5210.

Open Government

The GSA supports the Open Government initiative by promoting the principles of collaboration, participation, and transparency.

Per Diem Rates

The GSA sets the per diem rates for Federal travel within the continental United States. Per diem is the allowance for incidental expenses, lodging, and meals. The GSA Web site features a search tool for finding current rates in the continental United States by State or ZIP code or by clicking on a map.

The GSA offers regular travelers a mobile application that makes Federal per diem rates accessible on a smart phone. The application allows travelers to look up Federal Government per diem rates by city and State or ZIP code in locations throughout the United States and its territories.

Plain Language

The "Plain Writing Act of 2010" was passed by Congress and approved by the President to improve the effectiveness of Federal agencies and increase their accountability to the public "by promoting clear Government communication that the public can understand and use." The GSA is committed to writing agency documents and its Web site content in plain language.

Privacy Act

Privacy Act requests should be addressed to the GSA Privacy Act Officer, Office of the Chief Information Security Officer, Policy and Compliance Division, (ISP), General Services Administration, 1800 F Street, NW., Washington, DC 20405. Phone, 202-208-1317.

Publications

Government consumer publications on topics like avoiding scams and identity theft, managing finances and saving money, staying healthy, and understanding Government benefits are available on the USA.gov publications Web site.

The "Consumer Action Handbook" is a free resource guide that provides consumer rights tips and general information on shopping for goods and services. It is available in English and Spanish. A digital copy of the handbook in Portable Document Format (PDF) may be downloaded from the USA.gov Web site. A hardcopy may be ordered online; over the phone, weekdays, 8 a.m.–8 p.m., excluding Federal holidays; or by writing to USAGov–Handbook, Pueblo, CO 81009. Allow 4–6 weeks for delivery. Phone, 844-872-4681.

The GSA maintains an electronic forms library. The library features a collection of the most frequently downloaded forms: GSA, optional (OF), and standard (SF).

Real Property Disposal

Inquiries about the redistribution or competitive sale of surplus real property should be directed to the Office of Real Property Utilization and Disposal, Public Buildings Service, 1800 F Street NW., Washington, DC 20405. Phone, 202-501-0084.

The Office of Real Property Utilization and Disposal operates a resource center that provides information on the handling of excess real property and on properties that are being offered for sale.

Regional Offices

The GSA operates 11 regional offices. More information on these offices is available on the GSA Web site.

Site Map

The Web site map allows visitors to look for specific topics or to browse for content that aligns with their interests.

Speakers

Requests for speakers should be directed

to the nearest regional office or the Office of Communications and Marketing, General Services Administration, 1800 F Street NW., Washington, DC 20405. Phone, 202-501-1231.

Sustainable Facilities (SF) Tool

The SFTool supports the efforts of designers, facility managers, purchasing agents, tenants, and others to green buildings, operations, and purchases.

USA.gov

USA.gov is an online, Governmentwide guide to information and services.

Contact USA.gov by email, phone, or web chat for answers to Government-related questions. Web chat is available Monday–Friday, 8 a.m.–8 p.m., eastern standard time, excluding Federal Holidays. The same hours of operation apply to the USAGov contact center. Phone, 844-872-4681.

USA.gov tweets on Twitter.

For further information concerning the General Services Administration, contact the Office of Communications and Marketing, General Services Administration, Washington, DC 20417. Phone, 202-501-1231.

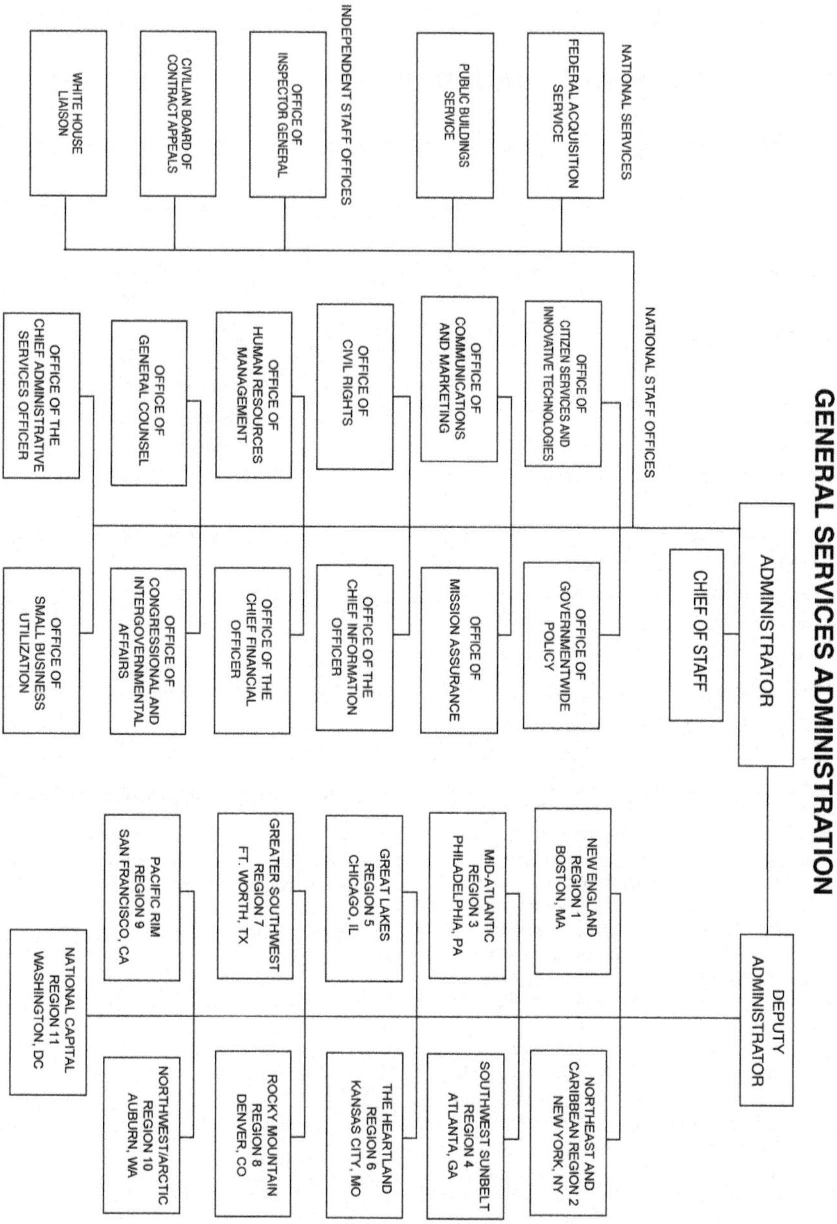
GENERAL SERVICES ADMINISTRATION
ADMINISTRATOR
CHIEF OF STAFF
DEPUTY ADMINISTRATOR
NATIONAL SERVICES
FEDERAL ACQUISITION SERVICE
PUBLIC BUILDINGS SERVICE
INDEPENDENT STAFF OFFICES
OFFICE OF INSPECTOR GENERAL
CIVILIAN BOARD OF CONTRACT APPEALS
WHITE HOUSE LIAISON
NATIONAL STAFF OFFICES
OFFICE OF CITIZEN SERVICES AND INNOVATIVE TECHNOLOGIES
OFFICE OF GOVERNMENTWIDE POLICY
OFFICE OF COMMUNICATIONS AND MARKETING
OFFICE OF MISSION ASSURANCE
OFFICE OF CIVIL RIGHTS
OFFICE OF THE CHIEF INFORMATION OFFICER
OFFICE OF HUMAN RESOURCES MANAGEMENT
OFFICE OF THE CHIEF FINANCIAL OFFICER
OFFICE OF GENERAL COUNSEL
OFFICE OF CONGRESSIONAL AND INTERGOVERNMENTAL AFFAIRS
OFFICE OF THE CHIEF ADMINISTRATIVE SERVICES OFFICER
OFFICE OF SMALL BUSINESS UTILIZATION
NEW ENGLAND REGION 1 BOSTON, MA
NORTHEAST AND CARIBBEAN REGION 2 NEW YORK, NY
MID-ATLANTIC REGION 3 PHILADELPHIA, PA
SOUTHWEST SUNBELT REGION 4 ATLANTA, GA
GREAT LAKES REGION 5 CHICAGO, IL
THE HEARTLAND REGION 6 KANSAS CITY, MO
GREATER SOUTHWEST REGION 7 FT. WORTH, TX
ROCKY MOUNTAIN REGION 8 DENVER, CO
PACIFIC RIM REGION 9 SAN FRANCISCO, CA
NORTHWEST/ARCTIC REGION 10 AUBURN, WA
NATIONAL CAPITAL REGION 11 WASHINGTON, DC

Inter-American Foundation

1331 Pennsylvania Avenue, NW., Suite 1200 North, Washington, DC 20004, 202-360-4530, *http://www.iaf.gov*

CHAIR	Eduardo Arriola
Vice Chair	(vacancy)
Secretary	Jack C. Vaughn, Jr.
Director	Juan Carlos Iturregui
Director	J. Kelly Ryan
Director	Luis A. Viada
Director	Roger W. Wallace
Director	(vacancy)
Director	(vacancy)
President / Chief Executive Officer	Robert N. Kaplan
Chief Operating Officer	Lesley Duncan
General Counsel	Paul Zimmerman
MANAGING DIRECTORS	
Grant-Making and Portfolio Management	Marcy Kelly
Networks and Strategic Initiatives	Stephen Cox
Office of External and Government Affairs	Manuel Nuñez

The Inter-American Foundation supports social and economic development in Latin America and the Caribbean.

The Inter-American Foundation (IAF) was created in 1969 (22 U.S.C. 290f) as an experimental U.S. foreign assistance program. The Foundation is governed by a nine-person Board of Directors whom the President appoints with the advice and consent of the Senate. Six members are drawn from the private sector and three from the Federal Government. The Board of Directors appoints the president of the Foundation.

In Latin America and the Caribbean, the IAF promotes equitable, participatory, and sustainable self-help development by awarding grants and giving other technical assistance directly to local organizations throughout the region. It also partners with the public and private sectors to build support and to mobilize local, national, and international resources for grassroots development.

Sources of Information

Employment

The IAF posts job vacancies online.

Freedom of Information Act (FOIA)

The IAF generally discloses documents or records upon receiving a properly submitted request in writing. Records, or parts of them, that one or more of the nine FOIA exemptions shield will not be released.

The IAF maintains an electronic FOIA reading room.

Grants

The IAF funds the self-help efforts of grassroots groups in Latin America and the Caribbean. It welcomes proposals for its grant program.

Internships

Information on student internships is available online.

Open Government

The IAF's Open Government Web page

has shortcuts to items of interest to the public.

Resources

The IAF makes available online a variety of informational resources: a blog, newsletter, and photo album, as well as news, publications, stories from the field, and videos.

Site Map

The Web site map allows visitors to look for specific topics or to browse content that aligns with their interests.

For further information, contact the Office of the President, Inter-American Foundation, 1331 Pennsylvania Avenue, NW., Suite 1200 North, Washington, DC 20004. Phone, 202-360-4530.

Merit Systems Protection Board

1615 M Street NW., Fifth Floor, Washington, DC 20419, 202-653-7200, 800-209-8960, 202-653-7130, *http://www.mspb.gov*

CHAIR	Susan Tsui Grundmann
Vice Chair	(vacancy)
Member	Mark A. Robbins
Director, Office of Equal Employment Opportunity	Jerry Beat
EXECUTIVE DIRECTOR	James M. Eisenmann
Clerk of the Board	Jennifer Everling, Acting
Director, Financial and Administrative Management	Kevin Nash
Director, Information Resources Management	William D. Spencer, Acting
Director, Office of Appeals Counsel	Susan M. Swafford
Director, Office of Policy and Evaluation	James M. Read
Director, Office of Regional Operations	Deborah Miron
General Counsel	Bryan G. Polisuk
Legislative Counsel	Rosalyn L. Coates

[For the Merit Systems Protection Board statement of organization, see the Code of Federal Regulations, Title 5, Part 1200]

The Merit Systems Protection Board protects the integrity of the Federal personnel merit systems and the rights of Federal employees.

The Merit Systems Protection Board (MSPB) is a successor agency to the United States Civil Service Commission, established by act of January 16, 1883 (22 Stat. 403). Reorganization Plan No. 2 of 1978 (5 U.S.C. app.) redesignated part of the Commission as the Merit Systems Protection Board. The Board comprises three members whom the President appoints with the advice and consent of the Senate.

Activities

The Board has responsibility for hearing and adjudicating appeals by Federal employees of adverse personnel actions, such as removals, suspensions, and demotions. It also resolves cases involving reemployment rights, denial of periodic step increases in pay, actions against administrative law judges, and charges of prohibited personnel practices, including charges in connection with whistleblowing.

The Board has the authority to enforce its decisions and to order corrective and disciplinary actions. An employee or applicant for employment involved in an appealable action that also involves an allegation of discrimination may ask the Equal Employment Opportunity Commission to review a Board decision. Final decisions and orders of the Board can be appealed to the U.S. Court of Appeals for the Federal Circuit.

The Board reviews regulations issued by the Office of Personnel Management and has the authority to require agencies to cease compliance with any regulation that could constitute a prohibited personnel practice. It also conducts special studies of the civil service and other executive branch merit systems and reports to the President and the Congress on whether the Federal workforce is being adequately protected against political abuses and prohibited personnel practices.

Sources of Information

Electronic Filing

An appeal may be filed online using the e-Appeal process.

Employment

The MSPB posts current job openings on USAJobs.

Freedom of Information Act (FOIA)

The MSPB participates in FOIAonline, which allows an information seeker to submit FOIA requests to participating agencies, track the status of requests, search for requests that others have submitted, access previously released records, and generate agency-specific FOIA processing reports.

Interviews

The MSPB posts external links to MSPB-related interviews on its Web site.

Public Affairs

The MSPB posts "Federal Register" notices, press releases, reports, and the results of its annual Federal Employee Viewpoint Survey online.

For further information, contact the Merit Systems Protection Board, 1615 M Street NW., Washington, DC 20419. Phone, 202-653-7200 or 800-209-8960. TDD, 800-877-8339. Fax, 202-653-7130.

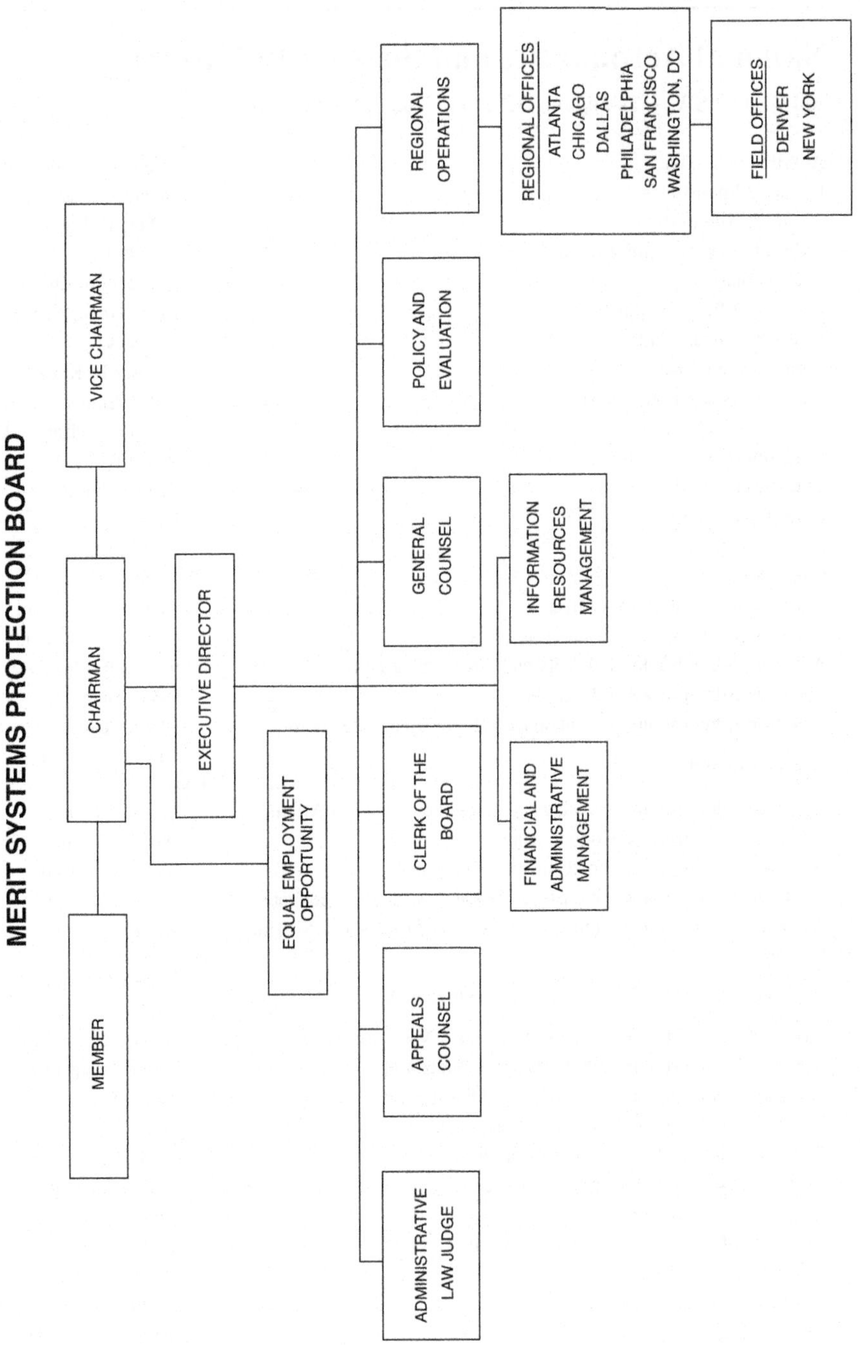
MERIT SYSTEMS PROTECTION BOARD
MEMBER
CHAIRMAN
VICE CHAIRMAN
EXECUTIVE DIRECTOR
EQUAL EMPLOYMENT OPPORTUNITY
ADMINISTRATIVE LAW JUDGE
APPEALS COUNSEL
CLERK OF THE BOARD
GENERAL COUNSEL
POLICY AND EVALUATION
REGIONAL OPERATIONS
FINANCIAL AND ADMINISTRATIVE MANAGEMENT
INFORMATION RESOURCES MANAGEMENT
REGIONAL OFFICES
ATLANTA
CHICAGO
DALLAS
PHILADELPHIA
SAN FRANCISCO
WASHINGTON, DC
FIELD OFFICES
DENVER
NEW YORK

National Aeronautics and Space Administration

300 E Street SW., Washington, DC 20546, 202-358-0000, *http://www.nasa.gov*

ADMINISTRATOR	Charles F. Bolden, Jr.
Deputy Administrator	Dava Newman
Associate Administrator	Robert M. Lightfoot
Associate Deputy Administrator	Lesa B. Roe
Chief of Staff	Michael French
Director, Office of Evaluation	Helen Grant, Acting
Director, Council Staff	(vacancy)
White House Liaison	Clarissa H. Kornell
Assistant Associate Administrator	Tom Cremins
Chief Financial Officer	David P. Radzanowski
Chief Information Officer	Renee Wynn
Chief Scientist	Ellen R. Stofan
Chief Technologist	David Miller
Inspector General	Paul K. Martin
Chief Engineer	Ralph R. Roe
Chief Health and Medical Officer	Richard S. Williams
Chief Safety and Mission Assurance Officer	Terrence W. Wilcutt
Associate Administrator, Diversity and Equal Opportunity	Brenda R. Manuel
Associate Administrator, Education	Donal James
Associate Administrator, International and Interagency Relations	Albert Condes
General Counsel	Sumara Thompson-King
Associate Administrator, Legislative and Intergovernmental Affairs	L. Seth Statler
Associate Administrator, Communications	David S. Weaver
Associate Administrator, Small Business Programs	Glenn A. Delgado
Associate Administrator, Aeronautics Research Mission Directorate	Jaiwon Shin
Associate Administrator, Human Exploration and Operations Mission Directorate	William H. Gerstenmaier
Associate Administrator, Science Mission Directorate	Geoffrey L. Yoder, Acting
Associate Administrator for Space Technology Mission Directorate	Stephen G. Jurczyk
Associate Administrator, Mission Support Directorate	Krista C. Paquin
Assistant Administrator, Human Capital Management	Lauren Leo
Assistant Administrator, Strategic Infrastructure	Calvin Williams
Executive Director, Headquarters Operations	Jay M. Henn
Executive Director, NASA Shared Services Center	Mark V. Glorioso
Assistant Administrator, Procurement	William McNally
Assistant Administrator, Protective Services	Joseph S. Mahaley
Director, NASA Management Office	Marcus Watkins
Director, Ames Research Center	Eugene Tue
Director, Armstrong Flight Center	David D. McBride
Director, Glenn Research Center	Janet L. Kavandi
Director, Goddard Space Flight Center	Christopher J. Scolese
Director, Johnson Space Center	Ellen Ochoa

Director, Kennedy Space Center	Robert D. Cabana
Director, Langley Research Center	David Bowles, Acting
Director, Marshall Space Flight Center	Todd A. May
Director, Stennis Space Center	Richard J. Gilbrech
Director, Jet Propulsion Laboratory	Charles Elachi

[For the National Aeronautics and Space Administration statement of organization, see the Code of Federal Regulations, Title 14, Part 1201]

The National Aeronautics and Space Administration advances aeronautic research, explores space, and makes scientific discoveries for the benefit of humankind.

The National Aeronautics and Space Administration (NASA) was established by the National Aeronautics and Space Act of 1958, as amended (42 U.S.C. 2451 et seq.).

Activities

Aeronautics Research Mission Directorate

The Aeronautics Research Mission Directorate conducts research, ground tests, and flight demonstrations to develop technologies and tools that reduce the adverse effects of aviation on the environment, increase efficiency while maintaining safety in skies that are becoming more crowded, and prepare the way for the emergence of new aircraft shapes and propulsion. The Directorate's four research programs partner with industry, other government agencies, and universities to develop technologies, converge breakthroughs from other fields, and ensure that the next generation workforce has the vision and skills for maintaining U.S. leadership in aviation.

For further information, call 202-358-2047.

Human Exploration and Operations Mission Directorate

The Human Exploration and Operations Mission Directorate oversees NASA space systems development and operations that support human exploration in and beyond low-Earth orbit. It also oversees low-level requirements development, policy, and programmatic oversight. The International Space Station represents the agency's exploration activities in low-Earth orbit. Beyond low-Earth orbit, exploration activities include the management of exploration systems development, human space flight capabilities, advanced exploration systems, and space life sciences research and applications. The Directorate also provides agency leadership and management of NASA space operations related to launch services and space communications and navigation in support of both human and robotic exploration programs.

For further information, call 202-358-1562.

Science Mission Directorate

The Science Mission Directorate explores Earth and space to advance Earth science, heliophysics, planetary science, and astrophysics. Using in situ and space-based observations, the Directorate seeks a better understanding of the Sun and its influence on the solar system, climate change, the solar system's origin and evolution, whether life is limited to Earth, and the universe beyond.

For further information, call 202-358-3889.

Space Technology Mission Directorate

The Space Technology Mission Directorate develops crosscutting and pioneering technologies and capabilities that the agency needs to carry out current and future missions. Through transparent, collaborative partnerships, the Directorate rapidly develops and demonstrates high-payoff technologies. It uses a merit-based competition model with a portfolio approach, spanning a range of discipline areas and technology readiness levels.

For further information, call 202-358-0454.

Mission Support Directorate

The Mission Support Directorate provides overall leadership, stewardship, advocacy, integration, and optimization of Agency institutional activities. These activities include management of human capital and strategic infrastructure, procurement, protective services, headquarters operations, shared services, partnerships, external audits, and management of Agency directives. To enable successful operations, the Directorate focuses on three major goals: to provide stewardship of major institutional operations; to integrate resources, infrastructure, and processes and to advocate for institutional capabilities and needs; and to optimize mission support services through strategic analysis and business services assessments to achieve greater operational efficiency.

For further information, call 202-358-2789.

NASA Centers

Ames Research Center

Located in California's Silicon Valley, the Center enables exploration through selected developments, innovative technologies, and interdisciplinary scientific discovery. It provides leadership in astrobiology; small satellites; technologies for CEV, CLV, and HLV; the search for habitable planets; supercomputing; intelligent-adaptive systems; advanced thermal protection; and airborne astronomy. The Center also develops tools for a safer, more efficient national airspace, and it cultivates partnerships that benefit NASA's mission.

Armstrong Flight Research Center

Located at Edwards Air Force Base, CA, the Center carries out flight research and technology integration, validates space exploration concepts, conducts airborne remote sensing and science missions, enables airborne astrophysics observation missions to study the universe, and supports International Space Station operations. It also supports activities of the Agency's four Mission Directorates.

Glenn Research Center

Located on two campuses—at Lewis Field, next to Cleveland Hopkins International Airport, and at Plum Brook Station in Sandusky, OH—the Center is associated with cutting edge technologies that will enable human exploration to Mars, the design of environmentally friendlier commercial hybrid electric aircraft, and the development of more advanced high-temperature materials. Its 3,200 scientists, engineers, and other specialized employees work in partnership with U.S. companies, universities, and other Government institutions to produce and improve new technologies that are useful on and above and beyond Earth. The Center's specialized staff focuses on air-breathing and in-space propulsion, power and energy storage, aerospace communications, extreme environment materials, biomedical technologies, and high-value space experiments in the physical sciences.

Goddard Space Flight Center

Located in Greenbelt, MD, the Center expands mankind's knowledge of Earth and its environment, the solar system, and the universe by observing them from space. It also conducts scientific investigations, develops and operates space systems, and advances essential technologies.

Johnson Space Center

Located in Houston, TX, the Center specializes in human space flight. It hosts and staffs program and project offices; selects and trains astronauts; manages and conducts projects that build, test, and integrate human-rated systems for transportation, habitation, and working in space; and plans and operates human space flight missions. This work requires a comprehensive understanding of space and planetary environments, as well as research into the effects of those environments on human physiology. It also requires development of technology to sustain and preserve life; maintenance of a supply chain to design, manufacture, and test flight products; selection, training, and provision of medical care to those who fly space missions; and ongoing administrative mission support services. The Center is currently hosting the International Space Station Program, the Multi-Purpose Crew Vehicle Program, and the Human Research Program. It plays a lead role in developing, operating, and integrating human exploration missions that include commercial, academic, international, and U.S. Government partners.

Kennedy Space Center

Located on Florida's east coast, the Center is responsible for space launch operations and spaceport and range technologies. Home to the launch services program, it manages the processing and launching of astronaut crews and associated payloads. Its management activities include the International Space Station segments, research experiments and supplies, and NASA's scientific and research spacecraft. These scientific and research spacecraft range from robotic landers to Earth observation satellites and space-based telescopes on a variety of launch vehicles.

Innovative technology experts at the Center support NASA's current programs and future exploration missions by developing new products and processes that benefit the Agency and consumers. The Center remains a leader in cutting-edge research and development in the areas of physics, chemistry, technology, prototype designing, engineering, environmental conservation, and renewable energy.

Langley Research Center

Located in Hampton, VA, and established in 1917 as an aeronautics lab, the Center is renowned for its scientific and technological expertise in aerospace research, atmospheric science, systems analysis and integration, and planetary entry, descent and landing. Its researchers and engineers conduct research in structures and materials, applied sciences, space technology development, and aerosciences across the hyper, super, and subsonic flight regimes. Langley researchers and engineers have developed and validated technologies to improve the effectiveness, safety, environmental compatibility, and efficiency of the Nation's air transportation system. The Center supports space exploration and operations, and it plays a major role in expanding science-based knowledge of Earth and its environment. By determining appropriate preventative and corrective action for problems, trends, and issues across agency programs and projects, its engineering and safety personnel at the NASA Engineering Safety Center have improved mission safety and execution.

Marshall Space Flight Center

Located in Huntsville, AL, the Center oversees complex engineering, technology development, and scientific research for making human space exploration a reality. The Center is building the space launch system and developing advanced technologies that are necessary for the human journey to Mars. It also manages a number of programs and projects: the International Space Station's environmental control and life support system, its payload operations, and numerous other facilities and experiments; the Chandra X-ray Observatory; the Discovery and New Frontiers programs; space technology demonstration missions; and the Michoud Assembly Facility, where space vehicles are manufactured and assembled.

Stennis Space Center

Located near Bay St. Louis, MS, the Center serves as the agency's rocket propulsion testing ground. It provides test services not only for America's space program, but also for the Department of Defense and private sector. Its unique rocket propulsion test capabilities will be used for testing the engines and stages of NASA's space launch system rocket. The Advanced Technology and Technology Transfer Branch develops and licenses state-of-the-art components, processes, sensors, and software.

Jet Propulsion Laboratory

The Laboratory is a Federally Funded Research and Development Center (FFRDC) managed under contract by the California Institute of Technology (Caltech) in Pasadena, CA. This FFRDC is a unique nongovernment entity sponsored and funded by the Agency to meet specific long-term technical needs that cannot be met by other organizations within the Agency. As part of this special relationship, the Laboratory must operate in the public interest with objectivity and independence, avoid organizational conflicts of interest, and fully disclose its affairs to NASA. The Laboratory develops and maintains technical and managerial competencies to perform the following missions in support of the Agency's strategic goals: to explore the solar system to understand its formation and evolution; to establish a continuous and permanent robotic presence on Mars to discover its history and habitability; to make critical measurements and models to understand the global and regional integrated Earth system; to conduct observations to search for neighboring solar systems and Earth-like planets and help understand formation, evolution, and composition of the Universe; to conduct communications and navigation for deep space missions; to provide support, particularly in robotic infrastructures and precursors, that enables human exploration of the Moon, Mars, and beyond; and, under Caltech's initiative, to collaborate with other Federal and State government agencies and commercial endeavors in areas synergistic with the Laboratory's work performed for NASA.

Sources of Information

Business Opportunities

Information on business opportunities is available on NASA's Office of Procurement Web site. NASA also offers small businesses opportunities to participate in prime contracts and subcontracts. Contact the Office of Small Business Programs. Phone, 202-358-2088.

Employment

In addition to astronauts, the agency relies on accountants, engineers, human resources specialists, IT specialists, scientists, technicians, writers, and other skilled professionals to carry out its mission. To learn more about employment opportunities and programs, visit the NASAJobs Web site or contact the NASA Shared Services Center at the Stennis Space Center. Phone, 877-677-2123.

Freedom of Information Act (FOIA)

FOIA requests may be submitted by email or fax, or delivered in person or mailed to NASA Headquarters, 300 E Street SW., Room 5Q16, Washington, DC 20546. Phone, 202-358-2462. Fax, 202-358-4332.

History

The NASA History Office publishes a quarterly newsletter and books, hosts social media, offers fellowships, and runs the historical reference collection to assist the public with finding information on aeronautical and space history. Phone, 202-358-0384.

Library

The NASA Headquarters Library welcomes visitors. Located in the East Lobby of NASA Headquarters in Washington, DC, the library is open Monday–Friday, 7:30 a.m.–5:00 p.m. It is closed on Federal holidays. Phone, 202-358-0168.

Hotline

The Office of Inspector General (OIG) prevents and detects abuse, fraud, mismanagement, and waste. To file a complaint, use the online complaint form; write to the NASA Office of Inspector General, P.O. Box 23089, L'Enfant Plaza Station, Washington, DC 20026; or call the OIG Hotline. Phone, 800-424-9183.

Publications

The NASA scientific and technical information program provides access to research papers.

Additional publications are available onsite at the NASA Headquarters Library. A "Find Publications" drop-down menu is available on the library Web page.

For further information, contact the Headquarters Information Center, National Aeronautics and Space Administration, Washington, DC 20546. Phone, 202-358-0000.

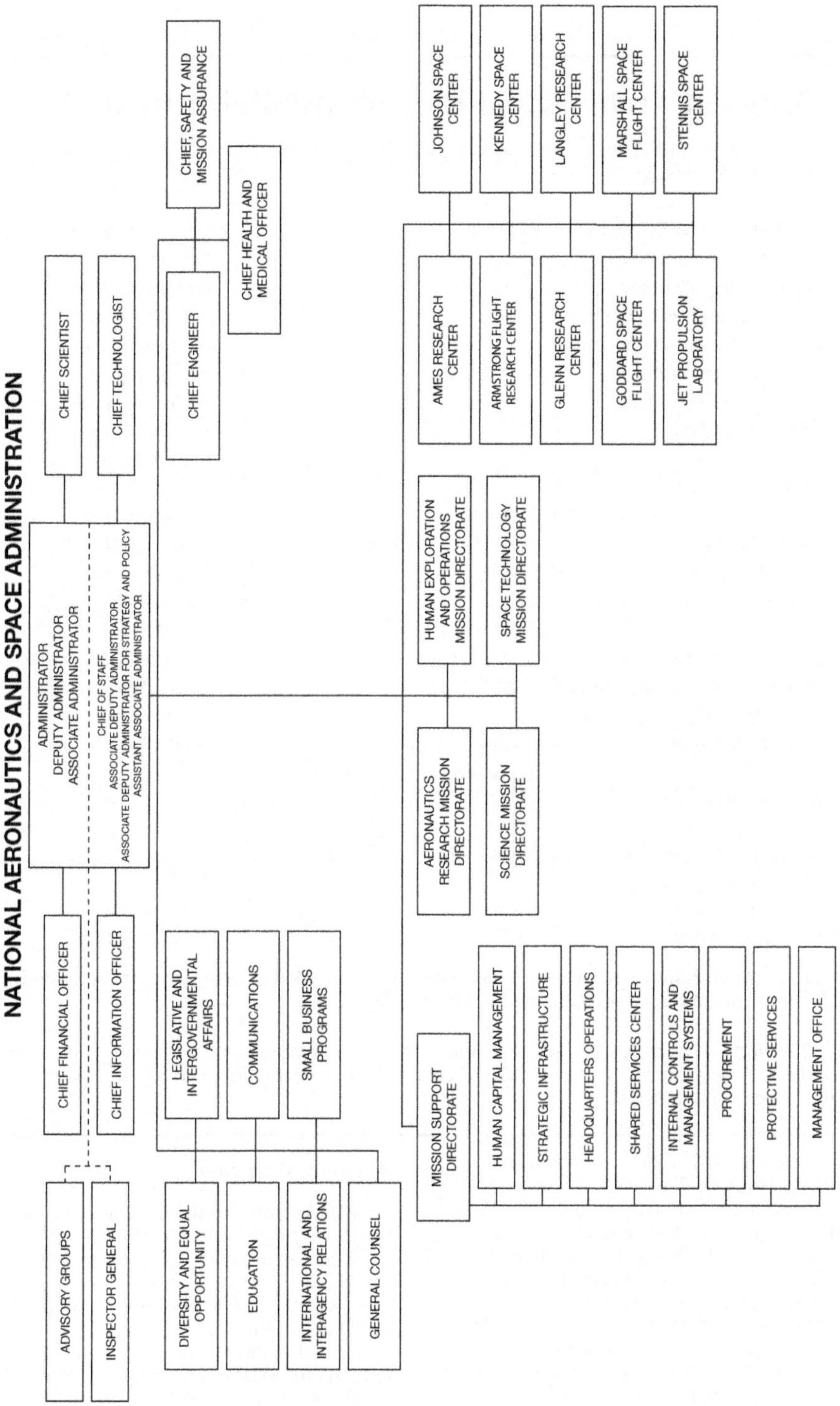
NATIONAL AERONAUTICS AND SPACE ADMINISTRATION
ADMINISTRATOR
DEPUTY ADMINISTRATOR
ASSOCIATE ADMINISTRATOR
CHIEF OF STAFF
ASSOCIATE DEPUTY ADMINISTRATOR
ASSOCIATE DEPUTY ADMINISTRATOR FOR STRATEGY AND POLICY
ASSISTANT ASSOCIATE ADMINISTRATOR
CHIEF SCIENTIST
CHIEF TECHNOLOGIST
CHIEF FINANCIAL OFFICER
CHIEF INFORMATION OFFICER
ADVISORY GROUPS
INSPECTOR GENERAL
CHIEF ENGINEER
CHIEF, SAFETY AND MISSION ASSURANCE
CHIEF HEALTH AND MEDICAL OFFICER
LEGISLATIVE AND INTERGOVERNMENTAL AFFAIRS
COMMUNICATIONS
SMALL BUSINESS PROGRAMS
DIVERSITY AND EQUAL OPPORTUNITY
EDUCATION
INTERNATIONAL AND INTERAGENCY RELATIONS
GENERAL COUNSEL
AERONAUTICS RESEARCH MISSION DIRECTORATE
HUMAN EXPLORATION AND OPERATIONS MISSION DIRECTORATE
SCIENCE MISSION DIRECTORATE
SPACE TECHNOLOGY MISSION DIRECTORATE
AMES RESEARCH CENTER
ARMSTRONG FLIGHT RESEARCH CENTER
GLENN RESEARCH CENTER
GODDARD SPACE FLIGHT CENTER
JET PROPULSION LABORATORY
JOHNSON SPACE CENTER
KENNEDY SPACE CENTER
LANGLEY RESEARCH CENTER
MARSHALL SPACE FLIGHT CENTER
STENNIS SPACE CENTER
MISSION SUPPORT DIRECTORATE
HUMAN CAPITAL MANAGEMENT
STRATEGIC INFRASTRUCTURE
HEADQUARTERS OPERATIONS
SHARED SERVICES CENTER
INTERNAL CONTROLS AND MANAGEMENT SYSTEMS
PROCUREMENT
PROTECTIVE SERVICES
MANAGEMENT OFFICE

National Archives and Records Administration

700 Pennsylvania Avenue NW., Washington, DC, 20408-0001, 866-272-6272, *http://www.archives.gov*

ARCHIVIST OF THE UNITED STATES	David S. Ferriero
Deputy Archivist of the United States	Debra Steidel Wall
Chief Financial Officer	Colleen Murphy, Acting
Chief Human Capital Officer	Sean M. Clayton
Chief Information Officer	Swarnali Haldar
Chief Innovation Officer	Pamela Wright
Chief Operating Officer	William J. Bosanko
Chief Records Officer	Laurence Brewer
Chief Strategy and Communications Officer	Maria Carosa Stanwich, Acting
Chief of Management and Administration	Micah Cheatham
Chief of Staff	Maria Carosa Stanwich
Director, Communications and Marketing	John Valceanu
Director, Congressional Affairs	John Hamilton
Director, Equal Employment Opportunity Office	Ismael Martinez
Director, Office of Government Information Services	Nikki Gramain, Acting
Director, Office of the Federal Register	Oliver Potts
Executive for Agency Services	Jay A. Trainer
Executive for Business Support Services	Donna Forbes, Acting
Executive for Legislative Archives, Presidential Libraries, and Museum Services	James B. Gardner
Executive for Research Services	Ann Cummings, Acting
Executive Director, National Historical Publications and Records Commission	Kathleen M. Williams
General Counsel	Gary M. Stern
Inspector General	James E. Springs

[For the National Archives and Records Administration statement of organization, see the Federal Register of June 25, 1985, 50 FR 26278]

The National Archives and Records Administration safeguards and preserves the records of the U.S. Government, ensuring that the American people can discover, use, and learn from their documentary heritage.

The National Archives and Records Administration (NARA) is the successor agency to the National Archives Establishment, which was created in 1934 and later, in 1949, incorporated into the General Services Administration as the National Archives and Records Service. NARA was established as an independent agency in the Federal Government's executive branch by act of October 19, 1984 (44 U.S.C. 2101 et seq.), effective April 1, 1985.

Archival Program

NARA maintains the U.S. Government's most historically valuable records, ranging from the Revolutionary War era to the recent past; arranges and preserves records and prepares finding aids to facilitate their use; makes records publicly accessible online and in its research rooms; answers requests for information contained in its holdings; and provides, for a fee, copies of records. NARA holdings include the records of the U.S. House of Representatives and Senate, which are preserved and administered by the Center for Legislative Archives. Many important records are available in microfilm and accessible online. Archival records are maintained in NARA facilities in the Washington, DC, area. Records of exceptional local or regional interest are maintained in NARA archives located in other parts of the country. There are also nine NARA-affiliated archives facilities that hold NARA-owned records and make them available to the public.

Records Management

To ensure proper documentation of the organization, policies, and activities of the Government, NARA develops standards and guidelines for nationwide management and disposition of recorded information. It appraises Federal records and approves disposition schedules. NARA also inspects agency records and management practices, develops records management training programs, provides guidance and assistance on records management, and stores inactive records.

Agency Services

Agency Services leads NARA's efforts to meet the ongoing records management needs of the Federal Government and to represent the public interest in the accountability and transparency of this management. Its components include the Office of the Chief Records Officer; the Federal Records Centers Program, including the National Personnel Records Center; the Information Security Oversight Office; the National Declassification Center; and the Office of Government Information Services.

Office of Innovation

The Office of Innovation finds innovative ways to serve its customers and to increase access to and delivery of records through all forms of media. Its mission includes demonstrating leadership in the archival and information access field. The Office coordinates NARA's efforts for Open Government and the National Digital Strategy. It comprises several divisions: digitization; digital engagement, including Internet, social media, and NARA's online catalog; business architecture, standards and authorities; and the Innovation Hub.

Office of the Chief Records Officer

The Office of the Chief Records Officer assists Government agencies with their records management programs and the lifecycle management of Federal records. The Office formulates recommendations for Governmentwide policies, procedures, regulations, and guidance on the creation, management, and disposition of records in various media. It conducts inspections, evaluations, and surveys of records and records management programs in agencies; reports its findings; and recommends improvements or necessary corrective actions. The Office also provides records management services, including appraisal and scheduling, technical assistance, training, consultation, and analysis regarding policy matters, as well as identifying permanent records eligible for transfer to the National Archives.

Federal Records Centers Program

NARA's Federal Records Centers Program (FRCP) stores and services active and inactive records for Federal agencies. A national network of 18 facilities, the FRCP system currently stores more than 30 million cubic feet of records. Since 1999, the FRCP system has operated as a reimbursable program that provides the Federal community with services on a fee-for-service basis. These services include storage of textual and special media records; management of classified and nonclassified records; retrieval of records needed by customers to conduct daily business or fulfill statutory requirements; expedited responses to congressional inquiries, litigation, and urgent business needs; disposition services, including the disposal of temporary records that have reached the end of their required retention period and the transfer of permanent records to the legal custody of the National Archives; and a variety of special projects based on customer needs.

The National Personnel Records Center (NPRC) in St. Louis, MO, is the largest facility in the FRCP system. This facility stores and services the civilian personnel, medical, and pay records of former U.S. Civil Service employees and the personnel, medical, and related records of discharged military personnel. The NPRC maintains research rooms where Federal employees and the general public can review official military and civilian personnel folders and other related records. It also provides services and technical advice relating to records disposition, filing and classification schemes, document conversion, and the protection of vital civilian and military records to Federal agencies.

To request military records, visit www.archives.gov/veterans. For information on the National Personnel Records Center, visit www.archives.gov/st-louis or call the NPRC. Phone, 314-801-0800. Fax, 301-801-9195.

For further information, contact the Federal Records Centers. Phone 314-801-9300.

Information Security Oversight Office

The Information Security Oversight Office (ISOO) oversees programs for Classified National Security Information and Controlled Unclassified Information in both Government and industry and reports their status to the President annually. ISOO receives policy and program guidance from the National Security Council and operates under the authority of Executive Orders 12829, 13549, 13587, 13526, and 13556. As a NARA organizational component, ISOO's goals are to hold classification activities to the minimum necessary standard to protect national security, promote consistency and transparency in the handling of Controlled Unclassified Information, safeguard Classified National Security Information in both Government and industry efficiently and cost-effectively, and promote declassification and public access to information as soon as security considerations permit.

ISOO is responsible for implementing and monitoring the National Industrial Security Program (NISP). The Director of ISOO also serves as the Chair of the NISP Policy Advisory Committee, a forum used to discuss policy issues in dispute and to recommend changes to those policies. ISOO acts as a consultant for policy guidance to the Executive Agent for Safeguarding Classified Information on Computer Networks. It also serves as the Chair of the State, Local, Tribal, and Private Sector Entities Policy Advisory Committee to discuss program-related policy issues, facilitate the resolution of disputes, and recommend policy and procedural changes to remove undue impediments to the sharing of information under the program. As a member of the Senior Information Sharing and Safeguarding Steering Committee and the Insider Threat Task Force, ISOO plays a leading role in the development, coordination, oversight, and promulgation of policies, objectives, and priorities for establishing and integrating security, counterintelligence, user audits and monitoring, and other safeguarding capabilities and practices within agencies.

The Office was also named the Executive Agent for administering Executive Order 13556, "Controlled Unclassified Information" (CUI). CUI establishes consistent information sharing and protection practices by replacing the ad hoc, agency-specific policies and procedures with an executive branchwide program to manage all unclassified information that requires safeguarding and/or dissemination controls pursuant to and consistent with applicable law, regulations, and Governmentwide policies.

For further information, contact the Information Security Oversight Office. Phone, 202-357-5250.

National Declassification Center

The National Declassification Center (NDC) was established by Executive Order 13526 and began operations in early January of 2010. The Center is responsible for the timely and appropriate processing of referrals between agencies for accessioned Federal records and transferred Presidential records; general interagency declassification activities necessary to fulfill the requirements of sections 3.3 and 3.4 of the Order; the exchange among agencies of detailed declassification guidance to support equity recognition; the development of effective, transparent, and standard declassification work processes, training, and quality assurance measures; the development of solutions to declassification challenges posed by electronic records, special media, and emerging technologies; and the linkage and effective utilization of existing agency databases and the use of new technologies to support declassification activities under the purview of the Center.

For further information, contact the National Declassification Center. Phone, 301-837-0405.

Office of Government Information Services

Established under the OPEN Government Act of 2007 (5 U.S.C. 101), the Office of Government Information Services (OGIS) works with agencies across the Executive branch to improve the Government's ability to respond to Freedom of Information Act (FOIA) requests. OGIS serves as liaison between individuals making FOIA requests and administrative agencies, providing mediation services to resolve disputes as an alternative to litigation. OGIS reviews policies and procedures of administrative agencies under FOIA. OGIS also reviews agency compliance with FOIA and recommends policy changes to the President and Congress.

For further information, contact the Office of Government Information Services. Phone, 202-741-5770.

Research Services

Research Services provides world-class services to customers seeking access to NARA's accessioned Federal records. Records are available for research purposes in reading rooms at the National Archives Building (Archives I) in Washington, DC; the National Archives (Archives II) in College Park, MD; and various regional facilities throughout the Nation.

A listing of Records Services facilities is available on the "Locations Nationwide" Web page.

Presidential Libraries

Through the Presidential Libraries, which are located at sites selected by the Presidents and built with private funds, NARA preserves and makes available the records, personal papers, and artifacts of a President's administration. Each Library operates a research room and provides reference services for Presidential papers and other historical materials. The Libraries display artifacts and other holdings in museum exhibits illustrating the life and times of a President. The Presidential Libraries also provide programming for students of all ages promoting citizen engagement. NARA operates the Libraries of Presidents Herbert Hoover through George W. Bush. While such records were once considered personal papers, all Presidential records created on or after January 20, 1981, are declared by law to be owned and controlled by the United States and are required to be transferred to NARA at the end of the administration, pursuant to the Presidential Records Act of 1978 (44 U.S.C. 2201 et seq.). The Office of Presidential Libraries within the National Archives oversees the archival, museum, and education programs of the 13 Presidential Libraries.

For further information, contact the Office of Presidential Libraries. Phone, 301-837-3250. Fax, 301-837-3199.

Office of the Federal Register

The Office of the Federal Register (OFR) prepares and publishes a variety of public documents.

After the Congress passes an act and the President approves it, the OFR assigns the new law a public or private law number and publishes its text in pamphlet form as a slip law. A slip law serves as the official publication of the new law and is admissible as legal evidence of its provisions. The OFR also publishes the "United States Statutes at Large," an annual compilation of all the laws passed during a congressional session.

Each Federal workday, the OFR publishes the "Federal Register," which contains current Presidential proclamations and Executive orders, Federal agency regulations having general applicability and legal effect, proposed agency rules, and documents required by statute to be published.

All Federal regulations in force are codified annually in the "Code of Federal

Regulations."

Presidential speeches, news conferences, messages, and other materials released by the White House Office of the Press Secretary are published online in the "Daily Compilation of Presidential Documents" and annually in the "Public Papers of the Presidents." The "Daily Compilation of Presidential Documents"—as well as electronic versions of its forerunner, the "Weekly Compilation of Presidential Documents," from 1993 onward—can be accessed on the Government Publishing Office's Federal Digital System (FDsys).

"The United States Government Manual," published annually, serves as the official handbook of the Federal Government. It contains extensive information on the legislative, judicial, and executive branches. The Manual is an online publication and is accessible on its Web site.

OFR publications are accessible online, and some are available in paper editions.

For further information, contact Information Services and Technology, Office of the Federal Register. Phone, 202-741-6000. TTY, 202-741-6086. Fax, 202-741-6012.

National Historical Publications and Records Commission

The National Historical Publications and Records Commission (NHPRC) is NARA's grant-making affiliate. NHPRC supports the preservation and promotes the use of America's documentary heritage that is essential for understanding American culture, democracy, and history. NHPRC grants help State and local archives, universities, historical societies, and other nonprofit organizations preserve and manage electronic records, improve training and techniques, strengthen archival programs, preserve and process records collections, and provide access to them through the publication of finding aids and documentary editions of the papers of the Founding Era and other themes and historical figures in American history. NHPRC works in partnership with a national network of State historical records advisory boards. It also provides Federal leadership in public policy affecting the preservation of and access to America's documentary heritage.

For further information, contact the National Historical Publications and Records Commission. Phone, 202-357-5010.

National Archives Trust Fund Board

The National Archives Trust Fund Board receives funds from the sale of historic document reproductions and publications based on historic records, as well as from gifts and bequests. The Board invests these funds and uses income to support archival functions such as the preparation of publications that make historic records information more widely available. Members of the Board are the Archivist of the United States, the Secretary of the Treasury, and the Chair of the National Endowment for the Humanities.

For further information, contact the Secretary, National Archives Trust Fund Board. Phone, 301-837-3165.

Sources of Information

Business Opportunities

Business opportunities with NARA are posted on the Federal Business Opportunities Web site.

Information also is available on the "Doing Business With NARA" Web page.

Calendar of Events

To be added to the mailing list for the monthly National Archives Calendar of Events or to hear a recorded announcement of events at National Archives locations in Washington, DC, and College Park, MD, call 202-357-5000. TDD, 301-837-0482. Or, visit the "Calendar of Events" Web page.

Center for Legislative Archives

The Center for Legislative Archives houses the official records of the U.S. House of Representatives and Senate from 1789 to the present. House and Senate records remain in the permanent legal custody of the House and Senate and are governed by their respective rules. The Center responds to requests from congressional committees for the timely delivery of records to support current congressional business needs. The Center is a full-service archive: It provides records management guidance to the House and Senate archivists; processes and provides public access to congressional and legislative branch records; and creates exhibits, public programs, and educational materials and workshops on the history of the Congress and representative government. The Center reports to the Advisory Committee on the Records of Congress on its programs, activities, and resources. For further information, contact the Center for Legislative Archives. Phone, 202-357-5350. Fax, 202-357-5911.

Communications

The Communications staff responds to inquiries from the media and maintains contact with them; issues press releases and other material online, in print, and through social media; produces the agency's magazine "Prologue"; and serves as the liaison with organizations representing the archival profession, scholarly organizations, and other groups served by NARA. Phone, 202-357-5300.

Congressional Affairs

The Congressional Affairs staff maintains contact with and responds to inquiries from congressional offices. Phone, 202-357-5100. Fax, 202-357-5959.

Employment

For job opportunities, contact the nearest NARA facility or the Office of Human Capital, Talent Management Division, Staffing and Classification Branch, Room 370, 1 Archives Drive, St. Louis, MO 63138. Phone, 800-827-0885.

Exhibits

There are permanent and temporary exhibits at the National Archives in Washington, DC, home of the Declaration of Independence, Constitution, and Bill of Rights, and as part of the museum facilities of the Presidential Libraries. Several of NARA's regional facilities regularly host exhibits, and the agency has national traveling exhibits that bring National Archives' records to communities across the Nation. For information on Presidential Library exhibits, call 301-837-3250. For information on programs and their hours at the National Archives, call 202-357-5000. For information on traveling and regional exhibits and exhibit loans, call the Exhibits Office at 202-357-5210.

Federal Register Public Inspection Desk

The Office of the Federal Register's public inspection desk is open every Federal business day for public inspection of documents scheduled for publication in the next day's "Federal Register." The Office is located at Suite 700, 800 North Capitol Street NW., Washington, DC 20001. Phone, 202-741-6000. Documents currently on public inspection may be viewed online.

Freedom of Information Act (FOIA) / Privacy Act

For NARA's operational records, contact the NARA Freedom of Information Act / Privacy Act Officer, Office of General Counsel, National Archives and Records Administration, 8601 Adelphi Road, College Park, MD 20740-6001. Phone, 301-837-3642. Fax, 301-837-0293. For archival records in the custody of Research Services in the Washington, DC, area, contact the Special Access / FOIA Staff, National Archives and Records Administration, 8601 Adelphi Road, College Park, MD 20740-6001. Phone, 301-837-3190. Fax, 301-837-1864. For archival records located at a NARA location outside the Washington, DC, metropolitan area, contact the facility holding the records. To determine the location of records, search NARA's online archival research catalog (www.archives.gov/research/arc). For archival records in the custody of a Presidential Library, contact the appropriate Library. For records in the physical custody of the Washington National Records Center or the regional Records Centers, contact the Federal agency that transferred the records to the facility. Records stored in the Records Centers remain in the legal custody of the agency that created them. For a listing of archival facilities, visit NARA's Web site.

Frequently Asked Questions (FAQs)

NARA posts answers to FAQs on its Web site.

Grants

For NHPRC grants, contact NHPRC, National Archives and Records Administration, 700 Pennsylvania Avenue NW., Washington, DC 20408-0001. Phone, 202-357-5010.

History

Congress established the National Archives in 1934 because Federal records were being housed at sites—abandoned buildings, attics, and basements—where security and storage conditions were inadequate. More of NARA's history is available on its Web site.

Institute for the Editing of Historical Documents / Archives Leadership Institute

For information on the Institute for the Editing of Historical Documents or the Archives Leadership Institute, contact NHPRC, National Archives and Records Administration, 700 Pennsylvania Avenue NW., Washington, DC 20408-0001. Phone, 202-357-5010.

Know Your Records Program

For information, contact the Customer Service Center, Room G–13, National Archives Building, 700 Pennsylvania Avenue NW., Washington, DC 20408-0001. Phone, 202-357-5260.

Laws, Regulations, and Presidential Documents

For information on public laws, regulations, and Presidential documents, contact the Office of the Federal Register, National Archives and Records Administration, Suite 700, 800 North Capitol Street NW., Washington, DC 20001. Phone, 202-741-6000. Internet, http://www.ofr.gov. To receive public inspection and publication notifications for the "Federal Register" by email, go to www.federalregister.gov/articles/current and click on the "SUBSCRIBE" box. To receive notifications when public law numbers are assigned to laws, subscribe to the Public Laws Electronic Notification Service (PENS) at www.archives.gov/federal-register/laws/updates.html.

Modern Archives Institute

The Modern Archives Institute is undergoing a program review. All 2015 sessions are cancelled. Please check the "Modern Archives Institute" Web page for the institute's future status.

Museum Shops

Publications, document facsimiles, and document-related souvenirs are available for sale at the National Archives in Washington, DC, and each Presidential Library. Phone, 202-357-5271.

Newsletter for Researchers

"Researcher News" offers the most important and up-to-date information for conducting research at the National Archives. The newsletter is accessible online. Join the "Researcher News" mailing list by sending an email request to the address below.

NHPRC Guidelines

NHPRC guidelines are available online and from the NHPRC, National Archives and Records Administration, 700 Pennsylvania Avenue NW., Washington, DC 20408-0001. Phone, 202-357-5010.

Open Government

NARA supports the Open Government initiative by promoting the principles of collaboration, participation, and transparency.

Publications

Free brochures, pamphlets, and agency finding aids to records are available from the Research Customer Support Division (RC), National Archives and Records Administration, 700 Pennsylvania Avenue NW., Washington, DC 20408-0001. Phone, 866-325-7208. Books, catalogs, research papers, teaching aids, and other resources are also available, many of them online.

Public Programs

The National Archives—in Washington, DC, and at eight field offices: Atlanta, GA; Chicago, IL; Ft Worth/Dallas, TX; Kansas City, MO; New York, NY; Philadelphia, PA; Seattle, WA; and Waltham, MA—conduct public programs that highlight NARA's holdings of documents, films, objects, and photographs. Topics are presented in a range of public program formats: family programs, featured authors, films, lectures, panel discussions, performances, and symposia. For more information on programs in the William G. McGowan Theater, Washington, DC, and at other field sites, visit the "Locations Nationwide" Web page.

Records Management Courses

For information on records management courses and training, contact the National Records Management Training Program.

Records Management Publications

Most records management publications are available on the NARA Web site. Limited quantities of some records management publications and posters are available in hardcopy from the National Records Management Training Program, National Archives and Records Administration, 8601 Adelphi Road, College Park, MD 20740-6001.

Research Facilities

Records are available for research purposes in reading rooms at the National Archives building, 700 Pennsylvania Avenue NW., Washington, DC (phone, 202-357-5400); at the National Archives at College Park, 8601 Adelphi Road, College Park, MD (phone, 866-272-6272); and at each Presidential Library, the National Personnel Records Center, and at NARA's 13 archives locations throughout the country. Written requests for information may be sent to any of these units, or they may be addressed to the Customer Services Division, National Archives at College Park, Room 1000, 8601 Adelphi Road, College Park, MD 20740-6001. Phone, 866-272-6272.

Email: *inquire@nara.gov* **Subject**

Index

NARA's Web site features a subject index that allows visitors to look for specific topics or to browse content that aligns with their interests.

Teacher Workshops / Teaching Materials

The National Archives education specialists offer professional development programs for teachers on the use of primary source materials in the classroom. Programs like Primarily Teaching instruct teachers on how to research NARA's holdings online, to use finding aids to conduct research using original documents, and to prepare lesson plans and activities that are featured on NARA's web-based education resource, DocsTeach. For more information, contact the Education Team. Phone, 202-357-5235. For information on teacher programs at various NARA locations, visit www.archives.gov/education.

Visits / Tours

Advance reservations for entry to the National Archives Experience are available through our partners at www.recreation.gov. The convenience fee for online reservations is $1.50 per person, and admission to all of the National Archives Experience exhibits is free. Individuals and groups may reserve up to 15 spaces for the guided tour conducted by a volunteer docent (available only at 9:45 a.m., weekdays). Individuals may reserve up to 20 spaces, and groups may reserve up to 100 spaces for a timed-visit entry. Visitors with advance reservations enter through the Special Events door at Constitution Avenue and 7th Street and must be in line at the entrance at least 10 minutes prior to the start time of their visit. Security screening will be conducted upon entry. There are no refunds on any ticket orders. For more details on tours, contact the Tour Office at 202-357-5450. Advance reservations for guided tours of the National Archives at College Park, MD, are available only Monday through Thursday between 10:30 a.m. and 2:30 p.m. Group size is limited to 20 people. For more information and reservations, contact the Volunteer Program staff. Phone, 301-837-3002.

Email: *volunteercp@nara.gov*

Volunteer Service

Volunteer service opportunities are available at the National Archives building and the National Archives at College Park, MD. Volunteers conduct tours, provide information in the exhibit halls, work with staff archivists in processing historic documents, and serve as research aides in the genealogical orientation room. For more information and a volunteer application, visit the "Volunteer at the National Archives" Web page. Volunteer Program staff may be reached in Washington, DC, or College Park, MD. Phone, 202-357-5272 (DC). Fax, 202-357-5925. Phone, 301-837-3002 (MD). Fax, 301-837-3603. The Presidential Libraries and NARA's regional locations nationwide offer opportunities for volunteers. Contact the closest NARA facility for more information.

For further information, write or visit the National Archives and Records Administration, 700 Pennsylvania Avenue NW., Washington, DC 20408-0001. Phone, 202-357-5400.

NATIONAL ARCHIVES AND RECORDS ADMINISTRATION

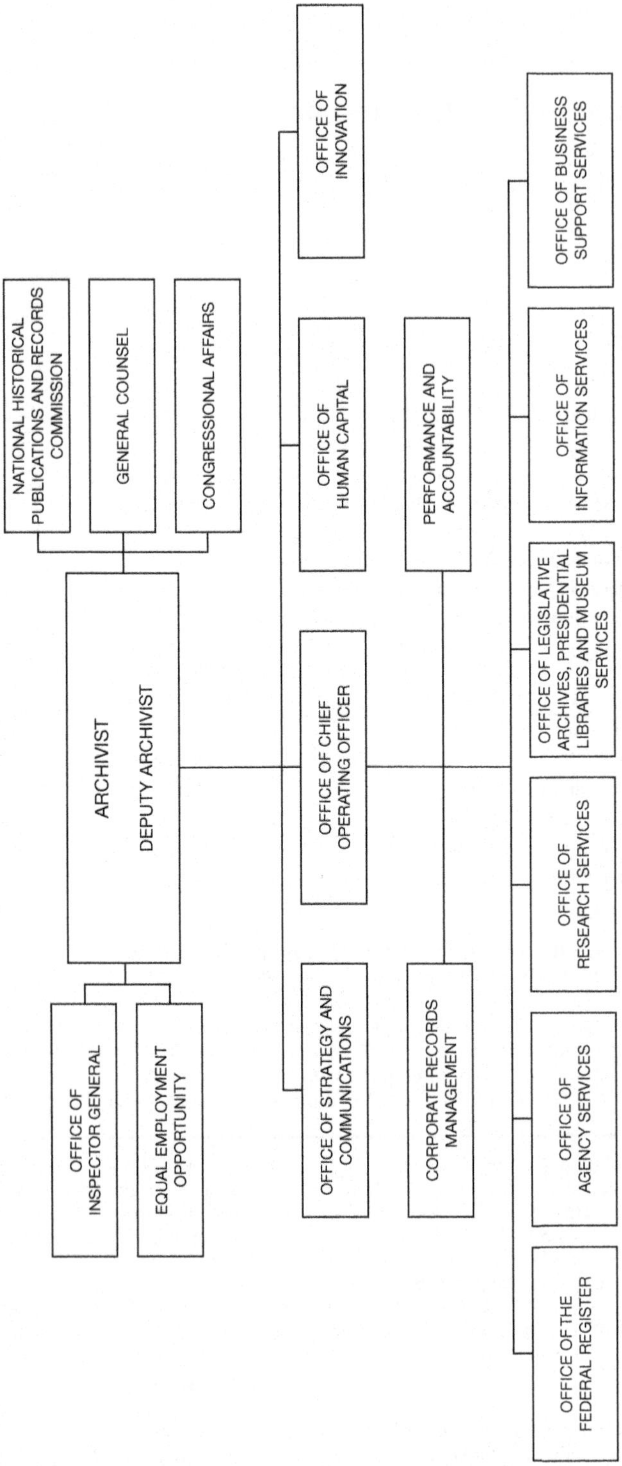

National Capital Planning Commission

401 Ninth Street NW., Suite 500, Washington, DC 20004, 202-482-7200, *http://www.ncpc.gov*

CHAIR	L. Preston Bryant, Jr.
Member	Arrington Dixon
Member	Thomas Gallas
Member	Geoffery Griffis
Member	Elizabeth White
Administrator of General Services (ex officio)	Denise Roth
Chair, Council of the District of Columbia (ex officio)	Philip Mendelson
Chair, House Committee on Oversight and Government Reform (ex officio)	Jason Chaffetz
Chair, Senate Committee on Homeland Security and Governmental Affairs (ex officio)	Ron Johnson
Mayor of the District of Columbia (ex officio)	Muriel Bowser
Secretary of Defense (ex officio)	Ashton Carter
Secretary of the Interior (ex officio)	Sarah M.R. Jewell

STAFF

EXECUTIVE DIRECTOR	Marcel C. Acosta
Chief Operating Officer	Barry S. Socks
Director, Office of Public Engagement / Secretary to the Commission	Julia A. Koster
Director, Physical Planning	Elizabeth Miller
Director, Policy and Research	Michael A. Sherman
Director, Urban Design and Plan Review	Lucy Kempf
Director, Office of Administration	Deborah B. Young
General Counsel	Anne R. Schuyler

[For the National Capital Planning Commission statement of organization, see the Code of Federal Regulations, Title 1, Part 456.2]

The National Capital Planning Commission conducts planning and development activities for Federal lands and facilities in the National Capital Region—the District of Columbia, the City of Alexandria, and all land areas within the boundaries of Montgomery, Prince George's, Fairfax, Loudoun, Prince William, and Arlington Counties.

The National Capital Planning Commission was established as a park planning agency by act of June 6, 1924, as amended (40 U.S.C. 8701 et seq.). Two years later, its role was expanded to include comprehensive planning. In 1952, the National Capital Planning Act designated the Commission as the central planning agency for the Federal and District of Columbia governments.

In 1973, the National Capital Planning Act was amended by the District of Columbia Home Rule Act, which made the mayor of the District of Columbia the chief planner for the District and gave the Commission specific authority for reviewing certain District decisions. The Commission continues to serve, however, as the central planning agency for the Federal Government in the National Capital Region.

The Commission comprises five appointed and seven ex officio members. Three citizen members, including the Chair, are appointed by the President. The mayor of the District of Columbia appoints the other two members. The Presidential appointees include one resident from Maryland, one resident from Virginia, and one from anywhere else in the United States. The two mayoral appointees must be District of Columbia residents.

Sources of Information

Business Opportunities

The Commission posts contracting opportunities on its Web site.

Employment

The Commission posts employment opportunities on its Web site.

Events

The Commission posts upcoming events that are open to the public online.

Freedom of Information Act (FOIA)

FOIA requests should be addressed to the Chief FOIA Officer, National Capital Planning Commission, 401 9th Street NW., Suite 500, Washington, DC 20004. Requests also may be submitted by fax or email. Fax, 202-482-7272

Internships

The Commission offers internships for students at accredited colleges and universities. Students with various educational backgrounds—architecture, communications, community planning, computer aided design, geography and geographic information systems, historic preservation, landscape architecture, law, urban design—are encouraged to apply.

Memorial Map

The Commission, in conjunction with the National Park Service, offers Internet users an interactive map of commemorative works in the Nation's capital.

Newsletters

Monthly newsletters are available online.

An archive of quarterly newsletters running from 1998 to 2009 is available online.

News

The Commission posts recent news releases on its Web site. Starting with the year 2001, an online archive contains releases from previous years.

Open Government

The Commission supports the Open Government initiative by promoting the principles of collaboration, participation, and transparency.

Plain Language

The Commission's writers and editors are committed to using plain language in new communications and revising confusing or unclear language in existing material. If a sentence or paragraph's clarity needs improvement, send them a note using the online form.

Publications

Recently released and frequently requested publications are accessible online.

Reports

Starting with the year 2004, the Commission's annual reports are accessible online.

Site Map

Web site visitors may use the site map to look for specific topics or to browse for content that aligns with their interests.

For further information, contact the National Capital Planning Commission, 401 Ninth Street NW., Suite 500, Washington, DC 20004. Phone, 202-482-7200. Fax, 202-482-7272.

NATIONAL CAPITAL PLANNING COMMISSION

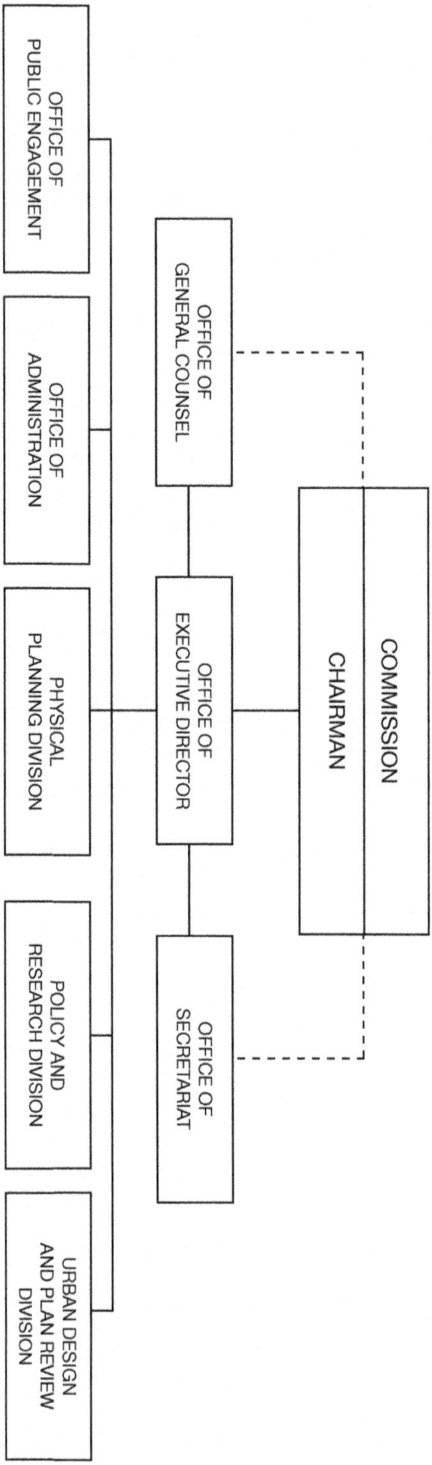

National Credit Union Administration

1775 Duke Street, Alexandria, VA 22314, 703-518-6300, *http://www.ncua.gov*

BOARD OF DIRECTORS

CHAIR	Richard T. Metsger
Member	J. Mark McWatters
Member	(vacancy)

HEADQUARTERS–Washington, DC

CHAIR	Richard T. Metsger
Member of the Board	J. Mark McWatters
Chief of Staff	Michael P. Radway
OFFICE HEADS	
Chief Economist	Ralph Monaco
Chief Financial Officer	Rendell L. Jones
Chief Information Officer	Edward Dorris
Director, Consumer Protection	Gail Laster
Director, Continuity and Security Management	Joy Miller
Director, Examination and Insurance	Larry Fazio
Director, Human Resources	Cheryl Eyre
Director, Minority and Women Inclusion	Monica Davy
Director, National Examinations and Supervision	Scott Hunt
Director, Public and Congressional Affairs	Todd M. Harper
Director, Small Credit Union Initiatives	Martha Ninichuk, Acting
Executive Director	Mark A. Treichel
General Counsel	Michael McKenna
Inspector General	James W. Hagen

[For the National Credit Union Administration statement of organization, see the Code of Federal Regulations, Title 12, Part 720]

The National Credit Union Administration provides a trustworthy credit union system that builds confidence in the Nation's system of cooperative credit.

The National Credit Union Administration (NCUA) was established by act of March 10, 1970 (12 U.S.C. 1752), and reorganized by act of November 10, 1978 (12 U.S.C. 226), as an independent agency in the executive branch of the Federal Government. It regulates and insures all Federal credit unions and insures State-chartered credit unions that apply and qualify for share insurance.

The Administration's Board comprises three members whom the President appoints and the Senate must confirm. Members serve staggered terms of 6 years, and no more than two of them can belong to the same political party.

Activities

Chartering

The NCUA grants Federal credit union charters to groups sharing a common bond of occupation or association or to groups within a well-defined neighborhood, community, or rural district. Before granting a Federal charter, the NCUA conducts a preliminary investigation to determine if certain standards are met.

Examinations

The NCUA regularly examines Federal credit unions to assess their solvency, to ensure their compliance with laws and regulations, and to assist credit union management and improve operations.

For further information, contact the Director, Office of Examination and Insurance. Phone, 703-518-6360.

Share Insurance

The act of October 19, 1970 (12 U.S.C. 1781 et seq.), provides for a program of share insurance, in which participation is mandatory for Federal credit unions. In some States, State-chartered credit unions must participate in the share insurance program. In other States, State-chartered credit unions may opt to participate in the insurance program. The National Credit Union Share Insurance Fund requires each participating credit union to place and maintain a 1-percent deposit of its insured savings with the Fund. Credit union members' accounts are insured up to $250,000.

Supervision

Supervisory activities are carried out through regular examiner contacts and by periodic policy and regulatory releases from the Administration. The NCUA also identifies emerging problems and monitors operations between examinations.

NCUA central offices include examination and supervision programs. Five regional offices manage the oversight of credit unions.

Sources of Information

Business Opportunities

The NCUA selects vendors who offer the best value to help the agency meet its mission. The Division of Procurement and Facilities Management is responsible for procuring goods and services. Phone, 703-518-6410. Fax, 703-518-6662.

Closed Credit Unions

The Asset Management and Assistance Center conducts credit union liquidations and performs asset management and recovery. It also participates in the operational phases of a failed credit union's conservatorship and assists with record reconstruction. The Center posts up-to-date information on closed, conserved, liquidated, and merged credit unions on the NCUA Web site.??

Consumer Assistance

For answers to questions on credit union insurance and other consumer matters or to submit a complaint, contact the NCUA Consumer Assistance Center on weekdays, 8 a.m.–5 p.m., eastern standard time. After regular business hours, callers may leave a recorded message. Phone, 800-755-1030.

Employment

Career information—including information on available positions, benefits, equal employment opportunity, pay structure, and the onboarding process—is available on the NCUA Web site. Career information is also available from the Office of Human Resources, National Credit Union Administration, 1775 Duke Street, Alexandria, VA 22314-3428.

The NCUA ranks among the top midsize Government agencies in the Best Places To Work Agency Rankings.

Federally Insured Credit Unions

A directory of federally insured credit unions that includes addresses, asset levels, and membership numbers is available online and for review at central and regional offices. Copies of the directory are available for a nominal fee: Write NCUA, Publications, 1775 Duke Street, Alexandria, VA 22314-3428. Phone, 703-518-6340.

Financial Literacy

The NCUA offers financial literacy and educational resources to help consumers increase their savings and achieve their financial goals.

Fraud Hotline

The NCUA operates a hotline for reporting illegal or suspicious activity associated with credit union employees, members, or officials in federally insured credit unions. Phone, 800-827-9650 or 703-518-6550 (Washington, DC, area).

Freedom of Information Act (FOIA)

The act allows any person to obtain records of a Federal agency. A record may be withheld only if it carries an exemption under the FOIA. The NCUA operates a FOIA requester service center to answer questions related to the FOIA process, to provide information on the status of a request, and to answer questions about documents that a requester has received from the NCUA. Phone, 703-518-6540. Fax, 703-518-6569.

Glossary

The NCUA maintains a glossary of the common terms associated with the corporate system resolution costs. ?

The NCUA maintains a glossary of the common terms associated with the share insurance coverage.

Learning Center

The Small Credit Union Learning Center, once it is completed, will provide a comprehensive training program with tracks for the basic, intermediate and advanced levels. Phone, 703-518-6610.

Locate a Credit Union

The NCUA Web site features a credit union locator tool, which complements the research a credit union tool. The locator provides a graphical map of credit unions based on an address search. The locator also allows the user to view a credit union's contact information, the services that it offers, and directions to it.

Newsroom

The NCUA posts annual reports, events, press releases, speeches, testimonies, and its newsletter "The NCUA Report" online.

The NCUA tweets announcements, news items, and other information on Twitter.

The NCUA posts educational videos, quarterly economic updates, and speeches on YouTube.

Open Government

NCUA supports the Open Government initiative by promoting the principles of collaboration, participation, and transparency. The NCUA regards openness, in terms of budget, policy, and operations, as essential to fulfilling its statutory mission and maintaining public trust.

Plain Language

The Plain Writing Act of 2010 promotes clear Government communication "to improve the effectiveness and accountability of Federal agencies to the public." Members of the public are welcome to comment on the NCUA's compliance with the act and to make suggestions for improving communication. Contact the NCUA via email if content in documents or on web pages is difficult to understand.

Proposed Regulations

The NCUA encourages the public to submit a comment on its proposed rules. Fax, 703-518-6319.

Publications

To order publications, contact the Office of the Chief Financial Officer. Payment by check, credit card, or money order is acceptable and prepayment is required. Phone, 703-518-6340.

Manuals and guides are available online to facilitate compliance with NCUA rules and regulations and with those from other agencies. The manuals and guides are not definitive and should be used in conjunction with other supervisory guidance and information provided by the NCUA and other Federal financial services regulators.

Research a Credit Union

The NCUA Web site features a credit union research tool, which complements the credit union locator. The research tool is text-based, and it can find a credit union and its profile by using a variety of search parameters.

Share Insurance Estimator

The NCUA Web site features a share insurance estimator to help consumers, credit unions, and their members know how NCUA share insurance rules apply to member share accounts—what is insured and what portion, if any, exceeds coverage limits.

Site Map

The Web site map allows visitors to look for specific topics or to browse for content that aligns with their interests.

Starting a Federal Credit Union

Groups interested in forming a Federal credit union may obtain free information from the appropriate regional office. Information is also available on the "How to Start a Credit Union" Web page.

For further information, contact the Office of Public and Congressional Affairs, National Credit Union Administration, 1775 Duke Street, Alexandria, VA 22314-3428. Phone, 703-518-6330.

National Foundation on the Arts and the Humanities

National Endowment for the Arts

400 7th Street SW., Washington, DC 20506, 202-682-5400, TDD, 202-682-5496, *http://www.arts.gov*

CHAIR	R. Jane Chu
Senior Deputy Chair	(vacancy)
Chief Information Officer	Carolyn Sanders
Chief of Staff	Mike Griffin
Deputy Chair, Management and Budget	Winona Varnon
Director, Accessibility	Beth Bienvenu
Director, Administrative Services	Kathy Daum
Director, Artist Communities and Presenting and Multidisciplinary Works / International Activities Coordinator	Michael Orlove
Director, Arts Education	Ayanna N. Hudson
Director, Budget	John Sotelo
Director, Civil Rights and Equal Employment Opportunity	Mike Griffin
Director, Dance	Douglas Sonntag
Director, Design Programs / Visual Arts Division Team Leader	Jason Schupbach
Director, Finance	Heidi Ren
Director, Folk and Traditional Arts	Clifford Murphy
Director, Grants and Contracts	Nicki Jacobs
Director, Guidelines and Panel Operations	Jillian L. Miller
Director, Human Resources	Craig M. McCord, Sr.
Director, Literature	Amy Stolls
Director, Local Arts Agencies and Challenge America	Michael Killoren
Director, Media Arts	Jax Deluca
Director, Museums, Visual Arts, and Indemnity	Wendy Clark
Director, Music and Opera	Ann Meier Baker
Director, Public Affairs	Jessamyn Sarmiento

Director, Research and Analysis	Sunil Iyengar
Director, State and Regional Partnerships	Laura Scanlan
Director, Theater and Musical Theater	Greg Reiner
Federal Partnerships Coordinator	Tony Tighe
General Counsel	India Pinkney
Inspector General	Ronald Stith

The National Endowment for the Arts supports artistic excellence and promotes creativity and innovation to benefit individuals and communities.

Through its grants and programs, the Arts Endowment brings art to all 50 States and six U.S. jurisdictions, including rural areas, inner cities, and military bases. The Arts Endowment awards competitive matching grants to nonprofit organizations, to units of State or local government, and to federally recognized tribal communities or tribes for projects, programs, or activities in the fields of artist communities, arts education, dance, design, folk and traditional arts, literature, local arts agencies, media arts, museums, music, musical theater, opera, presenting, theater, and visual arts. It also awards competitive, nonmatching individual fellowships in literature and honorary fellowships in jazz, folk and traditional arts, and opera. Forty percent of the Arts Endowment's grant funds go to the 56 State and jurisdictional arts agencies and their regional arts organizations in support of arts projects in thousands of communities nationwide.

Sources of Information

Employment

Job announcements are posted online.

Grants

Application forms and guidelines and listings of grants recently made to individuals and organizations are accessible online.

Podcasts

Podcasts feature actors, authors, composers, musicians, playwrights, poets, and other artists and professionals who support and strengthen the arts.

Publications

Publications, including annual reports and "NEA Arts" magazine, are available online.

For further information, contact the Public Affairs Office, National Endowment for the Arts, 400 7th Street SW., Washington, DC 20506-0001. Phone, 202-682-5400. TDD, 202-682-5496.

National Endowment for the Humanities

400 7th Street SW., Washington, DC 20506, 202-606-8400, 800-634-1121, *http://www.neh.gov* | Email: *info@neh.gov*

CHAIR	William D. Adams
Deputy Chair	Peggy Plympton
Assistant Chair, Partnership and Strategic Initiatives	Evagren O. Caldera
Assistant Chair, Planning and Operations	Jeffrey Thomas
Assistant Chair, Programs	Adam Wolfson
Chief Information Officer	Brett Bobley
Chief of Staff	Courtney Chapin
General Counsel	Michael McDonald
Inspector General	Laura M.H. Davis

The National Endowment for the Humanities supports research, education, preservation, and public programs in the humanities.

According to the agency's authorizing legislation, the term "humanities" includes, but is not limited to, the study of the following: language, both modern and classical; linguistics; literature; history; jurisprudence; philosophy; archeology; comparative religion; ethics; the history, criticism, and theory of the arts; and those aspects of the social sciences that employ historical or philosophical approaches.

To increase understanding and appreciation of the humanities, the Endowment makes grants to individuals, as well as to groups and institutions: colleges, libraries, museums, nonprofit private groups, public television stations and agencies, schools, and universities.

Challenge Grants

The Office of Challenge Grants offers matching funds to help nonprofit institutions develop new sources of long-term support for educational, scholarly, preservation, and public programs in the humanities.

For further information, call 202-606-8309.

Digital Humanities

The Office of Digital Humanities supports projects that use digital technology or study how it affects education, preservation, public programming, and research in the humanities.

For further information, call 202-606-8401.

Education Programs

The Division of Education Programs strengthens sustained, thoughtful study of the humanities at all educational levels. It makes grants to educational institutions and gives fellowships to teachers and scholars.

For further information, call 202-606-8500.

Federal/State Partnership

Humanities committees in each of the 50 States, the District of Columbia, Puerto Rico, the Virgin and Northern Mariana Islands, Guam, and American Samoa receive grants from the Endowment. These committees then make grants to humanities programs at the local level.

For further information, call 202-606-8254.

Preservation and Access

The Division of Preservation and Access supports creating, preserving, and increasing the availability of resources that are important for research, education, and public programming in the humanities.

For further information, call 202-606-8570.

Public Programs

The Division of Public Programs supports institutions and organizations that develop and present humanities programming for general audiences. Its activities center on the Endowment's mandate "to increase public understanding of the humanities."

For further information, call 202-606-8268.

Research Programs

The Division of Research Programs promotes original research in the humanities. It provides grants for significant research projects.

For further information, call 202-606-8389.

Sources of Information

Employment

The National Endowment for the Humanities posts job opportunities on USAJobs, the Federal Government's official source for Federal job listings and employment opportunity information.

Grants

Information on managing a grant, the application review process, and other topics is available on the "NEH Grants" Web page.

Publications

The Endowment's in-house, quarterly magazine "HUMANITIES" is available by subscription from the U.S. Government Publishing Office, P.O. Box 979050, St. Louis, MO 63197–9000. Phone, 202-512-1800.

For further information, contact the Office of Communications, National Endowment for the Humanities, 400 7th Street SW., Washington, DC 20506. Phone, 202-606-8400 or 800-634-1121. TDD, 202-606-8282 or 866-372-2930.

NATIONAL ENDOWMENT FOR THE HUMANITIES

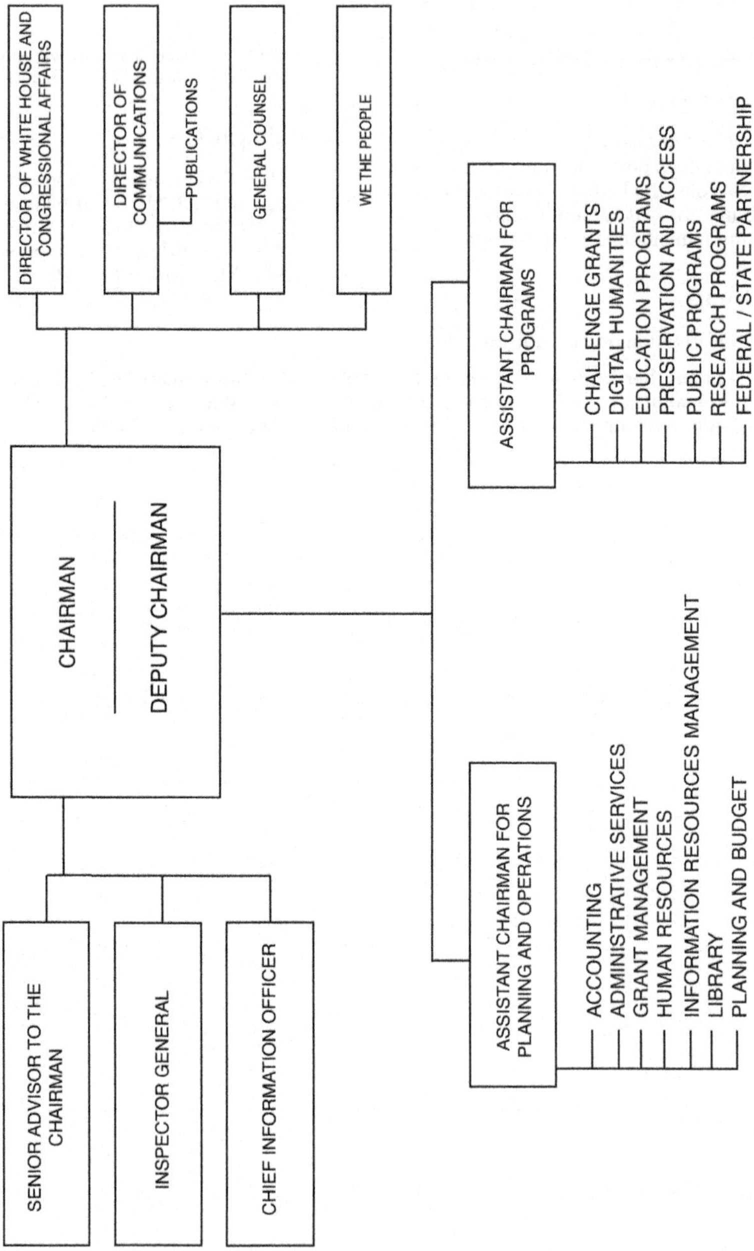

Institute of Museum and Library Services

955 L'Enfant Plaza North SW., Suite 4000, Washington, DC 20024-2135, 202-653-4657, *http://www.imls.gov* | Email: *imlsinfo@imls.gov*

DIRECTOR	Kathryn K. Matthew
Deputy Director for Library Services	Maura Marx
Deputy Director for Museum Services	Paula Gangopadhyay
Associate Deputy Director for Library Services	Robin Dale
Chief Financial Officer	Chris Catignani
Chief Information Officer	Stephanie Burwell
Chief Operating Officer	Michael D. Jerger
Deputy Director of Digital and Information Strategy	Ammie Farraj Feijoo
Director for Grants Administration	Mary E. Kennelly
Director of Communications and Government Affairs	Janelle Brevard
General Counsel	Nancy E. Weiss
Senior Museum Advisor	Christopher J. Reich

The Institute of Museum and Library Services helps libraries and museums enhance cultural and civic engagement, embrace innovation, and further lifelong learning.

The Institute of Museum and Library Services (IMLS) was established within the National Foundation on the Arts and the Humanities by the Museum and Library Services Act of September 30, 1996 (110 Stat. 3009), which amended the Museum Services Act (20 U.S.C. 961 et seq.). The Institute combines the administration of Federal museum programs, which the Institute of Museum Services formerly managed, and Federal library programs, which the Department of Education formerly managed. The Institute's Director, whom the President appoints with the advice and consent of the Senate, is authorized to make grants to museums and libraries. The Director receives policy advice on museum and library programs from the National Museum and Library Services Board. Its 20 voting members are appointed by the President; its three nonvoting members include the Director, Deputy Director for Museum Services, and Deputy Director for Library Services.

The IMLS is the primary source of Federal support for the Nation's 35,000 museums and 123,000 libraries. Its grant making, policy development, and research help museums and libraries offer services that make people and their communities prosper. The IMLS awards grants to art, children's, general, history, natural history, science, and technology museums, as well as to aquariums, arboretums, botanical gardens, nature centers, planetariums, zoos, and historic houses. It also awards grants to academic, public, research, school, and special libraries. IMLS grants improve electronic sharing of information and expand public access to information and services.

African American History and Culture Museum Grants

The IMLS awards these grants at two funding levels to improve care of collections, develop professional management, and provide internship and fellowship opportunities.

Laura Bush 21st Century Librarian Program

This program supports recruitment and education of library students, continuing education for those already working in the profession, and new programs and curricula.

Museum Assessment Program

The IMLS supports the cost of this program through a cooperative agreement with the American Alliance of Museums. The program helps museums strengthen operations, plan for the future, and meet national standards through self-study and a site visit from a peer reviewer.

Museums for America

The IMLS awards grants at two funding levels to help museums expand their role as lifelong learning resources, increase the vital contributions they make to livable communities, and become better stewards of the Nation's collections.

National Arts and Humanities Youth Program Awards

This is a project of the President's Committee on the Arts and the Humanities in partnership with the IMLS and the National Endowments for the Arts and for the Humanities. These awards acknowledge museums and libraries for their afterschool and out-of-school arts and humanities programs for young Americans.

National Leadership Grants for Libraries

These grants help library and archive professionals address the challenges and needs of their fields. Projects supported by these grants stimulate research, develop new tools, and produce innovative alliances, models, practices, and services that broadly affect the library and archival fields.

National Leadership Grants for Museums

These grants help museum professionals address the challenges and needs of their field. Projects supported by these grants promote innovation and collaboration and typically produce results that broadly affect the museum field.

National Medal for Museum and Library Service

This award acknowledges institutions for providing exceptional and meaningful public service in their communities.

Native American and Native Hawaiian Museum Services Program

These grants to federally recognized tribes and organizations that represent and serve Native Hawaiians help sustain indigenous culture, heritage, and knowledge through improved museum services.

Native American Library Services: Basic Grants and the Education/Assessment Option

These noncompetitive grants to federally recognized tribes help them purchase library materials, acquire computers and provide Internet connectivity, and fund salaries. The Education/Assessment option is supplemental to the basic grants and also noncompetitive. It funds library staff participation in continuing education courses, training workshops, and conferences. It also allows libraries to hire a consultant for an onsite professional assessment.

Native American Library Services: Enhancement Grants

These grants to federally recognized tribes expand services for access to information, learning, and partnerships.

Native Hawaiian Library Services

This program supports grants that implement new library services or enhance existing ones.

Sparks! Ignition Grants for Libraries

These grants promote exploration and expansion of the frontiers of archival and library practices and services.

Sparks! Ignition Grants for Museums

These grants promote exploration and expansion of the frontiers of museum practices and services.

State Program Grants

The Grants to States program is the largest Federal source of funding to support library services in the United States. The IMLS uses a population-based formula to distribute annual grants among the State

Library Administrative Agencies—official agencies charged by law with the extension and development of library services. Each year, thousands of Grants to States projects promote the priorities and assist the purposes of the Library Services and Technology Act.

Sources of Information

Employment

The IMLS offers a unique opportunity to work with the Nation's libraries and museums at the national level and in coordination with State and local organizations. The IMLS posts employment and internship opportunities on its Web site.

Freedom of Information Act (FOIA)

An online guide answers frequently asked FOIA-related questions.

Grants

Search tools are available online to search for available grants and awarded grants.

News

The IMLS posts news releases and project profiles online, as well as its "UpNext" blog and "Primary Source" monthly newsletter.

Open Government

The IMLS supports the Governmentwide initiative to promote openness in the work of Federal agencies. It posts datasets on Data.gov and maintains a data catalog that makes IMLS data accessible to developers, researchers, and to the general public.

Publications

Publications are accessible in Portable Document Format (PDF) on the "Publications List" Web page.

Videos

A collection of IMLS videos is available online.

For further information, contact the Office of Communications and Government Affairs, Institute of Museum and Library Services, 955 L'Enfant Plaza North SW., Suite 4000, Washington, DC 20024. Phone, 202-653-4757.

National Labor Relations Board

1015 Half Street SE., Washington, DC 20570, 202-273-1000, TDD, 202-273-4300, *http://www.nlrb.gov*

THE BOARD	
CHAIR	Mark G. Pearce
Member	Kent Y. Hirozawa
Member	Lauren McFerran
Member	Philip A. Miscimarra
Member	(vacancy)
THE GENERAL COUNSEL	
General Counsel	Richard F. Griffin, Jr.
Deputy General Counsel	Jennifer Abruzzo
Associate General Counsel, Division of Advice	Barry J. Kearney
Associate General Counsel, Division of Enforcement Litigation	John H. Ferguson
Associate General Counsel, Division of Legal Counsel	Barbara O'Neill
Associate General Counsel, Division of Operations-Management	Anne G. Purcell
Chief Financial Officer	Mehul Parekh
Chief Information Officer	Prem Aburvasamy
Chief Judge, Division of Judges	Robert A. Giannasi

Director, Division of Administration	Lasharn Hamilton
Director, Office of Congressional and Public Affairs	Celine McNicholas
Director, Office of Equal Employment Opportunity	Brenda V. Harris
Director, Office of Representation Appeals	Beverly Oyama, Acting
Executive Secretary	Gary W. Shinners
Inspector General	David P. Berry
Solicitor	William B. Cowen

[For the National Labor Relations Board statement of organization, see the Federal Register of June 14, 1979, 44 FR 34215]

The National Labor Relations Board remedies unfair labor practices and safeguards employees' rights to organize and to determine whether to have unions as their bargaining representative.

The National Labor Relations Board (NLRB) is an independent agency created by Congress to administer the National Labor Relations Act of 1935 (Wagner Act; 29 U.S.C. 167). The Board is authorized to designate appropriate units for collective bargaining and to conduct secret ballot elections to determine whether employees desire representation by a labor organization.

Activities

In addition to preventing and remedying unfair labor practices, the NLRB conducts secret ballot elections among employees in appropriate collective-bargaining units to determine whether or not they desire to be represented by a labor organization in bargaining with employers over wages, hours, and working conditions. It also conducts secret ballot elections among employees who have been covered by a union-security agreement to determine whether or not they wish to revoke their union's authority to make such agreements. In jurisdictional disputes between two or more unions, the Board determines which competing group of workers is entitled to perform the work involved.

The regional directors and their staffs process representation, unfair labor practice, and jurisdictional dispute cases. They issue complaints in unfair labor practice cases, seek settlement of unfair labor practice charges, obtain compliance with Board orders and court judgments, and petition district courts for injunctions to prevent or remedy unfair labor practices. The regional directors conduct hearings in representation cases, hold elections pursuant to the agreement of the parties or the decisionmaking authority delegated to them by the Board or pursuant to Board directions, and issue certifications of representatives when unions win or certify the results when they lose employee elections. The regional directors process petitions for bargaining unit clarification, for amendment of certification, and for rescission of a labor organization's authority to make a union-shop agreement. They also conduct national emergency employee referendums.

Administrative law judges conduct hearings in unfair labor practice cases, make findings of fact and conclusions of law, and recommend remedies for violations found. Their decisions can be appealed to the Board for a final agency determination. The Board's decisions are subject to review in the U.S. courts of appeals.

Sources of Information

Business Opportunities

Information is available online to assist businesses that seek to sell their products and services to the NLRB. Information is also available from the agency's Acquisitions Management Branch. Phone, 202-273-4047.

Electronic Filing

Parties or other persons may use the e-filing program to file selected documents in unfair labor practice and representation cases with the NLRB's Office of Executive Secretary, the Division of Judges, the General Counsel's Office of Appeals, and regional, subregional, and resident offices.

Electronic Mail Subscriptions

The NLRB uses email subscriptions to disseminate various types of information: administrative law judge decisions, appellate court branch briefs and motions, board decisions, general counsel memos, news releases, operations-management memos, personnel announcements, regional election decisions, regional news, social media feeds, and a weekly summary of decisions.

Employment

The Board appoints administrative law judges from a register established by the Office of Personnel Management. The Agency hires attorneys for all its offices, field examiners for its field offices, and administrative personnel for its Washington and field offices.

Freedom of Information Act (FOIA)

The NLRB makes available instructions online for submitting FOIA requests. Descriptions of the record types that the NLRB maintains and links to records that are accessible elsewhere on the Internet are also available on the NLRB Web site.

An e-FOIA request form is available on the NLRB Web site.

Inspector General Hotline

Violations of laws and regulations relating to NLRB programs may be reported to the Inspector General by email or phone or by using the online form. Phone, 800-736-2983.

Internships

At its Washington, DC, headquarters and its field offices, the NLRB offers opportunities, internships and student positions, for law and nonlegal students.

Open Government

The NLRB supports the Open Government initiative by incorporating the principles of collaboration, participation, and transparency in its plans for agency information and systems.

Publications

Case documents and agency publications are available on the NLRB's Web site. Or, visit the NLRB's headquarters in Washington, DC, or one of its field offices to inspect case documents and read agency publications. NLRB offices offer free informational leaflets in limited quantities.

Regional Offices

Contact information for NLRB regional, subregional, and resident offices is available on the "Regional Offices" Web pages.

Site Map

NLRB Web site visitors may use the site map to look for specific topics or to browse for content that aligns with their interests.

Speakers

To provide a better understanding of the National Labor Relations Act and NLRB policies, procedures, and services, NLRB experts are available to speak before labor and civic organizations, educational institutions, management organizations, bar associations, and other similar groups. Requests for speakers or panelists may be made online by using the online request form.

For further information, contact the Office of Congressional and Public Affairs, National Labor Relations Board, 1015 Half Street SE., Washington, DC 20570. Phone, 202-273-1991.

NATIONAL LABOR RELATIONS BOARD

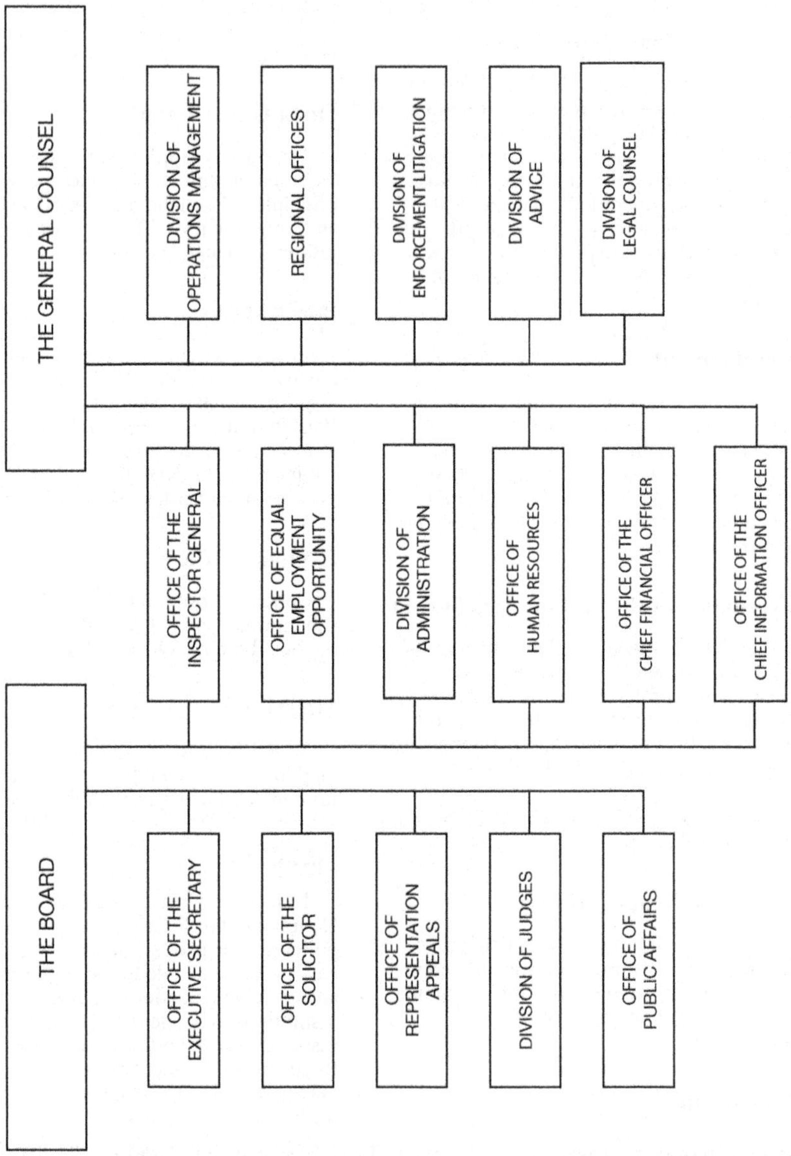

National Mediation Board

1301 K Street NW., Suite 250 East, Washington, DC 20005, 202-692-5000, *http://www.nmb.gov*

BOARD MEMBERS	
CHAIR	Linda A. Puchala
Member	Nicholas C. Geale
Member	Harry R. Hoglander
EXECUTIVE DIRECTORS	
Chief of Staff	Daniel Rainey
General Counsel, Office of Legal Affairs	Mary L. Johnson
Assistant Chief of Staff, Administration	Samantha T. Jones
Director, Arbitration Services	Roland Watkins
Deputy Chief of Staff, Mediation	Michael Kelliher

The National Mediation Board facilitates labor-management relations within the railroad and airline industries.

The National Mediation Board (NMB) is an independent agency established by the 1934 amendments to the Railway Labor Act of 1926 (45 U.S.C. 151-158, 160-162, 1181-1188). The Board comprises three members whom the President appoints and the Senate confirms. The Board designates a Chair on a yearly basis.

NMB dispute-resolution processes are designed to resolve disputes over the negotiation of new or revised collective bargaining agreements and the interpretation or application of existing agreements. The Board also effectuates employee rights of self-organization where a representation dispute exists.

Activities

Mediation and Alternative Dispute Resolution

Following receipt of an application for mediation, the NMB assigns a mediator to assist the parties in reaching an agreement. The NMB is obligated to use its best efforts to bring about a peaceful resolution to the dispute. If such efforts do not settle the dispute, the NMB advises the parties and offers interest arbitration as an alternative approach to resolve the remaining issues. If either party rejects this offer, the NMB releases the parties from formal mediation. This release triggers a 30-day cooling off period. During this period, the NMB continues to work with the parties to achieve a consensual resolution. If, however, an agreement is not reached by the end of the 30-day period, the parties are free to exercise lawful self-help, such as carrier-imposed working conditions or a strike by the union or organization.

In addition to traditional mediation services, the NMB also provides voluntary Alternative Dispute Resolution (ADR) services. ADR services include facilitation, training, grievance mediation, and an online dispute resolution component, which applies technology to the dispute resolution process. The purpose of the ADR program is to assist the parties in learning and applying more effective, less confrontational methods for resolving their disputes and to help them resolve more of them without outside intervention.

Presidential Emergency Board

If the NMB determines that a dispute threatens to deprive substantially any section of the country of essential transportation service, it notifies the President. The President, at his discretion, may establish a Presidential Emergency Board (PEB) to investigate and report back within 30 days. After the PEB has been created and for 30 days after it has made its report to the President, neither party to the dispute may exercise self-help.

There are also special emergency procedures for unresolved disputes affecting publicly funded and operated commuter railroads and their employees. If the mediation procedures are exhausted, the parties to the dispute or the Governor of any State where the railroad operates may request that the President establish a PEB. The President is required to establish such a board if requested. If no settlement is reached within 60 days following the creation of the PEB, the NMB is required to conduct a public hearing on the dispute. If there is no settlement within 120 days after the creation of the PEB, either party or the Governor of any affected state may request a second, final-offer PEB. No self-help is permitted pending the exhaustion of these emergency procedures.

Representation

When a labor organization or individual files an application with the NMB to represent employees, the Agency assigns an investigator to conduct a representation investigation. Should the applicant meet the requirements, the NMB continues the investigation, usually with a secret telephone or Internet election. The NMB is responsible for ensuring that the requirements for a fair election process have been maintained. If the employees vote to be represented, the NMB issues a certification that commences the carrier's statutory duty to bargain with the certified representative.

Arbitration

The NMB provides both grievance arbitration and interest arbitration. Grievance arbitration is a process for resolving disputes regarding the interpretation or application of an existing collective bargaining agreement. Grievances must be handled through grievance arbitration if not otherwise resolved, and they cannot be used by the parties to trigger self-help actions. The NMB has significant administrative responsibilities for grievance arbitration in the railroad industry, which includes those before the National Railroad Adjustment Board (NRAB), as well as the two types of arbitration panels established by the labor-management parties at each railroad: public law boards (PLBs) and special boards of adjustment (SBAs). Grievance arbitration in the airline industry is accomplished at the various system boards of adjustment created jointly by labor and management at the parties' expense. The NMB furnishes panels of prospective arbitrators for the parties' selection in both the airline and railroad industries. The NMB also pays the salary and travel expenses of the arbitrators for railroad arbitration proceedings. Grievance arbitration decisions are final and binding with very limited grounds for judicial review.

Interest arbitration is a process to establish the terms of a new or modified collective bargaining agreement through arbitration rather than through negotiations. Unlike grievance arbitration, its use is not statutorily required. The NMB offers the parties the opportunity to use binding interest arbitration when the agency has determined that further mediation efforts will not be successful. In addition, the parties may directly agree to resolve their collective bargaining dispute or portions of their dispute through interest arbitration. The NMB generally provides the parties with panels of potential arbitrators from which they choose an individual to resolve their dispute. In some instances, however, the parties agree to allow the NMB to appoint an arbitrator directly. Interest arbitration decisions are final and binding with very narrow grounds for judicial appeal.

Sources of Information

Employment

Job openings are posted online.

Knowledge Store

The Knowledge Store contains over 100,000 documents—including arbitration awards, representation decisions, annual reports, PEB reports, industry contracts, and union constitutions and bylaws—in an easily searchable format.

Open Government

The NMB supports the Open Government initiative, which requires Federal executive departments and agencies to implement principles of collaboration, participation, and transparency.

Publications

The annual reports of the National Mediation Board are available on its "NMB Documents On-Line" Web page and in the Knowledge Store.

Virtual Reading Room

Copies of collective bargaining agreements between labor and management of various rail and air carriers and NMB Determinations dating from October 1, 1998, and some even earlier, are available in the Knowledge Store.

For further information, contact the Public Information Officer, National Mediation Board, Suite 250 East, 1301 K Street NW., Washington, DC 20005-7011. Phone, 202-692-5050.

NATIONAL MEDIATION BOARD

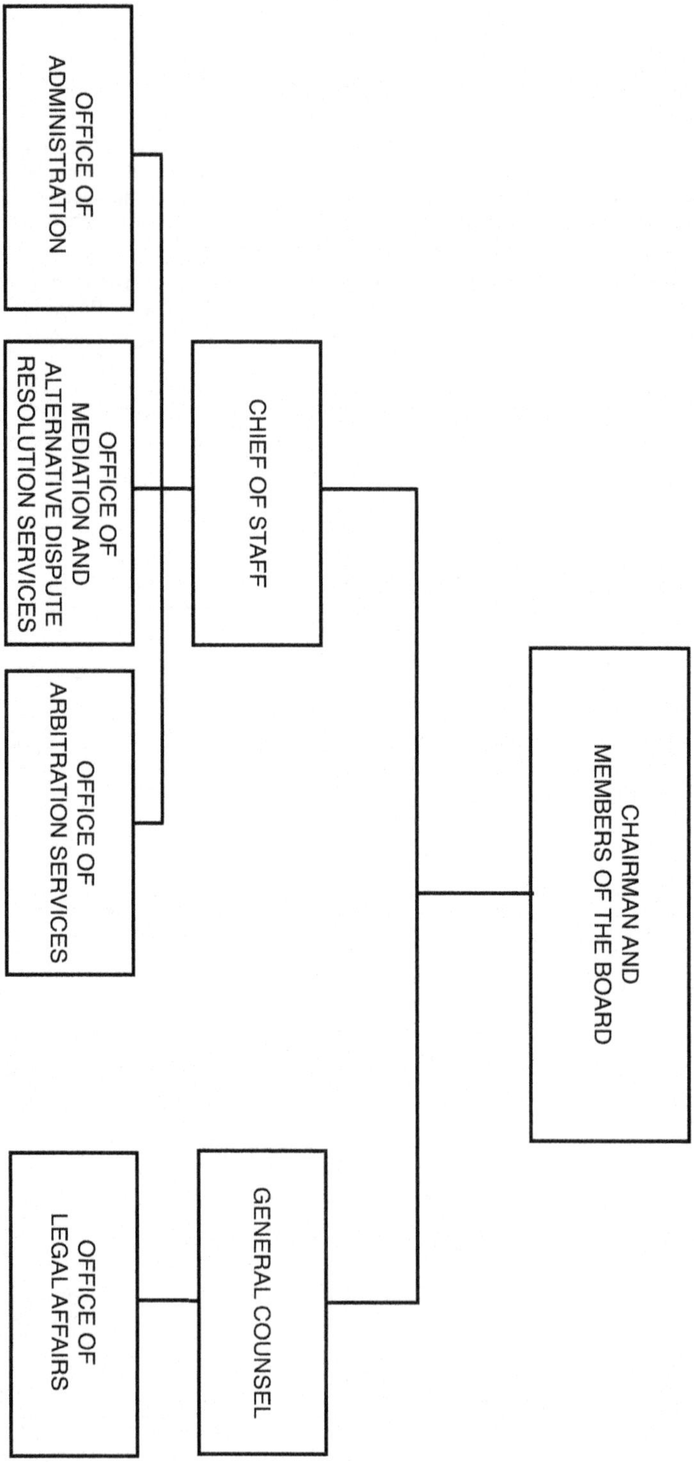

National Railroad Passenger Corporation (AMTRAK)

60 Massachusetts Avenue NE., Washington, DC 20002, 202-906-3000, *http://www.amtrak.com*

BOARD OF DIRECTORS

CHAIR	Anthony R. Coscia
Vice Chair	Jeffrey R. Moreland
Member	Christopher R. Beall
Member	Yvonne B. Burke
Member	Thomas C. Carper
Member	Albert DiClemente
Member	Derek Kan
Member	(vacancy)
Amtrak President / Amtrak Chief Executive Officer (ex officio)	Joseph H. Boardman
Secretary of Transportation (ex officio)	Anthony R. Foxx

OFFICERS

PRESIDENT / CHIEF EXECUTIVE OFFICER	Joseph H. Boardman
Executive Vice President / General Counsel / Corporate Secretary	Eleanor D. Acheson
Executive Vice President / Chief Financial Officer	Gerald Sokol, Jr.
Executive Vice President / Chief Human Capital Officer	Alex B. Melnkovic
Executive Vice President / Chief Information Officer	Jason Molfetas
Executive Vice President / Chief Marketing and Sales Officer	Matthew H. Hardison
Executive Vice President / Chief Northeast Corridor Business Development Officer	Stephen J. Gardner
Executive Vice President / Chief Operations Officer	Donald J. Stadtler
Inspector General	Thomas Howard
Senior Vice President / Chief of Police	Polly Hanson
Senior Vice President, Corporate Research and Strategy	Jeffrey K. Clements
Senior Vice President / Chief Government Affairs and Corporate Communications Officer	Joseph H. McHugh
Senior Vice President, Strategic Rail Initiatives and Strategic Fleet Initiatives	Mark Yachmetz
Vice President, Emergency Management and Corporate Security	Susan K. Reinertson

[For the National Railroad Passenger Corporation statement of organization, see the Code of Federal Regulations, Title 49, Part 700]

The National Railroad Passenger Corporation provides intercity rail passenger service in the United States.

The National Railroad Passenger Corporation (Amtrak) was created by the Rail Passenger Service Act of 1970, as amended (49 U.S.C. 241), and was incorporated under the laws of the District of Columbia. By developing, operating, and improving U.S. intercity rail passenger service, Amtrak provides a balanced nationwide transportation system.

Amtrak operates approximately 300 trains per day, serving over 500 stations in 46 States, over a system of 22,000 route miles. Of this route system, Amtrak owns about 530 route miles in the Northeast and several other small track segments elsewhere in the country.

Amtrak owns or leases its stations and owns its repair and maintenance facilities. The Corporation employs a total workforce of approximately 20,000 and provides all reservation, station, and onboard service staffs, as well as train and engine operating crews. Outside the Northeast Corridor, Amtrak may enter into contracts with privately or publicly owned railroads to operate on their track. These railroads are responsible for the condition of the roadbed and for coordinating the flow of traffic.

In fiscal year 2015, Amtrak transported nearly 31 million people, 85,000 passengers traveling per day. Amtrak also runs commuter trains under contract with several commuter agencies.

Although Amtrak's basic route system was originally designated by the Secretary of Transportation in 1971, modifications have been made to the Amtrak system and to individual routes that have resulted in more efficient and cost-effective operations. Increased capital funding in recent years has allowed Amtrak to reduce its debt load and make progress in bringing its network to a state of good repair.

Sources of Information

Business Opportunities

Amtrak provides an online procurement portal to foster business partnerships.

Employment

Amtrak employs more than 20,000 professionals in a variety of career fields.

Store

Official Amtrak merchandise—adult apparel, calendars, headwear, posters, and toys—may be purchased online.

For further information, contact the Government Affairs Department, Amtrak, 60 Massachusetts Avenue NE., Washington, DC 20002. Phone, 202-906-3918.

National Science Foundation

4201 Wilson Boulevard, Arlington, VA 22230, 703-292-5111, TDD, 800-281-8749, *http://www.nsf.gov* | Email: *info@nsf.gov*

NATIONAL SCIENCE BOARD

NATIONAL SCIENCE BOARD	
CHAIR	Maria T. Zuber
Vice Chair	Diane L. Souvaine
Member	John L. Anderson
Member	Deborah L. Ball
Member	Roger Beachy
Member	Vinton G. Cerf
Member	Vicki Chandler
Member	Ruth David
Member	Inez Fung
Member	Robert M. Groves
Member	James S. Jackson
Member	G. Peter Lepage
Member	Stephen L. Mayo
Member	Sethuraman Panchanathan

Member	George P. Peterson
Member	Geraldine Richmond
Member	(vacancy)
Member	(vacancy)
Member	(vacancy)
Member	(vacancy)
Member	(vacancy)
Member	(vacancy)
Member	(vacancy)
Member	(vacancy)
Member (ex officio)	France A. Córdova
Executive Officer (nonmember)	Michael L. Van Woert

NATIONAL SCIENCE FOUNDATION

DIRECTOR	France A. Córdova
Deputy Director	(vacancy)
Assistant Director, Biological Sciences	James L. Olds
Assistant Director, Computer and Information Sciences and Engineering	James F. Kurose
Assistant Director, Education and Human Resources	Joan Ferrini-Mundy
Assistant Director, Engineering	Grace Wang, Acting
Assistant Director, Geosciences	Roger M. Wakimoto
Assistant Director, Mathematical and Physical Sciences	F. Fleming Crim
Assistant Director, Social, Behavioral and Economic Sciences	Fay Cook
General Counsel	Lawrence Rudolph
Inspector General	Allison C. Lerner
Office Head, Office of Budget, Finance and Award Management / Chief Financial Officer	Martha A. Rubenstein
Office Head, Office of Diversity and Inclusion	Rhonda Davis
Office Head, Office of Information and Resource Management / Chief Human Capital Officer	Joanne S. Tornow
Office Head, Office of Integrative Activities	Suzanne Iacono
Office Head, Office of International Science and Engineering	Rebecca L. Keiser
Office Head, Office of Legislative and Public Affairs	Amanda H. Greenwell

[For the National Science Foundation statement of organization, see the Federal Register of February 8, 1993, 58 FR 7587-7595; May 27, 1993, 58 FR 30819; May 2, 1994, 59 FR 22690; and October 6, 1995, 60 FR 52431]

The National Science Foundation supports research and education to advance science and engineering.

The National Science Foundation (NSF) is an independent agency created by the National Science Foundation Act of 1950, as amended (42 U.S.C. 1861-1875).

The NSF increases the Nation's base of scientific and engineering knowledge; strengthens its ability to conduct research in all areas of science and engineering; develops and helps implement science and engineering education programs to meet the challenges of the future; and promotes international cooperation through science and engineering. As a leading Federal supporter of science and engineering, the Foundation also plays an important role in national policy planning.

With the advice and consent of the Senate, the President appoints the Director to a 6-year term and the Deputy Director to an unspecified term. The National Science Board (NSB) guides the NSF's activities. Including the chair and vice chair, the Board comprises 24 members—plus the Director of the NSF, who serves as an ex officio member. Members are appointed by the President to 6-year terms, one-third of the Members being appointed every 2 years. Appointees are known for distinguished service in science, engineering, education, research management, or public affairs, and for an outlook that broadly represents that of national science and engineering leadership. The NSB monitors national policy and makes recommendations to promote the health of U.S. science and engineering research and education.

The Foundation's Office of Inspector General conducts and supervises audits, inspections, and investigations on the programs and operations of the Foundation, including allegations of misconduct in science.

Activities

The NSF initiates and supports fundamental, long-term, merit-selected research in the scientific and engineering disciplines through grants, contracts, and other agreements awarded to universities, colleges, academic consortia, and nonprofit and small business institutions. Most of this research centers on answering scientific and engineering questions of fundamental life processes, natural laws and phenomena, fundamental processes influencing the human environment, and the forces affecting people as members of society as well as the behavior of society as a whole.

The Foundation encourages cooperative efforts involving universities, industries, and government. It also promotes research and development for better products and services that improve the quality of life and stimulate economic growth.

The Foundation cultivates talent by supporting undergraduate and graduate students and postdoctoral researchers. It administers special programs to identify and encourage participation of underrepresented groups in science and technology and to strengthen research capability at small institutions and businesses and at colleges and universities.

It supports major national and international science and engineering activities, including the U.S. Antarctic Program, Ocean Drilling Program, and global geoscience studies. Cooperative scientific and engineering research activities support exchange programs for American and foreign scientists and engineers, execution of jointly designed research projects, participation in international science and engineering organizational activities, and travel to international conferences.

Contracts and cooperative agreements with national centers allow qualified scientists and engineers use of large facilities. The Foundation supports national centers associated with astronomy and atmospheric sciences, biological and engineering research, science and technology, supercomputers, and long-term ecological research sites.

The Foundation's science and engineering education activities include grants for research and development of instructional materials for students and teachers and the application of advanced technologies to education. Grants also are available for teacher preparation and enhancement and informal science education activities. Funding is provided for college science instrumentation, course and curriculum improvement, faculty and student activities, and minority resource centers. The NSF also supports studies of the status of math, science, and engineering education.

The Vannevar Bush Award is given annually to an outstanding contributor to the welfare of the Nation and mankind through public service in science and technology. The Alan T. Waterman Award is given annually to a promising young scientist or engineer to support research and study. The Foundation also presents its Public Service Award to one individual and to one company, corporation, or organization for increasing public understanding of science or engineering through public service in areas other than research. The Foundation administratively supports the President's Committee on the National Medal of Science.

Sources of Information

Awards

The NSF funds science and engineering research and education through contracts, cooperative agreements, and grants. The Foundation provides approximately 20 percent of the Federal support that academic institutions receive for basic research.

Board and Committee Meetings

Webcasts of NSB open sessions and committee meetings that are held in Arlington, VA, remain available for at least 1 year after the event. Transcripts of closed sessions of the NSB, its committees, and other subentities are available upon request by email.

Business Opportunities

The NSF publicizes contracting and subcontracting opportunities in the "Commerce Business Daily" and other appropriate publications. Organizations seeking contract work should contact either the Division of Acquisition and Cooperative Support or the Division of Administrative Services, National Science Foundation, Arlington, VA 22230.

Division of Acquisition and Cooperative Support. Phone, 703-292-8240.

Division of Administrative Services. Phone, 703-292-8190.

Employment

To carry out its mission, the NSF relies on educators, engineers, mathematicians, program directors, and statisticians, as well as on professionals with administrative, business, and management backgrounds. The NSF also offers career opportunities—internship and recent graduates programs and the Presidential Management Fellows program—for students and recent graduates.

Fellowships

Consult the online "Guide to Programs / Browse Funding Opportunities" and appropriate announcements and brochures for postdoctoral fellowship opportunities that may be available through some NSF divisions. Beginning graduate and minority graduate students wanting to apply for fellowships should contact the Directorate for Education and Human Resources. Phone, 703-292-8600.

Freedom of Information Act (FOIA)

A request for agency records should be submitted in accordance with the NSF's FOIA regulation (45 CFR 612). A request should be clearly labeled as "FOIA REQUEST" and be addressed to the FOIA Officer, Office of General Counsel, National Science Foundation, Room 1265, Arlington, VA 22230. Phone, 703-292-8060. Fax, 703-292-9242.

Glossary

The NSF maintains a small glossary online.

Grants

The NSF makes the current guide for grant proposals available on its Web site.

Office of Inspector General (OIG)

The OIG investigates complaints of abuse, fraud, and waste; protects whistleblowers; and posts semiannual reports and other publications online. A hotline intake form is available online to submit allegations for review. Phone, 703-292-7100. Fax, 703-292-9159.

Privacy Act

A request for personal records should be submitted in accordance with the NSF's Privacy Act regulation (45 CFR 613). A request should be clearly labeled as "PRIVACY ACT REQUEST" and be addressed to the Privacy Act Officer, National Science Foundation, Room 1265, Arlington, VA 22230. Phone, 703-292-8060.

Publications

The NSF maintains an online document system to support the electronic dissemination of its documents. The online library contains thousands of documents that may be downloaded free of charge. Some NSF publications are available only in print, and others (e.g., the "Grant Proposal Guide" and "Award and Administration Guide") may be inconvenient to download. To obtain these publications in hardcopy, contact the NSF Publications Clearinghouse in Arlington, VA. Phone, 703-292-7827.

Search or browse the online document library.

Reading Room

NSF policy documents and staff instructions, as well as current indexes, are available to the public for inspection and copying. To gain access to the collection, a visitor must schedule an appointment in advance with the library, which is open on weekdays, excluding Federal holidays, 8:00 a.m.–4 p.m. The reading room is located in the National Science Foundation Library, Room 225, Arlington, VA 22230. Phone, 703-292-7830.

Email: **Small Business Support**

The Office of Small Business Research and Development informs small businesses with science and technology research capabilities about NSF support that could benefit them. The Office of Small and Disadvantaged Business Utilization oversees agency compliance with the provisions of the Small Business Act and the Small Business Investment Act of 1958, as amended. Phone, 703-292-8050.

The Small Business Innovation Research and Technology Transfer program helps startups and small businesses carry out scientific research and development.

For further information, contact the National Science Foundation Information Center, 4201 Wilson Boulevard, Arlington, VA 22230. Phone, 703-292-5111. TDD, 800-281-8749.

NATIONAL SCIENCE FOUNDATION

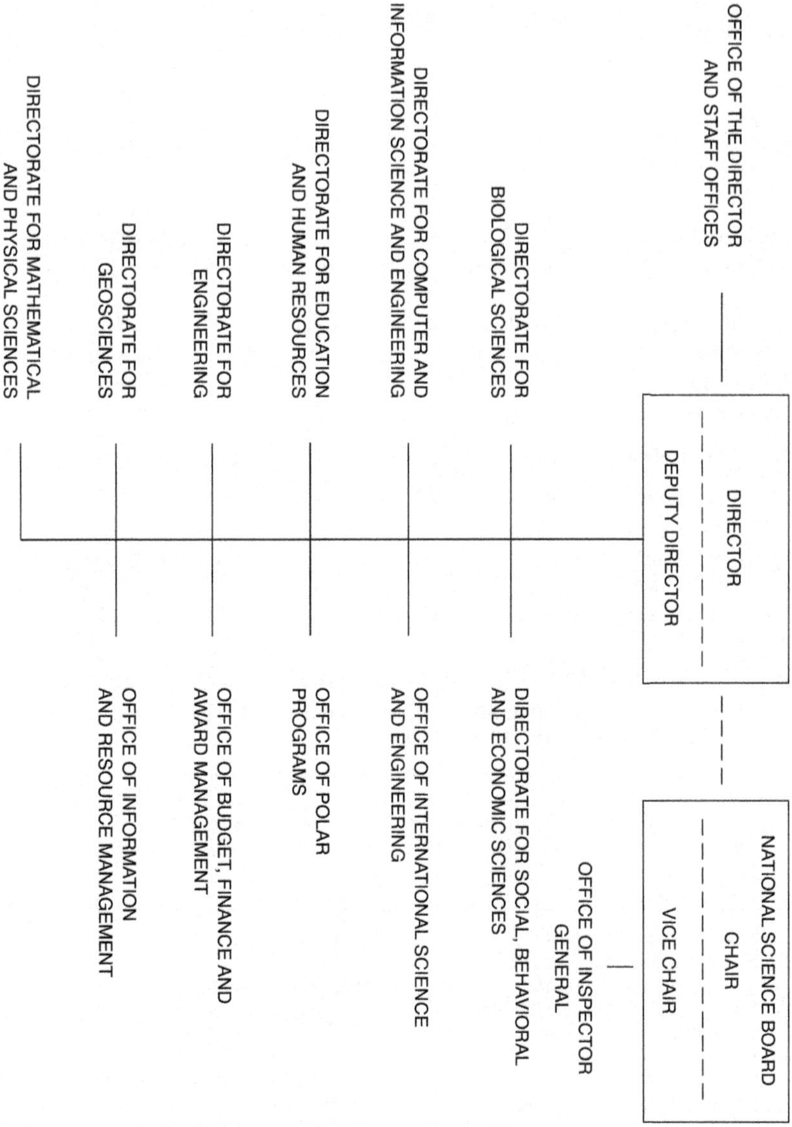

National Transportation Safety Board

490 L'Enfant Plaza SW., Washington, DC 20594, 202-314-6000, 202-314-6110, *http://www.ntsb.gov*

CHAIR	Christopher A. Hart
Vice Chair	Bella T. Dinh-Zarr
Member	Robert L. Sumwalt
Member	Earl R. Weener
Member	(vacancy)
Chief Financial Officer	Edward Benthall
Director, Office of Equal Employment Opportunity, Diversity, and Inclusion	Fara D. Guest
Director, Office of Safety Recommendations and Communications	Sharon Bryson
General Counsel	David K. Tochen
MANAGING DIRECTOR	Thomas E. Zoeller
Chief Administrative Law Judge	Alfonso J. Montaño
Chief Information Officer	Wanda E. Briggs, Acting
Director, Office of Administration	Susan Kantrowitz
Director, Office of Aviation Safety	John DeLisi
Director, Office of Highway Safety	Robert J. Molloy
Director, Office of Marine Safety	Brian Curtis, Acting
Director, Office of Railroad, Pipeline, and Hazardous Materials Investigations	Robert J. Hall
Director, Office of Research and Engineering	Joseph M. Kolly

[For the National Transportation Safety Board statement of organization, see the Code of Federal Regulations, Title 49, Part 800]

The National Transportation Safety Board investigates accidents, conducts studies, and makes recommendations on safety to Government agencies, the transportation industry, and others.

The National Transportation Safety Board (NTSB) was established in 1967. On April 1, 1975, the Independent Safety Board Act of 1974 (49 U.S.C. 1111) reestablished the NTSB as an independent agency outside the Department of Transportation.

The NTSB consists of five members whom the President appoints for 5-year terms with the advice and consent of the Senate. The President designates two of these members as Chair and Vice Chair of the Board for 2-year terms. The President designates the Chair also with the advice and consent of the Senate.

Activities

Accident Investigation

The NTSB investigates, determines probable cause, makes safety recommendations, and reports the facts and circumstances of the following types of accidents: U.S. civil aviation and certain public-use aircraft accidents; railroad accidents involving a fatality, substantial property damage, or a passenger train; pipeline accidents involving a fatality, substantial property damage, or significant harm to the environment; highway accidents (including railroad grade-crossing accidents) that the NTSB selects in cooperation with the States; major marine casualties and accidents involving a public vessel and a nonpublic vessel; certain accidents involving hazardous materials; and other transportation accidents that are catastrophic, caused by recurring problems, or otherwise should be investigated in the judgment of the Board.

Safety Problem Identification

The NTSB makes recommendations on matters of transportation safety. It reduces the severity and number of transportation accidents by conducting safety studies and special investigations; assessing accident investigation techniques and publishing recommended procedures; establishing regulatory requirements for reporting accidents; evaluating the transportation safety consciousness and efficacy of other Government agencies in accident prevention; evaluating safeguards and procedures for the transportation of hazardous materials and the performance of other Government agencies charged with ensuring the safe transportation of such materials; and reporting annually to the Congress on its activities.

Family Assistance for Aviation Disasters

The NTSB coordinates the resources of the Federal Government and other organizations to support the efforts of local and State governments and airlines to meet the needs of aviation disaster victims and their families. It assists in making Federal resources available to local authorities and airlines.

Certificate, Civil Penalty, and License Appeal

On appeal, the NTSB reviews the suspension, amendment, modification, revocation, or denial of certain certificates, licenses, and assessments of civil penalties issued by the Secretary of Transportation. The NTSB also reviews, on appeal from the orders of any administrative law judge, decisions of the Commandant of the Coast Guard that revoke, suspend, or deny certain licenses, certificates, documents, and registers.

Sources of Information

Business Opportunities

For information on contracting and procurement opportunities, contact the Contracting Officer, National Transportation Safety Board, Washington, DC 20594. Phone, 202-314-6102.

Employment

The NTSB relies on many types of skilled professionals to carry out its mission. Their areas of expertise include engineering, air safety, transportation safety, highway accidents, human performance, human resources, information technology, law, contracts, and writing-editing. Career information is available online and from the Human Resources Division. Phone, 202-314-6230.

Publications

Publications are free of charge for the following categories of subscribers: Federal, State, or local transportation agencies; international transportation organizations or foreign governments; educational institutions or public libraries; nonprofit public safety organizations; and the news media. To receive copies of NTSB publications, persons in these categories should contact the Records Management Division, National Transportation Safety Board, Washington, DC 20594. Phone, 202-314-6551. All other persons may download NTSB publications from the agency's Web site or purchase them from the National Technical Information Service, 5285 Port Royal Road, Springfield, VA 22161. To place an order, call the subscription unit at 703-487-4630 or the sales desk at 703-487-4768. More information is available on the NTSB Web site.

Reading Room

The NTSB's public reference room is available for record inspection and photocopying. It is located on the 6th floor at the Board's Washington, DC, headquarters and is open on weekdays from 8:45 a.m. to 4:45 p.m. Requests for access to public records should be made in person at the guard desk. Phone, 202-314-6551 or 800-877-6799.

Regional Offices and Response Operations Center

Contact information for regional offices is available on the NTSB Web site. To report an accident in any transportation mode, contact the Response Operations Center. Phone, 844-373-9922.

For further information, contact the Office of Public Affairs, National Transportation Safety Board, 490 L'Enfant Plaza SW., Washington, DC 20594. Phone, 202-314-6100. Fax, 202-314-6110.

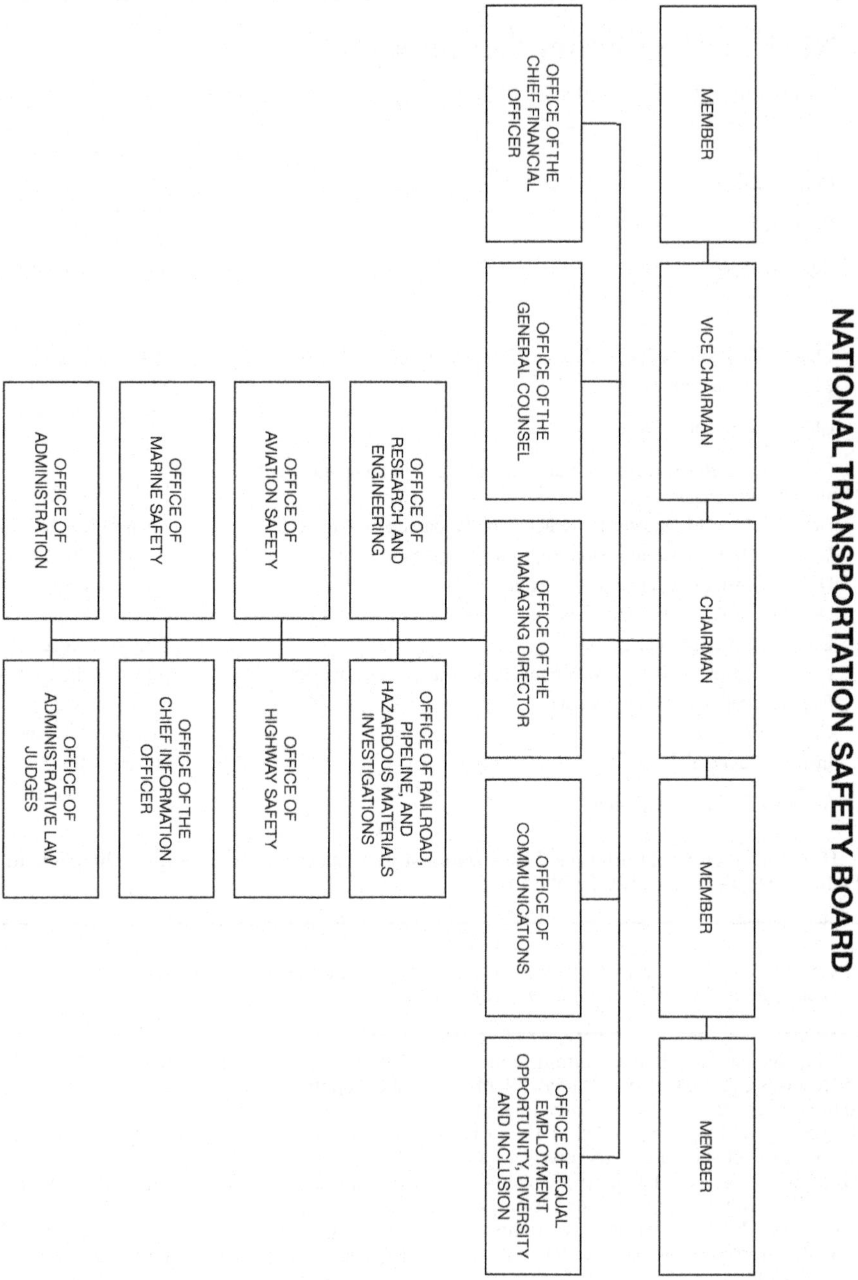
NATIONAL TRANSPORTATION SAFETY BOARD
MEMBER
VICE CHAIRMAN
CHAIRMAN
MEMBER
MEMBER
OFFICE OF THE CHIEF FINANCIAL OFFICER
OFFICE OF THE GENERAL COUNSEL
OFFICE OF THE MANAGING DIRECTOR
OFFICE OF COMMUNICATIONS
OFFICE OF EQUAL EMPLOYMENT OPPORTUNITY, DIVERSITY AND INCLUSION
OFFICE OF RESEARCH AND ENGINEERING
OFFICE OF RAILROAD, PIPELINE, AND HAZARDOUS MATERIALS INVESTIGATIONS
OFFICE OF AVIATION SAFETY
OFFICE OF HIGHWAY SAFETY
OFFICE OF MARINE SAFETY
OFFICE OF THE CHIEF INFORMATION OFFICER
OFFICE OF ADMINISTRATION
OFFICE OF ADMINISTRATIVE LAW JUDGES

Nuclear Regulatory Commission

Washington, DC 20555, 301-415-7000, *http://www.nrc.gov* | Email: *opa.resource@nrc.gov*

CHAIR	Stephen G. Burns
Commissioner	Jeffrey M. Baran
Commissioner	William C. Ostendorff
Commissioner	Kristine L. Svinicki
Commissioner	(vacancy)

Chief Administrative Judge, Atomic Safety and Licensing Board Panel	E. Roy Hawkens
Chief Financial Officer	Maureen E. Wylie
Chief Information Officer	Frederick D. Brown, Acting
Deputy Executive Director for Materials, Waste, Research, State, Tribal and Compliance Programs	Glen M. Tracy
Deputy Executive Director for Reactor and Preparedness Programs	Michael R. Johnson
Director, Office of Commission Appellate Adjudication	Brooke Poole Clark
Director, Office of Congressional Affairs	Eugene Dacus
Director, Office of International Programs	Nader L. Mamish
Director, Office of Public Affairs	Eliot B. Brenner
Executive Director, Advisory Committee on Reactor Safeguards	Edwin M. Hackett
Executive Director for Operations	Victor M. McCree
General Counsel	Margret M. Doane
Inspector General	Hubert T. Bell, Jr.
Secretary of the Commission	Annette L. Vietti-Cook

[For the Nuclear Regulatory Commission statement of organization, see the Code of Federal Regulations, Title 10, Part I]

The Nuclear Regulatory Commission licenses and regulates civilian use of nuclear energy to protect public health and safety and the environment.

The Nuclear Regulatory Commission (NRC) was established as an independent regulatory agency under the provisions of the Energy Reorganization Act of 1974 (42 U.S.C. 5801 et seq.) and Executive Order 11834 of January 15, 1975. All licensing and related regulatory functions formerly assigned to the Atomic Energy Commission were transferred to the Nuclear Regulatory Commission.

Five Commissioners whom the President appoints and Senate confirms for 5-year terms govern the NRC. The President appoints one of them to be the Commission's Chair and official spokesperson.

The NRC's major program components are the Office of Nuclear Reactor Regulation, the Office of New Reactors, the Office of Nuclear Material Safety and Safeguards, the Office of Federal and State Materials and Environmental Management Programs, and the Office of Nuclear Regulatory Research. Headquartered in Rockville, Maryland, the NRC has four regional offices.

The Commission ensures that nuclear

materials and facilities for civilian use are managed in a manner consistent with public health and safety, environmental quality, national security, and antitrust laws. The NRC centers most of its efforts on regulating the use of nuclear energy to generate electric power.

Activities

The NRC is primarily responsible for the following functions: licensing the construction, operation, and closure of nuclear reactors and other nuclear facilities, such as nuclear fuel cycle facilities, low-level radioactive waste disposal sites under NRC jurisdiction, the geologic repository for high-level radioactive waste, and nonpower test and research reactors; licensing the possession, use, processing, handling, and export of nuclear material; licensing the operators of nuclear power and nonpower test and research reactors; inspecting licensed facilities and activities; conducting the U.S. Government research program on light-water reactor safety; developing and implementing rules and regulations that govern licensed nuclear activities; investigating nuclear incidents and allegations concerning any matter regulated by the Commission; maintaining the NRC Incident Response Program; collecting, analyzing, and disseminating information on the operational safety of commercial nuclear power reactors and certain nonreactor activities; developing working relationships with the States regarding reactor operations and the regulation of nuclear material; and assuring that adequate regulatory programs are maintained by States exercising regulatory control over certain nuclear materials located within their borders.

Sources of Information

Active Regulatory Guides

Regulatory guides provide guidance to licensees and applicants for implementing parts of the Commission's regulations, techniques used by NRC staff to evaluate problems or postulated accidents, and data needed by NRC staff to review applications for permits or licenses. Regulatory guides are issued in 10 broad divisions: antitrust and financial review, environmental and siting, fuels and materials facilities, materials and plant protection, occupational health, power reactors, products, research and test reactors, transportation, and general. Active regulatory guides may be downloaded from the NRC's online library.

Business Opportunities

The NRC awards contracts to commercial firms, nonprofit organizations, and universities. The agency buys products and services, including technical assistance and research in nuclear fields, information technology, facility management, and administrative support.

Draft Regulatory Guides

The NRC issues regulatory guides in draft form to solicit public comment and participation in developing regulatory positions. Draft regulatory guides have not received complete staff review, and, therefore, they do not represent official NRC staff positions. The public may comment on draft guides and other documents issued in draft form online. NRC staff considers all comments received during the public comment period. Draft regulatory guides may be downloaded from the NRC's online library.

Employment

To carry out its mission, the NRC relies heavily on engineers, scientists, and security professionals.

Freedom of Information Act (FOIA)

To request copies of records, use the online "FOIA Request Submittal Form" or contact the FOIA / Privacy Act Officer, Mail Stop T–5 F09, Nuclear Regulatory Commission, Washington, DC 20555-0001. Phone, 301-415-7169. Fax, 301-415-5130.

Glossary

The NRC maintains an online glossary.

Microfiche Collections

Selected regional libraries of the U.S. Government Publishing Office Federal Depository Library Program maintain permanent microfiche collections of Nuclear Regulatory Commission documents released between January 1981 and October 1999. Contact the Public Document Room for more information. Phone, 301-415-4737 or

800-397-4209. Fax, 301-415-3548.

Publications

The NRC publishes information on licensing and regulation of civilian nuclear facilities and materials, as well as annual and periodic reports. Publications and many documents are accessible on the NRC Web site. The U.S. Government Publishing Office (GPO) and the National Technical Information Service (NTIS) sell single copies of and subscriptions to NRC publications. Contact the GPO bookstore (phone, 202-512-0132) or the NTIS (phone, 888-584-8332 or 703-605-6050) for more information.

http://www.ntis.gov **Public Documents**

The Public Document Room—located on the first floor at One White Flint North, 11555 Rockville Pike, Rockville, MD—is open on weekdays, 8 a.m.–4 p.m., except on Federal holidays. The NRC maintains a large collection of documents on licensing proceedings and other significant actions. Documents issued prior to October 1999 are available in paper or microfiche. After October 1999, documents are available online from the NRC's full-text document management system. Most public documents may be reproduced on CD–ROM, microfiche, or paper for a nominal fee. Phone, 301-415-4737 or 800-397-4209. Fax, 301-415-3548.

http://www.nrc.gov/reading-rm/adams.html http://www.nrc.gov/about-nrc/contactus.html

For further information, contact the Office of Public Affairs, Nuclear Regulatory Commission, Washington, DC 20555-0001. Phone, 301-415-8200.

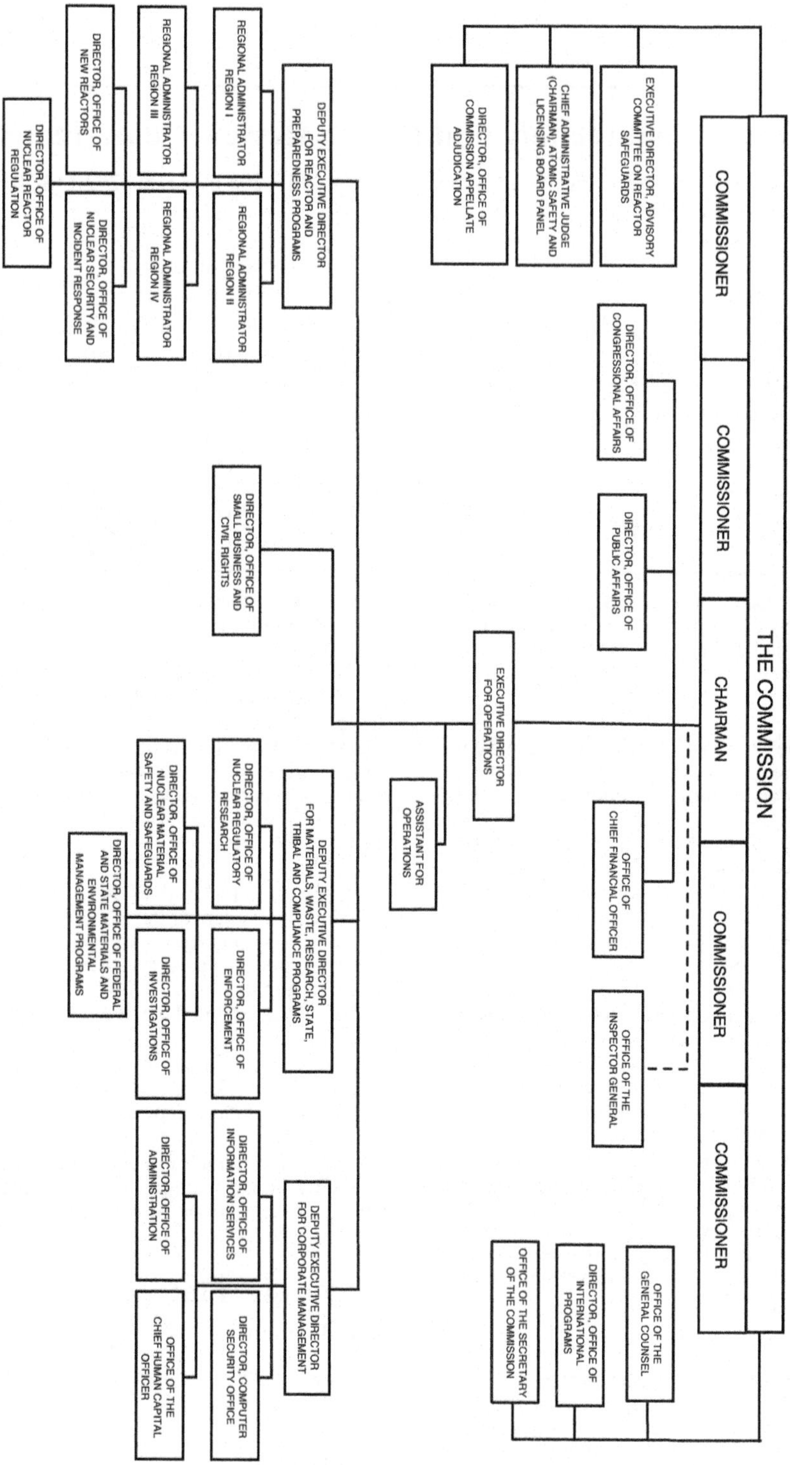
NUCLEAR REGULATORY COMMISSION
THE COMMISSION
COMMISSIONER
COMMISSIONER
CHAIRMAN
COMMISSIONER
COMMISSIONER
EXECUTIVE DIRECTOR, ADVISORY COMMITTEE ON REACTOR SAFEGUARDS
CHIEF ADMINISTRATIVE JUDGE (CHAIRMAN), ATOMIC SAFETY AND LICENSING BOARD PANEL
DIRECTOR, OFFICE OF COMMISSION APPELLATE ADJUDICATION
DIRECTOR, OFFICE OF CONGRESSIONAL AFFAIRS
DIRECTOR, OFFICE OF PUBLIC AFFAIRS
OFFICE OF CHIEF FINANCIAL OFFICER
OFFICE OF THE INSPECTOR GENERAL
OFFICE OF THE GENERAL COUNSEL
DIRECTOR, OFFICE OF INTERNATIONAL PROGRAMS
OFFICE OF THE SECRETARY OF THE COMMISSION
EXECUTIVE DIRECTOR FOR OPERATIONS
ASSISTANT FOR OPERATIONS
DIRECTOR, OFFICE OF SMALL BUSINESS AND CIVIL RIGHTS
DEPUTY EXECUTIVE DIRECTOR FOR REACTOR AND PREPAREDNESS PROGRAMS
REGIONAL ADMINISTRATOR REGION I
REGIONAL ADMINISTRATOR REGION II
REGIONAL ADMINISTRATOR REGION III
REGIONAL ADMINISTRATOR REGION IV
DIRECTOR, OFFICE OF NEW REACTORS
DIRECTOR, OFFICE OF NUCLEAR SECURITY AND INCIDENT RESPONSE
DIRECTOR, OFFICE OF NUCLEAR REACTOR REGULATION
DEPUTY EXECUTIVE DIRECTOR FOR MATERIALS, WASTE, RESEARCH, STATE, TRIBAL AND COMPLIANCE PROGRAMS
DIRECTOR, OFFICE OF NUCLEAR REGULATORY RESEARCH
DIRECTOR, OFFICE OF ENFORCEMENT
DIRECTOR, OFFICE OF NUCLEAR MATERIAL SAFETY AND SAFEGUARDS
DIRECTOR, OFFICE OF INVESTIGATIONS
DIRECTOR, OFFICE OF FEDERAL AND STATE MATERIALS AND ENVIRONMENTAL MANAGEMENT PROGRAMS
DEPUTY EXECUTIVE DIRECTOR FOR CORPORATE MANAGEMENT
DIRECTOR, OFFICE OF INFORMATION SERVICES
DIRECTOR, COMPUTER SECURITY OFFICE
DIRECTOR, OFFICE OF ADMINISTRATION
OFFICE OF THE CHIEF HUMAN CAPITAL OFFICER

Occupational Safety and Health Review Commission

1120 Twentieth Street NW., Washington, DC 20036-3457, 202-606-5380, 202-418-3017, *http://www.oshrc.gov*

CHAIR	Cynthia L. Attwood
Commissioner	Heather L. MacDougall
Commissioner	(vacancy)
EXECUTIVE DIRECTOR	Debra A. Hall
Chief Administrative Law Judge	Covette Rooney
Executive Secretary	John X. Cerveny
General Counsel	Nadine N. Mancini

The Occupational Safety and Health Review Commission ensures the timely and fair resolution of cases involving the alleged exposure of American workers to unsafe or unhealthy working conditions.

The Occupational Safety and Health Review Commission is an independent, quasi-judicial agency established by the Occupational Safety and Health Act of 1970 (29 U.S.C. 651-678).

The Commission rules on cases when disagreements arise over the results of safety and health inspections performed by the Department of Labor's Occupational Safety and Health Administration (OSHA). Employers have the right to dispute alleged job safety or health violations that OSHA inspectors find, the penalties that OSHA proposes, and the time given to correct a hazardous situation.

The Occupational Safety and Health Act covers virtually every employer in the country. Its purpose is to reduce employment-related injuries, illnesses, and deaths of working men and women in the United States. It requires employers to provide a work environment free from recognized hazards that cause or are likely to cause death or serious physical harm to their employees. It also requires employers to comply with occupational safety and health standards promulgated under the act.

Activities

The Commission adjudicates enforcement actions initiated under the act when they are contested by employers, employees, or representatives of employees. A case arises when a citation, issued to an employer as the result of an OSHA inspection, is contested within 15 working days of receipt of the report.

There are two levels of adjudication within the Commission. All cases are first assigned to an administrative law judge. A hearing is generally held in the community or as close as possible to where the alleged violation occurred. After the hearing, the judge issues a decision based on findings of fact and conclusions of law.

A substantial number of these decisions become final orders of the Commission. Commission members, however, will issue the final order if a party petitions the Commission members for review of the judge's decision and the petition is granted.

After a final order is issued, any party to the case may seek a review of the decision in the U.S. courts of appeals.

The Commission's principal office is in Washington, DC. Administrative law judges are also located in the Atlanta and Denver regional offices.

Sources of Information

Employment

Vacancy announcements are posted online.

Publications

The Commission's publications are

accessible online. Copies of them and decisions are also available from the Office of the Executive Secretary. Phone, 202-606-5400. Fax, 202-606-5050.

For further information, contact the Office of the Executive Director, Occupational Safety and Health Review Commission, 1120 Twentieth Street NW., Washington, DC 20036-3457. Phone, 202-606-5380. Fax, 202-418-3017.

Office of Government Ethics

1201 New York Avenue NW., Suite 500, Washington, DC 20005-3917, 202-482-9300, TTY, 800-877-8339, 202-482-9237, *http://www.oge.gov*

DIRECTOR	Walter M. Shaub, Jr.
Chief of Staff and Program Counsel	Shelley K. Finlayson
Deputy Director, Compliance	Dale A. Christopher
General Counsel	David J. Apol

[For the Office of Government Ethics statement of organization, see the Code of Federal Regulations, Title 5, Part 2600]

The Office of Government Ethics leads and oversees the executive branch program for preventing conflicts of interest.

The Office of Government Ethics (OGE) is an executive branch agency established under the Ethics in Government Act of 1978, as amended (5 U.S.C. app. 401).

With the advice and consent of the Senate, the President appoints the Director for a 5-year term.

Activities

The OGE provides overall leadership and oversight of the executive branch ethics program, which prevents and resolves conflicts of interest. To carry out its leadership and oversight responsibilities, the OGE promulgates and maintains enforceable standards of ethical conduct for approximately 2.7 million employees in over 130 executive branch agencies and the White House; oversees a financial disclosure system that reaches approximately 26,000 public and 380,000 confidential financial disclosure report filers; ensures that executive branch agency ethics programs are in compliance with applicable ethics laws and regulations; provides education and training to the more than 4,500 ethics officials throughout the executive branch; conducts outreach to the general public, the private sector, and civil society; and provides technical assistance to State, local, and foreign governments and international organizations.

Sources of Information

Advisories

Educational, legal, and program management advisories are available online.

Education

Educational resources—including Institute for Ethics in Government training videos posted on YouTube—are available online.

Employment

The OGE posts vacancy announcements on USAJobs. The Compliance Division, which oversees the agency ethics program, seeks agency ethics officials to participate in rotational details for increasing financial disclosure review proficiency. A detail assignment typically lasts 4–8 weeks, and arrangements can be made to accommodate commitment and schedule.

Financial Disclosure

Public financial disclosure reports and ethics agreements, executive branch agency ethics pledge waivers, and annual reports on Executive Order 13490 are available online.

Forms

All forms created by the OGE and instructions for downloading them are available online.

Freedom of Information Act (FOIA)

Information on how to submit a FOIA request is available online.

International Support

The OGE supports efforts to increase good governance and reduce corruption in the international environment. It posts online documents that international visitors to the OGE Web site request most frequently, that OGE staff prepares for anticorruption meetings, and that have been translated (Arabic, Chinese, French, Portuguese, Russian, and Spanish), as well as papers and speeches presented before international audiences.

Media

The OGE posts online documents and information—links to the schedule of important ethics dates and information on advisories, laws, and rules—that the media frequently request.

For further information, contact the Office of Government Ethics, Suite 500, 1201 New York Avenue NW., Washington, DC 20005-3917. Phone, 202-482-9300. TTY, 800-877-8339. Fax, 202-482-9237.

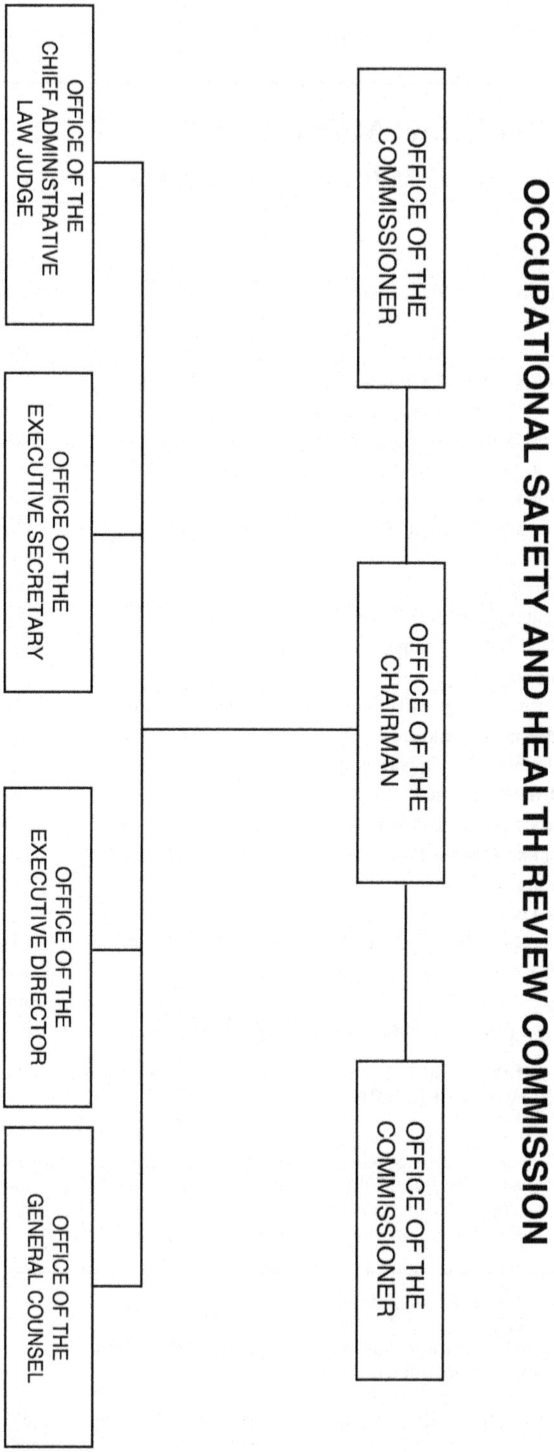
OCCUPATIONAL SAFETY AND HEALTH REVIEW COMMISSION
OFFICE OF THE COMMISSIONER
OFFICE OF THE CHAIRMAN
OFFICE OF THE COMMISSIONER
OFFICE OF THE CHIEF ADMINISTRATIVE LAW JUDGE
OFFICE OF THE EXECUTIVE SECRETARY
OFFICE OF THE EXECUTIVE DIRECTOR
OFFICE OF THE GENERAL COUNSEL

Office of Personnel Management

1900 E Street NW., Washington, DC 20415-0001, 202-606-1800, TTY, 202-606-2532, *http://www.opm.gov*

DIRECTOR	Beth F. Cobert, Acting
Chief of Staff / Director of External Affairs	Kiran Ahuja
Inspector General	Norbert Vint
Actuary	Steven M. Niu
Associate Director, Employee Services / Chief Human Capital Officer	Mark Reinhold
Associate Director, Federal Investigative Services	Merton Miller
Associate Director, Human Resources Solutions	Joseph Kennedy
Associate Director, Merit System Accountability and Compliance	Mark W. Lambert
Associate Director, Retirement Services	Kenneth Zawondy, Jr.
Chair, Federal Prevailing Rate Advisory Committee	Sheldon I. Friedman
Chief Financial Officer	Dennis D. Coleman
Chief Information Officer	Lisa Schlosser, Acting
Chief Management Officer	Kathleen McGettigan
Director, Combined Federal Campaign	Keith Willingham
Director, Communications	Michael Amato
Director, Congressional, Legislative, and Intergovernmental Affairs	Jason Levine
Director, Diversity and Inclusion	Sharon Wong, Acting
Director, Equal Employment Opportunity	Lashonn Woodland
Director, Executive Secretariat	Jozetta Robinson
Director, Facilities, Security, and Emergency Management	Dean Hunter
Director, Federal Executive Institute	Suzanne Logan
Director, Healthcare and Insurance	John O'Brien
Director, Internal Oversight and Compliance	Janet Barnes
Director, Planning and Policy Analysis	Jonathan Foley
Executive Director, Chief Human Capital Officers Council	Justin R. Johnson
General Counsel	Robin Jacobsohn
Senior Procurement Executive, Office of Procurement Operations	Nina Ferraro

[For the Office of Personnel Management statement of organization, see the Federal Register of Jan. 5, 1979, 44 FR 1501]

The Office of Personnel Management administers a merit system to ensure compliance with personnel laws and regulations and assists agencies in recruiting, examining, and promoting people on the basis of their knowledge and skills, regardless of their race, religion, sex, political influence, or other nonmerit factors.

The Office of Personnel Management (OPM) was created as an independent establishment by Reorganization Plan No. 2 of 1978 (5 U.S.C. app.), pursuant to Executive Order 12107 of December 28, 1978. Many of the functions of the former United States Civil Service Commission were transferred to OPM.

Activities

Employee Benefits

OPM manages numerous activities that directly affect the well-being of the Federal employee and indirectly enhance employee effectiveness. These include health benefits, life insurance, and retirement benefits.

Examining and Staffing

The Office of Personnel Management is responsible for providing departments and agencies with technical assistance and guidance in examining competitive positions in the Federal civil service for General Schedule grades 1 through 15 and Federal Wage system positions. In addition, OPM is responsible for the following duties: providing testing and examination services, at the request of an agency, on a reimbursable basis; establishing basic qualification standards for all occupations; certifying agency delegated examining units to conduct examining; providing employment information for competitive service positions; and providing policy direction and guidance on promotions, reassignments, appointments in the excepted and competitive services, reinstatements, temporary and term employment, veterans preference, workforce planning and reshaping, organizational design, career transition, and other staffing provisions.

Executive Resources

OPM leads in the selection, management, and development of Federal executives. OPM provides policy guidance, consulting services, and technical support on Senior Executive Service (SES) recruitment, selection, succession planning, mobility performance, awards, and removals. It reviews agency nominations for SES career appointments and administers the Qualifications Review Boards that certify candidates' executive qualifications. It manages SES, senior-level, and scientific and professional space allocations to agencies, administers the Presidential Rank Awards program, and conducts orientation sessions for newly appointed executives. In addition, OPM manages three interagency residential development and training centers for executives and managers.

Investigations

The Office of the Inspector General conducts comprehensive and independent audits, investigations, and evaluations relating to OPM programs and operations. It is responsible for administrative actions against health care providers who commit sanctionable offenses with respect to the Federal Employees' Health Benefits Program or other Federal programs.

For further information, contact the Office of the Inspector General. Phone, 202-606-1200.

Personnel Systems

OPM provides leadership and guidance to agencies on systems to support the manager's personnel management responsibilities. These include the following: white- and blue-collar pay systems, including SES and special occupational pay systems; geographical adjustments and locality payments; special rates to address recruitment and retention problems; allowances and differentials, including recruitment and relocation bonuses, retention allowances, and hazardous duty/environmental pay; and premium pay; annual and sick leave, court leave, military leave, leave transfer and leave bank programs, family and medical leave, excused absence, holidays, and scheduling of work, including flexible and compressed work schedules; performance management, covering appraisal systems, performance pay and awards, and incentive awards for suggestions, inventions, and special acts; classification policy and standards for agencies to determine the series and grades for Federal jobs; labor-management relations, including collective bargaining, negotiability, unfair labor practices, labor-management cooperation, and consulting with unions on Governmentwide issues; systems and techniques for resolving disputes with employees; quality of work-life initiatives, such as employee health and fitness, work and family, AIDS in the workplace, and employee assistance programs; human resources development, including leadership and administration of the Human Resources Development Council and the Government Performance and Results Act interest group; the Training and Management Assistance program, to help agencies develop training and human resources management solutions, including workforce planning and succession management strategies, e-learning applications, traditional classroom training materials, compensation and performance management systems, and other customized products; information systems to support and improve Federal personnel management decisionmaking; and Governmentwide instructions for personnel processing and recordkeeping and for release of personnel data under the Freedom of Information Act and the Privacy Act.

OPM also provides administrative support to special advisory bodies, including the Federal Prevailing Rate Advisory Committee, the Federal Salary Council, and the Presidential Advisory Committee on Expanding Training Opportunities.

Oversight

OPM assesses human capital management Governmentwide and within agencies to gather information for policy development and program refinement, ensure compliance with law and regulation, and enhance agency capability for human resources management accountability. Agency accountability systems help ensure that human capital decisions are consistent with merit principles and that human capital strategies are aligned with mission accomplishment. OPM also works with agencies to find better and more strategic ways to manage Federal human capital.

Workforce Diversity

OPM provides leadership, direction, and policy for Governmentwide affirmative recruiting programs for women, minorities, individuals with disabilities, and veterans. It also provides leadership, guidance, and technical assistance to promote merit and equality in systemic workforce recruitment, employment, training, and retention. In addition, OPM gathers, analyzes, and maintains statistical data on the diversity of the Federal workforce and prepares evaluation reports for Congress and others on individual agency and Governmentwide progress toward full workforce representation for all Americans in the Federal sector.

Other Personnel Programs

OPM coordinates the temporary assignment of employees between Federal agencies and State, local, and Indian tribal governments, institutions of higher education, and other eligible nonprofit organizations for up to 2 years, for work of mutual benefit to the participating organizations. It administers the Presidential Management Intern Program, which provides 2-year, excepted appointments with Federal agencies to recipients of graduate degrees in appropriate disciplines. In addition, the Office of Personnel Management administers the Federal Merit System Standards, which apply to certain grant-aided State and local programs.

Federal Executive Boards

Federal Executive Boards (FEBs) were established by Presidential memorandum on November 10, 1961, to improve internal Federal management practices and to provide a central focus for Federal participation in civic affairs in major metropolitan centers of Federal activity. They carry out their functions under OPM supervision and control.

FEBs serve as a means for disseminating information within the Federal Government and for promoting discussion of Federal policies and activities of importance to all Federal executives in the field. Each Board is composed of heads of Federal field offices in the metropolitan area. A chairman is elected annually from among the membership to provide overall leadership to the Board's operations. Committees and task forces carry out interagency projects consistent with the Board's mission.

Federal Executive Boards are located in 28 metropolitan areas that are important centers of Federal activity. These areas are as follows: Albuquerque-Santa Fe, NM; Atlanta, GA; Baltimore, MD; Boston, MA; Buffalo, NY; Chicago, IL; Cincinnati, OH; Cleveland, OH; Dallas-Fort Worth, TX; Denver, CO; Detroit, MI; Honolulu, HI; Houston, TX; Kansas City, MO; Los Angeles, CA; Miami, FL; Minneapolis-St. Paul, MN; New Orleans, LA; New York, NY; Newark, NJ; Oklahoma City, OK; Philadelphia, PA; Pittsburgh, PA; Portland, OR; St. Louis, MO; San Antonio, TX; San Francisco, CA; and Seattle, WA.

Federal Executive Associations or Councils have been locally organized in approximately 65 other metropolitan areas to perform functions similar to the Federal Executive Boards, but on a lesser scale of organization and activity.

For further information, contact the Director for Federal Executive Board

Operations, Office of Personnel Management, Room 5524, 1900 E Street NW., Washington, DC 20415-0001. Phone, 202-606-1000.

Sources of Information

Business Opportunities

The "Doing Business with OPM" Web site provides information—relevant for small, small disadvantaged, services-disabled-veteran-owned, women-owned, Historically Underutilized Business Zone, and 8(a) certified small disadvantaged businesses, as well as the general public—on contracting opportunities and registering to do business with OPM. For more information, contact the Contracting Division. Phone, 202-606-1984.

Employment

OPM consistently ranks among the best Federal agencies at which to work. Job satisfaction, results-oriented performance management, leadership and knowledge management, and talent management are agency priorities.

Information on Pathways opportunities and on internship, recent graduates, and Presidential Management Fellows programs is available online. For more information on employment opportunities, contact the Director of Human Resources. Phone, 202-606-2400.

Forms

The "Forms Management Program" Web site serves as the single source of information for forms belonging to and used by OPM.

Freedom of Information Act (FOIA)

A FOIA request must be made in writing and clearly labeled "Freedom of Information Act Request." Instructions for making a request are available online.

Insurance

Information on insurance-related topics—the Federal health benefits open season; flexible spending accounts; and dental and vision, health, life, and long-term care insurance programs—is available online.

A glossary of terms that are found on the "Federal Benefits Programs" Web site is available online to assist visitors. If a useful term is absent from the glossary, please email a request to include it.

News

Agency-related news items, blog posts, legislative proposals, memos to agencies, reports and publications, speeches and remarks, and testimonies, as well as links to social media sites, are available on the OPM Web site.

Open Government

OPM supports the Open Government initiative by promoting the principles of collaboration, participation, and transparency. It is committed to becoming more effective, efficient, and innovative; building trust with the American people; empowering the public; fostering a culture in which everyone's contributions are valued; increasing accountability; making better decisions; and tracking how agency money is used.

Publications

An online database allows users to search for OPM operating manuals, periodicals, and other publications. For more information on Federal personnel management publications, contact OPM Publications Management. Phone, 202-606-1822.

For further information, contact the Office of Communications, Office of Personnel Management, 1900 E Street NW., Washington, DC 20415-0001. Phone, 202-606-2402. TTY, 202-606-2532.

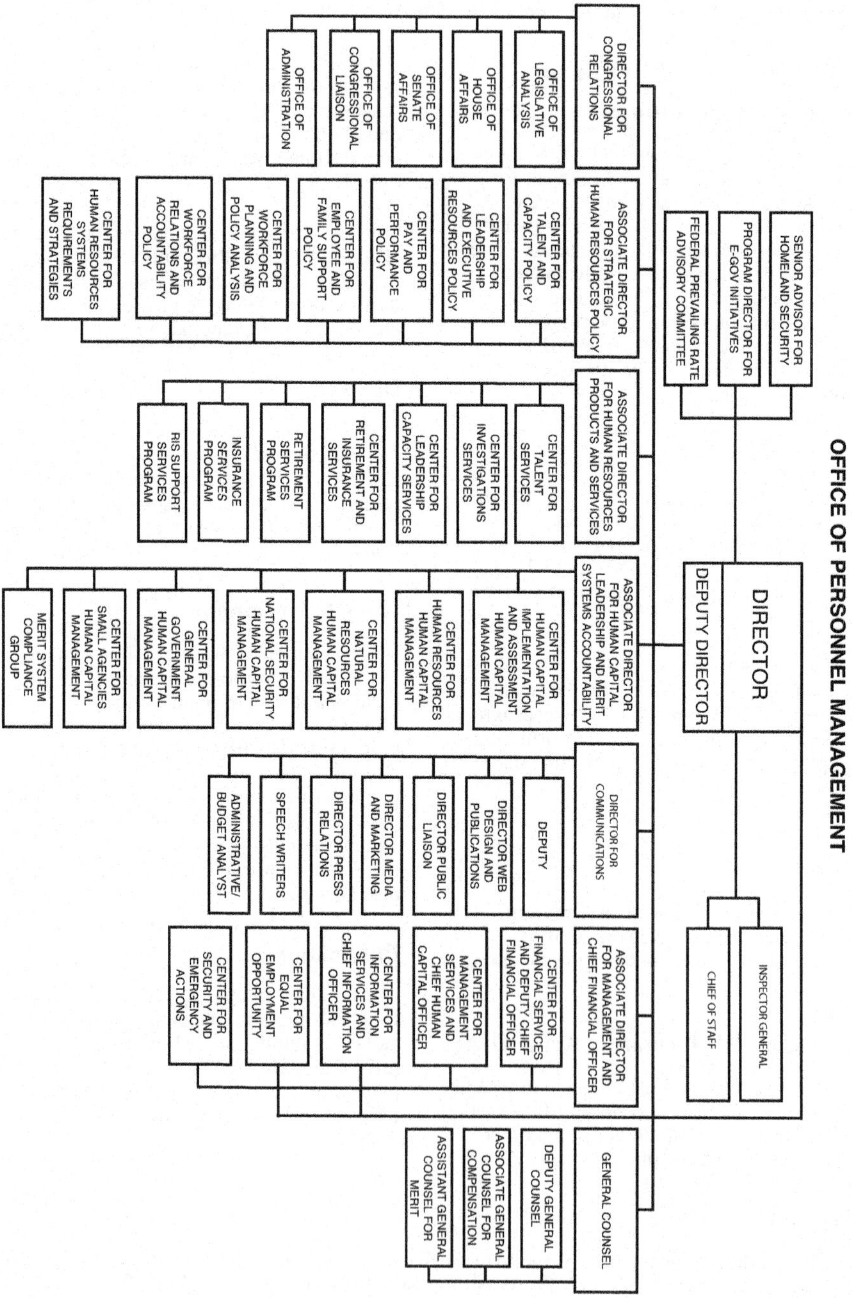
OFFICE OF PERSONNEL MANAGEMENT
DIRECTOR
DEPUTY DIRECTOR
SENIOR ADVISOR FOR HOMELAND SECURITY
PROGRAM DIRECTOR FOR E-GOV INITIATIVES
FEDERAL PREVAILING RATE ADVISORY COMMITTEE
INSPECTOR GENERAL
CHIEF OF STAFF
DIRECTOR FOR CONGRESSIONAL RELATIONS
OFFICE OF LEGISLATIVE ANALYSIS
OFFICE OF HOUSE AFFAIRS
OFFICE OF SENATE AFFAIRS
OFFICE OF CONGRESSIONAL LIAISON
OFFICE OF ADMINISTRATION
ASSOCIATE DIRECTOR FOR STRATEGIC HUMAN RESOURCES POLICY
CENTER FOR TALENT AND CAPACITY POLICY
CENTER FOR LEADERSHIP AND EXECUTIVE RESOURCES POLICY
CENTER FOR PAY AND PERFORMANCE POLICY
CENTER FOR EMPLOYEE AND FAMILY SUPPORT POLICY
CENTER FOR WORKFORCE PLANNING AND POLICY ANALYSIS
CENTER FOR WORKFORCE RELATIONS AND ACCOUNTABILITY POLICY
CENTER FOR HUMAN RESOURCES SYSTEMS REQUIREMENTS AND STRATEGIES
ASSOCIATE DIRECTOR FOR HUMAN RESOURCES PRODUCTS AND SERVICES
CENTER FOR TALENT SERVICES
CENTER FOR INVESTIGATIONS SERVICES
CENTER FOR LEADERSHIP CAPACITY SERVICES
CENTER FOR RETIREMENT AND INSURANCE SERVICES
RETIREMENT SERVICES PROGRAM
INSURANCE SERVICES PROGRAM
RIS SUPPORT SERVICES PROGRAM
ASSOCIATE DIRECTOR FOR HUMAN CAPITAL LEADERSHIP AND MERIT SYSTEMS ACCOUNTABILITY
CENTER FOR HUMAN CAPITAL IMPLEMENTATION AND ASSESSMENT HUMAN CAPITAL MANAGEMENT
CENTER FOR HUMAN RESOURCES HUMAN CAPITAL MANAGEMENT
CENTER FOR NATURAL RESOURCES HUMAN CAPITAL MANAGEMENT
CENTER FOR NATIONAL SECURITY HUMAN CAPITAL MANAGEMENT
CENTER FOR GENERAL GOVERNMENT HUMAN CAPITAL MANAGEMENT
CENTER FOR SMALL AGENCIES HUMAN CAPITAL MANAGEMENT
MERIT SYSTEM COMPLIANCE GROUP
DIRECTOR FOR COMMUNICATIONS
DEPUTY
DIRECTOR WEB DESIGN AND PUBLICATIONS
DIRECTOR PUBLIC LIAISON
DIRECTOR MEDIA AND MARKETING
DIRECTOR PRESS RELATIONS
SPEECH WRITERS
ADMINISTRATIVE/ BUDGET ANALYST
ASSOCIATE DIRECTOR FOR MANAGEMENT AND CHIEF FINANCIAL OFFICER
CENTER FOR FINANCIAL SERVICES AND DEPUTY CHIEF FINANCIAL OFFICER
CENTER FOR MANAGEMENT SERVICES AND CHIEF HUMAN CAPITAL OFFICER
CENTER FOR INFORMATION SERVICES AND CHIEF INFORMATION OFFICER
CENTER FOR EQUAL EMPLOYMENT OPPORTUNITY
CENTER FOR SECURITY AND EMERGENCY ACTIONS
GENERAL COUNSEL
DEPUTY GENERAL COUNSEL
ASSOCIATE GENERAL COUNSEL FOR COMPENSATION
ASSISTANT GENERAL COUNSEL FOR MERIT

Office of the Director of National Intelligence

Washington, DC 20511, 703-733-8600, *http://www.dni.gov*

DIRECTOR	James R. Clapper
Principal Deputy Director	Stephanie O'Sullivan
Deputy Director, Intelligence Integration	Michael Dempsey
Assistant Deputy Director, Intelligence Integration	Edward Gistaro
Assistant Director, Acquisition, Technology and Facilities	Kevin Meiners
Assistant Director, Partner Engagement	Lt. Gen. Theodore C. Nicholas
Assistant Director, Policy and Strategy	Dawn Eilenberger
Assistant Director, Systems and Resource Analyses	Troy Meink
Chief Financial Officer	Richard Fravel
Chief Human Capital Officer	Deborah Kircher
Chief Information Officer	Raymond Cook
Civil Liberties Protection Officer	Alexander W. Joel
Director, Cyber Threat Intelligence Integration Center	Tonya Ugoretz
Director, Equal Employment Opportunity and Diversity	Rita Sampson
Director, National Counterintelligence Security Center	William Evanina
Director, National Counterproliferation Center	Henry Hollatz
Director, National Counterterrorism Center	Nicholas Rasmussen
Director, Public Affairs	Brian Hale
General Counsel	Robert S. Litt
Inspector General	I. Charles McCullough III
Principal Deputy General Counsel	Susan Gibson
Program Manager, Information Sharing Environment	Kshemendra Paul

The Office of the Director of National Intelligence oversees and coordinates the foreign and domestic activities of the Intelligence Community across the Federal Government.

The Office of the Director of National Intelligence (ODNI) was established by the Intelligence Reform and Terrorism Prevention Act of 2004 (50 U.S.C. 403). It began operation on April 21, 2005.

The Office is headed by the Director of National Intelligence whom the President appoints with the advice and consent of the Senate. The Director reports directly to the President and is the principal intelligence adviser.

The ODNI ensures that the President, the heads of departments and agencies of the executive branch, the Chairman of the Joint Chiefs of Staff and senior military commanders, and the Congress receive timely and objective national intelligence. It also establishes goals and priorities for collection, analysis, production, and dissemination of national intelligence; ensures the availability of and access to intelligence information within the Intelligence Community; develops the annual budget for the National Intelligence Program; oversees coordination of relationships with the intelligence or security services of foreign governments and international organizations; ensures that accurate analysis of intelligence information is derived from all sources to support national security needs; develops personnel policies and programs to enhance the capacity for joint operations and to facilitate staffing of community management functions; and jointly oversees the development and implementation of an acquisition program management plan with the Secretary of Defense.

Sources of Information

Employment

The ODNI hires acquisitions and financial managers, engineers, foreign language experts, scientists, security experts, software and hardware developers, technology specialists, and other career professionals.

Publications

Reports and other publications are available online.

For further information, contact the Office of the Director of National Intelligence, Washington, DC 20511. Phone, 703-733-8600.

OFFICE OF THE DIRECTOR OF NATIONAL INTELLIGENCE

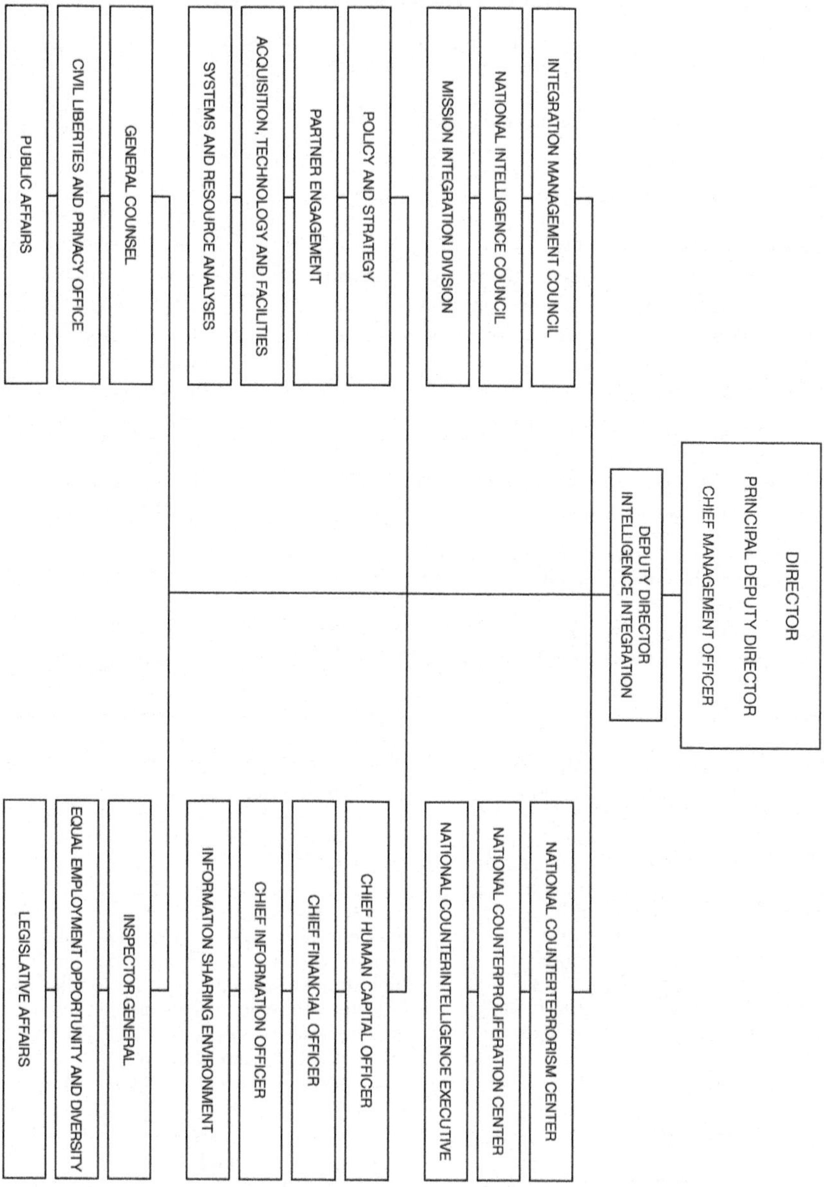

Overseas Private Investment Corporation

1100 New York Avenue NW., Washington, DC 20527, 202-336-8400, 202-336-7949, *http://www.opic.gov*

PRESIDENT / CHIEF EXECUTIVE OFFICER	Elizabeth L. Littlefield
Executive Vice President	(vacancy)
Chief Information Officer	Robert DeLuca
Chief of Staff	Cameron Alford
Director, Office of Accountability	William Kennedy
Vice President, Department of Legal Affairs / General Counsel	Kimberly Heimert
Vice President, Department of Management and Administration	Larry Spinelli, Acting
Vice President, Financial and Portfolio Management	Mildred Callear
Vice President, Human Resources	Rita Moss
Vice President, Investment Funds	Brooks Preston
Vice President, Office of External Affairs	Judith Pryor
Vice President, Office of Investment Policy	Margaret L. Kuhlow
Vice President, Small and Medium Enterprise Finance	James C. Polan
Vice President, Structured Finance and Insurance	Tracey Webb

[For the Overseas Private Investment Corporation statement of organization, see the Code of Federal Regulations, Title 22, Chapter VII]

The Overseas Private Investment Corporation promotes economic growth and job opportunities both at home and abroad by encouraging U.S. private investment in developing countries and emerging markets.

The Overseas Private Investment Corporation (OPIC) was established in 1971 as an independent agency by the Foreign Affairs Reform and Restructuring Act (112 Stat. 2681-790). The Corporation helps U.S. businesses invest overseas, fosters economic development in new and emerging markets, complements the private sector in managing risks associated with foreign direct investment, and supports U.S. foreign policy. It charges market-based fees for its products and operates on a self-sustaining basis at no net cost to American taxpayers.

Activities

The agency serves as the U.S. Government's development finance institution. It mobilizes private capital to help solve critical development challenges. This mobilization of capital advances U.S. foreign policy and national security objectives. Working with the U.S. private sector, the agency helps U.S. businesses gain footholds in emerging markets thereby catalyzing revenues, jobs, and growth opportunities both at home and abroad. Consistent with its mission, the Corporation provides financing guarantees, insures against political risk, and supports private equity investment funds to stimulate investment.

OPIC projects adhere to high environmental and social standards and uphold human rights. By its adherence to high standards, the agency tries to raise the industry and regional standards of the countries where it operates. OPIC services are available for new and expanding business enterprises in more than 160 countries.

Sources of Information

Eligibility

To determine whether a business owner or company is eligible for OPIC insurance or finance products, visit the online applicant screener. Some eligibility requirements are the same across all OPIC products; however, some vary by product.

Employment

Most OPIC career opportunities fall within the following professional categories: attorney-advisors, business development specialists, economists, finance specialists, and managers. New hires must be U.S. citizens.

Media

Annual reports, newsletters, and public notices, as well as the OPIC blog and media library are available online.

Workshops

Participants learn how American small businesses use OPIC finance and insurance products to gain access to emerging markets overseas, as well as how they can take advantage of OPIC products to expand their businesses abroad and support growth at home.

For further information, contact the Overseas Private Investment Corporation, 1100 New York Avenue NW., Washington, DC 20527. Phone, 202-336-8400. Fax, 202-336-7949.

Peace Corps

1111 Twentieth Street NW., Washington, DC 20526, 855-855-1961, 202-692-2000, 202-692-2231, *http://www.peacecorps.gov*

DIRECTOR	Carolyn Hessler-Radelet
Deputy Director	Carlos Torres
Chief of Staff	Laura M. Chambers
Chief Financial Officer	Joseph Hepp
Chief Information Officer	Francisco Reinoso
Director of Civil Rights and Diversity	Laara Manler, Acting
Director of Victim Advocacy	Da Shawna Townsend
General Counsel	Kathy Stroker, Acting
Inspector General	Kathy A. Buller
White House Liaison	Elizabeth Ogunwo
Associate Director for Global Operations	Ken Yamashita
Associate Director for Health Services	Paul Jung
Associate Director for Safety and Security	Shawn Bardwell
Associate Director for Volunteer Recruitment and Selection	Shelia Crowley, Acting
Director of Global Health and HIV	Marie McLeod
Director of Innovation	Patrick Choquette
Director of Office of Strategic Information, Research, and Planning	Cathryn Thorup
Director of Overseas Programming and Training Support	Sonia Stines Derenoncourt
Director of Peace Corps Response	Kathleen Beale
Regional Director, Africa	Richard Day
Regional Director, Europe, Mediterranean and Asia	Keri Lowry
Regional Director, Inter-America and the Pacific	Brian Riley
Associate Director for Management	Alan Price
Associate Director for Strategic Partnerships	Tonia Wellons
Chief Compliance Officer	Anne Hughes
Director of Communications	Melissa Silverman
Director of Congressional Relations	Jeremy Haldeman
Director of Third Goal and Returned Volunteer Services	B.J. Whetstine
Executive Secretariat	Melanie Wilhelm

The Peace Corps helps people of interested countries meet their need for trained men and women and promotes mutual understanding between Americans and citizens of other countries.

The Peace Corps was established by the Peace Corps Act of 1961, as amended (22 U.S.C. 2501), and was made an independent agency by title VI of the International Security and Development Cooperation Act of 1981 (22 U.S.C. 2501-1).

Activities

The Peace Corps consists of a Washington, DC, headquarters, eight area offices, and overseas operations in 63 countries, relying on more than 6,900 volunteers.

To fulfill the Peace Corps mandate, men and women are trained for a 9- to 14-week period in the appropriate local language, the technical skills necessary for their particular jobs, and the cross-cultural skills needed to adjust to a society with traditions and attitudes different from their own. Volunteers serve for a period of 2 years, living among the people with whom they work. Volunteers are expected to become a part of the community through their service.

Thousands of volunteers serve worldwide and work in six program areas: agriculture, business development, education, environment, health and HIV/AIDS, and youth development. Community-level projects are designed to match the skills of volunteers with the resources of host-country agencies and other international assistance organizations to solve specific development problems, often in conjunction with private volunteer organizations.

In the United States, the Peace Corps is working to promote an understanding of people in other countries. Through its World Wise Schools program, volunteers partner with elementary and junior high school students in the United States to encourage an exchange of letters, pictures, music, and artifacts. Participating students increase their knowledge of geography, languages, and different cultures, while gaining an appreciation for voluntarism.

The Peace Corps offers other domestic programs that rely on former volunteers. Working together with universities, local public school systems, and private businesses and foundations, these former volunteers help solve some of our Nation's most pressing domestic problems.

Sources of Information

Becoming a Volunteer

The volunteer program has an online application portal.

Employment

Peace Corps vacancy announcements are available online. Additional information is available from the Peace Corps, Office of Human Resource Management, Washington, DC 20526. Phone, 202-692-1200.

The Peace Corps consistently ranks high among midsize agencies in the Partnership for Public Service's "Best Places To Work Agency Rankings."

Freedom of Information Act (FOIA)

The Peace Corps posts certain types of records that it creates on its Web site. A formal FOIA request is not necessary to access them. The Peace Corps also maintains a FOIA requester service center that can provide information on the status of a person's FOIA request.

History

At 2 a.m., before a crowd of 10,000 students, then Senator and Presidential candidate John F. Kennedy launched a new experiment in public service from the steps of the Michigan Union at the University of Michigan in Ann Arbor. To learn more about what happened early that morning of October 14, 1960, visit the Peace Corps' "The Founding Moment" Web page.

Open Government

The Peace Corps supports the Open Government initiative by promoting the principles of collaboration, participation, and transparency.

Photos

The Peace Corps' Web site features a photo library.

Recruitment Offices

Contact information for Peace Corps recruitment offices is available online.

Social Media

The Peace Corps tweets announcements and other newsworthy items on Twitter.

The Peace Corps has a Facebook account.

The Peace Corps posts videos on its YouTube channel.

Stories

Peace Corps volunteers have stories to tell. Listen to and read them on the Peace Corps' Web site.

For further information, contact the Press Office, Peace Corps, 1111 Twentieth Street NW., Washington, DC 20526. Phone, 202-692-2230 or 855-855-1961. Fax, 202-692-2201.

PEACE CORPS

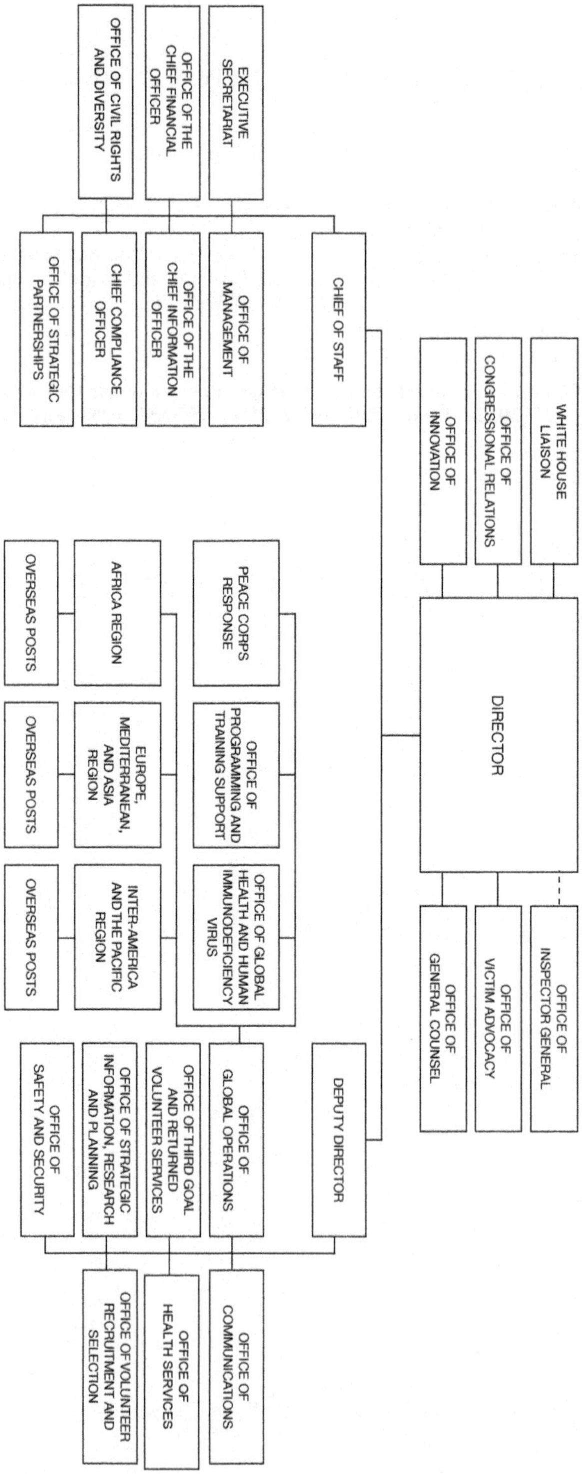
DIRECTOR
WHITE HOUSE LIAISON
OFFICE OF CONGRESSIONAL RELATIONS
OFFICE OF INNOVATION
OFFICE OF INSPECTOR GENERAL
OFFICE OF VICTIM ADVOCACY
OFFICE OF GENERAL COUNSEL
CHIEF OF STAFF
EXECUTIVE SECRETARIAT
OFFICE OF THE CHIEF FINANCIAL OFFICER
OFFICE OF CIVIL RIGHTS AND DIVERSITY
OFFICE OF MANAGEMENT
OFFICE OF THE CHIEF INFORMATION OFFICER
CHIEF COMPLIANCE OFFICER
OFFICE OF STRATEGIC PARTNERSHIPS
DEPUTY DIRECTOR
OFFICE OF GLOBAL OPERATIONS
OFFICE OF THIRD GOAL AND RETURNED VOLUNTEER SERVICES
OFFICE OF STRATEGIC INFORMATION, RESEARCH AND PLANNING
OFFICE OF SAFETY AND SECURITY
OFFICE OF COMMUNICATIONS
OFFICE OF HEALTH SERVICES
OFFICE OF VOLUNTEER RECRUITMENT AND SELECTION
PEACE CORPS RESPONSE
OFFICE OF PROGRAMMING AND TRAINING SUPPORT
OFFICE OF GLOBAL HEALTH AND HUMAN IMMUNODEFICIENCY VIRUS
AFRICA REGION
EUROPE, MEDITERRANEAN, AND ASIA REGION
INTER-AMERICA AND THE PACIFIC REGION
OVERSEAS POSTS
OVERSEAS POSTS
OVERSEAS POSTS

Pension Benefit Guaranty Corporation

1200 K Street NW., Washington, DC 20005, 202-326-4000, 800-400-7242, *http://www.pbgc.gov*

BOARD OF DIRECTORS

CHAIR (Secretary of Labor)	Thomas E. Perez
Member (Secretary of the Treasury)	Jacob J. Lew
Member (Secretary of Commerce)	Penny S. Pritzker

OFFICIALS

DIRECTOR	Thomas Reeder
Chief, Benefits Administration	Cathleen Kronopolus
Chief Counsel	Israel Goldowitz
Chief Financial Officer	Patricia Kelly
Chief Information Officer	Robert Scherer
Chief Investment Officer	John Greenberg
Chief Management Officer	Alice Maroni
Chief, Negotiations and Restructuring	Karen Morris, Acting
Chief of Staff	Ann Orr
Chief Policy Officer	(vacancy)
Deputy Chief, Benefits Administration	(vacancy)
Deputy Chief, Negotiations and Restructuring	(vacancy)
Deputy Chief Policy Officer	Michael Rae
Deputy General Counsel	Philip Hertz
Director, Department of Budget	Edgar Bennett
Director, Department of Communications Outreach and Legislative Affairs	Martha Threatt, Acting
Director, Department of Corporate Controls and Reviews	Martin Boehm
Director, Department of Corporate Finance and Restructuring	Adi Berger, Acting
Director, Department of Financial Operations	Theodore Winter
Director, Department of Human Resources	Arrie Etheridge
Director, Department of Information Technology and Business Modernization	Vidhya Shyamsunder
Director, Department of Information Technology Infrastructure Operations	Joshua Kossoy
Director, Department of Policy Research and Analysis	Christopher Bone
Director, Department of Procurement	Steve Block
Director, Department of Quality Management	Diane Braunstein
Director, Department of Workplace Solutions	Alisa Cottone
General Counsel	Judith Starr
Inspector General	Robert A. Westbrooks

The Pension Benefit Guaranty Corporation protects the retirement incomes of American workers in private-sector defined benefit pension plans.

The Pension Benefit Guaranty Corporation (PBGC) is a self-financing, wholly owned Government corporation subject to the Government Corporation Control Act (31 U.S.C. 9101-9109). The Corporation, established by title IV of the Employee Retirement Income Security Act of 1974 (29 U.S.C. 1301-1461), operates in accordance with policies established by its Board of Directors.

The Board comprises the Secretaries of Labor, Commerce, and the Treasury. The Secretary of Labor serves as Chair of the Board. A seven-member advisory committee, comprising two labor, two employer, and three general public representatives whom the President appoints, advises the PBGC on investment issues. The President also appoints the PBGC's Director, whom the Senate then confirms.

Activities

Coverage

The Corporation insures most private sector defined-benefit pension plans that provide a pension benefit based on factors such as age, years of service, and salary.

It administers two insurance programs, separately covering single-employer and multiemployer plans. More than 40 million workers and retirees participate in nearly 24,000 covered plans.

Single-Employer Insurance

Under the single-employer program, the Corporation guarantees payment of basic pension benefits if an insured plan terminates without sufficient assets to pay those benefits. The law limits, however, the total monthly benefit that the PBGC may guarantee for one individual to $5,011.36 per month for a 65-year-old individual in a pension plan that terminates in 2015. The law also sets other restrictions on PBGC's guarantee, including limits on the insured amount of recent benefit increases. In certain cases, the Corporation may pay some benefits above the guaranteed amount depending on the funding level of the plan and amounts recovered from employers.

A plan sponsor may terminate a single-employer plan in a standard termination if the plan has sufficient assets to purchase private annuities to cover all benefit liabilities. If a plan does not have sufficient assets, the sponsor may seek to transfer the pension liabilities to the PBGC by demonstrating that it meets the legal criteria for a distress termination. In either termination, the plan administrator must inform participants in writing at least 60 days prior to the date the administrator proposes to terminate the plan. Only a plan that has sufficient assets to pay all benefit liabilities may terminate in a standard termination. The Corporation also may institute termination of underfunded plans in certain specified circumstances.

Multiemployer Insurance

Under title IV, as revised in 1980 by the Multiemployer Pension Plan Amendments Act (29 U.S.C. 1001 note), which changed the insurable event from plan termination to plan insolvency, the Corporation provides financial assistance to multiemployer plans that are unable to pay nonforfeitable benefits. The plans are obligated to repay such assistance. The act also made employers withdrawing from a plan liable to the plan for a portion of its unfunded vested benefits.

Premium Collections

All defined-benefit pension plans insured by the PBGC are required to pay premiums to the Corporation according to rates set by Congress. The per-participant flat-rate premium for plans starting in 2015 is $57.00 for single-employer plans and $26.00 for multiemployer plans. Underfunded single-employer plans must also pay an additional premium equal to $24 per $1,000 of unfunded vested benefits. A termination premium of $1,250 per participant per year applies to certain distress and involuntary plan terminations, payable for 3 years after the termination.

Sources of Information

Blog

The PBGC Web site features the "Retirement Matters" blog.

Business Opportunities

The PBGC tries to give a fair share of its procurement awards and subcontracting opportunities to small businesses. The PBGC regularly procures accounting, actuarial, auditing, benefits administration, legal, and information technology services.

The agency utilizes various types of contract vehicles that are outlined in the "Federal Acquisition Regulation". These types of contract vehicles include agreements, commercial contracts, major contracts, orders against other Government contracts, and purchase orders.

Employment

The PBGC relies on accountants, actuaries, administrative personnel, analysts, attorneys, auditors, employee benefits law specialists, information technology experts, public affairs specialists, and other professionals to carry out its mission.

Fraud Alerts

The PBGC, with support from its Office of the Inspector General, posts fraud alerts to spread awareness of scams.

Freedom of Information Act (FOIA)

The PBGC participates in FOIAonline, which allows information seekers to submit electronic FOIA requests, to track the status of requests, to search for requests submitted by others, to access released records, and to generate agency-specific processing reports.

FOIA requests must be in writing and may be submitted also by email, fax, or by regular mail to the Disclosure Officer, Pension Benefit Guaranty Corporation, 1200 K Street NW., Suite 11101, Washington, DC 20005. Fax, 202-326-4042.

Glossary

The PBGC maintains a glossary of terms with simplified definitions. Some terms and their definitions are PBGC-specific in usage.

Insured Pension Plans

A list of pension plans that recently paid premiums to the PBGC is available online.

Open Government

The PBGC posts datasets that are useful for increasing agency accountability, public knowledge of the agency and its operations, and economic opportunity.

Plain Language

PBGC writers and editors are committed to using plain language in new communications and revising confusing or unclear language in existing material. Send them a note via email if a sentence or paragraph's clarity could be improved.

Press Room

The PBGC posts press releases on its Web site.

An online subscription form is available to sign up for the latest news, delivered via email, from the PBGC.

Site Map

PBGC Web site visitors may use the site map to look for specific topics or to browse for content that aligns with their interests.

For further information, contact the Pension Benefit Guaranty Corporation, 1200 K Street NW., Washington, DC 20005-4026. Phone, 202-326-4000 or 800-400-7242 .

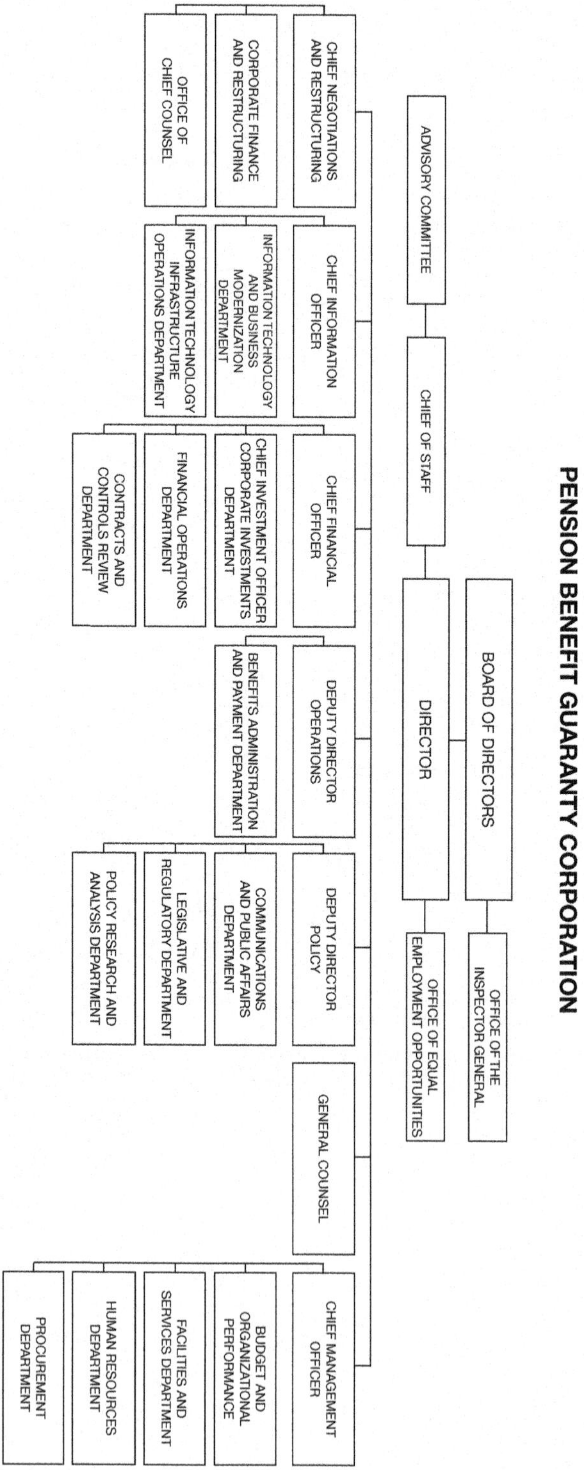
PENSION BENEFIT GUARANTY CORPORATION
BOARD OF DIRECTORS
OFFICE OF THE INSPECTOR GENERAL
ADVISORY COMMITTEE
CHIEF OF STAFF
DIRECTOR
OFFICE OF EQUAL EMPLOYMENT OPPORTUNITIES
CHIEF NEGOTIATIONS AND RESTRUCTURING
CORPORATE FINANCE AND RESTRUCTURING
OFFICE OF CHIEF COUNSEL
CHIEF INFORMATION OFFICER
INFORMATION TECHNOLOGY AND BUSINESS MODERNIZATION DEPARTMENT
INFORMATION TECHNOLOGY INFRASTRUCTURE OPERATIONS DEPARTMENT
CHIEF FINANCIAL OFFICER
CHIEF INVESTMENT OFFICER CORPORATE INVESTMENTS DEPARTMENT
FINANCIAL OPERATIONS DEPARTMENT
CONTRACTS AND CONTROLS REVIEW DEPARTMENT
DEPUTY DIRECTOR OPERATIONS
BENEFITS ADMINISTRATION AND PAYMENT DEPARTMENT
DEPUTY DIRECTOR POLICY
COMMUNICATIONS AND PUBLIC AFFAIRS DEPARTMENT
LEGISLATIVE AND REGULATORY DEPARTMENT
POLICY RESEARCH AND ANALYSIS DEPARTMENT
GENERAL COUNSEL
CHIEF MANAGEMENT OFFICER
BUDGET AND ORGANIZATIONAL PERFORMANCE
FACILITIES AND SERVICES DEPARTMENT
HUMAN RESOURCES DEPARTMENT
PROCUREMENT DEPARTMENT

Postal Regulatory Commission

901 New York Avenue NW., Suite 200, Washington, DC 20268-0001, 202-789-6800, 202-789-6861, *http://www.prc.gov*

CHAIR	Robert G. Taub, Acting
Vice Chair	Nanci E. Langley
Commissioner	Mark Acton
Commissioner	Tony Hammond
Commissioner	(vacancy)
Director, Office of Accountability and Compliance	Margaret Cigno
Director, Office of Public Affairs and Government Relations	Ann Fisher
Director, Office of Secretary and Administration	Stacy L. Ruble
General Counsel	David A. Trissell
Inspector General	John F. Callender

[For the Postal Regulatory Commission statement of organization, see the Code of Federal Regulations, Title 39, Part 3002]

The Postal Regulatory Commission develops and implements a modern system of postal rate regulation.

The Postal Regulatory Commission is the successor agency to the Postal Rate Commission, which was created by the Postal Reorganization Act, as amended (39 U.S.C. 101 et seq.). The Commission was established as an independent agency in the executive branch of Government by the Postal Accountability and Enhancement Act (39 U.S.C. 501). It comprises five Commissioners, appointed by the President with the advice and consent of the Senate, one of whom is designated as Chair.

The Commission promulgates rules and regulations, establishes procedures, and takes other actions necessary to carry out its obligations. It considers complaints received from interested persons relating to United States Postal Service rates, regulations, and services. The Commission also has certain reporting obligations, including a report on universal postal service and the postal monopoly.

Sources of Information

Case Information

Active cases and daily listings are accessible online. A docket search tool is also available.

Employment

The Commission relies on the professional services of accountants, attorneys, economists, industrial engineers, marketing specialists, statisticians, and administrative and clerical personnel to fulfill its mission.

Freedom of Information Act (FOIA)

A FOIA request form is available online.

Newsroom

The Commission posts congressional submissions, papers, press releases, speeches, and upcoming events online.

Reading Room

Facilities for inspection and copying of records, viewing automated daily lists of docketed materials, and accessing the Commission's Web site are located at 901 New York Avenue NW., Suite 200, Washington, DC. The room is open on weekdays, excluding legal holidays, 8 a.m.–4:30 p.m.

Practice and Procedure

Practice and procedure rules governing the conduct of proceedings before the Commission may be found in parts 3001, 3010, 3015, 3020, 3025, 3030, 3031, 3050, and 3060 of title 39 of the "Code of Federal Regulations."

For further information, contact the Secretary, Postal Regulatory Commission, 901 New York Avenue NW., Suite 200, Washington, DC 20268-0001. Phone, 202-789-6840.

Railroad Retirement Board

844 North Rush Street, Chicago, IL 60611-1275, 312-751-4777, 312-751-7154, *http://www.rrb.gov* | Email: *opa@rrb.gov*

CHAIR	(vacancy)
Labor Member	Walter A. Barrows
Management Member	Steven J. Anthony
Inspector General	Martin J. Dickman
Director, Administration	Keith B. Earley
Director, Equal Opportunity	Lynn E. Cousins
Director, Human Resources	Marguerite V. Daniels
Director, Public Affairs	Michael P. Freeman
Chief, Acquisition Management	Paul T. Ahern
Facility Manager	Scott L. Rush
General Counsel	Karl T. Blank
Director, Legislative Affairs / Legislative Counsel	Beverly Britton Fraser
Director, Hearings and Appeals	Rachel L. Simmons
Secretary to the Board	Martha P. Rico
Chief Actuary	Frank J. Buzzi
Chief Information Officer	Ram Murthy
Chief Financial Officer and Senior Executive Officer	George V. Govan
Director, Field Service	Daniel J. Fadden
Director, Programs	Michael A. Tyllas
Director, Policy and Systems	Kimberly Price-Butler
Director, Program Evaluation and Management Services	Janet M. Hallman
Director, Retirement and Survivor Benefits	Valerie F. Allen
Director, Disability Benefits	Sherita P. Boots
Director, Unemployment and Programs Support	Micheal T. Pawlak

[For the Railroad Retirement Board statement of organization, see the Code of Federal Regulations, Title 20, Part 200]

The Railroad Retirement Board administers comprehensive retirement-survivor and unemployment-sickness benefit programs for the Nation's railroad workers and their families.

The Railroad Retirement Board (RRB) was originally established by the Railroad Retirement Act of 1934, as amended (45 U.S.C. 201-228z-1).

The RRB derives statutory authority from the Railroad Retirement Act of 1974 (45 U.S.C. 231-231u) and the Railroad Unemployment Insurance Act (45 U.S.C. 351-369). It administers these acts and participates in the administration of the Social Security Act and the Health Insurance for the Aged Act insofar as they affect railroad retirement beneficiaries.

The RRB comprises three members

whom the President appoints with the advice and consent of the Senate: one upon the recommendations of representatives of railroad employees; one upon the recommendations of railroad employers; and one, the Chair, as a public member.

Activities

The Railroad Retirement Act provides for the payment of annuities to individuals who have completed at least 10 years of creditable railroad service, or 5 years if performed after 1995, and have ceased compensated service upon their attainment of specified ages or at any age if permanently disabled for all employment. In some circumstances occupational disability annuities or supplemental annuities are provided for career employees.

A spouse's annuity is provided, under certain conditions, for the wife or husband of an employee annuitant. Divorced spouses may also qualify.

Survivor annuities are awarded to the qualified spouses, children, and parents of deceased career employees, and various lump-sum benefits are also available under certain conditions.

Benefits based upon qualifying railroad earnings in a preceding 1-year period are provided under the Railroad Unemployment Insurance Act to individuals who are unemployed in a benefit year, but who are ready and willing to work, and to individuals who are unable to work because of sickness or injury.

The RRB maintains, through its field offices, a placement service for unemployed railroad personnel.

Sources of Information

Benefit Inquiries

The RRB provides personal assistance to railroad employees and railroad retirement beneficiaries through its field offices. Staff can explain benefit rights and responsibilities on an individual basis, assist employees in applying for benefits, and answer questions about benefit programs. (Railroad labor groups and employers also help railroad personnel stay informed about benefit programs.) Most field offices are open to the public during the week, 9 a.m.–3:30 p.m. They close at noon on Wednesdays, however, and do not open on Federal holidays. To locate an office, see "Field Offices" below and use the online Zip Code locator or call the automated phone system. Phone, 877-772-5772.

Congressional Inquiries

Members of Congress or their staff may inquire about constituents, benefit claims, and filed applications by contacting the Congressional Inquiry section of the Office of Administration. Phone, 312-751-4970. Fax, 312-751-7154.

Data

The RRB posts actuarial, financial, and statistical data on its Web site. It also publishes datasets on the Web site Data.gov.

Employment

Contact the RRB's Bureau of Human Resources. Phone, 312-751-4580.

Email:

The RRB posts online railroad job vacancies that have been reported to its field offices.

Field Offices

Field offices are located throughout the country. Staff members answer questions about Medicare and Social Security benefits for railroad workers and their families, retirement benefits, sickness and unemployment benefits, survivor benefits, and tax withholding and statements. A Zip Code locator is available online for finding the nearest field office.

Freedom of Information Act (FOIA)

A FOIA request may be made by fax, letter, or online request form. A record description must contain sufficient detail—author, date, subject matter, type of record—to allow RRB staff to locate the record with reasonable effort.

Glossary

A glossary of RRB terms is available online.

Hotline

To report the illegal receiving of RRB benefits or to file a complaint about misconduct relating to the RRB, its programs or employees, contact the Office of Inspector General. Phone, 800-772-4258. Fax, 312-751-4342.

Legislative Affairs

For information on legislative matters, contact the Office of Legislative Affairs. Phone, 202-272-7742. Fax, 202-272-7728. The office is open Tuesday–Thursday, 9 a.m.–3:30 p.m., eastern standard time, except on Federal holidays.

Publications

Booklets, pamphlets (English and Spanish), and forms of interest to beneficiaries and railroad workers are available online. Pamphlets also are available from the RRB's field offices and Chicago headquarters.

Telecommunications Devices for the Deaf (TDD)

The RRB provides TDD services: beneficiary inquiries (Phone, 312-751-4701); equal opportunity inquiries (Phone, 312-751-4334).

For further information, contact Public Affairs, Railroad Retirement Board, 844 North Rush Street, Chicago, IL 60611-1275. Phone, 312-751-4777. Fax, 312-751-7154.

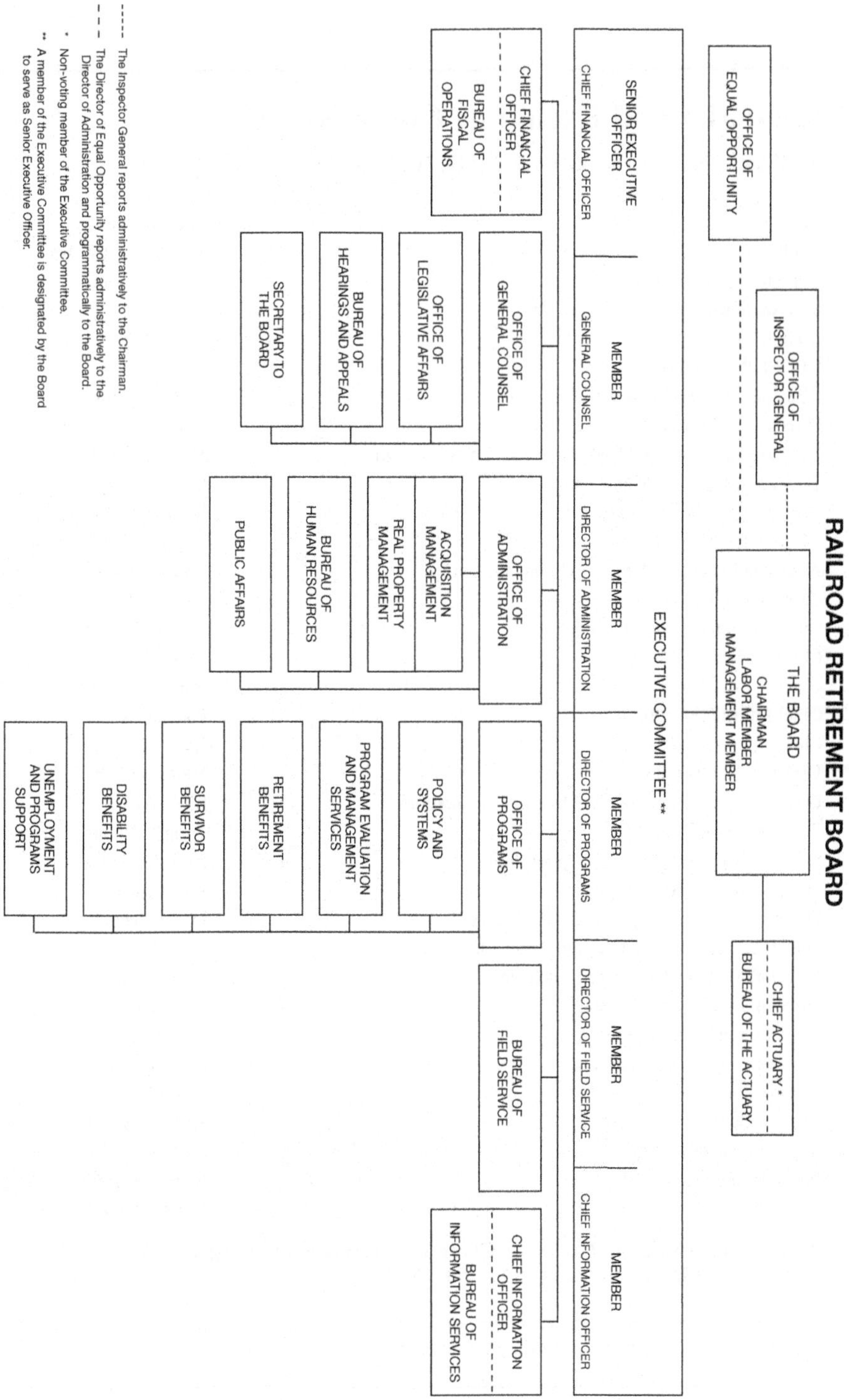
RAILROAD RETIREMENT BOARD
THE BOARD
CHAIRMAN
LABOR MEMBER
MANAGEMENT MEMBER
OFFICE OF EQUAL OPPORTUNITY
OFFICE OF INSPECTOR GENERAL
CHIEF ACTUARY *
BUREAU OF THE ACTUARY
EXECUTIVE COMMITTEE **
SENIOR EXECUTIVE OFFICER
CHIEF FINANCIAL OFFICER
MEMBER
GENERAL COUNSEL
MEMBER
DIRECTOR OF ADMINISTRATION
MEMBER
DIRECTOR OF PROGRAMS
MEMBER
DIRECTOR OF FIELD SERVICE
MEMBER
CHIEF INFORMATION OFFICER
CHIEF FINANCIAL OFFICER
BUREAU OF FISCAL OPERATIONS
OFFICE OF GENERAL COUNSEL
OFFICE OF LEGISLATIVE AFFAIRS
BUREAU OF HEARINGS AND APPEALS
SECRETARY TO THE BOARD
OFFICE OF ADMINISTRATION
ACQUISITION MANAGEMENT
REAL PROPERTY MANAGEMENT
BUREAU OF HUMAN RESOURCES
PUBLIC AFFAIRS
OFFICE OF PROGRAMS
POLICY AND SYSTEMS
PROGRAM EVALUATION AND MANAGEMENT SERVICES
RETIREMENT BENEFITS
SURVIVOR BENEFITS
DISABILITY BENEFITS
UNEMPLOYMENT AND PROGRAMS SUPPORT
BUREAU OF FIELD SERVICE
CHIEF INFORMATION OFFICER
BUREAU OF INFORMATION SERVICES
----- The Inspector General reports administratively to the Chairman.
- - - The Director of Equal Opportunity reports administratively to the Director of Administration and programmatically to the Board.
* Non-voting member of the Executive Committee.
** A member of the Executive Committee is designated by the Board to serve as Senior Executive Officer.

Securities and Exchange Commission

100 F Street NE., Washington, DC 20549, 202-551-7500, *http://www.sec.gov*

CHAIR	Mary Jo White
Commissioner	Michael S. Piwowar
Commissioner	Kara M. Stein
Commissioner	(vacancy)
Commissioner	(vacancy)
DIVISION HEADS	
Director, Corporation Finance	Keith Higgins
Director, Enforcement	Andrew Ceresney
Director, Economic and Risk Analysis / Chief Economist	Mark J. Flannery
Director, Investment Management	David Grim
Director, Trading and Markets	Stephen Luparello
OFFICE HEADS	
Associate Executive Director, Human Resources	Lacey Dingman
Chief Accountant	James Schnurr
Chief Administrative Law Judge	Brenda P. Murray
Chief Financial Officer	Kenneth Johnson
Chief FOIA Officer	Barry D. Walters
Chief Information Officer	Pamela Dyson
Chief Operating Officer	Jeffery Heslop
Director, Acquisitions	Vance Cathell
Director, Compliance Inspections and Examinations	Marc Wyatt
Director, Credit Ratings	Thomas Butler
Director, Equal Employment Opportunity	Alta Rodriguez
Director, International Affairs	Paul Leder
Director, Investor Education and Advocacy	Lori J. Schock
Director, Legislative and Intergovernmental Affairs	Keith Cassidy
Director, Minority and Women Inclusion	Pamela Gibbs
Director, Municipal Securities	Jessica Kane
Director, Public Affairs	John Nester
Director, Support Operations	Barry D. Walters
Ethics Counsel	Shira P. Minton
General Counsel	Anne K. Small
Inspector General	Carl W. Hoecker
Investor Advocate	Rick A. Fleming
Secretary	Brent J. Fields

[For the Securities and Exchange Commission statement of organization, see the Code of Federal Regulations, Title 17, Part 200]

The Securities and Exchange Commission protects investors, facilitates capital formation, and maintains efficient, fair, and orderly markets.

The Securities and Exchange Commission (SEC) was created under authority of the Securities Exchange Act of 1934 (15 U.S.C. 78a-78jj) and was organized on July 2, 1934. The Commission serves as adviser to United States district courts in reorganization proceedings for debtor corporations in which a substantial public interest is involved. The Commission also has certain responsibilities under section 15 of the Bretton Woods Agreements Act of 1945 (22 U.S.C. 286k-1) and section 851(e) of the Internal Revenue Code of 1954 (26 U.S.C. 851(e)).

The Commission is vested with quasi-judicial functions. Persons aggrieved by its decisions in the exercise of those functions have a right of review by the United States courts of appeals.

Activities

Full and Fair Disclosure

The Securities Act of 1933 (15 U.S.C. 77a) requires issuers of securities and their controlling persons making public offerings of securities in interstate commerce or via mail to file registration statements containing financial and other pertinent data about the issuer and the securities being offered with the SEC. There are limited exemptions, such as government securities, nonpublic offerings, and intrastate offerings, as well as certain offerings not exceeding $1.5 million. The effectiveness of a registration statement may be refused or suspended after a public hearing if the statement contains material misstatements or omissions, thus barring sale of the securities until it is appropriately amended.

Regulation of Investment Advisers

Persons who, for compensation, engage in the business of advising others with respect to securities must register with the Commission. The Commission is authorized to define what practices are considered fraudulent or deceptive and to prescribe means to prevent those practices.

Regulation of Mutual Funds and Other Investment Companies

The Commission registers investment companies and regulates their activities to protect investors. The regulation covers sales load, management contracts, composition of boards of directors, and capital structure. The Commission must also determine the fairness of various transactions of investment companies before they actually occur.

The Commission may institute court action to enjoin the consummation of mergers and other plans of reorganization of investment companies if such plans are unfair to securities holders. It may impose sanctions by administrative proceedings against investment company management for violations of the act and other Federal securities laws. It also may file court actions to enjoin acts and practices of management officials involving breaches of fiduciary duty and personal misconduct and to disqualify such officials from office.

Regulation of Securities Markets

The Securities Exchange Act of 1934 assigns to the Commission broad regulatory responsibilities over the securities markets, the self-regulatory organizations within the securities industry, and persons conducting a business in securities. Persons who execute transactions in securities generally are required to register with the Commission as broker-dealers. Securities exchanges and certain clearing agencies are required to register with the Commission, and associations of brokers or dealers are permitted to register with the Commission. The act also provides for the establishment of the Municipal Securities Rulemaking Board to formulate rules for the municipal securities industry.

The Commission oversees the self-regulatory activities of the national securities exchanges and associations, registered clearing agencies, and the Municipal Securities Rulemaking Board. In addition, the Commission regulates industry professionals, such as securities brokers and dealers, certain municipal securities professionals, Government securities brokers and dealers, and transfer agents.

Rehabilitation of Failing Corporations

In cases of corporate reorganization proceedings administered in Federal courts, the Commission may participate as a statutory party. The principal functions of the Commission are to protect the interests of public investors involved in such cases through efforts to ensure their adequate representation and to participate in legal and policy issues that are of concern to public investors generally.

Representation of Debt Securities Holders

The Commission safeguards the interests of purchasers of publicly offered debt securities issued pursuant to trust indentures.

Enforcement Activities

The Commission's enforcement activities are designed to secure compliance with the Federal securities laws administered by the Commission and the rules and regulations adopted thereunder. These activities include measures to do the following: compel compliance with the disclosure requirements of the registration and other provisions of the relevant acts; prevent fraud and deception in the purchase and sale of securities; obtain court orders enjoining acts and practices that operate as a fraud upon investors or otherwise violate the laws; suspend or revoke the registrations of brokers, dealers, investment companies, and investment advisers who willfully engage in such acts and practices; suspend or bar from association persons associated with brokers, dealers, investment companies, and investment advisers who have violated any provision of the Federal securities laws; and prosecute persons who have engaged in fraudulent activities or other willful violations of those laws.

In addition, attorneys, accountants, and other professionals who violate the securities laws face possible loss of their privilege to practice before the Commission.

To this end, private investigations are conducted into complaints or other indications of securities violations. Established evidence of law violations is used in appropriate administrative proceedings to revoke registration or in actions instituted in Federal courts to restrain or enjoin such activities. Where the evidence tends to establish criminal fraud or other willful violation of the securities laws, the facts are referred to the Attorney General for criminal prosecution of the offenders. The Commission may assist in such prosecutions.

Sources of Information

Business Opportunities

The Office of Acquisitions' Web page features links to help those who seek business opportunities with the SEC. Phone, 202-551-7300.

Electronic Data Gathering, Analysis, and Retrieval (EDGAR)

The EDGAR database provides free public access to corporate information such as prospectuses, registration statements, and quarterly and annual reports.

Employment

The SEC relies on accountants, attorneys, economists, examiners, industry specialists, information technology specialists, and other professionals to carry out its mission. Applicants must apply for a specific vacancy and complete a process of competitive selection. This process does not apply, however, to attorney vacancies. The Commission runs a college and law school recruitment program that relies on campus visits and student interviews.

For more information, contact the Office of Human Resources. Phone, 202-551-7500. Fax, 202-777-1028.

Events

A schedule of upcoming SEC meetings, public appearances by SEC officials, and public hearings is available online.

Fast Answers

The SEC maintains a list of the terms for which SEC Web site visitors search most frequently.

Freedom of Information Act (FOIA)

The Office of Freedom of Information Act Services makes SEC records available to the public to the greatest extent possible under the FOIA. The Office receives nearly 17,000 requests per year for Commission documents and records. For more information, contact the FOIA public service center. Phone, 202-551-7900. Fax, 202-772-9337.

Many records—no-action and interpretive letters, public comments on proposed rules, registration statements and reports filed by regulated companies and individuals, SEC decisions and releases, and staff manuals—can be read and printed for free by using the SEC online search feature. An electronic request form is available for obtaining nonpublic records: consumer complaints, records compiled in investigations, and staff comment letters. The SEC will release nonpublic records, except when they are protected by a FOIA exemption. The electronic request form may be used also for obtaining older records that the SEC has not posted on its Web site—records usually dated before 1996.

Glossary

The Office of Investor Education and Advocacy maintains an online glossary.

Investment Adviser Public Disclosure

The SEC provides an online tool to search for an investment adviser firm and to view the registration or reporting form (Form ADV) that the adviser filed. The tool also allows an investor to search for an individual investment adviser representative and to view his or her professional background and conduct.

Investor Education

The Office of Investor Education and Advocacy offers services to and provides tools for investors. The Office cannot tell an investor how or where to invest money, but it can help him or her invest knowledgeably and avoid fraud. Phone, 800-732-0330. Fax, 202-772-9295.

The Office of Investor Education and Advocacy tweets on Twitter.

The SEC maintains a list of external educational web sites.

The SEC maintains a list of investor calculators and tools that are available on external web sites.

Newsroom

The SEC posts press releases, public statements, speeches, testimonies, and web casts on its Web site. A subscription form is available online to receive news alerts via email.

The SEC maintains a presence on social media—Flickr, Twitter, YouTube—and uses RSS feeds to disseminate information and news.

Open Government

The SEC supports the Open Government initiative by promoting the principles of collaboration, participation, and transparency.

Plain Language

Like other Federal agencies, the SEC must compose documents in plain writing. According to the Plain Writing Act of 2010, writing should be "clear, concise, well-organized" and follow "other best practices appropriate to the subject or field or audience." SEC writers and editors want to know if agency documents and Web pages are difficult to understand. Contact them by email to leave a comment or make a suggestion.

Publications

SEC publications are available in Chinese, English, and Spanish in Portable Document Format (PDF).

Regional Offices

Regional offices can provide investors with information and assist them with complaints. Contact information for the SEC's 11 regional offices is available online.

Site Map

The Web site map allows visitors to look for specific topics or to browse for content that aligns with their interests.

Small Business Activities

Information for small businesses—information on legal obligations when they sell securities and on financial and other reporting obligations when their securities are traded publicly—is available online. Contact the Office of Small Business Policy for more information. Phone, 202-551-3460.

Tips and Complaints

Members of the public can inform the

SEC of possible violations of U.S. securities laws by completing the online questionnaire.

For further information, contact the Office of Public Affairs, Securities and Exchange Commission, 100 F Street NE., Washington, DC 20549. Phone, 202-551-4120. Fax, 202-777-1026.

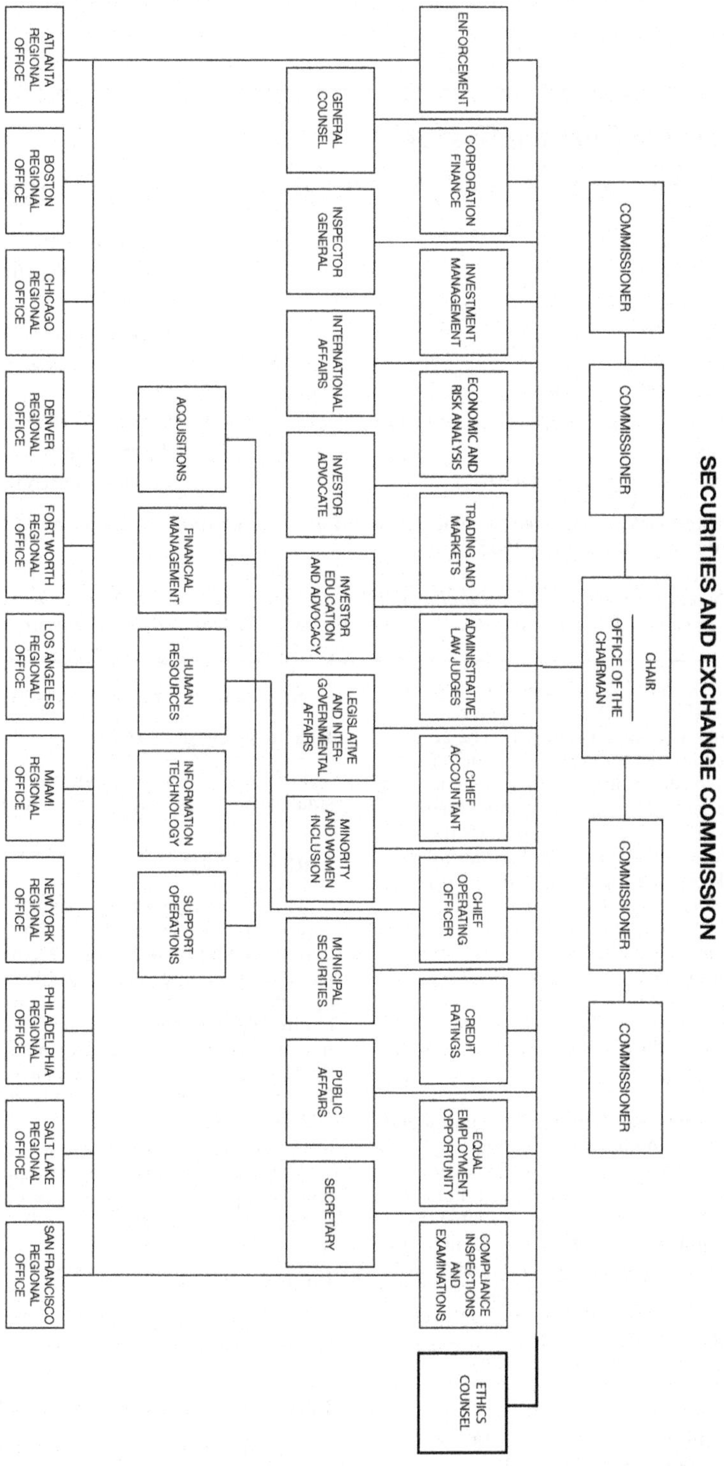
SECURITIES AND EXCHANGE COMMISSION
COMMISSIONER
COMMISSIONER
CHAIR
OFFICE OF THE CHAIRMAN
COMMISSIONER
COMMISSIONER
ENFORCEMENT
CORPORATION FINANCE
INVESTMENT MANAGEMENT
ECONOMIC AND RISK ANALYSIS
TRADING AND MARKETS
ADMINISTRATIVE LAW JUDGES
CHIEF ACCOUNTANT
CHIEF OPERATING OFFICER
CREDIT RATINGS
EQUAL EMPLOYMENT OPPORTUNITY
COMPLIANCE INSPECTIONS AND EXAMINATIONS
ETHICS COUNSEL
GENERAL COUNSEL
INSPECTOR GENERAL
INTERNATIONAL AFFAIRS
INVESTOR ADVOCATE
INVESTOR EDUCATION AND ADVOCACY
LEGISLATIVE AND INTER-GOVERNMENTAL AFFAIRS
MINORITY AND WOMEN INCLUSION
MUNICIPAL SECURITIES
PUBLIC AFFAIRS
SECRETARY
ACQUISITIONS
FINANCIAL MANAGEMENT
HUMAN RESOURCES
INFORMATION TECHNOLOGY
SUPPORT OPERATIONS
ATLANTA REGIONAL OFFICE
BOSTON REGIONAL OFFICE
CHICAGO REGIONAL OFFICE
DENVER REGIONAL OFFICE
FORT WORTH REGIONAL OFFICE
LOS ANGELES REGIONAL OFFICE
MIAMI REGIONAL OFFICE
NEW YORK REGIONAL OFFICE
PHILADELPHIA REGIONAL OFFICE
SALT LAKE REGIONAL OFFICE
SAN FRANCISCO REGIONAL OFFICE

Selective Service System

National Headquarters, Arlington, VA 22209-2425, 703-605-4100, *http://www.sss.gov*

DIRECTOR	Lawrence G. Romo
Deputy Director	Edward T. Allard III
Chief Information Officer	Jerry Klotz
Chief of Staff	Mario A. Garza
General Counsel	Rudy G. Sanchez, Jr.
ASSOCIATE DIRECTORS	
Financial Management / Chief Financial Officer	Roderick R. Hubbard
Operations	Adam J. Copp
Public and Intergovernmental Affairs	Richard S. Flahavan

[For the Selective Service System statement of organization, see the Code of Federal Regulations, Title 32, Part 1605]

The Selective Service System supplies the Armed Forces with manpower in an emergency and operates an Alternative Service Program for men classified as conscientious objectors.

The Selective Service System was established by the Military Selective Service Act (50 U.S.C. app. 451-471a). The act requires the registration of male citizens of the United States and all other male persons who are in the United States and who are ages 18 to 25. The act exempts members of the active Armed Forces and nonimmigrant aliens. Proclamation 4771 of July 20, 1980, requires male persons born on or after January 1, 1960, and who have attained age 18, but have not attained age 26 to register. Registration is conducted at post offices within the United States, at U.S. Embassies and consulates outside the United States, and online at the Selective Service System's Web site.

The act imposes liability for training and service in the Armed Forces upon registrants who are ages 18 to 26, except those who are exempt or deferred. Persons who have been deferred remain liable for training and service until age 35. Aliens are not liable for training and service until they have remained in the United States for more than 1 year. Conscientious objectors who are opposed to all service in the Armed Forces are required to perform civilian work in lieu of induction into the Armed Forces.

The authority to induct registrants, including doctors and allied medical specialists, expired on July 1, 1973.

Sources of Information

Business Opportunities

For information on opportunities for small businesses, call 703-605-4038.

Employment

The Selective Service System offers competitive wages, the Thrift Savings Plan with matching funds, health care benefits, paid vacation time, and work-life benefit options that include telework, as well as alternate and flexible work schedules for most positions. For more information, visit the "Careers" Web page or contact the Office of Human Resources. Phone, 703-605-4040.

The Selective Service System posts the results of past Federal employee viewpoint surveys on its Web site.

Forms

Frequently requested forms are available on the Selective Service System's Web site.

Freedom of Information Act (FOIA)

An information seeker should submit his or her request in writing; include his or her name, address, and telephone number;

indicate that the request is being made under the Freedom of Information Act; provide specific information for identifying the records sought; and send the request to the FOIA Officer, Selective Service System, National Headquarters, Arlington, VA 22209-2425.

The Selective Service System maintains a FOIA electronic reading room.

Newsletter

The Selective Service System's quarterly newsletter "The Register" is available online.

Plain Language

The Selective Service System adheres to Federal plain language guidelines. If a document or Web page is poorly written and difficult to understand, contact the agency by email.

Publications

The Selective Service System posts reports, including its "Annual Report to the Congress of the United States," online.

Registration

Men, age 18–25, with a valid social security number, may use the online registration form. A fillable registration form that can be returned by mail is also available for immigrant males (documented or undocumented), for men who cannot use the online registration form because of a faulty social security number, and for men without a social security number.

For further information, contact the Office of Public and Intergovernmental Affairs, Selective Service System, Arlington, VA 22209-2425. Phone, 703-605-4100.

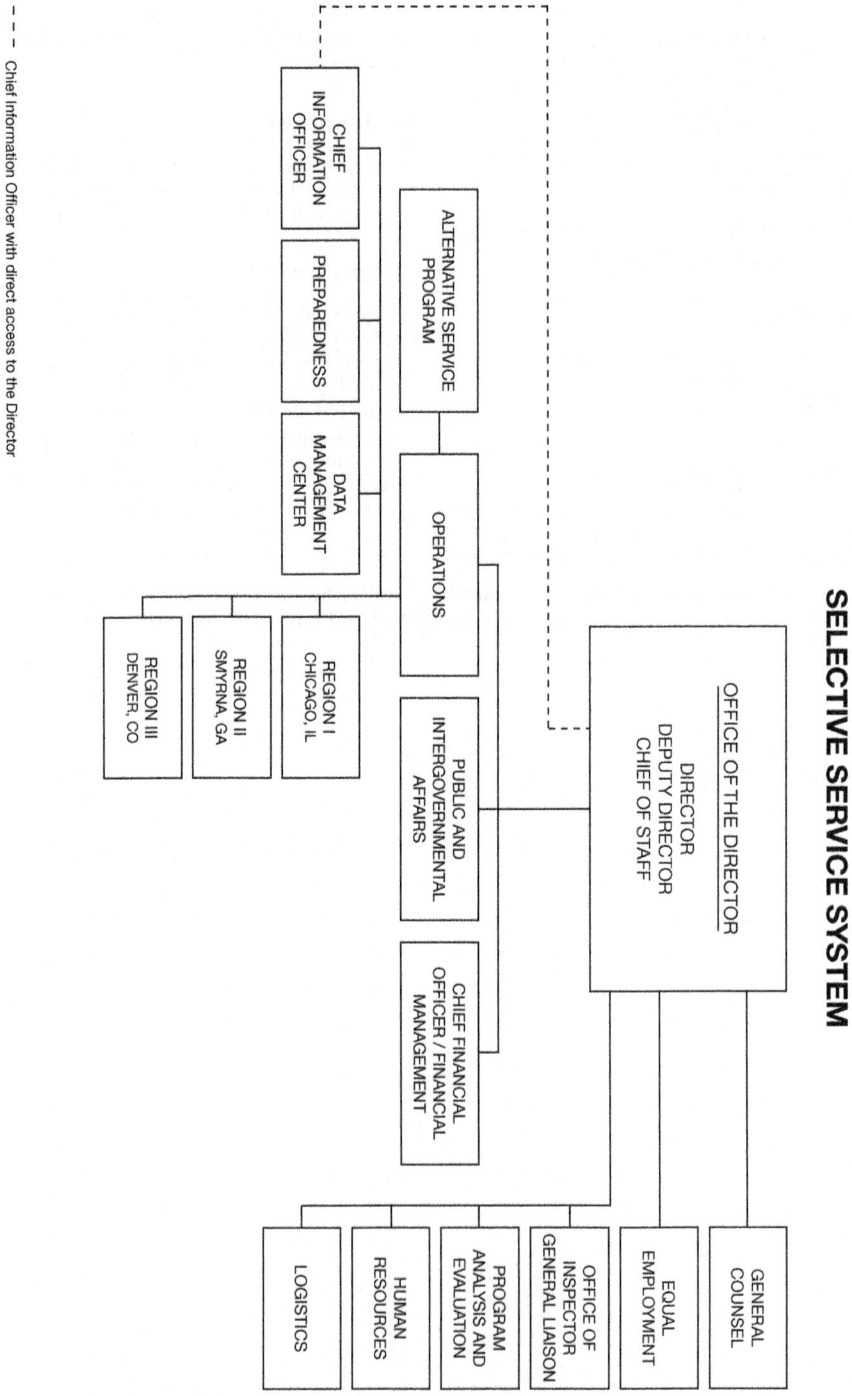
SELECTIVE SERVICE SYSTEM
OFFICE OF THE DIRECTOR
DIRECTOR
DEPUTY DIRECTOR
CHIEF OF STAFF
GENERAL COUNSEL
EQUAL EMPLOYMENT
OFFICE OF INSPECTOR GENERAL LIAISON
PROGRAM ANALYSIS AND EVALUATION
HUMAN RESOURCES
LOGISTICS
CHIEF FINANCIAL OFFICER / FINANCIAL MANAGEMENT
PUBLIC AND INTERGOVERNMENTAL AFFAIRS
OPERATIONS
ALTERNATIVE SERVICE PROGRAM
REGION I CHICAGO, IL
REGION II SMYRNA, GA
REGION III DENVER, CO
DATA MANAGEMENT CENTER
PREPAREDNESS
CHIEF INFORMATION OFFICER
Chief Information Officer with direct access to the Director

Small Business Administration

409 Third Street SW., Washington, DC 20416, 202-205-6600, 202-205-7064, *http://www.sba.gov*

ADMINISTRATOR	Maria Contreras-Sweet
Deputy Administrator	Douglas J. Kramer
ASSISTANT ADMINISTRATORS	
Office of Faith-Based Community Initiatives	(vacancy)
Office of Hearings and Appeals	Delorice Price Ford
Office of the National Ombudsman and Regulatory Enforcement Fairness	Earl L. Gay
ASSOCIATE ADMINISTRATORS	
Office of Capital Access	Ann Marie Mehlum
Office of Communications and Public Liaison	Brian Weiss
Office of Congressional and Legal Affairs	Danielle L. Jimenez
Officer of Disaster Assistance	James Rivera
Office of Entrepreneurial Development	Tameka Montgomery
Office of Field Operations	Christopher L. James
Office of Government Contracting and Business Development	John Shoraka
Office of International Trade	Eileen Sánchez
Office of Investment and Innovation	Mark L. Walsh
Office of Native American Affairs	Nathan Segal
Office of Veterans Business Development	Barbara Carson
Chief Counsel for Advocacy	Darryl L. DePriest
Chief Financial Officer	Tami Perriello
Chief Operating Officer	Matthew Varilek
General Counsel	Melvin F. Williams, Jr.
Inspector General	Peggy E. Gustafson

[For the Small Business Administration statement of organization, see the Code of Federal Regulations, Title 13, Part 101]

The Small Business Administration aids, assists, and counsels entrepreneurs and protects their business interests; preserves free and competitive enterprise; and maintains and strengthens the overall economy of the Nation.

The Small Business Administration (SBA) was created by the Small Business Act of 1953 and derives its present existence and authority from the Small Business Act (15 U.S.C. 631 et seq.) and the Small Business Investment Act of 1958 (15 U.S.C. 661).

Activities

Advocacy

The Office of Advocacy carries a congressional mandate to serve as an independent voice within the Federal Government for the approximately 28 million small businesses nationwide. The Chief Counsel for Advocacy, whom the President appoints with the advice and consent of the Senate, from the private sector, presents the concerns, interests, and views of the small business community to White House administrators, Members of the Congress, and Federal and State regulators.

The Office reports annually on Federal compliance with the Regulatory Flexibility

Act (RFA), which requires agencies to analyze the effect of their regulations on small businesses and to consider less burdensome alternatives. Executive Order 13272 requires Federal agencies to take the Office's comments into consideration before finalizing proposed regulations. It also requires the Office to train Federal staff on RFA compliance.

The Office serves as one of the best sources of information on the state of small businesses nationwide and on the issues that affect success and growth. It conducts economic and statistical research on jobs that small businesses create; on the effect of Federal laws, regulations, and programs; and on factors that influence their competitive strength. The Office then recommends measures that address the special needs of small businesses to policymakers.

Regional advocates facilitate communication between the Chief Counsel for Advocacy and the small business community. As the Chief Counsel's direct link to local business owners, State and local government agencies, State legislatures, and small business organizations, these advocates identify emerging problems and issues by monitoring the effect of Federal and State regulations and policies on business activity in their respective regions.

For further information, contact the Office of Advocacy. Phone, 202-205-6533.

Business and Community Initiatives

The Office of Business and Community Initiatives develops and cosponsors counseling, education, training, and information resources for small businesses. It partners with the private sector to promote entrepreneurial development. The Office supports the Service Corps of Retired Executives (SCORE) nationwide, nonprofit association (www.score.org). SCORE volunteers, who number over 11,000, help small businesses start and grow by providing free or low cost educational services: mentoring and business counseling, tools, and workshops. The Office also provides online information for young entrepreneurs (www.sba.gov/teens).

For further information, contact the Small Business Administration. Phone, 202-205-6600.

Business Development

The Office of Business Development oversees the 8(a) Business Development program. The Office assists with contracts and loans, counsels, expands access to capital and credit, gives technical guidance, and offers training workshops. One of its principal business development tools is the Mentor-Protégé program, which allows participants to benefit from business development assistance provided by successful companies.

For further information, contact the Office of Business Development. Phone, 202-205-5852.

Capital Access

The Office of the Associate Administrator for Capital Access increases the availability of capital through banks and other lending partners. It oversees SBA programs that help small businesses gain access to capital. These programs include the 7(a) general business guarantee, 504 Certified Development Company, SBA surety bond guarantee, and microlending.

For further information, contact the Office of Capital Access. Phone, 202-205-6657.

Disaster Assistance

The SBA serves as the Federal disaster bank for nonfarm, private sector losses. It lends money to disaster survivors for repairing or replacing their most damaged property. The agency makes direct loans with subsidized interest rates to individuals, homeowners, businesses of all sizes, and nonprofit organizations.

For further information, contact the Office of Disaster Assistance. Phone, 202-205-6734.

Field Operations

The Office of Field Operations is responsible for the provision of SBA services and availability of its products: It serves as the critical link between SBA policymakers and small businessmen and women. The Office provides policy guidance and oversight to regional administrators and district directors for achieving agency goals and objectives and for solving problems in specific operational areas. It plays a liaison role and expedites issues for the regional and district offices when dealing with the central office, coordinating the presentation of views from the field. It also establishes and monitors district performance goals and organizes reviews of the field offices.

A complete listing of the regional, district, and disaster field offices—including addresses, telephone numbers, and key officials—is available online.

For further information, contact the Office of Field Operations. Phone, 202-205-6808.

Financial Assistance

The SBA gives its guarantee to lending institutions and certified development companies that make loans to small businesses. These businesses can then use the money for working capital and financing the acquisition of land and buildings, constructing new and improving existing facilities, and purchasing equipment and machinery.

Under the SBA's microloan program, the Administration provides indirect, small-scale financial and technical assistance to very small businesses through loans and grants to intermediary nonprofit organizations (www.sba.gov/content/microloan-program).

For further information, contact the nearest Small Business Administration district office.

Government Contracting

Through various programs and services, the SBA assists small businesses—including HUBZone certified firms and disadvantaged, women-owned, and service-disabled veteran-owned small businesses—with receiving Government procurement. The contracting liaison helps small-scale entrepreneurs secure an equitable share of the natural resources that the Federal Government sells. The Administration also works with the Office of Management and Budget and other Federal agencies to establish policy and regulations affecting small business access to Government contracts.

For further information, contact the nearest Office of Government Contracting. Phone, 202-205-6460.

Historically Underutilized Business Zones

The Historically Underutilized Business Zone (HUBZone) program was enacted into law as part of the Small Business Reauthorization Act of 1997. The program fosters economic development and employment in HUBZones, which include Indian reservations, through the establishment of preferences. The program provides greater access to Federal contracting opportunities for qualified businesses. The SBA regulates and implements the program: It determines which businesses are eligible to receive HUBZone contracts, maintains a list of qualified businesses that Federal agencies can use to locate venders, adjudicates protests of contract eligibility, and reports to the Congress on the program's effect on employment and investment in the zones.

For further information, contact the HUBZone Help Desk. Phone, 202-205-8885.

International Trade

The Office of International Trade makes American small businesses more competitive in the global marketplace by developing international trade opportunities for small enterprises. It collaborates with other Federal agencies and public and private sector groups to promote small business exports and to help entrepreneurs who seek opportunities to export. The Office—through 19 U.S. Export Assistance Centers, SBA district offices, and service-provider partners—coordinates and directs the Administration's export initiatives.

For further information, contact the Office of International Trade. Phone, 202-205-6720.

Native American Affairs

The Office of Native American Affairs assists and encourages the creation, development, and expansion of small businesses owned by Native Americans. It develops and implements initiatives designed to address specific business challenges encountered by Native American entrepreneurs. The Office's Web page features information on programs and tools to promote reservation-based small business activity.

For further information, contact the Office of Native American Affairs. Phone, 202-205-7364.

Regulatory Fairness Program

Congress established the National Ombudsman and 10 Regulatory Fairness (RegFair) Boards in 1996 as part of the Small Business Regulatory Enforcement Fairness Act. The National Ombudsman assists small businessmen and women when they experience excessive or unfair Federal regulatory enforcement action. The National Ombudsman receives comments from small businesses and acts as a liaison between them and Federal agencies. These comments are forwarded to the appropriate Federal agencies for review and consideration of the fairness of their enforcement actions. The National Ombudsman sends a copy of an agency's response to the small business owner. In some cases, fines are reduced or eliminated and decisions changed in favor of the business owner.

Each of the RegFair Boards comprises five volunteer members who are owners, operators, or officers of small enterprises. The SBA Administrator appoints board members for 3-year terms. Each RegFair Board meets at least annually with the Ombudsman, reports to the Ombudsman on substantiated instances of excessive or unfair enforcement, and comments on the annual report to Congress prior to its publication.

For further information, contact the Office of the National Ombudsman. Phone, 888-734-3247.

Research Investment and Technology Transfer

The Office of Investment and Innovation manages the Small Business Investment Research (SBIR) and Small Business Technology Transfer (STTR) programs. These two programs together provide billions of dollars per year for small enterprises to participate in federally funded research and development and to cooperate with 11 Government agencies and hundreds of research institutions and universities. The SBIR and STTR programs stimulate the creation of intellectual property with potential for commercialization and with applications in a broad range of sectors in the Nation's economy.

For further information, contact the Office of Investment and Innovation. Phone, 202-205-6510.

Small Business Development Centers

The Office of Small Business Development Centers funds, oversees, and supports the nationwide Small Business Development Center (SBDC) network. The SBDC program provides one-stop management assistance to current and prospective small business owners in central and easily accessible branch locations. The program relies on the cooperation of the private sector, the educational community, and Federal, State, and local governments.

The SBDC program delivers up-to-date counseling, technical help, and training in all aspects of small business management. Its services include assistance with feasibility studies and with engineering, financial, marketing, organization, production, and technical challenges. Special SBDC activities include international trade assistance, procurement assistance, rural development, venture capital information, and technical assistance.

For further information, contact the Office of Small Business Development Centers. Phone, 202-205-6766.

Surety Bonds

The Surety Bond Guarantee program helps small and emerging contractors obtain the bonding necessary for bidding on and receiving contracts up to $5 million. The SBA guarantees bonds that participating surety companies issue and reimburses between 70–90 percent of losses and expenses incurred should a business default on the contract. Construction, service, and supply contractors are eligible for the program if they meet certain standards.

For further information, contact the Office of Surety Guarantees. Phone, 202-205-6540.

Venture Capital

The Small Business Investment Company (SBIC) program was created in 1958 to bridge the gap between venture capital availability and the needs of startups and expanding small businesses. SBICs are privately owned and managed venture capital funds, which the SBA licenses and regulates. They use their own capital combined with SBA guaranteed funds to make equity and debt investments in qualifying small businesses. Fund managers may invest only in small businesses having net worth of less than $18 million and average aftertax income for the previous 2 years of less than $6 million. The New Markets Venture Capital (NMVC) program is a sister program centering on low-income areas. It augments the contribution made by SBICs to small businesses in the United States.

The Federal Government neither invests directly in nor targets industries for inclusion in the SBIC program. Qualified private fund managers are responsible for fund portfolio management and investment decisions. To obtain an SBIC license, an experienced team of private equity managers must secure minimum commitments from private investors.

For further information, contact the Investment Division. Phone, 202-205-6510.

Veterans Business Development

The Office of Veterans Business Development (OVBD) formulates, executes, and promotes policies and programs that provide assistance to small businesses owned and controlled by veterans and service-disabled veterans, including reserve component members of the U.S. military. The Office also serves as an ombudsman, advocating for veterans. OVBD personnel are involved in every SBA program to ensure that veterans receive special consideration in the operation of that program.

The Office provides resources, services, and tools: the Vet Gazette newsletter, Reserve and Guard business assistance kits, program design assistance, training, and counseling. The Office manages five Veterans Business Outreach Centers to provide outreach, directed referrals, and tailored entrepreneurial development services to veterans, including service-disabled veterans, and reservists. The OVBD also coordinates SBA collaborative efforts with veterans service organizations; the Departments of Defense, Labor, and Veterans Affairs; the National Veterans Business Development Corporation; State veterans affairs departments; the National Committee for Employer Support of the Guard and Reserve; the Department of Defense Yellow Ribbon Reintegration Program; and other civic, private, and public organizations.

For further information, contact the Office of Veterans Business Development. Phone, 202-205-6773.

Women's Business Ownership

The Office of Women's Business Ownership (OWBO) enables and empowers women entrepreneurs through advocacy, outreach, education, and support. OWBO programs offer business training and counseling, access to credit and capital, and marketing opportunities, including Federal contracts.

In 1988, the SBA established the Women's Business Center (WBC) program to help women overcome barriers to success. Today, WBCs offer SBA services in almost every State. WBCs tailor their services to the needs of their communities. They provide financial, Internet, management, and marketing training, as well as offering access to SBA financial and procurement assistance programs.

For further information, contact the Women's Business Ownership representative in your SBA district office. Phone, 202-205-6673.

Sources of Information

Business Opportunities

Information on selling to the Government and qualifying for Government contracts is available online. The SBA also provides online resources for small businesses and posts information on Government contracting programs on its Web site.

The Office of Government Contracting maintains a glossary that defines program-related terms that may be unfamiliar.

Electronic Updates

An online subscription form is available to sign up for electronic updates on upcoming events and business tips.

Employment

The SBA offers Federal Government health benefits, flexible work schedules, and paid leave. It also promotes a work-life balance.

Freedom of Information Act (FOIA)

Instructions for submitting a FOIA request are available online.

Newsroom

The SBA newsroom features congressional testimonies, media advisories, press releases, speeches, and weekly lending reports.

Open Government

The SBA supports the Open Government initiative by promoting the principles of collaboration, participation, and transparency.

Plain Language

SBA writers and editors are committed to producing documents in plain language. If documents or Web pages are unclear or difficult to understand, contact the SBA by email.

Public Affairs

The SBA public affairs team responds to questions from the media and general public, arranges interviews with appropriate program staff, and provides referrals and other information. To find an SBA local or regional spokesperson, visit the "Regional and Local Media" Web page. For public inquiries and small business advocacy affairs, contact the Office of Public Communications and Public Liaison. Phone, 202-205-6740.

Resource Guide

English (2015) and Spanish (2012) versions of the "Resource Guide for Small Business" are available online in Portable Document Format (PDF).

For further information, contact the Office of Public Communications and Public Liaison, Small Business Administration, 409 Third Street SW., Washington, DC 20416. Phone, 202-205-6740.

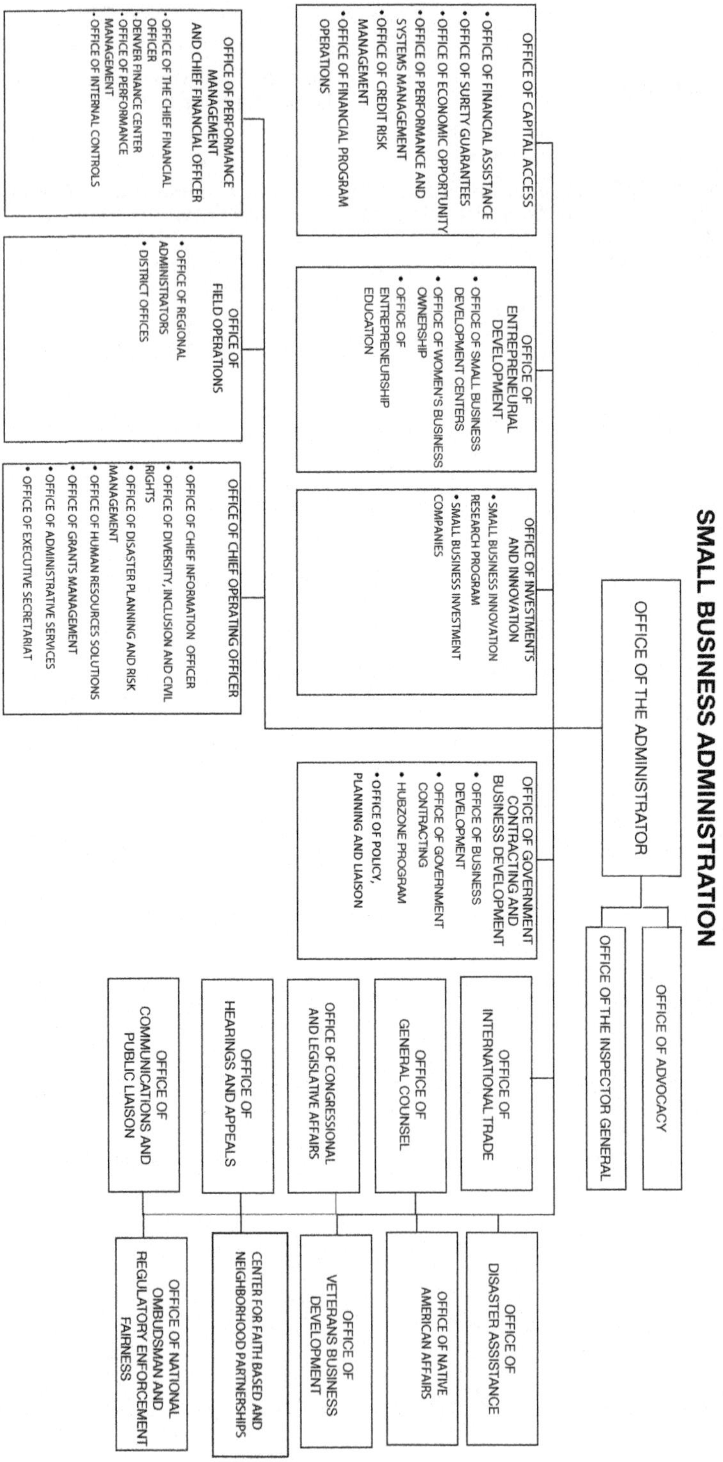
SMALL BUSINESS ADMINISTRATION
OFFICE OF THE ADMINISTRATOR
OFFICE OF ADVOCACY
OFFICE OF THE INSPECTOR GENERAL
OFFICE OF CAPITAL ACCESS
• OFFICE OF FINANCIAL ASSISTANCE
• OFFICE OF SURETY GUARANTEES
• OFFICE OF ECONOMIC OPPORTUNITY
• OFFICE OF PERFORMANCE AND SYSTEMS MANAGEMENT
• OFFICE OF CREDIT RISK MANAGEMENT
• OFFICE OF FINANCIAL PROGRAM OPERATIONS
OFFICE OF ENTREPRENEURIAL DEVELOPMENT
• OFFICE OF SMALL BUSINESS DEVELOPMENT CENTERS
• OFFICE OF WOMEN'S BUSINESS OWNERSHIP
• OFFICE OF ENTREPRENEURSHIP EDUCATION
OFFICE OF INVESTMENTS AND INNOVATION
• SMALL BUSINESS INNOVATION RESEARCH PROGRAM
• SMALL BUSINESS INVESTMENT COMPANIES
OFFICE OF GOVERNMENT CONTRACTING AND BUSINESS DEVELOPMENT
• OFFICE OF BUSINESS DEVELOPMENT
• OFFICE OF GOVERNMENT CONTRACTING
• HUBZONE PROGRAM
• OFFICE OF POLICY, PLANNING AND LIAISON
OFFICE OF PERFORMANCE MANAGEMENT AND CHIEF FINANCIAL OFFICER
• OFFICE OF THE CHIEF FINANCIAL OFFICER
• DENVER FINANCE CENTER
• OFFICE OF PERFORMANCE MANAGEMENT
• OFFICE OF INTERNAL CONTROLS
OFFICE OF FIELD OPERATIONS
• OFFICE OF REGIONAL ADMINISTRATORS
• DISTRICT OFFICES
OFFICE OF CHIEF OPERATING OFFICER
• OFFICE OF CHIEF INFORMATION OFFICER
• OFFICE OF DIVERSITY, INCLUSION AND CIVIL RIGHTS
• OFFICE OF DISASTER PLANNING AND RISK MANAGEMENT
• OFFICE OF HUMAN RESOURCES SOLUTIONS
• OFFICE OF GRANTS MANAGEMENT
• OFFICE OF ADMINISTRATIVE SERVICES
• OFFICE OF EXECUTIVE SECRETARIAT
OFFICE OF INTERNATIONAL TRADE
OFFICE OF GENERAL COUNSEL
OFFICE OF CONGRESSIONAL AND LEGISLATIVE AFFAIRS
OFFICE OF HEARINGS AND APPEALS
OFFICE OF COMMUNICATIONS AND PUBLIC LIAISON
OFFICE OF DISASTER ASSISTANCE
OFFICE OF NATIVE AMERICAN AFFAIRS
OFFICE OF VETERANS BUSINESS DEVELOPMENT
CENTER FOR FAITH BASED AND NEIGHBORHOOD PARTNERSHIPS
OFFICE OF NATIONAL OMBUDSMAN AND REGULATORY ENFORCEMENT FAIRNESS

Social Security Administration

6401 Security Boulevard, Baltimore, MD 21235, 410-965-1234 / 800-772-1213, 800-325-0778 (TTY), *http://www.socialsecurity.gov*

COMMISSIONER	Carolyn W. Colvin, Acting
Deputy Commissioner	Carolyn W. Colvin
Chief of Staff	Stacy L. Rodgers
DEPUTY COMMISSIONERS	
Budget, Finance, Quality, and Management	Michelle A. King
Communications	Douglas K. Walker
Disability Adjudication and Review	Theresa L. Gruber
Human Resources	Reginald F. Wells
Legislation and Congressional Affairs	Judy L. Chesser
Operations	Nancy A. Berryhill
Retirement and Disability Policy	Virginia P. Reno
Systems / Chief Information Officer	Robert Klopp
Chief Actuary	Stephen C. Goss
Chief Strategic Officer	Ruby D. Burrell
Counselor to the Commissioner	Frank A. Cristaudo
Director, Equality Employment Opportunity	Kojuan L. Almond
Executive Secretary	Darlynda K. Bogle
General Counsel	Andy Liu
Inspector General	Gale S. Stone, Acting

[For the Social Security Administration statement of organization, see the Code of Federal Regulations, Title 20, Part 422]

The Social Security Administration manages the retirement, survivors, and disability insurance programs that are known as Social Security; it administers the Supplemental Security Income program for the aged, blind, and disabled; and it assigns Social Security numbers to U.S. citizens and maintains earnings records based on those numbers.

The Social Security Administration (SSA) was established by Reorganization Plan No. 2 of 1946 (5 U.S.C. app.), effective July 16, 1946. It became an independent agency in the executive branch by the Social Security Independence and Program Improvements Act of 1994 (42 U.S.C. 901), effective March 31, 1995.

The SSA is headed by a Commissioner whom the President appoints with the advice and consent of the Senate.

The Deputy Commissioner assists in administering the programs necessary to accomplish the Administration's mission. The Deputy Commissioner performs duties that the Commissioner, Chief Financial Officer, Chief Information Officer, General Counsel, Chief Actuary, and Inspector General assign or delegate to him or her.

The Administration's operations are decentralized to provide local services. Each of the 10 SSA regions has a network of field offices and call centers. These offices and centers provide liaison between the SSA and public. The Administration operates 10 regional offices, approximately 1,230 field offices, 33 teleservice centers, 15 Social Security card centers, 6 processing centers, and 2 additional processing centers in its central office.

Activities

Black Lung

By agreement with the Department of

Labor, the SSA assists in the administration of the black lung benefits provisions of the Federal Coal Mine Health and Safety Act of 1969, as amended (30 U.S.C. 901).

Hearings and Appeals

The SSA administers a nationwide hearings and appeals program that offers a way for those who are dissatisfied with determinations affecting their rights to and amounts of benefits or their participation in programs to seek remedy through the Social Security Act. The act allows for administrative appeals of these determinations in accordance with the requirements of the Administrative Procedure and Social Security Acts. The SSA operates approximately 168 hearing offices, including 6 satellite offices; 5 national hearing centers; and 2 national case assistance centers within in its 10 administrative regions.

Medicare

While the administration of Medicare is the responsibility of the Centers for Medicare and Medicaid Services, the SSA provides Medicare assistance to the public through SSA field offices and call centers. It adjudicates requests for hearings and appeals of Medicare claims.

Old-Age, Survivors, and Disability Insurance

The SSA administers social insurance programs that provide monthly benefits to retired and disabled workers, to their spouses and children, and to survivors of insured workers. Financing is under a system of contributory social insurance, whereby employees, employers, and the self-employed pay contributions that are pooled in special trust funds. When earnings stop or decrease because the worker retires, dies, or becomes disabled, monthly cash benefits are paid to supplement the family's reduced income.

Supplemental Security Income

The SSA administers this needs-based program for the aged, blind, and disabled. A basic Federal monthly payment is financed by general revenue, rather than from a special trust fund. Some States, choosing to provide payments to supplement the benefits, have agreements with the Administration under which it administers the supplemental payments for those States.

Sources of Information

Business Opportunities

The Office of Acquisition and Grants serves as the SSA's principal procurement office. Phone, 410-965-7467.

Employment

The SSA offers opportunities for various career paths: acquisitions, contracts, and grants; administrative support; facilities and physical security; finance and accounting; human resources; information technology; law enforcement; legal; and public contact.

The SSA consistently ranks among the best large agencies at which to work in the Federal Government.

Fraud Hotline

The Office of the Inspector General (OIG) operates a toll-free hotline, 10 a.m.–4 p.m., eastern standard time, for reporting allegations of abuse, fraud, and waste affecting SSA programs and operations. Phone, 800-269-0271. TTY, 866-501-2101. Fax, 410-597-0118.

An online form also is available to file a report.

Freedom of Information Act (FOIA)

An online guide discusses important FOIA-related topics: how to request information and records, information that the SSA cannot disclose, and the fees associated with making a request.

Frequently Asked Questions (FAQs)

The SSA posts answers to FAQs and offers information on popular help-topics.

Glossary

A glossary of Social Security terms is available online.

Multilanguage Gateway

The SSA tries to eliminate or reduce, as

much as possible, barriers of language that impede the delivery of its services. Social Security information is available on the SSA Web site in the following languages: American Sign Language, Arabic, Armenian, Chinese, Farsi, French, Greek, Haitian Creole, Hmong, Italian, Korean, Polish, Portuguese, Russian, Somali, Spanish, Tagalog, and Vietnamese. The SSA provides free interpreter services for conducting Social Security-related business.

News

The SSA posts press releases on its Web site.

An online newsletter also is available.

Online Services

The SSA offers a growing number of services electronically through its Web site.

Open Government

The SSA supports the Open Government initiative to create a more open and transparent Government by promoting the principles of collaboration, participation, and transparency.

Plain Language

The Plain Writing Act of 2010 requires Federal agencies to communicate in a manner that the public can understand and use. SSA writers and editors welcome suggestions for improving agency forms, notices, pamphlets, or pages from its Web site.

Publications

Many SSA publications in English, Spanish, and other languages are accessible online.

Site Map

The Web site map allows visitors to look for specific topics or to browse content that aligns with their interests.

Speakers

Under certain circumstances, the SSA can provide a speaker free of charge, generally available during business hours, to explain benefits, programs, and services. An online form is available to initiate a request.

For further information, contact the Office of Public Inquiries, Social Security Administration, 6401 Security Boulevard, 1106 West High Rise Building, Baltimore, MD 21235. Phone, 410-965-0958. Fax, 410-965-0695.

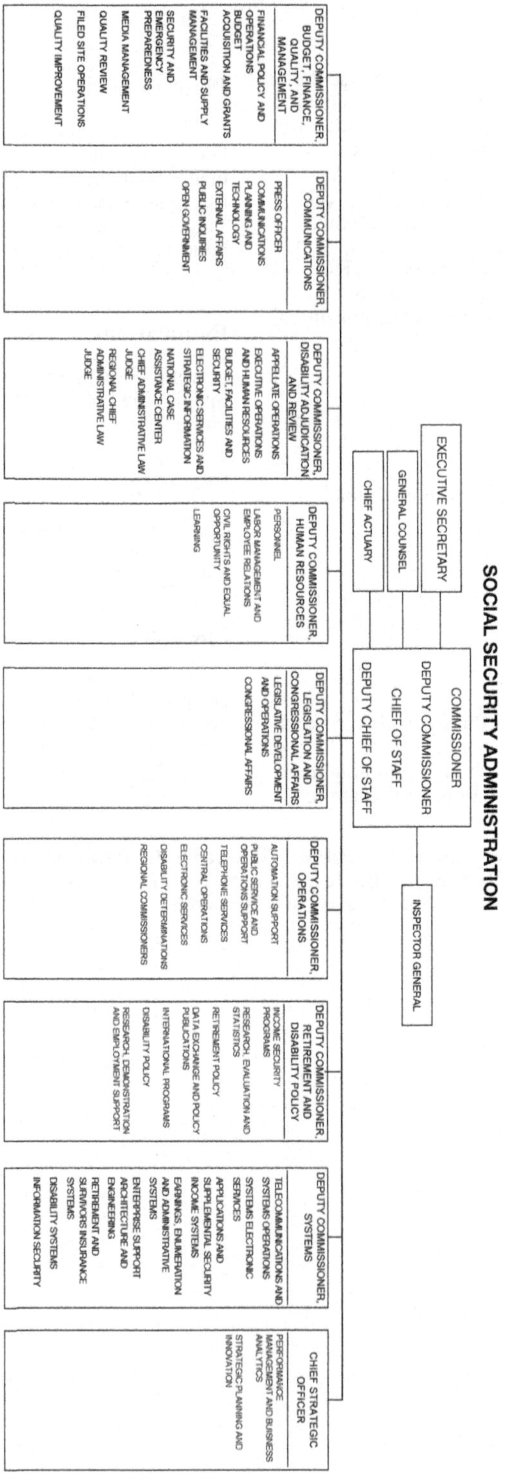
SOCIAL SECURITY ADMINISTRATION
EXECUTIVE SECRETARY
GENERAL COUNSEL
CHIEF ACTUARY
COMMISSIONER
DEPUTY COMMISSIONER
CHIEF OF STAFF
DEPUTY CHIEF OF STAFF
INSPECTOR GENERAL
DEPUTY COMMISSIONER, BUDGET, FINANCE, QUALITY, AND MANAGEMENT
FINANCIAL POLICY AND OPERATIONS
BUDGET
ACQUISITION AND GRANTS
FACILITIES AND SUPPLY MANAGEMENT
SECURITY AND EMERGENCY PREPAREDNESS
MEDIA MANAGEMENT
QUALITY REVIEW
FILED SITE OPERATIONS
QUALITY IMPROVEMENT
DEPUTY COMMISSIONER, COMMUNICATIONS
PRESS OFFICER
COMMUNICATIONS PLANNING AND TECHNOLOGY
EXTERNAL AFFAIRS
PUBLIC INQUIRIES
OPEN GOVERNMENT
DEPUTY COMMISSIONER, DISABILITY ADJUDICATION AND REVIEW
APPELLATE OPERATIONS
EXECUTIVE OPERATIONS AND HUMAN RESOURCES
BUDGET, FACILITIES AND SECURITY
ELECTRONIC SERVICES AND STRATEGIC INFORMATION
NATIONAL CASE ASSISTANCE CENTER
CHIEF ADMINISTRATIVE LAW JUDGE
REGIONAL CHIEF ADMINISTRATIVE LAW JUDGE
DEPUTY COMMISSIONER, HUMAN RESOURCES
PERSONNEL
LABOR MANAGEMENT AND EMPLOYEE RELATIONS
CIVIL RIGHTS AND EQUAL OPPORTUNITY
LEARNING
DEPUTY COMMISSIONER, LEGISLATION AND CONGRESSIONAL AFFAIRS
LEGISLATIVE DEVELOPMENT AND OPERATIONS
CONGRESSIONAL AFFAIRS
DEPUTY COMMISSIONER, OPERATIONS
AUTOMATION SUPPORT
PUBLIC SERVICE AND OPERATIONS SUPPORT
TELEPHONE SERVICES
CENTRAL OPERATIONS
ELECTRONIC SERVICES
DISABILITY DETERMINATIONS
REGIONAL COMMISSIONERS
DEPUTY COMMISSIONER, RETIREMENT AND DISABILITY POLICY
INCOME SECURITY PROGRAMS
RESEARCH, EVALUATION AND STATISTICS
RETIREMENT POLICY
DATA EXCHANGE AND POLICY PUBLICATIONS
INTERNATIONAL PROGRAMS
DISABILITY POLICY
RESEARCH, DEMONSTRATION AND EMPLOYMENT SUPPORT
DEPUTY COMMISSIONER, SYSTEMS
TELECOMMUNICATIONS AND SYSTEMS OPERATIONS
SYSTEMS ELECTRONIC SERVICES
APPLICATIONS AND SUPPLEMENTAL SECURITY INCOME SYSTEMS
EARNINGS, ENUMERATION AND ADMINISTRATIVE SYSTEMS
ENTERPRISE SUPPORT ARCHITECTURE AND ENGINEERING
RETIREMENT AND SURVIVORS INSURANCE SYSTEMS
DISABILITY SYSTEMS
INFORMATION SECURITY
CHIEF STRATEGIC OFFICER
PERFORMANCE MANAGEMENT AND BUSINESS ANALYTICS
STRATEGIC PLANNING AND INNOVATION

Surface Transportation Board

395 E Street SW., Washington, DC 20423, 202-245-0245, *http://www.stb.gov/stb/index.html*

CHAIR	Daniel R. Elliott III
Vice Chair	Debra L. Miller
Member	Ann D. Begeman
Member	(vacancy)
Member	(vacancy)
Director, Office of Economics	William F. Huneke
Director, Office of Environmental Analysis	Victoria J. Rutson
Director, Office of Proceedings	Rachel D. Campbell
Director, Office of Public Assistance, Governmental Affairs and Compliance	Lucille L. Marvin
General Counsel	Craig Keats
Managing Director	Leland L. Gardner

The Surface Transportation Board adjudicates and resolves railroad rate and service disputes and reviews proposals for railroad mergers.

The Surface Transportation Board (STB) is the successor agency to the Interstate Commerce Commission (ICC), which was created in 1887. The ICC Termination Act of 1995 established the STB as an independent adjudicatory body within the Department of Transportation. It remained administratively aligned with the Department for nearly two decades. On December 18, 2015, the Surface Transportation Board Reauthorization Act of 2015 established the STB as a wholly independent Federal agency (49 USC 1301 et seq.).

The STB comprises five members whom the President appoints and the Senate confirms for 5-year terms. The President also designates one of the members to serve as the Board's chair.

Activities

The STB adjudicates disputes and regulates interstate surface transportation through various laws governing the different modes of surface transportation. Its general responsibilities include the oversight of firms engaged in interstate and foreign commercial transportation—to the extent that it takes place within the United States, or between or among points in the contiguous United States and points in Alaska, Hawaii, or U.S. Territories or possessions. The STB's jurisdiction generally extends over railroad rate and service issues, rail restructuring transactions, including mergers and line abandonments, construction, and sales, and labor matters related thereto; some moving van, trucking, and noncontiguous ocean shipping company rate matters; some intercity passenger bus company financial, operational, and structural matters; and pipeline matters that the Federal Energy Regulatory Commission does not regulate.

The STB promotes substantive and procedural regulatory reform, provides a forum for the resolution of disputes, and facilitates appropriate market-based business transactions. Through rulemakings and case disposition, it develops improved and efficient ways of analyzing problems, reducing costs associated with regulatory oversight, and encouraging private sector negotiations and resolutions.

Sources of Information

Annual Reports

The STB posts activity reports that it prepares for Congress every few years and annual reports on its Web site.

Electronic Filing

As an alternative to submitting paper filings, consider filing electronically. E-filing may not be used for initial filings in a proceeding, filings requiring a fee (with the exception of recordations), and large evidentiary filings.

Employment

Current job openings are posted online.

The STB earned a place among the top small agencies in the Partnership for Public Service's "Best Places To Work in the Federal Government" rankings.

Environment

The Office of Environmental Analysis's Web page features links to cases, correspondence, rules, and other resources related to environmental matters.

Freedom of Information Act (FOIA)

The STB Web site features an online form for submitting FOIA requests. Phone, 202-245-0271. Fax, 202-245-0464.

Frequently Asked Questions (FAQs)

The STB posts answers to FAQs on its Web site.

Glossary

The STB Web site features a glossary of terms associated with environmental issues.

Historic Preservation

The National Environmental Policy and National Historic Preservation Acts and other Federal environmental laws require the STB to consider the impact of its licensing decisions on historic properties. The Office of Environmental Analysis develops guidance that clarifies the STB's historic preservation review requirements and posts it on the STB's Web site.

Industry Data

The STB posts financial and statistical reports containing economic data on its Web site.

Rail carriers must file a summary of each contract entered into for the transportation of agricultural products. Beginning with the first quarter of 2008, filed contract summaries are available on the STB's Web site in Portable Document Format (PDF) and grouped by railroad.

Library

The library is open to the public on weekdays, excluding Federal Holidays, 10 a.m.–3 p.m. Phone, 202-245-0406.

The STB's Web site features an electronic library whose resources can be accessed by opening the "E–Library" drop-down menu on the home page.

Maps

The Railroad Map Depot features links to railroad maps. The railroad map information is based on publicly available maps and data that government agencies, railroads, and other stakeholders produce.

News

The STB posts announcements and other noteworthy items on its "What's New" Web page.

Publications

Consumer pamphlets are available in Portable Document Format (PDF) from the electronic library.

Testimony / Speeches

The Office of Public Assistance, Governmental Affairs, and Compliance posts the testimony and speeches of STB officials online.

For further information, contact the Surface Transportation Board, Office of Public Assistance, Governmental Affairs, and Compliance, 395 E Street SW., Washington, DC, 20423. Phone, 202-245-0238.

Tennessee Valley Authority

400 West Summit Hill Drive, Knoxville, TN 37902, 865-632-2101, *http://www.tva.com*

CHAIR	Joseph H. Ritch
Director	Marilyn A. Brown
Director	V. Lynn Evans
Director	Richard C. Howorth
Director	Virginia T. Lodge
Director	C. Peter Mahurin
Director	Michael R. McWherter
Director	Eric M. Satz
Director	Ronald A. Walter
PRESIDENT / CHIEF EXECUTIVE OFFICER	William D. Johnson
Executive Vice President / Chief Financial Officer	John M. Thomas III
Executive Vice President / Chief Nuclear Officer	Joseph P. Grimes
Executive Vice President / Chief Operating Officer	Charles G. Pardee
Executive Vice President / General Counsel	Sherry A. Quick
Executive Vice President, External Relations	Van M. Wardlaw
Senior Vice President / Chief Human Resources Officer	Susan E. Collins
Senior Vice President, Communications	Janet J. Brewer
Senior Vice President, Nuclear Construction	Michael D. Skaggs
Senior Vice President, Shared Services	Ricardo G. Perez

The Tennessee Valley Authority conducts a unified program of resource development to advance economic growth in the Tennessee Valley region.

The Tennessee Valley Authority (TVA) is a wholly owned Government corporation created by the act of May 18, 1933 (16 U.S.C. 831-831dd). All functions of the Authority are vested in its nine-member Board of Directors, whose members the President appoints with the advice and consent of the Senate. The Board designates one of its members to serve as the Chair.

Activities

The TVA's activities are diverse: They range from economic development and environmental stewardship to electric power production and transmission, flood control, navigation, recreation improvement, and to water supply and water quality management.

The TVA's electric power program is financially self-supporting and operates as part of an independent system with the Authority's system of dams on the Tennessee River and its larger tributaries. These dams provide flood regulation on the Tennessee River and contribute to regulation of the lower Ohio and Mississippi Rivers. The system maintains a continuous 9-foot-draft navigation channel for the length of the 650-mile Tennessee River main stream, from Paducah, KY, to Knoxville, TN. The dams harness the power of the rivers to produce electricity. They also provide other benefits, notably outdoor recreation and water supply.

The Authority operates the river management system and provides assistance to State and local governments in reducing local flood problems. It also works with other agencies to encourage full and effective use of the navigable waterway by industry and commerce.

The TVA is the wholesale power supplier for 155 local municipal and cooperative electric systems serving customers in parts of 7 States. It supplies power to 56 industries and Federal installations whose power requirements are large or unusual. Power to meet these demands is supplied from dams, coal-fired powerplants, nuclear powerplants, natural gas combined-cycle powerplants, combustion turbine and diesel installations, solar energy sites, wind turbines, a methane gas facility, and a pumped-storage hydroelectric plant; U.S. Corps of Engineers dams in the Cumberland Valley; and Brookfield Renewable Energy Partners dams, whose operations are coordinated with the TVA's system.

Economic development is at the heart of the TVA's mission of making the Tennessee Valley a better place to live. A healthy economy means quality jobs, more investment in the region, sustainable growth, and opportunities for residents in the southeastern region to build more prosperous lives. TVA economic development takes a regional approach to economic growth by partnering with power distributors and both public and private organizations to attract new investments and quality jobs, supporting retention and growth of existing businesses and industries, preparing communities for leadership and economic growth, and providing financial and technical services.

Sources of Information

Business Opportunities

The TVA partners with power distributors, suppliers, and other individuals and organizations. It seeks business relationships with firms offering reliable products and services at competitive prices. The TVA encourages businessmen and women of diverse backgrounds—minorities, service-disabled-veterans, veterans, as well as small business owners and entrepreneurs in historically underutilized business zones—to learn about available opportunities. For more information, contact Supply Chain, BR 4A–C, 1101 Market Street, Chattanooga, TN 37402. Phone, 423-751-7903.

Economic Development

TVA Economic Development serves the seven States of the TVA service area—AL, GA, KY, NC, VA, as well as most of TN and parts of MS. Through partnerships with other economic development organizations, the TVA fosters capital investment and job growth in its service area. Information is available online, or contact TVA Economic Development, 26 Century Boulevard, Suite 100, Nashville, TN 37214. Phone, 615-232-6051.

Employment

The TVA is a service-oriented agency that relies on diverse and talented professionals to carry out its mission.

Environmental Reviews

The TVA conducts environmental reviews to consider the effects of its proposed projects on the human and natural environment before making final decisions. The TVA's environmental projects are open for public review.

Freedom of Information Act (FOIA)

The TVA operates a FOIA requester service center. Phone, 865-632-6945.

Library Services

Visitors may use the TVA Research Library by appointment. Contact the TVA Research Library, 400 W. Summit Hill Drive, Knoxville, TN 37902-1499. Phone, 865-632-3464.

Newsroom

The TVA posts news stories and press releases online.

Office of the Inspector General (OIG)

The OIG protects the confidentiality and rights of whistleblowers. To file a complaint of abuse, fraud, or waste online, use the TVA's EmPowerline. Phone, 855-882-8585.

Public Engagement

The TVA benefits from engaged citizens. It encourages comments, feedback, and input. Contact TVA Communications, 400 W. Summit Hill Drive, Knoxville, TN 37902-1499. Phone, 865-632-2101.

For further information, contact the Tennessee Valley Authority at 400 W. Summit Hill Drive, Knoxville, TN 37902-1499. Phone, 865-632-2101. Or, contact the Tennessee

Valley Authority at One Massachusetts Avenue NW., Washington, DC 20044. Phone, 202-898-2999.

Trade and Development Agency

1000 Wilson Boulevard, Suite 1600, Arlington, VA 22209-3901, 703-875-4357, 703-875-4009, *http://www.ustda.gov*

DIRECTOR	Leocadia I. Zak
Deputy Director	Enoh T. Ebong
Administrative Officer	Carolyn Hum
Chief of Staff	Devin Hampton
Chief, Office of Acquisition Management	Garth Hibbert
Director, Congressional Affairs and Public Relations	Thomas R. Hardy
Director, Finance	Monina Bantug
General Counsel	Michael Levitin

REGIONAL DIRECTORS

East Asia	Carl B. Kress
Latin America and Caribbean	Nathan Younge
Middle East, North Africa, Europe and Eurasia	Carl B. Kress
South and Southeast Asia	Henry D. Steingass
Sub-Saharan Africa	Lida Fitts
Director, Global Programs	Andrea Lupo
Director, Office of Program Monitoring and Evaluation	Diana Harbison

The Trade and Development Agency advances economic development and U.S. commercial interest in developing and middle-income countries.

The Trade and Development Program was established on July 1, 1980, as a component organization of the International Development Cooperation Agency. Section 2204 of the Omnibus Trade and Competitiveness Act of 1988 (22 U.S.C. 2421) made it a separate component agency. The organization was renamed the Trade and Development Agency (USTDA) and made an independent agency within the executive branch of the Federal Government on October 28, 1992, by the Jobs Through Exports Act of 1992 (22 U.S.C. 2421).

The USTDA is a foreign assistance agency that delivers its program commitments through overseas grants and contracts with U.S. firms. The Agency helps companies create U.S. jobs through the export of U.S. goods and services for priority development projects in emerging economies. The Agency links U.S. businesses to export opportunities by funding project planning activities, pilot projects, and reverse trade missions while creating sustainable infrastructure and economic growth in partner countries.

The USTDA provides grant funding to overseas project sponsors for the planning of projects that support the development of modern infrastructure and an open trading system. The hallmark of USTDA development assistance is building partnerships between U.S. companies and overseas project sponsors. These partnerships facilitate the application of proven private sector solutions to developmental challenges.

The Agency works with other U.S. Government agencies to bring their particular expertise and resources to a development objective. These agencies include the Departments of Commerce, Energy, State, Transportation, and the Treasury; Office of the U.S. Trade Representative; Export-Import Bank of the United States; and Overseas Private Investment Corporation.

TRADE AND DEVELOPMENT AGENCY

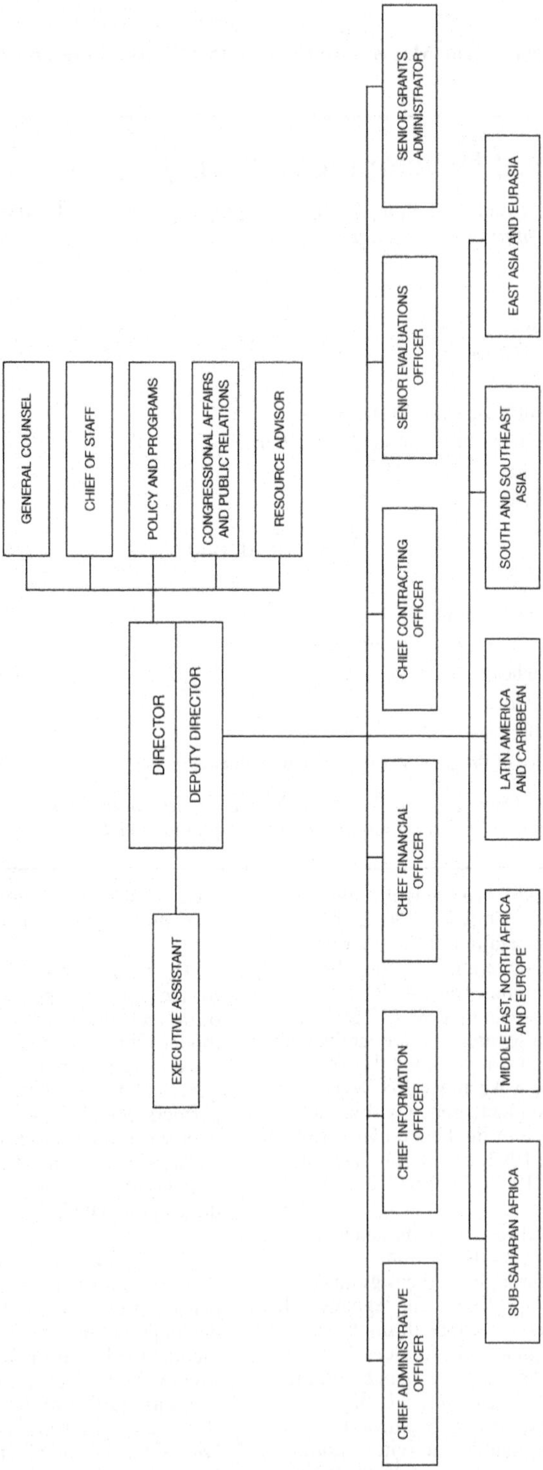

Activities

The USTDA funds various forms of technical assistance, training, early investment analysis, reverse trade missions, and business workshops that support the development of a modern infrastructure and a fair and open trading environment. The Agency works closely with foreign project sponsors and makes its funds available to them for contracting with U.S. businesses. This arrangement gives American firms market entry, exposure, and access to information. It helps them establish positions in markets that are otherwise difficult to penetrate. The USTDA is involved in many sectors, including energy, transportation, and information and communications technologies.

USTDA-funded studies evaluate the technical, economic, and financial aspects of a development project. They provide the host nation with information on the availability of U.S. goods and services. Financial institutions also use these studies for assessing the creditworthiness of an undertaking. Grants are based on an official request for assistance: Either the sponsoring government or a private sector organization in a developing or middle-income nation can make the request.

Sources of Information

Business Opportunities

Overseas project sponsors can select U.S. firms to carry out USTDA-funded work through a competitive proposal process that relies on the Federal Business Opportunities Web site (FedBizOpps.gov) or through "sole-source" grants, which allow an overseas project sponsor to identify a U.S. firm as a partner or preferred supplier. More information is available on the "Project Proposals" Web page.

Employment

Job openings and information on internships are posted online.

Freedom of Information Act (FOIA)

A FOIA request must be submitted in writing by email, fax, or mail, and clearly identified as a "FOIA REQUEST." Staff is available to answer questions and help formulate a request over the phone; however, the USTDA does not accept phone requests. Mail a request to the FOIA Requester Service Center, U.S. Trade and Development Agency, 1000 Wilson Boulevard, Suite 1600, Arlington, VA 22209-3901. Phone, 703-875-4357. Fax, 703-875-4009.

Library

The USTDA maintains a collection of reports on infrastructure development projects from emerging economies worldwide. Contact the library by email to obtain a report: Most reports can be sent electronically. These reports are accessible also online. Phone, 703-875-4357.

Newsletter

To provide timely information on Agency supported activities, the USTDA distributes an electronic newsletter containing business opportunities, events, and updates. A subscription form is available online.

Regional Programs

The USTDA is organized into five international regions. Information on each region is available on the Agency's Web site. Questions should be addressed to the appropriate regional director or country manager. Phone, 703-875-4357.

For further information, contact the U.S. Trade and Development Agency, 1000 Wilson Boulevard, Suite 1600, Arlington, VA 22209-3901. Phone, 703-875-4357. Fax, 703-875-4009.

United States African Development Foundation

1400 I Street NW., Suite 1000, Washington, DC 20005, 202-233-8800, 202-673-3810, *http://www.usadf.gov*

BOARD OF DIRECTORS

CHAIR	John W. Leslie, Jr.
Vice Chair	John O. Agwunobi
Board Member	Ward Brehm
Board Member	Morgan M. Davis
Board Member	Linda I. Etim
Board Member	Iqbal Paroo
Board Member	Linda Thomas-Greenfield

STAFF

PRESIDENT / CHIEF EXECUTIVE OFFICER	Constance Newman
Chief Financial Officer / Director of Finance and Administration	Mathieu Zahui, Acting
General Counsel	Doris Mason Martin

[For the United States African Development Foundation statement of organization, see the Code of Federal Regulations, Title 22, Part 1501]

The United States African Development Foundation promotes development in Africa to empower marginalized and underserved communities.

The United States African Development Foundation was established by the African Development Foundation Act (22 U.S.C. 290h) as a Government corporation to support African-led development. The Foundation is led by the Board of Directors, which comprises the Chair, the Vice Chair, and five Board Members whom the President nominates with the advice and consent of the Senate.

The Foundation invests in private and nongovernmental organizations in Africa to promote and support innovative enterprise development, generate jobs, and increase incomes of the poor. It seeks to expand local institutional and financial capacities to foster entrepreneurship, ownership, and community-based economic development among marginalized and underserved populations in sub-Saharan Africa.

Sources of Information

Employment

Vacancy announcements are posted online.

News

Press releases are available online.

For further information, contact the Office of the President, U.S. African Development Foundation, 1400 I Street NW., Suite 1000, Washington, DC 20005-2248. Phone, 202-673-3916. Fax, 202-673-3810.

United States Agency for International Development

1300 Pennsylvania Avenue NW., Washington, DC 20523, 202-712-0000, *http://www.usaid.gov*

ADMINISTRATOR	Gayle E. Smith
Deputy Administrator	Alfonso E. Lenhardt
Assistant Administrator, Bureau for Africa	Linda Etim
Assistant Administrator, Bureau for Asia	Jonathan Stivers
Assistant Administrator, Bureau for Democracy, Conflict and Humanitarian Assistance	Thomas Staal, Acting
Assistant Administrator, Bureau for Europe and Eurasia	Thomas Melia

Assistant Administrator, Bureau for Global Health / Child and Maternal Survival Coordinator	Ariel Pablos-Méndez
Assistant Administrator, Bureau for Latin America and the Caribbean	Elizabeth Hogan, Acting
Assistant Administrator, Bureau for Legislative and Public Affairs	T. Charles Cooper
Assistant Administrator, Bureau for Management	Angelique M. Crumbly
Assistant Administrator, Bureau for the Middle East	Paige Alexander
Assistant to the Administrator, Bureau for Economic Growth, Education and Environment	Charles North
Assistant to the Administrator, Bureau for Food Security / Deputy Coordinator for Development, Feed the Future	Beth Dunford
Assistant to the Administrator, Bureau for Policy, Planning and Learning	Wade Warren
Assistant to the Administrator, Office of Afghanistan and Pakistan Affairs	D. Larry Sampler, Jr.
Associate Administrator	Eric G. Postel
Chief Innovation Officer / Executive Director, U.S. Global Development Lab	Ann Mei Chang
Chief of Staff	Michele Sumilas
Counselor	Susan Reichle
Executive Secretary / National Security Advisor	Neilesh Shelat
General Counsel	John Simpkins

[For the Agency for International Development statement of organization, see the Federal Register of Aug. 26, 1987, 52 FR 32174]

The United States Agency for International Development works to eradicate extreme global poverty and to enable resilient and democratic societies to realize their potential.

The United States Agency for International Development (USAID) is an independent Federal agency established by 22 U.S.C. 6563. Its principal statutory authority is the Foreign Assistance Act of 1961, as amended (22 U.S.C. 2151 et seq.). The Agency serves as the focal point within the Government for economic matters affecting U.S. relations with developing countries. It administers international economic and humanitarian assistance programs. The Administrator is under the direct authority and foreign policy guidance of the Secretary of State.

Programs

The Agency works in over 100 countries to promote broadly shared economic prosperity, strengthen democracy and good governance, protect human rights, improve global health, advance food security and agriculture, increase environmental sustainability, further education, help societies prevent and recover from conflicts, and provide humanitarian assistance in the wake of natural and manmade disasters.

Democracy

The Agency promotes the transition to and consolidation of democratic regimes throughout the world. Programs focus on such problems as human rights abuses; misperceptions of democracy and free-market capitalism; lack of experience with democratic institutions; the absence or weakness of intermediary organizations; nonexistent, ineffectual, or undemocratic political parties; disenfranchisement of women, indigenous peoples, and minorities; failure to implement national charter documents; powerless or poorly defined democratic institutions; tainted elections; and inability to resolve conflicts peacefully.

Economic Growth

The Agency promotes broad-based economic growth by addressing factors that enhance the capacity for growth and by working to remove obstacles that obstruct individual opportunity. Programs concentrate on strengthening market economies, expanding economic opportunities for the disadvantaged in developing countries, and building human skills and capacities to facilitate broad-based participation.

Environment

Environmental programs support two strategic goals: 1) reducing long-term threats to the biosphere, particularly loss of biodiversity and change in climate; 2) promoting sustainable economic growth locally, nationally, and regionally by addressing shortsighted environmental, economic, and developmental practices. Globally, USAID programs focus on reducing sources and enhancing sinks of greenhouse gas emissions and on promoting innovative approaches to the conservation and sustainable use of the planet's biological diversity. The approach adopted to address national environmental problems differs from county to country, depending on its environmental priorities. Strategies may include improving agricultural, industrial, and natural resource management practices; strengthening public policies and institutions; dialoguing with governments and international agencies; and environmental research and education.

Global Health and Population

The Agency improves access and quality of services for maternal and child health, nutrition, voluntary family planning, and reproductive health. It prevents and treats HIV/AIDS, malaria, and tuberculosis. It assists countries in the design and implementation of state-of-the-art public health approaches to end preventable child-maternal deaths and achieve an AIDS-free generation. The Agency takes advantage of economies of scale in procurement, technical services, and commodities. To promote sustainability, the Agency helps expand health systems and the health workforce by adopting and scaling-up proven health interventions across programs and countries. It also contributes to a cooperative global effort to stabilize world population growth and support women's reproductive rights. The types of population and health programs supported vary with the particular needs of individual countries and the kinds of approaches that local communities initiate and support.

Humanitarian Assistance and Post-Crisis Transitions

The Agency gives humanitarian assistance to save lives, reduce suffering, help victims return to self-sufficiency, and reinforce democracy. Programs focus on disaster prevention, preparedness, and mitigation; timely delivery of disaster relief and short-term rehabilitation supplies and services; preservation of basic institutions of civil governance during a disaster crisis; support for democratic institutions during periods of national transition; and building and reinforcement of local capacity to anticipate disasters and better cope with their aftermath.

Overseas Organizations

USAID country organizations are located in countries where a bilateral program is being implemented. The in-country organizations are subject to the direction and guidance of the chief U.S. diplomatic representative in the country, usually the Ambassador. The organizations report to the appropriate assistant administrators according to geographic bureaus: Africa, Asia and the Near East, Europe and Eurasia, and Latin America and the Caribbean.

The overseas program activities that involve more than one country are administered by regional offices. These offices may also have country organizational responsibilities for assigned countries. Generally, the offices are headed by a regional development officer.

Coordination and representative offices for development assistance provide liaison with various international organizations and represent U.S. interests in development assistance matters. These offices may be only partially staffed by USAID personnel and may be headed by employees of other U.S. Government agencies.

Sources of Information

Business Opportunities

For information on contracting opportunities, contact the Office of Small and Disadvantaged Business Utilization, USAID, Washington, DC 20523-0001. Phone, 202-567-4730. Fax, 202-567-4740.

Comments

Comments, complaints, feedback, ideas, questions, and recommendations may be submitted by using an online form.

Congressional Affairs

Congressional inquiries should be directed to the Bureau for Legislative and Public Affairs. Phone, 202-712-4340.

Employment

USAID employs professionals with a variety of managerial, operational, and technical skills to achieve its international development goals. Its workforce includes direct-hire and contract employees based in the United States and at field missions worldwide.

Forms

An electronic forms page features a selection of up-to-date USAID forms that are arranged according to form number.

Freedom of Information Act (FOIA)

FOIA requests must be submitted in writing: email, fax, mail, or via the Public Access Link web portal. USAID Government information specialists are available to answer questions; however, the Agency does not accept verbal FOIA requests. Phone, 202-712-0960. Fax, 202-216-3070.

News

USAID posts news and information—congressional testimonies, events, factsheets, photographs, podcasts, speeches, and videos, as well as its "Frontlines" magazine, "Impact Newsletter", and "Impact" blog—online.

Open Government

USAID supports the Open Government initiative by posting data, records, and reports online.

For further information, contact the U.S. Agency for International Development, 1300 Pennsylvania Avenue NW., Washington, DC 20523-0001. Phone, 202-712-0000.

UNITED STATES AGENCY FOR INTERNATIONAL DEVELOPMENT

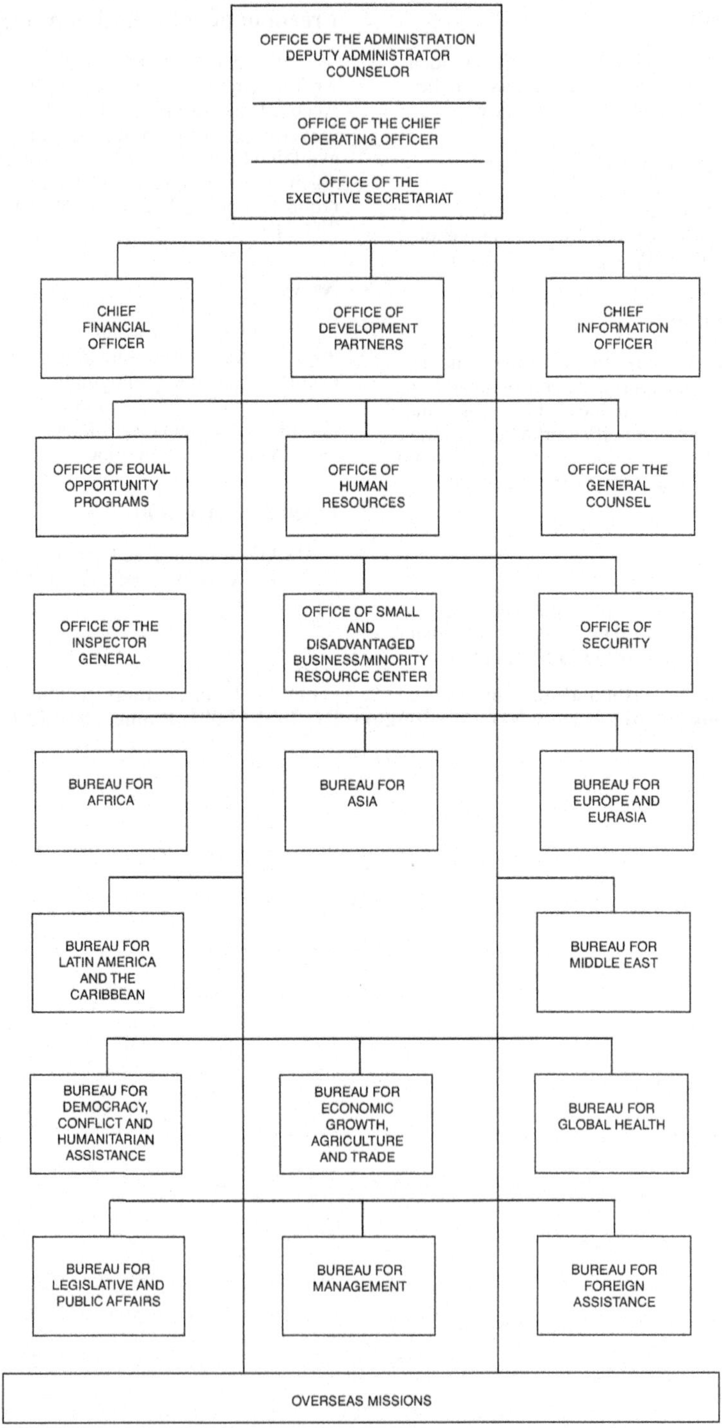

United States Commission on Civil Rights

1331 Pennsylvania Avenue NW., Suite 1150, Washington, DC 20425, 202-376-8128, 800-977-8339 (FedRelay), *http://www.usccr.gov*

CHAIR	Martin R. Castro
Vice Chair	Patricia Timmons-Goodson
Commissioner	Roberta Achtenberg
Commissioner	Gail Heriot
Commissioner	Peter N. Kirsanow
Commissioner	David Kladney
Commissioner	Karen Naraski
Commissioner	Michael Yaki
Staff Director	Mauro Morales

[For the Commission on Civil Rights statement of organization, see the Code of Federal Regulations, Title 45, Part 701]

The Commission on Civil Rights informs the development of national civil rights policy and enhances enforcement of Federal civil rights laws.

The Commission on Civil Rights was first created by the Civil Rights Act of 1957, as amended, and reestablished by the United States Commission on Civil Rights Act of 1994, as amended (42 U.S.C. 1975).

Activities

The Commission conducts hearings on important civil rights issues, including issuing subpoenas for the production of documents and the attendance of witnesses; publishes studies and reports on a wide range of civil rights issues to inform and advise policymakers; holds public briefings, issues press releases, makes information publicly available online, and provides a complaint referral service to promote greater public awareness of civil rights issues, protections, and enforcement; and sustains advisory committee involvement in the national program planning to strengthen factfinding.

Regional Programs

The Commission maintains 51 State Advisory Committees (SACs), one for each State and the District of Columbia. Each SAC is composed of citizen volunteers who are familiar with local and State civil rights issues. SAC members assist the Commission with factfinding, investigating, and disseminating information. The Commission ensures that advisory committees are diverse and represent a variety of backgrounds, skills, experiences, and perspectives. This diversity promotes debate and broadens exploration of the issues. All appointments are made in a nondiscriminatory manner.

Sources of Information

Complaints

The complaint referral service helps place individuals in contact with the appropriate office for obtaining information on the complaint process. Phone, 202-376-8513 or 800-552-6843.

Employment

Career opportunities—vacancy announcements and available internships—are posted online. Contact the Human Resources Division for more information. Phone, 202-376-8364.

Freedom of Information Act (FOIA)

Information on how to file a FOIA request is available online. A request may be sent by email or fax, or by mail to the FOIA Officer, U.S. Commission on Civil

Rights, 1331 Pennsylvania Avenue NW., Suite 1150, Washington, DC 20425. Phone, 202-376-8351. Fax, 202-376-1163.

Library

The Robert S. Rankin Memorial Library welcomes visitors. It is open on weekdays, 10 a.m.–4 p.m. (except on Federal holidays). For more information, contact the Robert S. Rankin Memorial Library, 1331 Pennsylvania Avenue NW., Washington, DC 20425. Phone, 202-376-8110. Fax, 202-376-7597.

Publications

For a complete list of Commission publications, consult the online catalog. It includes briefings; clearinghouse publications; hearings, consultations, and conferences; periodicals; publications in Spanish; staff reports; State advisory committee reports; and statutory and interim reports. To order a publication, contact the U.S. Commission on Civil Rights, 1331 Pennsylvania Avenue, NW., Suite 1150, Washington, DC 20425. Phone: 202-376-8128.

Regional Offices

A list of the six regional offices—including addresses, telephone numbers, and areas served—is available online.

For further information, contact the Office of the Staff Director, U.S. Commission on Civil Rights, 1331 Pennsylvania Avenue NW., Suite 1150, Washington, DC 20425. Phone, 202-376-7700. Phone, 800-977-8339 (FedRelay).

UNITED STATES COMMISSION ON CIVIL RIGHTS

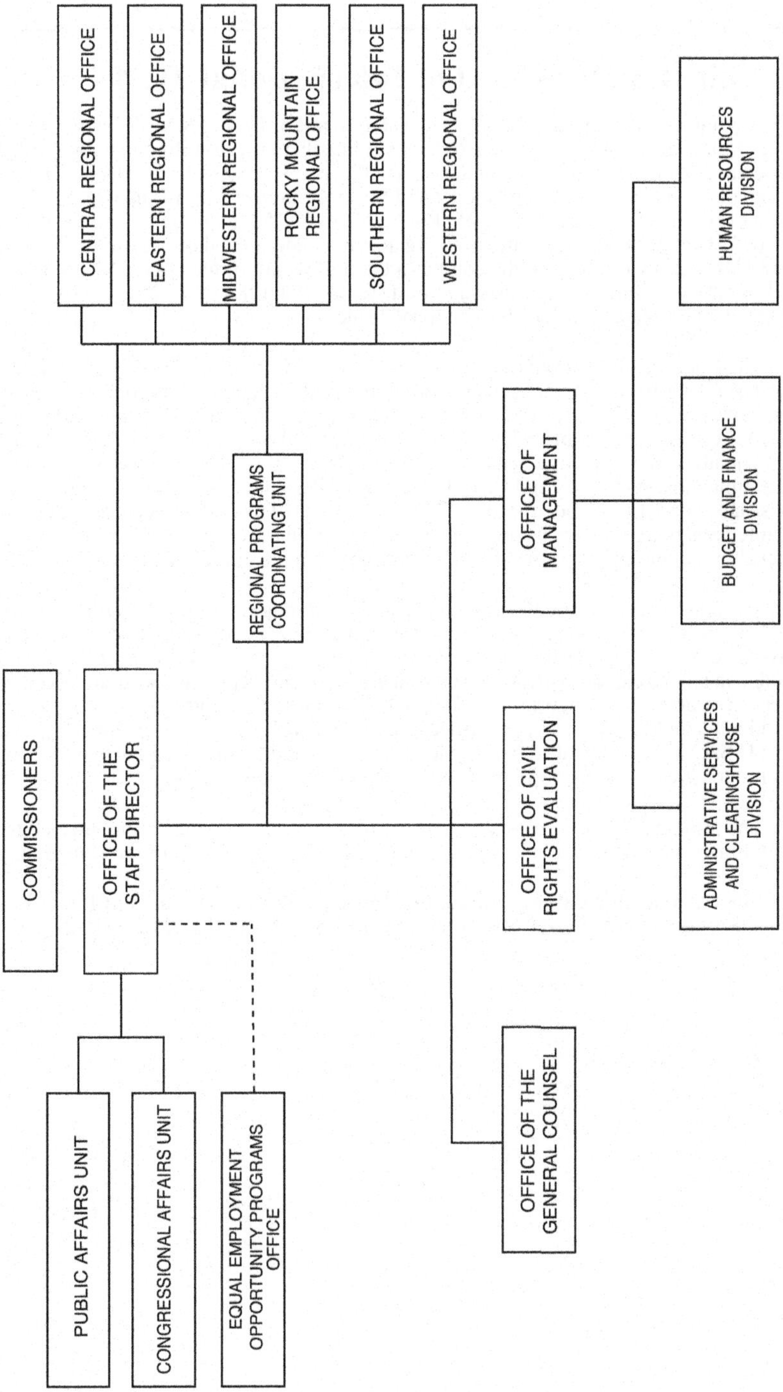

United States Court of International Trade

This court was originally established as the Board of United States General Appraisers by act of June 10, 1890, which conferred upon it jurisdiction theretofore held by the district and circuit courts in actions arising under the tariff acts (19 U.S.C. ch. 4). The act of May 28, 1926 (19 U.S.C. 405a), created the United States Customs Court to supersede the Board; by acts of August 7, 1939, and June 25, 1948 (28 U.S.C. 1582, 1583), the court was integrated into the United States court structure, organization, and procedure. The act of July 14, 1956 (28 U.S.C. 251), established the court as a court of record of the United States under Article III of the Constitution. The Customs Court Act of 1980 (28 U.S.C. 251) constituted the court as the United States Court of International Trade.

The Court of International Trade has jurisdiction over any civil action against the United States arising from Federal laws governing import transactions. This includes classification and valuation cases, as well as authority to review certain agency determinations under the Trade Agreements Act of 1979 (19 U.S.C. 2501) involving antidumping and countervailing duty matters. In addition, it has exclusive jurisdiction of civil actions to review determinations as to the eligibility of workers, firms, and communities for adjustment assistance under the Trade Act of 1974 (19 U.S.C. 2101). Civil actions commenced by the United States to recover customs duties, to recover on a customs bond, or for certain civil penalties alleging fraud or negligence are also within the exclusive jurisdiction of the court.

The court is composed of a chief judge and eight judges, not more than five of whom may belong to any one political party. Any of its judges may be temporarily designated and assigned by the Chief Justice of the United States to sit as a court of appeals or district court judge in any circuit or district. The court has a clerk and deputy clerks, a librarian, court reporters, and other supporting personnel. Cases before the court may be tried before a jury. Under the Federal Courts Improvement Act of 1982 (28 U.S.C. 1295), appeals are taken to the U.S. Court of Appeals for the Federal Circuit, and ultimately review may be sought in appropriate cases in the Supreme Court of the United States.

The principal offices are located in New York, NY, but the court is empowered to hear and determine cases arising at any port or place within the jurisdiction of the United States.

For further information, contact the Clerk, United States Court of International Trade, One Federal Plaza, New York, NY 10278-0001. Phone, 212-264-2814.

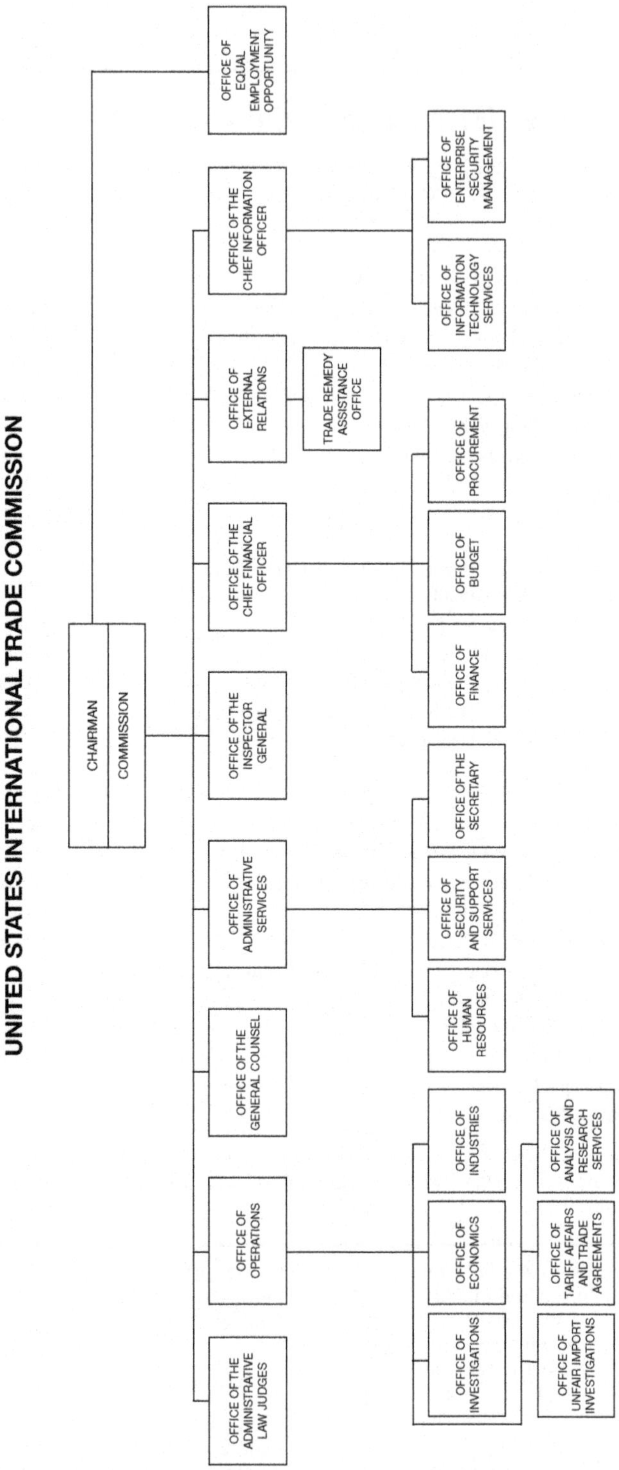
UNITED STATES INTERNATIONAL TRADE COMMISSION
CHAIRMAN
COMMISSION
OFFICE OF EQUAL EMPLOYMENT OPPORTUNITY
OFFICE OF THE ADMINISTRATIVE LAW JUDGES
OFFICE OF OPERATIONS
OFFICE OF THE GENERAL COUNSEL
OFFICE OF ADMINISTRATIVE SERVICES
OFFICE OF THE INSPECTOR GENERAL
OFFICE OF THE CHIEF FINANCIAL OFFICER
OFFICE OF EXTERNAL RELATIONS
TRADE REMEDY ASSISTANCE OFFICE
OFFICE OF THE CHIEF INFORMATION OFFICER
OFFICE OF INVESTIGATIONS
OFFICE OF ECONOMICS
OFFICE OF INDUSTRIES
OFFICE OF UNFAIR IMPORT INVESTIGATIONS
OFFICE OF TARIFF AFFAIRS AND TRADE AGREEMENTS
OFFICE OF ANALYSIS AND RESEARCH SERVICES
OFFICE OF HUMAN RESOURCES
OFFICE OF SECURITY AND SUPPORT SERVICES
OFFICE OF THE SECRETARY
OFFICE OF FINANCE
OFFICE OF BUDGET
OFFICE OF PROCUREMENT
OFFICE OF INFORMATION TECHNOLOGY SERVICES
OFFICE OF ENTERPRISE SECURITY MANAGEMENT

United States Office of Special Counsel

1730 M Street NW., Suite 218, Washington, DC 20036-4505, 202-254-3600, 800-872-9855, 202-653-5151, *http://www.osc.gov*

SPECIAL COUNSEL	Carolyn N. Lerner
PRINCIPAL DEPUTY SPECIAL COUNSEL	Mark P. Cohen
Deputy Special Counsel of Litigation and Legal Affairs	Eric Bachman
Deputy Special Counsel of Policy and Congressional Affairs	Adam Miles
Senior Communications Specialist	Nicholas Schwellenbach
ASSOCIATE SPECIAL COUNSEL OF GENERAL LAW DIVISION	Anne Wagner
Chief of Alternative Dispute Resolution	Jane Juliano
Chief of Complaints Examining Unit	Barbara J. Wheeler
Chief of Disclosure Unit	Catherine A. McMullen
General Counsel	(vacancy)
ASSOCIATE SPECIAL COUNSEL OF INVESTIGATION AND PROSECUTION DIVISION—Field	Bruce D. Fong
Chief of Field Office–Dallas	Anne Gullick
Chief of Field Office–Detroit	Christopher T. Tall
Chief of Field Office–San Francisco Bay Area	Joseph Siegelman
ASSOCIATE SPECIAL COUNSEL OF INVESTIGATION AND PROSECUTION DIVISION—Headquarters	Louis Lopez
Chief of Hatch Act Unit	Ana Galindo-Marrone
Chief of Investigation and Prosecution Division–Team A	Mariama Liverpool
Chief of Investigation and Prosecution Division–Team B	Rachel Venier
Chief of Investigation and Prosecution Division–Team C	Clarissa Pinheiro
Chief of Retaliation and Disclosure Unit	Karen Gorman
Chief of Retaliation and Disclosure Unit	Elizabeth McMurray
Director of Uniformed Services Employment and Reemployment Rights Act Enforcement / Senior Counsel	Patrick H. Boulay
CHIEF OPERATING OFFICER	Bruce Gipe
Chief Financial Officer	Karl P. Kammann
Chief Human Capital Officer	James J. Wilson
Chief Information Officer	Jennifer Li

The United States Office of Special Counsel investigates allegations of certain activities prohibited by civil service laws, rules, or regulations and litigates before the Merit Systems Protection Board.

The U.S. Office of Special Counsel (OSC) was established on January 1, 1979, by Reorganization Plan No. 2 of 1978 (5 U.S.C. app.). The Civil Service Reform Act of 1978 (5 U.S.C. 1101 note), which became effective on January 11, 1979, enlarged its functions and powers. Pursuant to provisions of the Whistleblower Protection Act of 1989 (5 U.S.C. 1211 et seq.), the OSC functions as an independent investigative and prosecutorial executive branch agency that litigates before the Merit Systems Protection Board.

Activities

The OSC safeguards the merit system in Federal employment by protecting employees and applicants from prohibited personnel practices, especially from reprisal for whistleblowing. The Office operates a secure channel for Federal whistleblower disclosures of gross waste of funds or mismanagement, substantial and specific danger to public health and safety, and violations of laws, regulations, or rules. The OSC also issues advice on the Hatch Act and enforces its restrictions on political activity by Government employees. It protects the civilian employment and reemployment rights of military servicemembers under the Uniformed Services Employment and Reemployment Act. The OSC enhances Government accountability and performance by the realization of a diverse, inclusive Federal workplace where employees embrace excellence in service, uphold merit system principles, are encouraged to disclose wrongdoing, and are protected against reprisals and other unlawful employment practices.

Sources of Information

Business Opportunities

The OSC relies on the Department of Interior for performing assisted procurements. The OSC posts contract opportunities online by using Government acquisition vehicles like GSA Ebuy. It posts open market opportunities on the Federal Business Opportunities Web site.

Electronic Filing

The E-Filing System makes filing a complaint with the OSC easier and faster.

Employment

The agency employs approximately 110 employees who work in Washington, DC, or in the Dallas, Detroit, and Oakland field offices. To carry out its mission, the OSC relies heavily on attorneys, investigators, and personnel management specialists.

The OSC seeks law students year-round for internships in Dallas, TX; Detroit, MI; Oakland, CA; and Washington, DC.

Freedom of Information Act (FOIA)

FOIA requests must be submitted in writing by email, fax, or U.S. postal mail or other delivery service. The OSC provides a Public Access Link portal that allows information seekers to submit a request online and to receive confirmation of and updates on a pending request.

Frequently Asked Questions (FAQs)

The OSC posts answers to FAQs on its Web site.

Hatch Act Advisory Opinions

Advice that the OSC has given to individuals on the Hatch Act is publicly accessible online.

News

The OSC posts news releases online.

Prohibited Personnel Practices

The OSC provides information on personnel practices that are prohibited within the Federal workplace.

Whistleblower Files

The OSC posts documents from closed investigations on its Web site. These documents are based on whistleblower disclosures.

2302(c) Program Certification

The White House has required all Federal agencies to certify that they are educating their employees about the rights of whistleblowers.

For further information, contact the U.S. Office of Special Counsel, 1730 M Street NW., Suite 218, Washington, DC 20036-4505. Phone, 202-254-3600 or 800-872-9855. Fax, 202-254-3711.

United States Postal Service

475 L'Enfant Plaza SW., Washington, DC 20260, 202-268-2000, *http://www.usps.gov*

BOARD OF GOVERNORS

CHAIR	James H. Bilbray, Acting
Vice Chair	(vacancy)
Governor	(vacancy)
Governor	(vacancy)
Governor	(vacancy)
Governor	(vacancy)
Governor	(vacancy)
Governor	(vacancy)
Governor	(vacancy)
Postmaster General / Chief Executive Officer	Megan J. Brennan
Deputy Postmaster General / Chief Government Relations Officer	Ronald A. Stroman
Inspector General	David C. Williams
Secretary	Julie S. Moore

OFFICERS

POSTMASTER GENERAL / CHIEF EXECUTIVE OFFICER	Megan J. Brennan
Deputy Postmaster General / Chief Government Relations Officer	Ronald A. Stroman
Chief Financial Officer / Executive Vice President	Joseph Corbett
Chief Human Relations Officer / Executive Vice President	Jeffrey Williamson
Chief Information Officer / Executive Vice President	Kristin Seaver
Chief Information Security Officer / Vice President, Digital Solutions	Randy Miskanic
Chief Marketing and Sales Officer / Executive Vice President	Jim Cochrane
Chief Operating Officer / Executive Vice President	David E. Williams
Chief Postal Inspector	Guy Cottrell
General Counsel / Executive Vice President	Thomas J. Marshall
Judicial Officer	Gary E. Shapiro
Vice President, Capital Metro Area Operations	Linda Malone
Vice President, Consumer and Industry Affairs	James Nemec
Vice President, Controller	Maura McNerney
Vice President, Corporate Communications	Janice Walker
Vice President, Delivery Operations	Kevin McAdams
Vice President, Employee Resource Management	Nancy Rettinhouse
Vice President, Engineering Systems	Michael J. Amato
Vice President, Enterprise Analytics	Isaac Cronkite
Vice President, Facilities	Tom Samra
Vice President, Finance and Planning	Luke Grossmann
Vice President, Global Business	Donald Ross, Acting
Vice President, Information Technology	Jeff Johnson
Vice President, Labor Relations	Douglas Tulino
Vice President, Mail Entry and Payment Technology	Pritha Mehra
Vice President, Network Operations	Robert Cintron
Vice President, New Products and Innovation	Gary Reblin
Vice President, Operations–Eastern Area	Joshua Colin

Vice President, Operations–Great Lakes Area	Jacqueline M. Krage Strako
Vice President, Operations–Northeast Area	Edward Phelan, Jr.
Vice President, Operations–Pacific Area	Dean Granholm
Vice President, Operations–Southern Area	Shaun Mossman
Vice President, Operations–Western Area	Greg Graves, Acting
Vice President, Pricing and Costing	Sharon Owens
Vice President, Retail and Customer Service Operations	Kelly M. Sigmon
Vice President, Sales	Cliff Rucker
Vice President, Supply Management	Susan M. Brownell

[For the United States Postal Service statement of organization, see the Code of Federal Regulations, Title 39, Part 221]

The United States Postal Service provides the American public with affordable, reliable, and universal mail service.

The Postal Service was created as an independent establishment of the executive branch by the Postal Reorganization Act (39 U.S.C. 101 et seq.), approved August 12, 1970. The present United States Postal Service commenced operations on July 1, 1971.

In Fiscal Year 2015, the Postal Service had approximately 492,000 career employees and handled over 154 billion pieces of mail. The chief executive officer of the Postal Service, the Postmaster General, is appointed by the nine Governors of the Postal Service. The President appoints the nine Governors with the advice and consent of the Senate. The Governors and the Postmaster General appoint the Deputy Postmaster General, and these 11 appointees constitute the Board of Governors.

In addition to the national headquarters, area and district offices oversee more than 35,000 post offices, branches, stations, contract postal units, village post offices, and community post offices throughout the United States.

Activities

To expand and improve service to the public, the Postal Service engages in customer cooperation activities, including the development of programs for both the general public and major customers. The consumer advocate, a postal ombudsman, represents the interests of the individual mail customer in matters involving the Postal Service. The advocate brings complaints and suggestions to the attention of top postal management and solves the problems of individual customers. To provide services responsive to public needs, the Postal Service operates its own planning, research, engineering, real estate, and procurement programs, and it maintains close ties with international postal organizations.

The Postal Service is the only Federal agency whose employment policies are governed by a process of collective bargaining under the National Labor Relations Act. Its Office of Human Resources, including the Labor Relations Division, administers labor contract negotiations that affect bargaining unit personnel, as well as personnel matters involving employees not covered by collective bargaining agreements.

The U.S. Postal Inspection Service, a Federal law enforcement agency, has jurisdiction in criminal matters affecting the integrity and security of the mail. Postal inspectors protect all postal employees and enforce more than 200 Federal statutes involving mail fraud, mail bombs, child pornography, illegal drugs, mail theft, and other postal crimes.

Sources of Information

Business Opportunities

Suppliers can learn about doing business with the Postal Service online. Information on rights and permissions (the use of trademarked material) and licensing products is also available online.

Consumer Information

For general information around the clock, call the "ASK USPS" line. Phone, 800-275-8777. To buy stamps, calculate postage prices, change addresses, find answers to frequently asked questions, locate ZIP Codes, print postage, shop at the Postal Store, and track packages, visit the Postal Service's Web site.

Employment

Information on careers—including information for veterans and reservists, for students and recent graduates—is available on the Postal Service's Web site or at the nearest post office.

The U.S. Postal Inspection Service posts career opportunities on its Web site.

Fraud and Theft

Postal inspectors can be located by Zip Code on the U.S. Postal Inspection Service's locator Web page.

Complaint forms to report identity and mail theft, mail fraud, and unsolicited sexually oriented advertising are accessible online. Phone, 800-275-8777.

Freedom of Information Act (FOIA)

Information and guidance on the Freedom of Information and the Privacy Acts and on Postal Service records management, as well as access to an electronic FOIA reading room are available online.

Inspector General

Information on the Office of Inspector General, on publicly available documents, and on certain Freedom of Information Act documents is available online. The Office of Inspector General has a toll-free hotline for reporting fraud, mismanagement, and waste. Phone, 888-877-7644 or 866-644-8398 (hearing impaired). Complaints also may be sent to the U.S. Postal Service, Office of Inspector General Hotline, 10th Floor, 1735 N. Lynn Street, Arlington, VA 22209-2020.

Newsroom

The Postal Service maintains an online newsroom that features broadcast and audio downloads, leadership biographies, national and local news, service alerts, testimonies and speeches, and a photo gallery.

Passports

Thousands of post offices accept passport applications on behalf of the Department of State. These post offices offer the products and services needed to acquire a first-time passport or renewal. At some locations, a passport photograph can be taken for an additional fee.

Philatelic Sales

For information on available stamps, philatelic items, and collectibles, visit the "Stamps" Web page.

Publications

Information on mailability, on postage rates and fees, and on other topics is available at the nearest post office. Most postal regulations affecting domestic and international mail, employee and labor relations, and purchasing can be found in Postal Service manuals. A wide range of publications—including annual reports to Congress, handbooks, manuals, notices, periodicals, and posters—is available online.

Reading Areas

Reading areas are maintained in the library at USPS Headquarters on the 11th Floor. The library's holdings include historic, legal, regulatory, and other documents. Visitors must schedule an appointment—weekdays, 9 a.m.–4 p.m. (except Federal holidays)—before accessing the library .Phone, 202-268-2906.

For further information, contact the U.S. Postal Service, 475 L'Enfant Plaza SW., Washington, DC 20260. Phone, 202-268-2000.

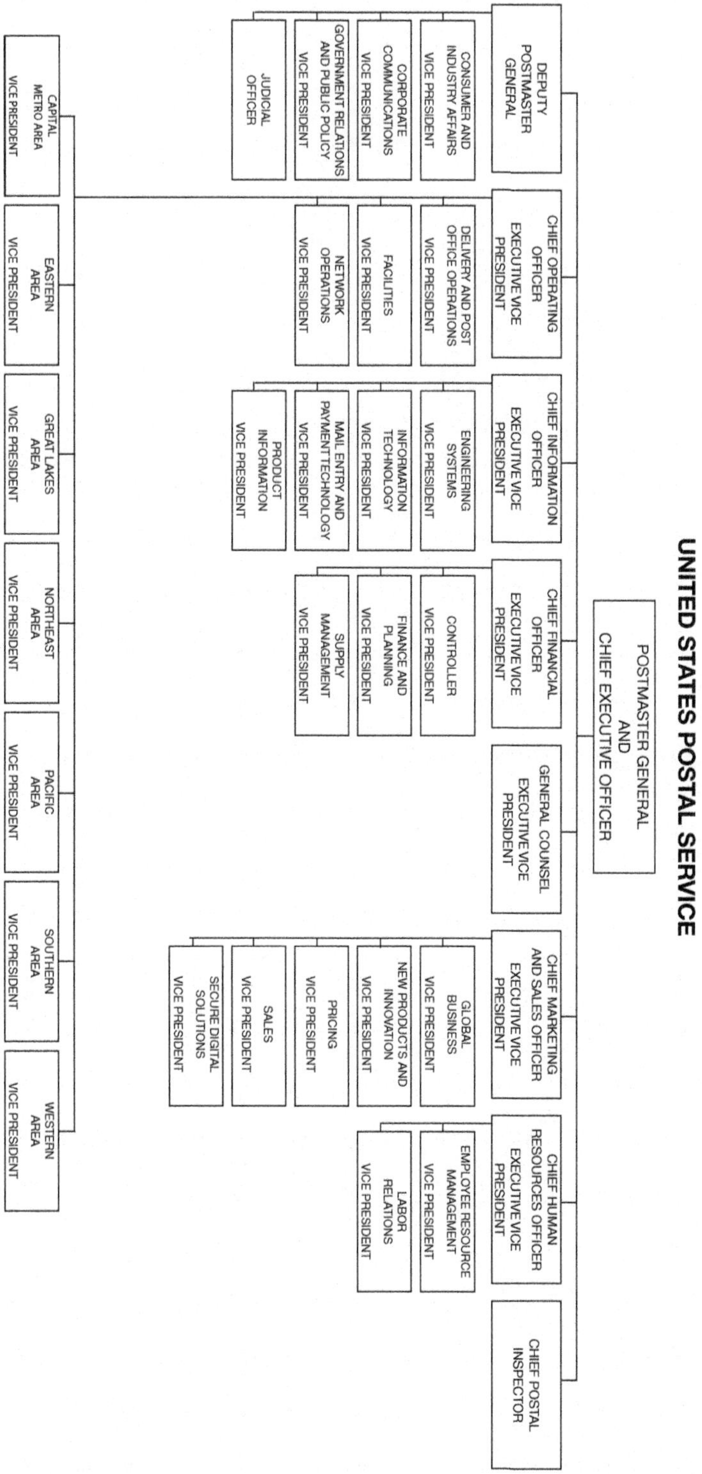
UNITED STATES POSTAL SERVICE
POSTMASTER GENERAL AND CHIEF EXECUTIVE OFFICER
DEPUTY POSTMASTER GENERAL
CONSUMER AND INDUSTRY AFFAIRS VICE PRESIDENT
CORPORATE COMMUNICATIONS VICE PRESIDENT
GOVERNMENT RELATIONS AND PUBLIC POLICY VICE PRESIDENT
JUDICIAL OFFICER
CHIEF OPERATING OFFICER EXECUTIVE VICE PRESIDENT
DELIVERY AND POST OFFICE OPERATIONS VICE PRESIDENT
FACILITIES VICE PRESIDENT
NETWORK OPERATIONS VICE PRESIDENT
CHIEF INFORMATION OFFICER EXECUTIVE VICE PRESIDENT
ENGINEERING SYSTEMS VICE PRESIDENT
INFORMATION TECHNOLOGY VICE PRESIDENT
MAIL ENTRY AND PAYMENT TECHNOLOGY VICE PRESIDENT
PRODUCT INFORMATION VICE PRESIDENT
CHIEF FINANCIAL OFFICER EXECUTIVE VICE PRESIDENT
CONTROLLER VICE PRESIDENT
FINANCE AND PLANNING VICE PRESIDENT
SUPPLY MANAGEMENT VICE PRESIDENT
GENERAL COUNSEL EXECUTIVE VICE PRESIDENT
CHIEF MARKETING AND SALES OFFICER EXECUTIVE VICE PRESIDENT
GLOBAL BUSINESS VICE PRESIDENT
NEW PRODUCTS AND INNOVATION VICE PRESIDENT
PRICING VICE PRESIDENT
SALES VICE PRESIDENT
SECURE DIGITAL SOLUTIONS VICE PRESIDENT
CHIEF HUMAN RESOURCES OFFICER EXECUTIVE VICE PRESIDENT
EMPLOYEE RESOURCE MANAGEMENT VICE PRESIDENT
LABOR RELATIONS VICE PRESIDENT
CHIEF POSTAL INSPECTOR
CAPITAL METRO AREA VICE PRESIDENT
EASTERN AREA VICE PRESIDENT
GREAT LAKES AREA VICE PRESIDENT
NORTHEAST AREA VICE PRESIDENT
PACIFIC AREA VICE PRESIDENT
SOUTHERN AREA VICE PRESIDENT
WESTERN AREA VICE PRESIDENT

Boards, Commissions, and Committees

Below is a list of Federal boards, commissions, councils, etc., not listed elsewhere in the Manual, which were established by congressional or Presidential action, whose functions are not strictly limited to the internal operations of a parent department or agency and which are authorized to publish documents in the Federal Register. While the editors have attempted to compile a complete and accurate listing, suggestions for improving coverage of this guide are welcome. Please address your comments to the Office of the Federal Register, National Archives and Records Administration, Washington, DC 20408. Phone, 202–741–6040. E-mail, fedreg.info@nara.gov. Internet, www.ofr.gov.

Federal advisory committees, as defined by the Federal Advisory Committee Act, as amended (5 U.S.C. app.), have not been included here. Information on Federal advisory committees may be obtained from the Committee Management Secretariat, General Services Administration, General Services Building (MC), Room G–230, Washington, DC 20405. Phone, 202–273–3556. Internet, www.gsa.gov/committeemanagement.

Administrative Committee of the Federal Register

Office of the Federal Register, National Archives and Records Administration, 8601 Adelphi Road, College Park, MD 20740–6001. Phone, 202–741–6000. E-mail, fedreg.info@nara.gov. Internet, www.ofr.gov.

Advisory Council on Historic Preservation

401 F. Street NW., Suite 308, Washington, DC 20001–2637. Phone, 202–517–0200. E-mail, achp@achp.gov. Internet, www.achp.gov.

American Battle Monuments Commission

2300 Clarendon Boulevard, Court House Plaza 2, Suite 500, Arlington, VA 22201. Phone, 703–696–6900. E-mail, info@abmc.gov. Internet, www.abmc.gov.

Appalachian Regional Commission

1666 Connecticut Avenue NW., Suite 700, Washington, DC 20009–1068. Phone, 202–884–7700. E-mail, info@arc.gov. Internet, www.arc.gov.

Architectural and Transportation Barriers Compliance Board[1]

1331 F Street NW., Suite 1000, Washington, DC 20004–1111. Phone, 202–272–0080, toll free, 800–872–2253 or TTY, 202–272–0082, toll free, 800–993–2822. Fax, 202–272–0081. E-mail, info@access-board.gov. Internet, www.access-board.gov.

Arctic Research Commission

4350 North Fairfax Drive, Suite 510, Arlington, VA 22203. Phone, 703–525–0111. Fax, 703–525–0114. E-mail, info@arctic.gov. Internet, www.arctic.gov.

[1] Also known as the Access Board.

Arthritis and Musculoskeletal Interagency Coordinating Committee

National Institutes of Health/NIAMS, Building 31—MSC 2350, Room 4C02, 31 Center Drive, Bethesda, MD 20892–2350. Phone, 301–496–8190. Fax, 301–480–2814. E-mail, NIAMSInfo@mail.nih.gov. Internet, www.niams.nih.gov.

Barry M. Goldwater Scholarship and Excellence in Education Program

Phone, 319–688–4335. Internet, www.act.org/goldwater.

Chemical Safety and Hazard Investigation Board

2175 K Street NW., Suite 400, Washington, DC 20037–1809. Phone, 202–261–7600. Fax, 202–261–7650. Internet, www.csb.gov.

Citizens' Stamp Advisory Committee

United States Postal Service c/o Stamp Development, 475 L'Enfant Plaza SW., Room 3300, Washington, DC 20260–3501. Internet, http://about.usps.com/who-we-are/csac.

U.S. Commission of Fine Arts

National Building Museum, 401 F Street NW., Suite 312, Washington, DC 20001–2728. Phone, 202–504–2200. Fax, 202–504–2195. E-mail, cfastaff@cfa.gov. Internet, www.cfa.gov.

Committee on Foreign Investment in the United States

Department of the Treasury, 1500 Pennsylvania Avenue NW., Washington, DC 20220. Phone, 202–622–1860. E-mail, CFIUS@treasury.gov. Internet, http://www.treasury.gov/resource-center/international/Pages/Committee-on-Foreign-Investment-in-US.aspx

Committee for the Implementation of Textile Agreements

Office of Textiles and Apparel, U.S. Department of Commerce, Washington, DC 20230. Phone, 202–482–5078. Fax, 202–482–2331. E-mail, OTEXA@trade.gov. Internet, otexa.ita.doc.gov/cita.htm.

Committee for Purchase From People Who Are Blind or Severely Disabled

1401 S. Clark Street, Suite 10800, Arlington, VA 22202–3259. Phone, 703–603–7740. Fax, 703–608–0655. E-mail, info@abilityone.gov. Internet, www.abilityone.gov.

Coordinating Council on Juvenile Justice and Delinquency Prevention

Department of Justice, Office of Juvenile Justice and Delinquency Prevention, 810 7th Street NW., Washington, DC 20531. Phone, 202–616–7567. Fax, 202–307–2819. E-mail, ddunston@aeioonline.com. Internet, www.juvenilecouncil.gov.

Delaware River Basin Commission

25 State Police Drive, P.O. Box 7360, West Trenton, NJ 08628–0360. Phone, 609–883–9500. Fax, 609–883–9522. E-mail, clarke.rupert@drbc.state.nj.us. Internet, www.nj.gov/drbc.

Endangered Species Program

4401 N. Fairfax Drive, Room 420, Arlington, VA 22203. Phone, 703–358–2171. Internet, www.fws.gov/endangered.

Export Administration Operating Committee

Department of Commerce, Bureau of Industry and Security, 14th Street and Constitution Avenue, NW., Washington, DC 20230. Phone, 202–482–4811. Internet, www.bis.doc.gov/index.htm.

Federal Financial Institutions Examination Council

3501 Fairfax Drive, D8073a, Arlington, VA 22226. Phone, 703–516–5590. Internet, www.ffiec.gov.

Federal Financing Bank

Department of the Treasury, 1500 Pennsylvania Avenue NW., Washington, DC 20220. Phone, 202–622–2470. Fax, 202–622–0707. E-mail, ffb@do.treas.gov. Internet, www.treasury.gov/ffb.

Federal Interagency Committee on Education

Department of Education, 400 Maryland Avenue SW., Washington, DC 20202. Phone, 202–401–3673. Internet, ed.gov/about/bdscomm/list/com.html.

Federal Laboratory Consortium for Technology Transfer

Washington, DC Liaison Office. Phone, 240–444–1383. E-mail, gkjones.ctr@federallabs.org. Internet, www.federallabs.org.

Federal Library and Information Center Committee

Library of Congress, 101 Independence Avenue SE., Washington, DC 20540–4935. Phone, 202–707–4800. Internet, www.loc.gov/flicc/.

Harry S. Truman Scholarship Foundation

712 Jackson Place NW., Washington, DC 20006. Phone, 202–395–4831. Fax, 202–395–6995. E-mail, office@truman.gov. Internet, www.truman.gov.

Indian Arts and Crafts Board

U.S. Department of the Interior, Room MS 2528–MIB, 1849 C Street NW., Washington, DC 20240. Phone, 202–208–3773. E-mail, iacb@ios.doi.gov. Internet, www.iacb.doi.gov.

J. William Fulbright Foreign Scholarship Board

Department of State, Bureau of Educational and Cultural Affairs, 2200 C Street NW., Washington, DC 20522–0500. Phone, 202–203–7010. E-mail, fulbright@state.gov. Internet, fulbright.state.gov.

James Madison Memorial Fellowship Foundation

1613 Duke Street Alexandria, VA 22314. Phone, 800–525–6928. Internet, www.jamesmadison.com.

Japan-US Conference on Cultural and Educational Interchange (CULCON)

1201 15th Street NW., Suite 330, Washington, DC 20005. Phone, 202–653–9800. Fax, 202–653–9802. E-mail, culcon@jusfc.gov. Internet, culcon.jusfc.gov.

Joint Board for the Enrollment of Actuaries

Internal Revenue Service, SE: RPO, REFM, 1111 Constitution Avenue, NW, Park 4, Floor 4, Washington, DC 20224. Fax, 703–414–2225. E-mail, nhqjbea@irs.gov. Internet, www.irs.gov/taxpros/actuaries/index.html.

Marine Mammal Commission

4340 East-West Highway, Suite 700, Bethesda, MD 20814. Phone, 301–504–0087. Fax, 301–504–0099. E-mail, mmc@mmc.gov. Internet, www.mmc.gov.

Medicare Payment Advisory Commission

425 Eye St., N.W. Suite 701 Washington, DC 20001. Phone, 202–220–3700. Fax, 202–220–3759. Internet, www.medpac.gov.

Migratory Bird Conservation Commission

Secretary, Migration Bird Conservation Commission, Mail Code: ARLSQ–622, 4401 North Fairfax Drive, Arlington, VA 22203–1610. Phone, 703–358–1713. Fax, 703–358–2223. Email, realty@fws.gov. Internet, www.fws.gov/refuges/realty/mbcc.html.

Mississippi River Commission

Mississippi River Commission, 1400 Walnut Street, Vicksburg, MS 39180–0080. Phone, 601–634–5757. E-mail, cemvd-pa@usace.army.mil. Internet, www.mvd.usace.army.mil/

Morris K. and Stewart L. Udall Foundation

130 South Scott Avenue, Tucson, AZ 85701–1922. Phone, 520–901–8500. Fax, 520–670–5530. Internet, www.udall.gov.

National Council on Disability

1331 F Street NW., Suite 850, Washington, DC 20004. Phone, 202–272–2004. TTY, 202–272–2074. Fax, 202–272–2022. E-mail, ncd@ncd.gov. Internet, www.ncd.gov.

National Indian Gaming Commission

90 K Street NE., Suite 200, Washington, DC 20002. Phone, 202–632–7003. Fax, 202–632–7066. E-mail, contactus@nigc.gov. Internet, www.nigc.gov.

National Park Foundation

1201 Eye Street NW., Suite 550B, Washington, DC 20005. Phone, 202–354–6460. Fax, 202–371–2066. E-mail, ask-npf@nationalparks.org. Internet, www.nationalparks.org.

Northwest Power and Conservation Council

851 SW. Sixth Avenue, Suite 1100, Portland, OR 97204. Phone, 503–222–5161 or 800–452–5161. Fax, 503–820–2370. E-mail, info@nwcouncil.org. Internet, www.nwcouncil.org.

Office of Navajo and Hopi Indian Relocation

201 East Birch Avenue, Flagstaff, AZ 86001. Phone, 928–779–2721. TTY, 800–877–8339. Fax, 928–774–1977. E-mail, webmaster@onhir.gov. Internet, http://onhir.gov

Permanent Committee for the Oliver Wendell Holmes Devise

Library of Congress, Manuscript Division, Washington, DC 20540–4680. Phone, 202–707–1082.

President's Intelligence Advisory Board

New Executive Office Building, Room 5020, Washington, DC 20502. Phone, 202–456–2352. Fax, 202–395–3403. Internet, www.whitehouse.gov/administration/eop/piab.

Presidio Trust

103 Montgomery Street, P.O. Box 29052, San Francisco, CA 94129–0052. Phone, 415–561–5300. TTY, 415–561–5301. Fax, 415–561–5315. E-mail, presidio@presidiotrust.gov. Internet, www.presidio.gov.

Social Security Advisory Board

400 Virginia Avenue SW., Suite 625, Washington, DC 20024. Phone, 202–475–7700. Fax, 202–475–7715. E-mail, ssab@ssab.gov. Internet, www.ssab.gov.

Susquehanna River Basin Commission

4423 North Front Street, Harrisburg, PA 17110. Phone, 717–238–0423. Fax, 717–238–2436. E-mail, srbc@srbc.net. Internet, www.srbc.net.

Trade Policy Staff Committee

Office of the United States Trade Representative, 600 17th Street NW.,Washington, DC 20508. Phone, 202–395–3475. Fax, 202–395–4549. Internet, www.ustr.gov.

United States Nuclear Waste Technical Review Board

2300 Clarendon Boulevard, Suite 1300, Arlington, VA 22201. Phone, 703–235–4473. Fax, 703–235–4495. Internet, www.nwtrb.gov.

Veterans Day National Committee

Department of Veterans Affairs, 810 Vermont Avenue NW., Mail Code 002C, Washington, DC 20420. Phone, 202–461–5386. E-mail, vetsday@va.gov. Internet, www1.va.gov/opa/vetsday.

White House Commission on Presidential Scholars

Department of Education, 400 Maryland Avenue SW., Washington, DC 20202–8173. Phone, 202–401–0961. Fax, 202–260–7464. E-mail, presidential.scholars@ed.gov. Internet, www.ed.gov/programs/psp/index.html.

QUASI-OFFICIAL AGENCIES

Legal Services Corporation

3333 K Street NW., Washington, DC 20007202-295-1500 202-337-6797

PRESIDENT	James J. Sandman
General Counsel / Corporate Secretary / Vice President, Legal Affairs	Ronald S. Flagg
Vice President, Grants Management	Lynn A. Jennings
Chief Information Officer	Peter S. Campbell
Director, Office of Compliance and Enforcement	Lora Rath
Director, Office of Data Governance and Analysis	Carlos A. Manjarrez
Director, Office of Program Performance	Janet LaBella
Treasurer / Comptroller	David L. Richardson
Director, Office of Human Resources	Traci Higgins
Director, Government Relations and Public Affairs	Carol A. Bergman
Director, Media Relations	Carl Rauscher
Inspector General	Jeffrey E. Schanz

The Legal Services Corporation promotes equal access to justice and provides civil legal assistance to low-income Persons

The Legal Services Corporation (LSC) is a private, nonprofit corporation established by the Legal Services Act of 1974, as amended (42 U.S.C. 2996), to promote equal access to justice under the law for all Americans.

Appointed by the President and confirmed by the Senate, the 11-member Board of Directors heads the LSC. By law, it is bipartisan and no more than six members may be of the same political party.

Congressional appropriations fund the LSC to provide legal services through grants to independent, local legal services provider programs. These programs are selected through a system of competition. In 2015, the LSC funded 134 programs. Together, they serve every county and congressional district in the Nation, as well as the U.S. Territories. Some of these programs address the particular needs of Native Americans and migrant farmworkers.

The legal services delivery system is based on several principles: local priorities, national accountability, competition for grants, and a strong public-private partnership. Local programs are governed by their own boards of directors, which set priorities and determine the types of cases that will be handled subject to restrictions set by Congress. A majority of each local board is appointed by local bar associations, and one-third of each local board is composed of client representatives appointed by client groups. Each board hires its own executive director. Programs may supplement their LSC grants with additional funds from State and local governments and other sources. They further leverage Federal funds by involving private attorneys in the delivery of legal services for the poor, mostly through volunteer pro bono work.

Programs that the LSC funds do not handle criminal cases, nor do they accept fee-generating cases that private attorneys are willing to accept on a contingency basis. In addition, in 1996 a series of new limitations were placed upon activities in which LSC-funded programs may engage on behalf of their clients, even with non-LSC funds. All programs must comply with laws enacted by Congress and the implementing regulations promulgated by the LSC.

Business Opportunities

The LSC regularly seeks the assistance of vendors and contractors for products and special projects. The LSC is eligible for General Services Administration schedule pricing and posts its request for proposals on eBuy and FedBizOpps.gov

Employment

The LSC is an organization of people who promote equal justice. Information on career opportunities and working at the LSC is available online.

Events

A list of upcoming events is available online

.http://www.lsc.gov/media-center/publications

Publications

Annual reports, budget requests, fact books, and reports are accessible online.

For further information, contact the Office of Government Relations and Public Affairs, Legal Services Corporation, 3333 K Street NW., Washington, DC 20007-3522. Phone, 202-295-1500. Fax, 202-337-6797.

Legal Services Corporation

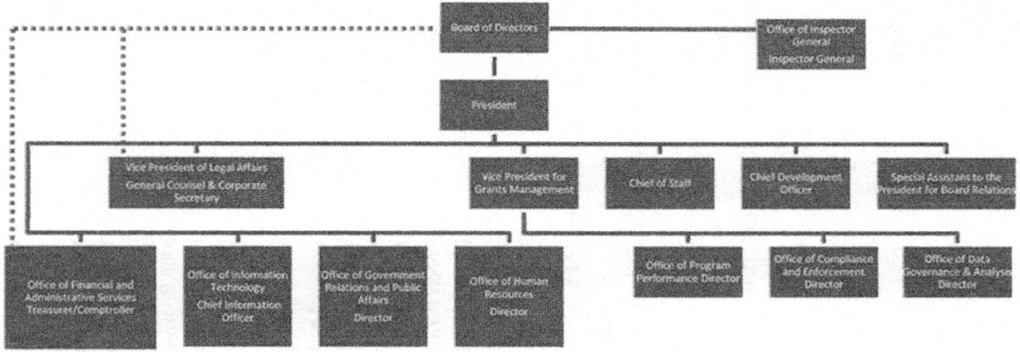

Smithsonian Institution

1000 Jefferson Drive SW., Washington, DC 20560, 202-633-1000, *http://www.si.edu*

BOARD OF REGENTS

Ex Officio	Chief Justice John G. Roberts, Jr.
Ex Officio	Vice President Joseph R. Biden, Jr.
CONGRESSIONAL REGENTS	
House of Representatives	Xavier Becerra
House of Representatives	Thomas J. Cole
House of Representatives	Samuel Johnson
Senate	John Boozman
Senate	Patrick J. Leahy
Senate	David Perdue
CITIZEN REGENTS	
Illinois	John W. McCarter, Jr.
New York	Shirley Ann Jackson
Arizona	Barbara M. Barrett
California	Michael M. Lynton
District of Columbia	John Fahey
District of Columbia	Robert P. Kogod
Maryland	David M. Rubenstein
Pennsylvania	Risa J. Lavizzo-Mourey
Virginia	Steve M. Case

OFFICIALS

SECRETARY	David J. Skorton
Under Secretary, Finance and Administration / Chief Financial Officer	Albert G. Horvath
Under Secretary, Museums and Research / Provost	Richard Kurin, Acting
Assistant Secretary, Advancement	Virginia B. Clark
Assistant Secretary, Communications and External Affairs	John K. Lapiana, Acting
Assistant Secretary, Education and Access	Patty Bartlett, Acting
Director, Equal Employment and Minority Affairs	Era L. Marshall
General Counsel	Judith E. Leonard
Inspector General	Cathy Helm
FINANCE / ADMINISTRATION	
Chief Information Officer	Deron Burba
Chief Investment Officer	Amy Chen
Director, Contracting and Personal Property Management	Dorothy A. Leffler
Director, Smithsonian Facilities	Nancy Bechtol
Director, Finance and Accounting	Jean Garvin
Director, Human Resources	James Douglas
Director, Planning, Management and Budget	David Voyles
Director, Policy and Analysis	H. Whitney Watriss, Acting
Director, Smithsonian Exhibits	Susan Ades
Director, Sponsored Projects	Tracey Fraser

President, Smithsonian Enterprises	Chris Liedel
MUSEUMS / RESEARCH	
Director, Anacostia Community Museum	Lori D. Yarrish, Acting
Director, Archives of American Art	Kate Haw
Director, Center for Astrophysics	Charles R. Alcock
Director, Center for Folklife and Cultural Heritage	Michael A. Mason
Director, Cooper Hewitt, Smithsonian Design Museum	Caroline Baumann
Director, Freer Gallery of Art and Arthur M. Sackler Gallery	Julian Raby
Director, Hirshhorn Museum and Sculpture Garden	Melissa Chiu
Director, Museum Conservation Institute	Robert J. Koestler
Director, National Air and Space Museum	John R. Dailey
Director, National Museum of African American History and Culture	Lonnie G. Bunch III
Director, National Museum of African Art	Johnnetta B. Cole
Director, National Museum of American History	John Gray
Director, National Museum of Natural History	Kirk Johnson
Director, National Museum of the American Indian	Kevin Gover
Director, National Portrait Gallery	Kim Sajet
Director, National Postal Museum	Allen R. Kane
Director, National Zoological Park	Dennis Kelly
Director, Smithsonian American Art Museum and Renwick Gallery	Elizabeth Broun
Director, Smithsonian Asian Pacific American Center	Lisa Sasaki
Director, Smithsonian Environmental Research Center	Anson H. Hines
Director, Smithsonian Institution Archives	Anne Van Camp
Director, Smithsonian Institution Traveling Exhibition Service	Myriam Springuel
Director, Smithsonian Latino Center	Eduardo Díaz
Director, Smithsonian Libraries	Nancy E. Gwinn
Director, Smithsonian Marine Station	Valerie Paul
Director, Smithsonian Tropical Research Institute	Matthew Larsen

The Smithsonian Institution increases the fund of human knowledge and diffuses that knowledge among people.

The Smithsonian Institution was created by an act of Congress on August 10, 1846 (20 U.S.C. 41 et seq.), to carry out the terms of the will of British scientist James Smithson (1765–1829), who in 1826 had bequeathed his entire estate to the United States "to found at Washington, under the name of the Smithsonian Institution, an establishment for the increase and diffusion of knowledge among men." On July 1, 1836, Congress accepted the legacy and pledged the faith of the United States to the charitable trust.

In September 1838, Smithson's legacy, which amounted to more than 100,000 gold sovereigns, was delivered to the mint at Philadelphia. Congress vested responsibility for administering the trust in the Secretary of the Smithsonian and the Smithsonian Board of Regents, composed of the Chief Justice, the Vice President, three Members of the Senate, three Members of the House of Representatives, and nine citizen members appointed by joint resolution of Congress. To carry out Smithson's mandate, the Institution executes the following functions: conducts scientific and scholarly research; publishes the results of studies, explorations, and investigations; preserves for study and reference more than 137 million artifacts, works of art, and scientific specimens; organizes exhibits representative of the arts, the sciences, American history, and world culture; shares Smithsonian resources and collections with communities throughout the Nation; and engages in educational programming and national and international cooperative research.

The Smithsonian Institution is an independent trust instrumentality of the

United States that comprises the world's largest museum and research complex. It includes 19 museums and galleries, the National Zoo, and nine research facilities in several States and the Republic of Panama. The Institution is dedicated to public education, national service, and scholarship in the arts, sciences, history, and culture. Smithsonian activities are supported by its trust endowments and revenues; gifts, grants, and contracts; and funds appropriated to it by Congress. Admission to the museums in Washington, DC, is free.

Activities

Anacostia Community Museum

The Museum, located in the historic Fort Stanton neighborhood of Southeast Washington, serves as a national resource for exhibitions, historical documentation, and interpretive and educational programs relating to the impact of history and contemporary social issues on urban communities.

For further information, contact the Anacostia Community Museum, 1901 Fort Place SE., Washington, DC 20020. Phone, 202-633-4820.

Archives of American Art

The Archives contains the Nation's largest collection of documentary materials reflecting the history of visual arts in the United States. On the subject of art in America, it is the largest archives in the world, holding more than 16 million documents. The Archives gathers, preserves, and microfilms the papers of artists, craftsmen, collectors, dealers, critics, and art societies. These papers include manuscripts, letters, diaries, notebooks, sketchbooks, business records, clippings, exhibition catalogs, transcripts of tape-recorded interviews, and photographs of artists and their work.

For further information, contact the Archives of American Art, Suite 2200, 750 Ninth Street NW., Washington, DC 20001. Phone, 202-633-7940.

Arthur M. Sackler Gallery

This Asian art museum opened in 1987 on the National Mall. Changing exhibitions drawn from major collections in the United States and abroad, as well as from the permanent holdings of the Sackler Gallery, are displayed in the distinctive below-ground museum. The Gallery's growing permanent collection is founded on a group of art objects from China, South and Southeast Asia, and the ancient Near East that were given to the Smithsonian by Arthur M. Sackler (1913–1987). The Museum's current collection features Persian manuscripts; Japanese paintings; ceramics, prints, and textiles; sculptures from India; and paintings and metalware from China, Korea, Japan, and Southeast Asia. The Sackler Gallery is connected by an underground exhibition space to the neighboring Freer Gallery.

For further information, contact the Arthur M. Sackler Gallery, 1050 Independence Avenue SW., Washington, DC 20560. Phone, 202-633-4880.

Center for Astrophysics

The Smithsonian Astrophysical Observatory and the Harvard College Observatory have coordinated research activities under a single director in a cooperative venture, Harvard-Smithsonian Center for Astrophysics. The Center's research activities are organized in the following areas of study: atomic and molecular physics, radio and geoastronomy, high-energy astrophysics, optical and infrared astronomy, planetary sciences, solar and stellar physics, and theoretical astrophysics. Research results are published in the Center Preprint Series and other technical and nontechnical bulletins and distributed to scientific and educational institutions around the world.

For more information, contact the Smithsonian Astrophysical Observatory, 60 Garden Street, Cambridge, MA 02138. Phone, 617-495-7463.

Center for Folklife and Cultural Heritage

The Center is responsible for research, documentation, and presentation of grassroots cultural traditions. It maintains a documentary collection and produces Smithsonian Folkways Recordings, educational materials, documentary films, publications, and traveling exhibits, as well as the annual Smithsonian Folklife Festival on the National Mall. Recent Folklife festivals have featured a range of American music styles, a number of State tributes, and performers from around the world. Admission to the festival is free. The 2-week program includes Fourth of July activities on the National Mall.

For further information, contact the Center for Folklife and Cultural Heritage, Capital Gallery, Suite 2001, 600 Maryland Avenue SW., Washington, DC 20024. Phone, 202-633-1000.

Cooper Hewitt, Smithsonian Design Museum

The Museum is the only museum in the country devoted exclusively to historical and contemporary design. Collections include objects in such areas as applied arts and industrial design, drawings and prints, glass, metalwork, wallcoverings, and textiles. Changing exhibits and public programs seek to educate by exploring the role of design in daily life.

For further information, contact the Cooper Hewitt, Smithsonian Design Museum, 2 East Ninety-First Street, New York, NY 10128. Phone, 212-849-8400.

Freer Gallery of Art

The building, the original collection, and an endowment were the gift of Charles Lang Freer (1854–1919). The Gallery houses one of the world's most renowned collections of Asian art, an important group of ancient Egyptian glass, early Christian manuscripts, and works by 19th- and early 20th-century American artists. The objects in the Asian collection represent the arts of East Asia, the Near East, and South and Southeast Asia, including paintings, manuscripts, scrolls, screens, ceramics, metalwork, glass, jade, lacquer, and sculpture. Members of the staff conduct research on objects in the collection and publish results in scholarly journals and books for general and scholarly audiences.

For further information, contact the Freer Gallery of Art, Jefferson Drive at Twelfth Street SW., Washington, DC 20560. Phone, 202-633-4880.

Hirshhorn Museum and Sculpture Garden

From cubism to minimalism, the Museum houses major collections of modern and contemporary art. The nucleus of the collection is the gift and bequest of Joseph H. Hirshhorn (1899–1981). Supplementing the permanent collection are loan exhibitions. The Museum houses a collection research facility, a specialized art library, and a photographic archive, available for consultation by prior appointment. The outdoor sculpture garden is located nearby on the National Mall. There is an active program of public service and education, including docent tours, lectures on contemporary art and artists, and films of historic and artistic interest.

For further information, contact the Hirshhorn Museum and Sculpture Garden, Seventh Street and Independence Avenue SW., Washington, DC 20560. Phone, 202-633-4674.

Museum Conservation Institute

The Institute researches preservation, conservation, and technical study and analysis of collection materials. Its researchers investigate the chemical and physical processes that are involved in the care of art, artifacts, and specimens and attempt to formulate conditions and procedures for storage, exhibit, and stabilization that optimize the preservation of these objects. In interdisciplinary collaborations with archeologists, anthropologists, and art historians, natural and physical scientists study and analyze objects from the collections and related materials to expand knowledge and understanding of their historical and scientific context.

For further information, contact the Museum Conservation Institute, Museum Support Center, Suitland, MD 20746. Phone, 301-238-1240.

National Air and Space Museum

Created to memorialize the development and achievements of aviation and spaceflight, the Museum collects, displays, and preserves aeronautical and space flight artifacts of historical significance as well as documentary and artistic materials related to air and space. Among its artifacts are full-size planes, models, and instruments. Highlights of the collection include the Wright brothers' Flyer, Charles Lindbergh's Spirit of St. Louis, a Moon rock, and Apollo spacecraft. The exhibitions and study collections record the human conquest of the air from its beginnings to recent achievements. The principal areas in which work is concentrated include flight craft of all types, spaceflight vehicles, and propulsion systems. The Museum's IMAX Theater and the 70-foot domed Einstein Planetarium are popular attractions. The Museum's Steven F. Udvar-Hazy Center, at Washington Dulles International Airport, opened in December 2003. Its featured artifacts include a space shuttle and the Enola Gay B–29 World War II bomber.

For further information, contact the National Air and Space Museum, Sixth Street and Independence Avenue SW., Washington, DC 20560. Phone, 202-633-2214.

National Museum of African American History and Culture

The Museum was established in 2003 and will be the only national museum devoted exclusively to the documentation of African American life, art, history, and culture. Recently completed, the new Museum has opened its doors to the public on the National Mall, adjacent to the Washington Monument.

For further information, contact the National Museum of African American History and Culture, Capital Gallery, Suite 7001, 600 Maryland Avenue SW., Washington, DC 20024. Phone, 202-633-1000.

National Museum of African Art

This is the only art museum in the United States dedicated exclusively to portraying the creative visual traditions of Africa. Its research components, collection, exhibitions, and public programs establish the Museum as a primary source for the examination and discovery of the arts and culture of Africa. The collection includes works in wood, metal, fired clay, ivory, and fiber. The Eliot Elisofon Photographic Archives includes slides, photos, and film segments on Africa. There is also a specialized library.

For further information, contact the National Museum of African Art, 950 Independence Avenue SW., Washington, DC 20560. Phone, 202-633-4600.

National Museum of American History

In pursuit of its fundamental mission to inspire a broader understanding of the United States and its people, the Museum provides learning opportunities, stimulates the imagination of visitors, and presents challenging ideas about the Nation's past. The Museum's exhibits provide a unique view of the American experience. Emphasis is placed upon innovative individuals representing a wide range of cultures, who have shaped our heritage, and upon science and the remaking of our world through technology. Exhibits draw upon strong collections in the sciences and engineering, agriculture, manufacturing, transportation, political memorabilia, costumes, musical instruments, coins, Armed Forces history, photography, computers, ceramics, and glass. Classic cars, icons of the American Presidency, First Ladies' gowns, the Star-Spangled Banner flag, Whitney's cotton gin, Morse's telegraph, the John Bull locomotive, Dorothy's ruby slippers from "The Wizard of Oz," and other American icons are highlights of the collection. During the remaining renovations of the West Wing, the Museum's core, its East Wing, and the first floor of the West Wing will be open to the public.

For further information, contact the National Museum of American History, Fourteenth Street and Constitution Avenue NW., Washington, DC 20560. Phone, 202-633-1000.

National Museum of Natural History

Dedicated to understanding the natural world and the place of humans in it, the Museum's permanent exhibitions focus on human cultures, Earth sciences, biology, and anthropology, with the most popular displays featuring gem stones such as the Hope Diamond, dinosaurs, insects, marine ecosystems, birds, and mammals. In 2010, the Museum celebrated its 100th anniversary with the opening of a new permanent exhibition, the David H. Koch Hall of Human Origins. An IMAX theater offers large-format films. The Museum's encyclopedic collections comprise more than 126 million specimens, making the Museum one of the world's foremost facilities for natural history research. The Museum's seven departments are anthropology, botany, entomology, invertebrate zoology, mineral sciences, paleobiology, and vertebrate zoology. Doctorate-level staff researchers ensure the continued growth and value of the collection by conducting studies in the field and laboratory.

For further information, contact the National Museum of Natural History, Tenth Street and Constitution Avenue NW., Washington, DC 20560. Phone, 202-633-1000.

National Museum of the American Indian

The Museum was established in 1989, and the building on the National Mall opened September 2004. Much of the collection of the Museum is comprised of the collection of the former Heye Foundation in New York City. It is an institution of living cultures dedicated to the collection, preservation, study, and exhibition of the life, languages, literature, history, and arts of the Native peoples of the Americas. Highlights include Northwest Coast carvings; dance masks; pottery and weaving from the Southwest; painted hides and garments from the North American Plains; goldwork of the Aztecs, Incas, and Maya; and Amazonian featherwork. The National Museum of the American Indian also operates the George Gustav Heye Center at the Alexander Hamilton U.S. Custom House in New York City.

For further information, contact the National Museum of the American Indian, Fourth Street and Independence Avenue SW., Washington, DC 20560. Phone, 202-633-1000.

National Portrait Gallery

The Gallery was established in 1962 for the exhibition and study of portraiture depicting men and women who have made significant contributions to the history, development, and culture of the United States. The Gallery contains more than 19,000 works, including photographs and glass negatives. The first floor of the Gallery is devoted to changing exhibitions from the Gallery's collection of paintings, sculpture, prints, photographs, and drawings as well as to special portrait collections. Featured on the second floor are the permanent collection of portraits of eminent Americans and the Hall of Presidents, including the famous Gilbert Stuart portrait-from-life of George Washington. The two-story American Victorian Renaissance Great Hall on the third floor of the Gallery houses an exhibit of 20th-century Americans and is used for special events and public programs. The Gallery shares a large library with the Smithsonian American Art Museum and the Archives of American Art. The education department offers public programs; outreach programs for adult groups; and walk-in and group tours.

For further information, contact the National Portrait Gallery, Eighth and F Streets NW., Washington, DC 20001. Phone, 202-633-8300.

National Postal Museum

The Museum houses the Nation's postal history and philatelic collection, the largest of its kind in the world, with more than 13 million objects. The Museum is devoted to the history of America's mail service, and major galleries include exhibits on mail service in colonial times and during the Civil War, the Pony Express, modern mail service, automation, mail transportation, and the art of letters, as well as displays of the Museum's priceless stamp collection. Highlights include three mail planes, a replica of a railway mail car, displays of historic letters, handcrafted mail boxes, and rare U.S. and foreign-issue stamps and covers.

For further information, contact the National Postal Museum, 2 Massachusetts Avenue NE., Washington, DC 20001. Phone, 202-633-1000.

National Zoological Park

The National Zoo is an international leader in wildlife conservation, education, and research. Home to more than 2,000 animals, the Zoo encompasses 163 acres along Rock Creek Park in Northwest Washington. Exhibits include the David M. Rubenstein Family Giant Panda Habitat, where the giant pandas Mei Xiang and Tian Tian reside with their cub Bao Bao. Built to mimic the animals' natural habitat in China, it is part of the Zoo's Asia Trail, which also takes visitors through the habitats of red pandas, Asian small-clawed otters, fishing cats, sloth bears, and clouded leopards. Other highlights include the Elephant Trails, home to the Asian elephant Kandula, who was born at the Zoo in 2001; Amazonia, a 15,000-square-foot rain forest habitat; the Reptile Discovery Center, featuring African pancake tortoises and the world's largest lizards, Komodo dragons; and the Great Ape House, home to gorillas, orangutans, and other primates.

For further information, contact the National Zoo, 3001 Connecticut Avenue NW., Washington, DC 20008. Phone, 202- 633-4888.

Renwick Gallery

The Gallery, a branch of the Smithsonian American Art Museum, is dedicated to exhibiting crafts of all periods and to collecting 20th-century American crafts. It offers changing exhibitions of American crafts and decorative arts, both historical and contemporary, and a rotating selection from its permanent collection. The Gallery's grand salon is elegantly furnished in the Victorian style of the 1860s and 1870s. The Gallery closes for a 2-year renovation beginning in early 2014.

For further information, contact the Renwick Gallery, Seventeenth Street and Pennsylvania Avenue NW., Washington, DC 20006. Phone, 202-633-7970.

Smithsonian American Art Museum

The Museum's art collection spans centuries of American painting, sculpture, folk art, photography, and graphic art. A major center for research in American art, the Museum has contributed to such resources as the Inventory of American Paintings Executed Before 1914, the Smithsonian Art Index, and the Inventory of American Sculpture. The library, shared with the National Portrait Gallery, contains volumes on art, history, and biography, with special emphasis on the United States. The Donald W. Reynolds Center for American Art and Portraiture is home to the Smithsonian American Art Museum, the National Portrait Gallery, and the Archives of American Art. Hundreds of images from the collection and extensive information on its collections, publications, and activities are available on the Museum's Web site.

For further information, contact the Smithsonian American Art Museum, Eighth and F Streets NW., Washington, DC 20006. Phone, 202-633-7970.

Smithsonian Asian Pacific American Center

The Center seeks to enrich the appreciation of America's Asian Pacific heritage and empower Asian Pacific American communities in their sense of inclusion within the national culture.

For further information, contact the Asian Pacific American Center's administrative office, Capital Gallery, Suite 7065, MRC 516, P.O. Box 37012, Washington, DC 20013-7012. Phone, 202-633-2691.

Smithsonian Environmental Research Center (SERC)

The Center is the leading national research center for understanding environmental issues in the coastal zone. SERC is dedicated to increasing knowledge of the biological and physical processes that sustain life on Earth. The Center, located near the Chesapeake Bay, trains future generations of scientists to address ecological questions of the Nation and the globe.

For further information, contact the Smithsonian Environmental Research Center, 647 Contees Wharf Road, Edgewater, MD 21037. Phone, 443-482-2200.

Smithsonian Institution Archives

The Smithsonian Institution Archives acquires, preserves, and makes available for research the official records of the Smithsonian Institution and the papers of individuals and organizations associated with the Institution or with its work. These holdings document the growth of the Smithsonian and the development of American science, history, and art.

For further information, contact the Smithsonian Institution Archives, Capital Gallery, Suite 3000, 600 Maryland Avenue SW., Washington, DC 20024. Phone, 202-633-5870.

Smithsonian Institution Traveling Exhibition Service (SITES)

Since 1952, SITES has been committed to making Smithsonian exhibitions available to millions of people who cannot view them firsthand at the Smithsonian museums. Exhibitions on art, history, and science travel to more than 250 locations each year.

For further information, contact the Smithsonian Institution Traveling Exhibition Service, Suite 7103, 470 L'Enfant Plaza SW., Washington, DC 20024. Phone, 202-633-3120.

Smithsonian Latino Center

The Center promotes Latino presence within the Smithsonian Institution. It is not represented in one physical location; rather, it works collaboratively with the Institution's museums and research centers to ensure that the contributions of the Latino community in the arts, history, national culture, and scientific achievement are celebrated, explored, presented, and preserved. The Center supports collections and archives, exhibitions, public and educational programs, research, and Web-based content and virtual platforms. It also manages leadership and professional development programs for emerging scholars, museum professionals, and Latino youth.

For further information, contact the Smithsonian Latino Center at Capital Gallery,

600 Maryland Avenue SW., MRC 512, Washington, DC 20013-7012. Phone, 202-633-1240.

Smithsonian Libraries

The Smithsonian Institution Libraries include more than 1 million volumes (among them, 40,000 rare books) with strengths in natural history, art, science, humanities, and museology. Many volumes are available through interlibrary loan.

For further information, contact the Smithsonian Institution Libraries, Tenth Street and Constitution Avenue NW., Washington, DC 20560. Phone, 202-633-2240.

Smithsonian Marine Station at Fort Pierce

The research institute features a state-of-the-art laboratory where Station scientists catalog species and study marine plants and animals. Among the most important projects being pursued at the site is the search for possible causes of fishkills, including Pfiesteria and other organisms.

For further information, contact the Smithsonian Marine Station–Fort Pierce, 701 Seaway Drive, Fort Pierce, FL 34949. Phone, 772-462-6220.

Smithsonian Tropical Research Institute (STRI)

The Institute is a research organization for advanced studies of tropical ecosystems. Headquartered in the Republic of Panama, STRI maintains extensive facilities in the Western Hemisphere tropics. It is the base of a corps of tropical researchers who study the evolution, behavior, ecology, and history of tropical species of systems ranging from coral reefs to rain forests.

For further information, contact the Smithsonian Tropical Research Institute, 1100 Jefferson Drive SW., Suite 3123, Washington, DC 20560. Phone, 202-633-4700. Phone, 011-507-212-8000 (Panama).

Sources of Information

Business Opportunities

Information on procurement of supplies, property management and utilization services for Smithsonian Institution organizations, and construction contracts may be obtained from the Director, Office of Contracting, Smithsonian Institution, 2011 Crystal Drive, Suite 350, Arlington, VA 22202. Phone, 202-633-7290.

Education / Research

Write to the Directors of the following offices at the Smithsonian Institution, Washington, DC 20560: Office of Fellowships and Internships, Smithsonian Center for Folklife and Cultural Heritage, Smithsonian Science Education Center, and Smithsonian Center for Learning and Digital Access.

Employment

Employment information for the Smithsonian is available from the Office of Human Resources, Smithsonian Institution, Capital Gallery, Suite 5060, 600 Maryland Avenue SW., Washington, DC 20560. Phone, 202-633-6370.

Events / Hours of Operation

The Office of Visitor Services records a weekly message announcing events and hours of operation. Phone, 202-633-1000.

Media Affairs

Members of the press may contact the Smithsonian Office of Public Affairs, 1000 Jefferson Drive SW., Washington, DC 20560. Phone, 202-633-2400.

Memberships

For information on the Friends of the Smithsonian, write to PO Box 37012, MRC 712 Washington, DC 20013-7012. Phone, 202-633-6300.

For information on the Resident

Associate Program, write to Smithsonian Associates, PO Box 23293, Washington, DC 20026-3293. Phone, 202-633-3030.

For information on the Smithsonian National Associate Program, call 800-766-2149.

For information on the National Air and Space Society, call 202-633-2603.

For information on the Friends of the National Zoo, call 202-633-3038.

For information on National Museum of the American Indian membership, call 800-242-6624.

Photographs

Photographs and slides from the Smithsonian photographic archives are available to researchers, publishers, Government agencies, and the general public. A searchable database of images is available online. Purchase or use of images may require permission from the Smithsonian curatorial unit that holds copyright. For assistance, contact Smithsonian Photographic Services. Phone, 202-633-1933.

Publications

The Smithsonian Institution's annual reports, starting with the year 2004, are available online as Portable Document Format (PDF) files. For information on acquiring hardcopies of reports, call 202-633-1000.

Smithsonian Books, in collaboration with the Smithsonian Institution, publishes narrative nonfiction books on culture, history, science and technology, and the arts, as well as signature illustrated books based on Smithsonian museums and their collections. Random House Publisher Services distribute these titles.

Smithsonian Institution Scholarly Press, in conjunction with Rowman and Littlefield Publishing Group, Inc., publishes the research and other scholarly contributions of Smithsonian authors.

Subscribe to the "Smithsonian Magazine" online. Phone, 800-766-2149.

Subscribe to "Air and Space Magazine" online. Phone, 800-513-3081.

The "Visitor Survival Guide" is available online as a Portable Document Format (PDF) file.

Tours

For information on museum and gallery tours, contact the Smithsonian Information Center, 1000 Jefferson Drive SW., Washington, DC 20560. Phone, 202-633-1000. School groups are welcome. The benefits of various memberships and their levels include special guided tours.

Visitor Information

The Smithsonian Information Center, located in the original Smithsonian building, commonly known as The Castle, provides general orientation through films, computer interactive programs, and visitor information specialists to help members and the public learn about the national collections, museum events, exhibitions, and special programs. Write to the Smithsonian Information Center, 1000 Jefferson Drive SW., Washington, DC 20560. Phone, 202-633-1000.

Volunteer Opportunities

The Smithsonian Institution welcomes volunteers and offers a variety of service opportunities. For information, write to the Office of Visitor Services, 1000 Jefferson Drive SW., Washington, DC 20560. Phone, 202-633-1000.

For further information, contact the Smithsonian Information Center, 1000 Jefferson Drive SW., Washington, DC 20560. Phone, 202-633-1000. TDD, 202-357-1729.

John F. Kennedy Center for the Performing Arts

John F. Kennedy Center for the Performing Arts, Washington, DC 20566, 202-467-4600, *http://www.kennedy-center.org*

CHAIR	David M. Rubenstein
President	Deborah F. Rutter

The Kennedy Center is the only official memorial to President John Kennedy in Washington, DC. Since its opening in 1971, the Center has presented a year-round program of the finest in dance, drama, music, and opera from the United States and abroad.

Sources of Information

Box Office

The Kennedy Center's box office is open daily: Monday–Saturday, 10 a.m.–9 p.m.; Sunday and Holidays, 12–9 p.m. General information and tickets are accessible online. Phone, 202-467-4600. TTY, 202-416-8524.

Business Opportunities

Opportunities are posted on the Federal Business Opportunities Web site. For more information, contact The John F. Kennedy Center for the Performing Arts, Washington, DC 20566.

Education and Research

For information on education programs, contact The John F. Kennedy Center for the Performing Arts, Washington, DC 20566. Phone, 202-416-8000.

Employment

For information on employment opportunities, visit the Center's Web site.

Free Performances

Free performances are given every day at 6 p.m. on the Millennium Stage in the Grand Foyer.

Memberships

For information on national and local activities, including the bimonthly "Kennedy Center News" for members, visit an information desk inside The John F. Kennedy Center for the Performing Arts. Or, contact Member Services, The John F. Kennedy Center for the Performing Arts, Washington, DC 20566. Phone, 202-416-8310.

Special Functions

For information on using the facilities for special functions, contact the Office of Special Events, The John F. Kennedy Center for the Performing Arts, Washington, DC 20566. Phone, 202-416-8000.

Theater Operations

For information on using the theaters, contact the booking manager at The John F. Kennedy Center for the Performing Arts, Washington, DC 20566. Phone, 202-416-8032.

Tours

The Friends of the Kennedy Center volunteers provide visitor services. Tours are available free of charge on weekdays, 10 a.m.–5 p.m., and on weekends, 10 a.m.–1 p.m.

Volunteer Opportunities

For information on volunteer opportunities, contact Friends of the Kennedy Center, 2700 F Street NW, Washington, DC 20566. Phone, 202-416-8000.

For further information, contact The John F. Kennedy Center for the Performing Arts. Phone, 202-467-4600.

National Gallery of Art

4th and Constitution Avenue NW., Washington, DC 20565, 202-737-4215, *http://www.nga.gov*

PRESIDENT	Frederick W. Beinecke
Director	Earl A. Powell III

Activities

The National Gallery of Art administers a world-class collection of painting, sculpture, and the graphic arts. The West Building includes European (13th–early 20th century) and American (18th–early 20th century) works. An extensive survey of Italian painting and sculpture, including the only painting by Leonardo da Vinci in the Americas, is on display in the Gallery. Rich in Dutch masters and French impressionists, the collection offers superb surveys of American, British, Flemish, Spanish, and 15th- and 16th-century German art, as well as Renaissance medals and bronzes, Chinese porcelains, and about 117,000 works of graphic art from the 12th century to the present day. The East Building collections and Sculpture Garden contain important works by major 20th-century artists. The Gallery relies on public and private resources. Federal appropriations support its operations and maintenance. Private donations and funds allow it to acquire artwork, as well as to offer a variety of special programs. For example, a fellowship program promotes graduate and postgraduate research, an extension service provides free education resources to millions of people each year, and other programs educate schoolchildren and the public.

Sources of Information

Business Opportunities

For more information, contact the National Gallery of Art, Office of Procurement and Contracts, 2000B South Club Drive, Landover, MD 20785. Phone, 202-842-6745. Fax, 202-312-2792.

Calendar of Events

The full calendar of events is available online. To subscribe to the quarterly brochure of seasonal exhibition and programming highlights, visit the Gallery's Web site or call 202-842-6662.

Concerts

Concerts by accomplished musicians are open to the public without charge. Seating starts 30 minutes before the performance on a first-come, first-seated basis. Phone, 202-842-6941.

Educational Resources

The Gallery's free loan program allows community groups, educational institutions, individuals, and nonprofit television stations nationwide to borrow teaching packets and DVDs. Dozens of lessons and activities are also accessible on the Gallery's Web site. For more information, including the free catalog of education resources, contact the Department of Education Resources, National Gallery of Art, 2000B South Club Drive, Landover, MD 20785. Phone, 202-842-6273.

Employment

For information on employment opportunities at the National Gallery of Art, contact the Personnel Office, National Gallery of Art, 601 Pennsylvania Avenue NW., South Building, Washington, DC 20004. Phone, 202-842-6282. Fax, 202-789-3011.

Family Programs

The Gallery offers free family programs—children's films, music performances, storytelling, and workshops—that are suitable for children ages 4 and up. Phone, 202-789-3030.

Fellowships

For information on research fellowship programs, contact the Center for Advanced Study in the Visual Arts. Phone, 202-842-6480. Fax, 202-842-6733.

Films

An ongoing program of classic cinema, documentary, avant-garde, and area premieres takes place each weekend. Seating is on a first-come, first-seated basis, and admission is free. Doors open approximately 30 minutes before each show. Visiting filmmakers and scholars discuss films with the audiences following some screenings. Phone, 202-842-6799.

Internships

For information on internship programs for college graduates and graduate students, contact the Department of Academic Programs, National Gallery of Art, 2000B South Club Drive, Landover, MD 20785. Phone, 202-842-6257.

Lectures

Lecture events are open to the public, and admission is free. Seating is available on a first-come, first-seated basis.

Library

The National Gallery of Art Library maintains a collection of more than 400,000 books and periodicals on the history, theory, and criticism of art and architecture. The collection's holdings emphasize Western art from the Middle Ages to the present and American art from the colonial era to the present. The library is accessible by appointment every Monday, noon–4:30 p.m., and Tuesday–Friday, 10 a.m.–4:30 p.m., except on Federal holidays. Phone, 202-842-6511.

Library Image Collections

The Department of Image Collections serves as the National Gallery of Art's research center for images of Western art and architecture. The collections now contain over 14 million digital images, microforms, negatives, photographs, and slides, making this resource one of the largest of its kind. Gallery staff, Center for Advanced Study in the Visual Arts members, visiting scholars, and serious adult researchers regularly use the collections. The library is accessible by appointment every Monday, noon–4:30 p.m., and Tuesday–Friday, 10 a.m.–4:30 p.m., except on Federal holidays. Phone, 202-842-6026.

Memberships

The Gallery offers three membership levels of annual giving: The Circle, The Tower Project, and The Exhibition Circle. Circle members contribute to conservation programs, special exhibitions, and research. Tower Project members promote contemporary artists by supporting modern and contemporary exhibitions in the Tower Gallery of the East Building. Exhibition Circle members provide funding for exhibitions. For more information on membership levels and their benefits, contact The Circle, National Gallery of Art, 2000B South Club Drive, Landover, MD 20785. Phone, 202-842-6450. Fax, 202 789-4577.

Newsletters

An online subscription form is available to sign up for announcements, newsletters, notifications, and updates on acquisitions and exhibitions; activities, projects, and programs; and other topics.

NGAkids

NGAkids offers interactive activities and adventures with artwork from the Gallery's collection and an animated tale set in the Gallery's Sculpture Garden.

Photographs

Photographs that are not on display may be viewed by appointment. Phone, 202-842-6144.

Email: Publications

The Gallery Shops sell publications on the Gallery's collections and quality reproductions of artwork. Purchases may be made online or by calling 800-697-9350.

Tours

The education division offers daily guided talks and tours in the galleries. Phone, 202-842-6247.

Visitor Services

The Visitor Services Office assists those with special needs, responds to written and telephone requests, and helps visitors plan their stay in the Washington, DC, area. For more information, contact the National Gallery of Art, Office of Visitor Services, 2000B South Club Drive, Landover, MD 20785. Phone, 202-842-6691.

Volunteer Opportunities

The Gallery offers a range of volunteer opportunities. Volunteers serve as docents, manage the information desks at the entrances to the East and West Buildings, work in the library, and help in the horticulture division. Local high school students can participate in the teen volunteer program. More information on volunteering is available on the Gallery's Web site.

Works on Paper

Works of art on paper that are not on display may be viewed by appointment. Phone, 202-842-6380 (European works). Phone, 202-842-6605 (American works).

For further information, contact the National Gallery of Art. Phone, 202-737-4215.

Woodrow Wilson International Center for Scholars

Scholar Administration Office, Woodrow Wilson Center, One Woodrow Wilson Plaza, 1300 Pennsylvania Avenue NW., Washington, DC 20004-3027, 202-691-4000, 202-691-4001, *http://www.wilsoncenter.org*

DIRECTOR	Jane Harman
Executive Vice President	Andrew S. Selee
Chair, Board of Trustees	Thomas R. Nides

Activities

Created by an Act of Congress in 1968, the Woodrow Wilson International Center for Scholars is a national, living memorial honoring the legacy of President Woodrow Wilson. The Wilson Center, headquartered in Washington, DC, and supported by both public and private funds, provides a strictly nonpartisan space for scholars and policymakers to interact. By conducting relevant, timely research and promoting dialogue from diverse perspectives, the Center works to address critical current and emerging challenges confronting the United States and the world.

Sources of Information

Donations

An online form is available for making tax-deductible contributions to support dialogue and scholarship in public policy. Gifts may be directed to a specific program by using the "Designation" dropdown menu. "Unrestricted" gifts allow the Center to build its overall capacity and meet areas of greatest need. Phone, 202-691-4171.

Employment

Career opportunities at the Center are posted online. For more information, contact the Office of Human Resources, One Woodrow Wilson Plaza, 1300 Pennsylvania Avenue NW., 3d Floor, Washington, DC 20004-3027.

Fellowships

The Center offers residential fellowships that allow academics, public officials, journalists, business professionals, and others to pursue their research and writing at the Center while interacting with policymakers in Washington. The Center also invites public policy scholars and senior scholars from a variety of disciplines to conduct research for varying lengths of time in residence. Phone, 202-691-4000.

Internships

The Center has a year-round need for interns to assist the program and projects staff and to act as research assistants for scholars and fellows. Phone, 202-691-4053.

Media Affairs

Members of the press may contact the Center at 202-691-4217.

Presidential Memorial Exhibit

The Center houses the Woodrow Wilson Presidential Memorial Exhibit, which features memorabilia, historical information, photographs, several short films, and a memorial hall with quotations. The exhibit is open weekdays, 8:30 a.m.–5 p.m. Admission is free. Phone, 202-691-4000.

Publications

The Center publishes policy briefs and research reports, as well as books written by staff and visiting scholars and fellows, through the Wilson Center Press. Phone, 202-691-4000.

Every 3 months, "The Wilson Quarterly" magazine releases a cluster of content exploring a single topic from diverse perspectives. The magazine examines culture, ideas, news, and the people affected by them.

Radio / Television

An award-winning weekly radio and television program, "Dialogue at the Wilson Center" explores the world of ideas through weekly, half-hour conversations with authors, journalists, public figures, and scholars. The program offers thoughtful commentary and informed discussion on important ideas and issues in national and international affairs, history, and culture.

Research

The Center's "Research" Web page allows visitors to explore the pressing global challenges confronting the U.S. policy community and general public today.

Social Media

The Center tweets announcements, news, and other noteworthy items on Twitter.

The Center maintains an account on Facebook.

The Center posts videos on its YouTube channel.

Visitor Services

Events, unless otherwise noted, are free and open to the public. Photo identification is required for entry. A listing of events at the Center is available online.

For further information, contact the Woodrow Wilson International Center for Scholars, One Woodrow Wilson Plaza, 1300 Pennsylvania Avenue NW., Washington, DC 20004-3027. Phone, 202-691-4000. Fax, 202-691-4001.

State Justice Institute

11951 Freedom Drive, Suite 1020, Reston, VA 20190, 571-313-8843, *http://www.sji.gov*

BOARD OF DIRECTORS

CHAIR	Daniel J. Becker, Acting
Vice Chair	(vacancy)
Member	David V. Brewer
Member	Isabel Framer
Member	Jonathan Lippman
Member	Wilfredo Martinez
Member	John B. Nalbandian
Member	Marsha J. Rabiteau
Member	Chase T. Rogers
Secretary	Gayle A. Nachtigal
Treasurer	Hernán D. Vera

OFFICERS

EXECUTIVE DIRECTOR	Jonathan D. Mattiello

The State Justice Institute supports the Nation's judicial system and the public that it serves.

The State Justice Institue (SJI) was established by the State Justice Institute

Authorization Act of 1984 (42 U.S.C. 10701 et seq.) as a private, nonprofit corporation to further the development and improvement of judicial administration in the State courts.

An 11-member Board of Directors supervises the SJI. The President appoints the members with the advice and consent of the Senate. By law, the Board is composed of six judges, a State court administrator, and four members of the public—no more than two of the four public members can be affiliated with the same political party.

The SJI develops solutions to common issues faced by State courts; provides practical products to judges and court staff; ensures that effective approaches in one State are quickly and economically shared with other courts nationwide; and supports national, regional, and instate educational programs to speed the transfer of solutions.

To accomplish these broad objectives, the SJI is authorized to provide funds through grants, cooperative agreements, and contracts to the State courts and to court support organizations.

Sources of Information

Forms

Documents to view and print are posted online in Portable Document Format (PDF). These documents include a number of forms: assurances, consultant rate, disclosure of lobbying activities, grant application, project budget, reimbursement request, and State approval certificate.

Grants

Information on various award and grant types—curriculum adaptation and training grants, the education support program, project grants, and technical assistance grants—is available online.

Newsletter

Readers may subscribe to the monthly "SJI Newsletter" online.

For further information, contact the State Justice Institute, 11951 Freedom Drive, Suite 1020, Reston, VA 20190. Phone, 571-313-8843.

United States Holocaust Memorial Museum

100 Raoul Wallenberg Place, SW., Washington, DC 20024-2126, 202-488-0400, TTY, 202-488-0406, *http://www.ushmm.org*

U.S. HOLOCAUST MEMORIAL COUNCIL

CHAIR	Tom A. Bernstein
Vice Chair	Allan M. Holt
MEMBERS	
	Laurence M. Baer
	Elisa Spungen Bildner
	Joshua B. Bolten
	Ethel C. Brooks
	Lee T. Bycel
	Michael Chertoff
	Diana Shaw Clark
	Sara Darehshori
	Shefali Razdan Duggal
	Norman L. Eisen
	Jonathan Safran Foer
	Amy R. Friedkin
	Nancy B. Gilbert

	Jordan T. Goodman
	Mark D. Goodman
	Samuel N. Gordon
	Sanford L. Gottesman
	Joseph D. Gutman
	Beth Heifetz
	Jane H. Jelenko
	Roman R. Kent
	Howard Konar
	Alan B. Lazowski
	Erica A. LeVine
	Susan G. Levine
	Deborah E. Lipstadt
	Susan E. Lowenberg
	Leslie Meyers
	Deborah A. Oppenheimer
	Cheryl Peisach
	Dana Perlman
	Richard S. Price
	Ronald Ratner
	Daniel J. Rosen
	Greg A. Rosenbaum
	Menachem Z. Rosensaft
	Michael P. Ross
	Kirk A. Rudy
	Elliot J. Schrage
	Maureen Schulman
	Irvin N. Shapell
	Cindy Simon Skjodt
	Andrea Lavin Solow
	Marc R. Stanley
	Michael Ashley Stein
	Michèle Taylor
	Howard D. Unger
	Clemantine Wamariya
	Daniel G. Weiss
	(vacancy)
	(vacancy)
	(vacancy)
	(vacancy)
CONGRESSIONAL MEMBERS	
House of Representatives	Theodore E. Deutch
House of Representatives	Steve Israel
House of Representatives	Patrick Meehan
House of Representatives	(vacancy)
House of Representatives	(vacancy)
Senate	Alan S. Franken
Senate	Orrin G. Hatch
Senate	Bernard Sanders

Senate	(vacancy)
Senate	(vacancy)
EX OFFICIO MEMBERS (Nonvoting)	
Department of Education	Philip H. Rosenfelt
Department of the Interior	Benjamin Milakofsky
Department of State	Thomas K. Yazdgerdi
General Counsel to the Council	Gerard Leval

COUNCIL STAFF

MUSEUM DIRECTOR	Sara J. Bloomfield
Internal Auditor	Mel Schwartz
Secretary	Jane M. Miller

MUSEUM ADMINISTRATION

MUSEUM DIRECTOR	Sara J. Bloomfield
Chief Development Officer	Jordan Tannenbaum
Chief Financial Officer	Polly Povejsil Heath
Chief Information Officer	Joseph Kraus
Chief Marketing Officer	Mark Irwin, Acting
Chief Museum Operations Officer	Tanell Colaman
Chief Program Officer	Sarah Ogilvie
Director, Collections	Michael Grunberger
Director, International Affairs	Paul Shapiro
Director, Levine Institute for Holocaust Education	Michael Abramowitz
Director, Mandel Center for Advanced Holocaust Studies	Wendy Lower, Acting
Director, Museum Operations and Administration	Tanell Coleman
Director, Planning	Dara Goldberg
Director, Simon-Skjodt Center for the Prevention of Genocide	Cameron Hudson
General Counsel	Ronald F. Cuffe
Senior Program Advisor for Institutional Projects	Arnold Kramer

The United States Holocaust Memorial Museum promotes documentation, study, and interpretation of the Holocaust and maintains a permanent living memorial to its victims.

The United States Holocaust Memorial Museum (USHMM) was established by the act of October 7, 1980 (36 U.S.C. 1401-1408). It received permanent authorization as an independent establishment by the act of October 12, 2000 (36 U.S.C. 2301 et seq.).

The United States Holocaust Memorial Council, which serves as a board of trustees, governs the USHMM. The Council's 55 members are appointed by the President to staggered 5-year terms. Additionally, five members are appointed from each Chamber of the Congress. There are also three nonvoting ex-officio members from the Departments of Education, State, and the Interior.

The USHMM operates as a public-private partnership. Its activities and programs are supported by planned giving, endowments, and revenues; gifts, grants, and contracts; and Federal funding.

Activities

Jack, Joseph and Morton Mandel Center for Advanced Holocaust Studies

The Center works with the United States Holocaust Memorial Council's Academic Committee to support research projects and publications on the Holocaust, provide access to Holocaust-related archival materials for study and new research, sponsor fellowship opportunities for pre- and postdoctoral researchers, and offer seminars, summer research workshops, conferences, lectures, and symposia.

For further information, contact the Jack, Joseph, and Morton Mandel Center for Advanced Holocaust Studies. Phone, 202-488-0400. TTY, 202-488-0406.

Simon-Skjodt Center for the Prevention of Genocide

The Center raises awareness of genocide, influences policymaking on genocide prevention, and stimulates worldwide action to prevent genocide and related mass atrocities. It seeks to make genocide prevention a national and international priority by increasing public awareness and mobilizing worldwide support to avert these crimes against humanity.

For further information, contact the Simon-Skjodt Center for the Prevention of Genocide. Phone, 202-488-0400. TTY, 202-488-0406.

William Levine Family National Institute for Holocaust Education

The Institute promotes a variety of resources and programs to help educators, professionals, and students increase their knowledge of Holocaust history and understand its relevance today. Educational outreach programs provide teachers with classroom strategies and resources for teaching students about the Holocaust.

For further information, contact the National Institute for Holocaust Education.

Programs

Law, Justice, and the Holocaust Program

This program examines the decisions German jurists made and the pressures they faced under the Nazi regime. This is a one-day program for judges, prosecutors, and court administrators.

For further information, contact the Law, Justice, and the Holocaust Program.

Civic and Defense Initiatives Program

This program explores the ways in which the military can work to prevent genocide today.

Lessons of the Holocaust Program

This program examines the role that law enforcement professionals played in the Holocaust. It also challenges them to reflect on their professional and personal responsibilities in a democracy today.

Law Enforcement and Society:

For further information, contact the Lessons of the Holocaust Program.

Programs on Ethics, Religion, and the Holocaust

These programs focus on the response of churches to the Holocaust and the ways in which religious institutions, leaders, and theologians have addressed this history and its legacy.

For further information, contact the Programs on Ethics, Religion, and the Holocaust.

Youth and Community Initiatives Program

This program introduces students to Holocaust history and helps them develop leadership skills for confronting hatred and promoting human dignity.

For further information, contact the Student Leaders Program.

Sources of Information

Cafe

The Museum Cafe is open daily, 8:30 a.m.–4:30 p.m., except on Yom Kippur and Christmas Day. Visitors may not bring food into the cafe or Museum. The cafe serves breakfast, salads, sandwiches, and soups, including vegetarian and kosher options. Kosher food is prepared and sealed offsite under rabbinical supervision.

Calendar of Events

For information on upcoming events, see the Museum's online calendar.

Collections / Exhibitions

The Museum's holdings include art, books, pamphlets, advertisements, maps, film and video historical footage, audio and video oral testimonies, music and sound recordings, furnishings, architectural fragments, models, machinery, tools, microfilm and microfiche of government documents and other official records, personal effects, personal papers, photographs, photo albums, and textiles. The self-guided permanent exhibition spans three floors and presents a narrative history of the Holocaust with historical artifacts, photographs, and film footage. Special exhibitions include Remember the Children: Daniel's Story (for children 8 and up) and Some Were Neighbors: Collaboration and Complicity in the Holocaust. The Museum's traveling exhibitions have gone to numerous cities, States, and countries. These exhibitions extend the history of the Holocaust beyond the Museum's walls. More information on the Museum's collections and exhibitions is available on its Web site.

Employment

The museum employs people with diverse professional experience: collections, education, exhibits, fundraising, marketing, programing, and other areas. A list of current job openings is available on the "Careers" Web page.

Frequently Asked Questions (FAQs)

The Museum posts answers to FAQs on its Web site.

Internships

Unpaid internship opportunities are available. More information on them is available on the Museum's Web site.

Multilingual Resources

At the top of the Museum's home page is a "Language" drop-down menu that allows non-English readers to access resources in a number of languages: Arabic, Bahasa, Chinese, French, Greek, Hungarian, Italian, Japanese, Korean, Portuguese, Russian, Spanish, and Turkish.

News

The Museum posts press releases on its Web site.

To receive electronic Museum news, invitations to special programs and exhibitions, and updates on genocide prevention and other initiatives, subscribe using the online form.

Plan a Visit

The Museum is open every day, except on Yom Kippur and Christmas. Admission is free; however, timed passes are required to enter the permanent exhibition from March through August. No passes are required for other Museum exhibitions. The "Plan Your Visit" Web pages contain a trove of useful information on accessibility, admission and tickets, group reservations, hours, location, transportation, and more.

Social Media

The Museum relies on social media to share information on its programs and resources; to memorialize the victims of Nazism; to launch discussion on the Holocaust and its relevance today; and to raise awareness that antisemitism, genocide, and hatred are persistent threats and that everybody has a role in combating them.

Support the Mission

Annual membership gifts help the Museum confront antisemitism and answer Holocaust denial, expand educational outreach, and preserve historical artifacts.

The Museum uses its resources to

confront hatred and genocide, to educate students and provide classroom resources for teachers, and to rescue Holocaust evidence and make additional historic documents available in digital format. An online contribution, one-time or monthly, supports these activities immediately and directly.

Volunteer Opportunities

The Museum welcomes volunteers and offers a variety of service opportunities. More information on volunteering is available on the Museum's Web site.

For further information, contact the U.S. Holocaust Memorial Museum, 100 Raoul Wallenberg Place, SW., Washington, DC 20024-2126. Phone, 202-488-0400. TTY, 202-488-0406.

United States Institute of Peace

2301 Constitution Avenue NW., Washington, DC 20037, 202-457-1700, 202-429-6063, *http://www.usip.org*

BOARD OF DIRECTORS

CHAIR	Stephen J. Hadley
Vice Chair	George E. Moose
Member	Judy Ansley
Member	Eric S. Edelman
Member	Joseph Eldridge
Member	Kerry Kennedy
Member	Ikram U. Khan
Member	Stephen D. Krasner
Member	John A. Lancaster
Member	Jeremy A. Rabkin
Member	J. Robinson West
Member	Nancy Zirkin
Secretary of State (ex officio)	John F. Kerry
Secretary of Defense (ex officio)	Ashton B. Carter
President, National Defense University (ex officio)	Maj. Gen. Frederick M. Padilla, USMC
President, U.S. Institute of Peace (ex officio)	Nancy Lindborg

OFFICIALS

PRESIDENT	Nancy Lindborg
Executive Vice President	William B. Taylor
Director, Congressional Relations	Anne Hingeley, Acting
Director, Public Affairs and Communications	Diane Zeleny
Vice President, External Relations	Salih Booker

The United States Institute of Peace prevents, mitigates, and resolves violent conflicts around the world.

The United States Institute of Peace (USIP) is an independent nonprofit corporation established by Congress pursuant to title XVII of the Defense Authorization Act of 1985, as amended (22 U.S.C. 4601-4611), to develop, apply, and foster cost-effective strategies and tools to prevent, mitigate, and resolve violent international conflicts, particularly those that threaten or harm America's strategic and security interests. The United States Institute of Peace Act defines the organization's mission: "to serve the people and the government through the widest possible range of education and training, basic and applied research opportunities, and peace information services on the means to promote international peace and the resolution of conflicts among nations and peoples of the world without recourse to violence."

With the confirmation of the Senate, the President appoints the Institute's bipartisan Board of Directors. It comprises 12 members from outside the Federal service—plus four ex officio members, three from the State Department, Department of Defense, and National Defense University, and the fourth is the President of the Institute. The Board governs the Institute and appoints its President. No more than eight voting members may be from the same political party.

Activities

The Institute supports U.S. national security and foreign affairs through conflict management and peacebuilding operations, training in conflict management and peacebuilding tradecraft and best practices, and conflict research and analysis. The USIP operates on the ground in conflict zones. It facilitates dialogue among parties in conflict, builds conflict management skills and capacity, identifies and disseminates best practices in conflict management, promotes the rule of law, reforms and strengthens education systems, strengthens civil society, and educates the public through media and other outreach activities. The USIP works in partnership with the State and Defense Departments, the U.S. Agency for International Development, nongovernmental organizations, higher and secondary educational institutions, foreign governments, and international organizations to promote collaborative problemsolving through conflict management operations, training and analysis, facilitated dialogue, Track 1.5 diplomacy, and special events. The Institute conducts practitioner training in conflict management, including mediation and negotiating skills for government and military personnel, civil society leaders, and staff of nongovernmental and international organizations. The Institute extends its reach through grants, fellowships, and scholarships to nonprofit organizations in the United States and overseas.

Sources of Information

Employment

The USIP relies on knowledgeable, talented professionals to carry out its mission. A recent graduate typically starts as a program assistant. The ideal candidate is a high academic achiever; has a background in international relations or a related field; and possesses administrative, computer, research, and writing skills. Regional specialization and language skills may be required for some positions.

Grants and Fellowships

Information on USIP grants and fellowship programs is available online.

Publications

USIP articles, publications, and tools are accessible online.

For further information, contact the U.S. Institute of Peace, Office of Public Affairs and Communications, 2301 Constitution Avenue NW., Washington, DC 20037. Phone, 202-457-1700.

International Organizaions

African Development Bank

Avenue Jean-Paul II, 01 BP 1387, Abidjan 01, Côte d'Ivoire, +225 20 26 10 20, *http://www.afdb.org* | Email: *afdb@afdb.org*

PRESIDENT Akinwumi Adesina

The African Development Bank stimulates sustainable economic development and social progress in regional member countries to mitigate poverty and its effects.

The African Development Bank (AFDB) was established in 1964. By charter amendment, the AFDB expanded its membership to include nonregional countries in 1982. The admission of nonregional countries boosted AFDB capital resources by more than twofold.

The Bank's mandate centers on the economic development and social progress of its regional members. On May 31, 2015, AFDB membership totaled 80 countries: 54 African and 26 nonregional countries. In 1998, at the time of the fifth general capital increase, African countries controlled 60 percent and nonregional countries controlled 40 percent of AFDB shares.

The African Development Fund, established in 1972 and operational in 1974, complements AFDB operations by providing concessional financing for high-priority development projects. Comprising 27 contributing countries, the Fund improves economic and social conditions in 40 beneficiary countries. These beneficiaries include countries that are increasing in economic capacity and en route to becoming the new emerging markets or that are regarded as fragile states and require special assistance for basics levels of service delivery.

Sources of Information

Employment

Grade and salary data and information on current job vacancies are available online.

Documents

The AFDB posts documents on its Web site.

Field Offices

Contact information for AFDB field offices is available online.

Frequently Asked Questions (FAQs)

The AFDB posts answers to FAQs on its Web site.

Glossary

The AFDB Web site features a glossary of acronyms.

News / Events

The AFDB Web site features events, interviews, loan and grant announcements, multimedia, news, press releases, project stories, and speeches.

Site Map

The Web site map allows visitors to look for specific topics or to browse content that aligns with their interests.

Web TV

The AFDB's Web TV features programs in English and French.

Where the AFDB Works

The AFDB's Web site features a list of African countries where the Bank is active.

Social Media

The AFDB tweets announcements and newsworthy items in English and French on Twitter.

The AFDB has a Facebook account.

Asian Development Bank

Headquarters: 6 ADB Avenue, Mandaluyong City, 1550 Metro Manila, Philippines, +632 632-4444, +632 636-2444, *http://www.adb.org* | Email: *information@adb.org*

ADB North American Representative Office: 900 17th Street NW., Suite 900, Washington DC 20006, 202-728-1500, 202 728 1505

PRESIDENT Takehiko Nakao

The Asian Development Bank stimulates sustainable economic development and social progress in member countries to mitigate poverty and its effects.

The Asian Development Bank (ADB) commenced operations on December 19, 1966. It comprises 67 members: 48 regional and 19 nonregional countries.

The ADB works to eradicate poverty in Asia and the Pacific. As a multilateral development finance institution, it provides grants, loans, and technical assistance. The Bank serves its member countries, which are also its shareholders. Through equity investments and loans, the ADB also provides direct assistance to private enterprises of developing member countries.

To maximize the effects of its assistance on development, the ADB facilitates policy dialogues, offers advisory services, and mobilizes financial resources through cofinancing operations involving official, commercial, and export sources of credit. ABD operations promote three complementary agendas: environmentally sustainable growth, inclusive economic growth, and regional integration. The Bank's core areas of development activity are education, environment, finance, infrastructure, and regional cooperation and integration.

Sources of Information

Business Opportunities

ADB projects rely on the goods and services of consultants, contractors, manufacturers, and suppliers.

Employment

The "Careers" Web page features access to the ABD career and employment system, information on its young professional program and internships, descriptions of current job vacancies, and a summary of what the ADB looks for in a potential employee.

Publications

The ADB Web site offers information on books, brochures and flyers, conference proceedings, guides, papers and briefs, policies and plans, reports, and statutory reports and official records.

European Bank for Reconstruction and Development

One Exchange Square, London EC2A 2JN, United Kingdom, +44 20 7338 6000, *http://www.ebrd.com*

PRESIDENT Sir Suma Chakrabarti

The European Bank for Reconstruction and Development develops open and sustainable market economies in democratic countries.

The European Bank for Reconstruction and Development (EBRD) is a multilateral development bank that supports economic development projects in 34 countries from central Europe to central Asia. Investing primarily in private sector clients whose needs cannot be fully met by commercial credit and equity markets, the EBRD promotes entrepreneurship and fosters transition towards open and democratic market economies.

Two intergovernmental institutions and 64 countries own the EBRD. The Bank is based in London.

Sources of Information

Business Opportunities

Information on opportunities for consultants, contractors, and suppliers is available on the EBRD Web site.

Contact Information

Department and country contacts are listed on the "EBRD Contacts" Web page.

Economic Data

Economic teams publish macroeconomic and structural data series, and they survey data affecting the Bank's countries of operation.

Environmental and Social Impact Assessment (ESIA)

ESIA documents for projects are available on the EBRD Web site.

Employment

Information on job locations and types, benefits and rewards, and internships is available on the EBRD Web site.

History

The EBRD's Web site features a history of the Bank.

Products / Services

Information on the EBRD's advisory services, policy reform dialogue services, and financial products is available online.

Reports

The EBRD posts annual, donor, financial, sustainability, and transition reports on its Web site.

Sectors / Topics

The EBRD Web site features a section that brings together the topics that most concern the Bank and the sectors in which it is most active.

Social Media

The EBRD tweets announcements and other newsworthy items on Twitter.

The EBRD maintains a Facebook account.

Where EBRD Works

The EBRD Web site features the list of countries where the Bank is active.

Inter-American Defense Board

2600 Sixteenth Street NW., Washington, DC 20441, 202-939-6041, 202-319-2791, *http://iadb.jid.org* | Email: *protocol@jid.org*

CHAIR Vice Adm. Gonzalo Nicolás Ríos Polastri

The Inter-American Defense Board is the oldest permanently constituted, international military organization in the world. It was founded by Resolution XXXIX of the Meeting of Foreign Ministers at Rio de Janeiro in January 1942. The Board is governed according to Statutes that the General Assembly of the Organization of American States approved in March 2006. Senior armed forces officers from the member nations staff the various agencies of the Board. Its three major components are the Council of Delegates, the Secretariat, and the Inter-American Defense College.

The Board studies and recommends to member governments measures it deems necessary for the safety and security of the hemisphere. It also acts as a technical military adviser for the Organization of American States and is involved in projects such as disaster preparedness and humanitarian demining programs in Central and South America.

Established in 1962, the Inter-American Defense College is located on Fort Lesley J. McNair, whose buildings and furnishings the United States Government donated. The United States hosts the College, which prepares senior military officers and civilian functionaries for positions in their respective governments. The College offers an 11-month, professionally-oriented, and fully accredited Masters of Science degree. Multidisciplinary in content, the curriculum centers on the Western Hemisphere's most pressing defense and security issues.

Sources of Information

Documents

Documents are posted online to increase the transparency of Inter-American Defense Board activities.

Events

Symposia and seminars are posted on the Board's Web site. A calendar of meetings also is available on the Web site's homepage.

News

News items are available on the homepage of the Board's Web site.

Regional Organizations

Links to regional organizations are accessible on the "Strategic Links" Web page.

For further information, contact the Inter-American Defense Board, 2600 Sixteenth Street NW., Washington, DC 20441. Phone, 202-939-6041. Fax, 202-319-2791.

Inter-American Development Bank

Headquarters: 1300 New York Avenue NW., Washington, DC 20577, 202-623-1000, 202-623-3096, *http://www.iadb.org*

PRESIDENT — Luis A. Moreno

The Inter-American Development Bank (IDB) was established in 1959 to help accelerate economic and social development in Latin America and the Caribbean.

The Bank has 48 member countries, 26 of which are borrowing members in Latin America and the Caribbean.

Sources of Information

Business Opportunities

IDB projects in Latin America and the Caribbean create contract opportunities for businesses and consultants.

Data

The IDB posts datasets on its Web site.

Employment

The IDB relies on professionals with expertise in economics, education, energy, environmental sustainability, financial markets, institutional capacity, investment funds, rural development and disaster risk, science and technology, social protection and health, transport, water and sanitation, and other fields to carry out its mission.

Glossary

The IDB maintains a glossary on its Web site.

Key Facts

To learn at glance who leads the IDB,

how many people it employs, how many countries are members, who are its clients, and recent annual levels of its approved lending, visit the "Key Facts" section.

Learning Resources

Online courses are accessible on the IDB Web site.

Looking for Something?

Try finding it by using the "What Are You Looking For" Web page.

Publications

A variety of publications—annual reports, books, catalogs and brochures, databases and datasets, discussion and working papers, journals, magazines, monographs, newsletters—is available online.

Social Media

The IDB tweets announcements and other newsworthy items on Twitter.

The IDB has a Facebook account.

Inter-American Investment Corporation

Headquarters: 1350 New York Avenue NW., Washington, DC 20577, 202-623-3901, *http://www.iic.org/en*

CHAIR, BOARD OF EXECUTIVE DIRECTORS	Luis A. Moreno
Chief Executive Officer	James P. Scriven

The Inter-American Development Bank promotes development in Latin America and the Caribbean through the private sector.

The Inter-American Investment Corporation (IIC), an affiliate of the Inter-American Development Bank based in Washington, DC, was established in 1985 to promote the economic development of its Latin American and Caribbean members by financing small- and medium-size private enterprises. The IIC provides project financing in the form of direct loans and equity investments, lines of credit to local financial intermediaries, and investments in local and regional investment funds.

The IIC has 45 member countries, of which 28 are in the Western Hemisphere, including the United States, and 17 are outside the region.

Sources of Information

Employment

The ICC relies on talent and experience to carry out its mission. It recruits, hires, and maintains a staff of diverse, motivated, and qualified professionals with expertise, leadership potential, and strong interpersonal and teamwork skills. Current job opportunities are posted online.

History

A three-part history, from 1985 to 1999, from 2000 to 2012, and from 2013 to the present, is available on the IIC's Web site.

Key Initiatives

The IIC's Web site features a section on its most important initiatives.

Library

The IIC's Web site features a photo library.

Member Countries

The IIC Web site features two lists of member countries: regional members and other members. An interactive map complements the two lists.

News

The IIC posts news items on its Web site.

Projects

IIC projects may be searched by country or year.

Publications

Brochures, factsheets, and reports—some in English and Spanish, some also in French and Portuguese—are available online.

Transaction Cycle

A description of the five stages of a successful IIC transaction—business origination, eligibility review, due diligence and approval, closing and disbursement, and supervision and evaluation—is available online.

Social Media

The IIC tweets announcements and other newsworthy items in Spanish on Twitter.

The IIC has a Facebook account.

International Monetary Fund

700 Nineteenth Street NW., Washington, DC 20431, 202-623-7000, 202-623-4661, *http://www.imf.org*

MANAGING DIRECTOR / CHAIR OF THE EXECUTIVE BOARD	Christine Lagarde
First Deputy Managing Director	David Lipton
Deputy Managing Director / Chief Administrative Officer	Carla Grasso
Deputy Managing Director	Mitsuhiro Furusawa
Deputy Managing Director	Min Zhu

The International Monetary Fund fosters global monetary cooperation, secures financial stability, facilitates international trade, promotes employment and sustainable economic growth, and reduces poverty worldwide.

The Final Act of the United Nations Monetary and Financial Conference, signed at Bretton Woods, NH, on July 22, 1944, set forth the original Articles of Agreement of the International Monetary Fund (IMF). The Agreement became effective on December 27, 1945, when the President, authorized by the Bretton Woods Agreements Act (22 U.S.C. 286), accepted membership for the United States in the IMF. The inaugural meeting of the Board of Governors was held in March 1946, and the first meeting of the Executive Directors was held May 6, 1946.

On May 31, 1968, the Board of Governors approved an amendment to the Articles of Agreement for the establishment of a facility based on Special Drawing Rights (SDR) and for modification of certain rules and practices. The amendment became effective on July 28, 1969, and the Special Drawing Account opened on August 6, 1969. The Special Drawing Rights Act (22 U.S.C. 286 et seq.) authorized the United States to accept the amendment and participate in the Special Drawing Account.

On April 30, 1976, the Board of Governors approved a second amendment to the Articles of Agreement, which became effective on April 1, 1978. This amendment gave members the right to adopt exchange arrangements of their choice while placing certain obligations on them regarding their exchange rate policies, which the IMF was to monitor closely. The official price of gold was abolished, and the Special Drawing Account was promoted as the principal reserve asset of the international monetary system. The Bretton Woods Agreements Act Amendments (22 U.S.C. 286e-5) authorized the United States to accept this amendment.

On June 28, 1990, the Board of Governors approved a third amendment to the Articles of Agreement, which became effective on November 11, 1992. Under this amendment, a member's voting rights and certain related rights may be suspended by a 70-percent majority of the executive board if the member country has been declared ineligible to use the Fund's general resources and persists in its failure to fulfill any of its obligations under the Articles.

The IMF has 189 member countries. It promotes international monetary cooperation through a permanent forum for consultation and collaboration on international monetary problems; facilitates the expansion and balanced growth of international trade; promotes exchange rate stability; assists in the establishment of an open multilateral system of payments for current transactions among members; and gives confidence to members by making IMF resources temporarily available to them under adequate safeguards.

The IMF helps member countries correct imbalances in their international balances of payments. It periodically examines the economic developments and policies of its members, offers policy advice, and at a member's request and upon executive board approval, provides financial assistance through a variety of financial facilities designed to address specific problems. These financing mechanisms provide access to the Fund's general resources and offer short-term assistance during crises of market confidence, compensatory financing to countries suffering declines in export earnings, emergency assistance for countries recovering from natural disasters or armed conflict, and low-interest rate resources to support structural adjustment and promote growth in the poorest countries. The IMF also provides technical assistance and training to member countries.

Sources of Information

Country Information

The IMF is an organization comprising 189 countries that, together, work to promote monetary cooperation, financial stability, international trade, employment and sustainable economic growth, and to reduce poverty. An alphabetical index of the participating countries and information on those countries are available on the IMF's Web site.

Employment

In addition to economists and research assistants, the IMF relies on professionals with skills and expertise in a range of other fields—communications, facilities management, finance and accounting, human resources, information technology, language services, legal, library and archives, office assistance, procurement, security, and transportation and hospitality. Information on careers, current job vacancies, and recruitment programs is available online.

Glossary

The IMF maintains an online glossary of financial terms and acronyms.

Publications

The IMF's "Finance and Development" magazine and "Fiscal Monitor" biannual report are available online in Portable Document Format (PDF). Its "New and Noteworthy" newsletter and other publications are also accessible online.

Videos

The IMF posts videos in Arabic, Chinese, English, French, Russian, and Spanish on its Web site.

For further information, contact the Chief of Public Affairs, International Monetary Fund–Communications Department, 700 Nineteenth Street NW., Washington, DC 20431. Phone, 202-623-7300. Fax, 202-623-6278.

International Organization for Migration

Headquarters: 17 Route des Morillons, C.P. 17, CH–1211 Geneva 19, Switzerland. Mailing address, P.O. Box 71, CH–1211, Geneva 19, Switzerland, 011-41-22-717-9111, *http://www.iom.int* | Email: *hq@iom.int*

Washington Office: Suite 700, 1752 N Street NW., Washington, DC 20036, 202-862-1826 Email: *IOMWashington@iom.int*

New York Office: 122 E. 42d Street, 48th Floor, New York, NY 10168, 212-681-7000 Email: *newyork@iom.int*

DIRECTOR GENERAL	William Lacy Swing
Deputy Director General	Laura Thompson
Chief of Mission–Washington, DC	Luca Dall'Oglio
Permanent Observer to the United Nations	Ashraf El Nour

The International Organization for Migration addresses the underlying issues of migration, answers the operational challenges of migration management, promotes economic and social development through migration, champions the dignity and well-being of migrants, and challenges the xenophobic narrative directed toward them.

Established in 1951, the International Organization for Migration (IOM) is the leading intergovernmental organization in the field of migration. With 162 member states, an additional 9 states holding observer status, and offices in over 100 countries, the IOM promotes humane and orderly migration for the benefit of all. It does so by providing services and advice to migrants and governments, while working in close cooperation with governmental, intergovernmental, and nongovernmental partners. The IOM has observer status to the United Nations.

The Organization works with its partners in the following areas: meeting the operational challenges of migration management, increasing understanding of migration issues, encouraging social and economic development through migration, and upholding the human dignity and well-being of migrants.

The Organization has been at the forefront of emergency response to ensure assistance and protection to stranded migrants and displaced persons. It has a lead role under the UN Cluster Approach in camp coordination and management in natural disasters and is a key partner in emergency shelter, logistics, health, protection, and early recovery.

IOM expertise and services support the following activities: secure, reliable, and cost-effective assistance for migrating persons; humane and orderly management of migration and the effective respect for migrants' human rights; technical cooperation and operational assistance for building national capacities and facilitating cooperation on issues relevant to migration; helping states to integrate migrants into their new environment and to engage diasporas as development partners; advising states in the development and delivery of programs and technical expertise to combat migrant smuggling and human trafficking; working with national health systems to reduce mortality, morbidity, and disabilities and to enhance access to rights-based health and well-being services throughout the migration cycle; and partnering with states to address labor migration.

Sources of Information

Business Opportunities

Information on procurement opportunities is available online.

Employment

Current job vacancies in various countries are posted online.

Glossary

A list of key migration terms that is based on the IOM's "Glossary on Migration" is available online.

Publications

Visit the online bookstore to see IOM publications in English, French, and Spanish.

Regional Offices

Regional Offices review and endorse projects and provide technical support to Country Offices. Descriptions of and contact information for the IOM's nine regional offices are available online.

United Nations

Information on the IOM's Office of Permanent Observer to the United Nations is available online.

For further information, contact the International Organization for

Migration–Headquarters, P.O. Box 71, CH–1211, Geneva 19, Switzerland.

Organization of American States

Seventeenth Street and Constitution Avenue NW., Washington, DC 20006, 202-370-5000, 202-458-3967, *http://www.oas.org/en*

SECRETARY GENERAL	Luis Almagro Lemes
Assistant Secretary General	Nestor Mendez

The Organization of American States seeks an order of peace and justice among its member states, promotes their solidarity and strengthens their collaboration, and defends their sovereignty, territorial integrity, and independence.

The Organization of American States (OAS) brings together the countries of the Western Hemisphere to strengthen cooperation and advance common interests. At the core of the OAS mission is a commitment to democracy. Building on this foundation, OAS works to promote good governance, strengthen human rights, foster peace and security, expand trade, and address the complex problems caused by poverty, drugs, and corruption. Through decisions made by its political bodies and programs carried out by its General Secretariat, OAS promotes greater inter-American cooperation and understanding.

OAS member states have intensified their cooperation since the end of the cold war, taking on new and important challenges. In 1994, the region's 34 democratically elected presidents and prime ministers met in Miami for the First Summit of the Americas, where they established broad political, economic, and social development goals. They have continued to meet periodically since then to examine common interests and priorities. Through the ongoing Summits of the Americas process, the region's leaders have entrusted the OAS with a growing number of responsibilities to help advance the countries' shared vision.

With four official languages—English, Spanish, Portuguese, and French—the OAS reflects the rich diversity of peoples and cultures across the Americas. The OAS has 35 member states: the independent nations of North, Central, and South America, and of the Caribbean. Since 1962, Cuba has been barred from participation by resolution of the Eighth Meeting of Consultation of Ministers of Foreign Affairs. Countries from all around the world are permanent observers, closely following the issues that are critical to the Americas and often providing key financial support for OAS programs.

Member states set major policies and goals through the General Assembly, which gathers the hemisphere's foreign ministers once a year in regular session. The Permanent Council, made up of ambassadors appointed by member states, meets regularly at OAS headquarters in Washington, DC, to guide ongoing policies and actions. The chairmanship of the Permanent Council rotates every 3 months, in alphabetical order of countries. Each member state has an equal voice, and most decisions are made through consensus.

Also under the OAS umbrella are several specialized agencies that have considerable autonomy: the Pan American Health Organization in Washington, DC; the Inter-American Children's Institute in Montevideo, Uruguay; the Inter-American Institute for Cooperation on Agriculture in San Jose, Costa Rica; and the Pan American Institute of Geography and History and the Inter-American Indian Institute, both in Mexico City.

In 1948, at the Ninth International Conference of American States, 21 nations of the hemisphere signed the OAS Charter: Argentina, Bolivia, Brazil, Chile, Colombia, Costa Rica, Cuba (barred from participation), Dominican Republic, Ecuador, El Salvador, Guatemala, Haiti, Honduras, Mexico, Nicaragua, Panama, Paraguay, Peru, United States of America, Uruguay, and Venezuela.

Subsequently, 14 other countries joined

the OAS by signing and ratifying the Charter. They were Barbados, Trinidad and Tobago, Jamaica, Grenada, Suriname, Dominica, Saint Lucia, Antigua and Barbuda, Saint Vincent and the Grenadines, the Bahamas, Saint Kitts and Nevis, Canada, Belize, and Guyana. This brings the number of member states to 35.

Sources of Information

Conferences

A calendar of conferences is available online.

Documents

The most important OAS documents, including its founding Charter and the Inter-American Democratic Charter, are available on its Web site. Along with these essential documents, links to other key reference material—such as annual reports of the Secretary General, OAS resolutions, agreements, and treaties—are also available.

Employment

Information on career opportunities, consultancies, and internships is available online.

History

A short history of the OAS is available on its Web site.

Language Assistance

The OAS maintains English and Spanish versions of its Web site. Some Web pages are also available in French and Portuguese. Language tags appear above the search box in the top right corner of most of the site's Web pages.

Members States

Information on the 35 independent states of the Americas—all of which have ratified the OAS Charter and are member states—is available on the OAS Web site.

News

The OAS posts press releases on its Web site.

The OAS posts newsletters on its Web site.

The OAS posts video news on its Vimeo channel.

The OAS posts speeches by OAS leadership on its Web site.

Permanent Representatives

A list of permanent representatives to the OAS is available on its Web site.

Publications

OAS publications in English and Spanish are available on its Web site.

Scholarships

Information on OAS scholarships is available online.

Social Media

The OAS tweets announcements, news, and other noteworthy items on Twitter.

The OAS has a Facebook account.

Staff Directory

The OAS Web site features an online staff directory. To see the complete directory, leave all fields blank and click on the search button.

Topics

The OAS Web site features a "Topics" Web page to help visitors find information that they seek or material that aligns with their interests.

For further information, contact the Organization of American States, Seventeenth Street and Constitution Avenue NW., Washington, DC 20006. Phone, 202-370-5000. Fax, 202-458-3967.

United Nations

United Nations, New York, NY 10017, 212-963-1234, *http://www.un.org*

United Nations Office at Geneva: Palais des Nations, 1211 Geneva 10, Switzerland

United Nations Office at Vienna: Vienna International Centre, P.O. Box 500, A–1400, Vienna, Austria

Washington, DC: United Nations Information Centre, Suite 400, 1775 K Street NW., Washington, DC 20006, 202-331-8670, 202-331-9191, *http://www.unicwash.org* | Email: *unicdc@unic.org*

SECRETARY–GENERAL	Ban Ki-moon
Director-General, United Nations Office at Geneva	Michael Møller
Director-General, United Nations Office at Vienna	Yury Fedotov
Director, Washington DC Information Centre	Robert Skinner

The United Nations supports tolerance and peaceful coexistence among the nations; seeks to maintain peace and security among them; opposes the use of armed force, except in the common interest; and promotes the economic and social advancement of all peoples.

The United Nations is an international organization that was set up in accordance with the Charter drafted by governments represented at the Conference on International Organization meeting at San Francisco. The Charter was signed on June 26, 1945, and came into force on October 24, 1945, when the required number of ratifications and accessions had been made by the signatories. Amendments increasing membership of the Security Council and the Economic and Social Council came into effect on August 31, 1965.

The United Nations now consists of 193 member states, of which 51 are founding members.

The purposes of the United Nations set out in the Charter are to maintain international peace and security; to develop friendly relations among nations; to achieve international cooperation in solving international problems of an economic, social, cultural, or humanitarian character and in promoting respect for human rights; and to be a center for harmonizing the actions of nations in the attainment of these common ends.

The principal organs of the United Nations are the General Assembly, Security Council, Economic and Social Council, Trusteeship Council, International Court of Justice, and the Secretariat.

General Assembly

All states that are members of the United Nations are members of the General Assembly. Its functions are to consider and discuss any matter within the scope of the Charter of the United Nations and to make recommendations to the members of the United Nations and other organs. It approves the budget of the organization, the expenses of which are borne by the members as apportioned by the General Assembly.

The General Assembly may call the attention of the Security Council to situations likely to endanger international peace and security, may initiate studies, and may receive and consider reports from other organs of the United Nations. Under the "Uniting for Peace" resolution adopted by the General Assembly in November 1950, if the Security Council fails to act on an apparent threat to or breach of the peace or act of aggression because of lack of unanimity of its five permanent members, the Assembly itself may take up the matter within 24 hours—in emergency special session—and recommend collective measures, including, in case of a breach of the peace or act of aggression, use of armed force when necessary to maintain or restore international peace and security.

The General Assembly normally meets in regular annual session from September through December. It also has met in special sessions and emergency special sessions.

Security Council

The Security Council consists of 15 members, of which 5—the People's Republic of China, France, Russia, the United Kingdom, and the United States of America—are permanent members. The 10 nonpermanent members are elected for 2-year terms by the General Assembly. The primary responsibility of the Security Council is to act on behalf of the members of the United Nations in maintenance of international peace and security. Measures that may be employed by the Security Council are outlined in the Charter.

The Security Council, together with the General Assembly, also elects the judges of the International Court of Justice and makes a recommendation to the General Assembly on the appointment of the Secretary-General of the organization.

The Security Council first met in London on January 17, 1946, and is so organized as to be able to function continuously.

Economic and Social Council

This organ is responsible, under the authority of the General Assembly, for the economic and social programs of the United Nations. Its functions include making or initiating studies, reports, and recommendations on international economic, social, cultural, educational, health, and related matters; promoting respect for and observance of human rights and fundamental freedoms for all; calling international conferences and preparing draft conventions for submission to the General Assembly on matters within its competence; negotiating agreements with the specialized agencies and defining their relationship with the United Nations; coordinating the activities of the specialized agencies; and consulting with nongovernmental organizations concerned with matters within its competence. The Council consists of 54 members of the United Nations elected by the General Assembly for 3-year terms; 18 are elected each year.

The Council usually holds two regular sessions a year. It has also held a number of special sessions.

Trusteeship Council

The Trusteeship Council was initially established to consist of any member states that administered trust territories, permanent members of the Security Council that did not administer trust territories, and enough other nonadministering countries elected by the General Assembly for 3-year terms to ensure that membership would be equally divided between administering and nonadministering members. Under authority of the General Assembly, the Council considered reports from members administering trust territories, examined petitions from trust territory inhabitants, and provided for periodic inspection visits to trust territories.

With the independence of Palau, the last remaining United Nations trust territory, the Trusteeship Council formally suspended operations after nearly half a century. The Council will henceforth meet only on an extraordinary basis, as the need may arise.

International Court of Justice

The International Court of Justice is the principal judicial organ of the United Nations. It has its seat at The Hague, the Netherlands. All members of the United Nations are ipso facto parties to the Statute of the Court. Nonmembers of the United Nations may become parties to the Statute of the Court on conditions prescribed by the General Assembly on the recommendation of the Security Council.

The jurisdiction of the Court comprises all cases that the parties refer to it and all matters specially provided for in the Charter of the United Nations or in treaties and conventions in force.

The Court consists of 15 judges known as members of the Court. They are elected for 9-year terms by the General Assembly and the Security Council, voting independently, and may be reelected.

Secretariat

The Secretariat consists of a Secretary-General and "such staff as the Organization may require." The Secretary-General, who is appointed by the General Assembly on the recommendation of the Security Council, is the chief administrative officer of the United Nations. He acts in that capacity for the General Assembly, the Security Council, the Economic and Social Council, and the Trusteeship Council. Under the Charter, the Secretary-General "may bring to the attention of the Security Council any matter that in his opinion may threaten the maintenance of international peace and security."

Sources of Information

Employment

United Nations Secretariat staff members work in a dynamic, multicultural environment that fosters a broader understanding of countries and cultures worldwide. The United Nations welcomes applications from nationals of all of its Member States and encourages women to apply.

Library

The Dag Hammarskjöld Library is accessible online.

News

The News Centre provides breaking news coverage of developments around the United Nations system, offering quick access to news-related products and resources.

Publications

Books, reports, and data are available from the online bookshop.

World Bank Group

Headquarters: 1818 H Street NW., Washington, DC 20433, 202-473-1000, 202-477-6391, *http://www.worldbank.org*

PRESIDENT	Jim Yong Kim

The World Bank Group promotes shared global prosperity and seeks to end extreme poverty.

The World Bank Group consists of five institutions: the International Bank for Reconstruction and Development (IBRD), the International Development Association (IDA), the International Finance Corporation (IFC), the Multilateral Investment Guarantee Agency (MIGA), and the International Centre for the Settlement of Investment Disputes (ICSID). The two primary economic and social development institutions are the IBRD and the IDA. Donor countries and countries with borrowing rights, a total of 189 countries, support and benefit from these two development banks. The other three institutions complement the activities of the IBRD and the IDA. These World Bank Group institutions are working collectively to end extreme poverty within a generation and boost shared prosperity and equality in the developing world.

Sources of Information

A–Z Topics

The World Bank's Web site features an alphabetical list of topics that helps visitors learn about the Banks many and diverse activities.

Blog

The World Bank posts items by featured bloggers on its Web site.

Countries / Regions

The Web site features a browse-by-country tool and roll-over-to-navigate world map to help visitors explore World Bank activities around the globe.

Data

The World Bank's Web site gives visitors free and open access to global development data.

The microdata library facilitates access to data collected through sample surveys of households, business establishments, and other facilities. These sets of microdata may also be derived from agricultural, housing, or population censuses or through an administrative data collection processes. The Library also contains supporting documentation from censuses and surveys that the World Bank and other international organizations, statistical agencies, and other agencies in low and middle-income countries conducted or supported.

Employment

The World Bank typically hires people with strong academic backgrounds, a broad understanding of development issues, and international work experience. In more than 170 countries, it employees professionals who specialize in economics, education, engineering, finance, public health, and many other fields. About 40 percent of World Bank staff members work in more than 110 developing countries.

History

The "World Bank Group Archives" Web site supports the institutional memory of the World Bank Group and provides access to records of the International Bank for Reconstruction and Development and the International Development Association. The Web site also features online historical resources and information products: exhibits on the Archives' collection and World Bank history, General International Standard Archival Description (ISAD(G)) finding aids, and transcripts of oral history interviews.

Libraries

The World Bank Group and International Monetary Fund libraries collaborate to provide information services and make available resources to World Bank Group and International Monetary Fund staff. These libraries provide limited services to external researchers and visitors.

News

The World Bank posts press releases and other newsworthy items on its Web site.

Open Learning Campus

The Open Learning Campus offers educational opportunities that allow diverse audiences to learn at their own pace. It helps prepare people seeking to address the tough development challenges of the 21st century.

Podcasts

The World Bank's features a trove of podcasts on a variety of topics: climate change, energy development, indigenous communities, immigration and forced displacement, sustainability, and more.

Projects

The World Bank's Web site allows visitors to browse or search for projects by country or area, sector, or theme.

Publications

The World Bank's Web site features an "Open Knowledge Repository" that allows users to browse and search for thousands of publications.

Research

The World Bank Web site features research program datasets and analytical tools on its Web site.

Social Media

The World Bank tweets announcements and other newsworthy items on Twitter.

The World Bank has a Facebook account.

The World Bank posts videos on its YouTube channel.

Speaker's Bureau

The Speaker's Bureau serves as the official liaison between the World Bank Group and its visitors, who include business leaders, governmental representatives, students and teachers, youth organizations, and other professionals.

International Bank for Reconstruction and Development

http://www.worldbank.org/en/about/what-we-do/brief/ibrd

The International Bank for Reconstruction and Development (IBRD) officially came into existence in 1944.

The Bank promotes economic, social, and environmental progress in developing nations by reducing poverty so that their people may live better and fuller lives. The Bank lends funds at market-determined interest rates, provides advice, and serves as a catalyst to stimulate outside investments. Its resources come primarily from funds raised in the world capital markets, its retained earnings, and repayments on its loans.

Sources of Information

Countries

The Governments of the 189 member countries own the IBRD.

Bonds

The IBRD issues World Bank bonds in the international capital markets to fund development projects in member countries.

International Centre for Settlement of Investment Disputes

Headquarters: 1818 H Street NW., MSN J2-200, Washington, DC 20433, 202-458-1534, 202-522-2615, *http://icsid.worldbank.org/ICSID* | Email: *ICSIDsecretariat@worldbank.org*

PRESIDENT	Jim Yong Kim
Secretary-General	Meg Kinnear

The International Centre for Settlement of Investment Disputes (ICSID), an autonomous international institution affiliated with the World Bank Group, was established under the Convention on the Settlement of Investment Disputes Between States and Nationals of Other States. The Convention sets forth ICSID's mandate, organization, and core functions. The primary purpose of ICSID is to provide facilities for conciliation and arbitration of international investment disputes.

The ICSID Convention is a multilateral treaty formulated by the Executive Directors of the International Bank for Reconstruction and Development (the World Bank). The treaty entered into force in 1966. There are currently 159 signatory states to the ICSID Convention of which 150 countries also deposited their instruments of ratification, acceptance, or approval of the Convention.

International Development Association

http://ida.worldbank.org

The International Development Association (IDA) came into existence in 1960 as an institution of the World Bank Group. The Association's resources consist of subscriptions and supplementary resources in the form of general replenishments on a 3-year revolving cycle, mostly from its more industrialized and developed members; special contributions by its richer members; repayments on earlier credits; and transfers from IBRD's net earnings.

The Association promotes economic development, reduces poverty, and raises the standard of living in the least developed areas of the world. It does this by financing their developmental requirements on concessionary terms, which are more flexible and bear less heavily on the balance of payments than those of conventional loans, thereby furthering the objectives of IBRD and supplementing its activities.

Sources of Information

Articles of Agreement

The IDA's Articles of Agreement became effective in 1960. They are available online in Portable Document Format.

Climate

Climate change threatens poorer people globally, with the potential to force more than 100 million people back into poverty by 2030. The IDA is making plans to help manage this threat of enormous scope and scale.

Countries

Seventy-seven countries are eligible to receive IDA resources. In addition, India is receiving transitional support.

A list of the approximately 50 contributor countries is available on the IDA's Web site.

History

A short history of the IDA is available on its Web site.

News / Publications

The IDA posts press releases and other newsworthy items on its Web site.

Results

The IDA's Web site features an overview of the results of the IDA's efforts in the world's poorest countries by country, theme, or topic.

International Finance Corporation

Headquarters: 2121 Pennsylvania Avenue NW., Washington, DC 20433, 202-473-7711, 202-974-4384, *http://www.ifc.org*

PRESIDENT	Jim Yong Kim
Executive Vice President / Chief Executive Officer	Philippe Le Houérou

The International Finance Corporation (IFC), a World Bank Group institution, was established in 1956 to promote productive private enterprise in developing member countries.

The Corporation pursues its objective principally through direct debt and equity investments in projects that establish new businesses or expand, modify, or diversify existing businesses. It also encourages cofinancing by other investors and lenders.

Additionally, advisory services and technical assistance are provided by IFC to developing member countries in areas such as capital market development, privatization, corporate restructuring, and foreign investment.

Sources of Information

Climate

The IFC is increasing its climate-related investments to address climate change—a fundamental threat to development, with the potential to impact millions, threatening agricultural livelihoods, increasing the incidence of natural disasters and affecting water, energy, and food supplies.

Contact Information

General information is available on the IFC's Web site.

Countries

The IFC operates in more than 100 countries. An online interactive map presents the scope of its activities.

Employment

The IFC posts career opportunities on its Web site.

History

Opened in 1956 with $100 million in capital, the IFC has been creating jobs and raising living standards for six decades.

Transparency / Accountability

The IFC provides information on its investment and advisory services activities to clients, partners, and stakeholders.

Multilateral Investment Guarantee Agency

Headquarters: 1818 H Street NW., Washington, DC 20433, 202-458-2538, 202-522-0316, *http://www.miga.org*

PRESIDENT	Jim Yong Kim
Executive Vice President / Chief Executive Officer	Keiko Honda

The Multilateral Investment Guarantee Agency (MIGA), a World Bank Group institution, was formally constituted in 1988.

Working with public and private insurers, MIGA promotes foreign direct investment in developing countries to support economic growth, reduce poverty, and improve the quality of people's lives. Due to its status as a World Bank Group institution, MIGA's guarantees protect investments against noncommercial risks and help investors gain access to funding sources with improved financial terms and conditions.

Sources of Information

Contact Information

General information is available on the MIGA's Web site.

Convention

The "Convention Establishing the Multilateral Investment Guarantee Agency" went into effect on April 12, 1988. The Council of Governors amended it in 2010. The Convention is available online in Portable Document Format (PDF).

Employment

The MIGA advertises available positions on the World Bank's job vacancies page.

Frequently Asked Questions (FAQs)

The MIGA posts answers to FAQs on its Web site.

History

A timeline and short history of the MIGA are available on its Web site.

Member Countries

The names of the 181 member countries—156 developing, 25 industrialized—are available on the MIGA's Web site.

News

The MIGA posts press releases on its Web site.

Other International Organizations

Below is a list of other international organizations that do not have separate entries elsewhere in the Manual. The United States participates in these organizations in accordance with the provisions of treaties, other international agreements, congressional legislation, or executive arrangements. In some cases, no financial contribution is involved.

Various commissions, councils, or committees subsidiary to the organizations listed here are not named separately on this list. These include the international bodies for drugs and crime, which are subsidiary to the United Nations.

This listing is provided for reference purposes and should not be considered exhaustive. For more information on international organizations and United States participation in them, contact the State Department's Bureau of International Organization Affairs. Phone, 202–647–9600. Internet, http://go.usa.gov/UjzR.

I. Specialized Agencies of the United Nations and Related Organizations

Food and Agricultural Organization
International Atomic Energy Agency
International Civil Aviation Organization
International Fund for Agriculture Development
International Labor Organization
International Maritime Organization
International Telecommunication Union
United Nations Educational, Scientific and Cultural Organization (UNESCO)
Universal Postal Union
World Health Organization
World Intellectual Property Organization
World Meteorological Organization

II. Peacekeeping and Political Missions Administered by the United Nations Department of Peacekeeping Operations

Africa

United Nations Hybrid Operation in Darfur (UNAMID)
United Nations Integrated Stabilization Mission in Mali (MINUSMA)
United Nations Interim Security Force for Abyei (UNISFA)
United Nations Mission for the Referendum in Western Sahara (MINURSO)
United Nations Mission in Liberia (UNMIL)
United Nations Mission in the Republic of South Sudan (UNMISS)
United Nations Operation in Côte d'Ivoire (UNOCI)
United Nations Organization Stabilization Mission in the Democratic Republic of the Congo (MONUSCO)
United Nations Stabilization Mission in the Central African Republic (MINUSCA)

Americas

United Nations Stabilization Mission in Haiti (MINUSTAH)

Middle East

United Nations Assistance Mission in Afghanistan (UNAMA)
United Nations Disengagement Observer Force (UNDOF)

United Nations Interim Force in Lebanon (UNIFIL)
United Nations Military Observer Group in India and Pakistan (UNMOGIP)
United Nations Truce Supervision Organization (UNTSO)

Europe

United Nations Interim Administration Mission in Kosovo (UNMIK)
United Nations Peacekeeping Force in Cyprus (UNFICYP)

III. Inter-American Organizations

Border Environment Cooperation Commission
Caribbean Postal Union
Inter-American Center of Tax Administrators
Inter-American Children's Institute
Inter-American Commission of Human Rights
Inter-American Commission of Women
Inter-American Committee Against Terrorism
Inter-American Committee on Natural Disaster Reduction
Inter-American Council for Integral Development
Inter-American Drug Abuse Control Commission
Inter-American Indian Institute
Inter-American Institute for Cooperation in Agriculture
Inter-American Institute for Global Change Research
Inter-American Investment Corporation
Inter-American Telecommunications Commission
Inter-American Tropical Tuna Commission
Pan American Health Organization
Pan American Institute of Geography and History
Pan American Railway Congress Association
Postal Union of the Americas, Spain and Portugal

IV. Regional Organizations

Antarctic Treaty System
Arctic Council
Asia-Pacific Economic Cooperation
Asia Pacific Energy Research Center
Colombo Plan for Cooperative Economic and Social Development in Asia and the Pacific
Commission for Environmental Cooperation
Commission for Labor Cooperation
International Commission for the Conservation of Atlantic Tunas
North Atlantic Assembly
North Atlantic Treaty Organization
North Atlantic Salmon Conservation Organization
North Pacific Anadromous Fish Commission
North Pacific Coast Guard Forum
North Pacific Marine Science Organization
Northwest Atlantic Fisheries Organization
Secretariat of the Pacific Community
South Pacific Regional Environment Program
Western and Central Pacific Fisheries Commission

V. Other International Organizations

Bioversity International
Center for International Forestry Research (CIFOR)
Commission for the Conservation of Antarctic Marine Living Resources
Community of Democracies
Comprehensive Nuclear Test Ban Treaty Organization
Consultative Group on International Agricultural Research (CGIAR)
COPAS–SARSAT (Search and Rescue Satellite System)
Global Biodiversity Information Facility
Global Environment Facility
Hague Conference on Private International Law
Human Frontier Science Program Organization
Integrated Ocean Drilling Program Council
International Agency for Research on Cancer (IARC)
International Bureau for the Permanent Court of Arbitration
International Bureau of Weights and Measures
International Center for Agricultural Research in the Dry Areas
International Center for the Study of the Preservation and the Restoration of Cultural Property

International Coffee Organization
International Committee of the Red Cross (ICRC)
International Cotton Advisory Committee
International Council for the Exploration of the Seas
International Court of Justice
International Criminal Police Organization (INTERPOL)
International Customs Tariffs Bureau
International Development Law Organization
International Energy Agency
International Energy Forum Secretariat
International Fertilizer Development Center
International Grains Council
International Hydrographic Organization
International Institute for Applied Systems Analysis
International Institute for Cotton
International Institute for the Unification of Private Law
International Mobile Satellite Organization
International Organization for Legal Metrology
International Organization of Supreme Audit Institutions
International Research and Training Institute for the Advancement of Women
International Rubber Study Group
International Science and Technology Center
International Seed Testing Association
International Sugar Council
International Telecommunications Satellite Organization
International Tropical Timber Organization
International Union of Credit and Investment Insurers (Berne Union)
International Whaling Commission
Inter-Parliamentary Union
Iran-United States Claims Tribunal
Multinational Force and Observers
Nuclear Energy Agency
Organization for Economic Cooperation and Development
Organization for the Prohibition of Chemical Weapons
Organization for Security and Cooperation in Europe
Permanent International Association of Navigation Congresses
Preparatory Commission for the Comprehensive Nuclear Test-Ban Treaty
Regional Environmental Center for Central and Eastern Europe
Science and Technology Center in Ukraine
Standards and Trade Development Facility
Wassenaar Arrangement
World Association of Investment Promotion Agencies
World Customs Organization
World Heritage Fund
World Organization for Animal Health
World Trade Organization

VI. Special Voluntary Programs

Asian Vegetable Research and Development Center
Convention on International Trade in Endangered Species of Wild Fauna and Flora (CITES)
Global Fund to Fight HIV/AIDS, Tuberculosis, and Malaria
International Council for Science
International Crop Research Institute for Semi-Arid Tropics
International Federation of the Red Cross and Red Crescent Societies
International Food Policy Research Institute
International Fund for Agricultural Development
International Institute of Tropical Agriculture
International Strategy for Disaster Reduction
Joint United Nations Program on HIV/AIDS (UNAIDS)
Korean Peninsula Energy Development Organization
Multilateral Fund for the Implementation of the Montreal Protocol
Ramsar Convention on Wetlands
United Nations Capital Development Fund
United Nations Children's Fund (UNICEF)
United Nations Conference on Trade and Development
United Nations Democracy Fund
United Nations Development Fund for Women (UNIFEM)
United Nations Development Program
United Nations Economic Commission for Europe
United Nations Environment Program

United Nations Framework Convention on Climate Change
United Nations Convention to Combat Desertification
United Nations High Commissioner for Human Rights Programs
United Nations High Commissioner for Refugees Programs
United Nations Human Settlements Program (UN HABITAT)
United Nations Population Fund (UNFPA)
United Nations Relief and Works Agency for Palestine Refugees (UNRWA)
United Nations Voluntary Fund for Technical Cooperation in the Field of Human Rights
United Nations Voluntary Fund for the Victims of Torture
United Nations World Food Program
World Agroforestry Center

Selected Bilateral Organizations

Below is a list of bilateral organizations in which the United States participates with its two neighbors, Mexico and Canada. This listing is for reference purposes only and should not be considered exhaustive.

Border Environment Cooperation Commission

United States Section: P.O. Box 221648, El Paso, TX 79913. Phone, 877–277–1703. Fax, 915–975–8280. E-mail, becc@cocef.org. Internet, www.becc.org.

Mexican Section: Bulevar Tomas Fernadez 8069, Ciudad Juarez, Chihuahua, 32470. Phone, 011–52–656–688–4600. Fax, 011–52–656–625–6180. Internet, www.cocef.org.

Great Lakes Fishery Commission

2100 Commonwealth Boulevard, Suite 100, Ann Arbor, MI 48105. Telephone, 734–662–3209. Fax, 734–741–2010. Email, info@glfc.org. Internet, www.glfc.org.

International Boundary Commission, United States and Canada

United States Section: 2000 L Street NW., Suite 615, Washington, DC 20036. Phone, 202–736–9102. Fax, 202–632–2008. E-mail, hipsleyk@ibcusca.org. Internet, www.internationalboundarycommission.org.

Canadian Section: 575–615 Booth Street, Ottawa, Ontario K1A 0E9 Canada. Phone, (613) 944–4515. Fax, (613) 992–1122. E-mail, ibc-cfi@nrcan.gc.ca. Internet, www.internationalboundarycommission.org.

International Boundary and Water Commission, United States and Mexico

United States Section: Suite C–100, 4171 North Mesa Street, El Paso, TX 79902. Phone, 800–262–8857. Internet, www.ibwc.state.gov.

Mexican Section: Avenue Universidad 2180, Zona Chamizal, C.P. 32310, Ciudad Juarez, Chihuahua, 32310. Phone, 011–52–656–639–7951 or 011–52–656–613–7311. Fax, 011–52–656–613–9943. E-mail, cilamex@cila.gob.mx. Internet, www.sre.gob.mx/cila.

International Joint Commission—United States and Canada

United States Section: 2000 L Street NW., Suite 615, Washington, DC 20440. Phone, 202–736–9009. Fax, 202–632–2007. E-mail: commission@washington.ijc.org. Internet, www.ijc.org.

Canadian Section: 234 Laurier Avenue West, 22d Floor, Ottawa, Ontario K1P 6K6. Phone, 613–995–2984. Fax, 613–993–5583. E-mail: commission@ottawa.ijc.org. Internet, www.ijc.org.

Great Lakes Regional Office: 100 Ouellette Avenue, 8th Floor, Windsor, Ontario N9A 6T3. Phone, 519–257–6700. Fax, 519–257–6740. E-mail: nevinj@windsor.ijc.org. Internet, www.ijc.org.

International Pacific Halibut Commission

2320 W. Commodore Way, Suite 300, Seattle, WA 98199–1287. Phone, 206–634–1838. Fax, 206–632–2983. Internet, www.iphc.int.

Joint Mexican-United States Defense Commission

United States Section: Room 2E773, The Pentagon, Washington, DC 20318. Phone, 703–695–8164.

Mexican Section: 6th Floor, 1911 Pennsylvania Avenue NW., Mexican Embassy, Washington, DC 20006. Phone, 202–728–1748.

Permanent Joint Board on Defense—United States and Canada

United States Section: Room 2E773, The Pentagon, Washington, DC 20318. Phone, 703–695–8164.

Canadian Section: Director of Western Hemisphere, 101 Colonel By Drive, Ottawa, ON K1A 0K2. Phone, 613–992–4423.

COMMONLY USED AGENCY ACRONYMS

ABMC	AMERICAN BATTLE MONUMENTS COMMISSION
ACF	ADMINISTRATION OF CHILDREN AND FAMILIES
ACFR	ADMINISTRATIVE COMMITTEE OF THE FEDERAL REGISTER
ADF	AFRICAN DEVELOPMENT FOUNDATION
AFRH	ARMED FORCES RETIREMENT HOME
AHRQ	AGENCY FOR HEALTHCARE RESEARCH AND QUALITY
AMS	AGRICULTURAL MARKETING SERVICE
AMTRAK	NATIONAL RAILROAD PASSENGER CORPORATION
AOA	ADMINISTRATION ON AGING
APHIS	ANIMAL AND PLANT HEALTH INSPECTION SERVICE
APPAL	APPALACHIAN STATES LOW LEVEL RADIOACTIVE WASTE COMMISSION
ARCTIC	ARCTIC RESEARCH COMMISSION
ARS	AGRICULTURAL RESEARCH SERVICE
ARTS	NATIONAL FOUNDATION ON THE ARTS AND THE HUMANITIES
ATBCB	ARCHITECTURAL AND TRANSPORTATION BARRIERS COMPLIANCE BOARD
ATF	ALCOHOL, TOBACCO, FIREARMS, AND EXPLOSIVES BUREAU
ATSDR	AGENCY FOR TOXIC SUBSTANCES AND DISEASE REGISTRY
BBG	BROADCASTING BOARD OF GOVERNORS
BEA	BUREAU OF ECONOMIC ANALYSIS
BGSEEF	BARRY M. GOLDWATER SCHOLARSHIP AND EXCELLENCE IN EDUCATION FOUNDATION
BIA	BUREAU OF INDIAN AFFAIRS
BIS	BUREAU OF INDUSTRY AND SECURITY
BLM	BUREAU OF LAND MANAGEMENT
BLS	BUREAU OF LABOR STATISTICS
BOP	FEDERAL PRISONS BUREAU
BOR	BUREAU OF RECLAMATION
BPA	BONNEVILLE POWER ADMINISTRATION
BPD	BUREAU OF PUBLIC DEBT
CBO	CONGRESSIONAL BUDGET OFFICE
CCC	COMMODITY CREDIT CORPORATION
CCJJDP	COORDINATING COUNCIL ON JUVENILE JUSTICE AND DELINQUENCY PREVENTION

CDC	CENTERS FOR DISEASE CONTROL AND PREVENTION
CDFI	COMMUNITY DEVELOPMENT FINANCIAL INSTITUTIONS FUND
CEQ	COUNCIL ON ENVIRONMENTAL QUALITY
CFTC	COMMODITY FUTURES TRADING COMMISSION
CFPB	CONSUMER FINANCIAL PROTECTION BUREAU
CIA	CENTRAL INTELLIGENCE AGENCY
CITA	COMMITTEE FOR THE IMPLEMENTATION OF TEXTILE AGREEMENTS
CMS	CENTERS FOR MEDICARE & MEDICAID SERVICES
CNCS	CORPORATION FOR NATIONAL AND COMMUNITY SERVICE
COE	CORPS OF ENGINEERS
COFA	COMMISSION OF FINE ARTS
COLC	COPYRIGHT OFFICE, LIBRARY OF CONGRESS
COPS	COMMUNITY ORIENTED POLICING SERVICES
CORP	CORPORATION FOR NATIONAL AND COMMUNITY SERVICE
CPPBSD	COMMITTEE FOR PURCHASE FROM PEOPLE WHO ARE BLIND OR SEVERELY DISABLED
CPSC	CONSUMER PRODUCT SAFETY COMMISSION
CRB	COPYRIGHT ROYALTY BOARD, LIBRARY OF CONGRESS
CRC	CIVIL RIGHTS COMMISSION
CSB	CHEMICAL SAFETY AND HAZARD INVESTIGATION BOARD
CSEO	CHILD SUPPORT ENFORCEMENT OFFICE
CSOSA	COURT SERVICES AND OFFENDER SUPERVISION AGENCY FOR THE DISTRICT OF COLUMBIA
CSREES	COOPERATIVE STATE RESEARCH, EDUCATION, AND EXTENSION SERVICE
DARPA	DEFENSE ADVANCED RESEARCH PROJECTS AGENCY
DARS	DEFENSE ACQUISITION REGULATIONS SYSTEM
DC	DENALI COMMISSION
DCAA	DEFENSE CONTRACT AUDIT AGENCY
DEA	DRUG ENFORCEMENT ADMINISTRATION
DEPO	DISABILITY EMPLOYMENT POLICY OFFICE
DFAS	DEFENSE FINANCE AND ACCOUNTING SERVICES
DHS	DEPARTMENT OF HOMELAND SECURITY
DIA	DEFENSE INTELLIGENCE AGENCY
DISA	DEFENSE INFORMATION SYSTEMS AGENCY
DLA	DEFENSE LOGISTICS AGENCY
DNFSB	DEFENSE NUCLEAR FACILITIES SAFETY BOARD
DOC	DEPARTMENT OF COMMERCE
DOD	DEPARTMENT OF DEFENSE
DOE	DEPARTMENT OF ENERGY
DOI	DEPARTMENT OF THE INTERIOR
DOJ	DEPARTMENT OF JUSTICE
DOL	DEPARTMENT OF LABOR
DOS	DEPARTMENT OF STATE
DOT	DEPARTMENT OF TRANSPORTATION
DRBC	DELAWARE RIVER BASIN COMMISSION
DSCA	DEFENSE SECURITY COOPERATION AGENCY
DSS	DEFENSE SECURITY SERVICE
DTRA	DEFENSE THREAT REDUCTION AGENCY
EAB	BUREAU OF ECONOMIC ANALYSIS
EAC	ELECTION ASSISTANCE COMMISSION

EBSA EMPLOYEE BENEFITS SECURITY ADMINISTRATION
ECAB EMPLOYEES' COMPENSATION APPEALS BOARD
ECSA ECONOMICS AND STATISTICS ADMINISTRATION
ED DEPARTMENT OF EDUCATION
EDA ECONOMIC DEVELOPMENT ADMINISTRATION
EEOC EQUAL EMPLOYMENT OPPORTUNITY COMMISSION
EERE ENERGY EFFICIENCY AND RENEWABLE ENERGY OFFICE
EIA ENERGY INFORMATION ADMINISTRATION
EIB EXPORT IMPORT BANK OF THE UNITED STATES
EOA ENERGY OFFICE, AGRICULTURE DEPARTMENT
EOIR EXECUTIVE OFFICE FOR IMMIGRATION REVIEW
EOP EXECUTIVE OFFICE OF THE PRESIDENT
EPA ENVIRONMENTAL PROTECTION AGENCY
ERS ECONOMIC RESEARCH SERVICE
ESA EMPLOYMENT STANDARDS ADMINISTRATION
ETA EMPLOYMENT AND TRAINING ADMINISTRATION
FAA FEDERAL AVIATION ADMINISTRATION
FAR FEDERAL ACQUISITION REGULATION
FAS FOREIGN AGRICULTURAL SERVICE
FASAB FEDERAL ACCOUNTING STANDARDS ADVISORY BOARD
FBI FEDERAL BUREAU OF INVESTIGATION
FCA FARM CREDIT ADMINISTRATION
FCC FEDERAL COMMUNICATIONS COMMISSION
FCIC FEDERAL CROP INSURANCE CORPORATION
FCSIC FARM CREDIT SYSTEM INSURANCE CORPORATION
FDA FOOD AND DRUG ADMINISTRATION
FDIC FEDERAL DEPOSIT INSURANCE CORPORATION
FEC FEDERAL ELECTION COMMISSION
FEMA FEDERAL EMERGENCY MANAGEMENT AGENCY
FERC FEDERAL ENERGY REGULATORY COMMISSION
FFIEC FEDERAL FINANCIAL INSTITUTIONS EXAMINATION COUNCIL
FHEO FAIR HOUSING AND EQUAL OPPORTUNITY
FHFA FEDERAL HOUSING FINANCE AGENCY
FHFB FEDERAL HOUSING FINANCE BOARD
FHWA FEDERAL HIGHWAY ADMINISTRATION
FINCEN FINANCIAL CRIMES ENFORCEMENT NETWORK
FINCIC FINANCIAL CRISIS INQUIRY COMMISSION
FISCAL FISCAL SERVICE
FLETC FEDERAL LAW ENFORCEMENT TRAINING CENTER
FLRA FEDERAL LABOR RELATIONS AUTHORITY
FMC FEDERAL MARITIME COMMISSION
FMCS FEDERAL MEDIATION AND CONCILIATION SERVICE
FMCSA FEDERAL MOTOR CARRIER SAFETY ADMINISTRATION
FNS FOOD AND NUTRITION SERVICE
FPPO FEDERAL PROCUREMENT POLICY OFFICE

FR OFFICE OF THE FEDERAL REGISTER
FRA FEDERAL RAILROAD ADMINISTRATION
FRS FEDERAL RESERVE SYSTEM
FRTIB FEDERAL RETIREMENT THRIFT INVESTMENT BOARD
FS FOREST SERVICE
FSA FARM SERVICE AGENCY
FSIS FOOD SAFETY AND INSPECTION SERVICE
FTA FEDERAL TRANSIT ADMINISTRATION
FTC FEDERAL TRADE COMMISSION
FTZB FOREIGN TRADE ZONES BOARD
FWS FISH AND WILDLIFE SERVICE
GAO GOVERNMENT ACCOUNTABILITY OFFICE
GEO GOVERNMENT ETHICS OFFICE
GIPSA GRAIN INSPECTION, PACKERS AND STOCKYARDS ADMINISTRATION
GPO GOVERNMENT PRINTING OFFICE
GSA GENERAL SERVICES ADMINISTRATION
HHS DEPARTMENT OF HEALTH AND HUMAN SERVICES
HHSIG INSPECTOR GENERAL OFFICE, HEALTH AND HUMAN SERVICES DEPARTMENT
HOPE BOARD OF DIRECTORS OF THE HOPE FOR HOMEOWNERS PROGRAM
HPAC HISTORIC PRESERVATION, ADVISORY COUNCIL
HRSA HEALTH RESOURCES AND SERVICES ADMINISTRATION
HST HARRY S. TRUMAN SCHOLARSHIP FOUNDATION
HUD DEPARTMENT OF HOUSING AND URBAN DEVELOPMENT
IAF INTER AMERICAN FOUNDATION
ICEB IMMIGRATION AND CUSTOMS ENFORCEMENT BUREAU
IHS INDIAN HEALTH SERVICE
IIO INTERNATIONAL INVESTMENT OFFICE
IRS INTERNAL REVENUE SERVICE
ISOO INFORMATION SECURITY OVERSIGHT OFFICE
ITA INTERNATIONAL TRADE ADMINISTRATION
ITC INTERNATIONAL TRADE COMMISSION
JBEA JOINT BOARD FOR ENROLLMENT OF ACTUARIES
LMSO LABOR MANAGEMENT STANDARDS OFFICE
LOC LIBRARY OF CONGRESS
LSC LEGAL SERVICES CORPORATION
MARAD MARITIME ADMINISTRATION
MBDA MINORITY BUSINESS DEVELOPMENT AGENCY
MCC MILLENNIUM CHALLENGE CORPORATION
MDA MISSILE DEFENSE AGENCY
MISS MISSISSIPPI RIVER COMMISSION
MKU MORRIS K. UDALL SCHOLARSHIP AND EXCELLENCE IN NATIONAL ENVIRONMENTAL POLICY FOUNDATION
MMC MARINE MAMMALCOMMISSION
MMS MINERALS MANAGEMENT SERVICE
MSHA MINE SAFETY AND HEALTH ADMINISTRATION
MSHFRC FEDERAL MINE SAFETY AND HEALTH REVIEW COMMISSION
MSPB MERIT SYSTEMS PROTECTION BOARD
NARA NATIONAL ARCHIVES AND RECORDS ADMINISTRATION

NASA	NATIONAL AERONAUTICS AND SPACE ADMINISTRATION
NASS	NATIONAL AGRICULTURAL STATISTICS SERVICE
NCA	NATIONAL CEMETERY ADMINISTRATION
NCD	NATIONAL COUNCIL ON DISABILITY
NCLIS	NATIONAL COMMISSION ON LIBRARIES AND INFORMATION SCIENCE
NCPPCC	NATIONAL CRIME PREVENTION AND PRIVACY COMPACT COUNCIL
NCS	NATIONAL COMMUNICATIONS SYSTEM
NCUA	NATIONAL CREDIT UNION ADMINISTRATION
NEC	NATIONAL ECONOMIC COUNCIL
NEIGHBOR	NEIGHBORHOOD REINVESTMENT CORPORATION
NHTSA	NATIONAL HIGHWAY TRAFFIC SAFETY ADMINISTRATION
NIFA	NATIONAL INSTITUTE OF FOOD AND AGRICULTURE
NIGC	NATIONAL INDIAN GAMING COMMISSION
NIH	NATIONAL INSTITUTES OF HEALTH
NIL	NATIONAL INSTITUTE FOR LITERACY
NIST	NATIONAL INSTITUTE OF STANDARDS AND TECHNOLOGY
NLRB	NATIONAL LABOR RELATIONS BOARD
NMB	NATIONAL MEDIATION BOARD
NNSA	NATIONAL NUCLEAR SECURITY ADMINISTRATION
NOAA	NATIONAL OCEANIC AND ATMOSPHERIC ADMINISTRATION
NPREC	NATIONAL PRISON RAPE ELIMINATION COMMISSION
NPS	NATIONAL PARK SERVICE
NRC	NUCLEAR REGULATORY COMMISSION
NRCS	NATURAL RESOURCES CONSERVATION SERVICE
NSA	NATIONAL SECURITY AGENCY/CENTRAL SECURITY SERVICE
NSF	NATIONAL SCIENCE FOUNDATION
NTIA	NATIONAL TELECOMMUNICATIONS AND INFORMATION ADMINISTRATION
NTSB	NATIONAL TRANSPORTATION SAFETY BOARD
NWTRB	NUCLEAR WASTE TECHNICAL REVIEW BOARD
OCC	COMPTROLLER OF THE CURRENCY
ODNI	OFFICE OF THE DIRECTOR OF NATIONAL INTELLIGENCE
OEPNU	OFFICE OF ENERGY POLICY AND NEW USES
OFAC	OFFICE OF FOREIGN ASSETS CONTROL
OFCCP	OFFICE OF FEDERAL CONTRACT COMPLIANCE PROGRAMS
OFHEO	FEDERAL HOUSING ENTERPRISE OVERSIGHT OFFICE
OFPP	OFFICE OF FEDERAL PROCUREMENT POLICY
OJJDP	JUVENILE JUSTICE AND DELINQUENCY PREVENTION OFFICE
OJP	JUSTICE PROGRAMS OFFICE
OMB	OFFICE OF MANAGEMENT AND BUDGET
ONDCP	OFFICE OF NATIONAL DRUG CONTROL POLICY
ONHIR	OFFICE OF NAVAJO AND HOPI INDIAN RELOCATION
OPIC	OVERSEAS PRIVATE INVESTMENT CORPORATION

OPM	OFFICE OF PERSONNEL MANAGEMENT
OPPM	OFFICE OF PROCUREMENT AND POLICY MANAGEMENT
OSC	OFFICE OF SPECIAL COUNSEL
OSHA	OCCUPATIONAL SAFETY AND HEALTH ADMINISTRATION
OSHRC	OCCUPATIONAL SAFETY AND HEALTH REVIEW COMMISSION
OSM	OFFICE OF SURFACE MINING RECLAMATION AND ENFORCEMENT
OSTP	OFFICE OF SCIENCE AND TECHNOLOGY POLICY
OTS	OFFICE OF THRIFT SUPERVISION
PACIFIC	PACIFIC NORTHWEST ELECTRIC POWER AND CONSERVATION PLANNING COUNCIL
PBGC	PENSION BENEFIT GUARANTY CORPORATION
PC	PEACE CORPS
PHMSA	PIPELINE AND HAZARDOUS MATERIALS SAFETY ADMINISTRATION
PHS	PUBLIC HEALTH SERVICE
PRC	POSTAL REGULATORY COMMISSION
PRES	PRESIDENTIAL DOCUMENTS
PT	PRESIDIO TRUST
PTO	PATENT AND TRADEMARK OFFICE
RATB	RECOVERY ACCOUNTABILITY AND TRANSPARENCY BOARD
RBS	RURAL BUSINESS COOPERATIVE SERVICE
RHS	RURAL HOUSING SERVICE
RISC	REGULATORY INFORMATION SERVICE CENTER
RITA	RESEARCH AND INNOVATIVE TECHNOLOGY ADMINISTRATION
RMA	RISK MANAGEMENT AGENCY
RRB	RAILROAD RETIREMENT BOARD
RTB	RURAL TELEPHONE BANK
RUS	RURAL UTILITIES SERVICE
SAMHSA	SUBSTANCE ABUSE AND MENTAL HEALTH SERVICES ADMINISTRATION
SBA	SMALL BUSINESS ADMINISTRATION
SEC	SECURITIES AND EXCHANGE COMMISSION
SIGIR	SPECIAL INSPECTOR GENERAL FOR IRAQ RECONSTRUCTION
SJI	STATE JUSTICE INSTITUTE
SLSDC	SAINT LAWRENCE SEAWAY DEVELOPMENT CORPORATION
SRBC	SUSQUEHANNA RIVER BASIN COMMISSION
SSA	SOCIAL SECURITY ADMINISTRATION
SSS	SELECTIVE SERVICE SYSTEM
STB	SURFACE TRANSPORTATION BOARD
SWPA	SOUTHWESTERN POWER ADMINISTRATION
TA	TECHNOLOGY ADMINISTRATION
TREAS	DEPARTMENT OF THE TREASURY
TSA	TRANSPORTATION SECURITY ADMINISTRATION
TTB	ALCOHOL AND TOBACCO TAX AND TRADE BUREAU
TVA	TENNESSEE VALLEY AUTHORITY
URMCC	UTAH RECLAMATION MITIGATION AND CONSERVATION COMMISSION
USA	ARMY DEPARTMENT
USAF	AIR FORCE DEPARTMENT
USAID	UNITED STATES AGENCY FOR INTERNATIONAL DEVELOPMENT
USBC	BUREAU OF THE CENSUS

USCBP	CUSTOMS AND BORDER PROTECTION BUREAU
USCC	U.S. CHINA ECONOMIC AND SECURITY REVIEW COMMISSION
USCERT	UNITED STATES COMPUTER EMERGENCY READINESS TEAM
USCG	COAST GUARD
USCIS	U.S. CITIZENSHIP AND IMMIGRATION SERVICES
USDA	DEPARTMENT OF AGRICULTURE
USEIB	EXPORT IMPORT BANK
USGS	U.S. GEOLOGICAL SERVICE
USHMM	UNITED STATES HOLOCAUST MEMORIAL MUSEUM
USIP	UNITED STATES INSTITUTE OF PEACE
USJC	JUDICIAL CONFERENCE OF THE UNITED STATES
USMINT	UNITED STATES MINT
USN	NAVY DEPARTMENT
USPC	PAROLE COMMISSION
USPS	POSTAL SERVICE
USSC	UNITED STATES SENTENCING COMMISSION
USSS	SECRET SERVICE
USTR	OFFICE OF UNITED STATES TRADE REPRESENTATIVE
USUHS	UNIFORMED SERVICES UNIVERSITY OF THE HEALTH SCIENCES
VA	DEPARTMENT OF VETERANS AFFAIRS
VCNP	VALLES CALDERA TRUST
VETS	VETERANS EMPLOYMENT AND TRAINING SERVICE
WAPA	WESTERN AREA POWER ADMINISTRATION
WCPO	WORKERS COMPENSATION PROGRAMS OFFICE
WHD	WAGE AND HOUR DIVISION

HISTORY OF AGENCY ORGANIZATIONAL CHANGES

NOTE: Italicized terms indicate obsolete agencies, organizations, and programs. Refer to the name of the obsolete entity in this index for more explanation. Some dates prior to March 4, 1933 are included to provide additional information.

Entries are indexed using the most significant term in their titles, or when there is more than one significant term, the entry uses the first significant term. Thus, **Bureau of the Budget** is found at **Budget, Bureau of the,** and **Annual Assay Commission** is found at **Assay Commission, Annual.**

Accounting Office, General Established by act of June 10, 1921 (42 Stat. 20). Renamed Government Accountability Office by act of July 7, 2004 (118 Stat. 814).

ACTION Established by Reorg. Plan No. 1 of 1971 (5 U.S.C. app.), effective July 1, 1971. Reorganized by act of Oct. 1, 1973 (87 Stat. 405). Functions relating to SCORE and ACT programs transferred to Small Business Administration by EO 11871 of July 18, 1975 (40 FR 30915). Functions exercised by the Director of ACTION prior to Mar. 31, 1995, transferred to the Corporation for National and Community Service (107 Stat. 888 and Proclamation 6662 of Apr. 4, 1994 (57 FR 16507)).

Acts of Congress *See* **State, Department of**

Administrative Conference of the United States Established by act of Aug. 30, 1964 (78 Stat. 615). Terminated by act of Nov. 19, 1995 (109 Stat. 480). Reauthorized in 2004, 2008, and 2009 by acts of Oct. 30, 2004 (118 Stat. 2255), July 30, 2008 (122 Stat. 2914), and March 11, 2009 (123 Stat. 656). Reestablished by Congress on Mar. 3, 2010 upon confirmation of chairman.

Advanced Research Projects Agency *See* Defense Advanced Research Projects Agency

Advisory Board. *See other part of title*

Advisory Committee. *See other part of title*

Advisory Council. *See other part of title*

Aeronautical Board Organized in 1916 by agreement of *War* and Navy Secretaries. Placed under supervision of President by military order of July 5, 1939. Dissolved by Secretary of Defense letter of July 27, 1948, and functions transferred to *Munitions Board* and *Research and Development Board.* Military order of July 5, 1939, revoked by military order of Oct. 18, 1948.

Aeronautics, Bureau of Established in the Department of the Navy by act of July 12, 1921 (42 Stat. 140). Abolished by act of Aug. 18, 1959 (73 Stat. 395) and functions transferred to *Bureau of Naval Weapons.*

Aeronautics, National Advisory Committee for Established by act of Mar. 3, 1915 (38 Stat. 930). Terminated by act of July 29, 1958 (72 Stat. 432), and functions transferred to National Aeronautics and Space Administration, established by same act.

Aeronautics Administration, Civil *See* **Aeronautics Authority, Civil**

Aeronautics Authority, Civil Established under act of June 23, 1938 (52 Stat. 973). Renamed *Civil Aeronautics Board* and Administrator transferred to the Department of Commerce by Reorg. Plan Nos. III and IV of 1940, effective June 30, 1940. Office of Administrator designated *Civil Aeronautics Administration* by Department Order 52 of Aug. 29, 1940. *Administration* transferred to *Federal Aviation Agency* by act of Aug. 23, 1958 (72 Stat. 810). Functions of *Board* under act of Aug. 23, 1958 (72 Stat. 775), transferred to National Transportation Safety Board by act of Oct. 15, 1966 (80 Stat. 931). Functions of *Board* terminated or transferred—effective in part Dec. 31, 1981; in part Jan. 1, 1983; and in part Jan. 1, 1985—by act of Aug. 23, 1958 (92 Stat. 1744). Most remaining functions transferred to Secretary of Transportation, remainder to U.S. Postal Service. Termination of *Board* finalized by act of Oct. 4, 1984 (98 Stat. 1703).

Aeronautics Board, Civil *See* **Aeronautics Authority, Civil**

Aeronautics Branch Established in the Department of Commerce to carry out provisions of act of May

20, 1926 (44 Stat. 568). Renamed *Bureau of Air Commerce* by Secretary's administrative order of July 1, 1934. Personnel and property transferred to *Civil Aeronautics Authority* by EO 7959 of Aug. 22, 1938.

Aeronautics and Space Council, National Established by act of July 29, 1958 (72 Stat. 427). Abolished by Reorg. Plan No. 1 of 1973, effective June 30, 1973.

Aging, Administration on Established by *Secretary of Health, Education, and Welfare* on Oct. 1, 1965, to carry out provisions of act of July 14, 1965 (79 Stat. 218). Reassigned to *Social and Rehabilitation Service* by Department reorganization of Aug. 15, 1967. Transferred to Office of Assistant Secretary for Human Development by Secretary's order of June 15, 1973. Transferred to the Office of the Secretary of Health and Human Services by Secretary's reorganization notice dated Apr. 15, 1991. Transferred to the Administration for Community Living by Department's notice of April 18, 2012 (77 FR 23250).

Aging, Federal Council on Established by Presidential memorandum of Apr. 2, 1956. Reconstituted at Federal level by Presidential letter of Mar. 7, 1959, to *Secretary of Health, Education, and Welfare*. Abolished by EO 11022 of May 15, 1962, which established *President's Council on Aging*.

Aging, Office of Established by *Secretary of Health, Education, and Welfare* June 2, 1955, as *Special Staff on Aging*. Terminated Sept. 30, 1965, and functions assumed by Administration on Aging.

Aging, President's Council on Established by EO 11022 of May 14, 1962. Terminated by EO 11022, which was revoked by EO 12379 of Aug. 17, 1982.

Agricultural Adjustment Administration Established by act of May 12, 1933 (48 Stat. 31). Consolidated into *Agricultural Conservation and Adjustment Administration* as *Agricultural Adjustment Agency*, Department of Agriculture, by EO 9069 of Feb. 23, 1942. Grouped with other agencies to form *Food Production Administration* by EO 9280 of Dec. 5, 1942. Transferred to *War Food Administration* by EO 9322 of Mar. 26, 1943. Administration terminated by EO 9577 of June 29, 1945, and functions transferred to Secretary of Agriculture. Transfer made permanent by Reorg. Plan No. 3 of 1946, effective July 16, 1946. Functions of *Agricultural Adjustment Agency* consolidated with *Production and Marketing Administration* by Secretary's Memorandum 1118 of Aug. 18, 1945.

Agricultural Adjustment Agency *See* **Agricultural Adjustment Administration**

Agricultural Advisory Commission, National Established by EO 10472 of July 20, 1953. Terminated Feb. 4, 1965, on resignation of members.

Agricultural Chemistry and Engineering, Bureau of *See* **Agricultural Engineering, Bureau of**

Agricultural Conservation and Adjustment Administration Established by EO 9069 of Feb. 23, 1942, consolidating *Agricultural Adjustment Agency, Sugar Agency, Federal Crop Insurance Corporation,* and *Soil Conservation Service*. Consolidated into *Food Production Administration* by EO 9280 of Dec. 5, 1942.

Agricultural Conservation Program Service Established by Secretary of Agriculture Jan. 21, 1953, from part of *Production and Marketing Administration*. Merged with *Commodity Stabilization Service* by Secretary's Memorandum 1446, supp. 2, of Apr. 19, 1961.

Agricultural Developmental Service, International Established by Secretary of Agriculture memorandum of July 12, 1963. Functions and delegations of authority transferred to Foreign Agricultural Service by Secretary's memorandum of Mar. 28, 1969. Functions transferred by Secretary to *Foreign Economic Development Service* Nov. 8, 1969.

Agricultural Economics, Bureau of Established by act of May 11, 1931 (42 Stat. 532). Functions transferred to other units of the Department of Agriculture, including *Consumer and Marketing Service* and Agricultural Research Service, under Secretary's Memorandum 1320, supp. 4, of Nov. 2, 1953.

Agricultural Engineering, Bureau of Established by act of Feb. 23, 1931 (46 Stat. 1266). Merged with *Bureau of Chemistry and Soils* by Secretarial order of Oct. 16, 1938, to form *Bureau of Agricultural Chemistry and Engineering.*

Agricultural and Industrial Chemistry, Bureau of *Bureau of Chemistry* and *Bureau of Soils,* created in 1901, combined into *Bureau of Chemistry and Soils* by act of Jan. 18, 1927 (44 Stat. 976). Soils units transferred to other agencies of the Department of Agriculture and remaining units of *Bureau of Chemistry and Soils* and *Bureau of Agricultural Engineering* consolidated with *Bureau of Agricultural Chemistry and Engineering* by Secretary's order of Oct. 16, 1938. In February 1943 agricultural engineering research made part of *Bureau of Plant Industry, Soils, and Agricultural Engineering,* and organization for continuing agricultural chemistry research relating to crop utilization named *Bureau of Agricultural and Industrial Chemistry,* in accordance with *Research Administration* Memorandum 5 issued pursuant to EO 9069 of Feb. 23, 1942, and in conformity with Secretary's Memorandums 960 and 986. Functions transferred to *Agricultural Research Service* under Secretary's Memorandum 1320, supp. 4, of Nov. 2, 1953.

Agricultural Library, National Established by Secretary of Agriculture Memorandum 1496 of Mar. 23, 1962. Consolidated into *Science and Education Administration* by Secretary's order of Jan. 24, 1978. Reestablished as National Agricultural Library by Secretary's order of June 16, 1981. Became part of Agricultural Research Service in 1994 under Department of Agriculture reorganization.

Agricultural Marketing Administration Established by EO 9069 of Feb. 23, 1942, consolidating *Surplus*

Marketing Administration, Agricultural Marketing Service, and *Commodity Exchange Administration. Division of Consumers' Counsel* transferred to *Administration* by Secretary's memorandum of Feb. 28, 1942. Consolidated into *Food Distribution Administration* in the Department of Agriculture by EO 9280 of Dec. 5, 1942.

Agricultural Marketing Service Established by the Secretary of Agriculture pursuant to act of June 30, 1939 (53 Stat. 939). Merged into *Agricultural Marketing Administration* by EO 9069 of Feb. 23, 1942. Renamed *Consumer and Marketing Service* by Secretary's Memorandum 1567, supp. 1, of Feb. 8, 1965. Reestablished as Agricultural Marketing Service by the Secretary of Agriculture on Apr. 2, 1972, under authority of Reorg. Plan No. 2 of 1953 (67 Stat. 633).

Agricultural Relations, Office of Foreign *See* **Agricultural Service, Foreign**

Agricultural Research Administration Established by EO 9069 of Feb. 23, 1942. Superseded by Agricultural Research Service.

Agricultural Research Service Established by Secretary of Agriculture Memorandum 1320, supp. 4, of Nov. 2, 1953. Consolidated into *Science and Education Administration* by Secretary's order of Jan. 24, 1978. Reestablished as Agricultural Research Service by Secretarial order of June 16, 1981.

Agricultural Service, Foreign Established by act of June 5, 1930 (46 Stat. 497). Economic research and agricultural attache´ activities administered by *Foreign Agricultural Service Division, Bureau of Agricultural Economics,* until June 29, 1939. Transferred by Reorg. Plan No. II of 1939, effective July 1, 1939, from the Department of Agriculture to the Department of State. Economic research functions of *Division* transferred to *Office of Foreign Agricultural Relations* June 30, 1939. Functions of *Office* transferred to Foreign Agricultural Service Mar. 10, 1953. Agricultural attache´s placed in the Department of Agriculture by act of Aug. 28, 1954 (68 Stat. 908).

Agricultural Stabilization and Conservation Service Established June 5, 1961, by the Secretary of Agriculture under authority of revised statutes (5 U.S.C. 301) and Reorg. Plan No. 2 of 1953 (5 U.S.C. app.). Abolished and functions assumed by the *Farm Service Agency* by Secretary's Memorandum 1010– 1 dated Oct. 20, 1994 (59 FR 60297, 60299).

Agricultural Statistics Division Transferred to *Bureau of Agricultural Economics* by EO 9069 of Feb. 23, 1942.

Agriculture, Division of *See* **Farm Products, Division of**

Air Commerce, Bureau of *See* **Aeronautics Branch**

Air Coordinating Committee Established Mar. 27, 1945, by interdepartmental memorandum; formally established by EO 9781 of Sept. 19, 1946. Terminated by EO 10883 of Aug. 11, 1960, and functions transferred for liquidation to *Federal Aviation Agency.*

Air Force, National Commission on the Structure of the Established by act of January 2, 2013 (126 Stat. 1703). Terminated 90 days after submission of final report to President on May 1, 2014.

Air Force Management Engineering Agency Established in 1975 in Air Force as separate operating unit. Made subordinate unit of Air Force Military Personnel Center (formerly Air Force Manpower and Personnel Center) in 1978. Reestablished as separate operating unit of Air Force, effective Mar. 1, 1985, by Secretarial order.

Air Force Manpower and Personnel Center Certain functions transferred on activation of Air Force Management Engineering Agency, which was made separate operating unit from Air Force Manpower and Personnel Center (later Air Force Military Personnel Center) in April 1985 by general order of Chief of Staff.

Air Force Medical Service Center Renamed Air Force Office of Medical Support by Program Action Directive 85–1 of Mar. 6, 1985, approved by Air Force Vice Chief of Staff.

Air Mail, Bureau of Established in Interstate Commerce Commission to carry out provisions of act of June 12, 1934 (48 Stat. 933). Personnel and property transferred to *Civil Aeronautics Authority* by EO 7959 of Aug. 22, 1938.

Air Patrol, Civil Established in *Civilian Defense Office* by Administrative Order 9 of Dec. 8, 1941. Transferred to *Department of War* as auxiliary of Army Air Forces by EO 9339 of Apr. 29, 1943. Transferred to the Department of the Air Force by Secretary of Defense order of May 21, 1948. Established as civilian auxiliary of U.S. Air Force by act of May 26, 1948 (62 Stat. 274).

Air Safety Board Established by act of June 23, 1938 (52 Stat. 973). Functions transferred to *Civil Aeronautics Board* by Reorg. Plan No. IV of 1940, effective June 30, 1940.

Airways Modernization Board Established by act of Aug. 14, 1957 (71 Stat. 349). Transferred to *Federal Aviation Agency* by EO 10786 of Nov. 1, 1958.

Alaska, Board of Road Commissioners for Established in *Department of War* by act of Jan. 27, 1905 (33 Stat. 616). Functions transferred to the Department of Interior by act of June 30, 1932 (47 Stat. 446), and delegated to *Alaska Road Commission.* Functions transferred to the Department of Commerce by act of June 29, 1956 (70 Stat. 377), and terminated by act of June 25, 1959 (73 Stat. 145).

Alaska, Federal Field Committee for Development Planning in Established by EO 11182 of Oct. 2, 1964. Abolished by EO 11608 of July 19, 1971.

Alaska, Federal Reconstruction and Development Planning Commission for Established by EO 11150 of Apr. 2, 1964. Abolished by EO 11182 of

Oct. 2, 1964, which established *President's Review Committee for Development Planning in Alaska* and *Federal Field Committee for Development Planning in Alaska.*

Alaska, President's Review Committee for Development Planning in Established by EO 11182 of Oct. 2, 1964. Superseded by *Federal Advisory Council on Regional Economic Development* established by EO 11386 of Dec. 28, 1967. EO 11386 revoked by EO 12553 f Feb. 25, 1986.

Alaska Communication System Operational responsibility vested in Secretary of the Army by act of May 26, 1900 (31 Stat. 206). Transferred to Secretary of the Air Force by Secretary of Defense reorganization order of May 24, 1962.

Alaska Engineering Commission *See* **Alaska Railroad**

Alaska Game Commission Established by act of Jan. 13, 1925 (43 Stat. 740). Expired Dec. 31, 1959, pursuant to act of July 7, 1958 (72 Stat. 339).

Alaska International Rail and Highway Commission Established by act of Aug. 1, 1956 (70 Stat. 888). Terminated June 30, 1961, under terms of act.

Alaska Natural Gas Transportation System, Office of Federal Inspector of Construction for the Established by Reorg. Plan No. 1 of 1979 (5 U.S.C. app.), effective July 1, 1979. Abolished by act of Oct. 24, 1992 (106 Stat. 3128) and functions and authority vested in the Inspector transferred to the Secretary of Energy. Functions vested in the Secretary of Energy transferred to the Federal Coordinator, Office of the Federal Coordinator for Alaska Natural Gas Transportation Projects by act of Oct. 13, 2004 (118 Stat. 1261).

Alaska Power Administration Established by the Secretary of the Interior in 1967. Transferred to the Department of Energy by act of Aug. 4, 1977 (91 Stat. 578).

Alaska Railroad Built pursuant to act of Mar. 12, 1914 (38 Stat. 305), which created *Alaska Engineering Commission.* Placed under the Secretary of the Interior by EO 2129 of Jan. 26, 1915, and renamed Alaska Railroad by EO 3861 of June 8, 1923. Authority to regulate tariffs granted to Interstate Commerce Commission by EO 11107 of Apr. 25, 1963. Authority to operate Railroad transferred to the Secretary of Transportation by act of Oct. 15, 1966 (80 Stat. 941), effective Apr. 1, 1967. Railroad purchased by State of Alaska, effective Jan. 5, 1985.

Alaska Road Commission *See* **Alaska, Board of Road Commissioners for**

Alcohol, Bureau of Industrial Established by act of May 27, 1930 (46 Stat. 427). Consolidated into *Bureau of Internal Revenue* by EO 6166 of June 10, 1933. Consolidation deferred until May 11, 1934, by EO 6639 of Mar. 10, 1934. Order also transferred to Internal Revenue Commissioner certain functions imposed on Attorney General by act of May 27, 1930, with relation to enforcement of criminal laws concerning intoxicating liquors remaining in effect after repeal of 18th amendment; personnel of, and appropriations for, *Bureau of Industrial Alcohol;* and necessary personnel and appropriations of *Bureau of Prohibition,* Department of Justice.

Alcohol, Drug Abuse, and Mental Health Administration Established by the *Secretary of Health, Education, and Welfare* by act of May 21, 1972 (88 Stat. 134). Redesignated as an agency of the Public Health Service from the *National Institute of Mental Health* Sept. 25, 1973, by the Secretary of Health, Education, and Welfare. Functions transferred to the Department of Health and Human Services by act of Oct. 17, 1979 (93 Stat. 695). Established as an agency of the Public Health Service by act of Oct. 27, 1986 (100 Stat. 3207–106). Renamed Substance Abuse and Mental Health Services Administration by act of July 10, 1992 (106 Stat. 325).

Alcohol Abuse and Alcoholism, National Institute on Established within the National Institute of Mental Health, *Department of Health, Education, and Welfare* by act of Dec. 31, 1970 (84 Stat. 1848). Removed from within the National Institute of Mental Health and made an entity within the Alcohol, Drug Abuse, and Mental Health Administration by act of May 14, 1974 (88 Stat. 1356). Functions transferred to the Department of Health and Human Services by act of Oct. 17, 1979 (93 Stat. 695). (*See also* act of Oct. 27, 1986; 100 Stat. 3207–106.) Abolished by act of July 10, 1992 (106 Stat. 331). Reestablished by act of July 10, 1992 (106 Stat. 359).

Alcohol Administration, Federal *See* **Alcohol Control Administration, Federal**

Alcohol Control Administration, Federal Established by EO 6474 of Dec. 4, 1933. Abolished Sept. 24, 1935, on induction into office of Administrator, *Federal Alcohol Administration,* as provided in act of Aug. 29, 1935 (49 Stat. 977). Abolished by Reorg. Plan No. III of 1940, effective June 30, 1940, and functions consolidated with activities of Internal Revenue Service.

Alcohol, Tobacco, and Firearms, Bureau of Established within Treasury Department by Treasury Order No. 221, eff. July 1, 1972. Transferred to Bureau of Alcohol, Tobacco, Firearms, and Explosives in Justice Department by act of Nov. 25, 2002, except some authorities, functions, personnel, and assets relating to administration and enforcement of certain provisions of the Internal Revenue Code of 1986 and title 27 of the U.S. Code (116 Stat. 2275).

Alexander Hamilton Bicentennial Commission Established by act of Aug. 20, 1954 (68 Stat. 746). Terminated Apr. 30, 1958.

Alien Property Custodian Appointed by President Oct. 22, 1917, under authority of act of Oct. 6, 1917 (40 Stat. 415). Office transferred to *Alien Property Division,* Department of Justice, by EO 6694 of May 1, 1934. Powers vested in President by act delegated to Attorney General by EO 8136 of May 15, 1939. Authority vested in Attorney General by EO's 6694 and 8136 transferred by EO 9142 of Apr. 21, 1942, to *Office of Alien Property Custodian, Office for Emergency Management,* as provided for by EO 9095 of Mar. 11, 1942.

American Forces Information Service Established by Secretary of Defense Directive 5122.10 of March 13, 1989. Dissolved by Secretary's Directive 5105.74 of Dec. 18, 2007 and functions transferred to Defense Media Activity effective Oct. 1, 2008.

American Republics, Office for Coordination of Commercial and Cultural Relations between the Established by *Council of National Defense* order approved by President Aug. 16, 1940. Succeeded by *Office of the Coordinator of Inter-American Affairs, Office for Emergency Management,* established by EO 8840 of July 30, 1941. Renamed *Office of Inter-American Affairs* by EO 9532 of Mar. 23, 1945. Information functions transferred to the Department of State by EO 9608 of Aug. 31, 1945. Terminated by EO 9710 of Apr. 10, 1946, and functions transferred to the Department of State, functioning as *Institute of Inter-American Affairs.* Transferred to *Foreign Operations Administration* by Reorg. Plan No. 7, effective Aug. 1, 1953.

American Revolution Bicentennial Administration *See* **American Revolution Bicentennial Commission**

American Revolution Bicentennial Commission Established by act of July 4, 1966 (80 Stat. 259). *American Revolution Bicentennial Administration* established by act of Dec. 11, 1973 (87 Stat. 697), to replace *Commission. Administration* terminated June 30, 1977, pursuant to terms of act. Certain continuing functions transferred to the Secretary of the Interior by EO 12001 of June 29, 1977.

Anacostia Neighborhood Museum Renamed Anacostia Museum by Smithsonian Institution announcement of Apr. 3, 1987.

Animal Industry, Bureau of Established in the Department of Agriculture by act of May 29, 1884 (23 Stat. 31). Functions transferred to Agricultural Research Service by Secretary's Memorandum 1320, supp. 4, of Nov. 2, 1953.

Apprenticeship, Federal Committee on Previously known as *Federal Committee on Apprentice Training,* established by EO 6750–C of June 27, 1934. Functioned as part of *Division of Labor Standards,* Department of Labor, pursuant to act of Aug. 16, 1937 (50 Stat. 664). Transferred to *Office of Administrator, Federal Security Agency,* by EO 9139 of Apr. 18, 1942. Transferred to *Bureau of Training, War Manpower Commission,* by EO 9247 of Sept. 17, 1942. Returned to the Department of Labor by EO 9617 of Sept. 19, 1945.

Archive of Folksong Renamed Archive of Folk Culture by administrative order of Deputy Librarian of Congress, effective Sept. 21, 1981.

Archives Council, National Established by act of June 19, 1934 (48 Stat. 1122). Transferred to General Services Administration by act of June 30, 1949 (63 Stat. 378). Terminated on establishment of Federal Records Council by act of Sept. 5, 1950 (64 Stat. 583).

Archives Establishment, National *Office of Archivist of the U.S.* and *National Archives* created by act of June 19, 1934 (48 Stat. 1122). Transferred to General Services Administration by act of June 30, 1949 (63 Stat. 381), and incorporated as *National Archives and Records Service* by order of General Services Administrator, together with functions of *Division of the Federal Register, National Archives Council, National Historical Publications Commission,* National Archives Trust Fund Board, *Trustees of the Franklin D. Roosevelt Library,* and Administrative Committee of the Federal Register. Transferred from General Services Administration to National Archives and Records Administration by act of Oct. 19, 1984 (98 Stat. 2283), along with certain functions of Administrator of General Services transferred to Archivist of the United States, effective Apr. 1, 1985.

Archives and Records Service, National *See* **Archives Establishment, National**

Archives Trust Fund Board, National *See* **Archives Establishment, National**

Area Redevelopment Administration Established May 8, 1961, by the Secretary of Commerce pursuant to act of May 1, 1961 (75 Stat. 47) and Reorg. Plan No. 5 of 1950, effective May 24, 1950. Terminated Aug. 31, 1965, by act of June 30, 1965 (79 Stat. 195). Functions transferred to Economic Development Administration in the Department of Commerce by Department Order 4–A, effective Sept. 1, 1965.

Arlington Memorial Amphitheater Commission Established by act of Mar. 4, 1921 (41 Stat. 1440). Abolished by act of Sept. 2, 1960 (74 Stat. 739), and functions transferred to the Secretary of Defense.

Arlington Memorial Bridge Commission Established by act of Mar. 4, 1913 (37 Stat. 885; D.C. Code (1951 ed.) 8–158). Abolished by EO 6166 of June 10, 1933, and functions transferred to *Office of National Parks, Buildings, and Reservations.*

Armed Forces, U.S. Court of Appeals for the *See* **Military Appeals, United States Court of**

Armed Forces, Industrial College of the Renamed Dwight D. Eisenhower School for National Security and Resource Strategy by act of Dec. 31, 2011 (125 Stat. 1701).

Armed Forces Medical Library Founded in 1836 as *Library of the Surgeon General's Office,* U.S. Army. Later known as *Army Medical Library,* then *Armed Forces Medical Library* in 1952. Personnel and property transferred to National Library of Medicine established in Public Health Service by act of Aug. 3, 1956 (70 Stat. 960).

Armed Forces Museum Advisory Board, National Established by act of Aug. 30, 1961 (75

Stat. 414). Functions discontinued due to lack of funding.

Armed Forces Staff College Renamed Joint Forces Staff College by act of Oct. 30, 2000 (144 Stat. 165A–230).

Armed Services Renegotiation Board Established by Secretary of Defense directive of July 19, 1948. Abolished by Secretary's letter of Jan. 18, 1952, and functions transferred to *Renegotiation Board.*

Arms Control and Disarmament Agency, U.S. Established by act of Sept. 26, 1961 (75 Stat. 631). Abolished by act of Oct. 21, 1998 (112 Stat. 2681– 767) and functions transferred to the Secretary of State.

Army Communications Command, U.S. Renamed U.S. Army Information Systems Command by Department General Order No. 26 of July 25, 1984.

Army Industrial College Established in *Department of War* by General Order No. 7 of February 25, 1924. Renamed The Industrial College of the Armed Forces by *Department of War* memorandum of April 11, 1946.

Army Materiel Development and Readiness Command, U.S. Renamed U.S. Army Materiel Command by Department General Order No. 28 of Aug. 15, 1984.

Army and Navy, Joint Board Placed under direction of President by military order of July 5, 1939. Abolished Sept. 1, 1947, by joint letter of Aug. 20, 1947, to President from Secretaries of *War* and Navy.

Army and Navy Staff College Established Apr. 23, 1943, and operated under Joint Chiefs of Staff. Redesignated the National War College, effective July 1, 1946.

Army Specialist Corps Established in *Department of War* by EO 9078 of Feb. 26, 1942. Abolished by the *Secretary of War* Oct. 31, 1942, and functions merged into central *Officer Procurement Service.*

Arts, National Collection of Fine Established within Smithsonian Institution by act of Mar. 24, 1937 (50 Stat. 51). Renamed *National Museum of American Art* in Smithsonian Institution by act of Oct. 13, 1980 (94 Stat. 1884).

Arthritis, Diabetes, and Digestive and Kidney Diseases, National Institute of *See* **Arthritis, Metabolism, and Digestive Diseases, National Institute of**

Arthritis, Metabolism, and Digestive Diseases, National Institute of Renamed *National Institute of Arthritis, Diabetes, and Digestive and Kidney Diseases* by Secretary's order of June 15, 1981, pursuant to act of Dec. 19, 1980 (94 Stat. 3184). Renamed National Institute of Diabetes and Digestive and Kidney Diseases and National Institute of Arthritis and Musculoskeletal and Skin Diseases by act of Nov. 20, 1985 (99 Stat. 820).

Arts, Advisory Committee on the Established under authority of act of Sept. 20, 1961 (75 Stat. 527). Terminated July 1973 by act of Oct. 6, 1972. Formally abolished by Reorg. Plan No. 2 of 1977, effective Apr. 1, 1978.

Arts, National Council on the Established in Executive Office of the President by act of Sept. 3, 1964 (78 Stat. 905). Transferred to National Foundation on the Arts and the Humanities by act of Sept. 29, 1965 (79 Stat. 845).

Assay Commission, Annual Established initially by act of Apr. 2, 1792 (1 Stat. 250) and by act of Feb. 12, 1873 (Revised Statute sec. 3647; 17 Stat. 432). Terminated and functions transferred to the Secretary of the Treasury by act of Mar. 14, 1980 (94 Stat. 98).

Assistance, Bureau of Public Renamed *Bureau of Family Services* by order of the *Secretary of Health, Education, and Welfare,* effective Jan. 1, 1962. Functions redelegated to *Social and Rehabilitation Service* by Secretary's reorganization of Aug. 15, 1967.

Assistance Coordinating Committee, Adjustment Established by act of Jan. 3, 1975 (88 Stat. 2040). Inactive since 1981.

Assistance Payments Administration Established by *Secretary of Health, Education, and Welfare* reorganization of Aug. 15, 1967. Transferred by *Secretary's* reorganization of Mar. 8, 1977 (42 FR 13262), from *Social and Rehabilitation Service* to Social Security Administration.

Athletics, Interagency Committee on International Established by EO 11117 of Aug. 13, 1963. Terminated by EO 11515 of Mar. 13, 1970.

Atlantic-Pacific Interoceanic Canal Study Commission Established by act of Sept. 22, 1964 (78 Stat. 990). Terminated Dec. 1, 1970, pursuant to terms of act.

Atomic Energy Commission Established by act of Aug. 1, 1946 (60 Stat. 755). Abolished by act of Oct. 11, 1974 (88 Stat. 1237) and functions transferred to *Energy Research and Development Administration* and Nuclear Regulatory Commission.

Aviation, Interdepartmental Committee on Civil International Established by Presidential letter of June 20, 1935. Terminated on organization of *Civil Aeronautics Authority.*

Aviation Agency, Federal Established by act of Aug. 23, 1958 (72 Stat. 731). Transferred to Secretary of Transportation by act of Oct. 15, 1966 (80 Stat. 931). *Agency* reestablished as Federal Aviation Administration by act of Jan 12, 1983 (96 Stat. 2416).

Aviation Commission, Federal Established by act of June 12, 1934 (48 Stat. 938). Terminated Feb. 1, 1935, under provisions of act.

Beltsville Research Center Established to operate with other agencies of the Department of Agriculture under *Agricultural Research Administration.*

Consolidated into *Agricultural Research Administration,* the Department of Agriculture, by EO 9069 of Feb. 23, 1942.

Bilingual Education and Minority Languages Affairs, Office of Renamed Office of English Language Acquisition, Language Enhancement, and Academic Achievement for Limited English Proficient Students by act of Jan. 8, 2002 (115 Stat. 2089).

Biobased Products and Bioenergy, Advisory Committee on Established by EO 13134 of June 3, 1999. Abolished by EO 13423 of Jan. 24, 2007.

Biobased Products and Bioenergy, Interagency Council on Established by EO 13134 of June 3, 1999. Abolished by EO 13423 of Jan. 24, 2007.

Biobased Products and Bioenergy Coordination Office, National Established by EO 13134 of June 3, 1999. Abolished by EO 13423 of Jan. 24, 2007.

Biological Service, National Established in the Department of the Interior in 1995 by Secretarial order. Transferred to U.S. Geological Survey as new Biological Resources Division by Secretarial Order No. 3202, Sept. 30, 1996.

Biological Survey, Bureau of Established by Secretary's order July 1, 1885, as part of *Division of Entomology,* Department of Agriculture. Made separate bureau by act of Apr. 23, 1904 (33 Stat. 276). Transferred to the Department of the Interior by Reorg. Plan No. II of 1939, effective July 1, 1939. Consolidated with *Bureau of Fisheries* into *Fish and Wildlife Service* by Reorg. Plan No. III of 1940, effective June 30, 1940.

Biological Survey, National Established in the Department of the Interior by Secretarial Order 3173 of Sept. 29, 1993. Renamed *National Biological Service* by Secretarial order in 1995.

Blind, Inc., American Printing House for the Established in 1858 as privately owned institution in Louisville, KY. Functions of the Secretary of the Treasury, except that relating to perpetual trust funds, transferred to *Federal Security Agency* by Reorg. Plan No. II of 1939, effective July 1, 1939. Functions performed by *Department of Health, Education, and Welfare* transferred to the Department of Education.

Blind-made Products, Committee on Purchases of Established by act of June 25, 1938 (52 Stat. 1196). Renamed *Committee for Purchase of Products and Services of the Blind and Other Severely Handicapped* by act of June 23, 1971 (85 Stat. 77). Renamed *Committee for Purchase from the Blind and Other Severely Handicapped* by act of July 25, 1974 (88 Stat. 392). Renamed Committee for Purchase From People Who Are Blind or Severely Disabled by act of Oct. 29, 1992 (106 Stat. 4486).

Blind and Other Severely Handicapped, Committee for Purchase of Products and Services of the *See* **Blind-made Products, Committee on Purchases of**

Board. *See other part of title*

Bond and Spirits Division Established as *Taxes and Penalties Unit,* as announced by Assistant to Attorney General in departmental circular of May 25, 1934, pursuant to EO 6639 of May 10, 1934. Abolished by administrative order of October 1942, and functions transferred to Tax, Claims, and Criminal Divisions, Department of Justice.

Bonneville Power Administration Established by the Secretary of the Interior pursuant to act of Aug. 20, 1937 (50 Stat. 731). Transferred to the Department of Energy by act of Aug. 4, 1977 (91 Stat. 578).

Boston National Historic Sites Commission Established by joint resolution of June 16, 1955 (69 Stat. 137). Terminated June 16, 1960, by act of Feb. 19, 1957 (71 Stat. 4).

Brazil-U.S. Defense Commission, Joint Established in May 1942 by agreement between the U.S. and Brazil. Terminated in September 1977 at direction of Brazilian Government.

Broadcast Bureau Merged with *Cable Television Bureau* to form Mass Media Bureau by Federal Communications Commission order, effective Nov. 30, 1982.

Broadcast Intelligence Service, Foreign *See* **Broadcast Monitoring Service, Foreign**

Broadcast Monitoring Service, Foreign Established in Federal Communications Commission by Presidential directive of Feb. 26, 1941. Renamed *Foreign Broadcast Intelligence Service* by FCC order of July 28, 1942. Transferred to *Department of War* by Secretarial order of Dec. 30, 1945. Act of May 3, 1945 (59 Stat. 110), provided for liquidation 60 days after Japanese armistice. Transferred to *Central Intelligence Group* Aug. 5, 1946, and renamed *Foreign Broadcast Information Service.*

Budget, Bureau of the Established by act of June 10, 1921 (42 Stat. 20), in the Department of the Treasury under immediate direction of President. Transferred to Executive Office of the President by Reorg. Plan No. I of 1939, effective July 1, 1939. Reorganized by Reorg. Plan No. 2 of 1970, effective July 1, 1970, and renamed Office of Management and Budget.

Buildings Administration, Public Established as part of *Federal Works Agency* by Reorg. Plan No. I of 1939, effective July 1, 1939. Abolished by act of June 30, 1949 (63 Stat. 380), and functions transferred to General Services Administration.

Buildings Branch, Public Organized in *Procurement Division,* established in the Department of the Treasury by EO 6166 of June 10, 1933. Consolidated with *Branch of Buildings Management,* National Park Service, to form *Public Buildings Administration, Federal Works Agency,* under Reorg. Plan No. I of 1939, effective July 1, 1939.

Buildings Commission, Public Established by act of July 1, 1916 (39 Stat. 328). Abolished by EO 6166 of June 10, 1933, and functions transferred to *Office of National Parks, Buildings, and Reservations,* Department of the Interior. Functions transferred to *Public Buildings Administration, Federal Works Agency,* under Reorg. Plan No. I of 1939, effective July 1, 1939.

Buildings Management, Branch of Functions of National Park Service (except those relating to monuments and memorials) consolidated with *Public Buildings Branch, Procurement Division,* Department of the Treasury, to form *Public Buildings Administration, Federal Works Agency,* in accordance with Reorg. Plan No. I of 1939, effective July 1, 1939.

Buildings and Public Parks of the National Capital, Office of Public Established by act of Feb. 26, 1925 (43 Stat. 983), by consolidation of *Office of Public Buildings and Grounds* under Chief of Engineers, U.S. Army, and *Office of Superintendent of State, War, and Navy Department Buildings.* Abolished by EO 6166 of June 10, 1933, and functions transferred to *Office of National Parks, Buildings, and Reservations,* Department of the Interior.

Bureau. *See other part of title*

Business, Cabinet Committee on Small Established by Presidential letter of May 31, 1956. Dissolved January 1961.

Business Administration, Domestic and International *See* **Business and Defense Services Administration**

Business and Defense Services Administration Established by the Secretary of Commerce Oct. 1, 1953, and operated under Department Organization Order 40–1. Abolished by Department Organization Order 40–1A of Sept. 15, 1970, and functions transferred to *Bureau of Domestic Commerce.* Functions transferred to *Domestic and International Business Administration,* effective Nov. 17, 1972. *Administration* terminated by Secretary's order of Dec. 4, 1977, and functions assumed by *Industry and Trade Administration.*

Business Economics, Office of Established by the Secretary of Commerce Jan. 17, 1946. Renamed *Office of Economic Analysis* Dec. 1, 1953. Transferred to the *Administration of Social and Economic Statistics* along with Bureau of the Census and renamed Bureau of Economic Analysis on Jan. 1, 1972.

Business Operations, Bureau of International Established by the Secretary of Commerce Aug. 8, 1961, by Departmental Orders 173 and 174. Abolished by Departmental Order 182 of Feb. 1, 1963, which established *Bureau of International Commerce.* Functions transferred to *Domestic and International Business Administration,* effective Nov. 17, 1972.

Cable Television Bureau Merged with *Broadcast Bureau* by Federal Communications Commission order to form Mass Media Bureau, effective Nov. 30, 1982.

California Debris Commission Established by act of Mar. 1, 1893 (27 Stat. 507). Abolished by act of Nov. 17, 1986 (100 Stat. 4229), and functions transferred to the Secretary of the Interior.

Canal Zone Government Established by act of Aug. 24, 1912 (37 Stat. 561). Abolished by act of Sept. 27, 1979 (93 Stat. 454).

Capital Housing Authority, National Established by act of June 12, 1934 (48 Stat. 930). Made agency of District of Columbia government by act of Dec. 24, 1973 (87 Stat. 779), effective July 1, 1974.

Capital Park Commission, National Established by act of June 6, 1924 (43 Stat. 463). *National Capital Park and Planning Commission* named successor by act of Apr. 30, 1926 (44 Stat. 374). Functions transferred to National Capital Planning Commission by act of July 19, 1952 (66 Stat. 781).

Capital Park and Planning Commission, National *See* **Capital Park Commission, National**

Capital Regional Planning Council, National Established by act of July 19, 1952 (66 Stat. 785). Terminated by Reorg. Plan No. 5 of 1966, effective Sept. 8, 1966.

Capital Transportation Agency, National Established by act of July 14, 1960 (74 Stat 537). Authorized to establish rapid rail transit system by act of Sept. 8, 1965 (79 Stat. 663). Functions transferred to Washington Metropolitan Area Transit Authority by EO 11373 of Sept. 20, 1967.

Career Executive Board Established by EO 10758 of Mar. 4, 1958. Terminated July 1, 1959, and EO 10758 revoked by EO 10859 of Feb. 5, 1960.

Caribbean Organization Act of June 30, 1961 (75 Stat. 194), provided for acceptance by President of Agreement for the Establishment of the Caribbean Organization, signed at Washington, June 21, 1960. Article III of Agreement provided for termination of *Caribbean Commission,* authorized by Agreement signed Oct. 30, 1946, on first meeting of Caribbean Council, governing body of *Organization.* Terminated, effective Dec. 31, 1965, by resolution adopted by Council.

Cemeteries and Memorials in Europe, National Supervision transferred from *Department of War* to American Battle Monuments Commission by EO 6614 of Feb. 26, 1934, which transfer was deferred to May 21, 1934, by EO 6690 of Apr. 25, 1934.

Cemeteries and Parks, National *Department of War* functions regarding National Cemeteries and Parks located in continental U.S. transferred to *Office of National Parks, Buildings, and Reservations,* Department of the Interior, by EO 6166 of June 10, 1933.

Cemetery System, National Established in the *Veterans' Administration* by act of June 18, 1973 (87 Stat. 75). Redesignated as the National Cemetery Administration by act of Nov. 11, 1998 (112 Stat. 3337).

Censorship, Office of Established by EO 8985 of Dec. 19, 1941. Terminated by EO 9631 of Sept. 28, 1945.

Censorship Policy Board Established by EO 8985 of Dec. 19, 1941. Terminated by EO 9631 of Sept. 28, 1945.

Census, Bureau of the *See* **Census Office**

Census Office Established temporarily within the Department of the Interior in accordance with act of Mar. 3, 1899. Established as a permanent office by act of Mar. 6, 1902. Transferred from the Department of the Interior to *Department of Commerce and Labor* by act of Feb. 14, 1903. Remained in the Department of Commerce under provisions of Reorganization Plan No. 5 of May 24, 1950, effective May 24, 1950.

Center. *See other part of title*

Central. *See other part of title*

Chemistry and Soils, Bureau of *See* **Agricultural and Industrial Chemistry, Bureau of**

Chesapeake Bay Center for Environmental Studies Established in 1965 in Annapolis, MD, as part of Smithsonian Institution by Secretarial order. Merged with *Radiation Biology Laboratory* by Secretarial Order July 1, 1983, to form Smithsonian Environmental Research Center.

Chief Information Officers Council Established by EO 13011 of July 16, 1996. Abolished by EO 13403 of May 12, 2006.

Chief People Officer, Office of the Renamed Office of the Chief Human Capital Officer by administrative order 5440.597 of June 16, 2006.

Chief Strategic Officer, Office of the Established by the Commissioner of Social Security Dec. 20, 2002. Abolished by Commissioner's memorandum of Jan. 14, 2008, and functions transferred to the Office of the Deputy Commissioner for Budget, Finance, and Management.

Child Development, Office of *See* **Children's Bureau**

Children's Bureau Established by act of Apr. 9, 1912 (37 Stat. 79). Placed in the Department of Labor by act of Mar. 4, 1913 (37 Stat. 737). Transferred, with exception of child labor functions, to *Social Security Administration, Federal Security Agency,* by Reorg. Plan No. 2 of 1946, effective July 16, 1946. Continued under *Administration* when *Agency* functions assumed by the *Department of Health, Education, and Welfare.* Reassigned to *Welfare Administration* by Department reorganization of Jan. 28, 1963. Reassigned to *Social and Rehabilitation Service* by Department reorganization of Aug. 15, 1967. Reassigned to *Office of Child Development* by Department reorganization order of Sept. 17, 1969.

Child Health and Human Development, National Institute of Established by act of Oct. 17, 1962 (76 Stat. 1072). Renamed Eunice Kennedy Shriver National Institute of Child Health and Human Development by act of Dec. 21, 2007 (121 Stat. 1826).

China, U.S. Court for Established by act of June 30, 1906 (34 Stat. 814). Transferred to the Department of Justice by EO 6166 of June 10, 1933, effective Mar. 2, 1934. Act of June 30, 1906, repealed effective Sept. 1, 1948 (62 Stat. 992).

Christopher Columbus Quincentenary Jubilee Commission Established by act of Aug. 7, 1984 (98 Stat. 1257). Terminated pursuant to terms of act.

Civil defense. *See* **Defense**

Civil Rights, Commission on Established by act of Sept. 9, 1957 (71 Stat. 634). Terminated in 1983 and reestablished by act of Nov. 30, 1983 (97 Stat. 1301). Renamed United States Commission on Civil Rights by act of Nov. 2, 1994 (108 Stat. 4683).

Civil Service Commission, U.S. Established by act of Jan. 16, 1883 (22 Stat. 403). Redesignated as Merit Systems Protection Board and functions transferred to Board and Office of Personnel Management by Reorg. Plan No. 2 of 1978, effective Jan. 1, 1979.

Civil War Centennial Commission Established by act of Sept. 7, 1957 (71 Stat. 626). Terminated May 1, 1966, pursuant to terms of act.

Civilian Conservation Corps Established by act of June 28, 1937 (50 Stat. 319). Made part of *Federal Security Agency* by Reorg. Plan No. I of 1939, effective July 1, 1939. Liquidation provided for by act of July 2, 1942 (56 Stat. 569), not later than June 30, 1943.

Civilian Health and Medical Program of the United States, Office of Established as field activity in the Department of Defense in 1974. Functions consolidated into the TRICARE Management Activity in November 1997 by Defense Reform Initiative.

Civilian Production Administration Established by EO 9638 of Oct. 4, 1945. Consolidated with other agencies to form *Office of Temporary Controls, Office for Emergency Management,* by EO 9809 of Dec. 12, 1946.

Civilian Service Awards Board, Distinguished Established by EO 10717 of June 27, 1957. Terminated by EO 12014 of Oct. 19, 1977, and functions transferred to *U.S. Civil Service Commission.*

Claims, U.S. Court of Established Feb. 25, 1855 (10 Stat. 612). Abolished by act of Apr. 2, 1982 (96 Stat. 26) and trial jurisdiction transferred to *U.S. Claims Court* and appellate functions merged with those of *U.S. Court of Customs and Patent Appeals* to form U.S. Court of Appeals for the Federal Circuit. *U.S. Claims Court* renamed U.S. Court of Federal Claims by act of Oct. 29, 1992 (106 Stat. 4516).

Claims Commission of the United States, International Established in the Department of State by act of Mar. 10, 1950 (64 Stat. 12). Abolished by

Reorg. Plan No. 1 of 1954, effective July 1, 1954, and functions transferred to Foreign Claims Settlement Commission of the United States.

Claims Settlement Commission of the United States, Foreign Established by Reorg. Plan No. 1 of 1954, effective July 1, 1954. Transferred to the Department of Justice by act of Mar. 14, 1980 (94 Stat. 96).

Clark Sesquicentennial Commission, George Rogers Established by Public Resolution 51 (45 Stat. 723). Expenditures ordered administered by the Department of the Interior by EO 6166 of June 10, 1933.

Classification Review Committee, Interagency Established by EO 11652 of Mar. 8, 1972. Abolished by EO 12065 of June 28, 1978.

Clemency Board, Presidential Established in Executive Office of the President by EO 11803 of Sept. 16, 1974. Final recommendations submitted to President Sept. 15, 1975, and *Board* terminated by EO 11878 of Sept. 10, 1975.

Coal Commission, National Bituminous Established under authority of act of Aug. 30, 1935 (49 Stat. 992). Abolished by Reorg. Plan No. II of 1939, effective July 1, 1939, and functions transferred to *Bituminous Coal Division,* Department of the Interior.

Coal Consumers' Counsel, Office of the Bituminous Established by act of Apr. 11, 1941 (55 Stat. 134), renewing provisions of act of Apr. 23, 1937 (50 Stat. 72) for 2 years to continue functions of *Consumers' Counsel Division,* Department of the Interior. Functions continued by acts of Apr. 24, 1943 (57 Stat. 68), and May 21, 1943 (57 Stat. 82). Terminated Aug. 24, 1943.

Coal Division, Bituminous Established July 1, 1939, by Secretary of the Interior Order 1394 of June 16, 1939, as amended by Order 1399, of July 5, 1939, pursuant to act of Apr. 3, 1939 (53 Stat. 562) and Reorg. Plan No. II of 1939, effective July 1, 1939. Administered functions vested in *National Bituminous Coal Commission* by act of Apr. 23, 1937 (50 Stat. 72). Act extended to Aug. 24, 1943, on which date it expired.

Coal Labor Board, Bituminous Established by act of July 12, 1921 (42 Stat. 140). Abolished as result of U.S. Supreme Court decision, May 18, 1936, in case of *Carter* v. *Carter Coal Company et al.*

Coal Mine Safety Board of Review, Federal Established by act of July 16, 1952 (66 Stat. 697). Inactive after Mar. 30, 1970, pursuant to act of Dec. 30, 1969 (83 Stat. 803).

Coal Mines Administration Established by the Secretary of the Interior July 1, 1943. Abolished by Secretary's Order 1977 of Aug. 16, 1944, as amended by Order 1982 of Aug. 31, 1944, and functions assumed by *Solid Fuels Administration for War. Administration* reestablished in the Department of the Interior by EO 9728 of May 21, 1946. Terminated June 30, 1947, by act of Mar. 27, 1942 (56 Stat. 176).

Coal Research, Office of Established in the Department of the Interior by act of July 7, 1960 (74 Stat. 336). Functions transferred to *Energy Research and Development Administration* by act of Oct. 11, 1974 (88 Stat. 1237).

Coalition Provisional Authority, Inspector General of the Established by act of Nov. 6, 2003 (117 Stat. 1234). Renamed Special Inspector General for Iraq Reconstruction by act of Oct. 28, 2004 (118 Stat. 2078.)

Coalition Provisional Authority, Office of the Inspector General of the Established by act of Nov. 6, 2003 (117 Stat. 1234). Renamed Office of the Special Inspector General for Iraq Reconstruction by act of Oct. 28, 2004 (118 Stat. 2078).

Coast and Geodetic Survey *See* **Coast Survey**

Coast Guard, U.S. Established by act of Jan. 28, 1915 (38 Stat. 800) as a military service and branch of the U.S. Armed Forces at all times and as a service in Treasury Department, except when operating as a service in the Navy. Transferred from the Department of the Treasury to the Department of the Navy by EO 8929 of Nov. 1, 1941. Returned to the Department of the Treasury by EO 9666 of Dec. 28, 1945. Transferred to the Department of Transportation by act of Oct. 15, 1966 (80 Stat. 931). Transferred to Homeland Security Department by act of Nov. 25, 2002 (116 Stat. 2249) with related authorities and functions of the Secretary of Transportation.

Coast Survey Established by act of Feb. 10, 1807 (2 Stat. 413). Redesignated as *Coast and Geodetic Survey* by act of June 20, 1878 (20 Stat. 206). Transferred to *Environmental Science Services Administration* by Reorg. Plan No. 2 of 1965, effective July 13, 1965.

Codification Board Established by act of June 19, 1937 (50 Stat. 304). Abolished by Reorg. Plan No. II of 1939, effective July 1, 1939, and functions transferred to *Division of the Federal Register.*

Coinage, Joint Commission on the Established by act of July 23, 1965 (79 Stat. 258). Expired Jan. 4, 1975, pursuant to act of Oct. 6, 1972 (88 Stat. 776).

Columbia Institution for the Instruction of the Deaf and Dumb, and the Blind Established by act of Feb. 16, 1857 (11 Stat. 161). Renamed *Columbia Institution for the Instruction of the Deaf and Dumb* by act of Feb. 23, 1865 (13 Stat. 436). Renamed *Columbia Institution for the Deaf* by act of Mar. 4, 1911 (36 Stat. 1422). Renamed *Gallaudet College* by act of June 18, 1954 (68 Stat. 265). Functions of the *Department of Health, Education, and Welfare* transferred to the Department of Education by act of Oct. 17, 1979 (93 Stat. 695). Renamed Gallaudet University by act of Aug. 4, 1986 (100 Stat. 781).

Commander in Chief, U.S. Fleet, and Chief of Naval Operations Duties of two positions prescribed by EO 8984 of Dec. 18, 1941. Combined under one officer by EO 9096 of Mar. 12, 1942.

Commerce, Bureau of Domestic *See* **Business and Defense Services Administration**

Commerce, Bureau of Foreign Established by the Secretary of Commerce Oct. 12, 1953, by Reorg. Plan No. 5 of 1950, effective May 24, 1950. Abolished by department order of Aug. 7, 1961, and functions vested in *Bureau of International Programs* and *Bureau of International Business Operations.*

Commerce, Bureau of Foreign and Domestic Established by act of Aug. 23, 1912 (37 Stat. 407). Functions reassigned to other offices of the Department of Commerce due to internal reorganizations.

Commerce, Bureau of International*See* **Business Operations, Bureau of International**

Commerce Service, Foreign Established in *Bureau of Foreign and Domestic Commerce,* Department of Commerce, by act of Mar. 3, 1927 (44 Stat. 1394). Transferred to the Department of State as part of Foreign Service by Reorg. Plan No. II of 1939, effective July 1, 1939.

Commercial Company, U.S. Established Mar. 27, 1942, as subsidiary of *Reconstruction Finance Corporation.* Transferred to *Office of Economic Warfare* by EO 9361 of July 15, 1943. *Office* consolidated into *Foreign Economic Administration* by EO 9380 of Sept. 25, 1943. Functions returned to *Corporation* by EO 9630 of Sept. 27, 1945, until June 30, 1948.

Commercial Policy, Executive Committee on Established by Presidential letter of Nov. 11, 1933, to Secretary of State. Abolished by EO 9461 of Aug. 7, 1944.

Commercial Standards Division Transferred with *Division of Simplified Trade Practice* from *National Bureau of Standards* to the Secretary of Commerce by Reorg. Plan No. 3 of 1946, effective July 16, 1946, to permit reassignment to *Office of Domestic Commerce.* Functions transferred to *National Bureau of Standards* by the Department of Commerce Order 90, June 7, 1963, pursuant to Reorg. Plan No. 5 of 1950, effective May 24, 1950.

Commission. *See other part of title*

Committee. *See also other part of title*

Committee Management Secretariat Established in the Office of Management and Budget Jan. 5, 1973, by act of Oct. 6, 1972 (86 Stat. 772). Functions transferred to General Services Administrator by Reorg. Plan No. 1 of 1977, effective Apr. 1, 1978. Reassigned to the *National Archives and Records Service* by GSA order of Feb. 22, 1979. Transferred in Archives to Office of the Federal Register by GSA order of Oct. 14, 1980. Transferred to Office of the Archivist of the United States by GSA order of Sept. 24, 1982. Reassigned to Office of Program Initiatives, GSA, by GSA order of May 18, 1984. Transferred to Office of Management Services, GSA, by GSA order of Apr. 7, 1986.

Commodities Corporation, Federal Surplus *See* **Relief Corporation, Federal Surplus**

Commodity Credit Corporation Organized by EO 6340 of Oct. 16, 1933, and managed in close affiliation with *Reconstruction Finance Corporation.* Transferred to the Department of Agriculture by Reorg. Plan No. I of 1939, effective July 1, 1939.

Commodity Exchange Administration *See* **Grain Futures Administration**

Commodity Exchange Authority *See* **Grain Futures Administration**

Commodity Exchange Commission Established by act of Sept. 21, 1922 (42 Stat. 998). Functions transferred to Commodity Futures Trading Commission by act of Oct. 23, 1974 (88 Stat. 1414).

Commodity Stabilization Service Established in the Department of Agriculture Nov. 2, 1953, by Secretary's Memorandum 1320, supp. 4. Renamed Agricultural Stabilization and Conservation Service by Secretary's Memorandum 1458 of June 14, 1961, effective June 5, 1961.

Communication Agency, International *See Information Agency, U.S.*

Communications Program, Joint Tactical Combined with *Joint Interoperability of the Tactical Command and Control Systems Programs* to form Joint Tactical Command, Control, and Communications Agency in July 1984, pursuant to DOD Directive 5154.28.

Community Development Corporation Established in the Department of Housing and Urban Development by act of Dec. 31, 1970 (84 Stat. 1791). Renamed *New Community Development Corporation* by act of Aug. 22, 1974 (88 Stat. 725). Abolished Nov. 30, 1983, by act of Nov. 30, 1983 (97 Stat. 1238), and functions transferred to Assistant Secretary for Community Planning and Development, Department of Housing and Urban Development.

Community Development Corporation, New *See* **Community Development Corporation**

Community Facilities, Bureau of Established in 1945 by *Federal Works Administrator.* Transferred by act of June 30, 1949 (63 Stat. 380), to General Services Administration, functioning as *Community Facilities Service.* Certain functions transferred to various agencies, including the Department of the Interior, *Housing and Home Finance Agency,* and *Federal Security Agency* by Reorg. Plans Nos. 15, 16, and 17 of 1950, effective May 24, 1950.

Community Facilities Administration Established in *Housing and Home Finance Agency* by Administrator's Organizational Order 1 of Dec. 23, 1954. Terminated by act of Sept. 9, 1965 (79 Stat. 667), and functions transferred to the Department of Housing and Urban Development.

Community Organization, Committee on Established in *Office of Defense Health and Welfare Services* Sept. 10, 1941. Functions transferred to *Federal Security Agency* by EO 9338 of Apr. 29, 1943.

Community Relations Service Established in the Department of Commerce by act of July 2, 1964 (78 Stat. 241). Transferred to the Department of Justice by Reorg. Plan No. 1 of 1966, effective Apr. 22, 1966.

Community Service, Commission on National and Established by act of Nov. 16, 1990 (104 Stat. 3168). Abolished by act of Sept. 21, 1993, and functions vested in the Board of Directors or the Executive Director prior to Oct. 1, 1993, transferred to the Corporation for National and Community Service (107 Stat. 873, 888).

Community Services Administration Established by act of Jan. 4, 1975 (88 Stat. 2291) as successor to *Office of Economic Opportunity*. Abolished as independent agency through repeal of act of Aug. 20, 1964 (except titles VIII and X of such act) by act of Aug. 13, 1981 (95 Stat. 519).

Community Services Administration Functions concerning Legal Services Program transferred to Legal Services Corporation by act of July 25, 1974 (88 Stat. 389). Renamed *Public Services Administration* by *Health, Education, and Welfare* departmental notice of Nov. 3, 1976. Transferred to *Office of Human Development* by Secretary's reorganization of Mar. 8, 1977 (42 FR 13262).

Community War Services Established in *Office of the Administrator* under EO 9338 of Apr. 29, 1943, and *Federal Security Agency* order. Terminated Dec. 31, 1946, by act of July 26, 1946 (60 Stat. 695).

Conciliation Service, U.S. Established by act of Mar. 4, 1913 (37 Stat. 738). Functions transferred to Federal Mediation and Conciliation Service, established by act of June 23, 1947 (61 Stat. 153).

Conference on Security and Cooperation in Europe Renamed Organization for Security and Cooperation in Europe by EO 13029, Dec. 3, 1996 (61 FR 64591).

Consolidated Farm Service Agency Established by act of Oct. 13, 1994 (108 Stat. 3214). Renamed Farm Service Agency (61 FR 1109), effective Jan. 16, 1996.

Constitution, Commission on the Bicentennial of the United States Established by act of Sept. 29, 1983, as amended (97 Stat. 722). Terminated by act of Dec. 3, 1991 (105 Stat. 1232).

Constitution, transfer of functions *See* **Statutes at Large and other matters**

Construction, Collective Bargaining Committee in Established by EO 11849 of Apr. 1, 1975. Inactive since Jan. 7, 1976. Formally abolished by EO 12110 of Dec. 28, 1978.

Construction, Equipment and Repairs, Bureau of Established in the Department of the Navy by act of Aug. 31, 1842 (5 Stat. 579). Abolished by act of July 5, 1862 (12 Stat. 510), and functions distributed among *Bureau of Equipment and Recruiting, Bureau of Construction and Repair,* and *Bureau of Steam Engineering*.

Construction Branch Established in the Department of the Treasury in 1853 and designated *Bureau of Construction* under control of *Office of Supervising Architect* by Sept. 30, 1855. *Office* incorporated into *Public Buildings Branch, Procurement Division,* by EO 6166 of June 10, 1933. Transferred to *Federal Works Agency* by Reorg. Plan No. I of 1939, effective July 1, 1939, when *Public Buildings Branch* of *Procurement Division, Bureau of Buildings Management,* National Park Service, Department of the Interior—so far as latter concerned with operation of public buildings for other departments or agencies—and *U.S. Housing Corporation* consolidated with *Public Buildings Administration, Federal Works Agency.*

Construction Industry Stabilization Committee Established by EO 11588 of Mar. 29, 1971. Abolished by EO 11788 of June 18, 1974.

Construction and Repair, Bureau of Established by act of July 5, 1862 (12 Stat. 510), replacing *Bureau of Construction, Equipment and Repairs.* Abolished by act of June 20, 1940 (54 Stat. 492), and functions transferred to *Bureau of Ships.*

Consumer Advisory Council Established by EO 11136 of Jan. 3, 1964. *Office of Consumer Affairs* established in Executive Office of the President by EO 11583 of Feb. 24, 1971, and Council reestablished in *Office.*

Consumer Affairs, Office of Established by EO 11583 of Feb. 24, 1971. Transferred to the *Department of Health, Education, and Welfare* by EO 11702 of Jan. 25, 1973.

Consumer Affairs Staff, National Business Council for Established in the Department of Commerce by departmental organization order of Dec. 16, 1971. Terminated by departmental order of Dec. 6, 1973, due to lack of funding.

Consumer agencies Consumer agencies of *National Emergency Council* and *National Recovery Administration* reorganized and functions transferred, together with those of *Consumers' Advisory Board, NRA,* and *Cabinet Committee on Price Policy,* to *Consumers' Division, NRA,* by EO 7120 of July 30, 1935. *Division* transferred to the Department of Labor by EO 7252 of Dec. 21, 1935. Transferred to *Division of Consumers' Counsel, Agricultural Adjustment Administration,* Department of Agriculture, by Secretary of Labor letter of Aug. 30, 1938, to the Secretary of Agriculture. Continued as *Consumer Standards Project* until June 30, 1941. Research on consumer standards continued by *Consumer Standards Section, Consumers' Counsel Division,* transferred to *Agricultural Marketing Administration* by administrative order of Feb. 28, 1942. Other project activities discontinued.

Consumer Cooperative Bank, National Established by act of Aug. 20, 1978 (92 Stat. 499). Removed from mixed-ownership, Government corporation status by acts of Sept. 13, 1982 (96 Stat. 1062) and Jan. 12, 1983 (96 Stat. 2478).

Consumer Information and Insurance Oversight, Office of Established by Health and Human Services Secretary's notice of April 19, 2010 (75 FR 20364). Abolished by Centers for Medicare & Medicaid's notice of Jan. 26, 2011 (76 FR 4703).

Consumer Interests, President's Committee on Established by EO 11136 of Jan. 3, 1964. Abolished by EO 11583 of Feb. 24, 1971.

Consumer and Marketing Service Established by the Secretary of Agriculture Feb. 2, 1965. Renamed Agricultural Marketing Service Apr. 2, 1972, by Secretary's order and certain functions transferred to Animal and Plant Health Inspection Service.

Consumers' Counsel Established in *National Bituminous Coal Commission* by act of Aug. 30, 1935 (49 Stat. 993). Office abolished by Reorg. Plan No. II of 1939, effective July 1, 1939, and functions transferred to Office of Solicitor, Department of the Interior, to function as *Consumers' Counsel Division* under direction of the Secretary of the Interior. Functions transferred to *Office of the Bituminous Coal Consumers' Counsel* June 1941 by act of Apr. 11, 1941 (55 Stat. 134).

Consumers' Counsel Division *See* **Consumers' Counsel**

Consumers' Counsel, Division of Established by act of May 12, 1933 (48 Stat. 31). Transferred by order of the Secretary of Agriculture from *Agricultural Adjustment Administration* to supervision of *Director of Marketing,* effective Feb. 1, 1940. Transferred to *Agricultural Marketing Administration* by administrative order of Feb. 28, 1942.

Consumers' Problems, Adviser on *See* **Consumer agencies**

Contract Committee Government *See* **Contract Compliance, Committee on Government**

Contract Compliance, Committee on Government Established by EO 10308 of Dec. 3, 1951. Abolished by EO 10479 of Aug. 13, 1953, which established successor *Government Contract Committee.* Abolished by EO 10925 of Mar. 6, 1961, and records and property transferred to *President's Committee on Equal Employment Opportunity.*

Contract Settlement, Office of Established by act of July 1, 1944 (58 Stat. 651). Transferred to *Office of War Mobilization and Reconversion* by act of Oct. 3, 1944 (58 Stat. 785). Terminated by EO 9809 of Dec. 12, 1946, and Reorg. Plan No. 1 of 1947, effective July 1, 1947, and functions transferred to the Department of the Treasury. Functions transferred to General Services Administration by act of June 30, 1949 (63 Stat. 380).

Contract Settlement Advisory Board Established by act of July 1, 1944 (58 Stat. 651). Transferred to the Department of the Treasury by EO 9809 of Dec. 12, 1946, and by Reorg. Plan No. 1 of 1947, effective July 1, 1947. Transferred to General Services Administration by act of June 30, 1949 (63 Stat. 380) and established as *Contract Review Board.* Renamed Board of Contract Appeals in 1961 by Administrator's order. Board established as independent entity within General Services Administration Feb. 27, 1979, pursuant to act of Nov. 1, 1978 (92 Stat. 2383).

Contract Settlement Appeal Board, Office of Established by act of July 1, 1944 (58 Stat. 651). Transferred to the Department of the Treasury by EO 9809 of Dec. 12, 1946, and by Reorg. Plan No. 1 of 1947, effective July 1, 1947. Functions transferred to General Services Administration by act of June 30, 1949 (63 Stat. 380). Abolished by act of July 14, 1952 (66 Stat. 627).

Contract Termination Board, Joint Established Nov. 12, 1943, by *Director of War Mobilization.* Functions assumed by *Office of Contract Settlement.*

Contracts Division, Public Established in the Department of Labor to administer act of June 30, 1936 (49 Stat. 2036). Consolidated with Wage and Hour Division by Secretarial order of Aug. 21, 1942. Absorbed by Wage and Hour Division by Secretarial order of May 1971.

Cooperation Administration, International Established by Department of State Delegation of Authority 85 of June 30, 1955, pursuant to EO 10610 of May 9, 1955. Abolished by act of Sept. 4, 1961 (75 Stat. 446), and functions redelegated to Agency for International Development pursuant to Presidential letter of Sept. 30, 1961, and EO 10973 of Nov. 3, 1961.

Cooperative State Research, Education, and Extension Service Established by act of Oct. 13, 1994 (108 Stat. 3178). Reorganized into the National Institute of Food and Agriculture by Secretary's Memorandum 1062–001 of Sept. 17, 2009.

Cooperative State Research Service Established in the Department of Agriculture. Incorporated into Cooperative State, Research, Education, and Extension Service under Department of Agriculture reorganization in 1995.

Coordinating Council for Comparative Effectiveness Research, Federal Established by act of Feb. 17, 2009 (123 Stat 187). Terminated by act of Mar. 23, 2010 (124 Stat. 747).

Coordinating Service, Federal *Office of Chief Coordinator* created by Executive order promulgated in *Bureau of the Budget* Circular 15, July 27, 1921, and duties enlarged by other *Bureau* circulars. Abolished by EO 6166 of June 10, 1933. Contract form, Federal traffic, and surplus property functions transferred to *Procurement Division* by order of the Secretary of the Treasury, approved by President Oct. 9, 1933, issued pursuant to EO's 6166 of June 10, 1933, and 6224 of July 27, 1933.

Copyright Arbitration Royalty Panels Established by act of Dec. 17, 1993 (107 Stat. 2304). Replaced by Copyright Royalty Judges under act of Nov. 30, 2004 (118 Stat. 2351).

Copyright Royalty Tribunal Established as an independent entity within the legislative branch by act of Oct. 19, 1976 (90 Stat. 2594). Abolished by act of Dec. 17, 1993 (107 Stat. 2304), and functions transferred to copyright arbitration royalty panels.

Copyrighted Works, National Commission on New Technological Uses of Established by act of Dec. 31, 1974 (88 Stat. 1873). Terminated Sept. 29, 1978, pursuant to terms of act.

Corporate Payments Abroad, Task Force on Questionable Established by Presidential memorandum of Mar. 31, 1976. Terminated Dec. 31, 1976, pursuant to terms of memorandum.

Corporation, Federal Facilities Established in the Department of the Treasury by EO 10539 of June 22, 1954. Placed under supervision of Director appointed by General Services Administrator by EO 10720 of July 11, 1957. Dissolved by act of Aug. 30, 1961 (75 Stat. 418), and functions transferred to Administrator of General Services.

Corregidor-Bataan Memorial Commission Established by act of Aug. 5, 1953 (67 Stat. 366). Terminated May 6, 1967, by act of Dec. 23, 1963 (77 Stat. 477).

Cost Accounting Standards Board Established by act of Aug. 15, 1970 (84 Stat. 796). Terminated Sept. 30, 1980, due to lack of funding. Reestablished by act of Nov. 17, 1988 (102 Stat. 4059).

Cost of Living Council Established by EO 11615 of Aug. 15, 1971. Abolished by EO 11788 of June 18, 1974.

Cotton Stabilization Corporation Organized June 1930 under laws of Delaware by *Federal Farm Board* pursuant to act of June 15, 1929 (46 Stat. 11). Certificate of dissolution filed with Corporation Commission of Delaware Dec. 27, 1934.

Cotton Textile Industry, Board of Inquiry for the Established by EO 6840 of Sept. 5, 1934. Abolished by EO 6858 of Sept. 26, 1934.

Council. *See other part of title*

Counterespionage Section Transferred from the Criminal Division to the National Security Division by act of Mar. 9, 2006 (120 Stat. 249).

Counterintelligence, Office of Established within the Department of Energy by Public Law 106–65 of Oct. 5, 1999 (113 Stat. 955). Merged with *Office of Intelligence* to form *Office of Intelligence and Counterintelligence* by memorandum of March 9, 2006 of the Secretary of Energy.

Counterterrorism Section Transferred from the Criminal Division to the National Security Division by act of Mar. 9, 2006 (120 Stat. 249).

Courts Under act of Aug. 7, 1939 (53 Stat. 1223), and revised June 25, 1948 (62 Stat. 913), to provide for administration of U.S. courts, administrative jurisdiction over all continental and territorial courts transferred to Administrative Office of the U.S. Courts, including U.S. courts of appeals and district courts, District Court for the Territory of Alaska, U.S. District Court for the District of the Canal Zone, District Court of Guam, District Court of the Virgin Islands, Court of Claims, Court of Customs and Patent Appeals, and Customs Courts.

Credit Unions, Bureau of Federal *See* **Credit Union System, Federal**

Credit Union System, Federal Established by act of June 26, 1934 (48 Stat. 1216), to be administered by *Farm Credit Administration.* Transferred to Federal Deposit Insurance Corporation by EO 9148 of Apr. 27, 1942, and Reorg. Plan No. 1 of 1947, effective July 1, 1947. Functions transferred to *Bureau of Federal Credit Unions, Federal Security Agency,* established by act of June 29, 1948 (62 Stat. 1091). Functions transferred to the *Department of Health, Education, and Welfare* by Reorg. Plan No. 1 of 1953, effective Apr. 11, 1953. Functions transferred to National Credit Union Administration by act of Mar. 10, 1970 (84 Stat. 49).

Crime, National Council on Organized Established by EO 11534 of June 4, 1970. Terminated by EO 12110 of Dec. 28, 1978.

Critical Materials Council, National Established within Executive Office of the President by act of July 31, 1984 (98 Stat. 1250). *Office* abolished in September 1993 due to lack of funding and functions transferred to the Office of Science and Technology Policy.

Crop Insurance Corporation, Federal Established by act of Feb. 16, 1938. Consolidated with the *Agricultural Stabilization and Conservation Service* and *Farmers' Home Administration* in 1995 to form the *Farm Service Agency* pursuant to act of Oct. 13, 1994 (108 Stat. 3178).

Crop Production Loan Office Authorized by Presidential letters of July 26, 1918, and July 26, 1919, to the Secretary of Agriculture. Further authorized by act of Mar. 3, 1921 (41 Stat. 1347). Transferred to Farm Credit Administration by EO 6084 of Mar. 27, 1933.

Cultural Center, National Established in Smithsonian Institution by act of Sept. 2, 1958 (72 Stat. 1698). Renamed John F. Kennedy Center for the Performing Arts by act of Jan. 23, 1964 (78 Stat. 4).

Customs, Bureau of Established under sec. 1 of act of Mar. 3, 1927 (19 U.S.C. 2071) in Treasury Department. Functions relating to award of numbers to undocumented vessels, vested in *Collectors of Customs,* transferred to Commandant of Coast Guard by EO 9083 of Feb. 27, 1942. Transfer made permanent by Reorg. Plan No. 3 of 1946, effective July 16, 1946. Redesignated U.S. Customs Service by the Department of the Treasury Order 165–23 of Apr. 4, 1973. Functions transferred to and agency established within Homeland Security Department by act of Nov. 25, 2002 (116 Stat. 2178).

Customs Court, U.S. Formerly established as Board of General Appraisers by act of June 10, 1890 (26 Stat. 136). Renamed *U.S. Customs Court* by act of May 26, 1926 (44 Stat. 669). Renamed U.S. Court of International Trade by act of Oct. 10, 1980 (94 Stat. 1727).

Customs and Patent Appeals, U.S. Court of Established by act of Mar. 2, 1929 (45 Stat. 1475). Abolished by act of Apr. 2, 1982 (96 Stat. 28) and functions merged with appellate functions of *U.S. Court of Claims* to form U.S. Court of Appeals for the Federal Circuit.

Dairy Industry, Bureau of *Bureau of Dairying* established in the Department of Agriculture by act of May 29, 1924 (43 Stat. 243). *Bureau of Dairy Industry* designation first appeared in act of May 11, 1926 (44 Stat. 499). Functions transferred to Agricultural Research Service by Secretary's Memorandum 1320, supp. 4, of Nov. 2, 1953.

Deepwater Horizon Oil Spill and Offshore Drilling, The National Commission on the Established by EO 13543 of May 21, 2010. Terminated March 11, 2011 pursuant to terms of order.

Defense, Advisory Commission to the Council of National *See* **Defense, Council of National**

Defense, Council of National Established by act of Aug. 29, 1916 (39 Stat. 649). *Advisory Commission*—composed of Advisers on Industrial Production, Industrial Materials, Employment, Farm Products, Price Stabilization, Transportation, and Consumer Protection—established by *Council* pursuant to act and approved by President May 29, 1940. *Commission* decentralized by merging divisions with newly created national defense units. Agencies evolved from *Commission,* except *Office of Agricultural War Relations* and *Office of Price Administration,* made units of *Office for Emergency Management. Council* inactive.

Defense, Office of Civilian Established in *Office for Emergency Management* by EO 8757 of May 20, 1941. Terminated by EO 9562 of June 4, 1945.

Defense Administration, Federal Civil Established in *Office for Emergency Management* by EO 10186 of Dec. 1, 1950; subsequently established as independent agency by act of Jan. 12, 1951 (64 Stat. 1245). Functions transferred to *Office of Defense and Civilian Mobilization* by Reorg. Plan No. 1 of 1958, effective July 1, 1958.

Defense Advanced Research Projects Agency Established as a separate agency of the Department of Defense by DOD Directive 5105.41 dated July 25, 1978. Renamed *Advanced Research Projects Agency* by order of the Secretary of Defense dated July 13, 1993. Reestablished by act of Feb. 10, 1996 (110 Stat. 406).

Defense Advisory Council, Civil Established by act of Jan. 12, 1951 (64 Stat. 1245). Transferred to *Office of Defense and Civilian Mobilization* by Reorg. Plan No. 1 of 1958, effective July 1, 1958.

Defense Aid Reports, Division of Established in *Office for Emergency Management* by EO 8751 of May 2, 1941. Abolished by EO 8926 of Oct. 28, 1941, which created *Office of Lend-Lease Administration.*

Defense Air Transportation Administration Established Nov. 12, 1951, by Department of Commerce Order 137. Abolished by Amendment 3 of Sept. 13, 1962, to Department Order 128 (revised) and functions transferred to *Office of the Under Secretary of Commerce for Transportation.*

Defense Atomic Support Agency Renamed *Defense Nuclear Agency* by General Order No. 1 of July 1, 1971.

Defense Audiovisual Agency Established by DOD Directive 5040.1 of June 12, 1979. Abolished by Secretary's memorandum of Apr. 19, 1985, and functions assigned to the military departments.

Defense Audit Service Established by DOD Directive of Oct. 14, 1976. Abolished by Deputy Secretary's memorandum of Nov. 2, 1982, and functions transferred to Office of the Inspector General.

Defense Civil Preparedness Agency Functions transferred from the Department of Defense to the Federal Emergency Management Agency by EO 12148 of July 20, 1979.

Defense and Civilian Mobilization Board Established by EO 10773 of July 1, 1938. Redesignated *Civil and Defense Mobilization Board* by act of Aug. 26, 1958 (72 Stat. 861). Abolished by *Office of Emergency Preparedness* Circular 1200.1 of Oct. 31, 1962.

Defense Communications Agency Established by direction of the Secretary of Defense on May 12, 1960. Renamed Defense Information Systems Agency by DOD Directive 5105.19 dated June 25, 1991.

Defense Communications Board Established by EO 8546 of Sept. 24, 1940. Renamed *Board of War Communications* by EO 9183 of June 15, 1942. Abolished by EO 9831 of Feb. 24, 1947, and property transferred to Federal Communications Commission.

Defense Coordinating Board, Civil Established by EO 10611 of May 11, 1955. EO 10611 revoked by EO 10773 of July 1, 1958.

Defense Electric Power Administration Established by Order 2605 of Dec. 4, 1950 of the Secretary of the Interior. Abolished June 30, 1953, by Secretary's Order 2721 of May 7, 1953. Reestablished by Departmental Manual Release No. 253 of Aug. 6, 1959. Terminated by Departmental Manual Release No. 1050 of Jan. 10, 1977.

Defense Fisheries Administration Established by Order 2605 of Dec. 4, 1950 of the Secretary of the Interior. Abolished June 30, 1953, by Secretary's Order 2722 of May 13, 1953.

Defense Health and Welfare Services, Office of Established by EO 8890 of Sept. 3, 1941. Terminated by EO 9338 of Apr. 29, 1943, and functions transferred to *Federal Security Agency.*

Defense Homes Corporation Incorporated pursuant to President's letter to the Secretary of the Treasury of Oct. 18, 1940. Transferred to *Federal Public Housing Authority* by EO 9070 of Feb. 24, 1942.

Defense Housing Coordinator Office established July 21, 1940, by *Advisory Commission to Council of National Defense.* Functions transferred to *Division of Defense Housing Coordination, Office for Emergency Management,* by EO 8632 of Jan. 11, 1941.

Defense Housing Division, Mutual Ownership Established by Administrator of *Federal Works Agency* under provisions of act of June 28, 1941 (55 Stat. 361). Functions transferred to *Federal Public Housing Authority, National Housing Agency,* by EO 9070 of Feb. 24, 1942.

Defense Intelligence College Established by DOD Directive 3305.1 of January 28, 1983. Renamed Joint Military Intelligence College by DOD Directive 3305.1 of January 14, 1998. *See also Defense Intelligence School.*

Defense Intelligence School Established by DOD Directive 5105.25 of November 2, 1962. Renamed Defense Intelligence College by DOD Directive 3305.1 of January 28, 1983.

Defense Investigative Service Established by the Secretary of Defense Jan. 1, 1972. Renamed Defense Security Service in November 1997 by Defense Reform Initiative.

Defense Manpower Administration Established by the Secretary of Labor by General Order 48, pursuant to EO 10161 of Sept. 9, 1950, and Reorg. Plan No. 6 of 1950, effective May 24, 1950. General Order 48 revoked by General Order 63 of Aug. 25, 1953, which established *Office of Manpower Administration* in Department.

Defense Mapping Agency Established as a the Department of Defense agency in 1972. Functions transferred to the National Imagery and Mapping Agency by act of Sept. 23, 1996 (110 Stat. 2677).

Defense Materials Procurement Agency Established by EO 10281 of Aug. 28, 1951. Abolished by EO 10480 of Aug. 14, 1953, and functions transferred to General Services Administration.

Defense Materials Service *See* **Emergency Procurement Service**

Defense Materiel Readiness Board Established by act of Jan. 28, 2008 (122 Stat. 260). Abolished by act of Jan. 2, 2013 (126 Stat. 2362).

Defense Mediation Board, National Established by EO 8716 of Mar. 19, 1941. Terminated on creation of *National War Labor Board, Office for Emergency Management* by EO 9017 of Jan. 12, 1942. Transferred to the Department of Labor by EO 9617 of Sept. 19, 1945. *Board* terminated by EO 9672 of Dec. 31, 1945, which established *National Wage Stabilization Board* in the Department of Labor. Terminated by EO 9809 of Dec. 12, 1946, and functions transferred to the Secretary of Labor and the Department of the Treasury, effective Feb. 24, 1947.

Defense Medical Programs Activity Functions consolidated into the TRICARE Management Activity in November 1997 by Defense Reform Initiative.

Defense Minerals Administration Established by Order 2605 of Dec. 4, 1950 of the Secretary of the Interior. Functions assigned to *Defense Materials Procurement Agency.* Functions of exploration for critical and strategic minerals redelegated to the Secretary of the Interior and administered by *Defense Minerals Exploration Administration* by Secretary's Order 2726 of June 30, 1953. Termination of program announced by Secretary June 6, 1958. Certain activities continued in *Office of Minerals Exploration,* Department of the Interior.

Defense Minerals Exploration Administration *See* **Defense Minerals Administration**

Defense Mobilization, Office of Established in Executive Office of the President by EO 10193 of Dec. 16, 1950. Superseded by *Office of Defense Mobilization* established by Reorg. Plan No. 3 of 1953, effective June 12, 1953, which assumed functions of former *Office, National Security Resources Board,* and critical materials stockpiling functions of Army, Navy, Air Force, and Interior Secretaries and of *Army and Navy Munitions Board.* Consolidated with *Federal Civil Defense Administration* into *Office of Defense and Civilian Mobilization* by Reorg. Plan No. 1 of 1958, effective July 1, 1958, and offices of Director and Deputy Director terminated.

Defense Mobilization Board Established by EO 10200 of Jan. 3, 1951, and restated in EO 10480 of Aug. 14, 1953. Terminated by EO 10773 of July 1, 1958.

Defense Nuclear Agency Established in 1971. Renamed *Defense Special Weapons Agency* by DOD Directive 5105.31 of June 14, 1995.

Defense Nuclear Counterintelligence, Office of Established by act of Oct. 5, 1999 (113 Stat. 960). Abolished by act of Oct. 17, 2006 (120 Stat. 2507) and functions transferred to the Secretary of Energy.

Defense Plant Corporation Established by act of June 25, 1940 (54 Stat. 572). Transferred from *Federal Loan Agency* to the Department of Commerce by EO 9071 of Feb. 24, 1942. Returned to *Federal Loan Agency* pursuant to act of Feb. 24, 1945 (59 Stat. 5). Dissolved by act of June 30, 1945 (59 Stat. 310), and functions transferred to *Reconstruction Finance Corporation.*

Defense Plants Administration, Small Established by act of July 31, 1951 (65 Stat. 131). Terminated July 31, 1953, by act of June 30, 1953 (67 Stat. 131). Functions relating to liquidation transferred to Small

Business Administration by EO 10504 of Dec. 1, 1953.

Defense Production Administration Established by EO 10200 of Jan. 3, 1951. Terminated by EO 10433 of Feb. 4, 1953, and functions transferred to *Office of Defense Mobilization.*

Defense Property Disposal Service Renamed Defense Reutilization and Marketing Service by Defense Logistics Agency General Order 10–85, effective July 1, 1985.

Defense Prisoner of War/Missing in Action Office Established by DOD Directive 5110.10, July 16, 1993. Renamed Defense Prisoner of War/Missing Personnel Office by Secretary of Defense memorandum of May 30, 1996.

Defense Public Works Division Established in *Public Works Administration.* Transferred to *Office of Federal Works Administrator* by administrative order of July 16, 1941. Abolished by administrative order of Mar. 6, 1942, and functions transferred to *Office of Chief Engineer, Federal Works Agency.*

Defense Purchases, Office for the Coordination of National Established by order of *Council of National Defense,* approved June 27, 1940. Order revoked Jan. 7, 1941, and records transferred to Executive Office of the President.

Defense Research Committee, National Established June 27, 1940, by order of *Council of National Defense.* Abolished by order of *Council* June 28, 1941, and reestablished in *Office of Scientific Research and Development* by EO 8807 of June 28, 1941. *Office* terminated by EO 9913 of Dec. 26, 1947, and property and records transferred to *National Military Establishment.*

Defense Resources Committee Established by Administrative Order 1496 of June 15, 1940. Replaced by *War Resources Council* by Administrative Order 1636 of Jan. 14, 1942. Inactive.

Defense Security Assistance Agency Established on Sept. 1, 1971. Renamed the Defense Security Cooperation Agency by DOD Directive 5105.38.

Defense Solid Fuels Administration Established by Order 2605 of Dec. 4, 1950 of the Secretary of the Interior. Abolished June 29, 1954, by Secretary's Order 2764.

Defense Special Weapons Agency Established by General Order No. 1 of July 1, 1971. Functions transferred to the Defense Threat Reduction Agency by DOD Directive 5105.62 of Sept. 30, 1998.

Defense Stockpile Manager, National Established by act of Nov. 14, 1986 (100 Stat. 4067). Functions transferred from the Administrator of General Services to the Secretary of Defense by EO 12626 of Feb. 25, 1988.

Defense Supplies Corporation Established under act of June 25, 1940 (54 Stat. 572). Transferred from *Federal Loan Agency* to the Department of Commerce by EO 9071 of Feb. 24, 1942. Returned to *Federal Loan Agency* by act of Feb. 24, 1945 (59 Stat. 5). Dissolved by act of June 30, 1945 (59 Stat. 310), and functions transferred to *Reconstruction Finance Corporation.*

Defense Supply Agency Renamed Defense Logistics Agency by DOD Directive 5105.22 of Jan. 22, 1977.

Defense Supply Management Agency Established in the Department of Defense by act of July 1, 1952 (66 Stat. 318). Abolished by Reorg. Plan No. 6 of 1953, effective June 30, 1953, and functions transferred to the Secretary of Defense.

Defense Technology Security Administration Established on May 10, 1985. Functions transferred to the Defense Threat Reduction Agency by DOD Directive 5105.62 of Sept. 30, 1998.

Defense Transport Administration Established Oct. 4, 1950, by order of Commissioner of *Interstate Commerce Commission* in charge of *Bureau of Service,* pursuant to EO 10161 of Sept. 9, 1950. Terminated by DTA Commissioner's order, effective July 1, 1955, and functions transferred to *Bureau of Safety and Service, Interstate Commerce Commission.*

Defense Transportation, Office of Established in *Office for Emergency Management* by EO 8989 of Dec. 18, 1941. Terminated by EO 10065 of July 6, 1949.

Deficit Reduction, Joint Select Committee on Established by act of Aug. 2, 2011 (125 Stat. 259). Terminated January 31, 2012, pursuant to the act (125 Stat. 263).

Director. *See other part of title*

Disarmament Administration, U.S. Established in the Department of State. Functions transferred to *U.S. Arms Control and Disarmament Agency* by act of Sept. 26, 1961 (75 Stat. 638).

Disarmament Problems, President's Special Committee on Established by President Aug. 5, 1955. Dissolved in February 1958.

Disaster Assistance Administration, Federal Functions transferred from the Department of Housing and Urban Development to the Federal Emergency Management Agency by EO 12148 of July 20, 1979.

Disaster Loan Corporation Grouped with other agencies to form *Federal Loan Agency* by Reorg. Plan No. I of 1939, effective July 1, 1939. Transferred to the Department of Commerce by EO 9071 of Feb. 24, 1942. Returned to *Federal Loan Agency* by act of Feb. 24, 1945 (59 Stat. 5). Dissolved by act of June 30, 1945 (59 Stat. 310), and functions transferred to *Reconstruction Finance Corporation.*

Disease Control, Center for Established within the Public Health Service by the *Secretary of Health, Education, and Welfare* on July 1, 1973. Renamed *Centers for Disease Control* by Health and Human

Services Secretary's notice of Oct. 1, 1980 (45 FR 67772). Renamed Centers for Disease Control and Prevention by act of Oct. 27, 1992 (106 Stat. 3504).

Displaced Persons Commission Established by act of June 25, 1948 (62 Stat. 1009). Terminated Aug. 31, 1952, pursuant to terms of act.

District of Columbia Established by acts of July 16, 1790 (1 Stat. 130), and Mar. 3, 1791. *Corporations of Washington and Georgetown* and *levy court of Washington County* abolished in favor of territorial form of government in 1871. Permanent commission government established July 1, 1878. District Government created as municipal corporation by act of June 11, 1878 (20 Stat. 102). Treated as branch of U.S. Government by various statutory enactments of Congress. District Government altered by Reorg. Plan No. 3 of 1967, effective Nov. 3, 1967. Charter for local government in District of Columbia provided by act of Dec. 24, 1973 (87 Stat. 774).

District of Columbia, Highway Commission of the Established by act of Mar. 2, 1893 (27 Stat 532). *National Capital Park and Planning Commission* named successor by act of Apr. 30, 1926 (44 Stat. 374). Functions transferred to National Capital Planning Commission by act of July 19, 1952 (66 Stat. 781).

District of Columbia, Reform-School of the Established by act of May 3, 1876 (19 Stat. 49). Renamed *National Training School for Boys* by act of May 27, 1908 (35 Stat. 380). Transferred to the Department of Justice by Reorg. Plan No. II of 1939, effective July 1, 1939, to be administered by Director of Bureau of Prisons.

District of Columbia Auditorium Commission Established by act of July 1, 1955 (69 Stat. 243). Final report submitted to Congress Jan. 31, 1957, pursuant to act of Apr. 27, 1956 (70 Stat. 115).

District of Columbia Redevelopment Land Agency Established by act of Aug. 2, 1946 (60 Stat. 790). Agency established as instrumentality of District Government by act of Dec. 24, 1973 (87 Stat. 774), effective July 1, 1974.

District of Columbia-Virginia Boundary Commission Established by act of Mar. 21, 1934 (48 Stat. 453). Terminated Dec. 1, 1935, to which date it had been extended by Public Resolution 9 (49 Stat. 67).

Division. *See other part of title*

Domestic Council Established in Executive Office of the President by Reorg. Plan No. 2 of 1970, effective July 1, 1970. Abolished by Reorg. Plan No. 1 of 1977, effective Mar. 26, 1978, and functions transferred to President and staff designated as *Domestic Policy Staff.* Pursuant to EO 12045 of Mar. 27, 1978, *Staff* assisted President in performance of transferred functions. Renamed Office of Policy Development in 1981. Abolished in February 1992 by President's reorganizational statement, effective May 1992.

Domestic Policy Staff *See* **Domestic Council**

Dominican Customs Receivership Transferred from *Division of Territories and Island Possessions,* Department of the Interior, to the Department of State by Reorg. Plan No. IV of 1940, effective June 30, 1940.

Drug Abuse, National Institute on Established within the National Institute of Mental Health, *Department of Health, Education, and Welfare* by act of Mar. 21, 1972 (86 Stat. 85). Removed from within the National Institute of Mental Health and made an entity within the Alcohol, Drug Abuse, and Mental Health Administration by act of May 14, 1974 (88 Stat. 136). Functions transferred to the Department of Health and Human Services by act of Oct. 17, 1979 (93 Stat. 695). (*See also* act of Oct. 27, 1986; 100 Stat. 3207–106.) Abolished by act of July 10, 1992 (106 Stat. 331). Reestablished by act of July 10, 1992 (106 Stat. 361).

Drug Abuse, President's Advisory Commission on Narcotic and Established by EO 11076 of Jan. 15, 1963. Terminated November 1963 under terms of order.

Drug Abuse Control, Bureau of Established in Food and Drug Administration, Department of Health and Human Services, to carry out functions of act of July 15, 1965 (79 Stat. 226). Functions transferred to *Bureau of Narcotics and Dangerous Drugs,* Department of Justice, by Reorg. Plan No. 1 of 1968, effective Apr. 8, 1968. Abolished by Reorg. Plan No. 2 of 1973, effective July 1, 1973, and functions transferred to Drug Enforcement Administration.

Drug Abuse Law Enforcement, Office of Established by EO 11641 of Jan. 28, 1972. Terminated by EO 11727 of July 6, 1973, and functions transferred to Drug Enforcement Administration.

Drug Abuse Policy, Office of Established in Executive Office of the President by act of Mar. 19, 1976 (90 Stat. 242). Abolished by Reorg. Plan No. 1 of 1977, effective Mar. 26, 1978, and functions transferred to President.

Drug-Free Schools, Office of Safe Abolished by the Secretary of Education on Sept. 25, 2011. Programs transferred to *Office of Safe and Healthy Students* within the Office of Elementary and Secondary Education.

Drug Abuse Prevention, Treatment, and Rehabilitation, Cabinet Committee on Established Apr. 27, 1976, by Presidential announcement. Terminated by Presidential memorandum of Mar. 14, 1977.

Drug Law Enforcement, Cabinet Committee for Established Apr. 27, 1976, pursuant to Presidential message to Congress of Apr. 27, 1976. Abolished by Presidential memorandum of Mar. 14, 1977.

Drug Law Enforcement, Cabinet Committee for Established Apr. 27, 1976, pursuant to

Presidential message to Congress of Apr. 27, 1976. Abolished by Presidential memorandum of Mar. 14, 1977.

Drugs, Bureau of Narcotics and Dangerous *See* **Drug Abuse Control, Bureau of**

Drugs and Biologics, National Center for Renamed *Center for Drugs and Biologics* by Food and Drug Administration notice of Mar. 9, 1984 (49 FR 10166). Reestablished as Center for Drug Evaluation and Research and Center for Biologics Evaluation and Research by Secretary's notice of Oct. 6, 1987 (52 FR 38275).

Drunk Driving, Presidential Commission on Established by EO 12358 of Apr. 14, 1982. Terminated Dec. 31, 1983, by EO 12415 of Apr. 5, 1983.

Dryden Research Center, Hugh L. Formerly separate field installation of National Aeronautics and Space Administration. Made component of Ames Research Center by NASA Management Instruction 1107.5A of Sept. 3, 1981.

Economic Administration, Foreign Established in *Office for Emergency Management* by EO 9380 of Sept. 25, 1943. Functions of *Office of Lend-Lease Administration, Office of Foreign Relief and Rehabilitation Operations, Office of Economic Warfare* (together with *U.S. Commercial Company, Rubber Development Corporation, Petroleum Reserves Corporation,* and *Export-Import Bank of Washington* and functions transferred thereto by EO 9361 of July 15, 1943), and foreign economic operations of *Office of Foreign Economic Coordination* transferred to *Administration.* Foreign procurement activities of *War Food Administration* and Commodity Credit Corporation transferred by EO 9385 of Oct. 6, 1943. Terminated by EO 9630 of Sept. 27, 1945, and functions redistributed to the Departments of State, Commerce, and Agriculture and the *Reconstruction Finance Corporation.*

Economic Analysis, Office of *See* **Business Economics, Office of**

Economic Cooperation Administration Established by act of Apr. 3, 1948 (62 Stat. 138). Abolished by act of Oct. 10, 1951 (65 Stat. 373), and functions transferred to *Mutual Security Agency* pursuant to EO 10300 of Nov. 1, 1951.

Economic Coordination, Office of Foreign *See* **Board of Economic Operations**

Economic Defense Board Established by EO 8839 of July 30, 1941. Renamed *Board of Economic Warfare* by EO 8982 of Dec. 17, 1941. *Board* terminated by EO 9361 of July 15, 1943, and *Office of Economic Warfare* established in *Office for Emergency Management. Office of Economic Warfare* consolidated with *Foreign Economic Administration* by EO 9380 of Sept. 25, 1943.

Economic Development, Office of Regional Established by the Secretary of Commerce Jan. 6, 1966, pursuant to act of Aug. 26, 1965 (79 Stat. 552). Abolished by Department Order 5A, Dec. 22, 1966, and functions vested in Economic Development Administration.

Economic Development Service, Foreign Established by order of the Secretary of Agriculture Nov. 8, 1969. Abolished by order of Secretary Feb. 6, 1972, and functions transferred to Economic Research Service.

Economic Growth and Stability, Advisory Board on Established by Presidential letter to Congress of June 1, 1953. Superseded by *National Advisory Board on Economic Policy* by Presidential direction Mar. 12, 1961. *Cabinet Committee on Economic Growth* established by President Aug. 21, 1962, to succeed *Board.*

Economic Management Support Center Established by Secretary of Agriculture Memorandum 1836 of Jan. 9, 1974. Consolidated with other Department units into *Economics, Statistics, and Cooperatives Service* by Secretary's Memorandum 1927, effective Dec. 23, 1977.

Economic Operations, Board of Established by Department of State order of Oct. 7, 1941. Abolished by departmental order of June 24, 1943, and functions transferred to *Office of Foreign Economic Coordination* established by same order. *Office* abolished by departmental order of Nov. 6, 1943, pursuant to EO 9380 of Sept. 25, 1943.

Economic Opportunity, Office of Established in Executive Office of the President by act of Aug. 20, 1964 (78 Stat. 508). All OEO programs except three transferred by administrative action to the Departments of *Health, Education, and Welfare,* Labor, and Housing and Urban Development July 6, 1973. Community Action, Economic Development, and Legal Services Programs transferred to *Community Services Administration* by act of Jan. 4, 1975 (88 Stat. 2310).

Economic Policy, Council on Established by Presidential memorandum of Feb. 2, 1973. Functions absorbed by *Economic Policy Board* Sept. 30, 1974.

Economic Policy, Council on Foreign Established Dec. 22, 1954, by Presidential letter of Dec. 11, 1954. Abolished by President Mar. 12, 1961, and functions transferred to Secretary of State.

Economic Policy, Council on International Established in Executive Office of the President by Presidential memorandum of January 1971. Reestablished by act of Aug. 29, 1972 (86 Stat. 646). Terminated Sept. 30, 1977, on expiration of statutory authority.

Economic Policy, National Advisory Board on *See* **Economic Growth and Stability, Advisory Board on**

Economic Policy Board, President's Established by EO 11808 of Sept. 30, 1974. Terminated by EO 11975 of Mar. 7, 1977.

Economic Recovery Advisory Board, President's Established by EO 13501 of February

6, 2009. Terminated February 12, 2011 pursuant to terms of order.

Economic Research Service Established by Secretary of Agriculture Memorandum 1446, supp. 1, of Apr. 3, 1961. Consolidated with other Department of Agriculture units into *Economics, Statistics, and Cooperatives Service* by Secretary's Memorandum 1927, effective Dec. 23, 1977. Redesignated as Economic Research Service by Secretarial order of Oct. 1, 1981.

Economic Security, Advisory Council on Established by EO 6757 of June 29, 1934. Terminated on approval of act of Aug. 14, 1935 (49 Stat. 620) Aug. 14, 1935.

Economic Security, Committee on Established by EO 6757 of June 29, 1934. Terminated as formal agency in April 1936, as provided in act, but continued informally for some time thereafter.

Economic Stabilization, Office of Established in *Office for Emergency Management* by EO 9250 of Oct. 3, 1942. Terminated by EO 9620 of Sept. 20, 1945, and functions transferred to *Office of War Mobilization and Reconversion.* Reestablished in *Office for Emergency Management* by EO 9699 of Feb. 21, 1946. Transferred by EO 9762 of July 25, 1946, to *Office of War Mobilization and Reconversion.* Consolidated with other agencies to form *Office of Temporary Controls* by EO 9809 of Dec. 12, 1946.

Economic Stabilization Agency Established by EO 10161 of Sept. 9, 1950, and EO 10276 of July 31, 1951. Terminated, except for liquidation purposes, by EO 10434 of Feb. 6, 1953. Liquidation completed Oct. 31, 1953, pursuant to EO 10480 of Aug. 14, 1953.

Economic Stabilization Board Established by EO 9250 of Oct. 3, 1942. Transferred to *Office of War Mobilization and Reconversion* by EO 9620 of Sept. 20, 1945. Returned to *Office of Economic Stabilization* on reestablishment by EO 9699 of Feb. 21, 1946. *Board* returned to *Office of War Mobilization and Reconversion* by EO 9762 of July 25, 1946. Functions terminated by EO 9809 of Dec. 12, 1946.

Economic Warfare, Board of *See* **Economic Defense Board**

Economic Warfare, Office of *See* **Economic Defense Board**

Economics, Bureau of Industrial Established by the Secretary of Commerce Jan. 2, 1980, in conjunction with Reorg. Plan No. 3 of 1979, effective Oct. 1, 1980, and operated under Department Organization Order 35-5B. Abolished at bureau level by Secretarial order, effective Jan. 22, 1984 (49 FR 4538). Industry-related functions realigned and transferred from Under Secretary for Economic Affairs to Under Secretary for International Trade. Under Secretary for Economic Affairs retained units to support domestic macroeconomic policy functions.

Economics, Statistics, and Cooperatives Service Renamed *Economics and Statistics Service* by Secretary of Agriculture Memorandum 2025 of Sept. 17, 1980. Redesignated as Economic Research Service and *Statistical Reporting Service* by Secretarial order of Oct. 1, 1981.

Economy Board, Joint Placed under direction of President by military order of July 5, 1939. Abolished Sept. 1, 1947, by joint letter of Aug. 20, 1947, from Secretaries of *War* and Navy to President.

Education, Federal Board for Vocational Established by act of Feb. 23, 1917 (39 Stat. 929). Functions transferred to the Department of the Interior by EO 6166 of June 10, 1933. Functions assigned to *Commissioner of Education* Oct. 10, 1933. *Office of Education* transferred from the Department of the Interior to the *Federal Security Agency* by Reorg. Plan No. I of 1939, effective July 1, 1939. *Board* abolished by Reorg. Plan No. 2 of 1946, effective July 16, 1946.

Education, National Institute of Established by act of June 23, 1972 (86 Stat. 327). Transferred to Office of Educational Research and Improvement, Department of Education, by act of Oct. 17, 1979 (93 Stat. 678), effective May 4, 1980.

Education, Office of Established as independent agency by act of Mar. 2, 1867 (14 Stat. 434). Transferred to the Department of the Interior by act of July 20, 1868 (15 Stat. 106). Transferred to *Federal Security Agency* by Reorg. Plan No. I of 1939, effective July 1, 1939. Functions of *Federal Security Administrator* administered by *Office of Education* relating to student loans and defense-related education transferred to *War Manpower Commission* by EO 9247 of Sept. 17, 1942.

Education, Office of Bilingual Abolished by act of Oct. 17, 1979 (93 Stat. 675), and functions transferred to Office of Bilingual Education and Minority Languages Affairs, Department of Education.

Education Beyond the High School, President's Committee on Established by act of July 26, 1956 (70 Stat. 676). Terminated Dec. 31, 1957. Certain activities continued by *Bureau of Higher Education, Office of Education.*

Education Division Established in the *Department of Health, Education, and Welfare* by act of June 23, 1972 (86 Stat. 327). Functions transferred to the Department of Education by act of Oct. 17, 1979 (93 Stat. 677).

Education Goals Panel, National Terminated by Congressional mandate, March 15, 2002.

Education Statistics, National Center for Established in the Office of the Assistant Secretary, Department of Health and Human Services, by act of Aug. 21, 1974 (88 Stat. 556). Transferred to the Office of Educational Research and Improvement, Department of Education, by act of Oct. 17, 1979 (93 Stat. 678), effective May 4, 1980. Renamed *Center for Education Statistics* by act of Oct. 17, 1986 (100 Stat. 1579). Renamed National

Center for Education Statistics by act of Apr. 28, 1988 (102 Stat. 331).

Educational and Cultural Affairs, Bureau of Established by Secretary of State in 1960. Terminated by Reorg. Plan No. 2 of 1977, effective July 1, 1978, and functions transferred to *International Communication Agency,* effective Apr. 1, 1978.

Educational and Cultural Affairs, Interagency Council on International Established Jan. 20, 1964, by Foreign Affairs Manual Circular, under authority of act of Sept. 21, 1961 (75 Stat. 527). Terminated Oct. 1973 following creation of Subcommittee on International Exchanges by National Security Council directive.

Educational Exchange, U.S. Advisory Commission on Established by act of Jan. 27, 1948 (62 Stat. 10). Abolished by act of Sept. 21, 1961 (75 Stat. 538), and superseded by U.S. Advisory Commission on International Educational and Cultural Affairs.

Efficiency, Bureau of Organized under act of Feb. 28, 1916 (39 Stat. 15). Abolished by act of Mar. 3, 1933 (47 Stat. 1519), and records transferred to *Bureau of the Budget.*

Elderly, Committee on Mental Health and Illness of the Established by act of July 29, 1975 (89 Stat. 347). Terminated Sept. 30, 1977.

Electoral votes for President and Vice President, transfer of functions *See* **State, Department of**

Electric Home and Farm Authority Incorporated Aug. 1, 1935, under laws of District of Columbia. Designated as U.S. agency by EO 7139 of Aug. 12, 1935. Continued by act of June 10, 1941 (55 Stat. 248). Grouped with other agencies in *Federal Loan Agency* by Reorg. Plan. No. I of 1939, effective July 1, 1939. Functions transferred to the Department of Commerce by EO 9071 of Feb. 24, 1942. Terminated by EO 9256 of Oct. 13, 1942.

Electric Home and Farm Authority, Inc. Organized Jan. 17, 1934, under laws of State of Delaware by EO 6514 of Dec. 19, 1933. Dissolved Aug. 1, 1935, and succeeded by *Electric Home and Farm Authority.*

Electricity Delivery and Energy Reliability, Office of Established by Secretary of Energy announcement of June 9, 2005. Position of director elevated to Assistant Secretary of Electricity Delivery and Energy Reliability by Secretary's memorandum EXEC-2007-010607 of Oct. 24, 2007.

Electricity Transmission and Distribution, Office of Renamed *Office of Electricity Delivery and Energy Reliability* by the Secretary of Energy's memo of Feb. 15, 2005.

Emergency Administration of Public Works, Federal Established by act of June 16, 1933 (48 Stat. 200). Operation continued by subsequent legislation, including act of June 21, 1938 (52 Stat. 816). Consolidated with *Federal Works Agency* as *Public Works Administration* by Reorg. Plan No. I of 1939, effective July 1, 1939. Functions transferred to *Office of Federal Works Administrator* by EO 9357 of June 30, 1943.

Emergency Conservation Work Established by EO 6101 of Apr. 5, 1933. Succeeded by *Civilian Conservation Corps.*

Emergency Council, National Established by EO 6433–A of Nov. 17, 1933. Consolidated with *Executive Council* by EO 6889–A of Oct. 29, 1934. Abolished by Reorg. Plan No. II of 1939, effective July 1, 1939, and functions (except those relating to *Radio Division* and *Film Service*) transferred to Executive Office of the President.

Emergency Council, Office of Economic Adviser to National Established by EO 6240 of Aug. 3, 1933, in connection with *Executive Council,* which later consolidated with *National Emergency Council.* Records and property used in preparation of statistical and economic summaries transferred to *Central Statistical Board* by EO 7003 of Apr. 8, 1935.

Emergency Management, Office for Established in Executive Office of the President by administrative order of May 25, 1940, in accordance with EO 8248 of Sept. 8, 1939. Inactive.

Emergency Management Agency, Federal Established in EO 12127 of Mar. 31, 1979. Functions transferred to Department of Homeland Security by act of Nov. 25, 2002 (116 Stat. 2213). Established as a distinct entity with the Department of Homeland Security by act of Oct. 4, 2006 (120 Stat. 1400).

Emergency Mobilization Preparedness Board Established Dec. 17, 1981, by the President. Abolished by Presidential directive of Sept. 16, 1985.

Emergency Planning, Office of Established as successor to *Office of Civil and Defense Mobilization* by act of Sept. 22, 1961 (75 Stat. 630). Renamed *Office of Emergency Preparedness* by act of Oct. 21, 1968 (82 Stat. 1194). Terminated by Reorg. Plan No. 2 of 1973, effective July 1, 1973, and functions transferred to the Departments of the Treasury and Housing and Urban Development and the General Services Administration.

Emergency Preparedness, Office of *See* **Emergency Planning, Office of**

Emergency Procurement Service Established Sept. 1, 1950, by Administrator of General Services. Renamed *Defense Materials Service* Sept. 7, 1956. Functions transferred to *Property Management and Disposal Service* July 29, 1966. *Service* abolished July 1, 1973, and functions transferred to Federal Supply Service, Public Buildings Service, and Federal Property Resources Service.

Emergency Relief Administration, Federal Established by act of May 12, 1933 (48 Stat. 55). Expired June 30, 1938, having been liquidated by *Works Progress Administrator* pursuant to act of May 28, 1937 (50 Stat. 352).

Employee-Management Relations Program, President's Committee on the Implementation of the Federal Established by EO 10988 of Jan. 17, 1962. Terminated upon submission of report to President June 21, 1963.

Employees' Compensation, Bureau of Transferred from *Federal Security Agency* to the Department of Labor by Reorg. Plan No. 19 of 1950, effective May 24, 1950. Functions absorbed by Employment Standards Administration Mar. 13, 1972.

Employees' Compensation Appeals Board Transferred from *Federal Security Agency* to the Department of Labor by Reorg. Plan No. 19 of 1950, effective May 24, 1950.

Employees' Compensation Commission, U.S. Established by act of Sept. 7, 1916 (39 Stat. 742). Abolished by Reorg. Plan No. 2 of 1946, effective July 16, 1946, and functions transferred to *Federal Security Administrator.*

Employment Board, Fair Established by *U.S. Civil Service Commission* pursuant to EO 9980 of July 26, 1948. Abolished by EO 10590 of Jan. 18, 1955.

Employment of People With Disabilities, President's Committee on Created by EO 12640 of May 10, 1988. Duties subsumed by the Office of Disability Employment within the Department of Labor as directed by Public Law 106–554 of Dec. 21, 2000.

Employment of the Physically Handicapped, President's Committee on Established by EO 10640 of Oct. 10, 1955, continuing *Committee* established by act of July 11, 1949 (63 Stat. 409). Superseded by President's Committee on Employment of the Handicapped established by EO 10994 of Feb. 14, 1962.

Employment Policy, President's Committee on Government Established by EO 10590 of Jan. 18, 1955. Abolished by EO 10925 of Mar. 6, 1961, and functions transferred to *President's Committee on Equal Employment Opportunity.*

Employment Practice, Committee on Fair Established in *Office of Production Management* by EO 8802 of June 25, 1941. Transferred to *War Manpower Commission* by Presidential letter effective July 30, 1942. Committee terminated on establishment of *Committee on Fair Employment Practice, Office for Emergency Management,* by EO 9346 of May 27, 1943. Terminated June 30, 1946, by act of July 17, 1945 (59 Stat. 743).

Employment Security, Bureau of Transferred from *Federal Security Agency* to the Department of Labor by Reorg. Plan No. 2 of 1949, effective Aug. 20, 1949. Abolished by order of Mar. 14, 1969 of the Secretary of Labor, and functions transferred to *Manpower Administration.*

Employment Service, U.S. Established in the Department of Labor in 1918 by departmental order. Abolished by act of June 6, 1933 (48 Stat. 113), and created as bureau with same name. Functions consolidated with unemployment compensation functions of *Social Security Board, Bureau of Employment Security,* and transferred to *Federal Security Agency* by Reorg. Plan No. I of 1939, effective July 1, 1939. *Service* transferred to *Bureau of Placement, War Manpower Commission,* by EO 9247 of Sept. 17, 1942. Returned to the Department of Labor by EO 9617 of Sept. 19, 1945. Transferred to *Federal Security Agency* by act of June 16, 1948 (62 Stat. 443), to function as part of *Bureau of Employment Security,* Social Security Administration. *Bureau,* including *U.S. Employment Service,* transferred to the Department of Labor by Reorg. Plan No. 2 of 1949, effective Aug. 20, 1949. Abolished by reorganization of *Manpower Administration,* effective Mar. 17, 1969, and functions assigned to *U.S. Training and Employment Service.*

Employment Stabilization Board, Federal Established by act of Feb. 10, 1931 (46 Stat. 1085). Abolished by EO 6166 of June 10, 1933. Abolition deferred by EO 6623 of Mar. 1, 1934, until functions of *Board* transferred to *Federal Employment Stabilization Office,* established in the Department of Commerce by same order. *Office* abolished by Reorg. Plan No. I of 1939, effective July 1, 1939, and functions transferred from the Department of Commerce to *National Resources Planning Board,* Executive Office of the President.

Employment Stabilization Office, Federal. *See* **Employment Stabilization Board, Federal**

Employment and Training, Office of Comprehensive Established in the Department of Labor. Terminated due to expiration of authority for appropriations after fiscal year 1982. Replaced by *Office of Employment and Training Programs.*

Employment and Training Programs, Office of Renamed Office of Job Training Programs by Employment and Training Administration reorganization in the Department of Labor, effective June 1984.

Endangered Species Scientific Authority Established by EO 11911 of Apr. 13, 1976. Terminated by act of Dec. 28, 1979 (93 Stat. 1228), and functions transferred to the Secretary of the Interior.

Energy Administration, Federal Established by act of May 7, 1974 (88 Stat. 96). Assigned additional responsibilities by acts of June 22, 1974 (88 Stat. 246), Dec. 22, 1975 (89 Stat. 871), and Aug. 14, 1976 (90 Stat. 1125). Terminated by act of Aug. 4, 1977 (91 Stat. 577), and functions transferred to the Department of Energy.

Energy Advisory Support Office, Secretary of Abolished by secretarial decision of Feb. 6, 2006.

Energy Assurance, Office of Abolished pursuant to Conference Report No. 108–729 on H.R. 4818, Consolidated Appropriations Act. Functions merged with *Office of Electricity Delivery and Energy Reliability.*

Energy Conservation, Office of Established by Interior Secretarial Order 2953 May 7, 1973. Functions transferred to *Federal Energy Administration* by act of May 7, 1974 (88 Stat. 100).

Energy Data and Analysis, Office of Established by Interior Secretarial Order 2953 of May 7, 1973. Functions transferred to *Federal Energy Administration* by act of May 7, 1974 (88 Stat. 100).

Energy Policy Office Established in Executive Office of the President by EO 11726 of June 29, 1973. Abolished by EO 11775 of Mar. 26, 1974.

Energy Programs, Office of Established by Department of Commerce Organization Order 25–7A, effective Sept. 24, 1975. Terminated by act of Aug. 4, 1977 (91 Stat. 581), and functions transferred to the Department of Energy.

Energy Research and Development Administration Established by act of Oct. 11, 1974 (88 Stat. 1234). Assigned responsibilities by acts of Sept. 3, 1974 (88 Stat. 1069, 1079), Oct. 26, 1974 (88 Stat. 1431), and Dec. 31, 1974 (88 Stat. 1887). Terminated by act of Aug. 4, 1977 (91 Stat. 577), and functions transferred to the Department of Energy.

Energy Resources Council Established in Executive Office of the President by act of Oct. 11, 1974 (88 Stat. 1233). Establishing authority repealed by act of Aug. 4, 1977 (91 Stat. 608), and *Council* terminated.

Energy Supplies and Resources Policy, Presidential Advisory Committee on Established July 30, 1954, by President. Abolished Mar. 12, 1961, by President and functions transferred to the Secretary of the Interior.

Enforcement Commission, National Established by General Order 18 of *Economic Stabilization Administrator,* effective July 30, 1952. Functions transferred to Director, *Office of Defense Mobilization,* and Attorney General by EO 10494 of Oct. 14, 1953.

Engineering, Bureau of *See* **Steam Engineering, Bureau of**

Entomology, Bureau of *See* **Entomology and Plant Quarantine, Bureau of**

Entomology and Plant Quarantine, Bureau of *Bureau of Entomology* and *Bureau of Plant Quarantine* created by acts of Apr. 23, 1904 (33 Stat. 276), and July 7, 1932 (47 Stat. 640), respectively. Consolidated with disease control and eradication functions of *Bureau of Plant Industry* into *Bureau of Entomology and Plant Quarantine* by act of Mar. 23, 1934 (48 Stat. 467). Functions transferred to Agricultural Research Service by Secretary's Memorandum 1320, supp. 4, of Nov. 2, 1953.

Environment, Cabinet Committee on the *See* **Environmental Quality Council**

Environmental Financing Authority Established by act of Oct. 18, 1972 (86 Stat. 899). Expired June 30, 1975, pursuant to terms of act.

Environmental Quality Council Established by EO 11472 of May 29, 1969. Renamed *Cabinet Committee on the Environment* by EO 11514 of Mar. 5, 1970. EO 11514 terminated by EO 11541 of July 1, 1970.

Environment, Safety, and Health, Office of Established by act of Aug. 4, 1977 (91 Stat. 570). Abolished by Secretary of Energy memorandum 2006–007929 of Aug. 30, 2006, and functions transferred to Office of Health, Safety, and Security.

Environmental Science Services Administration Established in the Department of Commerce by Reorg. Plan No. 2 of 1965, effective July 13, 1965, by consolidating *Weather Bureau* and *Coast and Geodetic Survey.* Abolished by Reorg. Plan No. 4 of 1970, effective Oct. 3, 1970, and functions transferred to National Oceanic and Atmospheric Administration.

Equal Employment Opportunity, President's Committee on Established by EO 10925 of Mar. 6, 1961. Abolished by EO 11246 of Sept. 24, 1965, and functions transferred to the Department of Labor and *U.S. Civil Service Commission.*

Equal Opportunity, President's Council on Established by EO 11197 of Feb. 5, 1965. Abolished by EO 11247 of Sept. 24, 1965, and functions transferred to the Department of Justice.

Equipment, Bureau of Established as *Bureau of Equipment and Recruiting* by act of July 5, 1862 (12 Stat. 510), replacing *Bureau of Construction, Equipment and Repairs.* Designated as *Bureau of Equipment* in annual appropriation acts commencing with fiscal year 1892 (26 Stat. 192) after cognizance over enlisted personnel matters transferred, effective July 1, 1889, to *Bureau of Navigation.* Functions distributed among bureaus and offices in the Department of the Navy by act of June 24, 1910 (61 Stat. 613). Abolished by act of June 30, 1914 (38 Stat. 408).

Ethics, Office of Government Established in the Office of Personnel Management by act of Oct. 26, 1978 (92 Stat. 1862). Became a separate executive agency status by act of Nov. 3, 1988 (102 Stat. 3031).

European Migration, Intergovernmental Committee for Renamed Intergovernmental Committee for Migration by Resolution 624, passed by Intergovernmental Committee for European Migration Council, effective Nov. 11, 1980.

Evacuation, Joint Committee on *See* **Health and Welfare Aspects of Evacuation of Civilians, Joint Committee on**

Exchange Service, International Established in 1849 in Smithsonian Institution. Renamed Office of Publications Exchange by Secretary's internal directive of Jan. 11, 1985.

Executive Branch of the Government, Commission on Organization of the Established by act of July 7, 1947 (61 Stat. 246). Terminated June 12, 1949, pursuant to terms of act. Second *Commission* *on Organization of the Executive Branch of the Government* established by act of July 10, 1953 (67 Stat. 142). Terminated June 30, 1955, pursuant to terms of act.

Executive Council Established by EO 6202–A of July 11, 1933. Consolidated with *National Emergency Council* by EO 6889–A of Oct. 29, 1934.

Executive Exchange, President's Commission on *See* **Personnel Interchange, President's Commission on**

Executive orders *See* **State, Department of**

Executive Organization, President's Advisory Council on Established by President Apr. 5, 1969. Terminated May 7, 1971.

Executive Protective Service *See* **Secret Service Division**

Executives, Active Corps of Established in ACTION by act of Oct. 1, 1973 (87 Stat. 404). Transferred to Small Business Administration by EO 11871 of July 18, 1975.

Export Administration, Bureau of Established as a separate agency within the Department of Commerce on Oct. 1, 1987 (50 USC app. 2401 *et seq.*). Renamed Bureau of Industry and Security by Department of Commerce internal organization order of Apr. 18, 2002 (67 FR 20630).

Export Control, Administrator of Functions delegated to Administrator by Proc. 2413 of July 2, 1940, transferred to *Office of Export Control, Economic Defense Board,* by EO 8900 of Sept. 15, 1941. Renamed *Board of Economic Warfare* by EO 8982 of Dec. 17, 1941. *Board* terminated by EO 9361 of July 15, 1943.

Export Control, Office of *See* **Export Control, Administrator of**

Export-Import Bank of Washington Organization of District of Columbia banking corporation directed by EO 6581 of Feb. 2, 1934. Certificate of incorporation filed Feb. 12, 1934. Grouped with other agencies to form *Federal Loan Agency* by Reorg. Plan No. I of 1939, effective July 1, 1939. Transferred to the Department of Commerce by EO 9071 of Feb. 24, 1942. Functions transferred to *Office of Economic Warfare* by EO 9361 of July 15, 1943. Established as permanent independent agency by act of July 31, 1945 (59 Stat. 526). Renamed Export-Import Bank of the U.S. by act of Mar. 13, 1968 (82 Stat. 47).

Export-Import Bank of Washington, DC, Second Authorized by EO 6638 of Mar. 9, 1934. Abolished by EO 7365 of May 7, 1936, and records transferred to *Export-Import Bank of Washington,* effective June 30, 1936.

Export Marketing Service Established by the Secretary of Agriculture Mar. 28, 1969. Merged with Foreign Agricultural Service by Secretary's memorandum of Dec. 7, 1973, effective Feb. 3, 1974.

Exports and Requirements, Division of Established in *Office of Foreign Economic Coordination* by the Department of State order of Feb. 1, 1943. Abolished by departmental order of Nov. 6, 1943, pursuant to EO 9380 of Sept. 25, 1943.

Extension Service Established by act of May 14, 1914 (38 Stat. 372). Consolidated into *Science and Education Administration* by Secretary's order of Jan. 24, 1978. Reestablished as *Extension Service* by Secretarial order of June 16, 1981. Became part of Cooperative State, Research, Education, and Extension Service under Department of Agriculture's reorganization in 1995.

Facts and Figures, Office of Established in *Office for Emergency Management* by EO 8922 of Oct. 24, 1941. Consolidated with *Office of War Information* in *Office for Emergency Management* by EO 9182 of June 13, 1942.

Family Security Committee Established in *Office of Defense Health and Welfare Services* Feb. 12, 1941, by administrative order. Terminated Dec. 17, 1942.

Family Services, Bureau of *See* **Assistance, Bureau of Public**

Family Support Administration Established on Apr. 4, 1986, in the Department of Health and Human Services under authority of section 6 of Reorganization Plan No. 1 of 1953, effective Apr. 11, 1953 (*see also* 51 FR 11641). Merged into Administration for Children and Families by Secretary's reorganization notice dated Apr. 15, 1991.

Farm Board, Federal Established by act of June 15, 1929 (46 Stat. 11). Renamed Farm Credit Administration and certain functions abolished by EO 6084 of Mar. 27, 1933. Administration placed under the Department of Agriculture by Reorg. Plan No. I of 1939, effective July 1, 1939. Made independent agency in the executive branch of the Government, to be housed in the Department of Agriculture, by act of Aug. 6, 1953 (67 Stat. 390). Removed from the Department of Agriculture by act of Dec. 10, 1971 (85 Stat. 617).

Farm Credit Administration *See* **Farm Board, Federal**

Farm Loan Board, Federal Established in the Department of the Treasury to administer act of July 17, 1916 (39 Stat. 360). Offices of appointed members of *Board,* except member designated as *Farm Loan Commissioner,* abolished by EO 6084 of Mar. 27, 1933, and *Board* functions transferred to *Farm Loan Commissioner,* subject to jurisdiction and control of Farm Credit Administration. Title changed to *Land Bank Commissioner* by act of June 16, 1933. Abolished by act of Aug. 6, 1953 (67 Stat. 393).

Farm Loan Bureau, Federal Established in the Department of the Treasury under supervision of *Federal Farm Loan Board* and charged with execution of act of July 17, 1916 (39 Stat. 360). Transferred to *Farm Credit Administration* by EO 6084 of Mar. 27, 1933.

Farm Loan Commissioner *See* **Farm Loan Board, Federal**

Farm Mortgage Corporation, Federal Established by act of Jan. 31, 1934 (48 Stat. 344). Transferred to the Department of Agriculture by Reorg. Plan No. I of 1939, effective July 1, 1939, to operate under supervision of Farm Credit Administration. Abolished by act of Oct. 4, 1961 (75 Stat. 773).

Farm Products, Division of (Also known as *Division of Agriculture*)

Established by *Advisory Commission to Council of National Defense* pursuant to act of Aug. 29, 1916 (39 Stat. 649). *Office of Agricultural Defense Relations* (later known as *Office for Agricultural War Relations*) established in the Department of Agriculture by Presidential letter of May 5, 1941, which transferred to the Secretary of Agriculture functions previously assigned to *Division of Agriculture.* Functions concerned with food production transferred to *Food Production Administration* and functions concerned with food distribution transferred to *Food Distribution Administration* by EO 9280 of Dec. 5, 1942.

Farm Security Administration *See* **Resettlement Administration**

Farm Service Agency Established by Secretary's Memorandum 1010–1 dated Oct. 20, 1994, under authority of the act of Oct. 13, 1994 (7 U.S.C. 6901), and assumed certain functions of the *Agricultural Stabilization and Conservation Service,* the *Farmers' Home Administration,* and the *Federal Crop Insurance Corporation.* Renamed *Consolidated Farm Service Agency* by Acting Administrator on Dec. 19, 1994.

Farmer Cooperative Service Established by Secretary of Agriculture Memorandum 1320, supp. 4, of Dec. 4, 1953. Consolidated with other Department of Agriculture units into *Economics, Statistics, and Cooperatives Service* by Secretary's Memorandum 1927, effective Dec. 23, 1977.

Farmers' Home Administration. *See* **Resettlement Administration**

Federal. *See also other part of title*

Federal Advisory Council Established in *Federal Security Agency* by act of June 6, 1933 (48 Stat. 116). Transferred to the Department of Labor by Reorg. Plan No. 2 of 1949, effective Aug. 20, 1949.

Federal Register, Administrative Committee of the *See* **Archives Establishment, National**

Federal Register, Division of the Established by act of July 26, 1935 (49 Stat. 500). Transferred to General Services Administration as part of *National Archives and Records Service* by act of June 30, 1949 (63 Stat. 381). Renamed Office of the Federal Register by order of General Services Administrator, Feb. 6, 1959. Transferred to National Archives and Records Administration by act of Oct. 19, 1984 (98 Stat. 2283).

Federal Register, Office of the *See* **Federal Register, Division of the**

Federal Reserve Board Renamed Board of Governors of the Federal Reserve System, and Governor and Vice Governor designated as Chairman and Vice Chairman, respectively, of Board by act of Aug. 23, 1935 (49 Stat. 704).

Federal Tax Reform, President's Advisory Panel on Established by EO 13369 of Jan. 7, 2005. Abolished by EO 13446 of Sept. 28, 2007.

Field Services, Office of Established by the Secretary of Commerce Feb. 1, 1963, by Department Organization Order 40–3. Terminated by Department Organization Order 40–1A of Sept. 15, 1970, and functions transferred to *Bureau of Domestic Commerce.*

Filipino Rehabilitation Commission Established by act of June 29, 1944 (58 Stat. 626). Inactive pursuant to terms of act.

Film Service, U.S. Established by *National Emergency Council* in September 1938. Transferred to *Office of Education, Federal Security Agency,* by Reorg. Plan No. II of 1939, effective July 1, 1939. Terminated June 30, 1940.

Films, Coordinator of Government Director of *Office of Government Reports* designated *Coordinator of Government Films* by Presidential letter of Dec. 18, 1941. Functions transferred to *Office of War Information* by EO 9182 of June 13, 1942.

Financial Capability, President's Advisory Council on Established by EO 13530 of January 29, 2010. Terminated on January 29, 2013 by sec. 3 of EO 13591 of November 11, 2011.

Financial Operations, Bureau of Government Renamed Financial Management Service by Order 145–21 of the Secretary of the Treasury, effective Oct. 10, 1984.

Fire Administration, U.S. *See* **Fire Prevention and Control Administration, National**

Fire Council, Federal Established by EO 7397 of June 20, 1936. Transferred July 1, 1939, to *Federal Works Agency* by EO 8194 of July 6, 1939, with functions under direction of *Federal Works Administrator.* Transferred with *Federal Works Agency* to General Services Administration by act of June 30, 1949 (63 Stat. 380). Transferred to the Department of Commerce by EO 11654 of Mar. 13, 1972.

Fire Prevention and Control, National Academy for Established in the Department of Commerce by act of Oct. 29, 1974 (88 Stat. 1537). Transferred to Federal Emergency Management Agency by Reorg. Plan No. 3 of 1978, effective Apr. 1, 1979.

Fire Prevention and Control Administration, National Renamed U.S. Fire Administration by act of Oct. 5, 1978 (92 Stat. 932). Transferred to Federal

Emergency Management Agency by Reorg. Plan No. 3 of 1978, effective Apr. 1, 1979

Fiscal Responsibility and Reform, National Commission on Established by EO 13531 of Feb. 18, 2010. Terminated 30 days after submission of final report to President on January 31, 2011.

Fish Commission, U.S. *Commissioner of Fish and Fisheries* established as head of *U.S. Fish Commission* by joint resolution of Feb. 9, 1871 (16 Stat. 594). *Commission* established as *Bureau of Fisheries* in *Department of Commerce and Labor* by act of Feb. 14, 1903 (32 Stat. 827). Department of Labor created by act of Mar. 4, 1913 (37 Stat. 736), and *Bureau* remained in the Department of Commerce. Transferred to the Department of the Interior by Reorg. Plan No. II of 1939, effective July 1, 1939. Consolidated with *Bureau of Biological Survey* into *Fish and Wildlife Service* by Reorg. Plan No. III of 1940, effective June 30, 1940.

Fish and Wildlife Service Established by Reorg. Plan No. III of 1940, effective June 30, 1940, consolidating *Bureau of Fisheries* and *Bureau of Biological Survey.* Succeeded by U.S. Fish and Wildlife Service.

Fisheries, Bureau of *See* **Fish Commission, U.S.**

Fisheries, Bureau of Commercial Organized in 1959 under U.S. Fish and Wildlife Service, the Department of the Interior. Abolished by Reorg. Plan No. 4 of 1970, effective Oct. 3, 1970, and functions transferred to National Oceanic and Atmospheric Administration.

Fishery Coordination, Office of Established in the Department of the Interior by EO 9204 of July 21, 1942. Terminated by EO 9649 of Oct. 29, 1945.

Flood Indemnity Administration, Federal Established in *Housing and Home Finance Agency* by Administrator's Organizational Order 1, effective Sept. 28, 1956, redesignated as Administrator's Organizational Order 2 on Dec. 7, 1956, pursuant to act of Aug. 7, 1956 (70 Stat. 1078). Abolished by Administrator's Organizational Order 3, effective July 1, 1957, due to lack of funding.

Flood Protection Structure Accreditation Task Force Established by act of July 6, 2012 (126 Stat. 942). Terminated upon submission of final report not later than July 6, 2013.

Food, Cost of Living Council Committee on Established by EO 11695 of Jan. 11, 1973. Abolished by EO 11788 of June 18, 1974.

Food, Drug, and Insecticide Administration Established by act of Jan. 18, 1927 (44 Stat. 1002). Renamed Food and Drug Administration by act of May 27, 1930 (46 Stat. 422). Transferred from the Department of Agriculture to *Federal Security Agency* by Reorg. Plan No. IV of 1940, effective June 30, 1940. Transferred to *Department of Health, Education, and Welfare* by Reorg. Plan No. 1 of 1953, effective Apr. 11, 1953.

Food Distribution Administration Established in the Department of Agriculture by EO 9280 of Dec. 5, 1942, consolidating *Agricultural Marketing Administration, Sugar Agency,* distribution functions of *Office for Agricultural War Relations,* regulatory work of *Bureau of Animal Industry,* and food units of *War Production Board.* Consolidated with other agencies by EO 9322 of Mar. 26, 1943, to form *Administration of Food Production and Distribution.*

Food and Drug Administration *See* **Food, Drug, and Insecticide Administration**

Food Industry Advisory Committee Established by EO 11627 of Oct. 15, 1971. Abolished by EO 11781 of May 1, 1974.

Food and Nutrition Service Established Aug. 8, 1969, by Secretary of Agriculture under authority of 5 U.S.C. 301 and Reorg. Plan No. 2 of 1953 (5 U.S.C. app.). Abolished by Secretary's Memorandum 1010–1 dated Oct. 20, 1994. Functions assumed by Food and Consumer Service.

Food Production Administration Established in the Department of Agriculture by EO 9280 of Dec. 5, 1942, which consolidated *Agricultural Adjustment Agency,* Farm Credit Administration, *Farm Security Administration,* Federal Crop Insurance Corporation, Soil Conservation Service, and food production activities of *War Production Board, Office of Agricultural War Relations,* and *Division of Farm Management and Costs, Bureau of Agricultural Economics.* Consolidated with other agencies by EO 9322 of Mar. 26, 1943, to form *Administration of Food Production and Distribution.*

Food Production and Distribution, Administration of Established by consolidation of *Food Production Administration, Food Distribution Administration,* Commodity Credit Corporation, and Extension Service, Department of Agriculture, by EO 9322 of Mar. 26, 1943, under direction of Administrator, directly responsible to President. Renamed *War Food Administration* by EO 9334 of Apr. 19, 1943. Terminated by EO 9577 of June 29, 1945, and functions transferred to the Secretary of Agriculture. Transfer made permanent by Reorg. Plan No. 3 of 1946, effective July 16, 1946.

Food Safety and Quality Service Renamed Food Safety and Inspection Service by Agriculture Secretary's memorandum of June 19, 1981.

Foods, Bureau of Renamed Center for Food Safety and Applied Nutrition by Food and Drug Administration notice of Mar. 9, 1984 (49 FR 10166).

Foreign. *See also other part of title*

Foreign Aid, Advisory Committee on Voluntary Established by President May 14, 1946. Transferred from the Department of State to the Director of the *Mutual Security Agency,* and later to Director of the *Foreign Operations Administration,* by Presidential letter of June 1, 1953.

Foreign Intelligence Advisory Board, President's Established by EO 12863 of Sept. 13, 1993. Abolished by EO 13462 of Feb. 29, 2008.

Foreign Operations Administration Established by Reorg. Plan No. 7 of 1953, effective Aug. 1, 1953, and functions transferred from *Office of Director of Mutual Security, Mutual Security Agency, Technical Cooperation Administration, Institute of Inter-American Affairs.* Abolished by EO 10610 of May 9, 1955, and functions and offices transferred to the Departments of State and Defense.

Foreign Scholarships, Board of Renamed J. William Fulbright Foreign Scholarship Board by act of Feb. 16, 1990 (104 Stat. 49).

Forest Reservation Commission, National Established by act of Mar. 1, 1911 (36 Stat. 962). Terminated by act of Oct. 22, 1976 (90 Stat. 2961), and functions transferred to the Secretary of Agriculture.

Forests, Director of Established by Administrative Order 1283 of May 18, 1938. Made part of *Office of Land Utilization,* Department of the Interior, by Administrative Order 1466 of Apr. 15, 1940.

Freedmen's Hospital Established by act of Mar. 3, 1871 (16 Stat. 506; T. 32 of D.C. Code). Transferred from the Department of the Interior to *Federal Security Agency* by Reorg. Plan No. IV of 1940, effective June 30, 1940.

Fuel Yards Established by act of July 1, 1918 (40 Stat. 672). Transferred from *Bureau of Mines,* Department of Commerce, to *Procurement Division,* Department of the Treasury, by EO 6166 of June 10, 1933, effective Mar. 2, 1934.

Fuels Coordinator for War, Office of Solid *See* **Fuels Administration for War, Solid**

Fuels Corporation, U.S. Synthetic Established by act of June 30, 1980 (94 Stat. 636). Terminated Apr. 18, 1986, by act of Dec. 19, 1985 (99 Stat. 1249), and functions transferred to the Secretary of the Treasury.

Fund-Raising Within the Federal Service, President's Committee on Established by EO 10728 of Sept. 6, 1957. Abolished by EO 10927 of Mar. 18, 1961, and functions transferred to *U.S. Civil Service Commission.*

Gallaudet College *See* **Columbia Institution for the Instruction of the Deaf and Dumb, and the Blind**

General Programs, Office of Renamed Office of Public Programs by the Chairman, National Endowment for the Humanities, in January 1991.

Geographic Board, U.S. Established by EO 27–A of Sept. 4, 1890. Abolished by EO 6680 of Apr. 17, 1935, and duties transferred to *U.S. Board on Geographical Names,* Department of the Interior, effective June 17, 1934. *Board* abolished by act of July 25, 1947 (61 Stat. 457), and duties assumed by *Board on Geographic Names.*

Geographical Names, U.S. Board on *See* **Geographic Board, U.S.**

Geography, Office of Function of standardizing foreign place names placed in the Department of the Interior conjointly with the *Board on Geographic Names* by act of July 25, 1947 (61 Stat. 456). Functions transferred to the Department of Defense by memorandum of understanding by the Departments of the Interior and Defense and the *Bureau of the Budget* Mar. 9, 1968.

Geological Survey Established in the Department of the Interior by act of Mar. 3, 1879 (20 Stat. 394). Renamed United States Geological Survey by acts of Nov. 13, 1991 (105 Stat. 1000) and May 18, 1992 (106 Stat. 172).

Germany, Mixed Claims Commission, U.S. and Established by agreement of Aug. 10, 1922, between U.S. and Germany. Duties extended by agreement of Dec. 31, 1928. Time limit for filing claims expired June 30, 1928. All claims disposed of by Oct. 30, 1939. Terminated June 30, 1941.

Global Communications, Office of Established within the White House Office by EO 13283 of Jan. 21, 2003. Abolished by EO 13385 of Sept. 29, 2005

Global Health Affairs, Office of Renamed Office o f Global Affairs by Secretary of Health and Human Services notice of June 22, 2011 (76 FR 36539).

Goethals Memorial Commission Established by act of Aug. 4, 1935 (49 Stat. 743). Placed under jurisdiction of *Department of War* by EO 8191 of July 5, 1939.

Government. *See other part of title*

Grain Futures Administration Established in the Department of Agriculture under provisions of act of Sept. 21, 1922 (42 Stat. 998). Superseded by *Commodity Exchange Administration* by order of Secretary, effective July 1, 1936. Consolidated with other agencies into *Commodity Exchange Branch, Agricultural Marketing Administration,* by EO 9069 of Feb. 23, 1942. Functions transferred to the Secretary of Agriculture by EO 9577 of June 29, 1945. Transfer made permanent by Reorg. Plan No. 3 of 1946, effective July 16, 1946. Functions transferred to *Commodity Exchange Authority* by Secretary's Memorandum 1185 of Jan. 21, 1947. Functions transferred to Commodity Futures Trading Commission by act of Oct. 23, 1974 (88 Stat. 1414).

Grain Inspection Service, Federal Established in the Department of Agriculture by act of Oct. 21, 1976 (90 Stat. 2868). Abolished by Secretary's Memorandum 1010–1 dated Oct. 20, 1994, and program authority and functions transferred to the Grain Inspection, Packers and Stockyards Administration.

Grain Stabilization Corporation Organized as Delaware corporation to operate in connection with *Federal Farm Board* pursuant to act of June 15, 1929 (46 Stat. 11). Terminated by filing of certificate of dissolution with Corporation Commission of State of Delaware Dec. 14, 1935.

Grant Administration, Office of Transferred from the Office of the General Council to the Deputy Director, U.S. Trade and Development Agency by administrative order of Apr. 25, 2007.

Grants and Program Systems, Office of Abolished and functions transferred to Cooperative State Research Service, Department of Agriculture, by Secretarial Memorandum 1020–26 of July 1, 1986.

Grazing Service Consolidated with *General Land Office* into Bureau of Land Management, Department of the Interior, by Reorg. Plan No. 3 of 1946, effective July 16, 1946.

Great Lakes Basin Commission Established by EO 11345 of Apr. 20, 1967. Terminated by EO 12319 of Sept. 9, 1981.

Great Lakes Pilotage Administration Established in the Department of Commerce to administer act of June 30, 1960 (74 Stat. 259). Administration of act transferred to the Secretary of Transportation by act of Oct. 15, 1966 (80 Stat. 931).

Greening the Government through Waste Prevention and Recycling, Steering Committee Established by EO 13101 of Sept. 14, 1998. Abolished by EO 13423 of Jan. 24, 2007.

Gulf Coast Ecosystem Restoration Council Task Force Established by EO 13554 of Oct. 5, 2010. Terminated by EO 13626 of Sept. 10, 2012.

Handicapped, National Center on Education Media and Materials for the Established by agreement between the *Secretary of Health, Education, and Welfare* and Ohio State University, pursuant to acts of Aug. 20, 1969 (83 Stat. 102) and Apr. 13, 1970 (84 Stat. 187). Authorization deleted by act of Nov. 29, 1975 (89 Stat. 795), and the Secretary was authorized to enter into agreements with non-Federal organizations to establish and operate centers for handicapped.

Handicapped, National Council on the Established in the *Department of Health, Education, and Welfare* by act of Nov. 6, 1978 (92 Stat. 2977). Transferred to the Department of Education by act of Oct. 17, 1979 (93 Stat. 677). Reorganized as independent agency by act of Feb. 22, 1984 (98 Stat. 26).

Handicapped Employees, Interagency Committee on Alternately renamed Interagency Committee on Employment of People with Disabilities by EO 12704 of Feb. 26, 1990.

Handicapped Individuals, White House Conference on Established by act of Dec. 7, 1974 (88 Stat. 1617). Terminated Dec. 30, 1977, pursuant to terms of act.

Handicapped Research, National Institute of Renamed National Institute on Disability and Rehabilitation Research by act of Oct. 21, 1986 (100 Stat. 1820).

Health, Cost of Living Council Committee on Established by EO 11695 of Jan. 11, 1973. Abolished by EO 11788 of June 18, 1974.

Health, Education, and Welfare, Department of Established by Reorganization Plan No. 1 of 1953 (5 U.S.C. app.), effective Apr. 11, 1953. Renamed Department of Health and Human Services by act of Oct. 17, 1979 (93 Stat. 695).

Health, Welfare, and Related Defense Activities, Office of the Coordinator of *Federal Security Administrator* designated as Coordinator of health, welfare, and related fields of activity affecting national defense, including aspects of education under *Federal Security Agency,* by *Council of National Defense,* with approval of President, Nov. 28, 1940. Office of Coordinator superseded by *Office of Defense Health and Welfare Services,* established in *Office for Emergency Services* by EO 8890 of Sept. 3, 1941.

Health Care Technology, National Council on Established by act of July 1, 1944, as amended (92 Stat. 3447). Renamed *Council on Health Care Technology* by act of Oct. 30, 1984 (98 Stat. 2820). Name lowercased by act of Oct. 7, 1985 (99 Stat. 493). Terminated by act of Dec. 19, 1989 (103 Stat. 2205).

Health Facilities, Financing, Compliance, and Conversion, Bureau of Renamed Bureau of Health Facilities by Department of Health and Human Services Secretarial order of Mar. 12, 1980 (45 FR 17207).

Health Industry Advisory Committee Established by EO 11695 of Jan. 11, 1973. Abolished by EO 11781 of May 1, 1974.

Health Manpower, Bureau of Renamed Bureau of Health Professions by Department of Health and Human Services Secretarial order of Mar. 12, 1980 (45 FR 17207).

Health and Medical Committee Established by *Council of National Defense* order of Sept. 19, 1940. Transferred to *Federal Security Agency* by *Council* order approved by President Nov. 28, 1940. Reestablished in *Office of Defense Health and Welfare Services, Office for Emergency Management,* by EO 8890 of Sept. 3, 1941. *Committee* transferred to *Federal Security Agency* by EO 9338 of Apr. 29, 1943.

Health Reform, White House Office of Established by EO 13507 of April 8, 2009. Revoked by EO 13569 of April 5, 2011.

Health Resources Administration Established in Public Health Service. Abolished by Department of Health and Human Services Secretarial reorganization of Aug. 20, 1982 (47 FR 38409), and functions transferred to Health Resources and Services Administration.

Health Service, Public Originated by act of July 16, 1798 (1 Stat. 605). Transferred from the Department of the Treasury to the *Federal Security Agency* by Reorg. Plan No. I of 1939, effective July 1, 1939.

Health Services Administration Established in Public Health Service. Abolished by Department of Health and Human Services Secretarial reorganization of Aug. 20, 1982 (47 FR 38409), and functions transferred to Health Resources and Services Administration.

Health Services Industry, Committee on the Established by EO 11627 of Oct. 15, 1971. Abolished by EO 11695 of Jan. 11, 1973.

Health Services and Mental Health Administration Established in Public Health Service Apr. 1, 1968. Abolished by *Department of Health, Education, and Welfare* reorganization order and functions transferred to *Centers for Disease Control, Health Resources Administration,* and *Health Services Administration,* effective July 1, 1973.

Health Services Research, National Center for Established by act of July 23, 1974 (88 Stat. 363). Transferred from *Health Resources Administration* to Office of the Assistant Secretary for Health by *Department of Health, Education, and Welfare* reorganization, effective Dec. 2, 1977. Renamed *National Center for Health Services Research and Health Care Technology Assessment* by Secretary's order, pursuant to act of Oct. 30, 1984 (98 Stat. 2817). Terminated by act of Dec. 19, 1989 (103 Stat. 2205).

Health Statistics, National Center for Established by act of July 23, 1974 (88 Stat. 363). Transferred from *Health Resources Administration* to Office of the Assistant Secretary for Health by the *Department of Health, Education, and Welfare* reorganization, effective Dec. 2, 1977. Transferred to *Centers for Disease Control* by Secretary's notice of Apr. 2, 1987 (52 FR 13318).

Health and Welfare Activities, Interdepartmental Committee to Coordinate Appointed by President Aug. 15, 1935, and reestablished by EO 7481 of Oct. 27, 1936. Terminated in 1939.

Health and Welfare Aspects of Evacuation of Civilians, Joint Committee on Established August 1941 as joint committee of *Office of Defense Health and Welfare Services* and *Office of Civilian Defense.* Reorganized in June 1942 and renamed *Joint Committee on Evacuation. Office of Defense Health and Welfare Services* abolished by EO 9388 of Apr. 29, 1943, and functions transferred to *Federal Security Agency. Committee* terminated.

Heart and Lung Institute, National Renamed National Heart, Lung, and Blood Institute by act of Apr. 22, 1976 (90 Stat. 402).

Heritage Conservation and Recreation Service Established by the Secretary of the Interior Jan. 25, 1978. Abolished by Secretarial Order 3060 of Feb. 19, 1981, and functions transferred to National Park Service.

Hemispheric Defense Studies, Center for Established by Department of Defense Directive 3200.12 of Sept. 3, 1997. Abolished by act of Oct. 17, 2006 (120 Stat. 2353).

Highway Safety Agency, National Established in the Department of Commerce by act of Sept. 9, 1966 (80 Stat. 731). Functions transferred to the Department of Transportation by act of Oct. 15, 1966 (80 Stat. 931). Functions transferred to *National Highway Safety Bureau* by EO 11357 of June 6, 1967. *Bureau* renamed National Highway Traffic Safety Administration by act of Dec. 31, 1970 (84 Stat. 1739).

Highway Safety Bureau, National *See* **Highway Safety Agency, National**

Home Economics, Bureau of Human Nutrition and *See* **Home Economics, Office of**

Home Economics, Office of Renamed *Bureau of Home Economics* by Secretary's Memorandum 436, effective July 1, 1923, pursuant to act of Feb. 26, 1923 (42 Stat. 1289). Redesignated *Bureau of Human Nutrition and Home Economics* February 1943 in accordance with *Research Administration* Memorandum 5 issued pursuant to EO 9069 of Feb. 23, 1942, and in conformity with Secretary's Memorandums 960 and 986. Functions transferred to Agricultural Research Service by Secretary's Memorandum 1320, supp. 4, of Nov. 2, 1953.

Home Loan Bank Administration, Federal *See* **Home Loan Bank Board, Federal**

Home Loan Bank Board *See* **Home Loan Bank Board, Federal**

Home Loan Bank Board, Federal Established by acts of July 22, 1932 (47 Stat. 725), June 13, 1933 (48 Stat. 128), and June 27, 1934 (48 Stat. 1246). Grouped with other agencies to form *Federal Loan Agency* by Reorg. Plan No. I of 1939, effective July 1, 1939. Functions transferred to *Federal Home Loan Bank Administration, National Housing Agency,* by EO 9070 of Feb. 24, 1942. Abolished by Reorg. Plan No. 3, effective July 27, 1947, and functions transferred to *Home Loan Bank Board, Housing and Home Finance Agency.* Renamed *Federal Home Loan Bank Board* and made independent agency by act of Aug. 11, 1955 (69 Stat. 640). Abolished by act of Aug. 9, 1989 (103 Stat. 354, 415), and functions transferred to Office of Thrift Supervision, Resolution Trust Corporation, Federal Deposit Insurance Corporation, and Federal Housing Finance Board. (*See also* **Thrift Supervision, Office of**).

Home Loan Bank System, Federal Grouped with other agencies to form *Federal Loan Agency* by Reorg. Plan No. I of 1939, effective July 1, 1939. Functions transferred to *Federal Home Loan Bank Administration, National Housing Agency,* by EO 9070 of Feb. 24, 1942. Transferred to *Housing and Home Finance Agency* by Reorg. Plan No. 3 of 1947, effective July 27, 1947.

Home Mortgage Credit Extension Committee, National Voluntary Established by act of Aug.

2, 1954 (68 Stat 638). Terminated Oct. 1, 1965, pursuant to terms of act.

Home Owners' Loan Corporation Established by act of June 13, 1933 (48 Stat. 128), under supervision of *Federal Home Loan Bank Board.* Grouped with other agencies to form *Federal Loan Agency* by Reorg. Plan No. I of 1939, effective July 1, 1939. Transferred to *Federal Home Loan Bank Administration, National Housing Agency,* by EO 9070 of Feb. 24, 1942. Board of Directors abolished by Reorg. Plan No. 3 of 1947, effective July 27, 1947, and functions transferred, for liquidation of assets, to *Home Loan Bank Board, Housing and Home Finance Agency.* Terminated by order of *Secretary of the Home Loan Bank Board,* effective Feb. 3, 1954, pursuant to act of June 30, 1953 (67 Stat. 121).

Homesteads, Division of Subsistence Established by act of June 16, 1933 (48 Stat. 205). Secretary of the Interior authorized to administer section 208 of act by EO 6209 of July 21, 1933. *Federal Subsistence Homesteads Corporation* created by Secretary's order of Dec. 2, 1933, and organization incorporated under laws of Delaware. Transferred to *Resettlement Administration* by EO 7041 of May 15, 1935.

Homesteads Corporation, Federal Subsistence *See* **Homesteads, Division of Subsistence**

Hospitalization, Board of Federal Organized Nov. 1, 1921. Designated as advisory agency to *Bureau of the Budget* May 7, 1943. Terminated June 30, 1948, by Director's letter of May 28, 1948.

Housing, President's Committee on Equal Opportunity in Established by EO 11063 of Nov. 20, 1962. Inactive as of June 30, 1968.

Housing Administration, Federal Established by act of June 27, 1934 (48 Stat. 1246). Grouped with other agencies to form *Federal Loan Agency* by Reorg. Plan No. I of 1939, effective July 1, 1939. Functions transferred to *Federal Housing Administration, National Housing Agency,* by EO 9070 of Feb. 24, 1942. Transferred to *Housing and Home Finance Agency* by Reorg. Plan No. 3, effective July 27, 1947. Functions transferred to the Department of Housing and Urban Development by act of Sept. 9, 1965 (79 Stat. 667).

Housing Administration, Public Established as constituent agency of *Housing and Home Finance Agency* by Reorg. Plan No. 3 of 1947, effective July 27, 1947. Functions transferred to the Department of Housing and Urban Development by act of Sept. 9, 1965 (79 Stat. 667).

Housing Agency, National Established by EO 9070 of Feb. 24, 1942, to consolidate housing functions relating to *Federal Home Loan Bank Board, Federal Home Loan Bank System, Federal Savings and Loan Insurance Corporation, Home Owners' Loan Corporation, U.S. Housing Corporation, Federal Housing Administration, U.S. Housing Authority, Defense Homes Corporation, Division of Defense Housing Coordination, Central Housing Committee, Farm Security Administration* with respect to nonfarm housing, *Public Buildings Administration, Division of Defense Housing, Mutual Ownership Defense Housing Division, Office of Administrator of Federal Works Agency,* and the Departments of *War* and the Navy with respect to housing located off military installations. Agency dissolved on creation of *Housing and Home Finance Agency* by Reorg. Plan No. 3 of 1947, effective July 27, 1947.

Housing Authority, Federal Public Established by EO 9070 of Feb. 24, 1942. Public housing functions of *Federal Works Agency, the Departments of War* and the Navy (except housing located on military installations), and *Farm Security Administration* (nonfarm housing) transferred to *Authority,* and *Defense Homes Corporation* administered by the Commissioner of the *Authority'.* Functions transferred to *Public Housing Administration, Housing and Home Finance Agency,* by Reorg. Plan No. 3 of 1947, effective July 27, 1947.

Housing Authority, U.S. Established in the Department of the Interior by act of Sept. 1, 1937 (50 Stat. 888). Transferred to *Federal Works Agency* by Reorg. Plan No. I of 1939, effective July 1, 1939. Transferred to *Federal Public Housing Authority, National Housing Agency,* by EO 9070 of Feb. 24, 1942. Office of Administrator abolished by Reorg. Plan No. 3 of 1947, effective July 27, 1947, and functions transferred to *Public Housing Administration, Housing and Home Finance Agency.*

Housing Corporation, U.S. Incorporated July 10, 1918, under laws of New York. Transferred from the Department of Labor to the Department of the Treasury by EO 7641 of June 22, 1937. Transferred from the Department of the Treasury to the *Public Buildings Administration, Federal Works Agency,* by EO 8186 of June 29, 1939. Functions transferred for liquidation to *Federal Home Loan Bank Administration, National Housing Agency,* by EO 9070 of Feb. 24, 1942. Terminated Sept. 8, 1952, by the *Secretary of the Home Loan Bank Board.*

Housing Council, National Established in *Housing and Home Finance Agency* by Reorg. Plan No. 3 of 1947, effective July 27, 1947. Terminated by Reorg. Plan No. 4 of 1965, effective July 27, 1965, and functions transferred to President.

Housing Division Established in *Public Works Administration* by act of June 16, 1933 (48 Stat. 195). Functions transferred to *U.S. Housing Authority* by EO 7732 of Oct. 27, 1937.

Housing Enterprise Oversight, Office of Federal Office and positions of Director and Deputy Director established within the Department of Housing and Urban Development by the act of October 28, 1992 (106 Stat. 3944). Abolished by the act of July 30, 2008 (122 Stat. 2794), and functions, personnel, and property transferred to Federal Housing Finance Agency.

Housing Expediter, Office of the Established in *Office of War Mobilization and Reconversion* by Presidential letter of Dec. 12, 1945, to *Housing Expediter.* Functions of *Housing Expediter* defined by EO 9686 of Jan. 26, 1946. *Housing Expediter* confirmed in position of *National Housing*

Administrator Feb. 6, 1946. *Office of the Housing Expediter* established by act of May 22, 1946 (60 Stat. 208). Functions of *Office* and *National Housing Administrator* segregated by EO 9820 of Jan. 11, 1947. Housing functions of *Civilian Production Administration* transferred to *Office* by EO 9836 of Mar. 22, 1947, effective Apr. 1, 1947. Rent control functions of *Office of Temporary Controls* transferred to *Office* by EO 9841 of Apr. 23, 1947. *Office* terminated by EO 10276 of July 31, 1951, and functions transferred to *Economic Stabilization Agency.*

Housing Finance Board, Federal Established by the act of August 9, 1989 (103 Stat. 354, 415), and certain functions transferred from Federal Home Loan Bank Board. Abolished by the act of July 30, 2008 (122 Stat. 2797), and functions, personnel, and property transferred to Federal Housing Finance Agency.

Housing and Home Finance Agency Established by Reorg. Plan No. 3 of 1947, effective July 27, 1947. Terminated by act of Sept. 9, 1965 (79 Stat. 667), and functions transferred to the Department of Housing and Urban Development.

Howard University Established by act of Mar. 2, 1867 (14 Stat. 438). Functions of the Department of the Interior transferred to *Federal Security Agency* by Reorg. Plan No. IV of 1940, effective June 30, 1940. Functions of the *Department of Health, Education, and Welfare* transferred to the Department of Education by act of Oct. 17, 1979 (93 Stat. 678).

Human Development, Office of Established in *Department of Health, Education, and Welfare.* Renamed Office of Human Development Services and component units transferred to or reorganized under new administrations in Office by Secretary's reorganization order of July 26, 1977. Merged into the Administration for Children and Families by Secretary of Health and Human Services reorganization notice dated Apr. 15, 1991.

Human Development Services, Office of *See* **Human Development, Office of**

Human Embryo Stem Cell Registry Approved by Presidential announcement of Aug. 9, 2001 and established through National Institute of Health's Departmental Notice NOT–OD–01–058 of Aug. 27, 2001. Renamed Human Pluripotent Stem Cell Registry by EO 13435 of June 20, 2007.

Hydrographic Office Jurisdiction transferred from *Bureau of Navigation* to Chief of Naval Operations by EO 9126 of Apr. 8, 1942, and by Reorg. Plan No. 3 of 1946, effective July 16, 1946. Renamed U.S. Naval Oceanographic Office by act of July 10, 1962 (76 Stat. 154).

Imagery and Mapping Agency, National Established by act of Sept. 23, 1996 (110 Stat. 2677). Renamed National Geospatial-Intelligence Agency by act of Nov. 24, 2003 (117 Stat. 1568).

Imagery Office, Central Established as a Department of Defense agency on May 6, 1992. Functions transferred to National Imagery and Mapping Agency by act of Sept. 23, 1996 (110 Stat. 2677).

Immigration, Bureau of Established as branch of the Department of the Treasury by act of Mar. 3, 1891 (26 Stat. 1085). Transferred to *Department of Commerce and Labor* by act of Feb. 14, 1903 (34 Stat. 596). Made *Bureau of Immigration and Naturalization* by act of June 29, 1906 (37 Stat. 736). Made separate division after the Department of Labor created by act of Mar. 4, 1913 (37 Stat. 736). Consolidated into Immigration and Naturalization Service, Department of Labor, by EO 6166 of June 10, 1933. Transferred to the Department of Justice by Reorg. Plan No. V of 1940, effective June 14, 1940. Abolished by act of Nov. 25, 2002 (116 Stat. 2205) and functions transferred to Homeland Security Department.

Immigration, Commissioners of Offices of commissioners of immigration of the several ports created by act of Aug. 18, 1894 (28 Stat. 391). Abolished by Reorg. Plan No. III of 1940, effective June 30, 1940, and functions transferred to *Bureau of Immigration and Naturalization,* Department of Labor.

Immigration and Naturalization, Bureau of *See* **Immigration, Bureau of**

Immigration and Naturalization, District Commissioner of Created by act of Aug. 18, 1894 (28 Stat. 391). Abolished by Reorg. Plan No. III of 1940, effective June 30, 1940. Functions administered by the Commissioner of Immigration and Naturalization, Department of Justice, through district immigration and naturalization directors.

Immigration and Naturalization Service *See* **Immigration, Bureau of**

Import Programs, Office of Established by the Secretary of Commerce Feb. 14, 1971. Functions transferred to *Domestic and International Business Administration,* effective Nov. 17, 1972.

Indian Claims Commission Established by act of Aug. 13, 1946 (60 Stat. 1049). Terminated by act of Oct. 8, 1976 (90 Stat. 1990), and pending cases transferred to *U.S. Court of Claims* Sept. 30, 1978.

Indian Commissioners, Board of Established by section 2039, Revised Statutes. Abolished by EO 6145 of May 25, 1933.

Indian Education Programs, Office of Established within the Bureau of Indian Affairs, Department of the Interior, by act of June 23, 1972 (86 Stat. 343). Renamed Bureau of Indian Education by Departmental Manual Release No. 3721 of Aug. 29, 2006.

Indian Medical Facilities Functions transferred from the Department of the Interior to the *Department of Health, Education, and Welfare,* to be administered by the Surgeon General of Public Health Service, by act of Aug. 5, 1954 (68 Stat. 674).

Indian Opportunity, National Council on Established by EO 11399 of Mar. 6, 1968. Terminated Nov. 26, 1974, by act of Nov. 26, 1969 (83 Stat. 220).

Indian Policy Review Commission, American Established by act of Jan. 2, 1975 (88 Stat. 1910). Terminated June 30, 1977, pursuant to terms of act.

Industrial Analysis, Committee of Established by EO 7323 of Mar. 21, 1936. Terminated Feb. 17, 1937.

Industrial Cooperation, Coordinator for Established by EO 7193 of Sept. 26, 1935. Continued by EO 7324 of Mar. 30, 1936. Terminated June 30, 1937.

Industrial Emergency Committee Established by EO 6770 of June 30, 1934. Consolidated with *National Emergency Council* by EO 6889–A of Oct. 29, 1934.

Industrial Pollution Control Council Staff, National Established by Department of Commerce Organization Order 35–3 of June 17, 1970. *Staff* abolished by departmental organization order of Sept. 10, 1973. Council inactive.

Industrial Recovery Board, National Established by EO 6859 of Sept. 27, 1934. Terminated by EO 7075 of June 15, 1935.

Industrial Recovery Board, Special Established by EO 6173 of June 16, 1933. Functions absorbed by *National Emergency Council* under terms of EO 6513 of Dec. 18, 1933.

Industrial Relations, Office of Activated in the Department of the Navy Sept. 14, 1945. Superseded June 22, 1966, by creation of *Office of Civilian Manpower Management.*

Industry and Trade Administration *See* **Business and Defense Services Administration**

Information, Committee for Reciprocity Established by EO 6750 of June 27, 1934; reestablished by EO 10004 of Oct. 5, 1948, which revoked EO 6750. Superseded by EO 10082 of Oct. 5, 1949; abolished by EO 11075 of Jan. 15, 1963, which revoked EO 10082.

Information, Coordinator of Established by Presidential order of July 11, 1941. Functions exclusive of foreign information activities transferred by military order of June 13, 1942, to jurisdiction of Joint Chiefs of Staff, *War Department,* as *Office of Strategic Services.* Foreign information functions transferred to *Office of War Information* by EO 9182 of June 13, 1942.

Information, Division of Established pursuant to Presidential letter of Feb. 28, 1941, to *Liaison Officer, Office of Emergency Management.* Abolished by EO 9182 of June 13, 1942. Functions relating to public information on war effort transferred and consolidated with *Office of War Information,* and publication services relating to specific agencies of OEM transferred to those agencies.

Information, Office of Coordinator of Transferred, exclusive of foreign information activities, to *Office of War Information* by EO 9182 of June 13, 1942. Designated *Office of Strategic Services* and transferred to jurisdiction of Joint Chiefs of Staff by military order of June 13, 1942. Terminated by EO 9621 of Sept. 20, 1945, and functions distributed to the Departments of State and *War.*

Information Administration, International Transferred from the Department of State to the *U.S. Information Agency* by Reorg. Plan No. 8 of 1953, effective Aug. 1, 1953.

Information Agency, U.S. Established by Reorg. Plan No. 8 of 1953, effective Aug. 1, 1953. Abolished by Reorg. Plan No. 2 of 1977, effective Apr. 1, 1978; replaced by and functions transferred to *International Communication Agency.* Redesignated *U.S. Information Agency* by act of Aug. 24, 1982 (96 Stat. 291). Abolished by act of Oct. 21, 1998 (112 Stat. 2681–761), and functions transferred to the Department of State, effective Oct. 1, 1999.

Information and Public Affairs, Office of Merged with *Office of Intergovernmental Affairs* to form Office of Public and Intergovernmental Affairs by Order 1–85 of June 5, 1985 of the Secretary of Labor.

Information Resources Management, Office of *See* **Telecommunications Service, Automated Data**

Information Resources Management Service Established in the General Services Administration. Renamed Information Technology Service in 1995.

Information Security Committee, Interagency Established by EO 12065 of June 28, 1978. Abolished by EO 12356 of Apr. 2, 1982.

Information Security Oversight Office Established in General Services Administration by EO 12065 of June 28, 1978. EO 12065 revoked by EO 12356 of Apr. 2, 1982, which provided for continuation of Office.

Information Service, Government *See* **Information Service, U.S.**

Information Service, Interim International Established in the Department of State by EO 9608 of Aug. 31, 1945. Abolished Dec. 31, 1945, pursuant to terms of order.

Information Service, U.S. Established in March 1934 as division of *National Emergency Council.* Transferred to *Office of Government Reports* by Reorg. Plan No. II of 1939, effective July 1, 1939. Consolidated, along with other functions of *Office,* into *Division of Public Inquiries, Bureau of Special Services, Office of War Information,* by EO 9182 of June 13, 1942. *Bureau of Special Services* renamed *Government Information Service* and transferred to *Bureau of the Budget* by EO 9608 of Aug. 31, 1945. *Service* transferred to *Office of Government Reports* by EO 9809 of Dec. 12, 1946.

Information Systems Council Established by EO 13356 of Aug. 27, 2004. Abolished by EO 13388 of Oct. 25, 2005 (70 FR 62025).

Information Technology Service Established in General Services Administration. Abolished by General Services Administrative Order No. 5440.492, Aug. 21, 1996, and functions transferred to Federal Telecommunications Service.

Insane, Government Hospital for the Established by act of Mar. 3, 1855 (10 Stat. 682). Renamed Saint Elizabeth's Hospital by act of July 1, 1916 (39 Stat. 309). Transferred from the Department of the Interior to *Federal Security Agency* by Reorg. Plan No. IV of 1940, effective June 30, 1940. Transferred to *Department of Health, Education, and Welfare* by Reorg. Plan No. 1 of 1953, effective Apr. 11, 1953. Functions redelegated to National Institute of Mental Health by Secretary's reorganization order of Aug. 9, 1967. Property and administration transferred to District of Columbia Government by act of Nov. 8, 1984 (98 Stat. 3369).

Installations, Director of Established in the Department of Defense by act of July 14, 1952 (66 Stat. 625). Abolished by Reorg. Plan No. 6 of 1953, effective June 30, 1953, and functions transferred to the Secretary of Defense.

Insular Affairs, Bureau of Transferred from *Department of War* to *Division of Territories and Island Possessions,* the Department of the Interior, by Reorg. Plan No. II of 1939, effective July 1, 1939.

Insurance Administrator, Federal Established by act of Aug. 1, 1968 (82 Stat. 567). Functions transferred to Federal Emergency Management Agency by Reorg. Plan No. 3 of 1978, effective Apr. 1, 1979.

Integrity and Efficiency, President's Council on Established by EO 12301 of Mar. 26, 1981 (46 FR 19211). Abolished and reestablished by EO 12625 of Jan 27, 1988 (53 FR 2812). Abolished and reestablished by EO 12805 of May 11, 1992 (57 FR 20627).

Intelligence, Office of Established within the Department of Energy by Public Law 106–65 of Oct. 5, 1999 (113 Stat. 955). Merged with *Office of Counterintelligence* to form Office of Intelligence and Counterintelligence by memorandum of March 9, 2006 of the Secretary of Energy.

Intelligence Activities, President's Board of Consultants on Foreign Established by EO 10656 of Feb. 6, 1956. EO 10656 revoked by EO 10938 of May 4, 1961, and *Board* terminated. Functions transferred to President's Foreign Intelligence Advisory Board.

Intelligence Advisory Board, President's Foreign Established by EO 11460 of Mar. 20, 1969. Abolished by EO 11984 of May 4, 1977. Reestablished by EO 12331 of Oct. 20, 1981.

Intelligence Authority, National Established by Presidential directive of Jan. 22, 1946. Terminated on creation of Central Intelligence Agency under National Security Council by act of July 26, 1947 (61 Stat. 497).

Intelligence Group, Central Terminated on creation of Central Intelligence Agency by act of July 26, 1947 (61 Stat. 497).

Intelligence Policy and Review, Office of Transferred from the Criminal Division to the National Security Division by act of Mar. 9, 2006 (120 Stat. 249).

Inter-American Affairs, Institute of *See* **American Republics, Office for Coordination of Commercial and Cultural Relations between the**

Inter-American Affairs, Office of *See* **American Republics, Office for Coordination of Commercial and Cultural Relations between the**

Inter-American Affairs, Office of the Coordinator of *See* **American Republics, Office for Coordination of Commercial and Cultural Relations between the**

Interagency. *See other part of title*

Interdepartmental. *See also other part of title*

Interdepartmental Advisory Council Established January 1941 to advise *Coordinator of Health, Welfare, and Related Defense Activities.* Terminated on creation of *Office of Defense Health and Welfare Service* Sept. 3, 1941.

Interest and Dividends, Committee on Established by EO 11695 of Jan. 11, 1973. Abolished by EO 11781 of May 1, 1974.

Intergovernmental Affairs, Office of Merged with *Office of Information and Public Affairs* to form Office of Public and Intergovernmental Affairs by Order 1–85 of June 5, 1985 of the Secretary of Labor. Renamed Office of Intergovernmental and External Affairs by Secretary of Health and Human Services notice of July 19, 2011 (76 FR 42710).

Intergovernmental and Interagency Affairs, Office of Abolished by decision of March 21, 2005 of the Secretary of Education under authority of section 413 of the Department of Education Organization Act.

Intergovernmental Relations, Advisory Commission on Established by act of Sept. 24, 1959 (73 Stat. 703). Terminated pursuant to act of Nov. 19, 1995 (109 Stat. 480). Continued in existence by act of Oct. 19, 1996 (110 Stat. 4004).

Intergovernmental Relations, Commission on Established by act of July 10, 1953 (67 Stat. 145). Final report submitted to Congress by June 30, 1955, pursuant to act of Feb. 7, 1955 (69 Stat. 7).

Intergovernmental Relations, Office of Established by EO 11455 of Feb. 14, 1969. Functions transferred to *Domestic Council* by EO 11690 of Dec. 14, 1972.

Interim Compliance Panel Established by Dec. 30, 1969 (83 Stat. 774). Terminated June 30, 1976, pursuant to terms of act.

Internal Revenue Service Functions relating to alcohol, tobacco, firearms, and explosives transferred to Bureau of Alcohol, Tobacco, and Firearms by Department of Treasury order of July 1, 1972.

Internal Security Division Established July 9, 1945, by transfer of functions from Criminal Division. Abolished Mar. 22, 1973, and functions transferred to Criminal Division, Department of Justice.

International *See also other part of title*

International Activities, Office of Renamed *Office of Service and Protocol* by Secretary of the Smithsonian Institution internal directive of Jan. 11, 1985.

International Development, Agency for Transferred from the Department of State to *U.S. International Development Cooperation Agency* by Reorg. Plan No. 2 of 1979, effective Oct. 1, 1979. Continued as agency within *IDCA* by IDCA Delegation of Authority No. 1 of Oct. 1, 1979. By act of Oct. 21, 1998 (112 Stat. 2681–790), became independent agency.

International Development Cooperation Agency, U.S. Established by Reorg. Plan No. 2 of 1979, effective Oct. 1, 1979. Abolished by act of Oct. 21, 1998 (112 Stat. 2681–790) and functions transferred to the Department of State, U.S. Agency for International Development, and Overseas Private Investment Corporation.

Interstate Commerce Commission Created by act of Feb. 4, 1887 (24 Stat. 379). Certain functions as cited in act of Oct. 15, 1966 (80 Stat. 931) transferred to the Secretary of Commerce. Functions relating to railroad and pipeline safety transferred to Federal Railroad Administrator and motor carrier safety to Federal Highway Administrator by act. Abolished by act of Dec. 29, 1995 (109 Stat. 932) and many functions transferred to the newly created Surface Transportation Board within the Department of Transportation.

Investigation, Bureau of Established by act of May 22, 1908 (35 Stat. 235). Functions consolidated with investigative functions of *Bureau of Prohibition, Division of Investigation,* Department of Justice, by EO 6166 of June 10, 1933, effective Mar. 2, 1934.

Investigation, Division of Designated as Federal Bureau of Investigation in the Department of Justice by act of Mar. 22, 1935 (49 Stat. 77).

Investigation and Research, Board of Established by act of Sept. 18, 1940 (54 Stat. 952). Extended to Sept. 18, 1944, by Proc. 2559 of June 26, 1942.

Investigations, Division of Established by administrative order of Apr. 27, 1933. Abolished Jan. 17, 1942, by administrative order and functions transferred to *Branch of Field Examination, General Land Office,* Department of the Interior.

Investments, Office of Foreign Direct Established in the Department of Commerce Jan. 2, 1968, by Departmental Organization Order 25–3 to carry out provisions of EO 11387 of Jan. 1, 1968. Controls on foreign investments terminated Jan. 29, 1974.

Iraq Reconstruction, Office of the Inspector General for Established by act of Nov. 6, 2003 (117 Stat. 1234). Abolished by act of Oct. 17, 2006 (120 Stat. 2397).

Iraq Transition Assistance Office Established by EO 13431 of May 8, 2007 (72 FR 26709). Personnel and administration transferred to Iraq Strategic Partnership Office by EO 13541 of May 7, 2010 (75 FR 26879).

Jamestown-Williamsburg-Yorktown National Celebration Commission Established by act of Aug. 13, 1953 (67 Stat. 576). Terminated upon submission of final report to Congress Mar. 1, 1958.

Job Corps, Office of Transferred from the Employment and Training Administration to the Office of the Secretary, U.S. Department of Labor by act of Dec. 30, 2005 (119 Stat. 2842). Transferred from the Office of the Secretary, U.S. Department of Labor to the Employment and Training Administration by act of Dec. 16, 2009 (123 Stat. 3238).

Joint. *See also other part of title*

Joint Resolutions of Congress *See* **State, Department of**

Judicial Procedure, Commission on International Rules of Established by act of Sept. 2, 1958 (72 Stat. 1743). Terminated Dec. 31, 1966, by act of Aug. 30, 1964 (78 Stat. 700).

Justice Assistance, Research, and Statistics, Office of Established in the Department of Justice by act of Dec. 27, 1979 (93 Stat. 1201). Abolished by act of Oct. 12, 1984 (98 Stat. 2091).

Kennedy, Commission To Report Upon the Assassination of President John F. Established by EO 11130 of Nov. 29, 1963. Report submitted Sept. 24, 1964, and *Commission* discharged by Presidential letter of same date.

Labor, President's Committee on Migratory Appointed by Presidential letter of Aug. 26, 1954. Formally established by EO 10894 of Nov. 15, 1960. Terminated Jan. 6, 1964, by the Secretary of Labor in letter to members, with approval of President.

Labor and Commerce, Department of Established by act of Feb. 14, 1903 (32 Stat. 825). Reorganized into separate Departments of Labor and Commerce by act of Mar. 4, 1913 (37 Stat. 736).

Labor Department, Solicitor for Transferred from the Department of Justice to the Department of Labor by EO 6166 of June 10, 1933.

Labor-Management Advisory Committee Established by EO 11695 of Jan. 11, 1973. Abolished by EO 11788 of June 18, 1974.

Labor-Management Policy, President's Advisory Committee on Established by EO 10918 of Feb. 16, 1961. Abolished by EO 11710 of Apr. 4, 1973.

Labor-Management Relations Services, Office of Established by Order 3–84 of May 3, 1984 of the Secretary of Labor. Renamed Bureau of Labor-Management Relations and Cooperative Programs by Secretarial Order 7–84 of Sept. 20, 1984 (49 FR 38374).

Labor-Management Services Administration *Office of Pension and Welfare Benefit Programs* transferred from *Administration* and constituted as separate unit by Order 1–84 of Jan. 20, 1984 of the Secretary of Labor (49 FR 4269). Remaining labor-management relations functions reassigned by Secretarial Order 3–84 of May 3, 1984.

Labor Organization, International Established in 1919 by Treaty of Versailles with U.S. joining in 1934. U.S. membership terminated Nov. 1, 1977, at President's direction. The U.S. rejoined the organization in February 1980.

Labor Relations Council, Federal Established by EO 11491 of Oct. 29, 1969. Abolished by Reorg. Plan No. 2 of 1978, effective Jan. 1, 1979, and functions transferred to Federal Labor Relations Authority.

Labor Standards, Apprenticeship Section, Division of Transferred to *Federal Security Agency* by EO 9139 of Apr. 18, 1942, functioning as *Apprentice Training Service.* Transferred to *War Manpower Commission* by EO 9247 of Sept. 17, 1942, functioning in *Bureau of Training.* Returned to the Department of Labor by EO 9617 of Sept. 19, 1945.

Labor Standards, Bureau of Established by Labor departmental order in 1934. Functions absorbed by Occupational Safety and Health Administration in May 1971.

Land Bank Commissioner *See* **Farm Loan Board, Federal**

Land Law Review Commission, Public Established by act of Sept. 19, 1964 (78 Stat. 982). Terminated Dec. 31, 1970, pursuant to terms of act.

Land Office, General Consolidated with *Grazing Service* into Bureau of Land Management, Department of the Interior, by Reorg. Plan No. 3 of 1946, effective July 16, 1946.

Land Office, Office of Recorder of the General Created in the Department of the Interior by act of July 4, 1836 (5 Stat. 111). Abolished by Reorg. Plan No. III of 1940, effective June 30, 1940, and functions transferred to *General Land Office.*

Land Policy Section Established in 1934 as part of *Program Planning Division, Agricultural Adjustment Administration.* Personnel taken over by *Resettlement Administration* in 1935.

Land Problems, Committee on National Established by EO 6693 of Apr. 28, 1934. Abolished by EO 6777 of June 30, 1934.

Land Program, Director of Basis of program found in act of June 16, 1933 (48 Stat. 200). *Special Board of Public Works* established by EO 6174 of June 16, 1933. Land Program established by *Board* by resolution passed Dec. 28, 1933, and amended July 18, 1934. *Federal Emergency Relief Administration* designated to administer program Feb. 28, 1934. Land Program transferred to *Resettlement Administration* by EO 7028 of Apr. 30, 1935. Functions of *Administration* transferred to the Secretary of Agriculture by EO 7530 of Dec. 31, 1936. Land conservation and land-utilization programs administered by *Administration* transferred to *Bureau of Agricultural Economics* by Secretary's Memorandum 733. Administration of land programs placed under Soil Conservation Service by Secretary's Memorandum 785 of Oct. 6, 1938.

Land Use Coordination, Office of Established by Secretary of Agriculture Memorandum 725 of July 12, 1937. Abolished Jan. 1, 1944, by General Departmental Circular 21 and functions administered by *Land Use Coordinator.*

Land Use and Water Planning, Office of Established in the Department of the Interior by Secretarial Order No. 2953 of May 7, 1973. Abolished by Secretarial Order No. 2988 of Mar. 11, 1976.

Law Enforcement Assistance Administration Established by act of June 19, 1968 (82 Stat. 197). Operations closed out by the Department of Justice due to lack of appropriations and remaining functions transferred to *Office of Justice Assistance, Research, and Statistics.*

Law Enforcement Training Center, Federal *See* **Law Enforcement Training Center, Consolidated Federal**

Law Enforcement Training Center, Consolidated Federal Established by Treasury Order No. 217, Mar. 2, 1970. Renamed Federal Law Enforcement Training Center by Amendment No. 1 to Treasury Order No. 217 on Aug. 14, 1975. Transferred to Department of Homeland Security by act of Nov. 25, 2002 (116 Stat. 2178).

Legislative Affairs, Office of Renamed Office of Intergovernmental and Legislative Affairs Feb. 24, 1984, by Attorney General's Order 1054–84 (49 FR 10177).

Lend-Lease Administration, Office of Established by EO 8926 of Oct. 28, 1941, to replace *Division of Defense Aid Reports.* Consolidated with *Foreign Economic Administration* by EO 9380 of Sept. 25, 1943.

Lewis and Clark Trail Commission Established by act of Oct. 6, 1964 (78 Stat. 1005). Terminated October 1969 by terms of act.

Libraries and Information Science, National Commission on Established by act of July 20, 1970 (84 Stat. 440). As per close out activities, the Commission was abolished by act of Dec. 26, 2007 (121 Stat. 2204), and functions transferred to the Institute of Museum and Library Services pursuant to instructions set forth in House Report 110–231 and Senate Report 110–107.

Library of Congress Police Established by act of Aug. 4, 1950 (64 Stat. 411). Personnel transferred to United States Capitol Police by acts of Dec. 26, 2007 (121 Stat. 2228) and Jan. 7, 2008 (121 Stat. 2546).

Lighthouses, Bureau of Established in the Department of Commerce by act of Aug. 7, 1789 (1 Stat. 53). Consolidated with U.S. Coast Guard by Reorg. Plan No. II of 1939, effective July 1, 1939.

Lincoln Sesquicentennial Commission Established by joint resolution of Sept. 2, 1957 (71 Stat. 587). Terminated Mar. 1, 1960, pursuant to terms of joint resolution.

Liquidation, Director of Established in *Office for Emergency Management* by EO 9674 of Jan. 4, 1946. Terminated by EO 9744 of June 27, 1946.

Liquidation Advisory Committee Established by EO 9674 of Jan. 4, 1946. Terminated by EO 9744 of June 27, 1946.

Literacy, National Institute for Established by act of July 25, 1991 (105 Stat. 333). Abolished by act of Dec. 16, 2009 (123 Stat. 3267).

Loan Agency, Federal Established by Reorg. Plan No. I of 1939, effective July 1, 1939, by consolidating *Reconstruction Finance Corporation*—including subordinate units of *RFC Mortgage Company, Disaster Loan Corporation, Federal National Mortgage Association, Defense Plant Corporation, Defense Homes Corporation, Defense Supplies Corporation, Rubber Reserve Company, Metals Reserve Company,* and *War Insurance Corporation* (later known as *War Damage Corporation*)—with *Federal Home Loan Bank Board, Home Owners' Loan Corporation, Federal Savings and Loan Insurance Corporation, Federal Housing Administration, Electric Home and Farm Authority,* and *Export-Import Bank of Washington. Federal Home Loan Bank Board, Federal Savings and Loan Insurance Corporation, Home Owners' Loan Corporation, Federal Housing Administration,* and *Defense Homes Corporation* transferred to *National Housing Agency* by EO 9070 of Feb. 24, 1942. *Reconstruction Finance Corporation* and its units (except *Defense Homes Corporation*), *Electric Home and Farm Authority,* and *Export-Import Bank of Washington* transferred to the Department of Commerce by EO 9071 of Feb. 24, 1942. *RFC* and units returned to *Federal Loan Agency* by act of Feb. 24, 1945 (59 Stat. 5). *Agency* abolished by act of June 30, 1947 (61 Stat. 202), and all property and records transferred to *Reconstruction Finance Corporation.*

Loan Fund, Development Established in *International Cooperation Administration* by act of Aug. 14, 1957 (71 Stat. 355). Created as independent corporate agency by act of June 30, 1958 (72 Stat. 261). Abolished by act of Sept. 4, 1961 (75 Stat. 445), and functions redelegated to Agency for International Development.

Loan Policy Board Established by act of July 18, 1958 (72 Stat. 385). Abolished by Reorg. Plan No. 4 of 1965, effective July 27, 1965, and functions transferred to Small Business Administration.

Longshoremen's Labor Board, National Established in the Department of Labor by EO 6748 of June 26, 1934. Terminated by Proc. 2120 of Mar. 11, 1935.

Low-Emission Vehicle Certification Board Established by act of Dec. 31, 1970 (84 Stat. 1701). Terminated by act of Mar. 14, 1980 (94 Stat. 98).

Lowell Historic Canal District Commission Established by act of Jan. 4, 1975 (88 Stat. 2330). Expired January 1977 pursuant to terms of act.

Loyalty Review Board Established Nov. 10, 1947, by *U.S. Civil Service Commission,* pursuant to EO 9835 of Mar. 21, 1947. Abolished by EO 10450 of Apr. 27, 1953.

Management, Budget and Evaluation, Office of Established within the Department of Energy pursuant to the Conference Report No. 107–258 on H.R. 2311, Energy and Water Development Appropriations Act, 2002. Abolished by memorandum of July 28, 2005 of the Secretary of Energy, and various functions transferred within the Department of Energy to the *Office of Management, Office of Chief Financial Officer,* and *Office of Human Capital Management.*

Management Improvement, Advisory Committee on Established by EO 10072 of July 29, 1949. Abolished by EO 10917 of Feb. 10, 1961, and functions transferred to *Bureau of the Budget.*

Management Improvement, President's Advisory Council on Established by EO 11509 of Feb. 11, 1970. Inactive as of June 30, 1973.

Manpower, President's Committee on Established by EO 11152 of Apr. 15, 1964. Terminated by EO 11515 of Mar. 13, 1970.

Manpower Administration Renamed Employment and Training Administration by Order 14–75 of Nov. 12, 1975 of the Secretary of Labor.

Manpower Management, Office of Civilian Renamed Office of Civilian Personnel by Notice 5430 of Oct. 1, 1976 of the Secretary of the Navy.

Marine Affairs, Office of Established by the Secretary of the Interior Apr. 30, 1970, to replace *Office of Marine Resources,* created by Secretary Oct. 22, 1968. Abolished by Secretary Dec. 4, 1970.

Marine Corps Memorial Commission, U.S. Established by act of Aug. 24, 1947 (61 Stat. 724). Terminated by act of Mar. 14, 1980 (94 Stat. 98).

Marine Debris Coordinating Committee Renamed Interagency Marine Debris Coordinating Committee by act of Dec. 22, 2006 (120 Stat. 3337).

Marine Inspection and Navigation, Bureau of *See* **Navigation and Steamboat Inspection, Bureau of**

Marine Resources and Engineering Development, National Council on Established in Executive Office of the President by act of June 17, 1966 (80 Stat. 203). Terminated Apr. 30, 1971, due to lack of funding.

Maritime Administration Established in the Department of Commerce by Reorg. Plan No. 21 of 1950, effective May 24, 1950. Transferred to the Department of Transportation by act of Aug. 6, 1981 (95 Stat. 151).

Maritime Advisory Committee Established by EO 11156 of June 17, 1964. Terminated by EO 11427 of Sept. 4, 1968.

Maritime Board, Federal *See* **Maritime Commission, U.S.**

Maritime Commission, U.S. Established by act of June 29, 1936 (49 Stat. 1985), as successor agency to *U.S. Shipping Board* and *U.S. Shipping Board Merchant Fleet Corporation.* Training functions transferred to Commandant of Coast Guard by EO 9083 of Feb. 27, 1942. Functions further transferred to *War Shipping Administration* by EO 9198 of July 11, 1942. Abolished by Reorg. Plan No. 21 of 1950, effective May 24, 1950, which established *Federal Maritime Board* and *Maritime Administration* as successor agencies. *Board* abolished, regulatory functions transferred to Federal Maritime Commission, and functions relating to subsidization of merchant marine transferred to the Secretary of Commerce by Reorg. Plan No. 7 of 1961, effective Aug. 12, 1961.

Maritime Labor Board Authorized by act of June 23, 1938 (52 Stat. 968). Mediatory duties abolished by act of June 23, 1941 (55 Stat. 259); title expired June 22, 1942.

Marketing Administration, Surplus Established by Reorg. Plan No. III of 1940, effective June 30, 1940, consolidating functions vested in *Federal Surplus Commodities Corporation* and *Division of Marketing and Marketing Agreements, Agricultural Adjustment Administration.* Consolidated with other agencies into *Agricultural Marketing Administration* by EO 9069 of Feb. 23, 1942.

Marketing and Marketing Agreements, Division of Established in the Department of Agriculture by act of June 3, 1937 (50 Stat. 246). Consolidated with *Federal Surplus Commodities Corporation* into *Surplus Marketing Administration* by Reorg. Plan No. III of 1940, effective June 30, 1940.

Mediation, U.S. Board of Established by act of May 20, 1926 (44 Stat. 577). Abolished by act of June 21, 1934 (48 Stat. 1193), and superseded by National Mediation Board, July 21, 1934.

Medical Information Systems Program Office, Tri-Service Renamed Defense Medical Systems Support Center by memorandum of the Assistant Secretary of Defense (Health Affairs) May 3, 1985.

Medical Services Administration Established by the *Secretary of Health, Education, and Welfare* reorganization of Aug. 15, 1967. Transferred from *Social and Rehabilitation Service* to Health Care Financing Administration by Secretary's reorganization of Mar. 8, 1977 (42 FR 13262).

Medicine and Surgery, Department of Established in the *Veterans Administration* by act of Sept. 2, 1958 (72 Stat. 1243). Renamed *Veterans Health Services and Research Administration* in the Department of Veterans Affairs by act of Oct. 25, 1988 (102 Stat. 2640). Renamed Veterans Health Administration by act of May 7, 1991 (105 Stat. 187).

Memorial Commission, National Established by Public Resolution 107 of Mar. 4, 1929 (45 Stat. 1699). Terminated by EO 6166 of June 10, 1933, and functions transferred to *Office of National Parks, Buildings, and Reservations,* Department of the Interior.

Mental Health, National Institute of Established by act of July 3, 1946 (60 Stat. 425). Made entity within the Alcohol, Drug Abuse, and Mental Health Administration by act of May 14, 1974 (88 Stat. 135). Functions transferred to the Department of Health and Human Services by act of Oct. 17, 1979 (93 Stat. 695). (*See also* act of Oct. 27, 1986; 100 Stat. 3207–106.) Abolished by act of July 10, 1992 (106 Stat. 331). Reestablished by act of July 10, 1992 (106 Stat. 364).

Metals Reserve Company Established June 28, 1940, by act of Jan. 22, 1932 (47 Stat. 5). Transferred from *Federal Loan Agency* to the Department of Commerce by EO 9071 of Feb. 24, 1942. Returned to *Federal Loan Agency* by act of Feb. 24, 1945 (59 Stat. 5). Dissolved by act of June 30, 1945 (59 Stat. 310), and functions transferred to *Reconstruction Finance Corporation.*

Metric Board, U.S. Established by act of Dec. 23, 1975 (89 Stat. 1007). Terminated Oct. 1, 1982, due to lack of funding.

Mexican-American Affairs, Interagency Committee on Established by Presidential memorandum of June 9, 1967. Renamed *Cabinet Committee on Opportunities for Spanish-Speaking People* by act of Dec. 30, 1969 (83 Stat. 838). Terminated Dec. 30, 1974, pursuant to terms of act.

Mexican Claims Commission, American Established by act of Dec. 18, 1942 (56 Stat. 1058). Terminated Apr. 4, 1947, by act of Apr. 3, 1945 (59 Stat. 59).

Mexican Claims Commission, Special Established by act of Apr. 10, 1935 (49 Stat. 149). Terminated by EO 7909 of June 15, 1938.

Mexico Commission for Border Development and Friendship, U.S. Established through exchange of notes of Nov. 30 and Dec. 3, 1966, between U.S. and Mexico. Terminated Nov. 5, 1969.

Micronesian Claims Commission Established by act of July 1, 1971 (85 Stat. 92). Terminated Aug. 3, 1976, pursuant to terms of act.

Migration, Intergovernmental Committee for European Renamed Intergovernmental Committee for Migration by Resolution 624, passed by *Intergovernmental Committee for European Migration Council,* effective Nov. 11, 1980.

Migration, International Committee for Created in 1951. Renamed International Organization for Migration pursuant to article 29, paragraph 2, of the ICM constitution, effective Nov. 14, 1989.

Migratory Bird Conservation Commission Chairmanship transferred from the Secretary of Agriculture to the Secretary of the Interior by Reorg. Plan No. II of 1939, effective July 1, 1939.

Military Air Transport Service Renamed *Military Airlift Command* in U.S. Air Force by HQ MATS/MAC Special Order G–164 of Jan. 1, 1966.

Military Airlift Command Inactivated June 1, 1992.

Military Appeals, United States Court of Established under Article I of the Constitution of the United States pursuant to act of May 5, 1950, as amended. Renamed United States Court of Appeals for the Armed Forces by act of Oct. 5, 1994 (108 Stat. 2831).

Military Establishment, National Established as executive department of the Government by act of July 26, 1947 (61 Stat. 495). Designated Department of Defense by act of Aug. 10, 1949 (63 Stat. 579).

Military Intelligence College, Joint Established by DoD Directive 3305.1 of January 14, 1998. Renamed *National Defense Intelligence College by DOD Instruction 3305.01 of Dec. 22, 2006. See also* Defense Intelligence College.

Military Purchases, Interdepartmental Committee for Coordination of Foreign and Domestic Informal liaison committee created on Presidential notification of Dec. 6, 1939, to the Secretaries of the Treasury and *War* and the Acting Secretary of the Navy. Committee dissolved in accordance with Presidential letter to the Secretary of the Treasury Apr. 14, 1941, following approval of act of Mar. 11, 1941 (55 Stat. 31).

Military Renegotiation Policy and Review Board Established by directive of the Secretary of Defense July 19, 1948. Abolished by Secretary's letter of Jan. 18, 1952, which transferred functions to *Renegotiation Board.*

Military Sea Transportation Service Renamed Military Sealift Command in U.S. Navy by COMSC notice of Aug. 1, 1970.

Militia Bureau Established in 1908 as *Division of Militia Affairs, Office of the Secretary of War.* Superseded in 1933 by National Guard Bureau.

Mine Health and Safety Academy, National Transferred from the Department of the Interior to the Department of Labor by act of July 25, 1979 (93 Stat. 111).

Minerals Exploration, Office of Established by act of Aug. 21, 1958 (72 Stat. 700). Functions transferred to *Geological Survey* by Order 2886 of Feb. 26, 1965 of the Secretary of the Interior.

Minerals Management Service Established on Jan. 19, 1982 by Secretarial order. Renamed as the *Bureau of Ocean Energy Management, Regulation and Enforcement* on June 18, 2010 by Secretarial order 3302. Reorganized into the Bureau of Ocean Energy Management and the Bureau of Safety and Environmental Enforcement by Secretarial order 3299 of May 19, 2010.

Minerals Mobilization, Office of Established by the Secretary of the Interior pursuant to act of Sept. 8, 1950 (64 Stat. 798) and EO 10574 of Nov. 5, 1954, and by order of *Office of Defense Mobilization.* Succeeded by *Office of Minerals and Solid Fuels* Nov. 2, 1962. *Office of Minerals Policy Development* combined with *Office of Research and Development* in the Department of the Interior May 21, 1976, under authority of Reorg. Plan No. 3 of 1950, to form *Office of Minerals Policy and Research Analysis.* Abolished Sept. 30, 1981, by Secretarial Order 3070 and functions transferred to Bureau of Mines.

Minerals Policy and Research Analysis, Office of *See* **Minerals Mobilization, Office of**

Minerals and Solid Fuels, Office of Established by the Secretary of the Interior Oct. 26, 1962. Abolished and functions assigned to Deputy Assistant Secretary—Minerals and Energy Policy, Office of the Assistant Secretary—Mineral Resources, effective Oct. 22, 1971.

Mines, Bureau of Established in the Department of the Interior by act of May 16, 1910 (36 Stat. 369). Transferred to the Department of Commerce by EO 4239 of June 4, 1925. Transferred to the Department of the Interior by EO 6611 of Feb. 22, 1934. Renamed United States Bureau of Mines by act of May 18, 1992 (106 Stat. 172). Terminated pursuant to act of Jan. 26, 1996 (110 Stat. 32). Certain functions transferred to Secretary of Energy by act of Apr. 26, 1996 (110 Stat. 1321–167).

Mining Enforcement and Safety Administration Established by Order 2953 of May 7, 1973 of the Secretary of the Interior. Terminated by departmental directive Mar. 9, 1978, and functions transferred to Mine Safety and Health Administration, Department of Labor, established by act of Nov. 9, 1977 (91 Stat. 1319).

Minority Business Enterprise, Office of Renamed Minority Business Development Agency by Commerce Secretarial Order DOO–254A of Nov. 1, 1979.

Minority Health and Health Disparities, National Center on Established by act of act of Nov. 22, 2000 (114 Stat. 2501). Renamed National Institute on

Minority Health and Health Disparities by act of Mar. 23, 2010 (124 Stat. 973).

Mint, Bureau of the Renamed U.S. Mint by Treasury Secretarial order of Jan. 9, 1984 (49 FR 5020).

Missile Sites Labor Commission Established by EO 10946 of May 26, 1961. Abolished by EO 11374 of Oct. 11, 1967, and functions transferred to Federal Mediation and Conciliation Service.

Missouri Basin Survey Commission Established by EO 10318 of Jan. 3, 1952. Final report of *Commission* submitted to President Jan. 12, 1953, pursuant to EO 10329 of Feb. 25, 1952.

Missouri River Basin Commission Established by EO 11658 of Mar. 22, 1972. Terminated by EO 12319 of Sept. 9, 1981.

Mobilization, Office of Civil and Defense *See* **Mobilization, Office of Defense and Civilian**

Mobilization, Office of Defense and Civilian Established by Reorg. Plan No. 1 of 1958, effective July 1, 1958. Redesignated as *Office of Civil and Defense Mobilization* by act of Aug. 26, 1958 (72 Stat. 861), consolidating functions of *Office of Defense Mobilization* and *Federal Civil Defense Administration.* Civil defense functions transferred to the Secretary of Defense by EO 10952 of July 20, 1961, and remaining organization redesignated *Office of Emergency Planning* by act of Sept. 22, 1961 (75 Stat. 630).

Mobilization Policy, National Advisory Board on Established by EO 10224 of Mar. 15, 1951. EO 10224 revoked by EO 10773 of July 1, 1958.

Monetary and Financial Problems, National Advisory Council on International Established by act of July 31, 1945 (59 Stat. 512). Abolished by Reorg. Plan No. 4 of 1965, effective July 27, 1965, and functions transferred to President. Functions assumed by National Advisory Council on International Monetary and Financial Policies, established by EO 11269 of Feb. 14, 1966.

Monument Commission, National Established by act of Aug. 31, 1954 (68 Stat. 1029). Final report submitted in 1957, and audit of business completed September 1964.

Monuments in War Areas, American Commission for the Protection and Salvage of Artistic and Historic Established by President June 23, 1943; announced by Secretary of State Aug. 20, 1943. Activities assumed by the Department of State Aug. 16, 1946.

Morris K. Udall Foundation Established by act of Mar. 19, 1992 (106 Stat 79). Renamed Morris K. Udall and Stewart L. Udall Foundation by act of Nov. 3, 2009 (123 Stat. 2977).

Mortgage Association, Federal National Chartered Feb. 10, 1938, by act of June 27, 1934 (48 Stat. 1246). Grouped with other agencies to form *Federal Loan Agency* by Reorg. Plan No. I of 1939, effective July 1, 1939. Transferred to the Department of Commerce by EO 9071 of Feb. 24, 1942. Returned to *Federal Loan Agency* by act of Feb. 24, 1945 (59 Stat. 5). Transferred to *Housing and Home Finance Agency* by Reorg. Plan No. 22 of 1950, effective July 10, 1950. Rechartered by act of Aug. 2, 1954 (68 Stat. 590) and made constituent agency of *Housing and Home Finance Agency.* Transferred with functions of *Housing and Home Finance Agency* to the Department of Housing and Urban Development by act of Sept. 9, 1965 (79 Stat. 667). Made Government-sponsored, private corporation by act of Aug. 1, 1968 (82 Stat. 536).

Motor Carrier Claims Commission Established by act of July 2, 1948 (62 Stat. 1222). Terminated Dec. 31, 1952, by acts of July 11, 1951 (65 Stat. 116), and Mar. 14, 1952 (66 Stat. 25).

Mount Rushmore National Memorial Commission Established by act of Feb. 25, 1929 (45 Stat. 1300). Expenditures ordered administered by the Department of the Interior by EO 6166 of June 10, 1933. Transferred to National Park Service, Department of the Interior, by Reorg. Plan No. II of 1939, effective July 1, 1939.

Mounted Horse Unit Transferred from the United States Capitol Police to the United States Park Police by Public Law 109–55 of Aug. 2, 2005 (119 Stat. 572).

Munitions Board Established in the Department of Defense by act of July 26, 1947 (61 Stat. 499). Abolished by Reorg. Plan No. 6 of 1953, effective June 30, 1953, and functions vested in the Secretary of Defense.

Munitions Board, Joint Army and Navy Organized in 1922. Placed under direction of President by military order of July 5, 1939. Reconstituted Aug. 18, 1945, by order approved by President. Terminated on establishment of *Munitions Board* by act of July 26, 1947 (61 Stat. 505).

Museum of American Art, National Renamed Smithsonian American Art Museum by Act of October 27, 2000 (114 Stat. 1463).

Museum of History and Technology, National Renamed National Museum of American History in Smithsonian Institution by act of Oct. 13, 1980 (94 Stat. 1884).

Museum Services, Institute of Established by act of June 23, 1972 (86 Stat. 327). Transferred to Office of Educational Research and Improvement, Department of Education, by act of Oct. 17, 1979 (93 Stat. 678), effective May 4, 1980. Transferred to National Foundation on the Arts and the Humanities by act of Dec. 23, 1981 (95 Stat. 1414). Functions transferred to the Institute of Museum and Library Services by act of Sept. 30, 1996 (110 Stat. 3009– 307).

Narcotics, Bureau of Established in the Department of the Treasury by act of June 14, 1930 (46 Stat. 585). Abolished by Reorg. Plan No. 1 of 1968, effective Apr. 8, 1968, and functions transferred to *Bureau of Narcotics and Dangerous Drugs,* Department of Justice.

Narcotics, President's Council on Counter- Renamed President's Drug Policy Council by EO 13023, Nov. 6, 1996 (61 FR 57767).

Narcotics Control, Cabinet Committee on International Established by Presidential memorandum of Aug. 17, 1971. Terminated by Presidential memorandum of Mar. 14, 1977.

National. *See other part of title*

Naval Material, Office of Established by act of Mar. 5, 1948 (62 Stat. 68). Abolished by the Department of Defense reorg. order of Mar. 9, 1966, and functions transferred to the Secretary of the Navy (31 FR 7188).

Naval Material Command *See* **Naval Material Support Establishment**

Naval Material Support Establishment Established by Department of the Navy General Order 5 of July 1, 1963 (28 FR 7037). Replaced by *Naval Material Command* pursuant to General Order 5 of Apr. 29, 1966 (31 FR 7188). Functions realigned to form Office of Naval Acquisition Support, and termination of *Command* effective May 6, 1985.

Naval Observatory Jurisdiction transferred from *Bureau of Navigation* to Chief of Naval Operations by EO 9126 of Apr. 8, 1942, and by Reorg. Plan No. 3 of 1946, effective July 16, 1946.

Naval Oceanography Command Renamed Naval Meteorology and Oceanography Command in 1995.

Naval Petroleum and Oil Shale Reserves, Office of Established by the Secretary of the Navy, as required by law (70A Stat. 457). Jurisdiction transferred to the Department of Energy by act of Aug. 4, 1977 (91 Stat. 581).

Naval Reserve Established by act of Mar. 3, 1915 (38 Stat. 940). Redesignated Navy Reserve by Public Law 109–163 of Jan. 6, 2006 (119 Stat. 3233).

Naval Weapons, Bureau of Established by act of Aug. 18, 1959 (73 Stat. 395), to replace *Bureau of Ordnance and Aeronautics.* Abolished by Department of Defense reorg. order of Mar. 9, 1966, and functions transferred to the Secretary of the Navy (31 FR 7188), effective May 1, 1966.

Navigation, Bureau of Created by act of July 5, 1884 (23 Stat. 118), as special service under the Department of the Treasury. Transferred to the *Department of Commerce and Labor* by act of Feb. 4, 1903 (32 Stat. 825). Consolidated with *Bureau of Navigation and Steamboat Inspection* by act of June 30, 1932 (47 Stat. 415).

Navigation, Bureau of Renamed Bureau of Naval Personnel by act of May 13, 1942 (56 Stat. 276).

Navigation and Steamboat Inspection, Bureau of Renamed *Bureau of Marine Inspection and Navigation* by act of May 27, 1936 (49 Stat. 1380). Functions transferred to *Bureau of Customs,* Department of the Treasury, and U.S. Coast Guard by EO 9083 of Feb. 28, 1942. Transfer made permanent and *Bureau* abolished by Reorg. Plan. No. 3 of 1946, effective July 16, 1946.

Navy, Department of Defense housing functions transferred to *Federal Public Housing Authority, National Housing Agency,* by EO 9070 of Feb. 24, 1942.

Navy Bureau of Medicine and Surgery, Dental Division of Renamed Dental Corps of the Navy Bureau of Medicine and Surgery by act of Oct. 17, 2006 (120 Stat. 2234).

Navy Commissioners, Board of Established by act of Feb. 7, 1815 (3 Stat. 202). Abolished by act of Aug. 31, 1842 (5 Stat. 579).

Neighborhoods, National Commission on Established by act of Apr. 30, 1977 (91 Stat. 56). Terminated May 4, 1979, pursuant to terms of act.

Neighborhoods, Voluntary Associations and Consumer Protection, Office of Abolished and certain functions transferred to Office of the Assistant Secretary for Housing—Federal Housing Commissioner and Office of the Assistant Secretary for Community Planning and Development. Primary enabling legislation, act of Oct. 31, 1978 (92 Stat. 2119), repealed by act of Aug. 13, 1981 (95 Stat. 398). Abolishment of *Office* and transfer of functions carried out by Housing and Urban Development Secretarial order.

New England River Basins Commission Established by EO 11371 of Sept. 6, 1967. Terminated by EO 12319 of Sept. 9, 1981.

Nicaro Project Responsibility for management of Nicaro nickel producing facilities in Oriente Province, Cuba, transferred from *Office of Special Assistant to the Administrator (Nicaro Project)* to *Defense Materials Service* by General Services Administrator, effective July 7, 1959. Facilities expropriated by Cuban Government and nationalized Oct. 26, 1960.

Noble Training Center Transferred from Public Health Service to the Center for Domestic Preparedness, Department of Homeland Security by act of Oct. 4, 2006 (120 Stat. 1433).

Northern Mariana Islands Commission on Federal Laws Created by joint resolution of Mar. 24, 1976 (90 Stat. 263). Terminated upon submission of final report in August 1985.

Nursing Research, National Center for Renamed National Institute of Nursing Research by act of June 10, 1993 (107 Stat. 178).

Nutrition Division Functions transferred from *Department of Health, Education, and Welfare* to the Department of Agriculture by EO 9310 of Mar. 3, 1943.

Ocean Mining Administration Established by Interior Secretarial Order 2971 of Feb. 24, 1975. Abolished by Department Manual Release 2273 of June 13, 1980.

Oceanography, Interagency Committee on Established by *Federal Council for Science and Technology* pursuant to EO 10807 of Mar. 13, 1959. Absorbed by *National Council on Marine Resources and Engineering Development* pursuant to Vice Presidential letter of July 21, 1967.

Office *See also other part of title*

Office Space, President's Advisory Commission on Presidential Established by act of Aug. 3, 1956 (70 Stat. 979). Terminated June 30, 1957, by act of Jan. 25, 1957 (71 Stat. 4).

Official Register Function of preparing *Official Register* vested in Director of the Census by act of Mar. 3, 1925 (43 Stat. 1105). Function transferred to *U.S. Civil Service Commission* by EO 6166 of June 10, 1933. Yearly compilation and publication required by act of Aug. 28, 1935 (49 Stat. 956). Act repealed by act of July 12, 1960 (74 Stat. 427), and last *Register* published in 1959.

Ohio River Basin Commission Established by EO 11578 of Jan. 13, 1971. Terminated by EO 12319 of Sept. 9, 1981.

Oil and Gas, Office of Established by the Secretary of the Interior May 6, 1946, in response to Presidential letter of May 3, 1946. Transferred to *Federal Energy Administration* by act of May 7, 1974 (88 Stat. 100).

Oil Import Administration Established in the Department of the Interior by Proc. 3279 of Mar. 10, 1959. Merged into *Office of Oil and Gas* Oct. 22, 1971.

Oil Import Appeals Board Established by the Secretary of Commerce Mar. 13, 1959, and made part of Office of Hearings and Appeals Dec. 23, 1971.

On-Site Inspection Agency Established on Jan. 26, 1988. Functions transferred to the Defense Threat Reduction Agency by DOD Directive 5105.62 of Sept. 30, 1998.

Operations Advisory Group Established by EO 11905 of Feb. 18, 1976. Abolished by Presidential Directive No. 2 of Jan. 20, 1977.

Operations Coordinating Board Established by EO 10483 of Sept. 2, 1953, which was superseded by EO 10700 of Feb. 25, 1957. EO 10700 revoked by EO 10920 of Feb. 18, 1961, and *Board* terminated.

Ordnance, Bureau of *See* **Ordnance and Hydrography, Bureau of**

Ordnance and Hydrography, Bureau of Established in the Department of the Navy by act of Aug. 31, 1842 (5 Stat. 579). Replaced under act of July 5, 1862 (12 Stat. 510), by *Bureau of Ordnance* and *Bureau of Navigation.* Abolished by act of Aug. 18, 1959 (73 Stat. 395), and functions transferred to *Bureau of Naval Weapons.*

Organization, President's Advisory Committee on Government Established by EO 10432 of Jan. 24, 1953. Abolished by EO 10917 of Feb. 10, 1961, and functions transferred to *Bureau of the Budget* for termination.

Organizations Staff, International Functions merged with Foreign Agricultural Service by memorandum of Dec. 7, 1973 of , effective Feb. 3, 1974.

Overseas Private Investment Corporation Transferred as separate agency to *U.S. International Development Cooperation Agency* by Reorg. Plan No. 2 of 1979, effective Oct. 1, 1979. Became an independent agency following the abolition of *IDCA* by act of Oct. 21, 1998 (112 Stat. 2681–790).

Oversight Board (for the Resolution Trust Corporation) Established by act of Aug. 9, 1989 (103 Stat. 363). Renamed *Thrift Depositor Protection Oversight Board* by act of Dec. 12, 1991 (105 Stat. 1767). Abolished by act of July 29, 1998 (112 Stat. 908). Authority and duties transferred to the Secretary of the Treasury.

Pacific Northwest River Basins Commission Established by EO 11331 of Mar. 6, 1967. Terminated by EO 12319 of Sept. 9, 1981.

Packers and Stockyards Administration Established by Memorandum 1613, supp. 1, of May 8, 1967 of the Secretary of Agriculture. Certain functions consolidated into Agricultural Marketing Service by Secretary's Memorandum 1927 of Jan. 15, 1978. Remaining functions incorporated into the Grain Inspection, Packers and Stockyards Administration by Secretary's Memorandum 1010–1 dated Oct. 20, 1994.

Panama Canal Operation of piers at Atlantic and Pacific terminals transferred to *Panama Railroad Company* by EO 7021 of Apr. 19, 1935. Panama Canal reestablished as *Canal Zone Government* by act of Sept. 26, 1950 (64 Stat. 1038).

Panama Canal Commission Established by act of Oct. 1, 1979, as amended (22 U.S.C. 3611). U.S. responsibility terminated by stipulation of the Panama Canal Treaty of 1977, which transferred responsibility for the Panama Canal to the Republic of Panama, effective Dec. 31, 1999. Commission terminated by act of Sept. 30, 2004 (118 Stat. 1140).

Panama Canal Company Established by act of June 29, 1948 (62 Stat. 1076). Abolished and superseded by *Panama Canal Commission* (93 Stat. 454).

Panama Railroad Company Incorporated Apr. 7, 1849, by New York State Legislature. Operated under private control until 1881, when original *French Canal Company* acquired most of its stock. *Company* and its successor, *New Panama Canal Company,* operated railroad as common carrier and also as adjunct in attempts to construct canal. In 1904 their shares of stock in *Panama Railroad Company* passed to ownership of U.S. as part of assets of *New Panama Canal Company* purchased under act of June 28,

1902 (34 Stat. 481). Remaining shares purchased from private owners in 1905. *Panama Railroad Company* reincorporated by act of June 29, 1948 (62 Stat. 1075) pursuant to requirements of act of Dec. 6, 1945 (59 Stat. 597). Reestablished as *Panama Canal Company* by act of Sept. 26, 1950 (64 Stat. 1038). The Secretary of the Army was directed to discontinue commercial operations of *Company* by Presidential letter of Mar. 29, 1961.

Paperwork, Commission on Federal Established by act of Dec. 27, 1974 (88 Stat. 1789). Terminated January 1978 pursuant to terms of act.

Park Service, National Functions in District of Columbia relating to space assignment, site selection for public buildings, and determination of priority in construction transferred to *Public Buildings Administration, Federal Works Agency,* under Reorg. Plan No. I of 1939, effective July 1, 1939.

Park Trust Fund Board, National Established by act of July 10, 1935 (49 Stat. 477). Terminated by act of Dec. 18, 1967 (81 Stat. 656), and functions transferred to National Park Foundation.

Parks, Buildings, and Reservations, Office of National Established in the Department of the Interior by EO 6166 of June 10, 1933. Renamed National Park Service by act of Mar. 2, 1934 (48 Stat. 362).

Parole, Board of Established by act of June 25, 1948 (62 Stat. 854). Abolished by act of Mar. 15, 1976 (90 Stat. 219), and functions transferred to U.S. Parole Commission.

Patent Office Provisions of first patent act administered by the Department of State, with authority for granting patents vested in board comprising Secretaries of State and *War* and Attorney General. Board abolished, authority transferred to Secretary of State, and registration system established by act of Feb. 21, 1793 (1 Stat. 318). *Office* made bureau in the Department of State in October 1802, headed by *Superintendent of Patents. Office* reorganized in 1836 by act of June 4, 1836 (5 Stat. 117) under *Commissioner of Patents. Office* transferred to the Department of the Interior in 1849. *Office* transferred to the Department of Commerce by EO 4175 of Mar. 17, 1925.

Patents Board, Government Established by EO 10096 of Jan. 23, 1950. Abolished by EO 10930 of Mar. 24, 1961, and functions transferred to the Secretary of Commerce.

Pay Board Established by EO 11627 of Oct. 15, 1971. Abolished by EO 11695 of Jan. 11, 1973.

Payment Limitations, Commission on Application of Established by act of May 13, 2002 (116 Stat. 216). Abolished by acts of May 22, 2008 (122 Stat. 1025) and June 18, 2008 (122 Stat. 1753).

Peace Corps Established in the Department of State by EO 10924 of Mar. 1, 1961, and continued by act of Sept. 22, 1961 (75 Stat. 612), and EO 11041 of Aug. 6, 1962. Functions transferred to ACTION by Reorg. Plan No. 1 of 1971, effective July 1, 1971. Made independent agency in executive branch by act of Dec. 29, 1981 (95 Stat. 1540).

Pennsylvania Avenue, Temporary Commission on Established by EO 11210 of Mar. 25, 1956. Inactive as of Nov. 15, 1969, due to lack of funding.

Pennsylvania Avenue Development Corporation Established by act of Oct. 27, 1972 (86 Stat. 1266). Terminated pursuant to act of Jan. 26, 1996 (110 Stat. 32) and act of Apr. 26, 1996 (110 Stat. 1321– 198). Functions transferred to General Services Administration, National Capital Planning Commission, and National Park Service (61 FR 11308), effective Apr. 1, 1996.

Pension and Welfare Benefit Programs, Office of *See* **Labor-Management Services Administration**

Pensions, Commissioner of Provided for by act of Mar. 2, 1833 (4 Stat. 668). Continued by act of Mar. 3, 1835 (4 Stat. 779), and other acts as *Office of the Commissioner of Pensions.* Transferred to the Department of the Interior as bureau by act of Mar. 3, 1849 (9 Stat. 395). Consolidated with other bureaus and agencies into *Veterans Administration* by EO 5398 of July 21, 1930.

Pensions, Office of the Commissioner of *See* **Pensions, Commissioner of**

Perry's Victory Memorial Commission Created by act of Mar. 3, 1919 (40 Stat. 1322). Administration of Memorial transferred to National Park Service by act of June 2, 1936 (49 Stat. 1393). *Commission* terminated by terms of act and membership reconstituted as advisory board to the Secretary of Interior

Perry's Victory Memorial Commission Created by act of Mar. 3, 1919 (40 Stat. 1322). Administration of Memorial transferred to National Park Service by act of June 2, 1936 (49 Stat. 1393). *Commission* terminated by terms of act and membership reconstituted as advisory board to the Secretary of Interior.

Personal Property, Office of *See* **Supply Service, Federal**

Personnel, National Roster of Scientific and Specialized Established by *National Resources Planning Board* pursuant to Presidential letter of June 18, 1940, to the Secretary of the Treasury. After Aug. 15, 1940, administered jointly by *Board* and *U.S. Civil Service Commission.* Transferred to *War Manpower Commission* by EO 9139 of Apr. 18, 1942. Transferred to the Department of Labor by EO 9617 of Sept. 19, 1945. Transferred with *Bureau of Employment Security* to *Federal Security Agency* by act of June 16, 1948 (62 Stat. 443). Transferred to the Department of Labor by Reorg. Plan No. 2 of 1949, effective Aug. 20, 1949, and became inactive. Roster functions transferred to National Science Foundation by act of May 10, 1950 (64 Stat. 154). Reactivated in 1950 as *National Scientific Register* by *Office of Education, Federal Security Agency,* through *National Security Resources Board* grant of funds, and continued by National Science Foundation funds until December 1952, when *Register* integrated into Foundation's National Register of Scientific and Technical Personnel project in Division of Scientific Personnel and Education.

Personnel Administration, Council of Established by EO 7916 of June 24, 1938, effective Feb. 1, 1939. Made unit in *U.S. Civil Service Commission* by EO 8467 of July 1, 1940. Renamed *Federal Personnel Council* by EO 9830 of Feb. 24, 1947. Abolished by act of July 31, 1953 (67 Stat. 300), and personnel and records transferred to *Office of Executive Director, U.S. Civil Service Commission.*

Personnel Council, Federal *See* **Personnel Administration, Council of**

Personnel Interchange, President's Commission on Established by EO 11451 of Jan. 19, 1969. Continued by EO 12136 of May 15, 1979, and renamed *President's Commission on Executive Exchange.* Continued by EO 12493 of Dec. 5, 1984. Abolished by EO 12760 of May 2, 1991.

Personnel Management, Liaison Office for Established by EO 8248 of Sept. 8, 1939. Abolished by EO 10452 of May 1, 1953, and functions transferred to *U.S. Civil Service Commission.*

Petroleum Administration for Defense Established under act of Sept. 8, 1950 (64 Stat. 798) by Order 2591 of Oct. 3, 1950 of the Secretary of the Interior, pursuant to EO 10161 of Sept. 9, 1950. Continued by Secretary's Order 2614 of Jan. 25, 1951, pursuant to EO 10200 of Jan. 3, 1951, and PAD Delegation 1 of Jan. 24, 1951. Abolished by Secretary's Order 2755 of Apr. 23, 1954.

Petroleum Administration for War *See* **Petroleum Coordinator for War, Office of**

Petroleum Administrative Board Established Sept. 11, 1933, by the Secretary of the Interior. Terminated Mar. 31, 1936, by EO 7076 of June 15, 1935. The Secretary of the Interior was authorized to execute functions vested in President by act of Feb. 22, 1935 (49 Stat. 30) by EO 7756 of Dec. 1, 1937. Secretary also authorized to establish *Petroleum Conservation Division* to assist in administering act. Records of *Petroleum Administrative Board* and *Petroleum Labor Policy Board* housed with *Petroleum Conservation Division, Office of Oil and Gas,* acting as custodian for the Secretary of the Interior.

Petroleum Coordinator for War, Office of Secretary of the Interior designated *Petroleum Coordinator for National Defense* pursuant to Presidential letter of May 28, 1941, and approved *Petroleum Coordinator for War* pursuant to Presidential letter of Apr. 20, 1942. *Office* abolished by EO 9276 of Dec. 2, 1942, and functions transferred to *Petroleum Administration for War,* established by same EO. *Administration* terminated by EO 9718 of May 3, 1946.

Petroleum Labor Policy Board Established by the Secretary of the Interior, as *Administrator of Code of Fair Competition for Petroleum Industry,* on recommendation of Planning and Coordination Committee Oct. 10, 1933. Reorganized by Secretary Dec. 19, 1933, and reorganization confirmed by order of Mar. 8, 1935. Terminated Mar. 31, 1936, when *Petroleum Administrative Board* abolished by EO 7076 of June 15, 1935.

Petroleum Reserves Corporation Established June 30, 1943, by *Reconstruction Finance Corporation.* Transferred to *Office of Economic Warfare* by EO 9360 of July 15, 1943. *Office* consolidated into *Foreign Economic Administration* by EO 9380 of Sept. 25, 1943. Functions transferred to *Reconstruction Finance Corporation* by EO 9630 of Sept. 27, 1945. *RFC's* charter amended Nov. 9, 1945, to change name to *War Assets Corporation. Corporation* designated by *Surplus Property Administrator* as disposal agency for all types of property for which *Reconstruction Finance Corporation* formerly disposal agency. Domestic surplus property functions of *Corporation* transferred to *War Assets Administration* by EO 9689 of Jan. 31, 1946. *Reconstruction Finance Corporation Board of Directors* ordered by President to dissolve *War Assets Corporation* as soon after Mar. 25, 1946, as practicable.

Philippine Alien Property Administration Established in *Office for Emergency Management* by EO 9789 of Oct. 14, 1946. Abolished by EO 10254 of June 15, 1951, and functions transferred to the Department of Justice.

Philippine War Damage Commission Established by act of Apr. 30, 1946 (60 Stat. 128). Terminated Mar. 31, 1951, by act of Sept. 6, 1950 (64 Stat. 712).

Photographic Interpretation Center, National Functions transferred to the National Imagery and Mapping Agency by act of Sept. 23, 1996 (110 Stat. 2677).

Physical Fitness, Committee on Established in *Office of Federal Security Administrator* by EO 9338 of Apr. 29, 1943. Terminated June 30, 1945.

Physical Fitness, President's Council on *See* **Youth Fitness, President's Council on**

Physician Payment Review Commission Established by act of Apr. 7, 1986 (100 Stat. 190). Terminated by act of Aug. 5, 1997 (111 Stat. 354). Assets, staff, and continuing responsibility for reports transferred to the Medicare Payment Advisory Commission.

Planning Board, National Established by *Administrator of Public Works* July 30, 1933. Terminated by EO 6777 of June 30, 1934.

Plant Industry, Bureau of Established by act of Mar. 2, 1902 (31 Stat. 922). Soil fertility and soil microbiology work of *Bureau of Chemistry and Soils* transferred to *Bureau* by act of May 17, 1935. Soil chemistry and physics and soil survey work of *Bureau of Chemistry and Soils* transferred to *Bureau* by Secretary's Memorandum 784 of Oct. 6, 1938. In February 1943 engineering research of *Bureau of Agricultural Chemistry and Engineering* transferred to *Bureau of Plant Industry, Soils, and*

Agricultural Engineering by Research Administration Memorandum 5 issued pursuant to EO 9069 of Feb. 23, 1942, and in conformity with Secretary's Memorandums 960 and 986. Functions transferred to Agricultural Research Service by Secretary's Memorandum 1320, supp. 4, of Nov. 2, 1953.

Plant Industry, Soils, and Agricultural Engineering, Bureau of *See* **Plant Industry, Bureau of**

Plant Quarantine, Bureau of *See* **Entomology and Plant Quarantine, Bureau of**

Policy Development, Office of *See* **Domestic Council**

Post Office, Department of *See* **Postal Service**

Postal Rate Commission Renamed Postal Regulatory Commission by act of Dec. 20, 2006 (120 Stat. 3241).

Postal Savings System Established by act of June 25, 1910 (36 Stat. 814). System closed by act of Mar. 28, 1966 (80 Stat. 92).

Postal Service Created July 26, 1775, by Continental Congress. Temporarily established by Congress by act of Sept. 22, 1789 (1 Stat. 70), and continued by subsequent acts. *Department of Post Office* made executive department under act of June 8, 1872 (17 Stat. 283). Offices of First, Second, Third, and Fourth Assistant Postmasters General abolished and Deputy Postmaster General and four Assistant Postmasters General established by Reorg. Plan No. 3 of 1949, effective Aug. 20, 1949. Reorganized as U.S. Postal Service in executive branch by act of Aug. 12, 1970 (84 Stat. 719), effective July 1, 1971.

Power Commission, Federal Established by act of June 10, 1920 (41 Stat. 1063). Terminated by act of Aug. 4, 1977 (91 Stat. 578), and functions transferred to the Department of Energy.

Preparedness, Office of Renamed *Federal Preparedness Agency* by General Services Administrator's order of June 26, 1975.

Preparedness Agency, Federal Functions transferred from General Services Administration to Federal Emergency Management Agency by EO 12148 of July 20, 1979.

President's. *See other part of title*

Presidential. *See other part of title*

Press Intelligence, Division of Established in August 1933. Made division of *National Emergency Council* July 10, 1935. Continued in *Office of Government Reports* by Reorg. Plan No. II of 1939, effective July 1, 1939. Transferred to *Office of War Information* by EO 9182 of June 13, 1942, functioning in *Bureau of Special Services. Office* abolished by EO 9608 of Aug. 31, 1945, and *Bureau* transferred to *Bureau of the Budget.* Upon reestablishment of *Office of Government Reports,* by EO 9809 of Dec. 12, 1946, *Division of Press Intelligence* made unit of *Office.*

Price Administration, Office of Established by EO 8734 of Apr. 11, 1941, combining *Price Division* and *Consumer Division* of *National Defense Advisory Commission.* Renamed *Office of Price Administration* by EO 8875 of Aug. 28, 1941, which transferred *Civilian Allocation Division* to *Office of Production Management.* Consolidated with other agencies into *Office of Temporary Controls* by EO 9809 of Dec. 12, 1946, except *Financial Reporting Division,* transferred to Federal Trade Commission.

Price Commission Established by EO 11627 of Oct. 15, 1971. Abolished by EO 11695 of Jan. 11, 1973.

Price Decontrol Board Established by act of July 25, 1946 (60 Stat. 669). Effective period of act of Jan. 30, 1942 (56 Stat. 23), extended to June 30, 1947, by joint resolution of June 25, 1946 (60 Stat. 664).

Price Stability for Economic Growth, Cabinet Committee on Established by Presidential letter of Jan. 28, 1959. Abolished by Presidential direction Mar. 12, 1961.

Price Stabilization, Office of Established by General Order 2 of *Economic Stabilization Administrator* Jan. 24, 1951. *Director of Price Stabilization* provided for in EO 10161 of Sept. 9, 1950. Terminated Apr. 30, 1953, by EO 10434 of Feb. 6, 1953, and provisions of acts of June 30, 1952 (66 Stat. 296) and June 30, 1953 (67 Stat. 131).

Prices and Costs, Committee on Government Activities Affecting Established by EO 10802 of Jan. 23, 1959. Abolished by EO 10928 of Mar. 23, 1961.

Priorities Board Established by order of *Council of National Defense,* approved Oct. 18, 1940, and by EO 8572 of Oct. 21, 1940. EO 8572 revoked by EO 8629 of Jan. 7, 1941.

Prison Industries, Inc., Federal Established by EO 6917 of Dec. 11, 1934. Transferred to the Department of Justice by Reorg. Plan No. II of 1939, effective July 1, 1939.

Prison Industries Reorganization Administration Functioned from Sept. 26, 1935, to Sept. 30, 1940, under authority of act of Apr. 8, 1935 (49 Stat. 115), and of EO's 7194 of Sept. 26, 1935, 7202 of Sept. 28, 1935, and 7649 of June 29, 1937. Terminated due to lack of funding.

Private Sector Programs, Office of Functions transferred to the Office of Citizen Exchanges within the Bureau of Educational and Cultural Affairs, USIA, by act of Feb. 16, 1990 (104 Stat. 56).

Processing tax *Agricultural Adjustment Administration's* function of collecting taxes declared unconstitutional by U.S. Supreme Court Jan. 6, 1936. Functions under acts of June 28, 1934 (48 Stat. 1275), Apr. 21, 1934 (48 Stat. 598), and Aug. 24, 1935 (49 Stat. 750) discontinued by repeal of these laws by act of Feb. 10, 1936 (49 Stat. 1106).

Processing Tax Board of Review Established in the Department of the Treasury by act of June 22, (49

Stat. 1652). Abolished by act of Oct. 21, 1942 (56 Stat. 967).

Proclamations *See* **State, Department of**

Procurement, Commission on Government Established by act of Nov. 26, 1969 (83 Stat. 269). Terminated Apr. 30, 1973, due to expiration of statutory authority.

Procurement and Assignment Service Established by President Oct. 30, 1941. Transferred from *Office of Defense Health and Welfare Services* to *War Manpower Commission* by EO 9139 of Apr. 18, 1942. Transferred to *Federal Security Agency* by EO 9617 of Sept. 19, 1945, which terminated *Commission.*

Procurement Division Established in the Department of the Treasury by EO 6166 of June 10, 1933. Renamed *Bureau of Federal Supply* by Department of the Treasury Order 73 of Nov. 19, 1946, effective Jan. 1, 1947. Transferred to General Services Administration as Federal Supply Service by act of June 30, 1949 (63 Stat. 380).

Procurement Policy, Office of Federal Established within Office of Management and Budget by act of Aug. 30, 1974 (88 Stat. 97). Abolished due to lack of funding and functions transferred to Office of Management and Budget by act of Oct 28, 1993 (107 Stat. 1236).

Product Standards Policy, Office of Formerly separate operating unit under Assistant Secretary for Productivity, Technology, and Innovation, Department of Commerce. Transferred to *National Bureau of*

Production Areas, Committee for Congested Established in Executive Office of the President by EO 9327 of Apr. 7, 1943. Terminated Dec. 31, 1944, by act of June 28, 1944 (58 Stat. 535).

Production Authority, National Established in the Department of Commerce Sept. 11, 1950, by EO's 10161 of Sept. 9, 1950, 10193 of Dec. 16, 1950, and 10200 of Jan. 3, 1951. Abolished by order of Oct. 1, 1953 of the Secretary of Commerce, and functions merged into *Business and Defense Services Administration.*

Production Management, Office of Established in *Office for Emergency Management* by EO 8629 of Jan. 7, 1941. Abolished by EO 9040 of Jan. 24, 1942, and personnel and property transferred to *War Production Board.*

Production and Marketing Administration Established by Secretary of Agriculture Memorandum 1118 of Aug. 18, 1945. Functions transferred under Department reorganization by Secretary's Memorandum 1320, supp. 4, of Nov. 2, 1953.

Productivity Council, National Established by EO 12089 of Oct. 23, 1978. EO 12089 revoked by EO 12379 of Aug. 17, 1982.

Programs, Bureau of International Established by the Secretary of Commerce Aug. 8, 1961, by Departmental Orders 173 and 174. Abolished by Departmental Order 182 of Feb. 1, 1963, which established *Bureau of International Commerce.* Functions transferred to *Domestic and International Business Administration,* effective Nov. 17, 1972.

Programs, Office of Public Established in the National Archives and Records Administration. Reorganized by Archivist under Notice 96–260, Sept. 23, 1996, effective Jan. 6, 1997. Functions restructured and transferred to Office of Records Services—Washington, DC.

Prohibition, Bureau of Established by act of May 27, 1930 (46 Stat. 427). Investigative functions consolidated with functions of *Bureau of Investigation* into *Division of Investigation,* Department of Justice. by EO 6166 of June 10, 1933, which set as effective date Mar. 2, 1934, or such later date as fixed by President. All other functions performed by *Bureau of Prohibition* ordered transferred to such division in the Department of Justice as deemed desirable by Attorney General.

Property, Office of Surplus Established in *Procurement Division,* Department of the Treasury, by EO 9425 of Feb. 19, 1944, and act of Oct. 3, 1944 (58 Stat. 765), under general direction of *Surplus Property Board* established by same legislation. Transferred to the Department of Commerce by EO 9541 of Apr. 19, 1945. Terminated by EO 9643 of Oct. 19, 1945, and activities and personnel transferred to *Reconstruction Finance Corporation.*

Property Administration, Surplus *See* **War Property Administration, Surplus**

Property Board, Surplus *See* **War Property Administration, Surplus**

Property Council, Federal Established by EO 11724 of June 25, 1973, and reconstituted by EO 11954 of Jan. 7, 1977. Terminated by EO 12030 of Dec. 15, 1977.

Property Management and Disposal Service *See* **Emergency Procurement Service**

Property Office, Surplus Established in *Division of Territories and Island Possessions,* Department of the Interior, under Regulation 1 of *Surplus Property Board,* Apr. 2, 1945. Transferred to *War Assets Administration* by EO 9828 of Feb. 21, 1947.

Property Review Board Established by EO 12348 of Feb. 25, 1982. EO 12348 revoked by EO 12512 of Apr. 29, 1985.

Protective Service, Federal Functions established in the *Federal Works* Agency by act of June 1, 1948 (62 Stat. 281). Functions transferred to General Services Administrator by act of June 30, 1949 (63 Stat. 380). Established as an agency within General Services Administration by GSA Administrator on Jan. 11, 1971 (ADM. 5440.46). Transferred to Homeland Security Department by act of Nov. 25, 2002 (116 Stat. 2178).

Prospective Payment Assessment Commission Established by act of Apr. 20, 1983 (97 Stat. 159). Terminated by act of Aug. 5, 1997 (111 Stat. 354). Assets, staff, and continuing responsibility for reports transferred to the Medicare Payment Advisory Commission.

Provisions and Clothing, Bureau of Established by acts of Aug. 31, 1842 (5 Stat. 579), and July 5, 1862 (12 Stat. 510). Designated *Bureau of Supplies and Accounts* by act of July 19, 1892 (27 Stat. 243). Abolished by Department of Defense reorg. order of Mar. 9, 1966, and functions transferred to the Secretary of the Navy (31 FR 7188).

Public *See other part of title*

Publications Commission, National Historical Established by act of Oct. 22, 1968 (82 Stat. 1293). Renamed National Historical Publications and Records Commission by act of Dec. 22, 1974 (88 Stat. 1734).

Puerto Rican Hurricane Relief Commission Established by act of Dec. 21, 1928 (45 Stat. 1067). No loans made after June 30, 1934, and *Commission* abolished June 3, 1935, by Public Resolution 22 (49 Stat. 320). Functions transferred to *Division of Territories and Island Possessions,* Department of the Interior. After June 30, 1946, collection work performed in *Puerto Rico Reconstruction Administration.* Following termination of *Administration,* remaining collection functions transferred to the Secretary of Agriculture by act of July 11, 1956 (70 Stat. 525).

Puerto Rico, U.S.-Puerto Rico Commission on the Status of Established by act of Feb. 20, 1964 (78 Stat. 17). Terminated by terms of act.

Puerto Rico Reconstruction Administration Established in the Department of the Interior by EO 7057 of May 28, 1935. Terminated Feb. 15, 1955, by act of Aug. 15, 1953 (67 Stat. 584).

Radiation Biology Laboratory *See* **Radiation and Organisms, Division of**

Radiation Council, Federal Established by EO 10831 of Aug. 14, 1959, and act of Sept. 23, 1959 (73 Stat. 688). Abolished by Reorg. Plan No. 3 of 1970, effective Dec. 2, 1970, and functions transferred to Environmental Protection Agency.

Radiation and Organisms, Division of Established by Secretarial order of May 1, 1929, as part of Smithsonian Astrophysical Observatory. Renamed *Radiation Biology Laboratory* by Secretarial order of Feb. 16, 1965. Merged with *Chesapeake Center for Environmental Studies* by Secretarial order of July 1, 1983, to form Smithsonian Environmental Research Center.

Radio Commission, Federal Established by act of Feb. 23, 1927 (44 Stat. 1162). Abolished by act of June 19, 1934 (48 Stat. 1102), and functions transferred to Federal Communications Commission.

Radio Division Established by *National Emergency Council* July 1, 1938. Transferred to *Office of Education, Federal Security Agency,* by Reorg. Plan No. II of 1939, effective July 1, 1939. Terminated June 30, 1940, by terms of act of June 30, 1939 (53 Stat. 927).

Radio Propagation Laboratory, Central Transferred from *National Bureau of Standards* to *Environmental Science Services Administration* by the Department of Commerce Order 2–A, effective July 13, 1965.

Radiological Health, National Center for Devices and Renamed Center for Devices and Radiological Health by Food and Drug Administration notice of Mar. 9, 1984 (49 FR 10166).

Rail Public Counsel, Office of Established by act of Feb. 5, 1976 (90 Stat. 51). Terminated Dec. 1, 1979, due to lack of funding.

Railroad Administration, U.S. *See* **Railroads, Director General of**

Railroad and Airline Wage Board Established by *Economic Stabilization Administrator's* General Order 7 of Sept. 27, 1951, pursuant to act of Sept. 8, 1950 (64 Stat. 816). Terminated Apr. 30, 1953, by EO 10434 of Feb. 6, 1953, and acts of June 30, 1952 (66 Stat. 296), and June 30, 1953 (67 Stat. 131).

Railroads, Director General of Established under authority of act of Aug. 29, 1916 (39 Stat. 645). Organization of *U.S. Railroad Administration* announced Feb. 9, 1918. Office abolished by Reorg. Plan No. II of 1939, effective July 1, 1939, and functions transferred to the Secretary of the Treasury.

Railway Association, U.S. Established by act of Jan. 2, 1974 (87 Stat. 985). Terminated Apr. 1, 1987, by act of Oct. 21, 1986 (100 Stat. 1906).

Railway Labor Panel, National Established by EO 9172 of May 22, 1942. EO 9172 revoked by EO 9883 of Aug. 11, 1947.

Reagan Centennial Commission, Ronald Established by act of June 2, 2009 (123 Stat. 1767). Terminated May 31, 2011, by act of May 12, 2011 (125 Stat. 215).

Real Estate Board, Federal Established by EO 8034 of Jan. 14, 1939. Abolished by EO 10287 of Sept. 6, 1951.

Reclamation, Bureau of *See* **Reclamation Service**

Reclamation Service Established July 1902 in *Geological Survey* by the Secretary of the Interior, pursuant to act of June 17, 1902 (32 Stat. 388). Separated from Survey in 1907 and renamed *Bureau of Reclamation* June 1923. Power marketing functions transferred to the Department of Energy by act of Aug. 4, 1977 (91 Stat. 578). *Bureau* renamed *Water and Power Resources Service* by Secretarial Order 3042 of Nov. 6, 1979. Renamed Bureau of Reclamation by Secretarial Order 3064 of May 18, 1981.

Reconciliation Service Established by Director of Selective Service pursuant to EO 11804 of Sept. 16, 1974. Program terminated Apr. 2, 1980.

Reconstruction Finance Corporation Established Feb. 2, 1932, by act of Jan. 22, 1932 (47 Stat. 5). Grouped with other agencies to form *Federal Loan Agency* by Reorg. Plan No. I of 1939, effective July 1, 1939. Transferred to the Department of Commerce by EO 9071 of Feb. 24, 1942. Returned to *Federal Loan Agency* by act of Feb. 24, 1945 (59 Stat. 5). *Agency* abolished by act of June 30, 1947 (61 Stat. 202), and functions assumed by *Corporation.* Functions relating to financing houses or site improvements, authorized by act of Aug. 10, 1948 (61 Stat. 1275), transferred to *Housing and Home Finance Agency* by Reorg. Plan No. 23 of 1950, effective July 10, 1950. *Corporation* Board of Directors, established by act of Jan. 22, 1932 (47 Stat. 5), abolished by Reorg. Plan No. 1 of 1951, effective May 1, 1951, and functions transferred to Administrator and *Loan Policy Board* established by same plan, effective Apr. 30, 1951. Act of July 30, 1953 (67 Stat. 230), provided for *RFC* succession until June 30, 1954, and for termination of its lending powers Sept. 28, 1953. Certain functions assigned to appropriate agencies for liquidation by Reorg. Plan No. 2 of 1954, effective July 1, 1954. *Corporation* abolished by Reorg. Plan No. 1 of 1957, effective June 30, 1957, and functions transferred to *Housing and Home Finance Agency,* General Services Administration, Small Business Administration, and the Department of the Treasury.

Records Administration, Office of Established in the National Archives and Records Administration. Reorganized by Archivist under Notice 96–260, Sept. 23, 1996, effective Jan. 6, 1997. Functions restructured and transferred to Office of Records Services—Washington, DC.

Records Centers, Office of Federal Established in the National Archives and Records Administration. Reorganized by Archivist under Notice 96–260, Sept. 23, 1996, effective Jan. 6, 1997. Functions restructured and transferred to Office of Regional Records Services.

Records and Information Management, Office of Functions transferred from *National Archives and Records Service* to *Automated Data and Telecommunications Service* by General Services Administrator's decision, effective Jan. 10, 1982, regionally and Apr. 1, 1982, in Washington, DC.

Recovery Administration, Advisory Council, National Established by EO 7075 of June 15, 1935. Transferred to the Department of Commerce by EO 7252 of Dec. 21, 1935, and functions ordered terminated not later than Apr. 1, 1936, by same order. *Committee of Industrial Analysis* created by EO 7323 of Mar. 21, 1936, to complete work of *Council.*

Recovery Administration, National Established by President pursuant to act of June 16, 1933 (48 Stat. 194). Provisions of title I of act repealed by Public Resolution 26 of June 14, 1935 (49 Stat. 375), and extension of *Administration* in skeletonized form authorized until Apr. 1, 1936. *Office of Administrator, National Recovery Administration,* created by EO 7075 of June 15, 1935. *Administration* terminated by EO 7252 of Dec. 21, 1935, which transferred *Division of Review, Division of Business Corporation,* and *Advisory Council* to the Department of Commerce for termination of functions by Apr. 1, 1936. *Consumers' Division* transferred to the Department of Labor by same order.

Recovery Review Board, National Established by EO 6632 of Mar. 7, 1934. Abolished by EO 6771 of June 30, 1934.

Recreation, Bureau of Outdoor Established in the Department of the Interior by act of May 28, 1963 (77 Stat. 49). Terminated by Secretary's order of Jan. 25, 1978, and functions assumed by *Heritage Conservation and Recreation Service.*

Recreation and Natural Beauty, Citizens' Advisory Committee on Established by EO 11278 of May 4, 1966. Terminated by EO 11472 of May 29, 1969.

Recreation and Natural Beauty, President's Council on Established by EO 11278 of May 4, 1966. Terminated by EO 11472 of May 29, 1969.

Recreation Resources Review Commission, Outdoor Established by act of June 28, 1958 (72 Stat. 238). Final report submitted to President January 1962 and terminated Sept. 1, 1962.

Regional Action Planning Commissions Authorized by act of Aug. 26, 1965 (79 Stat. 552). Federal role abolished through repeal by act of Aug. 13, 1981 (95 Stat. 766). At time of repeal, eight commissions—Coastal Plains, Four Corners, New England, Old West Ozarks, Pacific Northwest, Southwest Border, Southwest Border Region, and Upper Great Lakes—affected.

Regional Archives, Office of Special and Established in the National Archives and Records Administration. Reorganized by Archivist under Notice 96–260, Sept. 23, 1996, effective Jan. 6, 1997. Functions restructured and transferred between Office of Records Services—Washington, DC and Office of Regional Records Services.

Regional Councils, Federal Established by EO 12314 of July 22, 1981. Abolished by EO 12407 of Feb. 22, 1983.

Regional Operations, Executive Director of Established in Food and Drug Administration by order of May 20, 1971 of the *Secretary of Health, Education, and Welfare.* Merged into Office of Regulatory Affairs by order of Nov. 5, 1984 of the Secretary of Health and Human Services.

Regulations and Rulings, Office of Established in the U.S. Customs and Border Protection. Abolished by act of Oct. 13, 2006 (120 Stat. 1924) and functions transferred to the Office of International Trade.

Regulatory Council, U.S. Disbanded by Vice Presidential memorandum of Mar. 25, 1981. Certain functions continued in Regulatory Information Service Center.

Regulatory Relief, Presidential Task Force on Establishment announced in President's remarks Jan. 22, 1981. Disbanded and functions transferred to Office of Management and Budget in August 1983.

Rehabilitation Services Administration Functions transferred from *Department of Health, Education, and Welfare* to Office of Special Education and Rehabilitative Services, Department of Education, by act of Oct. 17, 1979 (93 Stat. 678), effective May 4, 1980.

Relief Corporation, Federal Surplus Organized under powers granted to President by act of June 16, 1933 (48 Stat. 195). Charter granted by State of Delaware Oct. 4, 1933, and amended Nov. 18, 1935, changing name to *Federal Surplus Commodities Corporation* and naming the Secretary of Agriculture, *Administrator of Agricultural Adjustment Administration,* and *Governor of Farm Credit Administration* as Board of Directors. Continued as agency under the Secretary of Agriculture by acts of June 28, 1937 (50 Stat. 323) and Feb. 16, 1938 (52 Stat. 38). Consolidated with *Division of Marketing and Marketing Agreements* into *Surplus Marketing Administration* by Reorg. Plan No. III of 1940, effective June 30, 1940. Merged into *Agricultural Marketing Administration* by EO 9069 of Feb. 23, 1942.

Relief and Rehabilitation Operations, Office of Foreign Established in the Department of State as announced by White House Nov. 21, 1942. Consolidated with *Foreign Economic Administration* by EO 9380 of Sept. 25, 1943.

Renegotiation Board Established by act of Mar. 23, 1951 (65 Stat. 7). Terminated Mar. 31, 1979, by act of Oct. 10, 1978 (92 Stat. 1043).

Rent Advisory Board Established by EO 11632 of Nov. 22, 1971. Abolished by EO 11695 of Jan. 11, 1973.

Rent Stabilization, Office of Established by General Order 9 of *Economic Stabilization Administrator* July 31, 1951, pursuant to act of June 30, 1947 (61 Stat. 193), and EO' s 10161 of Sept. 9, 1950, and 10276 of July 31, 1951. Abolished by EO 10475 of July 31, 1953, and functions transferred to *Office of Defense Mobilization. Office of Research and Development* combined with *Office of Minerals Policy Development* in the Department of the Interior May 21, 1976, under authority of Reorg. Plan No. 3 of 1950, effective May 24, 1950, to form *Office of Minerals Policy and Research Analysis.* Abolished Sept. 30, 1981, by Secretarial Order 3070 and functions transferred to *Bureau of Mines.*

Reports, Office of Government Established July 1, 1939, to perform functions of *National Emergency Council* abolished by Reorg. Plan No. II of 1939, effective July 1, 1939. Established as administrative unit of Executive Office of the President by EO 8248 of Sept. 8, 1939. Consolidated with *Office of War Information, Office for Emergency Management,* by EO 9182 of June 13, 1942. Reestablished in Executive Office of the President by EO 9809 of Dec. 12, 1946, which transferred to it functions of *Media Programming Division* and *Motion Picture Division, Office of War Mobilization and Reconversion,* and functions transferred from *Bureau of Special Services, Office of War Information,* to *Bureau of the Budget* by EO 9608 of Aug. 31, 1945. Subsequent to enactment of act of July 30, 1947 (61 Stat. 588), functions of *Office* restricted to advertising and motion picture liaison and operation of library. Terminated June 30, 1948.

Research, Office of University Transferred from *Office of Program Management and Administration,* Research and Special Programs Administration, to Office of Economics, Office of the Assistant Secretary for Policy and International Affairs, under authority of the Department of Transportation appropriation request for FY 1985, effective Oct. 1, 1984.

Research and Development Board Established in the Department of Defense by act of July 26, 1947 (61 Stat. 499). Abolished by Reorg. Plan No. 6 of 1953, effective June 30, 1953, and functions vested in the Secretary of Defense.

Research and Development Board, Joint Established June 6, 1946, by charter of Secretaries of *War* and Navy. Terminated on creation of *Research and Development Board* by act of July 26, 1947 (61 Stat. 506).

Research and Intelligence Service, Interim Established in the Department of State by EO 9621 of Sept. 20, 1945. Abolished Dec. 31, 1945, pursuant to terms of order.

Research and Special Programs Administration Established by act of Oct. 24, 1992 (106 Stat. 3310). Abolished and certain duties and powers transferred to both the Pipeline Hazardous Materials Safety Administration and the Administrator of the Research and Innovative Technology Administration, Department of Transportation, by act of Nov. 30, 2004 (118 Stat. 2424–2426).

Research Resources, Division of Established in National Institutes of Health, Department of Health and Human Services. Renamed National Center for Research Resources by Secretarial notice of Feb. 23, 1990 (55 FR 6455) and act of June 10, 1993 (107 Stat. 178).

Research Service, Cooperative State Established by Secretary of Agriculture Memorandum 1462, supp. 1, of Aug. 31, 1961. Consolidated into *Science and Education Administration* by Secretary's order of Jan. 24, 1978. Reestablished as Cooperative State Research Service by Secretarial order of June 16, 1981.

Research and Service Division, Cooperative Functions transferred to the Secretary of Agriculture in *Farmer Cooperative Service* by act of Aug. 6, 1953 (67 Stat. 390).

Resettlement Administration Established by EO 7027 of Apr. 30, 1935. Functions transferred to the Department of Agriculture by EO 7530 of Dec. 31, 1936. Renamed *Farm Security Administration* by Secretary's Memorandum 732 of Sept. 1, 1937.

Abolished by act of Aug. 14, 1946 (60 Stat. 1062) and functions incorporated into the *Farmers' Home Administration,* effective Jan. 1, 1947. *Farmers' Home Administration* abolished, effective Dec. 27, 1994, under authority of Secretary's Memorandum 1010–1 dated Oct. 20, 1994 (59 FR 66441). Functions assumed by the *Consolidated Farm Service Agency* and the *Rural Housing and Community Development Service.*

Resolution Trust Corporation Established by act of Aug. 9, 1989 (103 Stat. 369). Board of Directors of the Corporation abolished by act of Dec. 12, 1991 (105 Stat. 1769). Corporation functions terminated pursuant to act of Dec. 17, 1993 (107 Stat. 2369).

Resources Board and Advisory Committee, National Established by EO 6777 of June 30, 1934. Abolished by EO 7065 of June 7, 1935, and functions transferred to *National Resources Committee.*

Resources Committee, National Established by EO 7065 of June 7, 1935. Abolished by Reorg. Plan No. I of 1939, effective July 1, 1939, and functions transferred to *National Resources Planning Board* in Executive Office of the President. *Board* terminated by act of June 26, 1943 (57 Stat. 169).

Resources Planning Board, National *See* **Resources Committee, National**

Retired Executives, Service Corps of Established in ACTION by act of Oct. 1, 1973 (87 Stat. 404). Transferred to Small Business Administration by EO 11871 of July 18, 1975.

Retraining and Reemployment Administration Established by EO 9427 of Feb. 24, 1944, and act of Oct. 3, 1944 (58 Stat. 788). Transferred from *Office of War Mobilization and Reconversion* to the Department of Labor by EO 9617 of Sept. 19, 1945. Terminated pursuant to terms of act.

Revenue Sharing, Office of Established by the Secretary of the Treasury to administer programs authorized by acts of Oct. 20, 1972 (86 Stat. 919), and July 22, 1976 (90 Stat. 999). Transferred from the Office of the Secretary to Assistant Secretary (Domestic Finance) by Department of the Treasury Order 242, rev. 1, of May 17, 1976.

Review, Division of Established in *National Recovery Administration* by EO 7075 of June 15, 1935. Transferred to the Department of Commerce by EO 7252 of Dec. 21, 1935, and functions terminated Apr. 1, 1936. *Committee of Industrial Analysis* created by EO 7323 of Mar. 21, 1936, to complete work of *Division.*

RFC Mortgage Company Organized under laws of Maryland Mar. 14, 1935, pursuant to act of Jan. 22, 1932 (47 Stat. 5). Grouped with other agencies to form *Federal Loan Agency* by Reorg. Plan No. I of 1939, effective July 1, 1939. Transferred to the Department of Commerce by EO 9071 of Feb. 24, 1942. Returned to *Federal Loan Agency* by act of Feb. 24, 1945 (59 Stat. 5). Assets and liabilities transferred to *Reconstruction Finance Corporation* by act of June 30, 1947 (61 Stat. 207).

River Basins, Neches, Trinity, Brazos, Colorado, Guadalupe, San Antonio, Nueces, and San Jacinto, and Intervening Areas, U.S. Study Commission on Established by act of Aug. 28, 1958 (72 Stat. 1058). Terminated June 30, 1962.

River Basins, Savannah, Altamaha, Saint Mary's, Apalachicola-Chattahoochee, and Perdido-Escambia, and Intervening Areas, U.S. Study Commission on Established by act of Aug. 28, 1958 (72 Stat. 1090). Terminated Dec. 23, 1962.

Road Inquiry, Office of Established by the Secretary of Agriculture under authority of act of Aug. 8, 1894 (28 Stat. 264). Federal aid for highways to be administered by the Secretary of Agriculture through *Office of Public Roads and Rural Engineering* authorized by act of July 11, 1916 (39 Stat. 355), known as *Bureau of Public Roads* after July 1918. Transferred to *Federal Works Agency* by Reorg. Plan No. I of 1939, effective July 1, 1939, and renamed *Public Roads Administration.* Transferred to General Services Administration as *Bureau of Public Roads* by act of June 30, 1949 (63 Stat. 380). Transferred to the Department of Commerce by Reorg. Plan No. 7 of 1949, effective Aug. 20, 1949. Transferred to the Secretary of Transportation by act of Oct. 15, 1966 (80 Stat. 931), and functions assigned to Federal Highway Administration.

Roads, Bureau of Public *See* **Road Inquiry, Office of**

Roads Administration, Public *See* **Road Inquiry, Office of**

Roads and Rural Engineering, Office of Public *See* **Road Inquiry, Office of**

Rock Creek and Potomac Parkway Commission Established by act of Mar. 14, 1913 (37 Stat. 885). Abolished by EO 6166 of June 10, 1933, and functions transferred to *Office of National Parks, Buildings, and Reservations,* Department of the Interior.

Roosevelt Centennial Commission, Theodore Established by joint resolution of July 28, 1955 (69 Stat. 383). Terminated Oct. 27, 1959, pursuant to terms of act.

Roosevelt Library, Franklin D. Functions assigned to National Park Service by Reorg. Plan No. 3 of 1946, effective July 16, 1946, transferred to General Services Administration by Reorg. Plan No. 1 of 1963, effective July 27, 1963.

Roosevelt Library, Trustees of the Franklin D. Established by joint resolution of July 18, 1939 (53 Stat. 1063). Transferred to General Services Administration by act of June 30, 1949 (63 Stat. 381). Abolished by act of Mar. 5, 1958 (72 Stat. 34), and Library operated by *National Archives and Records Service,* General Services Administration.

Roosevelt Memorial Commission, Franklin Delano Established by joint resolution of Aug. 11, 1955 (69 Stat. 694). Terminated by act of Nov. 14, 1997 (111 Stat. 1601).

Rubber Development Corporation Establishment announced Feb. 20, 1943, by the Secretary of Commerce. Organized under laws of Delaware as subsidiary of *Reconstruction Finance Corporation.* Assumed all activities of *Rubber Reserve Company* relating to development of foreign rubber sources and procurement of rubber therefrom. Functions transferred to *Office of Economic Warfare* by EO 9361 of July 15, 1943. *Office* consolidated into *Foreign Economic Administration* by EO 9380 of Sept. 25, 1943. *Office* returned to *Reconstruction Finance Corporation* by EO 9630 of Sept. 27, 1945. Certificate of incorporation expired June 30, 1947.

Rubber Producing Facilities Disposal Commission Established by act of Aug. 7, 1953 (67 Stat. 408). Functions transferred to *Federal Facilities Corporation* by EO 10678 of Sept. 20, 1956.

Rubber Reserve Company Established June 28, 1940, under act of Jan. 22, 1932 (47 Stat. 5). Transferred from *Federal Loan Agency* to the Department of Commerce by EO 9071 of Feb. 24, 1942. Returned to *Federal Loan Agency* by act of Feb. 24, 1945 (59 Stat. 5). Dissolved by act of June 30, 1945 (59 Stat. 310), and functions transferred to *Reconstruction Finance Corporation.*

Rural Areas Development, Office of Established by Secretary of Agriculture memorandum in 1961 (revised Sept. 21, 1962). Renamed *Rural Community Development Service* by Secretary's Memorandum 1570 of Feb. 24, 1965.

Rural Business and Cooperative Development Service Established within the Department of Agriculture by Secretary's Memorandum 1020–34 dated Dec. 31, 1991. Renamed Rural Business-Cooperative Service (61 FR 2899), effective Jan. 30, 1996.

Rural Community Development Service Established by Secretary of Agriculture Memorandum 1570 of Feb. 25, 1965, to supersede *Office of Rural Areas Development.* Abolished Feb. 2, 1970, by Secretary's Memorandum 1670 of Jan. 30, 1970, and functions transferred to other agencies in the Department of Agriculture.

Rural Development Administration Established within the Department of Agriculture by Secretary's Memorandum 1020–34 dated Dec. 31, 1991. Abolished Dec. 27, 1994 (59 FR 66441) under authority of Secretary's Memorandum 1010–1 dated Oct. 20, 1994. Functions assumed by the Rural Business and Cooperative Development Service.

Rural Development Committee *See* **Rural Development Program, Committee for**

Rural Development Policy, Office of Established initially as *Office of Rural Development Policy Management and Coordination,* Farmers Home Administration, by Secretary of Agriculture Memorandum 1020–3 of Oct. 26, 1981. Abolished in 1986 due to lack of funding.

Rural Development Program, Committee for Established by EO 10847 of Oct. 12, 1959. Abolished by EO 11122 of Oct. 16, 1963, which established *Rural Development Committee. Committee* superseded by EO 11307 of Sept. 30, 1966, and functions assumed by the Secretary of Agriculture.

Rural Development Service Established by Agriculture Secretarial order in 1973. Functions transferred to *Office of Rural Development Coordination and Planning, Farmers Home Administration,* by Secretarial order in 1978.

Rural Electrification Administration Established by EO 7037 of May 11, 1935. Functions transferred by EO 7458 of Sept. 26, 1936, to *Rural Electrification Administration* established by act of May 20, 1936 (49 Stat. 1363). Transferred to the Department of Agriculture by Reorg. Plan No. II of 1939, effective July 1, 1939. Abolished by Secretary's Memorandum 1010–1 dated Oct. 20, 1994, and functions assumed by Rural Utilities Service.

Rural Housing and Community Development Service Established by act of Oct. 13, 1994 (108 Stat. 3219). Renamed Rural Housing Service (61 FR 2899), effective Jan. 30, 1996.

Rural Rehabilitation Division Established April 1934 by act of May 12, 1933 (48 Stat. 55). Functions transferred to *Resettlement Administration* by *Federal Emergency Relief Administrator's* order of June 19, 1935.

Saint Elizabeth's Hospital *See* **Insane, Government Hospital for the**

Saint Lawrence Seaway Development Corporation Established by act of May 13, 1954 (68 Stat. 92). Secretary of Commerce given direction of general policies of *Corporation* by EO 10771 of June 20, 1958. Transferred to the Department of Transportation by act of Oct. 15, 1966 (80 Stat. 931).

Salary Stabilization, Office of *See* **Salary Stabilization Board**

Salary Stabilization Board Established May 10, 1951, by *Economic Stabilization Administrator's* General Order 8. Stabilization program administered by *Office of Salary Stabilization.* Terminated Apr. 30, 1953, by EO 10434 of Feb. 6, 1953, and acts of June 30, 1952 (66 Stat. 296), and June 30, 1953 (67 Stat. 131).

Sales Manager, Office of the General Established by the Secretary of Agriculture Feb. 29, 1976. Consolidated with Foreign Agricultural Service by Secretary's Memorandum 2001 of Nov. 29, 1979.

Savings Bonds, Interdepartmental Committee for the Voluntary Payroll Savings Plan for the Purchase of U.S. Established by EO 11532 of June 2, 1970. Superseded by EO 11981 of Mar. 29, 1977, which established Interagency Committee for the Purchase of U.S. Savings Bonds.

Savings and Loan Advisory Council, Federal Established by act of Oct. 6, 1972 (86 Stat. 770). Continued by act of Dec. 26, 1974 (88 Stat. 1739). Terminated by act of Aug. 9, 1989 (103 Stat. 422).

Savings and Loan Insurance Corporation, Federal Established by act of June 27, 1934 (48 Stat. 1246). Grouped with other agencies to form *Federal Loan Agency* by Reorg. Plan No. I of 1939, effective July 1, 1939. Transferred to *Federal Home Loan Bank Administration, National Housing Agency,* by EO 9070 of Feb. 24, 1942. Board of Trustees abolished by Reorg. Plan No. 3 of 1947, effective July 27, 1947, and functions transferred to *Home Loan Bank Board.* Abolished by act of Aug. 9, 1989 (103 Stat. 354).

Savings Bonds Division, United States Established by Departmental Order 62 of Dec. 26, 1945, as successor to the War and Finance Division, War Savings Staff, and Defense Savings Staff. Functions transferred to Bureau of Public Debt by Departmental Order 101–05 of May 11, 1994, and *Division* renamed Savings Bond Marketing Office.

Science, Engineering, and Technology, Federal Coordinating Council for Established by act of May 11, 1976 (90 Stat. 471). Abolished by Reorg. Plan No. 1 of 1977, effective Feb. 26, 1978, and functions transferred to President. Functions redelegated to Director of the Office of Science and Technology Policy and Federal Coordinating Council for Science, Engineering, and Technology, established by EO 12039 of Feb. 24, 1978.

Science, Engineering, and Technology Panel, Intergovernmental Established by act of May 11, 1976 (90 Stat. 465). Abolished by Reorg. Plan No. 1 of 1977, effective Feb. 26, 1978, and functions transferred to President. Functions redelegated to Director of Office of Science and Technology Policy by EO 12039 of Feb. 24, 1978, which established Intergovernmental Science, Engineering, and Technology Advisory Panel.

Science Advisory Committee, President's Established by President Apr. 20, 1951, and reconstituted Nov. 22, 1957. Terminated with *Office of Science and Technology,* effective July 1, 1973.

Science Exhibit-Century 21 Exposition, U.S. Established Jan. 20, 1960, by Department of Commerce Order 167. Abolished by revocation of order on June 5, 1963.

Science and Technology, Federal Council for *See* **Scientific Research and Development, Interdepartmental Committee on**

Science and Technology, Office of Established by Reorg. Plan No. 2 of 1962, effective June 8, 1962. *Office* abolished by Reorg. Plan No. 1 of 1973, effective June 30, 1973, and functions transferred to National Science Foundation.

Science and Technology, President's Committee on Established by act of May 11, 1976 (90 Stat. 468). Abolished by Reorg. Plan No. 1 of 1977, effective Feb. 26, 1978, and functions transferred to President.

Scientific and Policy Advisory Committee Established by act of Sept. 26, 1961 (75 Stat. 631). Terminated Apr. 30, 1996 under terms of act.

Scientific Research and Development, Interdepartmental Committee on Established by EO 9912 of Dec. 24, 1947. EO 9912 revoked by EO 10807 of Mar. 13, 1959, which established *Federal Council for Science and Technology.* Abolished by act of May 11, 1976 (90 Stat. 472).

Scientific Research and Development, Office of Established in *Office for Emergency Management* by EO 8807 of June 28, 1941. Terminated by EO 9913 of Dec. 26, 1947, and property transferred to *National Military Establishment* for liquidation.

Scientists and Engineers, National Committee for the Development of Established by President Apr. 3, 1956. Renamed *President's Committee on Scientists and Engineers* May 7, 1957. Final report submitted Dec. 17, 1958, and expired Dec. 31, 1958.

Scientists and Engineers, President's Committee on *See* **Scientists and Engineers, National Committee for the Development of**

Screw Thread Commission, National Established by act of July 18, 1918 (40 Stat. 912). Terminated by EO 6166 of June 10, 1933, and records transferred to the Department of Commerce, effective Mar. 2, 1934. Informal Interdepartmental Screw Thread Committee established on Sept. 14, 1939, consisting of representatives of the Departments of *War,* the Navy, and Commerce.

Sea Grant Review Panel, National Established by act of Oct. 8, 1976 (90 Stat. 1967). Renamed National Sea Grant Advisory Board by act of Oct. 13, 2008 (122 Stat. 4207.

Secret Service, United States *See* **Secret Service Division**

Secret Service Division Established July 5, 1865, as a Bureau under Treasury Department. Acknowledged as distinct agency within Treasury Department in 1883. *White House Police Force* created on October 1, 1922, and placed under supervision of *Secret Service Division* in 1930. *White House Police Force* renamed *Executive Protective Service* by act of June 30, 1970 (84 Stat. 358). *Executive Protective Service* renamed U.S. Secret Service Uniformed Division by act of Nov. 15, 1977 (91 Stat. 1371). *Treasury Police Force* merged into Secret Service on Oct. 5, 1986. U.S. Secret Service transferred to Homeland Security Department by act of Nov. 25, 2002 (116 Stat. 2224).

Security and Safety Performance Assurance, Office of Established by Secretary of Energy memorandum of December 2, 2003. Abolished by Secretary's Memorandum 2006–007929 of Aug. 30, 2006 and functions transferred to the Office of Health, Safety and Security.

Security, Commission on Government Established by act of Aug. 9, 1955 (69 Stat. 595). Terminated Sept. 22, 1957, pursuant to terms of act.

Security, Office of the Director for Mutual *See* **Security Agency, Mutual**

Security Agency, Federal Established by Reorg. Plan No. I of 1939, effective July 1, 1939, grouping under one administration *Office of Education, Public Health Service, Social Security Board, U.S. Employment Service, Civilian Conservation Corps,* and *National Youth Administration.* Abolished by Reorg. Plan No. 1 of 1953, effective Apr. 11, 1953, and functions and units transferred to *Department of Health, Education, and Welfare.*

Security Agency, Mutual Established and continued by acts of Oct. 10, 1951 (65 Stat. 373) and June 20, 1952 (66 Stat. 141). *Agency* and *Office of Director for Mutual Security* abolished by Reorg. Plan No. 7 of 1953, effective Aug. 1, 1953, and functions transferred to *Foreign Operations Administration,* established by same plan.

Security and Individual Rights, President's Commission on Internal Established by EO 10207 of Jan. 23, 1951. Terminated by EO 10305 of Nov. 14, 1951.

Security Resources Board, National Established by act of July 26, 1947 (61 Stat. 499). Transferred to Executive Office of the President by Reorg. Plan No. 4 of 1949, effective Aug. 20, 1949. Functions of *Board* transferred to Chairman and *Board* made advisory to him by Reorg. Plan No. 25 of 1950, effective July 10, 1950. Functions delegated by Executive order transferred to *Office of Defense Mobilization* by EO 10438 of Mar. 13, 1953. *Board* abolished by Reorg. Plan No. 3 of 1953, effective June 12, 1953, and remaining functions transferred to *Office of Defense Mobilization.*

Security Training Commission, National Established by act of June 19, 1951 (65 Stat. 75). Expired June 30, 1957, pursuant to Presidential letter of Mar. 25, 1957.

Seed Loan Office Authorized by Presidential letters of July 26, 1918, and July 26, 1919, to the Secretary of Agriculture. Further authorized by act of Mar. 3, 1921 (41 Stat. 1347). Office transferred to Farm Credit Administration by EO 6084 of Mar. 27, 1933.

Selective Service Appeal Board, National Established by EO 9988 of Aug. 20, 1948. Inactive as of Apr. 11, 1975.

Selective Service Records, Office of *See* **Selective Service System**

Selective Service System Established by act of Sept. 16, 1940 (54 Stat. 885). Placed under jurisdiction of *War Manpower Commission* by EO 9279 of Dec. 5, 1942, and designated *Bureau of Selective Service.* Designated Selective Service System, separate agency, by EO 9410 of Dec. 23, 1943. Transferred for liquidation to *Office of Selective Service Records* established by act of Mar. 31, 1947 (61 Stat. 31). Transferred to Selective Service System by act of June 24, 1948 (62 Stat. 604).

Self-Help Development and Technical Development, Office of Established in *National Consumer Cooperative Bank* by act of Aug. 20, 1978 (92 Stat. 499). Abolished by act of Aug. 13, 1981 (95 Stat. 437), and assets transferred to Consumer Cooperative Development Corporation, Department of Commerce, Dec. 30, 1982.

Services, Bureau of Special *See* **Office of War Information**

Services, Division of Central Administrative Established by *Liaison Officer for Emergency Management* pursuant to Presidential letter of Feb. 28, 1941. Terminated by EO 9471 of Aug. 25, 1944, and functions discontinued or transferred to constituent agencies of *Office for Emergency Management* and other agencies.

Shipbuilding Stabilization Committee Originally organized by *National Defense Advisory Commission* in 1940. Established August 1942 by *War Production Board.* Transferred to the Department of Labor from *Civilian Production Administration,* successor agency to *Board,* by EO 9656 of Nov. 15, 1945. Terminated June 30, 1947.

Shipping Board, U.S. Established by act of Sept. 7, 1916 (39 Stat. 729). Abolished by EO 6166 of June 10, 1933, and functions, including those with respect to *U.S. Shipping Board Merchant Fleet Corporation,* transferred to *U.S. Shipping Board Bureau,* Department of Commerce, effective Mar. 2, 1934. Separation of employees deferred until Sept. 30, 1933, by EO 6245 of Aug. 9, 1933. Functions assumed by *U.S. Maritime Commission* Oct. 26, 1936, pursuant to act of June 29, 1936 (49 Stat. 1985).

Shipping Board Bureau, U.S. *See* **Shipping Board, U.S.**

Shipping Board Emergency Fleet Corporation, U.S. Established Apr. 16, 1917, under authority of act of Sept. 7, 1916 (39 Stat. 729). Renamed *U.S. Shipping Board Merchant Fleet Corporation* by act of Feb. 11, 1927 (44 Stat. 1083). Terminated Oct. 26, 1936, under provisions of act of June 29, 1936 (49 Stat. 1985), and functions transferred to *U.S. Maritime Commission.*

Shipping Board Merchant Fleet Corporation, U.S. *See* **Shipping Board Emergency Fleet Corporation, U.S.**

Ships, Bureau of Established by act of June 20, 1940 (54 Stat. 493), to replace *Bureau of Engineering* and *Bureau of Construction and Repair.* Abolished by Department of Defense reorg. order of Mar. 9, 1966, and functions transferred to the Secretary of the Navy (31 FR 7188).

Simpson Historical Research Center, Albert F. Renamed Headquarters USAF Historical Research

Center by special order of Dec. 16, 1983 of the Secretary of Defense.

Small and Disadvantaged Business Utilization, Office of Established within certain Defense Departments by act of Oct. 24, 1978 (92 Stat. 1770). Renamed Office of Small Business Programs by Public Law 109–163 of Jan. 6, 2006 (119 Stat. 3399).

Smithsonian Symposia and Seminars, Office of Renamed Office of Interdisciplinary Studies by Smithsonian Institution announcement of Mar. 16, 1987.

Social Development Institute, Inter-American Established by act of Dec. 30, 1969 (83 Stat. 821). Renamed Inter-American Foundation by act of Feb. 7, 1972 (86 Stat. 34).

Social Protection, Committee on Established in *Office of Defense Health and Welfare Services* by administrative order June 14, 1941. Functions transferred to *Federal Security Agency* by EO 9338 of Apr. 29, 1943.

Social and Rehabilitation Service Established by the *Secretary of Health, Education, and Welfare* reorganization of Aug. 15, 1967. Abolished by Secretary's reorganization of Mar. 8, 1977 (42 FR 13262), and constituent units—*Medical Services Administration, Assistance Payments Administration, Office of Child Support Enforcement, and Public Services Administration*—transferred.

Social Security Administration *See* **Social Security Board**

Social Security Board Established by act of Aug. 14, 1935 (49 Stat. 620). Incorporated into *Federal Security Agency* by Reorg. Plan No. I of 1939, effective July 1, 1939. *Social Security Board* abolished and Social Security Administration established by Reorg. Plan No. 2 of 1946 (5 U.S.C. app.), effective July 16, 1946, and functions of the *Board* transferred to *Federal Security Administrator.* Social Security Administration transferred from the *Federal Security Agency* by Reorganization Plan No. 1 of 1953 (5 U.S.C. app.), effective Apr. 11, 1953, to the *Department of Health, Education, and Welfare.* Social Security Administration became an independent agency in the executive branch by act of Aug. 15, 1994 (108 Stat. 1464), effective Mar. 31, 1995.

Soil Conservation Service *See* **Soil Erosion Service**

Soil Erosion Service Established in the Department of the Interior following allotment made Aug. 25, 1933. Transferred to the Department of Agriculture by Secretary of Interior administrative order of Mar. 25, 1935. Made *Soil Conservation Service* by order of the Secretary of Agriculture, Apr. 27, 1935, pursuant to provisions of act of Apr. 27, 1935 (49 Stat. 163). Certain functions of *Soil Conservation Service* under jurisdiction of the Department of the Interior transferred from the Department of Agriculture to the Department of the Interior by Reorg. Plan No. IV of 1940, effective June 30, 1940. *Soil Conservation Service* abolished by act of Oct. 13, 1994 (108 Stat. 3225) and functions assumed by the Natural Resources Conservation Service.

Soils, Bureau of *See* **Agricultural and Industrial Chemistry, Bureau of** and **Plant Industry, Bureau of**

Solicitor General, Office of Assistant Established in the Department of Justice by act of June 16, 1933 (48 Stat. 307). Terminated by Reorg. Plan No. 2 of 1950, effective May 24, 1950.

Southeastern Power Administration Established by the Secretary of the Interior in 1943 to carry out functions under act of Dec. 22, 1944 (58 Stat. 890). Transferred to the Department of Energy by act of Aug. 4, 1977 (91 Stat. 578).

Southwestern Power Administration Established by the Secretary of the Interior in 1943 to carry out functions under act of Dec. 22, 1944 (58 Stat. 890). Transferred to the Department of Energy by act of Aug. 4, 1977 (91 Stat. 578).

Space Access and Technology, Office of Established in the National Aeronautics and Space Administration. Abolished by Administrator's order of Feb. 24, 1997.

Space Communications, Office of Established in the National Aeronautics and Space Administration. Abolished by Administrator's order of Feb. 24, 1997.

Space Payload Technology Organization, Joint Operationally Responsive Established by act of Jan. 6, 2006 (119 Stat. 3408). Abolished by acts of Oct. 17, 2006 (120 Stat. 2358) and Dec. 20, 2006 (120 Stat. 3286).

Space Science, Office of *See* **Space and Terrestrial Applications, Office of**

Space Science Board Renamed Space Studies Board by authority of the National Research Council, National Academy of Sciences, effective May 8, 1989.

Space Station, Office of Established in the National Aeronautics and Space Administration. Abolished in 1990 and remaining functions transferred to the Office of Space Flight.

Space Technology Laboratories, National Renamed John C. Stennis Space Center by EO 12641 of May 20, 1988.

Space and Terrestrial Applications, Office of Combined with *Office of Space Science* to form Office of Space Science and Applications by National Aeronautics and Space Administrator's announcement of Sept. 29, 1981.

Space Tracking and Data Systems, Office of Renamed Office of Space Operations by National Aeronautics and Space Administrator's announcement of Jan. 9, 1987.

Space Transportation Operations, Office of Combined with *Office of Space Transportation Systems* to form Office of Space Transportation

Systems, National Aeronautics and Space Administration, effective July 1982.

Space Transportation Systems, Office of *See* **Space Transportation Operations, Office of**

Spanish-Speaking People, Cabinet Committee on Opportunities for *See* **Mexican-American Affairs, Interagency Committee on**

Special. *See other part of title*

Specifications Board, Federal Established by *Bureau of the Budget* Circular 42 of Oct. 10, 1921. Transferred from *Federal Coordinating Service* to *Procurement Division* by order of Oct. 9, 1933 of the Secretary of the Treasury. *Board* superseded by *Federal Specifications Executive Committee,* set up by *Director of Procurement* under Circular Letter 106 of July 16, 1935.

Sport Fisheries and Wildlife, Bureau of Established in the Department of the Interior by act of Aug. 8, 1956 (70 Stat. 1119). *Bureau* replaced by U.S. Fish and Wildlife Service pursuant to act of Apr. 22, 1974 (88 Stat. 92).

Standards, National Bureau of *See* **Weights and Measures, Office of Standard**

State, Department of Duty of Secretary of State of procuring copies of all statutes of the States, as provided for in act of Sept. 28, 1789 (R.S. 206), abolished by Reorg. Plan No. 20 of 1950, effective May 24, 1950. Functions of numbering, editing, and distributing proclamations and Executive orders transferred from the Department of State to the *Division of the Federal Register, National Archives,* by EO 7298 of Feb. 18, 1936. Duty of Secretary of State of publishing Executive proclamations and treaties in newspapers in District of Columbia, provided for in act of July 31, 1876 (19 Stat. 105), abolished by Reorg. Plan No. 20 of 1950, effective May 24, 1950. Functions concerning publication of U.S. Statutes at Large, acts and joint resolutions in pamphlet form known as slip laws, and amendments to the Constitution; electoral votes for President and Vice President; and Territorial papers transferred from the Department of State to the Administrator of the General Services Administration by Reorg. Plan No. 20 of 1950. (*See also* **Archives Establishment, National**)

State and Local Cooperation, Division of Established by *Advisory Commission to Council of National Defense* Aug. 5, 1940. Transferred to *Office of Civilian Defense.*

State and Local Government Cooperation, Committee on Established by EO 11627 of Oct 15, 1971. Abolished by EO 11695 of Jan. 11, 1973.

State Technical Services, Office of Established by the Secretary of Commerce Nov. 19, 1965, pursuant to act of Sept. 14, 1965 (79 Stat. 697). Abolished by Secretary, effective June 30, 1970.

Statistical Board, Central Organized Aug. 9, 1933, by EO 6225 of July 27, 1933. Transferred to *Bureau of the Budget* by Reorg. Plan No. I of 1939, effective July 1, 1939. Expired July 25, 1940, and functions taken over by *Division of Statistical Standards, Bureau of the Budget.*

Statistical Committee, Central Established by act of July 25, 1935 (49 Stat. 498). Abolished by Reorg. Plan No. I of 1939, effective July 1, 1939, and functions transferred to *Bureau of the Budget.*

Statistical Policy Coordination Committee Established by EO 12013 of Oct. 7, 1977. Abolished by EO 12318 of Aug. 21, 1981.

Statistical Reporting Service Established by Memorandum 1446, supp. 1, part 3, of 1961 of the Secretary of Agriculture. Consolidated with other departmental units into *Economics, Statistics, and Cooperatives Service* by Secretary's Memorandum 1927, effective Dec. 23, 1977. Redesignated as *Statistical Reporting Service* by Secretary's order of Oct. 1, 1981. Renamed National Agricultural Statistics Service.

Statistics Administration, Social and Economic Established Jan. 1, 1972, by the Secretary of Commerce. Terminated by Department of Commerce Organization Order 10–2, effective Aug. 4, 1975 (40 FR 42765). Bureau of Economic Analysis and Bureau of the Census restored as primary operating units of the Department of Commerce by Organization Orders 35–1A and 2A, effective Aug. 4, 1975.

Statutes at Large *See* **State, Department of**

Statutes of the States *See* **State, Department of**

Steam Engineering, Bureau of Established in the Department of the Navy by act of July 5, 1862 (12 Stat. 510). Redesignated as *Bureau of Engineering* by act of June 4, 1920 (41 Stat. 828). Abolished by act of June 20, 1940 (54 Stat. 492), and functions transferred to *Bureau of Ships.*

Steamboat Inspection Service President authorized to appoint *Service* by act of June 28, 1838 (5 Stat. 252). Secretary of Treasury authorized to establish boards of local inspectors at enumerated ports throughout the U.S. by act of Feb. 28, 1871 (16 Stat. 440). Authority to appoint boards of local inspectors delegated to *Secretary of Commerce and Labor* by act of Mar. 4, 1905 (33 Stat. 1026). Consolidated with *Bureau of Navigation and Steamboat Inspection* by act of June 30, 1932 (47 Stat. 415).

Stock Catalog Board, Federal Standard Originated by act of Mar. 2, 1929 (45 Stat. 1461). Transferred from *Federal Coordinating Service* to *Procurement Division* by order of Oct. 9, 1933 of the Secretary of the Treasury.

Strategic Defense Initiative Organization Established in 1986 as a separate agency of the Department of Defense. Renamed Ballistic Missile Defense Organization by Deputy Secretary's memorandum in May 1993.

Strategic Posture of the United States, Commission on the Implementation of the New Established by act of Jan. 6, 2006 (119 Stat. 3431). Terminated by act of Jan. 28, 2009 (122 Stat. 328)

Strategic Services, Office of *See* **Information, Office of Coordinator of**

Strategic Trade, Office of Established in the U.S. Customs and Border Protection pursuant to Customs Service Reorganization plan, effective Sept. 30, 1995. Abolished by act of Oct. 13, 2006 (120 Stat. 1924) and functions transferred to the Office of International Trade.

Subversive Activities Control Board Established by act of Sept. 23, 1950 (64 Stat. 987). Terminated June 30, 1973, due to lack of funding.

Sugar Division Created by act of May 12, 1933 (48 Stat. 31), authorized by act of Sept. 1, 1937 (50 Stat. 903). Taken from *Agricultural Adjustment Administration* and made independent division of the Department of Agriculture by Secretary's Memorandum 783, effective Oct. 16, 1938. Placed under *Agricultural Conservation and Adjustment Administration* by EO 9069 of Feb. 23, 1942, functioning as *Sugar Agency*. Functions transferred to *Food Distribution Administration* by EO 9280 of Dec. 5, 1942.

Sugar Rationing Administration Established by Memorandum 1190 of Mar. 31, 1947, of the Secretary of Agriculture under authority of act of Mar. 31, 1947 (61 Stat. 35). Terminated Mar. 31, 1948, on expiration of authority.

Supplies and Accounts, Bureau of *See* **Provisions and Clothing, Bureau of**

Supplies and Shortages, National Commission on Established by act of Sept. 30, 1974 (88 Stat. 1168). Terminated Mar. 31, 1977, pursuant to terms of act.

Supply, Bureau of Federal *See* **Procurement Division**

Supply, Office of Renamed Office of Procurement and Property by Smithsonian Institution announcement of Nov. 4, 1986.

Supply Committee, General Established by act of June 17, 1910 (36 Stat. 531). Abolished by EO 6166 of June 10, 1933, effective Mar. 2, 1934, and functions transferred to *Procurement Division,* the Department of the Treasury.

Supply Priorities and Allocations Board Established in *Office for Emergency Management* by EO 8875 of Aug. 28, 1941. Abolished by EO 9024 of Jan. 16, 1942, and functions transferred to *War Production Board.*

Supply Service, Federal Renamed *Office of Personal Property* by General Services Administration (GSA) order, effective Sept. 28, 1982; later renamed *Office of Federal Supply and Services* by GSA order of Jan. 22, 1983; then redesignated *Federal Supply Service*. Merged with *Federal Technology Service* to form Federal Acquisition Service by GSA Order No. 5440.591 of Sept. 9, 2005. *See also* act of Oct. 6, 2006 (120 Stat. 1735).

Surveys and Maps, Federal Board of *See* **Surveys and Maps of the Federal Government, Board of**

Surveys and Maps of the Federal Government, Board of Established by EO 3206 of Dec. 30, 1919. Renamed *Federal Board of Surveys and Maps* by EO 7262 of Jan. 4, 1936. Abolished by EO 9094 of Mar. 10, 1942, and functions transferred to Director, *Bureau of the Budget.*

Space System Development, Office of Established in the National Aeronautics and Space Administration. Renamed Office of Space Access and Technology in 1995.

Tariff Commission, U.S. Established by act of Sept. 8, 1916 (39 Stat. 795). Renamed U.S. International Trade Commission by act of Jan. 3, 1975 (88 Stat. 2009).

Tax Appeals, Board of Established as an independent agency within the executive branch by act of June 2, 1924 (43 Stat. 336). Continued by acts of Feb. 26, 1926 (44 Stat. 105) and Feb. 10, 1939 (53 Stat. 158). Renamed *Tax Court of the United States* by act of Aug. 16, 1954 (68A Stat. 879). Renamed United States Tax Court by act of Dec. 30, 1969 (83 Stat. 730).

Technical Advisory Board for First Responder Interoperability Established by act of Feb. 22, 2012 (126 Stat. 208). Terminated on July 6, 2012 by operation of law.

Technical Cooperation Administration Transferred from the Department of State to *Mutual Security Agency* by EO 10458 of June 1, 1953. Transferred to *Foreign Operations Administration* by Reorg. Plan No. 7 of 1953, effective Aug. 1, 1953.

Technical Services, Office of Designated unit of Office of the Secretary of Commerce by Department Order 179, July 23, 1962. Functions transferred to *National Bureau of Standards* by Order 90 of Jan. 30, 1964.

Technology Administration Established by act of Oct. 24, 1988 (102 Stat. 2593). Abolished by act of Aug. 9, 2007 (121 Stat. 587) and functions absorbed by National Institute of Standards and Technology, Department of Commerce.

Technology Assessment, Office of Created by act of Oct. 13, 1972 (86 Stat. 797). Office inactive as of Sept. 30, 1995.

Technology, Automation, and Economic Progress, National Commission on Established by act of Aug. 19, 1964 (78 Stat. 463). Terminated January 1966 pursuant to terms of act.

Technology Service, Federal Merged with *Federal Supply Service* to form Federal Acquisition Service by General Services Administration Order No. 5440.591

of Sept. 9, 2005. *See also* act of Oct. 6, 2006 (120 Stat. 1735).

Telecommunications Adviser to the President Established in Executive Office of the President by EO 10297 of Oct. 9, 1951. EO 10297 revoked by EO 10460 of June 16, 1953, and functions transferred to Director of *Office of Defense Mobilization.*

Telecommunications Management, Director of Established in *Office of Emergency Planning* by EO 10995 of Feb. 16, 1962. Assignment of radio frequencies delegated to Government agencies and foreign diplomatic establishments by EO 11084 of Feb. 16, 1963. Abolished by Reorg. Plan No. 1 of 1970, effective Apr. 20, 1970.

Telecommunications Policy, Office of Established in Executive Office of the President by Reorg. Plan No. 1 of 1970, effective Apr. 20, 1970. Abolished by Reorg. Plan No. 1 of 1977, effective Mar. 26, 1978, and certain functions transferred to President with all other functions transferred to the Department of Commerce.

Telecommunications Service, Automated Data Renamed *Office of Information Resources Management* by General Services Administration order of Aug. 17, 1982. Later renamed Information Resources Management Service.

Temporary Controls, Office of Established in *Office for Emergency Management* by EO 9809 of Dec. 12, 1946, consolidating *Office of War Mobilization and Reconversion, Office of Economic Stabilization, Office of Price Administration,* and *Civilian Production Administration.* Functions with respect to Veterans' Emergency Housing Program transferred to *Housing Expediter* by EO 9836 of Mar. 22, 1947. Functions with respect to distribution and price of sugar products transferred to the Secretary of Agriculture by act of Mar. 31, 1947 (61 Stat. 36). Office terminated by EO 9841 of Apr. 23, 1947, and remaining functions redistributed.

Temporary Emergency Court of Appeals Established by act of Dec. 22, 1971 (85 Stat. 749). Abolished by act of Oct. 29, 1992, effective Apr. 30, 1993 (106 Stat. 4507). Court's jurisdiction and pending cases transferred to the United States Court of Appeals for the Federal Circuit.

Territorial Affairs, Office of Established by Interior Secretarial Order 2951 of Feb. 6, 1973. Abolished by Departmental Manual Release 2270 of June 6, 1980, and functions transferred to Office of Assistant Secretary for Territorial and International Affairs.

Territorial papers *See* **State, Department of**

Territories, Office of Established by the Secretary of the Interior July 28, 1950. Functions reassigned to *Deputy Assistant Secretary for Territorial Affairs* in *Office of the Assistant Secretary—Public Land Management,* Department of the Interior, by Secretarial Order 2942, effective July 1, 1971.

Terrorism, Cabinet Committee To Combat Established by Presidential memorandum of Sept. 25, 1972. Terminated by National Security Council memorandum of Sept. 16, 1977.

Terrorist Threat Integration Center Established on May 1, 2003, pursuant to Presidential initiative. Transferred to the National Counterterrorism Center by act of Dec. 17, 2004 (118 Stat. 3697).

Textile National Industrial Relations Board Established by administrative order of June 28, 1934. Abolished by EO 6858 of Sept. 26, 1934, which created *Textile Labor Relations Board* in connection with the Department of Labor. *Board* terminated July 1, 1937, and functions absorbed by *U.S. Conciliation Service,* Department of Labor.

Textile National Industrial Relations Board, Cotton Established by original Code of Fair Competition for the Cotton Textile Industry, as amended July 10, 1934. Abolished by EO 6858 of Sept. 26, 1934.

Textile Work Assignment Board, Cotton Amendments to Code of Fair Competition for Cotton Textile Industry approved by EO 6876 of Oct. 16, 1934, and *Cotton Textile Work Assignment Board* appointed by *Textile Labor Relations Board. Board* expired June 15, 1935.

Textile Work Assignment Board, Silk Appointed by *Textile Labor Relations Board* following President's approval of amendments to Code of Fair Competition for Silk Textile Industry by EO 6875 of Oct. 16, 1934. Terminated June 15, 1935.

Textile Work Assignment Board, Wool Established by EO 6877 of Oct. 16, 1934. Terminated June 15, 1935.

Textiles, Office of Established by the Secretary of Commerce Feb. 14, 1971. Functions transferred to *Domestic and International Business Administration,* effective Nov. 17, 1972.

Thrift Depositor Protection Oversight Board. *See* **Oversight Board (of the Resolution Trust Corporation).**

Thrift Supervision, Office of Established by act of August 9, 1989 (103 Stat. 352). Abolished by act of July 21. 2010, (124 Stat. 1522), and functions transferred to Office of the Comptroller of the Currency, Federal Deposit Insurance Corporation, Federal Reserve Board of Governors, and Consumer Financial Protection Bureau.

Trade, Special Adviser to the President on Foreign Established by EO 6651 of Mar. 23, 1934. Terminated on expiration of *National Recovery Administration.*

Trade Administration, International *See* **Business and Defense Services Administration**

Trade Agreements, Interdepartmental Committee on Established by Secretary of State in 1934 and reestablished by EO 9832 of Feb. 25, 1947. Abolished by EO 11075 of Jan. 15, 1963.

Trade and Development Program Established by act of Sept. 4, 1961, as amended (88 Stat. 1804). Designated separate entity within the *U.S. International Development Cooperation Agency* by act of Sept. 4, 1961, as amended (102 Stat. 1329). Renamed Trade and Development Agency by act of Oct. 28, 1992 (106 Stat. 3657).

Trade Expansion Act Advisory Committee Established by EO 11075 of Jan. 15, 1963. Abolished by EO 11846 of Mar. 27, 1975, and records transferred to Trade Policy Committee established by same EO.

Trade Negotiations, Office of the Special Representative for Renamed Office of the U.S. Trade Representative by EO 12188 of Jan. 4, 1980.

Trade Policy Committee Established by EO 10741 of Nov. 25, 1957. Abolished by EO 11075 of Jan. 15, 1963.

Traffic Safety, President's Committee for Established by Presidential letter of Apr. 14, 1954. Continued by EO 10858 of Jan. 13, 1960. Abolished by EO 11382 of Nov. 28, 1967.

Traffic Safety Agency, National Established in the Department of Commerce by act of Sept. 9, 1966 (80 Stat. 718). Activity transferred to the Department of Transportation by act of Oct. 15, 1966 (80 Stat. 931). Responsibility placed in *National Highway Safety Bureau* by EO 11357 of June 6, 1967.

Training and Employment Service, U.S. Established in *Manpower Administration,* Department of Labor, Mar. 17, 1969. Abolished by Secretary's letter of Dec. 6, 1971, and functions assigned to *Office of Employment Development Programs* and *U.S. Employment Service.*

Training School for Boys, National *See* **District of Columbia, Reform-School of the**

Transportation, Federal Coordinator of Established by act of June 16, 1933 (48 Stat. 211). Expired June 16, 1936, under provisions of Public Resolution 27 (49 Stat. 376).

Transportation, Office of Established in the Department of Agriculture by Secretary's Memorandum 1966 dated Dec. 12, 1978. Abolished by Secretary's Memorandum 1030–25 dated Dec. 28, 1990.

Transportation and Communications Service Established by General Services Administrator Oct. 19, 1961. Abolished by Administrator's order, effective July 15, 1972. Motor equipment, transportation, and public utilities responsibilities assigned to Federal Supply Service; telecommunications function assigned to *Automated Data Telecommunications Service.*

Transportation and Public Utilities Service Abolished by General Services Administration order of Aug. 17, 1982. Functions transferred to various GSA organizations.

Transportation Safety Board, National Established in the Department of Transportation by act of Oct. 15, 1966 (80 Stat. 935). Abolished by act of Jan. 3, 1975 (88 Stat. 2156), which established independent National Transportation Safety Board.

Transportation Security Administration Established by act of Nov. 19, 2001 (115 Stat. 597). Functions transferred from Department of Transportation to Department of Homeland Security by act of Nov. 25, 2002 (116 Stat. 2178).

Transportation Statistics, Bureau of Established by act of Dec. 18, 1991 (105 Stat. 2172). Transferred to Research and Innovative Technology Administration, Transportation Department, by act of Nov. 30, 2004 (118 Stat. 2424).

Travel Service, U.S. Replaced by *U.S. Travel and Tourism Administration,* Department of Commerce, pursuant to act of Oct. 16, 1981 (95 Stat. 1014).

Travel and Tourism Administration, U.S. Established by act of Oct. 16, 1981 (95 Stat. 1014). Abolished by act of Oct. 11, 1996 (110 Stat. 3407).

Travel and Tourism Advisory Board Established by act of Oct. 16, 1981 (95 Stat. 1017). Abolished by act of Oct. 11, 1996 (110 Stat. 3407).

Treasury, Office of the Assistant Secretary of the—Electronics and Information Technology Established by Secretary's Order 114–1 of Mar. 14, 1983. Abolished by Secretary's Order 114–3 of May 17, 1985, and functions transferred to Office of the Assistant Secretary for Management. Certain provisions effective Aug. 31, 1985 (50 FR 23573).

Treasury, Solicitor of the Position established when certain functions of *Solicitor of the Treasury* transferred to the Department of Justice by EO 6166 of June 10, 1933. *Solicitor of the Treasury* transferred from the Department of Justice to the Department of the Treasury by same order. *Office of Solicitor of the Treasury* abolished by act of May 10, 1934 (48 Stat. 758), and functions transferred to General Counsel, the Department of the Treasury.

Treasury Police Force *See* **Secret Service Division**

Treasury Secretary, Assistant Office abolished by Reorg. Plan No. III of 1940, effective June 30, 1940, and functions transferred to Fiscal Assistant Secretary, Department of the Treasury.

Treasury Under Secretary for Enforcement, Office of Established by act of Oct. 28, 1993 (107 Stat. 1234). Office abolished by act of Dec. 8, 2004 (118 Stat. 3245), and functions transferred to the Office of the Under Secretary for Terrorism and Financial Crimes, Department of the Treasury.

Treaties *See* **State, Department of**

Typhus Commission, U.S. of America Established in *Department of War* by EO 9285 of Dec. 24, 1942. Abolished June 30, 1946, by EO 9680 of Jan. 17, 1946.

U.S. *See other part of title*

Uniformed Services University of the Health Sciences, School of Medicine of the Renamed F. Edward He´bert School of Medicine by act of Sept. 24, 1983 (97 Stat. 704).

United Nations Educational, Scientific and Cultural Organization U.S. membership in UNESCO authorized by act of July 30, 1946 (60 Stat. 712). Announcement of U.S. intention to withdraw made Dec. 28, 1983, in accordance with UNESCO constitution. Official U.S. withdrawal effective Dec. 31, 1984, by Secretary of State's letter of Dec. 19, 1984. The U.S. maintained status as an observer mission in UNESCO from 1984–2003, and rejoined the organization in October 2003.

Upper Mississippi River Basin Commission Established by EO 11659 of Mar. 22, 1972. Terminated by EO 12319 of Sept. 9, 1981.

Urban Affairs, Council for Established in Executive Office of the President by EO 11452 of Jan. 23, 1969. Terminated by EO 11541 of July 1, 1970.

Urban Mass Transportation Administration Functions regarding urban mass transportation established in the Department of Housing and Urban Development by act of July 9, 1964 (78 Stat. 302). Most functions transferred to the Department of Transportation by Reorg. Plan No. 2 of 1968, effective June 30, 1968 (82 Stat. 1369), and joint responsibility assigned to the Departments of Transportation and Housing and Urban Development for functions relating to research, technical studies, and training. Transportation and Housing and Urban Development Under Secretaries agreed in November 1969 that the Department of Transportation should be focal point for urban mass transportation grant administration; at which time functions transferred to the Department of Transportation. Renamed Federal Transit Administration by act of Dec. 18, 1991 (105 Stat. 2088).

Urban Renewal Administration Established in *Housing and Home Finance Agency* by Administrator's Organizational Order 1 of Dec. 23, 1954. Functions transferred to the Department of Housing and Urban Development by act of Sept. 9, 1965 (78 Stat. 667), and *Administration* terminated.

Utilization and Disposal Service Established July 1, 1961, by Administrator of General Services and assigned functions of Federal Supply Service and Public Buildings Service. Functions transferred to *Property Management and Disposal Service* July 29, 1966.

Veterans Administration Legal work in defense of suits against the U.S. arising under act of June 7, 1924 (43 Stat. 607), transferred to the Department of Justice by EO 6166 of June 10, 1933. Transfer deferred to Sept. 10, 1933, by EO 6222 of July 27, 1933. Established as an independent agency under the President by Executive Order 5398 of July 21, 1930, in accordance with the act of July 3, 1930 (46 Stat. 1016) and the act of Sept. 2, 1958 (72 Stat. 1114). Made an executive department in the executive branch and redesignated the Department of Veterans Affairs by act of Oct. 25, 1988 (102 Stat. 2635).

Veterans Appeals, U.S. Court of Established by act of Nov. 18, 1988 (102 Stat. 4113). Renamed U.S. Court of Appeals for Veterans Claims by act of Nov. 11, 1998 (112 Stat. 3341).

Veterans Education Appeals Board *See* **Veterans Tuition Appeals Board**

Veterans Employment and Training, Advisory Committee on Renamed Advisory Committee on Veterans Employment, Training, and Employer Outreach by act of June 15, 2006 (120 Stat. 403).

Veterans Employment Service Renamed Veterans' Employment and Training Service by Order 4–83 of Mar. 24, 1983 of the Secretary of Labor (48 FR 14092).

Veterans Health Administration *See* **Medicine and Surgery, Department of**

Veterans Health Services and Research Administration *See* **Medicine and Surgery, Department of**

Veterans Placement Service Board Established by act of June 22, 1944 (58 Stat. 293). Abolished by Reorg. Plan No. 2 of 1949, effective Aug. 20, 1949, and functions transferred to the Secretary of Labor.

Veterans Tuition Appeals Board Established by act of Aug. 24, 1949 (63 Stat. 654). Functions assumed by *Veterans Education Appeals Board* established by act of July 13, 1950 (64 Stat. 336). *Board* terminated by act of Aug. 28, 1957 (71 Stat. 474).

Veterinary Medicine, Bureau of Established in Food and Drug Administration, *Department of Health, Education, and Welfare*. Renamed Center for Veterinary Medicine by FDA notice of Mar. 9, 1984 (49 FR 10166).

Virgin Islands Public works programs under act of Dec. 20, 1944 (58 Stat. 827), transferred from General Services Administrator to the Secretary of the Interior by Reorg. Plan No. 15 of 1950, effective May 24, 1950.

Virgin Islands Company Established in 1934. Reincorporated as Government corporation by act of June 30, 1949 (63 Stat. 350). Program terminated June 30, 1965, and *Corporation* dissolved July 1, 1966.

Virgin Islands Corporation *See* **Virgin Islands Company**

Visitor Facilities Advisory Commission, National Established by act of Mar. 12, 1968 (82

Stat. 45). Expired Jan. 5, 1975, pursuant to act of Oct. 6, 1972 (86 Stat. 776).

Vocational Rehabilitation, Office of Established to administer provisions of act of July 6, 1943 (57 Stat. 374). Other duties delegated by acts of Aug. 3, 1954 (68 Stat. 652), Nov. 8, 1965 (79 Stat. 1282), July 12, 1960 (74 Stat. 364), and July 10, 1954 (68 Stat. 454). Redesignated *Vocational Rehabilitation Administration* Jan. 28, 1963. Made component of newly created *Social and Rehabilitation Service* as *Rehabilitation Services Administration* by *Department of Health, Education, and Welfare* reorganization of Aug. 15, 1967.

Vocational Rehabilitation Administration *See* **Vocational Rehabilitation, Office of**

Voluntary Citizen Participation, State Office of Renamed State Office of Volunteerism in ACTION by notice of Apr. 18, 1986 (51 FR 13265), effective May 18, 1986.

Volunteer Service, International, Secretariat for Established in 1962 by International Conference on Middle Level Manpower called by President. Terminated Mar. 31, 1976, due to insufficient funding.

Volunteers in Service to America Established by act of Nov. 8, 1966 (80 Stat. 1472). *Service* administered by *Office of Economic Opportunity* and functions transferred to ACTION by Reorg. Plan No. 1 of 1971, effective July 1, 1971.

Wage Adjustment Board Established May 29, 1942, by the Secretary of Labor at Presidential direction of May 14, 1942, to accomplish purpose of act of Mar. 3, 1931 (46 Stat. 1494), as amended by acts of Aug. 30, 1935 (49 Stat. 1011), and Jan. 30, 1942 (56 Stat. 23). Disbanded on termination of *National Wage Stabilization Board.*

Wage and Price Stability, Council on Established in Executive Office of the President by act of Aug. 24, 1974 (88 Stat. 750). Abolished by EO 12288 of Jan. 29, 1981. Funding ceased beyond June 5, 1981, by act of June 5, 1981 (95 Stat. 74), and authorization for appropriations repealed by act of Aug. 13, 1981 (95 Stat. 432).

Wage and Price Stability Program *See* **Wage and Price Stability, Council on**

Wage Stabilization Board Established by EO 10161 of Sept. 9, 1950. Reconstituted by EO 10377 of July 25, 1952. Terminated Apr. 30, 1953, by EO 10434 of Feb. 6, 1953, and acts of June 30, 1952 (66 Stat. 296), and June 30, 1953 (67 Stat. 131).

Wage Stabilization Board, National *See* **Defense Mediation Board, National**

Wallops Flight Center, Wallops Island, VA Formerly separate field installation of National Aeronautics and Space Administration. Made component of Goddard Space Flight Center by NASA Management Instruction 1107.10A of Sept. 3, 1981.

War, Solid Fuels Administration for Established in the Department of the Interior by EO 9332 of Apr. 19, 1943. Absorbed *Office of Solid Fuels Coordinator for War* (originally established as *Office of Solid Fuels Coordinator for National Defense*) pursuant to Presidential letter of Nov. 5, 1941; later changed by Presidential letter of May 25, 1942. Terminated by EO 9847 of May 6, 1947.

War Assets Administration Established in *Office for Emergency Management* by EO 9689 of Jan. 31, 1946. Functions transferred to *Surplus Property Administration* by Reorg. Plan No. 1 of 1947, effective July 1, 1947, and agency renamed *War Assets Administration.* Abolished by act of June 30, 1949 (63 Stat. 738), and functions transferred for liquidation to General Services Administration.

War Assets Corporation *See* **Petroleum Reserves Corporation**

War Claims Commission Established by act of July 3, 1948 (62 Stat. 1240). Abolished by Reorg. Plan No. 1 of 1954, effective July 1, 1954, and functions transferred to Foreign Claims Settlement Commission of the U.S.

War Commodities Division Established in *Office of Foreign Economic Coordination* by Department of State Order of Aug. 27, 1943. *Office* abolished by departmental order of Nov. 6, 1943, pursuant to EO 9380 of Sept. 25, 1943, which established *Foreign Economic Administration* in *Office for Emergency Management.*

War Communications, Board of *See* **Defense Communications Board**

War Contracts Price Adjustment Board Established by act of Feb. 25, 1944 (58 Stat. 85). Abolished by act of Mar. 23, 1951 (65 Stat. 7), and functions transferred to *Renegotiation Board,* established by same act, and General Services Administrator.

War Damage Corporation *See* **War Insurance Corporation**

War, Department of Established by act of Aug. 7, 1789 (1 Stat. 49), succeeding similar department established prior to adoption of the Constitution. Three military departments—Army; Navy, including naval aviation and U.S. Marine Corps; and Air Force—reorganized under *National Military Establishment* by act of July 26, 1947 (61 Stat. 495).

War Finance Corporation Established by act of Apr. 5, 1918 (40 Stat. 506). Functions and obligations transferred by Reorg. Plan No. II of 1939, effective July 1, 1939, to the Secretary of the Treasury for liquidation not later than Dec. 31, 1939.

War Food Administration *See* **Food Production and Distribution, Administration of**

War Information, Office of Established in *Office of Emergency Management* by EO 9182 of June 13, 1942, consolidating *Office of Facts and Figures; Office of Government Reports; Division of Information, Office for Emergency Management;* and

Foreign Information Service—Outpost, Publications, and Pictorial Branches, Coordinator of Information. Abolished by EO 9608 of Aug. 31, 1945. *Bureau of Special Services* and functions with respect to review of publications of Federal agencies transferred to *Bureau of the Budget.* Foreign information activities transferred to the Department of State.

War Insurance Corporation Established Dec. 13, 1941, by act of June 10, 1941 (55 Stat. 249). Charter filed Mar. 31, 1942. Renamed *War Damage Corporation* by act of Mar. 27, 1942 (56 Stat. 175). Transferred from *Federal Loan Agency* to the Department of Commerce by EO 9071 of Feb. 24, 1942. Returned to *Federal Loan Agency* by act of Feb. 24, 1945 (59 Stat. 5). *Agency* abolished by act of June 30, 1947 (61 Stat. 202), and functions assumed by *Reconstruction Finance Corporation.* Powers of *War Damage Corporation,* except for purposes of liquidation, terminated as of Jan. 22, 1947.

War Labor Board, National *See* **Defense Mediation Board, National**

War Manpower Commission Established in *Office for Emergency Management* by EO 9139 of Apr. 18, 1942. Terminated by EO 9617 of Sept. 19, 1945, and functions, except *Procurement and Assignment Service,* transferred to the Department of Labor.

War Mobilization, Office of Established by EO 9347 of May 27, 1943. Transferred to *Office of War Mobilization and Reconversion* by EO 9488 of Oct. 3, 1944.

War Mobilization and Reconversion, Office of Established by act of Oct. 3, 1944 (58 Stat. 785). Consolidated with other agencies by EO 9809 of Dec. 12, 1946, to form *Office of Temporary Controls. Media Programming Division* and *Motion Picture Division* transferred to *Office of Government Reports,* reestablished by same order. Certain other functions transferred to President and the Secretary of Commerce.

War Mobilization and Reconversion Advisory Board, Office of Established by act of Oct. 3, 1944 (58 Stat. 788). Transferred to *Office of Temporary Controls* by EO 9809 of Dec. 12, 1946.

War Plants Corporation, Smaller Established by act of June 11, 1942 (56 Stat. 351). Functions transferred by EO 9665 of Dec. 27, 1945, to *Reconstruction Finance Corporation* and the Department of Commerce. Abolished by act of June 30, 1947 (61 Stat. 202), and functions transferred for liquidation to General Services Administration by Reorg. Plan No. 1 of 1957, effective July 1, 1957.

War and Post War Adjustment Policies, Advisory Unit on Established in *Office of War Mobilization* by Presidential direction Nov. 6, 1943. Report submitted Feb. 15, 1944, and Unit Director and Assistant Director submitted letter to Director of *War Mobilization* ending their work May 12, 1944.

War Production Board Established in *Office for Emergency Management* by EO 9024 of Jan. 16, 1942. *Board* terminated and successor agency, *Civilian Production Administration,* established by EO 9638 of Oct. 4, 1945.

War Property Administration, Surplus Established in *Office of War Mobilization* by EO 9425 of Feb. 19, 1944. Terminated on establishment of *Surplus Property Board* by act of Oct. 3, 1944 (58 Stat. 768). *Surplus Property Administration* established in *Office of War Mobilization and Reconversion* by act of Sept. 18, 1945 (59 Stat. 533), and *Board* abolished. Domestic functions of *Administration* merged into *War Assets Corporation, Reconstruction Finance Corporation,* by EO 9689 of Jan. 31, 1946. Foreign functions transferred to the Department of State by same order. Transfers made permanent by Reorg. Plan No. 1 of 1947, effective July 1, 1947.

War Refugee Board Established in Executive Office of the President by EO 9417 of Jan. 22, 1944. Terminated by EO 9614 of Sept. 14, 1945.

War Relations, Agricultural, Office for *See* **Farm Products, Division of**

War Relief Agencies, President's Committee on Established by Presidential letter of Mar. 13, 1941. *President's War Relief Control Board* established by EO 9205 of July 25, 1942, to succeed *Committee. Board* terminated by EO 9723 of May 14, 1946, and functions transferred to the Department of State.

War Relief Control Board, President's *See* **President's Committee on War Relief Agencies**

War Relocation Authority Established in *Office for Emergency Management* by EO 9102 of Mar. 18, 1942. Transferred to the Department of the Interior by EO 9423 of Feb. 16, 1944. Terminated by EO 9742 of June 25, 1946.

War Resources Board Established in August 1939 as advisory committee to work with *Joint Army and Navy Munitions Board.* Terminated by President Nov. 24, 1939.

War Resources Council *See* **Defense Resources Committee**

War Shipping Administration Established in *Office for Emergency Management* by EO 9054 Feb. 7, 1942. Terminated by act of July 8, 1946 (60 Stat. 501), and functions transferred to *U.S. Maritime Commission,* effective Sept. 1, 1946.

Water, Office of Saline Established to perform functions vested in the Secretary of the Interior by act of July 29, 1971 (85 Stat. 159). Merged with *Office of Water Resources Research* to form *Office of Water Research and Technology* by Secretary's Order 2966 of July 26, 1974.

Water Commission, National Established by act of Sept. 26, 1968 (82 Stat. 868). Terminated Sept. 25, 1973, pursuant to terms of act.

Water Policy, Office of Established by Department of the Interior Manual Release 2374 of Dec. 29, 1981, under authority of Assistant Secretary.

Abolished by Secretarial Order No. 3096 of Oct. 19, 1983, and functions transferred to *Geological Survey* and *Office of Policy Analysis*.

Water Pollution Control Administration, Federal Established under the *Secretary of Health, Education, and Welfare* by act of Oct. 2, 1965 (79 Stat. 903). Transferred to the Department of the Interior by Reorg. Plan No. 2 of 1966, effective May 10, 1966. Renamed *Federal Water Quality Administration* by act of Apr. 3, 1970. Abolished by Reorg. Plan No. 3 of 1970, effective Dec. 2, 1970, and functions transferred to Environmental Protection Agency.

Water and Power Resources Service Renamed Bureau of Reclamation May 18, 1981, by Interior Secretarial Order 3064.

Water Quality Administration, Federal *See* **Water Pollution Control Administration, Federal Water**

Research and Technology, Office of Established by Interior Secretarial Order 2966 of July 26, 1974. Abolished by Secretarial order of Aug. 25, 1982, and functions transferred to Bureau of Reclamation, Geological Survey, and *Office of Water Policy*.

Water Resources Council Established by act of July 22, 1965 (89 Stat 575). Inactive as of Oct. 1, 1982.

Water Resources Research, Office of Established to perform functions vested in the Secretary of the Interior by act of July 17, 1964 (78 Stat. 329). Merged with *Office of Saline Water* to form *Office of Water Research and Technology* by Secretary's Order 2966 of July 26, 1974.

Watergate Special Prosecution Force Established by Attorney General order, effective May 25, 1973. Terminated by Attorney General order, effective June 20, 1977.

Waterways Corporation, Inland Incorporated under act of June 3, 1924 (43 Stat. 360). Transferred from the *Department of War* to the Department of Commerce by Reorg. Plan No. II of 1939, effective July 1, 1939. *Corporation* sold to *Federal Waterways Corporation* under contract of July 24, 1953. Renamed *Federal Barge Lines, Inc.* Liquidated by act of July 19, 1963 (77 Stat. 81).

Weather Bureau Established in the Department of Agriculture by act of Oct. 1, 1890 (26 Stat. 653). Transferred to the Department of Commerce by Reorg. Plan No. IV of 1940, effective June 30, 1940. Functions transferred to *Environmental Science Services Administration* by Reorg. Plan No. 2 of 1965, effective July 13, 1965.

Weather Control, Advisory Committee on Established by act of Aug. 13, 1953 (67 Stat. 559). Act of Aug. 28, 1957 (71 Stat. 426), provided for termination by Dec. 31, 1957.

Weed and Seed, Executive Office of Abolished by Public Law 109–162 of Jan. 5, 2006 (119 Stat. 3107). Functions transferred to Office of Weed and Seed Strategies, Office of Justice Programs, within the Department of Justice.

Weights and Measures, Office of Standard Renamed *National Bureau of Standards* by act of Mar. 3, 1901 (31 Stat. 1449). *Bureau* transferred from the Department of the Treasury to the *Department of Commerce and Labor* by act of Feb. 14, 1903 (32 Stat. 825). *Bureau* established within the Department of Commerce by act of Mar. 4, 1913 (37 Stat. 736). Renamed National Institute of Standards and Technology by act of Aug. 23, 1988 (102 Stat. 1827).

Welfare Administration Established by the *Secretary of Health, Education, and Welfare* reorganization of Jan. 28, 1963. Components consisted of *Bureau of Family Services, Children's Bureau, Office of Juvenile Delinquency and Youth Development,* and *Cuban Refugee Staff.* These functions reassigned to *Social and Rehabilitation Service* by Department reorganization of Aug. 15, 1967.

White House Police Force *See* **Secret Service Division**

Wilson Memorial Commission, Woodrow Established by act of Oct. 4, 1961 (75 Stat. 783). Terminated on submittal of final report to President and Congress Sept. 29, 1966.

Women, Interdepartmental Committee on the Status of Established by EO 11126 of Nov. 1, 1963. Terminated by EO 12050 of Apr. 4, 1978.

Women, President's Commission on the Status of Established by EO 10980 of Dec. 14, 1961. Submitted final report to President Oct. 11, 1963.

Women's Army Auxiliary Corps Established by act of May 14, 1942 (56 Stat. 278). Repealed in part and superseded by act of July 1, 1943 (57 Stat. 371), which established *Women's Army Corps. Corps* abolished by the Secretary of Defense Apr. 24, 1978, pursuant to provisions of 10 U.S.C. 125A.

Women's Business Enterprise Division Renamed *Office of Women's Business Enterprise* by Small Business Administrator's reorganization, effective Aug. 19, 1981. Renamed Office of Women's Business Ownership Aug. 19, 1982.

Women's Reserve Established in U.S. Coast Guard by act of Nov. 23, 1942 (56 Stat. 1020).

Women's Year, 1975, National Commission on the Observance of International Established by EO 11832 of Jan. 9, 1975. Continued by act of Dec. 23, 1975 (89 Stat. 1003). Terminated Mar. 31, 1978, pursuant to terms of act.

Wood Utilization, National Committee on Established by Presidential direction in 1925. Abolished by EO 6179–B of June 16, 1933.

Work Projects Administration *See* **Works Progress Administration**

Work-Training Programs, Bureau of Abolished by reorganization of *Manpower Administration* and functions assigned to *U.S. Training and Employment Service,* effective Mar. 17, 1969.

Working Group on Streamlining Paperwork for Executive Nominations Established by act of Aug. 10, 2012 (126 Stat. 1292). Terminated July 7, 2013, pursuant to terms of act.

Working Life, Productivity and Quality of, National Center for Established by act of Nov. 28, 1975 (89 Stat. 935). Authorized appropriations expired Sept. 30, 1978, and functions assumed by *National Productivity Council.*

Works, Advisory Committee on Federal Public Established by President Oct. 5, 1955. Abolished by President Mar. 12, 1961, and functions assigned to *Bureau of the Budget.*

Works Administration, Federal Civil Established by EO 6420–B of Nov. 9, 1933. Function of employment expired March 1934. Function of settling claims continued under *Works Progress Administration.*

Works Administration, Public *See* **Emergency Administration of Public Works, Federal**

Works Agency, Federal Established by Reorg. Plan No. I of 1939, effective July 1, 1939. Functions relating to defense housing transferred to *Federal Public Housing Authority, National Housing Agency,* by EO 9070 of Feb. 24, 1942. Abolished by act of June 30, 1949 (63 Stat. 380), and functions transferred to General Services Administration.

Works Emergency Housing Corporation, Public Established by EO 6470 of Nov. 29, 1933. Incorporated under laws of State of Delaware. Abolished and liquidated as of Aug. 14, 1935, by filing of certificate of surrender of corporate rights.

Works Emergency Leasing Corporation, Public Incorporated Jan. 3, 1934, under laws of Delaware by direction of Administrator of Public Works. Terminated with filed certificate of dissolution with secretary of state of Delaware Jan. 2, 1935.

Works Progress Administration Established by EO 7034 of May 6, 1935, and continued by subsequent yearly emergency relief appropriation acts. Renamed *Work Projects Administration* by Reorg. Plan No. I of 1939, effective July 1, 1939, which provided for consolidation of *Works Progress Administration* into *Federal Works Agency.* Transferred by President to *Federal Works Administrator* Dec. 4, 1942.

Works, Special Board of Public *See* **Land Program, Director of**

Yards and Docks, Bureau of Established by acts of Aug. 31, 1842 (5 Stat. 579), and July 5, 1862 (12 Stat. 510). Abolished by Department of Defense reorg. order of Mar. 9, 1966, and functions transferred to the Secretary of the Navy (31 FR 7188).

Youth Administration, National Established in *Works Progress Administration* by EO 7086 of June 26, 1935. Transferred to *Federal Security Agency* by Reorg. Plan No. I of 1939, effective July 1, 1939. Transferred to *Bureau of Training, War Manpower Commission,* by EO 9247 of Sept. 17, 1942. Terminated by act of July 12, 1943 (57 Stat. 539).

Youth Crime, President's Committee on Juvenile Delinquency and Established by EO 10940 of May 11, 1961. Terminated by EO 11529 of Apr. 24, 1970.

Youth Fitness, President's Council on Established by EO 10673 of July 16, 1956. Renamed *President's Council on Physical Fitness* by EO 11074 of Jan. 8, 1963. Renamed President's Council on Physical Fitness and Sports by EO 11398 of Mar. 4, 1968. Abolished and reestablished by EO 13265 of June 6, 2002. Renamed President's Council on Fitness, Sports, and Nutrition by EO 13545 of June 22, 2010.

Youth Opportunity, President's Council on Established by EO 11330 of Mar. 5, 1967. Inactive as of June 30, 1971; EO 11330 revoked by EO 12379 of Aug. 17, 1982.

Youth Programs, Office of Established in the Department of the Interior by Secretarial Order No. 2985 of Jan. 7, 1965. Functions moved to Office of Historically Black College and University Programs and Job Corps, Office of the Secretary, by Departmental Manual Release 2788 of Mar. 22, 1988.

CPSIA information can be obtained
at www.ICGtesting.com
Printed in the USA
LVOW03s1534160617
538389LV00001B/1/P

9 781598 048285